MCSA

MICROSOFT CERTIFIED SYSTEMS ADMINISTRATOR

MCSA Managing a Windows® 2000 Network Environment Study Guide

(Exam 70-218)

ABOUT THE AUTHORS

Alan Simpson (MCSA) is the author of over 80 computer books published throughout the world in over a dozen languages. His award-winning titles have sold hundreds of thousands of copies and are best known for their light, engaging style and clear, straightforward approach to technical subjects. Alan has written books on operating systems (DOS, Windows, Linux), the Internet (HTML, JavaScript), databases, spreadsheets, word processing programs, and more. Prior to becoming an author, Alan worked as a software consultant, programmer, and teacher. Alan lives in Pennsylvania with his wife and two children.

Rory McCaw (MCSE, MCT, CTT) is an independent certified technical trainer and an accomplished, published author of numerous technical books with more than five years of experience in information technology. Rory's interest in writing led him to courseware development where he has designed courses focused on different Microsoft technologies. Rory holds numerous designations, including MCSE, MCT, and CTT. An accomplished speaker, Rory developed and delivered presentations for Microsoft at COMDEX and designs custom courses to meet the needs of his growing list of corporate clients.

For the last three years, Rory has been providing technical instruction to IT professionals, and consulting for large organizations on enterprise implementations of IIS and active directory. Prior to training, Rory filled the role of systems administrator for an Internet startup after graduating from university with a bachelor's degree in business administration and a major in management information systems.

About LearnKey

LearnKey provides self-paced learning content and multimedia delivery solutions to enhance personal skills and business productivity. LearnKey claims the largest library of rich streaming-media training content that engages learners in dynamic media-rich instruction complete with video clips, audio, full-motion graphics, and animated illustrations. LearnKey can be found on the Web at www.LearnKey.com.

MCSA
MICROSOFT CERTIFIED SYSTEMS ADMINISTRATOR

MCSA Managing a Windows® 2000 Network Environment Study Guide

(Exam 70-218)

Rory McCaw
Alan Simpson

Microsoft is a registered trademark of Microsoft Corporation in the United States and other countries. McGraw-Hill/Osborne is an independent entity from Microsoft Corporation, and not affiliated with Microsoft Corporation in any manner. This publication may be used in assisting students prepare for a Microsoft Certified Professional Exam. Neither Microsoft Corporation nor McGraw-Hill/Osborne warrants that use of this publication will ensure passing the relevant exam.

McGraw-Hill/Osborne

New York Chicago San Francisco
Lisbon London Madrid Mexico City
Milan New Delhi San Juan
Seoul Singapore Sydney Toronto

McGraw-Hill/Osborne
2600 Tenth Street
Berkeley, California 94710
U.S.A.

To arrange bulk purchase discounts for sales promotions, premiums, or fund-raisers, please contact **McGraw-Hill**/Osborne at the above address. For information on translations or book distributors outside the U.S.A., please see the International Contact Information page immediately following the index of this book.

MCSA Managing a Windows® 2000 Network Environment Study Guide (Exam 70-218)

Copyright © 2002 by The McGraw-Hill Companies. All rights reserved. Printed in the United States of America. Except as permitted under the Copyright Act of 1976, no part of this publication may be reproduced or distributed in any form or by any means, or stored in a database or retrieval system, without the prior written permission of the publisher, with the exception that the program listings may be entered, stored, and executed in a computer system, but they may not be reproduced for publication.

1234567890 DOC DOC 01987654321

Book p/n 0-07-222434-7 and CD p/n 0-07-222435-5
parts of ISBN 0-07-222433-9

Publisher Brandon A. Nordin	**Acquisitions Coordinator** Jessica Wilson	**Indexer** Irv Hershman
Vice President & Associate Publisher Scott Rogers	**Technical Editor** Larry Passo	**Computer Designer** Carie Abrew Melinda Moore Lytle
Editorial Director Gareth Hancock	**Copy Editor** Bill McManus	**Illustrator** Michael Mueller, Lyssa Wald
Acquisitions Editor Tim Green	**Proofreaders** Mike McGee Nancy McLaughlin Paul Medoff	**Series Design** Roberta Steele
Project Editor Monika Faltiss		

This book was composed with Corel VENTURA™ Publisher.

Information has been obtained by McGraw-Hill/Osborne from sources believed to be reliable. However, because of the possibility of human or mechanical error by our sources, McGraw-Hill/Osborne, or others, McGraw-Hill/Osborne does not guarantee the accuracy, adequacy, or completeness of any information and is not responsible for any errors or omissions or the results obtained from use of such information.

CONTENTS

Acknowledgments . . . . *xxi*
Preface . . . . *xxiii*
Introduction . . . . *xxvii*

Part I
Configuring, Administering, and Troubleshooting the Network Infrastructure 1

1 Configuring and Troubleshooting TCP/IP 3

Configure TCP/IP on Servers and Clients 4
    Hardware Addresses 4
    IP Addresses 5
    Exercise 1-1: Configuring TCP/IP on Servers 12
    Converting Between Binary and Decimal 15
Determine Valid IP Addresses 17
    Subnetting 17
    Finding Valid IP Addresses 18
    Broadcasting 22
Configure Routing 23
    Building a Windows 2000 Router 27
    How Routing Works 30
    Viewing the Routing Table 30
    Exercise 1-2: Viewing a Computer's Routing Table 34
    Configuring Routing Tables 34
    How Routing Conflicts Are Handled 37
    Managing the Routing Table 38
Troubleshoot TCP/IP and Routing 39
    Troubleshooting with IPCONFIG 39
    Exercise 1-3: Checking an IP Configuration 42
    Troubleshooting with PING 42

		Troubleshooting with ARP	45
		Troubleshooting with Tracert	45
		Exercise 1-4: Tracing a Route	46
		Troubleshooting with PATHPING	48
	✓	Two-Minute Drill	51
	Q&A	Self Test	55
		Lab Question	58
		Self Test Answers	59
		Lab Answer	61

2 Implementing and Troubleshooting Name Resolution ... 63

Understand Name Resolution		64
Name Resolution Resources		65
Exercise 2-1: Check Out Your Computer Name		68
Configure NetBIOS Name Resolution		70
NetBIOS Names		71
NetBIOS Service Identifiers		72
NetBIOS Name Resolution Sequences		74
Creating an LMHOSTS File		74
Exercise 2-2: Peek at Some NetBIOS Names		76
Configure and Implement WINS		78
Installing a WINS Server		79
Configuring WINS Clients		80
Managing a WINS Database		82
Exercise 2-3: Viewing Records in a WINS Database		83
Supporting Non-WINS Clients		90
Setting Up Multiple WINS Servers		93
Troubleshoot NetBIOS Name Resolution		100
Troubleshooting WINS Servers		102
Exercise 2-4: Viewing WINS Server Statistics		102
Troubleshooting WINS Clients		102
✓ Two-Minute Drill		105
Q&A Self Test		108
Lab Question		112
Self Test Answers		113
Lab Answer		115

3 Configuring, Managing, and Troubleshooting DNS 117

Create and Configure DNS Zones 118
    How DNS Works 120
    DNS Zones of Authority 122
    Types of Zones 122
    Exercise 3-1: Installing AD-Integrated DNS 125
    Creating a Forward Lookup Zone 129
    Creating a Reverse Lookup Zone 130

Manage DNS Database Records 132
    Start of Authority (SOA) Record 133
    Name Server (NS) Records 133
    Exercise 3-2: Viewing Resource Records 134
    Host (A) Records 135
    Pointer (PTR) Records 136
    Other Resource Records 136

Configure DNS Server Properties 138
    Configuring DDNS 140
    Exercise 3-3: Configuring Dynamic DNS 141
    Supporting Downlevel Clients 143
    Subdomains and Delegation of Authority 145
    Multihomed DNS Name Servers 146
    Alternative DNS Server Roles 147

Configure Client Computer Name Resolution Properties 153
    Exercise 3-4: Configuring a DNS Client 154

Troubleshoot DNS Name Resolution 159
    Using the NSLOOKUP Command 160
    Exercise 3-5: Testing Forward and Reverse Lookups
        with NSLOOKUP 161
    Troubleshooting DNS with IPCONFIG 161
    Testing the Name Server 163
    Troubleshooting Zone Transfers 164

✓ Two-Minute Drill 166
Q&A Self Test 169
    Lab Question 174
    Self Test Answers 175
    Lab Answer 178

4 Configuring and Troubleshooting DHCP 179

Install and Authorize DHCP Servers 180
    DHCP Leases 181
    Installing DHCP 182
    Authorizing a DHCP Server 183
    Exercise 4-1: Installing and Authorizing the
        DHCP Service 184
Configure DHCP Servers and Scopes 186
    Exclusions 187
    Exercise 4-2: Defining a Scope 187
    DHCP Client Reservations 191
    Server Options vs. Scope Options 193
    DHCP Load Balancing and Redundancy 194
    DHCP-DDNS Integration 199
    Exercise 4-3: Configuring DHCP – DDNS Integration 201
Configure DHCP Clients 202
    Exercise 4-4: Configuring a Client to Use DHCP 203
    Commands for Managing Clients 205
    A Note on APIPA 207
Troubleshoot DHCP 207
    Detecting Rogue Servers 210
    Exercise 4-5: Checking for Rogue DHCP Servers 211
    ✓ Two-Minute Drill 214
  Q&A Self Test 216
    Lab Question 221
    Self Test Answers 223
    Lab Answer 225

Part II
Active Directory and Group Policy 227

5 Configuring and Implementing Active Directory 229

Understand Active Directory Concepts 231
    AD Physical Layout 231

	AD Logical Structure	232
	Organizational Units	237
	The Global Catalog	240
	Exercise 5-1: Enabling Global Catalog	241
Manage Active Directory Groups		243
	Security Group Scopes	244
	Exercise 5-2: Switching to Native Mode	245
	Predefined Groups	247
	Builtin Groups	248
	Nesting Groups	249
	Creating a Security Group	251
Administer AD Computers and Users		253
	Exercise 5-3: Adding a Computer Account	254
	Active Directory User Accounts	257
	Exercise 5-4: Create Two User Accounts	258
	Joining a Computer to the Domain	260
Create and Manage Organizational Units		261
	Creating Organizational Units	262
	Exercise 5-5: Create Some Organizational Units	262
	Creating Objects in an OU	264
	Exercise 5-6: Create a User Account in the Accounting OU	264
	Moving Objects to an OU	264
	Creating Contacts	266
	Finding Existing Objects	266
Delegate Control		268
	Exercise 5-7: Delegating Control to a User	270
	Managing AD Permissions	271
✓	Two-Minute Drill	279
Q&A	Self Test	283
	Lab Question	287
	Self Test Answers	288
	Lab Answer	290

6 Creating and Implementing Group Policies 291

Implement Group Policies 292
    Group Policy Concepts 293
    Viewing/Modifying an Existing GPO 296
    Managing Multiple Policy Links 301
    Exercise 6-1: Changing to Whom a
    Policy Applies (Filtering) 302
Create Group Policy Objects 304
    Software Settings 305
    Windows Settings 305
    Exercise 6-2: Allowing OU Admins to Log on Locally 312
    Administrative Templates 320
    Creating Stand-alone GPOs 322
    Exercise 6-3: Create a Stand-alone GPO 327
Link Group Policies to AD Objects 329
    Exercise 6-4: Linking the Start Menu Icons GPO to
    an OU 331
Filter Group Policies 333
    Exercise 6-5: Filter the Start Menu Icons GPO 336
Delegate Control of Group Policies 337
    Delegating Authority to Manage GPO Links 338
    Delegating Authority to Create GPOs 338
    Exercise 6-6: Delegate Control of the Start Menu
    Icons GPO 340
    Delegating Authority to Edit GPOs 342
    ✓ Two-Minute Drill 344
Q&A Self Test 346
    Lab Question 349
    Self Test Answers 350
    Lab Answer 352

7 Sharing and Publishing Folders and Printers 353

Sharing Folders and Files 355
    Exercise 7-1: Create and Share a Folder 356
    Shared Folder Permissions 357

	Combining Permissions	361
	File and Folder Inheritance	363
	Taking Ownership	364
	Hidden Shares	365
	Offline Files	367
Sharing and Configuring Printers		371
	Exercise 7-2: Sharing a Printer	372
	Setting Shared Printer Permissions	373
	Configuring Printers	373
	Finding Shared Printers in AD Users and Computers	376
Publishing Shared Resources in Active Directory		377
	Publishing Shared Folders	377
	Exercise 7-3: Publishing a Shared Folder	378
	Publishing Shared Printers	379
	Searching for AD Objects	379
✓	Two-Minute Drill	381
Q&A	Self Test	383
	Lab Question	387
	Self Test Answers	388
	Lab Answer	390

8 Managing Software with Group Policy 391

Deploying Applications with Group Policy		392
	Setting Up a Software Distribution Point	393
	Exercise 8-1: Creating a Distribution Point	393
	Creating the GPO	395
	Adding a Package to a Group Policy	398
	Testing the Deployment	402
Managing Software with Group Policy		402
	Upgrading Software	403
	Exercise 8-2: Creating and Filtering a GPO	405
	Redeploying Software	407
	Removing Software	407
Deploying Service Packs with Group Policy		409
	Installing Service Packs on New Computers	409

		Exercise 8-3: Testing Software Deployment	410
		A Note on Deploying Hotfixes	411
	✓	Two-Minute Drill	414
	Q&A	Self Test	416
		Lab Question	420
		Self Test Answers	421
		Lab Answer	423

9 Managing and Troubleshooting Active Directory 425

Managing Active Directory Objects		426
Exercise 9-1: Moving a Computer Object		428
Moving Objects Across Domains		428
Configuring Active Directory Replication		431
Implementing Intersite Active Directory Replication		433
Creating Site Links		434
Bridging Site Links		436
Defining Bridgehead Servers		437
Troubleshooting Active Directory Replication		438
Replication Between Sites Fails		439
Replication Has Slowed Down		439
Minimizing Replication Overhead		440
Checking Replication Topology		440
Exercise 9-2: Checking Replication Topology		441
✓ Two-Minute Drill		443
Q&A Self Test		445
Lab Question		448
Self Test Answers		450
Lab Answer		451

Part III
Creating, Configuring, Managing, Securing, and Troubleshooting File, Print, and Web Resources 453

10 Managing Data Storage 455

Configuring Disks and Volumes 456

Exercise 10-1: Converting a Basic Disk to a
Dynamic Disk 457

NTFS and FAT File Systems 458
Mount Points 458
Configuring and Enforcing Disk Quotas 459
Exercise 10-2: Enabling Disk Quotas 460
Enforcing Quota Limits Through Group Policy 461
Using the Encrypting File System (EFS) 463
Exercise 10-3: Encrypting a Folder 463
Implementing and Managing a Distributed File System (Dfs) 465
Exercise 10-4: Creating a Domain Dfs Root 467
✓ Two-Minute Drill 471
Q&A Self Test 473
Lab Question 477
Self Test Answers 478
Lab Answer 480

11 Configuring Internet Information Services (IIS) 481

Creating Web Sites 482
Defining Virtual Directories (Web Sharing) 483
Exercise 11-1: Creating a Virtual Directory 484
Accessing Local Sites 486
Managing Printers Remotely 487
Creating Virtual Web Servers 487
Tuning Web Site Performance 489
Creating FTP Sites 490
Exercise 11-2: Creating an FTP Site 490
Securing Web and FTP Sites 493
Authentication Methods 493
Controlling Site Access Through Permissions 496
Exercise 11-3: Enabling ISAPI Applications 497
Using Certificate Services and SSL 498
Maintaining and Troubleshooting IIS 499
Back Up and Restore IIS 499
Exercise 11-4: Backing Up Your IIS
Configuration Settings 500
Troubleshooting TCP/IP Filtering Problems 500
Troubleshooting Problems with Proxy Servers 501
✓ Two-Minute Drill 503
Q&A Self Test 505

	Lab Question	510
	Self Test Answers	511
	Lab Answer	513

12 Implementing and Analyzing Security 515

Configuring and Auditing Security	516
Auditing Security	518
Exercise 12-1: Set Up Auditing on Domain Controllers . . .	520
Configuring Event Viewer	523
Reviewing the Security Log	525
Administering Security Templates	525
Using the Security Templates Snap-in	527
Exercise 12-2: Opening the Security Templates Snap-in . . .	528
Creating a New Template	528
Analyzing Security Settings	530
Analyzing the Current Configuration	530
Exercise 12-3: Create a Security Database	533
Command-line Analysis and Configuration	534
✓ Two-Minute Drill	537
Q&A Self Test	539
Lab Question	543
Self Test Answers	544
Lab Answer	546

Part IV
Configuring, Securing, and Troubleshooting Remote Access 547

13 Configuring Remote Access and VPN Connections . . . 549

Configuring Client Computer Remote Access Properties	550
Remote Access Protocols	550
Dial-up Connections	552
Exercise 13-1: Configuring Dial-up Connections on a Remote Access Client	553

Contents **xv**

Exercise 13-2: Configuring a Direct Connection to Another Computer		557
Virtual Private Network Connections		558
Exercise 13-3: Creating a VPN Connection		559
Exercise 13-4: Configuring the VPN Client Settings		563
Configuring Remote Access Name Resolution and IP Address Allocation		571
Configuring IP Address Allocation in Windows 2000		571
Exercise 13-5: Configuring RRAS as a VPN Server		571
Configuring Remote Access Name Resolution		576
Exercise 13-6: Configuring the DHCP Relay Agent		577
Configuring and Troubleshooting Client-to-Server PPTP and L2TP Connections		579
Verifying VPN Connectivity Options		579
No-Answer Errors		581
Not Enough Available Ports		583
Authentication Protocol Problems		583
L2TP Connectivity Errors		586
Managing Existing Server-to-Server PPTP and L2TP Connections		588
Configuring PPTP and L2TP Filtering		588
Exercise 13-7: Configuring PPTP and L2TP Packet Filters		589
Configuring and Verifying the Security of a VPN Connection		594
Available Authentication Methods		594
Exercise 13-8: Configuring Authentication Protocols on RRAS		596
✓ Two-Minute Drill		600
Q&A Self Test		604
Lab Question		608
Self Test Answers		610
Lab Answer		612

14 Troubleshooting Remote Access ... 615

Create and Configurie Remote Access Policies and Profiles	616
Examining the RRAS Authentication Process	616
Creating a Remote Access Policy	626

Exercise 14-1:	Creating a RAS Policy	627
Exercise 14-2:	Configure RAS Policies	630
Select Appropriate Encryption and Authentication Protocols		637
Exercise 14-3:	Configuring Reversible Encryption	640
Diagnose RAS Policy Problems Caused by Nested Groups		642
Troubleshooting RAS Problems Related to Nested Groups		642
RAS Policy Storage		643
Identifying Troubleshooting Clues in the Event Viewer		643
Exercise 14-4:	Identifying RRAS Errors in the System Event Log	643
Diagnose Problems with Remote Access Policy Priority		644
Exercise 14-5:	Configuring the Order of RAS Policies	645
✓ Two-Minute Drill		647
Q&A Self Test		650
Lab Question		654
Self Test Answers		656

15 Implementing Terminal Services for Remote Access ... 661

Configure Terminal Services for Remote Administration or Application Server Mode		663
Installing Terminal Services		663
Exercise 15-1:	Installing Terminal Services	664
Exercise 15-2:	Installing TSAC	666
Exercise 15-3:	Switching Between Terminal Server Modes Using Add/Remove Programs	670
Client Installation Options and Requirements		671
Exercise 15-4:	Creating the Client Installation Disks	673
Exercise 15-5:	Installing the Terminal Services Client over the Network	674
Licensing		675
Establishing a Connection to the Terminal Server		677
Exercise 15-6:	Creating a Terminal Server Session	677
Configure Terminal Services for Local Resource Mapping		678
Clipboard Mapping		679

Contents xvii

      Exercise 15-7: Copying Text from an Application in
          a Terminal Services Session to an Application on the
          Terminal Services Client Computer 679
      Printer Redirection 680
      Exercise 15-8: Configuring Terminal Services Settings on
          a Per-Connection Basis 682
  Configure Terminal Services User Properties 690
    ✓ Two-Minute Drill 696
  Q&A Self Test 698
      Lab Question 702
      Self Test Answers 703

16 Configuring Network Address Translation and Internet Connection Sharing 707

  Configuring Internet Connection Sharing 708
      ICS and IP Address Configuration 711
      Installing ICS 711
      Exercise 16-1: Configuring ICS 711
      Service Publishing 713
      Application Publishing 716
  Troubleshooting Internet Connection Sharing Problems by Using
      the Ipconfig and Ping Commands 718
      Troubleshooting with Ipconfig 719
      Exercise 16-2: Determining a Computer's IP
          Configuration Using Ipconfig 721
      Troubleshooting Using PING 721
  Configuring Routing and Remote Access to Perform NAT 724
      Exercise 16-3: Installing NAT 726
      Configuring NAT Properties 729
      Exercise 16-4: Configuring NAT Interfaces 732
    ✓ Two-Minute Drill 737
  Q&A Self Test 740
      Lab Question 745
      Self Test Answers 746
      Lab Answer 749

Part V
Managing, Securing, and Troubleshooting Servers and Client Computers 751

17 Installing and Configuring Server and Client Hardware 753

Verifying Hardware Compatibility by Using the Qualifier Tools 755
    The Windows 2000 Readiness Analyzer 755
    Device Manager 756
    Exercise 17-1: Opening a Device's Properties Dialog Box in Device Manager 757
    Exercise 17-2: Creating a System Information File 761
Configuring Driver Signing Options 761
    Exercise 17-3: Configuring Driver Signing Options 764
    Exercise 17-4: Configuring Driver Signing Options Through Local Security Policy 765
Verifying Digital Signatures on Existing Driver Files 767
    Exercise 17-5: Using Sigverif.exe 768
    Exercise 17-6: Using SFC to Scan and Repair Protected System Files 770
Configuring Operating System Support for Legacy Hardware Devices ... 771
    Exercise 17-7: Installing a Legacy Device Through the System Properties Dialog Box 772
    ✓ Two-Minute Drill 779
    Q&A Self Test 781
    Lab Question 787
    Self Test Answers 788
    Lab Answer 791

18 Troubleshooting Startup Problems 793

The Hardware Startup Phase 794
The Software Startup Phase 795
Interpreting the Startup Log File 798
    Exercise 18-1: Booting a Computer Running Windows Using the Startup Log File Option 799

Repairing an Operating System by Using Various Startup Options 801
    Safe Mode 801
        Exercise 18-2:   Starting Your Computer in Safe Mode 803
    The Last Known Good Configuration 803
    Directory Services Restore Mode 804
Repairing an Operating System by Using the Recovery Console 807
        Exercise 18-3:   Installing the Recovery Console 807
        Exercise 18-4:   Accessing the Recovery Console from
    the Windows 2000 CD 809
    Recovery Console Commands 810
    Removing the Recovery Console 813
        Exercise 18-5:   Removing the Recovery Console 813
Recovering Data from a Hard Disk in the Event that the Operating
    System Will Not Start 815
    The Windows 2000 Boot Disk 816
        Exercise 18-6:   Creating a Windows 2000 Boot Disk 817
    The Emergency Repair Disk 818
        Exercise 18-7:   Creating an ERD 819
Restoring an Operating System and Data from Backup 821
        Exercise 18-8:   Backing Up Your Computer 822
    Backup Types 823
        Exercise 18-9:   Performing a Restore 825
  ✓   Two-Minute Drill 827
Q&A   Self Test 830
    Lab Question 834
    Self Test Answers 836
    Lab Answer 838

19 Monitoring and Troubleshooting Server Health and Performance 841

Monitoring and Interpreting Real-Time Performance by Using System
    Monitor and Task Manager 842
    Windows Task Manager 842
    System Monitor 846
        Exercise 19-1:   Using System Monitor to View
    Real-Time System Information 847
    Enabling Network Segment Monitors 850

Configuring System Monitor Alerts and Logging 851
    Counter Logs 851
        Exercise 19-2: Creating a Counter Log 852
        Exercise 19-3: Opening a Log with System Monitor 855
    Trace Logs 857
        Exercise 19-4: Creating a Trace Log 858
    Configuring Alerts 860
        Exercise 19-5: Configuring Alerts 861
Diagnosing Server Health Problems with Event Viewer 868
        Exercise 19-6: Examining Event Viewer Events 869
Identifying and Disabling Unnecessary Services 872
        Exercise 19-7: Disabling Services 876
    ✓   Two-Minute Drill 877
  Q&A Self Test 879
        Lab Question 883
        Self Test Answers 884
        Lab Answer 886

Appendix 889

    System Requirements 890
LearnKey Online Training 890
Installing and Running MasterExam and MasterSim 890
    MasterExam 891
    MasterSim 891
Electronic Book 891
CertCam 891
Help 892
Removing Installation(s) 892
Technical Support 892
LearnKey Technical Support 892

Index 893

ACKNOWLEDGEMENTS

We would like to thank the following people:

Every book is a team project, and this one is no exception. We'd like to give credit where credit is due, and thank the many people involved in turning this book from an idea to the finished product you now hold in your hands.

- At Osborne/McGraw Hill, many thanks to Tim Green, Jessica Wilson, Gareth Hancock, and those "behind the scenes" for their patience and support, and for giving us this opportunity.
- Many thanks to Matt Wagner, and everyone one at Waterside Productions, for bringing this opportunity to us.

To Susan, Ashley, and Alec, as always.

—Alan Simpson

PREFACE

This book's primary objective is to help you prepare for and pass the required core MCSA exam (70-218) so you can begin to reap the career benefits of certification. We believe that the only way we can accomplish this is to help you increase your knowledge and build your skills. After completing this book, you should feel confident that you have thoroughly reviewed all of the objectives that Microsoft has established for the exam.

In This Book

This book is organized in such a way as to serve as an in-depth review for the Microsoft Managing a Windows 2000 Network Environment exam for both experienced Windows NT and Windows 2000 professionals and newcomers to Microsoft networking technologies. Each chapter covers a major aspect of the exam, with an emphasis on the "why" as well as the "how to" of working with and supporting Windows 2000 as a network administrator or engineer.

In Every Chapter

We've created a set of chapter components that call your attention to important items, reinforce important points, and provide helpful exam-taking hints. Take a look at what you'll find in every chapter:

- **Certification Objectives** begin every chapter and tell you what you need to know to pass the section on the exam dealing with the chapter topic. The Objective headings identify the objectives within the chapter, so you'll always know an objective when you see it!

- **Exam Watch** notes call attention to information about, and potential pitfalls in, the exam. These helpful hints are written by authors who have taken the exams and achieved certification. Who better to tell you what to worry about? They know what you're about to go through!

- **Practice Exercises** are interspersed throughout the chapters. These are step-by-step exercises that allow you to get the hands-on experience you need to pass the exams. They help you master skills that are likely to be an area of focus on the exam. Don't just read through the exercises; they are hands-on practice that you should be comfortable completing. Learning by doing is an effective way to increase your competency with a product. The practical exercises will be very helpful for any simulation exercises you may encounter on the exam.

- **On the Job** notes describe the issues that come up most often in real-world settings. They provide a valuable perspective on certification- and product-related topics. They point out common mistakes and address questions that have arisen from on-the-job discussions and experience.

- **From the Classroom** sidebars describe the issues that come up most often in the training classroom setting. These sidebars highlight some of the most common and confusing problems that students encounter when taking a live Windows 2000 training course. You can get a leg up on those difficult-to-understand subjects by focusing extra attention on these sidebars.

- The **Certification Summary** is a succinct review of the chapter and a restatement of salient points regarding the exam.

- The **Two-Minute Drill** at the end of every chapter is a checklist of the main points of the chapter. It can be used for last-minute review.

- **Scenario and Solutions** sections lay out potential problems and solutions in a quick-to-read format:

SCENARIO & SOLUTION

I changed my default gateway address, and adjusted the 003 Routers option at the DHCP server to match that change. How do I get clients to use the new setting?	You'll either need to reboot the clients, or enter an **ipconfig /renew** command at each client to get the new default gateway address to the client.
How can I see which addresses are currently leased, and how many are still available?	In the DHCP console, right-click the server name or the name of a specific scope and choose Display Statistics.

- The **Self Test** offers questions similar to those found on the certification exams. The answers to these questions, as well as explanations of the answers, can be found at the end of each chapter. By taking the Self Test after completing each chapter, you'll reinforce what you've learned from that chapter while becoming familiar with the structure of the exam questions.

- The **Lab Question** at the end of the Self Test section offers a unique and challenging question format that requires the reader to understand multiple chapter concepts to answer correctly. These questions are more complex and more comprehensive than the other questions, as they test your ability to take all the knowledge you have gained from reading the chapter and apply it to complicated, real-world situations. These questions are aimed to be more difficult than what you will find on the exam. If you can answer these questions, you have proven that you know the subject!

On the CD-ROM

This book includes a CD-ROM with simulation assessment and training software. Be sure to look through the software—there is more than one hour of interactive instructional video training, hundreds of practice test questions found only using the CD-ROM, and CertCam audio-visual demonstrations of many of the exercises from the book. The CD-ROM with this book also contains a bonus Chapter 20, "Installing and Managing Service Packs and Hotfixes," and the Glossary for the book. These features can only be accessed through the CD-ROM. For more information about the CD-ROM, please see Appendix A.

Some Pointers

Once you've finished reading this book, set aside some time to do a thorough review. You might want to return to the book several times and make use of all the methods it offers for reviewing the material:

1. Reread all the Two-Minute Drills, or have someone quiz you. You also can use the drills as a way to do a quick cram before the exam. You might want to make some flash cards out of 3×5 index cards that have the Two-Minute Drill material on them.

2. Reread all the Exam Watch notes. Remember that these notes are written by authors who have taken the exam and passed. They know what you should expect—and what you should be on the lookout for.

3. Review all the S&S sections for quick problem solving.

4. Retake the Self Tests. Taking the tests right after you've read the chapter is a good idea, because the questions help reinforce what you've just learned. However, it's an even better idea to go back later and do all the questions in the book in one sitting. Pretend that you're taking the live exam. (When you go through the questions the first time, you should mark your answers on a separate piece of paper. That way, you can run through the questions as many times as you need to until you feel comfortable with the material.)

5. *Complete the Exercises.* Did you do the exercises when you read through each chapter? If not, do them! These exercises are designed to cover exam topics, and there's no better way to get to know this material than by practicing. Be sure you understand why you are performing each step in each exercise. If there is something you are not clear on, reread that section in the chapter.

INTRODUCTION

Welcome to *MCSA Managing a Windows® 2000 Network Environment Study Guide (Exam 70-218)*. The purpose of this book is to provide you with the skills and knowledge required to get a great score on Microsoft's Exam 70-218: *Managing a Microsoft® Windows® 2000 Network Environment*. The information is presented in an organized, "from the bottom up" manner, explaining important basic concepts and terms before moving on to more complex issues. Such an approach helps to avoid the confusion that results from being thrown a bunch of seemingly disconnected technical facts, and helps you better see the "big picture." And understanding the big picture is an important part of passing Exam 70-218.

Why MCSA?

The Microsoft Certified Systems Administrator (MCSA) credential is the latest addition to Microsoft's list of certification options. It's also the most controversial, and has caused quite a bit of confusion among individuals who are already certified, as well as those seeking certification. For those of you who are new to the certification game, let me explain.

Microsoft has offered the Microsoft Certified Systems Engineer (MCSE) credential for several years. That credential is largely about networking with Microsoft products. It's a grueling course of study, and candidates must pass seven rigorous exams to achieve certification. MCSA is also about networking with Microsoft products. However, candidates need only pass four (or perhaps fewer) equally rigorous exams to become certified.

Many existing MCSEs are concerned that candidates with the MCSA credential will be competing for their jobs, and will be willing to accept less pay. However, it's important to bear in mind that the two credentials actually reflect two different types of jobs within an IT organization. Whereas the MCSE credential qualifies its holder to design new networks from the ground up, the MCSA is all about managing existing Windows 2000 and .NET server networks.

According to Microsoft, its recent research has shown that there's a "demand gap" in organizations between the number of Microsoft Windows 2000 system administrators needed and the number of skilled individuals available to do the job. The MCSA certification covers the job skills defined by the National Workforce Center for Emerging Technologies (NWCET) for the positions of network administrator, network technician, technical support specialist, systems administrator, information systems administrator, network engineer, and IT engineer. The MCSA credential was developed to help close the gap between the number of people needed to fulfill those jobs and the number of people currently available to do so. Microsoft claims that it is committed to informing hiring managers of the differences between MCSE and MCSA, so that those managers can better determine which individuals are best suited to specific jobs within the organization.

Who Qualifies for MCSA?

Microsoft suggests that an MCSA candidate should have 6 to 12 months of experience implementing and administering a desktop operating system and network operating system, and managing clients and servers in networking environments that have most of the following characteristics and requirements:

- From 200 to 26,000 supported users
- From 2 to 100 distinct physical locations
- Typical networking services and resources, including messaging, file and print sharing, database access, proxy servers or firewalls, client computer management, and remote access
- Connectivity that includes intranets, such as connecting branch offices to a corporate network, as well as connecting corporate networks to the Internet

Of course, the experience part always presents something of a catch-22. If you can't get the credential without the job experience, and can't get the job experience without the credential, how are you going to get either one? Fortunately, one can acquire an MCSA credential without on-the-job experience. That's not to say that the exams are easy. In fact, the MCSA exams are as rigorous as the MCSE exams. But the student need only pass four exams for the MCSA, as opposed to seven for the MCSE.

The exams that the candidate must pass to qualify for the MCSA cover skills and concepts that can be learned by study, coupled with some hands-on experience with actual hardware. But that hardware need not be part of a production network in a large corporate environment. A small personal or classroom network can provide sufficient practice to pass all four exams. This allows younger students, and those with existing jobs outside of IT, the opportunity to get certified and accepted for a job within the IT industry.

MCSE vs. MCSA

Candidates seeking certification in Microsoft networking can achieve the MCSA first, and apply credits earned during that course of study to acquiring the more advanced MCSE credential. There are some advantages to going for the MCSA first:

- MCSA is more readily attainable, because the certification can be achieved with as few as four exams, as opposed to the seven exams required for MCSE.

- MCSA focuses on the modern Internet TCP/IP networking standards used in Windows 2000 and the .NET server products. Legacy systems, such as NetBIOS found in Windows NT, are de-emphasized in the MCSA track. So with MCSA, you'll be learning about technologies that have a long future ahead of them.

- The MCSA credential shows potential employers that you have sufficient knowledge to administer existing Windows 2000 and .NET TCP/IP networks, which in turn opens the door to getting a job and the additional experience needed to get the more advanced MCSE certification.

So in the long run, the MCSA credential is good for employers and employees alike. If you're new to the IT field, the MCSA is a great first step for a new career.

MCSA Requirements

Achieving the MCSA credential is no small feat. You must pass one Client Operating System exam, and two Network System Exams, as summarized in the following table.

Exam	Alternative
Client Operating System Exams (one required)	
Exam 70-210: Installing, Configuring, and Administering Microsoft Windows 2000 Professional or Exam 70-270: Installing, Configuring, and Administering Microsoft Windows XP Professional	As an alternative to exams 70-210 and 70-215, candidates who have passed Windows NT 4.0 Exams 70-067, 70-068, and 70-073 have the option to take Exam 70-240: Microsoft Windows 2000 Accelerated Exam for MCPs Certified on Microsoft Windows NT 4.0.
Network System Exams (two required)	
Exam 70-215: Installing, Configuring, and Administering Microsoft Windows 2000 Server or Exam 70-275: Installing, Configuring, and Administering Microsoft Windows .NET Server	Exam 70-240 as described earlier
Exam 70-218: Managing a Microsoft Windows 2000 Network Environment (available January 2002) or Exam 70-278: Managing a Microsoft Windows .NET Server Network Environment	None

In addition to the core exams, you must pass one of the following elective exams:

- Exam 70-028: Administering Microsoft SQL Server 7.0
- Exam 70-081: Implementing and Supporting Microsoft Exchange Server 5.5
- Exam 70-086: Implementing and Supporting Microsoft Systems Management Server 2.0
- Exam 70-088: Implementing and Supporting Microsoft Proxy Server 2.0

- Exam 70-216: Implementing and Administering a Microsoft Windows 2000 Network Infrastructure
- Exam 70-240: Microsoft Windows 2000 Accelerated Exam for MCPs Certified on Microsoft Windows NT 4.0
- Exam 70-224: Installing, Configuring, and Administering Microsoft Exchange 2000 Server
- Exam 70-227: Installing, Configuring, and Administering Microsoft Internet Security and Acceleration (ISA) Server 2000, Enterprise Edition
- Exam 70-228: Installing, Configuring, and Administering Microsoft SQL Server 2000 Enterprise Edition
- Exam 70-244: Supporting and Maintaining a Microsoft Windows NT Server 4.0 Network
- CompTIA A+ and CompTIA Network+ or CompTIA A+ and CompTIA Server+

The table lists the requirements at the time of this writing. Requirements and exam availability change from time to time—get in the habit of checking www.microsoft.com/ periodically so that you are aware of any program changes that might occur.

As you can see from the core exams and electives, certain candidates can use existing credentials as proven competence within an area of expertise. For example, MCPs who passed Exam 70-240: *Microsoft Windows 2000 Accelerated Exam for MCPs* before January 1, 2002 can use that credential as an alternative to taking the core exams 70-210 and 70-215 for MCSA, the reason being that accelerated exam 70-240 covers the most important elements of exams 70-210, 70-215, 70-216, and 70-217. Therefore, passing exam 70-240 shows that the candidate already possesses the skills needed to pass exams 70-210 and 70-215.

MCSEs who wish to acquire an MCSA credential might need to take only Exam 70-218: *Managing a Microsoft Windows 2000 Network Environment* to earn the MCSA certification, depending on which electives they passed to achieve MCSE status.

Professionals who have already attained CompTIA's A+, Server+, or Network+ certification will have a leg up on attaining their MCSA certification. A+ certification coupled with either the Server+ or Network+ certification can be used as an elective for the MCSA track, thereby reducing the number of Microsoft exams required to pass to three.

Professionals who currently hold non-Microsoft vendor-specific certifications aren't quite so lucky. As a rule, vendor-specific certifications such as Cisco's CCNA cannot be used as electives for the MCSA exam.

Exam Credit

When you pass Exam 70-218, you immediately achieve the status of Microsoft Certified Professional (MCP), and earn credit toward two other certifications:

- **Core credit** toward MCSA (Microsoft Certified System Administrator on Microsoft Windows 2000) certification
- **Elective credit** toward MCSE (Microsoft Certified Systems Engineer on Microsoft Windows 2000) certification

Skills Being Measured

Exam 70-218 is very broad in depth, measuring your ability to administer, support, and troubleshoot large-scale information systems that incorporate Microsoft Windows 2000. You can view the complete set of skills being measured at the MCSA web site at www.microsoft.com/traincert/mcp/mcsa/requirements.asp. According to Microsoft, the following is a quick summary of what you'll be faced with on the exam.

Configuring, Administering, and Troubleshooting the Network Infrastructure

- Configure and troubleshoot TCP/IP on servers and client computers including subnet masks, default gateways, network IDs, and broadcast addresses
- Configure client computer TCP/IP properties
- Troubleshoot routing and network connectivity using the **ipconfig**, **route**, **pathping**, and other commands

Managing Name Resolution on Client Computers

- Identify name resolution resources including DNS, WINS, NetBIOS, the HOSTS file, and the LMHOSTS file
- Configure client computer name resolution properties
- Troubleshoot name resolution problems using **nbtstat**, **ipconfig**, **nslookup**, and other commands

Configuring, Administering, and Troubleshooting DNS

- Install DNS and create DNS zones
- Configure Active Directory-integrated DNS zones
- Manage DNS database records including A, PTR, and CNAME records
- Configure dynamic DNS (DDNS) to automatically add new servers and clients to the DNS namespace
- Configure client computers to use DNS

Configuring, Administering, and Troubleshooting DHCP

- Install and authorize DHCP servers
- Configure DHCP server scopes
- Configure client computers to use dynamic IP addressing
- Detect unauthorized DHCP servers on a network

Configuring, Managing, and Securing Active Directory

- Create, manage, and troubleshoot Active Directory groups; considerations include nesting, scope, and type
- Create and manage user accounts in Active Directory Users and Computers
- Create and manage organizational units (OUs)
- Use the Delegation of Control Wizard to delegate tasks to OU administrators

Creating, Implementing, and Troubleshooting Group Policies

- Create and manage group policies at the domain, OU, and group levels
- Implement and manage security policies by using group policy
- Troubleshoot group policy problems involving precedence, inheritance, filtering, and the **No Override** option

Publishing Resources in Active Directory

- Configure a printer object
- Publish and assign network resources
- Deploy user applications, antivirus software, line-of-business applications, and software updates using group policy
- Configure and troubleshoot object permissions by using object access control lists (ACLs)
- Share folders and enable Web sharing
- Search for resources in Active Directory

Implementing Security Policies

- Create domain security policy to comply with corporate standards
- Use security templates to implement security policies
- Analyze the security configuration of a computer using Security Configuration and Analysis and the **secedit** command

Troubleshooting Active Directory

- Diagnose Active Directory replication problems and problems related to WAN links
- Recover lost user accounts
- Manually refresh group policy

Managing Data Storage

- Implement NTFS and FAT file systems
- Configure quotas
- Implement and configure Encrypting File System (EFS)
- Manage a domain-based Distributed File System (DFS)
- Manage file and folder compression
- Configure volumes and dynamic disks
- Configure file and folder permissions

Configuring and Troubleshooting Internet Information Services (IIS)

- Configure virtual directories and virtual servers
- Configure web sites and FTP services
- Troubleshoot Internet and intranet browsing from client computers
- Configure authentication and SSL for web sites
- Configure FTP services
- Configure access permissions for intranet web servers

Monitoring and Managing Network Security

- Audit and detect security breaches
- Configure user-account lockout settings
- Configure user-account password length, history, age, and complexity
- Configure group policy to run logon scripts
- Link Group Policy Objects
- Enable and configure auditing
- Monitor security using the system security log file

Configuring and Troubleshooting Remote Access and VPN

- Configure and verify the security of a VPN connection
- Configure client computer remote access properties
- Select appropriate encryption and authentication protocols
- Configure remote access name resolution and IP address allocation
- Configure and troubleshoot client-to-server PPTP and L2TP connections
- Manage existing server-to-server PPTP and L2TP connections
- Configuring Remote Access Policies and Profiles
- Troubleshoot Remote Access Policy Priority

Implementing Terminal Services for Remote Access

- Configure Terminal Services for Remote Administration
- Configure Terminal Services for Local Resource Mapping
- Configure Terminal Services User Properties

Configuring Network Address Translation (NAT) and Internet Connection Sharing

- Configure Internet Connection Sharing
- Troubleshoot Internet Connection Sharing
- Configure Routing and Remote Access to Perform NAT

Installing and Configuring Server and Client Hardware

- Verify hardware compatibility by using the qualifier tools
- Configure driver signing options
- Verify digital signatures on existing driver files
- Configure operating system support for legacy hardware devices

Troubleshooting Server and Client Startup Problems

- Use the startup log file to diagnose startup problems
- Repair an operating system by using Recovery Console and other tools
- Use Safe Mode and parallel installations
- Recover data from a hard disk in the event that the operating system will not start
- Restore an operating system and data from a backup

Monitoring and Troubleshooting Server Health and Performance

- Monitor and interpret real-time performance by using System Monitor and Task Manager
- Configure and manage System Monitor alerts and logging
- Diagnose server health problems by using Event Viewer
- Identify and disable unnecessary operating system services

Installing and Managing Service Packs, Hotfixes, and Security Hotfixes

- Use slipstreaming to update an installation source
- Apply and reapply service packs and hotfixes
- Verify service pack and hotfix installations
- Remove service packs and hotfixes

It's a lot to know, and a lot to learn. But learning the concepts involved in an organized, step-by-step manner, and getting some hands-on experience along the way, will greatly improve your chances of passing this broad and challenging exam.

Computer Adaptive Testing

Exam 70-218 is a computer adaptive test (CAT), whereby easy-to-moderate questions are presented first. If you answer the questions correctly, you're presented with questions of increasing difficulty. If you answer incorrectly, subsequent questions are easier. The CAT algorithm can then assess your chances of passing the exam early on, and give you a pass-fail score fairly quickly. The CAT approach saves your time and makes better use of test center resources. This approach also brings some security to the exam, because no single examinee sees the entire pool of questions from which the exam is drawn.

There's one major difference between traditional exam formats and CAT, of which you need to be aware. You cannot skip questions, or return to previous questions to change your answer. Be sure to study each question in depth as it's presented to you. And I do mean study each question, as you're likely to miss some important factors if you read through the question too quickly. Don't assume that the question is about a particular concept. For example, take a look at this hypothetical question:

You are a domain administrator for your company's Active Directory-integrated zone. You've configured a DHCP server, and configured clients to use dynamic addressing. You start a client and… (*some problem arises*).

Don't assume that a question like this is an Active Directory question or DHCP question. It could well be a DNS question, or even a question checking to see if you understand all the rights, and limitations, of the Domain Admins security group. As in real life, you need to take all factors into consideration before trying to solve a problem.

Performance-Based vs. Knowledge-Based Questions

The exam questions fall into two broad categories, knowledge-based and performance-based. Knowledge-based questions are designed to test your knowledge of specific facts. Performance-based questions are designed to measure your ability to perform on the job by presenting examples of situations and scenarios that an administrator might encounter in the real world.

Finally, be aware that your exam may consist of several different types of items, as summarized here:

- **Free Response items**   Traditional multiple-choice items, designed to test your basic knowledge of facts.
- **Select-and-Place items**   Designed to test your ability to synthesize information and assemble a solution to a problem graphically.

- **Case Study-based items**   Designed to simulate what administrators actually do on the job, these questions test your ability to analyze information and make decisions.
- **Simulation items**   Presents a scenario of dialog boxes and error messages, to test your ability to follow through on a procedure.

You can, and should, get some practice with different types of questions prior to taking the exam. Sample questions are available for download from the Exam and Testing Procedures web page at www.microsoft.com/traincert/mcpexams/faq/procedures.asp.

Study Strategies

Exam 70-218 will test your overall understanding of Windows 2000 networking, not just your ability to memorize facts. So you should use all the options available to you in preparation for your exam. Read the chapters in this book in the order they're presented. Doing so will allow you to start with the basics and work your way up to more complex concepts. It will also help you to keep the information organized "in your head," which further helps you remember the facts.

Review the two-minute drill at the end of each chapter, to reinforce the most important information presented in the chapter. And do take the practice test at the end of each chapter. The questions on the practice tests are very representative of the types of questions you'll encounter on the exam. Use your performance on the practice test to measure your understanding of the content, and identify weak points where some additional study might be required.

Experience is always the best teacher, and actually performing some task will greatly enhance your memory of how it works. The Exercises in this book are designed to be performed on a "minimal" network consisting of a Windows 2000 Server computer and a Windows 2000 Professional computer. While this is a far cry from a real-world corporate network, the techniques you use on even a tiny network are the same as the ones you'd use on an enormous network. So you should try to complete all exercises presented in the chapter.

Signing Up

When you feel you're ready to take the exam, signing up is easy. Call any Sylvan Prometrics or VUE center in your area to register. Optionally, you can go to the Register for an Exam web page at www.microsoft.com/traincert/mcpexams/register for an overview of the registration process and locations of testing centers near you.

I'd say "best of luck" to you on passing Exam 70-218, but unfortunately luck has nothing to do with it. The exam will test your overall knowledge of managing a Windows 2000 network. And there's no substitute for knowing your stuff before you sit for the exam. Let's get started.

Part I

MCSA — MICROSOFT CERTIFIED SYSTEMS ADMINISTRATOR

Configuring, Administering, and Troubleshooting the Network Infrastructure

CHAPTERS

1. Configuring and Troubleshooting TCP/IP
2. Implementing and Troubleshooting Name Resolution
3. Configuring, Managing, and Troubleshooting DNS
4. Configuring and Troubleshooting DHCP

MCSA
MICROSOFT CERTIFIED SYSTEMS ADMINISTRATOR

1

Configuring and Troubleshooting TCP/IP

CERTIFICATION OBJECTIVES

1.01	Configure TCP/IP on Servers and Clients
1.02	Determine Valid IP Addresses
1.03	Configure Routing
1.04	Troubleshoot TCP/IP and Routing
✓	Two-Minute Drill
Q&A	Self Test

The goal of Exam 70-218 is to test your ability to implement, manage, and troubleshoot an existing Windows 2000 network environment. It's a very broad exam, covering skills and concepts "from the ground up," so to speak. As such, it helps to understand how certain features are dependent on other features working properly. For example, a successful deployment of an application across multiple computers requires that Active Directory be working properly. A successful Active Directory implementation, in turn, requires a successful DNS installation. And DNS is part of a valid, working network infrastructure.

In this book, we'll take it from the ground up, starting with basic TCP/IP addressing in this chapter. We'll look at the "rhyme and reason" behind TCP/IP, as well as specific techniques for setting up, maintaining, and troubleshooting TCP/IP networks. As with all chapters in this book, we'll focus on the skills and concepts you're most likely to need to succeed on exam 70-218.

CERTIFICATION OBJECTIVE 1.01

Configure TCP/IP on Servers and Clients

TCP/IP (Transmission Control Protocol/Internet Protocol) is a set of protocols that enable computers to communicate with one another. It has been in use for over 20 years, and is the set of protocols used by the Internet, as well as countless smaller networks.

The protocols were developed by the Internet Engineering Task Force (IETF) using a system based on Requests for Comments (RFCs). The RFC system allows engineers to post technical papers describing new technologies to an electronic bulletin board for review and comments by peers. Today, there are over 3,000 RFCs published on IETF's web site at www.ietf.org.

A TCP/IP network is composed of *hosts*. A host, in turn, is any device or service that's connected to the network. The hosts use a couple of different addresses to identify and communicate with one another, a *hardware address* and an *IP address*.

Hardware Addresses

To connect to a network, a host must have a network interface card (NIC) installed. Every NIC that's manufactured is given a unique 48-bit hardware address. The hardware address is literally "burned into" the card during the manufacturing process, and as a rule cannot be changed by the user. (Actually, some devices do

Configure TCP/IP on Servers and Clients

allow you to change a card's hardware address, though it's unlikely you'd ever want to do this.)

exam
⍙atch

The terms "Ethernet board" and "Ethernet card" are often used as synonyms for "network interface card."

Before we go any further, I need to point out that the term "hardware address" could probably win some kind of award for having the most synonyms on the planet. While I'll stick to the term "hardware address" in this book, you may come across any of the following terms used as a synonym:

- Media Access Control (MAC) address
- Physical address
- Ethernet address
- Token Ring address
- NIC address

As mentioned, the hardware address is a 48-bit number, something along the lines of 000000001000000010101101011110111110000010110111, although it's far more common to see it expressed as six hexadecimal numbers separated by hyphens or periods, as in 00-80-AD-7B-E0-B7 or 00.80.AD.7B.E0.B7. You can view a machine's hardware address by entering the **ipconfig /all** command at a command prompt. (To get to the command prompt in Windows 2000, click the Start button and choose Programs | Accessories | Command Prompt.) The hardware address is next to Physical Address in the display, as in the example shown in Figure 1-1. (To close the Command Prompt window, type **exit** and press ENTER.)

IP Addresses

In addition to the hardware address that's physically burned into each NIC, each host on a TCP/IP network also has an *IP address* (sometimes called an *Internet address*). Unlike the hardware address, the IP address is a *logical address* that's assigned by a network administrator, or by DHCP (Dynamic Host Configuration Protocol), which can automatically assign an IP address when the host first connects to the network. We'll get into DHCP in detail in Chapter 4. For now, it's sufficient to keep in mind that the IP address is flexible in that it can be assigned or changed at any time.

FIGURE 1-1 The hardware address is listed as Physical Address in an **ipconfig /all** command's output.

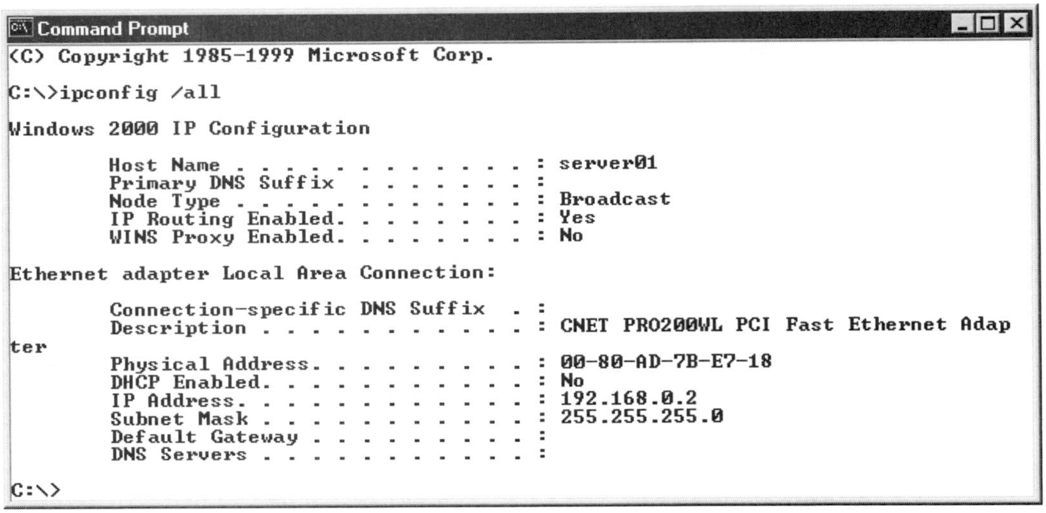

```
Command Prompt
(C) Copyright 1985-1999 Microsoft Corp.

C:\>ipconfig /all

Windows 2000 IP Configuration

        Host Name . . . . . . . . . . . . : server01
        Primary DNS Suffix  . . . . . . . :
        Node Type . . . . . . . . . . . . : Broadcast
        IP Routing Enabled. . . . . . . . : Yes
        WINS Proxy Enabled. . . . . . . . : No

Ethernet adapter Local Area Connection:

        Connection-specific DNS Suffix  . :
        Description . . . . . . . . . . . : CNET PRO200WL PCI Fast Ethernet Adap
ter
        Physical Address. . . . . . . . . : 00-80-AD-7B-E7-18
        DHCP Enabled. . . . . . . . . . . : No
        IP Address. . . . . . . . . . . . : 192.168.0.2
        Subnet Mask . . . . . . . . . . . : 255.255.255.0
        Default Gateway . . . . . . . . . :
        DNS Servers . . . . . . . . . . . :

C:\>
```

Each TCP/IP address is a 32-bit number, as in 11111111111111111010011 0111001110. You'll rarely see a TCP/IP address expressed in that binary notation. Instead, you'll see them expressed in *dotted quad* format (also called *dotted decimal notation*), where the address is divided into four *octets*. Each octet represents 8 bits of the address, and is expressed as a decimal number in the range of 0 to 255. Dots are used to separate the octets, as in the example 192.168.1.1.

Subnet Masks

Every host that has an IP address also has a subnet mask. The name "subnet mask" is a good one, because it "masks" the portion of the IP address that identifies the network to which a host belongs. Like IP addresses, a subnet mask is a 32-bit number. A series of 1's are used to identify the network portion of the address. The 0's are used to represent the host portion of the address. For example, Figure 1-2 shows an IP address expressed in binary format (1's and 0's). Beneath that is a subnet mask, also expressed in binary. The 1's "mask off" those digits in the IP address that identify the network as a whole. The 0's represent the portion of the address that identifies the host.

It's customary to display the subnet mask in dotted quad format, just as we usually do with IP addresses. The binary octet 11111111, when converted to

FIGURE 1-2 An IP address and subnet mask in binary format, where 1's "mask" the portion of the address that identifies the network

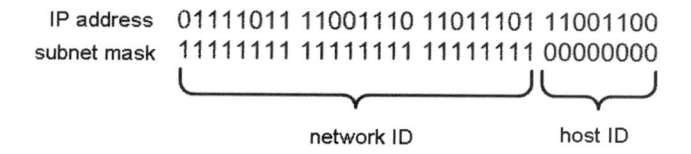

```
IP address   01111011 11001110 11011101 11001100
subnet mask  11111111 11111111 11111111 00000000
             _____/ _____/
                      network ID           host ID
```

decimal, is 255. The binary octet 00000000 is, of course, just 0 in decimal. Thus, we can display an IP address/subnet mask pair in the following more "human readable" format:

192.168.221.204

255.255.255.0

In English, we can say the preceding IP address/subnet mask combination identifies "host number 204 on network number 192.168.221." However, it would be more correct to say that it identifies host number 204 on the network 192.168.221.0 because host number 0 on a network isn't really a host at all. Rather, a 0 in the host portion of the address is the address of the network as a whole.

Here's another way to view it. Think of the network ID as the area code, and the host ID as the specific phone number. But, unlike telephone numbers, where all area codes are three digits, the number of digits used for the area code can vary. The subnet mask "masks" the bits that represent the area code (network ID). The unmasked bits are the telephone number (host ID).

Getting IP Addresses

Just as a person's Social Security Number uniquely identifies them among all the millions of U.S. citizens, an IP address uniquely identifies each host on the Internet. Which perhaps brings up the question, "With millions of IP addresses already taken, how do I know what IP addresses I can use for my network?" The answer to that question is a resounding "It depends." Every single computer that can *access* the Internet doesn't necessarily have its own unique IP address. However, the hosts that *serve* the Internet—that is, the hosts that can be reached from other computers on the Internet—all do have unique IP addresses. Each of those servers also has a unique *fully qualified domain name (FQDN)*. For example, the FQDN www.microsoft.com uniquely identifies the web site host, www, on the unique domain name microsoft.com.

> ### FROM THE CLASSROOM
>
> #### Who Controls IP Addresses?
>
> When reading about the various agencies involved in doling out globally unique IP addresses and domain names, you'll probably come across many agency names and acronyms including the Internet Corporation for Assigned Names and Numbers (ICANN), the Internet Assigned Numbers Authority (IANA), the American Registry for Internet Numbers (ARIN), Asia Pacific Network Information Center (APNIC), European IP Networks (RIPE), InterNIC, and others. To avoid confusing matters, I'll generally refer to ICANN as "the" organization in charge of allocating IP addresses, simply because they're at the top of the heap, so to speak. If you're interested in learning more about how it all works and the organizations involved, you can start by visiting ICANN's web site at www.icann.org. The first step involves finding and registering a unique domain name through an InterNIC accredited registrar. You can find a list of those at www.internic.net/regist.html.
>
> —*Alan Simpson, MA, MCSA*

Class A, B and C Addresses

There was a time when IP addresses were assigned to organizations based on their size—or roughly the number of computers that would be connected to the network. The largest organizations, such as IBM, General Electric, MIT, and Xerox, were assigned Class A addresses. Slightly smaller organizations received Class B addresses, and the smallest organizations got Class C addresses. Class A IP addresses all start with the number in the range of 1 to 126 and, by default, have a subnet mask of 255.0.0.0. Class B addresses have starting numbers in the range of 128 to 191, and use a standard subnet mask of 255.255.0.0. Class C network addresses all start with a number between 192 and 223, and have a default subnet mask of 255.255.255.0.

Some ranges of IP addresses, such as those starting with 127 and those starting with 224 through 255, aren't classified as A, B, or C. These addresses are reserved as follows:

- 127.*x.y.z* (reserved *loopback* address)
- 224.*x.y.z* through 239.*x.y.z* (Class D reserved *multicast* addresses)
- 240.*x.y.z* through 254.*x.y.z* (Class E reserved experimental addresses)

There are also ranges of *private* IP addresses, which can assigned to hosts that are clients to, but not servers on, the Web, as listed here:

- 10.0.0.0 through 10.255.255.255 (subnet mask 255.0.0.0)
- 172.16.0.0 through 172.31.255.255 (subnet mask 255.255.0.0)
- 192.168.0.0 through 192.168.255.255 (subnet mask 255.255.255.0)

> **exam** ⓦatch
>
> **While the private IP addresses can't be used for servers on the Internet, they can access the Internet through a proxy server or Network Address Translation (NAT).**

Table 1-1 summarizes what you've just learned about the *classed* (also called *classful*) IP addresses. Each class is defined by a certain range of IP addresses. Each class also has "set aside" some private addresses that can be used on a local network without approval from a governing body that assigns globally unique IP addresses.

Recall that the subnet mask identifies which portion of an IP address represents the address of the network as a whole versus the address of an individual host. In a subnet mask, each 255 value indicates 8 bits. The more bits there are in the host portion of the IP addresses, the more unique hosts you can identify on that network. Table 1-2 illustrates this by comparing Class A, B, and C networks. As you increase the number of bits used to identify the network, you increase the number of networks you can have within the class. But, at the same time, since you're taking away bits for identifying individual hosts, you decrease the maximum number of hosts a given network could contain.

TABLE 1-1 Ranges of Public and Private IP Addresses

Class	From...	To...	Default Subnet Mask	Private
Class A	1.*x.y.z*	126.*x.y.z*	255.0.0.0	10.*x.y.z*
Loopback	127.*x.y.z*			
Class B	128.*x.y.z*	191.*x.y.z*	255.255.0.0	172.16.*y.z* through 172.31.*y.z*
Class C	192.*x.y.z*	223.*x.y.z*	255.255.255.0	192.168.*y.z*
Class D	224.*x.y.z*	239.*x.y.z*	N/A	N/A
Class E	240.*x.y.z*	254.*x.y.z*	N/A	N/A

TABLE 1-2 Number of Networks and Hosts per Network for Each TCP/IP Address (Classes A–C)

Class	Subnet	Network Bits	Possible Networks	Host Bits	Hosts per Network
A	255.0.0.0	8	126	24	16,777,214
B	255.255.0.0	16	16,384	16	65,534
C	255.255.255.0	24	2,097,152	8	254

Subnet and Broadcast Addresses

As previously stated in our discussions of the network and host portions of IP addresses, you can use the bits to the right of the network portion of the address to identify individual hosts on the network. While that's true, there are a couple of exceptions. As mentioned, the lowest possible number is reserved as the *network ID* (also called the *subnet address,* the *subnet ID,* or *IP network address*). For example, if the IP address is 169.254.1.*x* with a subnet mask of 255.255.255.0, you cannot assign the address 169.254.1.0 to any specific host, because 169.254.1.0 is reserved as the network ID.

The highest possible address in the range of available addresses is reserved as the *broadcast address.* The broadcast address is used when a host needs to send a message to all other hosts on the network. Using the example 169.254.1.*x* with a subnet mask of 255.255.255.0, the highest possible host ID is 11111111, or 255 in binary. Hence, you cannot assign the address 169.254.1.255 to a host because that address is reserved for broadcasting. (We'll discuss broadcasting in depth a little later in this chapter.) So, when you break it all down, here's what you end up with, given 169.254.1.*x* with the subnet mask 255.255.255.0:

```
169.254.1.0         subnet address (network ID)
169.254.1.255       broadcast address
```

That leaves the following host addresses remaining, which you can assign to hosts:

```
169.254.1.1 to 169.254.1.254
```

It's not always quite as simple as that because *subnetting* would allow you to break that network into smaller subnets, as we'll discuss later in the chapter. But before we complicate matters, let's look at another address you're likely to assign to hosts in your network, the default gateway.

Configure TCP/IP on Servers and Clients

The Default Gateway

Every computer in a network is likely to have a *default gateway* address. This address represents an interface to computers outside the local subnet. The most common example is a NIC that connects the subnet to the Internet, as in the example shown in Figure 1-3. There, the address 192.168.100.2 identifies the NIC that connects the computer to other computers in the local subnet. The IP address 192.168.100.1 identifies the NIC that connects that computer to the Internet (in other words, computers not within the local subnet).

To understand how it works, you first need to be aware that all information sent across the network is divided into *packets* (also called *frames*), each of which contains the data to be sent, as well as the IP address of the destination. When the NIC is handed a packet, it compares the network portion of the destination address to the network portion of its own address. If it determines that the destination address is not the same as its own subnet address, it just sends the packet to the default gateway instead.

In the example shown in Figure 1-3, the server at the top of the subnet is playing the role of a router, in that it accepts messages that are intended for a host that's not in the current subnet and sends them out through the default gateway. Any Windows 2000 Server computer can play the role of a router, as you'll learn later. The important point to remember for now is that the default gateway address

FIGURE 1-3

The default gateway provides access to computers outside the local subnet.

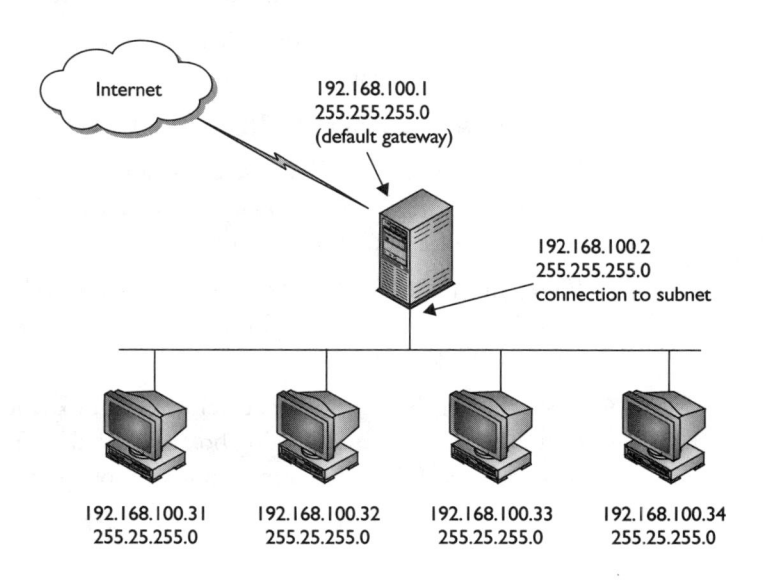

Internet

192.168.100.1
255.255.255.0
(default gateway)

192.168.100.2
255.255.255.0
connection to subnet

192.168.100.31
255.25.255.0

192.168.100.32
255.25.255.0

192.168.100.33
255.25.255.0

192.168.100.34
255.25.255.0

represents the place to which all "foreign" packets are sent. If any host in the subnet needs to send a packet to some host that's not in its own subnet, the packet gets shipped straight to the default gateway.

EXERCISE 1-1

Configuring TCP/IP on Servers

In this exercise, we'll look at the specific steps required to assign an IP address to a Windows computer on a LAN. We'll use an example of assigning a *static* IP address to a computer running Windows 2000 Server. A static IP address is one that's assigned by the administrator and never changes. Windows 2000 also supports dynamic IP addressing, where a host gets its IP address automatically from a DHCP server. We'll discuss all of that in Chapter 4. But since Microsoft recommends that all servers in a network use static IP addresses, we'll assign a static IP address to a server here. Here are the steps involved:

1. Open the Network and Dial-Up Connections window, either from the Settings menu on the Start menu, or by right-clicking My Network Places on the desktop and choosing Properties.
2. Right-click the icon for your Local Area Connection and choose Properties.
3. In the dialog box that opens, click Internet Protocol (TCP/IP) and then click the Properties button.
4. Choose Use The Following IP Address to set a static IP address.
5. Fill in this computer's IP address and subnet mask as in the example shown in Figure 1-4. Of course, you'll want to use an IP address and subnet mask appropriate for your own network.
6. If you already know the IP addresses of the default gateway and DNS servers for this network, you can fill those in as well. Otherwise, you can leave those options blank for now.
7. Click the OK button in the current dialog box, and then click the OK button in the remaining dialog box to close that. You can also close the Network and Dial-Up Connections window if you like.

Configure TCP/IP on Servers and Clients   13

FIGURE 1-4

The TCP/IP Properties dialog box

[Screenshot of Internet Protocol (TCP/IP) Properties dialog box with "Use the following IP address" selected, IP address: 192.168.100.2, Subnet mask: 255.255.255.0]

If you have access to two or more computers, and they're connected right now, you can repeat these steps on any other computers in the network. Generally, Microsoft recommends using dynamic IP addressing in client computers. But until you have a DHCP server set up to assign IP addresses automatically, you can just assign static IP addresses to all of your computers. For the purposes of the exercises in this book, be sure to make all the computers part of the same subnet.

exam ⓦatch

There's no rule that says you must use dynamic addresses on hosts and static IP addresses on servers. But since Microsoft recommends that approach, you should keep it in mind when answering any questions about assigning IP addresses to hosts.

Classless Inter-Domain Routing (CIDR)

The classed A, B, and C networks were fine in the early days of the Internet, when there were relatively few networks connected. But, as time went by and the Internet grew, it became clear that the powers that be were going to run out of globally unique IP Class A, B, and C addresses.

To gain some flexibility in doling out ranges of globally unique IP addresses, the registrars came up with Classless Inter-Domain Routing (CIDR, pronounced *cider*) addresses. CIDR addresses don't use traditional subnet masks to identify the network and host portions of an IP address. Rather, they use a /*x* at the end of the IP address, where *x* is the number of bits used to indicate the network portion of the address.

For example, the address 199.199.199.123/26 would be called a *slash 26* address. When viewing the address in binary format, the top (leftmost) 26 bits would be the ones assigned by the registrar, leaving the remaining 6 bits for the administrators assigned to hosts. Referring back to our discussion of subnet masks, if we write the address 199.199.199.5 in binary, and then use corresponding 1's and 0's to mask the network portion of the address, we end up with the address and mask shown in Figure 1-5.

You can easily convert a /*x* to a more traditional subnet mask, though you'll need to covert binary numbers to their decimal equivalents. You just have to jot down the 32-bit mask with *x* number of 1's, followed by enough 0's to make the number 36 bits in length. Divide that 32-bit number into four octets. Then convert each octet to a decimal number. For example, let's take the /26 designation. We jot down 26 ones, followed by 6 zeros:

```
11111111111111111111111111000000
```

Use dots to separate that into four 8-bit octets:

```
11111111.11111111.11111111.11000000
```

Now convert each binary octet to a decimal number, and you get the following:

```
255.255.255.192
```

FIGURE 1-5

The address 199.199.199.5/26 in binary with 1's representing the network portion in the lower mask

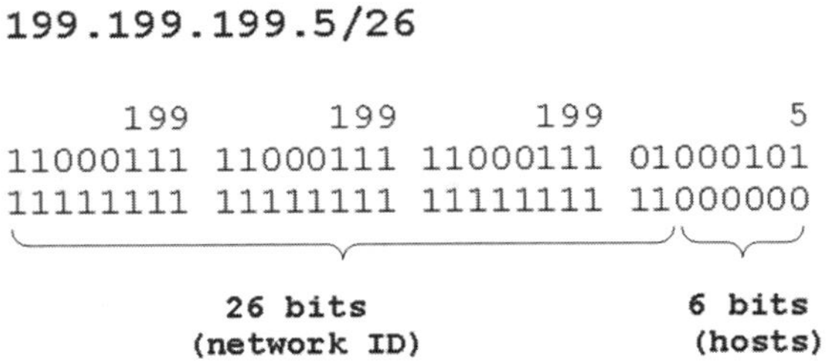

```
                199.199.199.5/26

           199       199       199        5
        11000111  11000111  11000111  01000101
        11111111  11111111  11111111  11000000
        _____/ _____/
                  26 bits              6 bits
               (network ID)            (hosts)
```

Thus, 255.255.255.192 and /26 are just two different ways of expressing the same thing—a subnet mask that, in binary, has 26 network bits and 6 host bits. If you take a look at Table 1-3, where I've converted a series of /x designations to binary and to subnet masks, you'll see the progression. The last number in the subnet mask is just the last octet converted from binary to decimal.

Before we get any deeper into this business of working with binary numbers, let's take a moment to look at some strategies you can use to convert decimal to binary, and vice versa.

Converting Between Binary and Decimal

The easiest way to convert a binary number to decimal, or a decimal number to binary, is to use the Windows Calculator. Click the Start button, choose Programs | Accessories | Calculator. From the Calculator's menu bar, choose View | Scientific to get to the view shown in Figure 1-6. Notice the Hex (hexadecimal), Dec (decimal), Oct (octal), and Bin (binary) options.

To convert from decimal to binary, first click the Dec option button to let the Calculator know that you're about to enter a decimal number. Then enter your decimal number and click the Bin option button to view that value in binary. For example, if you punch in the number 18 in decimal, and then click the Bin option button, the calculator displays 10010, which is the number 18 in binary. To convert that to the 8-bit chunk typically used in TCP/IP addressing, just pad the left side with leading 0's, such as 00010010.

TABLE 1-3   Some /x Designations, with Their Corresponding Subnet Masks in Binary and Decimal

/x Designation	Subnet Mask in Binary Format	Subnet Mask
/24	11111111.11111111.11111111.00000000	255.255.255.0
/25	11111111.11111111.11111111.10000000	255.255.255.128
/26	11111111.11111111.11111111.11000000	255.255.255.192
/27	11111111.11111111.11111111.11100000	255.255.255.224
/28	11111111.11111111.11111111.11110000	255.255.255.240
/29	11111111.11111111.11111111.11111000	255.255.255.248
/30	11111111.11111111.11111111.11111100	255.255.255.252

16 Chapter 1: Configuring and Troubleshooting TCP/IP

FIGURE 1-6

The Windows Calculator in scientific view

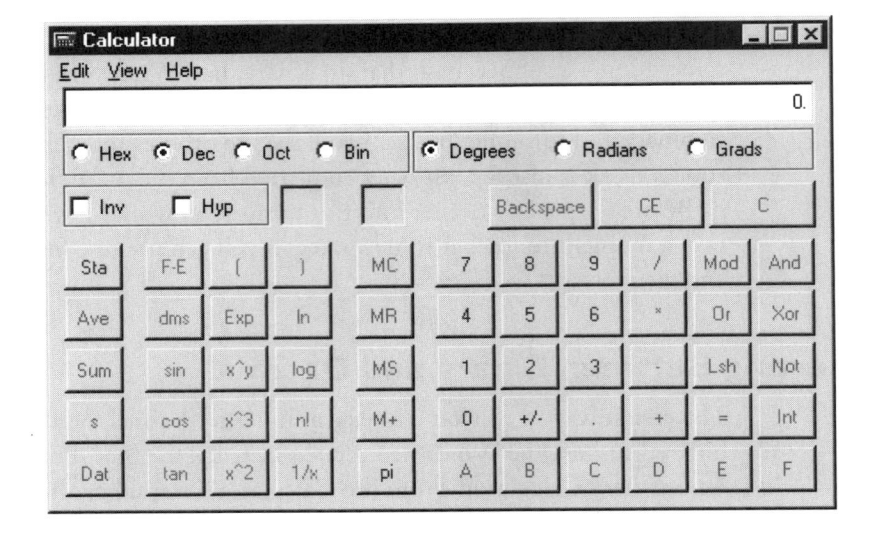

To convert decimal to binary, start by clicking the Bin option button. Then type in the binary number. Leading 0's will be ignored because they have no value, so just start typing at the first 1. For example, to convert 00110011 to decimal, you'd type or punch in 110011. Then click the Dec option button to see the result, 51.

SCENARIO & SOLUTION

My work PC's IP address is 24.0.2.5 (Class A) and has a subnet mask of 255.255.255.0 (Class C). What's up with that?	Your company has a Class A address. It's using the subnet mask 255.255.255.0 to break it down into smaller subnets. This illustrates the fact that it's really the IP address, and not the subnet mask, that defines Class A, B, or C.
Are hardware addresses used at all in TCP/IP?	Ethernet cards don't understand TCP/IP, they only understand hardware addresses. TCP/IP messages contain both the IP and hardware addresses of the sending and receiving machines. The protocol that resolves IP addresses to hardware addresses is called Address Resolution Protocol (ARP).
Do I have to get a globally unique domain name and IP address to set up my network?	Not at all. You can use a private address to set up your network. For example, if your subnet will have no more that 254 hosts, you can use 192.168.0.0 as your network address and 255.255.255.0 as your subnet mask. You can then assign addresses from 192.168.0.1 to 192.168.0.254 to hosts in your network. You'll still have basic Internet connectivity.

Now that we've been through some of the basics of TCP/IP addressing, let's take a look at some scenario questions and answers that might come up.

CERTIFICATION OBJECTIVE 1.02

Determine Valid IP Addresses

When you're working with a standard Class C address, it's easy to figure out the subnet address, broadcast address, and remaining addresses that are available to assign to hosts within the network. Recall that the subnet address is the last octet set to its lowest possible value, 0 in a Class C address; and the broadcast address is the last octet set to its highest possible value, 255 when you're talking about an octet (because 11111111 = 255). You can assign all the addresses between those two extremes to hosts within your network. Thus, we end up with this:

```
Subnet mask: 255.255.255.0
Subnet address: 192.168.0.0
Broadcast address: 192.168.0.255
Remaining addresses for hosts 192.168.0.1 to 192.168.0.254
```

Working with these same numbers in binary shows why this all makes sense. For example, using those same values, 192.168.1.0 and a subnet mask of 255.255.255.0 in binary, we can use the letter *n* to identify network bits, and *h* to identify host bits:

```
     192      168        0        0  IP Address (decimal)
11000000 10101000 00000000 00000000  IP address (binary)
nnnnnnnn nnnnnnnn nnnnnnnn hhhhhhhh  network or host
11111111 11111111 11111111 00000000  Subnet mask (binary)
     255      255      255        0  Subnet mask (decimal)
```

Subnetting

When we subnet a Class C address (in other words, break it down into two or more subnets), we're "swiping" host bits and making them into subnet bits. Let's see what happens when we change the subnet mask in the preceding example from 255.255.255.0 to 255.255.255.224. The bits that are affected by the change are indicated next by the letter *s*, to indicate that they're "swiped" bits now used to identify the subnet:

```
     192      168        0        0  IP address (decimal)
11000000 10101000 00000001 00000000  IP address (binary)
nnnnnnnn nnnnnnnn nnnnnnnn ssshhhhh  net, sub, or host
11111111 11111111 11111111 11100000  Subnet mask (binary)
     255      255      255      224  Subnet mask (decimal)
```

It's important to keep in mind that the subnet is a *mask*, not a number per se, and as such you must have a series of contiguous 1's for the network/subnet, followed by contiguous 0's for the host portion. Thus, only values that have leading 1's, like 10000000, 11000000, 11100000, and so forth, are valid. There are only nine possibilities, as summarized in Table 1-4.

It wouldn't actually make sense to have a /32 designation (for example, 255.255.255.255 subnet mask), since there wouldn't be any bits left in the host portion of the address. I've only included that in the table to show the progression.

Finding Valid IP Addresses

You can determine how many subnets, and how many hosts per subnet, you'll get from each /*x* designation as follows:

Number of subnets = 2^n
Number of hosts = $2^h - 2$

where *n* is the number of network bits, and *h* is the number of host bits. Since there are always 32 bits in the mask, and we're given the number of network bits

TABLE 1-4 The Full Range of Viable Subnet Octets in Binary and Decimal

/x	Last Octet (Binary)	Last Octet (Decimal)
/24	00000000	0
/25	10000000	128
/26	11000000	192
/27	11100000	224
/28	11110000	240
/29	11111000	248
/30	11111100	252
/31	11111110	254
/32	11111111	255

by the /x designation, we know there will always be 32 − n host bits available. (Incidentally, the reason you have to subtract 2 from the hosts calculation is because the highest and lowest addresses are reserved for the subnet address and broadcast address, respectively, so you can't assign those two addresses to hosts.)

With that in mind, Table 1-5 lists some /x designations, the number of subnets each provides, and the number of hosts you'll get per subnet. I've included /31 and /32 in the table just to illustrate the progression. These actually are invalid for practical use, though, because they don't leave a sufficient number of bits for addressing hosts.

Suppose you want to work with the IP address 192.168.0.1/25. You know you have two subnets to work with. But what are the ranges of available IP addresses to work with? Well, we know the network ID of the first subnet is

```
192.168.0.0
```

We know we have 126 host addresses to work with, and the first possible host address is 192.168.0.1. Therefore, the range of available addresses must be

```
192.168.0.1 to 192.168.0.126
```

TABLE 1-5 Number of Subnets and Possible Hosts per Subnet per /x Designation

/x Designation	n Bits in Last Octet (x-24)	Available Subnets (2^n)	h Bits (32 − n)	Hosts per Subnet ($2^h - 2$)	Subnet Mask (Decimal)
/24	0	1	8	254	255.255.255.0
/25	1	2	7	126	255.255.255.128
/26	2	3	6	62	255.255.255.192
/27	3	8	5	30	255.255.255.224
/28	4	16	4	14	255.255.255.240
/29	5	32	3	6	255.255.255.248
/30	6	64	2	2	255.255.255.252
/31*	7	128	1	0	Not valid
/32*	8	256	0	0	Not valid

*Invalid because they don't leave a sufficient number of host bits.

The broadcast address would be one higher than the last host address, so it must be

```
192.168.0.127
```

That covers the first subnet. The second subnet then starts right after the first subnet's broadcast address. Thus, the subnet address of the second subnet must be

```
192.168.0.128
```

Once again, we have 126 possible host addresses. The first valid host address would be one greater than the subnet address, so the range must be

```
192.168.0.129 to 192.168.0.254
```

because that's the range of numbers needed to address 126 hosts. The second subnet's broadcast address would be one greater than the last host address, so that address must be

```
192.168.0.129 to 192.168.0.254
```

Table 1-6 summarizes the preceding information. As you can see, we've actually taken a Class C address and split it right in half, making two equal-sized subnets.

If you use a /26 designation with a class C address of 192.168.9.9, you end up with 2^2 or 4 subnet bits. To determine the remaining host bits, we subtract 26 from 32, which tells us we have 6 host bits to work with. Thus, the maximum number of hosts per subnet would be $2^6 - 2$, or 62. Again, reserving the lowest and highest address within each of the four subnets for the network ID and broadcast address leaves us with the subnets and IP addresses listed in Table 1-7.

TABLE 1-6 IP Addresses and Subnet Masks for 192.168.0.0/25 (126 Hosts per Subnet)

Subnet	Subnet Address	First Host	Last Host	Broadcast Address	Subnet Mask
1	192.168.0.0	192.168.0.1	192.168.0.126	192.168.0.127	255.255.255.128
2	192.168.0.128	192.168.0.129	192.168.0.254	192.168.0.255	255.255.255.128

TABLE 1-7   IP Addresses and Subnet Masks for 192.168.0.0/26 (62 Hosts per Subnet)

Subnet	Subnet Address(es)	First Host	Last Host	Broadcast Address	Subnet Mask
1	192.168.0.0	192.168.0.1	192.168.0.62	192.168.0.63	255.255.255.192
2	192.168.0.64	192.168.0.65	192.168.0.126	192.168.0.127	255.255.255.192
3	192.168.0.128	192.168.0.129	192.168.0.190	192.168.0.191	255.255.255.192
4	192.168.0.192	192.168.0.193	192.168.0.254	192.168.0.255	255.255.255.192

In a nutshell, we've taken the Class C address 192.168.0.0 and divided it into four separate, equal-sized chunks. The starting address of each subnet is exactly 64 greater than the previous subnet's starting address, because we have 64 addresses per subnet (60 hosts plus the subnet and broadcast addresses).

Subnetting is simple to do with a good subnet calculator, like SolarWinds.Net Advanced Subnet Calculator, available from www.tucows.com—though, of course, you wouldn't be able to use that during your exam. But even without a subnet calculator, you can figure out anything as long as you know the network address and subnet mask. For example, suppose a senior administrator asks you to configure some new network using 192.168.0.160 with a subnet mask 255.255.255.240. What IP addresses can you assign to your host? Right off the bat, we know our network address, since that's a given:

```
192.168.0.160 subnet address (given)
```

So, how many hosts per subnet? First, we need to figure out how many subnet bits are available, so we convert the last octet in the subnet mask, 240, to binary, which yields 11110000. So, we have 4 host bits to work with, and hence $2^4 - 2$, or 14 hosts per subnet. We know that the IP address of the first host will be one greater than the subnet address, thus our range of IP addresses is

```
192.168.0.161 to 192.168.0.174 (14 hosts per subnet)
```

The broadcast address is one more than the last IP address, and thus is the following:

```
192.168.0.175 (broadcast address)
```

Broadcasting

Hosts on small subnets often use *broadcasting* to communicate with one another. Broadcasting is required when a given host doesn't know the address of some host with which it needs to communicate. To illustrate how broadcasting works, let's suppose a host named Igor needs to contact a host named Franz, but doesn't know Franz's hardware address or IP address. How's Igor going to get his message across? Easy. Since he doesn't know of a specific address to send the message to, he sends it to the broadcast address, which, in turn, automatically delivers the message to every host in the subnet. You might think of Igor sending his message to the subnet's broadcast address as being the same as Igor shouting "Igor at 192.168.0.2 here. If there is a Franz out there, please send me your address."

Every host on the network hears the broadcast message and checks to see who the message is intended for. Each host examines the message to see if the name Igor is looking for matches its own name. If the names don't match, the message is just ignored and no reply is sent back to Igor. However, when Franz sees that the message is addressed to him, he replies, "Hey Igor at 192.168.0.2, Franz here, and my address is 192.168.0.5," as illustrated in Figure 1-7. So now Igor and Franz know each other's addresses, and can send messages directly back and forth.

That all works just fine and dandy, but there's one big drawback. Igor has to pester every host in the LAN just to find the one host he's really trying to communicate with. That's not a big deal on a single small subnet. However, if you look at an extremely large network, like the Internet, you can see why broadcasting would create way too much traffic and take way too long. For example, suppose you type **www.GeneralSpecificX.com** into your web browser, which knows nothing about that site's IP address. If your browser had to go to every single host on the Internet asking "Are you www.GeneralSpecificX.com?," it would be pestering literally hundreds of millions of computers with this stupid question. And those other hundreds of millions of hosts would be pestering each other, and your computer, with similar stupid questions. There'd be so much bandwidth eaten up by all these broadcasts, it would be impossible to get anything else done.

So what's the solution to the broadcasting problem? In a word, *routing*. As you may recall, a router (or default gateway) connects a subnet to the "outside world." One side of the router has an IP address that makes it a member of the subnet to which it's connected. As such, the router "hears" all the broadcast messages going across the subnet. However, the one thing it won't do is send those broadcast messages through to the outside world. In other words, when the router gets a broadcast

Configure Routing **23**

FIGURE 1-7

Igor broadcasting a message to everyone, trying to find Franz

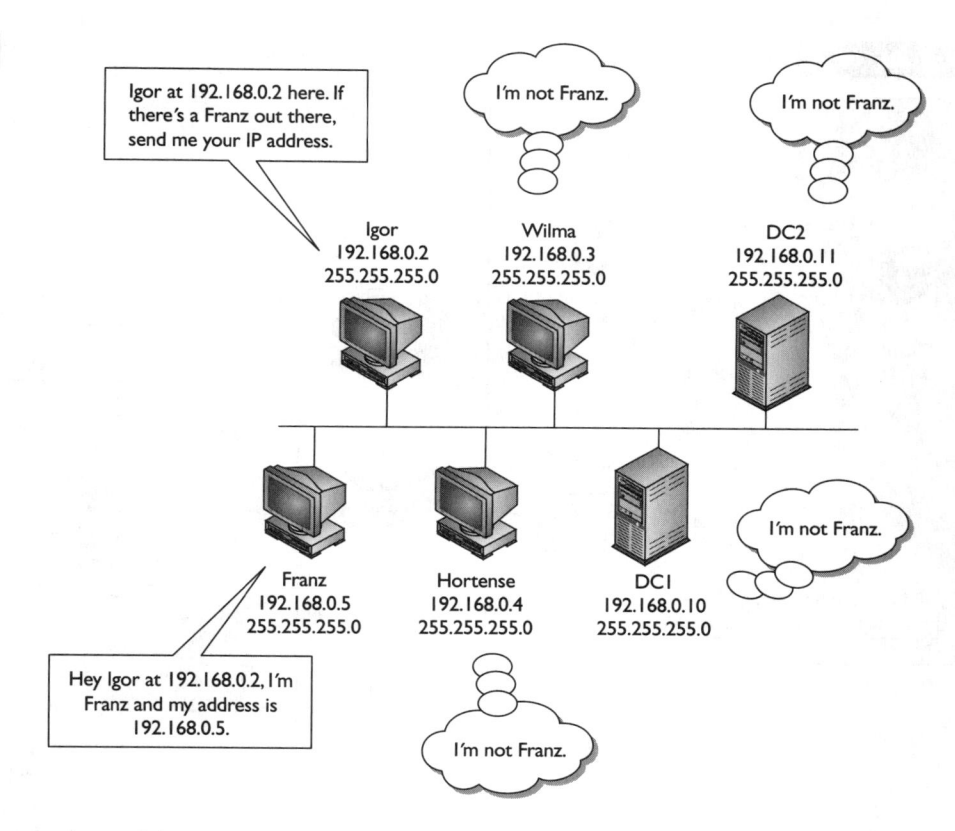

Igor at 192.168.0.2 here. If there's a Franz out there, send me your IP address.

I'm not Franz.

I'm not Franz.

Igor
192.168.0.2
255.255.255.0

Wilma
192.168.0.3
255.255.255.0

DC2
192.168.0.11
255.255.255.0

Franz
192.168.0.5
255.255.255.0

Hortense
192.168.0.4
255.255.255.0

DC1
192.168.0.10
255.255.255.0

I'm not Franz.

Hey Igor at 192.168.0.2, I'm Franz and my address is 192.168.0.5.

I'm not Franz.

message, it "shuts down the gateway," in essence saying "Broadcast messages stop here," as illustrated in Figure 1-8.

CERTIFICATION OBJECTIVE 1.03

Configure Routing

So now, armed with this information, let's look at the concept of *routing*, which is central to TCP/IP. The simplest form of routing is the network that's attached to the Internet via a router or modem and an Internet service provider (ISP). Hosts within the local subnet can communicate by broadcasts, and such messages stay within the subnet. Messages that are destined for hosts outside the local subnet are sent to the default gateway, which is the IP address of the device that connects the subnet to the Internet, as illustrated in Figure 1-9. That device then forwards the message to the ISP, who handles it from there.

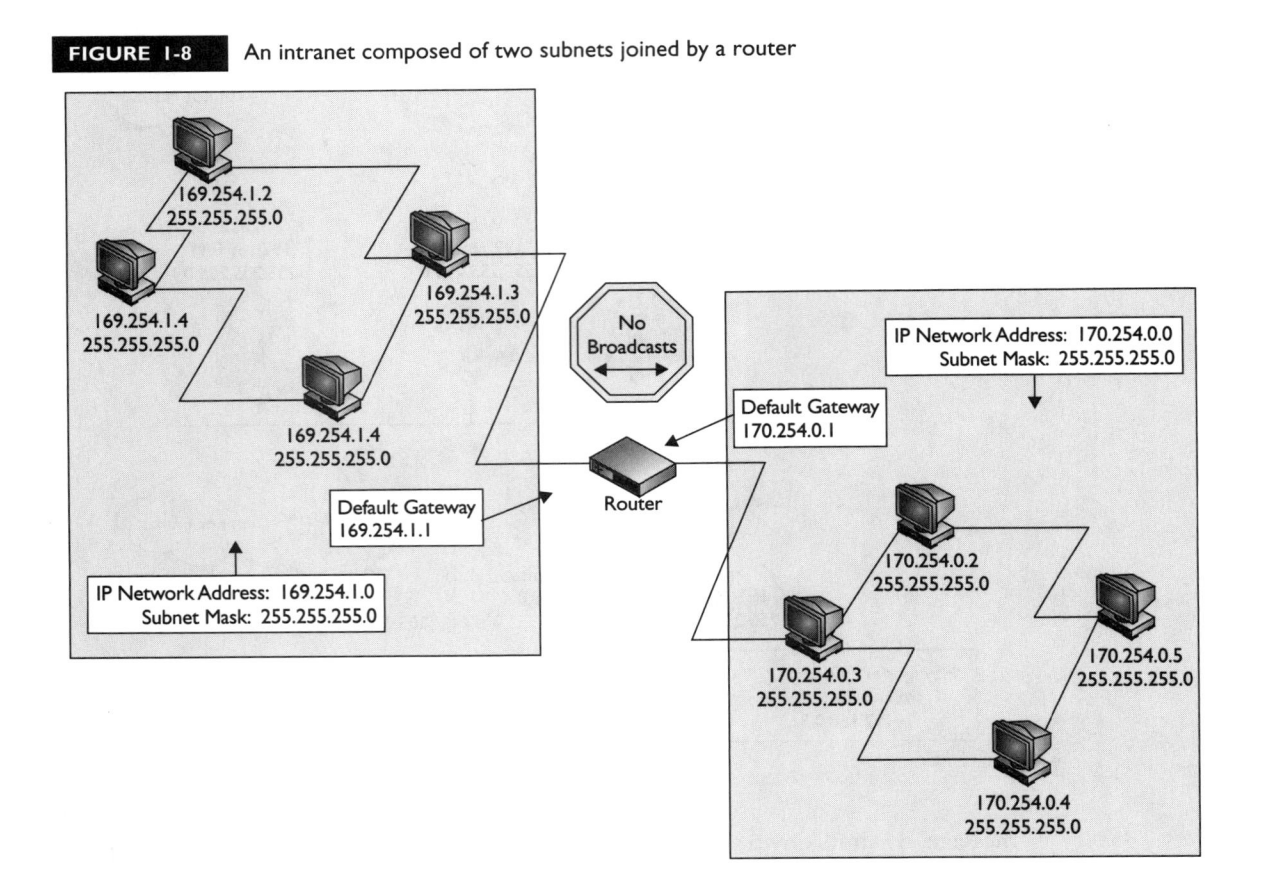

FIGURE 1-8 An intranet composed of two subnets joined by a router

Small Business Routing Scenario

In a small business, we might find multiple routers connecting multiple departmental subnets, as shown in Figure 1-10. In that scenario, Router1 connects the Marketing and Sales subnets, Router2 connects Sales to Accounting, and Router3 connects Accounting to Marketing. Any host in the company can contact any other host, since all the subnets are connected by routers.

In this scenario, computers within any given department can communicate with one another by broadcasting. But, for a message to reach a *remote network* (some other department's subnet), the message will have to cross one or two routers. For efficiency, we'd prefer messages to take the shortest path through one router. For example, we'd prefer a message being sent from Sales to Marketing to go through

Configure Routing 25

FIGURE 1-9

A small subnet that uses a default gateway to access the Internet

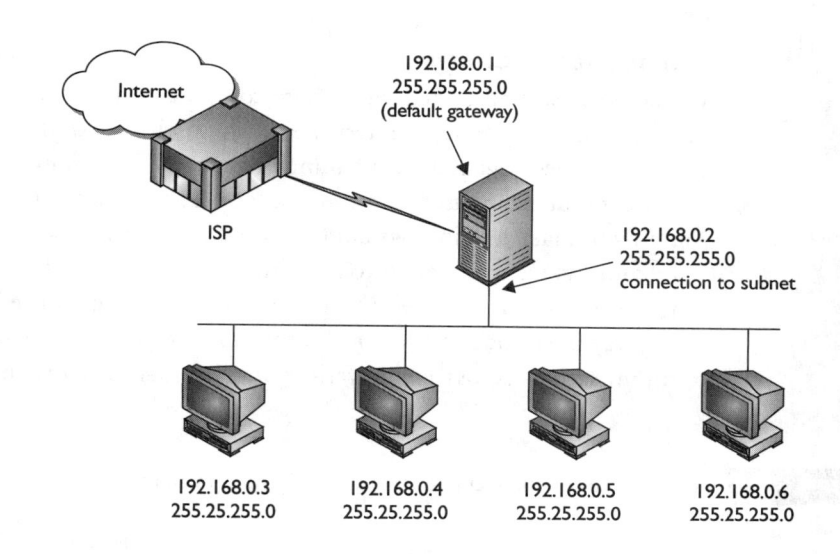

[Diagram: Internet/ISP connected to server at 192.168.0.1 255.255.255.0 (default gateway), with second interface 192.168.0.2 255.255.255.0 connection to subnet, connecting to four computers: 192.168.0.3, 192.168.0.4, 192.168.0.5, 192.168.0.6, all with 255.25.255.0]

Router1. However, if Router1 were unavailable, Sales could still get its message across to Marketing by going through Router2 and Router 3. Hence, we get some *fault tolerance* here in that if one router goes down, messages can still get through.

FIGURE 1-10

A small business scenario with routers connecting three departmental subnets

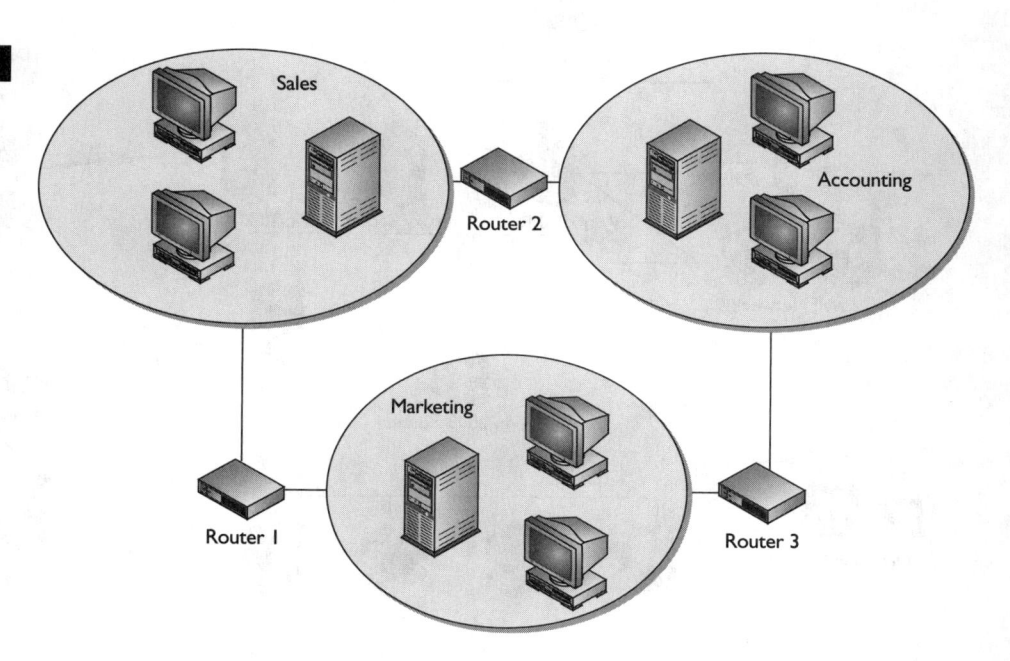

[Diagram: Three subnets—Sales, Accounting, and Marketing—connected by Router 1, Router 2, and Router 3]

Corporate Scenario

We can keep scaling up to larger, more complex scenarios. For example, Figure 1-11 shows a larger corporate or enterprise network with all kinds of networks and protocols joined together with a bunch of routers. In that example, Windows 2000 Server computers are used as routers (as opposed to "dedicated routers"). I'll show you how to make a Windows 2000 Server computer into a router momentarily.

Obviously, we won't get into all of the configuring needed to set up such a complex network right here. The point, though, is that a little bit of routing goes a long way in connecting all kinds of networks together, providing network communications across a wide variety of platforms. The Internet *is* exactly that,

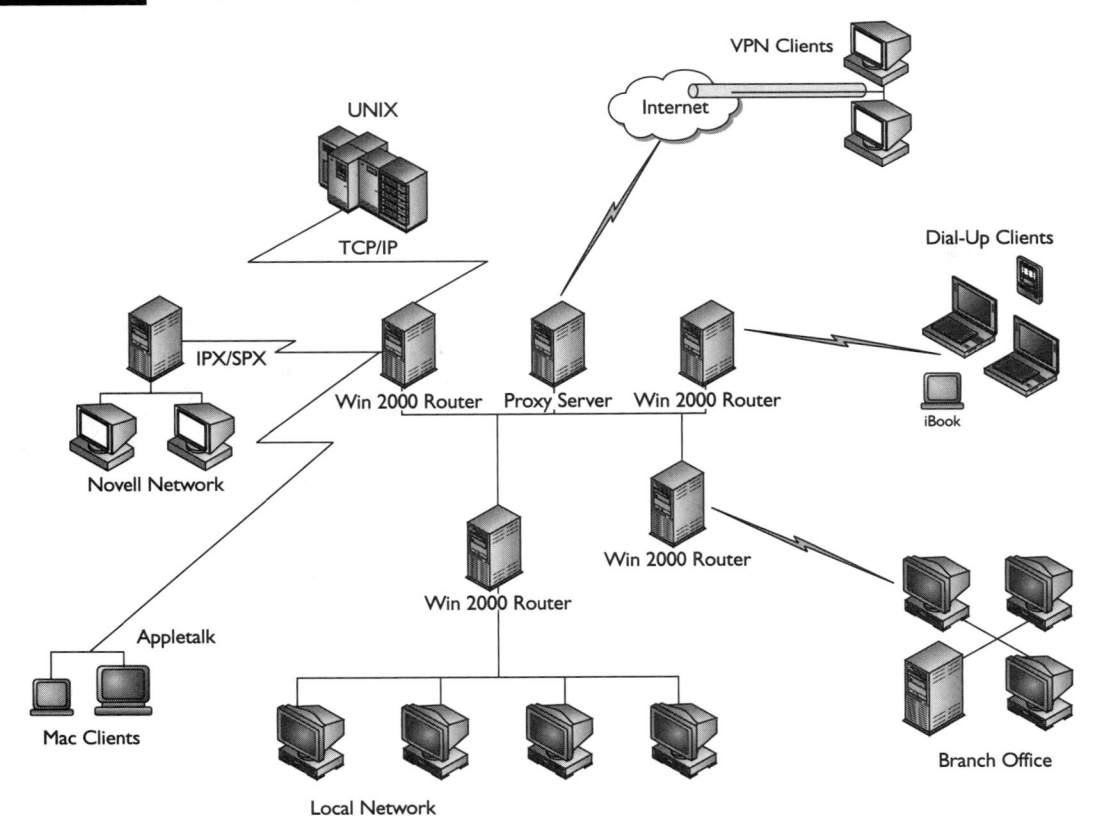

FIGURE 1-11 A corporate routing scenario involving many routers and protocols

a complex of computers, cables, networks, and routers connecting computers and networks around the globe.

Finally, bear in mind that there are no geographical boundaries here either. Any given subnet or network can be anywhere in the world. A large enterprise with offices in Europe, Asia, Mexico, and the United States would still use the same basic routing mechanisms to connect all these far-flung clients together into a (relatively) seamless network where any host could communicate with any other host, anywhere in the world.

Building a Windows 2000 Router

As you probably know, you can buy "dedicated" routers from manufacturers like Cisco and Lucent. But it's not entirely necessary to do so, as any Windows 2000 Server computer can easily play the role of router. Configuration is easy as well. First, you need to have two separate subnets to connect, of course. On the

SCENARIO & SOLUTION

What's the difference between a *network*, a *subnet*, a *physical segment*, and a *segment*?	The terms are used interchangeably, just as the terms *folder*, *subfolder*, and *directory* are. Any time you have two or more computers connected, you essentially have a network. Large networks, however, are often divided into smaller subnets (also called segments), largely for efficiency. Technically, a subnet (or segment) is any group of computers that can communicate with one another without the aid of a router.
What's the difference between a *router* and a *gateway*?	The terms tend to be used interchangeably, as a synonym for "the way out of this local subnet." However, the term *gateway* is a bit more generic, in that it can refer to a router; a computer that's acting as a router; or even the software used to provide communications between disparate networks, such as a Gateway Services for NetWare, which provides connectivity between Windows and Novell networks. The *default gateway* is where all "foreign" packets are sent—all packets that aren't addressed to a host that's within the current subnet.
What's the difference between the *Internet* and an *intranet*?	An intranet is composed of two or more subnets that use TCP/IP and routers to communicate with one another, though you'll sometimes hear these referred to as "internets." *The* Internet (with a capital *I*) is the big daddy of all internets that connects networks from all over the globe.

Windows 2000 Server computer that will be playing the role of router, you need to make sure the Routing and Remote Access Server is configured. Here's how:

1. Click the Start button, choose Programs | Administrative Tools | Routing And Remote Access. The Routing and Remote Access console opens.

2. Click the name of the server that will be acting as router. If you've never configured this service before, you'll see a message prompting you to configure the service now, as in Figure 1-12. Click the Action button and choose Configure Routing and Remote Access.

3. A wizard opens up and takes you through the steps required for the basic configuration. In this scenario, you'd choose Network Router when prompted for the configuration type, and click the Next button.

4. Follow the wizard through until you get to the Finish page.

When you've completed the wizard, you're ready to start the next phase, which involves installing the NICs. You would just go through the usual procedure. When both NICs are installed, each will have its own icon in Network and Dial-Up Connections, as in the example shown in Figure 1-13.

Since each NIC is a separate network interface, each can have its own unique TCP/IP settings. In this situation, you need to configure each NIC with a valid IP address for the subnet to which it connects. For example, take a look at Figure 1-14.

FIGURE 1-12

Routing and Remote Access Services, not yet configured

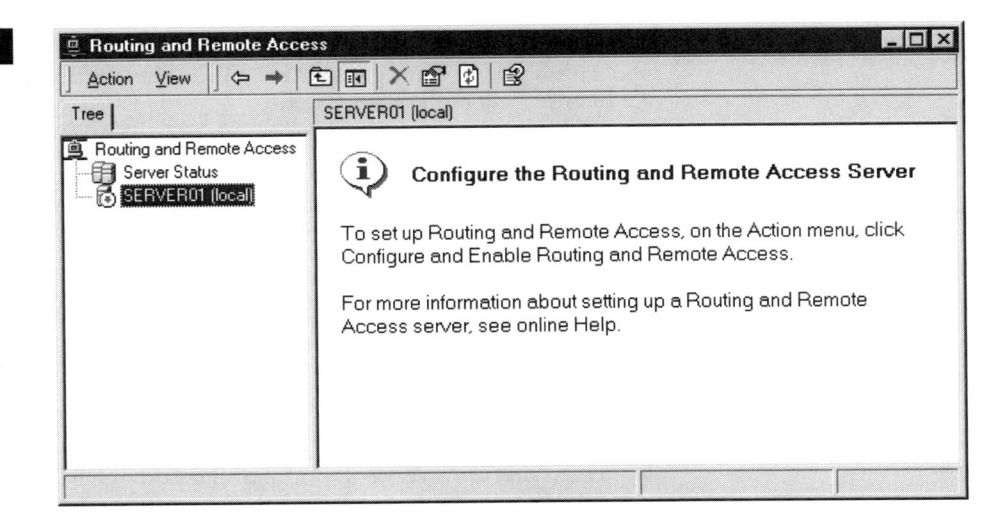

Configure Routing

FIGURE 1-13

Each installed NIC has its own icon in Network and Dial-Up Connections.

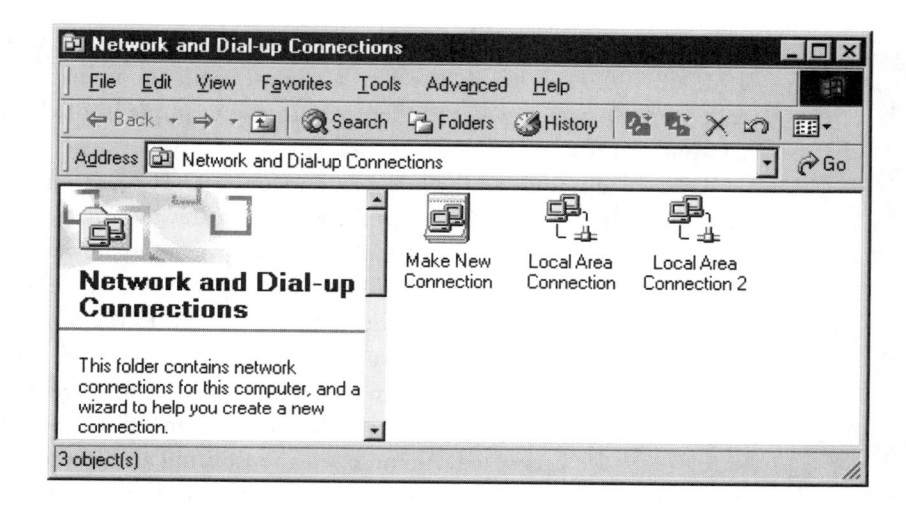

The subnet on the left has the address 192.168.0.0 subnet mask 255.255.255.0. The subnet on the right has the address 192.168.100.0 subnet mask 255.255.255.0. These are two separate subnets, since the network portions of their IP addresses clearly don't match.

To get routing to work, each NIC needs to be connected to and configured as a host within its subnet. For example, in the example shown in Figure 1-14, I've given NIC1 the IP address 192.168.0.1, thereby making it a host on the 192.168.0.0

FIGURE 1-14

Server01 playing the role of router between 192.168.0.0 and 192.168.100.0

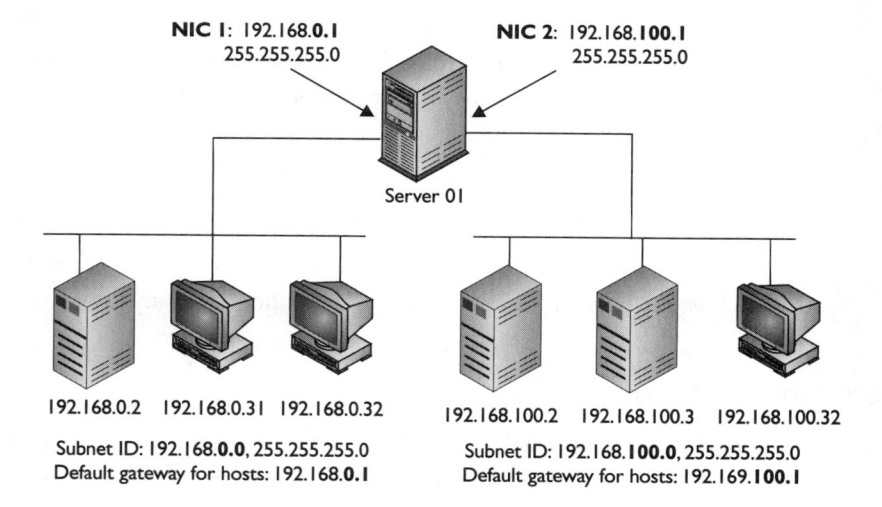

NIC 1: 192.168.**0**.1
255.255.255.0

NIC 2: 192.168.**100**.1
255.255.255.0

Server 01

192.168.0.2   192.168.0.31   192.168.0.32

Subnet ID: 192.168.**0.0**, 255.255.255.0
Default gateway for hosts: 192.168.**0**.1

192.168.100.2   192.168.100.3   192.168.100.32

Subnet ID: 192.168.**100.0**, 255.255.255.0
Default gateway for hosts: 192.169.**100**.1

subnet. I gave NIC2 the IP address 192.168.100.1, making it a host on the 192.168.100.0 subnet. By the way, a computer that contains two or more NICs is called a *multihomed computer*. Server01 in this example is, obviously, a multihomed computer at this point.

To use the router, all the hosts on network 192.168.0.0 would need to be configured to use 192.168.0.1 as their default gateway. All the hosts on subnet 192.168.100.0 would use 192.168.0.1 as their default gateway. Thus, broadcasts and other communications within each subnet stay in their respective subnets. Messages intended for "some other subnet" are sent to the interface on the router.

Finally, you'll want to make sure routing is enabled on the server. Typically, the wizard you ran earlier in this section would be sufficient to get that going. But just in case you have any problems with the router connection, you'll want to make sure the service is enabled. Again, open the Routing and Remote Access Services administrative tool, right-click the server's name in the console tree, and choose Properties. On the General tab, make sure routing is enabled. For this scenario, where you have only two subnets connected, you'll also want to make sure the Local Area Network (LAN) Routing Only option is selected, as shown in Figure 1-15.

How Routing Works

To understand the basics of routing, start with a single source host that's trying to get a message to some other destination host. The source host's own IP address is 192.168.100.33 with a subnet mask of 255.255.255.0. The destination host's IP address is 192.168.100.122 with a subnet mask of 255.255.255.0. If we stack the IP addresses and subnet mask one atop the other, we can see that the destination host is on the same network (or subnet) as the source host:

```
192.168.100.33      (source)
192.168.100.122     (destination)
255.255.255.0       (subnet mask)
```

The source host can "see" this same relationship. It "knows" that the destination host is on the same subnet. So it need not go through any routers to get to that host.

Viewing the Routing Table

Every computer on a TCP/IP network has a built-in routing table. The routing table is built automatically from known information. You can view the routing table by

FIGURE 1-15

Routing must be enabled for a Windows 2000 Server computer to function as a router.

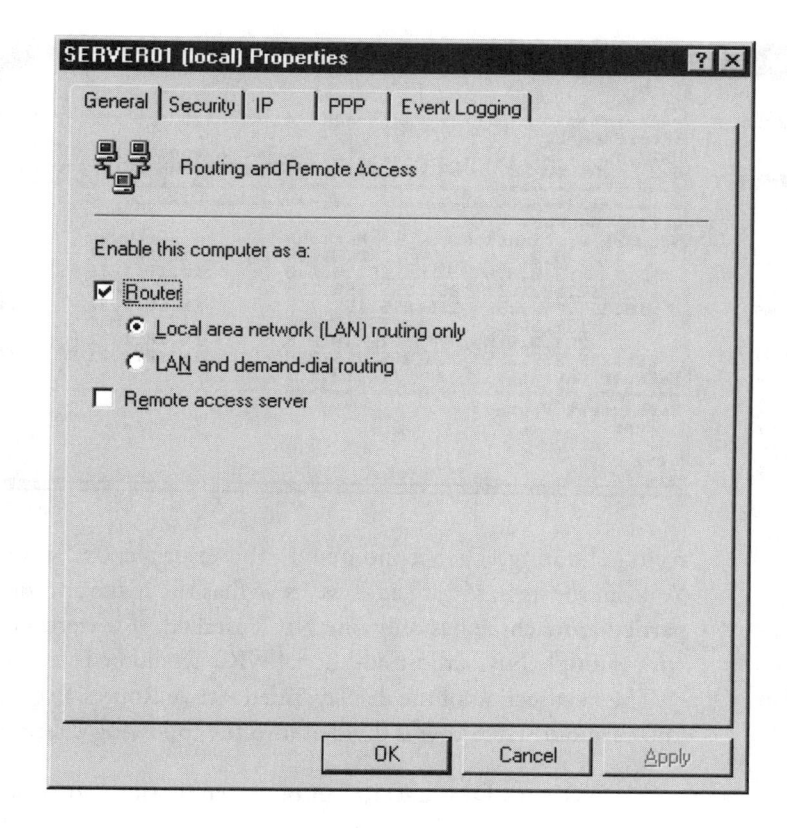

entering the command **route print** at the command prompt. The results might look something like the example in Figure 1-16.

To interpret the command's output in this example, you first need to know some things about the machine on which the command was entered. In this example, I entered the command at a Windows 2000 Professional computer that has the following TCP/IP configuration:

```
TCP/IP Address:     10.10.1.31
Subnet mask:        255.0.0.0
Default gateway:    10.10.1.1
```

The lines under Interface List indicate this computer's network interfaces. The first item, 0x1, is the TCP loopback interface used in conjunction with the loopback address for testing purposes. Every TCP/IP client has the same loopback address of 127.0.0.1; the loopback interface is just the address where loopback messages get sent. Later in this chapter, you'll see how you can use that address for testing and

FIGURE 1-16

Sample output from a **ROUTE PRINT** command

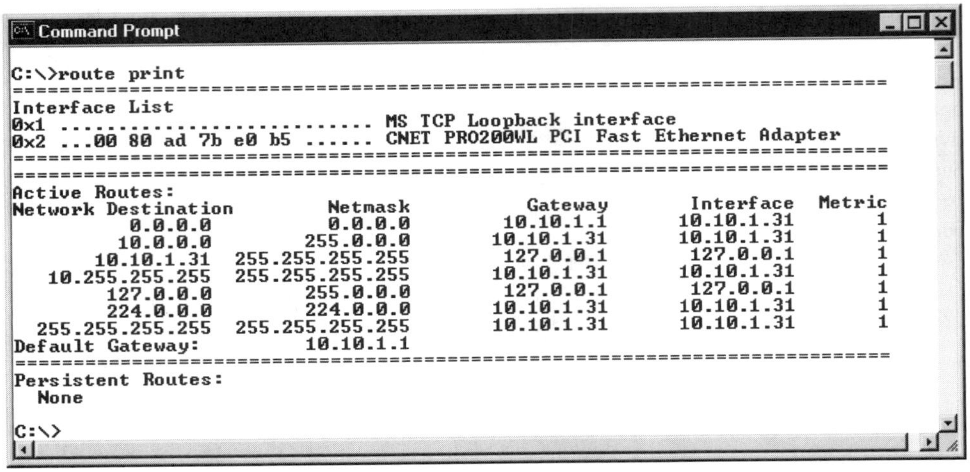

```
C:\>route print
===========================================================================
Interface List
0x1 ........................... MS TCP Loopback interface
0x2 ...00 80 ad 7b e0 b5 ...... CNET PRO200WL PCI Fast Ethernet Adapter
===========================================================================
===========================================================================
Active Routes:
Network Destination        Netmask          Gateway       Interface  Metric
          0.0.0.0          0.0.0.0       10.10.1.1     10.10.1.31       1
         10.0.0.0        255.0.0.0      10.10.1.31     10.10.1.31       1
       10.10.1.31  255.255.255.255       127.0.0.1      127.0.0.1       1
   10.255.255.255  255.255.255.255      10.10.1.31     10.10.1.31       1
        127.0.0.0        255.0.0.0       127.0.0.1      127.0.0.1       1
        224.0.0.0        224.0.0.0      10.10.1.31     10.10.1.31       1
  255.255.255.255  255.255.255.255      10.10.1.31     10.10.1.31       1
Default Gateway:        10.10.1.1
===========================================================================
Persistent Routes:
  None

C:\>
```

troubleshooting. The second item in this example, 0x2, is this computer's NIC. You can see its hardware address, as well as the make and model of the card. This particular machine has only one NIC installed. If it were a multihomed machine with multiple NICs, those additional NICs would be listed as 0x3, 0x4, and so forth.

The next section of the display, titled Active Routes, lists routes that this machine knows about. Each row is divided into the following columns:

- **Network Destination** A potential destination IP address, to which messages might be sent.
- **Netmask** A subnet mask for the network destination, which further defines which addresses will be included in this route.
- **Gateway** The IP address that provides access to the network destination addresses.
- **Interface** The local IP address that leads to the gateway.
- **Metric** The "cost" of a route in terms of "hops" across routers that will be required. The path from a host to its default gateway is also considered a hop, so there is always at least one hop, even when no routers are involved.

Now let's take a look at some of the routes listed in the sample output. The first line looks like this:

```
Network Destination    Netmask      Gateway      Interface     Metric
0.0.0.0                0.0.0.0      10.10.1.1    10.10.1.31    1
```

The address 0.0.0.0 with the netmask 0.0.0.0 translates roughly to "the place you should go if none of the lines in the routing table apply." In other words, this row defines the default gateway for all packets that aren't within broadcast range, and that don't meet any of the criteria in the other lines in the routing table.

Let's take a look at the next line now:

```
Network Destination        Netmask      Gateway      Interface      Metric
10.0.0.0                   255.0.0.0    10.10.1.31   10.10.1.31          1
```

This line says that "To get to any address that starts with 10. (in other words, 10.0.0.0 subnet 255.0.0.0), use your own NIC at 10.10.1.31. There will not be any router hops to make." This makes sense if you think about it for a minute. Recall that this is a machine on a Class A network. We know this because its own IP address and subnet mask are 10.10.1.31 and 255.0.0.0. So it stands to reason that in order to get a message out to another machine on this same network, the machine could use its own NIC (10.10.1.31) as the gateway to the local network, and there wouldn't be any routers involved.

The third route network destination, 10.10.1.31 netmask 255.255.255.255, refers to the local computer. This line essentially says "To get to yourself, use the loopback address 127.0.0.1." The next destination, 10.255.255.255 netmask 255.255.255.255, is the broadcast address. So this line says "To broadcast a message to all hosts on the 10.0.0.0 network, use your own 10.10.1.31 NIC." The next destination address, 127.0.0.0 netmask 255.0.0.0, is the reserved loopback address. Because the netmask uses 255.0.0.0, this line says "Any message sent to 127.*anything.anything.anything* gets sent to the IP address 127.0.0.1."

The network destination 224.0.0.0 netmask 224.0.0.0 is the reserved *multicast address*. We'll discuss multicasting in depth later in the book. For now, it's sufficient to know that multicasting is a means of sending a single stream of data to multiple IP addresses, sort of like a radio station that just sends out its show via an antenna, and any radio that happens to be tuned to that station hears the show. The 255.255.255.255 netmask 255.255.255.255 is the *limited broadcast address*, any alternative route used by some broadcasts to the local subnet.

The last section shown in Figure 1-16, titled Persistent Routes, lists static, permanent routes created by an administrator. In the sample output, there are none listed, simply because I haven't created any. I'm relying on the default gateway address to handle all messages with destinations outside my local subnet. But you can't always rely on that. We'll discuss why, and how to get around it, in the next section.

EXERCISE 1-2

Viewing a Computer's Routing Table

Like I said, every computer has a built-in routing table. So you can do this simple exercise on virtually any Windows machine. I didn't create an exercise that actually lets you change the routing table, as you wouldn't want to play around with that on a real, production network. Furthermore, you could only create a route to a viable network, and I don't know what, if any, networks you're connected to. But, anyway, to perform this simple exercise on a Windows 2000 machine, follow these steps:

1. Click the Start button and choose Programs | Accessories | Command Prompt.
2. Type **route print** and press ENTER.
3. That's it. If you'd like a printed copy, type **route print >prn** and press ENTER.
4. Type **exit** and press ENTER if you want to close the Command Prompt window.

The output of your **route print** command may not match the example shown in this chapter, but you should see many of the same default routes.

Configuring Routing Tables

Suppose you work in a company that has an intranet composed of three networks and two routers, as shown in Figure 1-17. Notice some features of this scenario. We have three separate Class C networks here. Network A's network address is 200.50.50.0, Network B's network address is 199.150.150.0, and Network C's address is 197.100.100.0. Networks A, B, and C could all be subnets of one Class C address, in which case you'd need a custom subnet mask. But for our current example, that wouldn't matter. Either way, you'd still need routers to connect the various networks or subnets.

Notice that Network C contains two routers, one at the address 197.100.100.101 and the other at 197.100.100.102. There is no Internet connection in this example, which means there is no default gateway to which Network C can just send all messages intended for hosts outside itself. So how does a host on Network C

Configure Routing 35

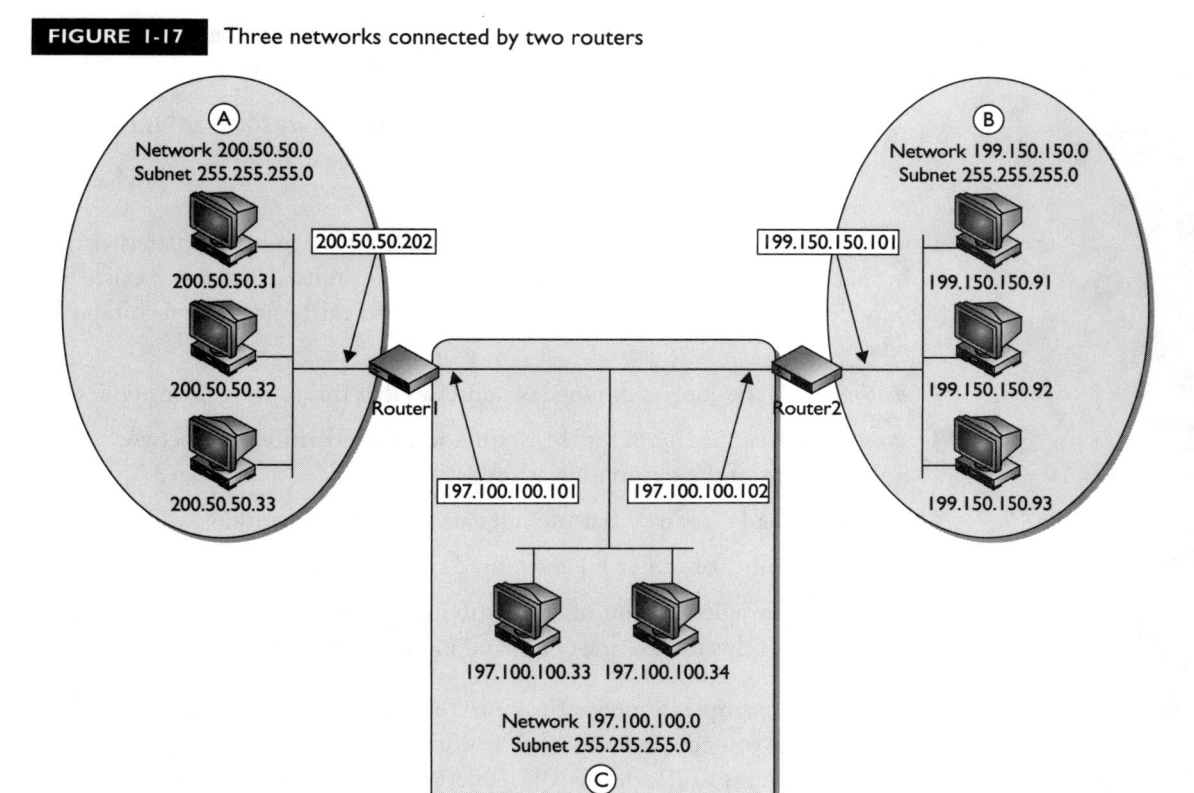

FIGURE 1-17 Three networks connected by two routers

(say, 197.100.100.33) get a message to a host on Network A (say, 200.50.50.31)? The obvious answer is through Router1. But the machine can only know this if its routing table tells it to go through Router1. You can manually add a route to a machine's routing table to handle a situation like this. In this example, in order for a host from Network C to get a message to Network A or B, it would need the following "instructions" placed in its routing table:

- To get a message to Network A (200.50.50.0), send it to Router1 at 197.100.100.101.
- To get a message to Network B (199.150.150.0), send it to Router2 at 197.100.100.102.

These "instructions," which are formally called *static routes*, can be added to the routing table using the ROUTE command with the following syntax

```
ROUTE [-p] ADD destination MASK subnet gateway METRIC m IF interface
```

where

- *−p* is an optional switch. If included, manually added routes are persistent, in that they exist from one reboot to the next. If omitted, the route exists only during the current session, and will cease to exist once the machine is rebooted.
- *destination* is the address or range of addresses that this routing table applies to.
- *subnet* is the subnet mask for the destination that identifies the network and host portions of the destination address.
- *gateway* is the IP address that provides access to the network.
- *m* is the number of router hops required to get to the destination.
- *interface* is a single-digit number identifying which NIC card interface to use. You can omit this to have the command locate the best interface automatically.

Let's look at an example. Suppose I want to tell one of the workstations in Network C "When you get a message that's addressed to any address starting with 200.50.50, send it to IP address 197.100.100.101." To do that, I get to the command prompt on that computer and enter the following command:

```
route -p ADD 200.50.50.0 MASK 255.255.255.0 197.100.100.101 METRIC 2
```

We'd also want to tell that computer to send all messages destined for any address starting with 199.150.150 to 197.100.100.102, the near-side IP address of the router that connects network C to network B. So we'd also enter this command:

```
route -p ADD 199.150.150.0 MASK 255.255.255.0 197.100.100.102 METRIC 2
```

The command will check the specified route before adding it to the routing table. If for some reason the specified network cannot be reached, the entry will be rejected and you'll see an error message to that effect. The problem could be a simple typo or a connection problem to the remote network.

Once you've successfully entered a route, it will appear in the output of the **route print** command. If you included the -p switch, the route will be listed under the

Persistent Routes heading. Otherwise, the new route just appears in the regular list of routes. In this example, the following lines would be added under Persistent Routes:

```
Network Destination    Netmask         Gateway          Interface        Metric
200.50.50.0            255.255.255.0   197.100.100.101  197.100.100.33   2
199.150.150.0          255.255.255.0   197.100.100.102  197.100.100.33   2
```

Notice that in both **route add** commands, I omitted the IF *interface* parameter. Since this machine has only one NIC, the **route add** command can test the connection and figure this out on its own.

How Routing Conflicts Are Handled

Recall that our small sample network contained no default gateway to the Internet. As such, there's no way for our sample host to communicate with the outside world beyond Networks A and B. But suppose we add another NIC to that machine, or an Internet connection through some other machine on the same subnet. For the sake of example, let's say that the default gateway address to the Internet is at 197.100.100.1. When we do a **route print** command on that machine, the output might include the following routes:

```
Network Destination    Netmask         Gateway          Interface        Metric
0.0.0.0                0.0.0.0         197.100.100.1    197.100.100.1    40
200.50.50.0            255.255.255.0   197.100.100.101  97.100.100.33    2
199.150.150.0          255.255.255.0   197.100.100.102  197.100.100.33   2
```

The large metric, 40, is somewhat typical of an Internet connection where many routers might have to be crossed to get to a specific destination on the Internet. But more importantly, there's also a conflict here. The default gateway address 0.0.0.0 says "Use 197.100.100.1 for all communications outside this subnet." But then, the next two lines say "Use 197.100.100.101 for communications to 200.50.50.0, and 197.100.100.102 for communications to 199.199.150.0." So, which will it be when it comes time to send a message to Network A, the default gateway address or the specified route?

For example, let's say some hypothetical routing table contains these two routes:

```
Network Destination    Netmask         Gateway          Interface        Metric
200.50.50.0            255.255.255.0   197.100.100.101  197.100.100.33   2
200.50.50.200          255.255.255.255 197.100.100.102  197.100.100.34   2
```

The first route tells the machine to send anything destined for the network 200.50.50.0 through 197.100.100.101." The second one tells the machine that a message specifically destined for 200.50.50.200 netmask 255.255.255.255 goes through 197.100.100.102. Since the second entry has the more specific netmask, 255.255.255.255 (in other words, "this particular host"), as opposed to an entire network (255.255.255.0), the second item wins. In the event that two routes have identical subnet masks, the route with the smallest metric will be chosen first.

on the Job

You can intentionally add some conflicting, static routes to a routing table for fault tolerance. Give the preferred route a low metric, such as 1; the "backup" route a higher metric, like 2; and so forth.

Managing the Routing Table

The **route** command offers two more options that you can use to manage a routing table. The **route delete** command allows you to delete static routes from the routing table. For example, entering the command

```
route delete 200.50.50 200
```

would delete the route that has the network destination address 200.50.50.200. If you have two routes with the same network destination address but different gateways, you can include the gateway address to specify the record you want to delete.

You can use the * wildcard character in both the **print** and **delete** versions of the command. For example **route print 200*** displays only routes whose network destination starts with 200. The **route delete 200*** command would delete all routes whose network destinations start with 200.

The **route change** command lets you change an existing static route, for example,

```
route change 199.150.150.0 MASK 255.255.255.0 197.100.100.102 METRIC 4
```

The **route** command alone on a line prints help for the command (same as entering the command **route /?**).

Now that I've told you all of this, let me first point out that it's very unlikely that you'll ever have to go from one machine to the next, setting up all these routes. Thanks to dynamic routing and modern routing protocols like RIP (Routing Information Protocol) and OSPF (Open Shortest Path First), routers can keep machines informed of available routes, and individual hosts can compare routing tables to one another and keep each other up to date. We'll get to these protocols in a later chapter. For now, the important thing is to understand that all machines have a routing table. And even if you don't specifically need to manually add static routes to a machine's table, it's good to be able to interpret the contents of the table for troubleshooting purposes.

Just because you might not have to use static routing much in the real world, that doesn't mean you can just ignore all this stuff. You may well need to analyze some routing tables and understand how ROUTE ADD works to answer some questions on your certification exam!

CERTIFICATION OBJECTIVE 1.04

Troubleshoot TCP/IP and Routing

As you probably know, there's a lot more to a TCP/IP network than just assigning IP addresses to machines. There are many things that can go wrong after the network is built, and even more things that can go wrong as you're building the network. For the rest of this chapter, we'll take a look at some diagnostic tools and troubleshooting techniques that you can use at any time to solve problems as they arise.

Troubleshooting with IPCONFIG

As the name implies, IPCONFIG is a command for checking a machine's IP configuration. Checking a host's IP configuration is always the best first step in troubleshooting connectivity problems. Entering just the command **ipconfig** at the command prompt displays basic IP configuration information (IP address, subnet mask, default gateway, and DNS suffix) for each network adapter in the computer. Settings that haven't been configured yet are left blank.

For more detailed information, use the **/all** switch by entering the command **ipconfig /all**. This command will display general information about the current computer's IP configuration, followed by detailed information about each installed NIC. Figure 1-18 shows an example of the display produced by an **ipconfig /all** command. Here's a brief description of what each line is about. Some items describe settings that we haven't discussed yet—but will over the next two chapters.

- **Host Name** This computer's hostname, which might be a single name like server01 if DNS hasn't been set up yet, or it might be a FQDN like server01.certifiable.net if DNS is set up.

FIGURE 1-18 Sample **ipconfig /all** command display

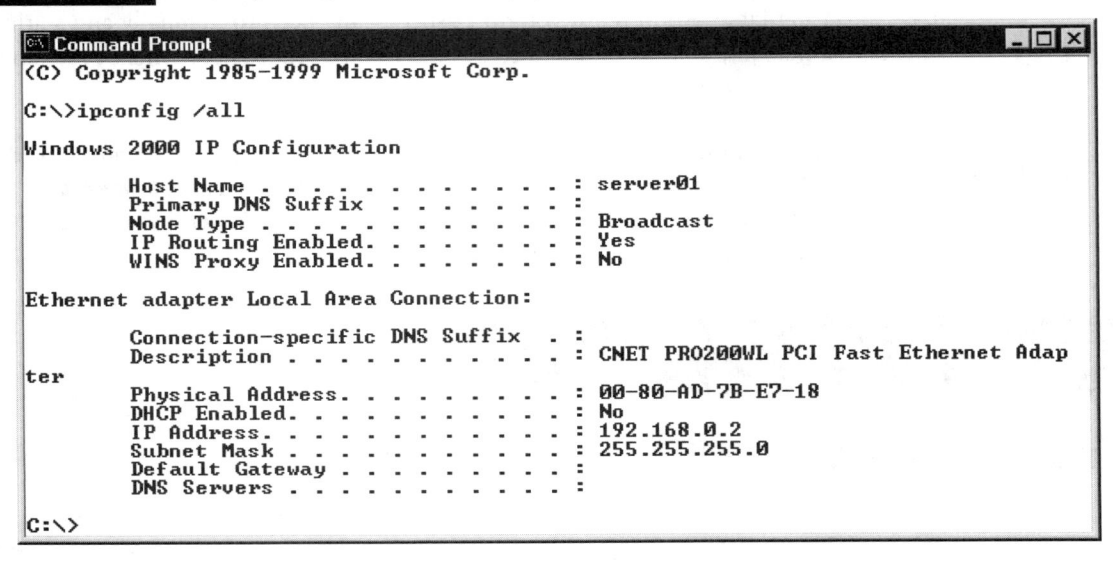

```
Command Prompt
(C) Copyright 1985-1999 Microsoft Corp.

C:\>ipconfig /all

Windows 2000 IP Configuration

        Host Name . . . . . . . . . . . . : server01
        Primary DNS Suffix  . . . . . . . :
        Node Type . . . . . . . . . . . . : Broadcast
        IP Routing Enabled. . . . . . . . : Yes
        WINS Proxy Enabled. . . . . . . . : No

Ethernet adapter Local Area Connection:

        Connection-specific DNS Suffix  . :
        Description . . . . . . . . . . . : CNET PRO200WL PCI Fast Ethernet Adap
ter
        Physical Address. . . . . . . . . : 00-80-AD-7B-E7-18
        DHCP Enabled. . . . . . . . . . . : No
        IP Address. . . . . . . . . . . . : 192.168.0.2
        Subnet Mask . . . . . . . . . . . : 255.255.255.0
        Default Gateway . . . . . . . . . :
        DNS Servers . . . . . . . . . . . :

C:\>
```

- **Primary DNS Suffix** If DNS has been set up, the domain portion of the DNS name (for example, certifiable.net) appears here.

- **Node Type** Describes the method used to resolve NetBIOS-style hostnames, like server01, to IP addresses, as will be discussed in Chapter 2.

- **IP Routing Enabled** A simple Yes or No answer describing whether or not this machine is functioning as a router.

- **WINS Proxy Enabled** Specifies whether WINS name resolution is enabled, as described in Chapter 2.

Information that's specific to network adapter cards is listed under the Ethernet Adapter heading. The name of the connection, as it appears in the Network and Dial-Up Connections window is followed by these lines:

- **Connection-Specific DNS Suffix** If DNS is enabled, shows the DNS domain name that's specific to this network interface card.

- **Description** The make and model of the network interface card.

- **Physical Address** The hardware address of the network interface card.

- **DHCP Enabled**   Determines whether or not this card's address can be assigned automatically by a DHCP server (Yes) or was manually entered (No). More information on DHCP is provided in Chapter 4.
- **IP Address**   The IP address of the network interface card.
- **Subnet Mask**   The subnet mask of the network interface card.
- **Default Gateway**   The IP address of the default gateway where messages outside the broadcast range will be sent.
- **DNS Servers**   If DNS is set up, lists the IP address of all available DNS servers.

In terms of what we've discussed so far in this chapter, what you're mainly looking for in IPCONFIG's output is to ensure that the computer has a valid IP address and subnet mask. If there is a gateway of some sort on the network, whether it be a dedicated router or just a computer that provides access to the Internet, the default gateway address for that router must be correct as well. If you find an error that needs correcting, you can make changes through the TCP/IP Properties dialog box, described previously in Exercise 1-1.

The IPCONFIG command works only on systems that have the TCP/IP networking protocols installed. If entering the **ipconfig /all** command returns an error message like "TCP/IP is not running on this system," there's a problem with the NIC or with the TCP/IP installation. To check to see if the NIC is working properly, open the Control Panel, open the System icon, and click the Hardware tab. Then click the Device Manager button and expand the Network Adapters category. Double-click the icon for your NIC to view its properties. If the dialog box doesn't indicate any problems, you know the problem lies outside the NIC.

on the job

Windows 2000 doesn't automatically install drivers for every NIC on the market, so it's a good idea to check the card and TCP/IP right after you install Windows, or install a new card.

If the Properties dialog box indicates, instead, that there is a problem with the card, first check to make sure the card is on the Windows 2000 Hardware Compatibility List. Optionally, you can search for updated drivers via the Internet, and use the Update Driver button on the Drivers tab of the Properties dialog box to install the updated driver.

EXERCISE 1-3

Checking an IP Configuration

You'll no doubt be using the **ipconfig /all** command often through this book, and in the real world as well. So, in this exercise, we'll go through the simple steps necessary to use the command:

1. Click the Windows Start button and choose Programs | Accessories | Command Prompt.

2. Type **ipconfig /all** and press ENTER. You should see output similar to the example shown in Figure 1-18, earlier in this chapter, but with the data from the current machine.

3. After viewing the output, type **exit** and press ENTER to close the Command Prompt window.

on the job

Just about all versions of Windows support the IPCONFIG command. However, Windows 95 and 98 use the command WINIPCFG instead.

Troubleshooting with PING

Whereas **ipconfig** is a good tool for checking a machine's IP configuration, **ping** (Packet Internet Groper) is the preferred tool for checking to see if a NIC is working, and for checking connectivity between two machines. Basically, **ping** sends an *echo request* message that basically asks "Are you there?" If the machine being pinged can be reached from the current machine, **ping** displays that machine's reply. Otherwise, it displays a list of "Request timed out" error messages.

A good strategy for troubleshooting TCP/IP problems with **ping** is to start with the local host, and then gradually work your way out to hosts that are increasingly distant from the local host, as discussed in the sections that follow.

Ping the Loopback Address

For testing and debugging purposes, you can start by pinging the loopback address, 127.0.0.1. That is, at the command prompt, type **ping 127.0.0.1** and press ENTER. You should get a reply, as in the example shown in Figure 1-19.

TABLE 1-19   Results of pinging the loopback address 127.0.0.1

```
C:\>ping 127.0.0.1

Pinging 127.0.0.1 with 32 bytes of data:

Reply from 127.0.0.1: bytes=32 time<10ms TTL=128
Reply from 127.0.0.1: bytes=32 time<10ms TTL=128
Reply from 127.0.0.1: bytes=32 time<10ms TTL=128
Reply from 127.0.0.1: bytes=32 time<10ms TTL=128

Ping statistics for 127.0.0.1:
    Packets: Sent = 4, Received = 4, Lost = 0 (0% loss),
Approximate round trip times in milli-seconds:
    Minimum = 0ms, Maximum =  0ms, Average =  0ms

C:\>
```

If pinging the loopback address results in an error message, there's likely a communication problem between Windows 2000 and your NIC. In that case, Microsoft recommends that you remove and reinstall TCP/IP.

Ping Your Own IP Address

If you can successfully ping the loopback address, try pinging the local PC's IP address. Once again, you should see some sort of successful feedback. If you get an error message instead, there's likely a communication problem between your NIC and Windows 2000. In that case, Microsoft recommends that you remove and then reinstall your NIC's driver.

Ping the Default Gateway Address

If your network has a functioning default gateway, you can ping its IP address to verify connectivity to the gateway. For example, if the default gateway address is 192.168.0.1, but pinging that address returns "Request timed out" errors, there's a problem with the address or the connection. If some other administrator already set up the default gateway, verify that you're using the correct default gateway address, and also have that administrator verify that the default gateway is properly connected to the network and functioning correctly.

Ping Nearby IP Addresses

Next, try pinging a host on the near side of the router (a computer on the same subnet) by its IP address. For example, let's say you have a computer named server01 configured as IP 192.168.0.1 and another set up as client01, IP 192.168.0.2. If you're sitting at 192.168.0.1 and want to check connectivity with the other machine, enter the **ping** command followed by that machine's address; for example, **ping 192.169.0.2**. If the connection works, you'll get a successful reply. If instead of a reply you get a "Destination host unreachable" error message, then obviously there's some problem.

If you were able to successfully ping the loopback address, but can't ping a separate machine, first check the network cabling. Many connectivity problems are nothing more than faulty cable connections. Another obvious but often overlooked potential cause should be checked—make sure the computer that you're trying to ping is up and running and connected to the network! Finally, if you have basic connectivity but still can't ping the other machine, the reason may lie in faulty ARP cache entries. You can use the ARP command, discussed in a moment, to view the contents of the cache, as well as to delete faulty entries.

Ping More Distant IP Addresses

If your network contains routers or you have an Internet connection, you can use the PING command to test connectivity to hosts on the far side of your router (outside your local subnet). The same basic syntax applies—**ping** *ipaddress*. For example, if you're connected to the Internet, you could try pinging a web site of mine by entering **ping 208.55.30.20**.

Be forewarned that some web sites, including www.microsoft.com, are designed not to respond to *ICMP Echo Requests*, which is the official name of the type of packet a **ping** command sends. So, if a first attempt fails, try some other sites. If you can't ping any web sites, trying pinging your default gateway address. If you can't ping your default gateway, check to make sure its IP address and subnet mask are set up correctly, and that you're pinging the correct address of the default gateway.

Pinging Hostnames

You can also ping another computer by its hostname. For example, if you're sitting at a computer named client01, which has a connection to a computer named server01, you can ping the server by entering the command **ping server01**. Once again, if the connection works, you'll get a positive response. If the ping fails, it could be a *name resolution problem*—a topic we'll discuss at length in Chapter 2.

> **exam**
> **Watch**
>
> *If you can ping a host by its IP address, but not its hostname, you should suspect a problem with your DNS configuration or name resolution.*

Troubleshooting with ARP

The Address Resolution Protocol (ARP) maintains a cache of IP address to hardware address mappings. Entering the command **arp -g** or **arp -a** displays the current mappings. Faulty ARP entries can cause PING echo requests to other computers in the network to fail. For example, if you can ping both the loopback address and your own IP address, but not any other IP addresses, you might be able to fix the problem by clearing out the ARP cache. You can clear individual entries using the syntax **arp -d** *IPaddress*, where *IPaddress* represents the entry you want to remove. You can delete all ARP entries by using the * wildcard with **-d** (for example, **arp -d ***) or by entering the command **netsh interface ip delete arpcache**.

Troubleshooting with Tracert

If you cannot ping a host outside your subnet, you can use the **tracert** (Trace Route) command to locate where the problem might lie. **tracert** provides information about each router or gateway that a message crosses when trying to reach another host. Each router that the message crosses is considered a *hop*.

The basic syntax for the command is **tracert** *IPaddress*, where *IPaddress* is the IP address of the destination you're trying to reach—just as in the PING command. For example, entering the command **tracert 208.55.30.20** would return a list of routers crossed on the way to that destination. The basic format of the display will look like this, where *name* represents the hostname of each router (as available) and *xxx.xxx.xxx.xxx* represents each router's IP address:

```
Tracing route to www.coolnerds.com [208.55.30.20]
over a maximum of 30 hops:

  1    <1 ms    <1 ms    <1 ms  name <xxx.xxx.xxx.xxx>
  2    12 ms    19 ms    19 ms  name <xxx.xxx.xxx.xxx>
  3     9 ms    15 ms    50 ms  name <xxx.xxx.xxx.xxx>

Trace complete.
```

By default, **tracert** is limited to testing 30 hops. But you can use the -h switch to test more or fewer maximum hops. For example, if 30 hops weren't enough to reach the destination host, you could try something like **tracert -h 40 208.55.30.20** to increase the maximum number of hops to 40.

EXERCISE 1-4

Tracing a Route

If you have Internet access from your current machine, you can try out the TRACERT command by following these simple steps:

1. Click the Windows Start button and choose Programs | Accessories | Command Prompt.

2. Type **tracert 208.55.30.20** to ping my web site. You should see output similar to the example shown in Figure 1-20, though the names and IP addresses of routers crossed will be different.

FIGURE 1-20 Results of a sample TRACERT command

```
C:\Documents and Settings\Alan>tracert 208.55.30.20

Tracing route to www.coolnerds.com [208.55.30.20]
over a maximum of 30 hops:

  1    <1 ms    <1 ms    <1 ms  cn780605-a.mshome.net [192.168.0.1]
  2   443 ms   510 ms   614 ms  10.87.14.1
  3   541 ms   283 ms   340 ms  r1-fe1-0.jamison1.pa.home.net [24.18.63.113]
  4   342 ms   183 ms   107 ms  r1-ge5-0.wyn1.pa.home.net [24.2.5.1]
  5   241 ms   323 ms   561 ms  bb1-srp2-0.rdc2.pa.home.net [216.197.151.81]
  6   380 ms    67 ms   391 ms  c1-pos4-0.phlapa1.home.net [24.7.74.57]
  7   779 ms   274 ms   353 ms  c1-pos6-0.cmdnnj1.home.net [24.7.65.225]
  8   121 ms   341 ms   442 ms  c1-pos2-0.bltmmd1.home.net [24.7.65.222]
  9   328 ms   181 ms   174 ms  c2-pos1-0.washdc1.home.net [24.7.65.89]
 10   889 ms   232 ms    57 ms  24.7.71.6
 11    41 ms    74 ms    27 ms  p16-0-0-0.r01.mclnva02.us.bb.verio.net [129.250.
5.253]
 12   229 ms   695 ms   477 ms  p16-0-0-0.r00.atlnga03.us.bb.verio.net [129.250.
2.49]
 13   679 ms   612 ms   494 ms  p4-0-2-0.r01.bcrtfl01.us.bb.verio.net [129.250.4
.54]
 14   288 ms   347 ms   594 ms  ge-1-1.r01.border.boca.verio.net [129.250.28.52]
 15   685 ms   588 ms   408 ms  ge-8-1.r01.edge.boca.verio.net [208.55.254.9]
 16   494 ms   270 ms   105 ms  www.coolnerds.com [208.55.30.20]

Trace complete.
```

3. After viewing the output, type **exit** and press ENTER to close the Command Prompt window.

Since you're tracing the route to an IP address that's on the Internet, the trace should complete successfully, provided your Internet connection is working.

If there is a problem with a router between your computer and the destination computer, you may receive feedback that looks more like this:

```
Tracing route to www.coolnerds.com [208.55.30.20]
over a maximum of 30 hops:

    1    <10 ms    <10 ms    <10 ms   <xxx.xxx.xxx.xxx>
    2     50 ms     50 ms     51 ms   <xxx.xxx.xxx.xxx>
    3   <xxx.xxx.xxx.xxx>   reports: Destination net unreachable.
```

Or perhaps like this:

```
Tracing route to www.coolnerds.com [208.55.30.20]
over a maximum of 30 hops:

    1    <10 ms    <10 ms    <10 ms   <xxx.xxx.xxx.xxx>
    2       *         *         *     Request timed out
    3       *         *         *     Request timed out
    4       *         *         *     Request timed out
```

If a router's IP address appears repeatedly in the display, that's called *looping*, and means the router is not forwarding to the next router. This is most often caused by an improper configuration at that specific router. Of course, whenever you encounter a problem tracing the route to an Internet address, it's very likely that the faulty router will be outside your company's internal network. The only thing to do, in that case, is to report the problem to your ISP. If the router is in-house, but outside your area of responsibility, you should report the problem to the administrator of that specific router.

Like PING, TRACERT will accept a hostname as well as an IP address. For example, you could enter the command **tracert www.coolnerds.com** to ping the host at 208.55.30.20. As with PING, if you're able to get to the host by its IP address but not by its hostname, then you know you have a name resolution problem on your hands. As mentioned, we'll start on name resolution in Chapter 2.

Finally, don't forget that when it comes to troubleshooting routing problems, the ROUTE PRINT command can be an ideal resource for seeing where a machine "thinks" it's supposed to route certain messages. Scan the table for conflicting routes, and remember that a route with a more specific netmask will take precedence over a conflicting route in the table that has a less specific netmask.

Troubleshooting with PATHPING

The PATHPING command combines features of PING and TRACERT, with some additional functionality. Whereas TRACERT can only point out places where these is no connectivity at all, PATHPING can point out routers that are slow or inconsistent in moving data along due to network congestion or dropped packets that need to be re-sent. To do this, PATHPING sends multiple PING echo requests to all the routers along a route for 25 seconds. Then it calculates the average time and percentage of lost packets encountered at each router. The resulting display helps you pinpoint which router along a path would be causing slow or inconsistent performance.

For example, suppose users are complaining the connection to a server named EgyptDC01 is slow or inconsistent. You enter the command **pathping EgyptDC01** from the source (any machine that's experiencing problems), and get the following results (I've boldfaced the information that's relevant to this example; your **pathping** command won't do that):

```
Tracing route to egyptdc01 [10.10.1.2]
over a maximum of 30 hops:
  0 myServer [172.16.87.35]
  1 aroute1 [180.10.20.22]
  2 aroute2 [192.168.52.1]
  3 aroute3 [192.168.80.1]
  4 aroute4 [10.10.20.22]
  5 egyptdc01 [10.10.1.2]

Computing statistics for 125 seconds...
           Source to Here   This Node/Link
Hop RTT    Lost/Sent = Pct  Lost/Sent = Pct Address
  0                                         myServer [172.16.87.35]
                              0/ 100 =  0% |
  1  46ms    0/ 100 =  0%     0/100 =  0% aroute1 [180.10.20.22]
```

Troubleshoot TCP/IP and Routing 49

```
                                    21/ 100 = 21% |
  2  21ms    16/ 100 = 16%    3/100 = 3% aroute2  [192.168.52.1]
                                     0/ 100 = 0% |
  3  20ms    10/ 100 = 10%    0/100 = 0% aroute3  [192.168.80.1]
                                     0/ 100 = 0% |
  4  21ms    12/ 100 = 12%    1/100 = 1% aroute4  [10.10.20.22]
                                     0/ 100 = 0% |
  5  20ms    12/ 100 = 12%    0/100 = 0% egyptdc01 [10.10.1.2]

Trace complete.
```

The **This Node/Link: Lost/Sent = Pct** and **Address** display the link between two router IP addresses. The value followed by the pipe character (|) is the loss rate for the specific link. In the example output, you can see that the link between 180.10.20.22 and 192.168.52.1 has a 21 percent loss rate. Dropped packets need to be retransmitted. So, with such a high drop rate, you can see that this link is the problem. So **pathping** has helped you locate the source of the problem. You could then go to that router, or contact its administrator, to try to resolve that problem. Most likely, the router is overloaded.

Now that you've learned about some basic network troubleshooting tools, let's take a look at some possible problem scenarios that might come up, and the solutions to those problems.

SCENARIO & SOLUTION

I can't get IPCONFIG, PING, or TRACERT to work at all. What should I do?	All three of those commands require a functioning TCP/IP stack. Check to make sure your NIC is properly installed (via Device Manager). If it is functioning, open the Dial-Up and Network Connections icon. Right-click the icon for your adapter and choose Properties. Make sure the Internet Protocol (TCP/IP) option under Components Checked Are Used By This Connection is selected.
IPCONFIG tells me that my computer already has an IP address of 169.254.0.10, but I've never assigned an IP address and I know there's not a DHCP server on this network.	If a Windows 2000 computer is set up to obtain an IP address automatically, but the computer can't find a DHCP server, Windows will automatically assign an IP address in the range of 169.254.0.1 through 169.254.255.254, with a subnet mask of 255.255.0.0. This capability is called Automatic Private IP Addressing (APIPA), and will be discussed in Chapter 4.

CERTIFICATION SUMMARY

In this chapter, we've looked at the ground level of the network infrastructure, the TCP/IP addresses that uniquely identify hosts on a network. You can assign either static or dynamic IP addresses to hosts. A static IP address is one that's assigned by an administrator, while a dynamic address is one that's assigned to a host automatically by a DHCP server. Microsoft recommends that you assign static IP addresses to all the servers in your network. Use dynamic IP addressing for all the clients. Doing so minimizes network administration headaches.

A TCP/IP address identifies both the network that a host belongs to and the specific host. The subnet mask tells you which part of the address identifies the network, and which part identifies the host. Standard addresses and subnet masks are categorized as Class A (subnet 255.0.0.0), Class B (255.255.0.0), and Class C (255.255.255.0). Any network can be divided into smaller subnets by using a custom subnet mask, like 255.255.255.128, to split the host portion of that address into a subnet ID and host ID.

You can use the command-line utilities IPCONFIG, PING, ARP, TRACERT, and PATHPING at any stage of a network's development to test and troubleshoot network connectivity problems. To check the IP configuration on the local host, use the **ipconfig /all** command. To test the connectivity between the local host and some other host, use **ping** *destination*. To check routing between the local host and a computer on the Internet or some other subnet, use **pathping** *destination* or **tracert** *destination*. Whereas **tracert** only lets you see "dead" connections, **pathping** lets you view packet-loss statistics, which can identify slow or inconsistent routers along a path. You can also use the **route print** command to view any computer's routing table, which lets you see where the host is actually sending messages for a given IP address or range of addresses.

✓ TWO-MINUTE DRILL

Configure TCP/IP on Servers and Clients

- ❑ TCP/IP is a suite of networking protocols, originally designed to solve problems on the Internet's precursor, ARPANet.
- ❑ Don't confuse IP addresses with hardware addresses. A hardware address is a unique 48-bit address that's hardwired into every network interface card (NIC) and usually cannot be changed by an administrator.
- ❑ The terms *Media Access Control (MAC) address*, *physical address*, *Ethernet address*, *Token Ring address*, and *NIC address* are all synonymous with the term *hardware address*.
- ❑ A TCP/IP address is a logical 32-bit address that can be assigned by an administrator.
- ❑ A TCP/IP address's subnet mask identifies which bits in the address represent the network, and which bits represent the host.
- ❑ TCP/IP addresses and subnet masks are usually displayed in *dotted quad format*, xxx.xxx.xxx.xxx, where xxx is any number from 0 to 255.
- ❑ The lowest host number in a range of IP addresses is reserved for the network ID, and cannot be assigned to a host. For example, the address 192.168.1.0 subnet mask 255.255.255.0 refers to the network 192.168.1.
- ❑ The highest available address in a range of IP addresses is reserved for the *broadcast address*. For example, 192.168.1.255 is the broadcast address for the network 192.168.1.x subnet mask 255.255.255.0.
- ❑ An IP address can be *static* (assigned by an administrator and permanent) or *dynamic* (assigned automatically by a DHCP server).

Determine Valid IP Addresses

- ❑ Subnetting allows you to subdivide a range of IP addresses into multiple subnets.
- ❑ To subnet, you "swipe" bits from the host portion of the subnet mask (the portion containing all 0's) and make them into network bits (or subnet bits).

- In binary, the subnet bits that define the network portion must be contiguous 1's, and the address must provide for some hosts to be valid.
- Valid, commonly used numbers for the host portion of a subnet mask include 128 (10000000), 192 (11000000), 224 (11100000), 240 (11110000), 248 (11111000), and 252 (11111100).
- The number of subnets you can get from a subnetted octet is 2^n where n is the number of network bits in the octet.
- The number of hosts per subnet is equal to $2^h - 2$ where h is the number of host bits the subnet mask provides.

Configure Routing

- Every computer on a TCP/IP network has a built-in routing table.
- Most entries in the routing table are dynamic, meaning they're created automatically from known data.
- You can view the routing table on a machine by entering the **route print** command at the command prompt.
- The network destination 0.0.0.0 netmask 0.0.0.0 tells where all traffic not destined for the current network (or subnet) will be sent. Hence, it identifies the default gateway.
- The Gateway column of the **route print** display identifies the IP address of the NIC used to reach machines within a network destination IP range.
- The Interface column indicates which NIC in the local machine is used to reach the IP address specified in the Gateway column.
- The Metric column indicates the *cost* of using a route in terms of hops across routers. The trip to the default gateway also counts as a hop, so the metric will never be less than 1.
- If there are conflicting routes in the routing table, the route with the most specific subnet mask will be chosen. If there is a tie between routes, the route with the smallest metric will be used.
- You can manually add *static routes* to a routing table by using the **route add** command.

- ❑ To create a persistent route—one that persists through reboots—use the **-p** switch in the **route add** command.
- ❑ It's rarely necessary to add static routes to a routing table, as the RIP and OSPF routing protocols do a good job of keeping the tables up-to-date automatically.

Troubleshoot TCP/IP and Routing

- ❑ The command **ipconfig /all** provides detailed information about the current machine's IP address, subnet mask, default gateway address, and related information for each of its logical connections.
- ❑ If the IPCONFIG command fails, either the NIC or the TCP/IP protocol isn't properly installed on the computer.
- ❑ To test the TCP/IP protocol on the current host, ping the loopback address by entering the command **ping 127.0.0.1**. If you get an error message, Microsoft recommends that you remove and reinstall the TCP/IP protocol.
- ❑ If you try to ping the local host's own IP address and get an error message, Microsoft recommends that you remove and reinstall, or update, the NIC's driver.
- ❑ To test connectivity between any two machines in a network, just ping the other machine's IP address. For example, if you're sitting at 192.168.0.1 and want to test connectivity to 192.168.0.2, enter the command **ping 192.168.0.2**.
- ❑ If you have trouble pinging another computer within your own subnet, always check the most obvious problems first. Are the cables connected correctly? Is the machine you're pinging running and online? Did you correctly type the machine's IP address in the PING command? If the physical connection is okay, try clearing the ARP cache by entering the command **arp –d ***.
- ❑ With the PING command, you can use a hostname, rather than an IP address, to identify the destination computer. If you're able to PING a host by its IP address, but not its name, you're probably looking at a name resolution problem.

- If you try to PING an address that's not on your subnet, and get an error message, you can use the TRACERT command to get information about each router that was contacted while trying to reach the destination address.
- If poor or inconsistent connections are the problem, PATHPING would be the preferred troubleshooting command because it calculates dropped-packet statistics for each path in the route.

SELF TEST

The following questions will help you measure your understanding of the material presented in this chapter. Read all the choices carefully because there might be more than one correct answer. Choose all correct answers for each question.

Configure TCP/IP on Servers and Clients

1. The 48-bit addresses expressed in the format *xx-xx-xx-xx-xx-xx*, as in 00-80-AD-7B-E0-B7, is referred to as which of the following? (Select three correct answers.)

    A. MAC address
    B. IP address
    C. Physical address
    D. Hardware address

2. You're tasked with adding a new server to a Windows 2000 network. Which of the following would be the best approach to giving the server an IP address?

    A. Use Automatic Private IP Addressing (APIPA) to assign an address automatically.
    B. Go to the Ethernet card's Internet Protocol (TCP/IP) Properties dialog box and choose Obtain An IP Address Automatically.
    C. Go to the Ethernet card's Internet Protocol (TCP/IP) Properties dialog box, choose Use The Following IP Address, and manually assign a static IP address.
    D. Manually assign a dynamic IP address through the Ethernet card's Internet Protocol (TCP/IP) Properties dialog box.

3. Which of the following would be the broadcast address for the network 192.168.0.1 with a subnet mask of 255.255.255.192?

    A. 192.168.1.0
    B. 192.168.1.1
    C. 192.168.1.62
    D. 192.168.1.63

Determine Valid IP Addresses

4. You want to subdivide the Class C network address 192.169.1.0 into four subnets. What would be the appropriate subnet mask?

    A. 192.255.255.255
    B. 255.192.0.0
    C. 255.255.192.0
    D. 255.255.255.192

5. You are the administrator for ABC Corp. One of the branch offices wants to create a subnet with the IP address 199.199.1.128 subnet 255.255.255.224. Which of the following would be the appropriate range of IP addresses that you could assign to hosts on the subnet?

    A. 199.199.1.128 to 199.199.1.159
    B. 199.199.1.128 to 199.199.1.191
    C. 199.199.1.129 to 199.199.1.158
    D. 199.199.1.129 to 199.199.1.255

Configure Routing

6. Client01 in Figure 1-21 cannot ping any sites on the Internet. However, it can ping other hosts within its own subnet. Which of the following would solve the problem? (Choose all that apply.)

    A. Change NIC1's IP address to 69.81.8.9.
    B. Change NIC2's IP address to 192.168.1.1.
    C. Change Client01's default gateway to 192.168.1.1.
    D. Change Client01's subnet mask to 255.0.0.0.

7. You are the administrator of one subnet in a large corporation. Another administrator asks you to configure a temporary static route to all hosts on the network 192.168.5.0 subnet 255.255.255.0 for testing purposes. Which of the following commands shows the appropriate network destination, subnet mask, and options for setting up such a route?

    A. **route add** 192.168.5.0 MASK 255.255.255.0
    B. **route -p** add 192.168.5.0 MASK 255.255.255.0
    C. **route add** 192.168.5.0 MASK 255.255.255.255
    D. **route -p** add 192.168.5.0 MASK 255.255.255.255

FIGURE 1-21

A server connected to the Internet and a local subnet

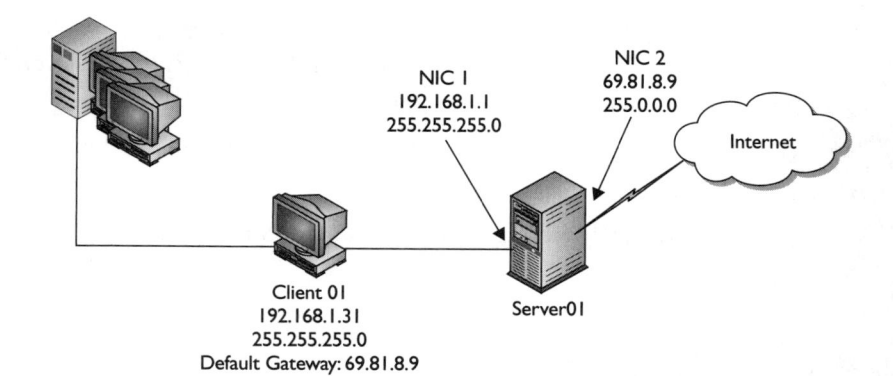

8. Which of the following routing table entries would be used first to get a message to the host at 201.202.203.101 subnet 255.255.255.0?

    A. Netmask 0.0.0.0 METRIC 30

    B. 201.202.203.0 Netmask 255.255.255.0 Metric 1

    C. 201.202.203.101 Netmask 255.255.255.255 Metric 1

    D. 201.202.203.101 Netmask 255.255.255.255 Metric 2

Troubleshoot TCP/IP and Routing

9. Which of the following commands would be best for testing connectivity to another computer within the same subnet?

    A. ipconfig

    B. tracert

    C. ping

    D. pathping

10. You are able to ping the local computer's loopback address and IP address. However, you are unable to ping any other computers within the subnet. Which of the following would be the best first step to resolving the problem?

    A. Check the network cabling to ensure the computer is connected to the network.

    B. Remove and reinstall the TCP/IP software.

    C. Update the NIC's driver.

    D. Assign a different IP address and subnet mask to the computer.

11. You are able to ping the loopback and a host's own IP address, but you're having problems pinging any other computers. You've checked all the connections and everything appears to be in place. What would be the appropriate next step?

A. Try reaching the other computers with the PATHPING command.

B. Clear the ARP cache using **arp -d** * and then try again.

C. Use the **nbtstat** command to check the NetBIOS name cache.

D. Replace the NIC.

LAB QUESTION

You are an administrator on the network shown in Figure 1-22. Users in the San Francisco office are complaining that they cannot reach DelDC01 from any clients. You run a TRACERT command to DelDC01 from a client in the San Francisco office. It gets as far as TXRouter and then times out. You run some additional PING tests and determine the following connections are valid:

- 176.17.1.1 (DelRouter) to 176.17.1.11 (DelDC01)
- 176.18.1.1 (TXRouter) to 176.17.1.1 (DelRouter)

What could you do at SFRouter to provide a consistent connection to DelDC01 for the San Francisco office?

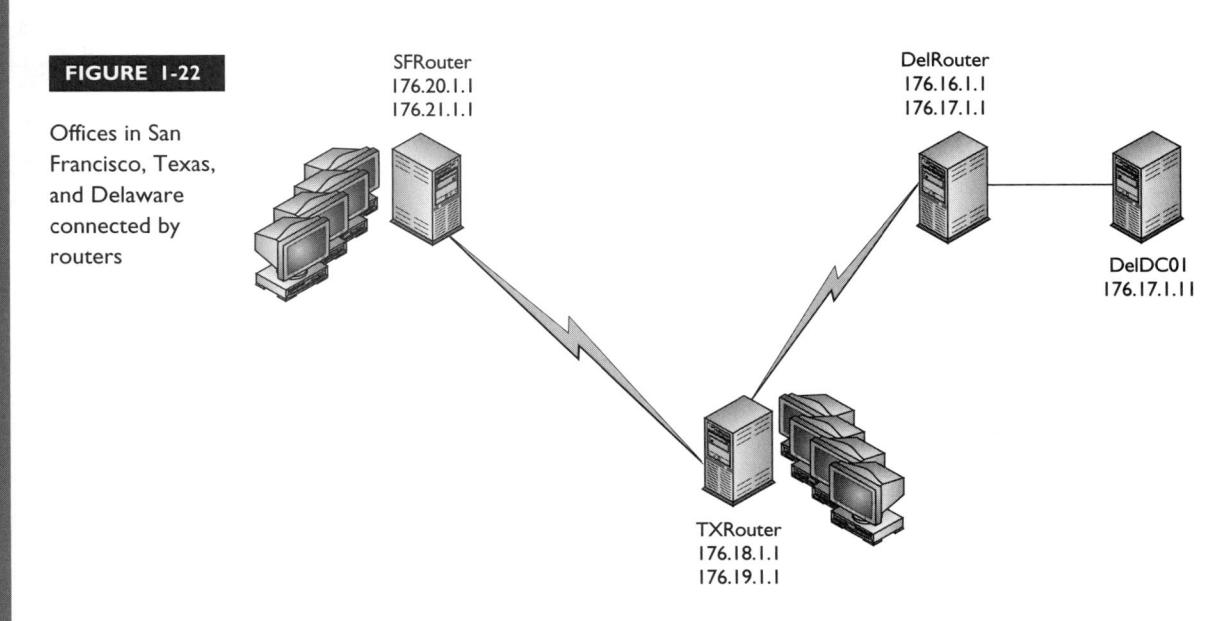

FIGURE 1-22

Offices in San Francisco, Texas, and Delaware connected by routers

SFRouter
176.20.1.1
176.21.1.1

DelRouter
176.16.1.1
176.17.1.1

DelDC01
176.17.1.11

TXRouter
176.18.1.1
176.19.1.1

SELF TEST ANSWERS

Configure TCP/IP on Servers and Clients

1. ☑ **A, C,** and **D** are all correct. The hardware address that's burned into the Ethernet card goes by many different names.
   ☒ **B** is incorrect because the logical, administrator-assigned TCP/IP address is always referred to as the *IP address* and (fortunately) doesn't have any synonyms.

2. ☑ **C** is correct. Microsoft recommends assigning static IP addresses to all the servers in a network. The reason for this is that if you let DHCP assign addresses dynamically, the server's IP address could change at some time, and then some clients might no longer be able to access the server.
   ☒ **A** is wrong because APIPA assigns an IP address automatically at startup when there is no DHCP server available to assign an IP address from an acceptable pool.
   ☒ **B** is wrong because Obtain An IP Address Automatically sets up a dynamic IP address that's assigned and managed by DHCP.
   ☒ **D** is wrong because a dynamic address is one that an administrator doesn't assign manually. DHCP assigns dynamic IP addresses automatically without administrator control.

3. ☑ **D** is correct. The host octet in the mask, 192, is 11000000, which means we have 6 host bits, and thus $2^6 - 2$, or 62 host addresses. Since the subnet ID is 192.168.1.0, hosts would be numbered 192.168.1.1 to 192.168.1.62. The broadcast address would be the next value, 192.168.1.63.
   ☒ **A** is incorrect because that's the lowest available number, and hence would be used as the network ID.
   ☒ **B** and **C** are incorrect because the highest address within the range is used as the broadcast address, and 192.168.1.63 is the highest available number in this range.

Determine Valid IP Addresses

4. ☑ **D** is correct. That's the only subnet mask that would apply to a Class C address. The answer here would have to be 255.255.255.*something*.
   ☒ **A, B,** and **C** are incorrect because they're not valid subnet masks for a Class C address.

5. ☑ **C** is correct. You were given the subnet address 199.199.1.128 to work with, so right off the bat, you know that the first available host address will be one greater than that—199.199.1.129. Converting the host portion of the mask, 224, to binary gives you 11100000.

So you know you can have $2^5 - 2$, or 30 hosts on the network. Thus, the range of valid host addresses is 199.199.1.129 to 199.199.1.158.

☒ A and B are wrong because you can't assign the network ID 199.199.1.128 to a host.

☒ C is wrong because 255 – 129 equals 126 possible host addresses. The host portion of the subnet mask only allows for 30 hosts per subnet.

Configure Routing

6. ☑ C is correct. The default gateway for all clients on that side of the router must match the connection that's on the same side of the router (Server01 is playing the role of a router here).

   ☒ A is incorrect because NIC1 is properly addressed for its side of the router.

   ☒ B is wrong because NIC2 is on the far side of the router, so its IP address wouldn't need to match the IP addresses on the other side of the router.

   ☒ D is wrong because Client01's subnet mask is already appropriate for its subnet.

7. ☑ A is correct. 192.168.5.0 netmask 255.255.255.0 would encompass all hosts on the 192.168.5.0 network.

   ☒ B is incorrect because we're looking to set up a temporary route. The **-p** switch would make this a persistent route.

   ☒ C and D are incorrect because the netmask is too specific. We want a route that will encompass all messages to 192.168.5.*x*.

8. ☑ C is correct. It has the most specific netmask and a lower metric than option D.

   ☒ A is incorrect because all the other options have a more specific netmask.

   ☒ B is incorrect because the netmask is less specific than those shown in C and D.

   ☒ D would not be chosen over C because D has a higher metric.

Troubleshoot TCP/IP and Routing

9. ☑ C is correct. **ping** is an easy tool for checking connectivity within the local subnet.

   ☒ A is wrong because **ipconfig** only tells you about the local host.

   ☒ B is wrong because **tracert** is for checking connectivity on the far side of the router (outside the local subnet).

   ☒ D is wrong because **pathping** is used for determining router statistics, not connectivity within a subnet.

10. ☑ **A** is correct. You know that the IP software on the local host is working correctly because you can **ping** the local host. Therefore, the first thing to check is the cable that connects the host to the network.
☒ **B** and **C** are wrong because you already know the NIC and IP software is functioning correctly.
☒ **D** is wrong because you'd only want to change the IP address and subnet mask after you've ascertained that the networking hardware is functioning, and have also determined that there's a problem with the local TCP/IP configuration.

11. ☑ **B** is correct. When connectivity between hosts within a subnet fails, even though everything appears to be in place, a faulty ARP cache could be the problem.
☒ **A** is incorrect because **pathping** tests across routers.
☒ **C** is incorrect because **nbtstat** and NetBIOS names aren't an issue here.
☒ **D** is incorrect because it's a lot more trouble to go to than entering **arp -d *** and trying again.

LAB ANSWER

This one takes some thinking, so let's look at what you know. The route to DelDC01 is reachable from 176.18.1.1 on TXRouter, as indicated from your ping tests. DelRouter is able to reach TXRouter, as indicated by **tracert**. But the hop from TXRouter to DelRouter isn't working. What's the most likely scenario in a situation like this? Either the routing table on SFRouter is wrong and needs to be corrected, or there just is no persistent route in the table for this path.

So let's say you check the routing table and there's nothing in there to direct packages addressed to 176.17.1.*x* to any particular IP address. You can create a persistent connection for all packets addressed to 176.17.1.*x* to 176.18.1.1 by entering this command in SFRouter's routing table:

```
route -p add 176.17.1.0 MASK 255.255.255.0 176.18.1.1
```

MCSA
MICROSOFT CERTIFIED SYSTEMS ADMINISTRATOR

2

Implementing and Troubleshooting Name Resolution

CERTIFICATION OBJECTIVES

2.01	Understand Name Resolution
2.02	Configure NetBIOS Name Resolution
2.03	Configure and Implement WINS
2.04	Troubleshoot NetBIOS Name Resolution
✓	Two-Minute Drill
Q&A	Self Test

Even though computers communicate with one another via numeric addresses, we humans prefer names. Names are just a lot easier to remember, because we can assign meaning to them. For example, you could type either **http://198.45.24.130** or **www.osborne.com** into the Address bar of any web browser and still end up at the same web page for Osborne/McGraw Hill. But clearly it's a lot easier to remember www.osborne.com than it is to remember the IP address. When users browse through local network resources via Network Neighborhood or My Network Places, they see names, not addresses, of those resources.

For we humans to be able to use names rather than numbers to find shared resources, the computer needs to translate, or *resolve,* the name to an IP address. The process of converting a name to an address is called *name resolution.* In a sense, name resolution is exactly what we do when we need to call someone on the phone, but don't know their phone number. In that case, we need to use the telephone directory, or call Directory Assistance, to be able to "resolve" the person's name into a telephone number that we can dial to reach the person.

There are a couple of name resolution services in Windows 2000 with which you'll need to be intimately familiar. In keeping with the goal of adhering to modern TCP/IP and Internet standards, Windows 2000 relies heavily on the Domain Name System (DNS) for resolving hostnames to IP addresses. However, to maintain backward compatibility, Windows 2000 still supports NetBIOS name resolution found in earlier Windows versions. In this chapter, we'll focus mainly on the older *NetBIOS name resolution.* We'll look at DNS in depth in Chapter 3.

exam
⍟atch

By today's standards, NetBIOS is a legacy network interface that's quickly being phased out by more modern TCP/IP protocols. Theoretically, one could build an entire Windows 2000 network without any NetBIOS support at all. Unfortunately, however, there is still quite a bit of NetBIOS software around. For that software to work, even a modern network needs to retain a complete NetBIOS infrastructure.

CERTIFICATION OBJECTIVE 2.01

Understand Name Resolution

Right off the bat, there are a couple of terms you need to become familiar with. The terms are similar, but represent two different approaches to resolving names to numeric addresses:

- **NetBIOS name resolution** Largely a remnant of earlier versions of Windows networking, but still in widespread use. Sometimes called *name resolution* for short.

- **Hostname resolution** Used by TCP/IP and most TCP/IP applications and programs.

Why two separate name resolution methods? Well, all network-capable applications use an *application programming interface (API)* to communicate with a network. This is to say that the programmers who write a specific application don't really need to write, from scratch, all the code necessary to allow networking. Instead, they can write to an API that provides the networking capabilities. Some applications (particularly older pre-TCP/IP-era ones) rely on NetBIOS for name resolution. Such programs "assume" they're being run on a NetBIOS-aware network, and would simply keel over and die if they found themselves running on a network with no NetBIOS capability.

By contrast, later TCP/IP-aware application programs are written to an entirely different API called *Windows Sockets*, or *Winsock* for short. Winsock is essentially an API that provides TCP/IP networking services to Windows applications. The vast majority of modern application programs—certainly Internet-aware apps—are written to the Winsock API.

Many of the networking utilities used in Windows 2000 networking are NetBIOS-based, while others are Winsock (TCP-IP) based. For example, the various NET commands that you may be familiar with from earlier versions of windows, including NET USE and NET VIEW, use the NetBIOS name resolution sequence to perform their tasks. By contrast, the TCP/IP utilities that you learned about in Chapter 1—IPCONFIG, PING, and TRACERT—are all Winsock-based.

on the job *Unlike the various NET commands found in Windows, the TCP/IP utilities IPCONFIG, PING, TRACERT, and such are available on all TCP/IP-enabled platforms, including UNIX, Linux, Macintosh, and VMS.*

Name Resolution Resources

Even though there are only two types of names that can be resolved to IP addresses in Windows 2000, each machine has many *resources* at its disposal to get the job done. Each resource offers a different means of providing name-to-address mappings.

A computer will try all the resources that are available to it to resolve the name. The resources available for resolving names to IP addresses are summarized here:

- **Local host (HOSTNAME)** The local machine's name.
- **NetBIOS name cache** A collection of recently resolved NetBIOS names, stored in memory (RAM).
- **Broadcast** A "shout" to all other computers in the LAN that in essence asks "Are you the machine I'm looking for?"
- **LMHOSTS file** A file of NetBIOS names and their IP addresses.
- **WINS** A centralized database of NetBIOS names and their IP addresses.
- **HOSTS file** A file of TCP/IP hostnames and their IP addresses.
- **DNS** The Domain Name System used in TCP/IP and the Internet.

In the sections that follow, we'll look at the various resources in more depth. As you'll see, some of them are geared toward resolving NetBIOS names, while others are geared toward resolving TCP/IP hostnames. TCP/IP and NetBIOS name resolution both use the same resources. Once again, the reason is that Windows 2000 needs to be able to resolve both types of names in order to be TCP/IP-oriented while maintaining backward compatibility with earlier versions of Windows.

Local Host (HOSTNAME)

Name resolution starts off its quest to resolve a name to an IP address by asking the simple, most straightforward question possible: "Is it me?" To complete this step, TCP/IP simply compares the name in question to the current machine's hostname. If the two are the same, the IP address of the local machine is returned as the IP address, and the search is over. This prevents the machine from going through more elaborate methods to try to resolve the name.

NetBIOS Name Cache

Each machine in a Windows network maintains a *NetBIOS name cache,* which is simply a list of NetBIOS names followed by their IP addresses, stored in memory (RAM). This cache is built, automatically, from recently resolved NetBIOS names. Whenever a computer successfully resolves a NetBIOS name, that name and address are automatically added to the NetBIOS names cache. The cache also contains name-to-IP address mappings from NetBIOS computers that have contacted your computer. Each time the machine encounters a new name to resolve, it does a quick check of the NetBIOS name cache to see if that name and address are already stored there. If so, the machine uses that address from the cache, which saves it from going through other, more elaborate methods to resolve the name.

To keep the cache from growing too large, each entry only remains in the cache for ten minutes from its creation. You can view the NetBIOS names currently stored in the cache, and the IP address associated with each name, by entering the command **nbtstat –c** at the command prompt.

Broadcast

Broadcasting is another means of resolving a computer name to an IP address. With this approach, the computer broadcasts a message to all the machines in the local subnet, essentially asking "Is there a machine named *whatever* here?" Each machine in the subnet compares the name being searched for (for example, *whatever*) to its own name. If a machine's name matches the requested name, that machine sends back its IP address, and hence the name is resolved.

LMHOSTS File

Like the HOSTS file, the LMHOSTS file is a text file that contains IP addresses and computer names. Unlike HOSTS, however, LMHOSTS contains only NetBIOS names (aka *computernames*), and no TCP/IP fully qualified domain names (FQDNs). NetBIOS names are single-label names up to 15 characters in length, such as THEODORE or ACCT_GROUP. Thus, an LMHOSTS file might contain entries that look like these:

192.168.0.1	Domain_Server
192.168.0.2	Backup_Server
192.168.0.3	Theodore
192.168.0.4	Wibble_Wobble

The LM in the filename stands for LAN Manager in reference to the earliest Microsoft networking products. In that regard, the LMHOSTS file is something of a relic. The LMHOSTS file is optional in a Windows 2000 network, so it won't exist on all machines. By default, it's placed in the same folder as the HOSTS file, %systemroot%\system32\drivers\etc. The folder also contains a sample LMHOSTS file named lmhosts.sam that describes the contents of an LMHOSTS file.

WINS

Windows Internet Naming Service (WINS) is a Microsoft-specific NetBIOS name server (NBNS). WINS evolved out of the need to have some sort of centralized name resolution service for NetBIOS networks. Don't let the name mislead you; WINS has nothing to do with the Internet. A *WINS server* is a database of NetBIOS names and IP addresses that's maintained automatically on a network, though it can also be administered manually. WINS still plays an important role in Windows 2000 networks, as we'll discuss later in this chapter. For now, it's sufficient to keep in mind that WINS is a step taken in both the NetBIOS and hostname resolution sequences.

EXERCISE 2-1

CertCam 2-1

Check Out Your Computer Name

Here's a simple exercise you can use to view your computer's NetBIOS name (computer name) and also change it if you need to:

1. On the Windows desktop, right-click My Computer and choose Properties.
2. Click on the Network Identification tab.
3. Click the Properties button to view the Identification Changes dialog box, shown in Figure 2-1.

The NetBIOS name appears in the text box under Computer Name. Beneath that you'll see the Full Computer Name (hostname), which will be the same as your domain membership, if the computer is already a domain member. Note that if you do this on a Windows 2000 Server computer that's already been promoted to a domain controller, the dialog box will look different, and you won't have the option of changing the computer name. The computer name, in that case, is just the hostname (Full Computer Name) with the domain name removed.

Go ahead and close the open dialog boxes when you're done.

FIGURE 2-1

The Identification Changes dialog box

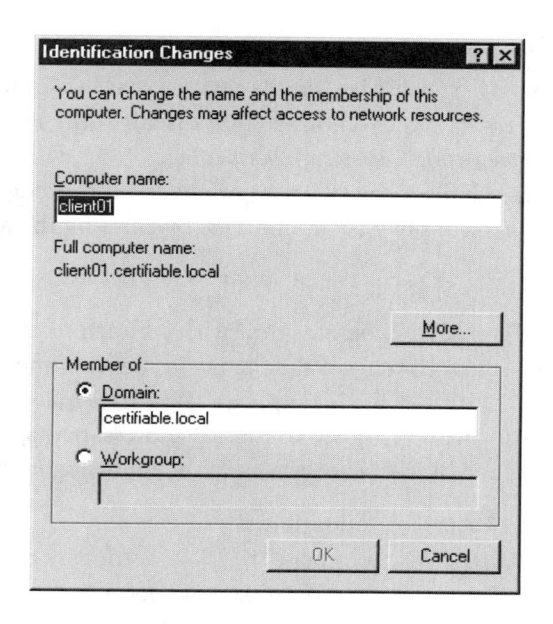

Domain Name System (DNS)

DNS is the name resolution system used by the Internet. It resolves a fully qualified domain name (FQDN) like www.osborne.com to an IP address. For DNS name resolution to take place, the local computer needs to know the IP address of a DNS *name server*. A simple example would be a single computer that connects to the Internet through an Internet service provider (ISP). The ISP automatically configures the computer with the IP address of one or two name servers. When name resolution reaches the DNS step of the procedure, it sends the name to the DNS server, which, hopefully, will return the IP address of the requested name.

DNS plays a major role in Windows 2000 networking. In fact, Active Directory depends on it. DNS is such a large and significant topic that it gets its own chapter in this book (Chapter 3). For the purposes of name resolution and this chapter, though, it's sufficient to know that when a client needs a name resolved, it simply sends a request to a DNS name server, something like "Hey name server, what's the IP address of www.osborne.com?" The DNS name server responds with one of two answers—either the IP address of the host, or "Beats me" (an error.)

The HOSTS File

The HOSTS file is a simple text file that lists hostnames and their corresponding IP addresses. On a Windows 2000 machine, the HOSTS file is usually stored in the %systemroot%\system32\drivers\etc folder with no filename extension. You can open the file using Notepad or any other text editor, or at the command prompt, you can simply view its contents by entering the following command:

```
type %systemroot%\system32\drivers\etc\hosts
```

The HOSTS file starts off with a bunch of comments preceded by # characters. The actual content of the file begins beneath the comments. Each line in the body of the HOSTS file is simply an IP address followed by a tab or space, followed by the hostname assigned to that IP address, perhaps followed by another comment preceded by a # character, as in the following example:

```
127.0.0.1        localhost
10.10.1.31       client01             #nearby client
192.168.2.1      Ahost.somenet.local  #host on somenet
208.55.32.20     www.coolnerds.com    #Web site
```

The HOSTS file is entirely optional. By default, the HOSTS file contains only the loopback address followed by the hostname *localhost*, as in the first line of the preceding example. As an administrator, you can add frequently accessed IP addresses and their hostnames to the file as you wish. There's no limit to how many items you can place in the file.

Be aware that the HOSTS file is entirely manual, meaning that if a host's IP address changes, that change will *not* be reflected in the HOSTS file. All attempts to connect to that host via the original IP address will fail. From a troubleshooting perspective, it's important to keep in mind that the HOSTS file is checked early in the name resolution process. If the HOSTS file contains a faulty IP address-to-hostname mapping, the name resolution will fail and return only an error message.

CERTIFICATION OBJECTIVE 2.02

Configure NetBIOS Name Resolution

The NetBIOS API in Windows 2000 can run atop NetBEUI, Novell IPX/SPX, and the TCP/IP transfer protocols. Any one transfer protocol will do. The most widely

Configure NetBIOS Name Resolution **71**

SCENARIO & SOLUTION

Isn't it terribly inefficient to have so many different resources available for name resolution?	As soon as a host successfully resolves a name to an IP address, it stops looking, so it won't go through all the resources, unless they all fail to resolve the name. If that happens, you get some sort of "…not found" error message.
What if a computer doesn't have a HOSTS file, LMHOSTS file, or some other resource?	That's not a problem. A client will use whatever resources it has at its disposal and simply ignore the rest.
If NetBIOS is so separate and distinct from TCP/IP, why do NetBIOS names get resolved to TCP/IP addresses?	Originally, NetBIOS used simple broadcasts and hardware addresses for communications. The widespread acceptance of TCP/IP forced NetBIOS to become compatible with TCP/IP. NetBIOS over TCP/IP was born from that need.

used is NetBIOS over TCP/IP, often abbreviated NetBT or NBT. Unlike the earliest implementations of NetBIOS, which used simple broadcasts to resolve NetBIOS names to Ethernet addresses, NetBT can resolve NetBIOS names to TCP/IP addresses. As such, NetBIOS can be used over routers. Unlike TCP/IP, NetBIOS names don't include any labels that identify the network to which a given host belongs. Instead, NetBIOS is a *flat namespace*, whereby each host is identified by a single, unique label.

NetBIOS Names

NetBIOS only recognizes *NetBIOS names* (also called *computernames*) like SERVER01 or HOWDYDOODY. Unlike fully qualified domain names, NetBIOS names have a maximum length of 15 characters and contain no dots.

exam
⑨atch
NetBEUI (NetBIOS Extended User Interface) is Microsoft's implementation of NetBIOS. Any exam question about NetBEUI is really a question about NetBIOS.

There are some potential conflicts between NetBIOS names and TCP/IP hostnames due to the fact that NetBIOS supports a wide range of punctuation characters, while TCP/IP does not. For example, NetBIOS names often contain an underscore, as in the name ACCOUNTING_SERV. The rules for composing NetBIOS names are as follows:

- Up to 15 characters in length
- Use any of the characters A-Z, a-z, 0-9, #$!-_@%()[]
- No blank spaces or periods
- Names are *not* case-sensitive (but will appear in uppercase in many applications)

When creating new hostnames for Windows 2000 machines, you should avoid all the punctuation characters—even the underscore, which was quite popular in NetBIOS names. Following the TCP/IP rule of "no punctuation" when assigning hostnames makes for smoother, simpler administration of networks that support both NetBIOS and TCP/IP.

NetBIOS Service Identifiers

A computer running NetBT will have several NetBIOS names divided into three main categories: a username, which identifies the user currently logged in to the machine, a unique computer name, which identifies the specific computer, and a group name, which identifies workgroup or domain memberships. When a NetBIOS process is communicating with a specific process on a remote computer, a unique name is used. When a NetBIOS process is communicating with multiple processes on multiple computers, a group name is used.

Within the computer and group names will be several nearly identical names in which the first 15 characters match, and the 16th character acts as a *service identifier*. The service identifier is used to inform other computers on the network of the services that are available on the local machine. You can use the **nbtstat –n** command to view all the NetBIOS names currently active on a given computer. The results of the command will look something like the example shown in Figure 2-2.

In the example, SERVER01 is the name of the machine, CERTIFIABLE is the name of the domain, and ADMINISTRATOR is the name I'm currently logged in as. The first column in the display lists NetBIOS names. The second column, which is a hex number in angle brackets (for example, <00>) is the service identifier. The third column tells whether the name represents a unique host or group. Table 2-1 lists some of the more common service identifiers for the various names that may appear in the **nbtstat –n** command's output.

The File and Printer Sharing for Microsoft Networks service provides a good example of a NetBIOS-based process and name resolution. When a client wants to

FIGURE 2-2   Sample results of an **nbtstat –n** command

```
C:\>nbtstat -n

Local Area Connection:
Node IpAddress: [10.10.1.1] Scope Id: []

            NetBIOS Local Name Table

       Name              Type         Status
    ---------------------------------------------
    SERVER01       <00>  UNIQUE       Registered
    SERVER01       <20>  UNIQUE       Registered
    CERTIFIABLE    <00>  GROUP        Registered
    CERTIFIABLE    <1C>  GROUP        Registered
    CERTIFIABLE    <1B>  UNIQUE       Registered
    SERVER01       <03>  UNIQUE       Registered
    CERTIFIABLE    <1E>  GROUP        Registered
    ADMINISTRATOR  <03>  UNIQUE       Registered
    INet~Services  <1C>  GROUP        Registered
    IS~SERVER01....<00> UNIQUE        Registered
    CERTIFIABLE    <1D>  UNIQUE       Registered
    .._MSBROWSE__. <01>  GROUP        Registered

C:\>_
```

get to the file and/or printing services of a client named, say, SERVER01, it actually looks for the following name:

SERVER01   <20>

where <20> represents the 16th character. The name is padded with enough blank spaces, automatically, to ensure that the service identifier is the 16th character in the name. It's that 16-character name that needs to be resolved to an address before communications can actually take place. Again, you'll rarely see that character in any sort of graphical interface to NetBIOS, but as you'll see, the service identifier will show up in some files and troubleshooting tools.

TABLE 2-1   Examples of Service Identifiers Used with NetBIOS Names

Name	16th Byte	Unique Service Identified
Computer	<00>	Workstation service: this is the *NetBIOS computer name*
Computer	<06>	Remote Access Server (RAS) service
Computer	<20>	Server service: identifies a machine that is a WINS client and has file and/or printer sharing enabled
Computer	<21>	Server service: identifies machines that have file and/or printer sharing enabled
Domain	<1B>	Primary domain controller name

NetBIOS Name Resolution Sequences

The order in which the various resources for name resolution are checked depends on a multitude of settings and options. Most importantly is the node type, which appears when you enter an **ipconfig /all** command at the command prompt. There are basically four mode types:

- **Broadcast (b-node)**   Uses broadcasts for NetBIOS name resolution; not ideal because of added network traffic, and because broadcasts won't cross routers.
- **Peer (p-node)**   Uses point-to-point communication whereby a specific NetBIOS name server (NBNS), such as WINS. Eliminates broadcasts but requires a centralized server.
- **Mixed (m-node)**   Tries a broadcast first, and if that fails, tries p-node.
- **Hybrid (h-node)**   Tries p-node first, and if that fails, tries a broadcast.

on the job

A fifth node type, called Microsoft-Enhanced b-Node, checks cached LMHOSTS entries prior to broadcasting.

Computers running Windows 2000 are b-node by default, but become h-node if you set up a WINS server. You can also assign a node type to a client via a DHCP server, as you'll learn in Chapter 4. There are numerous other settings and options that determine the behavior of the NetBIOS name resolution sequence, as you'll learn. For future reference, Figure 2-3 presents a flow chart of how NetBIOS name resolution works based on the node type, resources available, and various settings.

Creating an LMHOSTS File

Recall that both hostname resolution and NetBIOS name resolution use LMHOSTS as one of their resources in trying to resolve a name to an IP address. As such, the LMHOSTS file can be used as a backup for when other means of name resolution fail. It can also solve name resolution problems on any pre-Windows 2000 servers, and servers in networks that use both Windows 2000 and Windows NT domains.

The LMHOSTS file, like the HOSTS file, is a simple ASCII text file that you can create and modify using any simple text editor, such as Notepad. Like the HOSTS file, the LMHOSTS file (if it exists) is stored in the %systemroot%\system32\drivers\etc folder. Unlike the HOSTS files, which maps TCP/IP hostnames to IP addresses, the LMHOSTS file maps NetBIOS names to IP addresses. Also unlike the

Configure NetBIOS Name Resolution 75

FIGURE 2-3 Order of NetBIOS name resolution based on node type

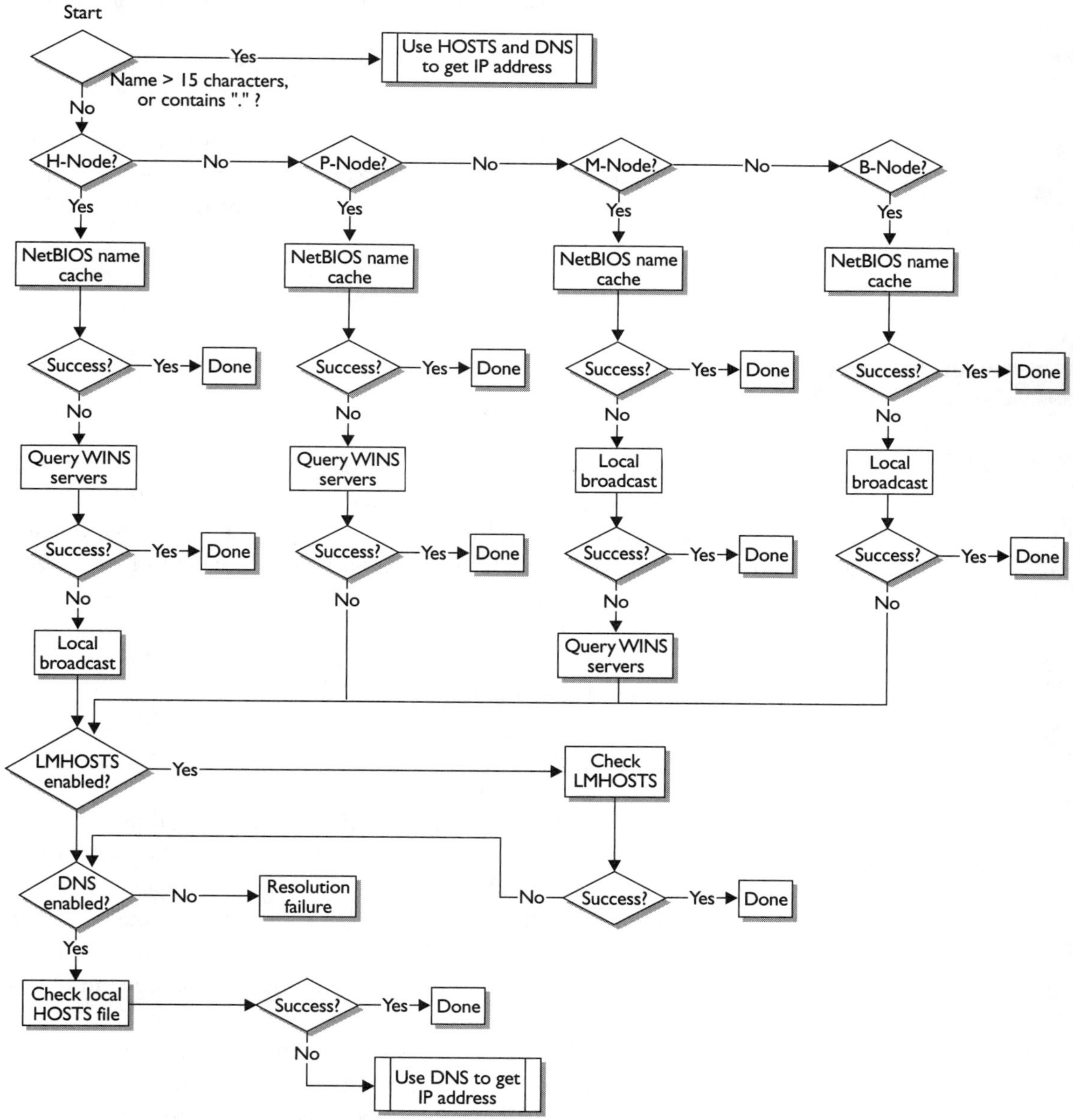

HOSTS file, the LMHOSTS file can contain several meaningful *tags* that allow it to interact with the NetBIOS name cache and the WINS database. The main tags are #DOM and #PRE.

The #DOM (Domain) Tag

The #DOM tag identifies domain controllers. Use the syntax #DOM:*domainName*, where *domainName* is the domain for which the machine is a controller. For example, the following line shows that the machine named Server01 is the domain controller for a domain named Certifiable:

199.198.0.1   Server01   #DOM:Certifiable

EXERCISE 2-2

Peek at Some NetBIOS Names

Here we'll go through some simple exercises that will let you view information about the current computer, but won't make any changes to the system. So, if you're trying this on a production machine, it's not necessary to get the permission of the network administrator. For starters, we'll take a look at your computer's local NetBIOS names. Follow these steps:

1. Click the Start button and choose Programs | Accessories | Command Prompt.
2. Type the command **nbtstat –n** and press ENTER.

Your computer will no doubt have several NetBIOS names, some different UNIQUE names for services that apply to this computer, as well as the other types of names we discussed earlier in this chapter.

Now, let's see if your local NetBIOS name cache has a list of any remote NetBIOS+ names. The list could well be empty, but we'll take a peek anyway just for the hands-on practice. You're already at a command prompt, so just type the command **nbtstat –c** and press ENTER.

You can also take a look to see what node type this computer is configured to use for NetBIOS name resolution. At the command prompt, type the command **ipconfig /all** and press ENTER. You'll see node type listed as the third item.

The #PRE (Preload) Tag

You can think of #PRE as either the PRELOAD or PRECEDENCE tag, because it *preloads* an entry into the NetBIOS name cache, and hence gives it *precedence* in a name-resolution scenario. If you have a WINS server for NetBIOS name resolution on the network, a #PRE entry in the LMHOSTS file will take precedence over the WINS entry. For example, let's say that a computer is looking for NetBIOS name resolution for the name ALBERTS_PC. If WINS returns one IP address, and LMHOSTS returns a different address, the IP address associated with a #PRE entry in the LMHOSTS file will be chosen. If there is no #PRE tag on the entry in the LMHOSTS file, the IP address returned by the WINS server will be used.

> **exam**
> **Watch**
>
> *Remember that even though the LMHOSTS file is one of the last resources that a name resolution sequence will use, those #PRE entries are actually evaluated early in the process when the NetBIOS name cache is scanned.*

To preload domain controllers, precede the #DOM tag with the #PRE tag as well. In the following example, both entries are preloaded into the NetBIOS name cache at bootup. The second entry identifies Server01 as the domain controller (*primary domain controller* or *PDC* in NT-speak) for the Certifiable domain:

```
199.198.0.31    Client01    #PRE
199.198.0.1     Server01    #PRE    #DOM:Certifiable
```

Remember that #PRE entries in LMHOSTS will be loaded into the NetBIOS name cache as soon as the computer starts. Thus, the corresponding #PRE entry in the LMHOSTS file is redundant at that point. For efficiency, it makes sense to put all #PRE entries at the bottom of the LMHOSTS file.

> **exam**
> **Watch**
>
> *In a non-WINS environment, it's important to ensure that the primary domain controller is clearly identified and preloaded within the LMHOSTS file. Remember the exact syntax is **IPaddress ServerName #PRE #DOM:domainName** in that order.*

Now that you have a better understanding of NetBIOS names and name resolution resources, let's take a moment to look at some possible scenario questions that might arise, and the answers to those questions.

SCENARIO & SOLUTION

I'm building a Windows 2000 network from scratch, and doubt I'll have any applications that are old enough to require NetBIOS. Would I still need to provide for NetBIOS name resolution in this case?	No, a pure Windows 2000 network can operate entirely on TCP/IP, but any older clients or programs that rely on NetBIOS wouldn't work on that network.
My LMHOSTS file contains a hostname that looks something like "Joe \0x1B" What's up with that?	The service codes associated with NetBIOS hostnames consist of nonprintable characters. Normally, you just see the code in the angle brackets, like <1B>. If you need to type a special service code into LMHOSTS, you need to type enough spaces after the name to make it exactly 15 characters long. Then type \01x and the hex code for the identifier (for example, \0x1B). Make sure the hostname and service identifier are enclosed in quotation marks.
How do I configure a computer's node type?	If you set up a DHCP server (see Chapter 4), you can assign a node type to all clients that use DHCP to get their IP addresses.

CERTIFICATION OBJECTIVE 2.03

Configure and Implement WINS

As mentioned, NetBIOS started out as a simple broadcast-based interface for small local area networks. As these small networks grew, it became obvious that some sort of centralized NetBIOS name server (NBNS) would greatly reduce traffic and administrative headaches. While the LMHOSTS file offered some relief, by allowing resolution of names across routers, it really didn't help to reduce the excess traffic caused by all the broadcasting involved. RFCs 1001 and 1002 specified some protocols that an NBNS would use, and Microsoft followed by creating its own, proprietary NBNS named Windows Internet Naming Service (WINS).

WINS consists of two primary components, *WINS servers* and *WINS clients.* A WINS server is a dynamic, centralized database of NetBIOS names and their corresponding IP addresses. Only "server" editions of Windows (Windows 2000 Server, Windows 2000 Advanced Server, or Windows 2000 DataCenter), can act as a WINS server. The advantages of WINS over other forms of NetBIOS name resolution are summarized as follows:

Configure and Implement WINS

- Improved response time through the reduction of NetBIOS name query traffic.
- A dynamically updated database of NetBIOS-to-IP address name mappings that handles name registration, resolution, and integration with DHCP IP address allocation.
- Centralized management of the WINS database for administrators, and automatic replication to other WINS servers.
- Support for clients running Windows 2000 Server and Professional, Windows NT Server and Workstation, Windows 98, Windows 95, Windows for Workgroups, and LAN Manager 2.*x*.
- Support for transparent browsing across routers for clients running any of the preceding operating systems *except* LAN Manager 2.*x*.

exam
Watch   *During the exam, you should consider DOS or any non-Microsoft operating system as being a non-WINS client. For example, a WINS question involving UNIX, Linux, or OS/2 is really a question about non-WINS clients.*

Installing a WINS Server

To set up a WINS server, you'll need Windows 2000 Server or NT Server. You can't install a WINS server on a Windows Workstation or Professional machine. Installing WINS is no different from installing any other Windows component software. You just have to make sure that you do it on a server-class computer, rather than a client. Also, unless you're working on a very small network, you don't want to choose a machine that will be busy playing the role of domain controller. That said, here are the steps required to install a WINS server:

1. Log in with administrative privileges, and open Control Panel.
2. Open Add/Remove Programs.
3. Click the Add/Remove Windows Components button.
4. In the Windows Components Wizard that opens, scroll down to and then click Networking Services.
5. Click the Details button, and then scroll down to and select the Windows Internet Name Service (WINS) option, as shown in Figure 2-4.

FIGURE 2-4 Windows Internet Name Service (WINS) selected in the Networking Services dialog box

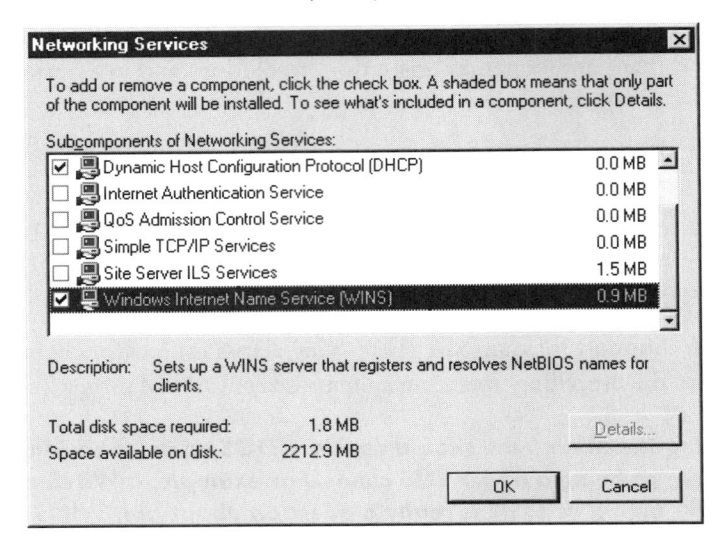

6. Click the OK button to return to the Windows Components Wizard and then click the Next button.

7. Click the Next button.

8. Follow the onscreen instructions and then click Finish to close the wizard. You can also close the Add/Remove Windows Components window and Control Panel at that point.

The server is installed and functioning when the wizard closes. There are, of course, quite a few options you can use to configure the server to your liking, and of course, you'll need to set up clients to use WINS.

Configuring WINS Clients

Once you've installed one or more WINS servers, you'll need to configure clients to use that service. You'll need to know the IP address of the primary WINS server (the main server you want the client to use for registration and renewal), plus the IP address of any additional secondary (backup) servers the client can use in the event that the first choice isn't available. To enable WINS on a WINS-capable client, follow these steps:

Configure and Implement WINS 81

1. Log in as administrator and open the Network and Dial-Up Connections window.
2. Right-click the Local Area Connection icon (or whichever icon represents your connection to the local network) and choose Properties.
3. Click Internet Protocol (TCP/IP) and then click the Properties button.
4. In the Internet Protocol (TCP/IP) dialog box that opens, click the Advanced button.
5. Click the WINS tab.
6. Click the Add button and enter the IP address of a WINS server, starting with the primary server and working your way down through backup servers. In the example shown in Figure 2-5, I've listed two WINS servers.
7. Optionally, you can rearrange WINS addresses in the list using the Up and Down buttons at the right side of the IP address list.
8. Click the OK button and close all remaining open dialog boxes.

FIGURE 2-5

Windows Internet Name Service (WINS) selected in the Networking Services dialog box

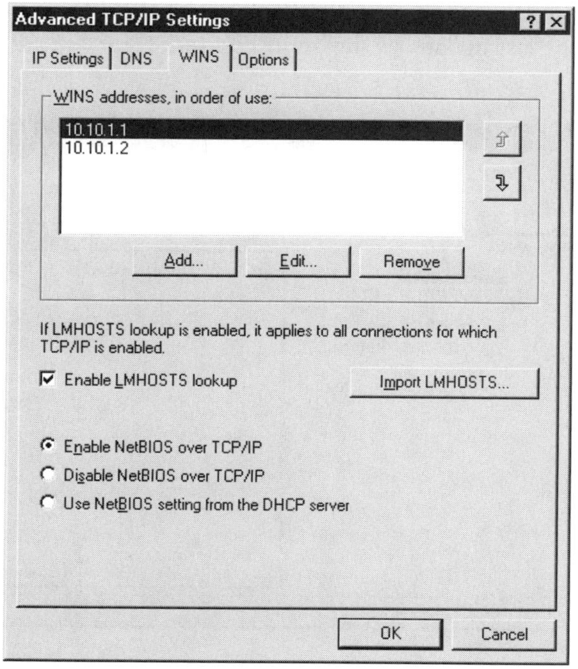

The WINS server itself can certainly be a WINS client as well. However (and this is important), when entering the IP address, you should enter only one—the server's own IP address. Otherwise, the server's WINS record might become *split*. A split occurs when names registered for a particular WINS server are owned by different WINS servers. The term "owner" in this context means the WINS database with which a machine originally registered its name. If you allow the WINS server the opportunity to register itself with some other machine, and it does so, the split is likely to lead to administrative headaches later down the road.

exam
⑩atch

Simply stated, a WINS server should point only to itself on the WINS tab of that computer's Advanced TCP/IP Settings dialog box.

Managing a WINS Database

Installing WINS also installs the *WINS management console,* which you can use for configuration and management. The tool is Microsoft Management Console (MMC) snap-in that you can get to by clicking the Start button and choosing Programs | Administrative Tools | WINS. When the management console opens, you'll see two nodes in the left pane. Clicking Server Status in the console tree displays the server's NetBIOS name, IP address, status, and the date and time of the last update, as shown in Figure 2-6.

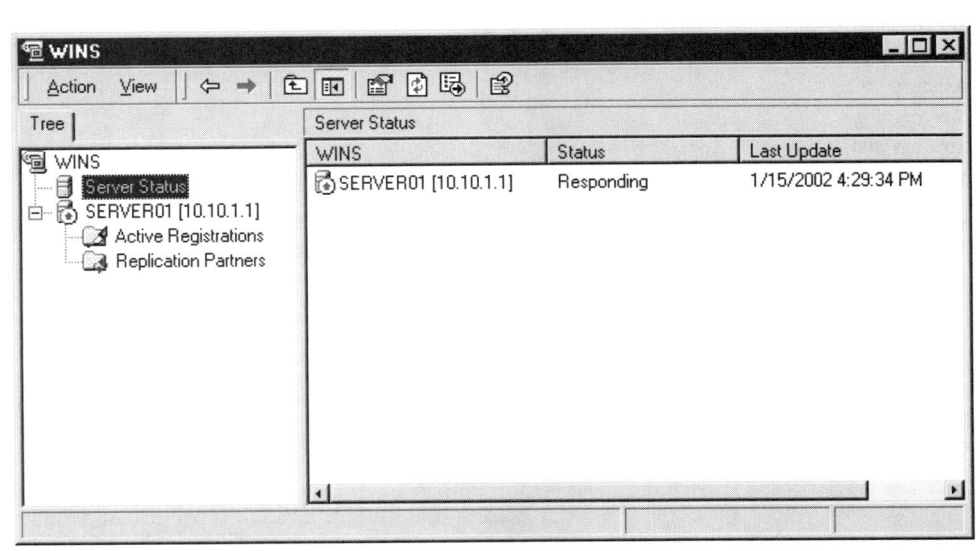

FIGURE 2-6

The WINS snap-in for the Microsoft Management Console showing the server's status

FIGURE 2-7

The All Tasks submenu lets you turn the WINS server service on and off.

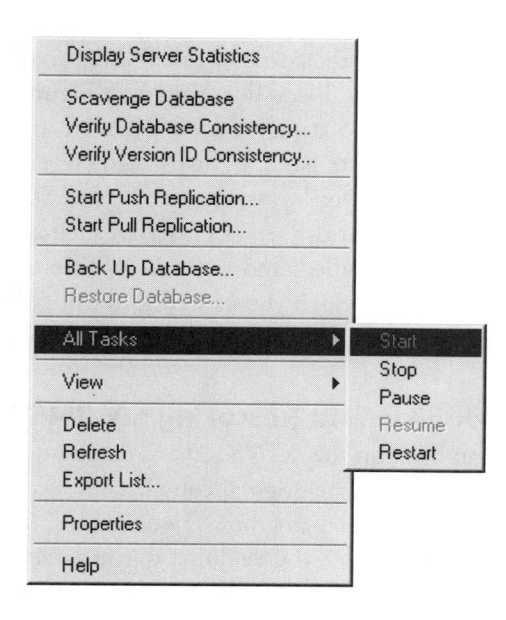

Display Server Statistics
Scavenge Database
Verify Database Consistency...
Verify Version ID Consistency...
Start Push Replication...
Start Pull Replication...
Back Up Database...
Restore Database...
All Tasks ▶
View ▶
Delete
Refresh
Export List...
Properties
Help

All Tasks submenu:
- Start
- Stop
- Pause
- Resume
- Restart

Once installed, the WINS service is started automatically. Occasionally, you might need to stop or pause the service to perform some maintenance activity. To do so, you can right-click the WINS server's name in the console tree, and point to All Tasks, as shown in Figure 2-7 above. Optionally, you can click the Actions button and point to All Tasks to get to the same options.

EXERCISE 2-3

Viewing Records in a WINS Database

If you have a Windows 2000 Server machine acting as a WINS server, you can try this exercise to view records in the WINS database:

1. Click the Start button and choose Programs | Administrative Tools | WINS.
2. Expand the server name and IP address node.
3. Right-click Active Registrations and choose Find By Owner.
4. Choose This Owner and click Find Now.

The resulting display will show all active name registrations.

Right-clicking the name of the WINS server and choosing Properties reveals the server's Properties dialog box, shown in Figure 2-8. Most of the tasks involved in managing a WINS database are available from various tabs in the dialog box, To view the server's statistics, right-click the sever name and IP address in the console tree and choose Display Server Statistics. A Statistics dialog box will open, displaying information about the server's activity, such as when it was started, the total number of queries it's handled, and so forth. Within that dialog box, you'll also find a Refresh button, which you can click to bring the server statistics up to date immediately.

Backing Up and Restoring a WINS Database

You can back up the WINS server's database as an extra copy for disaster recovery in the event that the original copy becomes corrupted. On the General tab of the server's Properties dialog box, choose a local folder for the backup file under Default Backup Path. Once you've done so, the database will be backed up automatically every three hours. To have the database backed up automatically whenever you stop the WINS service as well, just choose the Back Up Database During Server Shutdown option.

FIGURE 2-8

The General tab of a WINS server's Properties dialog box

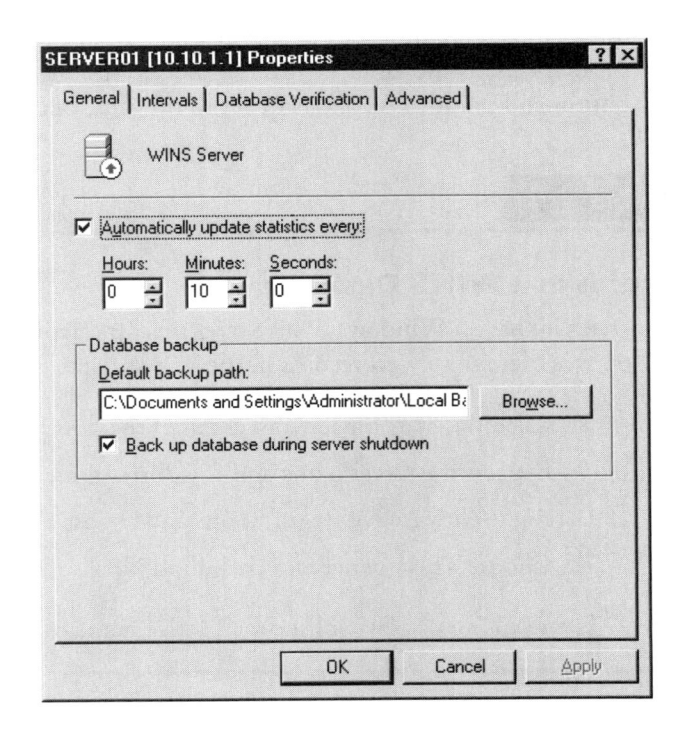

Configure and Implement WINS 85

exam ⓦatch

When choosing the default backup path, make sure you choose a local folder. If you choose a remote share, the backups will fail!

If you plan to do some sort of work on the WINS database and want to make an immediate backup, you can right-click the server name and IP address in the WINS console and choose Backup Database.

Should you ever need to restore the WINS database from the backup, you can follow these steps:

1. Stop the WINS service (right-click the server name and IP address in the WINS console and choose All Tasks | Stop).

2. Right-click the server name and IP address again and choose Restore Database.

3. In the Browse For Folder dialog box that appears, make sure the correct folder for your backup is selected and click OK.

Once the restoration is complete, the service is restarted automatically. There's no need to restart the WINS service manually.

Configuring WINS Intervals

Every NetBIOS name that's registered in the WINS database goes through a lifecycle of registration, renewal (to verify that it's still there), and eventually removal if it's taken off the network. The Intervals tab in the WINS server's Properties dialog box, shown in Figure 2-9, allows you to customize the various lifecycle intervals to your own needs. Microsoft recommends using the default intervals, but you can set your own intervals as summarized here:

- **Renew interval** Sets the renewal interval (TTL) for newly registered names. The first renewal request sent by a client occurs one half of the way through this duration, then every ten minutes until the name is renewed. In short, this setting determines how often each client renews its name.

- **Extinction interval** After a client logs off and releases its NetBIOS name, its WINS record is marked as "released" in the database, but the record is not physically removed. If another computer tries to register the same name as the one in the released record, no challenge is issued to the original holder of the name. Because the record is marked as released, it won't be replicated to other WINS servers. The extinction interval determines how long a record will be marked as "released." Once that extinction interval has transpired, the record is marked as "extinct."

- **Extinction timeout** A record that has been marked as "extinct" is said to be *tombstoned*. The record still exists in the database, though. The extinction timeout interval specifies how long the extinct record remains in the database before it's finally *scavenged* (physically removed from the database).

- **Verification interval** Specifies the amount of time after which a WINS server must verify that old names that it doesn't own are still active. For example, say a secondary WINS server got a registration for the name ACLIENT from a primary server. If the verification interval is set to 24 hours, the secondary server must check with the primary server every 24 hours to ensure that ACLIENT is still an active record in the primary server's database.

The default various time intervals involved in the release, extinction, and eventual removal of records from a WINS database allows records for disconnected clients to remain in the database for quite a long time. In the past, this has led some administrators to open up the WINS server database and start manually deleting records for computers that are no longer on the network. These same administrators were often surprised to see those deleted records "magically" reappear in the database at some time in the future. The reason for the reappearance has to do with replication among multiple WINS servers.

FIGURE 2-9

The Intervals tab of a WINS server's Properties dialog box

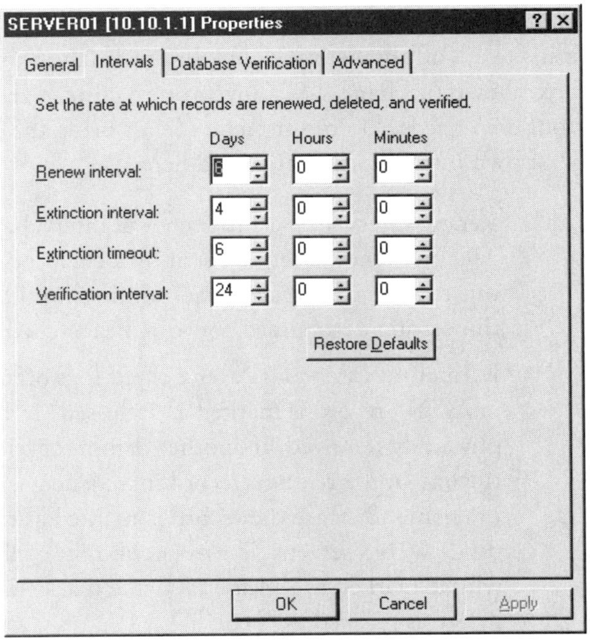

Manual Tombstoning and Scavenging

You can delete records from the WINS database simply by right-clicking a record, or group of selected records, and choosing Delete. However, if you have multiple WINS servers that replicate to one another, you may be surprised to see some of those deleted records reappear in the database at a later time. The reason for the reappearance is this: A "deleted record" isn't replicated to other WINS servers. In fact, quite the opposite happens. When another server verifies its records against the one with the deleted records, it sees that server's records as "missing," and writes them back into the WINS server's database.

To get around this problem, you should *manually tombstone* the records, not delete them. Doing so ensures that the tombstoned status is replicated to other WINS servers and the record expires normally. To tombstone a record, or multiple selected records, right-click and choose Delete. In the Delete Record dialog box that opens, choose the second option, Replicate Deletion Of The Record To Other Servers (Tombstone), as shown in Figure 2-10, and then click OK. Now the record will be marked for deletion across the board, so to speak, so you needn't worry about it magically reappearing within your database.

As mentioned, tombstoned records aren't physically removed until the database is scavenged. Optionally, you can scavenge the database at any time by right-clicking the server name and IP address in the console tree and choosing Scavenge Database.

Compacting a WINS Database

The WINS database uses the Extensible Storage Engine (ESE), a variant of Microsoft's Jet database engine. The files that make up the entire WINS database are stored in the %systemroot%\system32\wins folder. There's no physical limit to how many records a WINS database can hold—the database just continues to grow as new names are registered. As you've seen, old records are not deleted immediately, but rather are tombstoned and only removed when the database is scavenged. So there's the potential for a WINS database to become quite huge.

FIGURE 2-10

When deleting a record, you have the option to tombstone manually instead.

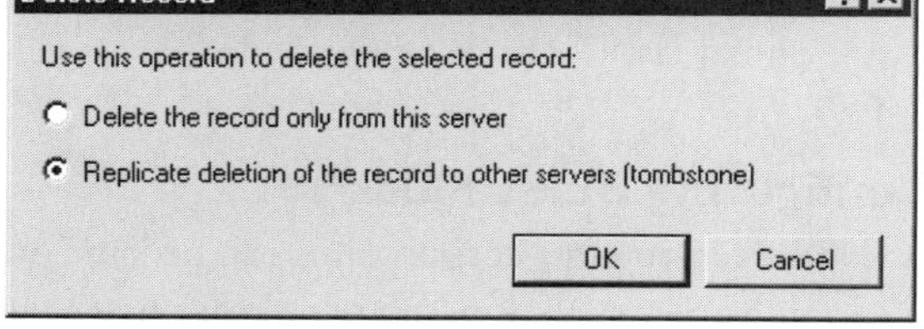

Like any database, a WINS database will be more efficient if it's compacted periodically. In Windows 2000, the database is automatically compacted as a background process during idle times through a process known as *online compaction*. However, online compaction isn't 100 percent efficient, and will fail altogether when a database is corrupted. So Microsoft recommends that if the size of the WINS database exceeds 30MB, you manually compact the database. This is called *offline compaction*.

---

on the job

Though WINS is a Jet database with an .mdb extension, you should never attempt to open a WINS database file with anything other than the WINS console. Opening the wins.mdb file with Microsoft Access will almost certainly corrupt the WINS database!

Since WINS uses Jet technology, you want to use the **jetpack** command (not the **compact** command) to compact the WINS database. The basic syntax is

```
jetpack <database name> <temporary database name>
```

where *database name* is the name of the main database file (wins.mdb by default), and *temporary database name* is the name of a nonexistent temporary file that will be used by the procedure. Do not use the name of an existing file for this temporary file, and don't use the name temp.mdb. The **jetpack** command actually uses two temporary files when compacting a database, one named temp.mdb (which is why you can't use that name), and another with the name you specify.

---

exam Watch

Some early Microsoft documentation recommended using the compact *command to compact a WINS database, but that was incorrect. You always use the* jetpack *command, not the* compact *command, to compact a WINS database (and DHCP databases as well).*

You'll need to stop the WINS service prior to compacting and then restart it when the compaction is complete. You can do everything at the command prompt by entering these commands:

```
cd %systemroot%\system32\wins
net stop wins
jetpack wins.mdb comptmp.mdb
net start wins
```

Configuring Burst Mode

WINS servers in large corporations can become overloaded with registration requests at certain times, such as when people are first logging on in the morning or just after recovering from a power outage. Historically, WINS servers would cache a number of requests but then start dropping requests once the cache was filled. *Burst handling,* which initially appeared in Windows NT Service Pack 3, fixes that by placing awaiting registration requests into a *burst cache* and then switching to *burst mode* once the burst cache is filled.

In burst mode, awaiting clients are given immediate positive acknowledgements to get onto the network with their requested names. However, the server doesn't verify the NetBIOS name, nor does it add the requested name to its database. It just tells the client "OK, you can log on" and gives it a reduced renewal interval.

You can enable or disable burst handling, and set the number of requests that the server can handle at one time, using the Advanced tab of the WINS server's Properties dialog box, shown in Figure 2-11. Your options are the following:

- **Low**   300
- **Medium**   500 (the default)
- **High**   1,000
- **Custom**   Any value from 50 to 5,000

The lower the setting you choose, the sooner WINS will go into burst mode. Since there are some risks involved in allowing NetBIOS computers onto the network without registering their names, you only want to use the lower settings if users are complaining of having to wait too long to log in to the network.

FIGURE 2-11

The Advanced tab of a WINS server's Properties dialog box

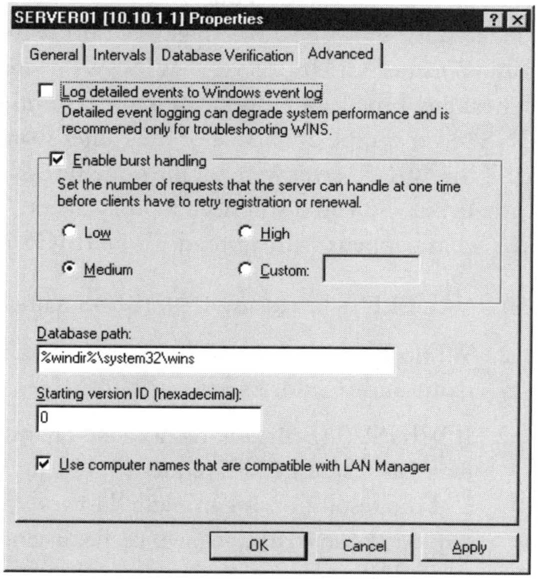

Supporting Non-WINS Clients

Though WINS is based on RFC standards, it is a Microsoft product, and largely limited to Microsoft Windows products. Any computer running Windows for Workgroups, Windows 95, 98, NT, 2000, or XP, or even LAN Manager 2.0, can function as a WINS client. DOS machines and many non-Microsoft products are oblivious to WINS. In fact, many products can only use b-node (broadcasts) for NetBIOS name resolution. Furthermore, they don't even attempt to register their NetBIOS names with a centralized NetBIOS name server. For such clients, WINS offers a WINS proxy service, and static mapping.

exam
⚠Watch

While taking your exam, it's safe to assume that any WINS-related question involving UNIX, Linux, AS/400, DOS, or any other operating system to be a question about non-WINS, b-node computers.

WINS Proxy: Name Resolution for B-Node Clients

WINS is the latest (and perhaps last) name resolution technology to come from the NetBIOS world. While most newer machines are capable of using WINS, there are still some older machines and applications out there that are strictly b-node (broadcast) capable. There's just no way to configure these machines to use anything other than b-node. To allow these machines to use WINS NetBIOS name resolution, you need to set up a WINS proxy agent on the same subnet, to intercept the broadcasts and then treat them as WINS requests.

Figure 2-12 shows how you might set up a WINS proxy agent. Note that the machines named CLUELESS and WINSWISE are on the same subnet, so WINSWISE will hear any broadcast request for name resolution coming from CLUELESS. The WINS server on the other side of the router won't hear those broadcasts. (Actually, even if the WINS server were on the same side of the router, it still wouldn't respond to broadcasts. So you'd still need a proxy agent.) When the proxy agent is working, here's what happens with a broadcast NetBIOS name request:

1. CLUELESS broadcasts a NetBIOS name query to its local subnet.
2. WINSWISE accepts the broadcast and checks its own cache for the NetBIOS name and IP address.
3. If WINSWISE already has a cached name-to-IP address mapping that matches CLUELESS's request, it returns the information to CLUELESS, and the resolution is complete. However, if WINSWISE can't resolve the requested name from its own cache, it sends a direct query to KNOWITALL, the WINS server.

Configure and Implement WINS **91**

4. When WINSWISE gets the IP address from KNOWITALL, it passes the information on to CLUELESS.

5. WINSWISE also caches the name-to-IP address mapping and will use it for future queries from b-node clients.

exam
🐊 **a t c h**
Since broadcasts rarely cross routers, it's important to put a WINS proxy agent on every subnet that contains b-node-only clients. Don't put multiple proxy agents on a single subnet, though, as they'll all respond to broadcasts, which just complicates matters and leads to unpredictable results.

To enable b-node clients to use WINS for NetBIOS name resolution, you need to pick one (and only one) WINS-enabled machine on the same subnet to act as the proxy agent. Oddly, there's no simple GUI method for doing this. You have to edit the Registry directly on the computer that will be acting as the proxy server. Using **regedit**, you need to navigate to HKEY_LOCAL_MACHINE\SYSTEM\CurrentControlSet\Services\Netbt\Parameters, create a new DWORD value named **EnableProxy**, and give it a value data of 1.

on the
🐊 **o b**
When a WINS proxy is used to answer a query for a multihomed client or a group record containing multiple IP addresses, only the first listed address is returned to the b-node client.

| FIGURE 2-12 | WINSWISE is a WINS proxy agent for CLUELESS. |

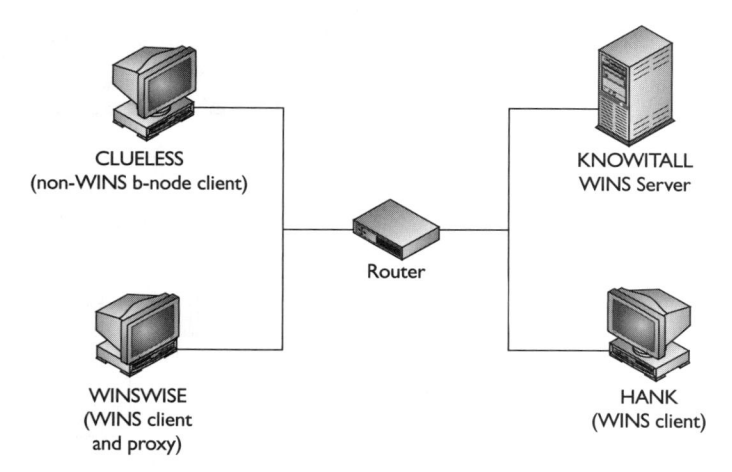

CLUELESS
(non-WINS b-node client)

KNOWITALL
WINS Server

Router

WINSWISE
(WINS client
and proxy)

HANK
(WINS client)

Static Mappings: Name Registration for non-WINS Clients

The proxy agent allows non-WINS clients to use a WINS server to resolve NetBIOS names to IP addresses. However, it doesn't allow those clients to register their names in the WINS server. When the non-WINS client first comes online, it makes no attempt to register its name with the WINS server, largely because it doesn't "know" the server exists and because the WINS server doesn't respond to its broadcasts. Since the b-node client isn't capable of registering its name with the WINS server on its own, you need to register that name for it. You do so by manually adding the machine's NetBIOS name and IP address to the WINS server's database. The best way to do so is through *static mapping*, as this ensures that the mapping stays put in the WINS database. Here's how it's done:

1. On the WINS server, open the WINS administrative tool.
2. Expand the node under the server name and IP address, right-click Active Registrations, and choose New Static Mapping. The New Static Mapping dialog box, shown in Figure 2-13, opens.

FIGURE 2-13

Making a WINS client into a WINS proxy agent

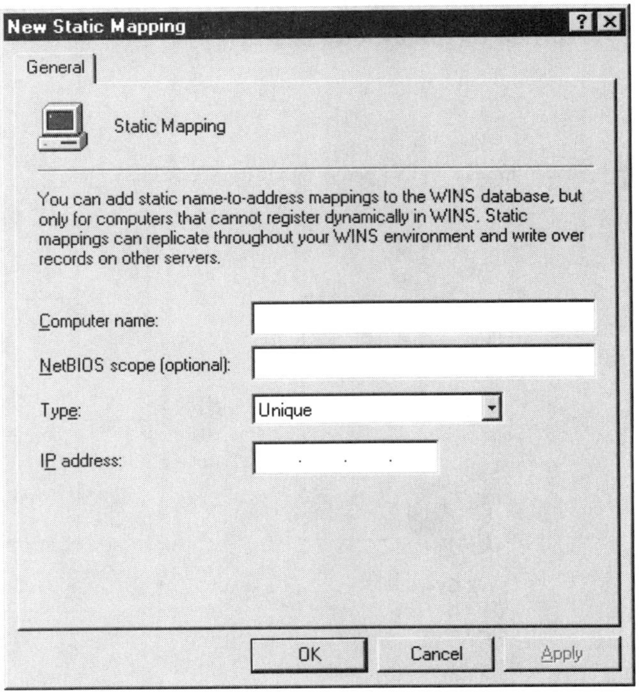

3. In the Computer Name text box, type in the NetBIOS name of the computer that's unable to register its name with the WINS server.

4. Leave the NetBIOS Scope option empty, unless your network specifically uses a NetBIOS scope. In that case, you'd type in the name of the NetBIOS scope to use for this mapping.

5. In the Type drop-down list box, choose the NetBIOS service identifier that best describes the client from the options shown in Table 2-3.

6. Type in the IP address(es) for the machine.

7. Click the Apply button.

8. Repeat Steps 3–7 for any additional static mappings.

9. Click OK when you're done.

You can close the WINS management console when you're finished. There's no need to reboot the computer.

Setting Up Multiple WINS Servers

For fault tolerance and efficient name resolution, a network can have two or more WINS servers. If one WINS server goes down or is unable to handle a sudden surge of requests, another server can take over seamlessly. To ensure that all the WINS

TABLE 2-3 Types Used for WINS Static Mapping

Type	Description
Unique	Associates the computer name with a single IP address. Three records representing three services are actually added to the database: WorkStation <00>, Messenger <03>, and File Server <20>.
Group	Adds an entry for the computer specified by name in another static mapping entry to a workgroup that's available on the network. If used, the IP address for the computer isn't stored in WINS, but rather is resolved through local subnet broadcasts.
Domain Name	Indicates a domain name <1C> or #DOM mapped entry for location domain controllers.
Internet Group	Used for special administrator-defined groups, such as a group of file or print servers. Each Internet group uses a shared group name identified by a <20> service identifier.
Multihomed	Registers a unique name for a multihomed computer and expands the dialog box to allow you to add multiple IP addresses.

servers in a network have reasonably up-to-date and consistent records, replication among the servers takes place automatically. Any WINS servers that share their information with one another are called *replication partners*.

Each WINS server maintains a *version ID*—a serial number that's incremented each time the contents of its database change. Thus, a replication partner can compare the version ID of the server from its most recent update, to the version ID that's currently on the server. If its own version ID is less than that of the originating server's, the replication partner knows it's out of sync, and it needs to update again. Replications are always incremental, meaning that the replication partner doesn't copy the entire database from its partner. Rather, it only copies information that has changed, or new records.

Exactly how, and when, WINS replication partners stay in sync depends on the types of relationships between them. There are basically three types of relationships the partners can use to replicate—pull, push, and push/pull—as discussed in the sections that follow.

Pull Relationship

A pull relationship typically involves a secondary WINS server "pulling" *replicas* (new or modified records) from a primary WINS server at regular time intervals. A pull relationship is always based on a time interval. When the time interval expires, the server contacts its partner and checks the version ID of its database. If the partner's version ID has increased since the last replication, the current partner knows its own records are out of date, and starts replicating.

Push Relationship

A push relationship is usually initiated from a primary WINS server and is based on the number of changes made since the last replication, as opposed to a time interval. The name is a little misleading, though, as the server doesn't actually "push" its changes onto the partner. Instead, it sends a message to the partner that says, "I don't know how long you were planning to wait to check me out, but I've made x changes to my database since your last visit. So I suggest you do a pull right now." The partner always agrees, and initiates its pull update.

Push/Pull Partners

Microsoft recommends that you set up both pull and push relationships among WINS servers to minimize inconsistencies between the partners. On a primary WINS server, set up a push relationship that's triggered after x number of changes. How large a number you choose for x is up to you. If you want to ensure that the secondary server is always up to date, you can set the number to 1. That means every time the version ID changes on the primary WINS server, the secondary WINS server is coaxed into doing a pull. Set up the secondary WINS server as a pull partner to the primary WINS server, as sort of a backup to the push.

Figure 2-14 shows a simple example using two WINS servers. WINSA is the primary server, in that each client has WINSA's IP address listed first in its Advanced TCP/IP Settings dialog box. Each client also has WINSB listed second in that same list. WINSA and WINSB are replication partners. WINSA can be configured to push its changes to WINSB, and WINSB can be configured to pull replicas from WINSA based on some time interval.

Configuring WINS Replication Partnerships

You can use the WINS management console to configure replication among WINS servers. Click the Start button and choose Programs | Administrative Tools | WINS. In the console tree, right-click Replication Partners and choose New Replication Partner. In the New Replication Partner dialog box that appears (see Figure 2-15), type the name or IP address of the WINS server to which you want to set up a

FIGURE 2-14 A simple push/pull relationship between two WINS server replication partners

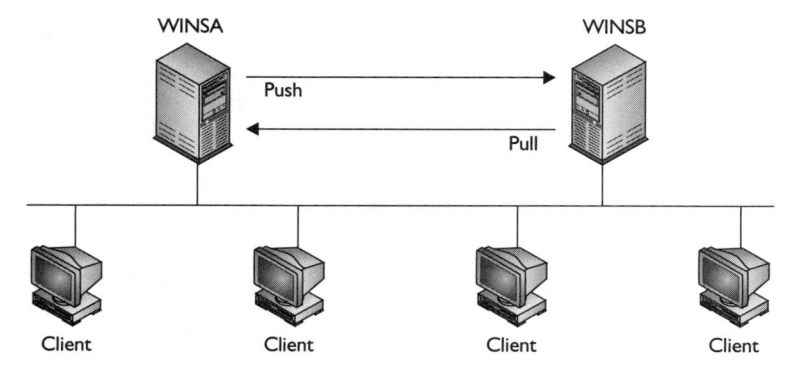

FIGURE 2-15

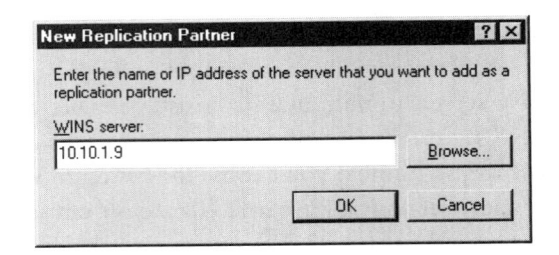

The New Replication Partner dialog box

replication partnership. Then click OK. The partner's name and IP address will appear on the pane on the right.

To set properties for replication at the local machine, right-click Replication Partners in the console tree and choose Properties. The Replication Partners Properties dialog box opens, as shown in Figure 2-16. On the General tab, choose from the following options:

- **Replicate only with partners**   If selected, this ensures that this server replicates directly only with defined partners.

- **Overwrite unique static mappings at this server (migrate on)**   If selected, this allows statically mapped unique and multihomed records to be overwritten in the database with dynamic entries when they conflict with a new registration or replica—best used when you have non-WINS clients that you plan to upgrade to WINS clients at some time in the future.

FIGURE 2-16

The General tab of the Replication Partners Properties dialog box

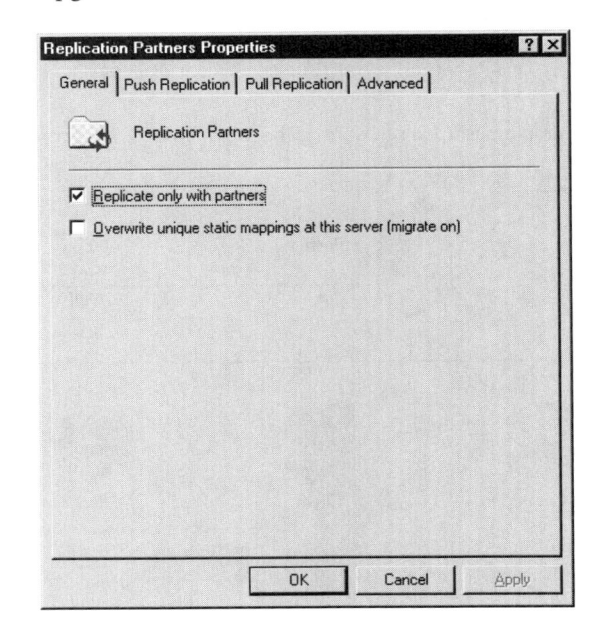

Configure and Implement WINS **97**

The Push Replication tab, shown in Figure 2-17, allows you to configure push replication from this server. Your options are the following:

- **At service startup** If selected, the server sends out a push trigger when the WINS server is first activated.
- **When address changes** If selected, the server informs pull partners whenever an address changes in a mapping record.
- **Number of changes in version ID before replication** Specifies how many updates need to be made to this server's database before it informs partners of these changes. Setting this value to 0 disables push replication, as no push triggers will ever be sent.
- **User persistent connections for push replication partners** If selected, this allows the server and its partners to remain connected persistently, which helps speed up replication. If not selected, the server must locate and set up a connection with replication partners before it can send a push trigger.

exam
Watch

Normally, the minimal update count for a push trigger is 20 records. However, with persistent connections enabled, the minimum is waived, and you can set the number of changes to as low as 1.

FIGURE 2-17

The Push Replication tab

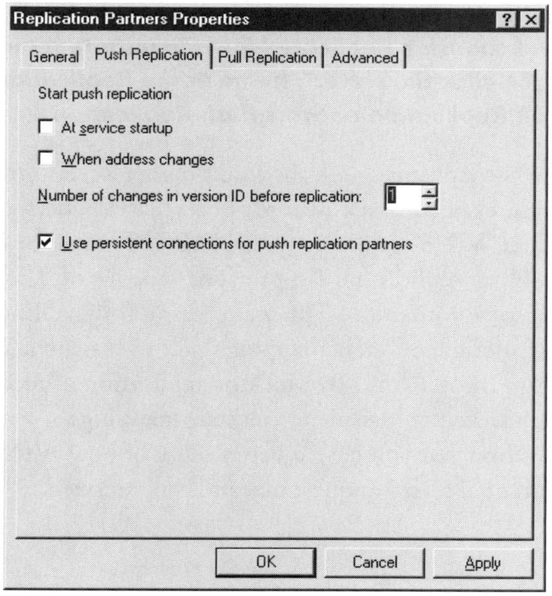

The Pull Replication tab lets you configure how often this server sends out a pull trigger to update its own database from its replication partners. Your options are the following:

- **Start time** The time of day at which you want to initiate the pull replication. For example, if you'll be doing a pull replication only once a day, you might want to set this to a time when traffic is at a minimum, as opposed to peak hours when the server is busy with name registration and resolution.

- **Replication interval** Specify how often you want this server to send a pull trigger to its replication partners.

- **Number of retries** Set the number of times the server will retry its connection with pull partners in case the first request fails.

- **Start pull replication at service startup** If selected, a pull request is sent as soon as the WINS service is started on this machine.

- **Use persistent connections for pull replication partners** As with push replication, uses persistent connections for pull replication, as opposed to opening a new connection each time.

on the Job

You can initiate a push, pull, or push/pull replication at any time by right-clicking the local server's name in the WINS management console tree and choosing Replicate Now. To initiate replication from a remote server, right-click the server's name in the Replication Partners list and choose Start Pull Replication or Start Push Replication.

The Advanced tab, shown in Figure 2-18, provides a couple of advanced WINS features. The Block Records For These Owners area allows you to create a list of other WINS servers by their NetBIOS names or IP addresses for which you want to block replication. (In previous versions of Windows, this feature was known as PersonaNonGrata.) The main reason for enabling this feature would be to minimize the lifetime of "stale mappings" left over from a WINS server that has been removed from the network. By blocking replication of records from inactive servers, you minimize the lifetime of the stale mappings.

Now that you have a better sense of how WINS works, let's review some potential scenario questions and their answers.

FIGURE 2-18

The advanced tab

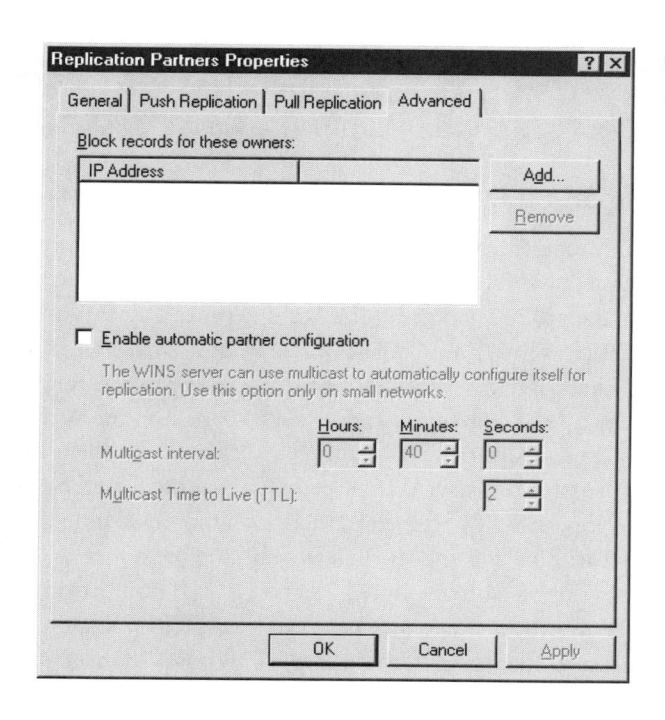

[Screenshot: Replication Partners Properties dialog, Advanced tab, showing "Block records for these owners:" list with Add/Remove buttons, "Enable automatic partner configuration" checkbox with explanatory text, Multicast interval (Hours: 0, Minutes: 40, Seconds: 0), and Multicast Time to Live (TTL): 2.]

SCENARIO & SOLUTION

If I have a pure TCP/IP network with no NetBIOS, would there be any advantage to having a WINS server?	No, because WINS is used strictly for NetBIOS name registration and resolution. For TCP/IP, the "big daddy" of name resolution is DNS, which you'll learn about in the next chapter.
How is a released WINS record different from an extinct (tombstoned) record?	When a host relinquishes its NetBIOS, its status is set to released, but it's not deleted immediately. After all, the same client may come back online in a day or two, but if a released record isn't reactivated for a long, long time, chances are that client isn't coming back. Tombstoning, rather than deleting, the old record gives the owner server a chance to tell its replication partners "This client has been gone for ages, so I'm dumping its record. You might as well dump its record too."
Would I gain a performance advantage by adding lots of WINS servers to my network?	Actually, you might degrade performance by adding lots of WINS servers. The goal is to use as few WINS servers as possible while maintaining acceptable performance. Each WINS server can handle hundreds of queries and registrations per second. Adding too many WINS servers just complicates replication and increases the likelihood of database corruption.

FROM THE CLASSROOM

Multicasting and IGMP

Internet Group Management Protocol (IGMP) is a protocol that allows one host to send a single stream of data to many hosts at the same time. Most TCP/IP connections consist of one host sending packets of data to another host, or all hosts in the case of a broadcast, and then waiting for an acknowledgement. Streaming is unique in that the stream is sent to multiple hosts (but not necessarily all hosts), and, there is no waiting for acknowledgements. You might liken it to a radio station's broadcast, where the show is sent out over the airways, and heard by whomever happens to be tuned to that radio station. The station doesn't wait for radios to respond with "I hear you" acknowledgements—it just broadcasts away with the hope that someone is listening.

The destination address for IGMP is called a *multicast address,* and is always within the Class D range of IP addresses 224.0.0.0 to 239.255.255.255. IGMP *multicasting* is often used for database replication. With multi-casting, a database can send a single stream of data to several replication partners all at the same time. This is much more efficient than updating one partner and starting all over to update the next partner. IGMP is also used for *streaming media* on the Web, where audio and/or video is sent to the client in a continuous stream without waiting for acknowledgement, to reduce the amount of time it takes for the content to reach the consumer.

IP multicasting was originally defined as a TCP/IP standard in RFC 1112, "Internet Group Management Protocol (IGMP)." RFC 2236, "Internet Group Management Protocol (IGMP), version 2" defines IGMP version 2. Be aware that not all routers are capable of forwarding multicasts. Routers that are capable of forwarding multicasts are often referred to as *multicast routers,* or routers that are *IGMP compliant, RFC-1112 compliant,* or *RFC-2236 compliant.*

—*Alan Simpson, MA, MCSA*

CERTIFICATION OBJECTIVE 2.04

Troubleshoot NetBIOS Name Resolution

Name resolution problems reveal themselves as an inability to connect to shared resources on a network. To make sure you have a name resolution problem, and not just a general connectivity problem, try using the PING command to contact the remote host by IP address. If you cannot PING the host by its IP address, you have a general connectivity problem, which isn't necessarily a name resolution problem. You'll need to check all connections between the local machine and the remote host.

If you're having trouble contacting a host that has a fully qualified domain name (in other words, the name contains dots), that's a DNS problem or perhaps a problem with one of the other resources for hostname resolution, such as the HOSTS file. If you start trying to troubleshoot for NetBIOS resolution, you'll probably get nowhere! (We'll talk about DNS in the next chapter.)

Finally, try to determine if the NetBIOS name resolution is system wide, or isolated to specific machines. If NetBIOS name resolution is a system-wide problem, or occurs on several (but not all) hosts, it's possible NetBT is disabled on the hosts. To verify that NetBT is enabled, open Network and Dial-Up Connections in Control Panel. Right-click the icon for the NIC that connects this computer to the network and choose Properties. Double-click Internet Protocol (TCP/IP) and click the Advanced button in the dialog box that opens. Make sure that Enable NetBIOS Over TCP/IP is selected or, if Use NetBIOS Setting From The DHCP Server is selected, make sure the DHCP server is enabling DHCP on new clients. (You'll learn about DHCP in Chapter 4.)

Make sure you know which node type the client is using for NetBIOS name resolution. You can find that by entering the **ipconfig /all** command. The node type will tell you which resources to check and in what order to check them, as illustrated in Figure 2-2 earlier in this chapter. Don't forget that any entries marked as #PRE in the LMHOSTS file are stored in the NetBIOS name cache automatically. As such, those entries will be detected when the NetBIOS name cache is used for resolution, *not* when the LMHOSTS file is used.

Finally, check to see what names are currently listed in the NetBIOS name cache. To do so, enter the command **nbtstat –c** to see the NetBIOS names and their IP addresses in the NetBIOS name cache. If you can't find the NetBIOS name that you're looking for, perhaps the remote client is incapable of NetBIOS name resolution. If that's the case, you'll need to enter a static mapping for the remote host.

If you're using WINS for NetBIOS name resolution, there are some additional techniques that you can use to troubleshoot WINS. Again, first try to assess how widespread the problem is. If NetBIOS name resolution isn't working at all, then there's probably a problem at the WINS server. If only one or a handful of clients are having problems with NetBIOS name resolution, the problem is more likely to be on the client side.

Troubleshooting WINS Servers

If you suspect that a WINS problem is based at the server, first start with the most obvious problem. Verify that the WINS service is running by opening the WINS management console and clicking Server Status in the console tree. The Status column will show "Responding" if the service is running and responding to requests. For a more detailed view of the server's activities, right-click the server name and choose Display Server Statistics. Use the information presented to verify that the server is responding to queries, releasing name registrations, and so forth.

EXERCISE 2-4

Viewing WINS Server Statistics

In this exercise, you'll use the WINS management console to view current WINS server statistics. Follow these steps (if you're already in the WINS management console, start at Step 2):

1. Click the Start button and choose Programs | Accessories | Administrative Tools | WINS.
2. Click the server name and IP address.
3. Click the Action button and choose View Server Statistics.

You'll see a display window like the example shown in Figure 2-19.

If NetBIOS name resolution is failing on one side of a router, verify that the router is configured properly and forwarding WINS queries. What appears to be a WINS server problem could actually be a lack of connectivity in the network itself.

You can also check the Event Viewer to see if there are any WINS-related messages logged. To do so, click the Start button, choose Programs | Administrative Tools | Event Viewer. Finally, click System Log. If you see a bunch of WINS errors, then there's definitely something wrong with the server. You can right-click any error message and choose Properties for a description of the error.

Troubleshooting WINS Clients

If WINS problems seem to be isolated to one or several clients, then the problem obviously isn't at the server side. First, try to determine if the troublesome clients

FIGURE 2-19

The server statistics for a WINS server

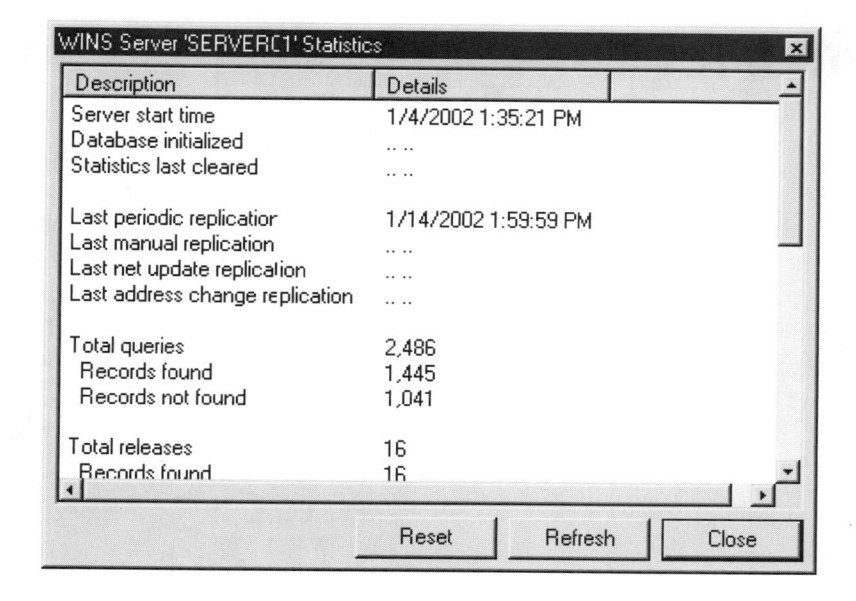

have something in common. For example, let's say all your WINS-enabled clients are working fine, but none of the UNIX machines on the network are able to resolve NetBIOS hostnames. In that case, you'll need to configure one of the WINS-enabled clients on the subnet to act as a WINS proxy agent to forward non-WINS name queries to the WINS server.

On the flip side, suppose all clients are able to reach all hosts except one—a UNIX server. In that case, the problem is most likely that the UNIX server isn't registered in the WINS database. You'll need to add a static mapping to the WINS database for any machines that aren't able to register their names with the WINS server automatically.

If the problem is isolated to a single client, or a few clients, check the advanced TCP/IP properties of the client(s). Verify that NetBIOS over TCP/IP and WINS are enabled, and that the list of WINS servers is appropriate. Check for basic connectivity by pinging the WINS servers by their IP addresses. If the WINS server fails to respond, you know you have a basic connectivity problem. If the WINS server does respond to a PING, the problem may be in the NetBIOS name cache. Use the **nbtstat –RR** (ReleaseRefresh) command at both the client and the server to purge cached NetBIOS names and force immediate renewal and re-registration of local NetBIOS names.

CERTIFICATION SUMMARY

In this chapter, we've looked at name resolution in general, with a focus on NetBIOS name resolution. Even though NetBIOS is gradually being phased out by more modern TCP/IP hostname resolution, there are still plenty of networks around that require a complete NetBIOS infrastructure. As such, Windows 2000 provides full support for both NetBIOS names and TCP/IP hostnames.

WINS provides a dynamic, centralized database used both for registering NetBIOS names and resolving NetBIOS names to IP addresses. For fault tolerance, a single client can access up to 12 WINS servers for registration and resolution. A network can have just about any number of WINS servers (though 20 is the recommended maximum). Replication across WINS servers is fully automated and can be tailored by a network administrator.

✓ TWO-MINUTE DRILL

Understand Name Resolution

- ❑ Name resolution is the process of converting a host's "friendly" name, preferred by humans, to the TCP/IP addresses the computers require.
- ❑ Windows 2000 supports both TCP/IP hostnames (for example, wanda.certifiable.net) and NetBIOS computer names (for example, WANDA_PC).
- ❑ Any computer has several resources at its disposal for resolving names, including broadcasting, LOCALHOST, the NetBIOS Name Cache, the HOSTS and LMHOSTS files, DNS, and WINS.
- ❑ The HOSTNAME command allows you to view the local host's NetBIOS name.
- ❑ LMHOSTS is a text file containing NetBIOS name-to-IP address mappings.
- ❑ HOSTS is a more generic text file that can map virtually any name to an IP address.
- ❑ DNS is the primary name resolution service for TCP/IP networks.
- ❑ WINS is the newest and easiest form of NetBIOS name resolution.
- ❑ NetBIOS is being pushed out by TCP/IP, but many networks still require a complete NetBIOS infrastructure to function properly.

Configure NetBIOS Name Resolution

- ❑ Unlike TCP/IP hostnames, NetBIOS names are a single label (no periods) up to 15 characters in length.
- ❑ NetBIOS names allow many punctuation characters, while TCP/IP hostnames do not.
- ❑ The command **nbtstat –n** lists local NetBIOS names and service identifiers.
- ❑ A NetBIOS client uses one of four node types for name resolution: b-node (broadcast), p-node (peer), m-node (mixed), and h-node (hybrid).
- ❑ Windows 2000 clients are b-node by default, but switch to h-node if the WINS service is enabled.

Configure and Implement WINS

- ❑ WINS (Windows Internet Naming Service) is the most modern, centralized, and easily managed tool for NetBIOS name resolution.
- ❑ A WINS server contains a dynamic database of NetBIOS name-to-IP address mappings, used both for name registration and name resolution.
- ❑ A WINS client is any Windows computer that can register its name with a WINS server, and use that WINS server for name resolution as well.
- ❑ Virtually all Windows computers, as well as LAN Manager 2.0 machines, can function as WINS clients.
- ❑ If you want non-WINS clients to be able to use WINS for name resolution, you must configure one WINS client on the local segment to act as a WINS proxy agent.
- ❑ Non-WINS clients don't register their names with a WINS server database. To add such a client to a WINS database requires a static mapping, in which you manually enter the hostname and IP address into the WINS database.
- ❑ WINS replication partners can replicate using push, pull, or push/pull replication.

Troubleshoot NetBIOS Name Resolution

- ❑ The first step to troubleshooting NetBIOS name resolution is to determine if the problem is network wide, or limited to a few machines.
- ❑ If there's a network-wide problem with NetBIOS name resolution, check for basic connectivity to the WINS server before assuming there's a problem with the WINS server itself.
- ❑ To verify that a name resolution problem isn't just a basic connectivity problem, try pinging the troublesome host by its IP address. If you can't connect via IP address, the problem is not one of name resolution.
- ❑ NetBIOS over TCP/IP must be enabled for NetBIOS name resolution to function properly on a client.
- ❑ If only non-WINS clients are having NetBIOS name resolution problems, verify that there's a WINS client on the segment that's acting as a WINS proxy.

❑ If there's a problem reaching a specific non-WINS server on the network, most likely that server's NetBIOS name and IP address aren't registered in the WINS server's database. You'll have to use a static mapping to add a record for that server to the WINS database.

❑ The System Log in Event Viewer maintains basic information about WINS name registrations.

❑ To clear out a machine's NetBIOS name cache, and reregister the computer with the WINS server, use the **nbtstat –RR** command.

SELF TEST

The following questions will help you measure your understanding of the material presented in this chapter. Read the question and all answers carefully, as there may be more than one correct answer per question. Choose *all* of the correct answers for each question.

Understand Name Resolution

1. As the administrator of Onion Republic, Inc.'s network, you need to add a new Windows 2000 client to the network. The network has a complete NetBIOS infrastructure in place because several applications require NetBIOS name resolution. Which of the following names would be the best candidate when entering the NetBIOS name for the new computer?

   A. BRANDNEW
   B. BRAND_NEW
   C. BRANDNEW.ONION.NET
   D. BRAND.NEW

2. Which of the following commands would allow you to view the name assigned to the computer at which you're currently seated?

   A. localhost
   B. ipconfig
   C. nbtstat -RR
   D. hostname

3. Windows Sockets (Winsock) is an application programming interface (API) that allows programs to interact with which of the following network transport protocols?

   A. NetBIOS
   B. TCP/IP
   C. NetEUI
   D. NetBT

Configure NetBIOS Name Resolution

4. You are the administrator of a network that includes eight Windows 2000 Server computers. Two of those servers provide DNS name resolution, and four of them act strictly as file and print servers. The network also houses 200 Windows 2000 Professional computers and 350 Windows 95 clients. To reduce overall network traffic, you split the network into four subnets connected by routers. All the servers remain on the original subnet. The remaining subnets each get some combination of Windows 2000 Professional and Windows 95 clients.

   After creating the subnets, you configure all clients to use DNS name resolution via the DNS name server on the original subnet. While users of the Windows 2000 Professional clients have no problem connecting to the file and print servers, Windows 95 users claim that they cannot access any of those servers. Which of the following would ensure that all users can access the shared file and print servers, with the least administrative effort on your part?

   A. Install a WINS proxy agent on each subnet.
   B. Configure each of the Windows 95 client computers to use b-node for NetBIOS name resolution.
   C. Create an LMHOSTS file on each client computer, and include mappings to all the Windows 2000 servers.
   D. Install WINS on one of the server computers, and configure the clients to use both WINS and DNS.

5. The Department of Motor Vehicles, for which you are the network administrator, gets enough funding to upgrade all of its existing servers to Windows 2000 Advanced Server and several clients to Windows 2000 Professional. Even after the upgrade, though, it'll still be using some OS/2 and Linux clients on the network. It hasn't gotten enough funding to upgrade some of its existing applications, either, which use the NetBIOS API. Your job requires that you come up with an efficient NetBIOS name resolution strategy that will be easy to administer, and simplify the task of upgrading some of the older clients to Windows 2000 as funding becomes available. Which of the following would be the best approach for meeting that goal?

   A. Use broadcasting for all NetBIOS name resolution.
   B. Create a centralized LMHOSTS file.
   C. Set up a WINS server.
   D. Rely solely on DNS for all NetBIOS name resolution.

Configure and Implement WINS

6. The company you work for has its corporate headquarters in New York and a branch office in San Diego. The offices are connected by a T1 line. The New York office contains a WINS server and numerous other servers providing file and print services. Users in the San Diego office all have Windows 98 computers. You want to ensure that users at both locations have access to all network resources. Which of the following would provide the most efficient and highest-performance name resolution?

   A. Configure the client computers in the San Diego office to use the WINS server in the New York office for name resolution.

   B. Create an LMHOSTS file on each client in the San Diego office that maps to resources in the New York office.

   C. Add a WINS server to the network in the San Diego office, and make it a replication partner to the WINS server in the New York office.

   D. Configure all the Windows 98 clients to use b-node for NetBIOS name resolution.

7. Users at your company are complaining that it seems to take forever to log on to their computers in the morning. Yet, once they are logged on, things move along smoothly and quickly. Which of the following would be the most cost-effective means of speeding up the morning logons on a Windows 2000 WINS server?

   A. Add another computer to the network and make it a backup WINS server.

   B. Enable manual tombstoning.

   C. Disable NetBIOS over TCP/P and enable LMHOSTS lookup.

   D. Enable burst handling.

8. You are the network administrator for Wambooli, Inc. Users are complaining of sporadic connectivity problems. You isolate the problem to NetBIOS name resolutions, but there doesn't seem to be any pattern to the failures. You suspect that the WINS database might be corrupted. Upon examining the database, you notice that it has ballooned up to over 100MB, more than ten times its normal size. Which of the following tasks should you perform at the server? (Choose all that apply.)

   A. Stop the WINS service.

   B. Compact the database using the **compact** command.

   C. Compact the database using the **jetpack** command.

   D. Restart the WINS service.

9. You are the administrator for a company that has branches in Seattle and New York. The Seattle branch office uses two local WINS servers, named SEAWINSA (primary) and SEAWINSB (secondary). The New York office uses two WINS servers, named NYWINSA (primary) and NYWINSB (secondary). Corporate wants the local servers at each office to be as concurrent as possible. Replication between offices should take place at least every 40 minutes. Which of the following activities should you perform to make the corporate folks happy? (Choose all that apply.)

   A. Configure SEAWINSA and SEAWINSB as push/pull replication partners with a persistent connection.

   B. Configure SEAWINSA and NYWINSA as push partners with persistent connections enabled and a replication interval of 40 minutes.

   C. Configure NYWINSA and NYWINSB as push/pull replication partners with a persistent connection.

   D. Enable persistent connections on the two primary servers, SEAWINSA and NYWINSA, and have them pull after every one record change.

   E. Configure SEAWINSB and NYWINSB as push/pull replication partners and specify a replication interval of 40 minutes.

   F. Configure SEAWINSB and NYWINSB as push partners with persistent connections and a push trigger set to one record change.

Troubleshoot NetBIOS Name Resolution

10. You are the administrator of a network consisting of 15 Windows 2000 Server computers, 250 Windows 2000 Professional computers, 150 Windows ME computers, and 20 UNIX computers. The network uses TCP/IP as its transport protocol. You need some NetBIOS name resolution so you set up some WINS servers. Everything seems to be running smoothly, except for the fact that the Windows clients can't access resources on the UNIX computers. How do you resolve this problem? (Choose all that apply.)

    A. Set up one WINS-enabled client on each subnet to act as a WINS proxy agent.
    B. Make all of the WINS servers act as WINS proxy agents.
    C. On the WINS servers, create static mappings for the UNIX machines.
    D. Create static mappings for the UNIX machines on each of the Windows client computers.

112 Chapter 2: Implementing and Troubleshooting Name Resolution

11. You are the administrator of a network containing a mix of Windows 2000 Server, Windows 2000 Professional, Windows 98, OS/2, and Linux computers on a single subnet. You set up WINS servers and enable WINS on Windows computers. What else must you do to enable WINS name resolution among the non-WINS clients?

   A. Create static mappings on all of the non-WINS clients.
   B. Configure each of the non-WINS clients as a WINS proxy agent.
   C. Configure one Windows 2000 Server machine as a WINS proxy agent.
   D. Configure one WINS client as a WINS proxy agent.
   E. Configure all of the WINS clients as WINS proxy agents.

LAB QUESTION

You have a network that looks something like the example shown in Figure 2-20 (though there could be any number of clients). You decide to implement WINS for NetBIOS name resolution. What are all the steps you would need to take to enable all the computers to communicate with one another via NetBIOS names?

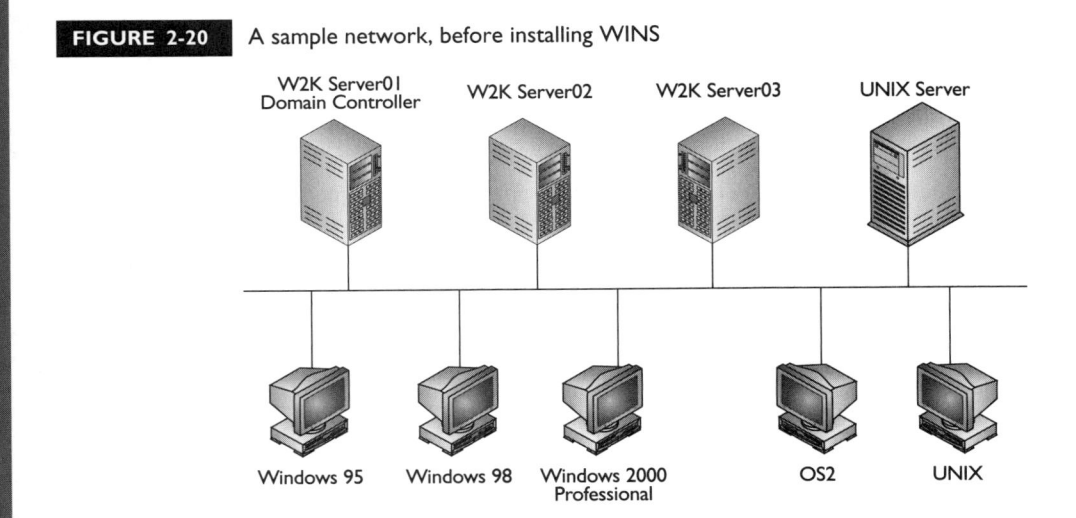

FIGURE 2-20 A sample network, before installing WINS

SELF TEST ANSWERS

Understand Name Resolution

1. ☑ **A** is correct. The name is "legal" for both NetBIOS and TCP/IP.
   ☒ **B** is wrong because even though it's a valid NetBIOS name, the underscore would not be a valid character for the TCP/IP hostname.
   ☒ **C** and **D** are wrong because NetBIOS names cannot contain periods.

2. ☑ **D** is correct. You enter the **hostname** command at the command prompt to view the name of the local host.
   ☒ **A** is wrong because there is no **localhost** command.
   ☒ **B** is wrong because the **ipconfig** command, by itself, displays only the local host's IP address, subnet mask, and default gateway.
   ☒ **C** is wrong because the **nbtstat –RR** command just sends name refresh packets to a WINS server and then refreshes those names.

3. ☑ **B** is correct. The WinSock API allows applications to communicate across a TCP/P network.
   ☒ **A, C,** and **D** are all incorrect because they're all NetBIOS related and Winsock is strictly a TCP/IP API.

Configure NetBIOS Name Resolution

4. ☑ **D** is correct. The downlevel Windows 95 clients will need to be able to resolve NetBIOS names to IP addresses. The easiest way to accomplish this would be to set up a WINS server on one of the Windows 2000 Server computers. Configuring all clients to use both WINS and DNS provides the most flexibility between the older Windows 95 clients and the newer Windows 2000 computers.
   ☒ **A** is incorrect because the WINS proxy agent allows non-WINS clients to access WINS clients. All the computers in this network can already function as WINS clients, so there's no need to add a WINS proxy agent.
   ☒ **B** is incorrect because using b-node (broadcasts) for NetBIOS name resolution wouldn't help the Windows 95 clients resolve names on the far side of their routers.
   ☒ **C** is incorrect because even though you could solve the problem in this manner, creating an appropriate LMHOSTS file and distributing it to all the clients would be a lot more administrative effort than creating a WINS server.

114 Chapter 2: Implementing and Troubleshooting Name Resolution

5. ☑ **C** is correct. WINS is always the easiest solution in terms of administrative effort. Since you have Windows 2000 Professional computers on this network, you can configure a WINS proxy agent to provide WINS name resolution to the non-WINS operating systems.
☒ **A** is incorrect because broadcasting isn't an efficient use of network resources.
☒ **B** is incorrect because unlike a dynamic WINS database, a centralized LMHOSTS file needs to be managed manually. WINS is always preferred over broadcasting and LMHOSTS.
☒ **D** is incorrect because DNS on its own can't handle NetBIOS names.

Configure and Implement WINS

6. ☑ **C** is correct. You have a fast WAN link between the two offices, which provides enough bandwidth to make WINS replication quick and easy. You also reduce name resolution traffic across the WAN link because clients can use their local WINS server for name resolution.
☒ **A** is incorrect because all the name resolution traffic will cross the WAN link. Even though you have a high-speed connection here, it would be more efficient to have the replications, rather than every individual name query, cross the link.
☒ **B** is incorrect because there's nothing "efficient" about using LMHOSTS. Remember, WINS was created to eliminate the administrative hassles of LMHOSTS.
☒ **D** is incorrect because you want to use WINS for name resolution, not broadcasts.

7. ☑ **D** is correct. Burst handling would speed up name registrations without the expense of adding another server to the network.
☒ **A** is incorrect because adding another computer is not the most cost-effective solution here.
☒ **B** and **C** are incorrect because neither would help speed up NetBIOS name registrations.

8. ☑ **A, C,** and **D** are correct (and need to be performed in that order).
☒ **B** is incorrect because you use the **jetpack** command, not the **compact** command, to compact a WINS database.

9. ☑ **A, C,** and **E** are correct. A and C allow the local replication partners to update to each other every one minute. C allows the two secondary servers to replicate every 40 minutes across a WAN link.
☒ **B** is incorrect because you want the secondary servers, not the primary servers, to perform the replication. Keep the primary servers freed up for name registrations and resolution.
☒ **D** and **F** are incorrect because you don't need to have the two distant primary servers update after every record change.

Troubleshoot NetBIOS Name Resolution

10. ☑ **C** is correct. The UNIX server cannot register its name with WINS, so you need to create a static mapping to that server in the WINS database.
    ☒ **A** is wrong because the problem here isn't with non-WINS clients using WINS for name resolution. The problem is that nobody can access the UNIX server because it isn't listed in the WINS database.
    ☒ **B** is wrong because WINS servers can't be proxies; only WINS clients can be proxies.
    ☒ **D** is wrong because you need to create the static mapping on the WINS servers, not the WINS clients.

11. ☑ **D** is correct because you need only configure one WINS client on the subnet to act as WINS proxy agent.
    ☒ **A** is incorrect because static mappings are used to *register* non-WINS clients, not to provide name resolution.
    ☒ **B** is wrong because you cannot configure non-WINS clients as WINS proxy agents.
    ☒ **C** is wrong because you don't configure a WINS server as a proxy; you configure a WINS client to play WINS proxy agent.
    ☒ **E** is wrong because you only want one WINS proxy agent per subnet.

LAB ANSWER

Your best bet would be to do the following:

1. Set up WINS on the two Windows 2000 servers, W2K Server02 and W2K Server03.
2. Make W2K Server02 and W2K Server03 replication partners, for fault tolerance.
3. Configure all the WINS clients to use W2K Server02 and W2K Server03 as their WINS servers.
4. To allow the non-WINS clients to use WINS for NetBIOS name resolution, configure the Windows 2000 Professional computer as a WINS proxy agent.
5. To ensure that all clients can find the computers that aren't able to register their names with WINS, add static mappings for the UNIX server, OS/2, and UNIX clients.

Figure 2-21 shows the end result.

FIGURE 2-21 Results of setting up WINS on the sample network

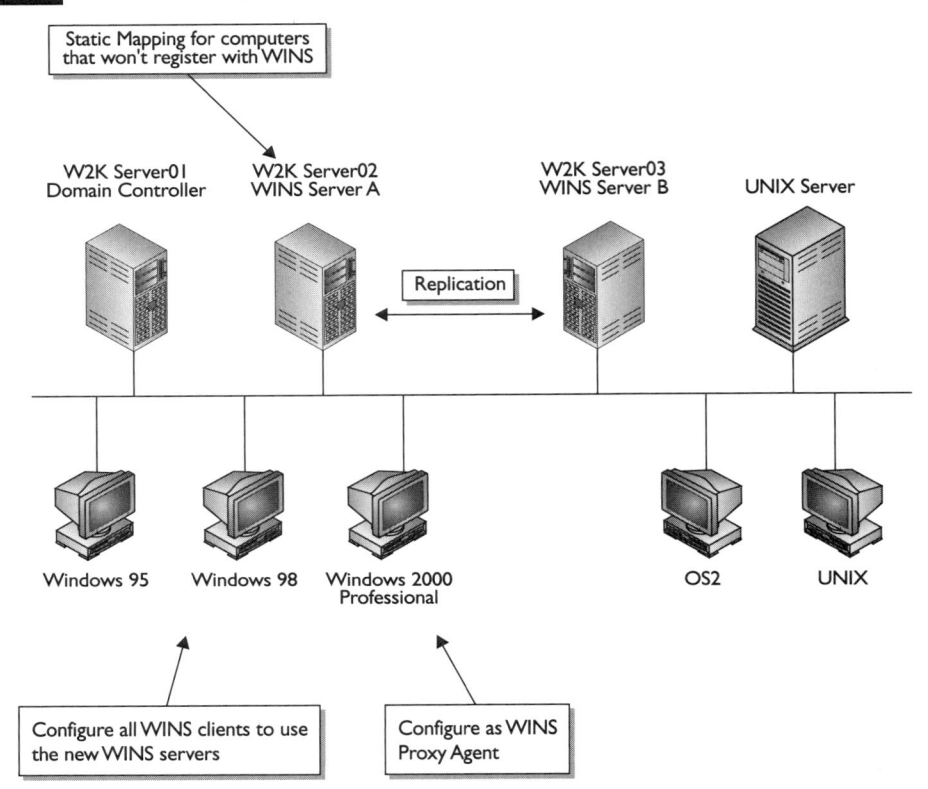

3
Configuring, Managing, and Troubleshooting DNS

CERTIFICATION OBJECTIVES

3.01	Create and Configure DNS Zones
3.02	Manage DNS Database Records
3.03	Configure DNS Server Properties
3.04	Configure Client Computer Name Resolution Properties
3.05	Troubleshoot DNS Name Resolution
✓	Two-Minute Drill
Q&A	Self Test

First and foremost, let me remind you that the Domain Name System (DNS) is a name resolution system, like those described in Chapter 2. I've given DNS its own chapter, though, because it's a large topic, and DNS plays a major role in a Windows 2000 network. In fact, Active Directory can't exist without DNS, and Active Directory is an important part of Windows 2000 networks (not to mention Exam 70-218!). DNS is also the name resolution method used by the Internet, and as such is quickly becoming the de facto standard for all modern networks.

In the early days of the Internet, when it was still quite small, name resolution was handled by a simple text file, named HOSTS.TXT, which was maintained by the Stanford Research Institute Network Information Center (SRI-NIC). Each time a new host came on, or left, the Internet, the HOSTS.TXT file needed to be updated manually with the host's name and IP address. Users needed to download the HOSTS.TXT file regularly to ensure they had the latest version. As the Internet grew, keeping the HOSTS.TXT file current became problematic, and a real bottleneck in the whole name resolution process. The solution to the HOSTS.TXT file was set forth in RFCs 1034 and 1035, which specified a distributed procedure we now know as the Domain Name System.

CERTIFICATION OBJECTIVE 3.01

Create and Configure DNS Zones

Unlike NetBIOS, which uses a flat namespace, DNS is based on a *hierarchical namespace*, where each hostname includes information about the network on which the specific host is located. A fully qualified domain name (FQDN) follows the format:

host.domain.tld

where

- *host* is the name of the specific host, such as JoesPC or www.
- *domain* is the name of the local network as a whole, such as microsoft or osborne.
- *tld* is the top-level domain name, such as .com, .net, .org, or whatever.

The hierarchical namespace provides for two major advantages over the flat namespace. For one, you can come up with a heck of a lot more unique names. Just think of all the web site URLs, ftp sites, and so forth that are out there, and you can see right off the bat that you can come up with literally millions of unique names using just the three labels separated by dots. (Though you could have even more labels separated by dots, as you'll see a little later.) Furthermore, the name provides information about the location of the host within the namespace hierarchy. For example, the hostname tells us that billsPC.microsoft.com is in the microsoft subdomain of the .com domain, whereas the name BILLSPC tells us nothing about the location of the host.

A second advantage of the hierarchical namespace is that it makes it easier to distribute the workload required to resolve hostnames across many different computers. The public domain namespace takes full advantage of this fact by organizing DNS name servers as in the example shown in Figure 3-1.

As a Windows 2000 network administrator, you don't have to worry about the public DNS root server or Top-Level Domain name servers. There are agencies that take care of those. Rather, your responsibility is likely to start at the Second-Level Domain—*YourCompanyName*.com. If *YourCompanyName*.com will be accessible to the public via the Internet, then you would need to register that name with an appropriate registrar, such as InterNIC, and then you'd need to get a globally unique IP address for that domain name, most likely via your ISP. Your ISP would then contact the appropriate agency to add your unique domain name and its IP address to the appropriate Top-Level Domain server.

FIGURE 3-1

The public DNS namespace

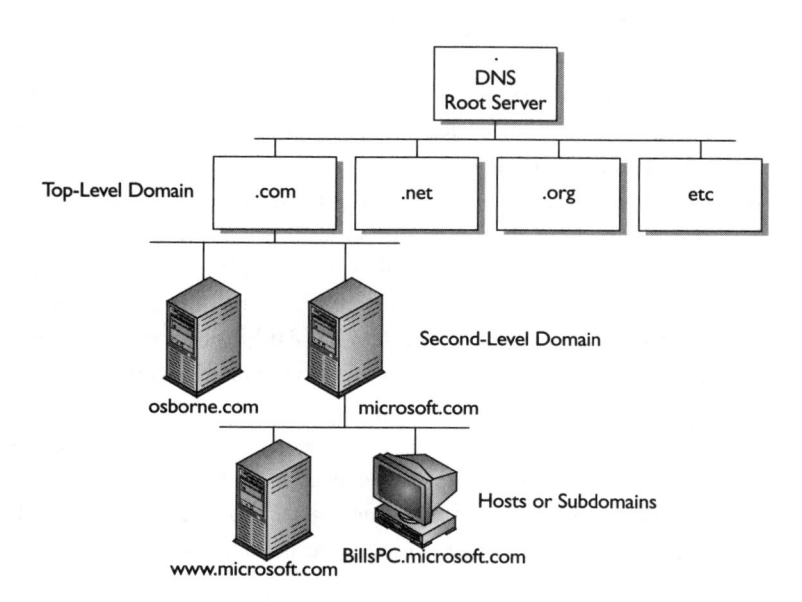

How DNS Works

Let's take a deeper look into the DNS name resolution procedure now and define some of the many buzzwords you'll come across. A *resolver* is any program that is capable of using DNS for name resolution. As such, any computer that can access the Internet is a resolver. Programs that rely on Winsock for name resolution (which would include things like Microsoft Internet Explorer) often use resolver software that's built right into that particular program. Windows 2000 also offers a system-wide resolver that any program can use for hostname resolution. A *DNS name server* (or just *name server* for short) is basically any computer that a resolver can contact when it needs to resolve a hostname to an IP address.

In order for a resolver to resolve a hostname to an IP address, it has to ask a DNS name server for help. It does so by sending a *recursive query* to the DNS root server. A recursive query is one that will only accept either of two answers: the IP address of the host or a "No such host" type of error message. For example, a request to resolve www.microsoft.com returns the IP address of that host. A request to resolve xyz.microsoft.com to an IP address is likely to return a "No such host" error message (unless Microsoft happens to add a name-to-IP address mapping for xyz.microsoft.com between now and the time you read this).

DNS name servers are more flexible than resolvers in that they're willing to accept a partial answer to a question. For example, when the root name server asks the .com server, "What's the IP address for www.microsoft.com," it's willing to accept a partial answer or a "forwarding address" like, "Don't ask me, go ask *some IP address.*" This type of DNS query, which is willing to accept a less-than-complete answer, is called an *iterative query.*

A *local DNS name server* is one that's local to your own network. A *remote DNS name server* is one that's not so local, most likely on the other side of a router. Any network can have any number of local DNS name servers, as we'll discuss later, but let's look at an example that has a network with one local DNS name server named NS1. Its IP address is 10.10.1.15. All hosts on that network have that server's IP address listed as their preferred DNS server within their local TCP/IP configurations, as shown in the example in Figure 3-2.

So now, let's say our resolver Client02 needs to resolve the name www.microsoft.com to an IP address. To do so, it sends a recursive query to its preferred DNS server, NS1 at 10.10.1.15. Since this is a recursive query, Client02 will accept only an IP address or "No such host" error as a response.

FIGURE 3-2

NS1 is the local preferred DNS server for Client01 and Client02.

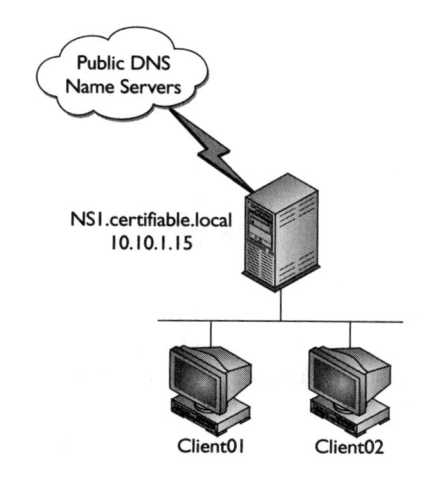

NS1.certifiable.local
10.10.1.15

Public DNS Name Servers

Client01   Client02

When NS1 receives the query, it might or might not know the answer to the question. For now, we'll say it doesn't know. Since NS1 can't answer the question, it puts the resolver's query "on hold" and then sends out an iterative query to a public DNS root domain name server on the Internet. There are 13 such servers in the world. NS1 can ask any one of them because it knows all of their IP addresses, as they're listed in the *root hints file* at %systemroot%\system32\dns\cache.dns on any Windows 2000 DNS server. When that root server gets the request, it responds with a partial answer like, "Beats me, but here's the IP address of a .com server that could help you find out." (Technically, this is called a *referral response*, since the answer is just a referral to some name server that's more suited to the task at hand.)

Before NS1 does anything else, it caches the information the referral response gave it. For example, if the referral response said something like, "Go to 10.15.20.1 to get .com IP addresses," NS1 adds something like, "All .com queries go to 10.15.20.1" to its cache. In the future, when some other name resolution request comes in asking for the IP address of *something*.com, NS1 now knows it can go straight to 10.15.20.1 for an answer. It won't need to go through the root name server just to get that same information again.

NS1 still can't answer the resolver's question, but now that it knows where to go for .com name resolution, it sends a query to the .com server, again asking, "What's the IP address of www.microsoft.com?" The process continues down the hierarchy until the final name server returns a complete answer, like "The IP address of www.microsoft.com is 207.46.230.219." NS1 can now answer Client02's recursive query. So Client02, the resolver, has resolved www.microsoft.com to an IP address (thanks to several helping DNS name servers).

DNS Zones of Authority

Now you know that DNS doesn't require one huge database of hostname-to-IP address mappings. Instead, each DNS name server is only responsible for a small "chunk" of names. The names for which a given DNS server has responsibility is called a DNS *zone*. We say that a DNS name server has *authority* over its own zone. A local domain can be broken down into subdomains, just as in the public hierarchy. With subdomains, you can either have a single name server resolve all names for hosts in the network or delegate name resolution responsibilities to name servers within subdomains. As an example of the first model, where a single name server covers a domain and all of its subdomains, take a look at Figure 3-3. There, the certifiable.com domain contains a couple of subdomains named NY.certifiable.com and Boston.certifiable.com. (By the way, I'm just using certifiable.com as a sample name here. This is not intended to reflect any actual domain named certifiable.com.)

In Figure 3-3, NS1.certifiable.com is the root server for all names that end in certifiable.com. NS1.certifiable.com *can* be authoritative for the subdomains because the namespace is *contiguous*, which is to say all names within the domain end in certifiable.com—even the subdomains. Thus, we have one big DNS zone shown within the gray oval.

Now, let's say you're the administrator for NS1.certifiable.com. Every time the people at NY.certifiable.com or Boston.certifiable.com make some change to their network, they call you on the phone asking you to make some change to the NS1 DNS name server to reflect *their change*. After a while, you get sick of these calls and want to say to them "Manage your own namespace." In other words, you want to *delegate* authority for DNS name resolution to those subdomains, so you can just worry about certifiable.com.

To do this, you give each subdomain its own DNS name server, and each name server has authority over its own subdomain, as shown in Figure 3-4. In this example, you now have three DNS zones (each marked by a gray oval). The NS1.certifiable.com name server at the top can now be configured to do name resolution only for machines named *something*.certifiable.com. Windows 2000 provides a simple Zone Delegation Wizard that makes it easy for you to delegate name resolution among zones.

Types of Zones

DNS is very much an industry standard, specified in numerous RFCs. With Windows 2000, you have the option of using *standard primary zones* and *standard*

FIGURE 3-3 The certifiable.com domain with two subdomains, NY.certifiable.com and Boston.certifiable.com

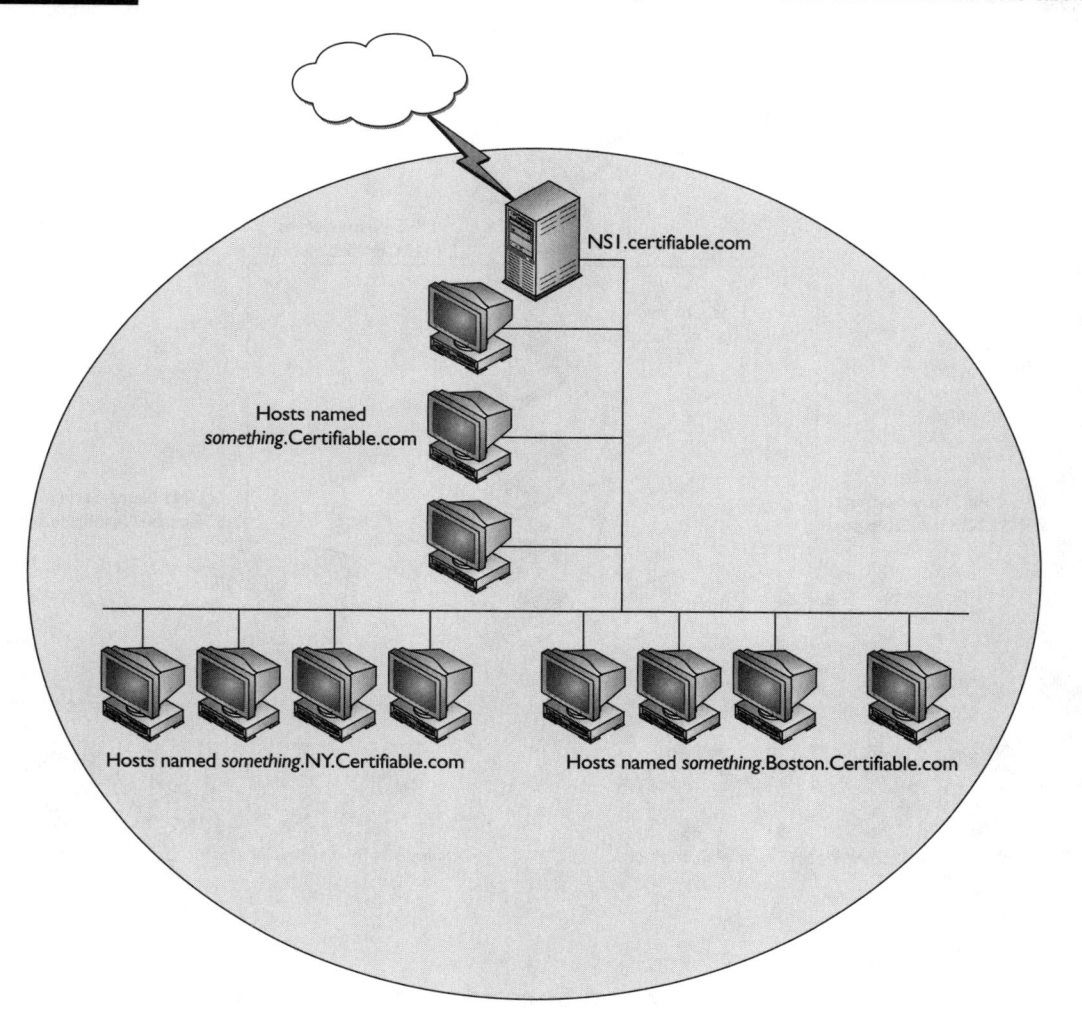

secondary zones (used for fault tolerance and load balancing), which are totally RFC compliant. You also have the option of using Windows 2000 *Active Directory–integrated zones* (AD-integrated zones), which are not RFC compliant. As the name implies, AD-integrated zones are very much tied into Active Directory, which is sort of what Windows 2000 is all about. We'll look at the features of each in the sections that follow.

FIGURE 3-4 The certifiable.com domain divided into three DNS zones

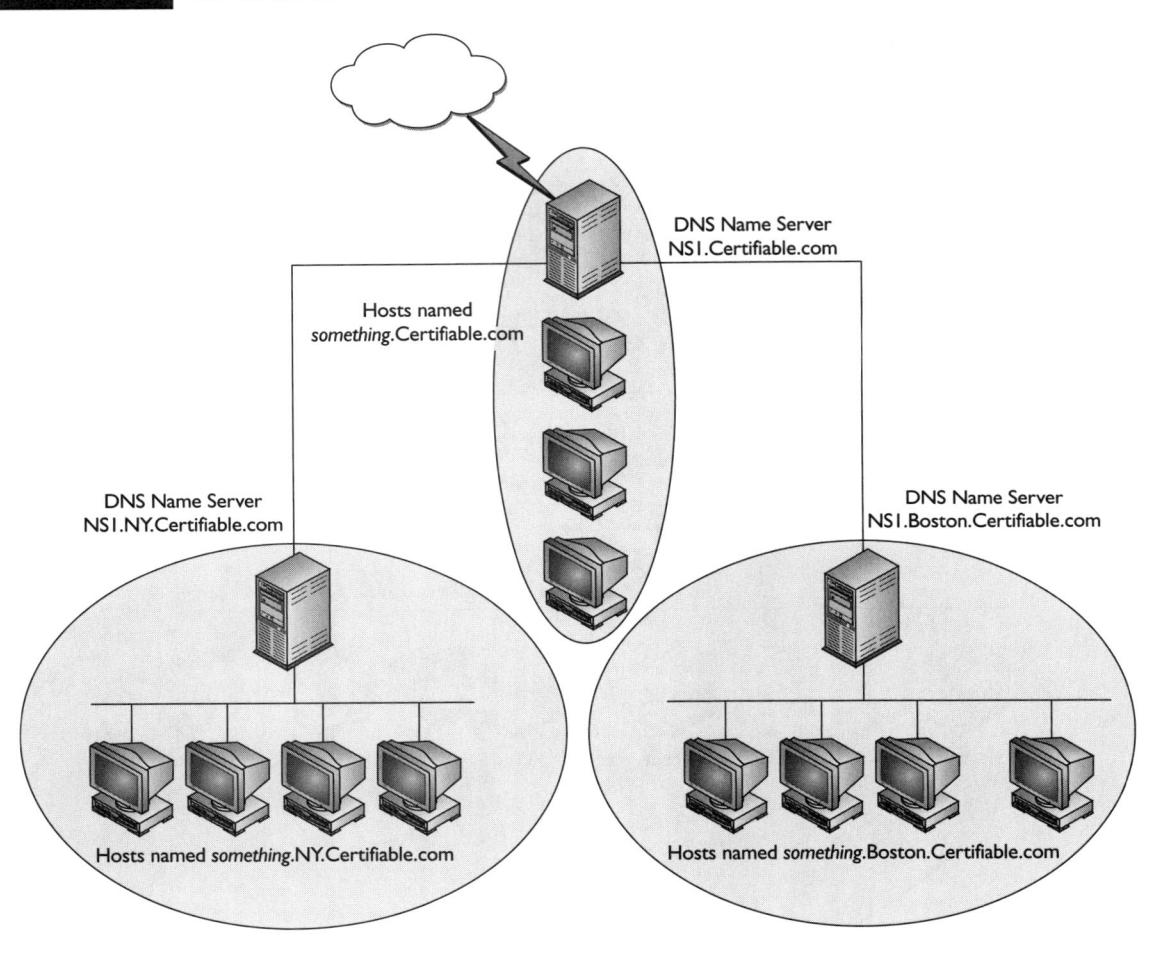

Standard Primary and Secondary Name Servers

The RFCs for DNS define standards for *primary name servers* and *secondary name servers*. A primary name server is one that maintains an actual database of hostname to IP addresses for a given zone. In this model, each domain has exactly one preferred DNS name server, and only that name server has a read/write copy of the zone database file. Thus, if a situation arises in which you need to manually alter the contents of the zone database file, you do so only on the primary DNS server.

The primary name server can also handle new *registrations*. For example, when a new client comes on, it can announce itself to the primary DNS server, essentially saying, "Hi, I'm wilbur.certifiable.com and my IP address is *whatever*. If anyone comes looking for wilbur.certifiable.com, just send them my way."

Standard secondary zones don't have read-write copies of the database. Instead, they get all their information from the primary name server through a type of replication known as *zone transfer*. Periodically, the secondary servers compare their version of the DNS zone database file against the master. If the master has changed, the secondary servers update their own copies of the zone database file with the new information. The secondary name servers cannot handle name registrations, nor can they be tweaked manually. They exist simply to handle name resolution based on the information they get from the primary name server.

Active Directory–Integrated Zones

As previously mentioned, Windows 2000 also offers a non-RFC type of zone called an Active Directory-integrated zone, which is neither primary nor secondary. As the name implies, this type of zone is integrated into Active Directory and provides a lot of conveniences that aren't found in the RFCs. For one thing, there's no need for a single, separate primary zone file that's used for all replication. Instead, with AD-integrated zones, you can use *multimaster zone replication*, whereby all servers are equal. AD-integrated zones also support secure DDNS, which you'll learn about later in this chapter.

The one caveat to AD-integrated zones is that only Windows 2000 domain controllers can host them. You can't separate your DNS name resolution from your domain controller, so the domain controllers are going to be quite busy handling authentications, registrations, and DNS name resolution. The solution, of course, is to use load balancing across multiple domain controllers so that no single machine gets stuck doing it all. As a general rule, Microsoft recommends creating at least two domain controllers with DNS enabled per subnet in your network.

exam
⚠ Watch

Because Active Directory is the major new feature of Windows 2000, Exam 70-218 is biased in the direction of AD-integrated zones.

EXERCISE 3-1

Installing AD-Integrated DNS

Promoting a Windows 2000 computer to a domain controller with Active Directory will automatically install and configure DNS, so one way to install DNS is to run the Active Directory Installation Wizard. In this exercise, we'll go through the steps to promote a server to a domain controller and install DNS in one fell swoop. There will be some questions about "trees" and "forests" along the way. For the purposes of this exercise, I'll assume that you're creating a new domain, tree, and forest. We'll talk about trees and forests in Chapter 5.

1. At the command prompt, type **DCPROMO** and press ENTER to start the Active Directory Installation Wizard. Click Next on the Welcome page to begin.

2. The first wizard page asks whether this domain controller will be for a new domain or an existing domain. Let's assume you're setting up a domain controller for a new domain, so you choose the first option and click Next.

3. The next page asks if you're creating a new domain tree or a new child within a tree. We'll talk about forests and trees in Chapter 5. For now, you can just choose the first option to create a new tree and click Next.

4. The next page asks if you want to create a new forest or join an existing one. Again, for this exercise, you can choose the first option, Create A New Forest Of Domain Trees, and click Next.

5. The next wizard page asks for the new domain name. If you have already registered a globally unique name with InterNIC or some other registrar, you can enter that name here. *Do not* just make up a .com, .net, or other domain name at random, as that name will likely conflict with a name that's already registered! If you don't have a registered name, you can use *.local* as your top-level domain name, as shown in the following illustration. Then click Next.

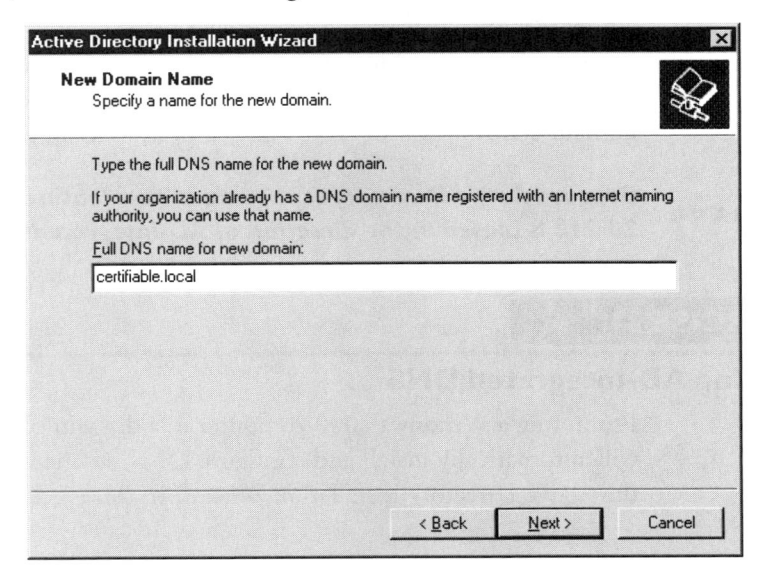

6. The next wizard page asks for the NetBIOS name for the domain. The suggested name is the domain name in all uppercase without the top-level domain name (for example, CERTIFIABLE if the domain name is certifiable.local). Click Next to accept the suggested name.

7. The next wizard page asks where you want to store the Active Directory database and log file. Unless you have multiple physical SCSI drives installed, and want to split the workload across the two drives, you can just accept the defaults at this point, C:\WINNT\NTDS for both. Click Next.

8. The next page asks where you want to store the Sysvol folder, which stores a copy of the domain's public files. Again, the default setting C:\WINNT\SYSVOL would be appropriate in most cases, so just click Next.

9. The next thing to pop up on your screen may be an informational message telling you that there is no root server "higher" than this server to be found that can be authoritative for this domain. It's just an informational message so you can click OK to proceed.

10. The next wizard page will ask if you want DNS to be installed and configured for you. You can accept the suggested option, Yes... and click Next.

11. The next wizard page asks if you need to allow "relaxed" permissions for pre-Windows 2000 servers. Choose an option and click Next.

12. The next wizard page asks for a password for the directory services administrator in the event of a crash that requires reinstallation of the services. Enter a password of your own choosing twice and click Next.

128 Chapter 3: Configuring, Managing, and Troubleshooting DNS

13. The next wizard page summarizes your selections, as in the following example. Click Next to begin the installation. Now you just follow the instructions on the screen to complete the installation.

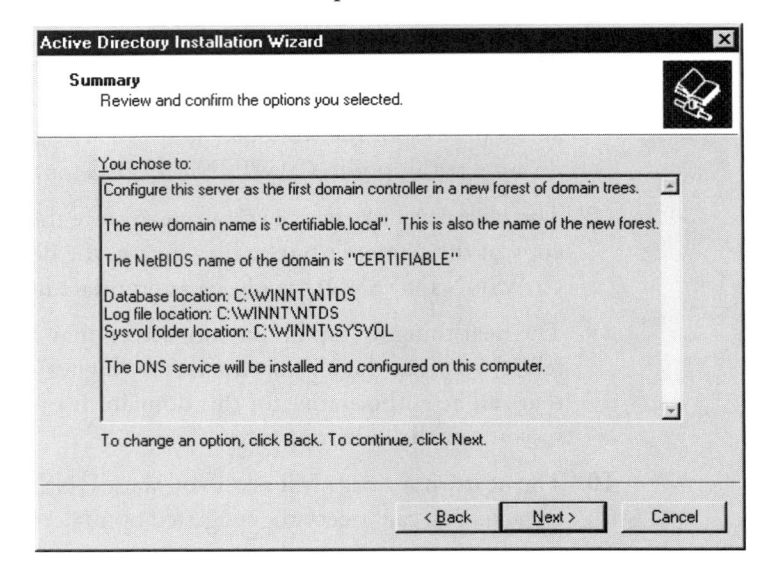

```
Active Directory Installation Wizard

Summary
Review and confirm the options you selected.

You chose to:
Configure this server as the first domain controller in a new forest of domain trees.

The new domain name is "certifiable.local". This is also the name of the new forest.

The NetBIOS name of the domain is "CERTIFIABLE"

Database location: C:\WINNT\NTDS
Log file location: C:\WINNT\NTDS
Sysvol folder location: C:\WINNT\SYSVOL

The DNS service will be installed and configured on this computer.

To change an option, click Back. To continue, click Next.

                                  < Back    Next >    Cancel
```

By using DCPROMO here, you've actually accomplished several tasks, including

- Making your server a domain controller and DNS name server
- Adding a DNS console (and several other snap-ins) to your Administrative tools
- Creating an AD-integrated forward lookup zone for your domain
- Enabling secure dynamic DNS updates to your DNS zone

As you read through the chapter, you won't actually have to make any changes to your existing zone to initiate these changes. You'll see that everything is in place as when you view the properties associated with your zone.

---

exam
⚠ watch

To install DNS without Active Directory, you'd use the traditional Add/Remove Programs applet in Control Panel. The DNS service is a subcomponent of the Networking Services component.

Creating a Forward Lookup Zone

Once DNS is installed on your server, you'll have access to the *DNS console* in the Microsoft Management Console (MMC). Your first task will be to tell the name server what domain it has authority over. (Well, actually, if you ran DCPROMO, that will have already been done for you, but for the purposes of the exam, you'll need to know how to do this, so I'll go ahead and explain how it's done here.)

A single name server can have authority over any number of zones. Each zone over which the server has authority is categorized as a *forward lookup zone* in DNS terminology. The name of the forward lookup zone will be the same as the domain over which the zone has authority, certifiable.local in my example. You can use the DNS console to modify an existing zone, as well as to create new forward lookup zones. To get to the DNS console

1. Click the Start button and choose Programs | Administrative Tools | DNS.

2. Expand the server name node, and click Forward Lookup Zones to see whether any forward lookup zones have already been created, as shown in Figure 3-5.

First, let me explain why there are already two forward lookup zones in the example shown in Figure 3-5. The first zone, named simply "." is the root zone. When I ran DCPROMO, that server wasn't connected to the Internet. As such, it

FIGURE 3-5

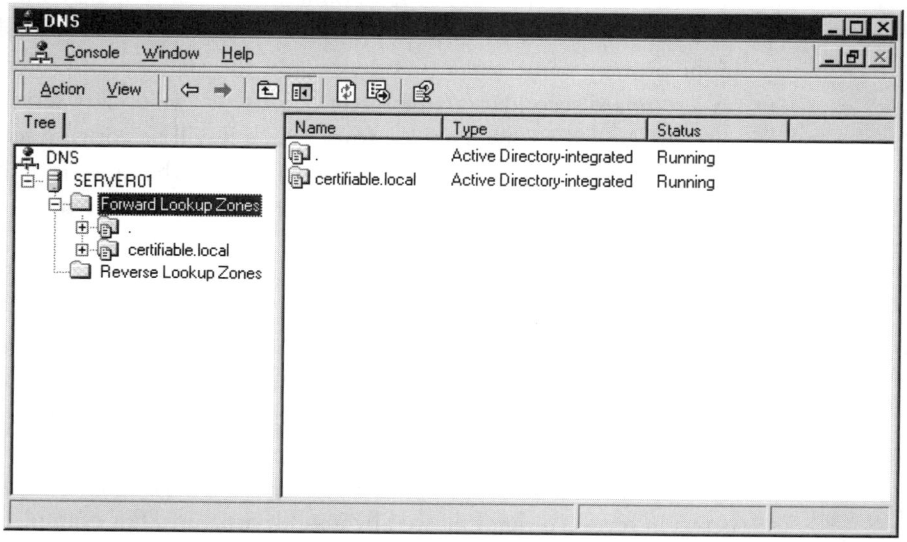

The DNS console with two forward lookup zones already created by DCPROMO

couldn't find a public DNS root server, so it created a root right here at the local server. If you run DCPROMO on a computer that is connected to the Internet, chances are it won't create that root zone. Either way, it doesn't matter much because even if you do end up with a root zone, you can always connect to the Internet later and get rid of the local root zone. The certifiable.local forward lookup zone was also created automatically by DCPROMO.

Should you ever need to add an entirely new zone to DNS, right-click Forward Lookup Zones in the console tree and choose New Zone. The New Zone Wizard starts. The first question will ask about the type of zone you want to create.

The next wizard page asks for the name of the zone. Once again, it's imperative that you not just make something up or pick a name out of a hat. If you want to use a .com, .net, or other publicly available top-level domain name, that name must be one you've already registered. If, on the other hand, the name server will be for a private network only, you can use any name you like followed by .local.

If you were to create a standard primary zone, another wizard page would appear asking you to name the zone database file. The suggested name, *yournamehere.yourtld*.dns, would be fine in most cases. However, you could import an existing zone database file, as instructed in the wizard, if you've already copied the zone database file from another server running DNS into the %systemroot%system32\dns folder of this server. This would be useful if you were replacing an existing name server and wanted to use the zone database file from the original server so as to not have to build a new zone database file from scratch.

If you're creating a standard secondary zone, the wizard will ask for the IP address of the primary name server (in other words, the master). This information is required on a standard secondary name server because the secondary server needs to know where to find the zone database from which it will be copying records. When you've completed the wizard, the new zone will appear in the right pane of the DNS console whenever you click Forward Lookup Zones in the console tree.

Creating a Reverse Lookup Zone

A reverse lookup zone does the opposite of normal name resolution. Rather than resolving a hostname to an IP address, it resolves an IP address to a hostname. The Internet authorities maintain an obscure domain that goes by the irritating and unpronounceable name *in-addr.arpa.dns* that maintains this reverse lookup information. Each reverse lookup zone is identified by the network portion of the IP address with the octets in reverse order, followed by in-addr-arpa.dns. For example, the reverse lookup zone for a class C address of 192.168.100.0 would be 100.168.192.in-addr.arpa.dns.

Create and Configure DNS Zones

on the job

RFC 2317, "Classless IN-ADDR-ARPA delegation," explains how you can configure DNS zones for custom subnet masks. Though not required for exam 70-218, I should point out that the Advanced tab of the Forward Lookup Zones node in the DNS console provides this option.

Truthfully, you hardly even need to know how to put together the name of the reverse lookup zone, because the New Zone Wizard will work that out for you when you follow these steps:

1. Right-click the Reverse Lookup Zones container and choose New Zone. The New Zone Wizard opens once again.

2. Click Next and choose the zone type once again. Then click Next.

3. On the next wizard page, enter the network ID portion of your IP address. For example, in Figure 3-6, I've entered **192.168.100** as the starting point for my sample network, though you'd enter the network ID portion of your own network's IP address. The wizard is clever enough to reverse the order of the octets all by itself, creating the reverse lookup zone for you.

4. The next wizard page asks for a filename. You can just choose Create A New File With This File Name to accept the default, which will be your network ID in reverse order with in-addr.arpa.dns appended to it. Click Next.

FIGURE 3-6

Creating a new reverse lookup zone

5. The last wizard page appears, summarizing your selections. Click Finish to complete the wizard.

When you expand the Reverse Lookup Zones node in the console tree now, you'll see your reverse lookup zone listed

Bear in mind that a DNS forward lookup zone is, ultimately, a database of hostname-to-IP address mappings (or vice versa in the case of a reverse lookup zone). Once you've created a zone, you can work with that database directly through the DNS console, as described in the next section.

CERTIFICATION OBJECTIVE 3.02

Manage DNS Database Records

Given that a DNS name server resolves hostnames to IP addresses, you'd probably assume that its zone database contains records of hostnames mapped to IP addresses, and you'd be correct in that assumption. However, it also contains a whole lot of

SCENARIO & SOLUTION

If I use .local as my top-level domain name, will I still be able to access the Internet?	A network that doesn't use a globally unique domain name that isn't registered with InterNIC can still use the Internet as a client, but Internet users outside that domain cannot reach servers within that domain.
If I set up AD-integrated zones, am I forever committed to using this Microsoft-specific implementation of DNS?	Not at all. If you right-click the name of a zone in the DNS manager and choose Properties, you'll see a Change button in the dialog box that opens. Clicking that button will present options for converting the zone to a standard primary or secondary zone.
Will AD-integrated zones work in a network that's also using standard and primary zones?	Yes, you can define additional name servers as standard secondary servers. Those secondary servers will receive zone transfers from AD-integrated zones in the same manner that they would a standard primary zone. In other words, the AD-integrated zone is the primary zone. In fact, unlike standard DNS, you can have any number of AD-integrated "primary" zones, not just one.

other useful information, divided into several different types of *resource records* (RR). The most commonly used record types are described in the sections that follow.

Start of Authority (SOA) Record

Every DNS zone database file contains a single Start of Authority (SOA) record. As the name implies, this record identifies the starting point of this zone file's authority, which is the DNS domain name. Creating a forward lookup zone automatically creates an SOA resource record for that zone. To view it, right-click the domain name under Forward Lookup Zones and choose Properties. Then, click the Start Of Authority (SOA) tab. The dialog box will look something like Figure 3-7.

Name Server (NS) Records

A DNS zone database also contains some Name Server (NS) records, which you can view by clicking the Name Servers tab in the zone database file's Properties dialog box. The list includes the primary name server for the domain, as well as any additional name servers. The list should include all name servers for the domain. In the

FIGURE 3-7

Start of Authority resource record

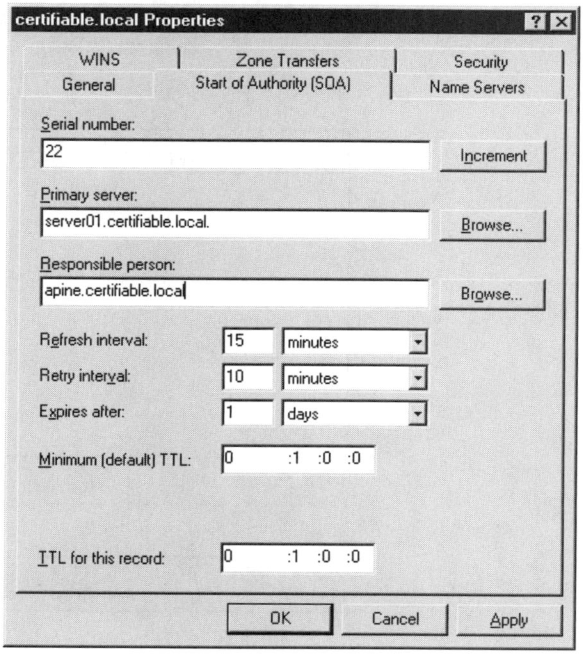

example shown in Figure 3-8, I've only created one name server so far, and its name and IP address appear in the list. As you add more name servers to your network, you'd need to add their names and IP addresses to this list as well.

EXERCISE 3-2

Viewing Resource Records

In this exercise, we'll take a look at existing RRs in a DNS zone database file. Note that you view or change the details of a record by right-clicking the record and choosing Properties. Delete a record by right-clicking and choosing Delete. To add a new record, right-click the zone name under Forward Lookup Zones or Reverse Lookup Zones and choose New. Assuming you're following along with the exercises, here's how you can view some RRs in your DNS zone database file:

1. Under Forward Lookup Zones in the DNS manager's console tree, right-click the name of a zone (for example, certifiable.local) and choose Properties.

FIGURE 3-8

The Name Servers tab of a zone file's Properties dialog box

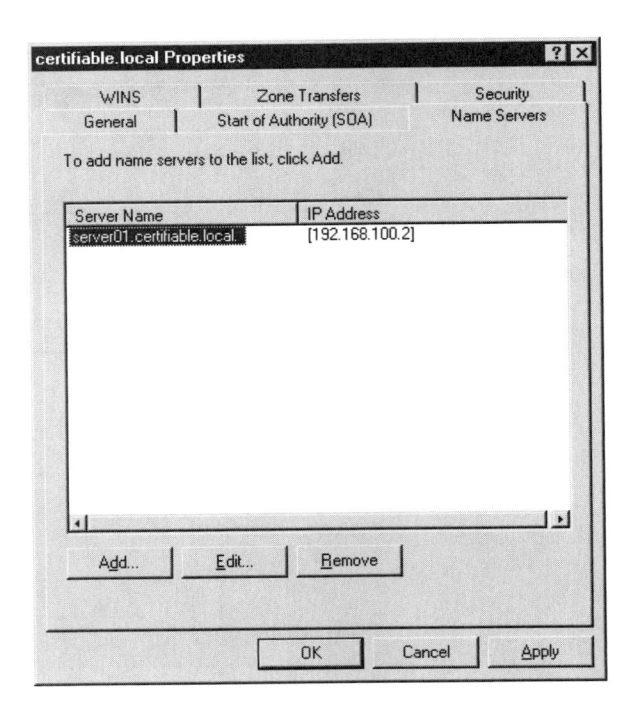

2. In the dialog box that opens, click the Start Of Authority (SOA) tab to view the SOA record for this zone.

3. To view the NS records, click the Name Servers tab. You should see at least one record representing your name server. If you've already set up additional name servers, you could use the Add button to specify their names and IP addresses here.

4. Since we're "just looking" in this exercise, you can close the Properties dialog box now by clicking its Cancel button.

Host (A) Records

The majority of records in a zone database file are *host records,* also called *address records* or just *A records* for short. These provide hostname-to-IP address resolution, which is the main task of DNS. Each host for which the name server has the authority to resolve names must have an A record in the zone database file. If automatic name registration is enabled, most hosts will create their own A records as they come into the domain. Clients that don't register with a Windows 2000 DHCP server may need to be entered manually. To manually add a new host record to a zone

1. In the console tree of the DNS console, right-click the name of the zone to which you want to add a new A record and choose New Host.

2. In the New Host dialog box that opens, type the hostname. Leave out the domain portion of the name if it's the same as the entry that appears as Location just above the text box.

3. Type the IP address of the host.

4. To automatically create a pointer record (used for reverse lookup), choose the Create Associated Pointer (PTR) Record option.

5. Click the Add Host button.

You'll see a message indicating that the operation was successful. You can continue to add more hosts or click the Done button when you're finished. Existing host records, if any, are listed in the right pane of the DNS console whenever you click the name of the zone database file.

Pointer (PTR) Records

Pointer (PTR) records are used for reverse lookups. Most of these records can be created automatically by choosing the Create Associated Pointer (PTR) Record option when creating a new record. You can view your current PTR records by clicking the name of the reverse lookup zone, as shown in Figure 3-9. In that example, you can see pointer records for server01 and client99 at the bottom of the list. The reverse lookup zone also has its own SOA and Name Server records, which are given the name *(same as parent folder)* by default.

---

exam
⍟atch

When you add a new host (A) record to a zone file, you must also add a corresponding pointer (PTR) record.

If you didn't select the option to create a pointer automatically when creating a new host record, you need to create one manually, just after creating the host record. To do so, right-click the name of the reverse lookup zone and choose New Pointer. Then just fill in the host portion of the IP address and hostname in the dialog box that opens and click OK.

Other Resource Records

Mail Exchanger records specify the location of mail servers where e-mail messages addressed to this domain should be sent. The name must resolve to a host that

FIGURE 3-9

Records in the reverse lookup zone are listed in the right pane when you click the zone's name in the console tree.

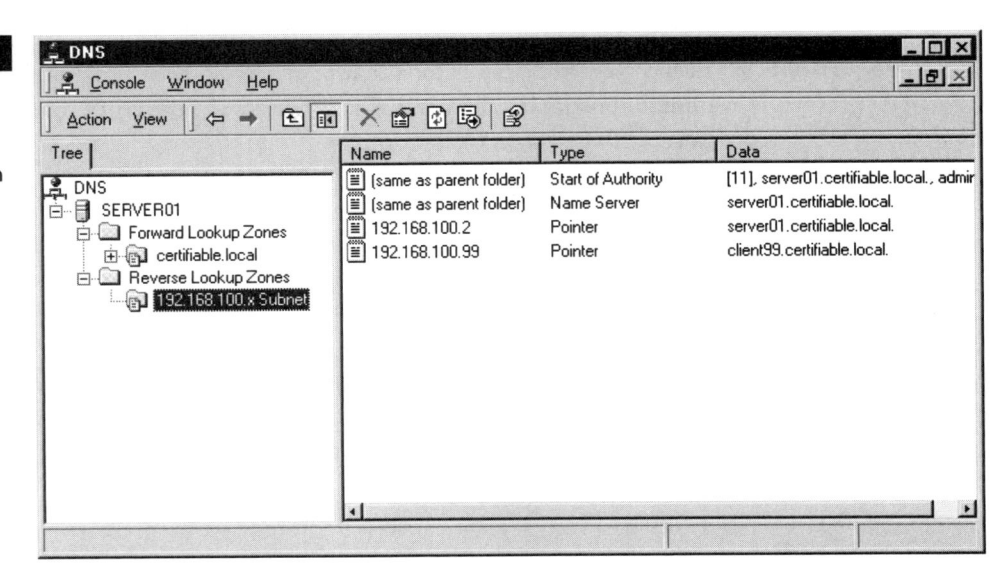

Name	Type	Data
(same as parent folder)	Start of Authority	[11], server01.certifiable.local., admir
(same as parent folder)	Name Server	server01.certifiable.local.
192.168.100.2	Pointer	server01.certifiable.local.
192.168.100.99	Pointer	client99.certifiable.local.

already has a corresponding A record. That is, if the host didn't register itself automatically, you'd first need to add an A (and PTR) record for that host. Then, you create an MX record to further define that host as the machine that's capable of accepting incoming e-mail messages. To add an MX record, right-click the domain name under Forward Lookup Zones in the DNS console and choose New Mail Exchanger. Fill in the blanks as instructed in the dialog box.

Alias records, also called *canonical name* or CNAME records, allow you to specify aliases for hosts. For example, let's say you have a web server at www.certifiable.local with the IP address 192.168.100.35, and there's already an A record for that host. However, you also have an FTP server on that same host. In that case, right-click the certifiable.com zone file in the DNS console and choose New Alias. In the new, blank CNAME record, type just the hostname (**ftp** in this example) and point it to the existing A record, www.certifiable.local, as in Figure 3-10.

Service Location (SRV) records are used to point clients to specific hosts for specific services and also allow an administrator to define primary and secondary hosts for services. DNS clients that can use SRV records will ask for a specific TCP/IP service and protocol within a domain and in return will receive a list of all servers within the

FIGURE 3-10

This CNAME record sends all ftp.certifiable.com traffic to www.certifiable.com.

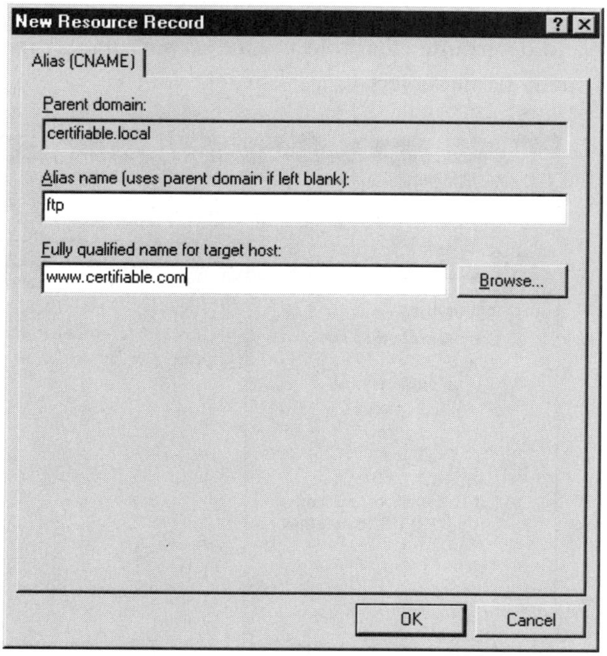

domain that are available to provide that service. If you used DCPROMO to install DNS, several SRV records have already been added to the _tcp and _udp folders within your domain. SRV records are indicated by the type Service Location, as shown in Figure 3-11.

The types of resource records covered so far will be sufficient for most settings (and the exam, of course!). For a complete list of supported record types, and a description of each, right-click the zone database filename under Forward Lookup Zones in the DNS console, and choose Other New Records. In the Resource Record Type dialog box that appears, click any listed record type to view its description. Most will also contain references to RFCs where additional information is available.

CERTIFICATION OBJECTIVE 3.03

Configure DNS Server Properties

The DNS console also has tools for managing DNS server properties as a whole, as well as properties for individual zones. As you'll learn in this section, you can use these properties to configure DDNS, set up and delegate authority to subdomains, and determine what role a name server will play in a large network that contains many name servers.

FIGURE 3-11

Service Location (SRV) records listed in _tcp on a domain controller using AD-integrated zones

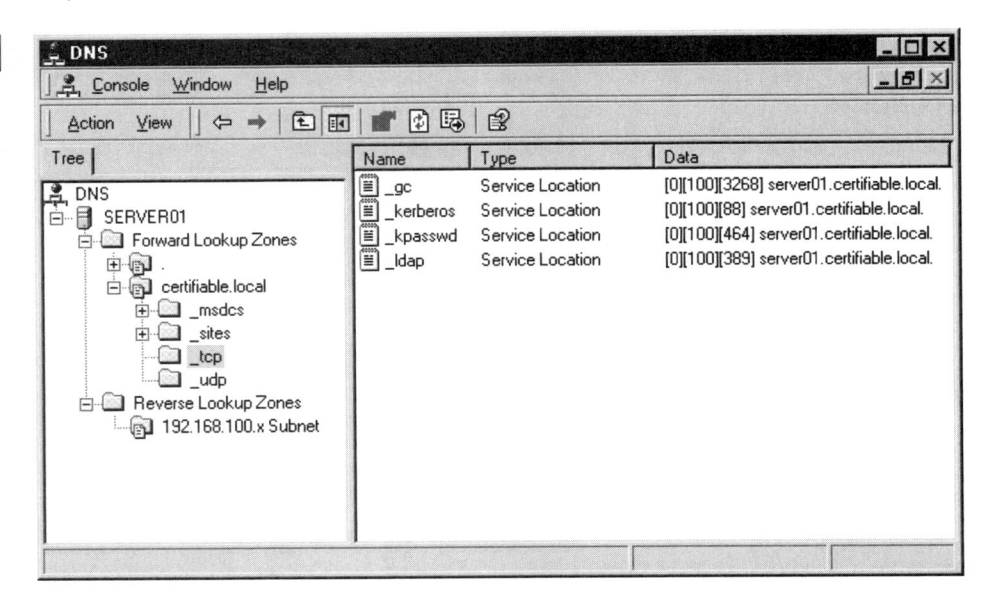

FROM THE CLASSROOM

Ports and UDP

A single IP address can support both TCP (Transmission Control Protocol) and UDP (User Datagram Protocol), each of which consists of 65,535 different ports. Most of the common services found on the Internet use certain *well-known ports*. For example, FTP uses port 21, SMTP uses port 25, DNS uses port 53, and the Web uses port 80 (all with the TCP protocol). Because all of these services use different ports, a single server (in other words, a single IP address) can provide all of these different services to clients. If there's a lot of traffic at the server, it might not be *practical* to use a single IP address to provide so many services. Nonetheless, it is *possible*.

The main difference between the TCP and UDP protocols is as follows: TCP communications are based on a connection between two specific IP addresses, and the protocol uses acknowledgements to guarantee successful transmissions. UDP, on the other hand, is *connectionless*. UDP just sends out packets without waiting for acknowledgements, and hence doesn't guarantee communications. UDP is used for communications that have no specific IP address to which a packet can be addressed. UDP communications are also faster than TCP communications, because there is no waiting around for acknowledgements.

—*Alan Simpson, MA, MCSA*

SCENARIO & SOLUTION

What characteristics should I look for in non-Microsoft DNS servers to best take advantage of the features found in Microsoft's DNS implementation.	First and foremost, you want to ensure that the DNS server supports SRV records, as those are critical to AD-integrated zones. Optionally, DNS servers that support dynamic updates, as per RFC 2136, and incremental transfers (IXFR records) will provide the best integration.
My network consists of five subnets and five domain controllers, as well as a number of member servers. All the computers are Windows 2000 based. I want all the computers to be able to find each other across all subnets. How many name servers do I need?	Technically, you could get away with just one Windows 2000 name server that is authoritative for all the machines in the network, but for fault tolerance and load balancing, you'd be better off setting up at least two AD-integrated zones on two of the domain controllers.

Configuring DDNS

Now, on to an altogether different subject, Dynamic DNS (DDNS) is a protocol that allows a DNS server to automatically accept new clients and add them to the domain. Without DDNS, an administrator would need to manually enter host (A) and pointer (PTR) records for every host in the network. In a large network, that would be a laborious task.

Bear in mind that a DNS server can be authoritative for any number of zones. As far as DNS goes, you can allow or disallow DDNS on any given zone. The procedure is pretty simple. In the console tree of the DNS manager, right-click the name of the zone for which you want to configure DDNS and choose Properties. Click the General tab, as shown in Figure 3-12. In the Allow Dynamic Updates? drop-down list, choose one of the following options:

- **No** This name server will not accept dynamic updates. All resource records must be created manually.
- **Yes** This machine will accept dynamic updates using the standard (relatively unsecure) DNS model.

FIGURE 3-12

The General tab of a DNS zone's Properties dialog box

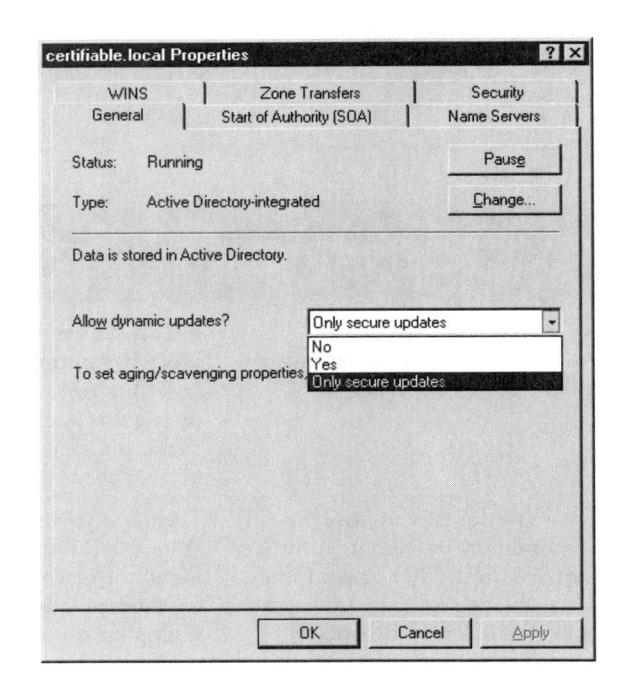

- **Only secure updates** This option is only available on AD-integrated zones. If selected, only machines that are capable of logging in to the domain will be registered with DNS. Machines outside that domain will not be allowed to register.

Note the Pause and Change buttons near the top of the tab. You can change a zone from one type to another at any time using those buttons. First, click the Pause button to stop the name service. Then, click the Change button. Choose the type of zone you want to convert to—Standard Primary, Standard Secondary, or Active Directory Integrated—and then click OK. To restart the DNS service, click the Start button that now appears where the Pause button was situated.

EXERCISE 3-3

Configuring Dynamic DNS

In this exercise, you'll go through the steps required to enable DDNS on your name server, so that when you start adding clients later in this chapter, the server will create host records for those clients automatically. You need to be logged in to the name server computer with administrative privileges. If the DNS console isn't already open, go ahead and open it now (click the Start button and choose Programs | Administrative Tools | DNS). Then follow these steps:

1. Under Forward Lookup Zones in the console tree, right-click the name of the zone for which you want to allow DDNS (certifiable.local in my example) and choose Properties.
2. On the General tab, choose Only Secure Updates from the drop-down list.
3. Click OK.

That's all that's needed on the server side. You'll configure clients to use DNS in a later exercise in this chapter.

DDNS Aging and Scavenging Properties

As you may recall from Chapter 2, WINS clients need to reregister their names from time to time to stay in the WINS database. If a client doesn't reregister within a certain amount of time, its name and IP address are removed from the WINS database, and another client can log in with that old name and/or IP address. It doesn't work that way with DDNS registrations. By default, once a client registers with DDNS, its host (A) and pointer (PTR) records stay in the zone database file "forever." To put it more accurately DDNS, by default, doesn't require clients to reregister their names periodically to stay in the zone database file.

You can change this default behavior by allowing the name server to periodically scavenge stale records from the zone database file. The first order of business along these lines takes place at the server level. That is, you right-click the name of the server in the DNS console manager (not the name of a specific zone) and choose Properties. Then, click the Advanced tab. Choose Enable Automatic Scavenging Of Stale Records, as shown in Figure 3-13.

That sets up scavenging of stale records for the server as a whole. However, to complete the job, you also need to set aging and scavenging within each DNS zone. To do so, you right-click the name of the zone in the console tree and choose Properties. On the General tab, as in Figure 3-14, click the Aging button to reveal the zone's Zone Aging/Scavenging Properties dialog box.

FIGURE 3-13

The Advanced tab of a name server's Properties dialog box

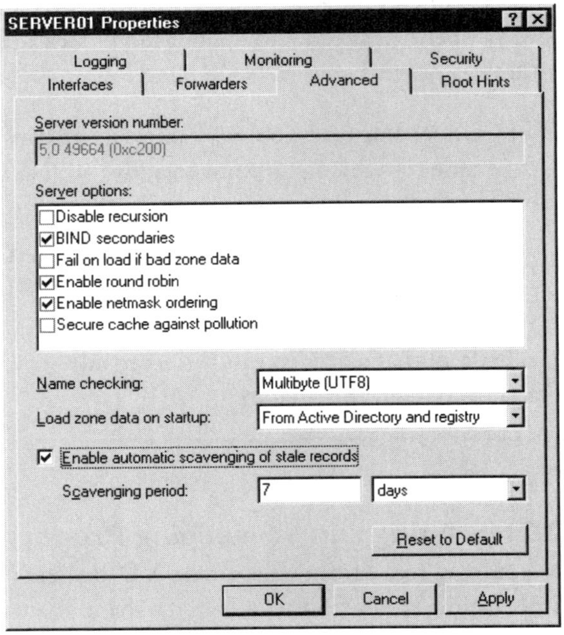

FIGURE 3-14

The Zone Aging/Scavenging Properties dialog box for a DNS zone

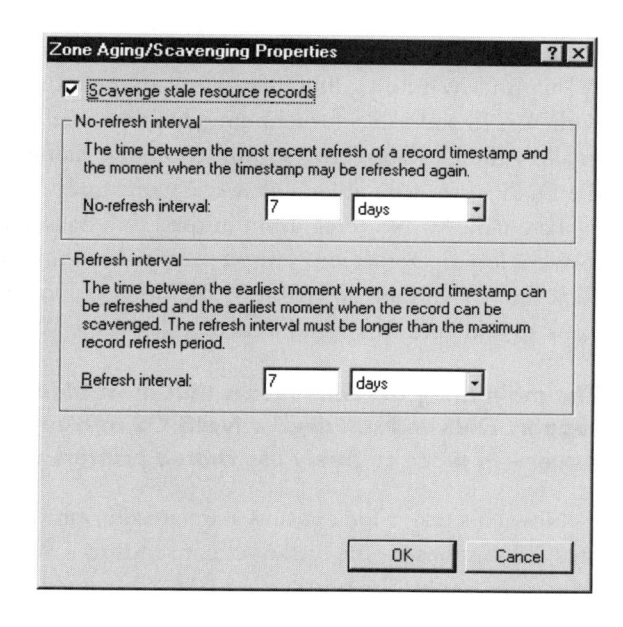

To ensure scavenging of records for the current zone, you first choose the Scavenge Stale Resource Records check box. Then you configure some time intervals that have some confusing names. First there's the No-Refresh Interval option, which specifies a period of time during which any client requests to reregister will be ignored. For example, let's say you set the No-Refresh Interval option to 2 days. A client registers itself at 8:00 A.M. on Monday morning. If that client tries to reregister its name any time before 8:00 on Wednesday morning, the reregistration will be ignored. Thus, you've set a limit on how often clients *can* reregister their names.

Once the no-refresh interval (the "no-registering-allowed period of time") has expired, a new interval called the refresh interval begins. This interval says something like, "OK, you can reregister now, but you only have x hours or x days to do so; otherwise, your resource record will be scavenged from the zone database file." You determine the value of x by setting the Refresh Interval options.

Supporting Downlevel Clients

As you learned in Chapter 2, Windows 95, NT, and other early Windows versions still rely on NetBIOS for name resolution. Windows 2000 provides support for both naming systems, but you need to provide the downlevel clients with a way to resolve

NetBIOS names to IP addresses. The most efficient way to do this is to install WINS on a Windows 2000 Server computer and configure all the clients to use both WINS and DNS for name resolution. Then you can use WINS integration to allow the DNS server to submit computer names or IP addresses to WINS when the DNS server isn't able to answer a name query from its own database.

To enable WINS integration in the DNS console, right-click the name of the forward lookup zone (for example, certifiable.com) and choose Properties. Then click the WINS tab. To enable WINS integration, choose Use WINS Forward Lookup and enter the IP address of at least one WINS server under IP Address.

> **exam**
> **Watch**
>
> *The main thing to remember is that most older Microsoft clients that don't support DNS will still need a NetBIOS infrastructure—preferably a WINS server—in place to freely use shared printers and folders on the network.*

Now let's take a look at how name resolution works with WINS integration enabled. Suppose some distant client sends to a WINS-integrated DNS server a request to resolve the hostname STACY.certifiable.local to an IP address. The DNS server scans its zone database to try to find a host (A) record matching that name. If no such record is found, the WINS-integrated server will then grab just the host portion of the name (STACY in this example) and send that off to the WINS server for name resolution. If the WINS server can convert STACY to an IP address, it then sends that IP address back to the DNS server. The DNS server, in turn, can send the IP address back to the original requesting client. That original client need not even "know" that STACY is a NetBIOS name or that WINS was used in the process of resolving the requested name to an IP address.

To provide this transparent NetBIOS-to-IP address name resolution to DNS clients, WINS-integrated DNS servers store WINS and WINS-R resource record types in the zone database file. These records are essentially forward (A) and reverse (PTR) records for the WINS server(s), though they're not 100 percent DNS-compatible. Rather, the WINS and WINS-R resource record types are unique to Microsoft's implementation of WINS.

If you have non-Microsoft DNS name servers in your network and these other servers receive zone transfers from the Microsoft DNS name server, the WINS and WINS-R records could cause the zone transfer to fail. To prevent such failures, you can choose the Do Not Replicate This Record option in the Properties dialog box.

Subdomains and Delegation of Authority

A DNS domain can be subdivided into subdomains, and you can delegate name resolution responsibilities to the subdomains. Doing so allows administrators of the subdomains to manage their own DNS zones and also reduces some of the demand placed on the primary domain server. Figure 3-15 shows an example where dc1.certifiable.com is domain controller and DNS name server for certifiable.com, and dc1.dev.certifiable.com is domain controller and DNS name server for dev.certifiable.com.

Zone delegation is pretty easy in Windows 2000 DNS, thanks to the Zone Delegation Wizard. Right-click the name of the parent domain (certifiable.com in this example) and choose New Delegation. In the wizard page that asks for the delegated domain name, enter just the first label of the name, which is **dev** in this example. Clicking Next then takes you to the Name Servers page of the wizard. Click the Add button to add a Name Server record for the new name server. Enter the FQDN of the name server for the subdomain, as well as its IP address, as shown in Figure 3-16. You can use the Add button to specify any number of name servers that are available in the subdomain.

After you complete the wizard, you're returned to the DNS console, where the new subdomain appears beneath the parent domain. When you click the subdomain's icon, you can see its Name Server record.

FIGURE 3-15

Here, dev.certifiable.com is a subdomain of certifiable.com.

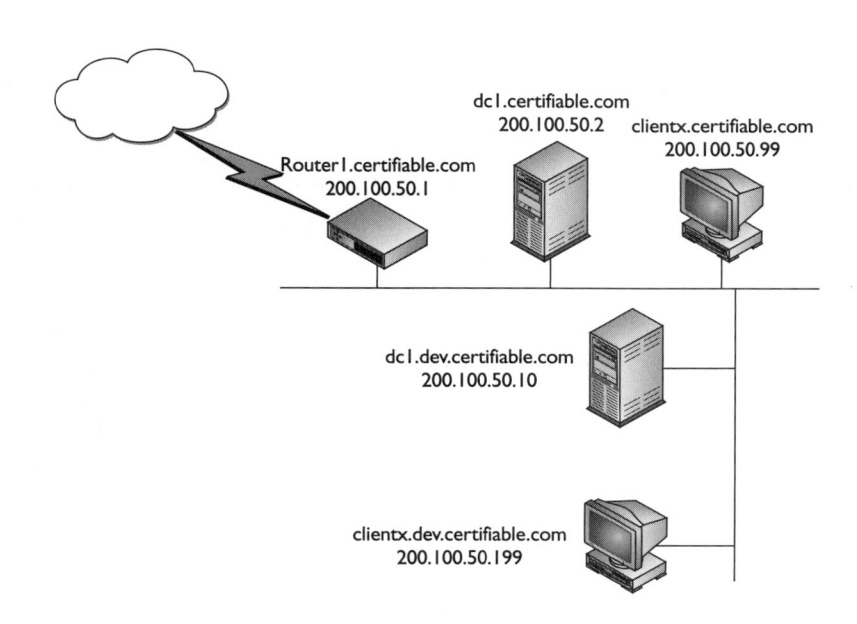

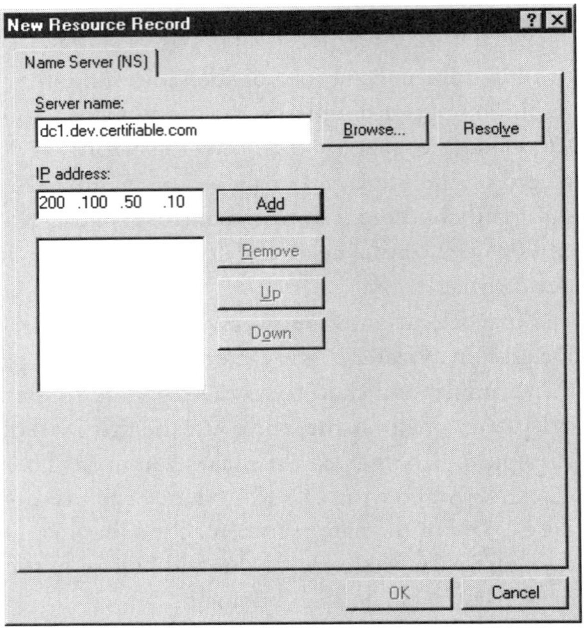

FIGURE 3-16

Adding Name Server records for a delegated domain

Multihomed DNS Name Servers

Any computer that contains more than one network interface card is referred to as a *multihomed computer*. A domain controller can certainly be multihomed, providing any number of services to clients on each network interface. If that multihomed server is a name server, you can control which interfaces the name server listens to and which it ignores. In the DNS console, right-click the name of the server and choose Properties. Then click the Interfaces tab, as shown in Figure 3-17.

As you can see, the default setting is to listen for DNS queries on all IP address (in other words, all NICs), but suppose you want the DNS service to apply to only one, or a few, of the network interfaces. In that case, you could choose the Only The Following IP Addresses option and then use the Add and Remove buttons to specify IP addresses on which to listen. For example, on the 192.168.100.2 NIC, you want to provide name resolution, but you don't want to provide name resolution for clients connected to the other NIC at 192.180.155.1. In that case, you could select Only The Following IP Addresses and specify 192.168.100.2 as the only interface on which to listen for DNS queries.

FIGURE 3-17

The Interfaces tab of a DNS name server's Properties dialog box

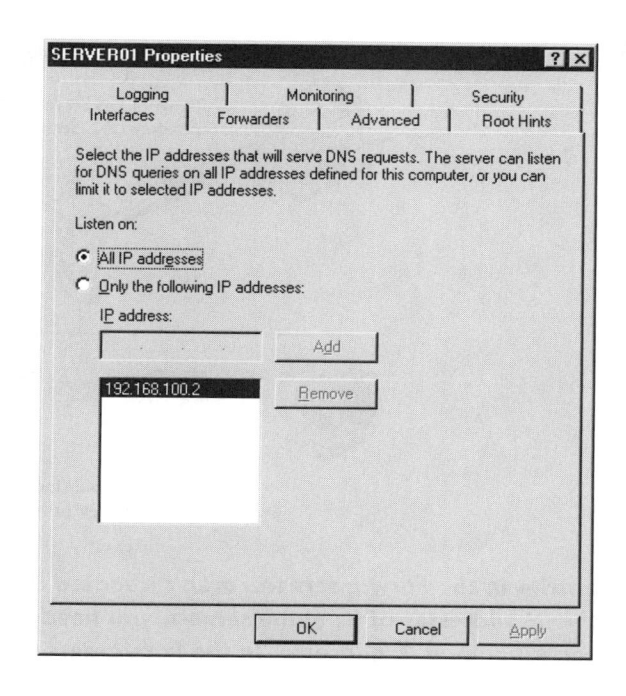

Alternative DNS Server Roles

If a DNS name server is to provide name resolution for both the domain over which it has authority and all the domains on the Internet, then that DNS server must have a WAN link connecting it to the Internet. To make this happen, the local name server needs to be authoritative for its own zone, of course. It also needs to be able to forward name resolution requests for which it doesn't have authority to some other name server. The simple scenario for this kind of setup is illustrated in Figure 3-18, where the name server is connected to an ISP. In this example, Server01.certifiable.local is not a root server. Thus, there should be no forward lookup zone named simply "." in the DNS console for the zone. If you originally set up this server without an Internet connection and DCPROMO created a root forward lookup zone, you'd want to right-click that zone and choose Delete to delete it.

Next, you need to tell the name server where to send name resolution requests for which it isn't authoritative. In this example, you'd use the IP addresses provided by the ISP—200.100.50.10 and 200.100.50.11 in this example. To plug in those values, right-click the local name server's name in the DNS console, and choose Properties. Click the Forwarders tab and choose Enable Forwarders. Then use the Add button to enter the IP addresses of the ISP's name servers, as shown in Figure 3-19.

148 Chapter 3: Configuring, Managing, and Troubleshooting DNS

FIGURE 3-18

A simple scenario of a name server connected directly to an ISP

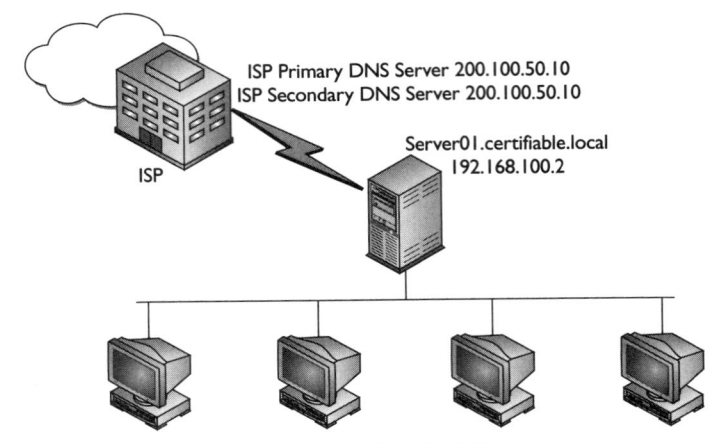

ISP Primary DNS Server 200.100.50.10
ISP Secondary DNS Server 200.100.50.10

Server01.certifiable.local
192.168.100.2

Clients in certifiable.local all point to
192.168.100.2 as their primary name server

exam
Watch

Entries in the Forwarders tab aren't updated dynamically. If the ISP changed the IP addresses of its name servers, you need to manually change the corresponding IP addresses in the Forwarders tab to match.

FIGURE 3-19

Name resolution requests outside the zone of authority will be forwarded to some other IP address.

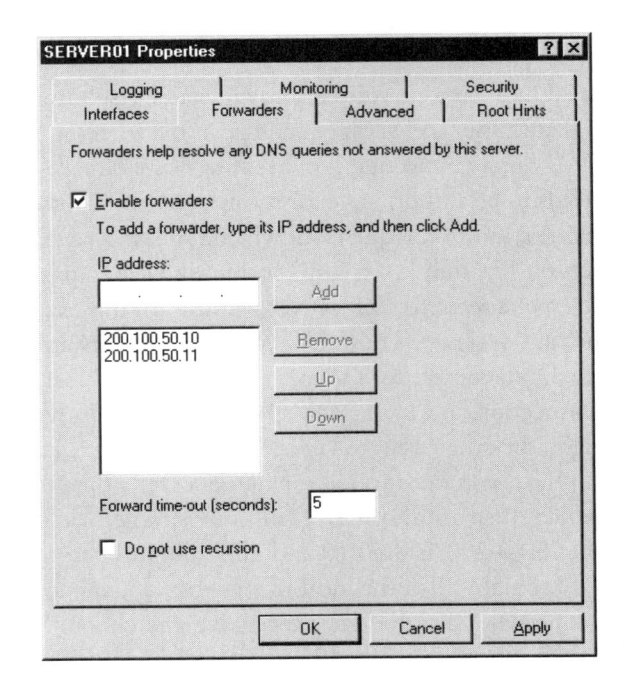

Finally, you'll also want to make sure your local name server can use the *root hints* file, which contains the IP addresses of the 13 public root servers on the Internet. If you deleted the root zone named "." in the DNS console, you should be able to click the Root Hints tab in that same dialog box to see a list of names and IP addresses of public DNS root servers. (If your local server is acting as a root server, all options on the Root Hints tab will be disabled and dimmed.)

Let's take a look at what happens when a client in certifiable.local sends a name resolution request to its primary, local name server Server01.certifiable.local:

1. Server01 receives the request and checks its local cache.
2. If it cannot find the name in its cache, it checks the zone(s) for which it has authority.
3. If it cannot find the name in its zone of authority, it forwards the request to the ISP's primary DNS server.

That all works out just fine, and there are some installations that use such setups because in that example, the setup is safe because certifiable.local is private (not in one of the public .com, .net, or other top-level domains). Now let's take a look at the situation in which the WAN link is a two-way street, where instead of certifiable.local, for example, we're working with certifiable.com, and certifiable.com has a public Internet presence and provides name resolution for requests coming in from the Internet. Now the company's entire DNS structure is be exposed to the Internet. If someone out there wanted to break into the local network, having that complete zone file at their disposal would certainly help their cause.

This security risk can be (and often is) eliminated by inserting a *DNS forwarder* between the name server and the WAN link, as shown in Figure 3-20. For this example, I've set up NS1.certifiable.com as a *forwarding server,* just as I did in the previous example, where I set up the local name server to forward locally irresolvable queries to the ISP's name servers. Only here, I can have NS1.certifiable.com forward those requests to the DNS forwarder, which is also a local machine.

Let's look at how a name resolution request would be handled with NS1 defined as a forwarding server and NS2 defined as the forwarder. NS1 gets a name resolution query from some client, checks its local cache and if it can't resolve from there, forwards the query to NS2. NS2 checks its local cache and if it can't resolve the query, sends the request out over the WAN link to the public DNS root for resolution.

150 Chapter 3: Configuring, Managing, and Troubleshooting DNS

FIGURE 3-20

Adding a DNS forwarder to .com network that serves the Internet

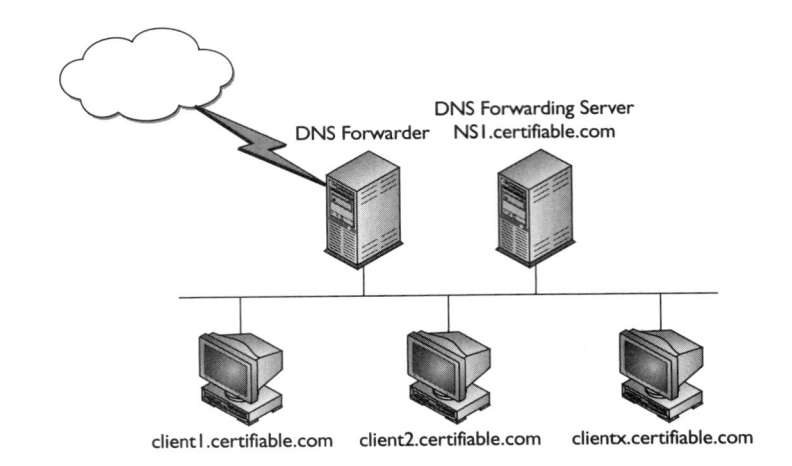

Of course, you'd look at that and say, "Yeah, but the DNS forwarder is connected to the WAN link, so its DNS zone files are every bit as vulnerable as they were on NS1." That would be true if the DNS forwarder contained vulnerable zone files, but there's really no reason for the DNS forwarder to have a zone file that exposes the entire internal DNS structure. The local clients can get that information from NS1.certifiable.com. The DNS forwarder needs to have only host records for hosts on the network that need to be accessible to the Internet, or, for that matter, the DNS forwarder could just be authoritative for no zones at all, thereby not providing any name resolution to outside clients.

exam
🕲 a t c h

Pay close attention to terminology when taking your exam. Remember, a DNS forwarder is the computer that's connected to the Internet (or some other kind of WAN link). Name servers that use that DNS forwarder for external name resolution are called DNS forwarding servers.

When you configure a forwarding server, you also have a Forward Time-Out (Seconds) option that determines how long the forwarding server will wait for a response from the forwarder before taking matters into its own hands. The default value is five seconds. This means that when NS1 gets a request to resolve a name from one of its own clients but has no authority to resolve the name, it will forward the request to the forwarder and wait five seconds for a positive response. If it gets no response in that time, NS1 will use its own query capabilities to try to resolve the name, perhaps bypassing the forwarder and querying a public DNS root server itself. If that happens, you've reopened the exposure that the forwarder initially had covered, but there's a simple way to plug up that hole as well. You make the forwarding server a *slave server.*

Configuring a Slave Server

A slave server is a DNS forwarding server that can pass on name resolution requests to a DNS forwarder, but *cannot* resolve those names without the forwarder. Here's how it works:

1. A client sends a name resolution request to its primary name server.
2. If the primary server doesn't have authority to resolve the name, it forwards the request to the DNS forwarder.
3. If the DNS forwarder doesn't respond within the Forward Time-Out (Seconds) interval (five seconds by default), the primary name server does not attempt to resolve the name on its own. Instead, it just sends a "Not found" response back to the client.

The primary name server still has authority to resolve names within its own zone of authority, but that's all it can do. When it comes to resolving names outside its zone, it's a "slave" to the DNS forwarder. If the DNS forwarder can't resolve the name, that's just tough luck. The client gets a "Not found" response.

Configuring a DNS forwarding server to be a slave is simple. Assuming you've already enabled forwarding and specified the IP address of one or more forwarders, all you need to do is select the Do Not Use Recursion option near the bottom of the Forwarders tab. If the five-second time limit starts causing too many unnecessary failed name resolution requests, you can increase the Forward Time-Out (Seconds) interval accordingly.

Caching-Only DNS Name Servers

As mentioned, all DNS name servers cache recently resolved names and IP addresses. It's also possible to set up a caching-only server, which does not contain a copy of a zone database file at all. Instead, it simply builds a database of hostnames and their IP addresses based on successful DNS resolution queries from its clients. The caching server starts by building its database from the root hints file, which contains mappings to the 13 public DNS servers on the Internet.

If you make a DNS forwarder a caching-only server, it need not have any zone files at all! Plus, there's another advantage. The caching-only server need not do zone transfers or replication with other servers, so all the available bandwidth can be used for name resolution. To really tighten up security, you could even put the caching-only DNS server on the far side of a firewall, as shown in Figure 3-21.

Creating a caching-only server is a simple matter of setting up a regular DNS name server, except that you don't give the server any zones over which it's authoritative. Since the server will have no authoritative zone to check for name resolution, it has only two resources to use for name resolution: its own local cache, and any root servers to which is has access (in other words, the public DNS root server).

on the job

If you add a firewall you need to open up port 53 to allow DNS messages to pass through the firewall. By default, messages are sent using UDP. However, since UDP packets are limited in size, messages that won't fit into a single UDP packet are automatically transferred in a fully connected TCP session.

Caching-only servers can also be useful in situations where speed, not just security, is a barrier to peak performance. For example, let's say you have a slow 56 Kbps connection to a branch office. Currently, name resolution requests for resources in the branch office are all traversing that slow WAN link, and taking forever. If you put a caching-only server on the near side of the WAN link, most name resolution requests will eventually be resolved by the local caching-only server.

exam watch

As far a speed goes on WAN links, slow WAN links can benefit from caching-only servers. With faster connections, like a T1 or T3, AD-integrated zones at both sides of the connection would be okay, because the zone replication wouldn't be hampered by a slow WAN link.

FIGURE 3-21

A caching-only forwarder, firewall, and internal slave server provide great security for the internal DNS zones.

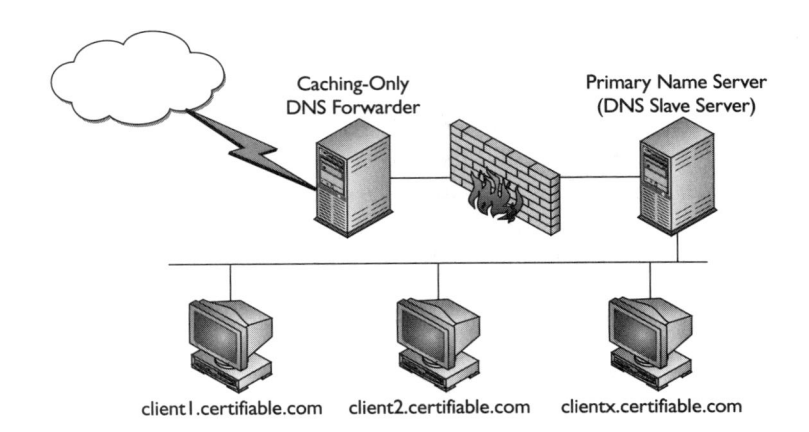

CERTIFICATION OBJECTIVE 3.04

Configure Client Computer Name Resolution Properties

Configuring a client to use a DNS server, and to register itself on startup, is an easy process. First, make sure the client has an IP address and subnet mask, and ping the server just to make sure you have basic connectivity. Then, you'll want to ensure that the client is a member of the domain over which the name server has authority. On the client, right-click the My Computer icon on the desktop and choose Properties. Click the Network Identification tab, as shown in Figure 3-22 to see the full computer name and the domain to which it belongs.

If you haven't joined the client to a domain yet, you can use the Properties button to join the client to a domain. Note that you must first create an account for the client on the domain controller using Active Directory Users and Groups. Since this is not your first Microsoft exam, I assume you already know how to do that, but in case you've forgotten how, here are the basic steps:

1. Log in to the domain controller (not the client) as administrator.

FIGURE 3-22

Network Identification tab of a client's System Properties dialog box

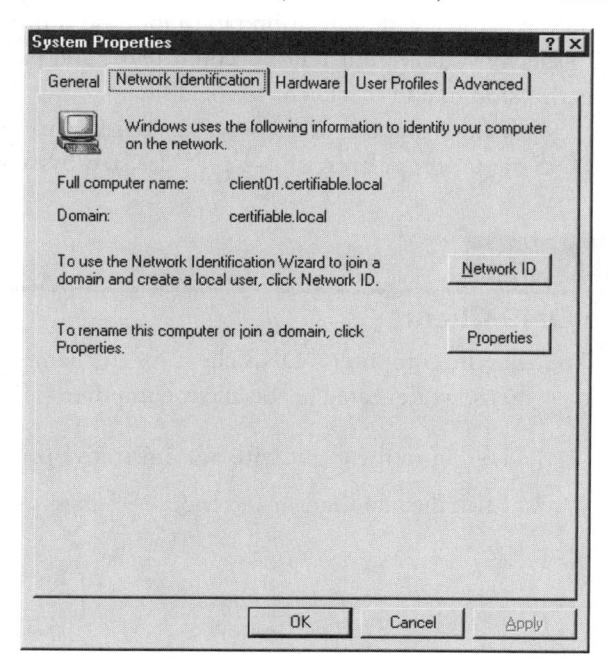

2. Click the Start button and choose Programs | Administrative Tools | Active Directory Users and Groups.

3. In the console tree, make sure the domain to which you want to add the client is selected.

4. Click the Action button and choose New | Computer.

5. Fill in the client name and click OK.

You can also create a user account for the name of the person who will be using that computer by following these steps

1. Click the Action button and choose New User.

2. Fill in the blanks, and make sure you type the user logon name exactly as you want the user to type it.

3. Click Next, fill in the password, and then follow the instructions to complete the wizard.

We'll discuss Active Directory in detail in Chapter 5. For our current purposes, the default permissions and such will be adequate. Once you've made the computer a member of the domain, you can go back to the client and use the Properties button on the Network Identification tab to join the computer to the domain. You'll need to specify your administrator account name and password when prompted to gain permission to add this client to the domain.

With all of that out of the way, you're ready to set up the client to use the local DNS name server. Exercise 3-4 provides step-by-step instructions.

EXERCISE 3-4

Configuring a DNS Client

To make the computer a DNS client for the name server(s) you've created, follow these steps, while seated at the client computer:

1. Log on to the client with administrative privileges.

2. Click the Start button and choose Settings | Network And Dial-Up Connections.

Configure Client Computer Name Resolution Properties

3. Right-click the icon that represents the connection to the network on which your local DNS name server is installed and choose Properties.
4. Click Internet Protocol (TCP/IP) and then click the Properties button.
5. Choose Use The Following DNS Server Addresses.
6. Type the IP address of your primary (or only) local DNS name server as the Preferred DNS Server.

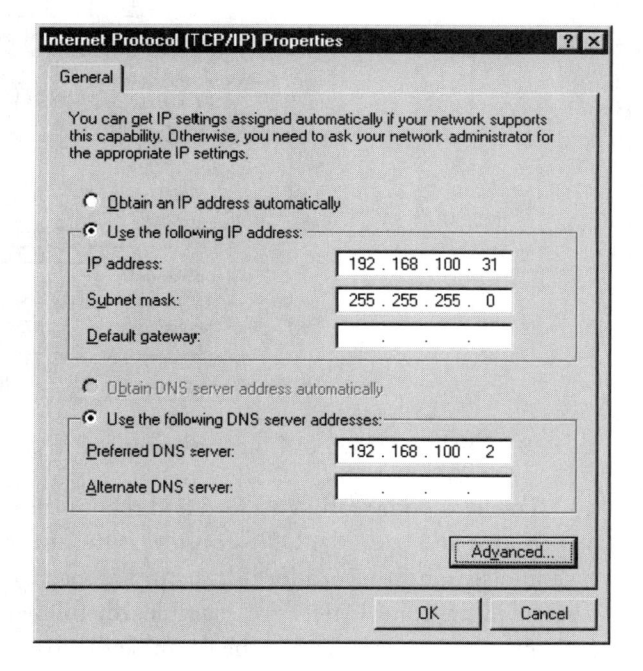

7. If you've already set up a second DNS name server, you can enter its IP address as the Alternate DNS Server.
8. Click the Advanced button and then click the DNS tab in the Advanced TCP/IP Settings dialog box that opens.

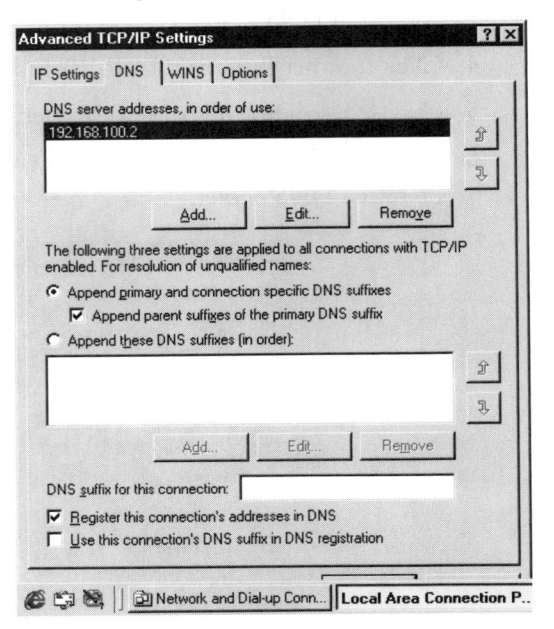

9. To use DDNS, choose Register This Connection's Addresses In DNS.

10. Click the three OK buttons required to close all three dialog boxes.

To check your work, go ahead and reboot the client. Once it's fully booted, go to the server and open the DNS console. If the client successfully registered itself, you should see a host record for it listed in the management pool after you click the zone name in the console tree. For example, the following illustration shows my client01 client's host record entry in the database file for the certifiable.local domain.

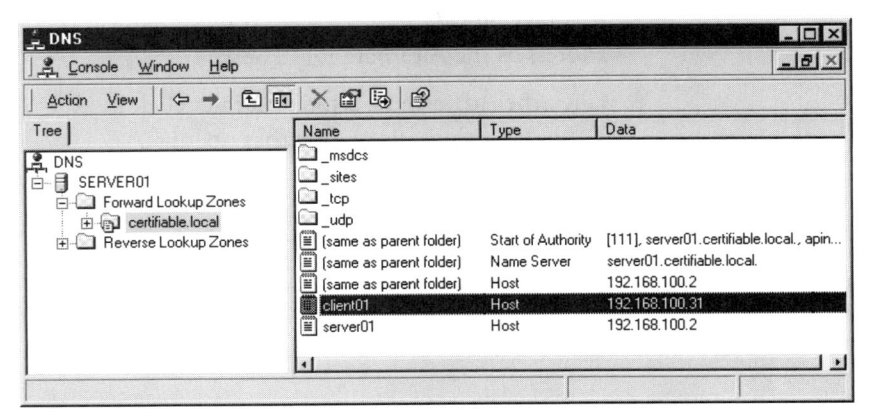

Configuring DNS Suffix Options on the Client

The Advanced TCP/IP Settings dialog box for a client offers some options that determine how the client will handle *unqualified domain names*. An unqualified name is usually just a hostname, such as devSite, as opposed to an FQDN like devSite.dev.certifiable.com. To get to the Advanced TCP/IP Settings dialog box on a client, just click the Advanced button on the TCP/IP Properties dialog box and click the DNS tab to see the options shown in Figure 3-23.

The options in the middle of the dialog box are relevant to handling unqualified domain names. To understand how those options work you first you need to know the definitions of a few other buzzwords:

- **Suffix** Everything after the hostname in an FQDN. For example, if MyPC.certifiable.local is the hostname, then the suffix is certifiable.local.

- **Primary DNS suffix** Usually the same as the name of the domain to which the client is a member. To view that, you can open the System Properties dialog box, click the Network Identification tab, and then click the Properties and More buttons.

FIGURE 3-23

The DNS tab of a client's Advanced TCP/IP Settings dialog box

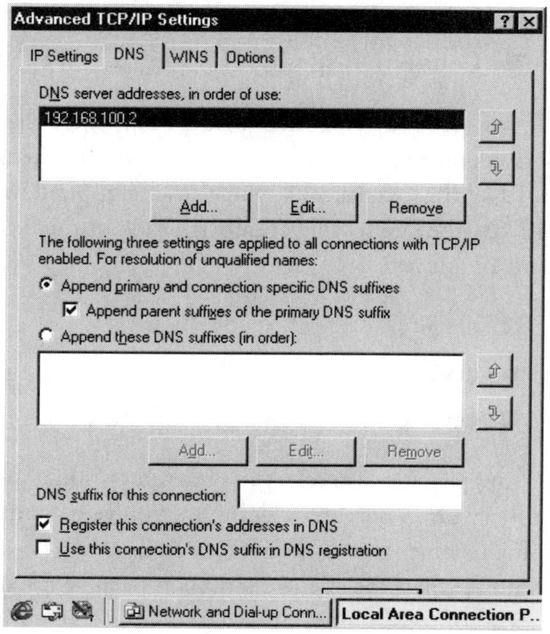

- **Connection-specific suffix**   A multihomed computer can have a separate DNS suffix for each NIC (connection). The DNS Suffix For This Connection option allows you to specify a DNS suffix that's specific to the NIC. If left blank, the connection-specific suffix will be the same as the primary DNS suffix.

To understand how the options work, you also need to be aware of the fact that whenever a request for name resolution comes into a DNS name server, that name server goes through three steps in attempting to resolve the name:

1. The name server checks its own cache.
2. If the cache doesn't help, the name server checks the zones for which it is authoritative.
3. If both steps fail, the name server queries a root server if one is available. This can be a public DNS root server.

With that in mind, let's take a look at the options for handling unqualified names in the Advanced TCP/IP Settings dialog box. Let's say you're sitting at a client computer that has the following configuration:

- **Primary DNS suffix**   dev.certifiable.com
- **Connection-specific DNS suffix**   WestWing.dev.certifiable.com

Now, let's say you select just the Append Primary And Connection Specific DNS Suffixes option. Your client wants to resolve the unqualified name http://devSite to an IP address. Given that you chose to append primary and connection-specific suffixes, the client will actually try each of the following names until one returns a valid IP address:

- devSite
- devSite.dev.certifiable.com
- devSite.dev.WestWing.certifiable.com

Suppose you also select the second option, Append Parent Suffixes Of The Primary DNS Server. In doing so, you've extended the search up to the second-level domain name. Hence, certifiable.com is now a potential candidate for name resolution. So now, when the client attempts to resolve the unqualified http://devSite name, it tries all of these names until it gets a valid IP address

- devSite
- devSite.dev.certifiable.com
- devSite.dev.WestWing.certifiable.com
- devSite.certifiable.com

because certifiable.com is the parent of dev.certifiable.com. Of course, if none of those names returns an IP address, the DNS name server will then try the parent name server, which might be the public DNS name server for the Internet.

As an alternative to applying just primary and parent DNS suffixes to unqualified names, you can choose the Append These DNS Suffixes (In Order) option and then use the Add button to list all the suffixes you want to apply to unqualified names.

The HOSTS file is just one way to make up "short names" for frequently accessed services. Appending DNS suffixes to unqualified domain names is another. Also, the latter method doesn't require mapping a name to a specific IP address.

Client DNS Registration Options

The bottom of the Advanced TCP/IP Settings dialog box provides some additional client-configuration options. The DNS Suffix For This Connection option, allows you to assign a DNS suffix to this specific NIC. The Register This Connection's Addresses In DNS option specifies that the client should register its name and IP address with its local DNS name server, using the primary domain suffix specified on the Network Identification tab of the System Properties dialog box. The Use This Connection's DNS Suffix In DNS Registration option registers the computer with the name server using the connection-specific suffix, if any. You can select both options, so the client registers with both the primary DNS suffix and the connection-specific suffix.

CERTIFICATION OBJECTIVE 3.05

Troubleshoot DNS Name Resolution

When it comes to troubleshooting DNS name resolution, you need to bear in mind that DNS name resolution uses all the resources described in Chapter 2. It just gives priority to DNS resources, using NetBIOS resources only if DNS resources fail. Figure 3-24 shows the order of DNS name resolution on a Windows 2000 client.

FIGURE 3-24

Hostname resolution sequence on a Windows 2000 DNS client

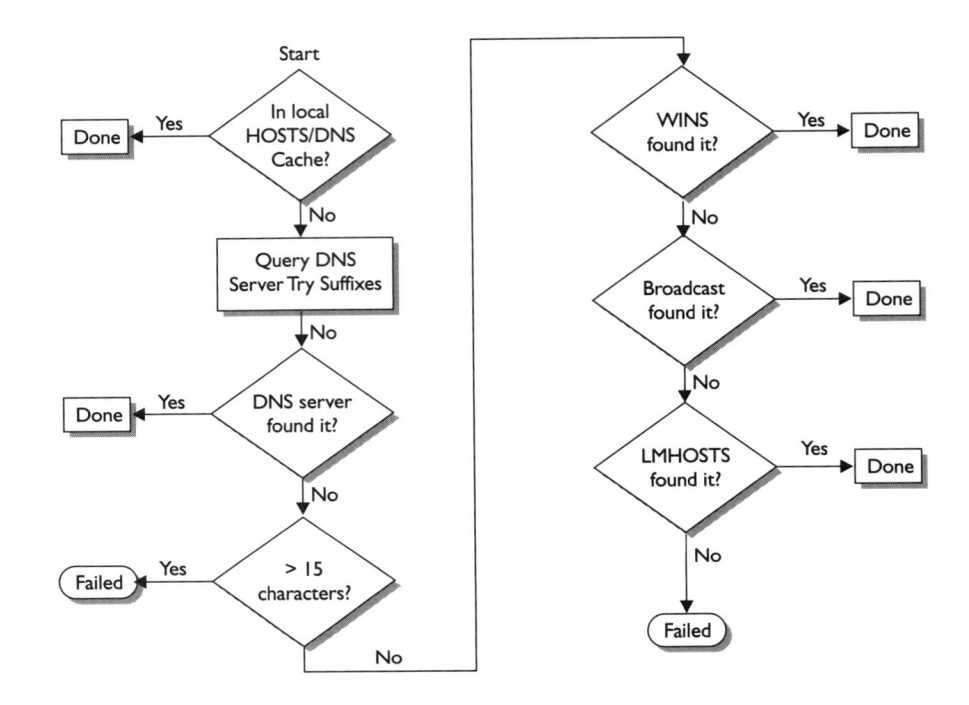

As always, the client will use only those resources that are available to the client. For example, if there is no WINS server specified on the client, then the whole WINS resource is just skipped over without generating any sort of error message. From a troubleshooting perspective, it's just important to know the basic order of hostname resolution, so you know all the places to check for faulty mappings or missing links.

Any time you're troubleshooting a networking problem, you want to start with basic connectivity issues, such as pinging a remote host by its IP address. You can also use **ipconfig /all** to verify that a client is pointing to the proper IP addresses for DNS and WINS name resolution. Finally, there are some DNS-specific commands you can use to troubleshoot DNS name resolution, as discussed in the sections that follow.

Using the NSLOOKUP Command

The NSLOOKUP (name server lookup) command provides options for testing a DNS server's zone database files. NSLOOKUP can be used as a stand-alone command using the following syntax

```
nslookup name/ipaddress
```

where *name/ipaddress* is an FQDN or IP address. For example, the command **nslookup client01** tells you which name server was used to find that host. The command **nslookup 192.168.100.31** does the same, though it has to do a reverse lookup.

EXERCISE 3-5

Testing Forward and Reverse Lookups with NSLOOKUP

If you've set up both a local DNS server and a client to use that name server, you can use NSLOOKUP to test for successful name resolution. For example, let's say you installed DNS on server01.certifiable.local (IP address 192.168.100.2), and you made it authoritative for the certifiable.local domain. If you enter the command **nslookup server01.certifiable.local** at a command prompt, you should see that hostname resolved to an IP address, as in the example shown in the following illustration.

```
C:\>nslookup server01.certifiable.local
Server:  server01.certifiable.local
Address: 192.168.100.2

Name:    server01.certifiable.local
Address: 192.168.100.2

C:\>_
```

To check for a reverse lookup, you'd enter a command like **nslookup 192.168.100.2**, substituting a valid IP address for your network, or an IP address on the Internet if you have Internet connectivity. If it succeeds, you'll see the hostname associated with that IP address.

Troubleshooting DNS with IPCONFIG

It's important to remember that a client will always check its local *resolver cache* for name resolution before it goes out to a DNS name server for help. Thus, if you have a name resolution problem, you'll want to take a look in the client's local cache to see if it contains any faulty mappings. You can use the command **ipconfig /displaydns** to do so. The resulting output might look something like Figure 3-25.

FIGURE 3-25

Sample output from an **ipconfig /displaydns** command

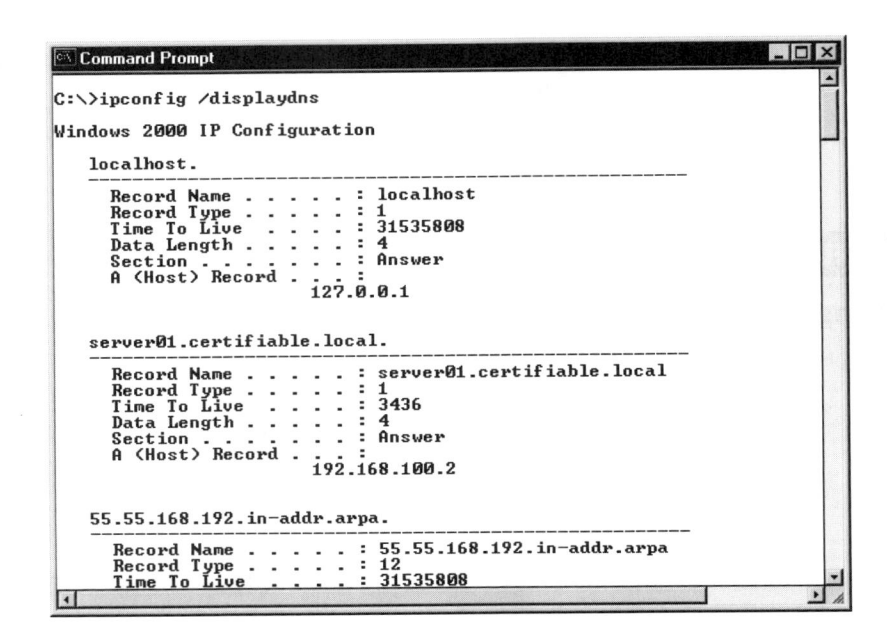

```
C:\>ipconfig /displaydns
Windows 2000 IP Configuration
    localhost.
    ----------------------------------------
        Record Name . . . . . : localhost
        Record Type . . . . . : 1
        Time To Live  . . . . : 31535808
        Data Length . . . . . : 4
        Section . . . . . . . : Answer
        A (Host) Record . . . :
                                127.0.0.1

    server01.certifiable.local.
    ----------------------------------------
        Record Name . . . . . : server01.certifiable.local
        Record Type . . . . . : 1
        Time To Live  . . . . : 3436
        Data Length . . . . . : 4
        Section . . . . . . . : Answer
        A (Host) Record . . . :
                                192.168.100.2

    55.55.168.192.in-addr.arpa.
    ----------------------------------------
        Record Name . . . . . : 55.55.168.192.in-addr.arpa
        Record Type . . . . . : 12
        Time To Live  . . . . : 31535808
```

The cache contains entries from the HOSTS file, as well as successful and failed DNS queries. Unsuccessful DNS queries are listed as *negative cache entries*. The client caches these to avoid repeatedly trying to resolve a name that cannot be resolved.

You can clear the local resolver cache by entering the command **ipconfig /flushdns**. If you then execute another **ipconfig /displaydns** command, any data that still appears originated from the HOSTS file. If you find a faulty entry that remains after flushing, you'll need to delete or correct that entry in the HOSTS file (which, as you may recall, is located in the %systemroot%\system32\drivers\etc folder).

Don't forget that the DNS name server also contains a cache, and if it contains any faulty A records, those too will cause name resolution to fail when clients use those faulty entries. To clear the cache on the name server, right-click the server's name in the DNS console and choose Clear Cache.

Finally, the command **ipconfig /registerdns** allows a DDNS client to reregister its name with a DNS name server. Use this command to refresh the connection to a name server if a client seems to have lost its connection.

Testing the Name Server

The DNS console lets you test the DNS name server's ability to resolve simple queries (names within its own zone of authority) and recursive queries (those requiring the server to go to an outside name server). To test your name server, open the DNS console, right-click the server name in the console tree, and choose Properties. Then click the Monitoring tab. Choose the type(s) of queries you want to test, as shown in Figure 3-26, and then click the Test Now button. In the example, the simple query passed, while the recursive query failed. (I knew the recursive query would fail because I haven't connected that computer to the Internet or any other outside DNS name server yet.)

on the job — *While you're in the DNS console, you can choose Help | Help Topics from the MMC menu bar. In the Contents pane of the help window, open the DNS book and click Troubleshooting for a more complete description of DNS troubleshooting options.*

FIGURE 3-26

The Monitoring tab of a name server's Properties dialog box

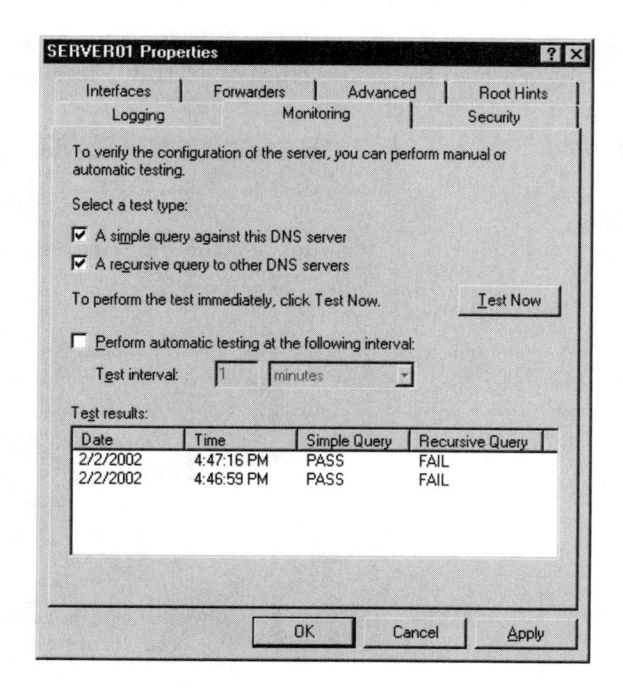

Troubleshooting Zone Transfers

For zone transfers, it's important to know that Windows 2000 and BIND DNS server versions after 4.9.4 all support *fast transfers*, where resource records are compressed before being transferred. If you attempt to use fast transfers with pre-4.9.4 versions of BIND, the transfers will fail. To fix the problem, you'll first need to ensure that Enable Zone Transfers is selected in the Properties dialog box for the zone on the Windows 2000 DNS server. (This option is selected by default, but it never hurts to double-check.) As you can see in Figure 3-27, you also have the option of allowing transfers to only servers listed in the Name Servers tab, or only specific servers.

To disable fast transfers to older DNS servers, and use the slower uncompressed method instead, right-click the DNS server name in the console tree, choose Properties, click the Advanced tab, and choose the BIND Secondaries option.

CERTIFICATION SUMMARY

Name resolution is the process of converting human-friendly names to IP addresses. Early versions of Windows relied on NetBIOS for name resolution, but the Internet has

FIGURE 3-27

The Zone Transfers tab of a DNS zone's Properties dialog box

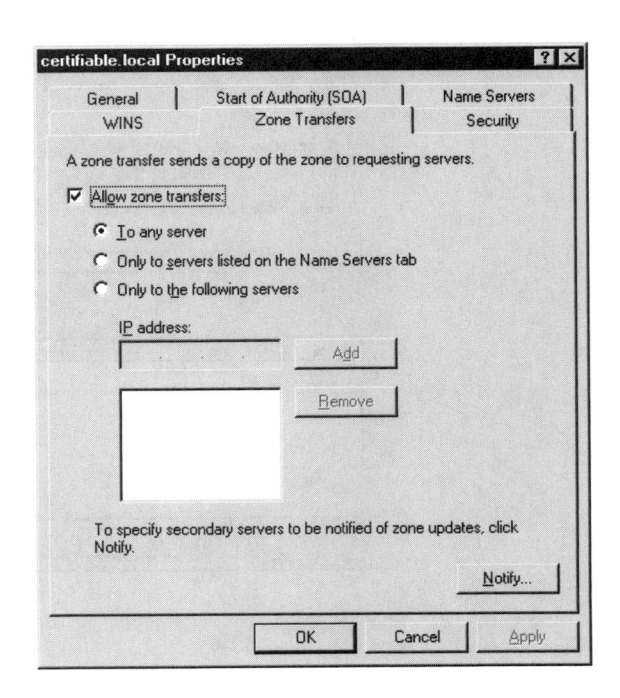

SCENARIO & SOLUTION

My network consists of several Windows 2000 Server and Professional computers, as well as numerous Windows 95 clients. All the clients send DNS requests to the same name server, but the Windows 95 clients are unable to access shared files and printers on the Windows 2000 servers. What do I do?	When you're dealing with older Windows clients, bear in mind that NetBIOS name resolution needs to be integrated into the network. Your best bet would be to set up at least one WINS server and have all the clients point to both the DNS name server and the WINS server for name resolution.
I have a subdomain named dev.certifiable.local beneath my main domain, certifiable.local, but all attempts to resolve names in the format something.dev.certifiable.local fail. What's the most likely cause?	The name server for certifiable.local needs to be configured to resolve names both for certifiable.local and dev.certifiable.local. Verify that you've created forward lookup zones for both domains in the DNS console.
My DNS name server forwards requests for irresolvable names to my ISP's DNS name servers. Everything was working fine. Then, all of a sudden, all the clients lost the ability to resolve Internet names. But they can still resolve names for the local zone. What's the most likely cause?	Since only external Internet names are failing, we know that your local server is working. However, queries that are being forwarded to the ISP's name server are failing. Therefore, you need to contact the ISP to see if its name servers are down or if it has changed the IP addresses of those servers. Then, make sure the local name server is forwarding queries to the appropriate IP addresses at the ISP's site.

made DNS name resolution something of a de facto standard in the industry, and Windows 2000 has followed suit by making DNS its primary means of name resolution.

DNS provides a hierarchical namespace based on FQDNs and a distributed database system for resolving names to IP addresses. Windows 2000 provides support for traditional, RFC-compliant DNS services in the form of standard primary zones, secondary zones, and zone transfers. Windows 2000 also offers a vendor-specific version of DNS that uses Active Directory for zone replication and other features that go beyond the capabilities provided by the RFCs.

The Microsoft DNS server offers several features that provide backward compatibility with downlevel clients. For example, WINS integration allows clients to find non-DNS Windows 95 and NT clients through a Windows 2000 DNS server. The Microsoft DNS server supports dynamic DNS (DDNS), wherein clients can register their names and IP addresses automatically, but you can still manually enter A and PTR records for any hosts that are unable to register their names dynamically.

✓ TWO-MINUTE DRILL

Create and Configure DNS Zones

- ❑ DNS is the hierarchical naming system used by the Internet and Windows 2000 networks.
- ❑ DNS name servers are computers that can resolve a fully qualified domain name (FQDN) to an IP address.
- ❑ DNS name resolution uses a distributed database, where name servers can forward requests to other servers.
- ❑ A recursive query is one that is sent to a name server and will accept only an IP address or a "Not found" error as a response.
- ❑ An iterative query is one that can accept a partial or incomplete answer and then contact another server in the distributed database system for more information.
- ❑ A DNS zone is the namespace for which a name server has the authority to provide IP addresses.
- ❑ Windows 2000 DNS supports standard RFC-compliant BIND-type primary and secondary zones, which use zone transfer to replicate from a single primary name server to any number of secondary name servers.
- ❑ Windows 2000 also supports Microsoft-specific Active Directory-integrated zones, which use *zone replication* to keep multiple master name servers in sync, and support secure dynamic registration of clients.

Manage DNS Database Records

- ❑ Information about the zone over which a name server has authority is stored in a zone file.
- ❑ A zone file consists of different types of resource records (RRs) that clients and other servers can use for name resolution, finding services, and zone transfers.
- ❑ The Start of Authority (SOA) record contains basic information about the server, settings used for zone transfers, and caching.
- ❑ Each shared resource in the domain contains a host or A (address) record identifying the hostname and its IP address.

- ❑ Each shared resource also contains a pointer (PTR) record, which provides IP address-to-name resolution.
- ❑ Name Server (NS) records provide the IP addresses of other name servers within the domain.
- ❑ CNAME (canonical name or *alias*) records allow you to create "nicknames" for available A records.

Configure DNS Server Properties

- ❑ Dynamic DNS (DDNS) allows clients to create their own A and PTR records when they connect to the network so you don't have to create those records manually.
- ❑ Unlike standard DNS zones, AD-integrated zones work only on domain controllers and support secure dynamic updates.
- ❑ DDNS also provides aging and scavenging options that you can use to periodically remove stale records from the zone database file.
- ❑ Microsoft's implementation of DNS provides WINS integration, where the DNS zone database file can work in harmony with a WINS database to provide resolution of NetBIOS names to non-NetBIOS clients.
- ❑ A forwarding server is one that can forward names outside its own zone of authority to another name server for resolution.
- ❑ A forwarder is a name server that accepts queries from a forwarding server.
- ❑ A slave server is one that is completely dependent on a forwarder for external name resolution. The slave cannot send recursive queries to external name servers.
- ❑ A caching-only server is one that doesn't have a zone of authority. Instead, it builds a cache of name-to-IP addresses over time. These can be used for security to shield an internal DNS structure from the public Internet, as well as to reduce name resolution traffic over slow WAN links.

Configure Client Computer Name Resolution Properties

- ❑ A client that is capable of reaching out to a DNS name server for name resolution is called a *resolver*. The term "resolver" is also used to describe the software that does the actual name resolution on the client.

- All DNS clients keep a cache of recently resolved hostnames. This cache is often referred to as the *resolver cache* and is separate from the cache that the DNS name server uses to store recent name resolutions.
- On a DNS client, you can use the TCP/IP Properties dialog box to specify the IP addresses of available name servers and to specify whether or not a client can register itself with a name server that accepts dynamic updates.
- You can have a client automatically append DNS suffixes to hostnames so that any given hostname can be queried against several different DNS domains.

Troubleshoot DNS Name Resolution

- The NSLOOKUP command provides information about the name server(s) that are available to a client.
- The **ipconfig /displaydns** command displays the client's resolver cache.
- The **ipconfig /flushdns** command clears the resolver cache and is often a first step in resolving name resolution problems caused by faulty cached records.
- On the DNS name server, you can use the Monitoring tab of the name server's Properties dialog box to test simple (local) and recursive (external) name resolution.
- Windows 2000 and BIND versions 4.9.4 and later all support *fast transfers*, whereby records being copied during a zone transfer are compressed for more rapid updating.
- To enable zone transfers to pre-version 4.9.4 BIND secondaries, you need to choose the BIND Secondaries option from the Advanced tab of the name server's Properties dialog box in the DNS console.

SELF TEST

The following questions will help you measure your understanding of the material presented in this chapter. Read the questions and answers carefully, and be aware that some questions will provide for more than one correct answer. Choose all correct answers for each question.

Create and Configure DNS Zones

1. You administer the domain controller/DNS name server for a domain named ZenithNadir.com. You've created an AD-integrated zone on the name server to provide local hostname resolution. ZenithNadir then buys ApexPits.com. The boss wants you to configure your name server to also resolve names for ApexPits.com, but ApexPits is using non-Microsoft servers. How can you do this?

   A. Create a second AD-integrated zone for ApexPits.com.

   B. Create a standard primary zone for ApexPits.com.

   C. Create a standard secondary zone for ApexPits.com.

   D. Make ApexPits.com a subdomain of ZenithNadir.com and delegate authority for that subdomain to a client computer in that domain.

2. You use DCPROMO to promote a Windows 2000 server to a domain controller with DNS. When all is done, you open the DNS console and notice a zone named simply ".". What does the very existence of that zone tell you about this server?

   A. This is a root server that cannot resolve Internet names or any other names outside its zone of authority.

   B. All zones for this name server are AD-integrated zones.

   C. This server is playing the role of a standard secondary name server.

   D. This server will automatically replicate with other AD-integrated zones that are within the same domain.

Manage DNS Database Records

3. You are the administrator for ColonelCob.com. Your network consists of 5 Windows 2000 server computers, 14 assorted member servers, and 350 clients. Another administrator adds a 15th member server, named mail5.ColonelCob.com, to the network. He's installed Microsoft Exchange on that server, and wants you to configure the DNS name server to identify mail5 as

being capable of accepting incoming e-mail messages. What do you need to do? (Choose all that apply.)

A. Create a Mail Exchanger (MX) record for mail5.ColonelCob.com.

B. Create a Name Server (NS) record for mail5.ColonelCob.com.

C. Create host (A) and pointer (PTR) records for mail5.ColonelCob.com.

D. Create a _ldap_udp service (SRV) record for mail5.Colonel.com.

4. You administer the GeneralSpecificX.com domain at IP address 11.10.9.0 subnet mask 255.0.0.0. One of the departments has created web and FTP sites on a new host at the IP address 11.10.9.200. The managers of this department would like to make these sites visible to the public via the names www.GeneralSpecificX.com and ftp.GeneralSpecificX.com. What do you need to do? (Choose all that apply.)

A. Create a Name Server (NS) record that delegates name resolution for www.GeneralSpecificX.com to the IP address 11.10.9.200.

B. Create host and pointer records for www.GeneralSpecificX.com at 11.10.9.200.

C. Create host and pointer records for ftp.GeneralSpecificX.com at 11.10.9.200.

D. Create an alias (CNAME) record that points the hostname ftp to www.GeneralSpecificX.com.

Configure DNS Server Properties

5. Your company's main office is in New York, in which it has a server named NYsrv01 that provides both DNS and WINS name resolution for all of its local clients and servers. NYsrv01 is a Windows 2000 domain controller and also uses an AD-integrated zone for local name resolution. Numerous member servers within that same network provide Windows file and printer shares.

   You work in the Rhode Island branch office, where you get a brand new Windows 2000 Server computer. You are instructed to configure that new server to provide seamless name resolution for all local resources, as well as resource at the New York office. Which of the following two options would provide for that?

   A. Make your WINS server a replication partner to the New York office's WINS server.

   B. Configure your server to forward DNS name resolution requests to the New York office.

   C. Set up an AD-integrated zone on your server and have it replicate with the New York office's AD-integrated zone.

   D. Configure your local server as a slave to the New York office's server.

6. You are the administrator for a branch office in San Diego, the main corporate office for which is in Pennsylvania. A T1 WAN link connects the two offices. Currently, the Pennsylvania office is using a Windows 2000 domain controller named PAsrv01, with an AD-integrated zone to provide name resolution for all clients, including clients in your branch office. Name resolution traffic is eating up bandwidth on the WAN link and slowing performance, so the corporate office sends you a Windows 2000 server named PAsrv02 that's preconfigured as a domain controller for the corporate network. You want to set up this new server to minimize traffic across the WAN link. Which of the following would be the best approach?

   A. Configure PAsrv02 with an AD-integrated zone that replicates across the WAN link with PAsrv01.

   B. Configure PAsrv02 as a standard secondary zone that gets zone transfers across the WAN link from PAsrv01.

   C. Configure PAsrv02 as a caching-only server.

   D. Configure PAsrv02 as a forwarding server for name resolution requests outside the current domain.

7. You have a network set up something like Figure 3-28, where multiple domain controllers named DC01 through DC034 provide name resolution services to IchthyPub.com. DC04 is multihomed, where NIC1 provides name resolution services to IchthyPub.com. NIC2 connects the server to the IchthyPriv.local domain on 192.1680.1. DC04 provides authentication services to clients on the 192.168.0.1 side of the box, but it does not provide name resolution on that side. The servers NS01 and NS02 provide name resolution for IchthyPriv.local. What would you need to do to have DC04 provide name resolution services on only the 200.100.50.1 interface?

   A. Configure DNS on DC04 so that it listens only to port 200.100.50.1.

   B. Configure NS01 and NS02 as zone replication partners to DC04.

   C. Make DC04 a forwarding server to some other name server in IchthyPub.com.

   D. Choose the option to append primary and connection-specific suffixes on clients in the ichthyPriv.local domain.

8. You are the administrator of your company's DNS name server. The server provides name resolution for local clients. That server also forwards any name resolution requests for which it is not authoritative to your ISP's name servers. Users complain that they've lost Internet connectivity. Upon inspection, you verify that this is true on all of the clients, but the clients are still able to resolve local hostnames. You call your ISP, who informs you that the server is

172 Chapter 3: Configuring, Managing, and Troubleshooting DNS

FIGURE 3-28   DC04 is multihomed and provides services to both IchthyPub.com and IchthyPriv.local.

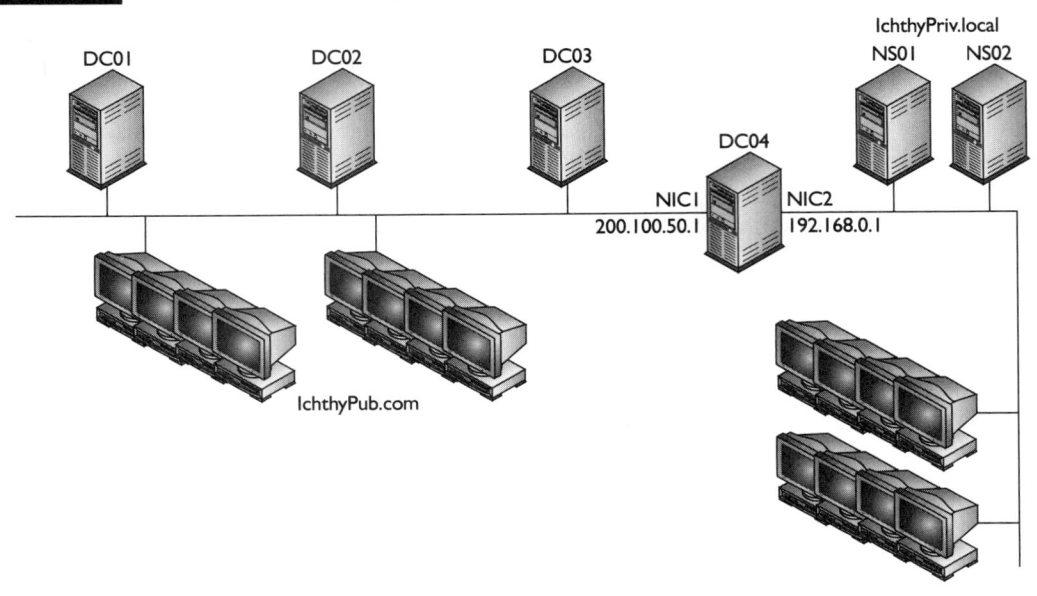

down, but you can use its name server at address 68.67.65.64 until the current servers are repaired. How can you quickly get your users reconnected to the Internet?

A. Create a centralized HOSTS file that points all name resolution requests to the new IP address.

B. Add the IP address 68.67.65.64 to the list of available forwarders in the name server's Properties dialog box.

C. In the Advanced TCP/IP Settings dialog box of each client computer, configure each of the clients to use the new 68.67.65.64 IP address as their primary DNS server.

D. In the Advanced TCP/IP Settings dialog box of the name server, set the primary DNS server's IP address to 68.67.65.64.

Configure Client Computer Name Resolution Properties

9. You are the network administrator for ABC Corp's Windows 2000 DNS server. The network also contains four other Windows 2000 member servers, which provide basic file and print servers. All the servers are on the same subnet. The network also contains 500 client computers spread across three separate subnets. These subnets are all connected to the servers' subnet via

routers. About half of the client computers are running Windows 2000 Professional. The other half are running Windows 95.

All the clients are configured to use your DNS name server for name resolution. However, the users of the Windows 95 clients complain that they cannot access file and print services on the member servers. What would be the easiest and most efficient way to correct the problem?

A. Configure all the Windows 95 computers to use b-node for NetBIOS name resolution.

B. Install WINS proxy agents on the Windows 95 computers to point to the DNS server.

C. Set up a WINS server on the network and set up WINS integration on the DNS name server.

D. Create an LMHOSTS file for each of the Windows 95 clients that provides suitable mappings.

Troubleshoot DNS Name Resolution

10. You administer a network for a domain named sub1.flaminghot.com, which consists of two Windows 2000 domain controllers and three UNIX servers. On the Windows server, you use an AD-integrated zone to provide name resolution and dynamic registration for all Windows 2000 clients in the network. UNIX hosts in the network are still using some older, standard BIND implementations for name resolution.

    To keep all the name servers in sync, you choose Allow Zone Transfers from the DNS console of the Windows 2000 name server and specify the UNIX servers as standard secondary zones. You expect the UNIX secondaries to update within a day or so (based on their transfer settings), but after a couple of days, you discover that no records have been transferred from the AD-integrated zones. How would you fix the problem?

    A. Convert all the AD-integrated zones to standard primary zones to allow replication to BIND servers.

    B. Check the version numbers of the BIND servers and if they're pre-version 4.9.4, disable fast transfers on the Windows 2000 name servers.

    C. Disable DDNS on the Windows 2000 servers and manually add resource records for all hosts.

    D. On the Windows 2000 name servers, choose the option that allows zone transfers to only those servers listed in the Name Servers tab.

11. You administer a network that provides local DNS name resolution for clients within the company, and also forwards name resolution requests to public root servers for Internet access. User Doris complains that she cannot access a specific web site by its URL, though she can connect to any other web site or local host. You verify the problem on Doris's computer but discover that other clients in the network don't have the same problem. It's isolated to Doris's

computer. You also verify that there is no faulty entry in the HOSTS file on Doris's computer. What else should you do at Doris's computer to try to resolve the problem?

A. Verify that the Use This Connection's DNS Suffix In DNS Registration option is selected in the client's TCP/IP Properties dialog box.

B. Use the **ipconfig /all** command to verify that the client is directly connected to the public root server.

C. Use the **ipconfig /registerdns** command to reregister this client with the local name server.

D. Use the **ipconfig /flushdns** command to flush out the local resolver cache and then try to connect again.

LAB QUESTION

You are the administrator of the ArborTreeX.com network shown in Figure 3-29. The Research and Mktg subdomains each have their own administrators and their own Windows 2000 servers. Currently, name resolution for all computers in the network is based on two domain controllers in the ArborTreeX.com domain. Those servers are currently getting bogged down with too many name queries. Furthermore, you're constantly dealing with failed name resolutions caused by changes that the other administrators make within their own subdomains. What would be a simple solution to the problem?

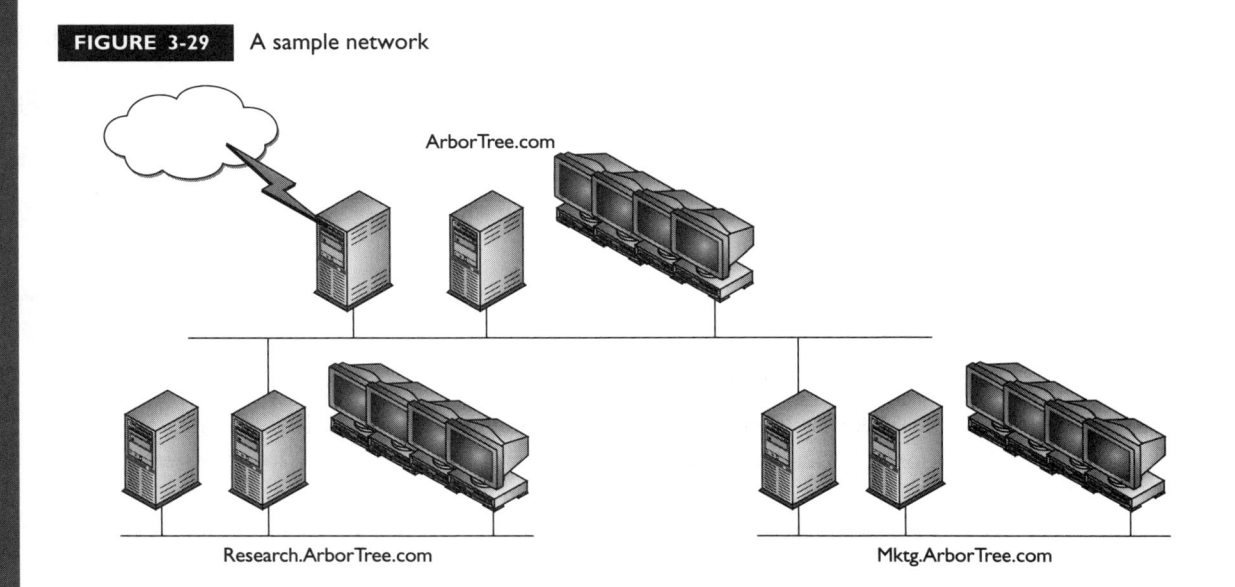

FIGURE 3-29 A sample network

SELF TEST ANSWERS

Create and Configure DNS Zones

1. ☑ **B** is correct. You could add a standard primary zone to the domain controller to resolve names for ApexPits.com.
   ☒ **A** is incorrect because the name server already belongs to ZenithNadir.com and cannot host an AD-integrated zone for an entirely separate domain.
   ☒ **C** is incorrect because you currently have only the one server and no primary zone for ApexPits.com. You need a whole new primary zone.
   ☒ **D** is incorrect because you'd need contiguous domain names for that; for example, *something*.ZenithNadir.com.

2. ☑ **A** is correct. The fact that there's a root zone here (".") specifies that there is no higher-level domain to which irresolvable queries can be sent.
   ☒ **B** and **C** are incorrect because the existence of a root zone doesn't tell you anything about the zone types.
   ☒ **D** is incorrect because the existence of a root zone tells you nothing about zone replication.

3. ☑ **A** and **C** are correct. Since this is a new host, you must create host and pointer records, and a Mail Exchanger (MX) record to identify the host as one that's capable of receiving incoming e-mail messages.
   ☒ **B** is wrong because NS records are only required for other name servers.
   ☒ **D** is incorrect because you don't need to create a service record for a mail server.

4. ☑ **B** and **D** are correct. You create host and pointer records for www.GeneralSpecificX.com at the appropriate IP address (though it's possible these records would be created dynamically when the host was added to the network). Since www.GeneralSpecificX.com and ftp.GeneralSpecificX.com share the same IP address, you then would create an alias (CNAME) record that sends queries for ftp.GeneralSpecificX.com to the host named www.GeneralSpecificX.com.
   ☒ **A** is wrong because name server records are required for other DNS name servers, not web or FTP sites.
   ☒ **C** is wrong because there's no need to create a service record for this FTP site.

Configure DNS Server Properties

5. ☑ **A** and **C** are correct. By making the WINS servers and AD-integrated zones replication partners across the WAN link, you keep their databases in sync. Clients will be able to resolve

names from their local WINS and zone database files, which reduces name resolution traffic across the WAN link.

☒ **B** is incorrect because it doesn't help with the larger task at hand. Rather, it would only help Rhode Island office clients resolve names for hosts in the New York office.

☒ **D** is incorrect because you'd only be making the Rhode Island name server dependent on the New York server for external name resolutions, which would not provide the type of seamless name resolution the task at hand requires.

6. ☑ **A** is correct. The computer is already configured as a domain controller for the company network. Since you have a fast WAN connection here, you can just set up an AD-integrated zone on that local server and use the WAN link for zone replication.

☒ **B** is incorrect because the standard zone transfer wouldn't be as fast as the AD-integrated zone replication, and besides, the computer is already configured as a domain controller so there'd be no reason not to use an AD-integrated zone.

☒ **C** is wrong because such a fast WAN link wouldn't warrant setting up a caching-only server. AD zone replication wouldn't burn up a lot of the available bandwidth.

☒ **D** is wrong because there really is no need to forward requests outside the zone of authority. Both PAsrv01 and PAsrv02 are members of the same domain, the corporate network.

7. ☑ **A** is correct. You don't want DC04 to listen for DNS queries from 192.168.0.1 if it won't be resolving names for hosts in that domain.

☒ **B** is wrong. The question didn't say anything about trying to resolve names for both domains, so there'd be no need to replicate or transfer zones across the DC04 server.

☒ **C** is incorrect because, once again, you're not trying to achieve any name resolution across the two domains. The private LAN just wants to use DC04 for authentication.

☒ **D** is incorrect because all you want to do is make sure that DC04 doesn't listen for name queries coming from the 192.168.0.1 interface.

8. ☑ **B** is correct. Since there's no problem with local name resolution, and the name server is already forwarding external names to your ISP's name server, you can simply add the new IP address to the list of available forwarders. Putting it at the top of the list would help, as this would prevent the server from trying the servers that are currently offline.

☒ **A** is wrong because there is no such thing as a centralized HOSTS file, and even if there were, it would be easier to just add the new IP address to the list of available forwarders.

☒ **C** is irrelevant. Clients are currently pointed to your local DNS name server, which is working just fine. Besides, manually adjusting any settings on each client in a network wouldn't be the most efficient way to make a change that could be configured at a server.

☒ D is incorrect because you just need to forward irresolvable name resolution requests to the new name server at 68.67.65.64.

Configure Client Computer Name Resolution Properties

9. ☑ C is correct. The Windows 95 clients require NetBIOS name resolution, while the Windows 2000 clients use DNS. WINS is always the most efficient way to deal with NetBIOS naming because it's centralized and easily integrated with the Windows 2000 DNS server.
☒ A is incorrect because b-node (broadcasts) wouldn't help in this multisubnet environment.
☒ B is incorrect because the WINS proxy agent is used to support non-WINS clients. Here, the Windows 95 computers are already WINS-enabled clients.
☒ D is incorrect because using an LMHOSTS file is not the most efficient way to solve the problem.

Troubleshoot DNS Name Resolution

10. ☑ B is correct. Whenever you have a zone transfer problem to a BIND server, always check to see if that BIND implementation is recent enough to support fast transfers. If it is not, you need to go to the Advanced tab of the Windows 2000 name server's Properties dialog box and choose BIND Secondaries to disable fast transfers.
☒ A is incorrect because it's not necessary to convert an AD-integrated zone to a standard primary zone in order to do zone transfers. AD-integrated zones use zone replication among themselves for replication, but also support standard BIND zone transfers.
☒ C is incorrect because this isn't a problem with name registration, it's a zone transfer problem.
☒ D is incorrect because limiting the number of secondaries used for zone transfers wouldn't solve the problem of failed transfers.

11. ☑ D is correct. Since the problem is isolated to this one computer, and one web site's URL, the most likely problem is a faulty entry in that computer's resolver cache. Flushing the resolver cache and trying again is a good way to quickly test for and solve that problem.
☒ A is incorrect because this problem isn't about DNS registrations. The problem is isolated to a single name-to-IP address mapping on a single computer.
☒ B is incorrect because Doris's computer has no problem resolving other hostnames, so there's no problem with the connection between the client and the name server.
☒ C is wrong because this isn't a problem of name registration. It's a name resolution problem

LAB ANSWER

Since each subdomain has its own Windows 2000 Server computers, the simple solution would be to set up AD-integrated DNS zones on the domain controllers for the subdomains and then delegate name resolution authority to each of those subdomains. That way, you don't need to keep up with changes that those administrators make within their own subdomains. Furthermore, the name servers in ArborTreeX.com won't be bothered with as many name queries, which would lighten their loads.

4
Configuring and Troubleshooting DHCP

CERTIFICATION OBJECTIVES

4.01	Install and Authorize DHCP Servers
4.02	Configure DHCP Servers and Scopes
4.03	Configure DHCP Clients
4.04	Troubleshoot DHCP
✓	Two-Minute Drill
Q&A	Self Test

Dynamic Host Configuration Protocol (DHCP) is a network infrastructure service that allows clients to be configured with valid IP addresses automatically as soon as they're connected to the network. DHCP can also assign other TCP/IP information to clients, including a subnet mask, default gateway address, DNS name server addresses, and more. Without DHCP, you'd need to sit at each client and assign all of these addresses manually. As clients come online and are configured with addresses, they can also register themselves with DNS automatically, making them available to other computers in the same network.

CERTIFICATION OBJECTIVE 4.01

Install and Authorize DHCP Servers

DHCP requires that at least one computer in the network act as the *DHCP server*. It's the job of the DHCP server to assign a unique, valid IP address to each host that requests access to the network. A *DHCP client* is a computer, or any other device, that's capable of receiving an IP address from a DHCP server. All Microsoft Windows versions since Windows for Workgroups, released in the early 1990s, include DHCP clients. The process a client goes through to get an IP address can be broken down into four steps: discover, offer, request, and acknowledge. Here's a brief overview of what each step does, and the type of packet that's sent during that step:

- **Discover (DHCPDISCOVER packet)** The client has no IP address yet and doesn't know any other hosts' IP addresses. So it broadcasts a packet containing its own hardware address to all hosts on the subnet asking, "Are you a DHCP server"?

- **Offer (DHCPOFFER packet)** Each host sees the packet, but only the DHCP server replies. The server picks an IP address from its pool of valid, available IP addresses and sends it back to the requester (it now knows the requester's hardware address). The packet essentially says, "Yes, I'm a DHCP server and I can offer you this IP address."

- **Request (DHCPREQUEST packet)** When the client receives the offer, it can return a DHCPREQUEST that essentially says, "That address looks good. I hereby officially request the IP address you've offered."

- **Acknowledge (DHCPACK packet)** The final message, sent from the DHCP server, clinches the deal by assigning the IP address to the client and removing the address from its list of available addresses.

So now the client has an IP address and is officially a host on the TCP/IP subnet. If you use DDNS integration, as we'll discuss later in the chapter, the host's name and IP address could be added to the DNS zone database file, and other hosts can resolve its name to its IP address through the DNS name server.

DHCP Leases

A DHCP client doesn't get a permanent IP address. Instead, it only *leases* the address provided by the DHCP server. That allows the DHCP server to reclaim addresses that it has assigned to hosts after they're no longer on the network. After all, it would be a waste to assign an IP address to some client that's on the network for only a few hours and then never assign that IP address to another client again, just because some host used it at some point in the past.

The duration of the lease that a DHCP server assigned to clients is called the Time To Live (TTL). When 50 percent of the TTL has lapsed, the client will request a lease renewal, sort of like saying, "I'm still here and want to keep my existing IP address." The DHCP server responds by refreshing the lease. If, on the other hand, the entire TTL expires and the host hasn't requested a lease extension, the DHCP server assumes the client is no longer on the network. In that case, it reclaims that old host's IP address, putting it back into the pool of available IP addresses. The DHCP server can then assign that reclaimed IP address to some other DHCP client in the future.

That 50 percent of the TTL after which the client starts trying to renew its lease is often called the *renewal interval,* or *T1*. Having a client try to renew its lease after only 50 percent of the TTL has expired gives the client plenty of time to renew its lease.

If 87.5 percent (7/8) of the lease duration expires before the client gets its lease renewed, the client sends out a broadcast request for renewal. The idea here being that perhaps the address of the DHCP server has changed, and hence the client better look elsewhere before its lease expires. The 87.5 percent period of the lease duration is called the *Rebinding Time Value,* and is often expressed as *T2*. When a client reaches this stage of the renewal process, it's said to be in the *Rebinding State*.

If the lease does expire before the client can renew, the client's IP address stays "reserved" within the DHCP server's pool for up to 24 hours. This "grace period" protects the client's lease just in case the client is off the network when the lease expires, the client and server are in different time zones, or their internal clocks are out of sync.

The network administration can determine the duration of DHCP leases. Perhaps the biggest factor in configuring the lease duration is the number of available IP addresses versus the number of clients contending for those addresses. For example, let's say the network has 200 possible IP addresses, and the network has 250 potential clients (including temporary notebook and dial-in connections, which are only on the network for brief periods of time). In this case, you'd want to keep the lease durations short, so that when a client disconnects, its IP address is returned to the pool of available IP addresses as quickly as possible.

At the other extreme, suppose you have 200 available addresses and relatively few clients, all or most of which are attached to the network all the time. In that case, there's really no need to force clients to renew their leases frequently. Setting a longer duration would reduce the network traffic caused by clients updating their leases.

That, in a nutshell, is how DHCP works and how you decide on a lease duration for dynamically assigned IP addresses.

Installing DHCP

The DHCP service is not installed automatically on a Windows 2000 Server computer, not even if you run DCPROMO to promote the server to a domain controller. Therefore, you'll need to install the service manually. You can do so on a domain controller or member server. The one catch is that the server must have a static IP address, though if you follow the general rule of assigning static IP addresses to all servers and use DHCP to assign dynamic IP addresses to clients only, this "catch" will already be covered.

Exercise 4-1 in this chapter will take you step by step through the process of installing DHCP on a Windows 2000 Server computer. The procedure is the same as installing most other networking components. Open Control Panel and click the Add/Remove Programs icon. Choose Add/Remove Windows Components, click Networking Services, and click the Details button. Select Dynamic Host Configuration Protocol (DHCP) as the service to install and click OK. You'll be taken back to the wizard, where you can click the Next button to complete the installation.

Once you've installed DHCP, you can manage your server using the *DHCP console,* an MMC console. To open the console:

1. Click the Start button and choose Programs | Administrative Tools.
2. Choose DHCP.

When all nodes are expanded, the name of the DHCP server appears in the console tree with a subfolder named Server Options, as in the example shown in Figure 4-1. A network can contain any number of DHCP servers. You can use the DHCP console to manage all the Windows 2000 DHCP servers on the network. After installing another DHCP server, choose Add Server from the Action button's menu to add another server to the console.

Authorizing a DHCP Server

If you use Active Directory, you'll need to authorize a DHCP server before it will start handing out IP addresses. This is a new feature in Windows 2000, designed to prevent *rogue DHCP servers* from gumming up the works. In those earlier versions, anyone could set up a DHCP server and have it start handing out IP addresses. That "anyone" could be someone who doesn't have a clue as to what they're doing and is just playing around. If that rogue DHCP server starts handing our invalid IP addresses, new clients coming online could get bad IP addresses that don't work on their subnet.

Exactly who can authorize a DHCP server depends on the role the sever computer is playing within the network. There are three possible roles a server computer can play:

- **Domain controller** The computer maintains a copy of the Active Directory database and provides security for domain members.

- **Member server** The computer is not a domain controller, but rather a member of a domain and as such has a membership account in Active Directory.

FIGURE 4-1

The DHCP console

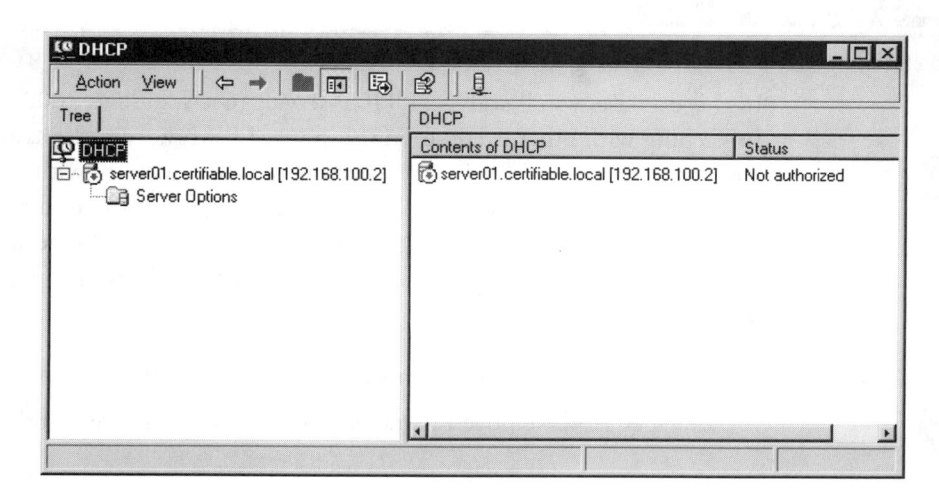

- **Stand-alone server** The computer is a member of a workgroup that doesn't have sophisticated security in place. The server does not provide secured logon or secured access to shared resources on the network.

Only DHCP servers on domain controllers or domain member servers can be authorized in Active Directory. Furthermore, only persons with Enterprise administrative privileges, or people who have been delegated appropriate permissions, can authorize DHCP servers. To authorize a DHCP server, assuming you're already logged in with appropriate privileges, just right-click the server's name in the console tree and choose Authorize.

---

exam
⒲atch

By default, only enterprise administrators can authorize DHCP servers. The enterprise administrator can delegate authority to non-enterprise administrators using the Active Directory Sites and Services console.

It can take several minutes for the authorization to complete. Unfortunately, you won't get any direct feedback when the process is done. You actually have to refresh the display to find out. You can do this by pressing the F5 key or clicking the Action button and choosing Refresh. If things seem to be taking too long, close the DHCP console and start it up again. Once the server is authorized, its icon will display a green up-arrow. If you click on DHCP at the top of the console tree, the status column will display Running for the server, as shown in Figure 4-2.

EXERCISE 4-1

Installing and Authorizing the DHCP Service

In this exercise, you'll add the DHCP service to a Windows 2000 Server computer. In keeping with other exercises in this book, I'll work from the assumption that you have only a single Windows 2000 Server computer to work with, so we'll install the service on the domain controller. In an actual working environment, you could install DHCP on any Windows 2000 Server computer in the network. *Do not install a DHCP server on a live, production network without the consent of the network administrator.*

1. Click the Start button and choose Settings | Control Panel.
2. Open Add/Remove Programs and click Add/Remove Windows Components.

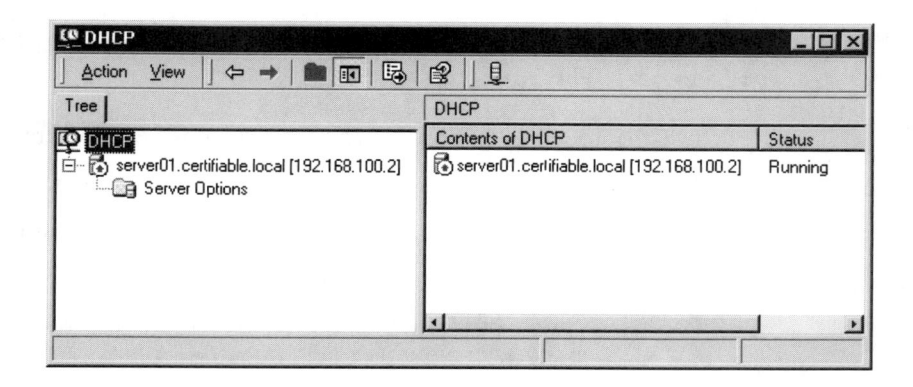

FIGURE 4-2

The DHCP service is authorized and running.

[Screenshot: DHCP console showing server01.certifiable.local [192.168.100.2] with Server Options in the tree, and Running status in the contents pane.]

3. In the Windows Components Wizard that opens, click Networking Services, and then click the Details button.

4. Choose Dynamic Host Configuration Protocol (DHCP).

[Screenshot: Networking Services dialog box with subcomponents listed, including Dynamic Host Configuration Protocol (DHCP) checked.]

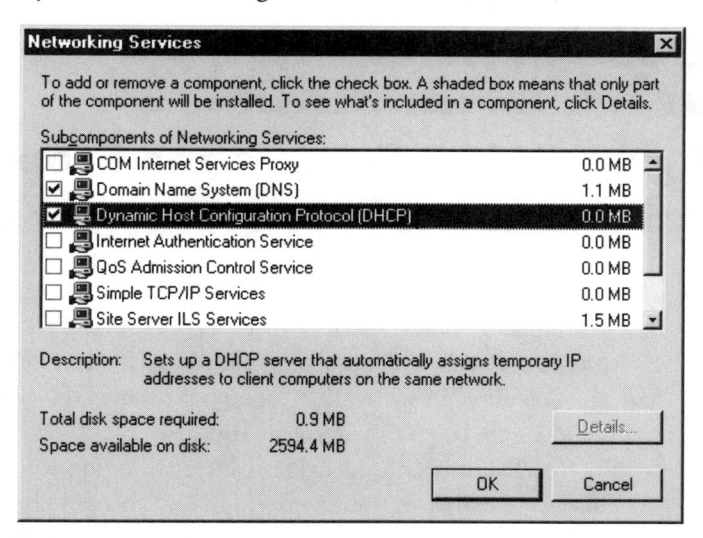

5. Click the OK button.

6. Click the Next button and follow the instructions on the screen. You may need to insert the Windows 2000 Server CD.

7. Close all open dialog boxes and Control Panel.

If you're using Active Directory, you'll need to authorize the server to hand out IP addresses. This is a simple task:

1. Click the Start button and choose Programs | Administrative Tools | DHCP.
2. Expand all the nodes in the DHCP console that opens.
3. Click the name of the DHCP server that you wish to authorize.
4. Click the Action button and choose Authorize.
5. Wait a couple of minutes, and then press F5 or click the Action button and choose Refresh.

Once the server is authorized and you've refreshed the display, the red down-arrow on the server's icon in the console will turn to a green up-arrow.

CERTIFICATION OBJECTIVE 4.02

Configure DHCP Servers and Scopes

Before your DHCP server can start handing out IP addresses, it needs to know what addresses are valid on your network. For example, let's say you're using 192.168.100.0 subnet mask 255.255.255.0 as your network address. That gives you IP addresses in the range of 192.168.100.1 to 192.168.100.254 to work with, but perhaps you'd like to set aside addresses 1–30 for static IP addresses to assign to servers and perhaps the default gateway. In that case, you'd want DHCP to assign addresses in the range of 192.168.100.31 to 192.168.100.254.

You'll also need to decide on a lease duration for your clients, using the criteria discussed earlier in this chapter. Finally, you can also have the DHCP server assign each client a default gateway address and the IP addresses of any DNS name servers and WINS servers on your network, if you already have those IP addresses defined in your network. This saves you the trouble of having to go to each client and assign these other server IP addresses manually.

Exclusions

If, for whatever reason, you need to reserve some IP addresses within your range of valid IP addresses to assign to clients, you can define those as *exclusions* to your range. For example, suppose you define your range of assignable IP addresses as 192.168.100.32 to 192.168.100.254, but then you remember some application programs used on client computers that use a server at 192.168.100.101. That server is already statically configured with that IP address, and on the client side, the IP address is hardwired into the application code. In short, it would be difficult to change the IP address of the server at 192.168.100.101. In that case, you'd just define 192.168.100.101 as an exclusion to your range. Once you do so, no clients will be assigned the excluded address(es).

You can define exclusions while running the wizard to define the scope (Exercise 4-2). Or, if you've already created the scope, you can expand the name of the scope in the console tree to reveal a number of subfolders, including one named Address Pool. To add a new exclusion to the scope, right-click that Address Pool folder and choose New Exclusion Range.

EXERCISE 4-2

Cert Cam 4-2

Defining a Scope

In this exercise, you'll go through the steps necessary to configure a scope for your DHCP server. I'll be using IP addresses in the range of 192.168.100.31 to 192.168.100.254, subnet mask 255.255.255.0, for this example. I'll also define a default gateway of 192.168.100.1 and a DNS server address of 192.168.100.2 in keeping with present IP addresses and future plans for my small sample network. Of course, if your network is using different IP addresses, you'll need to define your own scope, subnet mask, and optional IP addresses accordingly. Here are the steps:

1. If the DHCP console isn't already open, click the Start button and choose Programs | Administrative Tools | DHCP.

2. Right-click the name of the DHCP server and choose New Scope. The New Scope Wizard opens. Click Next.

3. Enter a name and description of your own choosing, as in the example shown in the next illustration. These entries are just to identify the scope in the event that you create multiple scopes.

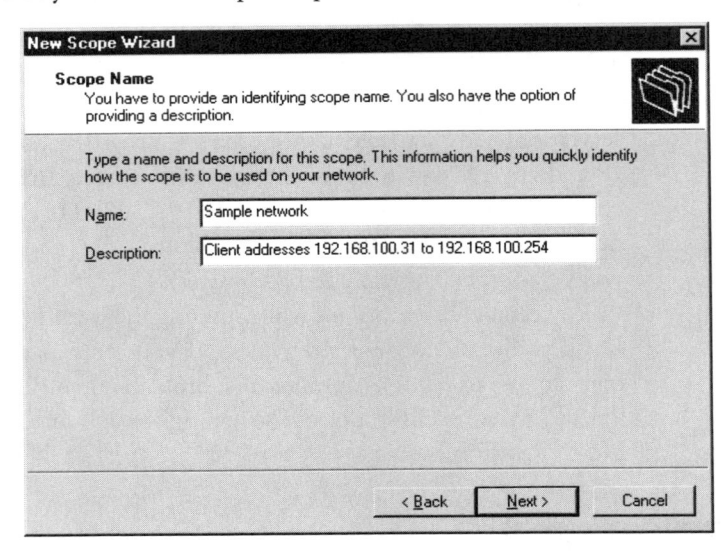

4. Click Next.

5. Enter the starting and ending IP addresses of your scope and then enter the appropriate subnet mask or /*x* designation for the subnet, as in the example shown here.

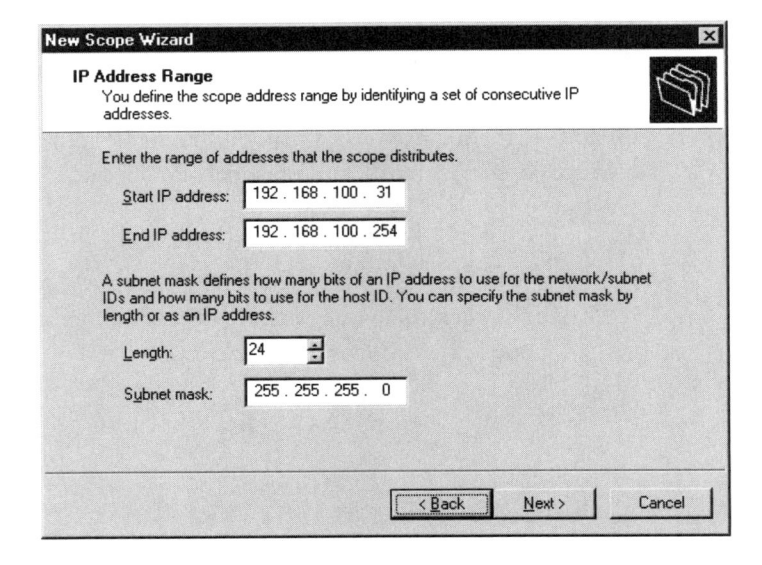

6. Click Next.

7. The next wizard page allows you to enter exclusions, IP addresses within the range that are already reserved for some other purpose. For the exercise, you can just click Next.

8. The Lease Duration page, shown in the following illustration, appears next. Specify your preferred duration and click Next.

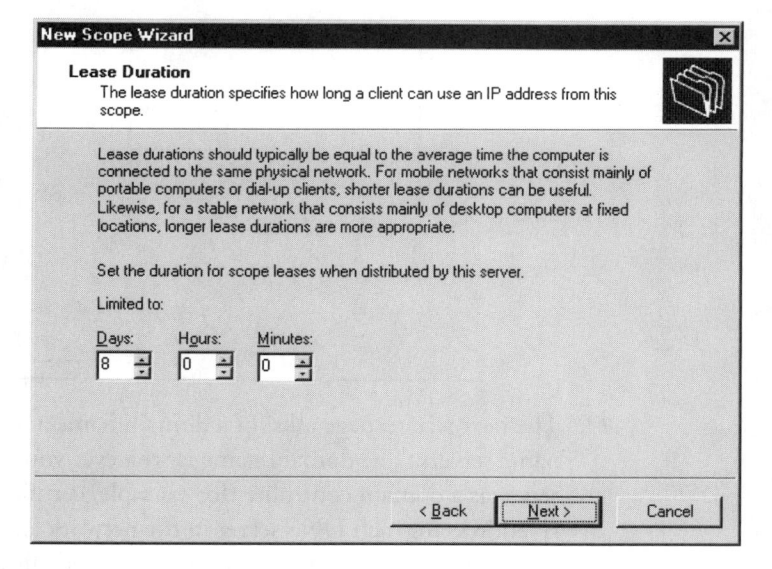

9. The next wizard page asks if you want to configure optional IP addresses for the default gateway and/or DNS name servers now. Choose Yes, I Want To Configure These Options Now and click Next.

10. If you already have a connection to a router or the Internet and know the IP address of the default gateway, you can add that IP address (or multiple IP

addresses if appropriate). If you don't know yet, you can leave this page blank. Click Next.

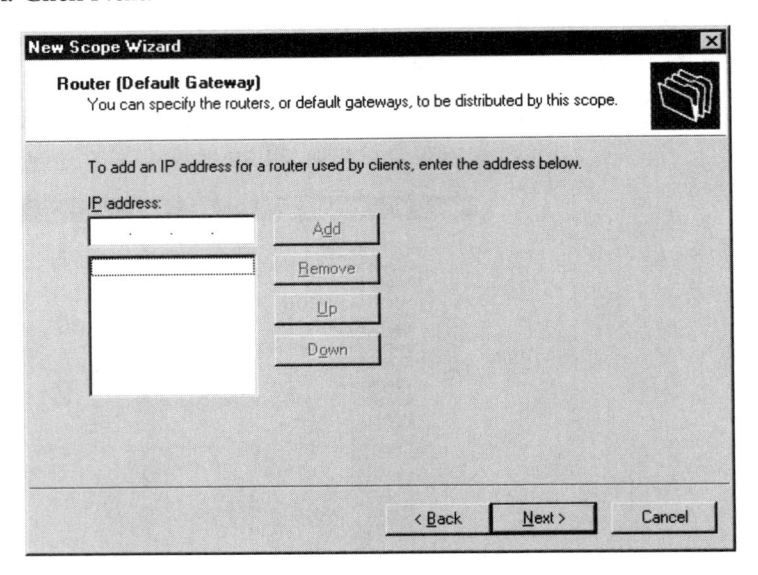

11. The next wizard page asks for a domain name and the IP address of any DNS name servers. The domain name is whatever you defined when setting up your server as a domain controller (for example, certifiable.local). You can type the IP address for each DNS server in the network and click the Add button. Optionally, you can type the server name and click the Resolve button to have the wizard automatically fill in the IP address. In my example, I configured DNS on Server01.certifiable.local, so I entered that name and clicked the Resolve button to enter that IP address. Click the Add button to enter each name server's IP address and click Next.

Configure DHCP Servers and Scopes

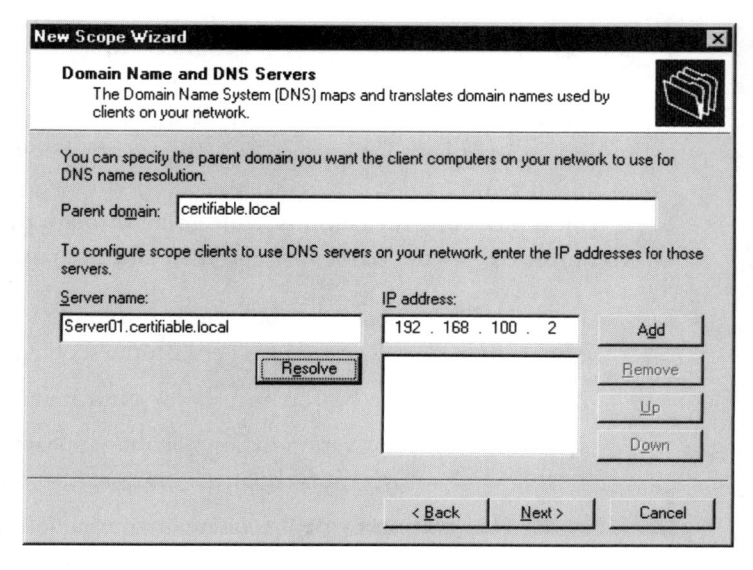

Screenshot of the New Scope Wizard "Domain Name and DNS Servers" page, with Parent domain set to "certifiable.local", Server name "Server01.certifiable.local", and IP address 192.168.100.2.

12. If you have any WINS servers in your network for NetBIOS name resolution, you can enter their IP addresses in the next wizard page, titled WINS Servers. If you don't have any WINS servers defined, you can leave the options empty. Click Next.

13. The next wizard page asks if you want to activate the scope now or later. Choose Yes, I Want To Activate This Scope Now and then click Next.

14. Click the Finish button to complete the job.

Done! Even if you opted to activate your new scope, nothing will actually *happen* until a new client that's configured to obtain an IP address automatically comes online. We'll talk about configuring DHCP clients a little later in this chapter.

DHCP Client Reservations

A DHCP reservation is sort of like a exclusion, in that you specify one or more IP addresses that are within the range of assignable IP addresses, but not handed out willy nilly. However, unlike exclusions, which are never handed out, reservations are handed out only to specific hosts. For example, suppose a mobile computer has its TCP/IP settings set to obtain an IP address automatically. You don't care what IP address that notebook uses when it connects to the Internet or some other network, but when it connects to *your* network, you want it to be assigned the IP address 192.168.100.99 (or whatever). In that case, you'd reserve the IP address 192.168.100.99 so that it can only be assigned to that mobile notebook when the notebook connects to your network.

You can't define reservations while going through the Add New Scope Wizard. You must create your scope first and then add reservations later. Here's how:

1. In the DHCP console, click the + sign to the left of any scope you've created, and then click Reservations beneath the scope name.
2. Click the Action button and choose New Reservation.
3. In the New Reservation dialog box that appears, as in Figure 4-3, fill in the following information about the reserved client address:

   - **Reservation name**   A name of your choosing that identifies this reservation. The name you enter here will not affect the name that's currently assigned to the client.
   - **IP address**   Enter the IP address that you want to assign to this client.
   - **MAC address**   Enter the hardware address of the client. You can view that on the client using the **ipconfig /all** command, as discussed in Chapter 1. The DHCP server uses this address to identify the host when it connects to the network.

FIGURE 4-3

The New Reservation dialog box

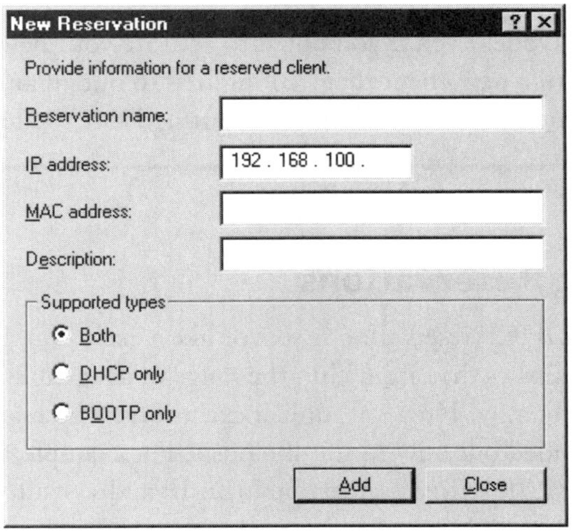

- **Description** A description of the reservation, in your own words.
- **Supported types** Specify whether this connection is for a DHCP client only, a BOOTP client only, or either type (BOOTP is discussed in a moment).

4. Click OK.

Server Options vs. Scope Options

Once you've defined a scope, you need to be aware that you can set options that apply to a specific scope or globally to all scopes. Each scope will be defined by its subnet address and the name you applied, as in the Scope [192.168.199.0] Sample Network entry. When you click Scope Options beneath the scope name, as I've done in Figure 4-4, options that are currently selected for that scope appear in the right pane. In the example, two options are currently selected. The 003 Router option is the default gateway, and 015 DNS Domain Name is the domain name that the client should use for resolving hostnames using DNS. Both of these options were created by the New Scope Wizard.

If you want to set, change, or delete options that apply to all scopes, use the Server Options folder at the bottom of the console tree. Be aware that if there's a conflict between a server option and a local scope option, the more specific scope option is given precedence over the server option. The main options to be aware of

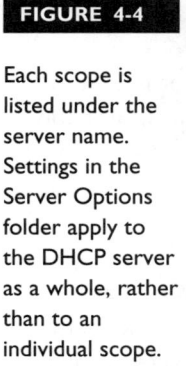

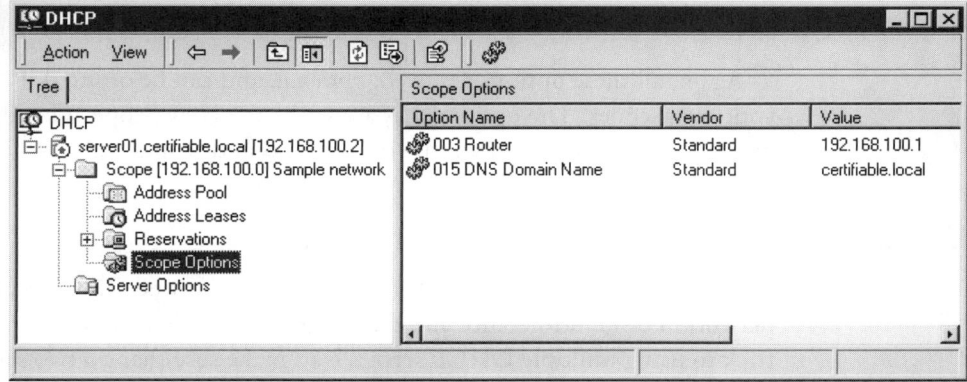

FIGURE 4-4

Each scope is listed under the server name. Settings in the Server Options folder apply to the DHCP server as a whole, rather than to an individual scope.

are those that are compatible with all Windows clients—all the way down to Windows 3.*x*. Those options are as follows:

- **003 Router**   Defines the IP address of the default gateway, and any additional routers, to be assigned to DHCP-enabled clients.
- **006 DNS Server**   Specifies the IP addresses of DNS name servers that clients should use for DNS name resolution.
- **015 DNS Domain Name**   Specifies the domain name that the client should use when resolving hostnames via DNS.
- **044 WINS Server**   Lists IP addresses of WINS servers to be used for NetBIOS computer name resolution.
- **046 NetBIOS node type**   Defines the node type for NetBIOS over TCP/IP (NetBT) to be assigned to DHCP clients.

exam
Watch

The main thing to keep in mind about DHCP in general and the preceding list of options is that they apply to downlevel clients like Windows 98 and 95, as well as Windows 2000.

Two additional noteworthy options, which apply only to Windows 2000 computers (not to downlevel computers), are the following:

- **031: Perform Router Discovery**   If selected (set to 1), configures DHCP-enabled clients to use the router discovery method described in RFC 1256.
- **033: Static Route**   Specifies any static routes to be places in DHCP clients' routing caches upon being assigned IP addresses.

Again, all these options are, well, *optional,* and can be omitted if not relevant to your own scopes. The options that are set by the New Scope Wizard will probably be sufficient for the vast majority of networks and scopes.

DHCP Load Balancing and Redundancy

There's certainly no rule that says you can only have one DHCP server on a network. For fault tolerance and redundancy, you might want several. The main trick to using multiple DHCP servers is to make sure that no two servers can assign the same IP address. Unlike WINS and DNS name servers, there is no replication or transfer between DHCP servers. So, for example, if DHCP01 assigns the IP address

Configure DHCP Servers and Scopes

SCENARIO & SOLUTION

What are the various vender class options on the Advanced tabs of the Scope Options and Server Options dialog boxes?	RFCs 2131 and 2132 define DHCP *vendor class options* that allow hardware and software vendors to add their own DHCP options that go beyond the basic DHCP standards. For example, Microsoft offers some vendor class options that apply only to Windows 2000, Windows 98, and Windows computers in general.
What about the user class options on the Advanced tab?	User class options let you define "classes" of computers in your network and assign options based on class membership. For example, you could create a class called Portables whose options are assigned only to portable computers. On the clients, you can use the **ipconfig /setclassid** *adapter* [**classID**] command to specify which class a specific NIC belongs to on the client.
If I set server, scope, vendor, and class options, and also set options on clients, what's the order of precedence in the event of a conflict? Are any options ignored?	The options you select are additive, so all will be applied. In the event of conflicts, the most specific setting takes precedence. Thus, settings on the client override all settings from the server. From the server, the order is vendor/user options, reserved client options, scope options, and then server options last.

10.10.10.50 to some host, DHCP02 has no way of knowing that. The only way to ensure that DHCP02 doesn't assign that same address to some other host is to define DHCP02's scope so that it *can't* assign that address to any hosts.

There's no hard-and-fast rule about what percentage of available addresses each server hands out. Some people go for an 80/20 balance, in which one DHCP server holds 80 percent of the available IP addresses, and the other server holds the remaining 20 percent. You could go for a 50/50 deal, in which each name server holds 50 percent of the IP addresses that are available for addressing. It's simply a matter of deciding what's best for your network. For example, if your "main" DHCP server is on a busy domain controller, you might want to put a larger proportion of IP addresses on the secondary DHCP server, so it picks up more of the load.

Again, the main thing is that the two servers not offer overlapping IP addresses. For example, in Figure 4-5 I've configured two separate DHCP servers. The full range of addresses that DHCP can hand out on this network is 192.168.100.31 to 192.168.100.254. I've split the workload roughly in half by giving the first server

FIGURE 4-5

Two DHCP servers, each serving about half of the available IP addresses in the range of 192.168.100.31 to 192.168.100.254

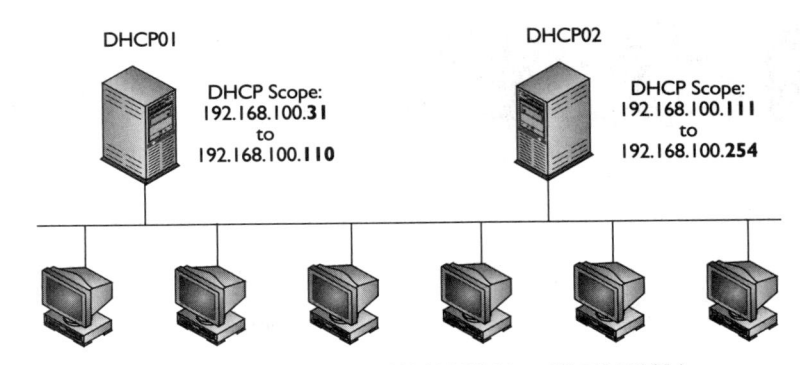

DHCP01 — DHCP Scope: 192.168.100.31 to 192.168.100.110

DHCP02 — DHCP Scope: 192.168.100.111 to 192.168.100.254

Full scope available to clients: 192.168.100.31 to 192.168.100.254

addresses in the range of 192.168.100.31 to 192.168.100.110, and the second DHCP server a scope consisting of the rest of the available IP addresses, 192.168.100.111 to 192.168.100.254.

As mentioned, a single DHCP server can house multiple scopes for multiple subnets. For instance, let's say your network consists of many subnets, each with few clients. You don't want to put a DHCP server on each subnet. Rather, you'd prefer to have one or two DHCP servers on one subnet providing addresses for all subnets, as in the example shown in Figure 4-6. To simplify the example, I've configured one DHCP server to assign IP addresses to hosts in the subnets 192.168.0.0/25 and 192.168.0.128/25. Sub1 Scope provides valid IP addresses for DHCP clients on Sub 1. The full range for that subnet could be 0–126, but I've left out some addresses to be assigned statically to servers on the subnet. Sub2 Scope provides addresses in the range of 150 to 254 for DHCP clients on Sub2. Again, the full range of addresses for the subnet would actually be 129 to 254, but I've omitted some addresses to use for static assignment to servers in that subnet.

There's just one problem with the scenario shown in Figure 4-6. As you may recall, when a client that's configured to obtain an IP address automatically comes online, it *broadcasts* a discovery packet to try to find a DHCP server. This poses a problem for subnets 2–4 in the sample network: how are they going to get those broadcasts across the routers that separate them from the DHCP server? There are two solutions to the problem, one called a BOOTP forwarder and the other a DHCP relay agent. We'll look at each in the sections that follow.

BOOTP Forwarding

BOOTP (Bootstrap Protocol) is the name for a protocol defined in RFC 1542 that allows DHCP Discover packets to be forwarded across routers. The

Configure DHCP Servers and Scopes **197**

FIGURE 4-6

A single DHCP server addressing some hosts across a router

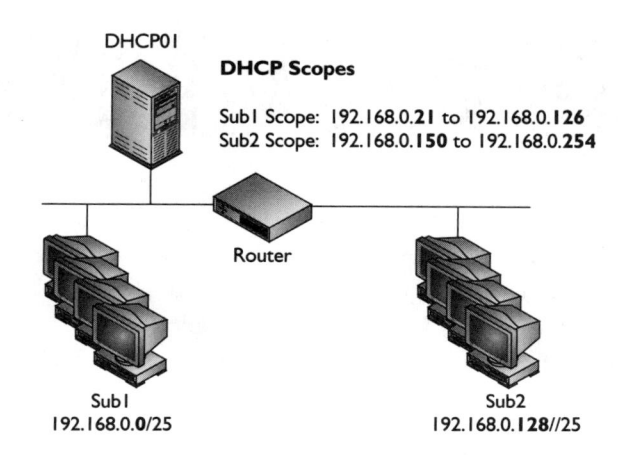

DHCP01

DHCP Scopes

Sub1 Scope: 192.168.0.**21** to 192.168.0.**126**
Sub2 Scope: 192.168.0.**150** to 192.168.0.**254**

Router

Sub1
192.168.0.**0**/25

Sub2
192.168.0.**128**//25

less-than-illuminating name stems from BOOTP's origins as a mechanism for allowing clients without their own operating systems to boot from boot image files on another computer. Both BOOTP and DHCP use UDP port 67 for messages from the client, and UDP port 68 for messages from the server. Even though BOOTP isn't used much anymore, the name lingers on.

_{exam}
🕲atch

Most modern routers are BOOTP compliant, though compliance isn't enough. You also need to ensure that BOOTP forwarding is enabled on the router if you intend to allow clients to get TCP/IP addresses from a DHCP server that's on the far side of the router.

Be aware that BOOTP merely forwards the DHCP request to the next subnet; it doesn't direct the request to the exact IP address of the DHCP server. Therefore, if there are multiple routers between the requesting client and the DHCP server, all those routers must have BOOTP forwarding enabled.

You might be wondering how the DHCP server knows which subnet a client belongs to, so it can assign an appropriate IP address. There's a relatively simple mechanism built into the protocol to handle that. When the router gets the broadcast request for an IP address, it doesn't just forward the broadcast. Rather, it creates a new packet that includes (among other things) a *gateway IP address,* which identifies which subnet the request came from. When the DHCP server receives the message, it chooses an IP address that's appropriate for the subnet from which the request originated.

FROM THE CLASSROOM

The relationship between BOOTP and DHCP is an evolutionary one, in that DHCP evolved from BOOTP. As mentioned, BOOTP was originally designed to allow diskless workstations to boot from an operating system image file stored on a remote computer. When it came to IP addressing clients, though, BOOTP wasn't very convenient. Administrators needed to create IP-address-to-hardware address mappings manually. When a BOOTP client started up, it would broadcast a request for an IP address. The BOOTP server would look up the client's hardware address in the file, and send back the appropriate IP address. So BOOTP wasn't really very dynamic. Every time a new client was added to the network, the administrator would need to add an IP address-to-hardware address mapping to the centralized file. In a sense, BOOTP was like DHCP, where every client has a reservation.

With time, it became apparent that a much simpler solution would be to have an administrator define a range, or scope, of IP addresses that could be handed out to clients on a first-come, first-serve basis. This created a new problem, though, in that any given computer's IP address could change, which is not good for servers. However, that problem was easily solved by assigning static IP addresses to server computers and omitting those addresses from the pool of assignable IP addresses. For good measure, DHCP also provides exclusions and client reservations which give administrators both the tight control offered by BOOTP and the convenience of DHCP's ability to assign IP addresses to nonserver clients on-the-fly.

—*Alan Simpson, MA, MCSA*

DHCP Relay Agents

As you know, any multihomed Windows 2000 Server computer can be configured as a router. If you're using such a computer as a router, you can activate the *DHCP relay agent* to allow broadcasts from a remote subnet to pass through to a subnet that has a DHCP server. Note that the DHCP server and DHCP relay agent cannot be one and the same; they must be separate computers, as in the example shown in Figure 4-7. If you were to configure the server as a relay agent, it wouldn't know whether to provide an IP address or try to forward the request to some other DHCP server!

Configure DHCP Servers and Scopes **199**

FIGURE 4-7

A Windows 2000 Server computer can forward broadcast requests for IP addresses to a DHCP server.

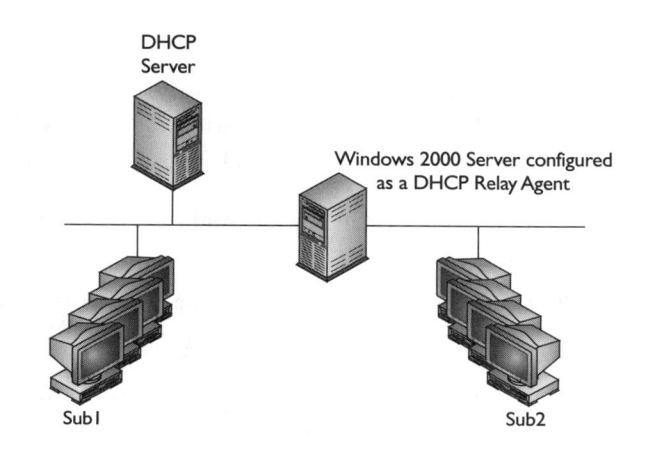

To configure a Windows 2000 Server computer that's acting as a router to play the role of a DHCP relay agent, follow these steps:

1. Click the Start button and choose Programs | Administrative Tools | Routing and Remote Access.
2. Click the + sign next to the name of the server that is acting as the forwarder to expand that node.
3. Expand the IP Routing node.
4. Right-click the DHCP Relay Agent node and choose Properties.
5. In the dialog box that appears, enter the IP address of the DHCP server.

on the job

Unlike BOOTP, which simply forwards DHCP requests to the next subnet, a Windows 2000 DHCP relay agent directs the request straight to the IP address of the DHCP server.

6. Click the Add button and click OK.

DHCP-DDNS Integration

You learned about dynamic DNS (DDNS) in Chapter 3, where a client that comes online automatically registers its name and IP address in the DNS name server so that other computers on the network are aware of its presence. When the client registers, the DDNS server automatically creates both forward lookup (A) and reverse lookup (PTR) records for the client. DHCP clients are no exception. Once a client gets its IP address and subnet mask from the DHCP server, it can then register itself with DDNS, just as a client with a static IP address would. You can configure if, and how, clients register with DDNS by following these steps:

1. Open the DHCP console, right-click the name of the DHCP server, and choose Properties.
2. Click the DNS tab to reveal the options, as shown in Figure 4-8.
3. Choose options as summarized here:

   - **Automatically update DHCP client information in DNS** Select this option if you want DHCP clients to register themselves with the DDNS name server.
   - **Update DNS only if DHCP client requests** Choosing this option limits DDNS updates to DHCP clients that specifically request registration during the lease process, as configured on the client.

FIGURE 4-8

The DNS tab with default settings

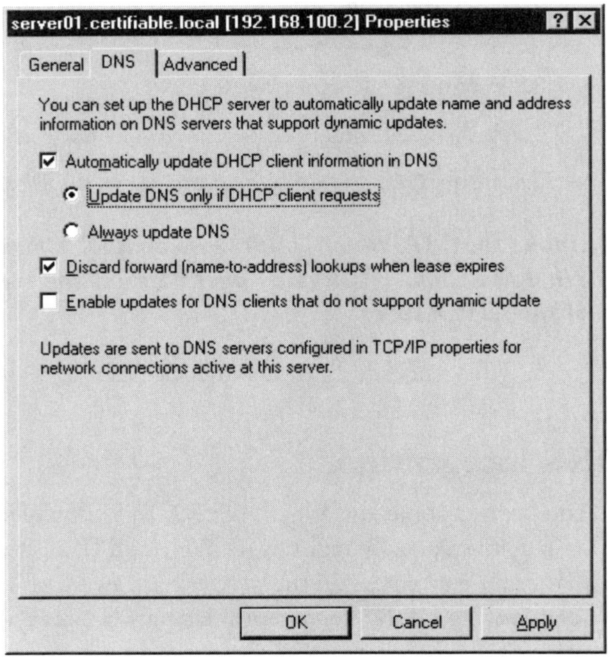

- **Always update DNS** Registers all DHCP clients with DDNS, regardless of the type of request the client made. This is your best bet for ensuring that the DHCP server creates address (A) and reverse lookup (PTR) records for all DHCP clients.

- **Discard forward (name-to-address) lookups when lease expires** If selected, host records for DHCP clients are removed from the DDNS zone file when the client's DHCP lease expires. If you don't select this option, the DHCP server removes only the PTR records.

- **Enable updates for DNS clients that do not support dynamic update** If selected, DHCP will automatically register downlevel clients with DNS, since they are not capable of registering themselves.

on the Job *Downlevel DHCP clients with static IP addresses won't be able to benefit from this last option, because the DHCP server will never see them, and hence won't be able to update DDNS on their behalf.*

EXERCISE 4-3

Configuring DHCP – DDNS Integration

In this exercise, you'll configure your DHCP server to automatically register all clients that obtain their IP addresses automatically:

1. If the DHCP console isn't already open, click the Start button and choose Programs | Administrative Tools | DHCP.

2. Right-click the server name in the console tree and choose Properties.

3. Click the DNS tab and choose the options that provide the widest range of DDNS registrations.

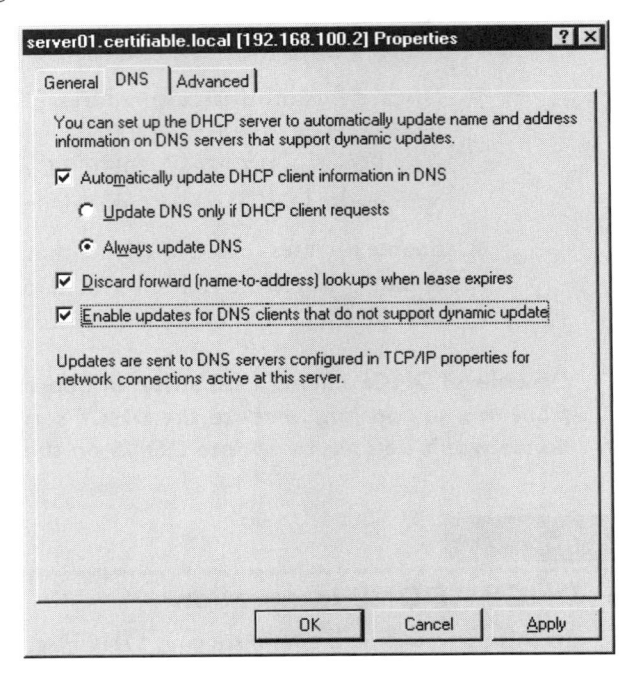

[Screenshot: server01.certifiable.local [192.168.100.2] Properties dialog, DNS tab, with "Automatically update DHCP client information in DNS", "Always update DNS", "Discard forward (name-to-address) lookups when lease expires", and "Enable updates for DNS clients that do not support dynamic update" checked.]

4. Click the OK button.

In a moment, you'll have a chance to test it all out.

CERTIFICATION OBJECTIVE 4.03

Configure DHCP Clients

Once you have a DHCP server running, configuring clients to use it is an easy process. Go to any client computer on which you want to enable DHCP and set the TCP/IP Properties to Obtain An IP Address Automatically. If you want the client to get the DNS name server IP address(es) from the DHCP server as well, choose Obtain DNS Server Address Automatically. Step-by-step instructions are presented in Exercise 4-4.

EXERCISE 4-4

Configuring a Client to Use DHCP

In this exercise, you'll configure a client computer to use DHCP to get an IP address. If you're working in a limited environment and have only one client computer to work with, you can still complete this exercise. You'll just be removing the client's static IP address and enabling it to get that from the DHCP server. Follow these steps:

1. Log on to the client computer with Administrative privileges.
2. Click the Start button and choose Settings | Network And Dial-Up Connections.
3. Right-click the icon for the NIC that connects you to the local network and choose Properties.
4. Click Internet Protocol (TCP/IP) and then click the Properties button.
5. Choose Obtain An IP Address Automatically.

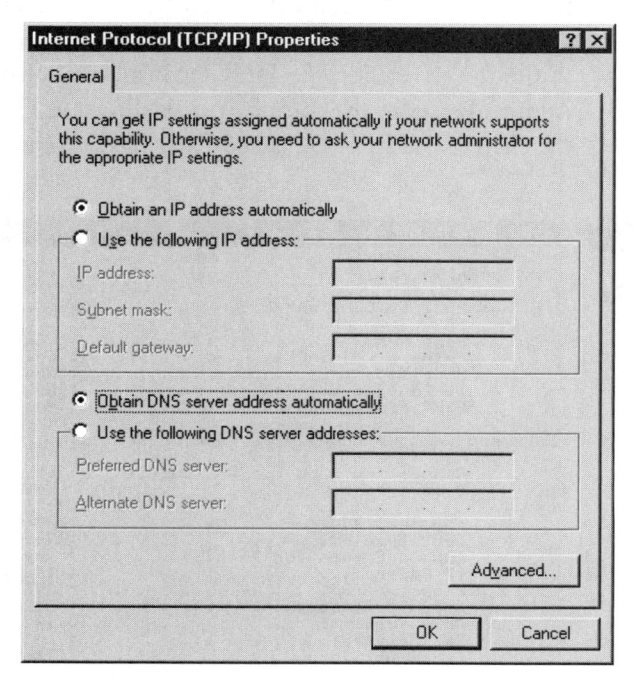

6. Choose Obtain DNS Server Address Automatically, as shown in the same figure.

204 Chapter 4: Configuring and Troubleshooting DHCP

7. Click OK to close all open dialog boxes, and follow any instructions that appear on the screen.

From this point on, whenever the computer first boots up, it will automatically get an IP address and name server addresses from the DHCP server.

Once the client has been configured to obtain an IP address automatically, you can test things out. To get the full effect of how DHCP really works, you may want to go to the command prompt on the client and enter the command **ipconfig /release** to release any previously assigned addresses. Then, reboot the computer to have the client obtain its IP address automatically. You won't see anything on the screen that tells you that the client is getting a dynamic IP address, but once you've rebooted, you can enter an **ipconfig /all** command to see what addresses the DHCP server has assigned to the client. Figure 4-9 shows an example where Client01 has been given the IP address 192.168.100.31 by the DHCP server. The display also shows the date the lease was obtained and when it will expire.

On the server side, the DHCP console will display the leased address under Address Leases in the console tree, as shown in Figure 4-10. There you can see that the client IP address 192.168.100.31 has been leased to client01.certifiable.local.

| FIGURE 4-9 | ```
C:\>ipconfig /all

Windows 2000 IP Configuration

        Host Name . . . . . . . . . . . . : client01
        Primary DNS Suffix  . . . . . . . : certifiable.local
        Node Type . . . . . . . . . . . . : Broadcast
        IP Routing Enabled. . . . . . . . : No
        WINS Proxy Enabled. . . . . . . . : No

Ethernet adapter Local Area Connection:

        Connection-specific DNS Suffix  . : certifiable.local
        Description . . . . . . . . . . . : CNET PRO200WL PCI Fast Ethernet Adapter
        Physical Address. . . . . . . . . : 00-80-AD-7B-E7-18
        DHCP Enabled. . . . . . . . . . . : Yes
        Autoconfiguration Enabled . . . . : Yes
        IP Address. . . . . . . . . . . . : 192.168.100.31
        Subnet Mask . . . . . . . . . . . : 255.255.255.0
        Default Gateway . . . . . . . . . : 192.168.100.1
        DHCP Server . . . . . . . . . . . : 192.168.100.2
        DNS Servers . . . . . . . . . . . :
        Lease Obtained. . . . . . . . . . : Thursday, February 14, 2002 10:58:52 AM
        Lease Expires . . . . . . . . . . : Friday, February 22, 2002 10:58:52 AM

C:\>
``` |
|---|---|
| Sample **ipconfig /all** command from a client that obtained its IP address automatically | |
```

The DNS console will also show a host record for the client, as shown in the bottom half Figure 4-10. (If either console seems to be lagging in its display, press the F5 key or click the Action button and choose Refresh to update the display.)

Commands for Managing Clients

The **ipconfig** command in Windows 2000 offers some switches especially designed for working with DHCP clients:

- **ipconfig /release**   Releases dynamically assigned IP addresses
- **ipconfig /renew**   Renews the IP address

FIGURE 4-10

Client has leased an address and registered a host record in DNS

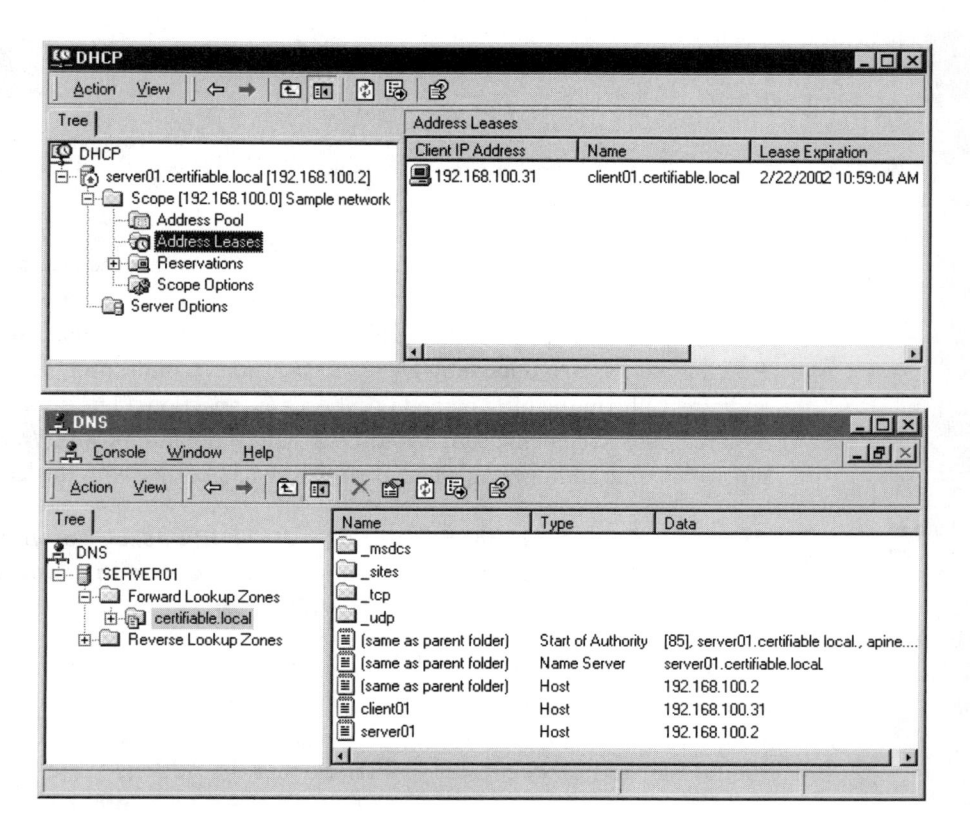

SCENARIO & SOLUTION

I configured by DHCP server to assign the IP address of my DNS servers to clients, but when I start the client and enter an **nslookup** command, the client says it can't find the name server. When I enter **ipconfig /all**, no DNS server addresses appear. How can I fix that?	Go back to the DHCP server console and configure a Scope Option or Server Option for service 006 DNS Servers. Enter the server name and click the Resolve button, or just enter the DNS server's IP address. Be sure to click the Add button, and then click OK. On the client, use the **ipconfig /release** and **ipconfig /renew** commands to get fresh IP address assignments.
I changed my default gateway address and adjusted the 003 Routers option at the DHCP server to match that change. How do I get clients to use the new setting?	You'll either need to reboot the clients or enter an **ipconfig /renew** command at each client to get the new default gateway address to the client.
How can I see which addresses are currently leased and how many are still available?	In the DHCP console, right-click the server name or the name of a specific scope and choose Display Statistics.

- **ipconfig /registerdns**   Refreshes all DHCP leases and reregisters the DNS names

If the client is a multihomed machine, you can follow the **/release** and **/renew** switches with the name of the specific connection to which you want to apply the command. You can also use the ? and * wildcards to cover multiple names. For example, entering the command **ipconfig /renew "Local Area Connection"** releases dynamic addresses only on the NIC named Local Area Connection. (The quotation marks are required only if the name contains spaces.) The command **ipconfig /renew loc*** would renew dynamic addresses on all adapters whose names start with the letters *loc*.

exam
🕒 *atch*

*After you change a client from using a static IP address to obtaining an IP address automatically, you can use **ipconfig /renew** on clients to get new IP address information from the DHCP server.*

You can enter the commands in that order to do the same as would happen during a reboot, without rebooting. Entering **ipconfig /release** releases the client's hold on the IP address. (If, on the server side, you then choose Action | Refresh from the DHCP and DNS consoles, you'll see that the Address Lease has been removed, and the client has been removed from the DNS zone.) Entering **ipconfig /renew** recontacts the DHCP server and obtains IP addresses, just as when booting up. Again, on the server side, you'd need to refresh this display in the consoles to see the change. If you've configured all DHCP clients to register with DDNS, you really won't need to enter an **ipconfig /registerdns** command to register. However, the command might be useful for debugging purposes if your clients are able to obtain IP addresses but not register themselves with DDNS.

A Note on APIPA

There was a time when, if a client that was configured to obtain an IP address automatically came online and was unable to find a DHCP server, an error message describing the problem would appear on the screen. In Windows 2000, however, you get no such feedback. Instead, Automatic Private IP Addressing (APIPA) kicks in, and assigns the client a class B IP address of 169.254.*x.y* subnet mask 255.255.0.0. About the only way you'll know this has happened is that when you enter an **ipconfig /all** command at the client, you'll see the class B IP address.

You can disable APIPA with a Registry hack. In the Registry Editor, go to HKEY_LOCAL_MACHINE\SYSTEM\CurrentControlSet\Services\Tcpip\ Parameters\Interfaces\adaptername. Create a new REG_DWORD value named IPAutoconfigurationEnabled and give it a value of 0.

APIPA is useful on home and small office networks where there is no DHCP server, since it allows the hosts to get *some* IP address, rather than no IP address at all, but on a client/server network that has a DHCP server, APIPA seems more of a problem than a feature. If you have any connectivity problems with a DHCP- enabled client after bootup, you'd do well to enter an **ipconfig /all** command to verify that the client has an IP address that's appropriate for the subnet. Which brings us to our next topic...

CERTIFICATION OBJECTIVE 4.04

Troubleshoot DHCP

When you're using a DHCP server, sometimes basic IP troubleshooting is really DHCP troubleshooting. This is especially true when a connection that used to work perfectly suddenly stops working. The sudden failure could be caused by the machine going offline, coming back online, and getting a new IP address from DHCP. Clients that "expect" to find a given service at some IP address no longer can find that IP address. This is the main reason Microsoft suggests using DHCP for clients only, never servers.

When you have a sudden failure, you need to check basic connectivity with PING as usual, just to make sure there's not a cabling problem. Then you need to think along the lines of the following questions:

- What is this server's IP address *supposed* to be?
- What is this server's IP address right now?
- Is this server DHCP enabled? (In other words, is it configured to obtain an IP address automatically?)

Once you've determined that the server has the wrong IP address and is DHCP enabled, you can go to the TCP/IP Properties dialog box on that server and assign it the appropriate static IP address. If that static IP address is within the range of IP addresses that can be assigned to clients, you'll need to go to the DHCP server and define that IP address as an exclusion so it doesn't get assigned to any other machines on the network.

Sometimes the reverse is true on DHCP-enabled clients, in that they're using static IP addresses when they should be using dynamic addresses. For example, suppose a given client cannot perform basic DNS name resolution or reach its default gateway. At first, you might think this is a DNS problem or basic connectivity problem, but you'd be wise to see where the client is looking for name servers and a default gateway before you go digging around in DNS.

For example, suppose you have a DHCP-enabled client that isn't resolving DNS names. You know you've configured the correct name server addresses at the DHCP server, and you know this client gets its configuration from DHCP. So why isn't DNS working? On that client, open up the TCP/IP Properties dialog box and see where it "expects" to find the name servers. If the client is configured with "hard" name server IP addresses, as in Figure 4-11, that could be the problem.

The cure here would be to select Obtain DNS Server Address Automatically on the client. Close the dialog box, and refresh all the dynamically assigned IP addresses using the **ipconfig /release** and **ipconfig /renew** commands (and perhaps an **ipconfig /registerdns** command, just for good measure!).

It all boils down to the basic rules of using static IP addresses for servers and dynamic IP addresses for clients, which I know I've repeated umpteen times in this book already. (It's not because I'm obsessed with the rule. Rather, it's because so many questions on Exam 70-218 present scenarios where these rules weren't followed, and you have to fix the problem!) Now that you know more about DHCP, I can more accurately define the rules that you want to follow as follows:

- Assign static IP addresses to servers, and exclude those addresses from your list of available IP addresses assigned to clients. You can do this by defining your DHCP scope so that the range of assignable IP addresses doesn't overlap with any statically assigned IP addresses. If it's too late for that, you can just exclude certain IP addresses from your range of assignable IP addresses.

- Define the default gateway and name server IP addresses that clients should use within your DHCP server to ensure that all clients get appropriate, current IP addresses.

- If a client fails to behave correctly after getting its dynamic IP addresses, open its TCP/IP Properties dialog box and make sure it's configured to obtain both its IP address and DNS name server addresses from the DHCP server. Then use **ipconfig /release** and **ipconfig /renew** to update the client's dynamic addresses.

When you think along those lines, some "complex" questions in Exam 70-218 suddenly look a little simpler. If it's a troubleshooting question involving DHCP, the problem is usually with a server using a dynamic IP address where it should be using a static IP address or a client using a static IP address where it should be using a dynamic address.

FIGURE 4-11

A DHCP-enabled client that is not getting DNS name server IP addresses from the DHCP server

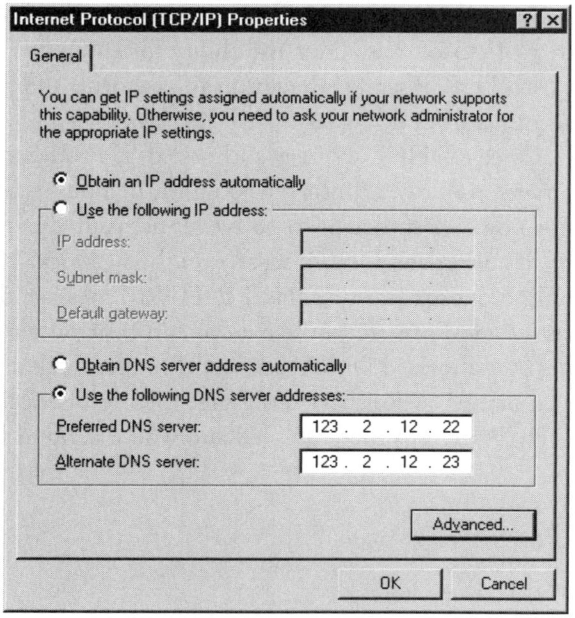

> **exam**
> **Watch**
> *The term "DHCP-enabled" on the exams means that the machine is configured to obtain its IP addresses automatically.*

Detecting Rogue Servers

It's important to remember that when a DHCP-enabled client first boots up, it has no IP address of its own, nor does it know the IP address of a DHCP server. As such, it must broadcast a message to all machines on the network in order to discover where the DHCP server is located—and here's the rub: if there are multiple DHCP servers within broadcast range, they'll *all* respond with an offer. The client will, basically, accept whichever offer it gets first.

> **on the**
> **Job**
> *Microsoft claims that when multiple DHCP servers respond to a client's DHCP request, the client will accept the "best" offer. However, most administrators will tell you that the client will actually accept whatever offer comes first and will ignore the other offers.*

The problem of "competing DHCP servers" has plagued many administrators in the past, who end up scratching their heads trying to figure out how DHCP-enabled "Client *X*" obtained some weird, invalid IP addresses. Often, the source of the problem turns out to be some *rogue* DHCP server that someone created on the network, perhaps just to try out an exercise in a book like this one. This is the reason that Microsoft has added the ability for enterprise administrators to pick and choose which DHCP servers they want to authorize and prevent users with more restrictive accounts from doing so.

Once a DHCP server is authorized, it's added to a list of all authorized DHCP servers in Active Directory. You'll learn about Active Directory in the next chapter. For now, it's sufficient to be aware that Active Directory automatically keeps track of all authorized DHCP servers on the network. Whenever a DHCP server comes online, it broadcasts a DHCPINFORM message that, in essence, says "I'm a DHCP server and I'm here." When a domain controller receives that message, it checks its list of authorized DHCP servers. If the server that just came online is not within that list, AD sends back a message that, in essence, says "Oh no you're not." That DHCP server is then disabled and won't respond to any more DHCP requests.

EXERCISE 4-5

Checking for Rogue DHCP Servers

The Event Viewer reports any rogue DHCP servers as DHCPServer errors in the System Log. If you want to see whether any rogue servers have been detected in your network, you can follow these steps:

1. Click the Start button and choose Programs | Administrative Tools | Event Viewer.

2. Click System Log in the tree view (left pane).

3. To limit the display to DHCP server events, click the View button, choose Filter, and choose DHCP Server from the Event Source drop-down list. Then click OK.

4. If any rogue servers were detected, they'll be listed as Error types. Double-click any error to see a detailed description, as in the following illustration.

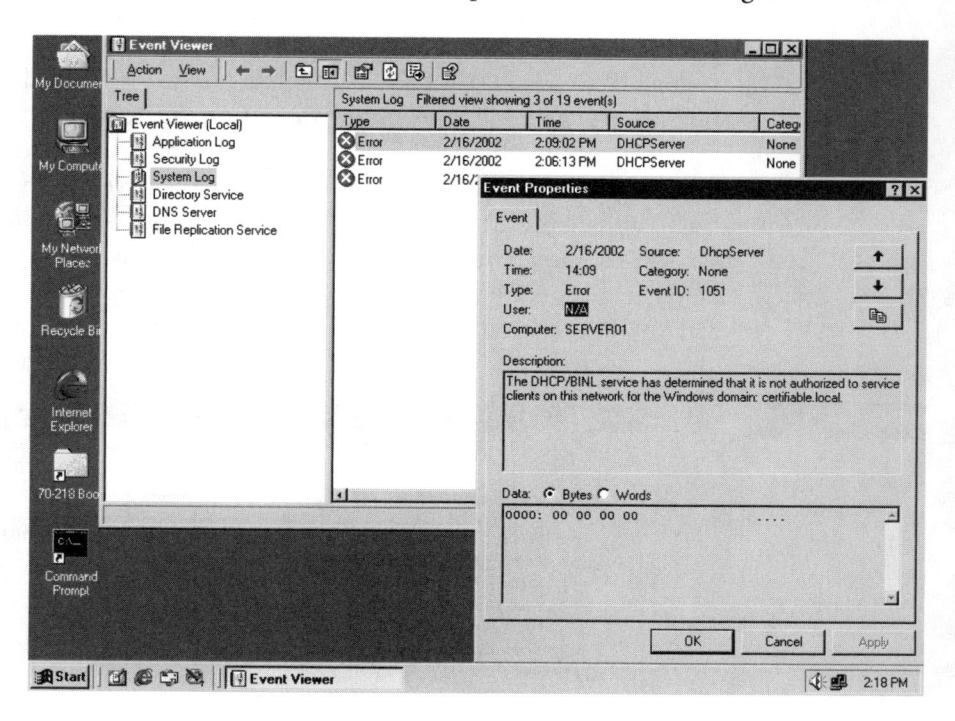

You can easily see which DHCP servers are currently authorized and running by opening the DHCP console and clicking the DHCP server at the top of the console tree. The Status column of the right pane will show "Running" for those DHCP servers that are currently authorized and working. For example, in Figure 4-12, I have one authorized DHCP server running in the certifiable.local domain.

To authorize or unauthorize a DHCP server, right-click its name in the DHCP console and choose Authorize or Unauthorize. Note too that you can start, stop, restart, pause, and resume a DHCP server by right-clicking its name in the DHCP console and choosing All Tasks.

CERTIFICATION SUMMARY

That wraps it up for DHCP. The basic goal of DHCP is simply to assign valid IP addresses to hosts as they come onto the network, the idea being to save you the trouble of having to manually assign an IP address to each host, create A and PTR records in DNS for each host, and so forth. DHCP is best used on clients, where a specific IP address isn't required. DHCP is not a good idea for servers, because the dynamic IP addresses that DHCP assigns are only "leased" and not permanent. Since many clients will be expecting to find specific servers and specific IP addresses, you don't want the IP addresses of those servers to change. Therefore, static IP addressing is the way to go on computers acting as servers in the network.

This also marks the end of Part I of this book and network infrastructure issues that are relevant to exam 70-218. Remember, infrastructure is all about getting the computers to communicate with one another, which entails ensuring that they have valid IP addresses, can resolve names to IP addresses, and so forth. In Part II, we'll

FIGURE 4-12

One DHCP server authorized and running in the certifiable.local domain

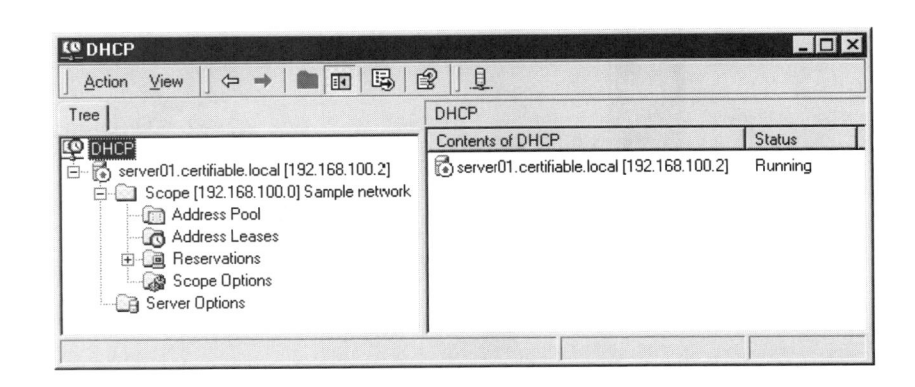

SCENARIO & SOLUTION

The **ipconfig** command doesn't work on my Windows 95 client computers. Is there an equivalent command I can use?	Windows 95 clients support the **winipcfg** command, which displays IP configuration settings and options in a graphical dialog box. Windows 98 supports both **ipconfig** and **winipcfg**.
I'm using a multihomed computer as a DHCP server. How can I specify which NIC provides the DHCP server?	In the DHCP console, right-click the DHCP server's name and choose Properties. Click the Advanced tab and then click the Bindings button. There you'll be able to specify the connections that the DHCP server supports for servicing clients.
Are there audit logs and events to help with troubleshooting DHCP?	Yes. By default, daily DHCP audit logs are kept in the $systemroot%\system32\dhcp folder, named DhcServLog.Mon (Monday), DhcServLog.Tue (Tuesday), and so forth. To enable or disable audit logs, right-click the server name in the DHCP console, choose Properties, and choose or clear the Enable DHCP Audit Logging option. The System Log in Event Viewer also tracks DHCP-related events, including reports of any rogue DHCP servers detected on the network.

turn our attention to *using* the network, with Active Directory as your centralized administrative tool for sharing resources, and controlling who exactly who has access to which shared resources.

✓ TWO-MINUTE DRILL

Install and Authorize DHCP Servers

- ❑ DHCP is all about automatically assigning IP addresses to client computers so that you don't have to configure every single host manually. (A daunting task when there are thousands of computers to contend with!)
- ❑ Dynamic addresses that are assigned by DHCP are leased, not permanent. Therefore, those addresses are subject to change and hence shouldn't be used on server computers.
- ❑ You can install a DHCP server on any Windows 2000 Server computer via the Add/Remove Programs icon in Control Panel.
- ❑ In a Windows 2000 Active Directory domain, only Windows 2000 DHCP servers that have been authorized by an enterprise administrator will function on the network.

Configure DHCP Servers and Scopes

- ❑ A *scope* is a range of IP addresses that the DHCP server can assign to hosts. An *exclusion* is an IP address within that range that cannot be assigned by DHCP.
- ❑ In the DHCP console, server options apply to all scopes, whereas scope options apply only to the scope to which they're applied. In the event of a conflict, the more localized scope option takes precedence.
- ❑ When using multiple DHCP servers for redundancy and load balancing, it's important to ensure that the IP addresses each server hands out do not overlap. That is, each DHCP server must have its own unique set of IP addresses to grant to clients.
- ❑ Because DHCP requests are broadcast, they normally are confined to the current subnet. However, you can install a DHCP relay agent or RFC 1542-compliant router with BOOTP forwarding enabled to get DHCP requests to cross the router.

Configure DHCP Clients

- ❑ To configure a client computer to use a DHCP server to obtain its IP address, subnet mask, and default gateway address, choose Obtain An IP Address Automatically in the client computer's TCP/IP Properties dialog box.

- ❑ To have the client receive IP addresses of DNS name servers from the DHCP server, choose Obtain DNS Server Addresses Automatically in the same dialog box.
- ❑ The best way to test a client's ability to use DHCP is to reboot the computer, to simulate exactly how the client will get its information in the future.
- ❑ You can use the regular **ipconfig /all** command to view the client's IP information after rebooting.
- ❑ On the server side, you can view address leases in the DHCP console to see which addresses have been allocated. However, you may need to refresh the console display to ensure it contains the most recent information.
- ❑ The command **ipconfig /release** instructs a client computer to release its dynamically assigned IP addresses.
- ❑ The command **ipconfig /renew** forces a client to renew its dynamically assigned IP addresses and lease.
- ❑ The command **ipconfig /registerdns** forces a client to register itself with a DDNS server.
- ❑ APIPA is an alternative automatic IP-addressing tool that's executed only if a DHCP-enabled client cannot find a DHCP server when first coming online.
- ❑ IP addresses assigned by APIPA are always Class B addresses starting with 169.254 and a subnet mask of 255.255.0.0.

Troubleshoot DHCP

- ❑ Connectivity problems with DHCP-enabled servers are often caused by the server's IP address having changed. The best way to avoid the problem is to assign static IP addresses to server computers.
- ❑ On client computers, connectivity problems can arise when the computer should be configured to obtain addresses automatically, but instead is using some outdated static IP address.
- ❑ If a DHCP server fails to function as a whole, there's a good chance that the server simply hasn't been authorized yet.
- ❑ You can use the DHCP console to see which DHCP servers are currently authorized and running.

SELF TEST

Install and Authorize DHCP Servers

1. Your company's domain consists of Windows 2000 Server, Windows 2000 Professional, and Windows NT Workstation 4.0 clients. You administer two Windows 2000 DHCP servers, two Windows 2000 DNS servers, and two Windows 2000 WINS servers. All of the servers have static IP addresses. All of the clients are DHCP, DNS, and WINS clients. You want to ensure that all client computers be dynamically registered in DNS. What should you do?

   A. Configure both DHCP servers to Automatically Update DHCP Client Information In DNS, and Enable Updates For DNS Clients That Do Not Support Dynamic Updates.

   B. Make the DHCP servers replication partners to one another.

   C. Configure the DNS zone that's authoritative for the domain to use WINS integration, and make sure the Do Not Replicate This Record option is not selected on the WINS tab.

   D. Configure each client computer with a static IP address and choose Register This Connection's Addresses In DNS in each client's Advanced TCP/IP Properties.

2. You are a domain administrator for MajorMinor.local in an enterprise. Your domain consists of several Windows 2000 Server computers running Active Directory. You install the DHCP service on a member server named Server04. You restart the server, and then test it out from a client that's configured to obtain its IP address automatically. The test fails. What should you do?

   A. Configure the client computer with a static IP address and forget it.

   B. Remove the DHCP service from Server04, and move it to a domain controller.

   C. Authorize, or get somebody with sufficient permissions to authorize, the new DHCP server.

   D. Get a user with a Local Administrator account to authorize the server.

Configure DHCP Servers and Scopes

3. You administer a network that consists of 50 Windows 2000 Server computers, 750 Windows Professional computers, and 35 UNIX clients. One of the Windows 2000 Server computers provides DHCP services for the entire network. All of the Windows 2000 clients are configured to obtain an IP address automatically.

   The UNIX clients run application programs with hard-coded IP addresses for each of the servers. Users of those applications complain that on some days, they're not able to connect to some of the servers. What can you do to ensure that servers will always be available to the UNIX clients?

- A. Create a DHCP scope for the servers that specifies a one month lease timeout.
- B. Create a DHCP scope for the servers that specifies a one week lease timeout.
- C. Create a DHCP client reservation for each server.
- D. Create a DHCP client reservation for each UNIX client.

4. You have four subnets connected by RFC 1542-compliant routers; the subnet IP addresses are 192.168.200.0, 192.168.200.64, 192.168.200.128, and 192.168.200.192, all with subnet masks of 255.255.255.192. You install and authorize a DHCP server on the first subnet and configure it to hand out addresses for all three subnets. When you test it out, only DHCP-enabled clients on the first subnet are able to get their IP addresses automatically. What should you do first to correct this problem?

- A. Enable BOOTP forwarding on all of the routers.
- B. Add a DHCP relay agent to each subnet.
- C. Create a HOSTS file on each client computer to help it find the DHCP server.
- D. Change the subnet mask to 255.255.255.0 to make all of the computers members of the same subnet.

5. You are the administrator for a network that uses Windows 2000 DHCP servers to automatically assign IP addresses to DHCP-enabled computers. You've also enabled automatic DDNS registrations on the server. Client computers are a mix of Windows 2000 Professional, Windows 98, and some non-Microsoft operating systems. When you test the network, you notice that only the Windows 2000 Professional computers are correctly registered in DNS. What should you do?

- A. Set up one of the Windows 2000 Professional computers as a WINS relay agent.
- B. Manually create A and PTR records for all hosts that were unable to register themselves with the DNS server.
- C. Choose Register This Connection's Addresses In DNS in the Advanced TCP/IP Properties dialog box for all the non-Windows 2000 client computers.
- D. Choose Enable Updates For DNS Clients That Do Not Support Dynamic Update at the DHCP server.

Configure DHCP Clients

6. You set up a small network consisting of a single Windows 2000 Server computer named Server01, and 15 Windows 2000 client computers. All of the computers in the network have static IP addresses. ServerA is configured as a DNS name server for name resolution within the network. The branch office gets its own administrator who adds a second Windows 2000 server, Server02. He installed both DNS and DHCP on the second server and configures it to assign IP addresses automatically and register all clients in the DNS zone defined on Server02. Once the change is completed, users complain that they cannot access any other hosts in their network. What must be done to correct the problem?

    A. Run the command **ipconfig /registerdns** on all of the client computers to give them new IP addresses and reregister their names.

    B. Run the command **ipconfig /renew** on each of the client computers to obtain new IP addresses.

    C. Enter the command **ipconfig /release L*** to release all client connections.

    D. Remove the DNS server from Server01, set up the DHCP server to assign IP addresses and DNS name server addresses to all clients, and then configure all clients to obtain an IP address and name server address automatically.

7. You administer a single subnet that consists of two Windows 2000 domain controllers offering DNS and DHCP services. DHCP assigns IP, default gateway, and DNS server IP addresses to all clients in the network. One user, Tom, is unable to access any network resources by name. You use PING commands to verify basic connectivity, and all tests pass. You open the TCP/IP Properties dialog box for Tom's connection to the network. His settings are shown in Figure 4-13. What should you do to get Tom's machine working properly? (Choose all that apply.)

    A. Change Tom's settings to Obtain DNS Server Address Automatically.

    B. Enter the command **ipconfig /renew** to assign new addresses to Tom's computer.

    C. Reconfigure the DHCP server to assign DNS server addresses that match those shown in Tom's TCP/IP Properties dialog box.

    D. Modify the LMHOSTS file on Tom's computer to point to the appropriate name servers.

Troubleshoot DHCP

8. You administer the network shown in Figure 4-14. Network A consists of multiple subnets all sharing a single DHCP server named DHCP01. Network B is configured in a similar manner, with DHCP02 providing DHCP services. NS01 is a multihomed DNS server providing name resolution for both networks. Each NIC's configuration is shown in the figure.

FIGURE 4-13

The TCP/IP Properties dialog box for Tom's computer

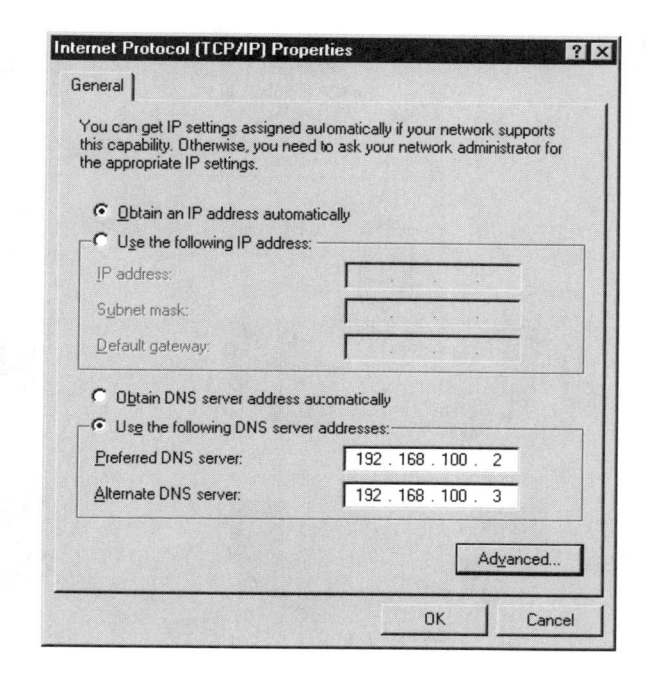

After working properly for several months, all the clients on Network B suddenly lose the ability to resolve hostnames. What can you do to fix the problem and ensure it doesn't happen again?

- A. Give NIC02 a static IP address of 192.168.6.1.
- B. Enable DHCP on NIC01.
- C. Use static IP addresses on all of the clients.
- D. Configure the DHCP servers to dynamically update DNS for the DHCP clients.

9. You are the administrator for GenerallyTired.com and are tasked with the problem of getting the network shown in Figure 4-15 to work. Currently, DHCP-enabled clients are able to get IP addresses from the DHCP server, but are unable to reach all network resources. What changes would you need to make to ensure that all the DHCP-enabled clients can access all local and remote network resources?

- A. Change the DHCP scope to something like 192.168.31.31 to 192.168.31.254 subnet mask 255.255.255.128.
- B. Change the 003 Router option in the DHCP server to 192.168.50.1/24.
- C. Reconfigure the remote servers to get their IP addresses automatically from Server02.
- D. Change the subnet mask assigned to the remote servers to 255.255.255.128.

220 Chapter 4: Configuring and Troubleshooting DHCP

FIGURE 4-14

NS01 is the name server for Network A and Network B.

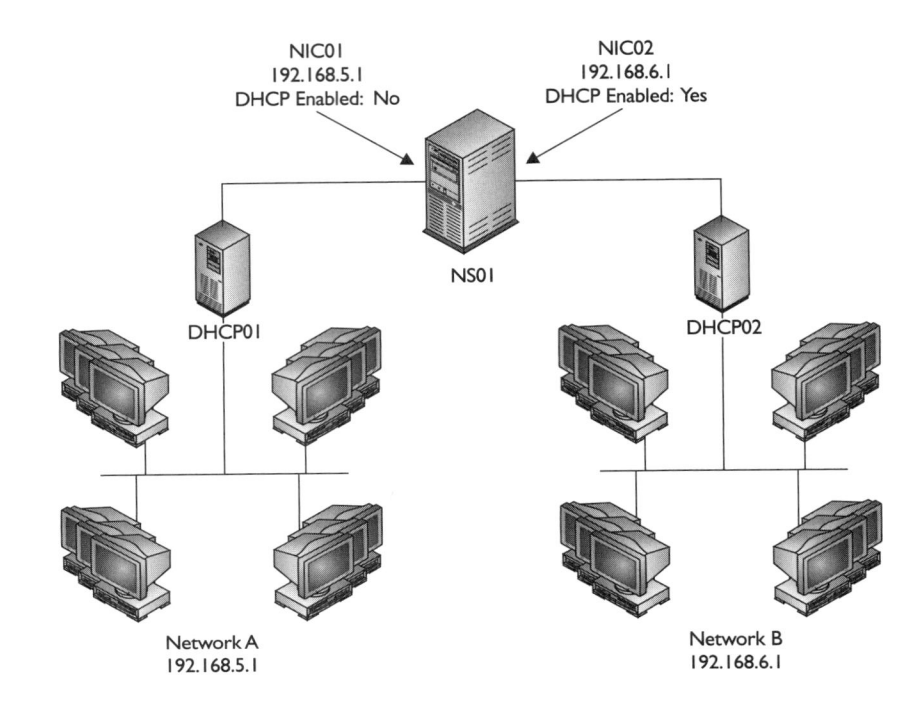

10. You administer a network containing Windows 2000 Server and Professional computers. Currently, Server01 provides DHCP, DNS, and WINS services. Server01 configures it clients with IP addresses, subnet masks, and its own IP address as the server for DNS and WINS name resolution. The company acquires some Windows 98 computers at a local yard sale and

FIGURE 4-15

DHCP-enabled clients get their IP information automatically from Server02.

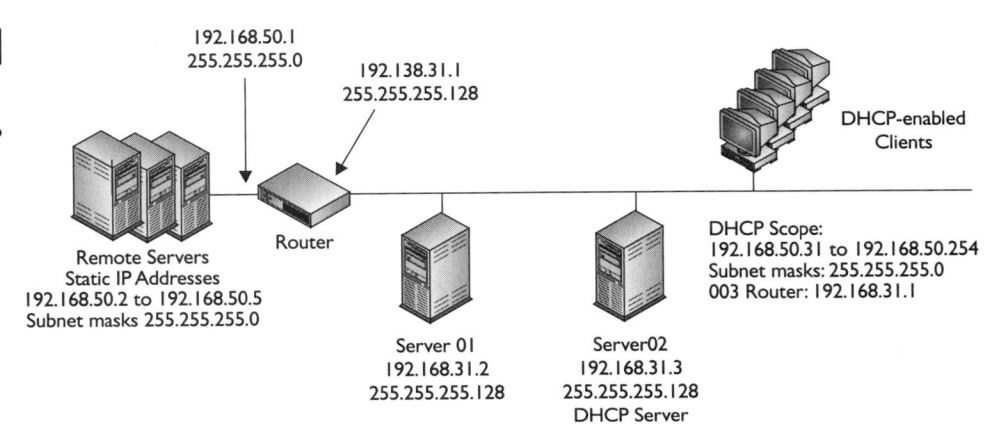

adds them to the network. Unfortunately, the new computers are unable to access any network resources, even after they've been properly connected to the network, largely because they're all configured with static IP addresses that aren't relevant to your network. You need to ensure that the Windows 98 clients will be able to obtain their IP addresses automatically and register themselves with the DNS name server on Server01. What do you need to do? (Choose all that apply.)

- **A.** Configure the Windows 98 computer to obtain their IP addresses automatically.
- **B.** Configure the Windows 98 computers to use Server01 for WINS name resolution.
- **C.** Configure the DNS server to perform WINS lookups.
- **D.** Configure the DHCP server on Server01 to register all clients using the DDNS update protocol.
- **E.** Upgrade all the Windows 98 computers to Windows 2000.

LAB QUESTION

Figure 4-16 shows a network consisting of two subnets. The servers are both multihomed with IP routing enabled to provide connectivity between the two subnets. Based on the information, you should be able to fill in the empty text boxes with the follow labels:

- Subnet 192.168.100.0
- Subnet 192.168.100.128
- Obtain IP address automatically (two boxes)
- DHCP Relay Agent

Then, fill in the blanks for DHCP server scopes. Leave set aside ten addresses at the start of each scope to be used for statically assigning to servers on each subnet.

222 Chapter 4: Configuring and Troubleshooting DHCP

FIGURE 4-16 Fill in the blanks to have clients on both subnets obtain IP addressing from the DHCP server.

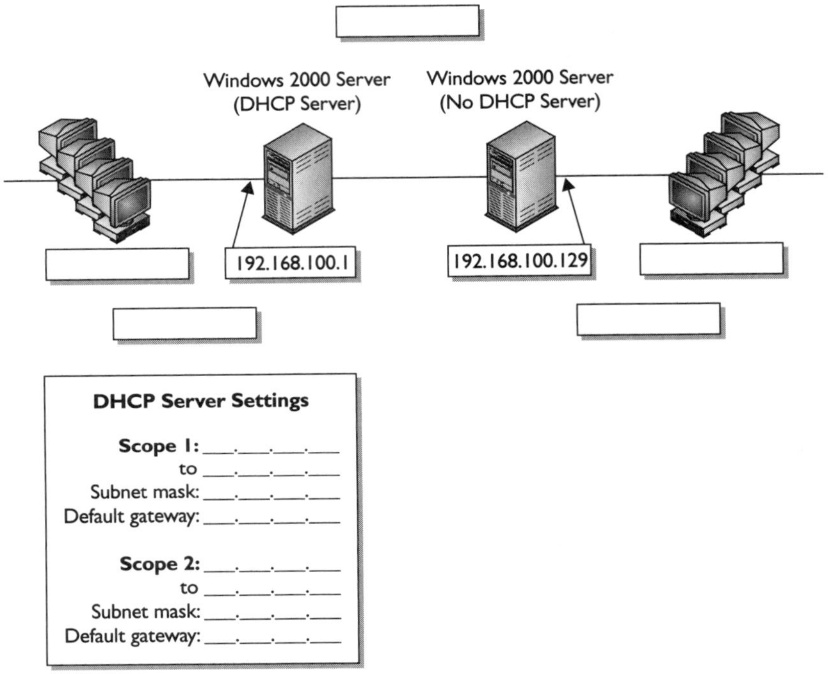

Windows 2000 Server (DHCP Server)   Windows 2000 Server (No DHCP Server)

192.168.100.1   192.168.100.129

DHCP Server Settings

Scope 1: ___.___.___.___
to ___.___.___.___
Subnet mask: ___.___.___.___
Default gateway: ___.___.___.___

Scope 2: ___.___.___.___
to ___.___.___.___
Subnet mask: ___.___.___.___
Default gateway: ___.___.___.___

SELF TEST ANSWERS

Install and Authorize DHCP Servers

1. ☑ **A** is correct. All that needs to be done here is to enable dynamic registration of all clients on the DHCP servers. Option A takes care of both the Windows 2000 clients and the downlevel clients.
   ☒ **B** and **C** are wrong because they have nothing to do with dynamic registration of DHCP clients.
   ☒ **D** is incorrect because it defeats the purpose of using DHCP, and preventing WINS record replication is only required when the DNS server is replicating with non-Windows 2000 name servers.

2. ☑ **C** is correct. The most likely scenario here is that the DHCP service isn't authorized within the domain. If you don't have permissions to authorize the server, get someone with higher-level Enterprise Administrator permissions to authorize the server.
   ☒ **A** is incorrect because it defeats the purpose of installing the DHCP server in the first place.
   ☒ **B** wouldn't help. The DHCP service can run from any server.
   ☒ **D** is incorrect because local administrators don't have permissions to authorize DHCP servers.

Configure DHCP Servers and Scopes

3. ☑ **C** is correct. Since the UNIX servers are using hard-coded IP addresses for servers and there are intermittent failures, you must ensure that the server IP addresses do not change. A simple solution would be to use static IP addresses on the servers, but the question doesn't say anything about static addresses. So the next best solution would be to create DHCP client reservations for each of the servers.
   ☒ **A** and **B** are incorrect because you don't want the servers to lease their IP addresses for any specific length of time. Rather, you want them to retain their IP addresses indefinitely.
   ☒ **D** is incorrect because the problem has nothing to do with the IP addresses of the clients. Rather, it's the programs using hard-coded IP addresses that are having problems because the IP addresses aren't static.

4. ☑ **A** is correct. The most likely cause of the problem is that BOOTP isn't enabled on the routers. This option also represents the easiest next step.
   ☒ **B** is incorrect because you already have routers that can forward DHCP requests, so there's no need to add DHCP relay agents.
   ☒ **C** is incorrect, largely because it would be a hassle to create all the HOSTS files.
   ☒ **D** is incorrect because you have routers that can forward the DHCP requests in place, so there's no need to reconfigure the entire network.

5. ☑ **D** is correct. You need to enable updates for DNS clients that do not support dynamic updates at the DHCP server, so that the downlevel clients can be registered "by proxy" by the DHCP server.
☒ **A** is incorrect because WINS is all about NetBIOS names, and there's nothing in the question that specifies that NetBIOS names are at issue here.
☒ **B** would work, but it's not an ideal solution. It would be much easier to allow the DHCP server to register those downlevel clients for you.
☒ **C** is wrong because only the Windows 2000 clients would have that option in their Advanced TCP/IP Properties dialog boxes.

Configure DHCP Clients

6. ☑ **D** is correct. The clients currently have static IP addresses, and static name server addresses pointing to Server01 for hostname resolution. Server02 won't do any good until the clients are reconfigured to obtain an IP address and name server addresses automatically, and use Server02 for name resolution.
☒ **A, B,** and **C** are all incorrect because they fail to take into consideration that all the clients are currently using static IP addresses, and aren't configured to use DHCP at all.

7. ☑ **A** and **B** are correct. Tom's machine should get name server addresses from the DHCP server. Once you've made that change in the dialog box, you can restart the client computer or enter an **ipconfig /renew** command to configure Tom's computer with appropriate IP addresses.
☒ **C** is wrong because Tom's computer is the only one that has name resolution problems, so the DNS name server addresses in his TCP/IP Properties dialog box are probably incorrect.
☒ **D** is incorrect because LMHOSTS is only valid for NetBIOS name resolution, which isn't an issue here.

Troubleshoot DHCP

8. ☑ **A** is correct. Since NIC2 is DHCP enabled, it will get its TCP/IP configuration settings dynamically from DHCP02. This means that the IP address for Network B could change and is therefore the most likely cause of the sudden name resolution failures.
☒ **B** is incorrect because if you do this, you expose Network A to the same problem Network B has.
☒ **C** is wrong because it's overkill. There's no need to manually configure every client with a static IP address. You just need to make sure that the IP address of Network B's interface remains constant.

☒ **D** is incorrect because the scenario here points out a sudden failure at one point in the network. You need to think in terms of "Where is the break, what IP address *is* at the break, what IP address *should be* at the break, and if there's a problem, where did this faulty IP address come from?"

9. ☑ **A** is correct. You need to change the DHCP server scope to assign DHCP-enabled clients with IP addresses and a subnet mask appropriate to their subnet.
☒ **B** is wrong because the default gateway assigned to clients via the 003 Router option is already correct.
☒ **C** is incorrect because there's no need to change the configuration of the remote servers.
☒ **D** is wrong because changing the subnet mask on the remote servers would have no effect on the computers on the far side of the router.

10. ☑ **A** and **D** are correct. The Windows 98 clients can be configured to get their IP addresses automatically, but since they won't be able to register themselves with DDNS, you'll need to configure the DHCP server to register them automatically.
☒ **B** is incorrect because the DHCP server will provide the Windows 98 clients with IP addresses for WINS servers once those clients are configured to obtain their IP addresses automatically.
☒ **C** is wrong because WINS isn't an issue here. Besides, according to the wording of the question, WINS name resolution is already handled by Server01 and the DHCP server.
☒ **E** isn't a bad idea, but the question asks how you'd get these Windows 98 computers to get their IP addresses automatically and register themselves with the DNS name server. Answers A and D are sufficient to meet that goal.

LAB ANSWER

Figure 4-17 shows the answers to the lab question. Here's an explanation of how you could figure it all out:

- The subnet on the left is 192.168.100.0, which you can figure out by the fact that the default gateway address on that server is 192.168.100.1.
- The subnet on the right is 192.168.100.128, which you can figure out by the fact that the default gateway address on that server is 192.168.100.129.
- The server on the right needs to be a DHCP relay agent so broadcast DHCP requests can reach the DHCP server.
- All clients can obtain their IP addresses automatically from the DHCP server once the DHCP relay agent is in place.

226 Chapter 4: Configuring and Troubleshooting DHCP

As far as the scopes go, you know that the subnet on the left is 192.168.100.0 and the subnet on the right is 192.168.100.128. So this must be a Class C address split into two subnets using a subnet mask of 255.255.255.128 (in other words, /25). You want to reserve ten IP addresses within each subnet's range, so you set the first stop to 192.168.100.11 to 192.168.100.126. (The address 192.168.100.127 is the broadcast address for that subnet, and hence cannot be assigned to clients.) The default gateway for that subnet is the connection to the server that's playing the role of router, 192.168.100.1.

The second scope needs to cover the subnet on the right, which is UP address 192.168.100.128 subnet mask 255.255.255.128. Again, you want to set aside ten IP addresses to assign to servers. So the scope for that subnet is 192.168.100.139 to 192.168.100.254. (The address 192.168.100.255 would be the broadcast address for that subnet.) The default gateway for that subnet is the router connection at 192.168.100.129.

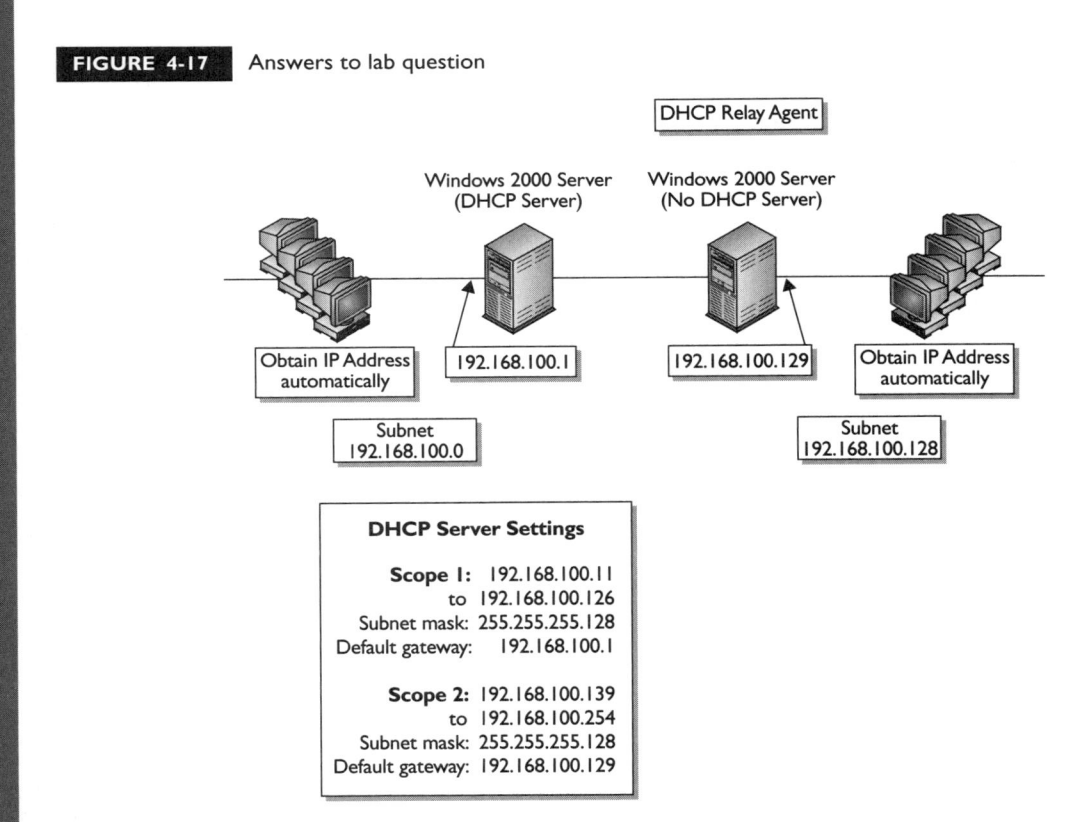

FIGURE 4-17 Answers to lab question

```
                              DHCP Relay Agent

              Windows 2000 Server    Windows 2000 Server
                 (DHCP Server)         (No DHCP Server)

  [Obtain IP Address]   192.168.100.1   192.168.100.129   [Obtain IP Address]
    automatically                                            automatically

        Subnet                                          Subnet
     192.168.100.0                                   192.168.100.128


              DHCP Server Settings

           Scope 1:  192.168.100.11
                 to  192.168.100.126
         Subnet mask: 255.255.255.128
         Default gateway:    192.168.100.1

           Scope 2: 192.168.100.139
                 to  192.168.100.254
         Subnet mask: 255.255.255.128
         Default gateway: 192.168.100.129
```

MCSA
MICROSOFT CERTIFIED SYSTEMS ADMINISTRATOR

Part II

Active Directory and Group Policy

CHAPTERS

5　Configuring and Implementing Active Directory

6　Creating and Implementing Group Policies

7　Sharing and Publishing Folders and Printers

8　Managing Software with Group Policy

9　Managing and Troubleshooting Active Directory

MCSA
MICROSOFT CERTIFIED SYSTEMS ADMINISTRATOR

5

Configuring and Implementing Active Directory

CERTIFICATION OBJECTIVES

5.01	Understand Active Directory Concepts
5.02	Manage Active Directory Groups
5.03	Administer AD Computers and Users
5.04	Create and Manage Organizational Units
5.05	Delegate Control
✓	Two-Minute Drill
Q&A	Self Test

Whereas the network infrastructure provides the basic connectivity of a network and low-level services like DHCP and DNS, Active Directory (AD) provides a higher-level means of administering and managing *objects* (in other words, computers, users, and shared resources) on the network. The term *directory* in this context has nothing to do with file directories (folders). Rather, Active Directory is a centralized and hierarchically organized store of information similar to a telephone directory, as illustrated in Figure 5-1. In a telephone directory, each person's name would equate to an object in Active Directory. The address and phone number for a given person would be considered *properties* or *attributes* of that person.

One beauty of Active Directory is that users can search for objects by name or by attributes, as opposed to scrolling through folders to try to find things the hard way. For example, suppose a network user needs to print something in color, but doesn't have a color printer attached to her own computer. She could search Active Directory for the "color printer" attribute to locate the names of all color printers that are available in the network. For the network administrator, Active Directory makes it easy to organize information into *containers* (folders) and then manage the containers as a whole.

FIGURE 5-1

Active Directory is a centralized store of information about all objects in the network.

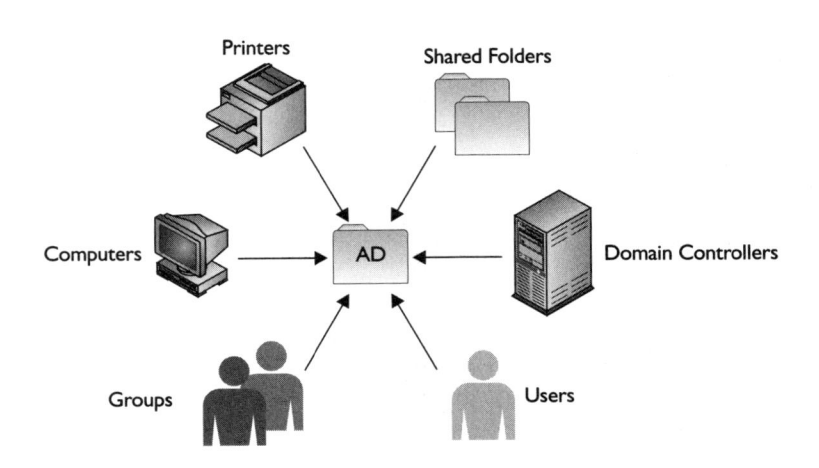

CERTIFICATION OBJECTIVE 5.01

Understand Active Directory Concepts

Active Directory is tightly integrated with DNS and shares the same namespace, which is to say that objects within the directory all have suffixes that end with the same name as the domain. Windows 2000 Active Directory Service (ADS) is based on the Lightweight Directory Access Protocol (LDAP), an industry-standard protocol. Active Directory also "borrows from" the X.500 naming standards defined in the RFCs, so it provides compatibility and interoperability with directory services that follow those standards.

AD Physical Layout

The physical layout of Active Directory relates to the actual hardware that defines the network, with a focus on two elements: domain controllers and Active Directory sites. As you probably know, any server computer in a network can play the role of *domain controller (DC)*, meaning that it provides logon and authentication services for the network (among other things). A *member server*, by contrast, is a server that doesn't provide logon and authentication, but instead "serves up" shared resources such as folders and printers. As you learned in Chapter 3, you can run the DCPROMO wizard to promote any Windows 2000 Server computer to the role of domain controller.

Domain Controllers

Microsoft generally recommends that you have at least two domain controllers per subnet in your network for fault tolerance and load balancing. Each domain controller maintains an identical copy of the Active Directory database in a file named NTDIS.DAT. Unlike NT 4.0, which used a primary domain controller (PDC) and backup domain controller (BDC) for fault tolerance, Windows 2000 uses *multimaster replication* to keep copies of the AD database in sync. As such, any domain controller can accept changes to the directory and replicate those changes to all other domain controllers. The relationships among the domain controllers, member servers, and client computers in a small network are illustrated in Figure 5-2.

FIGURE 5-2

Each domain controller stores an identical copy of the AD database.

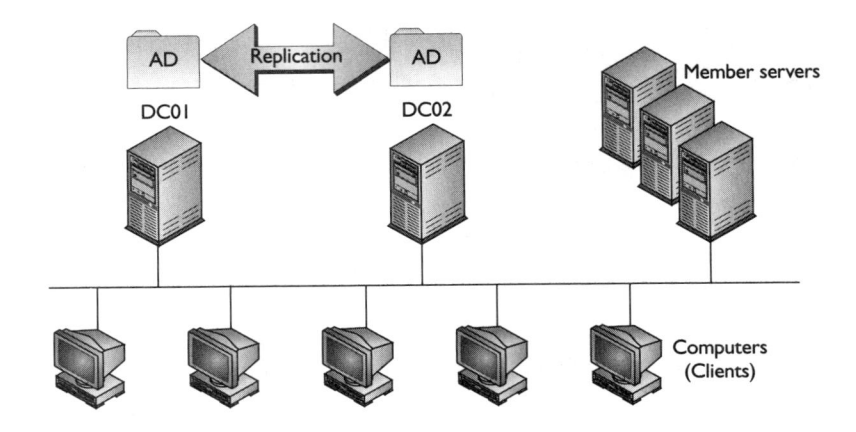

Active Directory Sites

A *site,* in Active Directory terminology, refers to any group of "well-connected" computers, such as those connected by 10 Mbps or 100 Mbps Ethernet connections. Or, put another way, a *site* is all the computers that can communicate without the aid of a WAN link. For example, the network shown in Figure 5-3 is divided into three sites joined by WAN links. The important point is that sites are not related to the namespace. A single domain namespace can be divided into any number of sites. You'll learn how to create and manage sites in Chapter 9.

AD Logical Structure

Whereas the domain controllers and sites make up the physical structure of Active Directory, the DNS namespace defines the logical structure. The logical structure of the directory is unrelated to the physical structure of the network. The major components of the logical structure are the domain, domain trees, forest, and organizational unit (OU).

Domains

The concept of a domain as a "security boundary," which you may have learned about from earlier NT versions of Windows, still applies as well. For example, let's say you are the network administrator for the mydomain.local domain. That only means you have administrative privileges for the mydomain.local domain, and

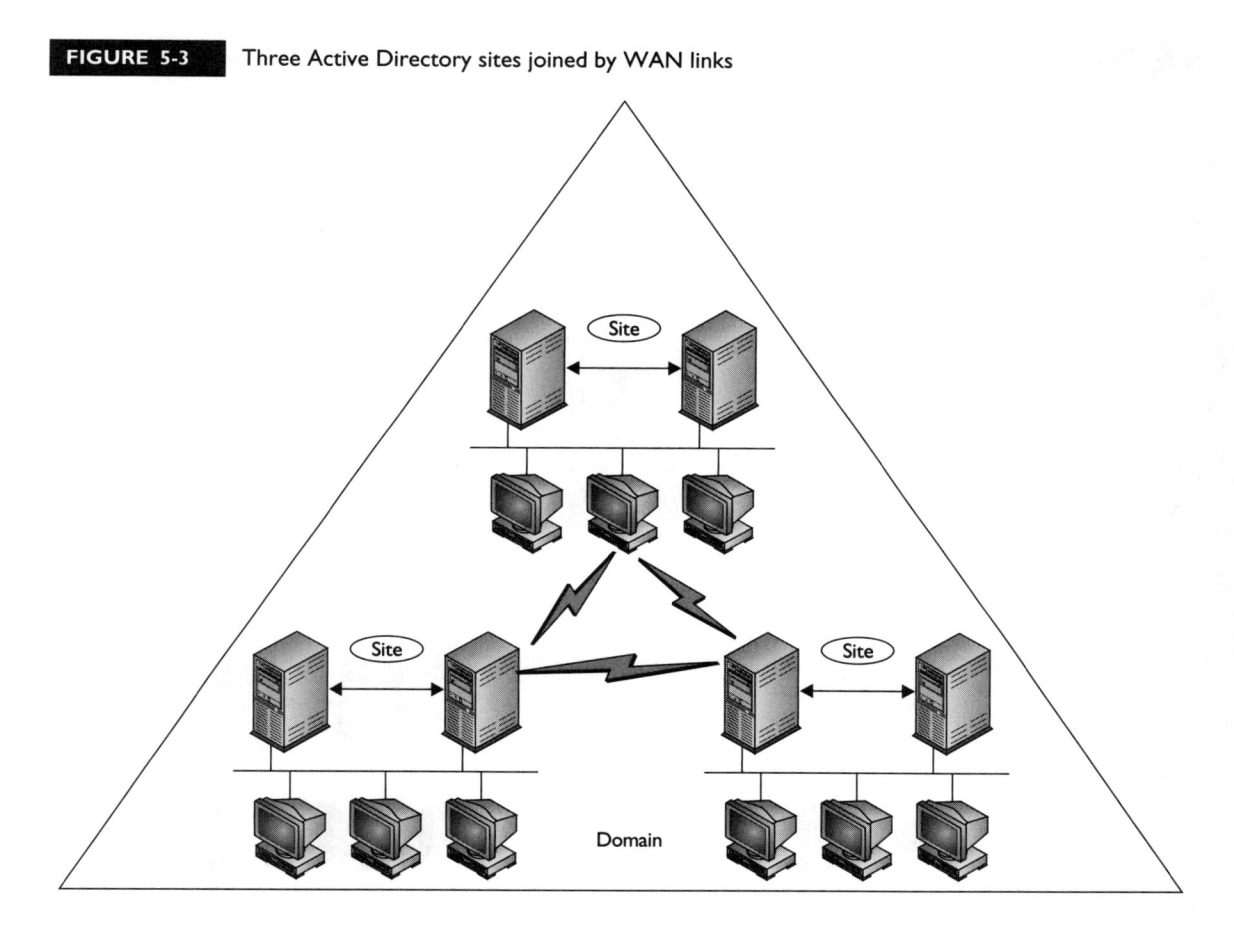

FIGURE 5-3 Three Active Directory sites joined by WAN links

grants you no additional privileges at microsoft.com, nasa.gov, or itef.org. In other words, your security privileges don't go beyond the boundaries of your own domain.

Trees

A *tree,* or *domain tree,* is a domain plus any subdomains (in other words, *child domains*) contained within that domain. Recall that the namespace of a subdomain is always *subnet.domainname.tld* and hosts within the subdomain have names like *something.subnet.domain.tld.* Many companies will create subdomains based on business unit or geographical location. For instance, Figure 5-4 shows a sample domain named xyz.com, which contains two child domains named biz.xyz.com and dev.xyz.com.

FIGURE 5-4 A sample domain tree

xyz.com domain

bix.xyz.com child domain

dev.xyz.com child domain

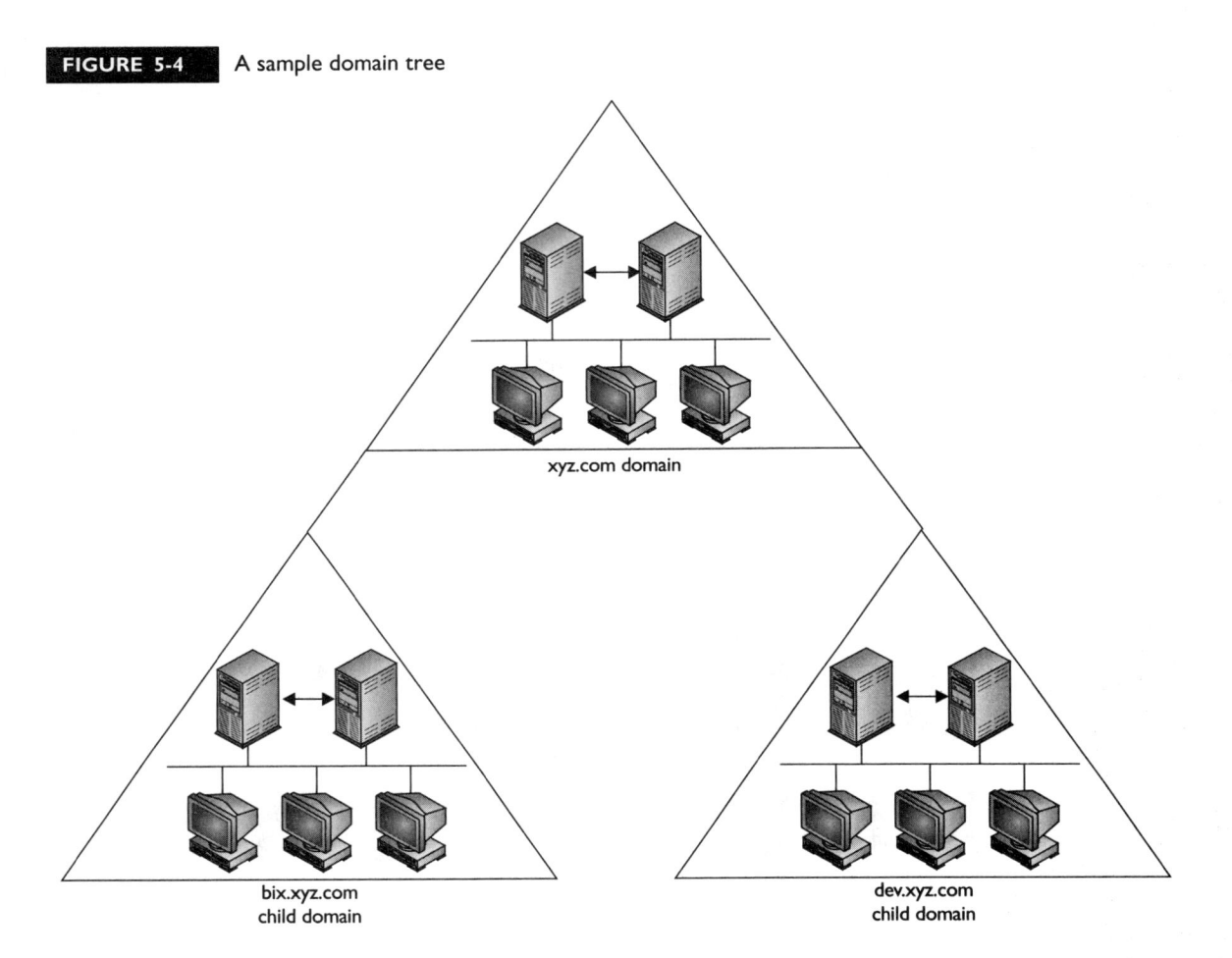

In the example, replication will still take place among all three domains (all six servers, since each domain has two servers). Figure 5-4 represents a logical *domain tree*. The physical hardware used to connect the domains is irrelevant when you're talking about the logical structure of the domain tree.

Forests

The term *forest* refers to all the objects that are managed by an Active Directory database. A forest can contain a single domain, domain trees, or even multiple domains. The ability to have multiple domains within a forest does away with the need to treat each domain as a separate unit of security. For example, let's say GeneralSpecificX.com buys MajorMinorX.com. GeneralSpecificX wants to keep the original name recognition of MajorMinorX, but would like to manage that network as part of its overall network. In that case, GeneralSpecificX need only add the MajorMinorX domain to their forest, as illustrated in Figure 5-5.

Transitive Trusts

In Windows NT, each domain represented a single security boundary, and any *trust* relationships between domains needed to be created manually. For example, if a user logged in to one domain, that login would not apply to any other domains. The user would have to log in to the second domain independently, unless the administrator set up a trust between the two domains. That's because NT used one-way NTLM trusts.

Active Directory uses Kerberos trusts, which are *transitive* (two-way). Thus, in Windows 2000, all domains in a tree, and all domain trees in a forest, automatically trust each other. For example, referring to Figure 5-5, let's say a user logs in to GeneralSpecific.com. Given appropriate permissions, the user could then access resources in all the domains and subdomains within the entire forest. The administrator need not take any additional steps to create the trusts.

Transitive trusts also pass through intermediate domains. For example, let's say Domain A trusts Domains B and C, as in Figure 5-6. Domains B and C will trust each other as well. There's no need to create an explicit trust there.

> **exam** ⓦatch
>
> *Transitive trusts work on all domains within a forest. If, for whatever reason, you prefer not to have so much trust between two domains, you can place them in separate forests, and then use NT-style explicit trusts to define security links between the domains.*

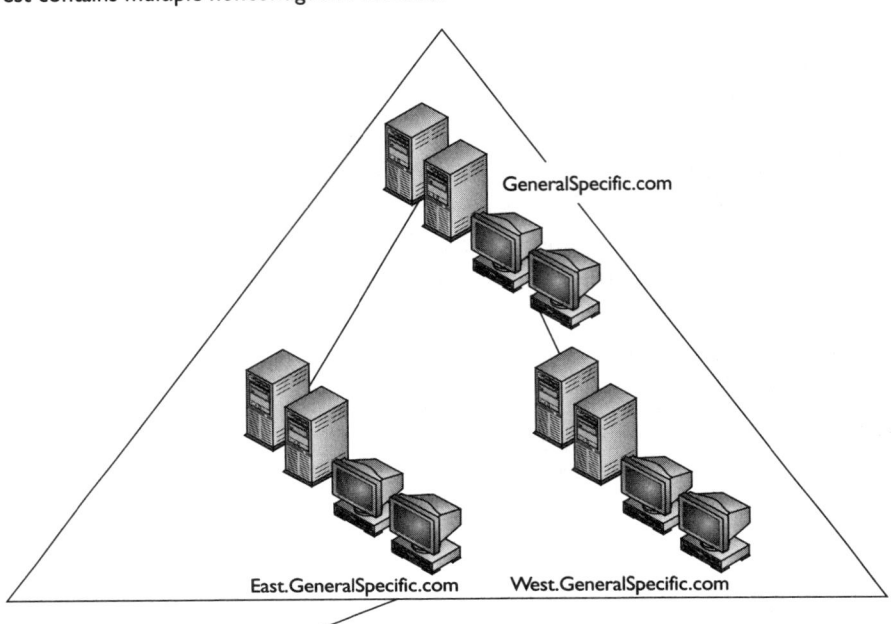

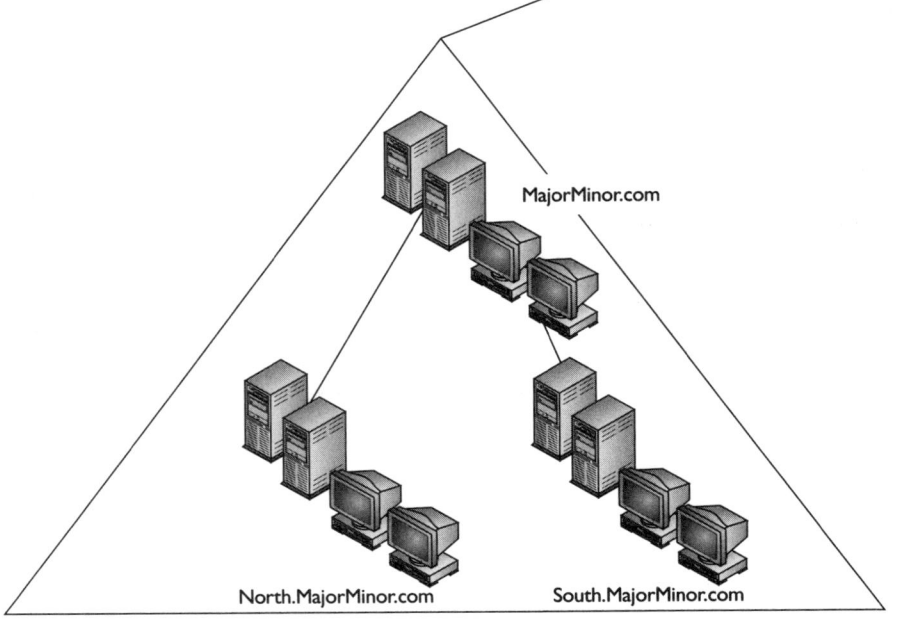

FIGURE 5-5   A forest contains multiple noncontiguous domains.

FIGURE 5-6

Transitive trusts are two-way.

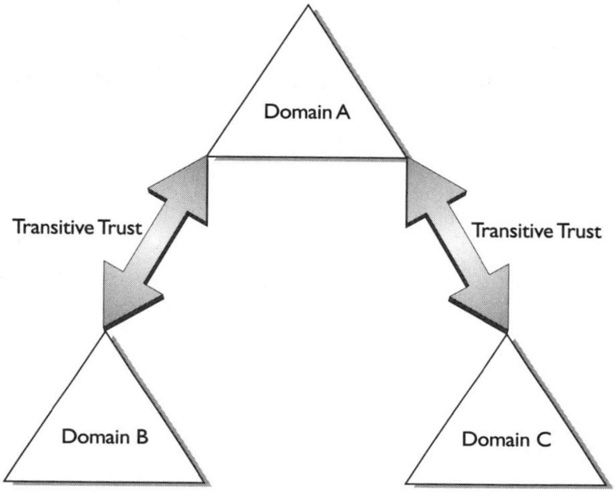

Organizational Units

In Windows NT, the domain was the smallest "unit of security" that you could create. Companies would set up multiple domains to delegate security to specific groups, and then suffer through the process of manually creating trusts to allow people to access resources on multiple domains. The process usually led to many administrative nightmares.

In Windows 2000, the domain is no longer the smallest unit of security, thanks to the *organizational unit,* or OU. An OU is a container object within Active Directory that, like a domain, defines administrative boundaries. An OU can contain any subset of computers, users, groups, printers, or even other OUs within the domain.

The beauty of OUs is that you can delegate administrative control to all objects within that OU. For example, let's suppose you want administrator "Josephine" to have administrative control over objects in her department, but not necessarily the entire domain. All you have to do is create an OU, place into it the items you wish to delegate control over, and give Josephine administrative control over that OU only.

Admittedly, you really wouldn't create an OU based on a particular user. It makes more sense to divide a domain up into OUs based on department, or geographical location. For example, let's say you have a single domain named GeneralSpecific.com. You want to delegate some responsibilities and privileges to administrators within various departments. You could just create an OU for each department, as shown in Figure 5-7.

FROM THE CLASSROOM

Benefits of Active Directory

Today's business networks have evolved well beyond the days of the simple file and printer sharing. Many corporations are now struggling with managing diverse, distributed networks, doing business over the Internet, and managing huge numbers of network resources and users. Active Directory was designed from the ground up to meet those needs. Experienced NT administrators need to be aware that, in many ways, Active Directory is a whole new ball game. Important features include

- **Simplified resource management** The ability to build hierarchical information structures makes it easier for administrators to manage network resources, and easier for users to find those resources.

- **Flexible authentication and authorization** Active Directory lowers the barriers to doing business over the Internet by supporting multiple authentication and authorization services including Kerberos Authentication v5 and x.509v3 certificates.

- **Group Policies** Active Directory allows you to create policies that define logon and password requirements, configure locked-down desktop settings, and more. Policy-based management also simplifies the installation of application programs and distribution of operating system updates.

- **Scalability** Active Directory can store millions of network objects per domain, and uses advanced indexing algorithms and multimaster replication to maximize performance.

- **Adherence to Internet standards** Active Directory uses a DNS-based namespace and follows LDAP standards for maximum interoperability with other systems. Active Directory Services Interface (ADSI) provides a powerful development environment to encourage third-party vendors to create AD-integrated applications.

Taking full advantage of these new features will require some serious planning. The planning phase should include upper and middle managers, IT personnel, systems, operations, security managers, and even users. The goal should be to create a structure that reflects the structure of the organization, and yet remains flexible enough to accommodate growth and changing needs.

—*Alan Simpson, MA, MCSA*

Understand Active Directory Concepts 239

FIGURE 5-7

A single domain containing multiple OUs based on department

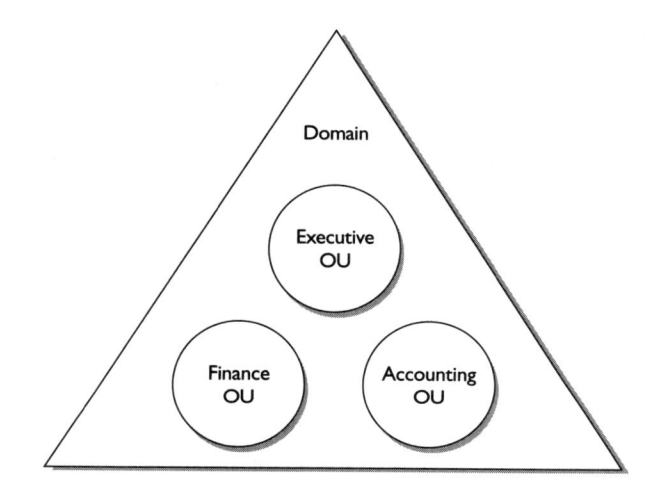

[Diagram: Triangle labeled "Domain" containing three circles: "Executive OU", "Finance OU", "Accounting OU"]

Optionally, you could create a single domain and then base OUs on geographical location, as shown in Figure 5-8.

It might help to think of an OU as being similar to a folder. Just as a folder can contain multiple documents, an OU can contain multiple network objects. An OU is also similar to a folder in that an OU can contain still more OUs, just as a folder can contain still more folders. For example, if you created a separate OU for each major corporate site, all of those OUs could contain still other OUs, as in the example shown in Figure 5-9.

FIGURE 5-8

A domain divided into OUs based on geographical location

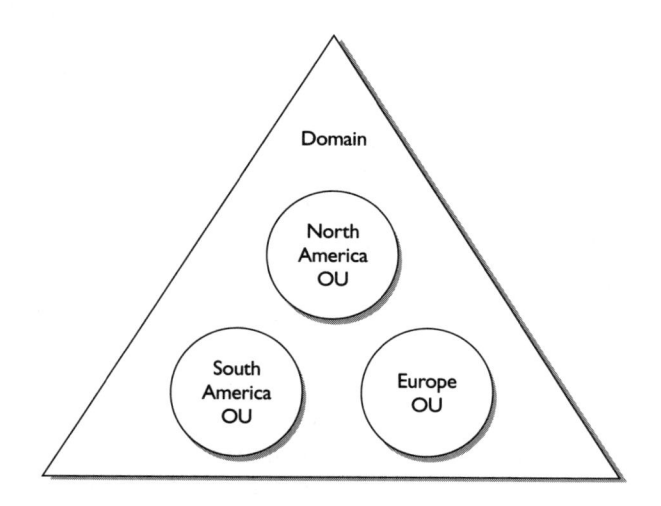

[Diagram: Triangle labeled "Domain" containing three circles: "North America OU", "South America OU", "Europe OU"]

FIGURE 5-9

An OU can contain other OUs.

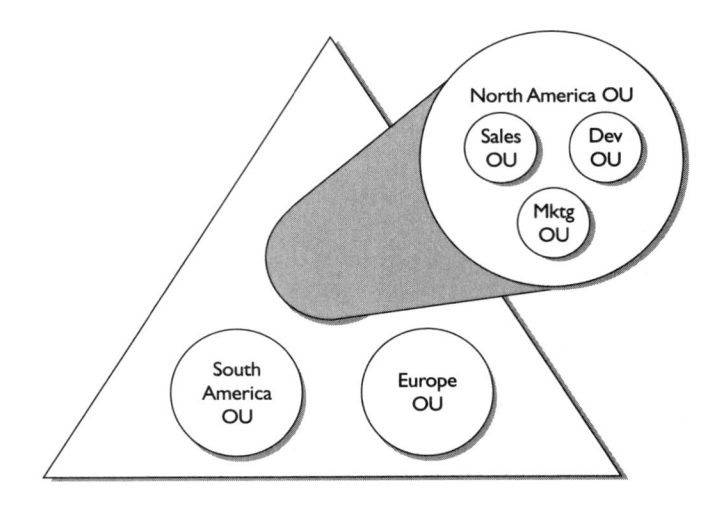

The Global Catalog

In a large Active Directory installation with multiple domains, there may be many thousands of objects stored in the directory, each with a considerable number of objects. When you start looking at multiple domains in a forest, each with its own directory, you can imagine that AD replication across all the domain controllers could become quite time and bandwidth intensive. To make replication across multiple domains, Windows 2000 stores replica information from the directory in the *global catalog*. The global catalog stores a full replica of every object from its own domain, and a partial replica of every object from other domains. The partial replicas contain some, but not all, of the properties of the objects from the other domains. The properties stored are those that are most likely to be used by people or programs searching for resources across domains.

The global catalog is also used to authenticate users and check group memberships during the logon process. Ideally, you'd probably want at least two of them because, if the one and only global catalog goes down, there won't be any way to log on to the domain. So, if you have two domain controllers, allow each to host a copy of the global catalog. On the other hand, if you have many domain controllers, you wouldn't necessarily want them all to host a global catalog, as that would add replication overhead.

By default, the first domain controller you create will host a global catalog. But you can easily enable or disable the global catalog on any domain controller using the Active Directory Sites and Services Snap-in. Just click the Start button and choose Programs | Administrative Tools | Active Directory Sites And Services. Expand all nodes under Sites until you get to the NTDS Settings under the name of the domain controller, as shown in Figure 5-10. Right-click NTDS Settings and choose Properties. On the General tab, you can select or clear the Global Catalog check box to enable or disable the global catalog on that domain controller.

EXERCISE 5-1

Enabling Global Catalog

In this exercise, you'll get some hands-on experience using the AD Sites and Services console, and verify that your domain controller is storing a global catalog. This exercise assumes you've already promoted the server to a domain controller using DCPROMO, as was discussed in Chapter 3. Also, the exercise assumes that you're currently logged in to the server with administrative privileges. As always, if you're working in a production network environment, check with the network administrator

FIGURE 5-10   The NTDS Settings option is highlighted.

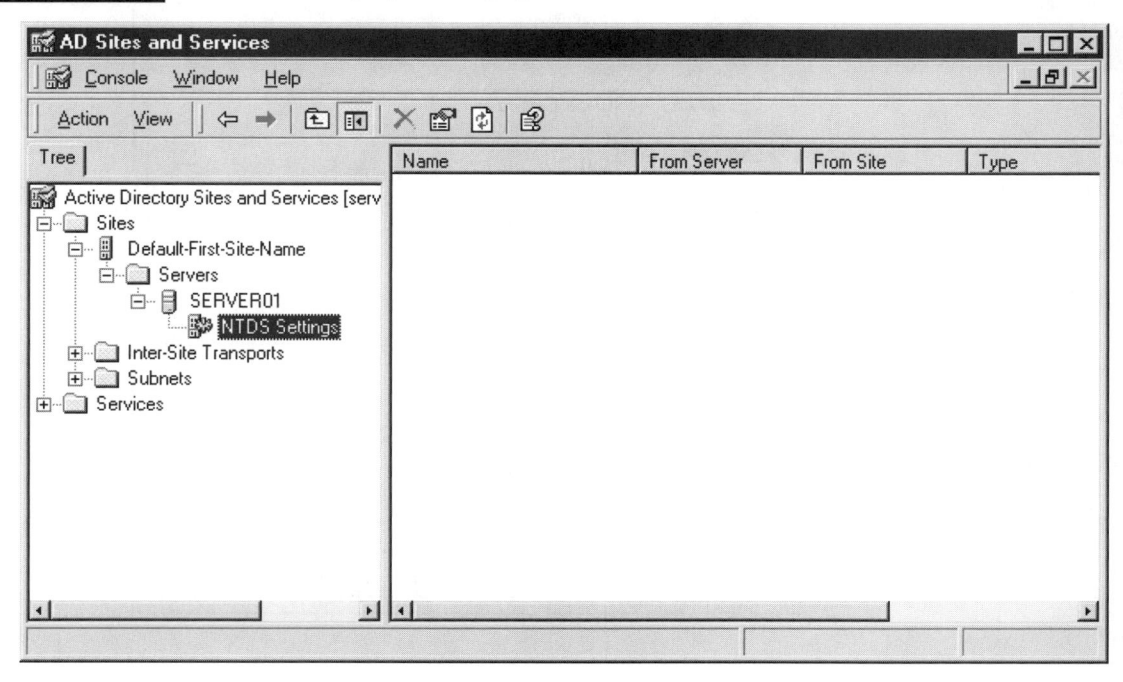

242 Chapter 5: Configuring and Implementing Active Directory

before changing the Global Catalog setting on your domain controller. Follow these steps:

1. Click the Start button and choose Programs | Administrative Tools | Active Directory Sites and Services.
2. Expand the Sites category and all subcategories, until you find NTDS Settings (NT Directory Services).
3. Right-click the NTDS Settings option and choose Properties.
4. On the General tab, verify that the Global Catalog option is selected, as shown in Figure 5-11.
5. Optionally, you can enter a reminder to yourself that the option is selected.

FIGURE 5-11

Global Catalog is selected (enabled).

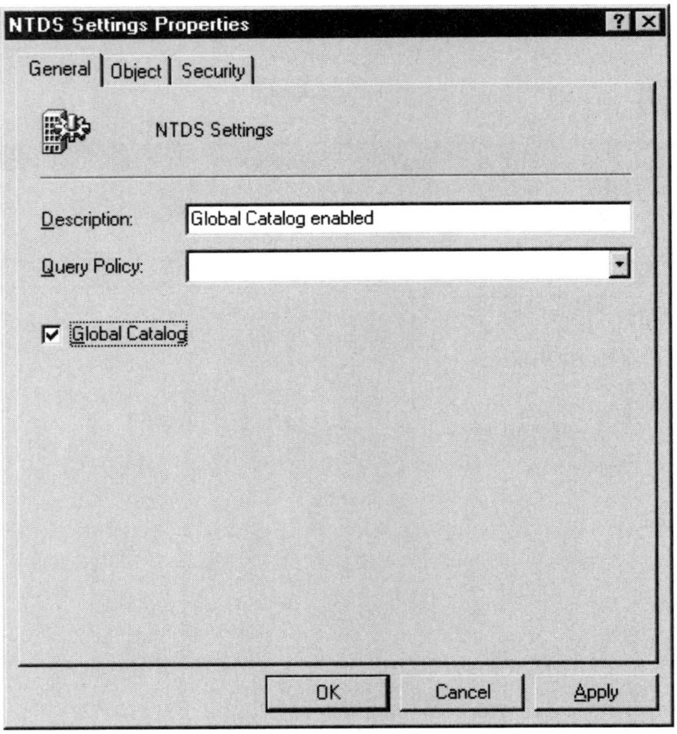

6. Click the OK button.

You can close the AD Sites and Services console as well.

CERTIFICATION OBJECTIVE 5.02

Manage Active Directory Groups

One class of network objects you can manage through Active Directory is *groups*. There are two major categories of groups you can create:

- **Security groups**   Each group defines a set of rights and permissions. Users who are members of that group automatically have all the rights and permissions that the security group provides. You might think of a security group as a "job description" that provides it members enough power to do their job, but not enough power to make a mess of things on the network.

- **Distribution groups**   Defines groups to be used by AD-aware applications such as Exchange 2000. You can make users members of distribution groups, but you cannot assign permissions to users through distribution groups.

As you probably know, assigning rights and permissions to users is a big part of the network administrator's job. So, we'll focus on security groups here for a while.

exam 🕑 **a t c h**   ***When you come across a question dealing with rights and permissions, keep in mind that distribution groups are for applications, not for people. You cannot grant permissions to users through distribution groups.***

Security groups will allow you to define rights and permissions. There's a subtle difference between the two. A *right* is the ability to perform some specific action, such as perform a backup or install new programs. A *permission,* on the other hand, has to do with accessing a shared resource. For example, you might create a shared folder on the network, give some users permission to access that folder, and deny other users permission to access the folder. Rights, on the other hand, have to do with things users can do. As you'll learn in Chapter 6, you can use Group Policies in Windows 2000 to assign rights.

Security Group Scopes

Security groups have *scopes*, which define how "far" the rights and privileges defined within the security extend throughout the network. If you open the Active Directory Users and Computers console from the Administrative Tools menu, open the Users folder, and sort existing groups by type, as shown in Figure 5-12, you'll notice that there are three types of security groups. (Though listed in the Type column, each actually defines a scope.) Here's what each scope represents:

- **Domain Local Security Group** Permissions apply to the local domain only, and will not extend to other domains. Users and groups from any domain can be added to the group. Example: Joe from the XYZ domain also has a domain local account in the ABC domain.

FIGURE 5-12 Active Directory Users and Computers sorted by Type

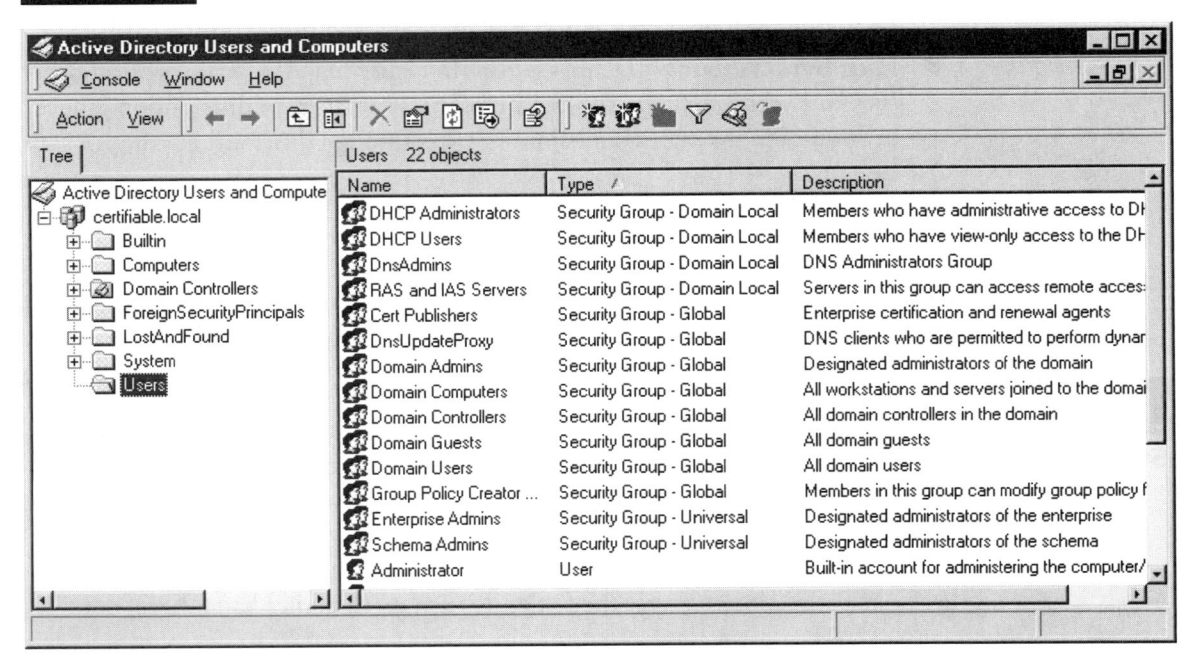

Name	Type	Description
DHCP Administrators	Security Group - Domain Local	Members who have administrative access to DH
DHCP Users	Security Group - Domain Local	Members who have view-only access to the DH
DnsAdmins	Security Group - Domain Local	DNS Administrators Group
RAS and IAS Servers	Security Group - Domain Local	Servers in this group can access remote acces
Cert Publishers	Security Group - Global	Enterprise certification and renewal agents
DnsUpdateProxy	Security Group - Global	DNS clients who are permitted to perform dynar
Domain Admins	Security Group - Global	Designated administrators of the domain
Domain Computers	Security Group - Global	All workstations and servers joined to the domai
Domain Controllers	Security Group - Global	All domain controllers in the domain
Domain Guests	Security Group - Global	All domain guests
Domain Users	Security Group - Global	All domain users
Group Policy Creator ...	Security Group - Global	Members in this group can modify group policy f
Enterprise Admins	Security Group - Universal	Designated administrators of the enterprise
Schema Admins	Security Group - Universal	Designated administrators of the schema
Administrator	User	Built-in account for administering the computer/

- **Global Security Group** Permissions apply to the entire forest. However, membership is limited to members of the domain to which the group belongs. Example: the ABC domain has a global security group that allows members of the ABC domain to use resources across the entire forest.
- **Universal Security Group** Permissions apply to any domain within the forest. Members can come from any domain in the forest. Example: ABC domain grants permissions to objects throughout the forest. Any user from any domain can log in and access resources throughout the forest. Available in native mode only.

Universal security groups only work in *native mode*, and not in *mixed mode*. You can use native mode only if all of the domain controllers in the network are Windows 2000 or later servers. If the network contains NT 4 (or earlier) domain controllers, then you must use mixed mode until all the domain controllers have been upgraded to Windows 2000. (The same doesn't apply to distribution groups. Universal distribution groups can exist in mixed mode, but those groups work only with AD-aware applications.)

on the Job

If you plan to upgrade all domain controllers with Windows 2000 in the future, you can stay in mixed mode and use domain local security groups. Later, when you've upgraded all the domain controllers, you can switch to native mode and convert domain local groups to universal groups at your convenience.

Mixed mode is the default setting for Windows 2000. Once you switch to native mode, there's no going back to mixed mode. So, you wouldn't want to switch to native mode unless you're certain that there are not, and will not be, any pre-Windows 2000 Server domain controllers in your network.

EXERCISE 5-2

Switching to Native Mode

To get some experience in working with universal security groups, you'll need to switch to native mode. If you're working in a live, production environment, you'll need to check with the network administrator before doing this. But, if you're using a small, personal network with one or two Windows 2000 domain controllers, there won't be any harm in switching to native mode. You must be logged in to the domain controller with administrative privileges to perform this exercise:

1. Click the Start button and choose Programs | Administrative Tools | Active Directory Domains And Trusts.
2. Right-click the name of your domain in the console tree and choose Properties.
3. In the Properties dialog box, verify that you are in mixed mode, as in the example shown in Figure 5-13.
4. Click the Change Mode button and follow the instructions on the screen.

FIGURE 5-13

This domain is currently operating in mixed mode.

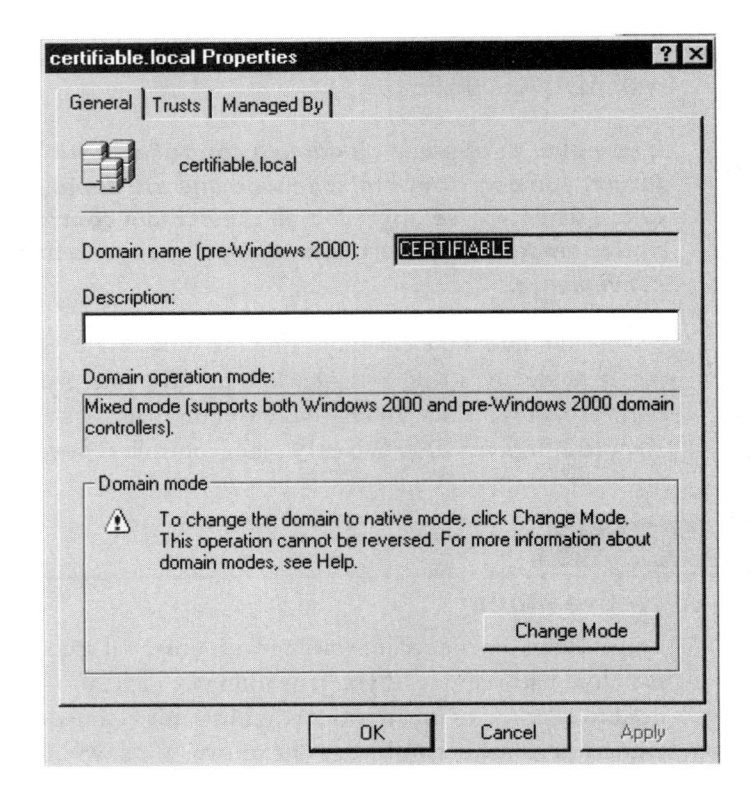

Predefined Groups

As mentioned, you can create security groups as appropriate for your network. However, as you may have noticed back in Figure 5-12, Windows 2000 comes with several predefined groups. Some users are added to some of these groups automatically. Some of the predefined groups might not be used at all. But you can use them if it's convenient to do so. The name, type, and a brief description of each predefined user group appears when you open the Users folder in Active Directory Users and Computers. Groups you'll want to be familiar with right off the bat are summarized here:

- **Domain Admins (Global)** Identifies users who have administrative privileges within the domain.
- **Domain Computers (Global)** Contains all computers and servers that are members of the domain.
- **Domain Guests (Global)** Guests of the domain who have very limited permissions.
- **Domain Users (Global)** Regular users of the domain who can log in and use resources, but do not have the broad range of rights and permissions of an administrator.
- **Enterprise Admins (Universal)** Administrators who have broad rights and permissions that extend across all domains in the forest.
- **Schema Admins (Universal)** Administrators with broad rights and permissions spanning all domains in the forest, with the additional right to modify the Active Directory schema. As you create accounts within the domain, some types of accounts will automatically be added to certain groups, as summarized next:
  - Any user account you create in a domain is automatically added to the Domain Users group.
  - Any computer account you create is automatically added to the Domain Computers group.

In a moment, you'll create a couple of accounts and be able to see this for yourself. First, we need to discuss the builtin groups that also exist on client and server computers.

Builtin Groups

In addition to the groups that appear in the Users folder of Active Directory Users and Computers, there are several *builtin* groups, which grant certain rights to their members automatically. These fall into two categories: local builtin and domain local builtin. The terminology is awful, especially since the domain local builtin groups show *Builtin Local* as their type in Active Directory Users and Groups. But, it's not as bad as it sounds once you see where the groups are located.

Local Builtin Groups

Local builtin groups exist on client computers, member servers, and stand-alone servers—not on domain controllers. They grant permissions to objects on the local computer only, such as a shared folder on that local computer's hard disk. To get to the local builtin groups on a Windows 2000 Professional computer, you open the Control Panel, open Administrative Tools, and click the Computer Management icon. In the console tree, expand the Local Users and Groups category and click Groups. Builtin groups appear in the details pane, as shown in Figure 5-14. There is no Type (scope) column because these are all local groups that have the same scope—they apply to resources on the current computer only.

on the job

As in NT 4, local users and groups on Windows 2000 Professional workstations, stand-alone servers, and member servers are stored in the Security Accounts Manager (SAM) file, in the system32\config folder of the system root. Domain-based accounts and groups are stored in the Active NTDS.DIT file, usually found in the NTDS folder of the system root. Windows 2000 domain controllers don't have a local SAM.

FIGURE 5-14 Local builtin groups on a Windows 2000 Professional computer

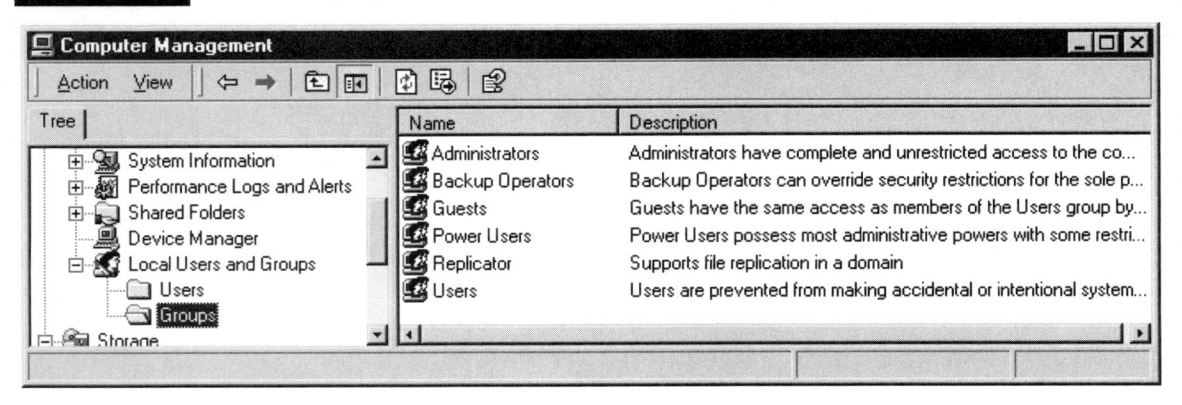

Domain Builtin Local Groups

On your domain controller, you'll find groups with similar builtin permissions for common administrative roles in the Builtin folder of Active Directory Users and Computers, as shown in Figure 5-15. But, unlike the groups on the Windows 2000 Professional computer, these builtin groups grant rights to the local domain. For example, a member of the Printer Operators group on a domain controller (in other words, in Active Directory Users and Groups) can administer printers throughout the domain.

The main point to keep in mind at this juncture is that groups exist primarily to allow you to work with groups of user accounts, as opposed to individual user accounts. As an example, let's say you have a shared printer on the network, and you want to give all domain users access to that printer. You could simply assign permissions for the printer within the Domain Users group, as opposed to granting permissions to each user account individually. Alternatively, you could put the Domain Users group into a domain local group that has permissions for the printer. Which brings us to the topic of nesting groups.

Nesting Groups

Groups can be *nested*, which is to say a group can contain still other groups. As an example of why you might want to nest groups, consider any organization that

FIGURE 5-15 AD Users and Computers Builtin groups

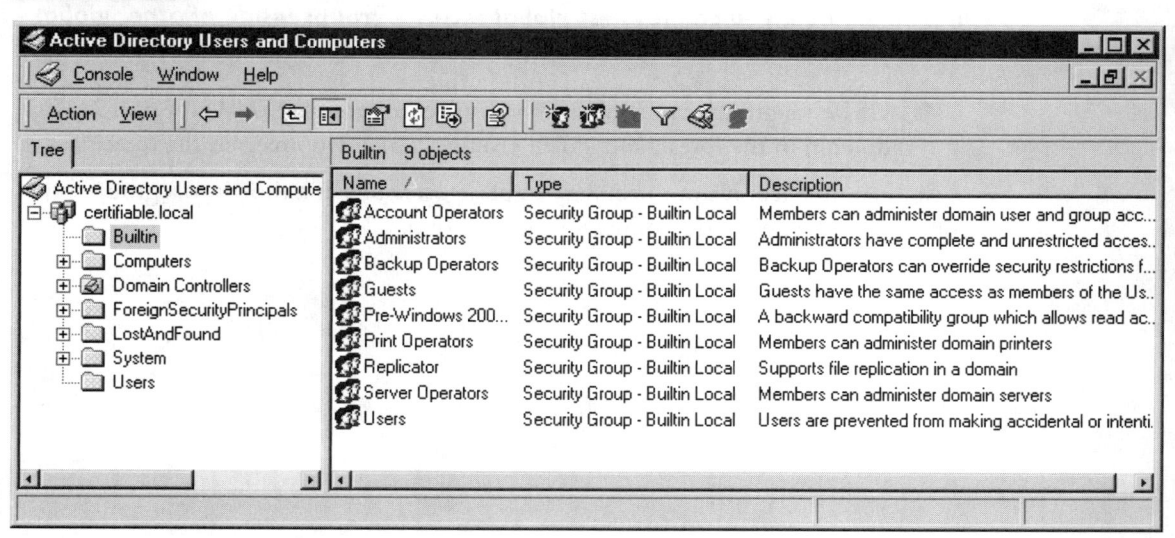

consists of divisions or departments. Let's say you create a separate security group for each department, so that you can individually grant permissions to users within each department to resources they need. But suppose there are some permissions that apply to all departments, such as permission to access resources in a company-wide shared folder. You *could* just add that permission to each departmental group. But it would be easier to create a group for the entire company that grants access to the company-wide shared folder, and then put all the departmental security groups inside that "company" security group.

There are some rules about what the different types of groups can contain, as summarized here:

- Local groups on a Windows 2000 Professional computer can contain domain local groups, global groups, and universal groups from the same domain. They can also contain global and universal groups from trusted domains, and global groups from trusted NT 4 domains.

- Domain local groups on a Windows 2000 domain controller can contain universal and global groups from any domain in the forest, global groups from the same domain, and user accounts from any domain in the forest. In native mode, domain local groups can contain other domain local groups from the same domain.

- Global groups can contain user accounts from the same domain, as well as other global groups from the same domain.

exam
Watch

In mixed mode, you cannot nest global security groups inside of other global security groups. That's only available in native mode.

- Universal groups can contain other universal groups, global groups from any domain in the forest, and global groups from any domain in the forest.

So, in a nutshell, it's not necessary to place users one at a time into a group, since you can put a whole group of users inside a group.

Creating a Security Group

Now that you have an idea of what security groups are all about, let's take a moment to go through the steps you'd follow to create a new security group. First, you'd want to open Active Directory Users and Computers, expand the node for the server, right-click the Users container, and choose New | Group. The New Object – Group dialog box appears. Then you'd fill in the blanks, summarized here, as shown in Figure 5-16.

- **Group name**   The name you want to give the group.
- **Group name (pre-Windows 2000)**   Automatically generated from the Group Name entry.
- **Group scope**   Choose how "far reaching" you want the account to be. The Universal option is only available in native mode.

FIGURE 5-16

The New Object – Group dialog box

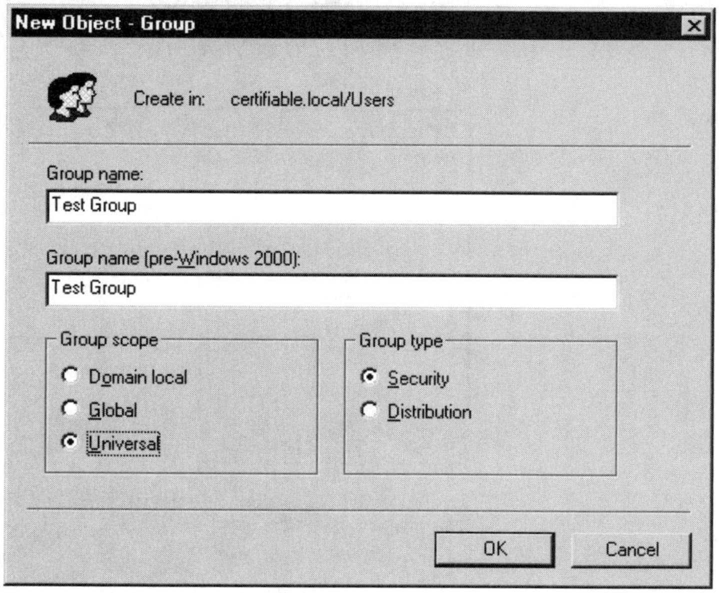

252 Chapter 5: Configuring and Implementing Active Directory

- **Group type** Obviously, you'd choose Security here to create a new security group. Distribution groups aren't related to security, but contain e-mail addresses and other information about users to whom you might want to distribute some file.

After you've filled in the blanks and clicked the OK button, the group name appears in the list of groups. To create members within the group, you'd right-click the group name, choose Properties, and click the Members tab. There you'll find a simple Add button that will allow you to specify who you want to be members of the group. The Member Of tab in that same dialog box, shown in Figure 5-17, would allow you to nest this group within some other group.

Now that you've learned about security groups, let's take a look at some potential scenarios and their solutions.

FIGURE 5-17

The Member Of tab lets you make a group a member of some other existing group.

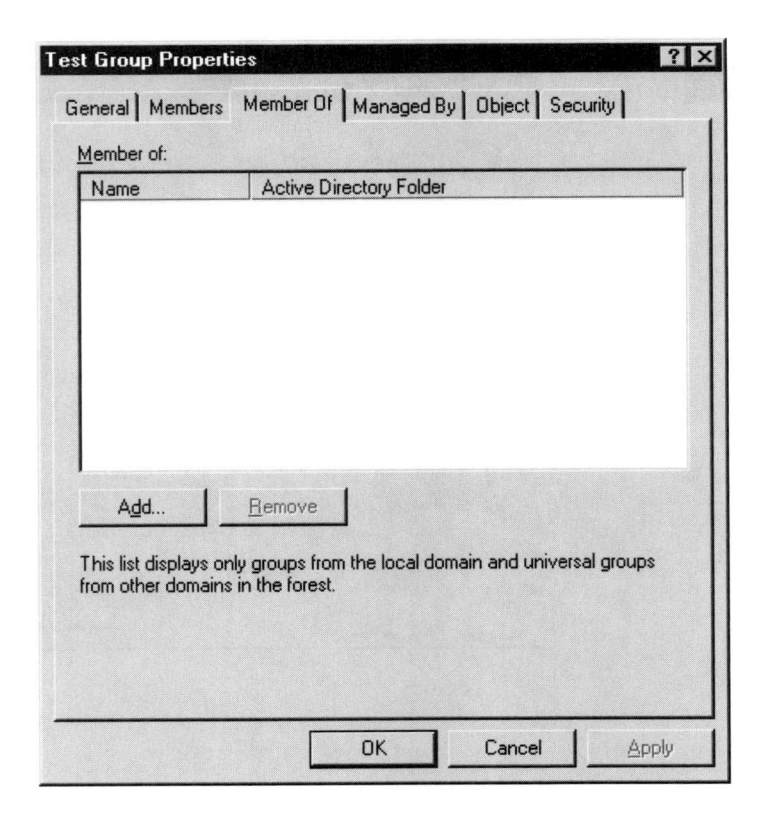

SCENARIO & SOLUTION

I've heard that Active Directory stores all kinds of properties for every object. But when I create an object, I don't see a whole lot of properties to fill in. Where are all these properties?	After you create an object, you can right-click its icon in Active Directory Users and Groups and choose Properties to get to the full set of properties for that object.
I created a domain local distribution group. Now I'm thinking it should have been a Universal security group. I'm using native mode. So how can I change a group's scope and type?	In Active Directory Users and Computers, right-click the group's icon and choose Properties. On the General tab of the Properties dialog box, you'll see options for changing the group's scope and type.
It seems as though global groups and universal groups are very similar. So why not just use universal groups for everything?	Remember that universal groups are available only in native mode. If you have any NT 4 domain controllers still in the network, you'll have to stick with global groups until you upgrade all the domain controllers.

CERTIFICATION OBJECTIVE 5.03

Administer AD Computers and Users

Every computer in a domain has a *computer account* that uniquely identifies that computer in the domain. Computer accounts are contained within the global security group named Domain Computers in Active Directory Users and Computers. Usually, the first step to add a new computer to an Active Directory domain is to create a Computer account for that computer. To do this, you need to log in to the domain controller with administrative privileges. Open Active Directory Users and Computers, right-click the Computers container in the console tree, and choose New | Computer. Type in a computer name (just the "host" portion, no dots). The dialog box will automatically generate a pre-Windows 2000 computer name from the first 15 characters of the name you specify.

You can choose which user or group can join the computer to the domain once the account is created. The default is to allow Domain Administrators to do this, although you can click the Change button and choose a different user or group if appropriate. If the computer for which you're adding the account is not running

254 Chapter 5: Configuring and Implementing Active Directory

Windows 2000, be sure to select the Allow Pre-Windows 2000 Computers To Use This Account option. Click OK. Once you've created the computer account, you can join the computer to the domain, as discussed later in this chapter.

EXERCISE 5-3

CertCam 5-3

Adding a Computer Account

In this exercise, you'll add a computer account to Active Directory. You'll need to log on to the domain controller with administrative privileges to do this. Follow these steps once you're logged on to the domain controller:

1. Click the Start button and choose Programs | Administrative Tools | Active Directory Users And Computers.

2. As necessary, expand the node that represents the domain to which you'll be adding an account, and then click the Computers container, as shown in Figure 5-18, to view any computers that already have accounts (there aren't any yet in the figure).

FIGURE 5-18 The Computers container open in Active Directory Users and Computers

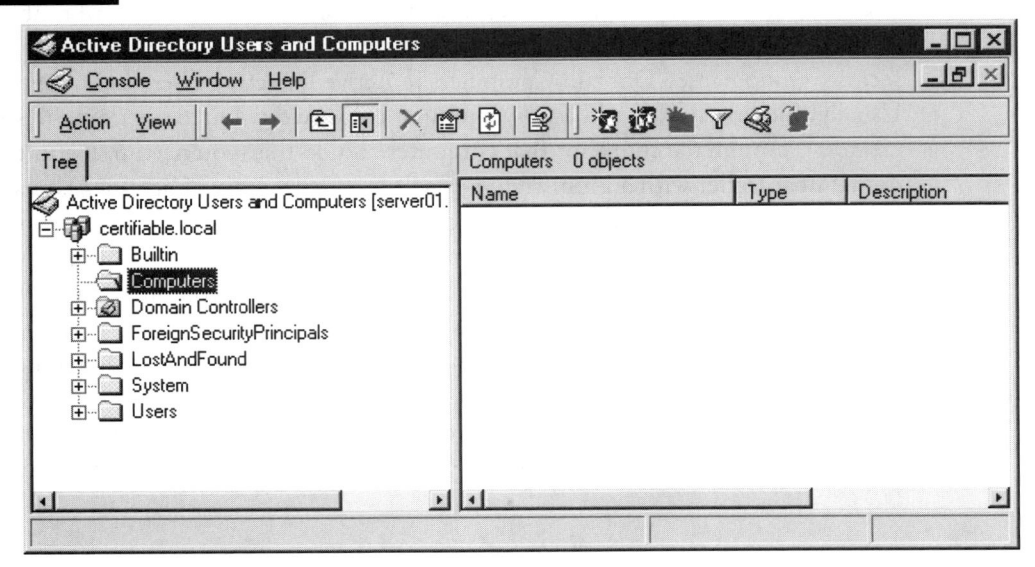

3. Type in the name of the computer you wish to add, as shown in Figure 5-19. The pre-Windows 2000 (NetBIOS) name will be the first 15 characters of the name you enter.

The computer account is added to the Computers container in Active Directory Users and Computers.

You can see which computers already have accounts in Active Directory Users and Computers by opening the Computers container in the console tree.

Adding a computer account is *usually* an easy task, though there is one peculiar issue that sometimes creeps up on people, leaving them somewhat stymied. Windows 2000 is preconfigured to allow members of the Authenticated Users group, who don't have administrative privileges, to add up to ten computer accounts to the domain. It does this by granting the Add Workstations To Domain privilege to the Authenticated Users group. You can use this to allow users to add their own workstations to the domain, so you don't have to do it yourself. The user can do this from his or her own workstation.

FIGURE 5-19

Adding a new computer account (object) to Active Directory

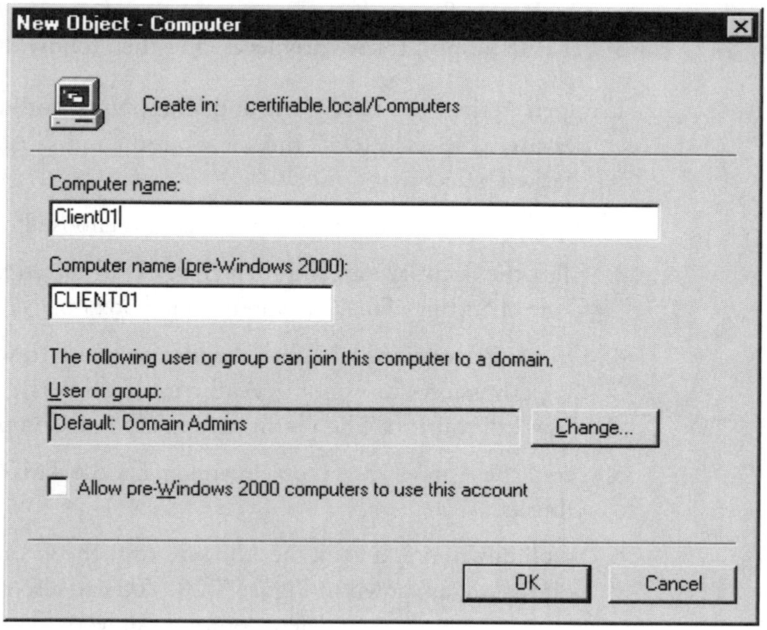

When trying to add an eleventh computer to the domain, an error message will appear. If the computer being added is a Windows 2000 Professional machine, the error message is fairly descriptive:

```
Your computer could not be joined to the domain. You have
exceeded the maximum number of computer accounts you are allowed
to create in this domain. Contact your system administrator to
have this limit reset or increased.
```

If the computer is a Windows NT 4 client, the error message that appears isn't quite so helpful:

```
The machine account for this computer either does not exist or
is unavailable.
```

There are a couple of ways around this problem. One is for the administrator to add computer accounts for all workstations, but that approach negates the convenience of having users create their own computer accounts. The second solution is to grant the Create Computer Objects and Delete Computer Objects permissions to appropriate groups or accounts in the Computers container. For example, you could allow Authenticated Users (a very broad group) to create computer objects. To use the latter method, you'd need to log on to the domain controller with administrative privileges, and then follow these steps:

1. Open Active Directory Users and Computers, and make sure that Advanced Features is selected (click the View button and, if Advanced Features is not checked, select that option).

2. Right-click the Computers container and choose Properties.

3. Click the Security tab, and then click its Advanced button. The Access Control Settings For Computers dialog box opens.

4. On the Permissions tab, click the user or group to which you want to apply the permission (for example, Authenticated Users), and then click the View/Edit button. The Permission Entry For Computers dialog box opens.

5. From the Apply Onto drop-down list, choose This Object And All Child Objects.

6. Scroll down to and click the Allow box for the Create Computer Objects permission, as shown in Figure 5-20. You can also choose the option to allow authenticated users to delete computer objects.

FIGURE 5-20

Permissions allowing authenticated users to create and delete computer objects (accounts)

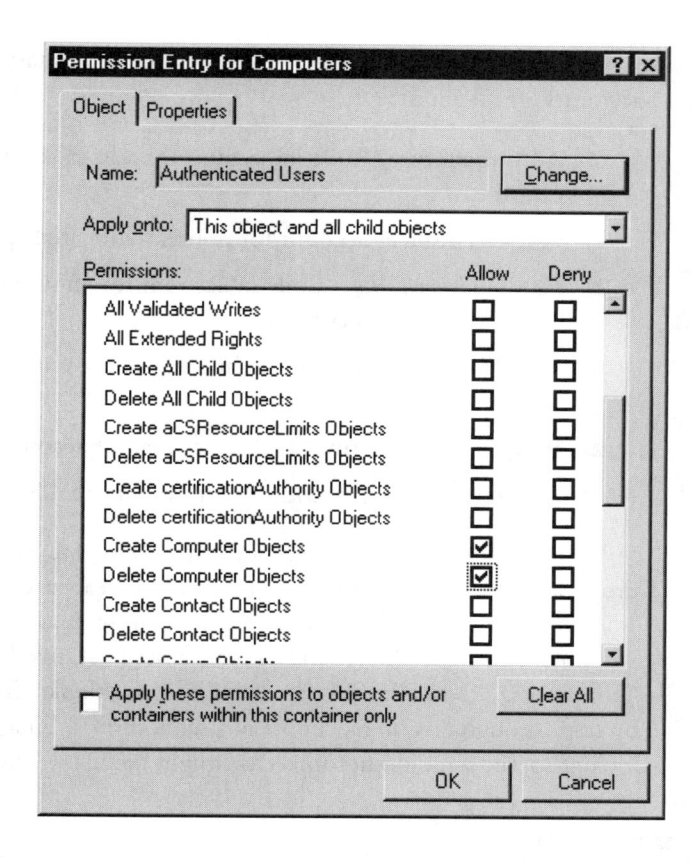

7. Click the OK buttons as necessary to close all open dialog boxes.

exam 🐶 **atch**

Don't forget about that limit of only ten computer accounts being created by authenticated users. It's such an esoteric bit of information, it's likely to show up in a question on your exam.

Active Directory User Accounts

User accounts generally define specific users. An authenticated user is one who has a user account on the domain, and has logged in with his or her username and password. As you've seen, some predefined user accounts are already defined in the Users folder of Active Directory Users and Computers. User accounts all have the "Type" User and sport a single person's profile in their icon, whereas groups sport an icon of two people's profiles. Here's a quick summary of what the predefined user accounts are all about:

- **Administrator**   Built-in account for administering the local computer or domain
- **Guest**   Built-in account for nonauthenticated "guest" users
- **IUSR_***servername*   Built-in account for anonymous access to Internet Information Services (IIS)
- **IWAM_***servername*   Built-in account for starting IIS out-of-process applications
- **krbtgt**   Key Distribution Center Service account
- **TsInternetUser**   Account used by Terminal Services

While each of the built-in accounts has a purpose, which you'll learn about as we progress through the chapters, you'll need to create accounts for individual users. The procedure is largely the same as for creating new groups and new computer accounts: you right-click the Users container in Active Directory Users and Computers, choose New | User, and fill in the blanks. Exercise 5-4 will take you step by step through creating a couple of user accounts. First, let's take a moment here to look at some scenario questions that might come up, and their solutions.

EXERCISE 5-4

Create Two User Accounts

In this exercise, you'll use Active Directory Users and Computers to add two new user accounts to the domain. One will be an "omnipotent" user account with Enterprise and Schema administrator privileges, the other will be a typical domain user account. You'll need to be logged in to the domain controller with appropriate permissions to do this. If you haven't already done so, open the Active Directory Users and Computer administrative tool, and then follow these steps:

1. In the console tree, right-click the Users container and choose New | User.
2. Type in the user's name, as in the example shown in Figure 5-21 (you can use your own name, of course).
3. Click the Next button.

SCENARIO & SOLUTION

I created a user account, but when I try to log in with it on the domain controller, I get an error message stating that I can't log in interactively. Why?	A new account will be a member of the Domain Users group, which doesn't have the right to log on to domain controllers. You can log on to client computers with that account. Optionally, you can change the logon policy for the domain controller, as discussed in the next chapter.
I logged in to my domain from a client computer. Why don't I see an icon for the domain controller when I open My Network Places?	You'll need to dig down a bit in My Network Places to find icons. The sequence is My Network Places	Entire Contents. From there, the Microsoft Windows Network icon takes you to icons for domains, and the Directory icon takes you to directories for domains.
How can I see, and perhaps change, the groups to which a user belongs?	In Active Directory Users and Computers, right-click the icon for the user account and choose Properties. Then click the Member Of tab.
I logged in to a computer at work and noticed there was no built-in Administrator account. Why is that?	Some companies rename the Administrator account because too many people know that once you "break into" that account, you have full access to the system. Most administrators give themselves both a powerful Administrators account and a less potent user account. They use the less-potent account for day-to-day stuff, which prevents them (and any programs that are running with their current permissions) from making harmful changes to the system.
If I don't log in as an administrator, but then need to run some program that requires administrative privileges, do I have to log out and log back in?	Typically not. Often, you can hold down the SHIFT key, right-click the icon for the program or MMC you want to run, and choose Run As. Fill in the administrator username and password.

4. Enter a password for the user, and choose password options.

5. Click the Next button. The new user account appears in the details pane when the Users container is selected in the console tree.

6. Next, we'll make this new user a member of the Enterprise Admins and Schema Admins group. Right-click the user account in the details pane and choose Properties.

7. In the Properties dialog box that opens, click the Member Of tab.

8. Click the Add button and select the Schema Admins and Enterprise Admins groups.

FIGURE 5-21

Creating a new User object in Active Directory

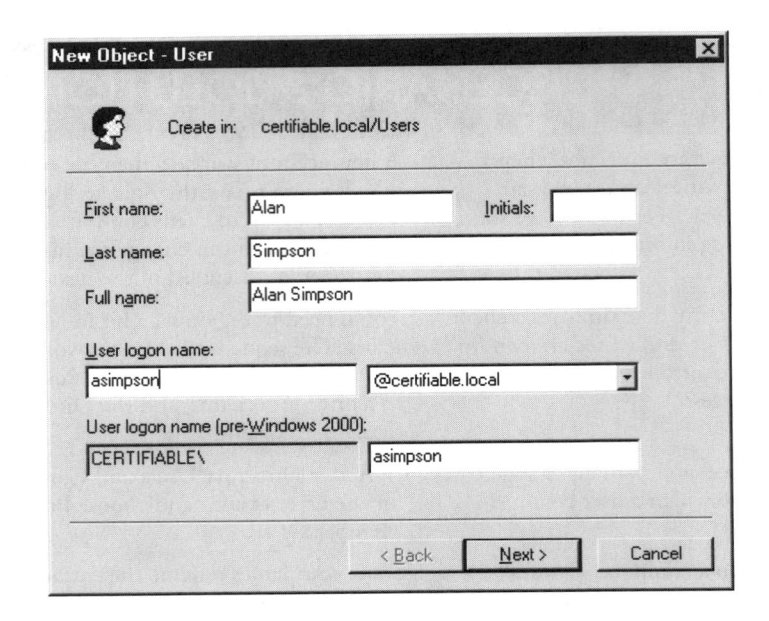

[New Object - User dialog box: Create in: certifiable.local/Users; First name: Alan; Initials: (blank); Last name: Simpson; Full name: Alan Simpson; User logon name: asimpson @certifiable.local; User logon name (pre-Windows 2000): CERTIFIABLE\ asimpson]

9. Click the OK button. The Member Of tab now lists all groups to which the user belongs.

10. To create a description for the new user, click the General tab and type in a description of your own wording.

11. Click the OK button.

The new account description appears in the Description column of the details pane of Active Directory Users and Computers. To add a second user account with Domain Users privileges, repeat the steps, but don't make the new account a member of any special groups. The account will be added to the Domain Users group by default. In Figure 5-22, I've added two accounts: one with username Alan Simpson, and a second, more limited, Domain User account for Alec Fraser.

Joining a Computer to the Domain

Suppose that you've created a computer account for Client01 (or some other nondomain computer in your network), and want to set up the nonadministrative

FIGURE 5-22   Accounts for users Alan Simpson and Alec Fraser added to the Users container

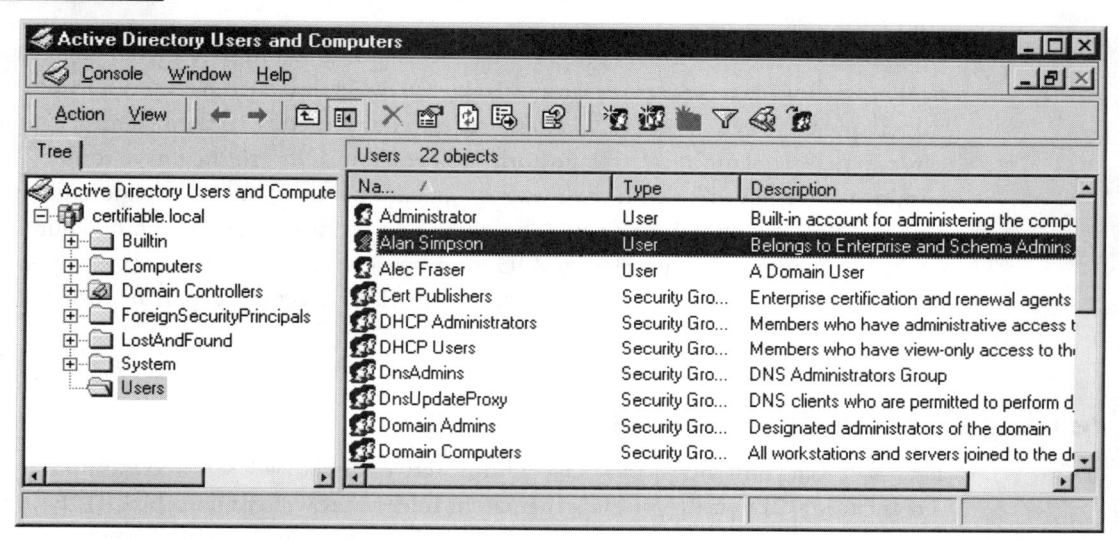

user account on that computer. The easiest way to do this would probably be to use the Network ID wizard that's available on Windows 2000 Professional computers. Log in to the client computer as Administrator, right-click the My Computer icon, and choose Properties. On the Network Identification tab, click the Network ID button. A wizard will take you step by step through the process of joining the client to the domain. When you complete the wizard, you'll need to reboot. When you log back in, make sure you log in to the domain, not the local computer.

CERTIFICATION OBJECTIVE 5.04

Create and Manage Organizational Units

As mentioned earlier in the chapter, you can use OUs to organize objects in Active Directory. To envision how this might be useful, image that you've created several hundred, or several thousand, user accounts. When you open the Users folder in Active Directory Users and Computers, you have this huge long list of User accounts to deal with. Instead of dealing with the long list, you could organize those user accounts into OUs, just like you can organize files into folders and subfolders on your hard disk.

Creating OUs is a simple task, but don't let that lull you into being complacent or sloppy about how you create and organize OUs. As discussed near the start of this chapter, the OUs you create should reflect your structure of the business. You can also delegate administrative authority to people in OUs, so they have some administrative powers within their own organizational unit, but not the domain as a whole. You should definitely take that into consideration when designing your OUs. For example, if you create an OU for each department in the company, you can group all of those user accounts into folders that reflect the department that the user works in.

Creating Organizational Units

Each OU is a container—a folder—within Active Directory Users and Computers. To create an OU, just right-click the parent folder that will contain the OU. For example, to create an OU at the "root" level of the domain controller, right-click the server name in the console tree and choose New | Organizational Unit.

A dialog box titled New Object – Organizational Unit will open. Just type in whatever name you want to give to the OU and click the OK button. The OU name appears in the console tree with all your other containers.

The procedure for creating an OU within an OU is the same. Right-click the name of the parent folder (the existing OU that will be the container for the new OU) and choose New | Organizational Unit.

EXERCISE 5-5

Create Some Organizational Units

In this exercise, you'll create a couple of OUs for practice. You'll create an OU named Corporate, and place a couple of smaller department OUs named Accounting and Sales within it. As always, if you're working in a live, production environment, check with your network administrator for permission. Also, you must be logged in to the domain controller to complete this exercise.

1. Click the Start button and choose Programs | Administrative Tools | Active Directory Users And Computers.

2. Right-click the domain name near the top of the console tree and choose New | Organizational Unit.

3. Type in **Corporate** as the OU's name, and then click the OK button.

4. To create the next OU, right-click the new Corporate container in the console tree and choose New | Organizational Unit.

5. Type in the name **Accounting** and click the OK button.

6. Once again, right-click the Corporate container in the console tree and choose New | Organizational Unit.

7. Type in **Sales** as the OU name and click the OK button.

When you click and expand the Corporate OU, you should be able to see the Accounting and Sales OUs contained within it, as shown in Figure 5-23.

FIGURE 5-23

Corporate OU contains OUs named Accounting and Sales

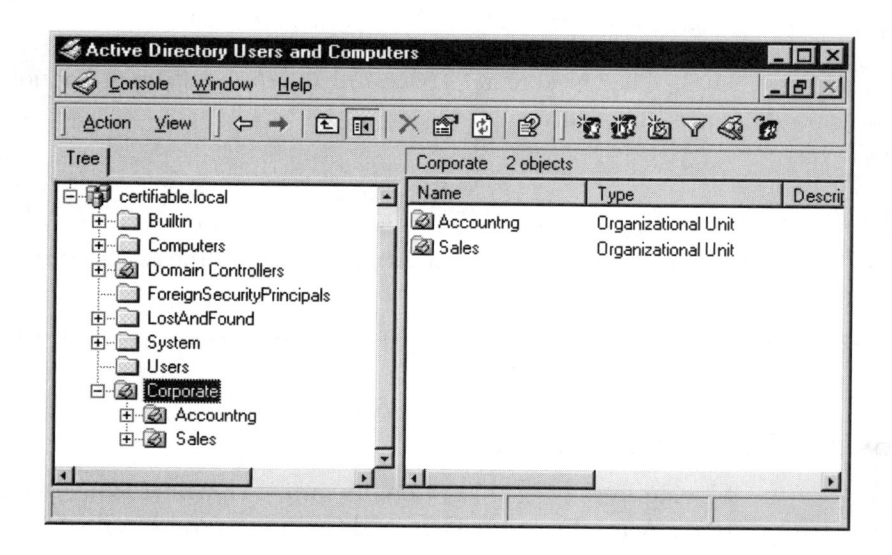

on the Job *You can apply group policies to OUs. So when you're planning your OUs, consider how you might apply different policies to different departments or divisions within the organization.*

Creating Objects in an OU

Creating an object within an OU is no different than creating one in some other folder. For example, to create a user account within an OU, right-click the OU's name in the console tree and choose New | User. Fill in the blanks in the New Object – User dialog box, and click OK.

EXERCISE 5-6

Create a User Account in the Accounting OU

In this exercise, you'll add a user account for an employee named Ashley Marie to the Accounting OU. Follow these steps:

1. Right-click the Accounting OU in the Active Directory Users and Computers console, and choose New | User.

2. Fill in the blanks as shown in Figure 5-24.

3. Click Next, enter a password and choose Password options, and then click Next.

4. Click Finish.

When the Accounting OU is selected in the console tree, you'll be able to see the new user account in the details pane whenever the Accounting OU is selected in the console tree.

Moving Objects to an OU

Moving an existing object from its current container to an OU is also a simple task. In the Active Directory Users and Computers console, first click the container that contains the object you want to move. Then, in the details pane, right-click the

FIGURE 5-24

Creating a new user account for amarie

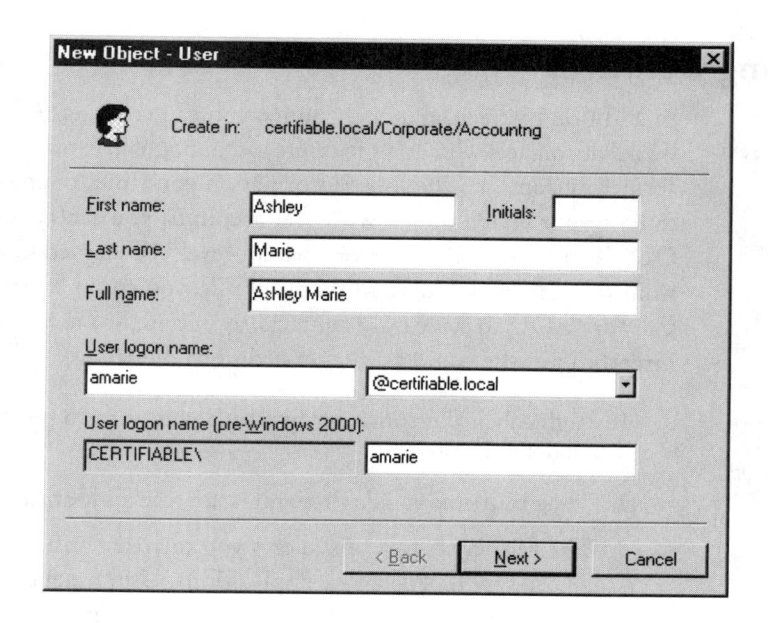

object and select Move. In the Move dialog box that appears (see Figure 5-25), click the name of the folder into which you want to move the object and click OK.

FIGURE 5-25

The Move dialog box

Creating Contacts

In addition to creating user accounts, you can create an Active Directory "address book" of contacts who don't have user accounts. You can store all kinds of information about any contact. The more information you store, the more properties you'll have to base your search on. As with user accounts, you can create contacts within an OU. For example, if you have a parent-level OU named Corporate, you might want to create all contacts in that OU. Or, you could create a new OU within the Corporate OU to store only contacts, as opposed to users. No matter where you intend to put the contacts, the procedure is the same:

1. Right-click the container in which you want to place the contact and choose New | Contact.
2. Type in the contact's first and last name and, optionally, a middle initial.
3. The Display Name box allows you to create an LDAP identifier that can be used by LDAP-aware applications. Use camel caps instead of spaces to separate names or words, such as aliciaMartinez or ralphCramden for display names.
4. Click the OK button.

Be aware that when you create a new user or contact, you're only asked for the bare minimum information necessary to identify the person. To really make Active Directory useful, you'll want to add information like address, phone number, e-mail address, and so forth. To do so, just right-click the user account or contact's icon and choose Properties. Use options on the General (shown in Figure 5-26), Address, Telephones, and Organization tabs to fill in whatever information about the user or contact you feel is useful.

Finding Existing Objects

Any user or administrator can easily search the Active Directory database to find network resources, including users and contacts. Perhaps the simplest way to do so is as follows:

1. Click the Start button, choose Search, and then select the type of object you want to search for (for example, select People to search for a user or contact).

FIGURE 5-26

The General tab of a contact's Properties dialog box

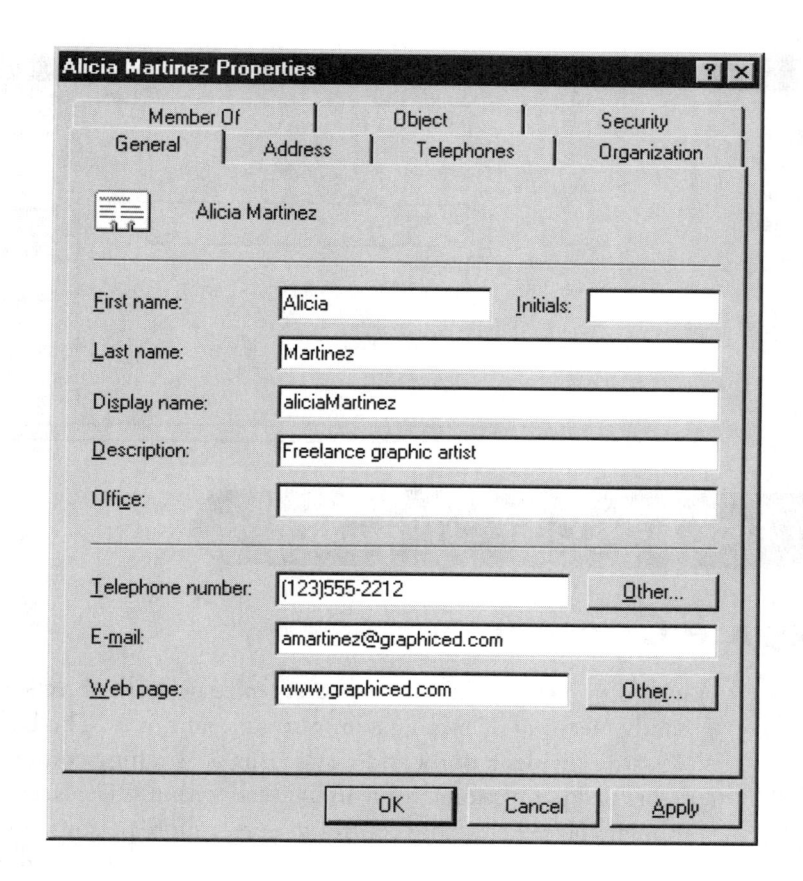

2. In the Find People dialog box that opens, choose Active Directory from the Look In drop-down list.

3. Type any known information about the user or contact, as shown in Figure 5-27.

4. Click the Find Now button.

Once the item is found, you can click it, and then click the Properties button to get to the properties for that object.

FIGURE 5-27

Preparing to search Active Directory for a person named Ashley

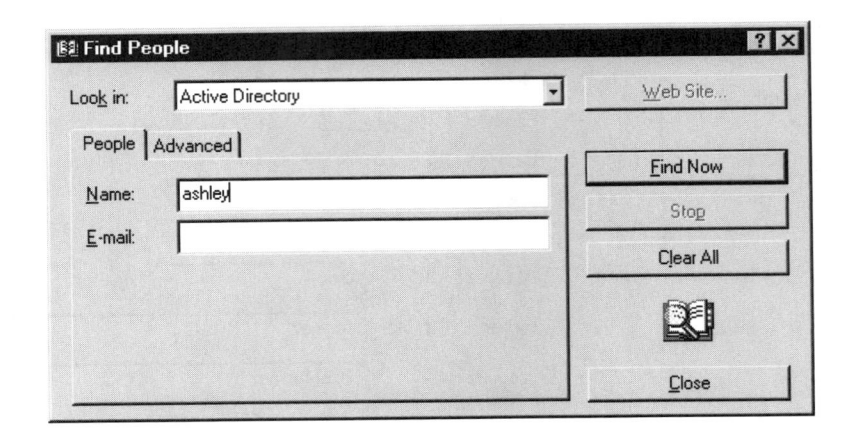

CERTIFICATION OBJECTIVE 5.05

Delegate Control

In addition to providing a way to organize network objects, OUs provide a very handy means of delegating administrative authority. The Delegation of Control Wizard provides a quick and easy means of assigning common administrative rights and permissions to key individuals within OUs. Keep in mind that even though you're delegating control to one or more persons, you *first* want to put that person's account into the appropriate OU, and you want to begin the operation by right-clicking the appropriate OU. Here are the steps:

1. Open Active Directory Users and Computers if it isn't already open.
2. In the console tree, right-click the OU to which you want to delegate control and choose Delegate Control. The first page of the Delegation of Control Wizard opens. Click Next.
3. A blank list of selected users and groups appears. Click the Add button.
4. If you're working with multiple domains, choose a domain from the Look In drop-down list.
5. Click the name of the person, or group, to whom you wish to delegate control, and then click Add. You can repeat this to add as many users or groups as appropriate.

Delegate Control **269**

6. Click OK to return to the list of selected users and groups, which will now contain whatever users and groups you chose in the previous step. Click Next.

7. On the Tasks To Delegate page, choose the tasks for which you want to delegate control. In Figure 5-28, I've selected all the available tasks.

8. Click Next to get to the last page of the wizard. You'll see a summary of what you've accomplished. Click the Finish button.

> **on the job** *You may want to cut and paste the explanatory information from the last wizard page into some simple text document for future reference. It never hurts to have a record of delegations on hand.*

Most of the options in the Tasks To Delegate page of the wizard are self-explanatory, but here's some more descriptive information on each one:

- **Create, delete, and manage user accounts** The user or group can add, change, and delete user accounts within the OU.

- **Reset passwords on all user accounts** The user or group can reset passwords that have expiration dates for all users in the OU.

FIGURE 5-28

The Tasks To Delegate page of the Delegation Of Control Wizard

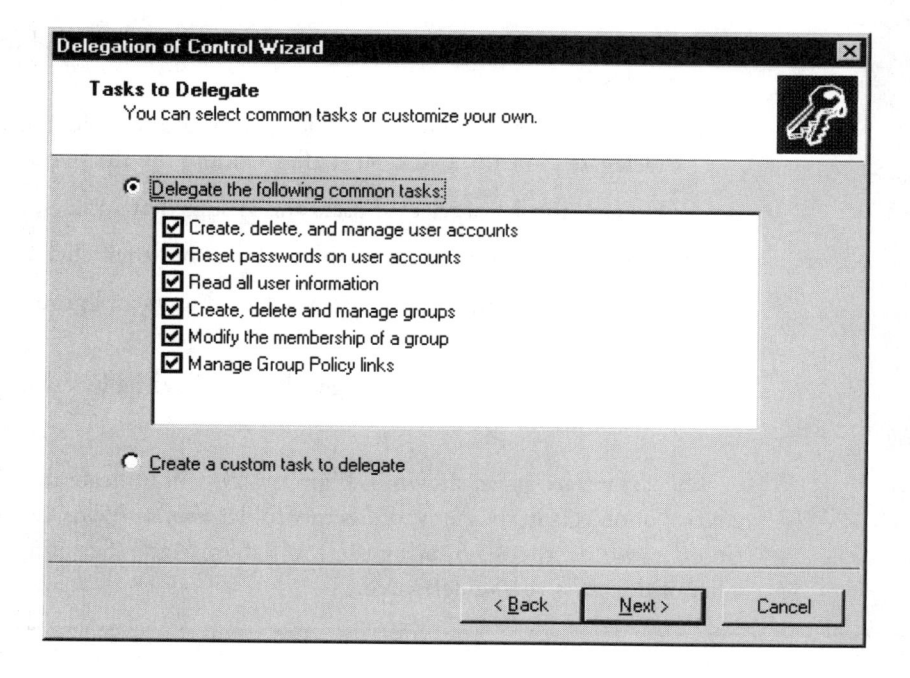

- **Read all user information**   The user or group can view all information about all users in the OU.

- **Create, delete, and manage groups**   The user or group who has this permission can create new security and distribution groups within the domain.

- **Modify the membership of a group**   The user or group who has this permission can change who belongs to which security group within the OU.

- **Manage Group Policy links**   The user or group can manage group polices within the OU, as discussed in Chapter 6.

EXERCISE 5-7

Delegating Control to a User

In this exercise, you'll delegate control to the user Ashley Marie in the Accounting OU. This exercise assumes you have already created the Corporate and Accounting OUs, and the user named Ashley Marie, from Exercises 5-5 and 5-6.

1. Open Active Directory Users and Computers.

2. In the console tree, expand the Corporate node to reveal the Accounting and Sales nodes.

3. Right-click the Accounting OU's icon in the console tree and choose Delegate Control. Click Next after reading the first wizard screen.

4. Beneath the list of selected users and groups that appears, click the Add button.

5. Click the user account for Ashley Marie, and then click the Add button.

6. Click OK to return to the list of selected users and groups, and then click the Next button.

7. In the Tasks To Delegate page, choose all available tasks. Then click the Next button.

The last wizard page, shown in Figure 5-29, will indicate that you've delegated control of objects in the Active Directory folder *domainName*\Corporate\Accounting (in other words, the Accounting OU) to Ashley Marie. Scrolling down will display a list of the tasks you've delegated.

FIGURE 5-29

Control of the Accounting OU has been delegated to user Ashley Marie.

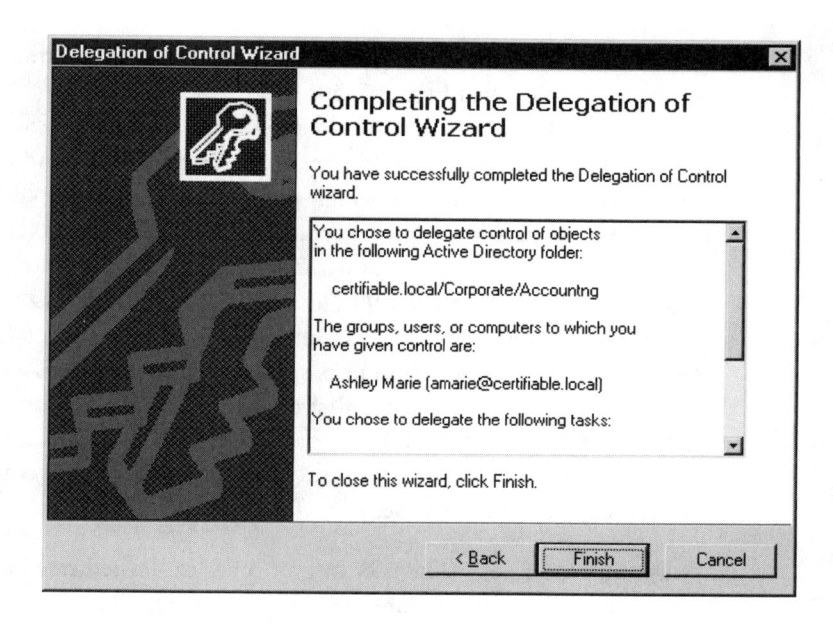

[Screenshot of Delegation of Control Wizard completion dialog showing delegation of certifiable.local/Corporate/Accountng to Ashley Marie (amarie@certifiable.local)]

Bear in mind that it's not entirely necessary to delegate control to individuals. In fact, in a large organization, you'll probably want to delegate control to groups. For example, you might create a group named Accounting Managers, assign certain rights to that group, and delegate some control to that group. Then, you can place managers from the Accounting department into that group. If an accounting manager quits, and someone else is promoted to that position, you simply have to delete the account for the ex-manager. Then, move the account for the promoted person into the Accounting Managers group to grant appropriate rights, permissions, and control to that new manager.

Managing AD Permissions

The Delegation of Control Wizard provides a small subset of permissions for performing common tasks, but the full range of assignable permissions is much larger. In fact, if you're accustomed to working with NTFS permissions, you'll find that you can apply many of the same permissions to objects and containers in Active Directory. When using the Delegation Of Control Wizard to delegate control to OU groups and users, you can get to the more advanced permissions by choosing the Create A Custom Task To Delegate option from the Tasks To Delete wizard page. When you do so, and click the Next button, you'll first be given the option to delegate control to everything in the container or just specific objects within the container, as shown in Figure 5-30.

Choosing the first option would allow you to set permissions for every object in the OU. Optionally, you could select the second option, and then choose specific objects to which you want to assign permissions. For example, in an OU, you could grant permissions specifically to creating Computer objects (computer accounts), Group objects (security groups within the OU), Organization objects (the ability to create new OUs within the OU), and User objects (user accounts within the OU).

After making your selection(s), clicking the Next button takes you to the list of Permissions to apply to the objects specified in the previous wizard page, as shown in Figure 5-31. There, you can first choose which permissions you want to be able to pick and choose among. The more check boxes you select, the lengthier the list of permissions you can assign to the selected objects. Some common permissions you can choose from include:

- **Full Control**   The user or group has unlimited freedom to create, change, and delete selected objects within the OU. Choosing this option is equivalent to choosing all the options that follow.

FIGURE 5-30

Choose objects to which you want to apply permissions.

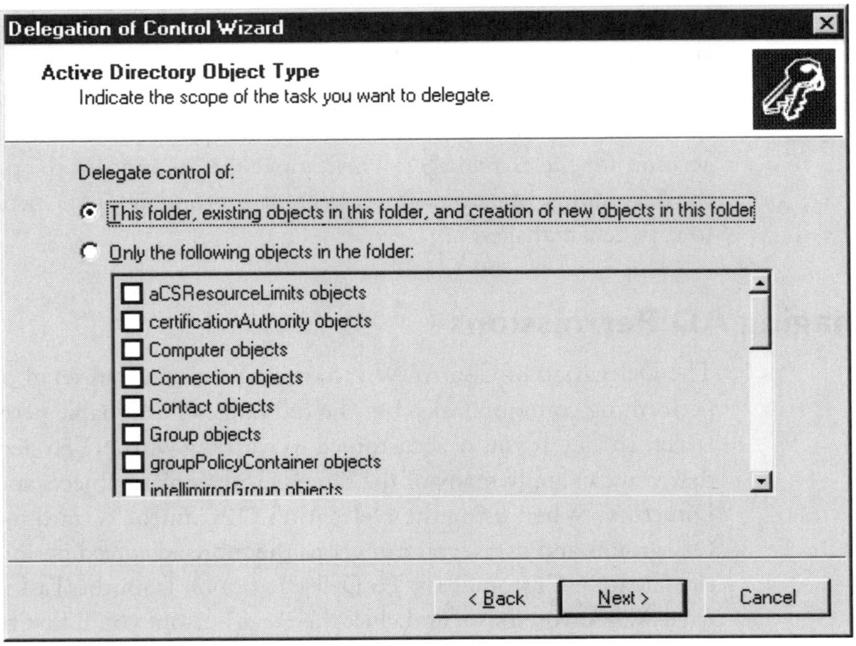

FIGURE 5-31

Choose the types of permissions you want to view and assign to objects.

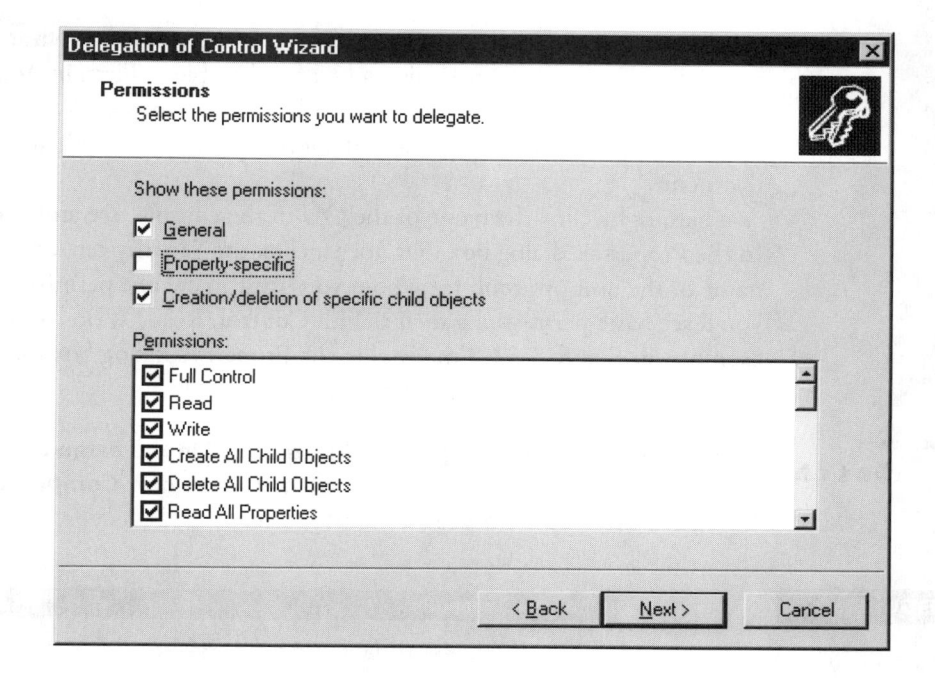

[Screenshot of Delegation of Control Wizard — Permissions dialog, showing "Show these permissions:" with General and Creation/deletion of specific child objects checked, Property-specific unchecked; Permissions list with Full Control, Read, Write, Create All Child Objects, Delete All Child Objects, Read All Properties all checked.]

- **Read** The user can view, but not necessarily change, objects in the OU.
- **Write** The user can read and change items in the OU, but not delete them.
- **Create All Child Objects** The user can create all the selected child objects in the OU (such as computer objects, user objects, and so forth).
- **Delete All Child Objects** The user can delete all selected Child objects.
- **Read All Properties** The user or group has permission to read the properties associated with each object, but not necessarily change properties.
- **Write All Properties** The user can view, and change, all properties associated with all selected objects.

Bear in mind that permissions are always additive. Thus, if you choose Full Control, you've chosen all options. If you choose only Read and Read All Properties, you've granted the user or group permission to read, but not change, information within the OU.

There are alternatives to using the Delegation of Control Wizard to assign specific permissions to specific objects. If you don't want to use the wizard, or you want to make some changes after running the wizard, or even if you just want to change existing permissions for some group or user, you can skip the wizard and change permissions in the Properties dialog box for the object. First, in Active Directory Users and Computers, make sure that Advanced options are available by clicking the View button and choosing Advanced View, if that option isn't already selected on the menu.

Then, right-click the name of the OU in the console tree and choose Properties. In the Properties dialog box that opens, click the Security tab, and then click the name of the user or group for whom you want to change permissions. Initially, you'll see basic permissions such as Full Control, Read, Write, and so forth. For example, in Figure 5-32, I'm viewing the Properties dialog box for the Accounting OU and have clicked the user Ashley Marie.

The phrase "run the Delegation Wizard on..." in the exam means to right-click the specific OU name in Active Directory Users and Computers and choose Delegate Control from the shortcut menu.

FIGURE 5-32

The Security tab of an OU's Properties dialog box

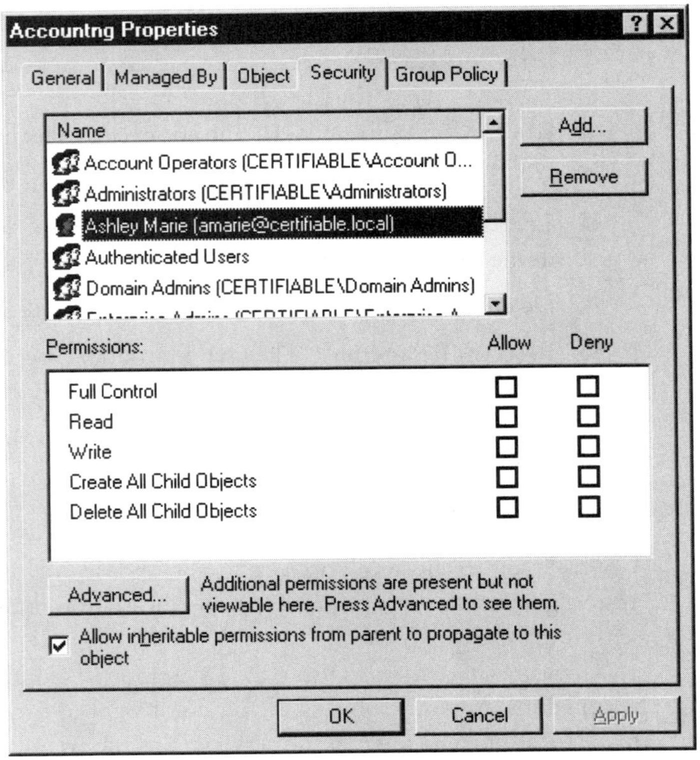

At first glance, it appears as though she has no permissions, as none of the Allow check boxes is selected. However, that doesn't necessarily mean she has no permissions. You need to look in the Advanced options to see exactly what permissions the user has. However, before we get to that, let's take a look at the meaning of the current status of the Allow and Deny check boxes:

- **Allow is selected**   Indicates the user or group is allowed the permission.

- **Allow is not selected**   If Allow is not selected, that's no guarantee that the user or group doesn't have that permission. That's because permissions are additive, in the sense a user's or group's permissions are based on the permissions defined in all groups to which the user (or group) belongs.

- **Check boxes are shaded**   Indicates that the permissions are inherited from some parent object, such as the group that contains the object. Clearing the Allow Inheritable Permissions From Parent To Propagate To This Object option will prevent the inheritance, clear the shading, and allow you to set permissions independent of the parent container's permissions.

- **Deny is selected**   Indicates that the user or group is specifically denied that permission. A Deny always takes precedence over an Allow. So if Deny is selected, the user or group does not have that permission, period. It doesn't matter what kinds of permissions the user is granted through other groups of which he or she is a member.

- **Deny is not selected**   Means that the user or group might have that permission if some other group membership allows it. In other words, the permission is not specifically denied.

- **Neither Allow nor Deny is selected**   The user or group *may* have the permission from membership in some other group, but the permission is not specifically allowed or denied for the current object.

As mentioned, to see the real nitty-gritty details of this user's permissions, you'll need to click the Advanced button. Doing so will take you to the Access Control Settings dialog box for the OU (or object), as shown in Figure 5-33.

The exact permissions available to you will vary with the type of object for which you're creating or changing permissions. There may also be numerous options per object. For example, in Figure 5-33, there are several rows of permission entries for the user Ashley Marie, such as Full Control for Group Objects (a permission she already has) and Create/Delete Group Objects (another permission she already has).

FIGURE 5-33

The Access Control Settings dialog box for an OU

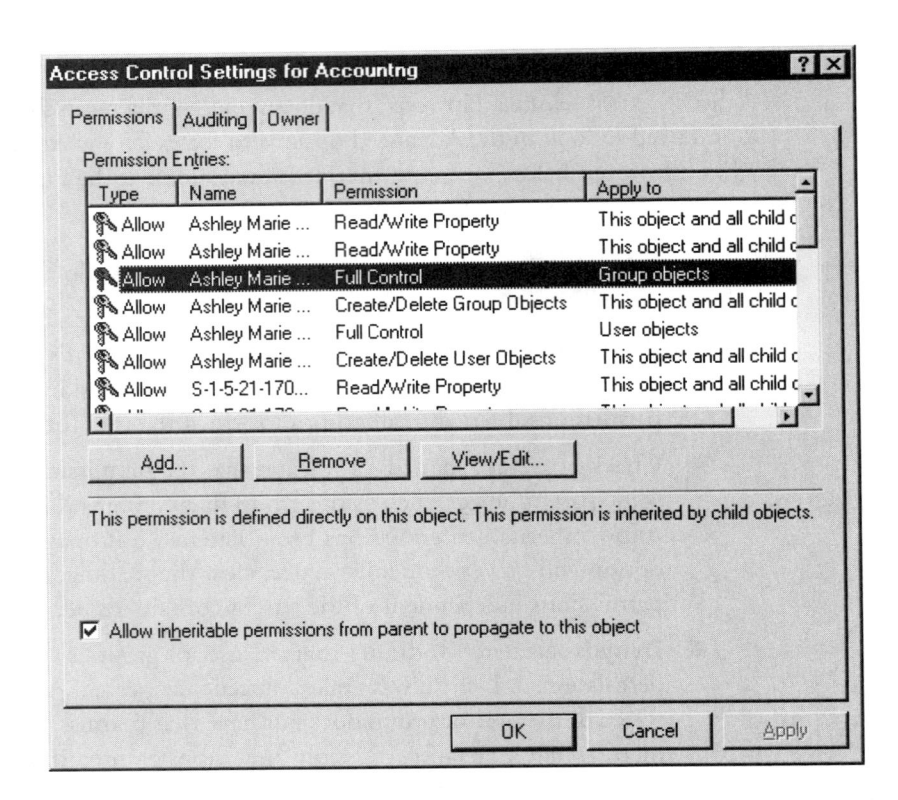

Note that different permissions apply to different objects. For example, Ashley Marie has Create/Delete User Objects for This Object And All Child Objects. Since the object at hand is the Accounting OU (as evidenced in the title bar), Ashley Marie can create and delete user accounts in the Accounting OU, as well as any OUs contained within the Accounting OU.

Some permissions are inherited from parent containers, though you could block that inheritance by clearing the Allow Inheritable Permissions From Parent To Propagate To This Object check box. But what you really want to do here is take an even closer look at the specific permissions. For example, clicking Ashley Marie's User Objects permissions, and then clicking the View/Edit button, takes you to the fine-grained set of permissions over user accounts to which you can allow or deny this user permission, as shown in Figure 5-34.

FIGURE 5-34

The full set of permissions for User objects

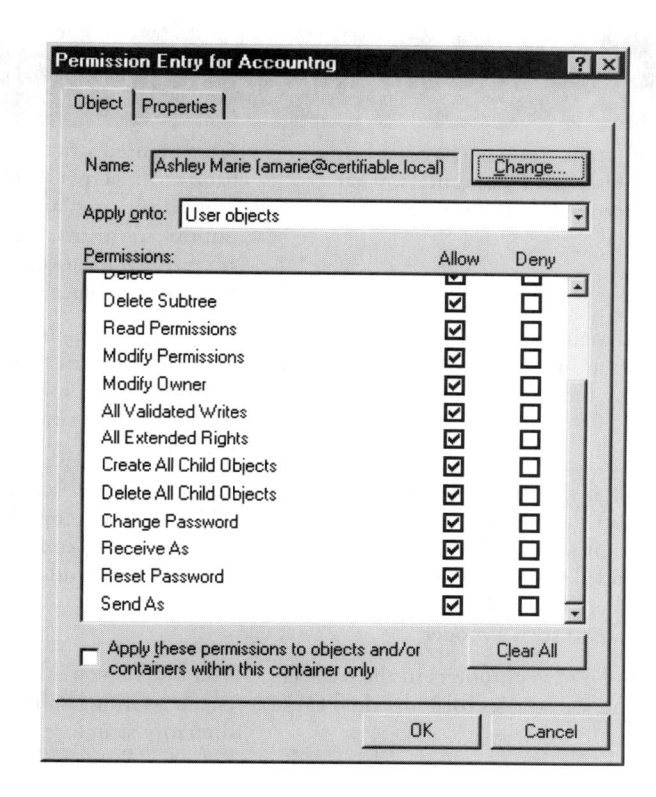

[Screenshot: Permission Entry for Accounting dialog box showing Object tab selected, Name: Ashley Marie (amarie@certifiable.local), Apply onto: User objects, with permissions list including Delete Subtree, Read Permissions, Modify Permissions, Modify Owner, All Validated Writes, All Extended Rights, Create All Child Objects, Delete All Child Objects, Change Password, Receive As, Reset Password, Send As — all with Allow checkboxes checked.]

Currently, the Allow check box for every permission is selected because Ashley Marie has Full Control of User Objects, though you could wrest control away from her for any permission by clearing the Allow box.

The Properties tab in that same dialog box allows you to select Read and Write permissions for all kinds of user account–related properties, like the ability to read and write logon hours, e-mail address, and so forth. In short, you can grant or deny permission for virtually everything having to do with creating, modifying, and deleting User accounts. Now that you have a sense of how Active Directory works, let's take a look at some last scenario and solution questions before closing this chapter.

SCENARIO & SOLUTION

With all these different containers available in Active Directory Users and Computers, what would be the purpose of defining an AD *site*?	Sites are used strictly to control replication and bandwidth across WAN links. A domain can consist of multiple sites, and a site can consist of all or part of multiple domains. The main distinction is that sites are physical locations, while everything else in Active Directory is logical grouping.
I have multiple domains to manage. Would there be any reason to put domains into separate forests, rather than one big forest?	Putting the domains into separate forests would break the automatic trust relationships defined by Active Directory. This might be useful if you want to keep the domains separate for security reasons, and control trusts explicitly.
My NT 4 network is divided into numerous subdomains for security reasons. From what you're saying here, it sounds like I could go to a single-domain model, and use OUs as security boundaries. Are there any tools that would help an NT user migrate to such a model?	Microsoft's free Active Directory Migration Tool will help you accomplish that. You can download the tool from TechNet at www.microsoft.com/technet/downloads.
I set local policies on my computers in the past. Is there any way I can set policies for individual OUs?	You bet! As you'll learn in the next chapter, you can create a Group Policy and apply it to any OU in your directory structure.

✓ TWO-MINUTE DRILL

Understand Active Directory Concepts

- ❑ Active Directory is a new feature of Windows 2000 that greatly simplifies the management of network objects, including users, groups, computers, and shared resources.

- ❑ You can use Active Directory to manage a single domain, a domain tree (a domain with subdomains), or a forest (multiple domains and domain trees).

- ❑ Active Directory is LDAP compliant, so it will work with non-Microsoft products that support the LDAP standard.

- ❑ An Active Directory *site* is generally a physical location that's separated from other resources by a WAN link or some other less-than-optimal connection. The official definition of a site is "one or more well-connected IP subnets."

- ❑ Active Directory redundancy and load balancing is based on multimaster replication among domain controllers.

- ❑ Trusts between domains in Active Directory is *transitive* (two-way), eliminating the administrative nightmares experienced by those trying to manage explicit trusts between domains in NT 4.

- ❑ Organizational units (OUs) provide a simple means to create security boundaries within a domain, without having to create subdomains.

- ❑ The global catalog is an exact copy of all the objects within the local domain and partial replicas of objects from other domains. Using partial replicas helps minimize replication overhead.

- ❑ The global catalog is also used in authentication, so each domain must maintain at least one copy of the global catalog.

Manage Active Directory Groups

- ❑ Security groups are a means of assigning rights to "job descriptions" and then granting those permissions to users simply by making them members of the group.

- Distribution groups are used by applications, not people, to distribute data to specific individuals.
- Native mode, whereby all domain controllers are Windows 2000 servers, allows for universal security groups.
- Local groups are groups that assign rights and permissions on a local computer only, but can accept virtually anyone as their members.
- Domain local groups assign rights across the domain as a whole. Members can come from any domain in the forest, or the same domain in native mode.
- Global groups can be applied to any object in the forest, not just objects in the current domain. But their membership is limited to members of the local domain, or global groups from other domains if operating in native mode.
- Universal groups are forest-wide. They can contain members from any group in the forest and can be applied to any object in the forest. Universal groups are available in native mode only.
- Rights and permissions are additive, meaning that a user has powers equal to the sum of all the groups of which she is a member.
- Deny permissions, which should be used sparingly, disrupt the normal additive properties of permissions, explicitly denying a privilege regardless of which groups a user belongs to.

Administer AD Computers and Users

- Active Directory Users and Computers is an MMC snap-in used to manage an Active Directory domain. It contains all network objects organized into containers, similar to folders on a disk.
- The Computers container is the default container for storing computer objects, computers that are members of the domain.
- As a rule, you must create a computer object for a client computer prior to joining that computer to the domain.
- The Domain Controllers container contains objects that represent domain controllers in the network.
- The Groups container is the default container for the security and distribution groups described earlier in this chapter.

- ❏ The Users container is the default container for storing user account objects.
- ❏ The Domain Administrators security group is automatically made a member of a local computer's Administrator account when the computer is joined to the domain.
- ❏ The Domain Users account is automatically made a member of the Users group on a local computer when that computer is joined to a domain.

Create and Manage Organizational Units

- ❏ The default containers in Active Directory Users and Groups are merely the defaults. You can place objects in any container.
- ❏ Organizational units (OUs) are a means of organizing network objects into units that can be managed as a whole.
- ❏ Organization units are containers within Active Directory Users and Computers.
- ❏ A proper OU design requires planning based on who you want to administer different objects, based on the structure of the organization.
- ❏ An OU can contain any type of network object, even other OUs.
- ❏ To create a new object in an OU, right-click the OU name, choose New, and then choose the type of object you want to create.
- ❏ To move an existing object into an OU, right-click the object and choose Move.
- ❏ To search Active Directory for a network object, click the Start button, choose Search, select the type of object you're looking for, and choose Active Directory from the Look In drop-down list.

Delegate Control

- ❏ A domain administrator can delegate the authority to perform certain tasks within an OU to any group or user.
- ❏ To use delegation of authority, first create an OU and place in it all the objects over which you want to delegate authority, such as user accounts, groups, and so forth.

- ❑ Then, create a security group that grants appropriate permissions as needed to effectively access resources in the OU.
- ❑ Run the Delegation of Control Wizard on the OU by right-clicking the OU name and choosing Delegate Control.
- ❑ The Delegation of Control Wizard will first allow you to choose to which users or groups you wish to delegate control.
- ❑ Then, the wizard will prompt you to choose which objects you wish to delegate control over.
- ❑ Last, the wizard will prompt you to select the permissions you wish to grant to the selected objects.
- ❑ You can modify the settings created by the Delegation of Control Wizard by right-clicking the name of the OU and choosing Properties. Click the Security tab to get to the security options.
- ❑ The Advanced security options for an OU allow the administrator to delegate very specific tasks to a delegated authority, such as only the right to reset passwords, or the right to create user accounts but not groups.

SELF TEST

Understand Active Directory Concepts

1. What does the triangle in Figure 5-35 represent?

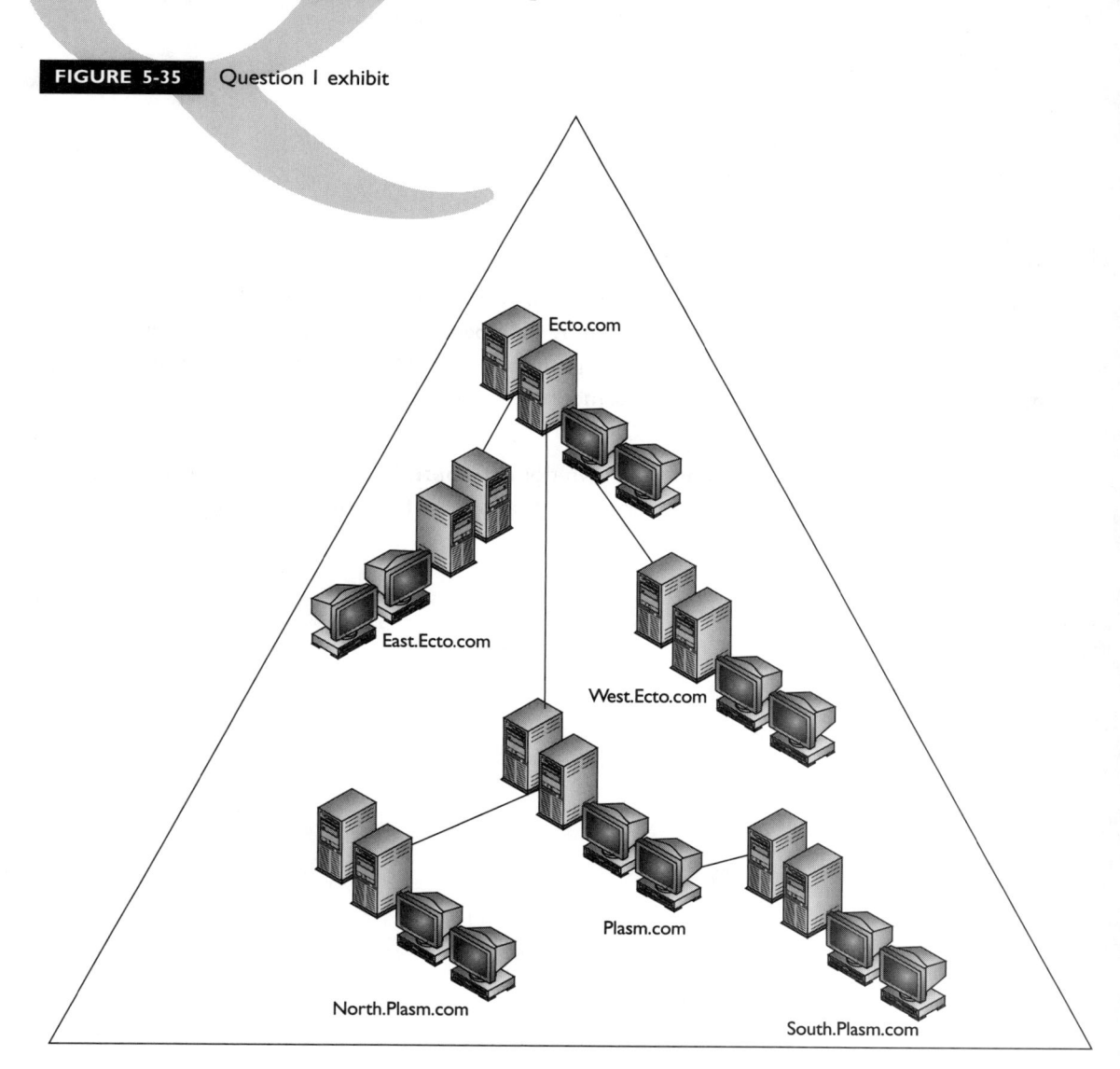

FIGURE 5-35 Question 1 exhibit

A. A domain
B. A subdomain
C. A tree
D. A forest

2. The global catalog stores which of the following? (Choose two.)

    A. A full replica of every object in all domains
    B. A partial replica of every object in its own domain
    C. A full replica of every object from other domains
    D. A partial replica of every object from other domains

Manage Active Directory Groups

3. You are a domain administrator for the LA.MajorMinor.com domain shown in Figure 5-36. The domain contains a shared resource used by members of the accounting department within your domain. You are instructed to create a group that will allow accounting members from other subdomains to have access to that same shared resource. Which of the following would accomplish this goal?

    A. Create a domain local group on your own domain controller, granting permissions to the local shared resource. Add appropriate groups and users from the accounting departments in other subdomains to that group.

FIGURE 5-36

Exhibit for Question 3

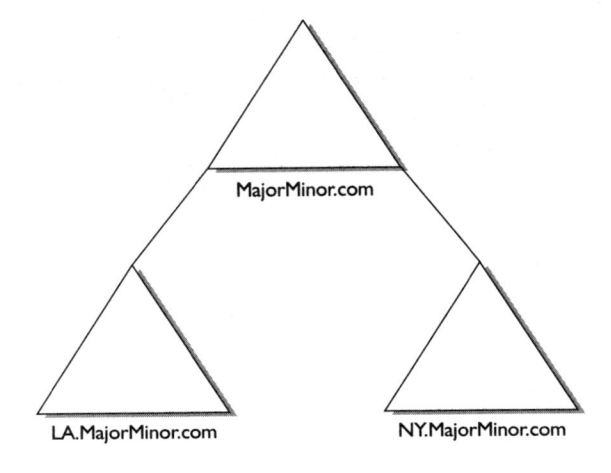

MajorMinor.com

LA.MajorMinor.com   NY.MajorMinor.com

B. Create a distribution group that has appropriate permissions for access to the shared resource. Then, add appropriate groups from other domains to that new group.

C. Create a universal distribution group that has appropriate permissions for access to the shared resource, and add all user accounts to that group.

D. Create a global group that provides appropriate permissions for the share. Then, add appropriate groups from other domains to the global group.

Administer AD Computers and Users

4. You are a desktop administrator for your company. You receive several new Windows 2000 Professional computers. Your job requires joining the computers to the domain. However, when you try to do so from each of the computers, you get an error message denying access to the domain. What should you do to get around this problem?

    A. On the domain controller, create a Computer account in Active Directory for each of the new computers. Then, you can go back and join the new computers to the domain.

    B. On the domain controller, create a User account in Active Directory for each person that will be using those computers, and then go back and log in to the workstations with those user accounts.

    C. Create an OU named New Workstations, create groups that provide Full Control of that OU, and then make yourself a member of the OU.

    D. Make yourself a member of the Enterprise Admins group, and then go back and join each computer to the domain.

5. Your company is migrating from a Windows NT 4.0 domain to a new Windows 2000 domain. You currently have two Windows 2000 domain controllers and four NT 4 domain controllers running. As part of the migration, you are removing Windows NT 4 computer accounts from the Windows NT domain and adding them to a Windows 2000 Active Directory domain. After adding ten NT computer accounts and clicking Add to enter an eleventh account, you get an error message that reads "The machine account for this computer either does not exist or is unavailable." What should you do to add this new account to the Active Directory domain?

    A. Ask the domain administrator to add the Create Computer Objects permission for the Computers container to your security settings.

    B. Log in to the local machine as Administrator, and then join the computer to the domain.

    C. Create a universal security group that grants permission to join workstations to the domain.

    D. Create an explicit trust between the NT 4 and Windows 2000 domains.

Create and Manage Organizational Units

6. You are the domain administrator for your company, which consists of a single Windows 2000 domain. Currently, each department has its own OU, and administrators within each department have full control over their own OUs. The departmental administrator for the Accounting domain is on vacation, so members of the Accounting department ask you to create a user account for a new staff member. When you try to add the new user account to the Accounting domain, you receive an Active Directory error message stating that you don't have sufficient access rights to perform the operation. What should you do?

   A. Assign the Domain Admins group the Allow–Write permission for the Accounting OU.

   B. Assign to the Domain Admins group the Allow–Read & Execute NTFS permission for the Accounting OU.

   C. Assign the Domain Admins group the Allow–Modify Owner share permission for the Accounting OU, and then take ownership of the OU.

   D. Assign the Domain Admins group the Allow–Create All Child Objects permission for the Accounting OU.

7. Bella Isagowa is a member of the Accounting Managers security group, which has been granted permissions to create child objects within the Accounting OU. She attempts to delete a user account from the Accounting OU, and receives an AD error message stating that her permissions are insufficient to perform this task. You want to give Bella appropriate permissions to remove user accounts, without giving any permissions that would extend beyond her OU. What should you do?

   A. Make Bella a member of the Domain Admins group.

   B. Make Bella a local Administrator on the domain controller.

   C. Assign the Allow–Delete Child Objects permission to the Accounting Managers security group.

   D. Grant ownership of the Users folder in the Accounting OU to Bella.

Delegate Control

8. You are a network administrator for your company. All user accounts and groups are in a single OU named Corp. One security group, Desktop Support, has as its members all employees from the desktop support staff. You need to allow desktop support staff to be able to create and manage user accounts, but you do not want them to be able to create or modify security groups. What should you do?

   A. Run the Delegation of Authority Wizard on the Corp OU, and delegate only the Create, Delete, And Manage User Accounts task to the Desktop Support group.

- **B.** Run the Delegation of Authority Wizard on the Corp OU, and delegate the Modify The Membership Of A Group right to members of the Desktop Support group.
- **C.** Run the Delegation of Authority Wizard on the Corp OU, and assign the Full Control permission for Contact Objects to the Desktop Support group.
- **D.** Run the Delegation of Authority Wizard on the Corp OU, and assign the Full Control permission for Computer Objects to the Desktop Support group.

9. You are the administrator for your company's Active Directory domain in the New York office. The company has created two new branch offices in Brisbane and Madrid. Currently, all user accounts are in the Users folder of Active Directory Users and Computers. To accommodate the two new offices, you create a security group for each of the three offices. You place all the network administrator accounts for each office within the appropriate group for the office.

   Management decides to adopt a new policy whereby network administrators can configure user accounts within their own office only. What can you do to ensure that each administrator group can administer only user accounts within their own office?

   - **A.** Create two new OUs, one for administrators in each office, and the other for staff in each office. Run the Delegation of Control Wizard on the Administrators OU, and delegate the Create, Delete, And Manage User Accounts task to appropriate OUs.
   - **B.** Create an OU for each office, and move administrator accounts to those OUs. Grant permissions to create and delete child objects within each OU to appropriate administrators for each office.
   - **C.** Create a universal security group for the administrators, and grant them permissions to create, delete, and manage groups.
   - **D.** Create an OU for each office, and move the user accounts into appropriate OUs. Then, delegate control of each OU to the appropriate administrators for that office.

LAB QUESTION

AnnaBanana, Inc., is a fast-growing company whose network has gotten out of control. To create some security boundaries, it originally divided its network into several NT 4 domains, each with its own administrators, and created explicit trusts between domains to provide users access across domains. The company has decided to upgrade all servers and computers to Windows 2000. Your job, as a new domain administrator, is to come up with a plan that will allow the company to delegate some authority to administrators in each department, but only as much authority as is needed. What would be a good approach, assuming there are no time restrictions?

SELF TEST ANSWERS

Understand Active Directory Concepts

1. ☑ **D** is correct. Since there are two separate namespaces involved, the figure represents a forest.
   ☒ **A** is wrong because either Ecto.com or Plasm.com would represent a domain.
   ☒ **B** is wrong because East.Ecto.com, West.Ecto.com, North.Plasm.com, and South.Plasm.com are subdomains.
   ☒ **C** is incorrect because Ecto.com plus its subdomains represent one tree, and Plasm.com and its subdomains represent a second tree.

2. ☑ **A** and **D** are correct. To minimize replication overhead, the global catalog stores all information about the directory from its own domain only, and partial replicas from other domains.
   ☒ **B** is wrong because the global catalog stores a full replica of every object in its own domain.
   ☒ **C** is wrong because the global catalog stores only partial replicas of objects from other domains.

Manage Active Directory Groups

3. ☑ **A** is correct. Since several people will be accessing the shared resource, the best thing to do would be to create a domain local security group that provides appropriate permissions for accessing that resource. Then, it's just a simple matter of adding appropriate groups (or users) from other domains to that group.
   ☒ **B** and **C** are incorrect because you cannot assign permissions to distribution groups.
   ☒ **D** is wrong because a global group can contain user accounts, computer accounts, or global groups from the same domain, but cannot contain global groups from other domains.

Administer AD Computers and Users

4. ☑ **A** is correct. If you create a Computer account for each computer in Active Directory, you'll then be able to join each computer to the domain.
   ☒ **B** is wrong because you need to create Computer accounts, not User accounts, to join the workstations to the domain.
   ☒ **C** is wrong because there is no need to create an OU here.
   ☒ **D** is incorrect because all that's needed here is to create an AD Computer account for each of the new workstations prior to joining them to the domain.

5. ☑ **A** is correct. Note that the question doesn't specify that you are a network or domain administrator. Windows 2000 allows each authenticated user to create up to ten new computer objects. So the solution here is to get a higher-level administrator to allow the Create Computer objects permission to the Computers container in AD Users and Computers. (A second approach would be to precreate the Computer accounts in AD Users and Computers, but that's not given as an option here.)
☒ **B** wouldn't help, as local Administrators don't have permissions to join a computer to a domain.
☒ **C** is wrong because universal groups are allowed only in native mode, and this network contains some NT 4 computers.
☒ **D** is wrong simply because this question deals with the ten-workstation limit applied to nonadministrative users trying to join computers to a domain. A trust is irrelevant.

Create and Manage Organizational Units

6. ☑ **D** is correct. Apparently, Domain Admins don't currently have permissions to create child objects in the Accounting OU, as evidenced by the Active Directory error message. But you can easily grant those permissions to yourself as a domain administrator.
☒ **A** is wrong because you need permission to create child objects in the Accounting OU, not just Write permissions.
☒ **B** is wrong because NTFS permissions aren't relevant to creating child objects within an OU.
☒ **C** is incorrect because you currently don't have Full Control permissions (as evidenced by the error message). Only current owners or users with Full Control permissions can assign the Allow–Modify Owner permission to an object.

7. ☑ **C** is correct. Apparently, the Accounting Managers group does not have permission to delete child objects in the OU. Assigning that permission for Accounting Managers for the Accounting OU would give Bella (and other members of Accounting Managers) the ability to delete objects within the Accounting OU, without adding any permissions that reach outside the OU.
☒ **A** is wrong because this would give Bella much broader permissions across the entire domain.
☒ **B** and **D** are incorrect because neither would enable Bella to delete child objects in the Accounting OU.

Delegate Control

8. ☑ **A** is correct. Delegating authority to Create, Delete, And Manage User Accounts to the Desktop Support group would give its members exactly the permissions they need.
☒ **B, C,** and **D** are wrong because none assigns exactly the permissions needed to create, manage, and delete user accounts.

9. ☑ **D** is correct. First and foremost, you need to create an OU for each office, and move user accounts into appropriate OUs so that each set of users can be managed independently. Then, you need to run the Delegation of Authority Wizard on each OU, delegating the Create, Delete, And Manage User Accounts task to appropriate administrators for each OU.
☒ **A** and **B** are wrong because you need to separate user accounts, not administrator accounts, into separate OUs.
☒ **C** is wrong because it doesn't provide a means of limiting each administrator's authority to her local office, and grants permissions for groups, not user objects.

LAB ANSWER

This is the perfect scenario for implementing Active Directory and organizational units. Simply create an OU for each department, and place all departmental user accounts within each domain. Create security groups that grant departmental administrators just enough authority to manage their own OUs. Then, run the Delegation of Authority Wizard on each OU, and delegate only as many tasks as necessary to the Administrators group for each OU.

MCSA™
MICROSOFT CERTIFIED SYSTEMS ADMINISTRATOR

6

Creating and Implementing Group Policies

CERTIFICATION OBJECTIVES

6.01	Implement Group Policies
6.02	Create Group Policy Objects
6.03	Link Group Policies to AD Objects
6.04	Filter Group Policies
6.05	Delegate Control of Group Policies
✓	Two-Minute Drill
Q&A	Self Test

Group policies are a major new feature of Windows 2000 and Active Directory. As the name implies, group policies allow you to create a set of policies and then apply them to a group of objects, such as all computers in a domain or all computers in an organizational unit. The kinds of things you can do with group policies include

- Define password, lockout, and audit policies for the domain.
- Enforce restrictions on users' desktops to prevent them from making changes that just confuse them.
- Assign startup, logon, logoff, and shutdown scripts.
- Publish (make available) or assign (enforce) software to specific computers.
- Redirect folders in users' profiles to some central location so that no matter what computer the user logs on to, she gets the same Start menu, desktop icons, and so forth.
- Configure and standardize policy settings and a wide range of other features, like disk quotas, offline folders, and more.

CERTIFICATION OBJECTIVE 6.01

Implement Group Policies

You're probably already familiar with *local security policies* on Windows 2000 and NT 4 computers. You set local policies on a Windows 2000 computer via the Local Security Policy option in Administrative Tools. Any policies you set apply locally to that computer only. Many of the options when you work with group policies will be the same as those you can set in the local policies. However, as the name implies, group policies allow you to define a set of policies that applies to multiple computers in the domain.

Group policies only work on Windows 2000 Server and Windows 2000 Professional (or higher) computers, and require that Active Directory be installed. As an administrator, you configure and deploy a group policy by building a Group Policy Object (GPO). The object is just a collection of settings that define the policy. You can then *link* (apply) the policy to any domain or OU. Before we get into the specific how-to's, though, you need to understand some concepts involving inheritance among group policies.

Group Policy Concepts

Like permissions, group policies are cumulative. For example, let's say you create a GPO that defines logon policies and link it to the entire certifiable.local domain. Then, you create a second policy and link it to a specific OU, such as the Accounting department's OU. The effective policy for the accounting OU will be the policy linked to that OU, plus the policy of the parent GPO that's linked to the domain. When a computer in the domain first starts up, its local policies are set first. Then, any group policies will be implemented. The order in which policies are applied is as follows (and often abbreviated as LSDOU):

- Local policy
- Site policy
- Domain policy
- OU policy
- Child OU's policy

For example, let's say there's a domain policy that has some setting set to Yes. (That's just an arbitrary example; not all settings are simple Yes/No toggles.) A user logs in to a computer in the Account Managers OU. In this simple scenario, the Yes setting is applied through all the subsequent policies, provided that no other policy changes the setting, as in Example 1 shown in Figure 6-1. However, if a lower, more localized setting conflicts with a higher-level setting, the more local setting is used. For instance, in Example 2 of Figure 6-1, the GPO for the Accounting Managers group changes the Yes setting from the domain level to a No setting for objects in the Accounting OU.

No Override and Block Inheritance Options

There are alternatives to the order of precedence shown in Figure 6-1. You can apply a No Override setting to any GPO to make it stick, no matter what child settings may attempt to do. For example, suppose you set a GPO option to Yes, plus the No Override option at the domain level. A subsequent setting of No would not be able

294 Chapter 6: Creating and Implementing Group Policies

FIGURE 6-1   By default, the last setting in a series of GPOs takes precedence.

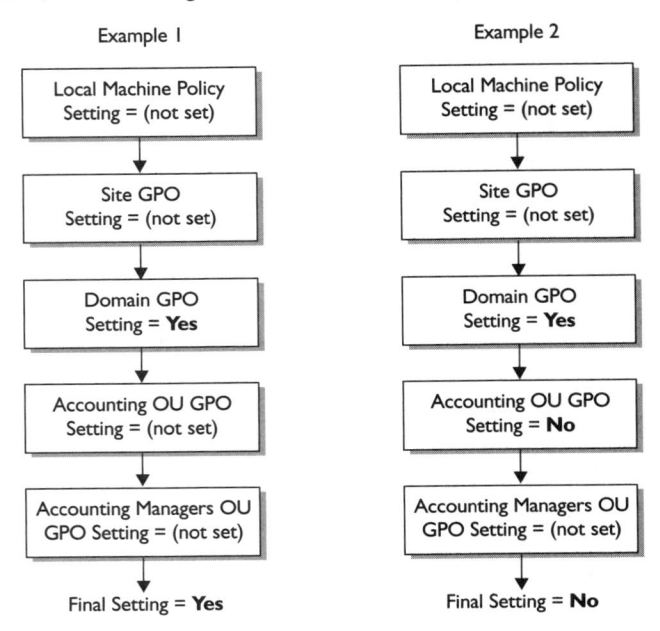

Example 1

Local Machine Policy
Setting = (not set)
↓
Site GPO
Setting = (not set)
↓
Domain GPO
Setting = **Yes**
↓
Accounting OU GPO
Setting = (not set)
↓
Accounting Managers OU
GPO Setting = (not set)
↓
Final Setting = **Yes**

Example 2

Local Machine Policy
Setting = (not set)
↓
Site GPO
Setting = (not set)
↓
Domain GPO
Setting = **Yes**
↓
Accounting OU GPO
Setting = **No**
↓
Accounting Managers OU
GPO Setting = (not set)
↓
Final Setting = **No**

to override the domain-level setting, so the final setting would be equal to that at the domain level, as illustrated in Figure 6-2.

The Block Inheritance option works in the opposite direction, blocking settings coming from a higher-level policy. For example, let's say you create a very restrictive policy at the domain level. People in the IT department can't live with those restrictive settings and need an altogether different policy. By turning on Block Inheritance at the IT Department level, you disable the domain policy for the IT department, and only its own policy settings apply, as shown in Figure 6-3.

So, what about conflicts between No Override and Block Inheritance? No Override always takes precedence, and for good reason. Suppose you're a domain administrator and need to set a policy that applies to every OU (even the IT group) in the domain. Then, you create OUs and grant administrative privileges to certain members of each OU. You want them to be able to manage certain aspects of their own OUs. However, you do not want them to be able to override policy settings defined at the OU level. By turning on the No Override option at the domain level, you prevent departmental managers from blocking that policy and making up their own policies.

Implement Group Policies **295**

FIGURE 6-2

The No Override option enforces a policy on all lower-level policies.

No Override Example

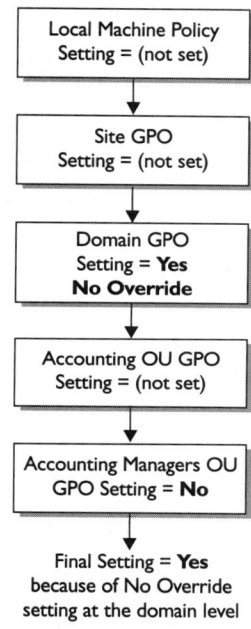

Local Machine Policy
Setting = (not set)
↓
Site GPO
Setting = (not set)
↓
Domain GPO
Setting = **Yes**
No Override
↓
Accounting OU GPO
Setting = (not set)
↓
Accounting Managers OU
GPO Setting = **No**
↓
Final Setting = **Yes**
because of No Override
setting at the domain level

---

exam
⑧atch

You may get some tricky questions that don't specifically tell you that a No Override or Block Inheritance setting is causing some problem. You have to figure out that one of those settings is causing a problem based on other facts stated in the question.

FIGURE 6-3

The Block Inheritance setting prevents restrictive policies from being applied to the IT OU.

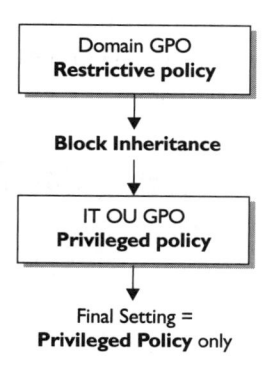

Domain GPO
Restrictive policy
↓
Block Inheritance
↓
IT OU GPO
Privileged policy
↓
Final Setting =
Privileged Policy only

Group Policy Timing and Refresh Intervals

Some group policies will apply to computers as a whole. Such polices are applied at system startup, before a user logs in. Other policies will apply to specific users. Those are applied when the user logs in. Once instantiated, group policies are refreshed every 90 minutes, with a 30-minute randomization between policies to prevent the domain controller from getting hit by all refreshes at the same time. Rather than waiting for a group policy to be applied, you can use the **secedit** command to enforce the policy immediately. To enforce policies that are applied to computers, use the syntax

```
secedit /refreshpolicy machine_policy /enforce
```

To enforce policies that are applied to users, use the syntax

```
secedit /refreshpolicy user_policy /enforce
```

You'll learn more about the differences between computer (machine) configuration policies a little later in this chapter.

When a question specifies that you need to immediately apply a policy to users, the user_policy *parameter is required. If the question specifies applying a policy to computers or machines, the* machine_policy *parameter is required.*

Group policies are stored in Active Directory. As such, they're replicated across domain controllers at the same rate as all other AD replications. By default, AD replicates every 5 minutes within a site, and every 180 minutes between sites. We'll talk more about AD replication in Chapter 9. For now, it's sufficient to keep in mind that every GPO you create will, at some point, be replicated to all the Active Directory domain controllers in your network, which, in turn, means that the GPO will be applied no matter which domain controller is used to authenticate a user's login.

Viewing/Modifying an Existing GPO

You can use Active Directory Sites and Services, as well as Active Directory Users and Computers, to create GPOs. Bear in mind that sites are defined and used

SCENARIO & SOLUTION

What's the relationship between group policies and user profiles?	User profiles contain personal settings, such as a user's desktop environment. Group policies have a much wider scope, and can be applied to computers as well as users. In a situation where a user profile conflicts with a group policy, the group policy takes precedence, overriding settings in the user profile.
I created a GPO that locks down users' desktops and linked it to the domain. Now my OU administrators are complaining that their desktops are locked down as well. How do I fix this?	By default, GPOs are applied to the Authenticated Users group, of which your OU administrators are probably members. You should remove the Authenticated Users group from the GPO link's Security Properties. Then, add only those groups to which you want the policy applied. Assign Allow–Read and Allow–Apply Group Policy for those security groups.
I created a GPO and linked it to my OU. I applied it to the appropriate security groups. I even blocked policy inheritance. But some of the settings aren't being applied. Why?	If a higher-level policy has its No Override option enabled, settings from your more local GPO will be ignored, even if you block policy inheritance.

primarily to control replication across WAN links. Since we haven't really discussed replication issues in any detail yet, we'll use AD Users and Computers for all examples in this chapter. Here are the steps:

1. Log in to the domain controller with administrative privileges.
2. Open Active Directory Users and Computers.
3. Right-click the object to which you want to apply a group policy, such as the domain name, an OU, or child OU, and choose Properties.
4. Click the Group Policy tab.

Figure 6-4 shows the dialog box that opened when I right-clicked the certifiable.local domain name and chose Properties. The dialog box shows the properties for the entire domain. The Default Domain Policy that's listed under Group Policy Object Links is a default GPO that comes with Windows 2000. Note that the Block Policy Inheritance check box is cleared here, meaning that policies from a higher-level Site object would trickle down to the policies defined in this dialog box.

FIGURE 6-4

The Default Domain Policy in the domain's Properties dialog box

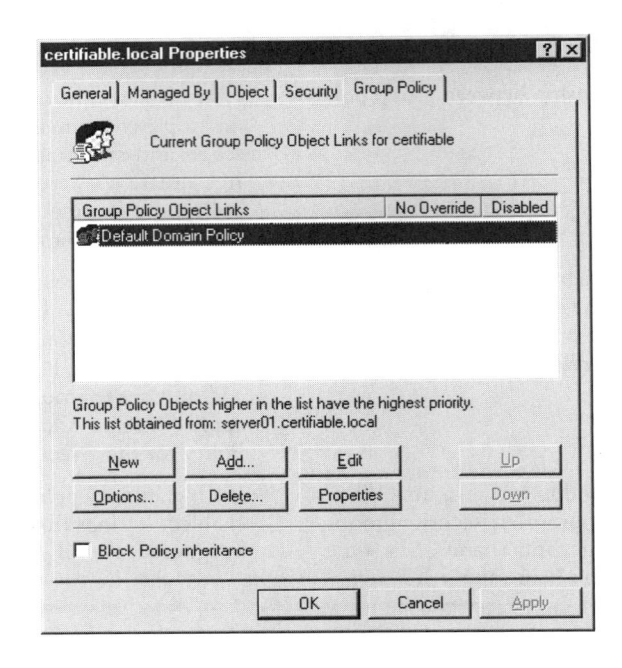

Clicking the Default Domain Policy and then clicking the Edit button opens the Group Policy window, as shown in Figure 6-5. Notice that the policy options fall into two main categories, Computer Configuration and User Configuration. As mentioned, Computer Configuration policies are activated at system startup, whereas User Configuration policies are activated when a user logs in.

If you wanted to turn on the No Override option for the currently selected GPO, you would just click the Options button to get to the options shown in Figure 6-6. Remember, activating No Override would prevent lower-level policies from changing settings defined in the current GPO. Thus, any policies you set here at the domain level would be applied to all lower-level OUs, even if the administrators from lower-level OUs attempted to block inheritance from this policy. Selecting the Disabled option would disable the GPO, thereby making its settings null and void. You might use that option if you were troubleshooting and wanted to find out if some problem was being caused by a setting in the GPO.

Clicking the Properties button for a given Group Policy displays properties relevant to just that policy. The General tab, shown on the left side of Figure 6-7, provides general information about the policy, as well as options to disable the Computer Configuration and User Configuration settings independently. You can

FIGURE 6-5

The Default Domain Policy

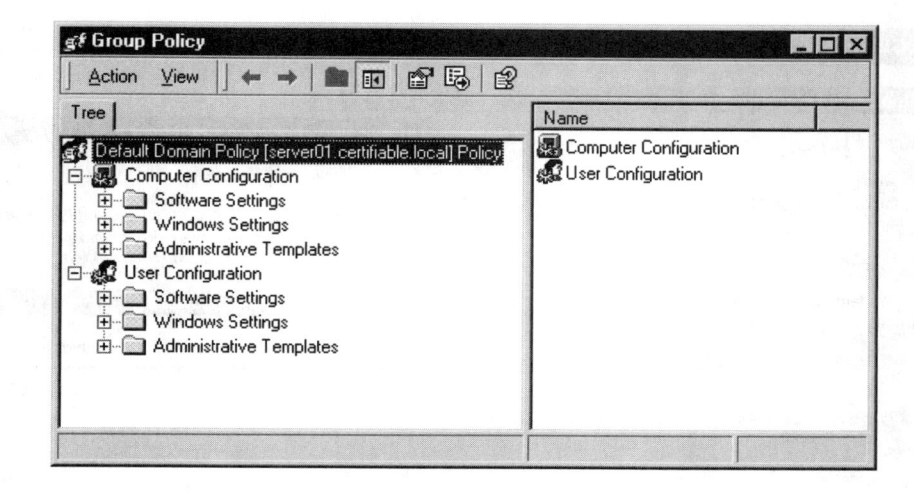

use those to improve the performance of a GPO. For example, if you create a new GPO that only changes a few User Configuration settings, you could disable Computer Configuration settings to prevent objects that are subject to the policy from spending the time required to process all the settings in Computer Configuration.

The Links tab, shown in that same dialog box, provides a quick and easy way to see what containers a GPO is currently linked to. The Default Domain Policy in this example is currently linked only to the certifiable.local domain.

The Security tab, shown in Figure 6-8, shows the discretionary access control list (permissions) for the GPO. While you can't specifically link a GPO to a security group, you can filter how a GPO affects different security groups by adjusting settings in the Security tab. Any group that has Allow–Read and Allow–Apply Group Policy permissions will be subject to restrictions defined within the policy.

FIGURE 6-6

Options for a Group Policy

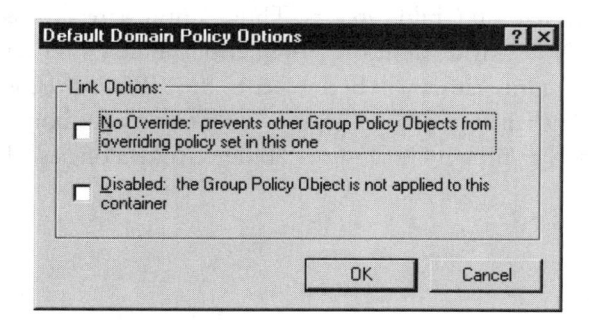

Chapter 6: Creating and Implementing Group Policies

FIGURE 6-7 The General and Links tabs for a GPO's Properties dialog box

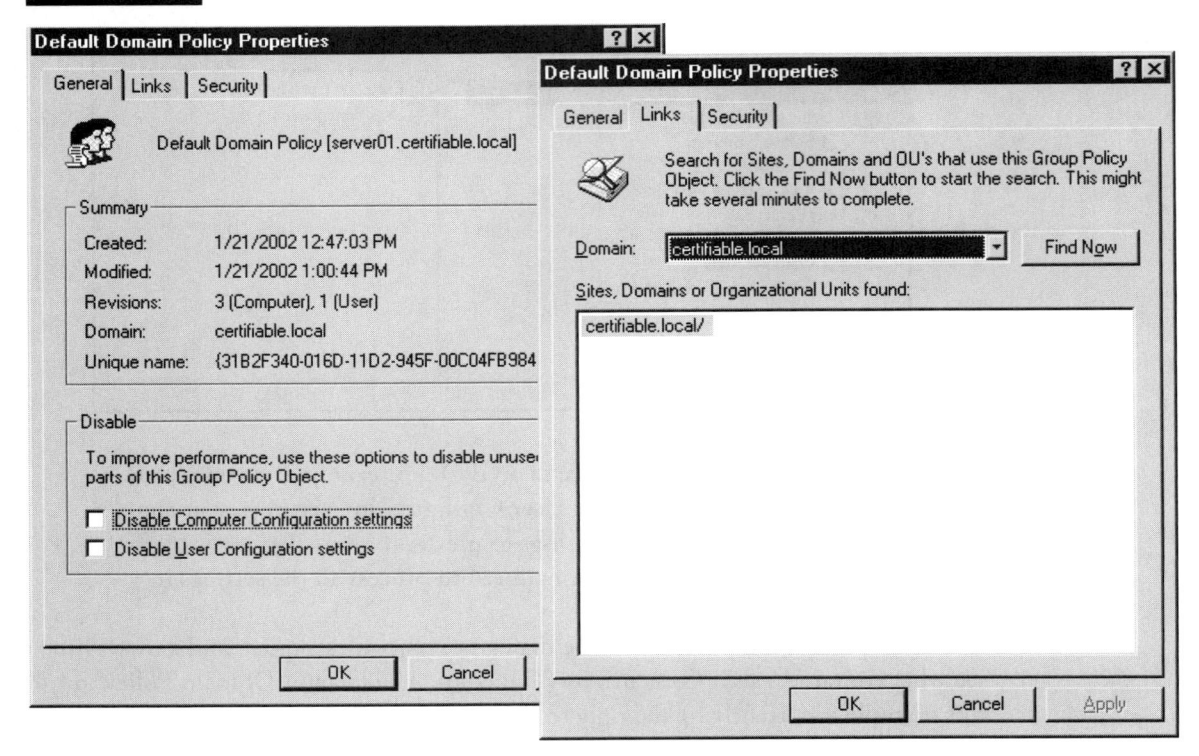

By default, the Authenticated Users group has those settings. So, everyone except anonymous logins will be subject to the policies defined in the GPO.

If you choose Domain Admins or Enterprise Admins from the upper list, you'll see that the administrators have permissions to Read and Write, as well as Create or Delete All Child Objects. Thus, Admins are allowed to create, change, and delete GPOs. By default, the Apply Group Policy isn't set for administrators. However, administrators will be subject to the GPO by virtue of their membership in the Authenticated Users group. We'll talk more about how you can use the Security tab to filter a GPO under "Filter Group Policies," later in this chapter.

FIGURE 6-8

The Security tab for a GPO

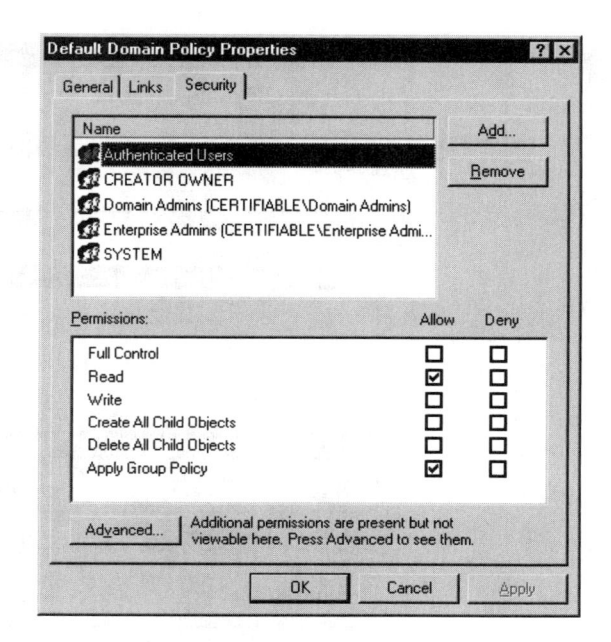

Managing Multiple Policy Links

You can create any number of group policies, and you can link a single group policy to any number of Active Directory containers. For example, suppose you create a second group policy named Password GPO that defines password policies, and link it to the domain. In that case, you'd see both policies listed for the domain as shown in Figure 6-9. As stated beneath the list in the dialog box, higher-level policies take precedence over lower-level policies. Or, stated another way, policies are applied from the bottom of the list up. So, if there are any conflicts, the first-listed items take precedence over items lower in the list. You can control the order of items in the list using the Up and Down buttons in the dialog box.

To delete a group policy from the list, just click its name and click the Delete button. You'll be given the option to remove just the link, or both the link and the actual GPO. If you remove just the link, the policy will no longer be applied to the selected object, but the GPO itself will continue to exist so that it can be applied to other objects. Choosing the second option removes both the link and the GPO itself.

302 Chapter 6: Creating and Implementing Group Policies

FIGURE 6-9

Multiple policies linked to a single object

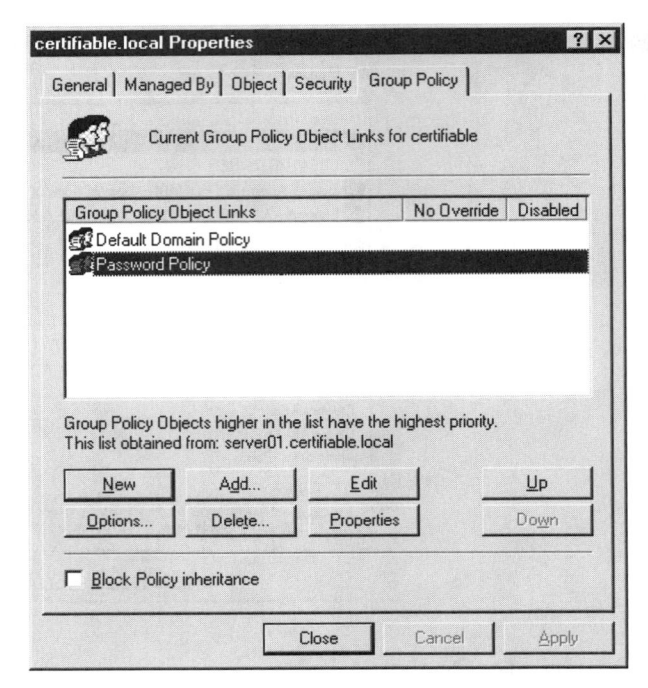

EXERCISE 6-1

Changing to Whom a Policy Applies (Filtering)

As mentioned, the default domain policy is applied to Authenticated Users. Domain and Enterprise Administrators are subject to the policy not by virtue of their status as administrators, but rather by the fact that they are members of the Authenticated Users group. In this exercise, you'll prevent the default domain policy from being applied to the Enterprise Admins group by specifically denying the Apply Group Policy permission for that group. Follow these steps:

1. Log in to the domain controller with your Enterprise Administrators account name and password.

2. Open Active Directory Users and Computers in Administrative Tools.

3. Right-click the name of the domain at the top of the tree and choose Properties.

4. Click the Group Policy tab.

Implement Group Policies 303

5. Click the Default Domain Policy link, and then click the Properties button.
6. Click the Enterprise Admins group in the access control list (ACL) for the domain, as shown in Figure 6-10.
7. Select Deny for the Apply Group Policy permission.
8. Click Yes in response to the warning prompt.
9. Click Domain Admins, and select Deny for the Apply Group Policy permission.
10. Click OK to close the dialog box and save the change.

The default domain permissions will no longer be applied to Domain Admins or Enterprise Admins. Of course, another way to avoid making the default domain policies apply to administrators would be to remove the Authenticated Users security group from the ACL. Then, add only those security groups to which you want the policy applied, and choose the Allow–Read and Allow–Apply Group Policy for those groups.

FIGURE 6-10

Policy won't be applied to Enterprise Admins.

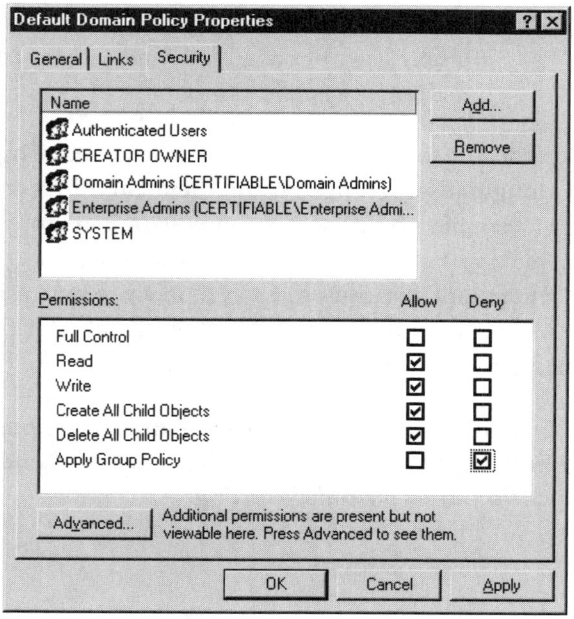

CERTIFICATION OBJECTIVE 6.02

Create Group Policy Objects

When creating GPOs, you have an enormous number of policy settings to choose from. As mentioned, you get to the settings by clicking the name of any existing policy and then clicking the Edit button. Doing so opens the Group Policy snap-in. That snap-in, in turn, consists of a number of snap-in extensions divided into two major categories: Computer Configuration and User Configuration. Each of those categories offers similar snap-in extensions, such as Software Settings, Windows Settings, and Administrative Templates. Here's a quick overview of what each snap-in extension offers:

- **Software Settings** Lets you specify how applications are installed and maintained.
- **Windows Settings** Contains two nodes, one for defining startup and shutdown scripts on computers, and another for defining security settings on computers.
- **Administrative Templates** Allows you to change Registry key settings for multiple users or computers, and thereby control access to operating system functions and applications.

There is considerable overlap between the Computer Configuration and User Configuration settings. Again, the main difference is how the setting is applied. For example, you'd use Computer Configuration settings to create polices that are applied to a computer regardless of who logs in to that computer. You'd use User Configuration settings to apply a policy to a user, regardless of which computer that user happened to log in to. Next, we'll look over the various snap-in extensions so you can get a feel for the "big picture."

exam
Watch

Exam 70-218 is more focused on how you apply and filter GPOs than on where you'll find specific settings, so there's no need to memorize the exact location of every policy setting.

Software Settings

The Software Settings node (in other words, the Software Settings snap-in extension) in Group Policy allows you to assign or publish software to user or computer groups. Each application program you install is referred to as a *package* in Group Policy. Any program that ships with an MSI (Microsoft Software Installer) file can be deployed through a GPO. You can also create custom MSI files using a variety of authoring kits, such as VERITAS's WinINSTALL, which comes with Windows 2000. The difference between assigning and publishing a package is as follows:

- **Publish**   Makes the program available to the users, but does not require that they install it. Users can then install the package using Add/Remove Programs in the Control Panel.
- **Assign**   When you install an application to a computer, the program is installed immediately, and the user has no choice. When you assign an application to users, the application becomes available through a shortcut on the Start menu, as well as when the user clicks a document type that's associated with the program.

We'll get into the specific how-to steps in Chapter 8. For now, let's look at the other major categories of policy settings.

Windows Settings

The Windows Settings node allows you to define policies that apply to Windows. Figure 6-11 shows the Windows Settings nodes expanded under both the Computer Configuration and User Configuration nodes. As always, there is some overlap of settings. But policies set under Computer Configuration are applied to computers, and policies set under User Configuration are applied to users. The sections that follow will describe the various nodes under Windows Settings.

Scripts

You can specify scripts to execute at startup and shutdown, as well as scripts that are applied to users at logon and logoff. The scripts can be written in any Windows Script Host–supported language you might use, including Microsoft VBScript, JavaScript, and MS-DOS batch files (BAT and CMD). And you can assign multiple

FIGURE 6-11 The Windows Settings nodes expanded under Computer Configuration and User Configuration

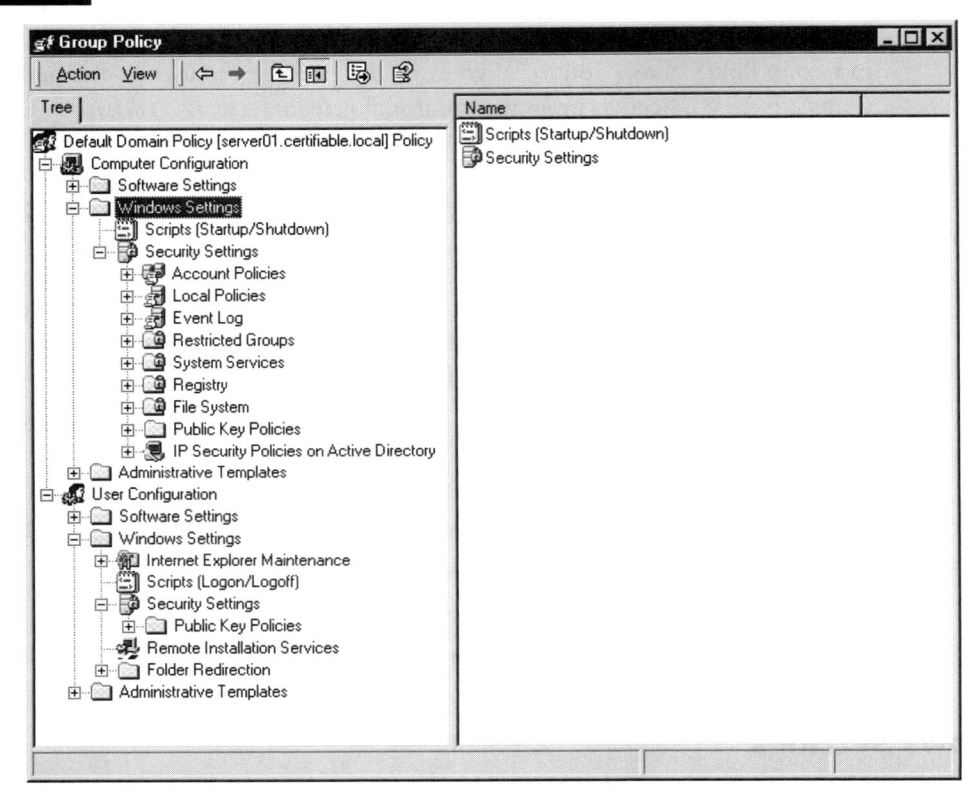

scripts to Startup/Shutdown (under Computer Configuration), as well as to Logon/Logoff (under User Configuration).

All scripts you assign to GPOs should be copied to the SYSVOL folder using the path %systemroot%\SYSVOL\SysVol*domain.name**guid*\. Startup and shutdown scripts should be stored in the \MACHINE\Scripts subfolder, and logon and logoff scripts should be stored in the \USER\Scripts folder. When you assign a script, you'll see a Show Files button that will open the appropriate folder in Windows Explorer.

Once you've assigned a script, you can use options under Administrative Templates to control how scripts are executed. By default, script processing is *synchronous,* meaning that each script process is dependent on the outcome of the previous process, and a process will not begin until the previous process is completed. You also have the option to run scripts *asynchronously,* which allows the processes to run in parallel. Asynchronous processing is faster, though it should only be used when there are no dependencies among multiple scripts. Furthermore, if you run logon scripts asynchronously, it's possible that the users will be able to get to their desktops before the script finishes running. You'll also find options to run scripts visibly or invisibly in the Administrative Templates.

Security Settings

The Security Settings node gives you fine-grained control over security options. Most of the options are presented under Computer Configuration, since they naturally apply to machines rather than users. We'll look at each of the subnodes in the sections that follow.

Account Policies   The Account Policies node provides options for setting password, account lockout, and Kerberos authentication policies. Under Password Policy, shown in Figure 6-12, you'll find the following settings:

- **Enforce password history**   Enable this option to prevent users from reusing the same password. For example, setting this to a value of 4 would require that a user's new password not match any of her previous four passwords.

- **Maximum password age**   Specifies how long a password can be used before the user must create a new password.

- **Minimum password age**   Specifies how long a password must be used before the user is allowed to change the password.

- **Minimum password length**   Sets the minimum length, in characters, for passwords. For example, setting this to 8 would prevent a user from creating a password that is less than eight characters in length.

- **Passwords must meet complexity requirements**   A password filter sets requirements such as "the password must contain at least one digit" or "the password cannot contain the username." Selecting this option forces all passwords to meet the requirement of the filter.

on the job   *The best way to prevent hackers from using brute-force methods of gaining access to the network is to enable "Password must meet complexity requirements" and increase the minimum length of passwords.*

FIGURE 6-12 Password policies shown in the details pane

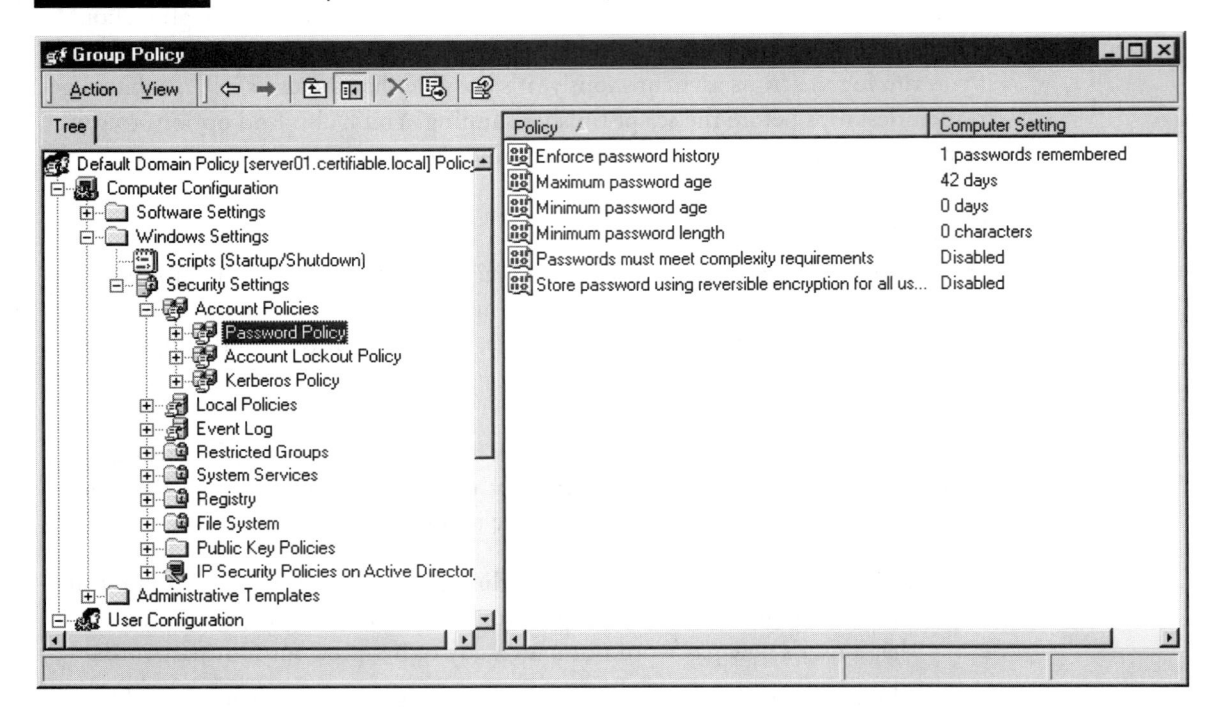

- **Store passwords using reversible encryption...** If selected, allows the use of digest authentication by IIS.

The Account Lockout Policy node provides settings that prevent users from trying to break into an account by guessing at passwords. The options include:

- **Account lockout duration** Specifies how long a user is locked out of an account once the account lockout threshold has been reached.

- **Account lockout threshold** Specifies how many times a user can attempt to log in with an invalid password before being locked out of the account altogether.

- **Reset account lockout counter after** Specifies the duration, in minutes, between the moment the account lockout threshold is reached and when the counter for counting failed attempts is reset to zero.

Both Windows 2000 and Windows XP implement the Kerberos Key Distribution Center (KDC) as a domain service. The KDC is a single process that provides authentication services and ticket-granting services. When a user successfully logs in to a domain, the KDC issues a Ticket-Granting Ticket (TGT). To access a specific service, the user needs to be granted a session ticket for that service. The Kerberos Policy node lets you set policies as follows:

- **Enforce user logon restrictions**   Forces the user rights policy to be examined for either Log On Locally or Access This Computer From The Network rights on the target computer before issuing a service ticket.
- **Maximum lifetime for service ticket**   Specifies how long, in minutes, a session ticket that's been issued by the KDC remains active.
- **Maximum lifetime for user ticket**   Specifies how long a TGT issued by the KDC remains active.
- **Maximum lifetime for user ticket renewal**   Specifies the duration, in days, during which a TGT may be renewed.
- **Maximum tolerance for computer clock synchronization**   Kerberos uses timestamps as part of its authentication to prevent "replay attacks." This policy specifies how large a time difference will be tolerated between a client's clock and the server's clock before the clocks are considered out of sync.

When it comes to Exam 70-218, it's important to keep in mind that account policies *must* be set at the domain level. Furthermore, Windows 2000 allows only one domain account policy per domain. There's nothing to prevent you from applying account policies to an OU, and no warning telling you not to do this. Instead, the account policies just don't work! Account policies applied at the domain level will still be in effect, no matter what account policies you apply to the OU.

> *Exam 70-218 will test your ability to troubleshoot failed account policies by moving them from OUs to the domain level. The question might not specifically use the term "account policies," so remember that policies involving password requirements, account lockout, and Kerberos authentication are account policies that need to be linked at the domain level.*

Local Policies   Local policies apply to security settings on the local computer—that is, the computer being used by an application or user. Thus, the vast majority of policies appear under the Computer Configuration node as opposed to the User Configuration node. The selected events will be tracked in the Security Log, which you can access via Event Viewer in Administrative Tools. When you opt to keep track of a particular type of event, you'll be given the option to audit successful attempts, failed attempts, or both.

As shown in Figure 6-13, the Local Policies node offers three categories of options titled Audit Policy, User Rights Assignment, and Security Options. Under Audit Policy, you find options for auditing security events. You'll learn more about those in Chapter 12.

The User Rights Assignment node is where you assign user rights to computers. When you double-click an option, the dialog box shown in Figure 6-14 appears. There, you can select the Define These Policy Settings option to activate the policy, and then use the Add and Remove buttons to assign rights to users and groups. Most of the rights are self-explanatory, but I've listed a few here as examples:

- **Access this computer from the network** Determines which users and groups are allowed to connect to the computer over the network.

- **Add workstations to the domain** Determines which groups or users can add workstations to a domain. Valid only on domain controllers.

- **Backup files and directories** Determines which users and groups can circumvent file and directory permissions for the purposes of backing up files.

- **Change the system time** Determines which users and groups can change the computer's internal date and time.

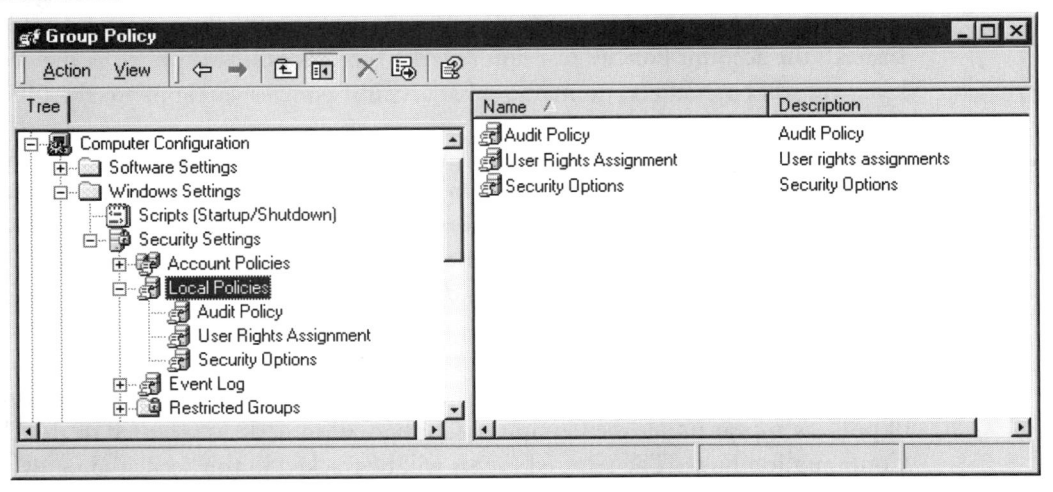

FIGURE 6-13 Local Policies expanded in the Group Policy console

- **Create permanent shared objects**   Determines which accounts can be used by processes to create a directory object in the Windows 2000 Server or Windows 2000 Professional object manager.
- **Deny access to this computer from the network**   Determines which users are prevented from accessing a computer over the network. Takes precedence over Access This Computer From The Network policy setting.
- **Log on locally**   Determines which users can log on locally to the computer.
- **Manage auditing and security policy**   Determines which users can specify object access auditing for individual resources, and also view and clear the security log in Event Viewer.
- **Restore files and directories**   Determines which users can circumvent file and directory permissions when restoring from backups. Also allows users to set any valid security principal as the owner of an object.
- **Shut down the system**   Determines which locally logged on users can shut down the operating system.
- **Take ownership of files or other objects**   Determines which users can take ownership of any securable objects in the system, files, folders, printers, Active Directory objects, Registry keys, processes, and threads.

FIGURE 6-14

Dialog box for assigning Log On Locally rights

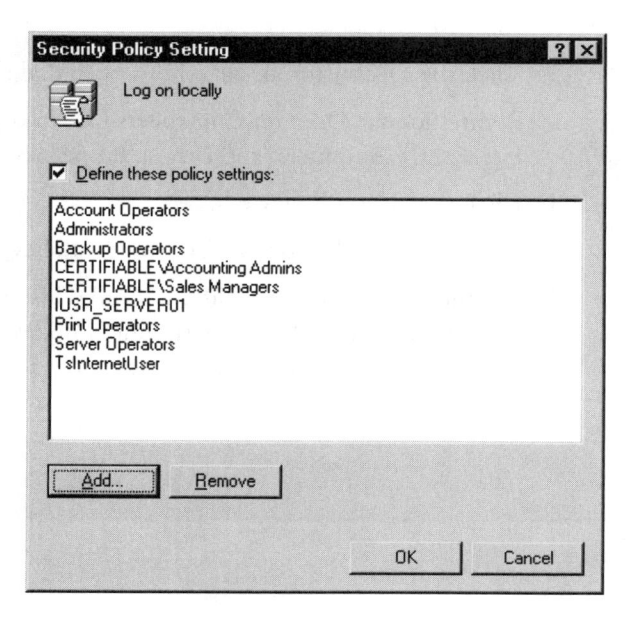

EXERCISE 6-2

Allowing OU Admins to Log on Locally

In Chapter 5, you created some user accounts. If you tried logging on to a domain controller using one of those accounts, you were no doubt denied access. This is because the default Domain Controllers GPO only allows administrators to log on locally. In this exercise, you'll create a new security group named OU Admins, and add a user account to it. Then, you'll allow members of that group to log on locally via User Rights Assignment. Here are the steps:

1. Log on to the domain controller with administrative privileges.
2. Open Active Directory Users and Computers.
3. Right-click the Corporate OU container and choose New | Group.
4. Enter **OU Admins** as the group name, and make it a Global Security group. Then click OK.
5. Right-click the new group in the details pane and choose Properties.
6. Click the Members tab, and then click the Add button.
7. Click on Ashley Marie, and then click the Add button.
8. You can repeat Steps 6 and 7 to add additional user accounts to this group if you wish.
9. Click the OK button to close both open dialog boxes.
10. Right-click the Domain Controllers OU in the left pane of Active Directory Users and Computers, and choose Properties.
11. Click the Group Policy tab.
12. Click the Default Domain Controllers Policy, and then click the Edit button.
13. Expand the Computer Configuration\Windows Settings\Security Settings\Local Policies\User Rights Assignment nodes, and then click Log On Locally in the details pane, as shown in Figure 6-15.

FIGURE 6-15 Log On Locally policy in User Rights Assignment

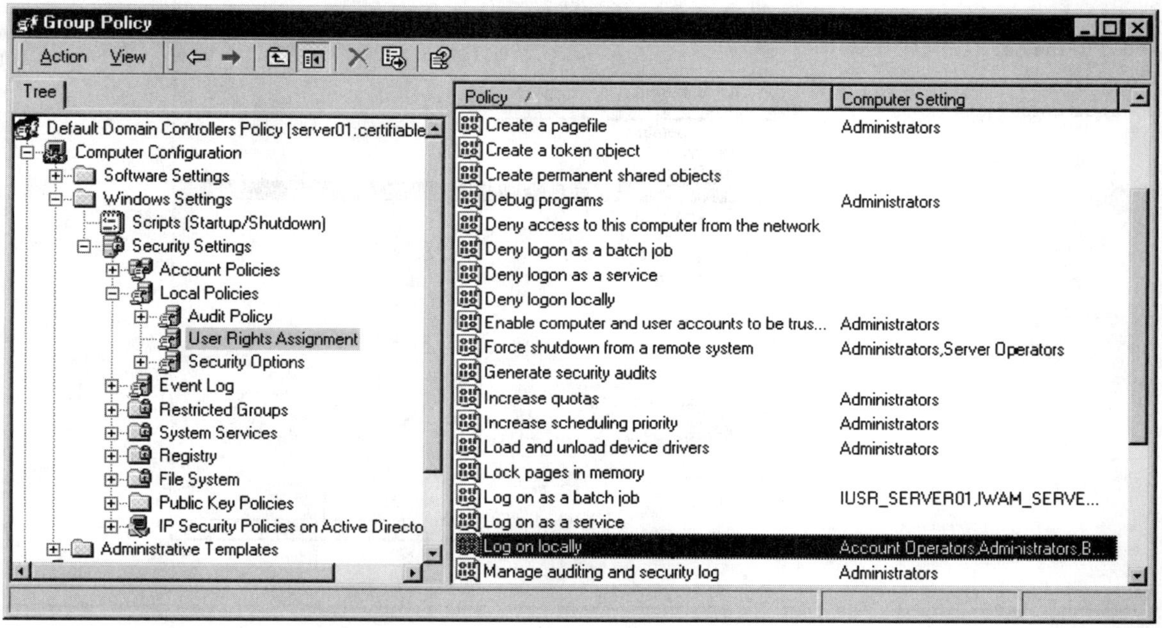

14. Right-click the Log On Locally policy and choose Security.
15. Click the Add button, and use the Browse button to select the OU Admins group.
16. Click the OK buttons to close the Add and Select dialog boxes. The new OU Admins group will appear in the access control list, as shown in Figure 6-16.
17. Click OK to close the Security Policy Setting dialog box.

Before you can test the new policy, you'll need to wait at least five minutes for the security policy to refresh, or use a **secedit /refreshpolicy** command to refresh immediately. Then, to test the new setting, close all remaining dialog boxes and windows, and log out. Then, try to log in to the domain controller using the amarie account, or any other users you added to the OU Admins security group.

FIGURE 6-16

OU Admins added to the Log On Locally policy settings

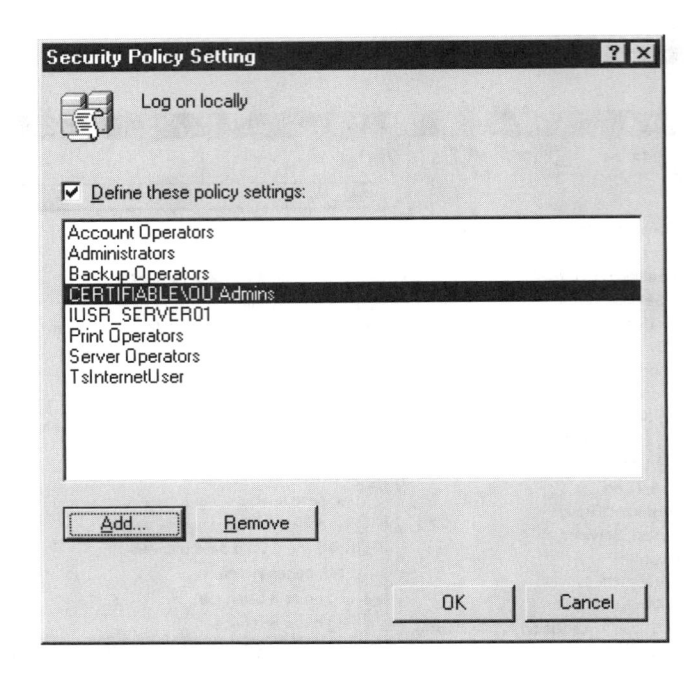

[Screenshot: Security Policy Setting dialog for "Log on locally" with "Define these policy settings" checked, showing list: Account Operators, Administrators, Backup Operators, CERTIFIABLE\OU Admins (highlighted), IUSR_SERVER01, Print Operators, Server Operators, TsInternetUser, with Add/Remove and OK/Cancel buttons.]

The Security Settings node provides a long list of policy settings, as shown in Figure 6-17. Most are self-explanatory, so I won't list them here. As always, you can double-click any item to see a description.

The remaining Security Settings categories are summarized next. Chapter 12 will discuss security settings in more detail.

- **Event Log** Provides policy settings for managing the size, permissions, and methods used by event logs (see Chapter 12).

- **Restricted Groups** Provides a container for controlling permanent memberships in special groups like Power Users, Backup Operators, and so forth. Used primarily to configure local groups on workstations and member servers (see Chapter 12).

- **System Services** Allows you manually to control startup and permissions of various system services including DHCP, file replication services, or RRAS to eliminate unauthorized modems.

Create Group Policy Objects 315

FIGURE 6-17 Security Options under Computer Configuration in Group Policy

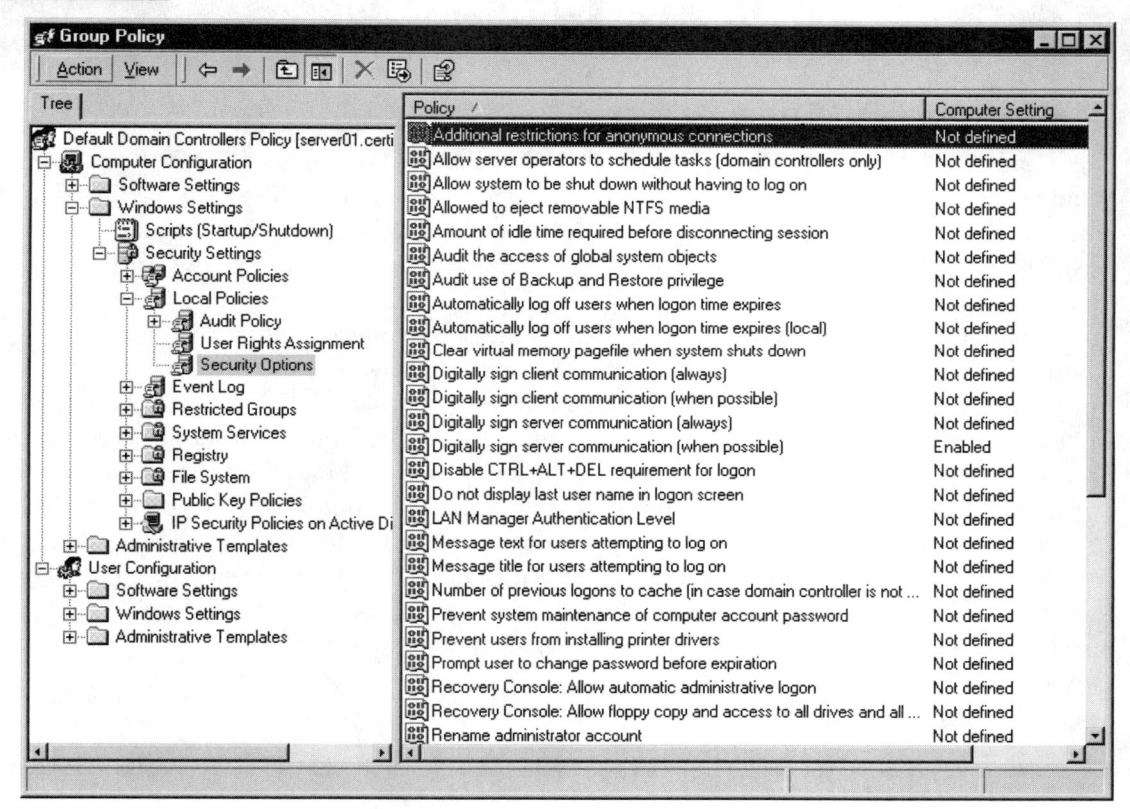

Policy	Computer Setting
Additional restrictions for anonymous connections	Not defined
Allow server operators to schedule tasks (domain controllers only)	Not defined
Allow system to be shut down without having to log on	Not defined
Allowed to eject removable NTFS media	Not defined
Amount of idle time required before disconnecting session	Not defined
Audit the access of global system objects	Not defined
Audit use of Backup and Restore privilege	Not defined
Automatically log off users when logon time expires	Not defined
Automatically log off users when logon time expires (local)	Not defined
Clear virtual memory pagefile when system shuts down	Not defined
Digitally sign client communication (always)	Not defined
Digitally sign client communication (when possible)	Not defined
Digitally sign server communication (always)	Not defined
Digitally sign server communication (when possible)	Enabled
Disable CTRL+ALT+DEL requirement for logon	Not defined
Do not display last user name in logon screen	Not defined
LAN Manager Authentication Level	Not defined
Message text for users attempting to log on	Not defined
Message title for users attempting to log on	Not defined
Number of previous logons to cache (in case domain controller is not ...	Not defined
Prevent system maintenance of computer account password	Not defined
Prevent users from installing printer drivers	Not defined
Prompt user to change password before expiration	Not defined
Recovery Console: Allow automatic administrative logon	Not defined
Recovery Console: Allow floppy copy and access to all drives and all ...	Not defined
Rename administrator account	Not defined

- **Registry** Allows you to set access permissions to Registry keys.
- **File System** Allows you to set access permissions to files and folders, including inheritance, auditing, and the right to take ownership.
- **Public Key Policies** Allows you to configure and manage public key certificate settings.
- **IP Security Policies on Active Directory** Allows you to specify which types of TCP/IP traffic will use IPSec (Internet Protocol Security).

FROM THE CLASSROOM

The Importance of Group Policies

Group policies are the key to managing a Windows 2000 network, and one of the most difficult concepts to grasp. The name itself, "*Group* Policy," is confusing because, for experienced administrators, the word "group" conjures up the idea of security groups. But you cannot link group policies to security groups, only the AD containers (sometimes generically referred to as *network objects*).

Remember that a GPO is a collection of settings that define a user's computing environment. The idea is to stipulate a user environment once, and then rely on the operating system to enforce those policies.

A group policy affects the domain, site, or OU to which it is linked. By default, the policy affects all the computers and users in the site, domain, or OU to which it is linked. It doesn't affect anything outside that container, and it does not affect security groups. However, you can use security groups to filter group policies—that is, to alter the scope of the policy.

So, if you create a GPO named My Policy and link it to the Domain Controllers OU, the policy applies to all the objects in the Domain Controllers OU. But, if you only want domain users, and not administrators, to be subjected to the policy, then you can filter the policy so that it is applied only to members of the Domain Users group.

—*Alan Simpson, MA, MCSA*

Remote Installation Services

Under User Configuration, the Windows Settings folder offers an additional option titled Remote Installation Services. You can use that to set policies that affect the options that are available to users who are using the RIS Client Installation Wizard to install Windows 2000 from a RIS server. The "choice" options, shown in Figure 6-18, are as follows:

- **Automatic Setup** Most installation options provided by the wizard will be configured by the administrator, and the user will have very few choices to make.

- **Custom Setup** Allows the user to create a unique name for the computer and specify where the account will be created within Active Directory.
- **Restart Setup** Restarts the operating system installation if, for whatever reason, it fails prior to completion.
- **Tools** Provides the ability to access tools in the RIS Client Installation Wizard.

The options associated with each choice are as follows:

- **Allow** If selected, offers the installation option to everyone who is subject to this GPO.
- **Don't Care** Same as "no setting," and means that the policy settings of the parent, if any, will be applied.
- **Deny** If selected, explicitly denies access to Client Installation Options to everyone who is subject to this GPO.

FIGURE 6-18

Choosing options that users will see when using the Client Installation Wizard with RIS

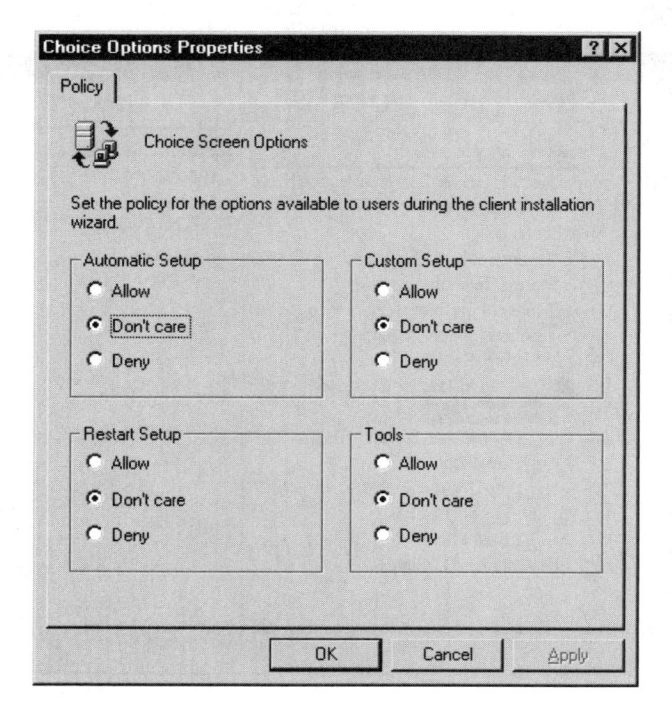

Folder Redirection

The User Configuration node also offers a Folder Redirection node, as shown in Figure 6-19. This option allows you to place a user's Application Data, Desktop, My Documents, My Pictures, and Start Menu folders on some centralized share, and follow the user around no matter which computer she logs in to.

Folder redirection provides benefits to administrators as well. For example, placing users' Start Menu, Desktop, and Application Data folders in a single share ensures that all users will have identical configurations, which greatly simplifies support by help desk personnel. It also allows an administrator to place items in these folders, as necessary, to provide standardized options across the domain or OU. Placing users' My Documents and My Pictures folders at a centralized location greatly simplifies that task of backing up those items on a regular schedule.

FIGURE 6-19 Folder Redirection is available under Windows Settings in the User Configuration node.

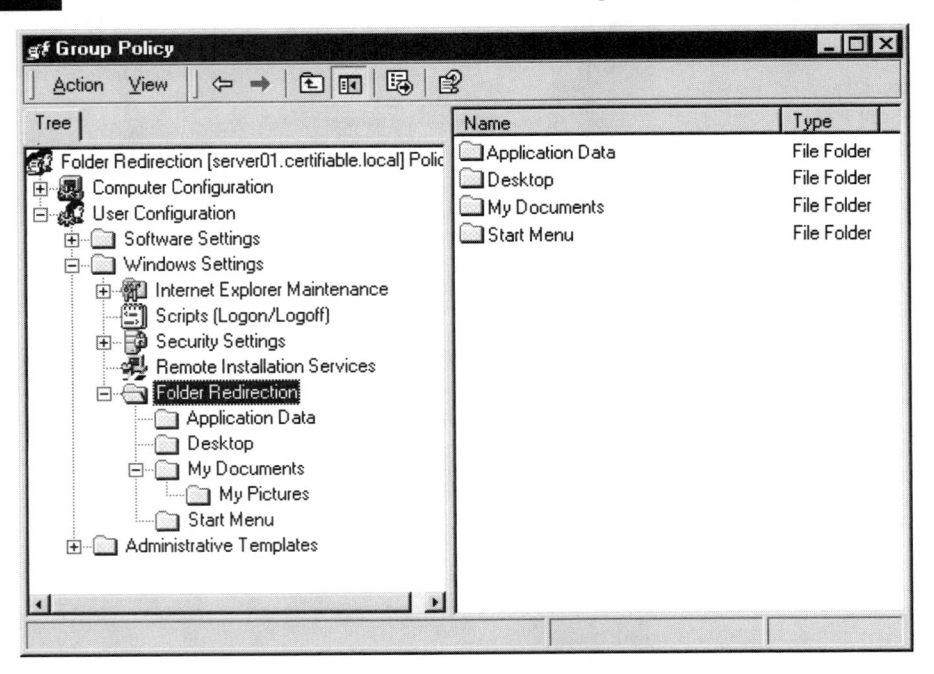

To set a location and specify policies for a folder, right-click the folder and choose Properties. On the Target tab, shown on the left side of Figure 6-20, you can choose from two different methods of redirecting the folder:

- **Basic**   Redirects all users who are subject to the policy to the same location
- **Advanced**   Allows you to choose a location for the object based on membership in security groups

Once you've chosen an option, you can specify the target location in standard UNC format: in other words, *servername**sharename*. If each user will have a separate folder within the share, you can use %username% as a placeholder for the specific user's name (for example, *server**share*\\%username%).

Options on the Settings tab, shown on the right side of Figure 6-20, vary slightly from object to object, but are self-explanatory. Options include things like granting the user exclusive rights to the folder, moving the current contents of the folder to the new location, and choosing what to do in the event the policy is removed.

FIGURE 6-20   Properties for redirecting folders

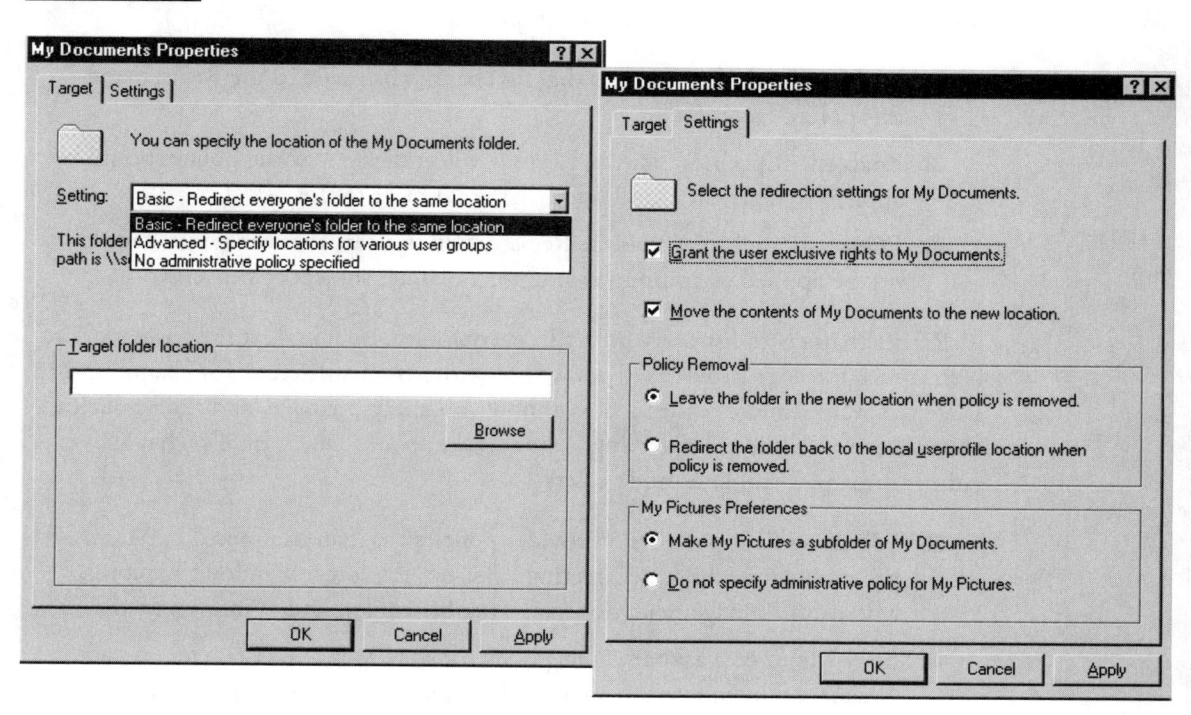

Administrative Templates

The Administrative Templates container contains all Registry-based policy information, similar to System Policies in Windows NT. The settings are based on *template files* (ADM files) that adjust users' machine configurations and environment, thereby allowing you to lock down users' computers and gain fine control over exactly what users can and cannot do. The settings defined in Administrative Templates under the Computer Configuration container are applied to HKEY_LOCAL_MACHINE\Software\Policies keys. Settings defined under User Configuration are written to HKEY_CURRENT_USER\Software\Policies.

There are a ton of policy settings under Administrative Templates\Windows Components, grouped into folders such as NetMeeting, Internet Explorer, Windows Explorer, and so forth. Those allow you to set policies for specific Windows programs.

The Start Menu & Taskbar node, shown in Figure 6-21, provides options for customizing users' Start menus. All the policies are currently set to the default Not Configured setting. Double-clicking any policy allows you to change that setting, and also provides an explanation of what the policy does. For the vast majority of policies, you'll be given three simple options:

- **Not Configured**   Specifies that no changes be made to the Registry for this policy
- **Enabled**   Specifies that the Registry will indicate that the policy should be applied to computers and users that are subject to this GPO
- **Disabled**   Specifies that the Registry will indicate that the policy should not be applied to computers and users that are subject to this GPO

Rather than try to list every policy in every folder, we'll look at the basic types of settings each folder provides. This will be more than sufficient for Exam 70-218, since the exam is more concerned with how you apply, manage, and filter policies than where each and every setting is stored. So, in a nutshell, here's what the Administrative Templates node offers:

- **Windows Components**   Provides policies that can be applied to Microsoft programs, including NetMeeting, Internet Explorer, Windows Explorer, Microsoft Management Console, Task Scheduler, and Windows Installer.
- **Start Menu & Taskbar**   Sets policies for the Windows Start menu and Taskbar, allowing you to choose what appears on those objects and to prevent users from making changes to those objects.

FIGURE 6-21 The Start Menu & Taskbar policies in the details pane

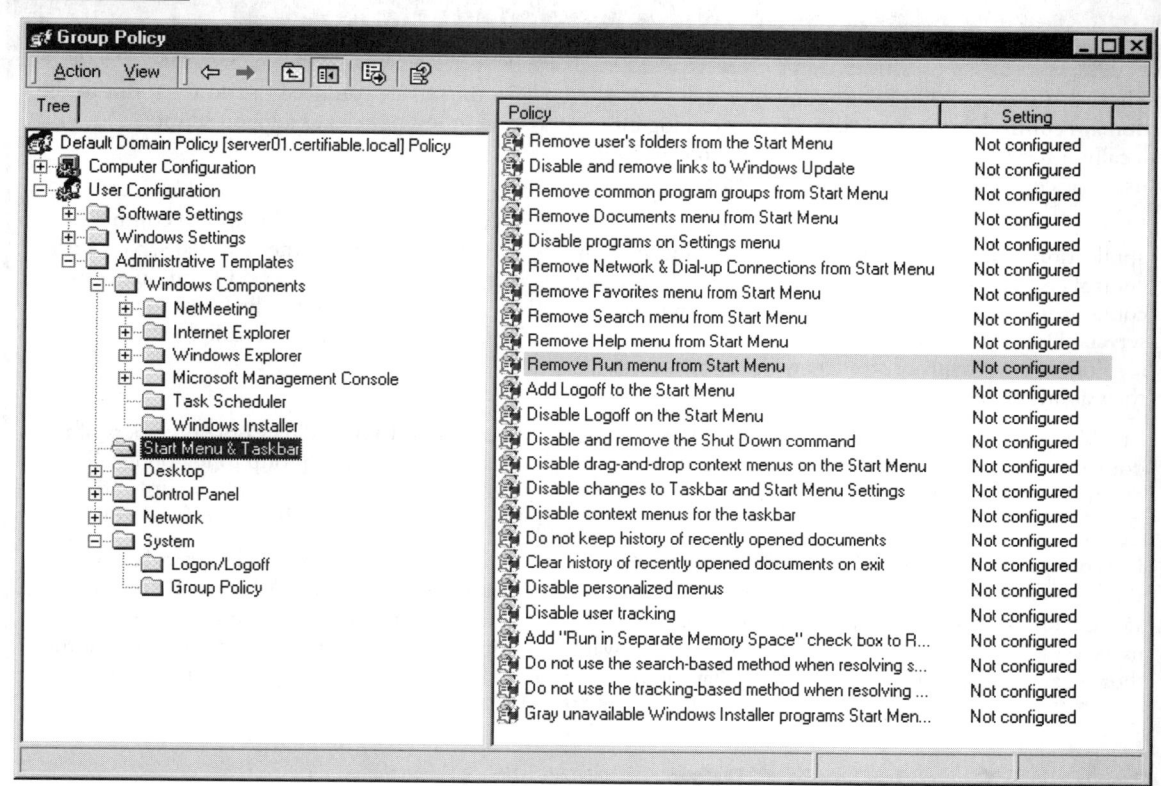

![Group Policy window showing Start Menu & Taskbar policies. Tree pane on left shows Default Domain Policy [server01.certifiable.local] Policy expanded to Computer Configuration and User Configuration, with User Configuration expanded to Software Settings, Windows Settings, Administrative Templates (expanded to Windows Components with NetMeeting, Internet Explorer, Windows Explorer, Microsoft Management Console, Task Scheduler, Windows Installer; Start Menu & Taskbar highlighted; Desktop, Control Panel, Network, System expanded to Logon/Logoff and Group Policy). Details pane lists policies all marked "Not configured":
- Remove user's folders from the Start Menu
- Disable and remove links to Windows Update
- Remove common program groups from Start Menu
- Remove Documents menu from Start Menu
- Disable programs on Settings menu
- Remove Network & Dial-up Connections from Start Menu
- Remove Favorites menu from Start Menu
- Remove Search menu from Start Menu
- Remove Help menu from Start Menu
- Remove Run menu from Start Menu
- Add Logoff to the Start Menu
- Disable Logoff on the Start Menu
- Disable and remove the Shut Down command
- Disable drag-and-drop context menus on the Start Menu
- Disable changes to Taskbar and Start Menu Settings
- Disable context menus for the taskbar
- Do not keep history of recently opened documents
- Clear history of recently opened documents on exit
- Disable personalized menus
- Disable user tracking
- Add "Run in Separate Memory Space" check box to R...
- Do not use the search-based method when resolving s...
- Do not use the tracking-based method when resolving ...
- Gray unavailable Windows Installer programs Start Men...]

- **Desktop** Controls the appearance and behavior of the Windows desktop, and can be used to prevent users from making and saving changes to the desktop.

- **Control Panel** Gives you precise control over users' ability to use the Control Panel, ranging from no access at all to the ability to access only specific Control Panel icons and capabilities.

- **Network** Provides policy settings for using Offline Files and Network and Dial-Up Connections.

- **System** Provides policies for controlling a wide range of Windows operating system features, including Logon/Logoff policies and policies that determine the user's ability to manage GPOs.

Before we go any further here, let's take a look at some scenario questions and answers that might arise.

SCENARIO & SOLUTION

I have a Windows 2000 Server computer that's not a domain controller, to which several users can log on locally. I need a script to be run each time one of those users logs on. How would I configure that?	On the server, you need to add the script to the local group policies as a logon script.
I have a group of servers that act strictly as application-based terminal servers; they are not domain controllers. I have a security group named TSUsers that contains user accounts for all users that log on to those servers. How do I prevent the members of TSUsers from logging on to domain controllers without restricting their ability to log on to the terminal servers?	You could create an OU named Terminal Servers, and move all the terminal servers into that OU. Then, create a GPO and link it to the new OU. Configure the GPO to allow the TSUsers group to log on locally.
My AD forest consists of a root domain with two child domains. I need to restrict the Log On Locally right to members of the local Administrators group. How can I do this?	Create a GPO that allows only members of the local Administrators group to log on locally. Link the GPO to the parent domain, and choose the No Override option for that link.
I've configured roaming profiles for Windows 2000 Professional client users, and placed all profiles in the \servername\Profiles\%username% path. I've allowed users to make changes to their desktops, but I don't want those changes saved when they log off. What should I do?	This is really a matter of using mandatory profiles more than a GPO issue. If you simply rename the ntuser.dat files for each user to ntuser.man, any changes the user makes to their desktop will not be saved when they log off.

Creating Stand-alone GPOs

When you first create a new GPO, it's linked to whatever container you right-clicked to start the process. However, you can link a GPO to any number of AD containers. You might find it convenient to create *stand-alone* GPOs for this purpose. A stand-alone GPO is one that can be managed within its own MMC console. Initially, you can create the GPO by right-clicking any site, domain, or OU in Active Directory Users and Computers. Click the Group Policy tab, and then click the New button. Type in a new name for the GPO and press ENTER. For example, in Figure 6-22, I've created a new GPO named Start Menu Icons GPO. When you've finished, just click the Close button to return to the console.

Once the new GPO is created, you can create a custom console that focuses on just the new GPO, making it easy to manage and link the GPO as required. To create the custom GPO console, follow these steps:

1. Click the Start button and choose Run.

Create Group Policy Objects 323

FIGURE 6-22

A new GPO

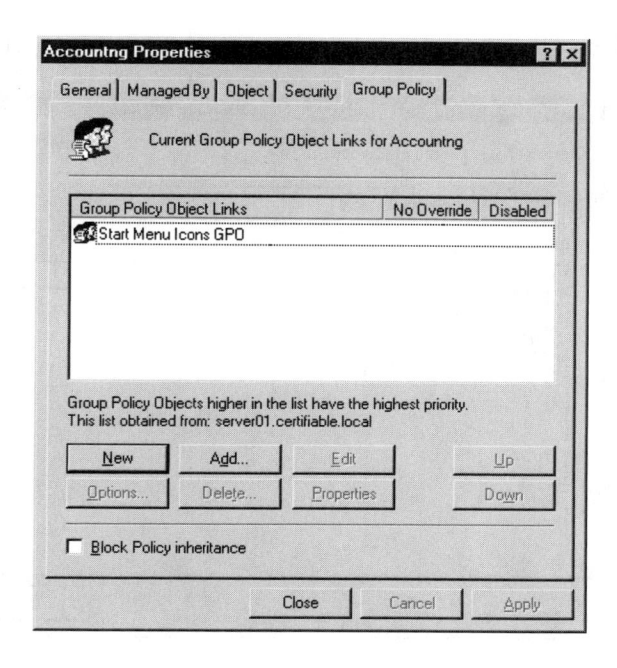

2. Type **mmc** in the Open dialog box and click OK to open the Microsoft Management Console.
3. From the Console menu, choose Add/Remove Snap-In.
4. In the Add/Remove Snap-In dialog box that opens, click Add. The Add Standalone Snap-In dialog box opens.
5. In the list of available stand-alone snap-ins, click Group Policy and click Add. The Select Group Policy Object Wizard opens.
6. Click the Browse button to open the Browse For A Group Policy Object dialog box.
7. Navigate to the name of the GPO you wish to open. For example, in Figure 6-23, I clicked the All tab, and then clicked Start Menu Icons GPO.
8. Click the OK button to return to the wizard, and then click the Finish button.
9. Click Close to close the Add Standalone Snap-In dialog box, and then click OK to close the Add/Remove Snap-In dialog box.
10. From the Console menu, choose Save As, type in a name for the GPO, and click the Save button.

324 Chapter 6: Creating and Implementing Group Policies

FIGURE 6-23 Start Menu Icons GPO selected in the Browse For A Group Policy Object dialog box

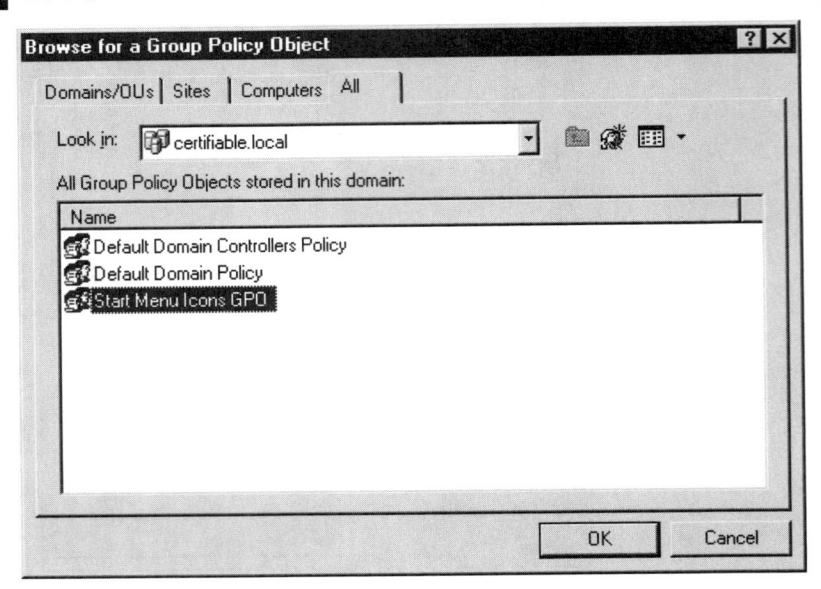

From now on, you'll be able to open this GPO as a stand-alone object from the Administrative Tools menu.

Choosing Policy Settings for the GPO

When the stand-alone GPO is open, you're ready to start choosing policy settings. Expand nodes as required to get to the settings you want to change. By default, most will initially be set to Not Configured. To set a policy, just double-click the policy in the details pane to get to its Properties dialog box. Then, choose whichever option you wish. For example, in Figure 6-24, I've expanded User Configuration and Administrative Templates, and opened the Start Menu & Taskbar folder. Then, in the details pane, I double-clicked Remove Run Menu From Start Menu and enabled that policy. After clicking OK to close the dialog box, the Enabled setting is visible in the details pane.

You could, of course, specify any combination of policies you wish. For example, the Start Menu Icons GPO could also disable the Control Panel by enabling the Disable Control Panel policy in the Control Panel node, as shown in Figure 6-25.

Create Group Policy Objects **325**

FIGURE 6-24 The Remove Run Menu From Start Menu policy enabled

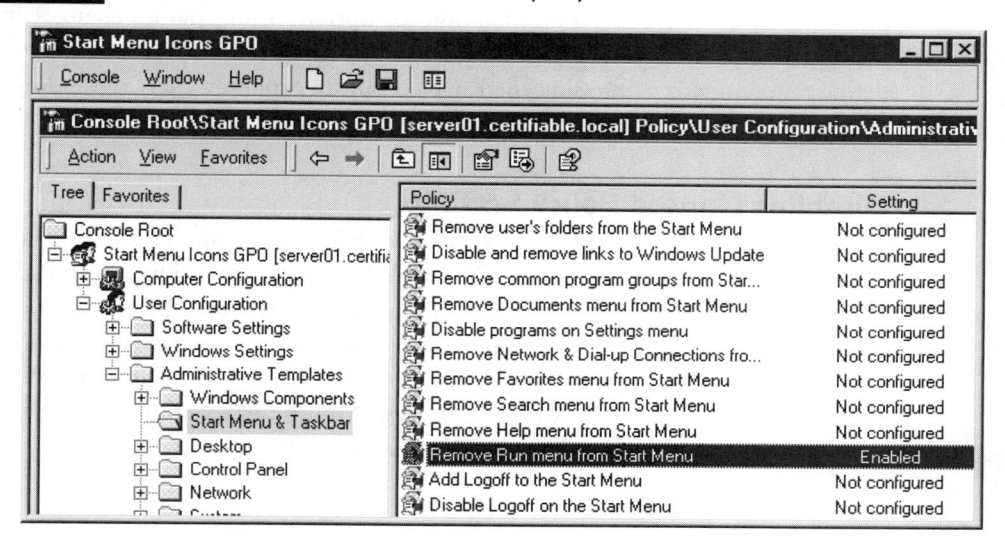

FIGURE 6-25 Control Panel disabled

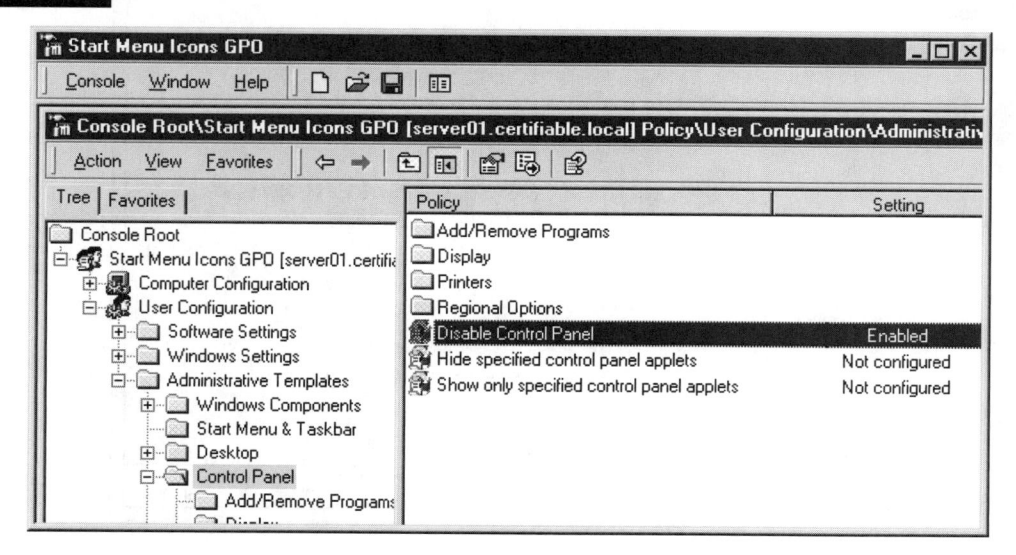

When choosing policies that have Enabled, Disabled, and Not Configured options, bear in mind that a Not Configured option means that no changes are made to the client computer's existing Registry settings. Whatever its local policies define remain intact. Choosing the Enabled option explicitly changes the Registry setting. Choosing Disabled explicitly removes the Registry setting.

Disabling Unused Policy Settings

When you create a stand-alone GPO using only a few settings, there's no need to have the client process all the Not Configured options that you have left unchanged. Disabling those options will speed the client startup and logon process. For example, if you've only set options under User Configuration, you could disable Computer Configuration settings for the GPO by right-clicking the GPO name and choosing Properties. Use the check box to disable either Computer Configuration or User Configuration, as shown in Figure 6-26, and click OK.

FIGURE 6-26

Computer Configuration settings disabled for this GPO

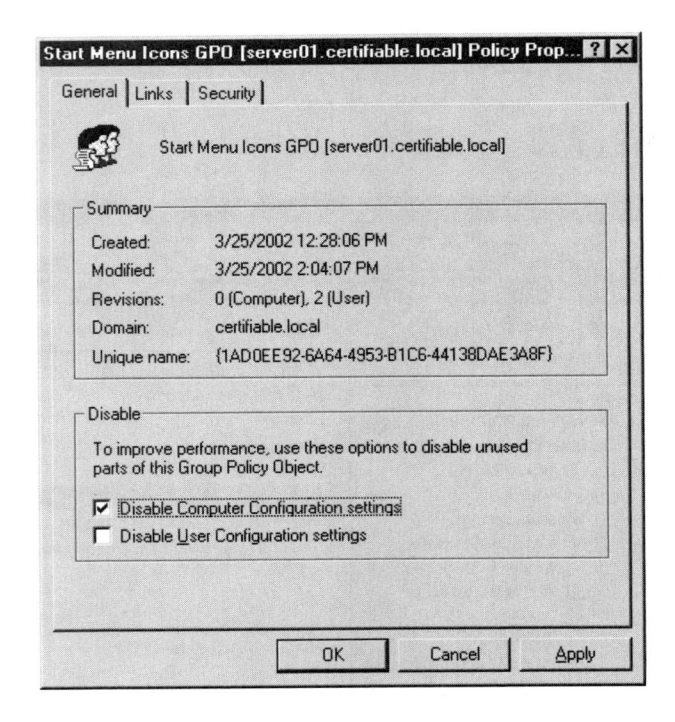

EXERCISE 6-3

Create a Stand-alone GPO

In this exercise, you'll create a stand-alone GPO like the Start Menu Icons GPO described earlier in the text. In later exercises, you'll link, filter, and delegate control of this same GPO. To get started, follow these steps:

1. Log in to the domain controller with administrative privileges.
2. Open Active Directory Users and Computers.
3. Right-click the domain name and choose Properties. Then, click the Group Policy tab in the dialog box that opens.
4. Click the New button and name the new GPO **Start Menu Icons GPO**.
5. Click the Close button, and then close Active Directory Users and Computers.
6. Click the Start button, choose Run, type **mmc**, and click the OK button.
7. From the Console menu, choose Add/Remove Snap-In.
8. Click the Add button in the Add/Remove Snap-In dialog box to open the Add Standalone Snap-In dialog box.
9. Click Group Policy in the dialog box that opens, and then click Add.
10. Click the Browse button, select the Start Menu Icons GPO, and click OK.
11. Click the Finish button; then click the Close button in the Add Standalone Snap-In dialog box.
12. Click the OK button.
13. From the Console menu, choose Save.
14. Type **Start Menu Icons GPO** as the filename, and click the Save button.
15. Close the MMC and choose Yes when asked about saving your changes.

Now you can try opening the stand-alone GPO from the menu. Follow these steps:

1. Click the Start button.
2. Choose Programs | Administrative Tools. You should be able to open the new GPO by clicking its name in the Administrative Tools menu, as shown in Figure 6-27.

328 Chapter 6: Creating and Implementing Group Policies

FIGURE 6-27 Stand-alone GPO is available in the Administrative Tools menu

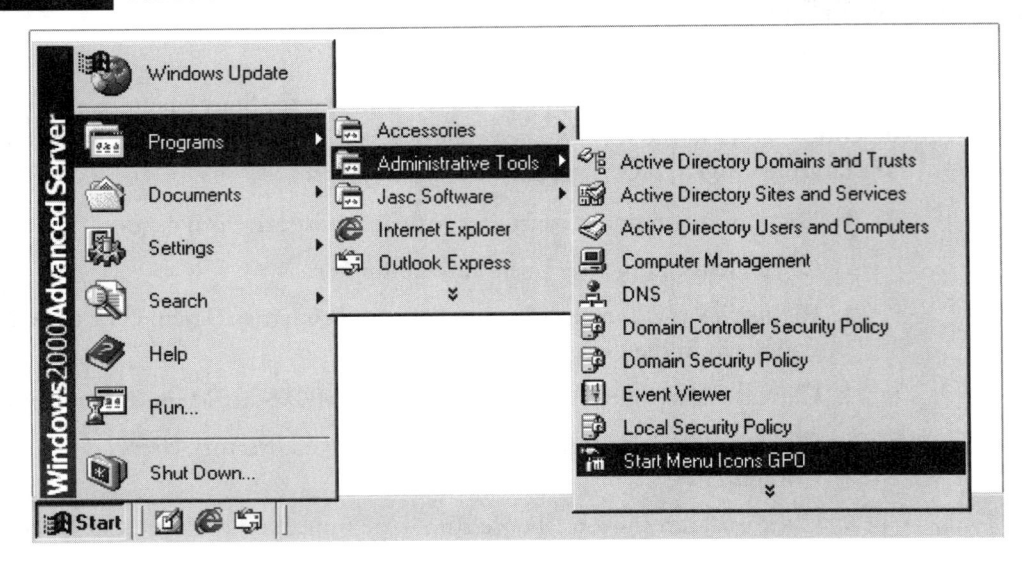

3. Click the name of the GPO to open it.

Finally, you'll want to make this GPO do something. To make it behave like the example presented in text, follow these steps:

1. In the console tree, expand User Configuration\Administrative Template, and click Start Menu & Taskbar.

2. Double-click Remove Run Menu From Start Menu, choose Enabled, and click OK.

3. Click the Control Panel node, double-click Disable Control Panel, choose Enabled, and click OK.

In a later exercise, we'll link this GPO to an OU rather than the default domain GPO, and filter it so that it only applies to specific security groups.

CERTIFICATION OBJECTIVE 6.03

Link Group Policies to AD Objects

As discussed earlier in this chapter, GPOs are linked to specific AD containers, such as the domain or a specific OU. Unless you block inheritance, policies are automatically applied to child objects. For example, let's say you have an OU named Corporate that, in turn, contains two child OUs named Accounting and Sales. If you link a GPO to the Corporate OU, its policies will be inherited by the child domains, as illustrated in Figure 6-28.

Suppose now that you've delegated administrative control of the Accounting OU to some other group of administrators. Those administrators decide that they don't want the Corporate policies applied to them, so they create their own GPO and block policy inheritance. This would not be a good thing if the Corporate policy needs to be applied to all child domains. The "fix" is to enable the No Override option for the Corporate GPO so that the child OUs can't block policy inheritance.

FIGURE 6-28

A GPO linked to the Corporate OU would be inherited by the child OUs named Accounting and Sales.

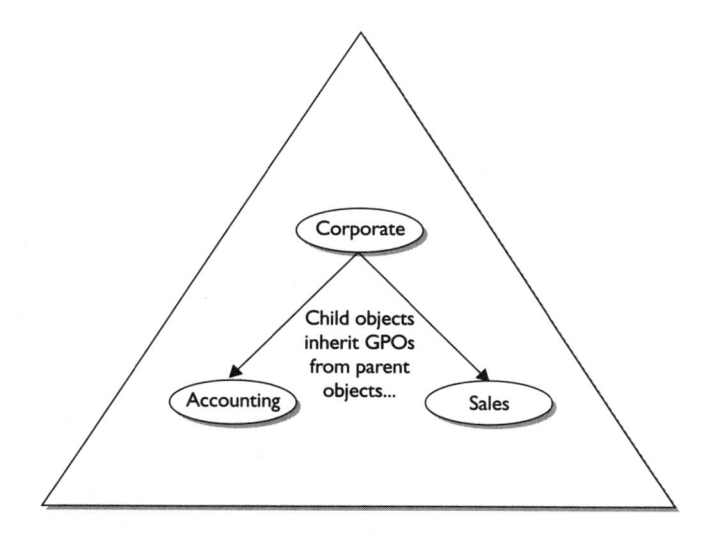

exam
Watch

Remember that account policies are the one exception to linking GPOs to OUs. Account policies (which include options such as account lockout, password, and Kerberos authentication policies) must be linked at the domain level. Account policies that are linked to OUs are ignored.

Bear in mind that if a GPO affects computer Registry settings, the object that the OU is linked to must contain some computer objects. Otherwise, there won't be any machines to which the policy can be applied. So, to link a GPO to a group of machines, you would first need to move the computer objects from the Computers container into an OU. Then, link the GPO to that OU.

When you first create a GPO, it exists within the container in which it was created. (Well, it exists in the container logically. Physically, they exist in the %systemroot%\SYSVOL\sysvol*domainname*\Policies folder.) But you can link a GPO to any number of containers you wish. The procedure for linking a GPO to a container is similar to that of creating a new GPO from scratch.

on the
Job

If you want to link a GPO at the Site level, you start by opening Active Directory Sites and Services. Otherwise, open Active Directory Users and Computers.

Next, right-click the object to which you want to link the GPO. Choose Properties, and click the Group Policy tab. Any GPOs that are already linked to the container will be listed in the dialog box. For example, Figure 6-29 shows a hypothetical example where several GPOs are already linked to a container.

To link an existing GPO to the container, click the Add button. The Add A Group Policy Object Link dialog box opens. Clicking the All tab will display a list of all available GPOs. Just click any GPO name, and click OK to add the GPO to the list.

Remember that when multiple GPOs are linked to a container, as in Figure 6-29, they're processed from the bottom up, so those that are highest in the list have the highest priority. You can use the Up and Down buttons to move any GPO up or down within the list.

The Block Policy Inheritance check box, if selected, prevents the settings from GPOs that are linked to parent objects from being enforced on the current OU. However, if those higher-level GPOs have their No Override option set, blocking policy inheritance will have no effect. Those higher-level settings will still be applied.

You can also disable a GPO, to prevent its settings from being applied at all. Disabling a GPO is handy for testing and debugging purposes. For example, if you suspect a GPO is causing a problem, you can disable it without removing the link altogether.

Link Group Policies to AD Objects **331**

FIGURE 6-29

An example of multiple GPOs linked to a container

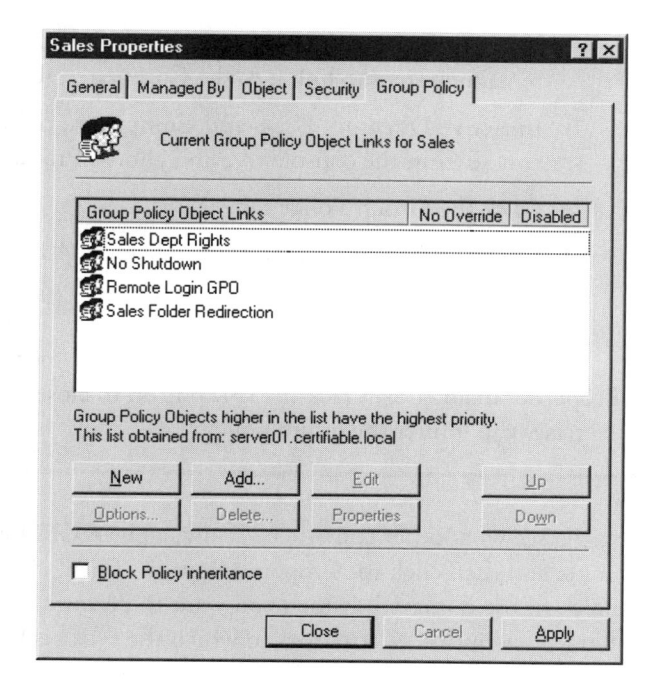

EXERCISE 6-4

Linking the Start Menu Icons GPO to an OU

When you created the Start Menu Icons GPO in the previous exercise, you linked it to the domain. Let's suppose you've changed your mind about that, and now want to link it to the OU Admins container. Here's how you can do that:

1. Log in to the domain controller with administrative privileges.
2. Open Active Directory Users and Computers from the Administrative Tools menu.
3. Right-click the domain name in the console tree, choose Properties, and click the Group Policy tab.
4. Click Start Menu Icons GPO and choose Delete.
5. Choose Remove The Link From The List and click OK.
6. Click Close to close the dialog box.

Chapter 6: Creating and Implementing Group Policies

7. Now the Start Menu Icons GPO isn't linked to any container. Follow the remaining steps to link it to the Corporate OU you created back in Chapter 5.
8. In Active Directory Users and Computers, right-click the Corporate container in the console tree and choose Properties.
9. Click the Group Policy tab.
10. Click the Add button, and then click the All tab.
11. Click Start Menu Icons GPO.

The GPO now appears in the Group Policy Object Links list in the Corporate Properties dialog box. Click the OK button to close the dialog box. In the next exercise, you'll filter the group policy.

To see what other containers, if any, a given GPO is linked to, click the GPO name and then click the Properties button. Then, click the Links tab. Choose the name of the domain in which you want to perform the search, and then click the Find Now button. Containers to which the GPO is linked will be listed.

SCENARIO & SOLUTION

I created a GPO and linked it to a branch office OU named SeattleOU. Now users of offline files for that office are complaining that they can't synchronize their offline files. What should I do?	The new GPO is preventing the use of offline files. You need to change the Prevent Use Of Offline Files Folder setting within that GPO to Not Configured. You'll find that under Computer Configuration\Administrative Templates\Network\Offline Files.
Can I create "Group Policy policies"? For example, could I create a GPO that disables the Group Policy tab in Active Directory tools?	Yes. You'll find policy settings under User Configuration\Administrative Tools\Windows Components\Microsoft Management Console\Restricted/Permitted Snap-Ins\Group Policy.
Can I create a GPO that adds a Registry key to computers within its container?	Yes, under Computer Configuration\Windows Settings\Security Settings\Registry. Remember, though, that the Administrative Templates nodes provides an easy configuration interface for the vast majority of Registry settings.

CERTIFICATION OBJECTIVE 6.04

Filter Group Policies

GPOs are applied to network objects, not people. But, as mentioned earlier in the chapter, you can *filter* a GPO's scope by setting permissions on the Security tab of the GPO's Properties dialog box. In a stand-alone GPO, you just right-click the name of the GPO, choose Properties, and click the Security tab. From Active Directory Users and Computers, right-click the container to which the GPO has been linked and choose Properties. Click the Group Policy tab to see all GPOs that are linked to that container. Then, in the list of Group Policy Object Links that appears, click the name of the policy you wish to filter, click the Properties button, and then click the Security tab.

Different groups will have different permissions by default. For example, the left side of Figure 6-30 shows default permissions for the Authenticated Users group in a sample GPO. By default, group policies are applied to all authenticated users, as evidenced by the Allow–Read and Allow–Apply Group Policy permissions. The right side of Figure 6-30 shows the default permissions for the Domain Admins group.

Administrators have Read, Write, Create All Child Objects, and Delete All Child Objects permissions, as shown in the right half of Figure 6-30. These permissions grant administrators the ability to administer the GPO. Since Apply Group Policy is not selected for administrators, by default, administrators are not subject to the restrictions placed by the GPO. However, administrators could be subject to the policies of a GPO by virtue of their membership in the Authenticated Users group.

on the Job

If a group neither is subject to a GPO nor has any administrative authority over the GPO, you should clear the Read permission as well. This will prevent subject machines from even reading the GPO, which can speed startup time.

If you want to be selective in whom a GPO applies to, you'll probably want to remove Authenticated Users from the access control list. Just click the Authenticated Users group and click the Remove button. Then, you can use the Add button to add new groups to the list, and set permissions as appropriate for each group. When it

334 Chapter 6: Creating and Implementing Group Policies

FIGURE 6-30 The Security tab of a GPO's Properties dialog box

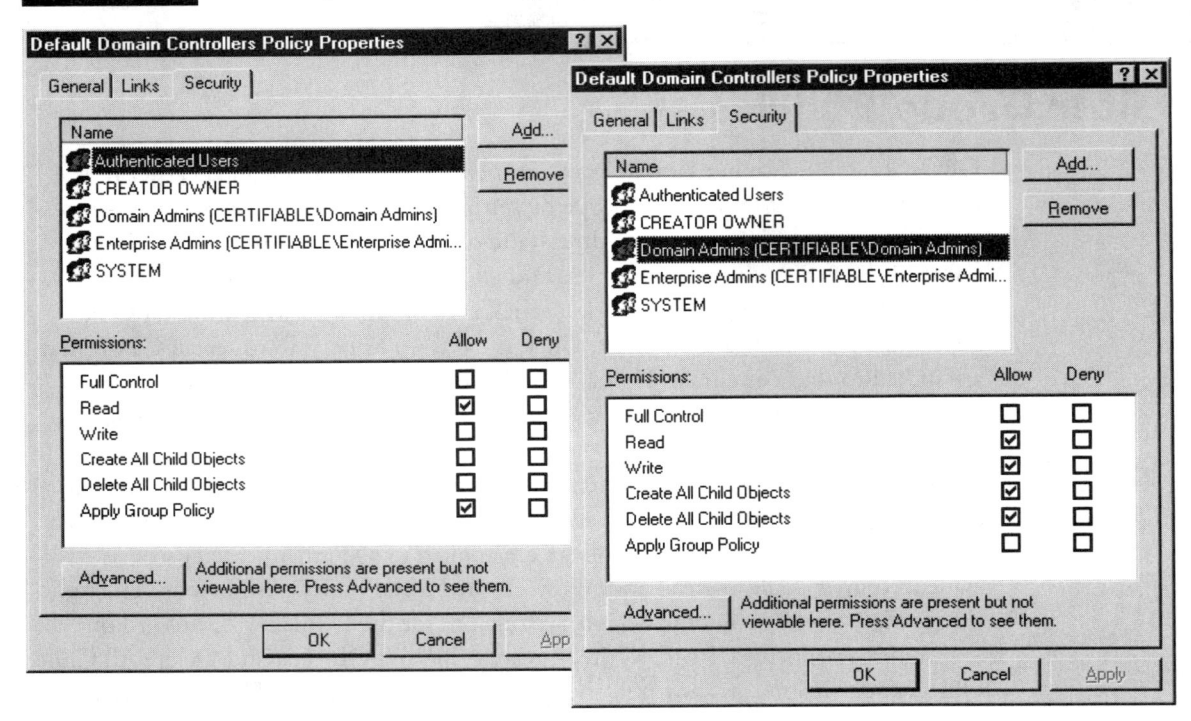

comes to making a security group subject to a GPO, the Read and Apply Group Policy options are really the only ones that count, as follows:

- **Allow–Read** and **Allow–Apply Group Policy**   Choosing both these options would force the GPO to be applied to the selected security group, unless they are members of at least one other security group that has either, or both, of these settings explicitly set to Deny.

- **Deny–Apply Group Policy**   Members of this group are exempt from the policy, no matter what other groups they belong to.

- **Neither configured** If neither Read nor Apply Group Policy is set to Allow or Deny, the GPO is irrelevant to the selected group. Any Apply or Deny settings defined in other groups to which a member belongs will remain intact and not be altered by the current GPO.

The permissions that appear for a group in the list are only the most basic ones. You can get to a more detailed list by clicking the Advanced button on the Security tab. Initially, you'll be taken to the Access Control Settings dialog box for the GPO, where you'll see a list of permission entries and groups. Some will already have "Special" permissions applied. To view or change the special permissions for a group, click the group name and then click the View/Edit button. There you'll find a more extensive list of permissions that you can allow or deny, as shown in Figure 6-31.

FIGURE 6-31

The Security tab of a GPO's Properties dialog box

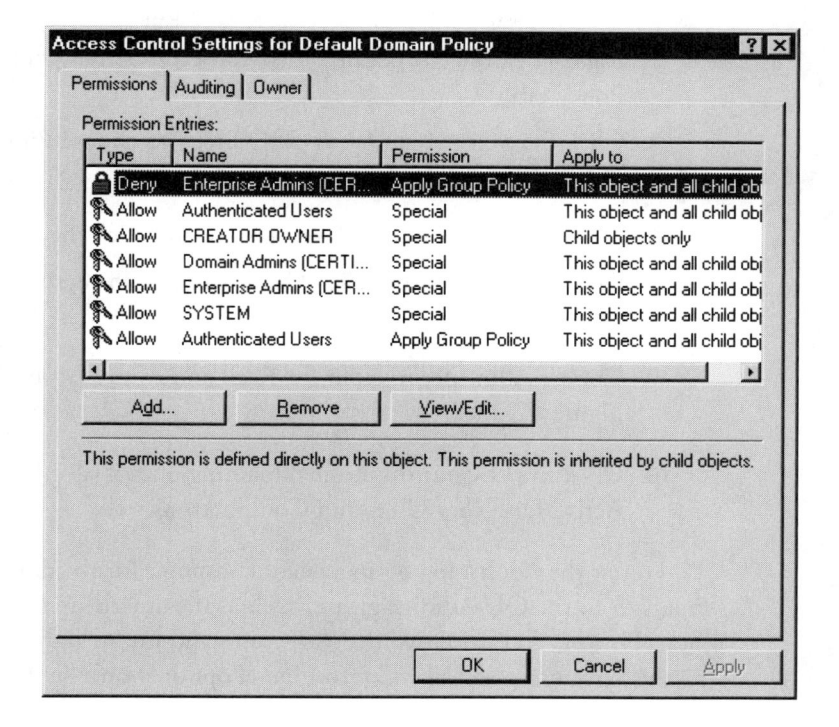

So, the bottom line on applying group policies is simply this: choose the Allow permission for Read, and Apply Group Policy for any group to which you want the policy applied. If you give a security group any more permissions than that, you're actually allowing them to administer group policies, as discussed next.

EXERCISE 6-5

Filter the Start Menu Icons GPO

In this exercise, you'll change the scope of (filter) the Start Menu Icons GPO so that it only applies to members of the OU Admins group. Follow these steps:

1. Log in to the domain controller with administrative privileges.
2. Open Active Directory Users and Computers.
3. Right-click the Corporate OU, choose Properties, and then click the Group Policy tab.
4. Click the Start Menu Icons GPO link and choose Properties.
5. Click the Security tab.
6. Click the Authenticated Users group, and click the Remove button.
7. Click the Add button, click OU Admins, and then click the Add button.
8. Click the OK button.
9. Choose Allow permissions for Read and Apply Group Policy, as shown in Figure 6-32.
10. Click the OK button in the remaining open dialog boxes. You can close Active Directory Users and Computers as well.

To test the results, log on to a client computer (or the domain controller) as a member of the OU Admins group, such as the amarie user account. Then click the Start button. You won't see the Run command in the Start menu. When you point to the Settings option, the Control Panel option won't be there.

FIGURE 6-32

Access Control Settings dialog box for a GPO

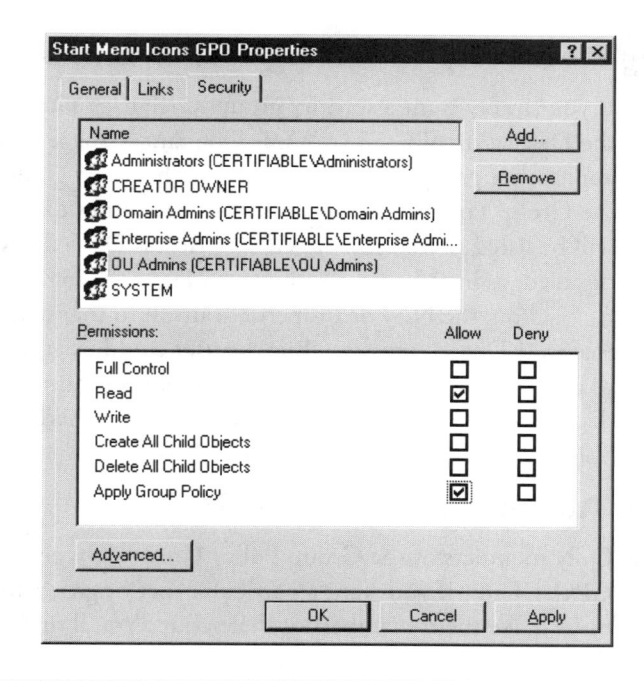

CERTIFICATION OBJECTIVE 6.05

Delegate Control of Group Policies

As you've seen, network administrators (members of the Domain Admins and Enterprise Admins groups) automatically have permissions to create and manage GPOs. Administrators can also use the permissions on the Security tab to delegate control of GPOs to other security groups. As a network administrator, you can delegate the following tasks independently:

- Manage Group Policy links only
- Create new Group Policy Objects
- Edit existing Group Policy Objects

We'll look at how you delegate these tasks in the sections that follow.

Delegating Authority to Manage GPO Links

If you simply want a security group to Manage Group Policy links, you can use the Delegation of Control Wizard to grant Manage Group Policy Links to the appropriate group. When the user who has been granted this permission opens the Group Policy tab in a container's Properties dialog box, existing GPOs will be listed as Inaccessible GPO – Access Denied and the Edit button will be disabled, as in the example shown in Figure 6-33.

Clicking the New or Properties button in that dialog box would display an Access Is Denied message. But the user could use the Add and Delete buttons to alter the list of GPO links, use the Options button to set No Override or to disable a GPO, and choose the Block Policy Inheritance option.

Delegating Authority to Create GPOs

Only members of the Group Policy Creator Owners security group can create new GPOs. Thus, if you want a particular user or group to have this permission, you must make them members of that group. You'll find the group in the Users

FIGURE 6-33

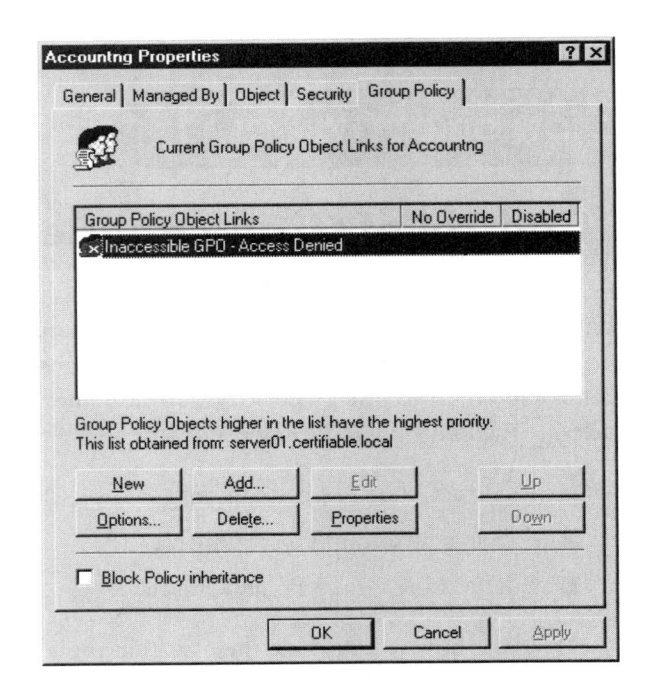

Read and Apply Group Policy permissions for the OU Admins group

container of Active Directory Users and Computers. For example, in Figure 6-34, I right-clicked the Group Policy Creator Owners group, chose Properties, and clicked the Members tab. Then, I used the Add button to make OU Admins a member of that group.

When a nonadministrator who is a member of the Group Policy Creator Owners group creates a new GPO, she becomes the Creator Owner of that GPO. She also will have the ability to edit that object, as well as any other objects she creates. But being a member of the Group Policy Creator Owners group does not grant her full control over all GPOs. Instead, the user can edit only those GPOs she creates herself. In and of itself, membership in the Group Policy Creator Owners group doesn't grant permission to link GPOs to sites, domains, or OUs. The aforementioned Manage Group Policy Links permission is required for that.

FIGURE 6-34 Making OU Admins members of the Group Policy Creator Owners security group

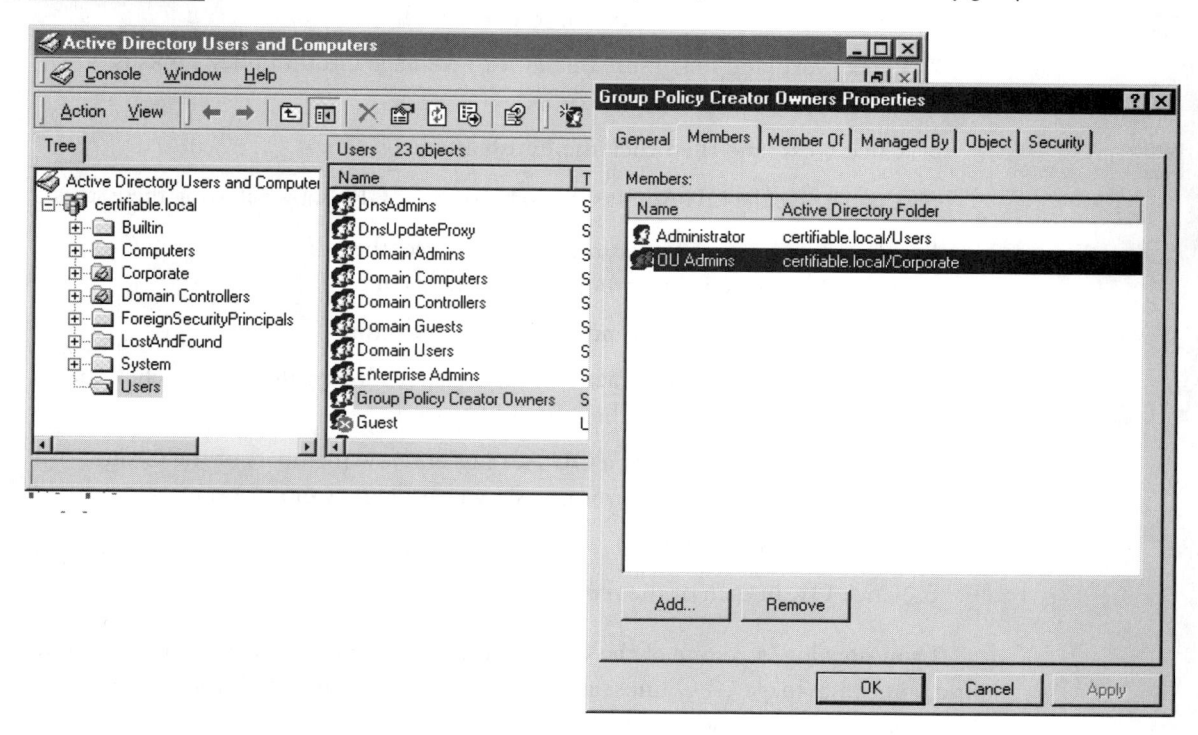

EXERCISE 6-6

Delegate Control of the Start Menu Icons GPO

In this exercise, you'll delegate the ability to manage GPO links and create new GPO links in the Corporate OU to the OU Admins security group. Follow these steps:

1. Log in to the domain controller with full administrative privileges.
2. Open Active Directory Users and Computers.
3. Right-click the Corporate OU and choose Delegate Control.
4. Click Next on the first wizard page. On the second wizard page, click the Add button.
5. In the Select Users, Computers, or Groups dialog box that opens, click OU Admins as the group to whom you want to delegate control, and then click the Add button.
6. Click the OK button to return to the wizard.
7. Click Next, and make sure that at least Manage Group Policy Links is selected, as shown in Figure 6-35.
8. Click Next, and then click the Finish button.

Next, you'll give the OU Admins the right to create GPOs, by following these steps:

1. Click the Users container in the console tree, then double-click the Group Policy Creator Owners group in the details pane.
2. Click the Members tab, and click the Add button.
3. In the Select Users, Contacts, Computers, or Groups dialog box, click the OU Admins group and click the Add button.
4. Click the OK button. The OU Admins are now members of the Group Policy Creator Owners group, as shown in Figure 6-36.
5. Click the OK button.
6. Click OK in each of the remaining open dialog boxes.

If you now log in to one of the OU Admins user accounts, such as amarie, you'll find you can manage GPO links, as well as create GPOs, in the Corporate OU. However, you still cannot edit GPOs that you didn't create.

Delegate Control of Group Policies 341

FIGURE 6-35

Making OU Admins members of the Group Policy Creator Owners security group

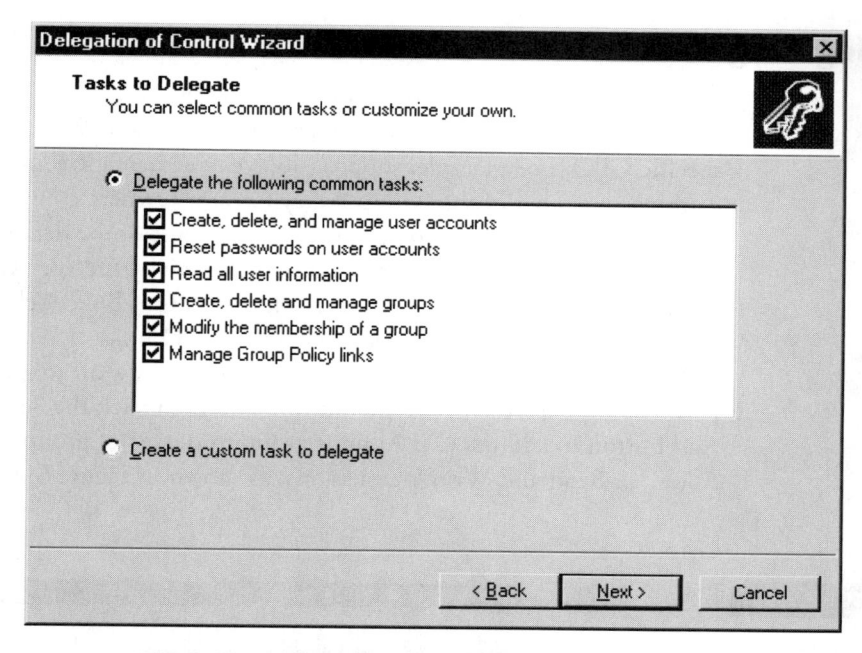

FIGURE 6-36

Make sure that Manage Group Policy Links is selected.

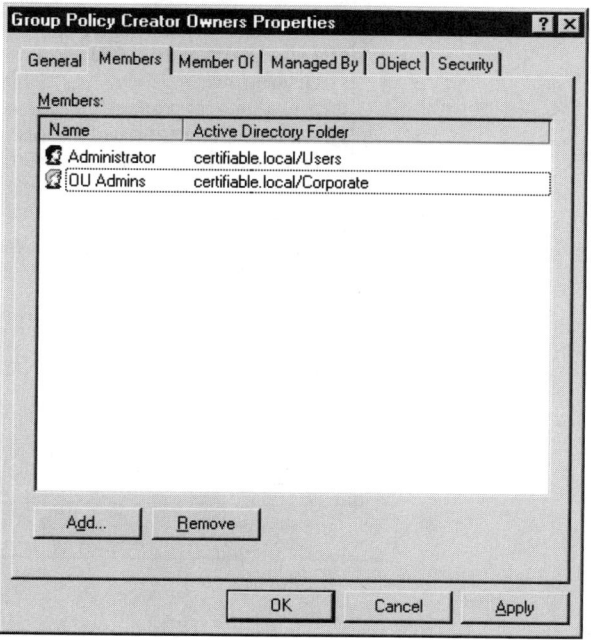

Delegating Authority to Edit GPOs

To edit a GPO that a user does not own, that user must be a member of the Group Policy Creator Owners group, and have both Read and Write permissions on the specific GPO. For example, suppose you've already made a group named OU Admins a member of the Group Policy Creator Owners group. Now you'd like to give members of that group permission to edit one of the default security policies, or a GPO that you created as administrator. In Active Directory Users and Computers, you'd right-click any container to which the GPO is linked, choose Properties, and click the Group Policy tab to see all current GPO links.

Next, you'd click the specific GPO to which you want to grant editing permissions, click the Properties button, and then click the Security tab. Use the Add button to add the OU Admins group to the list of groups, and then choose Allow for Read and Write permissions, as shown in Figure 6-37.

FIGURE 6-37

OU Admins are now members of the Group Policy Creator Owners group.

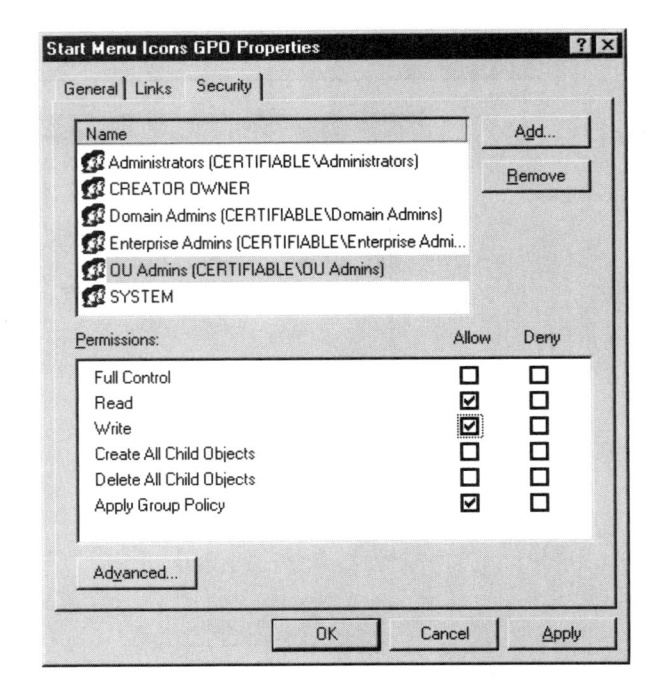

CERTIFICATION SUMMARY

In this chapter, you learned what group policies are all about. We started by looking at how group policies are implemented, and how policy settings trickle down from the domain level to lower levels. The Block Policy Inheritance option allows you to prevent a higher-level policy from trickling down to the current level, though administrators can use the No Override option to prevent lower-level policies from blocking inheritance.

Next, we looked at how you create GPOs and outlined the enormous number of policy settings available to you. We looked at how you can filter a GPO (change its scope) by choosing which security groups the policy will be applied to. You also learned how you can delegate authority to manage GPOs to specific security groups.

There's plenty more on GPOs coming up in future chapters, but you've covered a lot of ground here already. Be sure to read through the Two-Minute Drill, and use the Self Test to check your mastery of the topics discussed in this chapter before moving on to Chapter 7.

✓ TWO-MINUTE DRILL

Implement Group Policies

- ❏ Group policies allow you to create policy settings that can be applied to sites, domains, and OUs.
- ❏ By default, group policy settings are applied to the AD object to which they're linked, as well as all child objects.
- ❏ Blocking policy inheritance is a means of preventing higher-lever policy settings from being applied at, and below, the current level.
- ❏ Administrators can enforce higher-level policies by selecting the No Override option at the GPO link.
- ❏ You can manually refresh group policies using the **secedit /refreshpolicy** [*machine_policy* | *user_policy*] **/enforce** command.

Create Group Policy Objects

- ❏ You can create domain- and OU-level GPOs by right-clicking the domain name or an OU name in Active Directory Users and Computers and then choosing Properties.
- ❏ In the Group Policy snap-in, policies are divided into two main categories named Computer Configuration and User Configuration.
- ❏ Each main category offers Software Settings, Windows Settings, and Administrative Templates nodes.
- ❏ The Software Settings node allows you to assign and publish application software through a GPO.
- ❏ The Windows Settings node lets you assign startup, shutdown, logon, and logoff scripts, as well as a wide range of security settings including account policies and local policies.
- ❏ The Administrative Templates node offers an easy interface for defining Registry settings to be applied to computers and users.

Link Group Policies to AD Objects

- ❑ By default, a GPO is linked to whatever container object you right-click in Active Directory Users and Computers to create the policy.
- ❑ If a policy contains Computer Configuration settings, it must be linked to an object that contains computers, not just users and groups.
- ❑ You can link a single GPO to multiple AD objects.
- ❑ A single AD object can also be linked to multiple GPOs. GPO links that are highest in the list have the highest priority.

Filter Group Policies

- ❑ Group policies are applied to any security groups to which you set Allow–Read and Allow–Apply Group Policy permissions.
- ❑ To prevent a group policy from being applied to all authenticated users, remove the Authenticated Users security group from the Security tab of the link's Properties dialog box.
- ❑ Don't forget that administrators are members of the Authenticated Users group, and therefore are subject to any policies that are applied to that group.

Delegate Control of Group Policies

- ❑ To allow security groups to manage group policy links, use the Delegation of Control Wizard to grant the Manage Group Policy Links task to appropriate security groups.
- ❑ To allow users to create group policies, make them members of the Group Policy Creator Owner security group.
- ❑ Members of the Group Policy Creator Owners group can edit only the group policies they create, unless granted additional permissions to edit others' policies.
- ❑ To allow a user or group to edit an existing GPO, assign Read and Write permissions to that user or group.

SELF TEST

Implement Group Policies

1. You are the network administrator for your company. The network consists of an OU named Corporate that, in turn, contains several child OUs. Corporate IT policy dictates that strict password security policy settings must be applied throughout the organization. You create a GPO named PasswordPoliciesGPO that meets the requirements, and link it to the domain. Later, you discover that the policy isn't being enforced in all the OUs. You need to ensure that the password settings are applied to all users in the company. What should you do?

   A. Go to the Default Domain GPO for each child domain, and clear the Block Policy Inheritance check box.
   B. Delete the Default Domain GPO in each of the child domains.
   C. Enable the No Override option for the PasswordPoliciesGPO.
   D. Create a new site that contains all the domains, and link the PasswordPolicyGPO to that site.

2. You create some policies under User Configuration in the Group Policy window. You want to apply those policies immediately to try them out. What should you do?

   A. Execute a **secedit /refreshpolicy machine_policy /enforce** command.
   B. Execute a **secedit /refreshpolicy user_policy /enforce** command.
   C. Execute a **secedit /enforce /refresh_policy** command.
   D. Execute a **secedit /gpupdate /refreshpolicy** command.

Create Group Policy Objects

3. You create a script named LockdownDesktop.vbs that configures users' desktops. You want this script to run whenever someone logs on to the domain, and you want to ensure that the script finishes running before the user sees his or her desktop. What should you do?

   A. Create a GPO that runs the script asynchronously at logon, and link this GPO to the domain.
   B. Create a GPO that runs the script synchronously at logon, and link this GPO to the domain.
   C. Create a GPO that runs the script asynchronously at startup, and link this GPO to the domain.
   D. Create a GPO that runs the script synchronously at startup, and link this GPO to the domain.

4. You create a GPO that sets some policies under the Computer Configuration category of the Group Policy snap-in. You've made no changes to policy settings in the User Configuration category. You link the GPO to the domain. What should you do to maximize the performance of the GPO when it's being applied?

A. Choose Disable User Configuration Settings from the GPO's Properties dialog box.
B. Choose Disable Computer Configuration Settings from the GPO's Properties dialog box.
C. Link the GPO to individual OUs rather than to the domain.
D. Remove Allow–Read permissions for the GPO from the Authenticated Users group.

Link Group Policies to AD Objects

5. You are the network administrator for your company. During a routine review of the security log, you notice that someone is attempting to break into the Finance OU using a brute-force method. To increase security on the OU, you create a GPO named PasswordPolicy that increases the minimum password length to eight characters, requires all passwords to meet certain complexity requirements, and defines an account lockout policy that gives users only two attempts to log in. You link this GPO to the Finances OU. Later, you discover that users in the Finance OU are able to log in with simple passwords, and are not being locked out after two bad attempts. What should you do?

   A. In the Properties dialog box for the Finance OU, clear the Allow Inheritable Permissions From Parent To Propagate To This Object check box.
   B. Enable the No Override option on the PasswordPolicy GPO.
   C. Verify that in the list of GPOs linked to the Finance OU, the PasswordPolicy GPO has the highest priority.
   D. Remove the GPO link to the Finance OU, link it instead to the domain, and ensure it has the highest priority.

6. You are a domain administrator for your company. You want to apply a GPO to all domain controllers in your domain. To which container in AD Users and Computers would you link the GPO?

   A. Domain
   B. Domain Controllers
   C. Computers
   D. Users

Filter Group Policies

7. You create two GPOs named DevelopersGPO and HTMLAuthorsGPO, and link both to the domain. DevelopersGPO provides access to resources needed by programmers, while HTMLAuthorsGPO provides access to resources required by web page developers. Developers are all members of a security group named Developers, and HTML authors are all members of a security group named WebAuthors.

Upon implementing the GPO, you discover that all users have access to all the resources. What should you do to ensure that only the developers and HTML authors have access to their required resources? (Choose all that apply.)

- A. Remove the Authenticated Users security group from both GPOs.
- B. Add the Developers security group to DevelopersGPO and grant Allow–Read and Allow–Apply Group Policy permissions to that group.
- C. Add the WebAuthors security group to HTMLAuthorsGPO and grant Allow–Read and Allow–Apply Group Policy permissions to that group.
- D. Ensure that the default domain group policy has the highest priority in the domain.

8. You are the network administrator for a network that consists of a single domain and an OU named Philly. All user accounts are contained within the Philly OU. You configure a GPO named StartMenuIcons that redirects the Start menu to a shared network folder, and link the GPO to the Philly OU. You want all user accounts in the Philly OU, except Domain Admin accounts, to have the StartMenuIcons GPO applied. Furthermore, you need to ensure that all domain administrators can administer all GPOs. What should you do?

- A. Set the permissions on the StartMenuIcons GPO Deny–Apply Group Policy for the Domain Admins group.
- B. Remove the GPO link from the Philly OU and link it at the domain level.
- C. Move all user accounts into the Users container and then filter the GPO permissions to Allow–Read and Allow–Apply Group Policy for the Authenticated Users group.
- D. Create a new GPO that grants Domain Admins Allow–Read and Allow–Write permissions to the StartMenuIcons GPO.

Delegate Control of Group Policies

9. How can you allow OU administrators to create new GPOs?

- A. Run the Delegation of Control Wizard and grant the task Create New GPOs to the appropriate security groups.
- B. Grant Allow–Read and Allow–Write permissions to appropriate security groups at the domain level.
- C. Create a custom security template that provides the right to create GPOs, and import that template into each of the OUs.
- D. Make the appropriate administrator accounts members of the Group Policy Creator Owners security group.

10. Which of the following permissions are required to allow users to manage GPO links, create new GPOs, and edit GPOs that they don't own? (Choose all that apply.)

   A. Manage Group Policy Links, as granted by the Delegation of Control Wizard.
   B. Membership in the Group Policy Creator Owners group.
   C. Allow–Apply Group Policy permissions on specific GPO links.
   D. Allow–Read and Allow–Write permissions.

LAB QUESTION

You are the network administrator for your company. The company has numerous branch offices, each with a couple of domain controllers, as well as application-based terminal servers, as illustrated in Figure 6-38. Traveling sales representatives need to connect to the application servers using Terminal Services over the Internet to run corporate application programs. You need to ensure that remote users can log on to the terminal servers, but not log on to domain controllers. You want to ensure that if any new terminal servers are added to the domain, the same policies will be applied automatically. What should you do?

FIGURE 6-38

Exhibit for the Lab Question

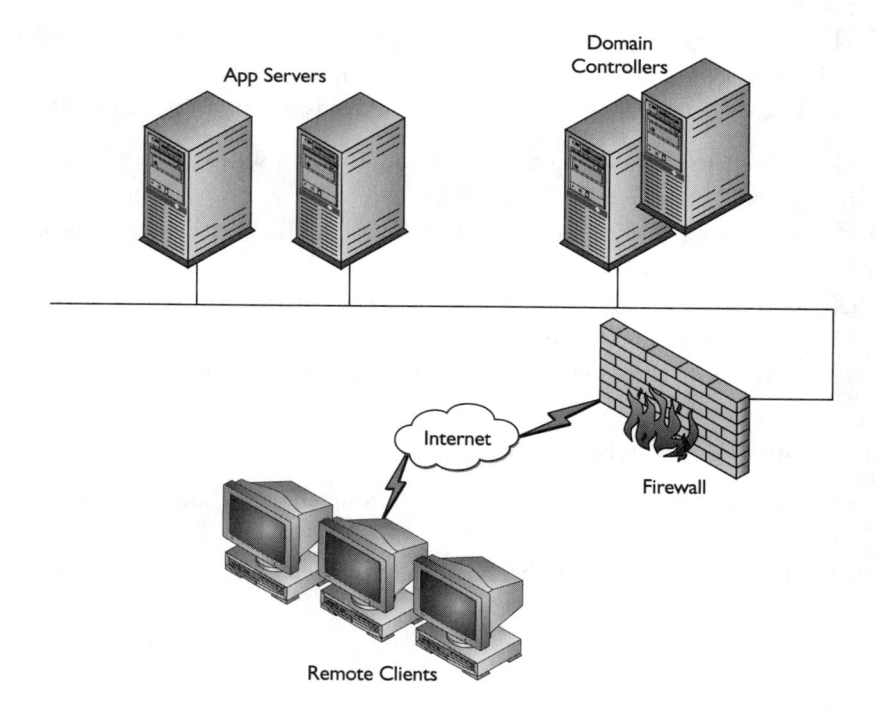

SELF TEST ANSWERS

Implement Group Policies

1. ☑ **C** is correct. Enabling the No Override option on the PasswordPoliciesGPO would ensure that the password policies are enforced throughout the OUs.
   ☒ **A** and **B** are incorrect because neither enforces the policy from the domain level. To ensure that the password settings are applied throughout the company, you need to prevent lower-level policies from overwriting the domain settings.
   ☒ **D** is incorrect because there is no need to create a site.

2. ☑ **B** is correct. That's the correct command for refreshing the user policies.
   ☒ **A** is wrong because it would refresh machine policies, and your policy applies to users.
   ☒ **C** and **D** are the wrong syntax for the **secedit** command.

Create Group Policy Objects

3. ☑ **B** is correct. Running the script synchronously at logon for the entire domain will ensure that the script is executed before users see their desktops.
   ☒ **A** is wrong because running the script asynchronously wouldn't ensure that the entire script is executed before the user's desktop appears.
   ☒ **C** and **D** are wrong because the script needs to run at login, not at startup.

4. ☑ **A** is correct. Disabling the User Configuration settings would prevent those settings from being read when the GPO is applied.
   ☒ **B** is wrong because the Computer Configuration settings must be enabled for the GPO to work.
   ☒ **C** is wrong because there would be no performance advantage to linking the GPO to OUs rather than the domain.
   ☒ **D** is wrong since denying Read permissions would prevent the policy from being applied.

Link Group Policies to AD Objects

5. ☑ **D** is correct. Password policies are account policies, and must be applied at the domain level.
   ☒ **A**, **B**, and **C** are wrong because Account Policies applied to an OU will be ignored, no matter what you do at the OU level.

6. ☑ B is correct—link the policy to the Domain Controllers container.
   ☒ A and C are wrong because you want the policy applied to domain controllers.
   ☒ D is wrong because you can't link any GPOs to the Users container.

Filter Group Policies

7. ☑ A, B, and C are correct. Currently, all users are having the policies applied to them by virtue of membership in the Authenticated Users group. You need to remove that security group from both GPOs, and then filter DevelopersGPO and HTMLAuthorsGPO so they apply only to members of the appropriate groups.
   ☒ D is wrong because changing the priority of the GPO links wouldn't filter to whom the policies are applied.

8. ☑ A is correct. Domain Admins members already have permissions to administer GPOs, so you just have to prevent the StartMenuIcons GPO from being applied to the Domain Admins group.
   ☒ B is wrong because you need to filter to whom the policy is applied, not link it to a different AD object.
   ☒ C is incorrect because there is no need to move the user accounts from the Philly OU.
   ☒ D is wrong because Domain Admins members already have permissions to create and modify GPOs.

Delegate Control of Group Policies

9. ☑ D is correct. Only members of the Group Policy Creator Owners security group can create new GPOs.
   ☒ A, B, and C are incorrect because membership in the Group Policy Creator Owners group is sufficient.

10. ☑ A, B, and D are correct.
    ☒ C is wrong because Apply Group Policy isn't related to administration of GPOs.

LAB ANSWER

As complex as the scenario in the question appears to be, it's really a question about group policies. Terminal Server clients need the right to log on locally to use Terminal Server. So, to configure a policy, you need to do two things. First, you need to get all of the terminal servers into an OU so they can be managed as a whole. Second, you need a security group to which you can provide Log On Locally rights for the servers. So the first step is to create an OU, perhaps named TerminalServers, and move all appropriate computer account objects into that OU. Any new terminal servers that the company adds in the future should be created within that OU as well.

Next, you need to create a GPO that grants the Log On Locally right, and link it to the TerminalServers OU. Then, create a security group, perhaps named TSUsers, and make as its members all sales representatives that need to access the application servers. Filter the GPO to give members of the TSUsers security group Allow–Read and Allow–Apply Group Policy permissions for the GPO link.

7
Sharing and Publishing Folders and Printers

CERTIFICATION OBJECTIVES

7.01	Sharing Folders and Files
7.02	Sharing and Configuring Printers
7.03	Publishing Shared Resources in Active Directory
✓	Two-Minute Drill
Q&A	Self Test

354 Chapter 7: Sharing and Publishing Folders and Printers

If you've gotten this far in your networking career, you're no doubt familiar with the concept of shared folders. In Windows 2000, you can view current shares through the Computer Management tool, available in the Administrative Tools of the Control Panel. To see folders that are already shared on a computer, you can open the Computer Management tool and navigate to System Tools\Shared Folders\Shares, as shown in Figure 7-1.

Several folders are shared automatically. *Administrative shares* are visible only to administrators, and their names always end with a $. Some examples of shares that are created automatically include:

- **ADMIN$**   The system root folder (usually c:\WINNT) used during remote administration. Administrators have Full Control permissions by default.
- **C$**   The root of each volume is shared to allow administrators to remotely connect to the computer and perform administrative tasks.
- **IPC$**   Shared named pipes used for communications between programs.
- **NETLOGON**   A resource used by the Net Logon service for processing domain logon requests, available only on domain controllers.

FIGURE 7-1   Sample shares on the Windows 2000 Server computer

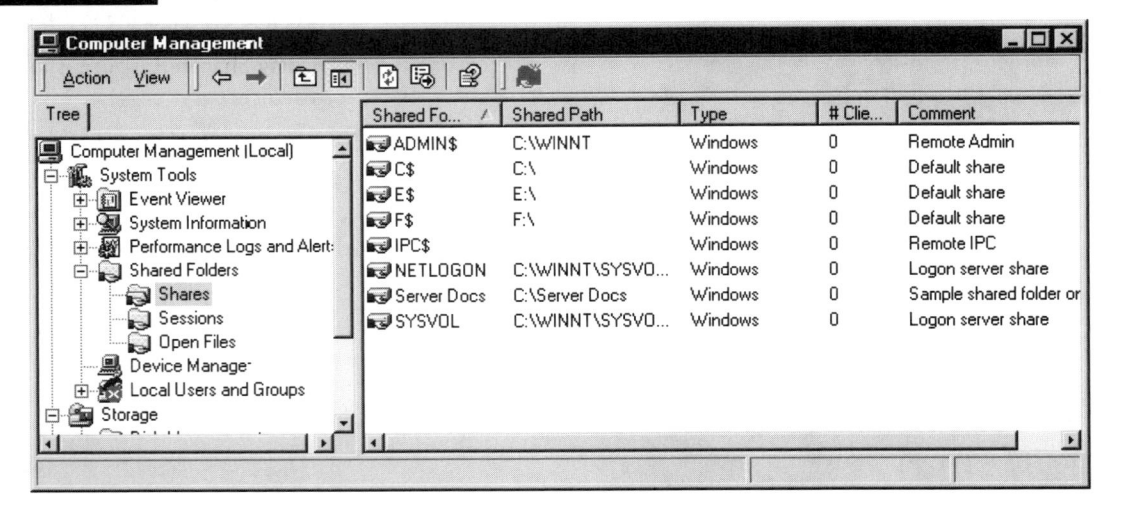

CERTIFICATION OBJECTIVE 7.01

Sharing Folders and Files

There are two ways to create a new shared folder. One method is to choose Action | New File Share. The second method is to use Windows Explorer. To use Windows Explorer, open My Computer and create or navigate to the folder you want to share. Right-click the folder's icon and choose Properties, and then click the Sharing tab. Choose Share This Folder, and give the folder a short share name and a longer description. If there will be older DOS LAN Manager clients, they won't be able to recognize share names over eight characters. Otherwise, you can use longer names with blank spaces. Use the Comment field to enter a description of the share, as in the example shown in Figure 7-2.

The User Limit option allows you to set a limit on how many users can simultaneously access the shared folder. The Permissions button and Security tab allow you to set permissions for the share, as discussed in a moment. The Caching option refers to caching of files for the Offline Files feature, as will also be discussed later in this chapter.

FIGURE 7-2

Sharing a folder

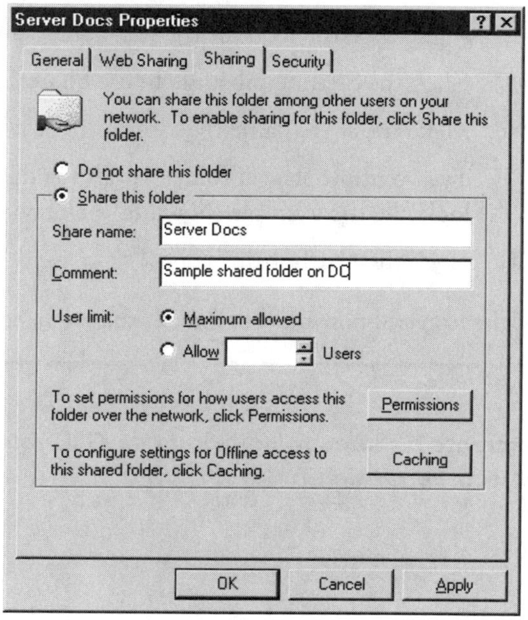

exam watch

The maximum number of users who can simultaneously access a shared folder on a Windows 2000 Professional computer is ten. Increasing the limit on such a computer has no effect. If you need more than ten simultaneous users, you must move the folder to a server and set the limit there.

EXERCISE 7-1

Create and Share a Folder

In this exercise, you'll create a shared folder on the C drive of your server. You could create the share on any drive, or any computer for that matter, but we'll stick with drive C on the domain controller here, because many of you will be working with minimal hardware, and I know you have a drive C on your domain controller. Here are the steps:

1. Log in to the domain controller with administrative privileges.
2. Open My Computer and click Folders in the toolbar to view the Folders list.
3. Expand the My Computer node and click the icon for drive C.
4. Choose File | New | Folder from My Computer's menu bar.
5. Name the new folder **Server Docs** and press ENTER.
6. Right-click the icon for the new folder and choose Properties.
7. Click the Sharing tab and choose Share This Folder.
8. Make the share name the same as the folder name, **Server Docs**.
9. Type **Sample shared folder on DC** as the comment. Your dialog box should look like the example shown in the previous illustration.
10. Click the OK button.

The icon will now show the small "sharing hand" indicating that the folder is shared.

on the job

To create a shared folder within an OU, you must have Allow–Create Child Objects permission for that OU.

Shared Folder Permissions

To control the level of access that various security groups will have to a shared folder, you configure permissions for the shared folder. There are two "categories" of permissions you can assign to shared folders:

- **Share permissions** Apply to all shared folders.
- **File and directory (NTFS) permissions** Additional permissions available only on NTFS volumes, and not available on FAT volumes.

We'll look at the two different types of permissions and how they interact in the sections that follow.

Share Permissions

Share permissions are available in both NTFS and FAT file systems. They provide access to the folder as a whole. To view the current share permissions for a shared folder, do either of the following:

- In Windows Explorer, right-click the folder's icon and choose Properties. Then, click the Sharing tab and click the Permissions button.
- In the Computer Management tool, right-click the shared folder's icon and choose Properties. Then, click the Share Permissions tab.

On a new share, you'll notice that the security level is, basically, no security at all, because the Everyone group has Full Control, as shown in Figure 7-3.

If you're working on an NTFS volume, your best bet would be to just leave the permissions as they are, then use NTFS permissions (described in a moment) to control access to the folder. On the other hand, if the folder were on a FAT or FAT32 volume, you'd have no NTFS permissions to work with, so you'd want to set share permissions here. You can use the Add and Remove buttons to add and remove security groups, and assign permissions to each group as follows:

- **Read** Groups with this permission can view folder names, filenames, and attributes, open documents, and run programs within the shared folder.
- **Change** Groups with this permission have Read permissions, plus they can create folders, add files to folders, change data in files, append data to files, change file attributes, delete folders and files.

■ **Full Control** Groups with this permission have Read and Change permissions, plus they can change file permissions and take ownership of files.

Let's look now at that other set of permissions, often referred to as *file and directory permissions,* or *NTFS permissions.*

File and Directory (NTFS) Permissions

Whereas share permissions apply to the entire folder and everything within it, NTFS permissions can be set at a more granular level, such as specific files and folders within the shared folder. Again, these permissions aren't available on FAT file systems, because they're applied to the access control list (ACL) for the specific object, and FAT files don't have ACLs.

NTFS permissions provide a much more detailed level of control over objects. To get to a shared folder's NTFS permissions, right-click the shared folder's icon in Windows Explorer or Computer Management and choose Properties, and then click the Security tab. The initial set of NTFS permissions you'll see are shown in

FIGURE 7-3

Everyone has Full Control of new shares by default.

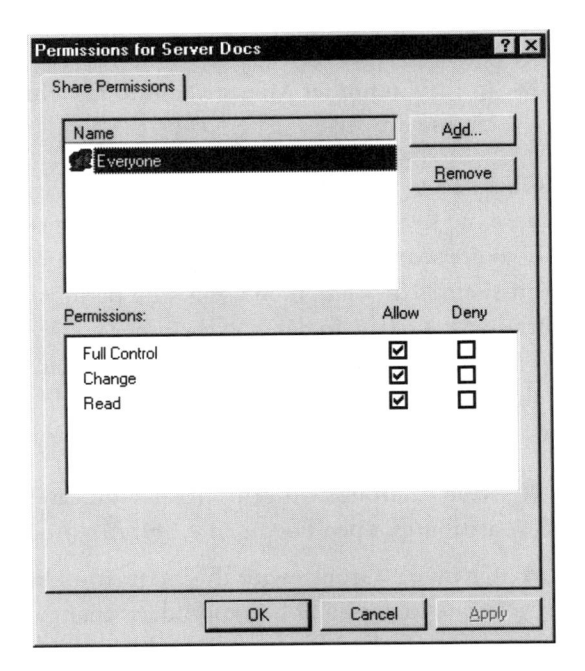

Figure 7-4 and summarized as follows (initially, they're all disabled for the Everyone group, as will be discussed in a moment):

- **Full Control** Groups with this level of access have unlimited access to the file or folder.
- **Modify** Groups with this permission can read, execute, write, and delete the object or objects within the folder.
- **Read & Execute** Groups with this permission can read files and execute programs, as well as traverse folders.
- **List Folder Contents** Groups with this permission can view the contents of a folder, but not necessarily be able to read files and execute programs within the folder. (This permission cannot be applied to files—only to folders.)
- **Read** Groups with this permission can view the contents, permissions, and attributes of an object, but not make any changes to the object. In the case of a folder, the permission applies to all objects within the folder.
- **Write** Groups with this permission on a folder can create new files or folders within the shared folder.

FIGURE 7-4

File and Directory (NTFS) permissions for a shared folder

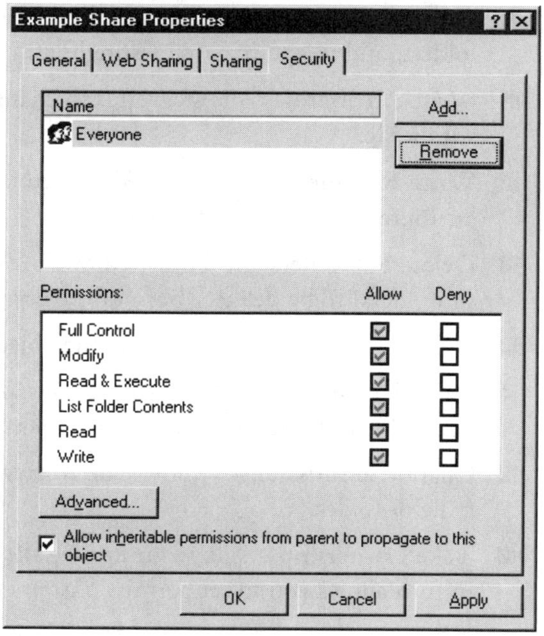

Each permission on the Security tab is actually a collection of smaller, *special permissions*. To view the more special permissions, click the Advanced button. You'll be taken to the Access Control Settings dialog box for the shared folder. Permissions for groups will be listed. You can click any group name, then click the View/Edit button to see the special NTFS permissions, as shown in Figure 7-5. Here's a brief description of what each of the special permissions controls do:

- **Traverse Folder/Execute File**   Allows groups (and programs) to traverse to other folders contained within the shared folder.

- **List Folder/Read Data**   Allows groups to view the contents of folders and read the contents of files.

- **Read Attributes**   Allows groups to read *basic attributes,* such as Read-Only, Hidden, Archive, and System, associated with a file.

- **Read Extended Attributes**   Allows groups to read the *extended attributes* offered by some file types, such as the Author, Title, Artist, Subject, and Genre attributes available on some multimedia file types.

- **Create Files/Write Data**   Allows groups to create folders within the folder, and to overwrite existing files with new data.

- **Create Folders/Append Data**   Allows groups to create folders within folders, and to add data to existing files.

- **Write Attributes**   Allows groups to change the basic attributes associated with a file.

- **Write Extended Attributes**   Allows groups to change the extended attributes associated with a file.

- **Delete Subfolders and Files**   Allows the contents of a folder (files and subfolders) to be deleted, but not the object itself.

- **Delete**   Allows groups to delete the object.

- **Read Permissions**   Allows you to view all the NTFS permissions associated with a file or folder, but not change them.

- **Change Permissions**   Allows you to view and change NTFS permissions of a file or folder.

- **Take Ownership**   Allows groups to take ownership of a file or folder, which in turn allows you to set permissions on the object.

FIGURE 7-5

NTFS special permissions

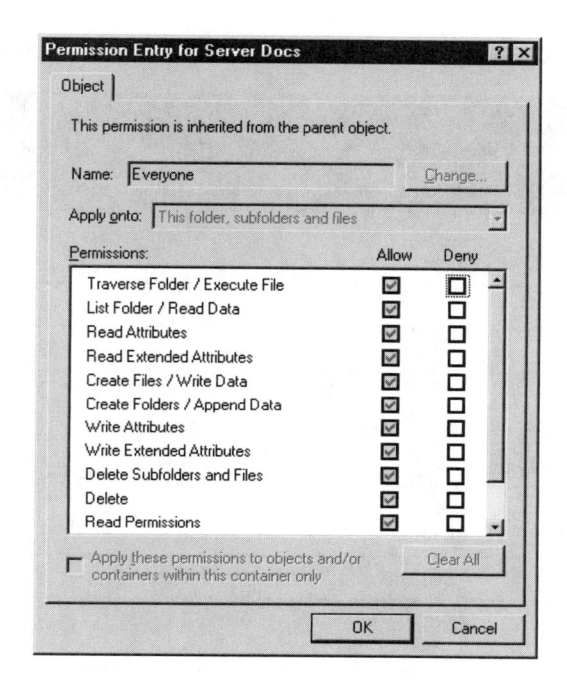

The relationship between the basic NTFS permissions and special permissions is summarized in Table 7-1.

Combining Permissions

As always, multiple permissions combine to form effective permissions. For example, let's say a user is a member of the Employees security group, and that group has Read permissions for a shared folder. That same user is also a member of the Managers group, which has Write permissions for the folder. Since the permissions combine, the user's effective permissions would be Write. Deny permissions always override Allow permissions. So, let's say the same user is also a member of a group named RandomClickers, which is denied Write permissions for the folder. In that case, the Deny permission takes precedence over the Write permission granted by the Managers group. Thus, the user's effective permissions are Read.

Share permissions for NTFS volumes work in combination with NTFS permissions. The most restrictive permissions will apply. For example, on an NTFS volume, users need both share permissions and NTFS permissions to access the share. To access folders

TABLE 7-6 Relationship Between Basic Permissions and Advanced Permissions

	Write	Read	List Folder Contents	Read and Execute	Modify	Full Control
Traverse Folder/ Execute File			X	X	X	X
List Folder/Read Data		X	X	X	X	
Read Attributes		X	X	X	X	X
Read Extended Attributes		X	X	X	X	X
Create Files/ Write Data	X				X	X
Create Folder/ Append Data	X				X	X
Write Attributes	X				X	X
Write Extended Attributes	X				X	X
Delete Subfolders and Files						X
Delete					X	X
Read Permissions	X	X	X	X	X	X
Change Permissions						
Take Ownership						X

and files within the shared folder, they also need appropriate NTFS permissions for that folder and file. This is in contrast to FAT volumes, where share permissions are all that is required to gain access to the folder and everything within it.

When trying to figure out a given user's effective permissions, calculate the cumulative NTFS permissions, then add that to the share permissions. The most restrictive permissions are the effective permissions. For example, if share permissions grant Full Control, and NTFS permissions grant Read, that's Full Control+Read. Since Read is the most restrictive, the effective permission is Read.

Sharing Folders and Files **363**

> *exam*
> *⍺atch*
>
> *On an NTFS volume, you need both share and NTFS permissions to access a folder. For example, Full Control share permissions with no NTFS permissions results in no permissions at all. In other words, even nonexistent NTFS permissions are more restrictive than share permissions.*

File and Folder Inheritance

Permissions set for a folder are automatically inherited by all folders and files within that folder. Permissions that an object acquires from its parent object(s) are called *inherited permissions*. Permissions that are defined directly on the object are called *explicit permissions*.

Sometimes, to change the permissions of an object, you need to break away from the inherited permissions coming from the parent. You can do so by clearing the Allow Inheritable Permissions From Parent To Propagate To This Object option in the shared folder's Properties dialog box. When you do so, you'll see the Security dialog box, shown in Figure 7-6, which allows you to copy the permissions from the parent to the current object, or to remove the permissions altogether. Either way, you'll then be able to set permissions independently of the parent folder.

Remember that NTFS permissions can be assigned at both the folder level and the file level. Sometimes, the actions that users can perform might seem a little mysterious when you set both. For example, suppose you have a shared folder named SharedFolder. Within that folder is a file named SomeFile. You grant Full Control to the folder to some group or user, and then deny Full Control for the file. The user or group can still delete SomeFile because the Full Control permission for SharedFolder's special permissions includes Delete Subfolders And Files. That special permission allows the group or user to delete files within the shared folder, even if the special permission Delete has not been granted (or even denied) on SomeFile.

If you wanted to prevent SomeFile from being deleted, you would need to ensure that the user or group is not granted the Delete Subfolders And Files

FIGURE 7-6

Message that appears when you clear permission inheritance

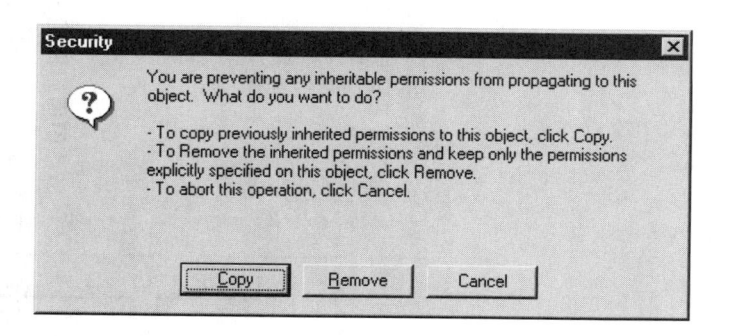

special permission on the parent folder (SharedFolder). If the group has Full Control of the folder, by way of either inherited or explicit permissions, you could do either of the following to prevent a group from being able to delete objects within the folder:

- Remove inheritance from the folder, and then reset all permissions for that one security group.
- Explicitly deny the Delete Subfolders And Files special permission for either the group or the individual user.

Taking Ownership

Sometimes, in the course of assigning permissions, you end up in a situation where nobody—not even administrators—can access the folder to change its permissions. By default, the person who created the folder is the *owner* of the folder, and only that user can change permissions on the folder. For example, let's say user amarie has created a shared folder, and has granted Full Control to herself, and no permissions at all to anybody else, as shown in Figure 7-7.

FIGURE 7-7

Only one user, amarie, has permission to use this folder.

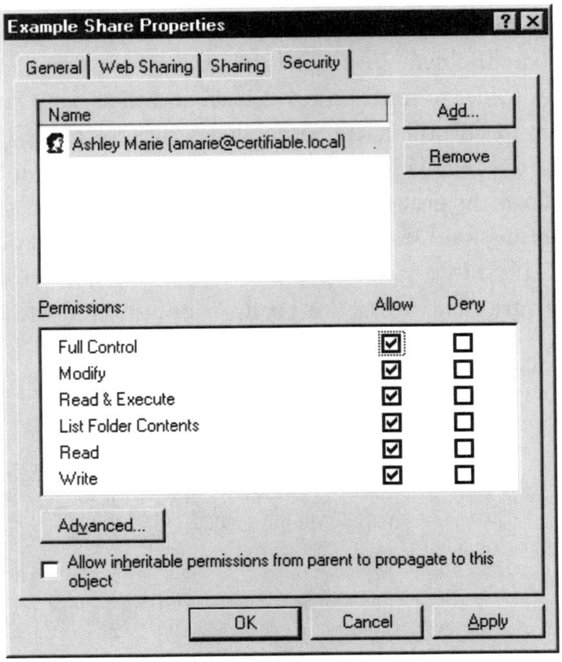

Suppose now that, for whatever reason, you need to change the permissions to allow other groups access to this folder. You couldn't really do this at the moment because you, as administrator, have no permissions at all on this folder. When you attempt to make some change, though, you'll see a Security dialog box like the one shown in Figure 7-8.

Clicking the OK button takes you to the Security tab of the folder's Properties dialog box, but all options are disabled. So, how the heck do you get ownership of this thing with a bunch of disabled controls? You click the Advanced button, then click the Owner tab in the Access Control Settings dialog box that appears, as shown in Figure 7-9.

Now, it's a simple matter of clicking a user or group name to take ownership. If you want ownership to propagate through all child objects within the folder, select the check box beneath the list. Then click the OK button. Just keep following the prompts on the screen and work your way back to the folder's icon. This time, when you right-click the folder's icon and choose Properties, you'll be able to get to the Security tab with all options enabled, where you can set all permissions in the usual manner.

on the Job *Taking ownership is often required when dealing with folders that inexperienced users have created and shared without really knowing what they're doing.*

Hidden Shares

You saw some examples of administrative shares that are created by default, such as C$ and Admin$, earlier in this chapter. You can create your own hidden shares simply by sharing a folder in the usual manner, and adding a dollar sign ($) to the end of the share name, as shown in Figure 7-10.

The shared folder won't be visible to clients using normal browser tools like My Network Places. Though, as an administrator, you can map a network drive to the share by manually entering its UNC name after choosing Map Network Drive from a Windows Explorer menu bar (such as the My Computer window).

FIGURE 7-8

Security dialog box offering to grant ownership

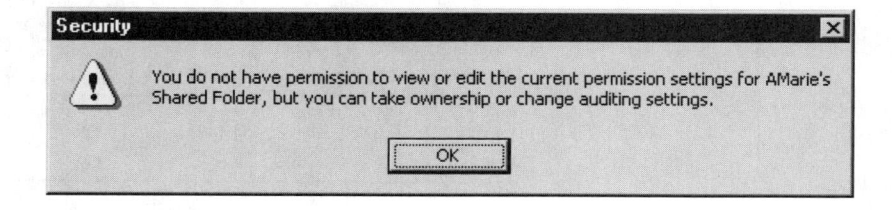

Security

You do not have permission to view or edit the current permission settings for AMarie's Shared Folder, but you can take ownership or change auditing settings.

OK

FIGURE 7-9

Owner tab of a folder's Access Control Settings dialog box

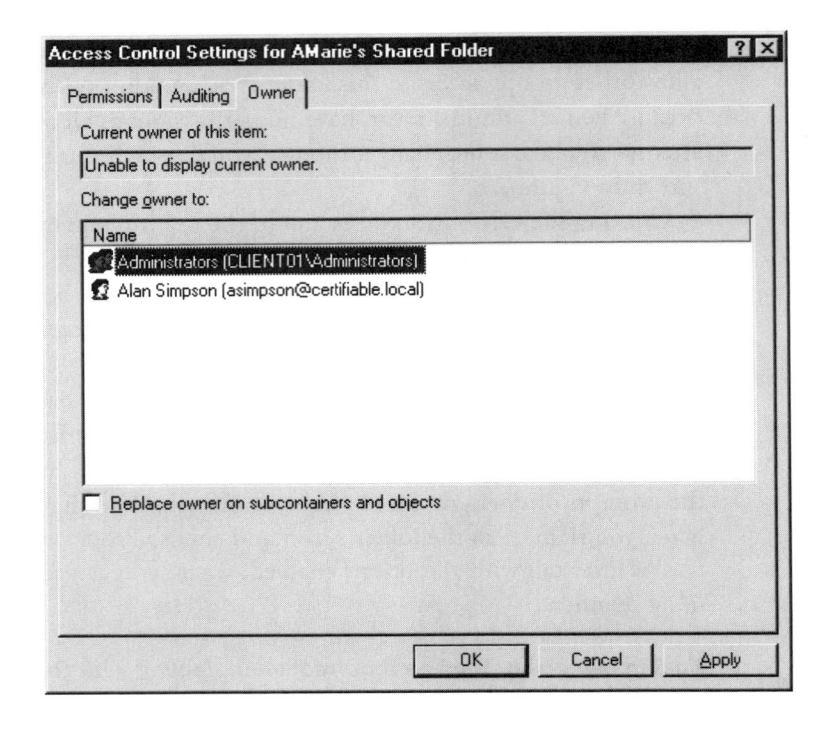

FIGURE 7-10

Adding a $ to a share name to hide the share

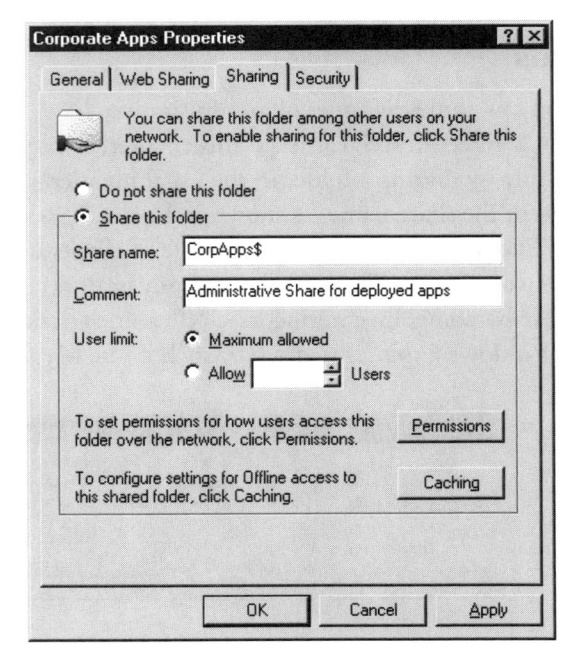

FROM THE CLASSROOM

Shared Folder Strategies

In Exercise 7-1, earlier in this chapter, I had you create a Server Docs folder on drive C of your domain controller, simply because I know drive C is available. In the real world, it would make more sense to store shared data folders on a volume that's separate from the operating system. Doing so will make it easier to back up just the data (documents) frequently. Grant Full Control to administrators only. Then, you can create subfolders for various types of data based on department, project, or whatever. Grant permissions to those subfolders based on which groups actually need to read or change the contents of those subfolders.

For shared network applications, consider organizing all the applications under one shared folder. Doing so will give you a central location from which you can install and upgrade programs. Assign Full Control permission to administrators who will be managing the software. Then, remove the Full Control permission from the Everyone group, and grant Read permissions to a more restricted group, such as the Users group. This allows members of user accounts that you've created to run the applications, but not make any changes. It also prevents anonymous users, such as the guests, from running the applications.

—*Alan Simpson, MA, MCSA*

on the Job — *If you wanted to give a specific user the right to access a shared folder, but prevent other users from even seeing the shared folder, you could share the folder with a hidden $ name. Then, map a persistent drive connection to \the hidden share on the specific user's computer.*

Offline Files

Offline Files is a feature that allows clients to access network files when offline. It works by automatically caching often-used network files in a folder named Offline Files on clients' local hard drives. Remote users work with the cached copies on their local drives, thereby reducing network transfer time, and even allowing users to work with the files while they're offline. To ensure that the server and the client computer copies of cached files are in sync, Offline Files compares the timestamp and size of the two copies of the files. If they're the same, then no copies are transmitted across the network. If the copies are out of sync, Offline Files does whatever is necessary to get them in sync. It's all automatic and invisible to the users.

Offline Files also solves the problem of not being able to access a file that's stored on a server. If the user needs to access a shared file on the network, but the network is down or the user is offline, Offline Files switches to Offline mode, where the local cached copy is served up automatically. The whole process can be automated so that users don't even need to resynchronize files that they've modified while offline. When the user eventually does connect to the network, the synchronization takes place automatically as a background process that's transparent to the user.

Offline Files can be configured on any Windows 2000 Professional computer. It's a simple matter of opening the Folder Options dialog box in the Control Panel, or by choosing Tools | Folder Options from Windows Explorer's menu bar. Clicking the Offline Files tab displays the options shown in Figure 7-11. The options are self-explanatory. But, of course, you must select the Enable Offline Files option for any of this to work.

On the server side, it's up to the administrator to determine which shared folders can use the Offline Folders feature. Right-click the shared folder's icon and choose Properties. On the General tab, click the Caching button to open the Caching Settings dialog box, shown in Figure 7-12. The first option, Allow Caching Of Files In This Shared Folder, must be selected if users are to be able to work with files contained within the folder while they're offline.

The drop-down list provides three options for determining how offline files are cached:

- **Manual Caching for Documents** Users must manually choose which files to add to their local Offline Files folder by *pinning* the documents within that folder. This is a simple matter of right-clicking the document's icon and choosing Make Available Offline.

- **Automatic Caching for Documents** When the user opens a document on the server, the server automatically places a cached copy of the document in the user's Offline Files folder. Documents that are cached automatically are flagged as *temporary offline files* (as opposed to files that have been manually "pinned" by the user).

- **Automatic Caching for Programs**   The same idea as the preceding option, but used on shared folders that contain executable files rather than documents. The client computer will run the local, cached copy of the program rather than downloading the entire program from the server.

Whenever users are online, they can get their locally cached copies of documents in sync with the server's copies by choosing Tools | Synchronize from the menu bar in the Offline Files folder.

If there's a GPO that affects users of offline files, enabling Prevent Use Of Offline Files under Administrative Templates\Network\Offline Files would prevent users from using this feature no matter what other settings you define. The policy must be Disabled or Not Configured for offline files to be available to users.

FIGURE 7-11

Offline Files options on a Windows 2000 Professional client

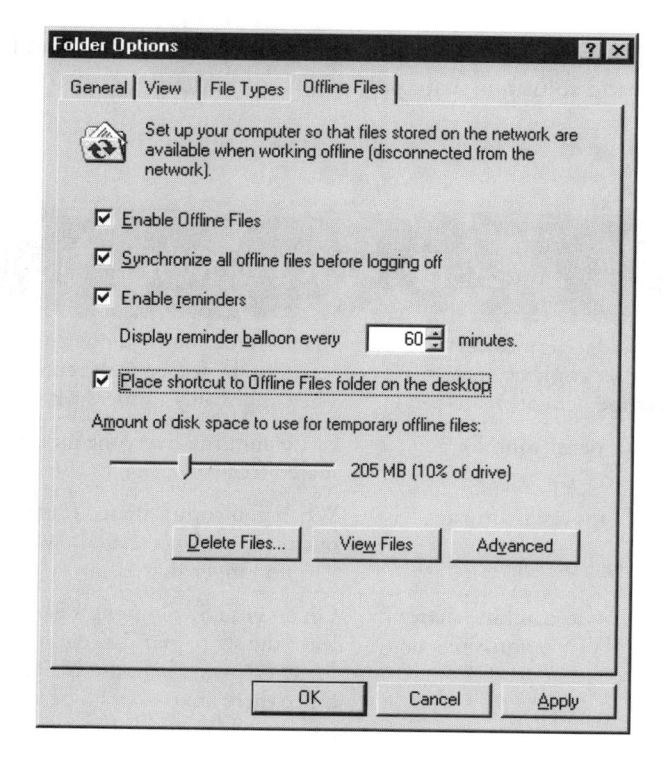

FIGURE 7-12

Caching Settings dialog box for a shared folder on a server

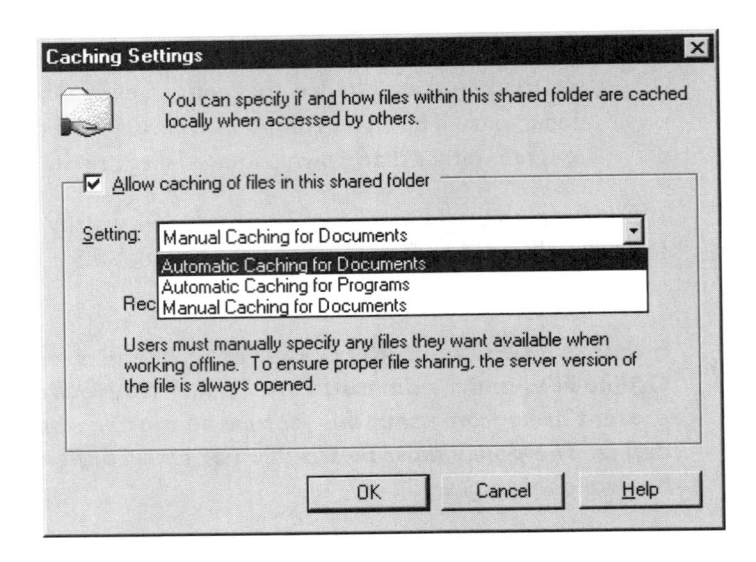

Next, we'll look at how to share printers. But first, let's look at some scenarios and solutions that apply to shared folders.

SCENARIO & SOLUTION

How do shared folder permissions affect a folder when a user connects locally rather than over the network?	Shared folder permissions don't restrict access to users who gain access to the folder at the computer where the folder is stored. They apply only to users who gain access over the network.
What's the default permission for a shared folder?	By default, the Everyone group has full control of a newly shared folder.
What happens if I move or copy a shared folder?	When you copy a shared folder, the original remains shared, but the copy isn't shared. When you move a shared folder, it is no longer shared.
What's the best way to combine share permissions and NTFS permissions on a shared folder?	On an NTFS volume, it's generally recommended that you leave the share permissions at the default setting of Full Control for Everyone. Then, use NTFS permissions to restrict access. Since there are no NTFS permissions on a FAT volume, you'll have to rely on share permissions.

CERTIFICATION OBJECTIVE 7.02

Sharing and Configuring Printers

Windows 2000 supports Plug and Play, and also automatically shares installed printers. So, there may not be much for you to do when it comes to sharing a printer. Just plug the printer into the appropriate port on the printer server, turn on the printer, boot up the computer, and wait for Windows 2000 to detect and install the printer.

exam ⓦatch

If Windows 2000 is unable to detect a plug-and-play printer/scanner that uses an EPP connection, enable the Enhanced Parallel Port (EPP) support in the computer's system BIOS.

Once the printer is installed, sharing it is a simple matter. Log on to the computer to which the printer is physically attached, with administrative privileges, open the Control Panel, and open the Printers icon. Each installed printer will have an icon. If the printer is already shared, its icon will sport the "sharing hand." If the printer is not already shared, you can easily share it by right-clicking the printer's icon and choosing Sharing. Choose Shared As, enter a short descriptive name for the printer, and choose the List In The Directory option, as shown in Figure 7-13. Click OK, and you're done as far as sharing the printer goes.

So far, I've been using the term "printer" in the traditional sense. As you probably know, in Windows 2000, the term *print device* is used to describe a physical printer. The term *printer* actually refers to a logical printer. You can define multiple logical printers for a single print device. Doing so allows you to configure different options for different people. For example, if you want a print device to be available to one group of people in the morning, and a different group of people in the afternoon, you could create a second printer for the one print device, then configure each printer to be available at different times of the day.

Making another printer for a print device is a simple matter. Open the Control Panel and open the Add Printer icon. Let the wizard guide you through the steps. Use the same port, and the same drivers as the first printer. Just give this new printer definition a different name. You'll end up with two icons for the print device in the Printers folder. From now on in this chapter, when I use the term "printer," I'm actually referring to a printer icon in the Printers folder. Any number of icons might refer to the same print device.

FIGURE 7-13

Sharing a printer

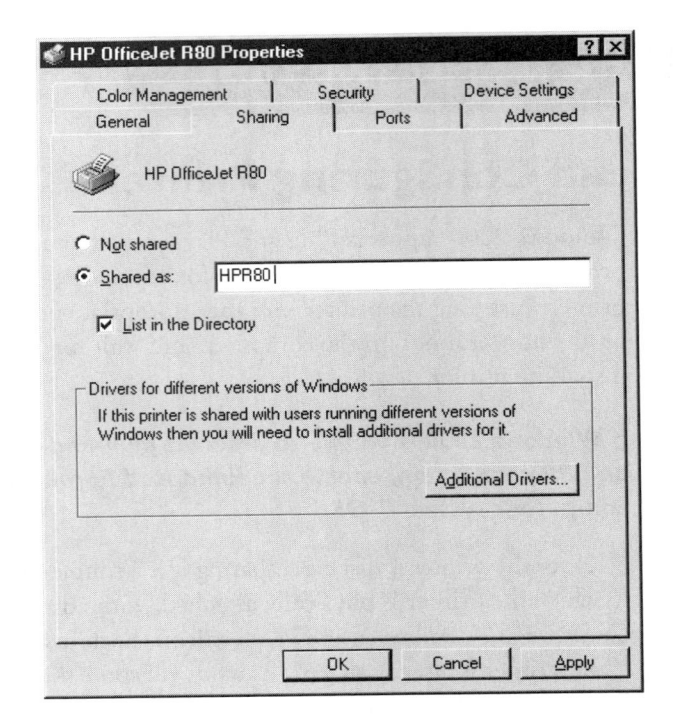

EXERCISE 7-2

Sharing a Printer

In this exercise, you'll share a printer. You'll need to have a printer already installed on one of the Windows 2000 computers in your network. Log on to the computer to which the printer is physically connected, then follow these simple steps to share the printer:

1. Click the Start button and choose Settings | Printers. The Printers folder opens.
2. Right-click the icon for the printer you want to share and choose Sharing.
3. Choose Shared As, and enter a brief name that's appropriate for your make and model of printer.
4. Make sure List In The Directory is selected, then click OK.

The printer's icon will now sport the sharing hand, indicating that it's now shared.

Setting Shared Printer Permissions

Like shared folders, you can control access to printers through permissions. To get to a printer's access control list, right-click its icon in the Printers folder, and choose Properties. Then, click the Security tab. The following are the basic permissions for a printer:

- **Print**   Users with this permission can send print jobs to the printer, but not change printer properties or permissions.
- **Manage Printers**   Users can print, read permissions, change permissions, and take ownership of the printer.
- **Manage Documents**   Users can pause, resume, delete, and restart print jobs and modify document-specific settings.

By default, the security groups are granted printer permissions as follows:

- **Administrators, Server Operators, Printer Operators**   Print, Manage Printers, Manage Documents
- **Everyone**   Print
- **Creator Owner**   Manage Documents

Configuring Printers

One of the beauties of having multiple printers (in other words, printer icons on the Printers folder) is that you can set priorities and schedules for different groups of people. Just right-click the printer of interest and choose Properties. Use the Security tab to define which groups can send print jobs to the printer. For example, in Figure 7-14, I've removed the Everyone group from the access control list, and given members of the Accounting Admins group permission to print instead.

The Advanced tab, shown in Figure 7-15, provides options that allow you to further refine the printer's behavior and availability. You can choose a range of time during which the printer will be available by choosing Available From and then setting a start and end time. For example, suppose you've given the Accounting Admins security permission to send print jobs to this printer, but want to restrict their access to some time range like 8:00 A.M. to 12:00 P.M. Just set the appropriate time range in the printer icon for which you've granted Print permissions to the Accounting Admins group.

374 Chapter 7: Sharing and Publishing Folders and Printers

FIGURE 7-14

Permissions changed to allow Accounting Admins to print

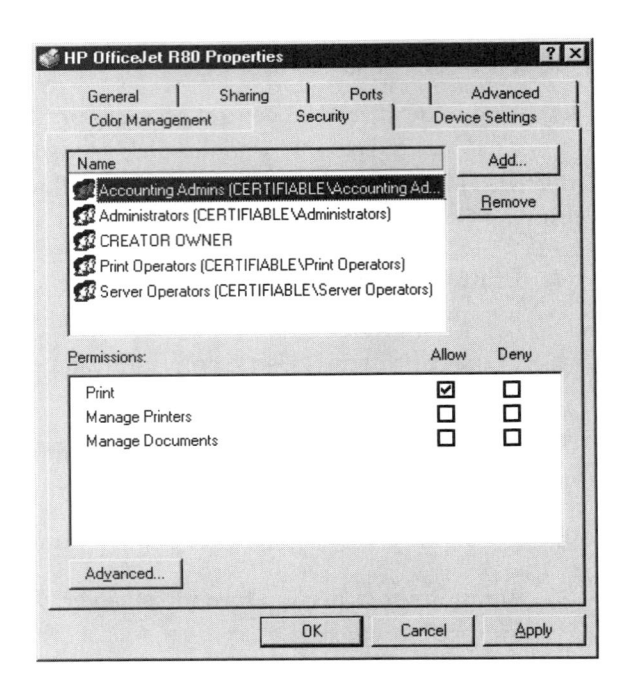

If you then wanted to give Everyone permission to use the printer from noon on, you'd open the printer icon for which you granted Print permissions to Everyone, and limit availability to the appropriate time range.

When multiple print jobs are sent to a printer faster than the print device can print them, the print jobs are organized into a print queue. You can also set a priority in the range of 1 to 99, where the higher the number, the higher the priority within the queue. Using the example of the Accounting Admins group once again, let's say that on the printer icon for which they have Printer permissions, you assign a priority of 99. On the printer icon for which you've granted Everyone print permissions, you've assigned a priority of 1. (In this example, let's say you didn't put an availability time on either printer.) When members of the Accounting Admins group send a print job to the printer, their documents will be printed before documents of members of the Everyone group.

Sharing and Configuring Printers **375**

FIGURE 7-15

The Advanced tab of a printer's Properties dialog box

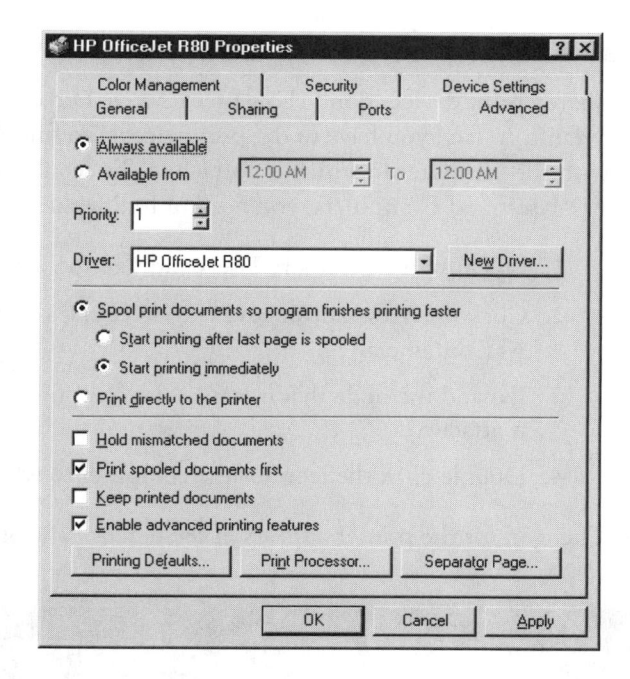

The spooling options let you decide whether or not print jobs from programs are spooled to a temporary file before actually being printed. Those options are summarized as follows:

- **Spool print documents so program finishes printing faster** If selected, print jobs from programs are sent to the print spooler, rather than directly to the printer, so that the program finishes printing sooner. If you opt to spool documents, you can choose from one of the following two options:

    - **Start printing after last page is spooled** The print job isn't sent to the print device until the program has finished spooling the job.

    - **Start printing immediately** The print job is sent to the print device as soon as the program starts spooling.

- **Print directly to the printer** Deactivates print spooling so print jobs are sent directly to the print device.

Finding Shared Printers in AD Users and Computers

Shared print devices don't show up in Active Directory Users and Computers by default. In fact, you have to dig pretty deeply to find them. Each printer is associated with the computer to which it's attached. To see the icon for a shared print device in AD Users and Computers, you need to follow these steps:

1. Open Active Directory Users and Computers.
2. Click the View button and choose Users, Groups, And Computers As Containers.
3. Expand the node that contains the computer object to which the printer is attached.
4. Double-click the icon for the computer to which the printer is attached.

The icon for the printer appears in the details pane of AD Users and Computers.

SCENARIO & SOLUTION

I connected a plug-and-play combination printer/scanner to my computer, but Windows 2000 didn't detect it at all. What should I do?	Printers that require use of an EPP (Enhanced Printer Port) won't be detected unless you set the system BIOS Parallel Port setting to EPP.
I would like users to be able to install their own printers, but some of the printers require unsigned drivers that the users cannot install. How do I give users permissions to install those drivers?	Log in locally to the user's machine, open the System Properties dialog box, and click the Hardware tab. Click the Driver Signing button, choose the Warn or Block option, and make sure Apply Setting As System Default is selected.
I shared a printer on a server, but when I choose File	Print from a program on a client computer, there's no sign of the printer. How do I fix that?	On the client computer, open the Printers folder in the Control Panel, and then open the Add Printer icon. In the Add Printer Wizard that opens, choose Network Printer. If the printer has already been published to Active Directory, you can choose Find A Printer In The Directory when prompted. Otherwise, you can browse for the printer, or just enter its name in UNC format.

That should be sufficient for what you'll need to know for Exam 70-218. Three printer-related issues that you should also be aware of are included in the Scenario and Solutions grid to follow.

CERTIFICATION OBJECTIVE 7.03

Publishing Shared Resources in Active Directory

As you know, one of the big advantages to Active Directory is that anyone can search the directory for shared resources. When you publish an object, be sure to include any attributes that a user might enter in searching for the object. The larger the network, the more important it is to provide detailed information about each object, so that users can be certain that they're selecting an appropriate object from the directory.

Publishing Shared Folders

Publishing shared folders in Active Directory is simply a means of making the shared folders easily accessible to users. You'll use the Active Directory Users and Computers console for this job. You can place the shared folder in any existing OU, at the domain level, or create a new OU for organizing printers. It all depends on what makes sense for your organization. In AD Users and Computers, just right-click the container of choice and choose New | Shared Folder. The New Object – Shared Folder dialog box opens. Type in the name of the shared folder, exactly as you want it to appear in the directory. Then, type in the path to the printer in UNC format, as in the example shown in Figure 7-16. Click OK, and the shared folder appears as an icon within the container.

To make the shared folder easier to find, you can right-click its icon in AD Users and Computers, choose Properties, and enter a description. You can also click the Keywords button to add additional keywords that a user might enter when attempting to locate this shared folder.

FIGURE 7-16

Publishing the shared folder \\Server01\Server Docs as "Public Documents"

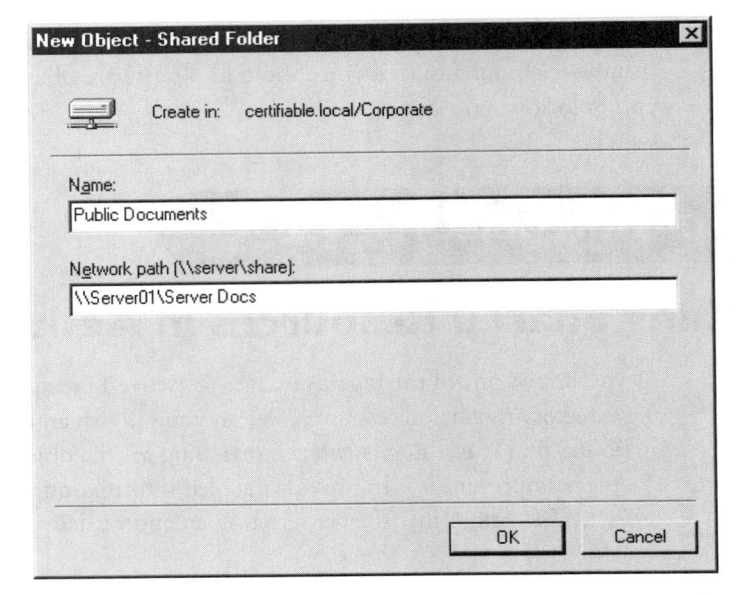

[Screenshot of "New Object - Shared Folder" dialog box. Create in: certifiable.local/Corporate. Name: Public Documents. Network path (\\server\share): \\Server01\Server Docs. OK and Cancel buttons.]

EXERCISE 7-3

CertCam 7-3

Publishing a Shared Folder

In this exercise, you'll publish the Server Docs folder that you created in Exercise 7-1 to Active Directory. I'll use the Corporate OU as the container for this object, though you can use any container you wish. You'll need to be logged in to the domain controller with administrative privileges to complete this exercise.

1. On the domain controller, open Active Directory Users and Computers from the Administrative Tools menu.

2. Right-click the Corporate OU and choose New | Shared Folder.

3. Type **Public Documents** as the share name.

4. Type **\\Server01\Server Docs** as the network path, as in the example shown in the previous illustration.

5. Click the OK button.

The shared folder is added to the OU. Its icon looks like a network drive icon, and its Type is Shared Folder.

exam Watch   *Whenever you want users to be able to find a shared object without knowing which server it's on, you must publish that object to Active Directory.*

Publishing Shared Printers

Shared printers on Windows 2000 are automatically published to Active Directory if you chose List In Directory as mentioned earlier in this chapter. Shared printers on non-Windows 2000 computers need to be published manually. Once again, you can accomplish this using Active Directory Users and Computers. Right-click the Computers container, and choose New | Printer. Type the path to the printer (for example, \\ServerXY\HPColor) and click OK.

Searching for AD Objects

Once you've published shared folders and printers in Active Directory, you can use the Find options available through Windows 2000 to locate objects in the directory. For example, you could right-click the domain icon in AD Users and Computers. Or, on a client computer, open My Network Places, drill down to the icon for the domain within the Directory icon, right-click it, and choose Find. Choose the type of object you want to search for from the Find drop-down list, shown in Figure 7-17, and then enter any keywords or other information about the object for which you're searching and click the Find Now button.

Now that you know about sharing and publishing resources through Active Directory, let's look at some scenarios and their solutions before closing this chapter.

FIGURE 7-17

The Find dialog box for locating Active Directory objects

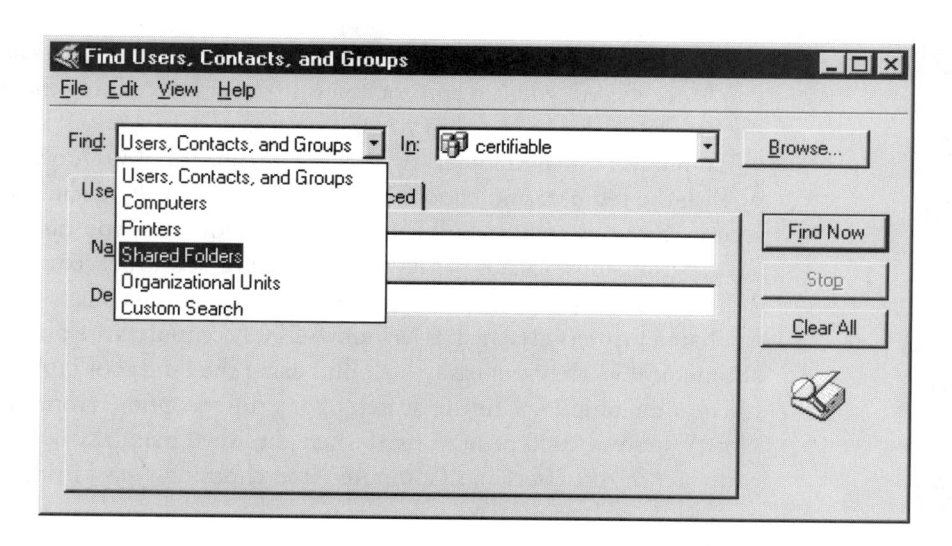

Chapter 7: Sharing and Publishing Folders and Printers

SCENARIO & SOLUTION

I shared a printer and opted to list it in the directory, but I don't see it in Active Directory Users and Computers. Where should I look?	By default, printers are created in the computer object to which they're physically connected. To see a printer's entry, choose View | Users, Groups, And Computers As Containers. Then, expand the Computers container and double-click the icon for the computer to which the printer is physically connected. You'll see the printer listed as an object in the details pane.
How can I control users' ability to manage printers?	Right-click the domain name or any OU in AD Users and Computers, click Properties, then create a new GPO from the Group Policy tab. Then, edit the new policy and look under User Configuration\Administrative Templates\Control Panel\Printers to find general policies related to the addition, deletion, and browsing of printers.
Are there group policies that affect the ability to publish printers in Active Directory?	Yes, you'll find them under Computer Configuration\Administrative Templates\Printers in AD Users and Computers.

CERTIFICATION SUMMARY

Active Directory is your central location for storing information about all resources that are available in the network. Once you share and publish a resource, users can search the directory for resources without knowing which server is offering the resource.

Sharing a folder or printer is a simple job—just right-click the object's icon and choose Sharing. Or, right-click and choose Properties, and then click the Sharing tab. Once shared, you can control access to the resource using the Security tab in the Properties dialog box.

To publish a shared folder, right-click the domain or OU to which you want to publish the resource and choose New | Shared Folder. By default, the Everyone security group is granted Full Control of the folder. But you can restrict access using share permissions. On an NTFS volume, you can control access to the folder and individual objects within the folder using NTFS permissions.

Shared printers attached to Windows 2000 computers are published automatically. They can easily be found using the Find tool in Active Directory Users and Computers, or the Search | For Printers options from the Start menu. Non-Windows 2000 printers need to be published manually by right-clicking a container in AD Users and Computers and choosing New | Printer.

✓ TWO-MINUTE DRILL

Sharing Folders and Files

- ❏ Administrative shares are shared folders that are visible only to administrators. Their share names end with a dollar sign character ($).
- ❏ You can chare a folder by right-clicking its icon in Windows Explorer and choosing Sharing.
- ❏ You can set user limits on shared folders.
- ❏ The maximum number of users who can simultaneously access a shared folder on a Windows 2000 Professional computer is ten, no matter how high you set the user limit.
- ❏ Share permissions are the only ones you can use on FAT and FAT32 volumes.
- ❏ File and Directory Permissions (also called NTFS Permissions) are additional permissions you can set on NTFS volumes only.
- ❏ By default, the Everyone security group has Full Control of all newly shared folders.
- ❏ Permissions set for a folder are automatically inherited by all child folders and files.
- ❏ Permissions that an object acquires from its parent object(s) are called *inherited permissions*.
- ❏ Permissions that are defined directly on the object are called *explicit permissions*.
- ❏ Deny permissions expressly deny a permission, regardless of conflicting inherited permissions.
- ❏ The Offline Files feature allows clients to access network files when offline.

Sharing and Configure Printers

- ❏ The term *print device* refers to the actual physical printer. The term *printer* refers to any icon used to represent that print device.
- ❏ A single print device might be identified by several different printer icons or names.

- ❏ When using a print device with EPP cabling, you must enable PPP mode in the system BIOS. Otherwise, Windows 2000 won't detect the printer.
- ❏ When configuring permissions for a shared printer, you can specify times during which the printer is, and isn't, available.
- ❏ You can also assign print job priorities to security groups, whereby the groups with the highest priority get their print jobs done first.
- ❏ Shared printers are visible in AD Users and Computers only when View | Users, Groups, And Computers As containers is selected, and the computer to which the printer is physically attached is highlighted in the console tree.

Publishing Shared Resources in Active Directory

- ❏ To publish a shared folder in Active Directory, right-click the container of choice, choose New | Shared Folder, and fill in the blanks.
- ❏ Shared printers are automatically published to Active Directory no extra steps are required.
- ❏ To search for AD objects from AD Users and Computer, right-click the domain name and choose Find.
- ❏ To search for AD objects from the Windows desktop, open My Network Places, right-click the icon that represents the domain, and choose Find.

SELF TEST

Sharing Folders and Files

1. You are a domain administrator for your company. The network consists of a single Windows 2000 domain with 400 Windows 2000 Professional client computers. One of the client computers contains a shared folder with the default permissions assigned. You publish the folder to Active Directory where other users are able to find it. However, many users complain that they cannot access the folder or map a persistent drive to the folder. What should you do to solve the problem?

    A. Increase the User Limit on the shared folder to 400 users.
    B. Grant the Everyone group Read permissions for the folder.
    C. Move the folder to a Windows 2000 Server computer.
    D. Create a new GPO that grants Read permissions to the Authenticated Users security group, and link it to the shared folder.

2. You are the network administrator for your company. A shared folder on the network, named Sales Docs, contains shared resources for the Sales department, with permission inheritance enabled. Each employee within the Sales department has their own folder and Modify permissions on that folder, as summarized in Table 7-2.

    Hobart is promoted to a supervisor position, and needs to be able to view the contents of Jack's and Jill's folders, but not make any changes to those folders. How can you give Jack appropriate permissions, but no more than what's needed for this situation?

    A. Grant Hobart Allow–Read & Execute share permission on the Sales Department folder.
    B. Grant Hobart Allow–Read NTFS permission on the Sales Department folder.
    C. Make Hobart a member of the Everyone group.
    D. Make Hobart a member of the Administrators group.

3. You are the administrator of a Windows 2000 file server named ITServer, which is a member of the company's Windows 2000 domain. You create and share folders for the IT department on drive I, which is an NTFS volume. Managers are all members of the ITManagers Security group, and need full control over all subfolders and files within the department's folders. Users named Mandy, Maureen, and Jack need to be able to read files in the I:\IT\Public folder,

384 Chapter 7: Sharing and Publishing Folders and Printers

| TABLE 7-2 | Permissions on a Folder and Subfolder |

Resource	Permission Type	Permissions
Sales Department share	Share	Everyone–Full Control
Sales Department folder	NTFS	Administrators–Full Control
Jack's folder	NTFS	Administrators–Full Control Jack–Modify
Jill's folder	NTFS	Administrators–Full Control Jill–Modify
Hobart's folder	NTFS	Administrators–Full Control Hobart–Modify

and have Full Control of only their own personal folders. You configure folder and share permissions as shown in the following table (where FC stands for "Full Control").

Folder	Share Name	Share Permission	NTFS Permissions
I:\ITfolder	IT	ITManagers–FC	ITManagers–Read
I:\ITFolder\Public	Public	Everyone–Read	Everyone–Read
I:\ITFolder\Public\Mandy	Mandy	Mandy–FC	Mandy–FC
I:\ITFolder\Public\Maureen	Maureen	Maureen–FC	Maureen–FC
I:\ITFolder\Public\Jack	Jack	Jack–FC	Jack–FC

IT managers report that while they're able to read the contents of all folders, they are unable to modify the contents of the folders. How can you correct the problem?

  A. Change the share permission for ITManagers on the IT share to Modify.

  B. Change the NTFS permissions for ITManagers to Full Control.

  C. Add ITManagers–Modify permissions to the Public share.

  D. Add the ITManagers–FC permissions to the Mandy, Maureen, and Jack shares' permissions.

4. You are the domain administrator for your company. You create a shared folder named GroupDocs with default share permissions. You grant the Authenticated Users group NTFS

Full Control permissions. Within the GroupDocs folder, you create a file named Handbook. You grant the Authenticated Users group Read permissions on the file. Later, you discover that members of the Authenticated Users group are able to delete the file. How could you prevent users from deleting that file, as well as all other files and subfolders within the GroupDocs folder?

A. Assign the Deny–Read Permissions permission to Authenticated Users on the GroupDocs folder.

B. Assign the Deny–Read Permissions permission to Authenticated Users on the Handbook file.

C. Assign the Deny–Delete Subfolders And Files permission to Authenticated Users on the Handbook file.

D. Assign the Deny–Delete Subfolders And Files permission to Authenticated Users on the GroupDocs folder.

Sharing and Configure Printers

5. User Frank, who has permission to install new printers on his computer, connects a multipurpose plug-and-play printer/scanner/copier to his computer through a USB port. His Windows 2000 computer doesn't detect the printer. He scans for hardware changes in the Device Manager, but cannot find any reference to the printer anywhere. What could you do to solve his problem?

    A. Enable printer sharing on his computer.
    B. Update the usbhub.sys driver in his computer.
    C. Enable EPP mode in the system BIOS.
    D. Publish the printer in Active Directory.

6. User Hank successfully installs a new printer on his Windows 2000 Professional computer. He is able to print documents from his printer. He wants other users to be able to locate his printer in Active Directory and send print jobs to it. However, no other users are able to locate or send jobs to his printer. What must you do to correct the problem?

    A. Search the manufacturer's web site for an updated printer driver.
    B. Share the printer on Hank's computer.
    C. Grant the Everyone security group Print permissions to the printer.
    D. Make Hank a member of the Domain Admins group and have him publish the shared printer to Active Directory.

Chapter 7: Sharing and Publishing Folders and Printers

7. You are the domain administrator for your company's network. You install a high-speed color laser print device on a member server named PrnServer and share it with the default settings. You want all users to have access to the printer, but you want print jobs from the Graphics domain local group to always have the highest priority. What should you do?

   A. For the Graphics Security group, set a printing priority of 99 on the printer.

   B. Deny Print permissions to the Everyone group, and allow Print permissions for the Graphics group.

   C. Create and share a second printer for the print device and set its priority to 1. Assign the Everyone group Deny–Print permission, and the Graphics group Allow–Print permission. Instruct the Graphics group to use the second printer.

   D. Create and share a second printer for the print device, and give the printer a priority level of 99. Remove permissions for the Everyone group, and grant Allow–Print permission to the Graphics group. Instruct the Graphics group to use the second printer.

8. You are the domain administrator for a Windows 2000 network that includes a high-speed laser printer. You want all users in the company to be able to use the printer throughout the day, except from 11:00 A.M. to 1:00 P.M. During that time, you want the Finance department to have exclusive use of the printer. Finance department members who need exclusive use of the printer are all members of a security group named FinanceGroup. What should you do?

   A. Configure the printer so that the Everyone group has Allow–Print permissions from 1:00 P.M. to 10:00 A.M. Create a second printer icon for the print device, and grant the FinanceGroup security group Allow–Print permissions. Remove the Everyone group from this second printer icon, and instruct members of the FinanceGroup group to use the second printer for all printing.

   B. Configure the printer so that the Everyone group has Allow–Print permissions, and members of the FinanceGroup group have a priority of 1 from 10:00 A.M. to 1:00 P.M.

   C. Add a second print device and assign Allow–Print permissions to FinanceGroup from 10:00 A.M. to 1:00 P.M.

   D. Create a second printer and configure it so that the Everyone group has Deny–Print permissions, and the FinanceGroup security group has Allow–Print permissions from 10:00 A.M. to 1:00 P.M. Instruct members of FinanceGroup to always use the second printers.

9. You are the network administrator for your company's network, which consists of a single Windows 2000 domain. You create and share a folder at I:\AcctApps and share it using the share name AccountingApps. You grant Read & Execute permissions to the folder to a security group named AccountingAdmins. Accounting administrators report that they are unable to find the folder in the directory. What should you do?

   A. Grant the AccountingAdmins group Full Control permissions on the folder.
   B. Publish the shared folder to Active Directory.
   C. Rename the share to AccountingApps$.
   D. Move the folder to the C drive on a domain controller.

10. You are a print operator for your company's network. You share and publish a printer named ColorInkjet on a Windows NT computer named Client99. You are able to find the printer by name when searching the directory, but when you open AD Users and Computers, you see no sign of the printer. How could you view the icon that represents the printer in AD Users and Computers? (Choose all that apply.)

    A. Look in the Printers container of AD Users and Computers.
    B. Look in the LostAndFound folder.
    C. Select Users, Groups, And Computers As Containers from the View menu in AD Users and Computers.
    D. Double-click the icon that represents the computer to which the printer is attached.

LAB QUESTION

You are the domain administrator for your company's Windows 2000 domain. You want to provide users with a central, publicly accessible set of folders and files that they can use to share information with others. Domain administrators should have full control of the folder and all of its contents. Authenticated users should be able to create, change, and delete files and folders within the share. You want everyone to be able to find the shared folder using the name PublicData, and you want more than ten users to be able to use the folder simultaneously. What should you do?

SELF TEST ANSWERS

Sharing Folders and Files

1. ☑ **C** is correct. The fact the *some*, but not all, users are able to access the shared folder indicates that the user limit is likely to blame. Since this shared folder is on a Windows 2000 Professional computer, the limit will be ten users, no matter what you do.
   ☒ **A** is wrong because increasing the user limit won't help on a Windows 2000 Professional computer.
   ☒ **B** is wrong because the Everyone group already has Full Control of the folder, and it's not doing them any good because of the user limit.
   ☒ **D** is wrong because there's no need to create a GPO here, and doing so wouldn't get you past the ten-user limit.

2. ☑ **B** is correct. If Hobart has Allow–Read permissions on the Sales Department folder, he'll be able to read the contents of Jack's and Jill's subfolders.
   ☒ **A** is wrong because Hobart already has Full Control permissions on the share. He needs NTFS permissions that will allow him to read the contents of subfolders within the share.
   ☒ **C** is wrong because Hobart is already a member of the Everyone group.
   ☒ **D** is incorrect because it gives Hobart far more permission than necessary.

3. ☑ **B** is correct. ITManagers needs NTFS Full Control permissions to the entire shared folder. The NTFS Read permissions are canceling out the Full Control share permissions.
   ☒ **A** is wrong because changing the share permissions wouldn't override the NTFS permission on the shared folder.
   ☒ **C** and **D** are wrong because the ITManagers group needs Full Control of the entire folder, not just Modify permissions on subfolders.

4. ☑ **D** is correct. Users are able to delete the file because of permissions on the GroupDocs folder. Denying them permission to delete subfolders and files in the GroupDocs folder would prevent them from deleting all files within the folder.
   ☒ **A** and **B** are incorrect because the Read Permissions permission has nothing to do with the ability to delete the contents of the folder.
   ☒ **C** is incorrect because you need to set the Deny–Delete Subfolders And Files permission on the GroupDocs folder, not the Handbook file.

Self Test Answers **389**

Sharing and Configure Printers

5. ☑ **C** is correct. Whenever Windows 2000 is incapable of detecting a newer printer, your best bet is to enable EPP mode on the parallel port, even if the printer connects through a USB port.
☒ **A** is incorrect because there's no need to enable printer sharing, and the printer isn't installed yet anyway.
☒ **B** is incorrect because this would not help Windows 2000 detect the printer.
☒ **D** is wrong because the printer needs to be installed and shared before it can be published in Active Directory.

6. ☑ **B** is correct. There's nothing in the question that states that Hank has shared the printer. Since this printer is on a Windows 2000 computer, sharing the printer will be sufficient to publish the printer in Active Directory and give Everyone Print permissions.
☒ **A** is wrong because the printer is working for Hank, so this is a sharing problem, not a driver problem.
☒ **C** is wrong because the printer hasn't been shared yet. Once it is shared, the Everyone group will be granted Print permissions to the printer.
☒ **D** is incorrect because it gives Hank a lot more privileges than he needs, and doesn't help him to share the printer.

7. ☑ **D** is correct. You want to copy the printer icon, but give this second printer a high priority (99). Allow only the Graphics group to use this printer, and instruct its members to use it so that they'll get that higher priority. Leave the original printer intact, whereby everyone else can print, but with a low priority of 1. Everyone still gets to use the print device, but jobs from the Graphics department will get the highest priority.
☒ **A** is wrong because you can't set different priorities for different groups within a single printer icon. You must create a separate printer icon for each priority setting you want.
☒ **B** is wrong because nobody would be able to print if you were to set Deny–Print to the Everyone group.
☒ **C** is wrong because you want to give the Graphics group a high priority like 99, not a low priority like 1.

8. ☑ **A** is correct. Giving the Everyone group Print permissions from 1:00 P.M. to 11:00 A.M. makes the printer available to everyone during that timeframe. Having a second icon that gives Print permissions only to the FinanceGroup group lets them print whenever they want. But since nobody else has Print permissions from 11:00 A.M. to 1:00 P.M., the FinanceGroup will have exclusive use of the printer during that timeframe.
☒ **B** is incorrect because this isn't about priority. FinanceGroup members need exclusive use of the printer from 11:00 A.M. to 1:00 P.M.

☒ C is wrong because the question states that you must configure the existing print device—adding another print device isn't an option.
☒ D is wrong because assigning a Deny–Print permission to the Everyone group would prevent everybody from using the printer.

9. ☑ B is correct. After you've shared the folder, you must manually publish it to Active Directory for users to find it there.
☒ A, C, and D are wrong because none of those actions would lead to the shared folder being published in Active Directory.

10. ☑ C and D are correct. When you view those objects as containers and double-click the host computer's icon, the printer's icon appears in the details pane.
☒ A is wrong because there is no folder named Printers in AD Users and Computers.
☒ B is incorrect because the LostAndFound container contains only objects that failed during a move operation using a command like MoveTree.

LAB ANSWER

You can accomplish all of these goals in a few easy steps:

1. On a Windows 2000 Server computer, create the folder on an NTFS volume other than the operating system volume. You'd be stuck with the ten-user limit if you did this on a Windows 2000 Professional computer. Putting the shared folder on a separate volume keeps it separate from the operating systems.

2. Share the folder, and leave the Everyone–Full Control share permission in place. You'll use NTFS permissions to control access to the share.

3. For NTFS permissions, grant Allow–Full Control to the Domain Admins group, grant Allow–Modify to the Authenticated User group, and remove the Everyone group. Now you have proper permissions in place.

4. Publish the shared folder in Active Directory with the share name **PublicData** so people can find it in the directory.

8
Managing Software with Group Policy

CERTIFICATION OBJECTIVES

8.01	Deploying Applications with Group Policy
8.02	Managing Software with Group Policy
8.03	Deploying Service Packs with Group Policy
✓	Two-Minute Drill
Q&A	Self Test

In Chapter 6, you learned the basics of working with group policies. As you saw, you create a Group Policy Object (GPO) that defines a policy as a collection of policy settings. You can then link that GPO to any Active Directory site, domain, or OU object (category). You can also define to whom the policy does, and doesn't, apply, and delegate authority to manage GPOs to security groups as appropriate to your organization. In Chapter 7, you saw how to share and publish folders. In this chapter, we'll focus on using group policies and shared folders to install and manage software on multiple computers.

There was a time when bringing a new application to all users' desktops required the administrator to sit down at each machine and install the software. This was no small feat when it involved hundreds, or thousands, of workstations. In Windows 2000, you can automate the entire process using the Group Policy Software Installation extension and the Windows Installer Service.

The Windows Installer Service relies on installer *packages,* which are usually MSI (Microsoft Software Installation) files that come with a given application, although a package can use other types of files as well, including MSP (Microsoft Patch) and MST (Microsoft Transform). If a package comes with the application, it's referred to as a *native package.* Applications that don't contain built-in Windows Installer files can be *repackaged* using a third-party tool like Veritas's WinInstall.

on the Job

Windows 2000 ships with a limited version of WinInstall, which you can find in the installation CD under valueadd\3rdParty\mgmt\winstle.

CERTIFICATION OBJECTIVE 8.01

Deploying Applications with Group Policy

The Software Installation Group Policy extension is the primary tool for centrally managing client application software. There are two ways to deploy software. When you *assign* an application, you make it mandatory to the user. When a user to whom you've assigned a package logs on, the assigned application will already be available on the user's Start menu. The application will automatically be installed when the user starts the program or opens a document that's associated with the assigned application.

Publishing an application is different from assigning an application in that installing the application isn't mandatory. When you publish software, you simply make it available to users as an option. The published applications advertise themselves in Active Directory, and can be installed by the user when she opens Add/Remove

Deploying Applications with Group Policy **393**

Programs in Control Panel, or opens a document that's associated with the published application.

You have a lot of flexibility when deploying software with group policies. You can create as many GPOs as you wish, and link each GPO to the domain or a specific OU. As always, you can filter the group policy so that the software deployment is applied only to specific security groups. A single GPO can be used to install a single package, or multiple packages.

exam
⍟atch

Don't forget that to create group policies, an OU administrator needs to be a member of the Group Policy Creator Owners group.

Setting Up a Software Distribution Point

You'll need to create a shared folder for each application to be deployed. Your best bet might be to create a single folder, name it something like Packages, and grant administrators Read and Write access to the file. Users only need Read permissions to the folder. Within that single folder, you can create a separate subfolder for each application to be deployed.

Exactly what you need to copy to the application's subfolder will vary somewhat from one application to the next, so you'll need to check the documentation that came with the application for further instructions and options. For example, to deploy Microsoft Office 2000, you can enter the command **setup /a** on the distribution CD. Doing so will allow you to enter the CD Key just once, and copy all the appropriate files to a distribution folder of your choosing.

EXERCISE 8-1

CertCam 8-1

Creating a Distribution Point

In this chapter, you'll deploy the administrative tools, collectively known as AdminPak, to client computers. Don't do this in a production environment without the permission of the network administrator. The first step will be to create a shared folder to act as a central distribution point, assign appropriate permissions, and copy adminpak.msi from the system32 folder to the distribution point. Follow these steps:

1. Log in to your domain controller (or any other server in the domain) with administrative privileges.

2. Open My Computer, and open a drive icon.

3. Right-click within the drive's folder and choose New | Folder.

4. Name the folder **Packages**.
5. Right-click the folder and choose Sharing. Share it with the name **Packages** and the description **Windows Installer Packages**.
6. Optionally, set permissions to allow administrators full control, and users Read permissions. (Though, if you're practicing on a small private network, it's okay to just use the default permissions.)

Now you can create a subfolder for AdminPak by following these steps:

1. Open the new Packages folder.
2. Right-click within the folder and choose New | Folder.
3. Name the new folder **AdminPack**.
4. Copy the file adminpak.msi from %system%\root system32 to the new AdminPack folder, as shown in Figure 8-1.

In Exercise 8-2, you'll create the GPO for publishing the AdminPack programs.

FIGURE 8-1 The adminpak.msi file added to the new AdminPack folder

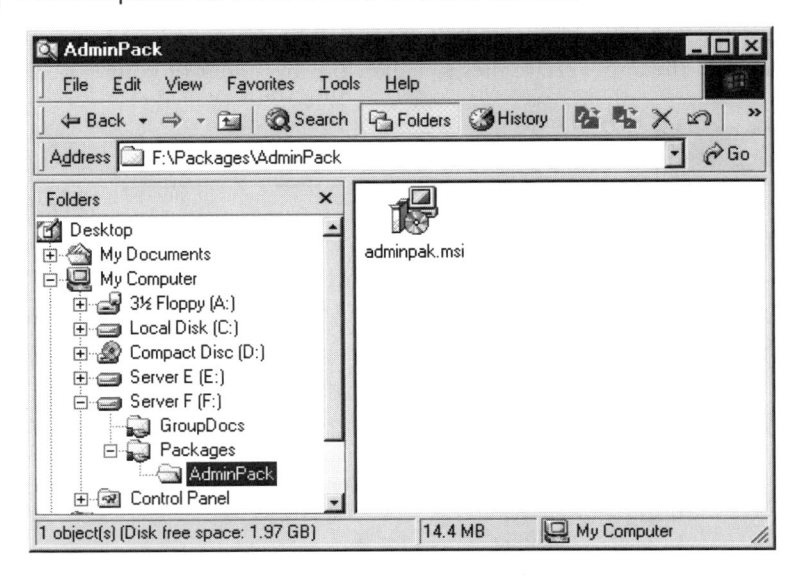

Creating the GPO

Creating a software deployment GPO is like creating any other GPO. In Active Directory Users and Computers, right-click the domain or OU to which you want to link the GPO, choose Properties, then click the Group Policy tab. You can use the New button to create a new GPO. To filter the GPO, click its name in the list of Group Policy Object Links and choose Properties. Then click the Security tab. Add and remove groups as applicable to your situation, and choose Allow–Apply Group Policy for *only* those groups for which you want the software installed. For example, if you're deploying software to be used only by yourself and other administrators, you could choose Allow–Apply Group Policy for the Domain Admins and Enterprise Admins groups only, and clear the Allow check box for all other security groups.

on the Job
Group policies not only save you time in installing new software, but simplify all management tasks at all stages of the software lifecycle.

To define the packages that the GPO will install, and various options, click the GPO name in the list of GPO links and click the Edit button to get to the Group Policy snap-in. You can define packages to be installed under either Computer Configuration or User Configuration, as shown in Figure 8-2. If you choose Computer Configuration, you'll only have the option to assign the software to computers. If you add packages under User Configuration, you'll then be given the option to either publish or assign the software. The differences between using Computer Configuration and User Configuration are summarized in Table 8-1.

You can choose default settings for Software Installation from either container. The default settings you choose will be applied to all packages that you add to the GPO later, and can easily be overwritten at that time. To get to the default settings, just right-click Software Installation under either container and choose Properties. On the General tab, you'll see the options shown in Figure 8-3, which are summarized here:

- **Default package location** Enter the network path, in UNC format, to the shared folder in which you'll be installing packages. This is just the starting point for finding packages, so you can specify the parent folder if you wish.
- **Display the Deploy Software dialog box** If selected, you'll be prompted to Assign, Publish, or Configure new packages that you add to the GPO.

Chapter 8: Managing Software with Group Policy

FIGURE 8-2 Software Installation is available under Computer Configuration and User Configuration.

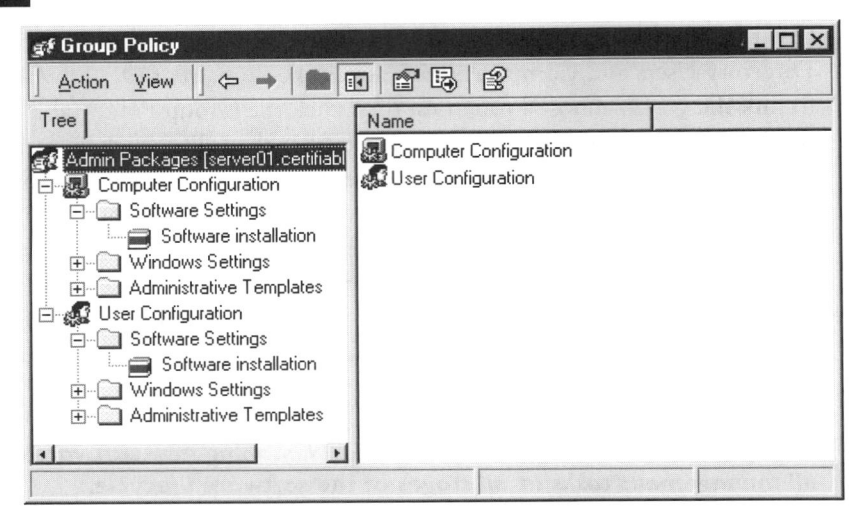

TABLE 8-1 Installation Options for Computers and Users

Consideration	User–Publish	User–Assign	Computer–Assign
When is software available?	After the next logon	After the next logon	Next time the computer is started
How does user install?	Add/Remove Programs in the Control Panel	By opening the program from the Start menu or desktop icon	No action required by the user; software is already installed
What happens when the user opens an associated document?	Software is installed only if AutoInstall is turned on	Software is installed	Document opens because software is already installed
Can user remove software in Add/Remove Programs?	Yes	Yes	No, only administrators can remove the software
Which installation files are supported?	Windows Installer packages and down-level ZAP files	Windows Installer packages	Windows Installer packages

- **Publish**   If selected, new applications that you add will be published by default. This setting is disabled under Computer Configuration, which only supports Assign, not Publish.
- **Assign**   If selected, new applications that you add will be published by default.
- **Advanced published or assigned**   When selected, a Configure Package Properties dialog box will appear when you add a new package.

on the Job

If you plan to run any transforms (MST) files with the deployment, choose the Advanced Published Or Assigned option.

- **Basic**   If selected, only basic options will be displayed to users when they install the package. This is the preferred setting for nonadministrative users who might not know how to select more advanced options.
- **Maximum**   If selected, a full set of options will be displayed when the user installs the application. This is the preferred setting for more sophisticated users and administrators who need more control over how the application is installed.
- **Uninstall the applications when they fall out of the scope of management**   If selected, ensures that if a user gets "demoted," the application will be uninstalled for that user.

As an example of the last option, suppose that your company frequently assigns employees to different departments based on whatever project they're working on. You create GPOs linked to various departmental OUs. When a user moves from one department to another and you move his user account, he'd normally still have the same software installed. If you select the last option, however, the deployed application will be removed when the user's account is moved to another OU.

exam Watch

Remember, you want to select, not clear, the Uninstall The Applications When They Fall Out Of The Scope Of Management option to prevent applications from following users when you move their accounts from one OU to another.

FIGURE 8-3

Software installation properties for Computer Configuration

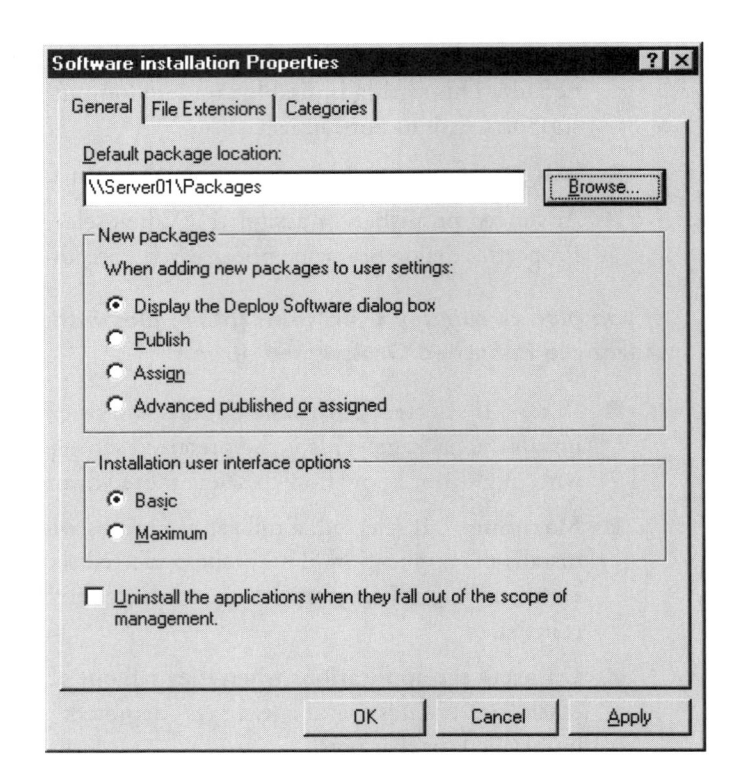

Adding a Package to a Group Policy

Once you've defined your distribution point, and created and filtered a GPO, you're ready to start adding packages to that GPO. Click the name of the policy under Group Policy Object Links in the Properties dialog box for the domain or OU to which you linked the group policy. Then, click the Edit button to open the Group Policy snap-in. Expand either the Computer Configuration or User Configuration node, expand Software Settings, right-click Software Installation, and choose New | Package. An Open dialog box will appear, initially displaying the contents of the default shared folder for packages. Open the folder that contains the package MSI file, as shown in Figure 8-4. Click the Open button.

FIGURE 8-4 About to add adminpak.msi to Software Installation under User Configuration

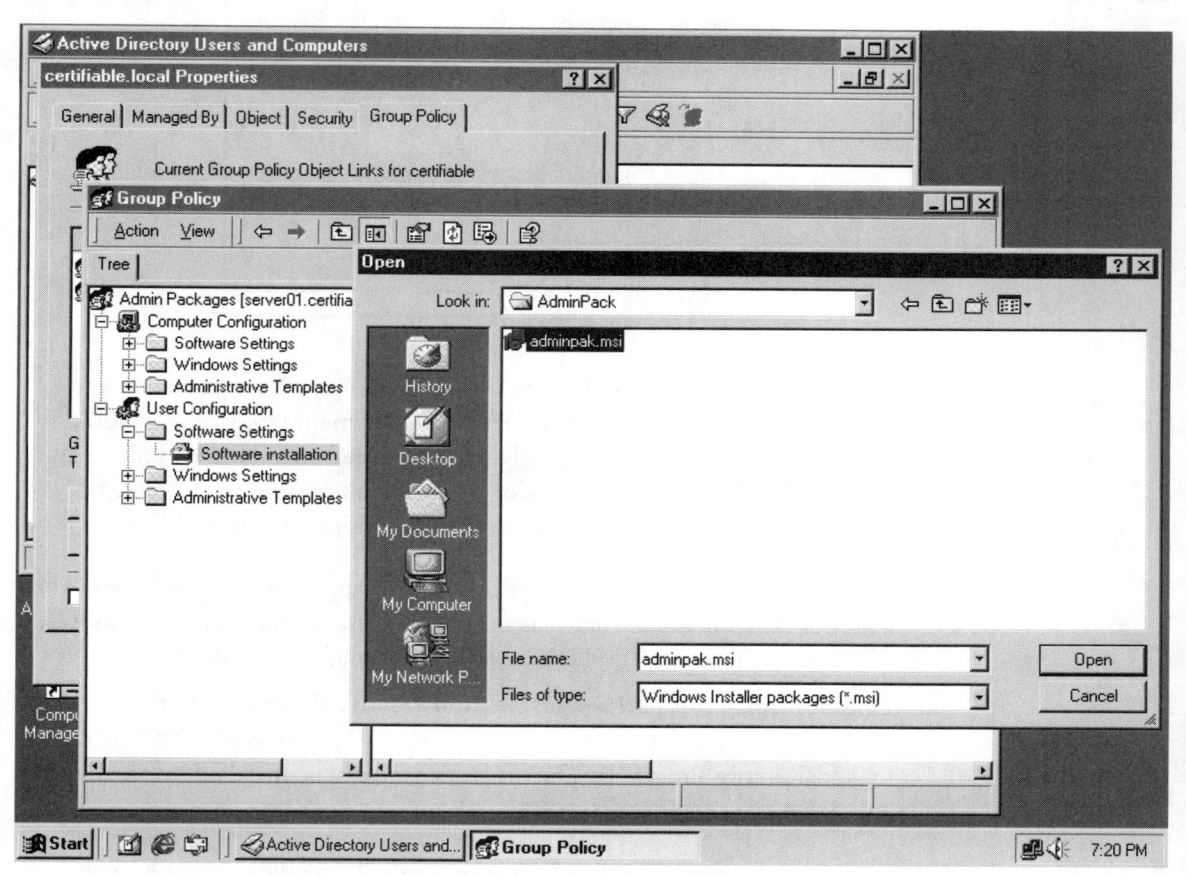

If you chose Display The Deploy Software Dialog Box as the default Software Installation setting, the Deploy Software dialog box shown in Figure 8-5 opens. There, you can choose Published, Assigned, or Advanced Published Or Assigned. If you choose the Published or Assigned option, the package will just be published or assigned, and that's the end of it.

FIGURE 8-5

The Deploy Software dialog box

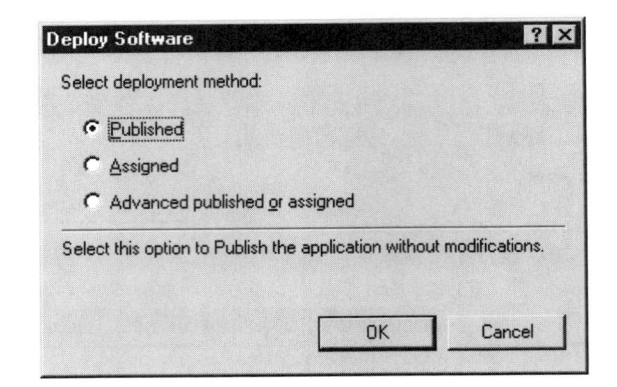

*[Deploy Software dialog box showing:
Select deployment method:
• Published (selected)
• Assigned
• Advanced published or assigned
Select this option to Publish the application without modifications.
OK / Cancel]*

If you choose the Advanced Published Or Assigned option, you'll be taken to a dialog box like the one in Figure 8-6. On the Deployment tab, you'll see some familiar options—the ones you previously selected as default values to apply to all packages in the GPO. Here, you can tailor those default options to this specific package, if you wish. You also get a couple of new options here, including:

- **Auto-install this application by file extension application**   If selected, when a user clicks a document that's associated with the application (for example, an XLS file), the Excel application will be installed automatically.

- **Do not display this package in the Add/Remove Programs control panel**   If selected, the option to add or remove the program won't be visible in Add/Remove Programs. The program can only be installed by opening an associated document type.

on the Job   *You can use the Categories tab of the package's Properties dialog box to categorize applications to your liking. Use the Modifications tab to specify any transforms (MST files) that need to be used to customize applications during deployment.*

Clicking the Advanced button provides a couple of other useful options, as shown in Figure 8-7. The first option, if selected, will deploy the package in its native language, even if that language conflicts with language settings on the target machine. The second option is great for gaining control over applications that were installed locally. When a user installs an application locally, it falls outside the control of group policy, and hence cannot be managed centrally. Choosing the second option will remove the locally installed copy of the application and replace it with the group policy-installed version, so you regain centralized administrative control.

Deploying Applications with Group Policy 401

FIGURE 8-6

The Properties dialog box for a package

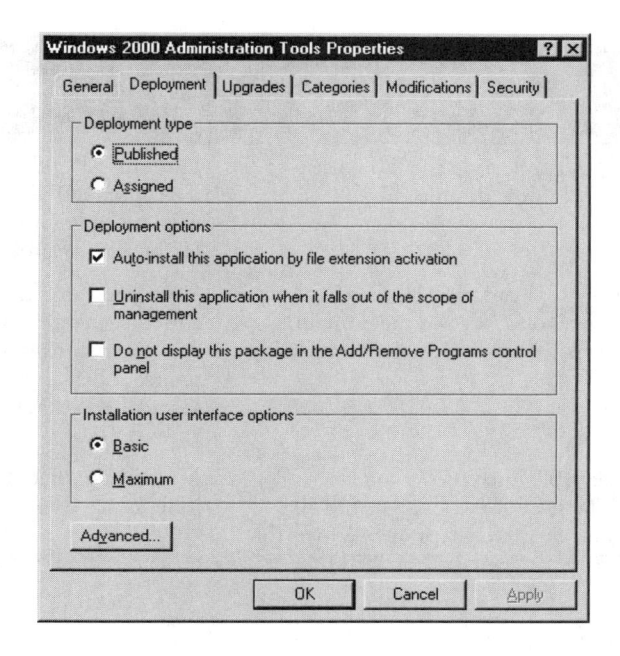

Click the Close button to return to the Group Policy snap-in. When you click the Software Installation node there, you'll see the package listed in the details area.

FIGURE 8-7

Still more advanced deployment options

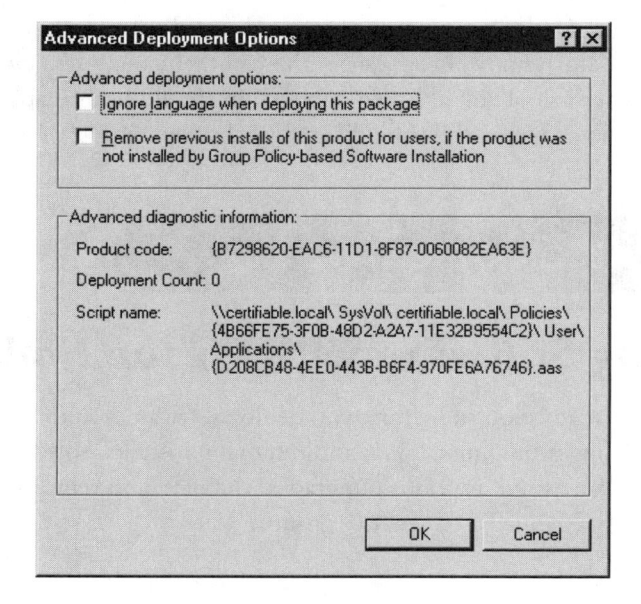

SCENARIO & SOLUTION

I need to publish an application to all the users within a specific OU. How do I do this?	Link the GPO that publishes the software to the appropriate OU. When you filter the policy, choose Allow–Apply Group Policy for the Authenticated Users security group.
I need to deploy an application to all the client computers in my network, but not the domain controllers or servers. How can I accomplish this?	Since you can't link a GPO to the Computers container, you'd have to put all the appropriate computer icons into some other OU, perhaps one named Clients. Exclude domain controllers and servers from that OU, and link the GPO to the Clients OU.
I linked a software deployment GPO to my Corporate OU. The software was assigned to all departments within the OU, except one. Why is that?	Most likely, that child OU is blocking policy inheritance from the parent OU.

Testing the Deployment

To verify the deployment, you just need to go to a client computer to which the deployment applies, and log in as a user to whom the deployment applies. If you assigned the software, the icon for starting the program should already be on the Start menu. If you published the program, you can install it by opening Add/Remove Programs in the Control Panel, then clicking the Add New Programs button. The published application should be available under Add Programs From Your Network in the dialog box that opens.

CERTIFICATION OBJECTIVE 8.02

Managing Software with Group Policy

In addition to helping you deploy software, group policy provides options for upgrading, managing, and removing installed software. As with deployments, you can assign or publish upgrades, changes, and removals, and filter policies to apply only to selected security groups.

Upgrading Software

Group policies can also aid in upgrading software. There are two types of upgrades you can deploy. A *mandatory* upgrade is one that is automatically installed the next time a user opens the application. An *optional* upgrade is one that the user can voluntarily install from Add/Remove Programs in the Control Panel.

Deploying a mandatory upgrade is similar to deploying a new package. Copy the MSI file, and any other files needed for the upgrade, to a shared folder at your normal distribution point. Create a GPO, or add the upgrade to an existing GPO. Right-click the GPO's name in the Group Policy Object Links list on the Group Policy tab and choose Properties. In the Properties dialog box for the package, clickthe Upgrades tab, as shown in Figure 8-8.

FIGURE 8-8

The Upgrades tab in a package's Properties dialog box

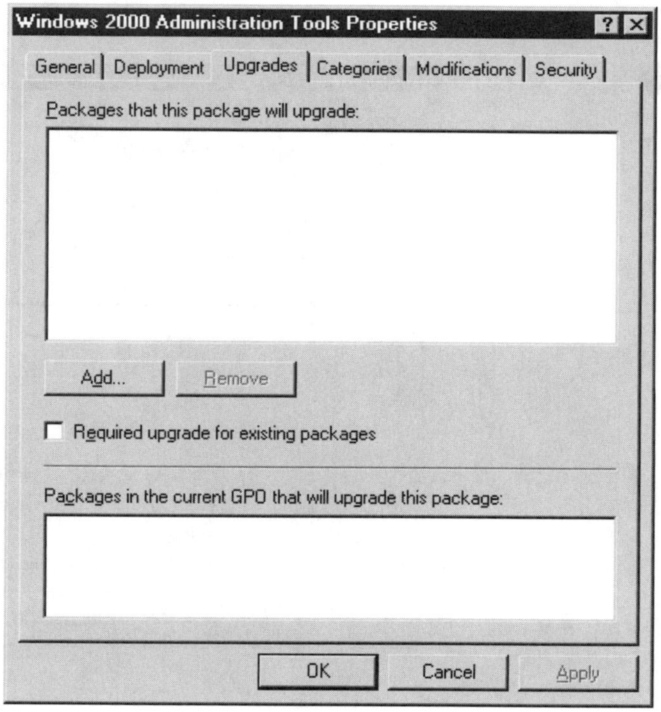

If the MSI package is native to the upgrade, chances are the Packages That This Package Will Upgrade list will already be populated with programs that will be upgraded. But you can use the Add and Remove buttons to choose any packages to upgrade. When you click the Add button, you'll be taken to the Add Upgrade Package dialog box, shown in Figure 8-9. There, you can specify the GPO that contains the package you're upgrading, and choose whether you want to uninstall the existing package before installing the new one, or install the current package over the existing installation. Click OK after making your selections.

Back on the Upgrades tab, choose the Required Upgrade For Existing Packages option. Otherwise, clear that option to make the upgrade optional. The rest is automatic. Just close everything and the upgrade will be installed, or made available to all users when they log on. Or, in the case of a deployment through Computer Configuration, the upgrade will be installed the next time the client is started.

FIGURE 8-9

The Add Upgrade Package dialog box

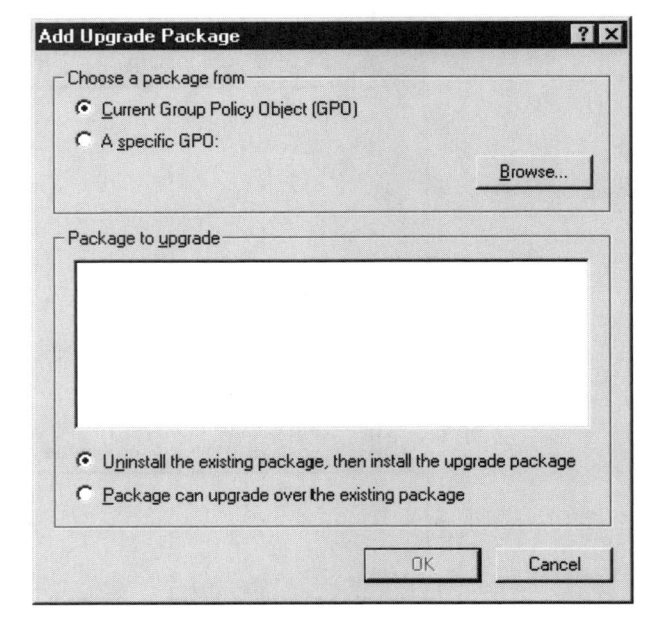

EXERCISE 8-2

Creating and Filtering a GPO

In this exercise, you'll pick up where you left off in Exercise 8-1. You'll create a new GPO to publish AdminPack (and any other apps) to users (as opposed to computers). You'll filter the GPO so that it applies only to members of the Domain Admins and Enterprise Admins groups, so that only they can install the package. I'll assume you're still logged in to the domain controller or server from the previous exercise. Follow these steps:

1. Open Active Directory Users and Computers.
2. Right-click the name of your domain and choose Properties.
3. Click the Group Policy tab, click the New button, and name this GPO **Admin Packages**.
4. To filter the new GPO, click its name and click the Properties button.
5. Click the Security tab.
6. Go through each listed group, and choose the Allow–Apply Group Policy permission only for Domain Admins and Enterprise Admins. Clear the Allow check box for all other groups, so that the package is published to the administrators only.
7. Click the OK button to close the dialog box.

Next, you'll set the default software installation defaults for User Configuration\Software Installation. Follow these steps:

1. In the console tree of the Group Policy snap-in, expand User Configuration\Software Settings.
2. Right-click Software Installation and choose Properties.
3. Under Default package location, type the UNC path to the shared Packages folder. For example, if that folder is on Server01, type **\\Server01\Packages**.

4. Click OK.

5. Right-click the Software Installation node again and choose New | Package.

6. In the Open dialog box, navigate to the adminpak.msi file, click its name, and choose Open.

7. Choose Published from the Deploy Software dialog box that appears and click OK.

Now when you click Software Installation under User Configuration, you'll see Windows 2000 Administration Tools listed as a package, as in the example shown in Figure 8-10.

Now you can close the Group Policy window, Properties dialog box, and Active Directory Users and Computers.

FIGURE 8-10 The Windows 2000 Administration Tools package is added.

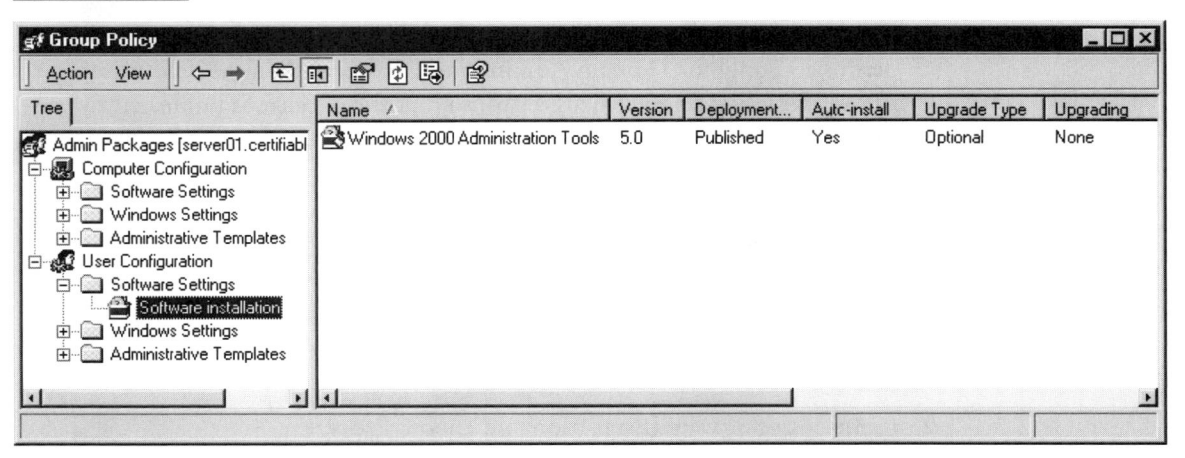

Redeploying Software

If you make some change to an installed application, such as adding or removing some component after the initial deployment, you can easily deploy that change to all appropriate clients, providing you used group policy to install the application in the first place. Add any required files to the package in the Group Policy snap-in, using the same Software Installation node you used for the original package. Then, in the details pane, right-click the name of the package and choose All Tasks | Redeploy Application. You'll see a warning reminding you that the package will be reinstalled on all relevant client computers. Since that's your intent, you can bypass the warning to initiate the redeployment.

Removing Software

When you deploy software using group policy, you can just as easily remove it. Open the original GPO, right-click the package name, choose All Tasks | Remove. You'll be given the self-explanatory options shown in Figure 8-11. Choose either option, and the software will be uninstalled the next time the user logs on, or the next time the computer is started.

exam
Watch
Do be aware that, unlike other policy settings, simply removing or disabling a GPO that installs software is not sufficient to remove the application. If you really want to uninstall a deployed application, you must go through the removal process described here.

Be aware that this procedure only removes copies of the application that were deployed with group policy. If an application was installed locally on a given client computer, it won't be uninstalled by a group policy.

FIGURE 8-11

The Remove Software dialog box

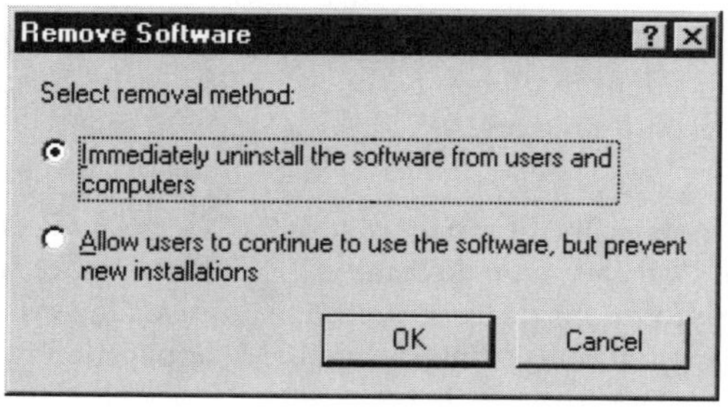

FROM THE CLASSROOM

Planning Software Deployments

When you start to plan software deployments, think about your organization's software requirements in relation to its organizational structure. Which organizational units need a particular package? Which users in the department need access to the package? Who will administer the software that's deployed to a specific GPO?

When you come up with a strategy for how you'll organize your deployments, test each deployment in a couple of phases. In the first phase, limit the deployment to a couple of users or computers, and publish the software so it can be installed optionally. Log in as one of those users, and test everything yourself, or have one of the existing users test it and provide feedback. If all goes well during phase 1, you can reconfigure the package to be applied to all appropriate users or computers.

—*Alan Simpson, MA, MCSA*

Now that you know more about maintaining software with GPOs, let's take a look at some scenarios and their solutions.

SCENARIO & SOLUTION

I received an upgrade for an application that I've already deployed to over 1,000 computers. I need to get this upgrade deployed right away. What's my best strategy?	Configure the GPO that performs the upgrade to assign the software to each computer. Have all users restart their computers so the upgrade is installed automatically without any further intervention on their part.
I need to assign an upgrade to users, but need to assign different modifications to different groups of users. How can I accomplish that?	Check the transform (MST) file that came with the package. Create a separate installation package for each group of users, with a transform that specifies the options needed for each group.
I deployed an application to one of my OUs, only to discover that there's a major upgrade coming out next month. I don't mind if the users who've already installed the application continue to use it but I would like to prevent those who haven't installed it from doing so. What should I do?	Create a GPO to remove the application. In the Remove Software dialog box, choose the option that allows those who have already installed the application to continue using it.

CERTIFICATION OBJECTIVE 8.03

Deploying Service Packs with Group Policy

You can use group policy to install service packs on computers throughout the network. For the sake of example, let's say you want to deploy a service pack to all computers in the domain. The first step would be to create the shared distribution point folder, as usual. For example, you might name this folder **SP2Files**. Then, you need to copy all the service pack files to the distribution folder. If you ordered the service pack on CD-ROM, you can copy its contents to the shared distribution folder. If you downloaded the service pack in archive format, you can extract the files to the distribution folder using the /x switch. For example, if you downloaded Service Pack 2 for Windows 2000, entering the command **W2ksp2 /x** would allow you to extract all the files to your SP2Files folder.

Next, you'd want to create a GPO that executes the update.msi file that came with the service pack. Since you want to deploy the service pack to all computers, you could right-click the domain name in Active Directory Users and Computers to link the GPO at the domain level. Choose Properties, click the Group Policy tab, and then create a new GPO or edit an existing one. Expand the Computer Configuration\Software Settings node to ensure that the GPO will be executed at computer startup.

exam
Watch
When you encounter a question about deploying software, remember that you cannot link a GPO to the default Computers container. You can only link GPOs to a site, domain, or OU.

Right-click the Software Settings node, choose New, and choose Package. When the Open dialog box appears, navigate to the service pack share (SP2Files in our example), open the \Update subfolder, and click the update.msi file. Click the Open button and, when the Deploy Software dialog box opens, be sure to choose Assign. Click OK, and the group policy is ready to go. The service pack will be deployed to each computer at restart.

Installing Service Packs on New Computers

If you add new computers after a service pack has been released, and want to ensure that all the new computers have the latest service packs installed, you can perform *slipstream* installations, where Windows 2000 and the service pack are installed together. To accomplish this, you would install Windows 2000 on the first new computer, and create a distribution folder for all the Windows 2000 installation files. For the sake of example, let's say you name this folder **Win2KInstall**.

Copy all the files from the Windows 2000 product CD-ROM into the distribution folder. Then, apply the service pack(s) to the Windows 2000 installation files in the distribution folders using the syntax **update.exe –s:***distributionFolder*. The –s switch slipstreams the service pack changes into the specified folder. For our example, if the Win2KInstall folder is on drive C, the command would be **update.exe –s:c:\Win2KInstall**.

As new computers arrive, install Windows 2000 from the shared distribution folder, Win2KInstall in this example. Optionally, you could create a new Windows 2000 Installation CD-ROM from the Win2KInstall folder, and use that to install Windows 2000 on all the new computers.

EXERCISE 8-3

Testing Software Deployment

In this exercise, you'll test the deployment you created in Exercises 8-1 and 8-2. You'll need to log in to a client computer as an administrator, and see if the program is available in Add/Remove Programs. Follow these steps:

1. Go to a client computer and log in as an Enterprise or Domain Administrator.
2. Click the Start button and choose Settings | Control Panel.
3. Open the Add/Remove Programs icon.
4. Click the Add New Programs button in the left column. You should see Windows 2000 Administration Tools listed, as shown in Figure 8-12.

If you want to install AdminPak, just click the Add button and follow the instructions on the screen. Once the program is installed, you can get to the administrative tools by clicking the Start button and choosing Programs | Administrative Tools. You'll have access to the same tools that you have on the server, such as Active Directory Users and Computers.

FIGURE 8-12 Administration Tools available for installation on a Windows 2000 Professional computer

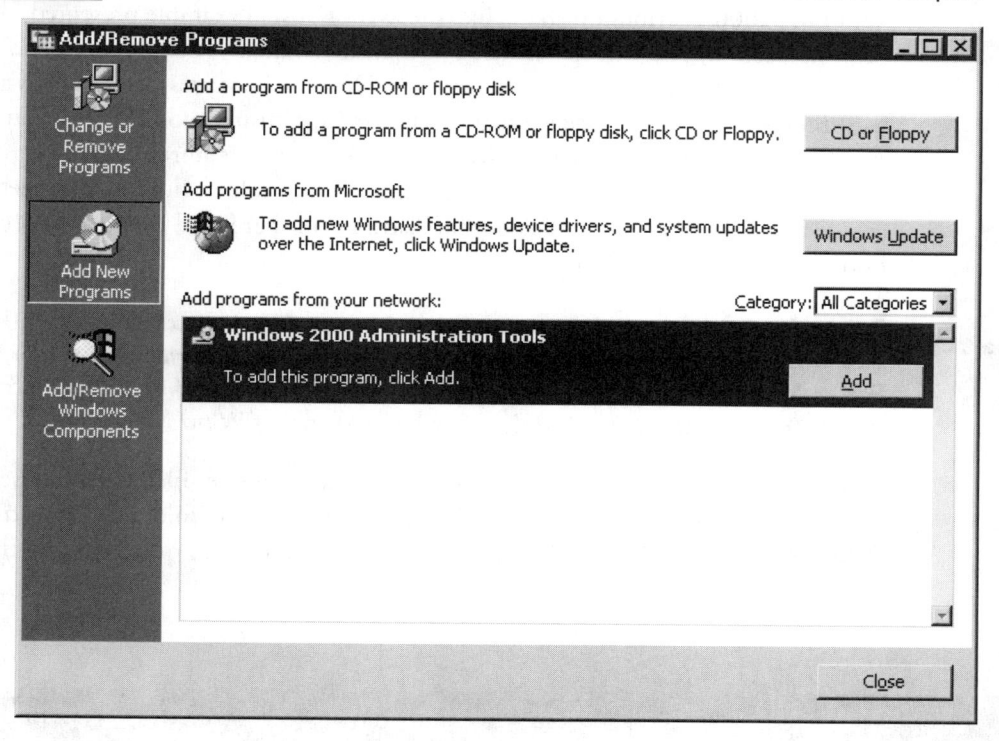

> **on the job** Don't try to install AdminPak from Windows 2000 on Windows XP, because you need the version from .NET Server.

A Note on Deploying Hotfixes

A *hotfix* is a software update released between major service pack releases. Typically, a hotfix will plug up a security hole, so Microsoft will release it immediately rather than waiting for the next service pack release. Not all hotfixes are appropriate to all installations. Before installing a hotfix, you should check its purpose to determine if it's appropriate for your network.

For this chapter, it's important to know that you can slipstream hotfixes into a Windows 2000 distribution share, like the Win2KInstall example presented in the previous section. You can also install a hotfix.exe file in any shared folder, and run it locally from any computer in the network. However, hotfixes don't come with MSI files, so there is no package that can be deployed using a GPO. Also, you need to rename all the hotfixes, because Windows 2000 Setup requires 8.3 naming conventions for all files and folders in the distribution folder. Finally, you need to create the appropriate subfolders on the distribution share, and copy the appropriate hotfix binaries into the folders.

exam
Watch

To deploy hotfixes on new computers without affecting existing computers, and without user intervention, copy the hotfixes to a distribution folder. Use Setup Manager to create an answer file, and edit the cmdlines.txt file to install the hotfixes immediately after installation of Windows 2000.

You can, however, use Setup Manager to create an answer file, and add lines to the cmdlines.txt file to install the files from a distribution folder during setup. Before we close this chapter, let's take a look at some scenario questions and their solutions.

SCENARIO & SOLUTION

I went to the WindowsUpdate site and found quite a few new hotfixes. Should I install them all right now, or wait until the next service pack release?	You need to decide on a case-by-case basis by referring to the Microsoft Knowledgebase Article associated with the hotfix. The hotfix filename will start with the appropriate article number, for example Q123456.
Are service packs cumulative?	Yes, each service pack includes all the fixes from the previous service packs, as well as all hotfixes released since that preceding service pack.
How can I see which service packs, if any, have already been applied to a computer?	Right-click the My Computer icon on the Windows desktop and choose Properties to open the System Properties dialog box. The version number under the computer name will include the name of the latest installed service pack.

CERTIFICATION SUMMARY

Group policies are an effective way to deploy and maintain software throughout your organization. Because you can link GPOs to specific OUs, and filter policies to apply to specific users, you can precisely control who gets which software packages. Most modern applications come with a native Microsoft Software Installer (MSI) file that you can use to deploy the application. For other applications, you can create a package using a variety of third-party tools.

It's important to remember that when you *assign* a program to a computer, you essentially leave the user of that program out of the installation loop. The application is installed automatically at startup. The appropriate icons for starting the application appear on the Start menu, and perhaps the desktop as well. When you *assign* a package to users, the package advertises its presence to the users, and is installed the first time they use it. When you *publish* an application, you simply make it available to users. The users need to find the application in Add/Remove Programs, and perform the installation themselves.

You can use GPOs to upgrade and remove applications. You can configure upgrades as mandatory or optional. When removing applications, you have the option of removing existing installations, or simply preventing future installations without removing existing installations. Service packs can be deployed and managed using the same techniques you use to deploy and manage application software.

✓ TWO-MINUTE DRILL

Deploying Applications with Group Policy

- ❏ Group policies provide an excellent means of deploying and managing software across an entire domain, or to specific OUs within a domain.
- ❏ For convenience, you can create a single shared folder to act as a distribution point for all software to be deployed. Make sure all users have at least Read permissions on the shared folder.
- ❏ Before deploying an application, copy all necessary files to the distribution files, including the native MSI file if one is provided.
- ❏ When creating the GPO, if you use the Software Installation node under Computer Configuration, the software will be assigned to the computer at the next startup. You don't have the option to Publish when deploying to computer objects.
- ❏ If you use the Software Installation node under User Configuration in your GPO, you can choose to assign, or publish, the application. The application is deployed, or made available, at logon.
- ❏ Remember that assigned software is mandatory, while published software is just made available to users.
- ❏ Software deployed through a GPO will only be deployed to those security groups for whom you've assigned Allow–Apply Group Policy permission in the Security tab of the GPO's Properties dialog box.
- ❏ To have an application installed automatically when a user attempts to open a document that's associated with the application, choose the Auto-install This Application By File Extension Activation option in the package's Properties dialog box.
- ❏ If you want an application to be uninstalled from a user's account when the user is moved to a different OU, choose the Uninstall This Application When It Falls Out Of The Scope Of Management option in the package's Properties dialog box.

Managing Software with Group Policy

- ❏ When upgrading an application, you have the option to uninstall the existing package first, which will completely remove the existing application, and all user preferences, prior to upgrading.

- Optionally, you can upgrade over the existing package. This approach will allow users to keep their existing preferences.
- You can configure an upgrade to be mandatory, so that it is performed without user intervention.
- Optionally, you can configure an upgrade to be optional so users can decide for themselves whether or not to upgrade.
- To change an existing deployment's settings, you can make the appropriate changes to the application's files, then redeploy the package using the All Tasks options on the package's shortcut menu.
- When you create a GPO to remove an application, choosing Immediately Uninstall The Software From Users And Computers removes the software so that no users will have access to it anymore.
- When you create a GPO to remove an application, and you choose Allow Users To Continue To Use The Software, But Prevent New Installations, you don't remove the application from computers. However, users who have not yet installed that application will no longer be able to install it.

Deploying Service Packs with Group Policy

- You can deploy service packs to multiple computers by ordering the service pack on CD-ROM, or by downloading the Network Installation version (archive) of the service pack.
- To deploy a service pack, extract the archive to a distribution folder, or copy all the files from the CD-ROM to the distribution folder.
- Use the update.msi file that came with the service pack as the package to be deployed.
- Hotfixes are small patch files that are released prior to the next service pack, usually to fix a security hole or a problem with a specific type of installation.
- You should review the Microsoft Knowledgebase article associated with a hotfix prior to deciding whether or not you want to install that hotfix.
- Hotfixes ship as stand-alone EXE files. There is no native MSI file that you can use to deploy a hotfix.

SELF TEST

The following questions will help you measure your understanding of the material presented in this chapter. Read the question and all answers carefully, as there may be more than one correct answer per question. Choose *all* of the correct answers for each question.

Deploying Applications with Group Policy

1. You are the network administrator for a Windows 2000 network. You've created several departmental OUs. You create a GPO to assign an application to all users. When the deployment is complete, users in the Executive OU report that the icon for starting the application isn't visible in their Start menus. When verifying, you discover that the application has been assigned to all OUs except the Executive OU. What should you do to ensure that the application is deployed to all child OUs?

    A. Use Remote Installation Services (RIS) to deploy the application.

    B. Prevent the Executive OU from blocking policy inheritance.

    C. Change the GPO so that it publishes, rather than assigns, the application.

    D. Delegate authority for managing GPOs to administrators of the Executive OU.

2. You are the network administrator for your company. The domain is organized into OUs based on projects in progress. The user accounts for members of a project team are stored in the project OU. Employees are frequently moved from one project to another, and their user accounts are moved to the appropriate OU with each change. You need to ensure that the applications assigned to a user are removed when a user is moved to a different project OU. What should you do?

    A. Configure GPOs that assign software to uninstall the applications when they fall out of the scope of management.

    B. Create a script that runs a removal policy whenever a user logs off.

    C. Choose the Do Not Display This Package In The Add/Remove Programs Control Panel option.

    D. Create a GPO that removes installed applications the next time the user logs on.

3. You want to ensure that all computers in the Accounting OU have an application named AcctWhiz installed on them. You want members of the DesktopSupport OU to have the option of installing the application on their computers. What should you do? (Choose all that apply.)

   A. Create a GPO that assigns the AcctWhiz application to all computers in the Accounting OU.
   B. Create a GPO that publishes the AcctWhiz application to all computers in the Accounting OU.
   C. Create a GPO that assigns the AcctWhiz application to all users in the DesktopSupport OU.
   D. Create a GPO that publishes the AcctWhiz application to all users in the DesktopSupport OU.

4. You are the domain administrator for your company's Windows 2000 network. Several users have installed Microsoft Office 2000 on their local computers. You want to deploy and manage Windows 2000 from a central location. What should you do?

   A. Manually remove the program from all computers prior to creating a group policy to deploy Microsoft Office 2000.
   B. When configuring the package, choose the Remove Previous Installs Of This Product For Users, If The Product Was Not Installed By Group Policy-based Software Installation option.
   C. Create a GPO that uninstalls Microsoft Office 2000 from all computers in the domain at logon.
   D. When configuring the package, choose the Uninstall This Application When It Falls Out Of The Scope Of Management option.

5. You need to deploy an application to all Windows 2000 Professional computers in the domain. The application should not be installed on servers or domain controllers. How can you accomplish this task with minimal administrative effort?

   A. Link the GPO that installs the software to the Computers container in Active Directory Users and Computers.
   B. Link the GPO that installs the software to the Domain Controllers container in Active Directory Users and Computers.
   C. Create an OU that contains an icon for each Windows 2000 Professional computer in the domain, and link the GPO to that OU.
   D. Create a script that runs the installation program from a distribution share. Install the script on each Windows 2000 Professional computer in the domain.

Managing Software with Group Policy

6. You are a domain administrator for your company's Windows 2000 network. The company uses ProductX as its word processing software. You originally installed ProductX using a GPO named WP. The company has discovered that ProductZ is better suited to the company's needs, and wants to perform an upgrade that installs ProductZ on all computers, and removes ProductX. How can you accomplish this goal with the least administrative effort?

   A. Create one GPO to remove ProductX from all computers. Create a second GPO to install ProductZ. Link both GPOs to the domain object in Active Directory Users and Computers.

   B. Configure the WP package to upgrade to ProductZ. Choose ProductX as the package to upgrade, and choose the Uninstall The Existing Package, Then Install The Upgrade Package option from the package's Properties dialog box.

   C. Create a transform file that removes ProductX while installing ProductZ.

   D. On the Security tab for the package's Properties dialog box, grant Allow–Change permissions to the Everyone group.

7. You create and deploy a package to allow users to upgrade an existing software product. Several users successfully install the upgrade, while others complain that they cannot. You determine that the people who cannot perform the upgrade are all members of a security group named RandomExpectations. What should you do?

   A. Verify that the GPO filter assigned Allow–Apply Group Policy permission to the RandomExpectations security group.

   B. Create a new GPO to install the upgraded package, and link it to the RandomExpectations OU.

   C. Verify that Authenticated Users have Read permissions on the distribution folder.

   D. Verify that Authenticated Users have Read & Execute permissions on the distribution folder.

Deploying Service Packs with Group Policy

8. You are the network administrator for your company. The network contains 100 Windows 2000 Server computers, all of which are in an OU named Servers in Active Directory. The network also contains 2,000 Windows 2000 Professional computers, which are in the Computers container in Active Directory. You need to deploy the most recent Windows 2000 Service Pack to servers only. You download the archive and extract it to a shared distribution folder named SPxFiles. What should you do to deploy the service pack to the servers?

   A. Create a GPO that uses Computer Configuration to assign the service pack, and link the GPO to the Servers container. Restart each of the server computers.

B. Create a GPO that uses Computer Configuration to assign the service pack, and link it to the Computers GPO. Restart all the server computers.

C. Create a GPO that uses Computer Configuration to publish the service pack, and link it to the Servers OU. Log in to each of the server computers to install the service pack.

D. Create a GPO that uses Computer Configuration to assign the service pack, and link the GPO to the Domain Controllers container. Restart each of the server computers.

9. You are the domain administrator for your company. All computers in the company have all the latest service packs installed. Executives are planning to add 100 more Windows 2000 Professional computers over the next three months. Company policy requires that all new computers have all current service packs installed as soon as Windows 2000 Professional is installed. Which of the following would allow you to accomplish that goal with the least administrative effort?

   A. Install Windows 2000 on all new computers, then deploy a startup script that downloads and installs all service packs from WindowsUpdate.com as soon as each computer is started.

   B. Create a GPO to install all service packs, and link the GPO to the Computers container in Active Directory.

   C. Create a GPO to upgrade all computers to the latest service pack at startup, without overwriting existing files. Link the GPO to the Computers container in Active Directory.

   D. Put all the Windows 2000 installation files in a shared file. Slipstream all service packs to the installation files using the –s switch with the **update** command. Install Windows 2000 on new computers using the slipstreamed installation files in the distribution folder.

10. You are the network administrator for your company's Windows 2000 network. You download and install 50 hotfixes on all computers in the domain. The company plans to install 100 new member servers and 50 new domain controllers within two months. All new computers must have all the hotfixes installed before they're deployed. What would be the most efficient way to get the hotfixes installed on the new computers?

    A. Create a GPO based on all the hotfix update.msi files, and link the GPO to the Domain Controllers and Server OUs in Active Directory.

    B. Create a GPO based on all the hotfix update.exe files, and link the GPO to the Domain Controllers and Server OUs in Active Directory.

    C. Install the hotfixes in a shared distribution folder. Configure an answer file to support unattended installations, and configure cmdlines.txt to install the hotfixes automatically during setup.

    D. Create an answer file that runs each hotfix from the distribution folder.

LAB QUESTION

You are the OU administrator for the Corporate OU shown in Figure 8-13. Domain administrators have given you full control of the OU, including permission to create, link, and edit group policies within the domain. All user accounts and computer accounts have already been moved from their default containers into the appropriate OUs.

An administrator hands you a CD containing all the files for an application named OpWiz, including a network install package named OpWiz.msi. You need to ensure that the OpWiz application is installed on all computers in the Operations domain. You also need to make that same application available to users in the HelpDesk OU. What should you do?

TABLE 8-13

Exhibit for the Lab Question

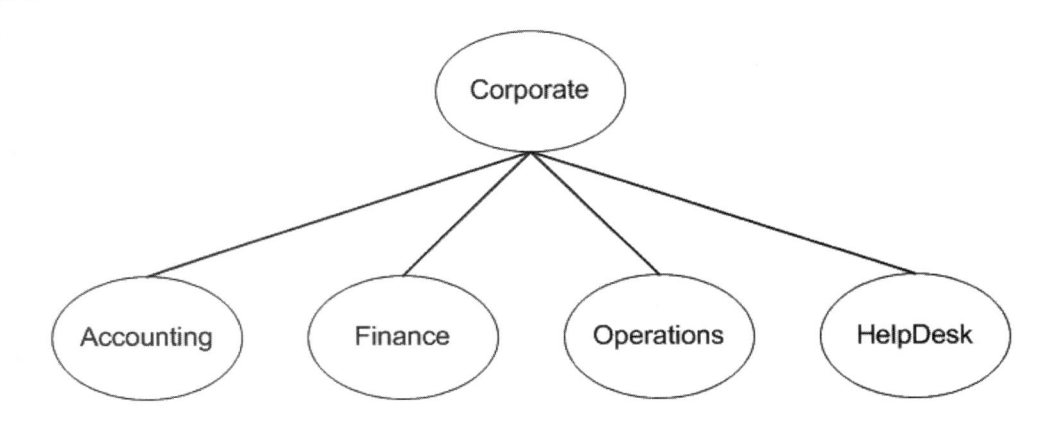

SELF TEST ANSWERS

Deploying Applications with Group Policy

1. ☑ **B** is correct. Since the application was successfully deployed to other OUs, the most likely scenario is that the Executive OU is blocking policy inheritance from the parent OU.
   ☒ **A** is wrong because RIS is used for remote operating system installations, not software deployment.
   ☒ **C** is incorrect because publishing the application wouldn't fix the problem.
   ☒ **D** is incorrect because delegating authority wouldn't ensure that the application is deployed.

2. ☑ **A** is correct. Simply selecting that option when creating the package will uninstall the application automatically when the user account is moved outside the OU to which the application was assigned.
   ☒ **B** is incorrect because we don't want applications removed every time a user logs off, just when they're moved to another OU.
   ☒ **C** is wrong because that option wouldn't remove the installed application.
   ☒ **D** is wrong because the goal here isn't to remove all installed applications for the user. The goal is to automatically remove an application when a user account is moved to another OU.

3. ☑ **A** and **D** are correct. You want to assign the application to Accounting computers, and publish it to Desktop Support users so that they have a choice of whether they want to install the program or not.
   ☒ **B** is wrong because you need to assign, not publish, the application to the Accounting OU.
   ☒ **C** is wrong because you need to publish, not assign, the application to Desktop Support personnel.

4. ☑ **B** is correct. Choosing that option will automatically remove local installations prior to installing the group policy–based version of the program.
   ☒ **A** is wrong because there is no need to go from machine to machine to manually remove the software.
   ☒ **C** is wrong because a GPO that removes software can only remove copies that were installed through group policies.
   ☒ **D** is wrong because that option removes the application when a user's account is deleted or moved to another OU. It has nothing to do with applications that were installed locally.

5. ☑ **C** is correct. You can put all the appropriate computers in an OU, and link the GPO to that OU.
☒ **A** is wrong because you can't link a GPO to the Computers container.
☒ **B** is wrong because that would install the application on the domain controllers, not the Windows 2000 Professional clients.
☒ **D** is wrong because it's a lot of administrative effort.

Managing Software with Group Policy

6. ☑ **B** is correct. A GPO that removes the original package then installs the upgrade package would accomplish all goals with a single deployment.
☒ **A** is wrong because, even though it would work, it's not the option with the least administrative effort.
☒ **C** is wrong because a transform file allows you to fine-tune an installation based on groups to which the application is being deployed, and there's no need to create a transform file in this scenario.
☒ **D** is wrong because filtering the GPO won't remove the existing application.

7. ☑ **A** is correct. Since only that one security group is unable to install the upgrade, the most likely scenario is that the GPO wasn't applied to the RandomExpectations security group.
☒ **B** is wrong because RandomExpectations is a security group, not an OU.
☒ **C** and **D** are wrong because, apparently, authenticated users already have Read permissions on the distribution folder, by virtue of the fact that other users were able to install the upgrade.

Deploying Service Packs with Group Policy

8. ☑ **A** is correct. You can configure the GPO to assign the service pack to computers, and link that GPO to the Servers OU.
☒ **B** is wrong because it's the wrong OU, and you cannot link a GPO to the Computers container anyway.
☒ **C** is wrong because you cannot publish software using the Computer Configuration node.
☒ **D** is wrong because you want to assign the software to all servers, not just domain controllers.

9. ☑ **D** is correct. Slipstreaming the service packs to the installation files prior to installing Windows 2000 would ensure that all new computers have the latest service packs when Windows 2000 is installed.
☒ **A** is wrong because it's not as efficient as slipstreaming the service pack to the

installation files.

☒ B and C are wrong because you can't link GPOs to the Computers container in Active Directory.

10. ☑ C is correct. Hotfixes don't come with MSI files, so the closest you can get would be to set up an answer file to run the hotfixes unattended, and configure cmdlines.txt to execute the hotfixes from the shared distribution file.

☒ A and B are wrong because hotfixes don't come with MSI files, and EXE files don't work as installation packages.

☒ D is wrong because an answer file can only answer questions posed by an installation GUI. Answer files can't run scripts or programs.

LAB ANSWER

First, you need to create a shared folder to act as your distribution point. Then, copy all the OpWiz files from the CD to that distribution folder. Then, create two group policies. Name the first group policy something like AssignOPWiz, linked to the Operations OU. Under Computer Configuration\Software Settings\Software Installation, create a new package that assigns OpWiz.msi.

Create a second GPO, linked to the HelpDesk OU. Name the second one something like PublishOpWiz. Create a new package that publishes (not assigns) OpWiz.msi under User Configuration. Make sure that the appropriate people have Allow–Apply Group Policy permission for the package.

By assigning the application to computers in the Operations OU, you ensure that the application is installed automatically and will be available on the Start menu the next time the machine starts up. By publishing the application to the HelpDesk OU, you make the application available to people in that OU, but don't force it upon them.

9
Managing and Troubleshooting Active Directory

CERTIFICATION OBJECTIVES

9.01	Managing Active Directory Objects
9.02	Configuring Active Directory Replication
9.03	Troubleshooting Active Directory Replication
✓	Two-Minute Drill
Q&A	Self Test

Active Directory is both flexible and scalable. You can create new container objects as needed, create new objects within those containers, and move existing objects among containers. If your company has offices throughout the country or world, and you connect them all with some sort of WAN link, you can define each geographical location as a site, and precisely control how and when AD replication takes place between those sites. In this chapter, you'll learn how to move AD objects to new containers, and to different domains. You'll learn how to set up sites and control replication between those sites. And finally, you'll learn troubleshooting techniques for some of the more common problems that arise with AD replication.

CERTIFICATION OBJECTIVES 9.01

Managing Active Directory Objects

As your organization grows and changes, you may want to rearrange objects in Active Directory to reflect those changes. In some cases, you might simply want to move an object to a new location within its current domain. For example, you might need to move a user account from one OU to another when that user moves to a new department. The main point to keep in mind is that when you move an object within a domain, but from one OU to another OU, the permissions set at the destination OU are applied. The permissions that the object inherited from the original source OU are lost. When you simply move an object from one container to another, where there are no OU permissions involved, the object retains all of its existing permissions.

Moving an object within a domain is a simple process, though not as simple as a drag-and-drop action. In Active Directory Users and Computers, simply right-click the object you want to move, and choose Move from the shortcut menu, as in the example shown in Figure 9-1.

The Move dialog box opens, as shown in Figure 9-2. Just click the container to which you want to move the object and then click OK.

Managing Active Directory Objects **427**

FIGURE 9-1 To move an AD object, right-click it and choose Move.

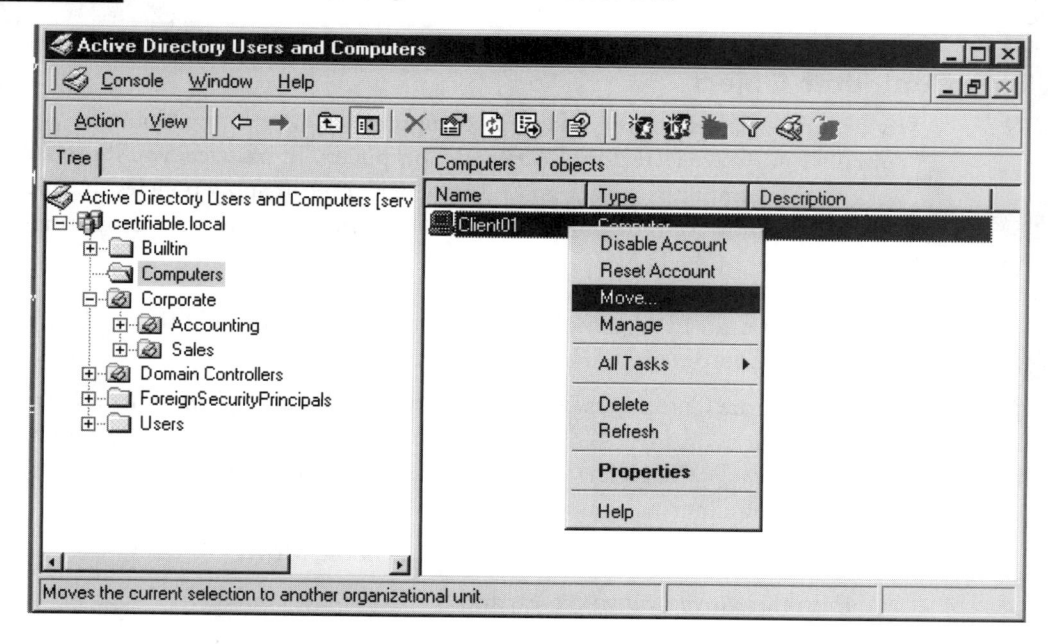

FIGURE 9-2 The Move dialog box

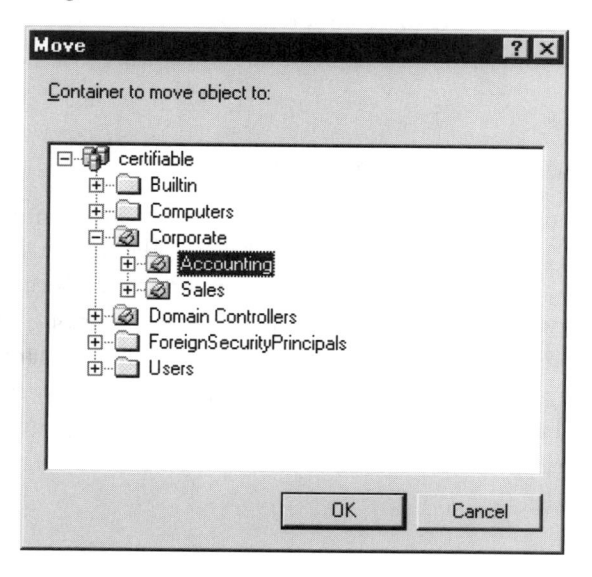

EXERCISE 9-1

Moving a Computer Object

By default, Active Directory places all computer accounts in the Computers container in Active Directory Users and Computers. In practice, you'll probably want to put computers within an OU to which you can apply policies. In this exercise, you'll move the sample Client01 computer object to the Accounting OU created earlier in the book.

1. Select Start | Programs | Administrative Tools | Active Directory Users And Computers.

2. Click the Computers container. If the details pane shows an icon for a printer connected to that computer, rather than an icon for the computer object, click the View button and clear the Users, Groups, And Computers As Containers option.

3. Right-click the icon for Client01 and choose Move.

4. In the Move dialog box, expand the Corporate container.

5. Click the Accounting OU container and then click OK.

Any machine policies that you apply to the Corporate OU or Account OU will now be applied to the Client01 computer.

Moving Objects Across Domains

To move an object from one domain to another, you can use the movetree command, provided in the \Support\Tools folder on the Windows 2000 Server CD-ROM. Bear in mind the users and groups have a security identifier (SID) that is unique to the domain. When you move a user or group to another domain, a new SID is generated. If you're working in Windows native mode, however, the SIDHistory feature of Windows 2000 will retain security settings, even with the new SID. However, if you're working in mixed mode, you'll need to create new security settings on the moved object.

There are several restrictions and conditions that apply to using the movetree command, as follows:

- Movetree can only be used to move objects from one domain to another within the same AD forest.
- Global security groups at the domain level with member user accounts cannot be moved. Likewise, local groups that have members cannot be moved.
- Users with global security group membership cannot be moved.
- Objects contained within the System, Built-in, and Foreign SecurityPrincipals containers cannot be moved.
- Locked objects cannot be moved.
- Domain controllers (DCs) and objects whose parent is a domain controller cannot be moved.
- Group policies that are associated with an object are not moved with the object. You'll need to apply new policies at the destination.

Even when all conditions and restrictions are met, there will still be conditions that will cause a movetree command to fail, including the following:

- There isn't sufficient storage capacity at the destination computer.
- The destination computer already contains an object with the same name as the object you're trying to move.
- User accounts whose account policies, such as minimum password length, would be changed by a move to another domain will not be moved.
- Replication delays can cause a movetree command to fail. For example, an object that has been deleted at the destination domain through replication won't be able to subsequently move that object.

The following is the syntax of the movetree command:

```
movetree [/start | /startnocheck | /continue | /check] /s SrcDSA
[/d DstDSA] [/sdn SrcDN] [/ddn DstDN] [/u Domain\Username] [/p
password] [/verbose]
```

where the individual elements are described as follows:

- **/start** Performs a test run (same as /check), then performs the move if the check is successful.
- **/startnocheck** Starts the operation without first checking its viability.
- **/continue** Continues a previously failed Movetree command.
- **/check** Checks for viability without performing the command.
- **/s** *SrcDSA* The source server's fully qualified primary DNS name (required).
- **/d** *DstDSA* The destination server's fully qualified primary DNS name (required).
- **/sdn** *SrcDN* The source subtree's root domain name, required when using /start or /check.
- **/ddn** *DstDN* The destination subtree's root domain name.
- **/u** *Domain\UserName* Domain name and user account name (optional).
- **/p** *password* Password (optional).
- **/verbose** Verbose mode with output piped to the screen (optional).

For example, suppose you wanted to do a test run to see if there would be any problems moving an OU named SampleOU from Server01 in the Research.myDomain.com domain to Server02 in the Dev.myDomain.com domain, and rename the OU to ProjectXOU in its new location. The syntax of the command would be as follows:

```
movetree /check /s:Server01.Research.myDomain.com
/d:Server02.Dev.myDomain.com
/sdn:OU=SampleOU,DC=Research,DC=myDomain,DC=com
/ddn:OU=ProjectXOU,DC=Dev,DC=myDomain,DC=com
```

The LostAndFound container in AD Users and Computers contains all objects whose containers were deleted elsewhere at the same time that the object was created. If an object has been moved to a location that is missing after replication, the lost object is placed in the LostAndFound container.

SCENARIO & SOLUTION

Since I can't link GPOs to the Computers container in AD Users and Computers, could I just move computer objects into some OU and link GPOs to that OU?	Sure. The Computers and Users containers are really just default "placeholders." You can move those objects to any OU you create so you can apply policies to them.
How can I move server objects from one site to another site?	When you need to move AD objects between sites, use AD Sites and Services, rather than AD Users 4and Computers.

exam
Watch *Deleted objects are not placed in the LostAndFound container, only objects that failed during a move operation are.*

CERTIFICATION OBJECTIVE 9.02

Configuring Active Directory Replication

Replication is an important element of Active Directory, because you need multiple DCs for fault tolerance, and those DCs must stay in sync. AD supports two major categories of replication: intrasite replication and intersite replication. *Intrasite replication* refers to the replication that takes place between all the DCs within a site. Intrasite replication takes place automatically at five-minute intervals in a bidirectional ring topology. For example, Figure 9-3 shows a replication topology among four DCs within a site.

Each replication arrow in Figure 9-3 is a single, unidirectional *connection object*. The replication topology in a site is created and maintained automatically by the Knowledge Consistency Checker (KCC), which runs every 15 minutes to verify that all DCs are available for replication. If the KCC determines that a given DC is not available for replication (such as when it is shut down), the KCC automatically adjusts the replication topology to accommodate the change and keep replication accurate and efficient. In short, when it comes to managing replication within a site, there's not a whole lot for an administrator to worry about.

FIGURE 9-3

Multimaster replication among domain controllers in a site

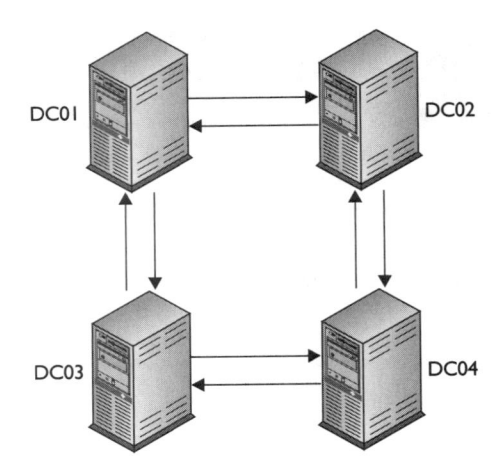

FROM THE CLASSROOM

How Replication Takes Place

Remember that AD is a database that contains many objects and attributes of those objects. You might wonder what happens if, say, you change a single attribute of a single object. For example, suppose you open a particular user account and change one attribute, such as the user's fax number. When you change that one attribute, that attribute gets a new update sequence number (USN). During replication, only the new fax number, not the entire user account, will be replicated to other DCs.

The USN helps replication partners estimate how much replication they have to do. When a DC needs to replicate from another DC, it starts with a query like "What's your high-water mark?" (which is basically the same as asking "What's your highest USN at the moment?"). The other DC sends back its highest USN, which the first DC can compare to its own high-water mark. If the two are already in sync, there's no need to replicate.

On the other hand, let's say DC1 tells DC2 "My current high-water mark is 8932." DC2 looks at its own high-water mark, and sees it's at 8800. In that case, DC2 knows it needs to replicate changes 8801 through 8932 to get in sync with CD1.

—*Alan Simpson, MA, MCSA*

on the Job *If you want to change the replication schedule for a KCC-created connection object, you must first take ownership of that object. Once you do that, though, the connection becomes a manual object that won't be managed automatically by the KCC.*

Intersite replication—that is, replication between Active Directory sites—is not so automatic. In fact, replication between sites won't take place at all until an administrator manually defines an appropriate connection object between the sites.

Implementing Intersite Active Directory Replication

As you may recall, an Active Directory *site* is a set of *well-connected* computers and subnets, where the term "well-connected" refers to fast, low-cost connections such as Ethernet or Token Ring. When you first install Active Directory, Windows 2000 automatically creates a site named Default-First-Site on the DC. It appears in the Active Directory Sites and Services snap-in when you expand the Sites node, as shown in Figure 9-4. You can rename that site as appropriate to your network simply by right-clicking the site name and choosing Rename, though for this book, I'll keep the default name to avoid any potential confusion.

FIGURE 9-4

Default-First-Site in AD Sites and Services

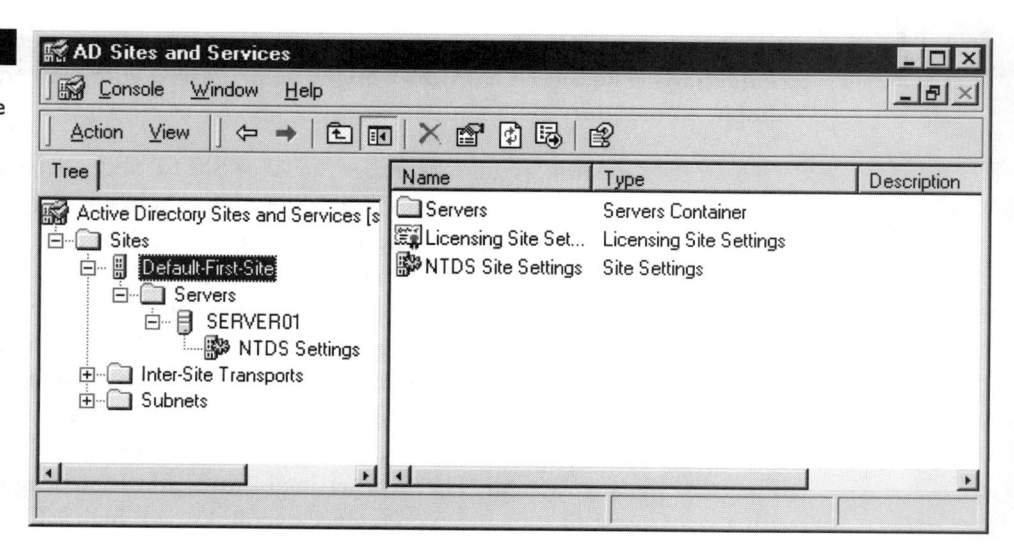

The Sites folder in AD Sites and Services also contains a couple of subfolders, named Inter-Site Transports and Subnets. Any given site can contain multiple subnets. For example, suppose the network in the New York office consists of three subnets, and the London office's network consists of two subnets. There would be no need to create five sites in this case. Rather, you could create two sites, one for each office. You would then use the Subnets container to identify which subnets belong to which sites.

exam
Watch

Sites are strictly for controlling replication across slow, unreliable, or expensive links.

Creating Site Links

A *site link* is an Active Directory object that you configure to determine how and when replication takes place between AD sites. A default site link, named DEFAULTIPSITELINK, is created automatically when you first install AD on a DC, but you can create your own site links based on either the IP or SMTP protocol. The IP protocol is the same protocol used for replication among DCs within a site, and relies on remote procedure calls (RPCs). SMTP transport can be used between two DCs only if they are in different sites, and in different domains. Also, SMTP requires that you install certificate authority (CA), which the replication will use for authentication.

on the
Job

The IP transport is preferred when you're using fast, reliable network connections. The SMTP transport might be preferred with slower, less reliable connections.

To create a site link, right-click either the IP or SMTP node, depending on which protocol you want to use, and choose New Site Link. Fill in a name for the link and click OK. If you have multiple connections between sites, for fault tolerance, you can create a separate site link for each connection. You can then assign to each link a *cost* to give them priority. For example, suppose you have a T1 connection between two sites, and also a standard 56 Kbps modem connection you use as a backup. You could give the T1 connection a lower cost value of, say, 1 to make it the preferred link. Give the backup connection a higher cost, such as 10, to give it a lower priority. The actual number you enter is somewhat arbitrary in that it doesn't need to relate to speed or dollar cost at all. The Cost setting is just a priority setting where links with lower Cost values are given preference over links with higher Cost values.

To configure a site link's cost, replication frequency, and schedule, right-click the site link name and choose Properties. In the Properties dialog box, enter a Cost and replication frequency in the spin boxes near the bottom of the dialog box, shown in Figure 9-5. The replication interval can be any value between 15 and 10,800 minutes (the latter value being one week).

You can also use the Change Schedule button to specify when the connection is available. If the replication interval expires during a time when the replication link is flagged as "not available," no replication takes place. By default, the IP transport adheres to schedules, and SMTP ignores them. You can change that default behavior, though, by right-clicking either the IP or SMTP node in the console tree and choosing Properties. You'll see a check box that allows you to ignore schedules, as shown in Figure 9-6.

There are a couple of ways to associate sites with site links. If you've already created some sites, you can use the Add and Remove buttons in the site link's

FIGURE 9-5

Properties for a site link

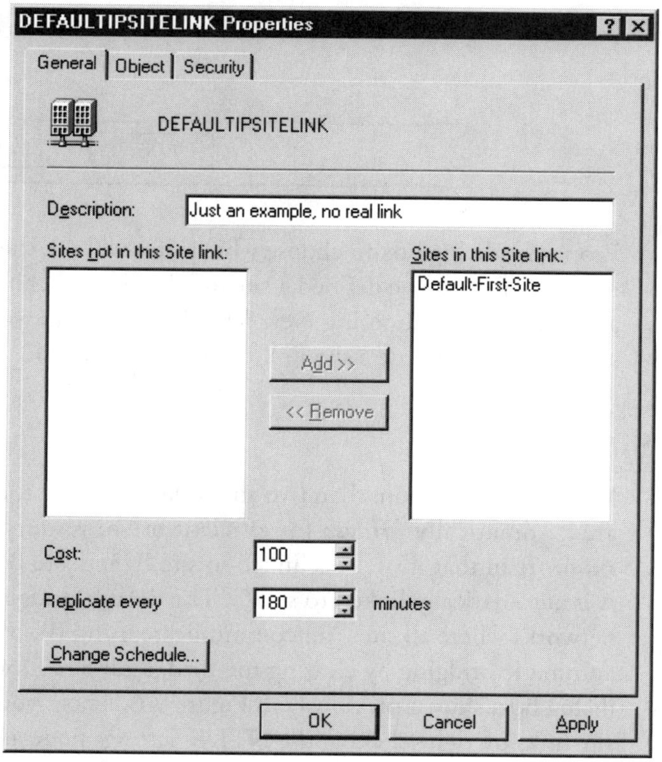

FIGURE 9-6

Properties for IP intersite transports

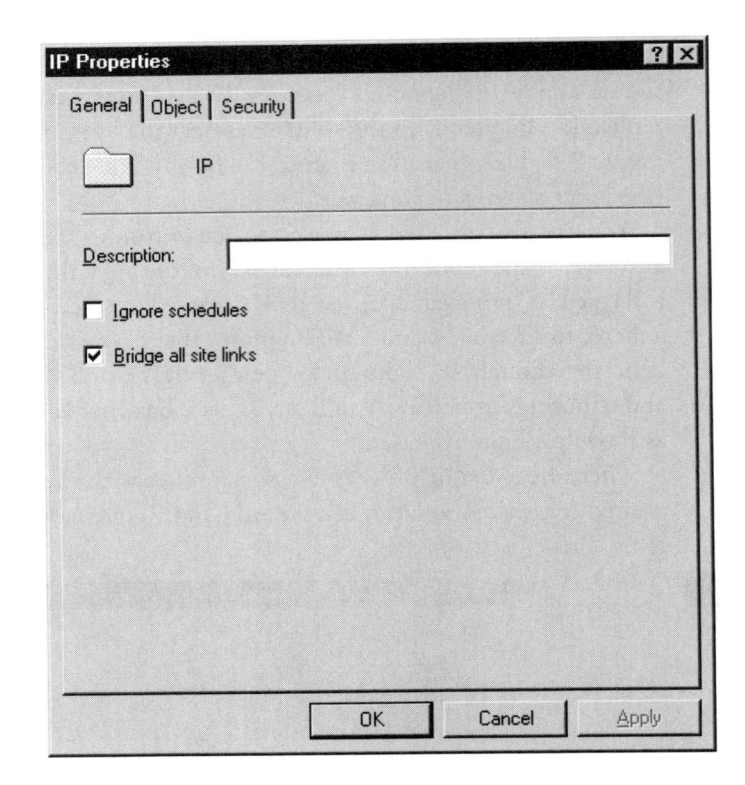

Properties dialog box to choose which sites will use the site link. You also create a new site after you've defined a site link by right-clicking the Sites node in AD Sites and Services and choosing New Site. When you do, you'll be prompted to enter a site name and choose a site link to use for replication.

Bridging Site Links

When you have more than two site links that share the same protocol, the site links are automatically *bridged* for efficient use of resources. Bridged site links are *transitive* in that if site A is linked to site B, and site B is linked to site C, then site A is automatically linked to site C. The default bridging, however, works only in networks where all sites can communicate using IP. If necessary, you can disable automatic bridging by clearing the Bridge All Site Links option in the Properties dialog box, shown previously in Figure 9-6. Then, you can manually configure site links by right-clicking the NTDS Settings node and choosing New Active Directory Connection.

Defining Bridgehead Servers

You can define any DC within a site as a *bridgehead server,* which makes it the preferred point of contact for intersite replication. For example, if you have a DC that's directly connected to a high-speed WAN connection, you might want to make that computer the preferred bridgehead server. If your network uses a firewall to protect a site, creating a bridgehead server is mandatory, not optional. You'll want to specify your firewall proxy server as the bridgehead server to ensure that replicated directory information is transmitted through the firewall.

> **exam**
> **Watch**
>
> *Keep in mind that bridgehead servers are only required when firewalls are involved, to allow replication traffic between specific DCs. Otherwise, bridgehead servers are optional.*

To define a bridgehead server for a site, expand the Sites node in AD Sites and Services, then expand the site for which you want to designate a bridgehead server. Expand the Servers node, and right-click the DC that you want to designate as a bridgehead server and choose Properties. Use the Add and Remove buttons, shown in Figure 9-7, to specify for which transports this server will act as a bridgehead.

If, for whatever reason, the bridgehead server isn't available for replication when a scheduled transfer is initiated, Active Directory will attempt to use another DC for replication. If you have several DCs that you prefer to use for intersite replication, you can designate all of them as bridgehead servers. When the preferred bridgehead server is unavailable, AD will give preference to other bridgehead servers when choosing the DC to use for the intersite replication.

SCENARIO & SOLUTION

I have several subnets in my local office. Should each subnet be defined as a separate site?	Not necessarily. If you have high-speed, reliable connections between the subnets, then there would be no reason to define each subnet as a separate site.
I noticed that when manually creating a connection object for intrasite replication, I can choose from three transports, RPC, IP, and SMTP. What's the difference?	RPC and IP are basically the same, except that IP uses some data compression. As far as intrasite replication goes, the default transport, RPC, is probably your best bet, assuming the DCs are "well-connected."
I have several site links with different costs set up. How do the costs determine how replication takes place?	The KCC will examine all available site links, and automatically use the least-expensive route for replication between sites.

FIGURE 9-7

Use this dialog box to define a bridgehead server.

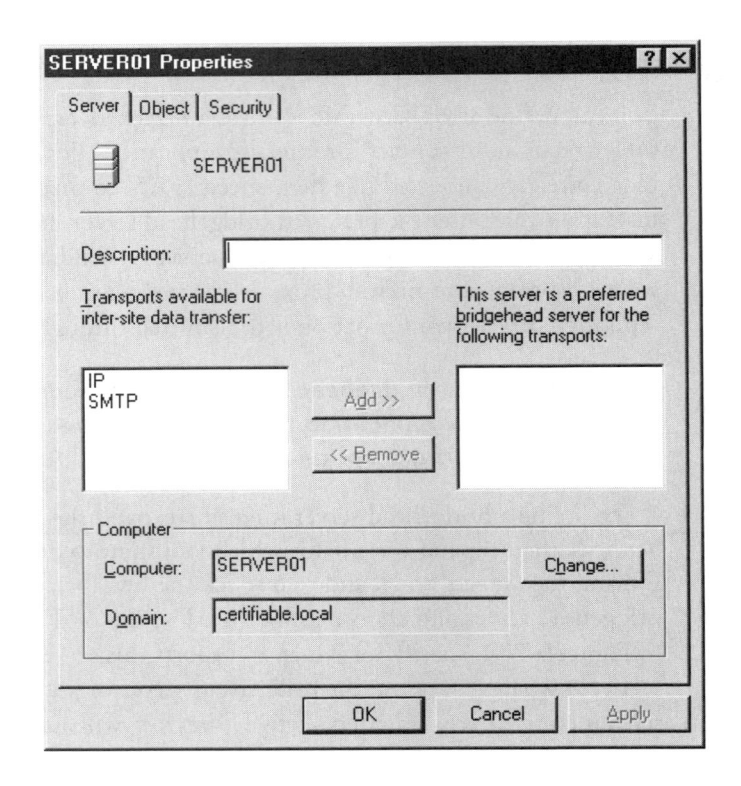

[Screenshot of SERVER01 Properties dialog box with Server, Object, and Security tabs. Shows Description field, Transports available for inter-site data transfer (IP, SMTP), This server is a preferred bridgehead server for the following transports, Add and Remove buttons, Computer section with Computer: SERVER01 and Domain: certifiable.local, and OK/Cancel/Apply buttons.]

CERTIFICATION OBJECTIVE 9.03

Troubleshooting Active Directory Replication

When Active Directory replication problems arise, the result is erratic and inconsistent behavior, such as new user accounts not being recognized, password changes not being updated, and so forth. The first thing you'll want to do is check your basic network connectivity between the replicating DCs. A simple PING would do the trick. Ideally, you'll want at least one DC that is acting as the global catalog, and one DNS server at each site. This will help reduce overhead by keeping "day-to-day" traffic, like authentication requests, within each site.

Remember that Active Directory is closely integrated with DNS. If there's a problem with replication, verify that the DNS servers are set up correctly at each site. Active Directory replication also relies on the remote procedure call (RPC) service. When Active Directory replication fails due to RPC errors, you first want to ensure that the RPC service is running on all replicating machines. The RPC service can also fail if the machines are unable to resolve host names correctly due to improper DNS configuration.

> **exam**
> **Watch**
>
> *In addition to replication, RPCs are used for authentication and other basic networking services. Regardless of the specific service that's failing due to RPC errors, DNS must always be considered a primary suspect.*

Once you've determined that all the basic infrastructure components are working, you can start looking at other issues, based on the nature of the replication problem, as discussed in the sections that follow.

Replication Between Sites Fails

If you find that replication within a site is working fine, but that DCs at different sites aren't replicating, then you know the problem is somewhere in the site link. Remember that unlike replication within a site, which happens without any intervention on your part, replication between sites needs to be configured manually. At each site, you need to create an Active Directory site link object that's connected to other sites within the network.

Replication Has Slowed Down

If replication was originally working fine, but seems to be slowing down as traffic on the network grows, it's time to consider taking a look at all the site links to determine whether there's a way to start bridging them. You'll get the best performance if you can bridge all of the site links.

> **on the**
> **Job**
>
> *Unlike intrasite connection objects that are automatically created by the KCC, you can change the frequency of replication on any site link at any time. You already have ownership of manually created site links.*

If Active Directory information at the DCs at one site is taking too long to get to DCs at some other site, you may need to increase the frequency of replication between those two sites. Configuring bridgehead servers at each site might help too, especially if you can use a DC that isn't already busy performing other tasks, like basic authentication and name resolution services.

If client services, like basic logon authentication, have slowed, check to make sure that the clients aren't having to traverse any slow WAN links to get that job done.

Ideally, you want at least one DC at each site that handles all the local DC tasks for that site. Keeping basic client services off of the WAN link will not only speed those services to clients, it will also free up bandwidth that, in turn, can be used by replication.

Minimizing Replication Overhead

How you set up your security groups can have an impact on the speed of replication across sites. As you may recall, much of the data to be replicated among DCs is stored in the global catalog. Every change that impacts the global catalog must be replicated to every global catalog in the forest.

Security groups that have universal scope, as well as all the members of those universal groups, are listed in the global catalog. Whenever you change even one member of a universal security group, the entire group membership must be replicated to all global catalogs in the domain tree or forest.

Security groups that have global or domain local scope are also listed in the global catalog. However, members of those groups are not listed in the global catalog. Using global or domain local groups reduces the size of the global catalog, which in turn reduces the replication traffic needed to keep the global catalog up to date.

Within a single site, the replication overhead caused by using universal security groups is generally not likely to slow replication within the site. However, if your network consists of many sites separated by slower WAN links, you can improve replication performance by using groups with global or domain local scope for any Active Directory objects that need to be changed frequently.

When faced with exam questions that deal with security groups and replication overhead, the best approach is to use a domain local group, and make as its members appropriate groups and users from the local domain as well as any other domains.

Checking Replication Topology

The KCC mentioned earlier in this chapter keeps track of DCs, as well as the costs of various site link bridges. It uses this information to automatically create an efficient replication topology based on the current status of DCs and available connections. You can use Active Directory Sites and Services to run a quick check of the current topology by following the steps in Exercise 9-2.

Troubleshooting Active Directory Replication   **441**

EXERCISE 9-2

Checking Replication Topology

In this exercise, you'll get a little hands-on experience checking the replication topology. I realize that many of you are working in a limited environment with a single DC, in which case there's no real replication topology to concern yourself with. But you can still perform the exercise just to get a little experience with the steps. Here's how:

1. Select Start | All Programs | Administrative Tools | Active Directory Sites And Services.

2. Expand the Sites node and all nodes within it until you get to the NTDS Settings node.

3. Right-click the NTDS Settings node and choose All Tasks | Check Replication Topology.

4. If there is no problem, you'll get a simple informational message like the one shown in the following illustration.

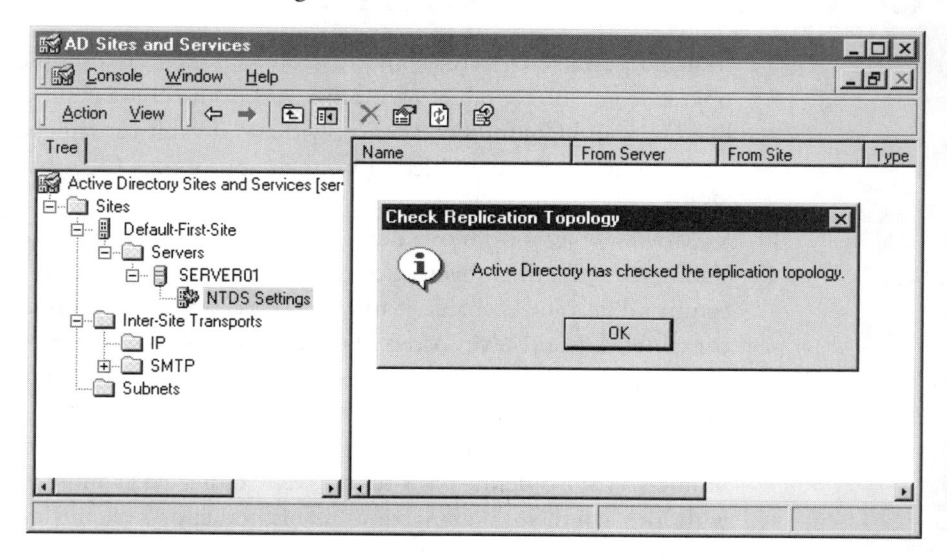

If there are any problems with the topology, the message box will describe the problem.

SCENARIO & SOLUTION

I've planned my sites based on our company's physical locations, but now I'm not sure how to set up the domains to avoid running into replication problems. What should I do?	You need to remember that sites and domains aren't really related. A domain can span two or more sites. A site can contain multiple domains. So you can define your domains as needed for "security boundaries" without regard to the physical location of each site.
I have a high-speed connection between my local and overseas sites, but the connection isn't very reliable and often causes replication problems. How could I get better performance from that link?	If you're using an IP transport, try using SMTP instead. SMTP can have outstanding transactions pending, but still continue to work, which is ideal for unreliable links. IP transports must wait for each transaction to be completed prior to sending the next transaction.
What tools can I use to force AD replication to take place immediately?	If you install the Resource Kit tools from the \Support\ Tools folder of the Windows 2000 installation CD, you'll find a repadmin tool, which you can use to force immediate AD replication. Optionally, you can use the GUI-based replmon tool.

CERTIFICATION SUMMARY

Managing Active Directory objects within a domain is a simple matter of moving objects from one container to another within the domain. The default containers, like Users and Computers, are simply that—default containers. You can move user accounts and computer objects into their appropriate OUs just by right-clicking the object and choosing Move.

Moving objects from one domain to another within a forest isn't quite so simple. You need to use the **movetree** command with the appropriate syntax. If a **movetree** command fails and is unable to move an object, the object ends up in the LostAndFound container. Once you've corrected the problem that prevented the move from taking place, you can then move the object from the LostAndFound container to its intended destination.

Replication of Active Directory within a site takes place, automatically, every five minutes. A *site* is defined as a set of "well-connected" computers—that is, objects with high-bandwidth connections like Ethernet or Token Ring. Replication across sites needs to be configured and managed separately. You create site link bridges to manage intersite replication. To make intersite replication as efficient as possible, you can bridge site links, and specify DCs at each site to play the role of *bridgehead server*. A bridgehead server will be the preferred computer to be used for intersite replication.

✓ TWO-MINUTE DRILL

Managing Active Directory Objects

- ❏ Organizing AD objects within a domain is a simple matter of right-clicking an object, choosing Move, and then specifying the OU (or other container) in which to place the object.

- ❏ Moving objects across domains within an OU is more complex, and requires the movetree command.

- ❏ You can use the /check option in a movetree command to test a move before actually implementing the move.

- ❏ The /start switch in the movetree command will automatically test the operation as well, and move the objects only if the test is successful.

- ❏ Any objects that movetree is unable to move will be placed in the LostAndFound container in AD Users and Computers.

Configuring Active Directory Replication

- ❏ A site is defined as a group of *well-connected* computers or subnets, where "well-connected" implies high-speed, reliable, and low-cost connectivity.

- ❏ The Knowledge Consistency Checker (KCC) automatically creates and maintains *connection objects* for replication between DCs within a site.

- ❏ AD replication between sites needs to be configured manually in Active Directory Sites and Services.

- ❏ A *site link* (also called a *site link object*) is an AD replication link between two sites.

- ❏ A *site link bridge* is a collection of two or more site link objects that provides a structure for evaluating a least-cost path between two sites.

- ❏ By default, all site links are bridged in Windows 2000.

- ❏ A *bridgehead server* is a server that's been designated as the preferred server for handling intersite replication.

Troubleshooting Active Directory Replication

- ❑ Problems with AD replication manifest themselves as failed or excessively delayed synchronization among DCs.
- ❑ The first step to resolving AD replication problems is to check basic network connectivity.
- ❑ AD replication depends on proper DNS configuration, so a replication problem could actually be a problem with a misconfigured DNS server.
- ❑ IP replication links rely on remote procedure calls (RPCs). Chronic RPC errors will occur if the RPC service is halted on a server.
- ❑ Intermittent replication errors and RPC errors are likely to be the result of faulty DNS configuration.
- ❑ Excessive delays in AD replication can be caused by too little bandwidth or a replication frequency that's set too low.
- ❑ Basic client services such as authentication can be slowed if the required DC is in a separate site. Each site should have at least one DC and DNS server to minimize traffic across a WAN link.

SELF TEST

The following questions will help you measure your understanding of the material presented in this chapter. Read each question and possible answer thoroughly, as you would on the actual exam. Choose all correct answers for each question.

Managing Active Directory Objects

1. When you move an object from one OU to another OU within a domain, what happens to the permissions that the object originally inherited at the source OU?
   A. The original inherited permissions stay with the moved object.
   B. The original inherited permissions are lost, and the object inherits the permissions of the destination OU.
   C. The original inherited permissions are combined with the permissions inherited at the destination OU, with the least restrictive permissions taking precedence in a conflict.
   D. The original inherited permissions are combined with the permissions inherited at the destination OU, with the most restrictive permissions taking precedence in a conflict.

2. You use a movetree command to move some AD objects from one container to another. The move fails because the destination computer had insufficient available disk space. What happens to the moved objects?
   A. They remain in their original containers.
   B. They are deleted and lost forever.
   C. They're placed in the LostAndFound container in AD Users and Computers.
   D. They're placed in the LostAndFound container in AD Sites and Services.

3. You are the network administrator for your company. You've created a Group Policy Object and linked it to an OU named ProjectX. During a major reorganization, you are asked to move the ProjectX OU to a different domain. After you complete the move, you discover that everyone has full control over the object. What must you do to reinstate the former policies applied to the object?
   A. Use the movetree command to move the GPO link to the new domain.
   B. Use the movegpolink command to move the GPO link to the new domain.
   C. Create a new GPO at the destination domain and link it to the moved object.
   D. Enable the GPO at the new domain, because moving an object automatically disables any linked GPOs.

Configuring Active Directory Replication

4. You are the network administrator for your company's Windows 2000 network. Your company sets up a new branch office that connects to the corporate network through a leased line. You create a new site for the branch office in Active Directory Sites and Services. You notice, however, that no replication is taking place between the two sites. What should you do?

   A. Designate one DC at each site as a bridgehead server.
   B. Create a site link object that defines how the two sites will replicate.
   C. Use a single DNS server to provide name resolution services for both sites.
   D. Move all user and computer accounts from the branch office into containers in AD Users and Computers at the home office.

5. Which of the following best defines an Active Directory site?

   A. A single subnet within a domain.
   B. A group of computers that share the same default domain policy.
   C. Any group of well-connected computers and subnets.
   D. A forest containing two or more domains.

6. Which of the following best describes the concept of "cost" for an intersite replication link?

   A. An arbitrary number you assign to a link to define a "preferred" link when multiple links are available.
   B. The bandwidth of the link in Kbps.
   C. The unit cost, in dollars, of moving data across the link.
   D. The annual fee paid to the provider of the link.

7. You are the network administrator for your company's Windows 2000 network. Your company adds a new branch office and asks you to configure AD replication between the new office and existing sites. The new branch office is protected by a firewall. When you create the site link, you discover that replication isn't taking place. What else must you do?

   A. Define a bridgehead server.
   B. Disable the firewall.
   C. Define a port through which AD replication can take place.
   D. Bridge site links among all sites.

Troubleshooting Active Directory Replication

8. You are the network administrator for your company's Windows 2000 network. You've created several sites in AD Sites and Services. You discover that while intrasite replication within each site is working perfectly, you're not getting any replication between sites. What must you do?

    A. Wait for the KCC to create appropriate site link bridges.

    B. Enter an **ipconfig /registerdns** command at each site's DC to update all the DNS servers.

    C. At each site, create an Active Directory site link object that's connected to other sites within the network.

    D. Define a bridgehead server at each site.

9. You are the network administrator for your company's Windows 2000 network. The main office houses all DCs for the company. Branch offices have their own servers, but use the DCs at the main office for authentication. Users at the branch offices complain that it's taking far too long to log in to their machines. What can you do to speed things along?

    A. Create one or more DCs at each site and configure each site to use its local DCs for authentication.

    B. Increase the frequency of intersite replications among the sites.

    C. Copy the global catalog from the DC at the main office to member servers at each site.

    D. Bridge all site links to improve intersite replication performance.

10. You are a domain administrator for the Windows 2000 network shown in Figure 9-8. Recently, you've created a shared folder named CorpNews in the East.MajorMinorX.com domain. You need to create a security group that will allow users whose accounts are in global from other domains to access the shared folder. You must accomplish this goal while minimizing replication overhead. What should you do?

    A. Create a universal group that has permissions for the share, then add appropriate groups from other domains to the universal group.

    B. Create a global group that has permissions for the share, then add appropriate groups from other domains to the global group.

    C. Create a domain local group that has permissions for the share, then add appropriate groups from other domains to the domain local group.

    D. Create a distribution group that has permissions for the share, then add appropriate groups from other domains to the distribution group.

FIGURE 9-8

Exhibit for Question 10

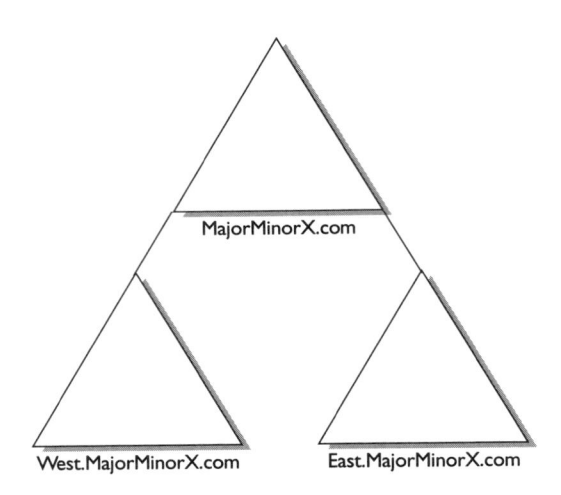

```
              MajorMinorX.com


    West.MajorMinorX.com    East.MajorMinorX.com
```

LAB QUESTION

You are a network administrator for the Windows 2000 network shown in Figure 9-9. The DC named DC1 is a multihomed computer that provides DNS and DHCP services for BizNet, but only DHCP services for RnDNet.

DC1 does not route between the two networks, and computers in RnDNet are not members of the domain. DC1 hosts an AD integrated DNS zone, and is configured as summarized in Table 9-1.

FIGURE 9-9 Exhibit for the Lab Question

RnDNet
192.168.0.0

BizNet
10.10.0.0

DC01

DC02   DC03

TABLE 9-1 Configuration for DC1

NIC	IP Address	Subnet Mask	DNS Server Address	DNS Interfaces
Local Connection 1	10.10.0.1	255.255.255.0	127.0.0.1	10.10.0.1
Local Connection 2	192.168.0.1	255.255.255.0	127.0.0.1	192.168.0.1

You discover that Active Directory replication between DC2 and the other DCs occasionally fails, displaying the error message "RPC server is unavailable." You test for basic connectivity between DCs, and all tests pass. What would be the next step to resolving the problem?

SELF TEST ANSWERS

Managing Active Directory Objects

1. ☑ **B** is correct. When you move an object from one OU to another within a domain, the object inherits the permissions of the new OU, and the original inherited permissions are lost.
   ☒ **A**, **C**, and **D** are all inaccurate descriptions of permissions inheritance on objects moved from one OU to another within a domain.

2. ☑ **C** is correct. The objects are placed in the LostAndFound folder in AD Users and Computers.
   ☒ **A** and **B** are incorrect because they don't describe what happens to the objects.
   ☒ **D** is wrong because the LostAndFound container is in AD Users and Computers, not AD Sites and Services.

3. ☑ **C** is correct. GPOs are not moved with objects, and must be re-created and linked in the new domain.
   ☒ **A** is wrong because you can't use movetree to move GPO links.
   ☒ **B** is wrong because there is no movegpolink command.
   ☒ **D** is incorrect because the GPO link is not moved at all during a movetree operation.

Configuring Active Directory Replication

4. ☑ **B** is correct. Intersite replication links are not created automatically when you define a site. You'll need to define an appropriate site link after creating the new site.
   ☒ **A** is wrong because it's not necessary to define bridgehead servers; those are optional.
   ☒ **C** and **D** are incorrect because they wouldn't fix a replication problem.

5. ☑ **C** is correct. Any group of computers and subnets that are connected by fast, reliable connections could be defined as a site.
   ☒ **A** is wrong because a site could contain any number of subnets.
   ☒ **B** is wrong because that would define a domain, and a domain can contain multiple sites.
   ☒ **D** is wrong because a forest could contain any number of sites.

6. ☑ **A** is correct. The cost needn't be an exact measure of bandwidth or dollar cost. It's simply a number you assign to give preference when multiple links are available.
   ☒ **B**, **C**, and **D** are incorrect because the cost you assign to a link need not be an exact number that matches bandwidth or dollar cost.

7. ☑ **A** is correct. When a site is protected by a firewall, defining a bridgehead server is mandatory.
   ☒ **B** is incorrect because it's not necessary to disable the firewall.
   ☒ **C** is wrong because what's really needed here is a bridgehead server.
   ☒ **D** is wrong because it wouldn't allow replication to take place through the firewall.

Troubleshooting Active Directory Replication

8. ☑ **C** is correct. You must create site links at each site.
   ☒ **A** is wrong because the KCC won't automatically create intersite replication links.
   ☒ **B** is wrong because the command isn't related to AD replication.
   ☒ **D** is wrong because, unless there's a firewall involved, defining bridgehead servers is optional.

9. ☑ **A** is correct. You need to ensure that each site has at least one DC to be used for authentication at that site.
   ☒ **B** and **D** are incorrect because you'd need to have DCs at each site to even set up the replication.
   ☒ **C** is wrong because the global catalog isn't something you can just manually copy from one computer to another.

10. ☑ **C** is correct. A domain local group could provide access for appropriate groups, while keeping replication overhead to a minimum.
    ☒ **A** is wrong because universal groups do not provide for minimal replication overhead.
    ☒ **B** wouldn't work because a global security group can contain only user accounts, computer accounts, and global groups from the same domain.
    ☒ **D** wouldn't work because you can't configure permissions with distribution groups.

LAB ANSWER

When AD replication fails with an "RPC server is unavailable" error, and basic network connectivity is in place, DNS is the next place to look for the problem. In this scenario, DC1 is supposedly providing DNS name resolution services for BizNet. However, it's currently configured to service that network, which is the most likely cause of the problem. Resolving the problem would require that you do the following:

- Disable DNS name resolution for RnDNet.
- Remove the 192.168.0.1 address from the Interfaces tab in the DNS console.

- Disable dynamic DNS registration for RnDNet.
- Remove all host records from the DNS zone for the address 192.168.1.1.

Once the DNS zone database is cleaned up and configured properly, the intermittent RPC errors should be resolved.

Part III

MCSA — MICROSOFT CERTIFIED SYSTEMS ADMINISTRATOR

Creating, Configuring, Managing, Securing, and Troubleshooting File, Print, and Web Resources

CHAPTERS

10 Managing Data Storage
11 Configuring Internet Information Services (IIS)
12 Implementing and Analyzing Security

MCSA
MICROSOFT CERTIFIED SYSTEMS ADMINISTRATOR

10

Managing Data Storage

CERTIFICATION OBJECTIVES

10.01	Configuring Disks and Volumes
10.02	Configuring and Enforcing Disk Quotas
10.03	Implementing Encrypting File System (EFS)
10.04	Implementing and Managing a Distributed File System (Dfs)
✓	Two-Minute Drill
Q&A	Self Test

456 Chapter 10: Managing Data Storage

Managing data storage is an important element of network administration, for many reasons. First, it's important to ensure that users have sufficient hard disk space to store all their files. Second, it's important to ensure that users have access to all of the shared files and folders necessary to perform their jobs. On the other side of the coin, the administrator might also need to limit users' storage space to prevent them from filling up disks with files that aren't relevant to their job, such as large multimedia files used purely for personal entertainment.

An administrator also needs to ensure that users can easily find and use the resources available to them. If users will be allowed to make their files and folders "private" by encrypting them, the administrator needs to be able to decrypt those files and folders in case a user leaves the job. If the network is large, containing many shares spread across multiple servers, the administrator needs to find a way to simplify things for less-experienced users who aren't able to browse through network resources to see what's available. You'll learn about these and other issues pertaining to data storage in this chapter.

CERTIFICATION OBJECTIVE 10.01

Configuring Disks and Volumes

Windows 2000 supports two kinds of disk storage known as *basic disks* and *dynamic disks*. Basic disks are the ones that have been around since DOS days, allowing you to create primary and extended disk partitions and logical drives, mirror sets, volume sets, and stripe sets. You can create up to four partitions on a basic disk.

Dynamic disks are relatively new. Unlike basic disks, which are partition-oriented, dynamic disks are volume-oriented. Dynamic disks remove the four-partition limit imposed by basic disks. When you use dynamic disks, you can extend volumes by adding free space to them.

A disk must be either basic or dynamic—you can't combine basic partitions with dynamic volumes on a single physical disk. Only Windows 2000 can read dynamic disks directly, but any computer with appropriate permissions can access shared data on dynamic disks across the network.

On multiple disk systems, you can combine storage from two or more drives to appear as a single volume. Table 10-1 summarizes the various volume configurations supported by Windows 2000, as well as equivalent volume types from Windows NT 4.0.

TABLE 10-1 Volume Types Supported by Windows 2000 Dynamic Disks

Volume Type	Description	Windows NT Equivalent
Simple volume	A single disk.	Primary partition or logical drive
Spanned volume	Enables you to combine multiple small areas of free space on up to 32 disks into a single volume. Data fills the first disk, then the next, and so forth.	Volume set
Mirrored volume	Two disks, each containing an identical copy of a volume for fault-tolerance purposes.	Mirror set
Striped volume	Increases disk performance by allowing you to spread data across as many as 32 physical disks.	Stripe set
RAID-5 volume	Three or more disks for fault tolerance.	Stripe set with parity

There are two major caveats to be aware of with dynamic disks: (1) Windows 2000 dynamic disks are invisible to pre-Windows 2000 operating systems on the same machine, and (2) they cannot be used on laptops. You can convert a basic disk to a dynamic disk and vice versa, but there's a hefty caveat there, too. If the dynamic disk contains any volumes, you'll need to delete those volumes before reverting to a basic disk.

EXERCISE 10-1

Converting a Basic Disk to a Dynamic Disk

This exercise will show you, step-by-step, how to convert a basic disk to a dynamic disk. You can perform this exercise on any Windows 2000 Server or Professional computer, provided you log in with administrative privileges.

1. Open the Control Panel, open Administrative Tools, then open Computer Management.
2. Expand the Storage node and click Disk Management. The Disk Management tool displays a bar for each physical disk in the system (Disk 0, Disk 1, and so forth).
3. Right-click the disk number and choose Upgrade To Dynamic Disk.
4. When prompted, choose the physical disks you want to upgrade and click OK. Follow the remaining instructions that appear on the screen.

458 Chapter 10: Managing Data Storage

FIGURE 10-1

The Disk Management tool and a dynamic disk

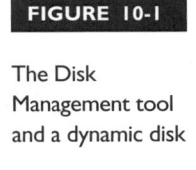

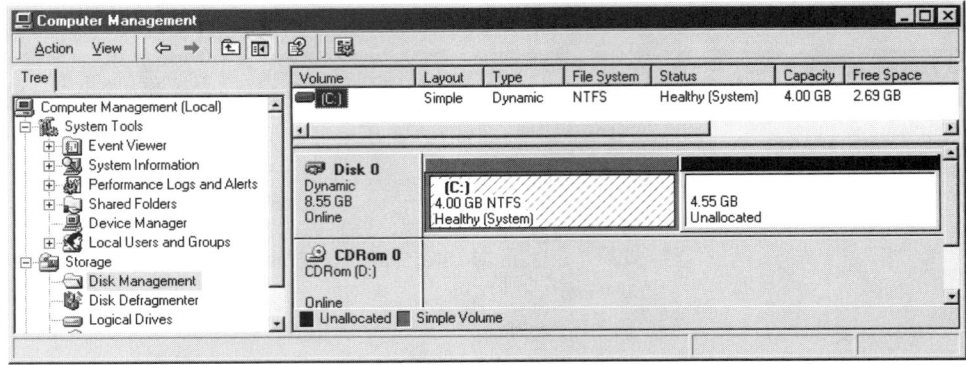

After reboot, you can reopen the Disk Management tool to check your work. The disk Type will show Dynamic rather than Basic, as in Figure 10-1.

NTFS and FAT File Systems

As you probably know, DOS and the 16-bit versions of early versions of Windows relied on the FAT (File Allocation Table) and FAT32 file systems. Windows 2000 retains support for FAT for backward compatibility. But you need only concern yourself with that when a single computer is used to dual-boot between Windows 2000 and an older version of Windows. For example, if you have a computer that boots in both Windows 98 and Windows 2000, you'd have to use the FAT file system to store any data that you want to be available to Windows 98.

The preferred file system for Windows 2000 is NTFS, which supports compression, encryption, access control, and other features described in this chapter. Note that a Windows 95 or 98 client can read data from NTFS volumes across a network. They just can't read NTFS partitions on the same physical computer.

exam 🕲 *atch*
FAT partitions are required only on computers that dual-boot to Windows 9x, and only on partitions that Windows 9x needs access to. NTFS partitions will be invisible to Windows 9x.

Mount Points

Windows 2000 also supports the concept of *mount points* or *mounted drives,* which can be a lifesaver when you've run out of space in a basic disk partition. Rather than repartitioning everything, you can mount a partition to that existing drive, where it

Configuring and Enforcing Disk Quotas **459**

SCENARIO & SOLUTION

My network included several Windows 95 and 98 client computers. I need to set up a file server that all clients can access. Do I need to format partitions as FAT or FAT32 on the server to provide Windows 9*x* access to the server shares?	No, you only need to use FAT on dual-boot systems where one of the installed operating systems is Win 9*x*. Those clients are capable of reading NTFS volumes across a network, so you wouldn't need to use FAT on the file server.
I already have several FAT partitions on file servers that I'd like to convert to NTFS. How can I do that?	Use the convert command with the syntax **convert** *volume* **/FS:NTFS**, where *volume* represents the drive you want to convert (such as D:).
What's the difference between FAT and FAT32?	FAT32 is an enhancement to the original FAT file system that supports large drives and improves storage efficiency. FAT32 is part of Windows 98 and Windows 95 OSR2.
Can I use spanned volumes or striped volumes for fault tolerance?	Definitely not—these are used to improve read performance. If any disk in a spanned or striped volume fails, the data in the entire volume will be lost!

appears as just another folder on the drive. Applications can then refer to the contents of that new folder as drive C:, even though technically it's an entirely separate partition.

exam
🕘 *atch*
The easiest way to add more space to an existing volume is to create a partition from unallocated space, and configure it as a mount point on the drive that needs the extra space.

As far as Exam 70-218 goes, the main features of NTFS that are covered include disk quotas and encryption, discussed in the sections that follow.

CERTIFICATION OBJECTIVE 10.02

Configuring and Enforcing Disk Quotas

Disk quotas provide a means to control the amount of disk storage allocated to users. The total amount of space charged to a user is the sum of the length of all data streams. Compressing or decompressing files does not affect the calculation. As illustrated in Exercise 10-2, you can easily enable disk quotas from a drive's Properties dialog box.

460 Chapter 10: Managing Data Storage

EXERCISE 10-2

CertCam 10-2

Enabling Disk Quotas

This exercise can be performed on any Windows 2000 Server or Professional computer on which you want to enable disk quotas. Of course, you wouldn't want to do this on a live production computer without the consent of the network administrator. The procedure for enabling disk quotas is pretty simple and straightforward:

1. Open My Computer, right-click the icon for the drive on which you want to enable disk quotas, and choose Properties.
2. Click the Quota tab.
3. Choose Enable Quota Management to enable the other options in the dialog box, as in Figure 10-2.
4. Choose whichever options best describe how you want to manage disk quotas.
5. Click the Apply button and follow the instructions on the screen.

FIGURE 10-2

The Quota tab in a drive's Properties dialog box

Once quota management is enabled, the traffic light icon in the dialog box turns from red to green. Note that the policies won't be enforced until you enable the enforcement of disk quota limits.

The options available on the Quota tab of a drive's Properties dialog box are described next:

- **Deny disk space to users exceeding their quota limit**   If selected, a user who exceeds her quota limit will not be able to store any more data on the hard disk unless she deletes some files.

- **Do not limit disk usage**   If selected, new users automatically get unlimited storage on the volume.

- **Limit disk space to**   If selected, allows you to define the hard quota limit—the amount of storage space each user can consume.

- **Set warning levels to**   Allows you to set a level at which users will be warned when they are approaching their quota limit.

- **Log event when a user exceeds their quota limit** and **Log event when a user exceeds their warning**   If selected, will generate a system logfile entry when users exceed their limits or warning levels.

Quotas are calculated per user, per partition. If you want to set a quota limit strictly for users' home folders, you'll need to create a separate partition for those folders and set quota limits on that partition. If necessary, you can use the Quota Entries button in the dialog box to configure quota limits on a user-by-user basis. However, that's only necessary if you want different users to have different limits.

Enforcing Quota Limits Through Group Policy

Disk quotas can be enabled, disabled, defined, and enforced through group policies. To get the policies, go to the Group Policy window, expand the Computer Configuration \ Administrative Templates \ System nodes, and click Disk Quotas, as in Figure 10-3. Settings you choose here will override any settings defined on local machines whenever the user is logged in to the domain.

462 Chapter 10: Managing Data Storage

FIGURE 10-3

Group policies for disk quotas

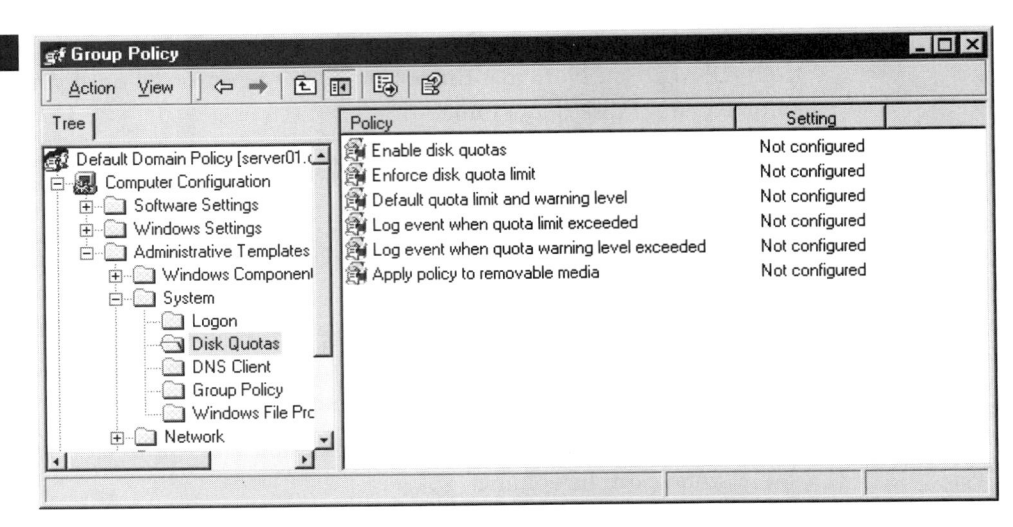

Policy	Setting
Enable disk quotas	Not configured
Enforce disk quota limit	Not configured
Default quota limit and warning level	Not configured
Log event when quota limit exceeded	Not configured
Log event when quota warning level exceeded	Not configured
Apply policy to removable media	Not configured

Tree:
- Default Domain Policy [server01.c...]
  - Computer Configuration
    - Software Settings
    - Windows Settings
    - Administrative Templates
      - Windows Components
      - System
        - Logon
        - Disk Quotas
        - DNS Client
        - Group Policy
        - Windows File Protection
      - Network

The first two policies affect quotas as a whole, and can be set independently. The first policy, Enable Disk Quotas, enables or disables disk quota management on all NTFS volumes of the computer and affects user capabilities as follows:

- **Enable disk quotas – Enabled**   Disk quota management is enabled, users cannot disable it.

- **Enable disk quotas – Disabled**   Disk quota management is disabled, users cannot enable it.

- **Enable disk quotas – Not Configured**   Disk quota management is disabled by default, but administrators can enable it.

It's important to note that the Enable Disk Quotas policy affects only quota management, not enforcement. The second option, Enforce Disk Quota Limit, allows you to control enforcement of quotas as follows:

- **Enforce disk quota limit – Enabled**   Disk quota limits are enforced.

- **Enforce disk quota limit – Disabled**   Disk quota limits are not enforced.

- **Enforce disk quota limit – Not Configured**   Disk quota limits are not enforced by default, but administrators can change the setting.

exam
Watch

If you configure quota limits, only to discover that they're not being applied, make sure the Enforce Disk Quota Limit policy is enabled.

CERTIFICATION OBJECTIVE 10.03

Using the Encrypting File System (EFS)

Encrypting File System (EFS) is an NTFS feature that allows users to secure files through encryption. Encrypting a file or folder is a simple matter of right-clicking the object's icon in Windows Explorer, choosing Properties, and clicking the Advanced button, as described in Exercise 10-3.

EXERCISE 10-3

Encrypting a Folder

This exercise takes you through the process of encrypting a folder. Make sure you only encrypt personal folders because once encrypted, you'll be the only person who can open it (well, you and an EFS Recovery Agent). The steps are simple:

1. Open My Documents, My Computer, or any other Explorer window and navigate to the icon for the folder you want to encrypt.
2. Right-click the folder's icon and choose Properties.
3. On the General tab, click the Advanced button to get to the Advanced Attributes dialog box shown in Figure 10-4.
4. Choose Encrypt Contents To Secure Data.
5. Click the OK button in each open dialog box.

You'll be given the option to encrypt only the current folder, or all subfolders and files contained within the folder. The encryption will be transparent to you as the owner of the folder. If you log in under a different username and try to open the folder, you'll be denied access.

Once encrypted, only the person who encrypted the file or folder will be able to access its contents normally. In the event that a given user leaves the company before decrypting his files, the only way to decrypt the files is through the EFS Recovery Agent.

464 Chapter 10: Managing Data Storage

FIGURE 10-4

Advanced attributes support encryption on NTFS volumes

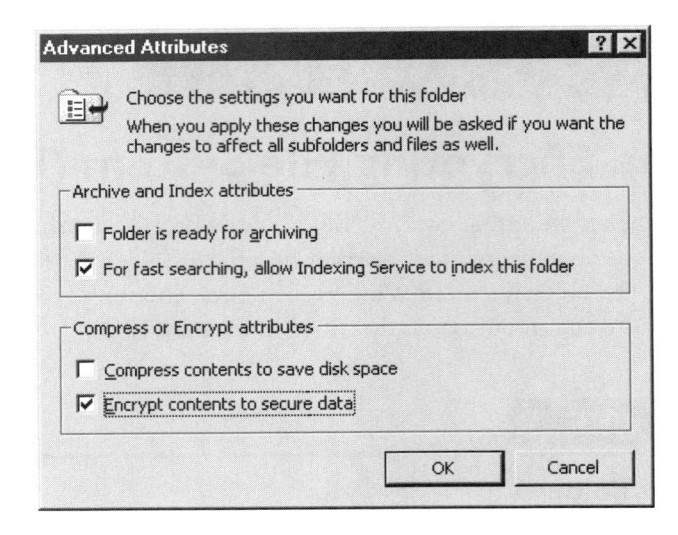

[Advanced Attributes dialog box showing options to choose folder settings, with Archive and Index attributes (Folder is ready for archiving unchecked, For fast searching allow Indexing Service to index this folder checked) and Compress or Encrypt attributes (Compress contents to save disk space unchecked, Encrypt contents to secure data checked)]

exam
Watch

Disk quotas and EFS are features of NTFS, and don't require dynamic disks or any special volume sets.

Because only NTFS supports encryption, encrypted files or folders that are moved or copied to FAT partitions will be decrypted.

on the job

A file can be compressed or encrypted, but not both.

SCENARIO & SOLUTION

Is there a command line tool I can use to encrypt and decrypt files and folders?	You can use the cipher command for that. To view the command's syntax, enter the command **cipher /?**.
One of my users keeps getting "Out of disk space" errors, even though there appears to be plenty of space left on the drive. What's up with that?	When users exceed their quota limit, "Out of disk space" is the error message they'll see. There is no separate message stating that the quota limit has been reached.
Can I use EFS to encrypt files for transmission over a network?	No, you must use a protocol that's specifically designed for that purpose, such as Internet Protocol Security (IPSec) or Secure Sockets Layer (SSL).

CERTIFICATION OBJECTIVE 10.04

Implementing and Managing a Distributed File System (Dfs)

Distributed File System (Dfs) is a tool that you can use to make files that are distributed across multiple servers appear to be all in one place on the network. This is a great boon to users, as they don't need to know the actual physical location of a file to get at it. In Windows 2000, Dfs can be implemented as stand-alone or domain-based. *Domain-based Dfs* (also called *fault-tolerant Dfs*) offers several advantages of stand-alone implementations found in NT, including:

- Automatic publishing to Active Directory, making the shares visible and accessible to all users with appropriate permissions.

- Dfs roots can be replicated to multiple servers in the domain for fault-tolerance. Thus, users can get to files even if one of the physical servers goes offline.

On the server side, any domain controller or member server can be used to host the Dfs root. The Dfs root can be placed on a FAT partition. However, NTFS is preferred because of its superior security and the synchronization of Dfs shared folders. Windows 2000 includes support for both stand-alone and domain-based Dfs. Windows NT 4.0 with SP 3 and Dfs software supports stand-alone Dfs only.

on the job

You can access the Dfs root from My Network Places by choosing Entire Network | Microsoft Windows Network | and the domain name.

Clients need appropriate software to use Dfs shares. The Active Directory client for Windows 95, 98, and Windows NT 4.0 includes a client-side Dfs component that provides access to domain-based Dfs shares. The standard Dfs clients, known as Dfs 4.x and the Dfs 5.0 add-on, will allow access with Dfs in non-AD environments. For Windows 95 clients to access domain-based Dfs folders, both the client for Dfs 4.x and the 5.0 add-on can be installed. Windows 98 clients require only the Dfs 5.0 add-on to be able to access Dfs shares. Table 10-2 summarizes the server- and client-side Dfs components available for different Windows platforms.

TABLE 10-2 Server-Side and Client-Side Dfs in Various Windows Versions

Platform	Host Dfs Root?	Host Dfs Client?
Windows 2000	Stand-alone and domain-based	Yes, both stand-alone and domain-based Dfs access
Windows NT 4 SP 3 with Dfs	Stand-alone server only	Stand-alone client only
Windows 98	No	Stand-alone client only; AD client required for domain-based access
Windows 95	No	No, requires client for Dfs 4.x and 5.0 add-on for stand-alone access; AD client for domain-based Dfs
DOS, NetWare, Windows 3.x/Workgroups	No	No

FROM THE CLASSROOM

Dfs Replication

Dfs can use replication to ensure that shares remain available to users even if the server hosting the Dfs root or specific shares fails. To replicate a Dfs root, you need to right-click its node in the Distributed File System console and choose New Root Replica. A wizard titled New Dfs Root Wizard opens. Simply follow the instructions presented by the wizard to specify where you want to place the replicated Dfs root.

For each Dfs link, you can also create up to 32 replicated shares to which the link points. To create a replica, right-click the Dfs link in the Distributed File System console and choose New Replica. In the Add A New Replica dialog box that appears, specify the name of the share to which you want to direct users should the original share be unavailable. You'll also be given the option to perform replication manually or automatically. If you choose manual replication, it becomes your responsibility to ensure that the shared folders are in sync.

If you choose to replicate shared folders automatically, you'll need to configure the Windows 2000 File Replication Service (FRS) as well. Right-click any Dfs share for which you've chosen automatic replication and choose Replication Policy. In the Replication Policy dialog box that opens, click the shared folder that will act as the master copy, then click the Set Master button. Then, select each of the shared folders listed in the dialog box and click the Enable button.

—*Alan Simpson, MA, MCSA*

> **exam**
> **⚠ Watch** *Only the Active Directory client is needed to give Windows 95 and 98 computers access to domain-based Dfs.*

EXERCISE 10-4

Creating a Domain Dfs Root

This exercise will take you through the steps required to set up a domain-based Dfs root. You must log in to a Windows 2000 domain controller (or member server) to complete this exercise. If you're working in a live production environment, do not complete this exercise until you get clearance from the network administrator. You can create a shared folder to act as the root ahead of time, or while creating the Dfs root. The steps to setting up a Dfs root are as follows:

1. Click the Start button and choose Programs | Administrative Tools | Distributed File System.
2. On the Action menu, choose New Dfs Root. The New Dfs Root Wizard opens.
3. Click the Next button, choose Create A Domain Dfs Root, and then click the Next button.
4. The next wizard page will ask you to choose the host domain. If you're working with a single domain, the default settings are sufficient. Click Next.
5. Choose the host name for the Dfs root. You can choose the current computer or any other server in the network.
6. In the Specify Dfs Root Share window, choose an existing shared folder, or specify the path and name of a new shared folder to create, then click the Next button.
7. In the next wizard page, you can accept the default name for the root, or specify a new name. Then click Next.
8. Click Finish to create the new Dfs root.

The path to the shared Dfs root appears in the console tree with a green check mark. You'll need to reboot the computer to finalize the setup. Opening the Distributed File System administrative tool at that point will display each shared folder as a node beneath the root node, with the UNC path to the selected share shown in the Details pane, as in the example shown in Figure 10-5. In this view, you can add more shares to the Dfs root by clicking the Action button and choosing New Dfs Link.

468 Chapter 10: Managing Data Storage

FIGURE 10-5

The Distributed File System snap-in with a Dfs root in place

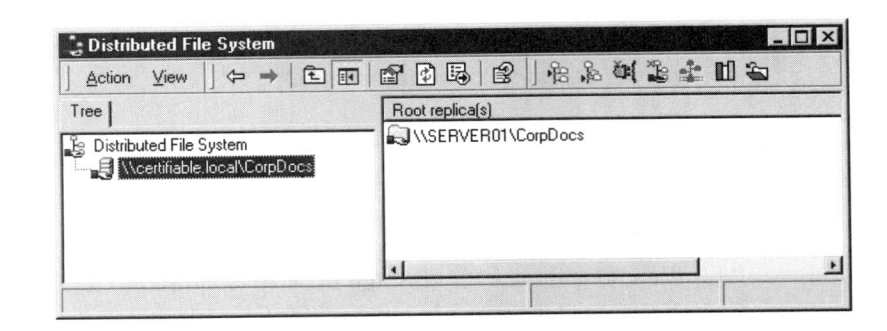

Once you've created a Dfs root, you can add Dfs links to it. The links can point to shared folders anywhere on the network. Each share will have a Share Name and a Link Name. Table 10-3 shows some examples using hypothetical shares. The first step to adding such shares to a distributed file system would be to simply create the shared folders in Windows Explorer.

Once the folders are created, you create links to them in the Distributed File System root. Right-click the name of the DFS root in the console tree and choose New Dfs Link. Fill in the blanks for a single shared folder, as in the example shown in Figure 10-6. After you've created links for all appropriate folders, they'll appear beneath the Dfs root name in the console tree, as in Figure 10-7.

on the Job

A Dfs topology is essentially a single Domain Name System (DNS) namespace where the names for Dfs roots resolve to the host server for the root.

Users will now be able to locate any share in the root by its link name, either through My Network Places, or by searching for the link name.

TABLE 10-3 Examples of Dfs Links—Users Need Only Know the Link Name to Access Shares

Server	Folder	Share Name	Link Name
Server01	E:\Apps\WP	\\Server01\WP	Word Processing
Server01	E:\Apps\Database	\\Server01\DB	Database
Server01	E:\Data\Corp	\\Server01\CorpData	Corporate Data
Server01	E:\Data\UserShares	\\Server01\UserShares	Public Folders

FIGURE 10-6

Creating a Dfs link for a shared folder

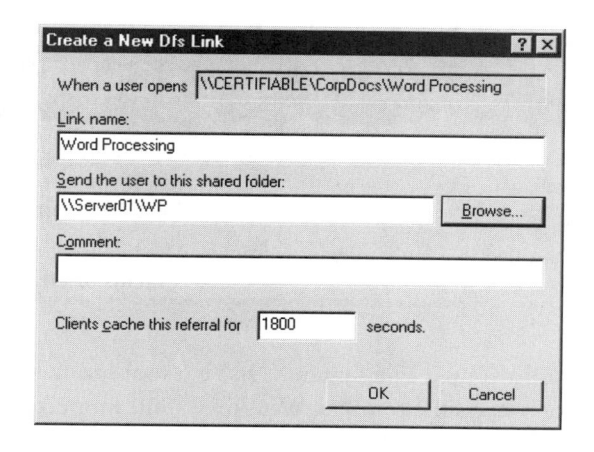

CERTIFICATION SUMMARY

While Exam 70-218 focuses heavily on Windows 2000 networking, there are some questions dealing with basic disk storage issues. The main points to remember about disk storage are that Windows 95, 98, and other downlevel clients cannot read NTFS permissions directly. So if you'll be dual-booting with one of those downlevel clients, make sure you use the FAT (or FAT32) file system for formatting any volumes to which those platforms will need access.

Disk quotas, compression, and encryption are features of the NTFS file system. To use disk quotas, you must set quota limits and also enable quota management either through the Quota tab of a disk's Properties dialog box, or via group policies. EFS allows the owner of a file or folder to encrypt the object, thereby denying access to all other users. Owners can decrypt their own files and folders by turning off compression. Administrators can decrypt users' files and folders using an EFS Recovery Agent.

FIGURE 10-7

Four new Dfs links added to the Dfs root

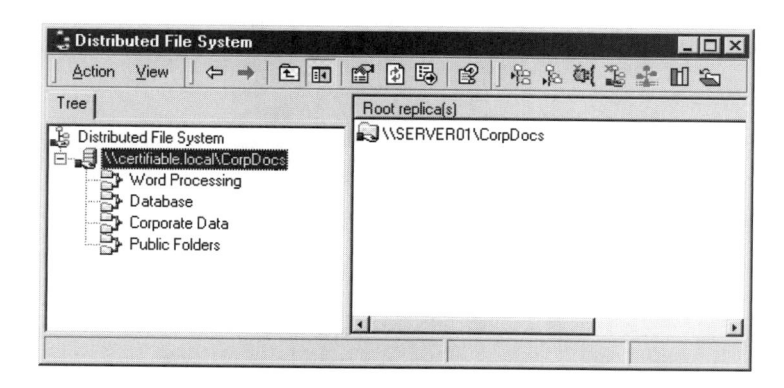

SCENARIO & SOLUTION

When would I want to use Dfs client as opposed to Active Directory client with Dfs?	Active Directory client works only with domain-based Dfs. If you implement a stand-alone Dfs topology, downlevel clients will need the Dfs client.
How is replication handled in a fault-tolerant Dfs implementation?	The File Replication Service (FRS) replicates the contents of Dfs shared folders at 15-minute intervals.

Distributed File System (Dfs) is a tool for making shared files and folders more accessible to users. Windows 2000 supports domain-based Dfs (also called fault-tolerant Dfs), where shares can be located anywhere in the domain, and replicated for redundancy. To access domain-based Dfs shares, Windows 9x and NT 4 clients need to have the Active Directory client installed.

✓ TWO-MINUTE DRILL

Configuring Disks and Volumes

- ❑ A physical disk is a single hard disk drive.
- ❑ A physical disk can be configured as a basic disk, which uses traditional DOS-style partitions.
- ❑ A physical disk can also be configured as a dynamic disk, which is volume-oriented rather than partition-oriented.
- ❑ When using dynamic disks, you can create a single volume from multiple physical disks.
- ❑ NTFS is the preferred file system for Windows 2000 because of its fine-grained security and permissions.
- ❑ Downlevel Windows 9x clients can only read data from FAT (and FAT32) volumes on the local system.
- ❑ If you plan to dual-boot Windows 2000 with Windows 9x, all volumes to which the downlevel clients need access must be formatted as FAT or FAT32.

Configuring and Enforcing Disk Quotas

- ❑ Disk quotas are a means of setting limits on each user's storage allotment.
- ❑ Disk quotas are available on NTFS volumes only.
- ❑ Enforcing disk quotas is a two-step process. You must set quota limits and also enable the enforcement of disk quotas.
- ❑ You can enable disk quotas through the Quota tab of a disk's Properties dialog box, or through group policies.
- ❑ When you first set quota limits, they're applied equally to all users.
- ❑ You can set individual quota limits through the Quota Entries button in a disk's Properties dialog box.

Implementing Encrypting File System (EFS)

- Encrypting File System (EFS) is a feature of NTFS that allows users to encrypt their own folders and files for security.
- Encryption is transparent to the person who encrypted the file and to applications.
- You can enable encryption through a file or folder's Properties dialog box. Click the Advanced button on the General tab of the Properties dialog box.
- Users who encrypt shared objects will prevent other users from accessing those objects.
- If a user encrypts a shared folder that others need access to, the simplest solution is to have that user decrypt the files.
- If the owner of an encrypted file or folder leaves the company, an administrator can regain access to the object using an EFS Recover Agent.
- A file or folder can be compressed or encrypted, but not both.

Implementing and Managing a Distributed File System (Dfs)

- Distributed file system (Dfs) allows an administrator to create a single container for multiple shared folders. Users can access those folders without knowing the specific location of the folder.
- Stand-alone Dfs, which was introduced in Windows NT 4.0, stores the Dfs topology on a single computer. It provides no fault-tolerance and isn't part of Active Directory.
- Domain-based Dfs makes the Dfs topology part of the Active Directory service, provides fault-tolerance, and can be used with multiple servers and domain controllers.
- To set up a Dfs topology, you first create a Dfs root in the Distributed File System administrative tool.
- Once you have a Dfs root in place, you can add Dfs links to it.
- Each Dfs link is simply a pointer to some shared folder in the network.
- Downlevel Windows 9*x* and NT clients will need to have the Active Directory client installed to access domain-based Dfs shares.

SELF TEST

Configuring Disks and Volumes

1. You are an administrator of a Windows 2000 network. Your boss asks you to configure his computer to dual-boot between Windows 2000 and Windows 98. The computer has a single hard disk that contains two partitions—a system partition and a data partition—each 4GB in size. Both partitions must be formatted so they are accessible to both Windows 2000 and Windows 98. What should you do? (Choose all that apply.)

    A. Format the system partition as FAT32.
    B. Format the system partition as NTFS.
    C. Format the data partition as FAT32.
    D. Format the data partition as NTFS.

2. You are an administrator of a Windows 2000 network. All of the client computers on the network have been upgraded from Windows NT Workstation 4.0 to Windows 2000 Professional. Each client computer contains a single basic disk formatted as an NTFS volume, drive C:. One of the computers needs to run a large custom application that's hard-coded to use only drive C:. Currently, there isn't sufficient space available for the application. Upon inspection, you discover that there is still some unallocated space on the drive. How could you extend the amount of space available on drive C: without deleting the existing partition?

    A. Create a partition from the unallocated space, and configure the partition as a mount point on drive C:.
    B. Convert the disk from a basic disk to a dynamic disk.
    C. Create a mirrored volume from the unallocated space on the disk.
    D. Create a stripe set from the unallocated space on the disk.

3. Which of the following would be the correct file system arrangement?

    A. Format all partitions as NTFS.
    B. Format all partitions as FAT32.
    C. Format C:, D:, F:, and G: as FAT32, E: as NTFS.
    D. Format C:, D:, and G: as FAT32, E: and F: as NTFS.

Configuring and Enforcing Disk Quotas

4. Which of the follow is required for using disk quotas?

   A. Basic disk
   B. Dynamic disk
   C. FAT or FAT32
   D. NTFS

5. You are the network administrator for your company's Windows 2000 network. To prevent users from storing excessive amounts of data on the hard disk, you create disk quotas on users' home folders. Shortly thereafter, users complain that they are no longer able to create new folders. Upon inspection, you discover that none of the users have reached their quota limits yet in their home folders. What can you do to enforce quotas on the home folders and still allow users to create folders and store data up to their quota limits?

   A. Create a separate partition for each user's home folder, then configure quotas on each partition.
   B. Place all of the home folders on a single, separate partition and configure quotas on that partition.
   C. Instruct each user to take ownership of his or her own home folders, and compress them.
   D. Create a separate quota limit for each individual user using the Quota Entries window.

6. You are an administrator of a Windows 2000 Server computer that acts as a file and print server. You have recently enabled and configured quota limits for all users. After time passes, you discover that several users have already exceeded their limits and are still able to save files to the server. What should you do?

   A. Upgrade the hard disks on the server to dynamic disks.
   B. Enable the enforcement of quota limits.
   C. Set a quota limit for each individual user.
   D. Use the secedit command to enforce the quota immediately.

7. Which of the following best describes the effect of setting the Enable Disk Quotas policy to Enabled?

   A. Disk quota management is enabled, users cannot disable it.
   B. Disk quota management is enabled, users can disable it.
   C. Disk quota limits are enforced, users can disable the enforcement.
   D. Disk quota limits are enforced, users cannot disable the enforcement.

Implementing Encrypting File System (EFS)

8. Which of the following best describes the purpose of EFS?
   A. EFS compresses folders and files so they consume less disk space.
   B. EFS automatically encrypts files and folders just before they're sent as e-mail attachments.
   C. EFS allows a user to encrypt a file or folder so only that user can access it.
   D. EFS allows a single file or folder to span multiple physical disks.

9. You are the network administrator for your company's Windows 2000 network. A user named Hilda has created a folder named CorpDocs on a file server. She has encrypted about half of the files in that folder. You are instructed to make all of Hilda's files accessible to all users in her department. You share the folder and assign appropriate users Allow-Read share permission and Allow-Read NTFS permission. Users report that they are able to access only about half the files in the new share. What must you do to grant appropriate users the ability to read all files in the shared folder?
   A. Change the share permission to Full Control.
   B. Change the NTFS permission to Full Control.
   C. Share Hilda's public key with all of the users who need access to the files.
   D. Instruct Hilda to decrypt the files.

10. Which of the following is required if you wish to use EFS?
    A. Mirrored volumes
    B. Dynamic disks
    C. NTFS
    D. FAT 32

11. You are the administrator of your company's Windows 2000 file servers. A user named Hank leaves the company, and you need to allow other users to access his files to take over some of his responsibilities. You grant all appropriate users Full Control of the files Hank has left behind. Users report that when trying to access some of Hank's old files, they receive an "Access is denied" error message. Which of the following is the most likely cause of the problem?
    A. Hank compressed the files.
    B. Hank secured the files with EFS.
    C. The files are in a Dfs location.
    D. The files are protected by special permissions that Full Control cannot override.

12. You are an administrator of a Windows 2000 Server computer that acts as a file and print server. Users store their files on the server and occasionally use EFS to secure their files. An employee named Chang left the company and has been replaced by an employee named Juan. When Juan tries to open some of the files that Chang has left behind, he is denied access to some of them. Upon inspection, you discover that Chang has left some of his files encrypted. What must you do to give Juan access to the encrypted files?

    A. Use an EFS Recovery Agent to decrypt the files.

    B. Take ownership of the files and grant Juan Full Control of those files.

    C. Assign Juan the Allow-Take Ownership permission for the files.

    D. Move all the encrypted files to a FAT32 partition and instruct Juan to access the files on that partition.

Implementing and Managing a Distributed File System (Dfs)

13. What is the primary purpose of Dfs?

    A. To compress files and folders so they take up less space.

    B. To provide security for sensitive files and folders.

    C. To allow users to access shares without knowing specifically where those shares are located.

    D. To allow Windows 9*x* computers to access shared files and folders on a Windows 2000 file server.

14. Which of the following best describes a *Dfs link*?

    A. A central storage container for shared folders throughout the domain.

    B. A pointer to a shared folder located somewhere in the domain.

    C. A shared folder on a domain controller.

    D. A shared folder on a stand-alone Dfs implementation.

15. You are an administrator of a Windows 2000 domain with Active Directory implemented. All client computers on the network are either Windows 95 or Windows 98. You plan to set up a domain-based Dfs topology that will make it easy for users to find resources. What should you do to ensure that all client computers will be able to access resources on the Distributed File System? (Choose two.)

    A. Install the Windows 2000 Administration Pack on all of the client computers.

    B. Install the standard DFS client on all of the client computers.

    C. Install the Active Directory client on all of the client computers.

    D. Upgrade all client computers to Windows 2000 Professional.

LAB QUESTION

You are the domain administrator for your company network, which consists of some 3000 users. You've discovered that many users are downloading huge multimedia files for their personal use, which in turn is causing hard disks to fill up to capacity. All user accounts use folder redirection to allow users to roam. You need to find a way to prevent users from piling up these multimedia files in their home folders, without restricting their access to the Internet. What should you do?

SELF TEST ANSWERS

Configuring Disks and Volumes

1. ☑ **A and C** are correct. Both partitions must be formatted as FAT32 to be accessible to both operating systems.
   ☒ **B and D** are incorrect because Windows 98 would be unable to access the NTFS volumes.

2. ☑ **A** is correct. The simple solution here is to create a new partition from the unallocated space and configure it as a mount point so it appears as a folder on drive C:.
   ☒ **B** is wrong because converting the basic disk to a dynamic disk wouldn't increase the storage space available on drive C:.
   ☒ **C** is wrong because you need two physical disks to create a mirrored volume, and even if you did so, that wouldn't increase the amount of space available on drive C:.
   ☒ **D** is incorrect because a stripe set would do nothing to increase the amount of space available on drive C:.

3. ☑ **C** is correct. All partitions should be formatted as FAT32, except for the partition that specifically needs NTFS security capabilities.
   ☒ **A** is wrong because Windows 98 wouldn't be able to access the NTFS permissions.
   ☒ **B** is wrong because drive E: needs NTFS. **D** is wrong because the swap partition, F:, must be FAT32.

Configuring and Enforcing Disk Quotas

4. ☑ **D** is correct because NTFS is the only required option for using disk quotas.
   ☒ **A and B** are wrong because either basic or dynamic disks will allow you to use NTFS, which is the only requirement here.
   ☒ **C** is wrong because FAT does not support disk quotas.

5. ☑ **B** is correct. Since quota limits are calculated on a per user and partition basis, placing all the home folders in a separate partition, then setting quota limits on just that partition would ensure that only files and folders within that partition would be charged against the users' limits.
   ☒ **A and D** are wrong because neither would ensure that only files and folders within the home folder are charged against the users' quota limits.
   ☒ **C** is wrong because the users haven't reached their limits yet, and compressing objects wouldn't reduce the charges against their limits anyway.

Self Test Answers

6. ☑ **B** is correct. You've already enabled disk quotas and set limits for all users; they're just not being enforced. You need to enable Enforce Disk Quota Limit to enforce the quota limits.
   ☒ **A** is wrong because converting a basic disk to a dynamic disk would not enforce quota limits.
   ☒ **C** is wrong because there is nothing in the question that asks you to configure different limits for different users.
   ☒ **D** is wrong because there's no mention of ever having enabled the enforcement of quota limits.

7. ☑ **A** is correct. Enabling quota management prevents users from disabling it.
   ☒ **B** is wrong because once disk quotas are enabled from a group policy, users can no longer disable quotas.
   ☒ **C and D** are wrong because enforcement of quotas is always optional and disabled unless you explicitly enforce those limits.

Implementing Encrypting File System (EFS)

8. ☑ **C** is correct. EFS is used for security purposes to make a file or folder accessible only to the person who encrypted the file.
   ☒ **A** is wrong because encryption has nothing to do with compression.
   ☒ **B** is wrong because EFS encrypts a file or folder immediately.
   ☒ **D** is wrong because encryption is used strictly for security and has nothing to do with spanning physical disks.

9. ☑ **D** is correct. Other users won't be able to read Hilda's encrypted files until she decrypts them.
   ☒ **A and B** are incorrect because granting Full Control would do nothing toward giving users access to Hilda's encrypted files.
   ☒ **C** is wrong because you cannot decrypt files with a public key.

10. ☑ **C** is correct. EFS is available in any NTFS file system.
    ☒ **A and B** are wrong because all that's required is the NTFS file system.
    ☒ **D** is wrong because FAT does not support EFS.

11. ☑ **B** is correct. The most likely scenario is that Hank secured the files using EFS, preventing other users from opening them.
    ☒ **A** is wrong because even if Hank had compressed the files, that wouldn't prevent other users from accessing them.
    ☒ **C** is wrong because storing the files in a Dfs location wouldn't prevent users with appropriate permissions from opening the files.
    ☒ **D** is incorrect because Full Control wouldn't be restricted by special permissions.

12. ☑ **A** is correct. You'll need to use an EFS Recovery Agent to decrypt the files.
    ☒ **B** and **C** are wrong because they won't allow Juan to decrypt the files.
    ☒ **D** is wrong because you'd need to take ownership of the files before moving them. Furthermore, you'd lose all the other features of NTFS by moving the files to a FAT partition.

Implementing and Managing a Distributed File System (Dfs)

13. ☑ **C** is correct. The main function of Dfs is to give users easy access to shares without having to browse the network to locate those resources.
    ☒ **A** and **C** are wrong because Dfs has nothing to do with encryption or compression.
    ☒ **D** is wrong because Windows 9*x* computers are able to access shared folders without a Dfs implementation in place.

14. ☑ **B** is correct. A DFS link is a pointer to a shared folder that could be anywhere on the network.
    ☒ **A** is wrong. It more accurately describes a Dfs root.
    ☒ **C** and **D** are wrong because links are not folders, they're pointers to folders.

15. ☑ **C** is correct. You need only install the Active Directory client on the Windows 95 and Windows 98 clients to enable them to use Dfs.
    ☒ **A** is wrong, as the AdminPak would not be required on the client computers.
    ☒ **B** is wrong, as the standard Dfs client wouldn't allow those computers to access a domain-based Distributed File System.
    ☒ **D** is wrong, as the upgrade would not be required.

LAB ANSWER

Disk quotas are clearly the solution to this problem. For starters, you can create a partition on which to store users' home folders. Format the partition with NTFS, enable disk quotas, and set limits to be applied to all users. Move all users' home folders to the new volume, and enable the enforcement of disk quotas on the volume.

11
Configuring Internet Information Services (IIS)

CERTIFICATION OBJECTIVES

11.01	Creating Web Sites
11.02	Creating FTP Sites
11.03	Securing Web and FTP Sites
11.04	Maintaining and Troubleshooting IIS
✓	Two-Minute Drill
Q&A	Self Test

Windows 2000 Server ships with Microsoft's Internet Information Services (IIS) version 5. As the name implies, IIS allows you to set up web sites, as well as File Transfer Protocol (FTP) and Network News Transfer Protocol (NNTP) sites. The sites can be made available to the public through the Internet, or just used privately within your own network. (Sites that are used only internally are referred to as *intranet sites* or *intrasites* in Exam 70-218.) You can host as many web and FTP sites as you wish using a single installation of IIS on a single Windows 2000 Server computer. As you'll see, the actual site content can be placed anywhere in your network—the content doesn't have to physically reside on the server.

A basic Windows 2000 Server installation will automatically set up the components you need for creating basic web sites. Be aware, however, that there are some additional components available to you. We'll install what's needed as we progress through the chapter. However, if you discover that something's missing on your own server, you can install the missing component as you would any other. That is, open Add/Remove Programs in the Control Panel and click Add/Remove Windows Components. When the Windows Components Wizard opens, click Internet Information Services (IIS), and then click the Details button to see all the available IIS components.

CERTIFICATION OBJECTIVE 11.01

Creating Web Sites

Windows 2000 automatically creates a single, default web site on your server, in the folder c:\inetpub\wwwroot. It's not necessary to put all of your web content into that one folder, though. You can use any folder in any computer in the domain to store web content. In fact, you can create as many web sites as you wish, all in different locations throughout the domain, using virtual directories. Then, use the default web folder as the "root folder" from which all of your web content is available. This is the most common scenario, so let's take it from the top, starting with creating folders for your web content.

Defining Virtual Directories (Web Sharing)

A *virtual directory* is a folder that contains web or FTP content for a site, but that isn't contained within the home directory. It's "virtual" in that, to a user visiting the site, the virtual directory appears to be just a subfolder within the site. In truth, the virtual directory could be a folder located on an entirely separate drive or computer. For example, let's say your default web site (C:\Inetpub\wwwroot) is located on Server01. The URL for that site would be http://Server01.

Now let's say you want to create numerous web sites that appear as folders within that site. Each virtual directory would have a physical location, which could be expressed as either a standard Windows path or a UNC path. Each virtual directory could also have an *alias,* which is just a short name that's used as an alternative to the entire path. The URL that points to each site would be http://*servername/alias,* where *servername* is the name of the server that's hosting the default web site.

Folders that are contained within the default web site need not have aliases assigned to them. In that case, the folder name can still be used in the URL to identify the folder from a URL, as in the examples listed in Table 11-1, where the server name is assumed to be Server01.

Creating a virtual directory is an easy process. Basically, you share the folder using the Web Sharing tab (as opposed to the standard Sharing tab) in the folder's Properties dialog box. Exercise 11-1 takes you through all the required steps.

TABLE 11-1   Examples of URLs for Accessing Local Sites

Physical Location	Assigned Alias	URL
c:\inetpub\wwwroot	None; this is the home directory	http://Server01
e:\SalesFolder	Sales	http://Server01/Sales
e:\PR\PublicInfo	Public	http://Server01/Public
\\Server02\AnotherSite\WildSide	Wild	http://Server01/Wild
c:\inetpub\wwwroot\notVirtual	Not needed because folder is contained within the default web site folder	http://Server01/notVirtual

EXERCISE 11-1

Creating a Virtual Directory

In this exercise, you'll create a virtual directory on a server computer. You'll need to log in to your domain controller (or any other server) with administrative privileges, and then follow these steps:

1. Open My Computer, and navigate to the drive and folder in which you want to place the new folder.

2. Choose File | New | Folder from My Computer's menu bar, and give the folder a meaningful name (I'll be creating a folder named E:\Practice Web on Server01, but you can do this on any server and drive on your domain).

3. Right-click the new folder and choose Properties.

4. Click the Web Sharing tab and choose Share This Folder. The Edit Alias dialog box appears.

5. In the Alias text box, type a brief name you'll use as the alias for the folder, such as **Practice**.

6. Leave all the other options at their default values. Click OK to return to the Web Sharing tab. The alias you specified appears in the Aliases list, as in Figure 11-1. Note that you could create additional aliases for the virtual directory using the Add button, but we'll stick with one alias for this example.

7. Click OK to close the Properties dialog box. Note that the web-shared folder's icon doesn't display the "sharing hand" that other shares display.

Now let's create a simple web page so you have something to browse to in this new web site.

1. Open the folder you just shared.

2. Right-click within the empty folder and choose New | Text Document.

3. Name the new file **default.htm** and skip the warning message about changing the extension.

4. Right-click the new icon and choose Open With | Notepad.

Creating Web Sites **485**

FIGURE 11-1

A folder named Practice web-shared with the alias *Practice*

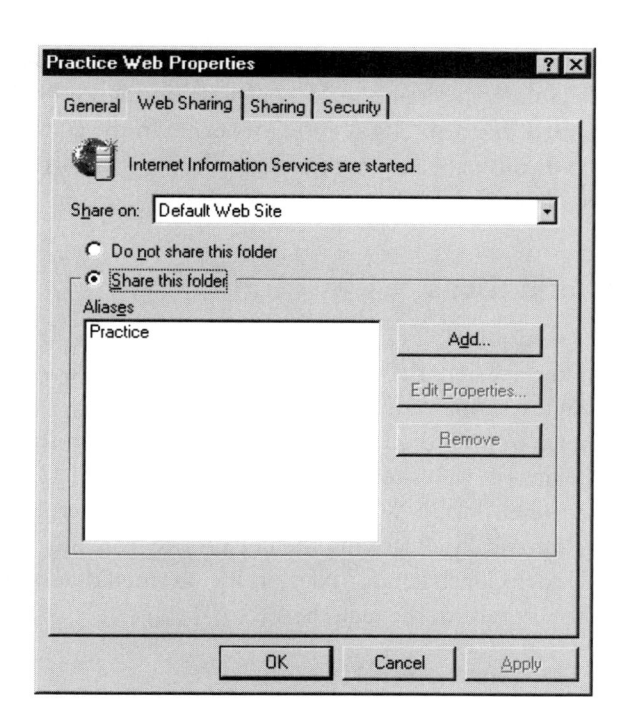

5. Type some basic HTML and text, as follows:

```
<html>
<head></head>
<body>

I am default.htm in the Practice site.

</body>
</html>
```

6. Close and save the document.
7. Close the folder and My Computer.

You should be able to view the sample web page right now, from any computer in the domain, by typing **http://Server01/Practice** in the Address bar of your web browser or Windows Explorer.

In the IIS snap-in, virtual directories appear as folders contained within the Default Web Site node. For example, in Figure 11-2, I've created a virtual directory named Practice. Highlighting its name in the console tree displays its contents in the details pane. In that example, the Practice virtual directory contains only a single file, named default.htm.

Accessing Local Sites

As mentioned, local users can access sites using simple URLs—they don't need to know where the site is physically located to open the site. The default web site that's at c:\inetpub\wwwroot can be accessed by just the server name, the domain name, or even the IP address of the server, as in the following examples (where the default web site is on server01, IP address 192.168.100.2, domain name certifiable.local). When accessed from the server itself, some IIS documents open automatically. Accessing the default site from any other computer just displays an "Under Construction" page, as it's assumed that other users are visiting to view content, not to manage the site.

- http://server01
- http://certifiable.local
- http://192.168.100.2

FIGURE 11-2

The Practice virtual directory within the Default Web Site

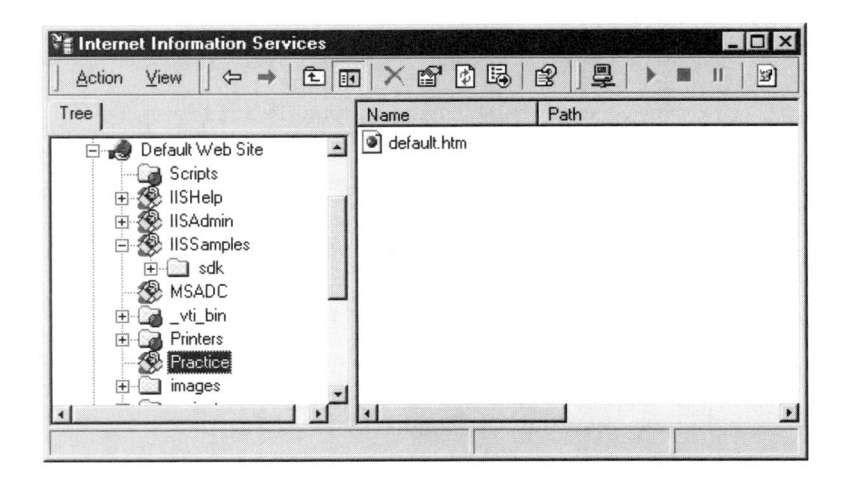

Managing Printers Remotely

In Figure 11-2, a folder named Printers appears in the console tree, just above the Practice folder. The Printers folder represents a fringe benefit of IIS 5—it can be used to manage printers remotely. For example, let's say you create a print server that hosts one or more printers. If you install IIS on that server, you can easily administer printers remotely from any web browser. Just enter the URL **http://*servername*/printers**, where *servername* is the name of the print server. You'll then be able to manage printers from the "All Printers on *servername*" web page that opens.

Creating Virtual Web Servers

In the early days of the Internet, every web site URL, such as www.microsoft.com, essentially represented a single web server. IIS 5 supports *virtual servers,* whereby each web site appears to clients to be hosted on an entirely different machine. For example, rather than have multiple folders contained within a single site with URLs like http://*servername*/sales, http://*servername*/freebies, and so forth, each site could just have a name like http://sales or http://freebies. This approach also allows the web sites to be moved to other web servers as a domain changes over time. You can keep the same name, and just point to a different web server when necessary.

Unlike virtual directories, which are contained within the Default Web Site folder, a new virtual web site will be listed at the same level as the Default Web Site folder. As such, it can be managed independently of the Default Web Site. Also, like the Default Web Site, this new site could contain its own virtual directories.

The first step to creating a virtual server is to create a home directory for the site. This can be any folder on any drive in your system, or any drive on any computer in the network for that matter. Once you've created the folder, go ahead and run the IIS snap-in by clicking the Start button and choosing Programs | Administrative Tools | Internet Services Manager.

In the IIS console, right-click the server name and choose New | Web Site. This launches the Web Site Creation Wizard. You'll be prompted to enter a description of the site. Then, you'll need to select one of three possible methods of distinguishing the virtual site, as shown in Figure 11-3. You need only choose one option to uniquely identify the virtual site—a unique IP address, a unique port, or a host header. We'll look at each option in the sections that follow.

FIGURE 11-3

Options for uniquely identifying the virtual web server

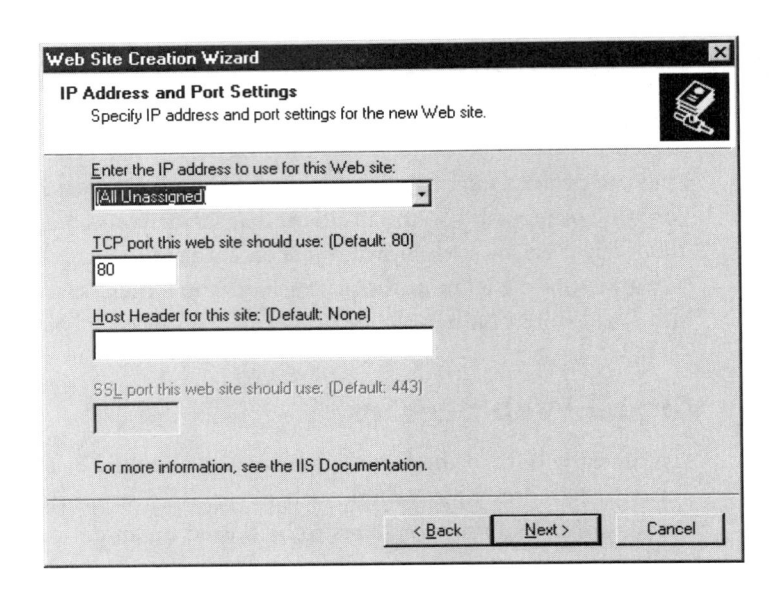

Distinguishing Sites by IP Address

The Enter The IP Address To Use For This Web Site drop-down list contains all IP addresses that the server is currently configured to use. You can use any available IP address to uniquely identify this web site. If you plan to use a unique port number or host header to uniquely identify the site, just leave this first option at the default setting of (All Unassigned).

Distinguishing Sites by Port

TCP port 80 is the *well-known port* used by all web browsers when no other port is specified in a URL. You can use different port numbers to distinguish among multiple sites in your network. To access these sites, users have to add *:number* to their URLs. For example, let's say you create a site at port TCP 91 on Server01. To access that site, users would enter the URL http://Server01:91.

Distinguishing Sites by Host Header

Host headers provide a means of using a single IP address and port to access multiple sites. Rather than specifying a unique IP address or port for the site, just enter a brief name for the site under Host Header For This Site. For the sake of example, let's say you enter **Virtuality** as the host header. The rest of the wizard will post questions similar to those you saw when creating a virtual directory, including the path to the home directory and permissions for accessing the site.

Using a host header has the advantage of giving the site a URL with a simple name without an IP address or port number. The user can just access it by its name, such as http://virtuality. But there's a catch. You need to provide name resolution by creating a DNS host (A) record that maps the name to the TCP/IP address of the web server.

exam
🐘 **watch**
If you want to use a short name like http://virtsite to access a virtual web server, you must define a host header and *add an appropriate name resolution record to the DNS server.*

Tuning Web Site Performance

To tune the performance of a site, right-click its name in the IIS console and choose Properties. Then, click the Performance tab to reveal the options shown in Figure 11-4. The first option is simple enough—drag the slider to indicate the number of hits you expect your site to receive each day.

Bandwidth throttling gives you control over how much bandwidth each of your web sites is allowed to consume. For example, let's say you're hosting six web sites on a single server, some of which are intrasites, others of which are public web sites.

FIGURE 11-4

Performance tuning options

Local users of the intrasite complain that it's taking too long to access company web sites. You could set throttles on the public web sites to limit the amount of bandwidth they consume, thereby conserving bandwidth for the intrasites. Process throttling is the same idea, though with the focus on CPU usage rather than bandwidth.

on the job

The white paper titled "Deploying Windows 2000 with IIS 5.0 for Dot Coms: Best Practices" at www.microsoft.com/windows2000/docs/iisbprac2.doc provides planning, testing, deployment, and management guidelines for setting up a public web site with IIS.

CERTIFICATION OBJECTIVE 11.02

Creating FTP Sites

File Transfer Protocol is an Internet service used for downloading files from, or uploading files to, some central location. To create an FTP site, you need to install the File Transfer Protocol (FTP) Server component from IIS using Add/Remove Programs, as described earlier in this chapter. Once installed, IIS displays a node titled Default FTP Site, which will act as the root. The URL for the default site will be FTP://*computername*, where *computername* is, as usual, the name of the computer on which IIS is running.

As with web sites, you can use virtual directories to create folders within the root. Like web sites, the virtual directories will be accessible through URLs, with the same syntax, FTP://*computername/alias*. Exercise 11-2 takes you through the steps necessary to create a virtual directory and use it as an FTP site.

EXERCISE 11-2

Creating an FTP Site

In this exercise, you'll create an FTP site. To complete this exercise, you must have already installed the File Transfer Protocol (FTP) Server component of IIS. You'll need to log in to the server that's the default web site server for your network (I'll use Server01, as usual):

1. Open My Computer, and open the drive on which you want to place the FTP site. Create a folder and give it a name (I'll use **E:\FTPSite** as the folder name for this example).

2. Click the Start button and choose Programs | Administrative Tools | Internet Services Manager. The Internet Information Services snap-in opens.

3. Right-click the Default FTP Site node and choose New | Virtual Directory. The Virtual Directory Creation Wizard opens. Click Next to bypass the Welcome screen.

4. Enter an alias for the site (I'll use **FTPPractice** for this example) and click the Next button.

5. On the next wizard page, type the path (or use the Browse button to navigate to the path) to the folder you created in Step 1 (E:\FTPSite in my example). Then, click the Next button.

6. For this exercise, we'll allow users to upload and download, so select both the Read and Write options in the next wizard page, then click Next.

7. Click the Finish button to close the wizard.

If you expand the Default FTP Site node in IIS, you'll see the site listed by its alias. The URL for this new virtual directory will be ftp://*comptername/alias*. For example, if you created the virtual directory on Server01, and provided the alias FTPPractice, the URL will be ftp://Server01/FTPPractice.

To control access to an existing FTP site, right-click the site's node in the console tree and choose Properties. On the Security Accounts tab, shown in Figure 11-5, you'll see some basic authentication options. If you disable anonymous access, users will be required to enter a valid username and password to access the FTP site. If you choose to disable anonymous access, you'll see a warning message that *basic authentication* will be used to send the user's password, along with the warning that the unencrypted passwords aren't secure and can be hacked. As you'll see in a moment, you'll have more flexibility than that when working with web sites.

FIGURE 11-5

The Security Accounts tab of an FTP site

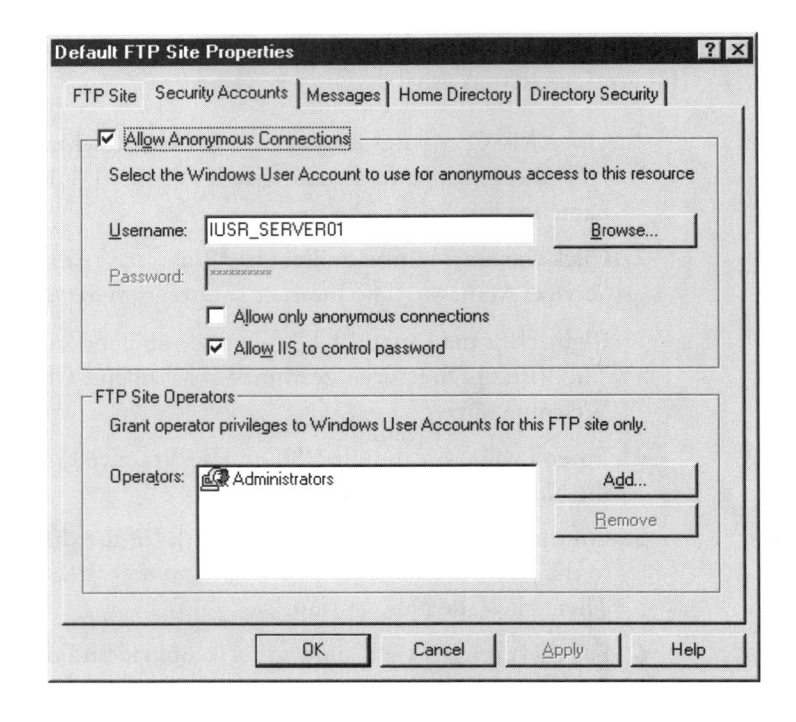

exam 🕭 **atch** With FTP, you only get two authentication options: anonymous access (no passwords transmitted) or basic authentication (passwords transmitted in clear text).

On the Home Directory tab, you'll see Read and Write access permissions. As you might expect, Write permissions allow users to upload files to the site. Read permissions allow users to download files from the site.

SCENARIO & SOLUTION

Must I use default.htm as the name of the home page on IIS?	You can specify default document names on the Documents tab of the Web Site Properties dialog box.
Does inheritance apply to IIS sites?	Yes, settings at the root level are inherited by child objects. For example, settings at the Default Web Site node propagate to any virtual directories within the root. If you right-click the server name and choose Properties, you'll find a Master Properties option, which can be used to set properties that will be inherited by all sites.

CERTIFICATION OBJECTIVE 11.03

Securing Web and FTP Sites

IIS offers many options for securing web sites, and Exam 70-218 will expect you to know which type of security is best for different scenarios. Unlike FTP sites, web sites offer several authentication options for you to choose from. You can also control access to resources using permissions, and create secure web sites that use Secure Sockets Layer (SSL) to encrypt all transmissions. Let's take a look at the various authentication options for web sites first.

Authentication Methods

Most web sites and FTP sites that you visit in your daily use of the Internet rely on simple *anonymous authentication,* which is basically no authentication at all. Anonymous authentication is the default setting for sites you create with IIS, though it can be changed. In the IIS snap-in, right-click the site or virtual directory for which you want to change the authentication method and choose Properties. In the dialog box that opens, click the Directory Security tab. Under Anonymous Access And Authentication Control, click the Edit button to get to the Authentication Methods dialog box, shown in Figure 11-6.

FIGURE 11-6

The Authentication Methods dialog box

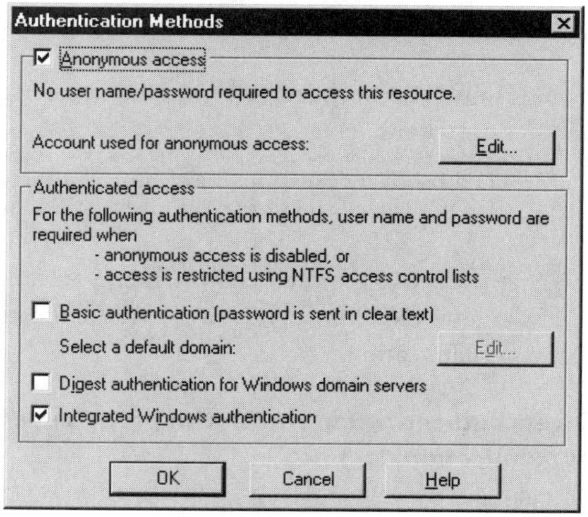

If you click the Edit button you'll see a small dialog box that shows the username and password used for anonymous access. Each anonymous user that accesses the site is given the username IUSR_*computername*, where *computername* is the NetBIOS name on which IIS is stored. By default, IIS generates a random password that's used to "authenticate" all anonymous users.

Basic Authentication

Basic authentication provides simple authentication where each user who wants to access a site must have a user account and password on the web server. These users can also log on locally to the server, provided they have the right to log on locally. The biggest advantage of basic authentication is that it's supported by all web browsers. The biggest disadvantage is that authentication information is transmitted in *clear text* format. Thus, anyone running a protocol analyzer could capture usernames and passwords, thereby compromising the overall security of the web site. Thus, if you must use basic authentication, you want the user accounts on the server to have many restrictions placed upon them. That way, if security is compromised, the unauthorized user won't have administrative privileges on the network. Optionally, you can use basic authentication with SSL (as described a little later in this chapter) to encrypt passwords.

Digest Authentication

Digest authentication allows web clients to send authentication data in encrypted form, thereby offering protection from protocol analyzers. Digest authentication can also be used with proxy servers. There are some prerequisites to using digest authentication:

- All user accounts must be located in an Active Directory domain, not a stand-alone server.
- Each user account must have Store Password Using Reversible Encryption enabled through AD Users and Computers.

Once those two requirements are met, you can choose Digest Authentication For Windows Domain Servers in the Authentication Methods dialog box to activate digest authentication.

Digest authentication works with proxy servers, whereas Integrated Windows authentication does not.

Integrated Windows Authentication

Integrated Windows authentication is best suited for intrasites, where there is no public access. This is the authentication method that most resembles earlier Windows NT Challenge/Response (NT CHAP). The web client uses the same credentials that authenticated the user when logging on to the domain to authenticate itself to the IIS server, so users don't have to continually enter their username and password to access sites. If the logon credentials aren't sufficient to access the web site, the user is automatically prompted to enter a password, and the password is then transmitted in encrypted form.

Getting Around FTP's Authentication Limitations

After learning about all the authentication options that are available for web sites, you might be wondering whether there's a way to get some of that into your FTP sites. The simple solution to that problem is to not create a web site at all. Rather, place all the documents that need to be made accessible offline in a folder, and then create a *document web site* by not defining a default home page for the site. Then, enable directory browsing for the shared folder.

The other approach is the use Web Distributed Authoring and Versioning (WebDAV), which extends the HTTP 1.1 protocol to allow clients to publish, manage, and lock resources in a WebDAV publishing directory on the server. Users can access and manage documents in the site using Internet Explorer 5 (or later), Microsoft Office 2000 (or later) applications, and My Network Places. The procedure for creating a publishing directory is the same as that for creating a virtual directory. You first create a folder, and then use the IIS snap-in to create a virtual directory. Grant Read, Write, and Browsing permissions to the virtual directory.

Clients will be able to access the site like any other web site, using an HTTP URL (for example, http://*computername*). But, with no default web page defined, and directory browsing enabled, users will see the contents of the folder in a hyperlinked directory display. Those users can then use their web browsers to download documents from the site.

exam
🐶 **atch**

Using a document web site with Integrated Windows authentication provides a quick and easy means of providing local employees access to a document web site without granting any access to the public at large.

FROM THE CLASSROOM

How to Remotely Administer IIS

By default, IIS administration can only be performed on the local host. But with some simple configuration, you can use the browser-based version of Internet Services Manager (HTML) to remotely administer IIS over the Internet or through a proxy server. First, you need to open the IIS snap-in. Right-click the Administration Web Site node, choose Properties, and click the Web Site tab. Jot down the TCP Port listed under Web Site Identification (for example, 8736).

Next, click the Directory Security tab, and then click the Edit button under IP Address And Domain Name Restrictions. Use the options to grant access to specific computers or domains from which you'll want to access IIS, or even grant access to all computers.

To access the administration web site remotely, specify the port number in the URL. For example, if the site is on Server01, port 8736, and you want to access it from another site in the same domain, enter the URL http://Sever01:8736. If you've registered a domain name for the site, and want to gain access from the Internet, just add the appropriate port number to the standard URL, as in http://www.MySite.com:8736.

—*Alan Simpson, MA, MCSA*

Controlling Site Access Through Permissions

You can also control access to sites and virtual directories using the various permissions that appear when defining a site or virtual directory, or after the fact by right-clicking the site or directory name in the IIS console and choosing Properties. Permissions will be accessible from the Home Directory or Virtual Directory tab, as shown in Figure 11-7.

Basic permissions include the following:

- **Read** Allows users to read and download files and folders.
- **Write** Allows users to upload files and change content in Write-enabled documents.
- **Directory Browsing** Allows users to view a hypertext listing of directories.
- **Script source access** Allows users to view the source code of scripts on the server for which Read or Write permissions are set.

FIGURE 11-7

The Home Directory tab of a site's Properties dialog box

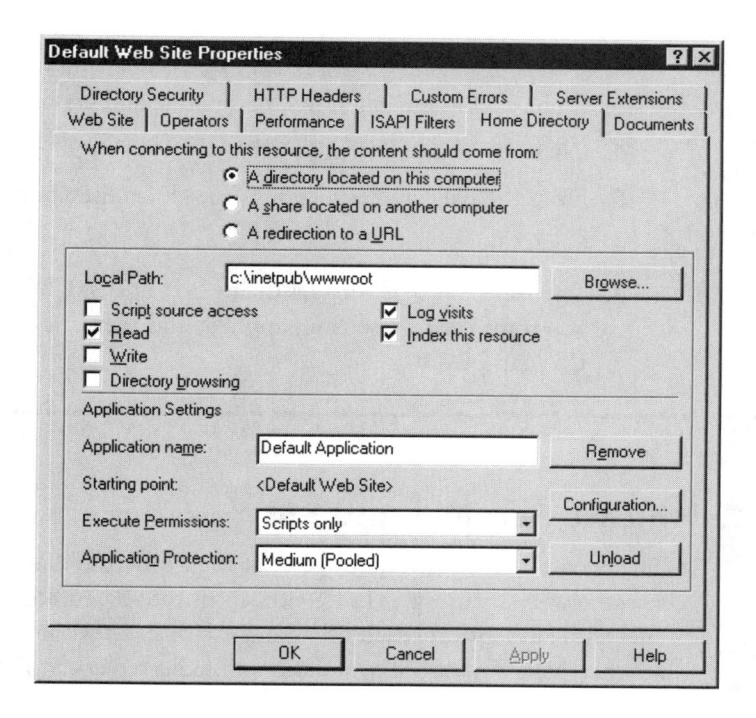

Under Application Settings, the Execute Permissions option lets you choose whether users are permitted to run scripts only, scripts and executable, or neither.

If you want users to be able to run ISAPI scripts, you must set the Execute Permissions option to Scripts And Executables from the drop-down list.

EXERCISE 11-3

Enabling ISAPI Applications

This exercise gives you a little hands-on practice in administering a web site. You'll be taken through the steps to configure the Default Web Site to allow execution of ISAPI applications. But once you're in the Properties dialog box, you could choose whatever settings are realistic for your web server. You must log in to the web server with administrative privileges to complete this exercise.

1. If the IIS snap-in isn't already open, click the Start button and choose Programs | Administrative Tools | Internet Services Manager.

2. Expand the server name node.
3. Right-click the Default Web Site node and choose Properties.
4. Click the Home Directory tab.
5. From the Execute Permissions drop-down list, choose Scripts And Executables.
6. Click OK.
7. The Inheritance Overrides dialog box opens. Choose child objects to which you want the new settings applied, and then click OK. You're returned to the IIS snap-in.

Using Certificate Services and SSL

The Secure Communications pane of the Properties dialog box allows you to set up a secure web site using SSL. IIS uses certificate-based SSL, which allows servers and clients to authenticate each other and establish a session whereby all transmissions are encrypted. To use SSL, you need to install a server certificate that uniquely identifies your web site. You can create certificates by clicking Server Certificate button in the Secure Communications pane. You can also obtain certificates from a third-party certificate authority (CA) such as VeriSign.

on the Job

At first glance, SSL might seem to just duplicate the capabilities of other security protocols, such as IPSec and TLS. The differences, however, are in where they operate. IPSec works at the IP layer, and as such is totally transparent to applications. Applications must be specifically written or modified to support SSL or TLS, which operate at the Transport layer.

SCENARIO & SOLUTION

Where can I find a complete list of well-known ports?	Check out www.iana.org/assignments/port-numbers.
Why might I want to use basic authentication on a site when there are so many other options?	Basic authentication has one (and only one) advantage over other forms of authentication: it's supported by virtually all web browsers.

The main points to remember about SSL are that it is supported by virtually all web browsers and that it's the only method of web security that provides both authentication and encryption of all traffic across the connection. So, when you're thinking about totally secure web sites for e-commerce, think certificate services and SSL.

CERTIFICATION OBJECTIVE 11.04

Maintaining and Troubleshooting IIS

For disaster prevention and recovery, IIS provides its own built-in backup and restore commands. For troubleshooting, the main issues addressed on Exam 70-218 revolve around conflicts with other TCP/IP matters, such as TCP/IP filtering and proxy servers. In this section, we'll look at the most common maintenance and troubleshooting scenarios you'll encounter in real life, as well as on the exam.

Back Up and Restore IIS

The IIS snap-in has its own backup and restore options for settings and configuration. Note that this approach only backs up configuration settings, *not* content. The site content should be backed up independently using whatever backup strategy your company uses for all other content. To back up your IIS configuration, click the server name (Server01 in my example), click the Action button, and choose Backup/Restore Configuration. The Configuration Backup/Restore dialog box opens. Click the Create Backup button and give the backup a name, as prompted on the screen. Click the OK button, and your IIS configuration settings will be saved in a backup file in the %systemroot%\system32\inetsrv\MetaBack folder.

If the IIS file becomes corrupted and unusable, you can reinstall it from scratch. Then, to restore your previous configuration settings, click the server name, and choose Action | Backup/Restore Configuration once again. A list of all previous backups appears in the Configuration Backup/Restore dialog box. Click the backup you want to restore, then click the Restore button.

on the Job

You cannot restore configuration settings from a remote computer; you can do so only on the local host.

EXERCISE 11-4

Backing Up Your IIS Configuration Settings

This exercise gives you the chance to back up any configuration settings you've made so far. You must log in to the web server with administrative privileges to complete this exercise.

1. If the IIS snap-in isn't already open, click the Start button and choose Programs | Administrative Tools | Internet Services Manager.
2. In the console tree, click the server name node.
3. Click the Action button and choose Backup/Restore Configuration.
4. Click the Create Backup button.
5. Type in a name for this backup.
6. Click OK.
7. Click Close.

The settings are backed up without any further feedback. You'll want to back up your configuration settings any time you make a significant change to those settings.

Troubleshooting TCP/IP Filtering Problems

TCP/IP filtering is a tool for managing inbound traffic. You set TCP/IP filtering at the NIC. In the Network and Dial-Up Connections window in the Control Panel, right-click the icon for the NIC and choose Properties. Right-click Internet Protocol (TCP/IP) in the components list and choose Properties. Click the Advanced button, and then click the Options tab to get to the optional settings. Click TCP/IP Filtering, and then click the Properties button. By default, all traffic will be permitted, as shown in Figure 11-8.

It's important to know that FTP uses ports 20 and 21, nonsecure HTTP uses port 80, and secure HTTP over SSL uses port 443 for transmissions. So, if any of those ports are blocked, the corresponding service will be unavailable to users. Thus, if you use TCP/IP filtering and IIS or FTP, make sure the appropriate ports for your services are open.

FIGURE 11-8

The TCP/IP Filtering dialog box

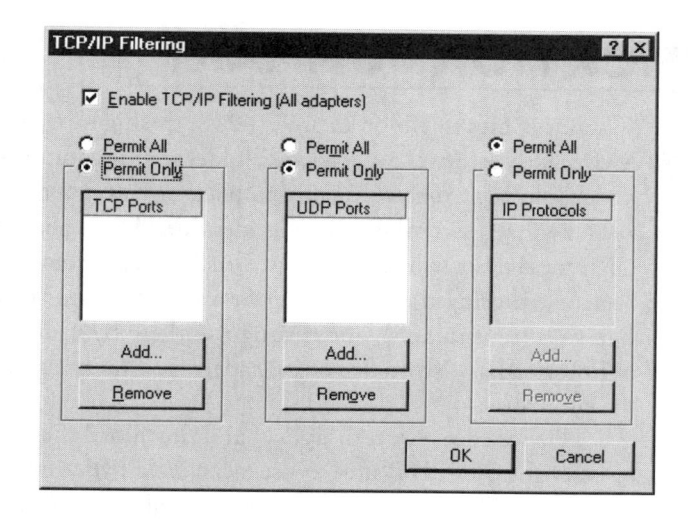

Troubleshooting Problems with Proxy Servers

Proxy servers can also block access to web sites. The most common problem is when local users try to access a local intrasite, and the proxy server rejects them with an "Error 401.2 Unauthorized access…" message. If you have a proxy server and your users experience this problem, the solution lies on the client side, not the server side. You'll need to go to the client, start Internet Explorer, and choose Tools | Internet Options. Click the Connections tab, then click the LAN Settings button. In the Proxy Server pane of the Local Area Network (LAN) Settings dialog box that opens, choose Bypass Proxy Server For Local Addresses.

SCENARIO & SOLUTION

How do I start and stop IIS services?	In the IIS console tree, right-click the default site or any virtual site to get to the Start, Stop, and Pause options.
Can I use redirection in IIS? For example, when someone connects to a site, can I forward them to a completely different URL?	Yes. On the Home Directory tab of the site's Properties dialog box, choose A Redirection To A URL.

CERTIFICATION SUMMARY

When it comes to IIS on Exam 70-218, the big topics are web sites and FTP sites. A virtual directory is a *web-shared* folder that is contained within a web site's root folder (or *home directory*). You can place any number of virtual directories within a web site. Each virtual directory is identified by an alias, which users append to the URL for the site. For example, a virtual directory named VirtSite on Server01 could be accessed using the URL http://Server01/VirtSite. You can also create multiple web sites (root folders), and distinguish them by using IP addresses, port numbers, or host headers. If you use host headers, you must also provide name resolution for the site's alias.

FTP sites allow users to upload and download files. Directory browsing needs to be enabled on FTP sites so users can see a hyperlinked listing of files within the site's folder. Write permissions are required if you want to allow users to upload files. FTP supports only anonymous access and basic authentication. Web sites provide a variety of authentication options, including basic authentication, digest authentication, and Integrated Windows authentication. To build a secure web site where all transmissions are encrypted, use SSL.

If clients have problems accessing a site, and you're using TCP/IP filtering, make sure appropriate ports are open. Common port numbers include port 80 for HTTP, port 443 for secure HTTP, and ports 20 and 21 for FTP. If your network includes a proxy server, and local users have problems accessing local sites, enable the Bypass Proxy Server For Local Addresses option on client computers.

✓ TWO-MINUTE DRILL

Creating Web Sites

- ❏ Windows 2000 comes with Internet Information Services (IIS) 5 partially preinstalled. Additional IIS components can be installed through Add/Remove Windows Components in Add/Remove Programs.
- ❏ IIS automatically creates a Default Web Site at c:\inetpub\wwwroot. You can use that default site as the root for any number of web sites within your domain.
- ❏ Any folder can be made into a *virtual directory* within a web site's root. Just right-click the folder's icon, choose Properties, and use the Web Sharing tab to share the folder.
- ❏ To access the default web site from a web browser, use the address http://*computername*, where *computername* is the name of the server on which IIS is installed.
- ❏ To access a virtual directory from a web browser, use the URL syntax http://*computername/alias*, where *alias* is the name you provided while creating the virtual directory.
- ❏ You can remotely manage printers that are connected to a server hosting IIS using the URL http://*computername/*printers.
- ❏ A *virtual server* is a folder on any computer in the domain that's configured as a web site at the root level in IIS.
- ❏ You can distinguish multiple web sites on the same server by using port numbers, TCP/IP addresses, or host headers.
- ❏ If you use host headers to uniquely identify web sites, you must create DNS host records that map aliases to IP addresses.
- ❏ Bandwidth throttling allows you to specify how much bandwidth each web site in a domain is allowed to use.

Creating FTP Sites

- ❏ You can also use IIS to host File Transfer Protocol (FTP) sites, generally used for uploading and downloading files to/from the server.
- ❏ Read permissions on an FTP site allow users to download, but not upload, files.

- Write permissions allow users to upload files to an FTP server.
- FTP supports only anonymous access or basic authentication using unencrypted passwords.

Securing Web and FTP Sites

- Unlike FTP sites, which support only basic authentication and anonymous access, web sites can be configured to use a variety of authentication methods.
- Basic authentication is the least secure method as it transmits passwords in clear text (unencrypted) format.
- Digest authentication encrypts passwords in compatible browsers, such as Internet Explorer, but it does not encrypt data.
- Integrated Windows authentication works best for private intrasites, because it uses a client's domain login credentials to access local sites.
- A certificate and SSL allow you to create secure web sites in which all transmissions between server and client are encrypted.
- Directory browsing allows users to view a hypertext listing of files and folders contained within a site.
- ISAPI applications on a web site will work only if you set the Execute Permissions drop-down list box to Scripts And Executables.

Maintaining and Troubleshooting IIS

- To back up IIS configuration settings, click the server name in the IIS console, click the Action button, and choose Backup/Restore Configuration.
- In the event of a problem that requires reinstalling IIS, you can use the Backup/Restore Configuration option in IIS to restore an earlier backup.
- If you use TCP/IP filtering on a TCP/IP connection, you need to ensure that the appropriate ports are open for web and FTP access.
- Unsecured HTTP uses port 80, secure HTTP uses port 443, and FTP uses ports 20 and 21.
- If local users can't access a local intranet site through a proxy server, you need to enable the Bypass Proxy Server For Local Addresses option on client computers.

SELF TEST

Creating Web Sites

1. You are the network administrator for your company's Windows 2000 network. Server01 is a web server for the domain, and contains a folder named E:\Web\Content. You want users to be able to access this folder using either the URL http://Server01/Local or the URL http://Server01/Loc. What should you do?

   A. Use the Web Sharing tab in the folder's Properties dialog box to share the folder with two aliases, Local and Loc.

   B. Create two new web virtual servers named Local and Loc, and copy the contents of the E:\Web\Content folder to those servers' home directories.

   C. Share the E:\Server01\Content folder with the share name Local, and configure a host header that points Loc to that share.

   D. Define E:\Web\Content as two separate sites, one with TCP port 80, the other with TCP port 443.

2. You are the administrator of a Windows 2000 print server computer named PrnServ01. The server has several printers attached to it, all of which you'd like to be able to manage remotely without using Terminal Services or any third-party programs. How can you accomplish this goal?

   A. Make sure IIS is installed and running on the print server. From any web browser, connect to http://PrnServ01/DefaultWebSite/Printers.

   B. Make sure IIS is installed and running on the print server. From any web browser, connect to http://PrnServ01/ Printers.

   C. Make sure IIS is installed and running on your client computer. From any web browser, connect to http://PrnServ01/ Printers.

   D. Place all printer icons in a folder named Printers. Move all the printer icons into that folder, and then web-share the folder with the alias Printers. In any web browser, enter the URL http://Printers to manage the printers remotely.

3. You are a domain administrator for your company's network, which contains some 5,000 user accounts. You are installing a new Windows 2000 Server computer named WebServer with Internet Information Services (IIS) installed. You create a corporate intrasite on the server, to be accessed only by employees within the company. You want clients to be able to access the

site with the simple URL http://CompanyNews. Which of the following would allow you to accomplish that goal with minimal administrative effort? (Choose all that apply.)

- A. Create a virtual web server named CompanyNews, and use a unique IP address to identify the site.
- B. Create a virtual web server named CompanyNews, and assign it a unique port number.
- C. Create a virtual web server named CompanyNews, and assign a host header to it.
- D. In DNS, create a mapping that links CompanyNews to the IP address of WebServer.
- E. On each client computer, create a mapping in the HOSTS file that resolves to the IP address of WebServer.

4. You are the domain administrator for your company's network, which has about 200 employees. You have a Windows 2000 Server computer named IntServ that uses IIS to provide four web sites to the public through a T1 connection. Company employees use the same T1 connection to access the Internet and other outside resources. Users are starting to complain that their network connections are slowing down. An analysis of bandwidth usage shows you that the public web sites are getting more hits than anticipated, and using a substantial amount of bandwidth in the process. What can you do to reserve a portion of the bandwidth for company employees?

- A. In the TCP/IP Properties dialog box for the NIC in IntServ, set a bandwidth throttle that limits the amount of bandwidth available to outside clients.
- B. In the TCP/IP Properties dialog box for the NIC in IntServ, use TCP/IP filtering to limit the number of users who can access the public web sites.
- C. On the Performance tab of the default web site's Properties dialog box, set the web site Performance Tuning slider to Fewer Than 10,000 hits per day.
- D. Set a bandwidth throttle on each of the public web sites.

Creating FTP Sites

5. You are a domain administrator for your company's Windows 2000 network. You want to use one of your Windows 2000 Server computers to set up an FTP site that will allow business partners, but not the general public, to upload and download documents. Which of the following options would allow you to accomplish that goal? (Choose all that apply.)

- A. Configure the FTP server to use only anonymous access.
- B. Disable anonymous access on your FTP server.
- C. Configure Default FTP Site on ServerA to enable SSL for all connections.
- D. Create user accounts for those business partners who will be allowed to access the site.
- E. Configure the FTP server to grant Read and Write permissions to each business partner.

6. You are the administrator of a Windows 2000 Server computer named ServerX, which functions as a file and web server in your Windows 2000 domain. ServerX contains a folder named E:\Graphics\ShareDocs that's shared with the default NTFS and share permissions. Employees in the Graphics department use this folder to store documents they share with one another. You'd like to offer other employees read-only access to the shared folder via the URL ftp://ServerX/Graphics. How can you accomplish this with the least administrative effort?

   A. Change the NTFS permissions on the shared folder to allow members of the Graphics group Full Control of the folder, and all other employees Read permission.

   B. Create a new FTP site at the root level in IIS, making E:\Graphics\ShareDocs its home folder. Add a host record to your DNS server that points the alias Graphics to that folder name.

   C. Configure the E:\Graphics\ShareDocs folder as virtual directory under the Default FTP Site node with the alias Graphics, assigning the Read and Directory Browsing permissions to the folder.

   D. Create a new virtual web site named Graphics on ServerX, with an alias of Graphics.

7. Which FTP site authentication method provides the best security against hackers stealing usernames and passwords of people accessing the site?

   A. Anonymous access
   B. Basic authentication
   C. Digest authentication
   D. Integrated Windows authentication

Securing Web and FTP Sites

8. You are the administrator of a Windows 2000 Server computer that uses IIS to offer web sites to the public. You'd like to use that same server to allow company employees to download documents while they're out of the office. But, you cannot allow the public access to those same folders. You need to make the download area as secure as possible. Which of the following would allow you to accomplish this goal?

   A. Create an FTP site on the server, and configure it for anonymous access.
   B. Create an FTP site on the server, and configure it to use basic authentication.
   C. Create a document web site and configure it to use basic authentication. Then, enable directory browsing on the site.
   D. Create a document web site and configure it to use Integrated Windows authentication. Then, enable directory browsing on the site.

9. You are the administrator of a Windows 2000 web server named ServerX. Programmers from the software development department have supplied you with a new ISAPI-based web application that's to be added to the company web site. You install the application in a virtual directory and enable the Read and Scripts Only permissions. When the developers attempt to access the application, they receive an error message stating that the application cannot be started. What must you do to fix the problem?

    A. Configure the site to enable Scripts Only.
    B. Configure the site to enable Scripts and Executables.
    C. Create a secure web site with SSL to host the application.
    D. Enable Write permissions on the site.

10. You are the network administrator for your company's network. Management informs you that they are planning to offer e-commerce capabilities on the company's public web site, wherein customers will be transmitting credit card information over the Internet. Which of the following would provide the best security for such a site?

    A. Basic authentication
    B. Windows Integrated authentication
    C. Digest authentication
    D. Secure Sockets Layer (SSL)

11. Which of the following statements about digest authentication are true? (Choose all that apply.)

    A. Digest authentication was previously known as Windows NT Challenge/Response.
    B. Digest authentication requires that all user accounts be defined in AD Users and Computers, not a stand-alone server.
    C. Digest authentication requires that each user account have the Store Password Using Reversible Encryption option enabled.
    D. Digest authentication does not encrypt passwords, but it is supported by the vast majority of web browsers.

12. Which of the following is most likely to be used on a secure e-commerce web site that's open to the public and must support the widest range of web browsers?

    A. Digest authentication
    B. Integrated Windows authentication
    C. SSL
    D. PPTP

Maintaining and Troubleshooting IIS

13. Your web server is host to several web sites. For disaster recovery, you back up all content on a regular basis, back up your configuration settings, and use the IIS snap-in. Your installation becomes corrupted, requiring that you completely reinstall IIS from scratch. How could you restore all of your previous IIS configuration settings?

    A. Use System Restore to restore the system state to an earlier time.

    B. Invoke the Internet Information Services Manager HTML version and perform the restore.

    C. In the IIS snap-in, click the server name and choose Backup/Restore Configuration from the Action menu.

    D. Restore the system state data of the server using Windows 2000's Backup utility.

14. You are the domain administrator for your company's Windows 2000 network, which includes a proxy server. On a Windows 2000 Server computer named OurSite, you create an intrasite to be used only by company employees. When the employees attempt to access the site, they all get "Unauthorized access" error messages. What can you do to enable all employees to access the local web site?

    A. Change the NTFS permissions on the site to grant Read permissions to the Authenticated Users group.

    B. Change the NTFS permissions on the site to Allow–Write and Allow–Directory Browsing.

    C. On client computer web browsers, set the web browsers' security level to Low.

    D. On client computers, enable Bypass Proxy Server For Local Addresses.

15. You have enabled TCP/IP filtering on a NIC in a web server. Users have no problem accessing the company FTP site. However, when they attempt to connect to the company's secure web site, they get an error message saying the page cannot be opened. Which port do you need to enable in TCP/IP filtering to allow users to access the secure web site?

    A. Port 5000

    B. Port 443

    C. Port 80

    D. Port 21

LAB QUESTION

You are the administrator for your company's Windows 2000 Active Directory domain. Your company is installing a new Windows 2000 Server computer with IIS installed. Your company wants you to use this new server to provide two private intrasites, each with its own URL and access permissions. One of the sites will be used to publish an employee handbook and related materials for all personnel. The second site will publish data for managers, and only managers should be able to access the site. The server will contain only a single NIC. How can you set up these sites to meet the requirements?

SELF TEST ANSWERS

Creating Web sites

1. ☑ **A** is correct. A virtual directory can have any number of aliases, so the simple solution here is to web-share the folder with two aliases, Local and Loc.
   ☒ **B** is incorrect because creating a separate virtual server for each site isn't required and wouldn't allow the sites to be accessed by the names specified in the question.
   ☒ **C** and **D** are incorrect because there's no need to define separate sites with unique host headers or port assignments in this scenario.

2. ☑ **B** is correct. IIS automatically creates a folder for accessing printers remotely. So, as long as IIS is installed and running on PrnServ01, you can get to those printers from Internet Explorer via the URL http://PrnServ01/Printers.
   ☒ **A** is incorrect because it's displaying the wrong URL.
   ☒ **C** is incorrect because IIS needs to be running on the server, not the client.
   ☒ **D** is incorrect because there is no need to create a new folder or move printer icons.

3. ☑ **C** and **D** are correct. The goal would require the two-step process of using a host header to uniquely identify the site, and creating a DNS host record to map the name to the server's IP address.
   ☒ **A** and **B** are incorrect because the question requires that the site be identified by a single short name, not an IP address or port number.
   ☒ **E** is incorrect because changing the HOSTS file on each client computer would require substantial administrative effort.

4. ☑ **D** is correct. Placing bandwidth throttles on the public web sites will conserve bandwidth for local employees.
   ☒ **A** is incorrect because you don't place bandwidth throttles on a NIC, you define them in IIS.
   ☒ **B** is incorrect because TCP/IP filtering restricts access to certain ports, and doesn't do anything to conserve bandwidth.
   ☒ **C** is incorrect because the Performance Tuning slider wouldn't conserve bandwidth for internal users.

Creating FTP Sites

5. ☑ **B, D,** and **E** are correct. You need to disable anonymous access on the FTP site to enable basic authentication. Then, you need to create user accounts for people who are allowed to

access the FTP site. To ensure that business partners can upload and download documents, you need to enable both Read and Write permissions.
☒ A is incorrect because the question calls for authentication, not anonymous access.
☒ C is incorrect because SSL isn't available for FTP.

6. ☑ C is correct. The virtual directory created in this answer would meet all goals posed in the question.
☒ A, B, and D are incorrect because none of them achieves the goal of being able to access the folder using the URL ftp://ServerX/Graphics.

7. ☑ A is correct. Anonymous access doesn't require usernames or passwords, so there would be nothing for hackers to capture.
☒ B is incorrect because basic authentication actually exposes unencrypted account credentials to hackers.
☒ C and D are incorrect because FTP does not support either of those authentication methods.

Securing Web and FTP Sites

8. ☑ D is correct. This is the best solution because Integrated Windows authentication provides the security you're looking for, and directory browsing provides the hyperlinked directory listing that employees need.
☒ A, B, and C are incorrect because none of them achieves the goal of making the site as secure as possible.

9. ☑ B is correct. You must enable Scripts and Executables on the site to get the ISAPI application to run.
☒ A is incorrect because you need to enable executables, not scripts.
☒ C and D are incorrect because neither option would solve the problem at hand.

10. ☑ D is correct. Certification services and SSL would be the most secure, as they encrypt all transmissions.
☒ A, B, and C are incorrect because none offers the level of security and widespread browser support of SSL.

11. ☑ B and C are correct. Digest authentication works with Active Directory and requires AD user accounts and reversible password encryption.
☒ A is incorrect because Integrated Windows authentication, not digest authentication, was previously known as Windows NT Challenge/Response.
☒ D is incorrect because digest authentication does encrypt passwords, but is not supported in all web browsers.

12. ☑ **C** is correct. Most secure web sites use Secure Sockets Layer (SSL) to encrypt transaction data.
☒ **A** and **B** are incorrect because neither is supported by a wide range of browsers.
☒ **D** is incorrect because Point-to-Point Tunneling Protocol is used for virtual private networks, but not to secure e-commerce web sites.

Maintaining and Troubleshooting IIS

13. ☑ **C** is correct. Use the Backup/Restore Configuration option in IIS to restore the most recent configuration settings backup.
☒ **A** is incorrect because System Restore would not restore IIS configuration settings.
☒ **B** is incorrect because even though you can use an HTML version of IIS to create backups, you cannot use that version to restore configuration settings.
☒ **D** is incorrect because a system state backup would not include IIS configuration settings.

14. ☑ **D** is correct. When there's a proxy server involved, enabling Bypass Proxy Server For Local Addresses will allow clients to access the local site.
☒ **A** and **B** are incorrect because this isn't an NTFS permissions problem.
☒ **C** is incorrect because setting the security level lower in the web browser wouldn't help with the proxy server problem.

15. ☑ **B** is correct. Secure HTTP uses port 443.
☒ **A, C,** and **D** are incorrect because they are the wrong port numbers (80 is used for unsecured HTTP, and 21 is used for FTP).

LAB ANSWER

Your best bet here would be to use host headers to uniquely identify each site. You'll need to create a DNS entry for each site to map it to the server's IP address. There's no need for any special security on the employees' site, since it's open to everyone. But to limit access to managers on the other site, you need to come up with a means of authenticating users. Since this is a Windows 2000 AD domain, you can use digest authentication, provided all user accounts are defined in Active Directory. Don't forget, though, that with digest authentication, user passwords must be stored using reversible encryption. You'll also want to ensure that all users have current versions of Microsoft Internet Explorer.

12
Implementing and Analyzing Security

CERTIFICATION OBJECTIVES

12.01	Configuring and Auditing Security
12.02	Administering Security Templates
12.03	Analyzing Security Settings
✓	Two-Minute Drill
Q&A	Self Test

In previous chapters, you've seen examples of linking GPOs to objects to apply policies. In this chapter, you'll expand your knowledge of working with security settings by learning how to create and audit security, as well as how to analyze a computer's current configuration against a baseline database that defines what the security settings should be. Such analyses are useful for checking up on a machine's current security settings to see if any security breaches have opened up over time.

You'll be introduced to some security features that are new to Windows 2000 (and, therefore, are also prime candidates for questions on Exam 70-218), such as Restricted Groups, and the ability to automatically shut down a computer when its security log is filled. You'll also learn about the security templates, and the Security Configuration Tool Set, which consists of several tools for creating and managing those templates.

CERTIFICATION OBJECTIVE 12.01

Configuring and Auditing Security

As you learned in Chapter 6, group policies provide an enormous number of settings that allow you to clearly define security settings on computers throughout the domain. In this section, you'll see an example of using Restricted Groups policies. Restricted Groups is a new feature of Windows 2000 designed to govern security group membership. This feature automatically provides security memberships for default Windows 2000 groups that have predefined capabilities, such as local Administrators, Domain Admins, Power Users, Print Operators, and Server Operators.

To see how using Restricted Groups can be useful in managing security, let's look at a fairly common scenario. Let's assume that the local Administrators group on some member server or workstation contains two user accounts named aMarie and bDooley. User bDooley is going on vacation, so he adds user cShore to the local Administrators group to cover for him while he is away. However, no one remembers to remove cShore from the Administrators group when bDooley returns from his vacation, so cShore retains his supposedly temporary privileges.

If you imagine that scenario being played out among dozens of users, you can see where users could end up having permanent privileges that were supposed to be temporary. Configuring security through Restricted Groups can prevent this buildup of inappropriate group memberships. By defining aMarie and bDooley as the only members of the Administrators group through a Restricted Groups policy, cShore would automatically be removed from the local Administrators group the next time the policy is applied.

Like all group policy settings, you can restrict group memberships though GPOs. So, you could add this policy to an existing GPO, or create a new GPO. The most likely scenario would be to apply the GPO or an OU that already contains all the member servers and/or workstations to which you want to apply the policy. Or, create a new OU and move the appropriate computer objects into that OU.

> **exam**
> **Watch**
>
> *Restricted Groups doesn't prevent people from logging on to a computer. For example, if you wanted to ensure that only members of the local Administrators group could log on to a machine, you'd create a GPO that restricts Log On Locally rights to members of the local Administrators group.*

Next, you could go to any Windows 2000 workstation or member server that has the AdminPak installed, open AD Users and Groups, right-click the OU you created, and choose Properties. On the Group Policy tab, click New and give the policy a name (we'll use RestrictGroups in this example). Click the new policy name and choose Edit. Expand the Computer Configuration\Windows Settings\Security Settings nodes, right-click Restricted Groups, then click Add Group. Click the Browse button. With the focus on the local computer, add the users and/or groups that are allowed to be members of this group, and click OK. You can see the Administrators group listed in the details pane window now. Right-click that group name and choose Security. You'll be taken to the dialog box shown in Figure 12-1.

The dialog box displays the current settings under Members Of This Group (called the *members list*) and This Group Is A Member Of (called the *member of list*). By default, both lists are empty. It's important to note that an empty list isn't the same as "not configured." The comment in each empty list describes what happens if you leave the list empty. The effect of an empty list varies, as follows:

- If the Members Of This Group list is empty, that means that when the policy is applied, any users or groups that are currently members of that group will be removed—meaning nobody will have the rights and permissions of that group after the policy is enforced.

- If the This Group Is A Member Of list is empty, that translates to "no restrictions." When the policy is applied with this list empty, the restricted group is not removed from any other group's memberships.

To restrict who can belong to the group, use the Add button to specify users (or groups) who are allowed to be members of this group. When the policy is applied, the members you specify here will be enforced. That is, anyone who is currently in

FIGURE 12-1

The Configure Membership dialog box

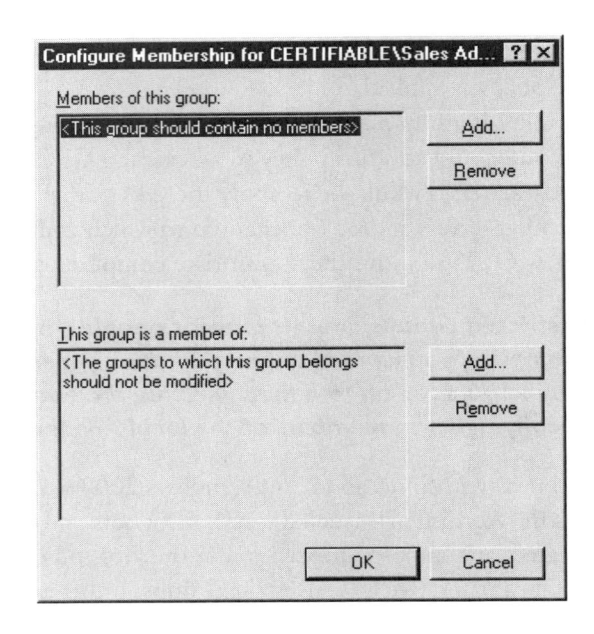

the group but shouldn't be will be removed from the group. Anyone who is supposed to be in the group but isn't will be added to the group when the policy is applied.

Under This Group Is A Member Of, specify which other groups this restricted group is allowed to belong to. If you don't want to place any restrictions on which groups the current group belongs to, leave the This Group Is A Member Of list blank.

on the job

Restricted groups are available in group policies that are linked to domains, sites, or OUs. They are available in a Windows 2000 computer's Local Security Policy.

When you're done, just close all open dialog boxes and windows. To apply the policy immediately, you can enter the command **secedit /refreshpolicy machine_policy /enforce** at the command prompt. Note that you can view the local groups and see whether the global group is a member of the local Administrators group from any workstations or servers in the OU.

Auditing Security

Auditing is the process whereby you track security-related events to the security log in Event Viewer. Basically, auditing allows you to keep track of what users are doing, and what they're attempting to do. There are two steps to setting up auditing. First, you must enable auditing on the local machine or in a GPO that's linked to a container that hosts the appropriate objects (discussed next). Once auditing is enabled, you can then choose specific objects to audit.

Enabling Auditing

To enable auditing, you first define an *audit policy*. You must be a member of the Administrators group on the local computer, or have the Manage Auditing and Security Log right. To set an audit policy for a group of machines, you can set the policy on the appropriate container. For example, to audit account logons, you could set a policy on the Domain Controllers OU, as in the example presented in Exercise 12-1. In the Group Policy window for the OU, you'll find audit policies under Computer Configuration\Windows Settings\Security Settings\Local Policies\Audit Policy, as shown in Figure 12-2. The following are the audit policies available to you:

- **Audit account logon events**   Audits each instance of a user logging on or logging off of another computer where the local computer was used to validate the account.

- **Audit account management**   Audits account management activities such as creating, changing, and deleting groups, enabling, disabling, and renaming user accounts, and setting and changing passwords.

- **Audit directory service access**   Audits users' access to Active Directory objects.

- **Audit logon events**   Keeps track of each instance of a user logging on, logging off, or making a network connection to this computer.

- **Audit object access**   Audits events of a user accessing an object, including files, folders, printers, and Registry keys.

exam
⑦atch

To create an audit policy that determines which user is deleting files on an NTFS volume, you would audit object access for successful deletion of objects.

- **Audit policy change**   Keeps track of every change to audit policies, user rights assignment, and trust policies.

FIGURE 12-2 Audit policies

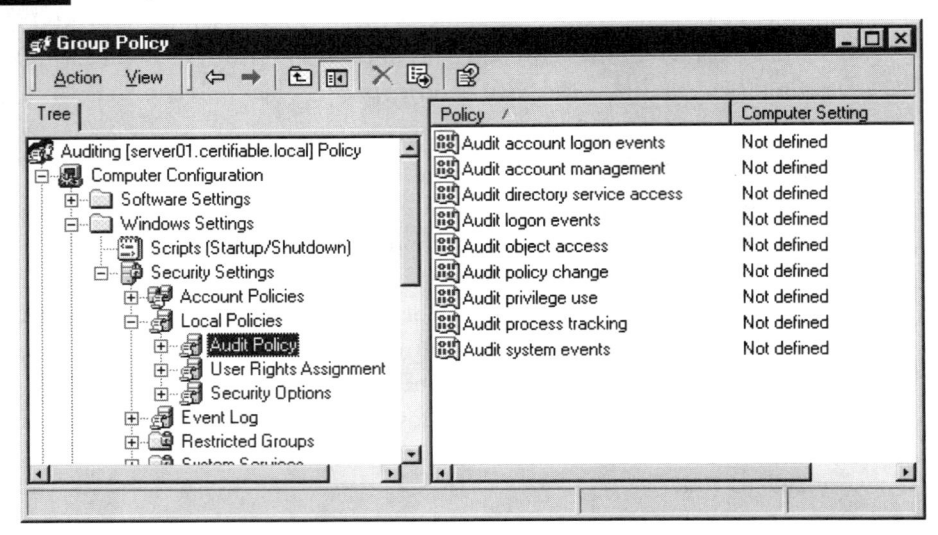

- **Audit privilege use**   Audits each instance of a user exercising rights that are granted to that user though membership in special groups like Administrators, Power Users, or Server Operators.

- **Audit process tracking**   Keeps track of process events such as programs attempting to perform some action, and indirect object access.

- **Audit system events**   Audits when a user restarts or shuts down a computer, and when an event has occurred that affects either the system security or the security log.

EXERCISE 12-1

Set Up Auditing on Domain Controllers

In this exercise, you'll create an audit policy for the Domain Controllers OU to track successful and failed logon attempts. You must log on to a domain controller with administrative privileges to complete this exercise:

1. Open Active Directory Users and Computers.
2. Right-click the Domain Controllers OU and choose Properties.

3. Click the Group Policy tab.
4. To create a new GPO for auditing, click the New button and give the policy a name. I'll use **Tracker** as the name in this example.
5. Click the new GPO's name and click the Edit button to get to the Group Policy snap-in.
6. Expand the Computer Configuration\Windows Settings\Security Settings\Local Policies nodes and click Audit Policy. Audit policies appear in the details pane.
7. To enable auditing, double-click the policy you want to enable, which is Audit Account Logon Events in this example.
8. Choose Define These Policy Settings and then select the attempts you want to audit, which are Success and Failure in this example.
9. Click OK. Your selections appear in the Computer Setting column of the details pane.
10. Close the Group Policy window.
11. Close the Domain Controllers Properties dialog box and AD Users and Computers.

It's not necessary to specify specific objects to audit when implementing a logon audit policy, so you're basically done. After logging off and logging on (and perhaps trying a couple of fake log-on attempts with bogus usernames and passwords), you can open Event Viewer and view the security log to see a record of the logon attempts.

Choosing Objects to Audit

If you opt to audit access to objects, you must also take a second step whereby you specify the specific items you want to audit. For example, let's say you have a shared folder named Group Stuff in which multiple users can create and delete files and folders. One user is deleting things seemingly at random, and you want to find out who it is. To set up auditing on that folder, browse to it via Windows Explorer, right-click its icon, and choose Properties. Click the Security tab, then click the Advanced button. You're taken to the Access Control Settings dialog box for the folder. Click the Auditing tab.

Once you're at the Auditing tab, click the Add button to first determine whom you want to audit. The Select User, Computer, or Group dialog box will appear. Choose the security group(s) and/or user(s) you want to audit. To audit all access to the folder, you can choose the Everyone group. Click OK to get to the Auditing Entry dialog box. There, you can choose which events and attempts you want to audit. For example, to audit successful and failed attempts at creating and deleting files and folders, you would make the selections shown in Figure 12-3.

on the Job

Auditing does eat up some resources, so you'll want to use it sparingly in actual practice.

Click OK in each open dialog box to save your settings, and you'll see the auditing entry in the list.

exam Watch

Auditing Failure events only tells you when someone attempts to do something they can't. To see who is actually performing some task, you need to audit Success events.

FIGURE 12-3

Auditing successful and failed attempts to create and delete objects in a shared folder

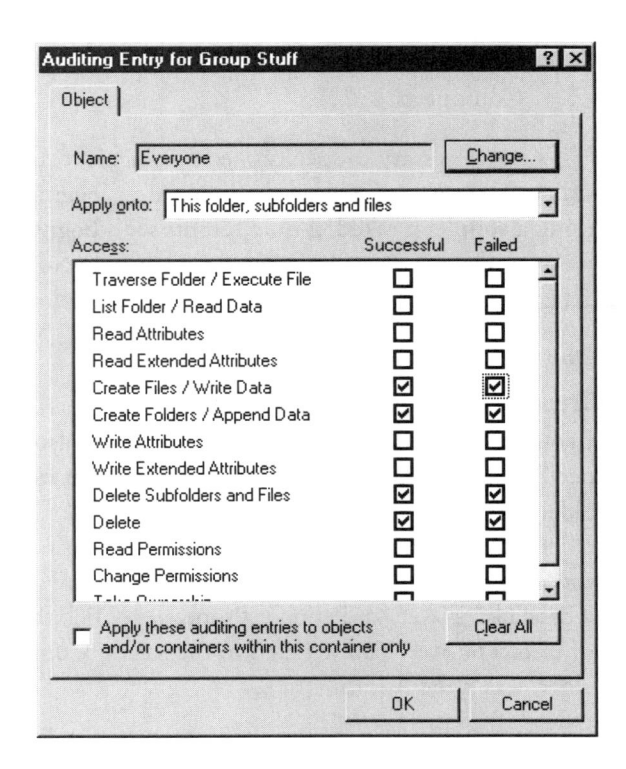

If you've enabled auditing of access to directory objects, you can use a similar procedure to choose which objects and events you want to audit. But rather than going through Windows Explorer, you can use AD Users and Computers. Click the View button in the toolbar and choose Advanced Features. Then, right-click the object you wish to audit and choose Properties. Click the Security tab, then click the Advanced button. The rest of the process is identical to that of setting auditing on a folder through Windows Explorer.

Remember, audited events are tracked in the security log of Event Viewer. To finalize your auditing policies, you may need to configure Event Viewer as discussed next.

Configuring Event Viewer

Auditing is tracked in Event Viewer's security log, along with the system and application logs. You can configure Event Viewer through security templates if the default settings aren't appropriate for your situation. In any security template or Group Policy window, expand the Event Log node under Local Policies, and click Settings For Event Logs. You'll see options for the application, security, and system logs, as shown in Figure 12-4.

For each log, you can configure the following:

- **Maximum size**   Specify the maximum size of the log file.
- **Restrict guest access**   Enable or disable guest account access to the log. If enabled, only authenticated users can access the log.
- **Retain log**   Specifies the amount of time, in days, that logged events remain in the log before being overwritten by newer events.
- **Retention method for log**   Specifies how events in the log are overwritten: by day, as needed, or never. If never is selected, you must manually delete old entries to make room for new ones.
- **Shut down the computer when the security audit log is full**   Shuts down the system when the security log has reached its maximum allowed size.

The last option applies only to security logs. Shutting down the system when the security log is full may seem like a radical thing to do. You'd only use this in a high-security setting where you need to lock out all users when it's no longer possible to track security events. If you're going to enable that option, you need to set maximum size and retention options on the security log in such a way as to prevent the computer from shutting down all the time!

FIGURE 12-4   Policy settings for event logs

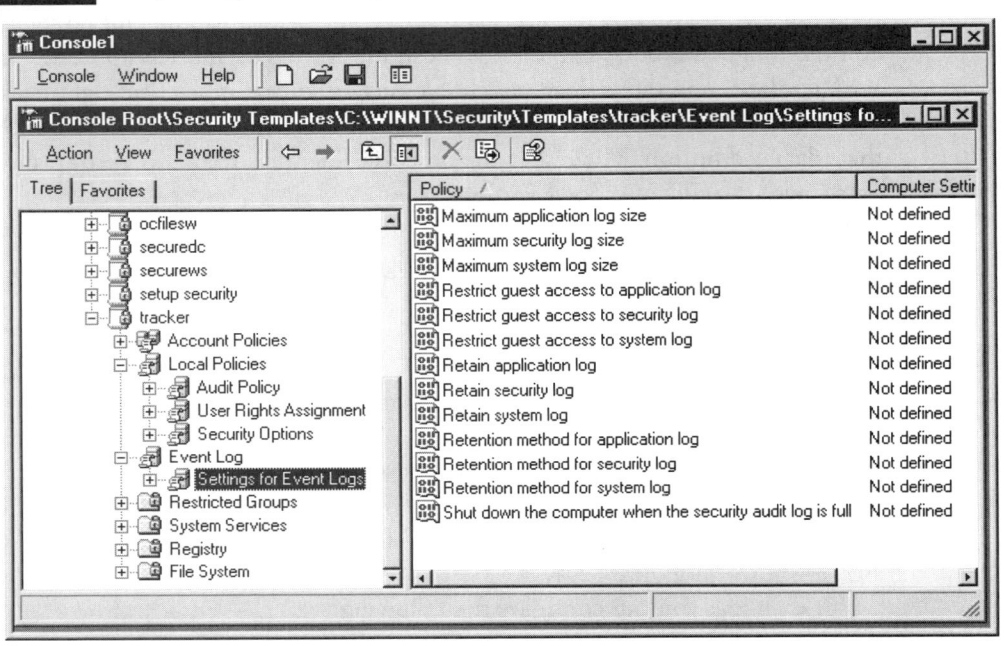

SCENARIO & SOLUTION

Some of my OU administrators also have the ability to create computer and user accounts. I'd like to be able to audit that activity. How can I do so?	Create an audit policy that tracks successful Audit Account Management events.
I also have some users who keep trying to "help" each other by sharing their Internet connections. They don't understand that they can't do that with our network and local DNS server. Can I create a policy to prevent them from enabling ICS?	Yes, you can, but not through a security template. You'll need to create a GPO that disables Allow Configuration Of Connection Sharing under User Configuration\Administrative Templates\Network\Network and Dial-up Connections, and filter the GPO for the appropriate security group.

Reviewing the Security Log

Once you've initiated auditing, you can check the security log at any time to review audited events. Just open Event Viewer from the Administrative Tools menu or the Control Panel. Double-click the Security Log node, and the details pane will display all audited events. You can double-click any event in the details pane to view detailed information about the event.

CERTIFICATION OBJECTIVE 12.02

Administering Security Templates

A *security template* is a collection of security settings stored in a simple text file so you can manage the settings as a whole. Windows 2000 comes with several predefined security templates that define an overall level of security ranging from basic to high security. The templates are stored in the %systemroot%\Security\Templates folder, each with an .inf filename extension. The templates are named according to the level of security they apply:

- **Basic (basic*.inf)** The basic settings that are initially provided during a clean install of Windows 2000 to an NTFS volume. You can import these to revert to the basic security settings at any time. Templates include Default Workstation (basicwk.inf), Default Server (basicsv.inf), and Default Domain Controller (basicdc.inf).

- **Compatibility (compatws.inf)** Lowers security levels on specific files, folders, and Registry keys that are used by applications, which in turn allows members of the Users security group to run applications that are not certified with Windows 2000. Also removes all members of the Power Users group, making them members of the Users group.

- **Secure (secure*.inf)** These templates increase security in all areas except files, folders, and Registry keys, which are secured by default. Templates are provided for workstations and member/stand-alone servers (securews.inf) and domain controllers (securedc.inf).

- **High Security (hisec*.inf)** These templates define strong protection for network traffic and protocols between computers running Windows 2000. With these settings in place, the Windows 2000 computer cannot communicate with computers running Window 95, 98, or NT. Templates provided include hisecws.inf for workstations and member/stand-alone servers, and hisecdc.inf for domain controllers.

on the Job

The %systemroot%\inf folder may be hidden on some systems. To make it visible, choose Show Hidden Files And Folders in the Folder Options dialog box, available in the Control Panel or on the Tools menu in Windows Explorer.

Clean installs of Windows 2000 to NTFS permissions automatically get the basic template installed (such as basicws.inf or basicdc.inf). Upgrades or clean installs to FAT or FAT32 volumes automatically get the compatible template installed. When upgrading a Windows NT 4 computer, existing policies on the NT machine are retained so as not to disrupt your existing security policy. When installation is complete, the Local Computer Policy stores the security settings. You can export the Local Computer Policy to a security template file to preserve those initial system security settings in case you ever need to restore those settings at a later time.

The tools for creating and managing security templates are collectively referred to as the *Security Configuration Tool Set*. The specific tools are summarized here:

- **Security Templates snap-in** A stand-alone Microsoft Management Console (MMC) snap-in that lets you edit and create security template files (INI files).

- **Security Configuration and Analysis snap-in** Another stand-alone MMC snap-in that can analyze and configure Windows 2000 security based on a security template.

- **Secedit.exe** The command-line version of the Security Configuration and Analysis snap-in that allows security analysis and configuration to be performed as a scheduled task.

- **Security Settings extension to Group Policy** An extension snap-in used to configure local security policies as well as security policies for domains or OUs. Local security policies include only the Account Policy and Local Policy security areas. Security policies defined for domains, OUs, or sites can include all security areas.

In the sections that follow, you'll learn how to use the various components to analyze and implement Windows 2000 operating system security.

Using the Security Templates Snap-in

The Security Templates snap-in is a useful tool for managing security templates. You can open it as a stand-alone snap-in by following the steps presented in Exercise 12-2. Once the snap-in is open, you'll see a node titled Security Templates in the console tree. If you expand the Security Templates folder, you'll see the default templates folder (C:\WINNT\Security\Templates on most computers). Expanding that node will display a list of predefined security templates that come with Windows 2000, as shown in Figure 12-5.

FIGURE 12-5 The Security Templates snap-in

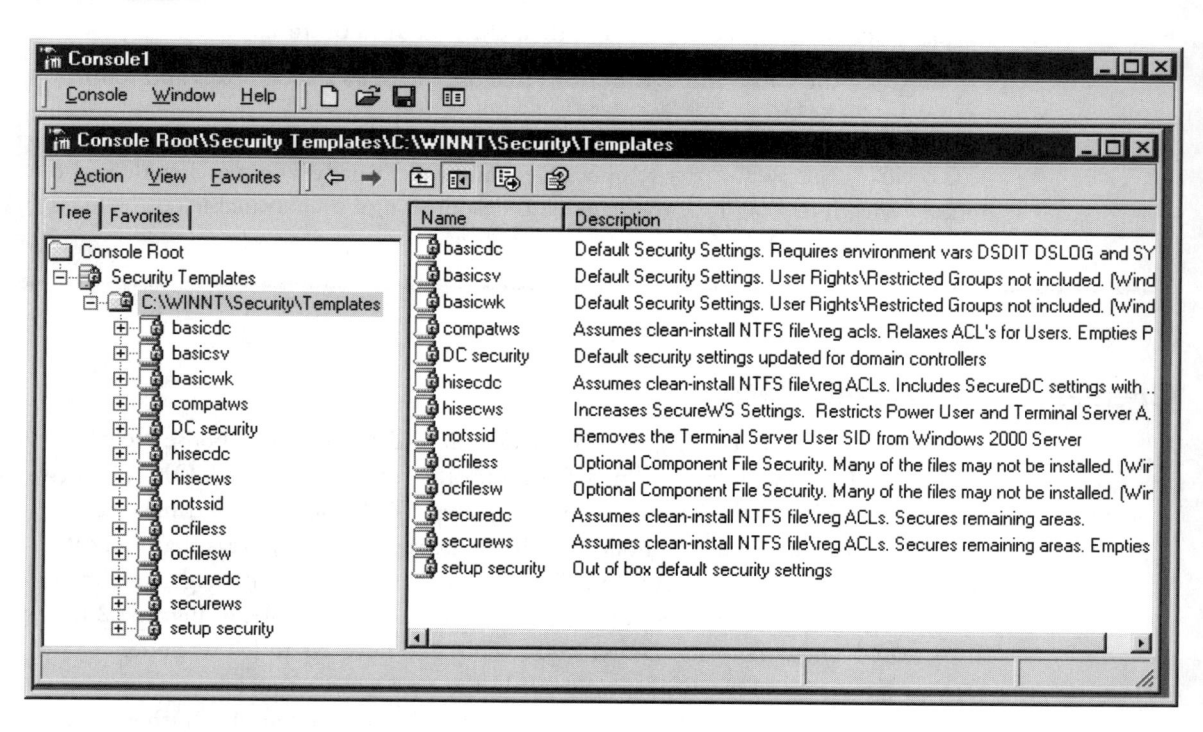

EXERCISE 12-2

Opening the Security Templates Snap-in

In this exercise, you'll go through the steps required to open the Security Templates snap-in:

1. Click the Start button and choose Run.
2. Type **mmc** and click OK.
3. Click the Console button in the toolbar and choose Add\Remove Snap-in.
4. Click the Add button to reveal the Add Standalone Snap-in dialog box.
5. Click Security Templates and then click the Add button.
6. Click the Close and OK buttons to close the open dialog boxes and return to the MMC.

To view available security templates, expand the Security Templates node and the folder beneath it. You'll see the name and description of each available template, as shown in Figure 12-5.

Creating a New Template

To create a new template, right-click the default folder name and choose New | Template. Type in a name and description for the template and click OK. The new template is added to the list of existing templates. To define policy settings within the new template, expand its node. You'll see the seven security areas that you can define through templates—Account Policies, Local Policies, Event Log, Restricted Groups, System Services, Registry, and File System. For example, in Figure 12-6, I've created a new template named MySecTmp and have expanded its node.

You can view and modify settings within the new template just as you can a predefined template or GPO. The beauty of working with a template rather than working directly in a GPO is that the settings aren't actually applied to any computer, object, or OU. They're just stored in a template (INF) file. As you'll learn in the next section, you can use that template to analyze the current security of a given computer. Often, the analysis will help you fine-tune the template before you actually apply it to a computer.

FIGURE 12-6 A new security template named MySecTmp

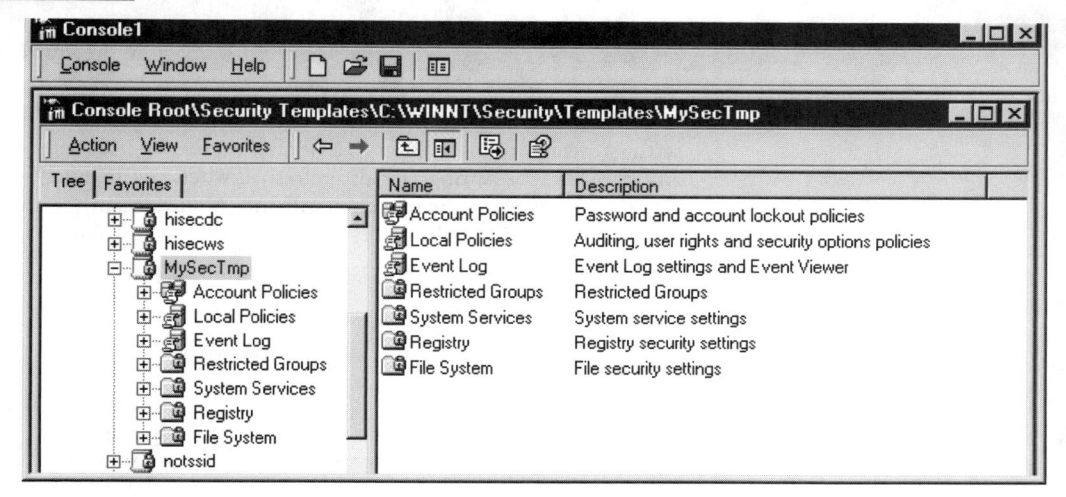

One way to apply a security template is to simply import it to an existing GPO by following these steps:

1. Open AD Users and Computers.
2. Right-click the container to which you want to import the security template and choose Properties.
3. Click the Group Policy tab.
4. Click Edit to open the Group Policy object into which you want to import the template. Or, click the New button to create a new GPO, name the GPO, and then click the Edit button.
5. In the Group Policy window, expand the Computer Configuration and Windows Settings nodes.
6. Right-click the Security Settings folder and choose Import Policy.
7. If you want to incrementally add the imported template's settings to current settings, leave the Clear This Database Before Importing check box empty. Otherwise, you can choose that option to keep current security settings and have the new settings added incrementally.
8. Click the security template you want to import, then click the Open button.

Those are the basic steps for importing a security template to a GPO. There are other ways to work with security templates, as you'll learn in the next section.

SCENARIO & SOLUTION

When are security settings applied?	Security settings are refreshed every 90 minutes on a workstation or member server, and every 5 minutes on a domain controller. The settings are also refreshed every 16 hours, whether or not there are any changes. The settings are also refreshed when you manually refresh policies using the **secedit** command. Non-domain controllers are refreshed roughly every 60 minutes by default.
I need to set policies on a group of remote users who connect by dialing in. I can't seem to find them in any templates or GPOs. Where should I look?	Remote access policies are available in Routing and Remote Access.
When users dial in to domain controllers, not all policies are applied. Why?	By default, certain policies, like disk quotas and application deployment, are not applied across slow links. You can control which policies are, and are not, applied across slow links using Computer Configuration\Administrative Templates\System\Group Policy in any Group Policy window.

CERTIFICATION OBJECTIVES 12.03

Analyzing Security Settings

The Security Configuration and Analysis snap-in is a tool for analyzing and applying security. You can open the snap-in as you would any other. Assuming you're starting from the desktop, click the Start button, choose Run, type **mmc**, and click OK. Then, click the Console button, and choose Add\Remove Snap-in. Click the Add button. Choose Security Configuration and Analysis, and click the Add button. Now you can click the Close and OK buttons to close all open dialog boxes. You'll see a single node named Security Configuration and Analysis under the Console Root.

Analyzing the Current Configuration

Security analysis works by comparing the machine's current security settings against a baseline database. By comparing a machine's configuration settings against the baseline database, you can find out where the system deviates from desired settings.

Analyzing Security Settings

FROM THE CLASSROOM

Comparing Policy Settings to Local Settings

Every computer has a local, machine-specific security database named secedit.sdb that contains all currently enforced policy settings. (The file is also called the security analysis configuration and analysis database, or local computer policy database.) When you do a clean install of Windows 2000 to an NTFS volume, that database is created with the basic, default security settings that are applied to all new installations. When you upgrade from Windows NT 4, however, the file is not overwritten, as doing so would replace any security settings already in place on the computer.

You can use that secedit.sdb file as "the current configuration" for comparison during an analysis. But, you have to work with a copy of the file, not the original, because the snap-in won't open secedit.sdb directly. For example, you might copy the secedit.sdb file from a machine named client01 to a shared folder on a domain controller, and name the copy client01.sdb. After you right-click the Security Configuration and Analysis node and choose Open Database, you could then open that copied database for comparison.

—*Alan Simpson, MA, MCSA*

The information can be useful for troubleshooting, fine-tuning, and, perhaps most importantly, detecting any security holes that may have opened up over time.

To analyze security on a given machine, you first generate a baseline security configuration database (SDB file). To do so, right-click the Security Configuration and Analysis node and choose Open Database. Type in a name of your own choosing (I'll use the generic name MySecDB.sdb as an example), and click Open.

The Import Template dialog box appears next. As when working with the Security Templates snap-in, you can choose the Clear This Database Before Importing option to replace all current settings with those from the imported template. Otherwise, you can leave that option unselected to incrementally add the imported template's settings to the baseline database settings. Click the name of the template you want to import, and click the Open button. The snap-in now changes to show you instructions on analyzing and configuring the security settings, as shown in Figure 12-7.

Chapter 12: Implementing and Analyzing Security

FIGURE 12-7 The Security Configuration and Analysis snap-in with a security database open

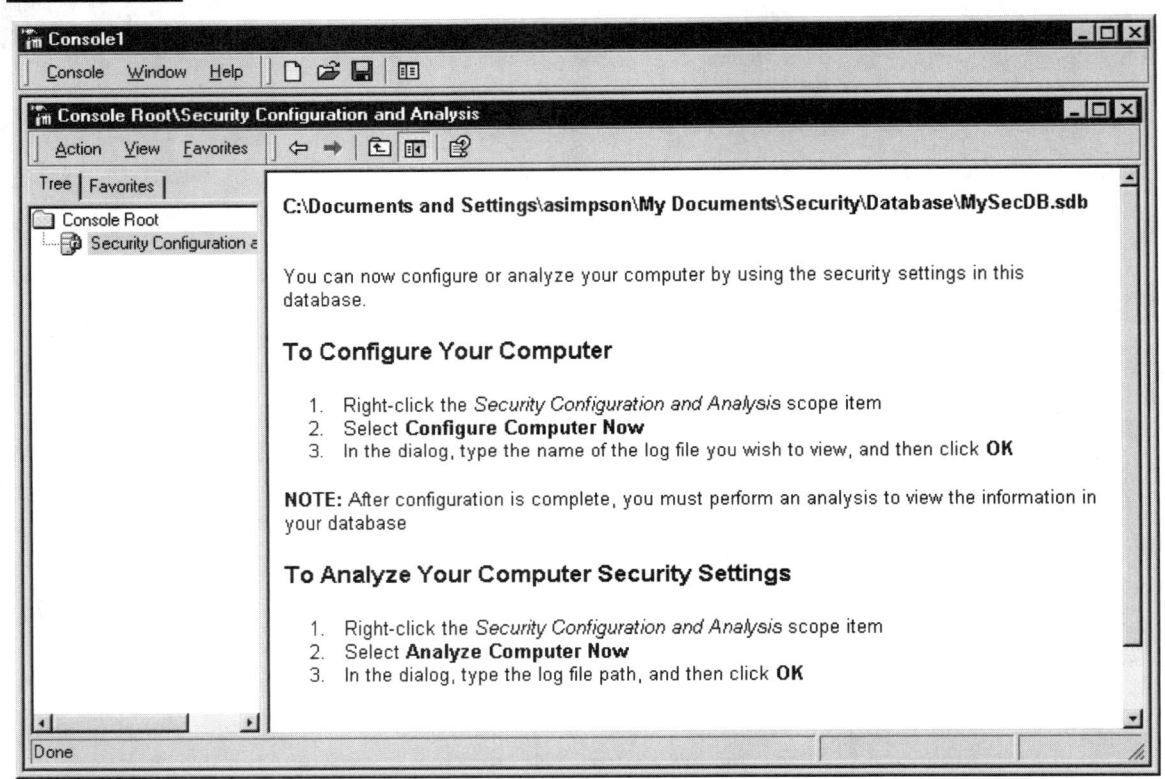

```
C:\Documents and Settings\asimpson\My Documents\Security\Database\MySecDB.sdb

You can now configure or analyze your computer by using the security settings in this
database.

To Configure Your Computer

    1. Right-click the Security Configuration and Analysis scope item
    2. Select Configure Computer Now
    3. In the dialog, type the name of the log file you wish to view, and then click OK

NOTE: After configuration is complete, you must perform an analysis to view the information in
your database

To Analyze Your Computer Security Settings

    1. Right-click the Security Configuration and Analysis scope item
    2. Select Analyze Computer Now
    3. In the dialog, type the log file path, and then click OK
```

To perform the analysis, right-click the Security Configuration and Analysis node again, and choose Analyze Computer Now. In the Error Log File Path dialog box that opens, specify a log file for the analysis results. For example, you might enter something like %windir%\security\logs\MySecDB.log as the path to the log file. When you click OK, the analysis begins. You'll see a progress dialog box during the analysis.

When the analysis is completed, choose View | Customize from the MMC toolbar. Select the Description Bar option. Expand the Security Configuration and Analysis node and any node you're interested in viewing. The details pane will display database settings and actual computer settings in two columns, as shown in Figure 12-8. Any conflicts between the database setting and the computer setting are marked with a red X, and consistencies are marked with a green check mark. If neither the check mark nor red X appears, the security setting isn't specified in the database—the security setting isn't configured in the security template that you imported to the database.

FIGURE 12-8 Results of a security analysis

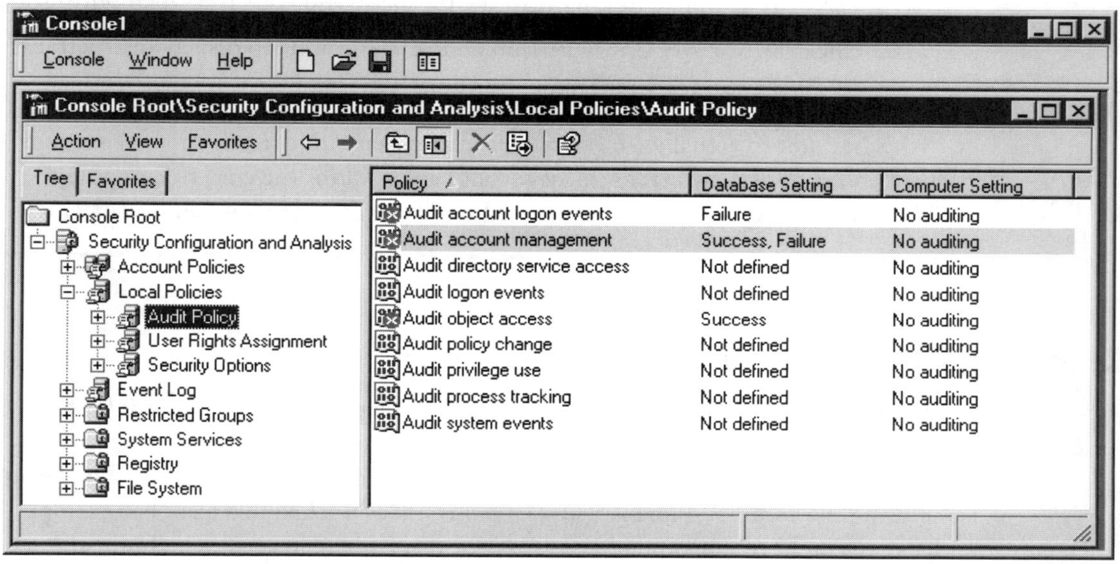
Console1
Console Window Help
Console Root\Security Configuration and Analysis\Local Policies\Audit Policy
Action View Favorites
Tree Favorites
Console Root
Security Configuration and Analysis
Account Policies
Local Policies
Audit Policy
User Rights Assignment
Security Options
Event Log
Restricted Groups
System Services
Registry
File System
Policy
Database Setting
Computer Setting
Audit account logon events
Failure
No auditing
Audit account management
Success, Failure
No auditing
Audit directory service access
Not defined
No auditing
Audit logon events
Not defined
No auditing
Audit object access
Success
No auditing
Audit policy change
Not defined
No auditing
Audit privilege use
Not defined
No auditing
Audit process tracking
Not defined
No auditing
Audit system events
Not defined
No auditing

EXERCISE 12-3

Create a Security Database

In this exercise, you'll go through the basic steps of opening the Security Configuration and Analysis snap-in, and defining a database, just to get started using that tool. You can perform this exercise on any Windows 2000 computer that has the AdminPak installed.

1. Starting from the desktop, click the Start button, choose Run, type **mmc**, and click OK.
2. Click the Console button, and choose Add\Remove Snap-in.
3. Click the Add button and choose Security Configuration and Analysis.
4. Click the Add button, and then click the Close and OK buttons to close all open dialog boxes.
5. Right-click Security Configuration and Analysis under the Console Root.
6. Type in a name for the new database (if you had previously created a database, you could open that here instead) then click the Open button.

7. In the Import Template Database dialog box that opens, click the name of a security template to import to the database, and click the Open button.

8. Click the Security Configuration and Analysis node to display instructions for configuring and analyzing the computer.

It's best not to actually configure your computer with current database settings until you're absolutely certain those settings are valid for the current computer. But you can analyze current settings without committing to any new settings.

Command-line Analysis and Configuration

While the Security Configuration and Analysis snap-in provides a nice GUI for working with security templates, it's not the only tool available. You can also perform analyses and configure a computer using the **secedit** command. The beauty of using the command line is that you can run it as a scheduled task. For example, let's say you have some member servers out there where lower-level administrators are forever changing security settings, granting more access than necessary to other users. You want to automate the security analysis and configuration on those computers so you can keep track of changes and reapply a template's settings when needed. You could schedule **secedit** to run and apply a custom security template at regular intervals to ensure the settings don't drift too far from what you intended.

The syntax for using the **secedit** command to analyze security is as follows:

```
secedit [/analyze] [/configure] /db FileName [/cfg FileName]
[/log FileName] [/quiet | /verbose]
```

The parameters are as follows:

- **/analyze, /configure**   Use /analyze if you want to analyze the current configuration against a template; use /configure to configure the computer with the template's settings.

- **/db *file***   Required parameter. Specifies the path and filename of the security database (SDB file) that contains the settings that will be applied, or that the analysis will use for comparison.

- **/cfg** *file* Specifies the path and filename of the security template (INF file) that will be imported into the database for comparison. Required for /analysis; optional for /configure.
- **/log** *file* Specifies the path and filename of the log file used for the analysis.
- **/quiet, /verbose** Suppresses/displays verbose screen and log output. The /quiet switch is best for running **secedit** as a scheduled task.
- **/overwrite** Used only with /configure; specifies that the security template in the database will overwrite, rather than be added to, existing settings on the computer.
- **/areas** *area1 area2* Used only with /configure; can be used to specify which security areas of the template to apply. Options are SECURITYPOLICY (account and audit policies), GROUP_MGMT (Restricted Groups area), USER_RIGHTS (User Rights Assignment), REGKEYS (Registry key settings), FILESTORE (File System area), and SERVICES (System Services area). Multiple security areas should be separated by a space.

So, let's say you want to analyze the computer's current security against a security template named tightship.inf. You plan to run this as a scheduled task. The syntax of the command would be as follows:

```
secedit /analyze /DB databasename.sdb /CFG templatefile.inf
/quiet
```

To apply the template settings quietly, you'd use this syntax:

```
secedit /configure /DB databasename.sdb /quiet
```

When configuring security, the /CFG parameter is optional. If omitted, only the current database settings are applied.

> **exam**
> **Watch**
>
> Don't forget that the /refreshpolicy switch can be used with the secedit command to quickly apply a changed policy setting.

SCENARIO & SOLUTION

I want the upgraded workstations in my domain to have the same basic security configuration as the workstations with clean installs of Windows 2000 Professional. I'd like to create a detailed log of changes as well. What should I do?	You can apply the basicwk.inf template to all the workstations. The default (basic*.inf) templates are not incremental—they replace existing policies on the target machine. To apply one of those policies, go to the %systemroot%\security\templates folder and run this command on workstations: **secedit /configure /cfg basicwk.inf /db basicwk.sdb /log basicwk.log /verbose**
If I apply the basicwk.inf security template to a computer, will that affect group memberships and user rights assignments?	No. When you apply a basic*.inf template, the User Rights Assignment and Restricted Groups security areas aren't applied.
Is there any reason why I shouldn't just apply a basic*.inf template through a group policy?	Yes. Those basic*.inf default policies are usually applied during installation. Applying them through group policies could take a very long time.

CERTIFICATION SUMMARY

Security is a big part of a network administrator's job, and a sizable chunk of Exam 70-218. The main things to remember in terms of general issues regarding security is that Exam 70-218 does lean slightly toward the newer features, such as Restricted Groups and the ability to shut down the computer when the security log is filled. For auditing, remember that when it comes to auditing object access and access to directory objects, there are a couple of steps involved. First, you need to create an audit policy. Then, you need to activate auditing on specific objects. That second step isn't required for auditing logon events, as there are no specific objects involved when auditing logons.

For security templates, be aware that you can import security templates into GPOs. You can also use the **secedit** command to apply a security database to a computer, even as a scheduled task. Finally, there's always the little bugaboo about the Account Policies node in the Group Policy window. You need to remember that, whether you're using security templates or just configuring policies within a GPO, account policies such as password length and lockout policy will work only when applied at the domain level. If you apply those policies to an OU, they will be ignored.

✓ TWO-MINUTE DRILL

Configuring and Auditing Security

- ❑ Restricted Groups allow you to control security group memberships through policies.
- ❑ You can audit security to verify that settings are in place, and to review users' successful and failed attempts to log on, access objects, and exercise privileges.
- ❑ Auditing object access and AD object access requires enabling the policy, plus enabling auditing of specific objects.
- ❑ You can configure Event Viewer policies through security templates.
- ❑ When configuring Event Viewer, you can opt to have the computer shut down when the security log is full.

Administering Security Templates

- ❑ A security template is a collection of security settings stored in a text file to make it easy to manage the settings as a unit.
- ❑ Security templates have the filename extension .inf.
- ❑ Predefined templates that come with Windows 2000 include the basic*.inf templates, which contain basic configuration settings, and hi*.inf templates, which contain higher-security settings.
- ❑ The Security Templates snap-in provides a graphical user interface for defining custom security templates.
- ❑ To import a custom security template to a group policy, open the Group Policy window, right-click the Security Settings node under Computer Configuration\Security Settings, and choose Import Policy.

Analyzing Security Settings

- ❑ A security database is a collection of security settings stored in an SDB file.
- ❑ You can use the Security Configuration and Analysis snap-in to analyze and configure security.

- Analysis allows you to compare settings in a security database to settings defined on the current computers.
- Policies are only compared, not applied, during an analysis.
- To analyze a computer's security configuration from a scheduled task, use the **secedit /analyze...** command.
- To configure a computer's security configuration from a scheduled task, use the **secedit /configure...** command.

SELF TEST

The following questions will help you measure your understanding of the material presented in this chapter. Read the question and all answers carefully, as there may be more than one correct answer per question. Choose *all* of the correct answers for each question.

Configuring and Auditing Security

1. You are a domain administrator for a Windows 2000 network. You've created a shared folder on a member server, and given everyone permissions to use it freely. Some users are complaining that their files are being deleted. You want to find out who is deleting the files. What should you audit?

    A. Directory service access

    B. Privilege use

    C. Object access

    D. Policy change

2. Which of the following best describes the effect of leaving the This Group Is A Member Of list empty on a Restricted Groups policy?

    A. This restricted group must immediately be removed from membership in all other groups.

    B. This restricted group can only be a member of those groups defined by the computer's local policy settings.

    C. This restricted group cannot be made a member of any other group, even by administrators.

    D. This restricted group can be a member of any other group. There's no need to change existing memberships when applying this policy.

3. You are the domain administrator for your company's network. A user complains that she's no longer able to log on. Upon inspection, you discover that the user's account has been deleted. In the future, you want to audit changes to user and computer accounts to find out who is deleting them. How would you configure an audit policy?

    A. Audit Object Access – Failure

    B. Audit Object Access – Success

    C. Audit Account Management – Failure

    D. Audit Account Management – Success

4. Which of the following would you open to review the results of an applied audit policy?
   A. The application log in Event Viewer
   B. The system log in Event Viewer
   C. The security log in Event Viewer
   D. The audit.log file in %systemroot%\security\database

5. You are the domain administrator for your company's Windows 2000 network. You have delegated authority to create and manage user and computer accounts to administrators within OUs. Which of the following security policies would you activate to audit the activities of those OU administrators?
   A. Object access
   B. Directory service access
   C. Process tracking
   D. Account management

6. You are the network administrator for your company's Windows 2000 network. The network contains several OUs, each with one or more member servers administered by its own local group of administrators. While checking group memberships, you notice that a lot of inappropriate users have been added to the local Administrators group in an OU named Accounting. You create a security template that restricts membership in the local Administrators account to personnel you've deemed appropriate for the task. What must you do after creating the security template?
   A. Import the template to the Default Domain Policy GPO.
   B. Import the template to the Default Domain Controllers Policy GPO.
   C. Place all member servers for the Accounting department in a child OU, create a GPO for that child OU, and import the security template to that new GPO.
   D. Create a new OU named Servers that contains all the member servers in the domain. Create and link a GPO to that Servers OU, and import the security template to that GPO.

7. You are the domain administrator for your company's Windows 2000 network. A member server named ServerJ contains highly confidential information and requires constant security auditing. You create and apply an appropriate policy. In the event that the security log is filled, you want to deny access to all users. What should you do?
   A. Configure the audit policy to shut down the computer when the security log is full.
   B. Configure the event log to shut down the computer when the security log is full.

C. Schedule a task to check the size of the security log at regular intervals, and apply an empty restricted group to ServerJ when the log reaches its maximum size.

D. Configure IP Security Policies to empty the appropriate security group when the security log reaches its maximum size.

Administering Security Templates

8. What is the filename extension for security templates?

    A. .adm
    B. .inf
    C. .sdb
    D. .stf

9. Which of the following security areas are not available through security templates? (Choose all that apply.)

    A. Public Key Policies
    B. IP Security for Active Directory
    C. Event Log
    D. Account Policies

10. You are a domain administrator for a Windows 2000 network that contains on OU named Corporate. That OU contains child OUs named Executive, Operations, Finance, Accounting, and Sales. All Computer and User accounts are contained within their appropriate OUs. Each OU has a GPO linked to it named after the OU—in other words, CorpGPO, ExecGPO, OpsGPO, FinanceGPO, AcctGPO, and SalesGPO. You create two security templates named CorpSec.inf and HighSec.inf. The CorpSec.inf security policy contains security settings that must be applied to all computers and users in the company. The HighSec.inf template contains more- restrictive security settings required for the Finance and Executive OUs. How would you import the security templates to apply the settings correctly? (Choose all that apply.)

    A. Import the CorpSec.inf template to the Default Domain GPO.
    B. Import the CorpSec.inf template to the Default Domain Controllers GPO.
    C. Import the CorpSec.inf template to CorpGPO.
    D. Import the CorpSec.inf template to OpsGPO, AcctGPO, and SalesGPO.
    E. Import the HighSec.inf template to CorpGPO.
    F. Import the HighSec.inf template to ExecGPO and FinanceGPO.

11. You've created a custom security template, and now want to add its settings to the default Domain Controllers OU. Which method would allow you to do that?

    A. Use the Security Analysis and Configuration snap-in to link the security template to the GPO.

    B. Import the security template to the Security Settings node of the GPO linked to the Domain Controllers OU contained in AD Users and Computers.

    C. Rename the template to match the name of the group policy.

    D. Copy the security template to the SYSVOL folder.

Analyzing Security Settings

12. You are the domain administrator for your company's Windows 2000 network, which consists of 50 domain controllers and 2,500 users, grouped into 20 OUs. You need to increase security on all the domain controllers. You create a security template named HighDC.inf and test it on one of the domain controllers. After verifying that the template works as desired, you need to apply it to all the domain controllers in the network. Which of the following methods would allow you to do so with the least administrative effort?

    A. Schedule a task to configure the template on each domain controller.

    B. Import the HighDC.inf security template to the Default Domain Controllers GPO in AD Users and Computers.

    C. Copy the HighDC.inf template to the SYSVOL folder on one domain controller.

    D. Use the Security Configuration and Analysis snap-in to apply the template to each of the domain controllers in the network.

13. Your network consists of a mix of Windows 2000 Professional clients with clean installs and Windows 2000 Professional clients that have been upgraded from NT 4. You want all clients to have the same basic configuration as the computers with the clean installs. Which security template could you use to accomplish that goal?

    A. compatws.inf

    B. secedit.sdb

    C. hisecws.inf

    D. basicws.inf

14. You are the administrator of your company's Windows 2000 domain. You create and implement a security template and apply it to all Windows 2000 client computers in the

network. You discover that some other administrators are occasionally changing security settings on client computers, against company policy. You want to automate security analysis and configuration to keep track of changes and enforce your company's standard policy. You don't want to take away any of the other administrators' privileges because there are some settings that they need to be able to change. What should you do?

A. Import your security template to a group policy that's linked to the Computers container in Active Directory Users and Groups.

B. Use the Security and Configuration Analysis tool on each of the client computers to analyze and configure the security policy.

C. Schedule the secedit command to run on the client computers to analyze and configure their security policies.

D. Import your security template to the Default Domain Policy GPO link and set the No Override option.

15. What's the filename extension for a security database?

A. .inf
B. .adm
C. .sec
D. .sdb

LAB QUESTION

You are the domain administrator for your company's network, which contains an OU named Corporate, which in turn creates several child OUs. One of the child OUs, named Research, requires high security. You create two security templates named General.inf and hiSec.inf that enable security settings as summarized here:

General.inf	Minimum password length Account lockout policies Software installation
HiSec.inf	Audit policies Event log shut-down when full

How could you apply the templates so that the settings in General.inf are applied companywide, and settings in HiSec.inf are applied only to the Research OU?

SELF TEST ANSWERS

Configuring and Auditing Security

1. ☑ **C** is correct. By tracking successful object access events on the shared folder, you'll generate a security log that shows you who is deleting the files.
   ☒ **A, B**, and **D** are wrong because they won't track file deletions.

2. ☑ **D** is correct. An empty This Group Is A Member Of list in a Restricted Groups policy basically translates to "I don't care."
   ☒ **A, B**, and **C** are wrong because they don't accurately describe the effect of an empty This Group Is A Member Of list.

3. ☑ **D** is correct. You want to audit successful account management events.
   ☒ **A** and **B** are wrong because they're the wrong events.
   ☒ **C** is wrong because you want to audit successful account deletions.

4. ☑ **C** is correct. The security log in Event Viewer maintains audited events.
   ☒ **A** and **B** are wrong because they're the wrong logs.
   ☒ **D** is wrong because audit policies don't create an audit.log file.

5. ☑ **D** is correct. The Audit Account Management security policy allows you to audit the management of computer and user accounts.
   ☒ **A** is wrong because object access audits basic NTFS file and folder management.
   ☒ **B** is wrong because that policy audits access to specific objects in the directory.
   ☒ **C** is wrong because process tracking is used to audit processes.

6. ☑ **C** is correct. Since the Restricted Groups policy specifically limits local Administrators memberships on member servers in the Accounting OU, you need to isolate those servers and apply the security template just to those servers.
   ☒ **A** and **B** are wrong because the Default Domain and Default Domain Controllers policies are too high-level for restricting group memberships in this question.
   ☒ **D** is incorrect because you're trying to control membership on servers within the Accounting OU, not all member servers in the domain.

7. ☑ **B** is correct. You configure the Event Log security settings to shut down the computer when the security log is full.
   ☒ **A** is wrong because the setting is under Settings for Event Log, not Audit Policies.
   ☒ **C** and **D** are wrong because they don't represent the correct approach. You need to apply the policy to the event log.

Administering Security Templates

8. ☑ **B** is correct. Security template files have an .inf extension.
   ☒ **A** is wrong because administrative templates have an .adm extension.
   ☒ **C** is wrong because .sdb is the extension used on a security database.
   ☒ **D** is incorrect because there are no security files that have an .stf extension.

9. ☑ **A** and **B** are correct. Neither of those security areas can be configured through a custom security template.
   ☒ **C** and **D** are wrong because you can configure the Event Log and Account Policies in custom security templates.

10. ☑ **C** and **F** are correct. Applying the CorpSec policy to the CorpGPO covers all users and computers within the domain. Importing HighSec to ExecGPO and FinanceGPO adds the extra security needed for those OUs.
    ☒ **A** and **B** are wrong because the templates need to be applied to all computers and users, not to domain controllers or "everything."
    ☒ **D** is wrong because the CorpSec policy must be applied companywide, not just to Operations, Accounting, and Sales.
    ☒ **E** is wrong because HiSec only needs to be applied to the two child OUs, not the entire OU.

11. ☑ **B** is correct. You right-click the Security Settings node under Computer Configuration\Windows Settings and choose Import Policy.
    ☒ **A, C,** and **D** are wrong because they will not import a security template.

Analyzing Security Settings

12. ☑ **B** is correct. Importing the security template into the Default Domain Controllers GPO would get the job done with the least administrative effort.
    ☒ **A** is wrong because there's no need to run the configuration as a scheduled task.
    ☒ **C** is incorrect because copying the security template to the SYSVOL folder wouldn't apply to the template.
    ☒ **D** is wrong because importing the template to a GPO link would be easier.

13. ☑ **D** is correct. The basicws.inf security template is the default security template for Windows 2000 Professional computers with clean installs on NTFS volumes.
    ☒ **A, B,** and **C** are wrong because they're not the correct filenames for the default template.

14. ☑ **C** is correct. A scheduled task would be the easiest approach.
☒ **A** is wrong because you can't link a GPO to the Computers container in AD Users and Computers.
☒ **B** is wrong because the goal is to automate the analysis and configuration, not run it manually.
☒ **D** is wrong because you want to give the other administrators some flexibility, not deny them the ability to make any changes.

15. ☑ **D** is correct. The extension is .sdb.
☒ **A** is wrong because .inf is the extension used for security templates.
☒ **B** is wrong because .adm is the extension used for administrative templates.
☒ **C** is just the wrong filename extension.

LAB ANSWER

The General.inf template needs to be imported at the domain level, because it contains account policies. Applying that at the Corporate OU level would cause those account policies to be ignored. The HiSec.inf policy can be imported to a GPO that's linked to the Research OU, so that its settings affect only that OU.

Part IV

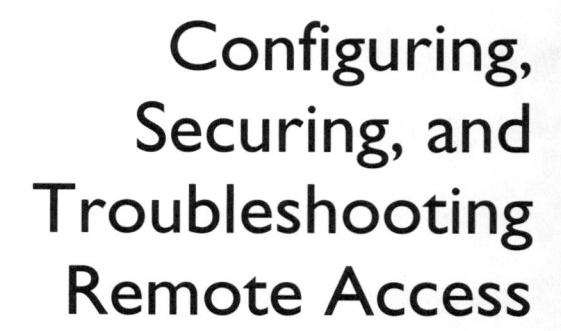

MCSA
MICROSOFT CERTIFIED SYSTEMS ADMINISTRATOR

Configuring, Securing, and Troubleshooting Remote Access

CHAPTERS

13 Configuring Remote Access and VPN Connections

14 Troubleshooting Remote Access

15 Implementing Terminal Services for Remote Access

16 Configuring Network Address Translation and Internet Connection Sharing

MCSA
MICROSOFT CERTIFIED SYSTEMS ADMINISTRATOR

13

Configuring Remote Access and VPN Connections

CERTIFICATION OBJECTIVES

13.01	Configuring Client Computer Remote Access Properties
13.02	Configuring Remote Access Name Resolution and IP Address Allocation
13.03	Configuring and Troubleshooting Client-to-Server PPTP and L2TP Connections
13.04	Managing Existing Server-to-Server PPTP and L2TP Connections
13.05	Configuring and Verifying the Security of a VPN Connection
✓	Two-Minute Drill
Q&A	Self Test

Routing and Remote Access Service (RRAS) is the service included and installed by default with all installations of Windows 2000 Server operating systems. Although RRAS is installed by default, you must configure and enable it. Once configured and enabled, RRAS allows you to use Windows 2000 as a router, remote access server, Internet Connection Server (ICS), Network Address Translation (NAT) Server, DHCP relay agent, or any combination of these. RRAS also includes the ability to configure packet filtering for increased security and set strict RAS policies that define user access and are stored on individual RAS servers. RAS policy is discussed in Chapter 14, but in this chapter, you are going to learn how to configure virtual private networks (VPNs) from both the client and server perspectives. Remote access and VPN support are not new features in Windows 2000, but how they are configured differs greatly from Windows NT 4. Because of the popularity and use of VPNs by many organizations and the enhancements that have been made to the RRAS service in Windows 2000, count on these being significant components on the certification exam.

Well, let's begin our look at configuring remote access and VPN connections with a look at configuring the properties of a remote access client for dial-up, computer-to-computer, and VPN connections.

CERTIFICATION OBJECTIVE 13.01

Configuring Client Computer Remote Access Properties

There are really two sides to remote access connections: the server side, which allows incoming connections to be established, and the client side, which initiates remote access connections. In this section, you will learn about client-side configuration, specifically the two types of client connections available in Windows 2000—dial-up connections and VPN connections, both of which are shown in Figure 13-1. Before we get into a discussion of these two types of connections, we will begin with a look at the remote access and LAN protocols supported by RRAS.

Remote Access Protocols

Windows 2000 supports four remote access protocols: Point-to-Point Protocol (PPP), Microsoft RAS, Serial Line Internet Protocol (SLIP), and AppleTalk Remote Access Protocol (ARAP). ARAP is only configurable on the server side and cannot

FIGURE 13-1 The two types of client connections

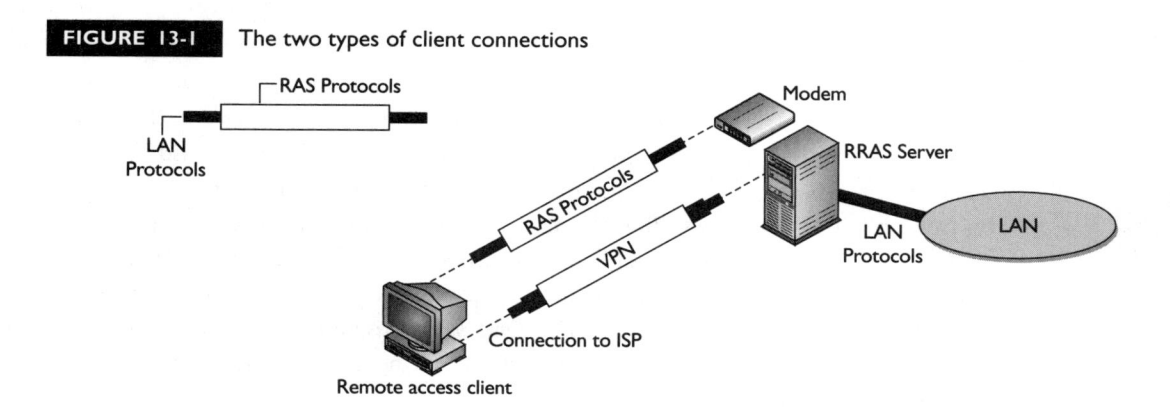

be used from a Windows 2000 client computer. SLIP is only configurable on the client side and cannot be configured on a computer running Windows 2000 Server to accept incoming SLIP connections. Let's take a look at what each of these protocols has to offer and where it generally is used.

Point to Point Protocol

PPP allows remote access clients and servers to communicate with one another regardless of the underlying OSs. In other words, an Apple notebook user is able to dial in to a Windows 2000 RRAS server using a protocol such as TCP/IP, which then encapsulates the data into the PPP protocol, which is what is sent between the client's modem and the RRAS server's modem, allowing the two computers to communicate. PPP is the most commonly used remote access protocol.

Microsoft RAS

The Microsoft Remote Access Service protocol is a proprietary protocol to Microsoft. I know, I cringe too when I hear the word proprietary, because when used in a technology context, it tends to mean complicated and frustrating configuration is required. The Microsoft RAS protocol supports a LAN protocol that Microsoft is working diligently to get rid of, Network Basic Input/Output System (NetBIOS). The Microsoft RAS protocol is included and supported in Windows 2000 for Microsoft down-level, legacy client support, such as computers running Microsoft NT 3.1, MS-DOS, and Windows for Workgroups. It is included to support legacy clients such as those previously mentioned that are only able to use NetBIOS for remote access connectivity.

Serial Line Internet Protocol

SLIP is an older remote access protocol that is generally used by legacy remote access services running on UNIX. Most modern UNIX remote access services use PPP, but on occasion, you may run into a SLIP server. Windows 2000 Network and Dial-up Connections supports SLIP but it is not supported in RRAS, meaning that a computer running Windows 2000 RRAS cannot be configured to accept incoming SLIP connections. When you establish a connection to a SLIP server, the Windows Terminal dialog box appears, allowing for interactive logon sessions to be established with the UNIX SLIP server. This UNIX logon overrides and prevents the remote access logon session from appearing, thereby preventing a user's logon name and password to be used for authentication.

exam
Watch
Windows 2000 clients are only able to dial out using SLIP if the port for the phonebook entry is a serial COM port.

AppleTalk Remote Access Protocol

Support for ARAP is included in Windows 2000 to allow Apple Macintosh clients to connect to a computer running Windows 2000 and RRAS. Windows 2000 remote access clients cannot be configured to connect to a remote access server using AppleTalk over PPP.

Dial-up Connections

Users can establish dial-up connections using a common phone line over the Public Switched Telephone Network (PSTN), which will allow them to create a physical connection to a port on a remote access server. This type of connection is generally made using a modem or ISDN adapter, which allows a connection to the remote access server to be established. This allows for a direct connection to be made from a remote access client to a remote access server from anywhere that has a local phone line. This has been and continues to be, a very popular way of establishing remote access connections while working remotely, as is the case with many employees who are required to travel. Using the phone line in their hotel room, remote users can connect to the remote access server back at the office to update files, send in reports, connect to internal mail servers, and generally conduct business. The downside to this type of connectivity is that it can be very costly when long-distance charges, incoming telephone lines, and multiple hardware devices are required to support this type of configuration. An alternative to this is the use of VPNs.

Dial-up connections are initiated by the remote access client, as described in Exercise 13-1, and allow a remote access client to communicate with a remote access server. This type of connection requires the use of a remote access protocol.

EXERCISE 13-1

Configuring Dial-up Connections on a Remote Access Client

This exercise teaches you how to establish a dial-up connection in Windows 2000 that will allow you to dial into a remote access server. The remote access server does not have to be a Windows 2000 server running RRAS, but rather can be any remote access server, including a hardware RAS solution.

1. Select Start | Settings | Network And Dial-up Connections, and double-click Make New Connection. If it is your first time using this, you will be prompted with the Location Information dialog box. Enter the required information accordingly and click OK, and then click OK again to avoid having this dialog box pop up in the future.

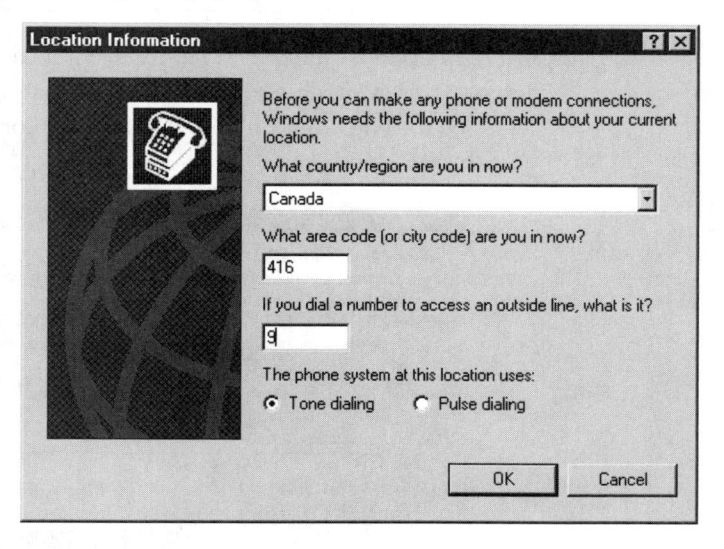

2. Click Next on the Welcome page of the Network Connection Wizard page to reveal the Network Connection Type page. To create a remote access connection to a RRAS server, leave the default selection Dial-up To Private

554 Chapter 13: Configuring Remote Access and VPN Connections

Network selected and click Next. Some of the other options available on the Network Connection Type page will be explored later in this chapter.

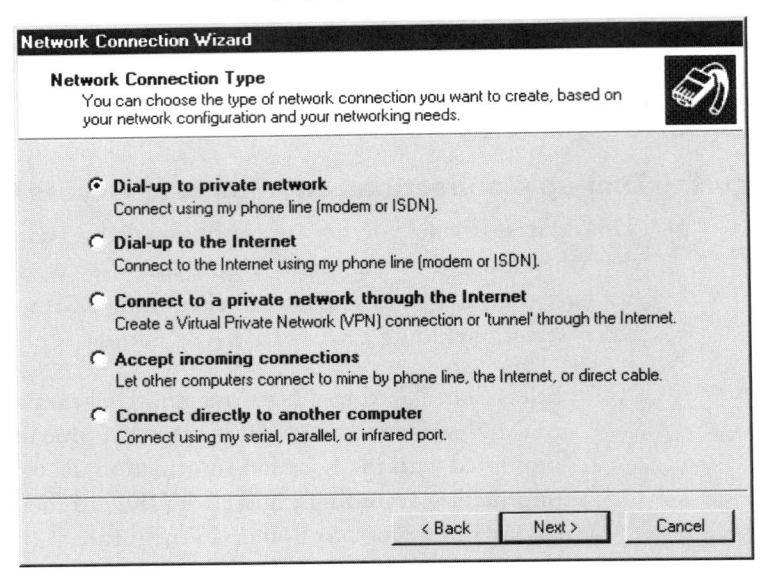

3. On the Phone Number To Dial page, enter the phone number of the remote access server or modem pool that you are dialing into, check the Use Dialing Rules box if you would like to use your preconfigured dialing rules, and click Next.

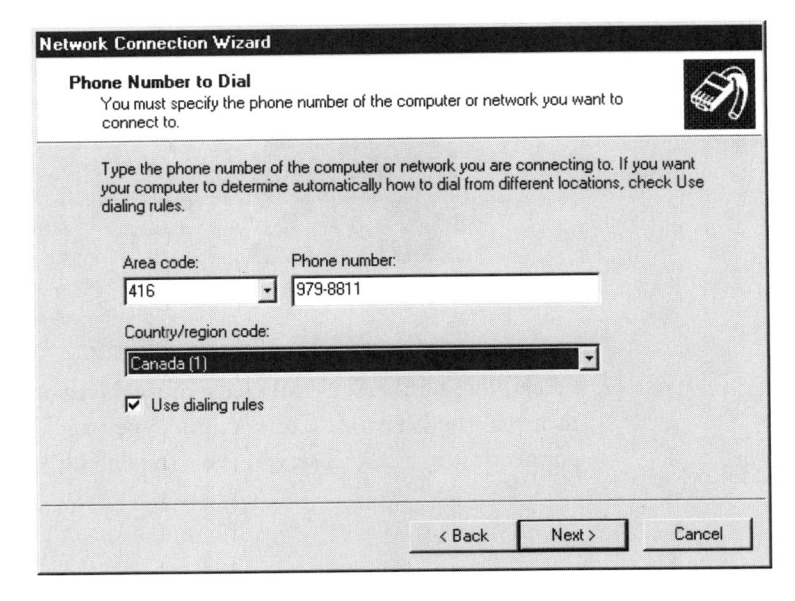

4. On the Connection Availability page, select whether to create this connection for all users of the computer or only for yourself. Create the connection only for yourself if this is a private connection and more than one user uses the computer. If you select the For All Users option and click Next, the Internet Connection Sharing page opens, which allows other users on the network to share this dial-up connection. Selecting the Only For Myself option and clicking Next takes you to the last page of the wizard.

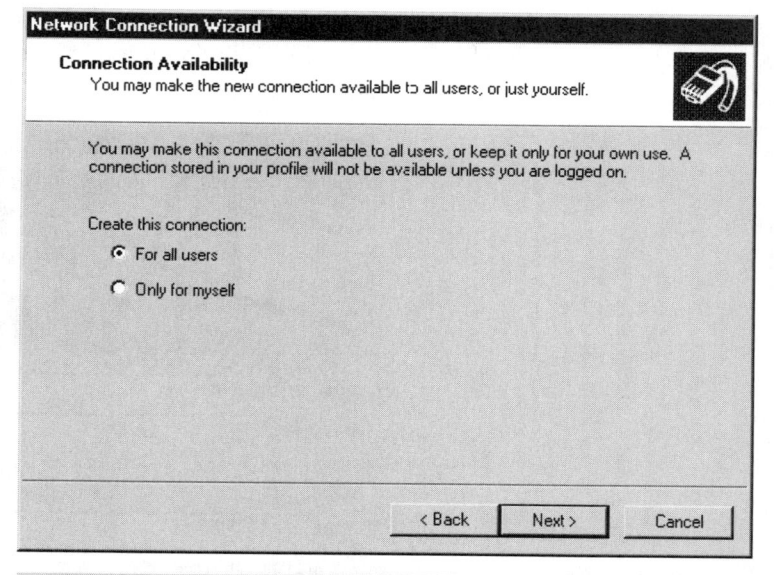

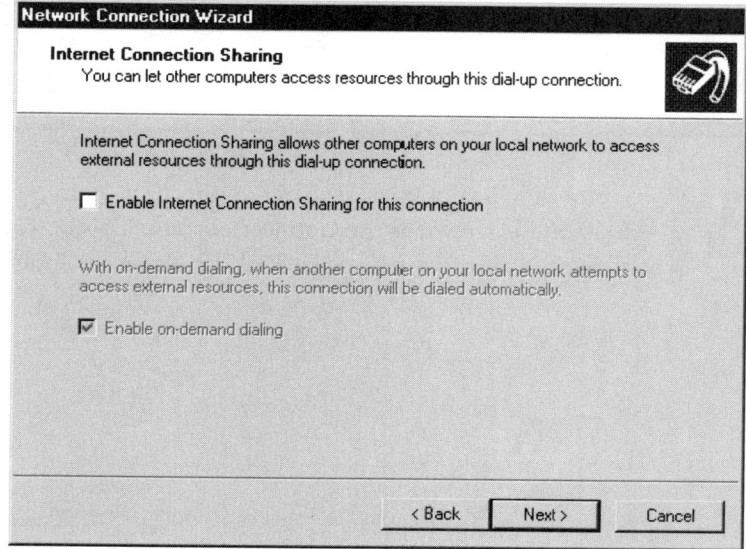

5. On the last page of the Network Connection Wizard, type the name that you would like to assign to the connection. This is simply the friendly name that will be used to identify the connection to you in the Network and Dial-up Connections dialog box. Click Finish and you now have a new dial-up connection.

6. Upon clicking Finish, the Connect Dial-up Connection dialog box opens, in which you enter your username and password, confirm the other information, and click Dial to initiate the connection. It is also in this dialog box that you can modify the properties of the connection via the Properties button or make changes to the dialing rules through the Dialing Rules button.

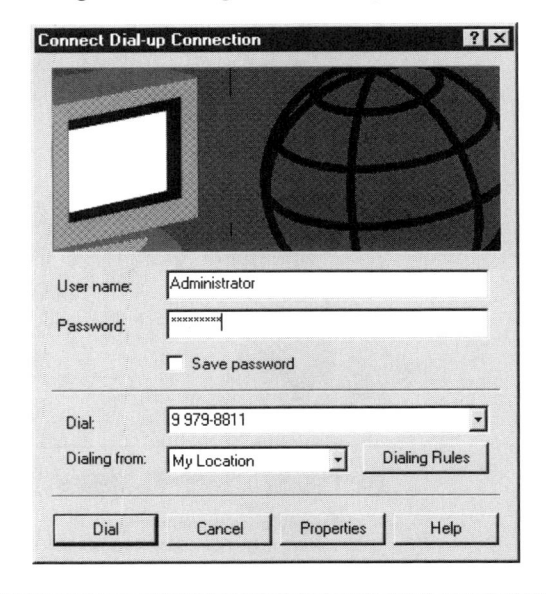

Another, less-popular type of dial-up connection is also supported in Windows 2000 and is known as the Connect Directly To Another Computer option on the Network Connection Type page of the Network Connection Wizard. This allows you to establish a connection between two computers using a serial or parallel cable or an infrared port. This type of connectivity is generally not required in a corporate environment where routers, hubs, switches, and networking equipment exist but enables you to communicate between two computers at home without the expense of a hub, networking cables, and network cards. These types of connectivity options do vary in speed, but for the most part, all generally are slower than a network connection on a LAN.

When configuring this type of connection, you are required to identify which computer is the host computer and which is the guest. The host is the computer that will be receiving the connection, and the guest is the computer that will be attempting to establish the connection. Exercise 13-2 looks at the configuration of the guest, as that is the client side in this type of configuration.

EXERCISE 13-2

Configuring a Direct Connection to Another Computer

This exercise teaches you how to create the guest connection when looking to connect directly to another computer. This type of remote connection is usually in a small, unnetworked environment as an alternate to copying information onto removable media to share it with another computer.

1. Select Start | Settings | Network And Dial-up Connections, and double-click Make New Connection. Click Next on the Welcome page.

2. On the Network Connection Type page, select the last option, Connect Directly To Another Computer, and click Next.

3. On the Host or Guest page, click the Guest radio button and click Next.

4. On the Select A Device page, select a device from the drop-down menu and click Next. The range of options in this drop-down box will depend on the configuration of your computer.

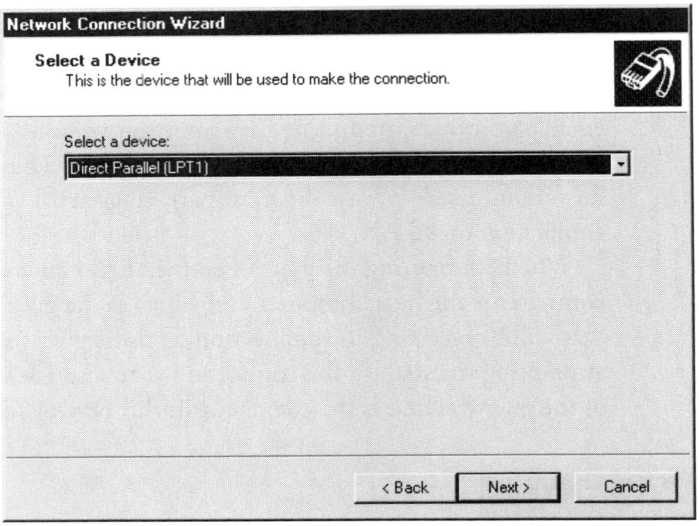
Network Connection Wizard
Select a Device
This is the device that will be used to make the connection.
Select a device:
Direct Parallel (LPT1)
< Back
Next >
Cancel

5. On the Connection Availability tab, select either For All Users to allow you to share the connection through Internet Connection Sharing or Only For Myself, and click Next.
6. Enter a name for the connection and click Finish.
7. In the Connect Direct dialog box, enter the username and password that you wish to connect with. Remember that in the case of a workgroup, you have to use a local account that exists on the host computer to authenticate successfully. In the case of a domain, the remote access server will have to be able to successfully query a domain controller.

Now that you are familiar with the first remote access connection type, the dial-up connection, let's take a look at how to configure VPN connections.

Virtual Private Network Connections

VPNs allow remote users to dial up to a local Internet service provider (ISP) and establish a local connection to the Internet. Once a connection with the Internet has been established, the remote user can connect to the corporate network through a

VPN server. A VPN connection provides secure remote access through the Internet over a TCP/IP connection. This type of configuration scenario reduces the required server hardware in the form of modem pools, costly phone lines, and long-distance charges for the remote user. VPNs have grown exponentially in popularity and use thanks to these cost-saving advantages and their relatively simple configuration requirements. Most organizations already have the required infrastructure in place to support VPNs, which consists of a persistent Internet connection and internal server hardware and software to run remote access services. Our discussion and the focus of the exam will concentrate on the software remote access solutions available in Windows 2000. As you will see in Exercise 13-3, creating a VPN connection is quite easy once you have an existing connection to the Internet.

EXERCISE 13-3

Creating a VPN Connection

This exercise teaches you how to create a client-side VPN connection that will allow you to connect to a remote VPN server either across a private LAN or across a public network such as the Internet.

1. Select Start | Settings | Network And Dial-up Connections, and double-click Make New Connection. Click Next on the Welcome page.

2. On the Network Connection Type page, select the last option, Connect To A Private Network Through The Internet, and click Next.

3. If you have been following along with the previous exercises, you will be presented with the Public Network page. This page only appears if other connections already exist, and it allows you to instruct the OS to establish another connection first, prior to establishing the VPN connection, by choosing the option Automatically Dial This Initial Connection and selecting the connection from the drop-down list. This is a useful option for remote users who are traveling and must establish a connection to their ISP prior to establishing a VPN connection to a remote VPN server. If you have an existing connection, such as a routed connection to the Internet,

you can choose Do Not Dial The Initial Connection. This will allow you to use the existing network to establish the VPN. Click Next.

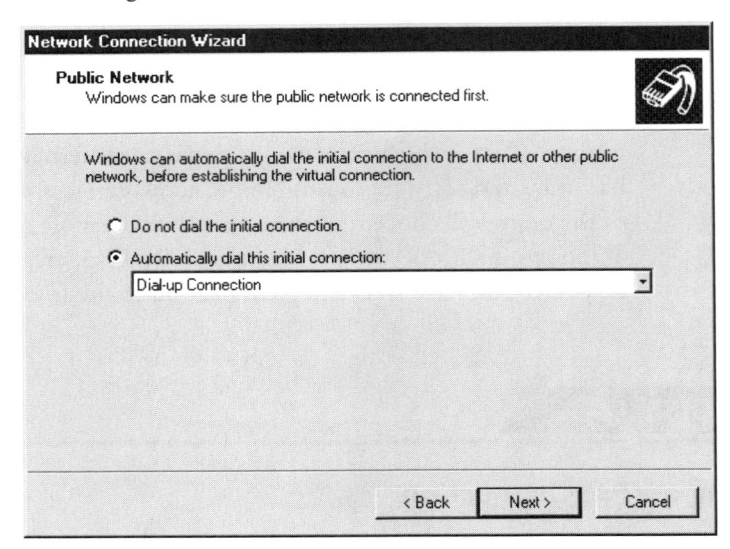

4. On the Destination Address page, enter the fully qualified domain name or IP address of the remote VPN server and click Next. Remember that using the IP address avoids the requirement for name resolution, and this IP address will be the IP address of the external network adapter of the remote VPN server.

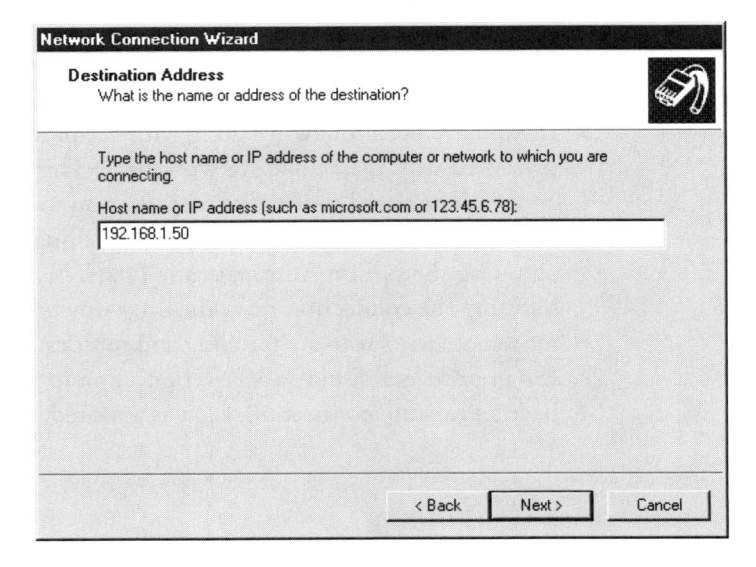

5. On the Connection Availability page, select the For All Users or Only For Myself option and click Next. Selecting For All Users allows the connection to be shared with other users on the same local network, but data is only encrypted inside the VPN tunnel, not between the LAN client and the VPN client that is sharing the connection, as shown in the following illustration.

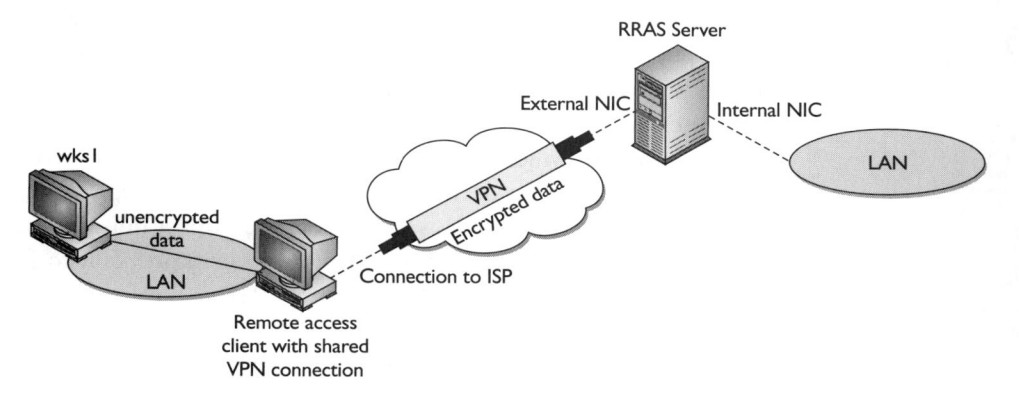

6. Enter the name of the VPN connection and click Finish. The Connection dialog box appears. Enter the username and password and click Connect.

Now that you are familiar with the client-side configuration of a VPN connection, we are going to look a little deeper into the technologies that support this type of communication. The first place to start is with the two VPN protocols supported in Windows 2000: Point-to-Point Tunneling Protocol (PPTP) and Layer Two Tunneling Protocol (L2TP). Looking back to Figure 13-1, and specifically looking at the VPN connection, you see that there are really three layers of protocols involved in this type of communication. The bottommost layer is represented by the thinnest pipe and represents the PPP connection established by the remote access service on the client to the RRAS server. The middle layer represents the LAN protocol that is used for communication across the network, which in the case of Internet communications is TCP/IP. The third layer represents the VPN protocols and can be either PPTP or L2TP. VPN protocols encapsulate TCP/IP data packets inside PPP data packets, providing data encryption, security checks, and validation at the point of transmission and receipt, making the data much more secure than if it were to be sent using TCP/IP. Sending data using TCP/IP guarantees delivery but also allows anyone with connectivity on any of the network segments over which the data is sent to use a packet sniffer to pull off the packets and recompile the data. Overall, very unsecure!

PPTP

PPTP is one of two VPN protocols supported in Windows 2000. PPTP is included with Windows 2000 for a number of reasons, but primarily because it is currently the most popular VPN protocol. Older Microsoft client OSs such as Windows NT 4 and Windows 98 only support PPTP, so it is also included for down-level support. Like everything, PPTP has both benefits and drawbacks. The benefits are that it has widespread support, which allows it to be used by a number of different clients, OSs, and hardware vendors. Its drawbacks, however, can be enough to make you want to choose L2TP, particularly when security is of the utmost importance.

PPTP is less secure than L2TP because it uses Microsoft Point-to-Point Encryption (MPPE) as its built-in encryption technology. PPTP also offers no header compression or tunnel authentication. This means that PPTP consumes more bandwidth and does not offer you the ability to prove through authentication that the remote VPN server is the server that you think it is and not an imposter. Using an imposter server is a common hacker trick strategy, sometimes referred to as a man-in-the-middle attack, that allows a hacker to receive and decrypt the data. The other potential drawback to PPTP is that it requires the internetwork to be IP-based. This prevents you from using PPTP over other internetworks such as ATM, G3 Fax, X.25, X.75, or frame relay.

L2TP

L2TP is more secure than PPTP but has less industry support at this point, though this is quickly changing. PPTP's drawbacks are part of the reason that L2TP was included with Windows 2000 and is where the industry is progressing to. Taking a look at the available Microsoft OSs, L2TP is only supported in Windows 2000, Windows XP, and Windows .NET at the current time. The benefits of L2TP are that it can operate over a number of different internetworks, supports header compression and tunnel authentication, and uses Internet Protocol Security (IPSec) for encryption. This means that L2TP offers you more configuration options and more network type options, uses less bandwidth, and allows you to prove that the computer you are communicating with is the computer that you think it is.

exam
Watch

L2TP cannot be used when the communication between the two computers that wish to establish the secure VPN crosses a NAT server, because NAT encrypts the header portion of the IP datagram, which contains the UDP port number. To perform translation, NAT needs to change the information in the datagram header, and when it does, it invalidates the checksum that IPSec has calculated. This causes the recipient to think the packet has been tampered with and request a retransmission.

From a VPN client configuration perspective, you have the ability to configure the types of LAN and VPN protocols that you wish to use. Exercise 13-4 teaches you how to make these client-side VPN configuration changes.

EXERCISE 13-4

Configuring the VPN Client Settings

This exercise teaches you how to configure the client VPN settings. This allows you to increase the level of security in your VPN connection as well as change any of the options you configured during the VPN connections creation.

1. Select Start | Settings | Network And Dial-up Connections, right-click your VPN connection, and click Properties.

2. The VPN connection's properties dialog box opens, which has five tabs. On the General tab, you can change the IP address or FQDN of the remote VPN server and configure the VPN connection icon to appear in the taskbar, which is the default setting.

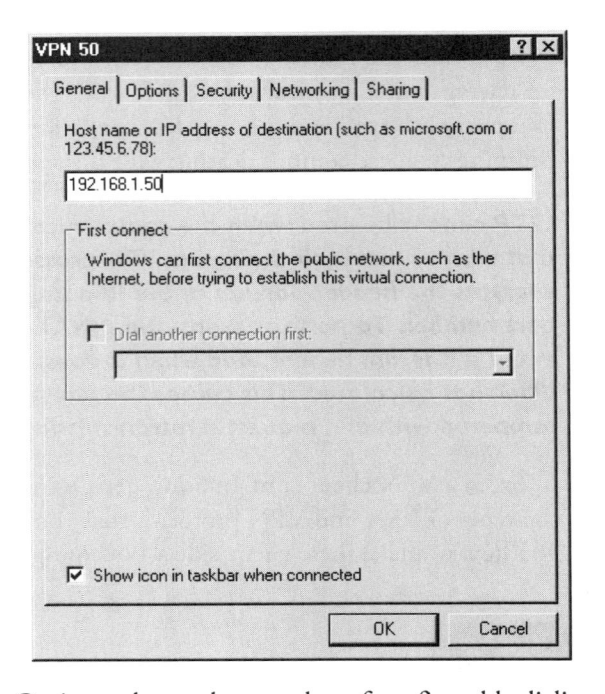

3. Clicking the Options tab reveals a number of configurable dialing and redialing options. You can customize the dialing settings to include the Windows logon domain; prompt for name and password, certificate, and so forth; display the calling progress; and specify the redial attempts, time between these attempts, and idle time before hanging up. The last option can be a lifesaver on your finances if you pay for the time you are connected, as is the case with some ISPs. Speaking from personal experience, this option has saved me a small fortune. My 85-year-old grandmother asked me to connect her to the Internet about two years ago and she sometimes forgets that she is connected and walks away while the connection is active for long periods, sometimes even days.

You can imagine the potential costs if I hadn't configured the Idle Time Before Hanging Up setting to ten minutes, as her connection was billed by the hour. Once you have configured the options, click the Security tab.

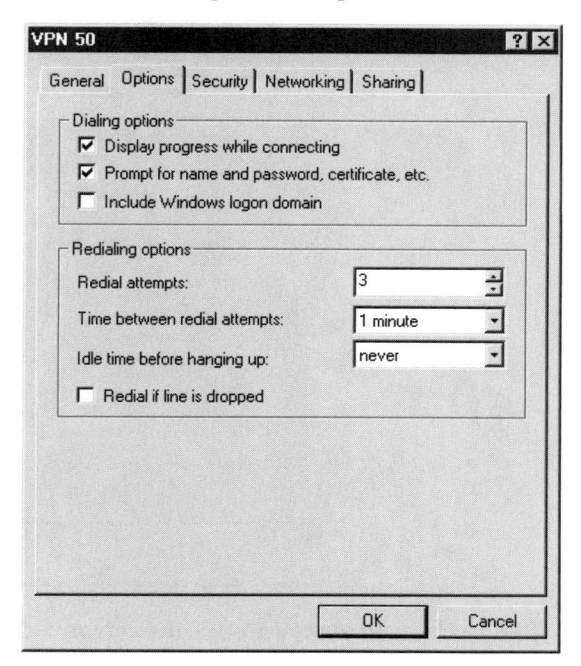

4. The Security tab allows you to configure the security options for the connection to use either typical (the default) or advanced settings. The drop-down box in the Typical setting options allows you to choose between requiring a secure password or using a smart card. You can also configure the connection to automatically use your Windows logon name and password and to require data encryption when sending data.

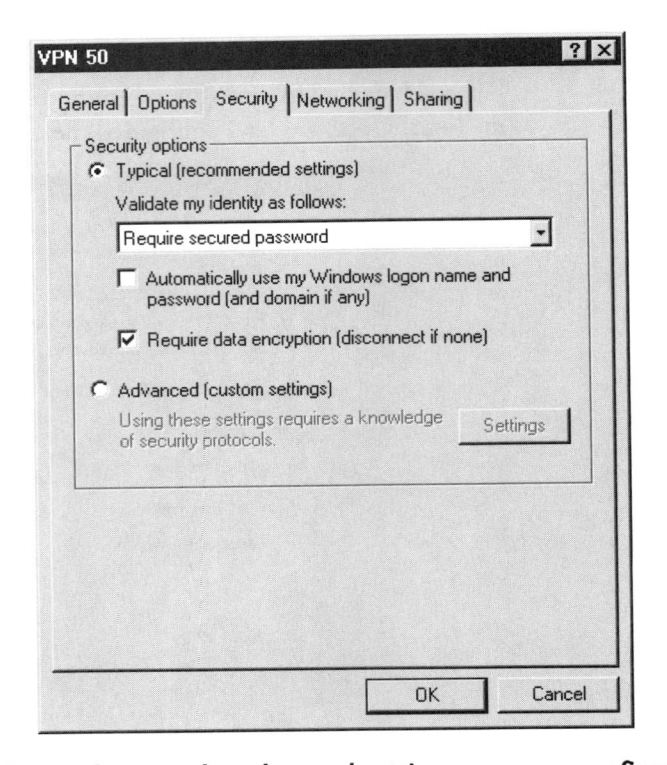

566 Chapter 13: Configuring Remote Access and VPN Connections

author's note
If you select Advanced to use the advanced settings, you can configure these settings by clicking the Settings button, which opens the Advanced Security Settings dialog box. You can set the data encryption level from the drop-down box, with the default being Require Encryption. You can also choose to customize the logon security, which we will cover in the last section of this chapter, "Configuring and Verifying the Security of a VPN Connection."

Advanced Security Settings

Data encryption: Require encryption (disconnect if server declines)

Logon security:
- ○ Use Extensible Authentication Protocol (EAP)
- ● Allow these protocols
  - ☐ Unencrypted password (PAP)
  - ☐ Shiva Password Authentication Protocol (SPAP)
  - ☐ Challenge Handshake Authentication Protocol (CHAP)
  - ☑ Microsoft CHAP (MS-CHAP)
    - ☐ Allow older MS-CHAP version for Windows 95 servers
  - ☑ Microsoft CHAP Version 2 (MS-CHAP v2)
- ☐ For MS-CHAP based protocols, automatically use my Windows logon name and password (and domain if any)

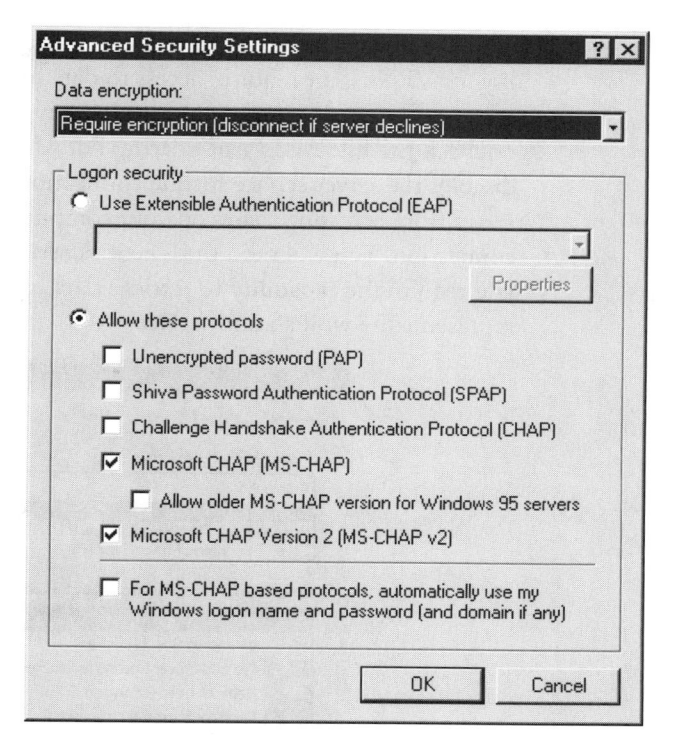

5. The Networking tab allows you to select the VPN protocol that you wish to use for the connection. The default setting of Automatic allows Windows 2000 to negotiate the most secure protocol. Windows 2000 always attempts to use L2TP first, but if the RRAS server doesn't support L2TP, then it tries PPTP. Obviously, if neither is accepted, the connection fails. It is also on the Networking tab that you can define the components used by this connection.

This can also be useful when you are worried about security. For example, if your VPN client requires access to data on the VPN server but the VPN server will never require access to data on the VPN client, you should uncheck the File And Print Sharing For Microsoft Networks box, which disables the server service for the connection, preventing anyone on the VPN server from accessing shares on your computer through the established VPN connection. You will need the Client For Microsoft Networks connection if you require the capability to retrieve data from the VPN server, as this represents the workstation service.

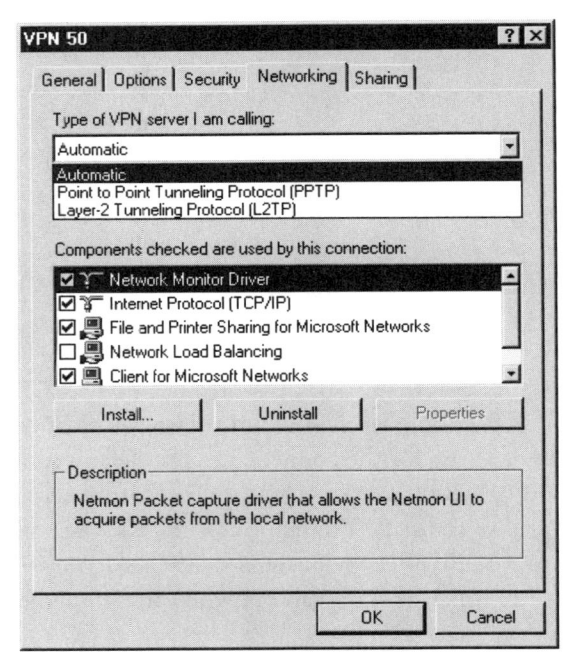

6. Selecting the Settings button on the Networking tab reveals the PPP Settings dialog box, where all three settings are enabled by default. LCP extensions should be disabled if you are connecting to VPN servers that use older PPP software. Software compression allows for the compression of data in addition to hardware compression and does not require that hardware compression be enabled. Using the Negotiate Multi-link For Single-link Connections option

may help to improve audio quality and transmission speed but may not allow you to connect to remote access servers other than those running on Windows 2000.

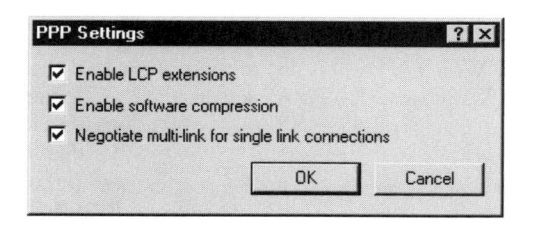

PPP Settings dialog box showing: Enable LCP extensions, Enable software compression, Negotiate multi-link for single link connections

exam
Watch

You are likely to run into a question regarding the Link Control Protocol (LCP) extensions. LCP extensions may cause problems if you are attempting to connect to servers using older PPP software. Should connectivity problems arise, disable the LCP extensions option. Without the LCP extensions, time-remaining and identification packets, as well as callback, are not supported during the PPP negotiation.

7. The Sharing tab is the last of the connection configuration tabs and allows you to enable ICS. If you enable ICS, you must select the network adapter to enable it on. This will always be the internal network adapter. Think of the enabling of ICS as being similar to crossing an international border. I lived in Switzerland once, on the French-Swiss border. If you liken the country of Switzerland to a LAN and the Swiss border post as the internal NIC, then the French border post would be the external NIC. If you want to configure ICS or allow people from Switzerland into France, you would configure the Swiss border post to allow this. The Swiss border post or internal NIC should be the gateway to the French border post or external NIC and remote network. Once you are finished configuring the connection options, click OK to close the Connection Properties dialog box.

You now have the knowledge to tackle the certification objective of configuring client computer remote access properties.

SCENARIO & SOLUTION

What are the four remote access protocols that are available to you in Windows 2000 when configuring a client connection? Which of these is not supported when configuring a Windows 2000 RRAS server connection?	Windows 2000 supports four remote access protocols: PPP, SLIP, Microsoft RAS, and ARAP. Only three of these remote access protocols can be used when configuring a Windows 2000 remote access client to establish a dial-up connection: PPP, SLIP, and Microsoft RAS. Windows 2000 Server can be configured through RRAS to accept incoming PPP, Microsoft RAS, and ARAP connections, but not SLIP connections.
You have been asked to describe some of the benefits of using L2TP over PPTP. What are the benefits that you would describe?	L2TP has many benefits over PPTP but the key is increased security. L2TP uses IPSec to encrypt the data and to allow mutual authentication, which allows you to confirm that the computer that you are sending data to is in fact the computer that you think it is. Other benefits include the ability to use a number of different types of internetworks, such as ATM, frame relay, and x.25. L2TP also uses header compression and tunnel authentication.
You would like to create a VPN connection from a computer running Windows 2000 that is configured with a modem to a Windows 2000 RRAS server configured to accept incoming VPN calls. You have a dial-up package from your local ISP. What are the basic steps involved in accomplishing this?	The first step is to create a dial-up connection to your local ISP and test this to ensure that it works properly and allows you to connect. Once this is complete, the next step is to create a VPN connection to the remote VPN server. Now, if you want to simplify the connection process and allow the VPN to connect by first establishing the dial-up connection, select the Automatically Dial This Initial Connection option on the Public Network page of the Network Connection Wizard and, from the drop-down menu, select the dial-up connection to your ISP. This combines the two connection steps into one and requires only that you double-click the VPN connection shortcut.
You are the administrator of a small corporate network with ten client computers. You have added a second network adapter to one of the computers running Windows 2000 so that it can be connected to both the LAN and the cable modem used for Internet access through cable. Where on the Network Connection Type page of the Internet Connection Wizard do you choose to configure Internet Connection Sharing (ISC)?	Configuring this type of configuration (multiple network adapters) for ICS is generally not something that you would do through the Network Connection Wizard even though there is an option to do it. Selecting the Dial-up To The Internet option on the Network Connection Type page launches the Internet Connection Wizard, which allows you to configure ICS.

CERTIFICATION OBJECTIVE 13.02

Configuring Remote Access Name Resolution and IP Address Allocation

I weighed the order of the first two remote access certification objectives heavily while plotting out the flow of this chapter. It really came down to the old adage about which came first, the chicken or the egg. When looking at remote access, do you talk about the client side first, and then the server side, because the client-side configuration isn't of much value if the server side isn't configured? In the end, as you can see, I decided to go with the client side first followed by the server side. My reasoning was, the remainder of the chapter and the certification objects really focuses on the server-side configuration, so the chapter seemed to flow a lot smoother when it started with the client-side configuration and then transitioned and finished with the server side. I hope you agree and have found it easy to follow. Well, enough semantics, let's begin with a look at configuring IP address allocation.

Configuring IP Address Allocation in Windows 2000

The first step in the configuration of IP address allocation in Windows 2000 is to configure and enable the RRAS service in Windows 2000, which we look at in Exercise 13-5.

EXERCISE 13-5

Configuring RRAS as a VPN Server

This exercise teaches you how to configure a Windows 2000 server as a VPN server that allows both PPTP and L2TP incoming connections. When you configure a RRAS server, the configuration wizard offers you a number of different configuration choices, but with VPNs being such a significant focus on the certification exam, I decided to discuss that configuration option.

572 Chapter 13: Configuring Remote Access and VPN Connections

1. Select Start | Programs | Administrative Tools, and click Routing And Remote Access. In the RRAS snap-in, right-click the name of your server and click Configure And Enable Routing And Remote Access.

exam
🕲atch

Notice that RRAS is installed by default in Windows 2000. Unlike earlier versions of Windows NT, however, it is not enabled. Therefore, it must be enabled and configured.

2. Click Next on the Welcome page, click the Virtual Private Network (VPN) Server radio button, and click Next.

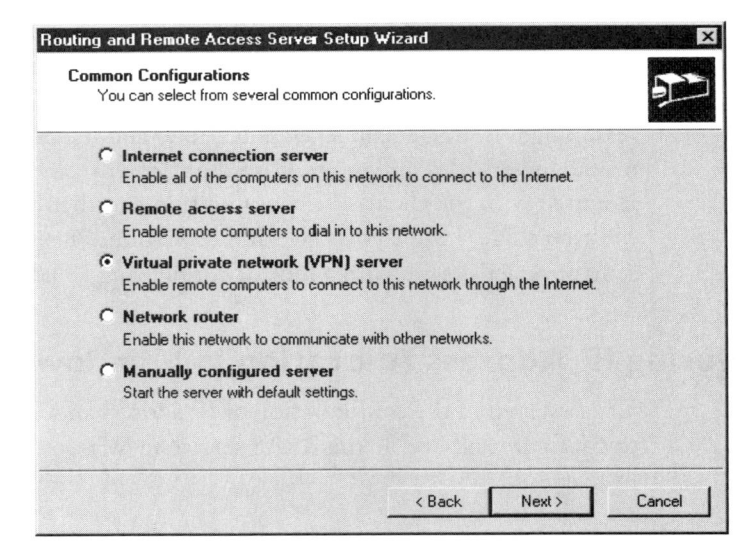

3. On the Remote Client Protocols page, verify that TCP/IP is listed in the Protocols list and click Next. TCP/IP should be listed, as it is installed by default.

Configuring Remote Access Name Resolution and IP Address Allocation **573**

4. On the Internet Connection page, select the external network adapter and click Next.

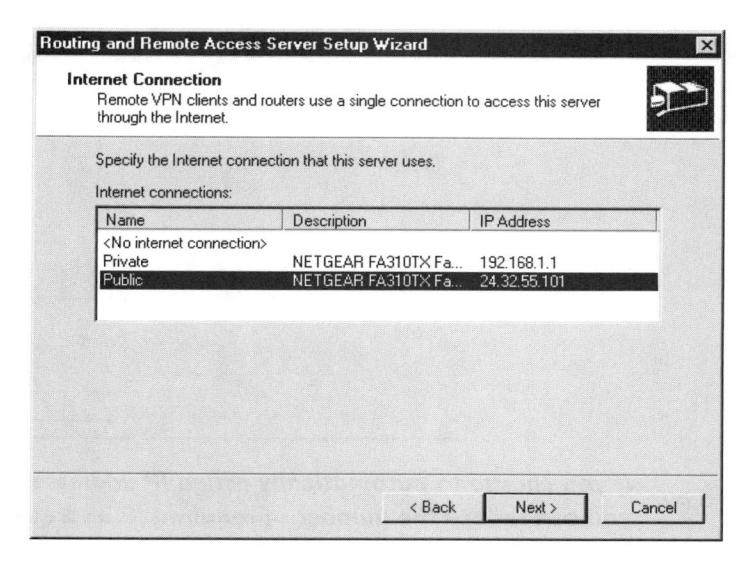

5. On the IP Address Assignment page, select to either Automatically assign IP addresses or to assign them From A Specified Range Of Addresses. If you already have a DHCP server on the network that handles IP address assignment, choose the Automatically option. Selecting to use a specified range allows you to define an IP address range on the Address Range Assignment page, shown in the following illustration. Click Next.

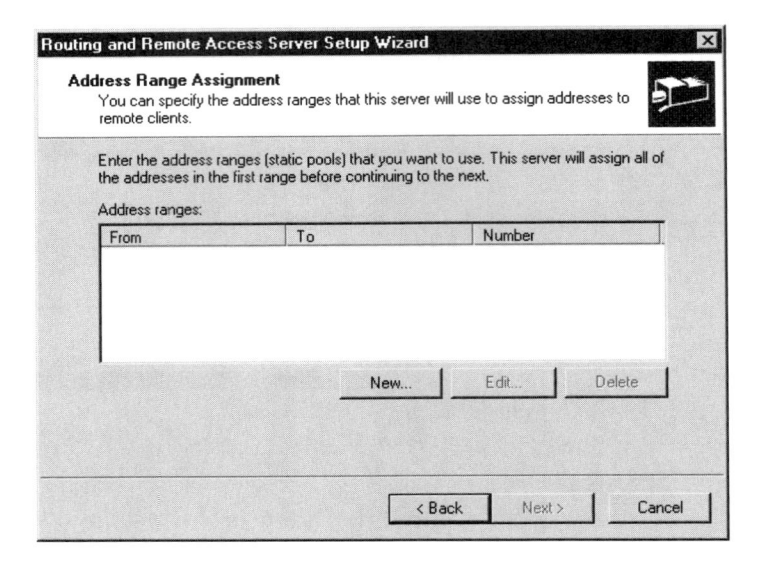

Chapter 13: Configuring Remote Access and VPN Connections

[Screenshot: Routing and Remote Access Server Setup Wizard — Address Range Assignment dialog]

on the Job

If you choose to automatically assign IP addresses for remote access clients, you can reduce the number of required IP addresses by configuring a shorter lease duration. Your remote access server only requires IP addresses for the number of simultaneous connections you have configured to allow in RRAS.

6. The Managing A Multiple Remote Access Servers page appears, asking if you want to use a RADIUS server. In this example, the default of No is acceptable, so click Next and click Finish.

Now that you have RRAS enabled and configured, you are able to edit and change your IP address allocation settings. This is done through the properties of the RRAS server in the RRAS snap-in. It is on the IP tab of the server's Properties dialog box, shown in Figure 13-2, that you can change and configure the IP address assignment options. When you are configuring your IP address assignment for dial-up clients, the Adapter option at the bottom of the IP tab allows you to select the adapter from which to obtain DHCP, DNS, and WINS server addresses for your dial-up clients. By default, RRAS randomly picks a LAN adapter to use. This adapter should be one that is connected to the network on which DHCP-allocated addresses can be obtained. In other words, this adapter should be on the same segment as the DHCP server.

FIGURE 13-2

Configuring the IP address assignment options

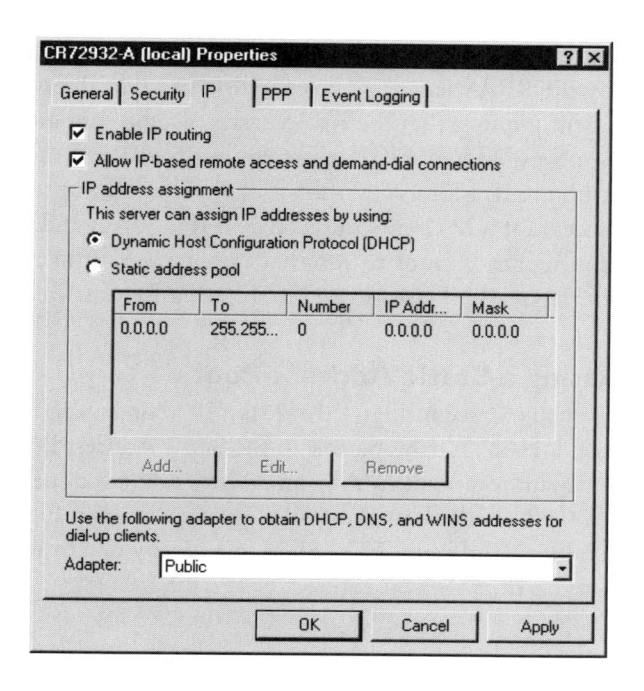

exam 😊 *Watch*

If you select to use a DHCP server and the server is not available when RRAS is started, Automatic Private IP Addressing (APIPA) will assign addresses to remote access clients on the 169.254.0.0/16 network. This will prevent remote access clients from accessing computers on the LAN through the RRAS server.

Automatic IP Address Assignment

Choosing to automatically assign IP addresses using DHCP requires that a DHCP server exist on the network. When RRAS starts, it obtains a block of ten IP addresses for lease to remote access clients, plus one IP address for its remote access adapter. When the first block of ten IP addresses has been leased, RRAS will continue to obtain IP addresses in blocks of ten and manage the IP address lease process between the RRAS server and the remote access clients. The IP addresses, obtained in blocks of ten, are only released by the DHCP server when the RRAS service is stopped.

The DHCP server is never directly involved in the individual lease process when remote access clients are installed. This means that when a remote access client releases its IP address, the address becomes available on the RRAS server but is not returned to the DHCP server to be made available to other clients; it remains held by the RRAS server. This separation of DHCP server from remote access DHCP client requires that the RRAS server also be configured as a DHCP relay agent if you would like DHCP scope options forwarded to the remote access DHCP client with the IP address and subnet mask. Configuring a DHCP relay agent allows remote access DHCP clients to receive an IP address and subnet mask and additional configuration information that can be used for name resolution. This is covered in the upcoming section, "Configuring Remote Access Name Resolution."

Using a Static Address Pool

As you can see in Figure 13-2, the IP address assignment is currently configured to use DHCP. Changing this to the Static Address Pool option allows you to add your own address pool. Adding an address range is done by clicking the Add button and, in the New Address Range dialog box shown in Figure 13-3, entering a starting and ending IP address. This will automatically determine the number of addresses based on the IP range you entered.

Configuring Remote Access Name Resolution

Name resolution in remote access scenarios is not that different from name resolution in a routed network. The key to success is getting name resolution information in the form of DNS and WINS server IP addresses to the remote access clients. When the RRAS server is configured to automatically assign IP addresses to remote access clients, it is recommended that a DHCP relay agent be installed and configured.

FIGURE 13-3

Adding an IP address range

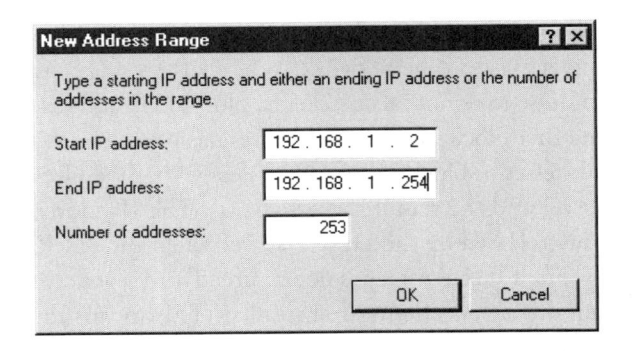

This is done in RRAS and allows the RRAS server to forward DHCP scope options from the DHCP server to the remote access clients. Exercise 13-6 teaches you the steps involved in configuring a DHCP relay agent.

> **exam**
> **⟨Watch⟩**
>
> *If you have chosen to automatically assign IP addresses in RRAS, you can configure your Windows 2000 DHCP server to use the default Routing and Remote Access user option class to assign different options to your remote clients than you assign to your LAN clients, such as DNS and WINS server and gateway information.*

EXERCISE 13-6

Configuring the DHCP Relay Agent

Configuring the DHCP relay agent is accomplished in the RRAS snap-in and allows you to forward DHCP scope information to your remote access clients through the RRAS server. This type of configuration can be further enhanced by using the Routing and Remote Access user option class to configure special options only for remote access clients.

1. Select Start | Programs | Administrative Tools, and click Routing And Remote Access.
2. In the RRAS snap-in, expand IP Routing, right-click General, and click New Routing Protocol.
3. Select DHCP relay agent and click OK.
4. Right-click DHCP relay agent under IP Routing and click New Interface.
5. Select the internal interface that is able to access the DHCP server, click OK, and click OK again.
6. Right-click DHCP relay agent under IP Routing and click Properties. This opens the DHCP relay agent Properties dialog box. Enter the IP address of the DHCP server, click Add, and click OK.

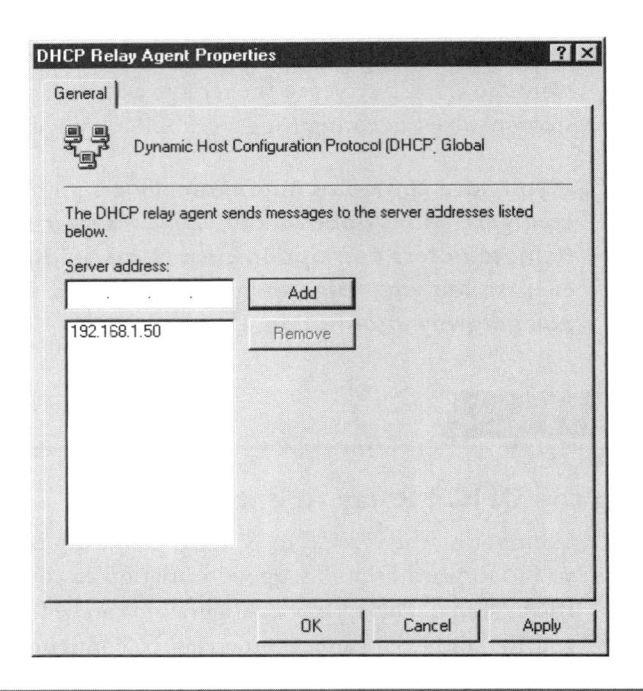

SCENARIO & SOLUTION

You are the administrator of a number of RRAS servers, most of which are configured for different purposes. You have noticed that the number of VPN ports created differs. Why is this, and when do these differences occur?	You are very observant to notice this difference in the number of VPN ports. When you configure RRAS to be a VPN server through the wizard, 128 PPTP and L2TP ports are configured. However, when RRAS is installed for remote access, only five ports are configured. More ports are configured when you configure RRAS as a VPN server, as it is assumed that more will be required if this is the purpose of the server.
What new DHCP feature can you use in conjunction with RRAS to help simplify and organize the scope options that are obtained by your remote access clients?	The Routing and Remote Access user option class can be used in conjunction with RRAS to assign different scope options that will apply only to your remote access clients.

Configuring and Troubleshooting Client-to-Server PPTP and L2TP Connections **579**

SCENARIO & SOLUTION

You have configured your RRAS server to automatically assign IP addresses through DHCP. You have noticed that upon starting RRAS, a number of new DHCP leases occur, but there are currently no remote access client connections. What is causing this?	When configured to use DHCP to automatically assign IP addresses, RRAS grabs a block of ten IP addresses from DHCP upon initialization. This block of IP addresses is managed by RRAS and used to lease IP addresses to remote access clients as required. RRAS also grabs one additional address for itself and assigns this to its PPP adapter. When a remote access client releases its IP address, the address becomes available for other remote access clients but is not returned to the DHCP pool of available IPs.

CERTIFICATION OBJECTIVE 13.03

Configuring and Troubleshooting Client-to-Server PPTP and L2TP Connections

Configuring a VPN connection by following step-by-step instructions is one thing, but where you really earn your stripes as an administrator is solving problems that occur when trying to establish a connection. That is what this section of the chapter will teach you. You will learn about a number of potential errors you could see when configuring client-to-server VPN connections. We will also explore how to find more-detailed information about established VPN connections, which will allow you to confirm that the settings you think are in use are actually in use.

Verifying VPN Connectivity Options

When you are successful in establishing a connection, it is useful to know how you have connected and what authentication and encryption methods the connection is using. This information can be found by right-clicking the VPN Connection icon in the taskbar and clicking Status. In the Status dialog box, select the Details tab to reveal the detailed connection information shown in Figure 13-4.

FIGURE 13-4

Viewing VPN connection details

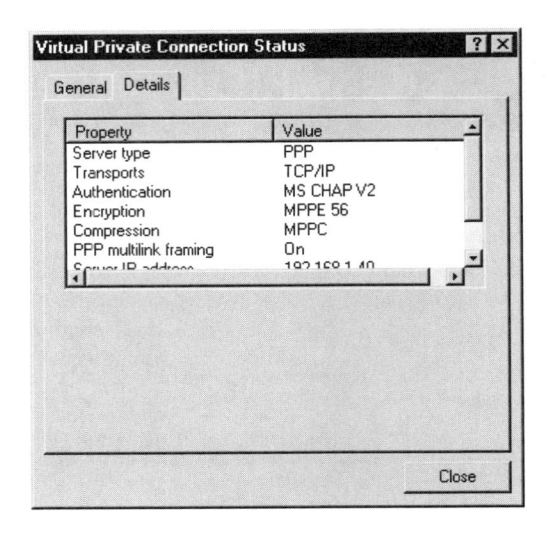

From the detailed connection information, you can see that PPP is the remote access protocol used to establish the connection, the LAN protocol is TCP/IP, and the authentication method was the most secure of the standard authentication methods, MC-CHAP v2. The data sent through the VPN is encrypted with 56-bit MPPE, and Microsoft Point-to-Point Compression (MPPC) is also used. Other information that is available if you were to scroll down is the server and client IP addresses used in the remote access VPN connection. All this information can be used to determine if the connection was established as you intended. For example, if you wanted the VPN to use L2TP but the information on the Details tab indicates that it is using PPTP, then you have a place to start your troubleshooting and you know what is working. Sometimes you might not be this lucky in having a functioning connection to start from, but regardless, the System event log can also provide you with some excellent troubleshooting information.

Looking to the System event log reveals a warning message with Event ID 20192, shown in Figure 13-5, which describes why the L2TP connection failed but PPTP succeeded. What you see in the event message is that a valid machine certificate could not be found, which prevented the connection from using L2TP over IPSec. Until a machine certificate is installed, no L2TP calls will be accepted. The installation and configuration of certificates is beyond the scope of this exam, but you can find information on this by searching for **certificates** at www.microsoft.com/windows2000.

FIGURE 13-5

Examining Event ID 20192 to determine why L2TP failed to connect

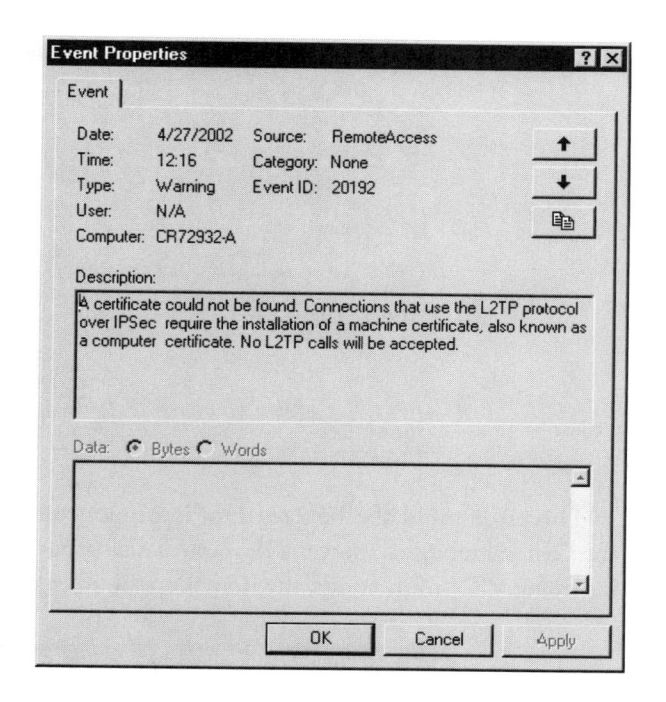

[Event Properties dialog showing:
Date: 4/27/2002 Source: RemoteAccess
Time: 12:16 Category: None
Type: Warning Event ID: 20192
User: N/A
Computer: CR72932-A
Description: A certificate could not be found. Connections that use the L2TP protocol over IPSec require the installation of a machine certificate, also known as a computer certificate. No L2TP calls will be accepted.]

No-Answer Errors

Another common error you are likely to run into is shown in Figure 13-6. This error could be a result of the PPTP and L2TP ports not being configured to accept incoming connections. By checking the Remote Access Connections (Inbound Only) check box, shown in Figure 13-7, and configuring the number of required ports, this problem is solved. You will require a minimum of one port per incoming connection.

FIGURE 13-6

Error 678: No Answer

[Error Connecting to Virtual Private Connection dialog:
Connecting to 192.168.1.1...
Error 678: There was no answer.
Redial = 48   Cancel   More Info]

582 Chapter 13: Configuring Remote Access and VPN Connections

FIGURE 13-7

Configuring the PPTP ports

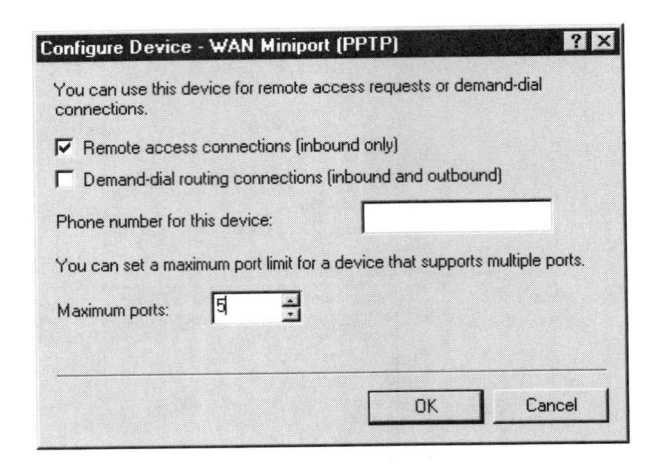

This error could also be a result of improper configuration of the RRAS server on the General tab of the server's Properties dialog box, shown in Figure 13-8. To allow incoming VPN connections, the Router option must be enabled, as must the sub option

FIGURE 13-8

Improper RRAS server configuration for VPN connectivity

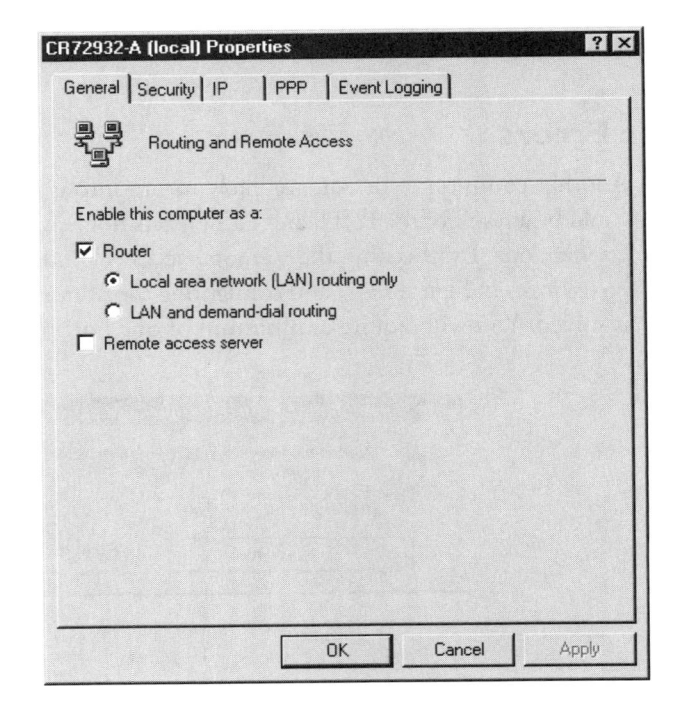

LAN And Demand-Dial Routing. Another alternative is to enable the Remote Access Server option. Both of these options will add the L2TP and PPTP ports required to establish incoming VPN connections.

Not Enough Available Ports

Another common error that you might come across is Error 651, shown in Figure 13-9. This error message can be one of the more misleading messages, as it suggests that the modem is the problem. When I generated this error, there was no modem involved in the attempted communication, which left the problem related to another connecting device. The connecting device in question was the port configuration. If all of the available PPTP or L2TP ports are active, this is the message a user attempting to connect is likely to see. This can be easily resolved by increasing the number of available ports. A good rule of thumb is to create as many ports as you have a need for at your peak connectivity time. This type of information can be collected by initially opening more ports than you require and then configuring logging to log the access for a period of time in order to establish a baseline.

Authentication Protocol Problems

Authentication protocol problems are another likely source of error messages. These generally occur when the remote VPN client and the VPN server are unable to agree on an authentication protocol that both can use. By default, both the client and server connections are configured to use MS-CHAP v2 first, followed by MS-CHAP, but if these defaults have been changed, you are likely to receive Error 919, shown in Figure 13-10. These types of problems can be easily rectified by editing the authentication protocol properties on both the client and the VPN server and configuring a similar authentication protocol on each computer.

FIGURE 13-9

Modem error message

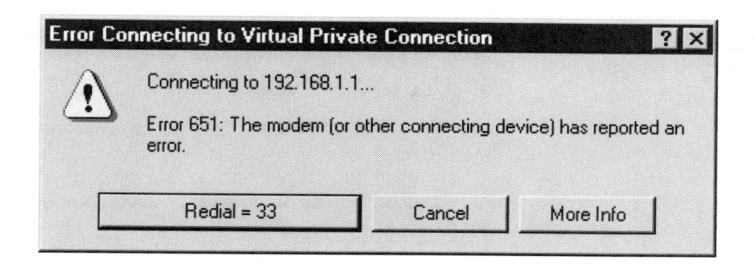

584 Chapter 13: Configuring Remote Access and VPN Connections

FIGURE 13-10

Authentication errors

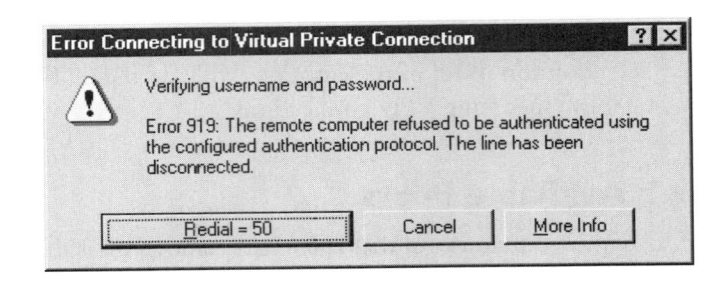

In addition to authentication problems, there are also permission-related problems. To establish a connection to a remote VPN server, you must be granted Allow dial-in permission or be granted permission through the remote access policy. Chapter 14 delves into the configuration of remote access policy, so we will leave the specifics for that chapter. Suffice it to say that your user account must be granted dial-in permission and you must meet the conditions and profile settings found within the applicable RAS policy in order to be granted access.

If your user dial-in permission was set to Deny access, you would be denied and receive the Error 649, shown in Figure 13-11. This type of problem can be corrected by changing the user's dial-in permission to Allow access or to Control access through remote access policy on the Dial-in tab of the user's Properties dialog box. Selecting the latter option of controlling access through RAS policy might require further configuration in the RAS policy (but again, this is covered in detail in Chapter 14). Another way around this error message can be tried by clicking the Redial button. Upon redial, the Connect Virtual Private Connection dialog box opens, shown in Figure 13-12, allowing you to try another username and password that do have the required dial-in permission.

Another useful feature that is include in RRAS to assist you in troubleshooting is the PPP logging option. PPP logging can be configured on the Event Logging tab of the RRAS server's Properties dialog box, as shown in Figure 13-13. When

FIGURE 13-11

Permission problems

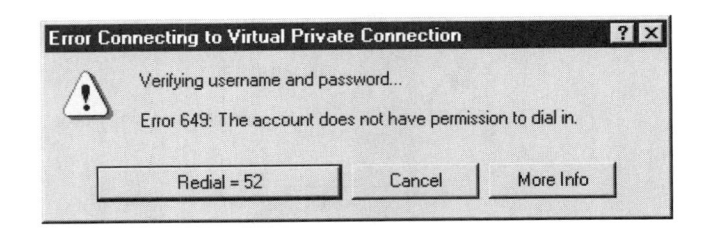

Configuring and Troubleshooting Client-to-Server PPTP and L2TP Connections **585**

FIGURE 13-12

Specifying a different user in the Connect Virtual Private Connection dialog box

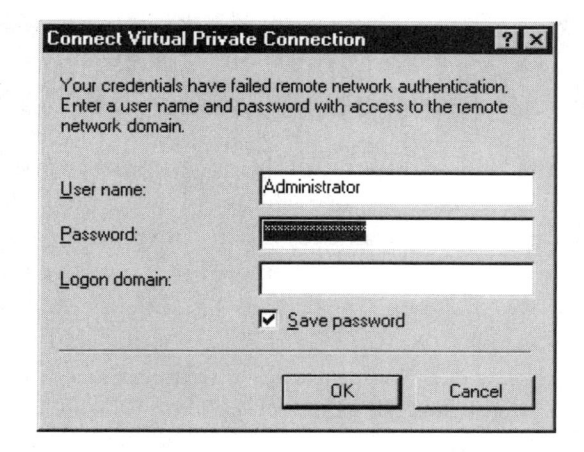

enabled, a ppp.log file will be created and stored in the %systemroot%\tracing folder. This can be used to help you determine where in the connection or authentication process things failed.

FIGURE 13-13

Configuring PPP logging

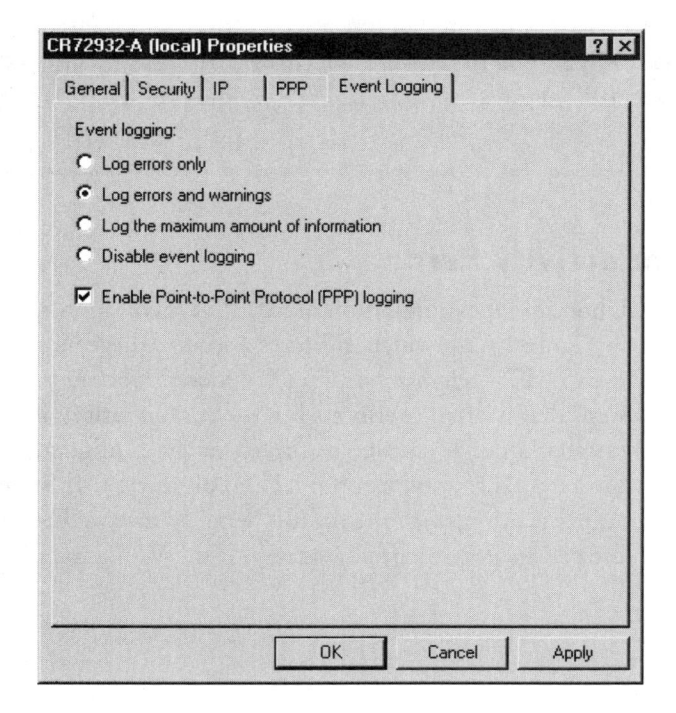

> ### FROM THE CLASSROOM
>
> Another documented, and frustrating problem with VPNs in Windows 2000 is that enabling a VPN in RRAS may cause all traffic to be sent over the VPN and prevent traffic from being sent to remote networks through the default gateway. The problem here is that RRAS doesn't forward packets over the network interface that is configured as the Internet (VPN) interface. When you configure the Internet Connection page of the RRAS Setup Wizard (as shown earlier) during the configuration of a VPN server, all network traffic is forwarded over the VPN connection, because RRAS secures this Internet interface through the configuration of default filters that only accept PPTP or L2TP traffic. This prevents any packets other than PPTP and L2TP from being forwarded on the Internet interface.
>
> To resolve this problem, you must configure your RRAS server to also perform routing, which can be done by right-clicking the name of the server in RRAS and selecting the Routing check box and the LAN And Demand-Dial Routing radio button. Then, once the RRAS server restarts, right-click Ports, select Properties, select WAN Miniport PPTP, and select the Remote Access Connections (Inbound Only) check box. Repeat this last step, but select WAN Miniport L2TP, and you have now solved the problem.
>
> —*Rory McCaw*

L2TP Connectivity Errors

Upon initial configuration of L2TP, it is common to receive Error 792, shown in Figure 13-14, which indicates a security negotiation failure. This has to do with L2TP's reliance on IPSec for encryption and authentication. One of the steps that is often overlooked in the configuration of an L2TP VPN server is the installation of a machine certificate or the configuration of an IPSec policy that can be used to establish the L2TP connection. IPSec offers three choices for authentication, with the default being Kerberos. The other two options are to use certificates or a preshared key. If the VPN server is not configured with an

FIGURE 13-14

Failed security negotiation

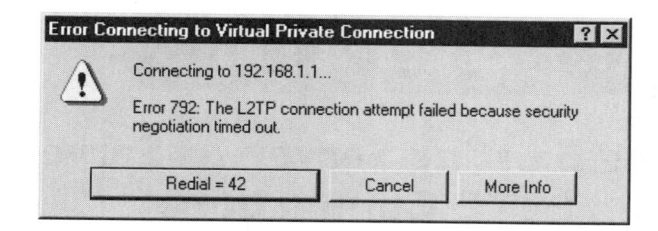

[Dialog box: Error Connecting to Virtual Private Connection — Connecting to 192.168.1.1... Error 792: The L2TP connection attempt failed because security negotiation timed out. Redial = 42 / Cancel / More Info]

IPSec policy, then it will not be able to allow incoming L2TP connections. This problem can be resolved by obtaining and installing a machine certificate to be used for IPSec.

SCENARIO & SOLUTION

You have just finished the configuration on your first Windows 2000 VPN server. You have successfully established a connection from a VPN client and now you would like to verify that the characteristics of the connection are as you think they are. How will you do this?	Once you have established the connection, right-click the connection icon in the taskbar and select Status. In the Connection dialog box, click the Details tab to view the connection characteristics.
What is the default MPPE encryption level used to encrypt data that is sent through a PPTP VPN?	56-bit encryption is the default MPPE level used to encrypt data sent through a PPTP VPN.
You are having problems with the functionality of your RRAS server. You have decided to try to identify the problem using Event Viewer. Which log file will you look in?	Messages related to RRAS can be found in the System event log. RRAS is a system service, as opposed to an application, and therefore its event messages are found in the System log.
You have been making changes to your RRAS server's configuration in an attempt to familiarize yourself with the service. Some of the configuration changes you made on the General tab of the RRAS server's Properties dialog box resulted in the Ports section disappearing, which is preventing all remote VPN users from accessing the server. How should the General tab be configured to reenable VPN connectivity to the RRAS server?	The General tab of the RRAS server's Properties dialog box should have both the Router option and the LAN And Demand-Dial Routing suboption selected. Selecting the Remote Access Server option would also result in the Ports section being added back and allowing for VPN connectivity.

CERTIFICATION OBJECTIVE 13.04

Managing Existing Server-to-Server PPTP and L2TP Connections

This section assumes that you have already established a server-to-server VPN that uses either PPTP or L2TP and now requires you to manage the configuration. More often than not in corporate environments, your RRAS server will sit behind a firewall for security purposes. This will require you to open the required ports on the firewall to allow incoming and outgoing traffic. The types of traffic you need to configure through the firewall will depend on the VPN protocols that you have selected to use. Once the appropriate firewall ports have been opened, security can be further enhanced by configuring inbound and outbound packet filters on the VPN server to only allow the specific VPN protocols in and out of the VPN server.

Configuring PPTP and L2TP Filtering

There are two ways in which to configure the architecture of your VPN server. The first is to connect the VPN server directly to the Internet, in front of the firewall. This network architecture is the least popular method, because it is the less secure option and exposes the VPN to the Internet, leaving it open to attack. The second architectural design places the VPN server behind the firewall either on the LAN or in a DMZ, which is isolated from the LAN. This is the more popular and more secure architecture, but requires that additional security configuration steps be taken to allow VPN protocol traffic through the firewall.

To allow PPTP traffic through your firewall, you have to allow IP protocol 47, which represents Generic Routing Encapsulation (GRE), and TCP port 1723, which is used for tunnel creation, maintenance, and termination.

To allow L2TP and IPSec traffic through your firewall, you have to allow UDP port 500 and IP protocol 50 or 51. IP protocol 50 represents the Encapsulating Security Payload (ESP) protocol, and IP protocol 51 represents the Authentication

Header (AH) protocol. UDP port 500 is used for the IPSec security negotiation, and IP protocol 50 or 51 is used to allow IPSec ESP and/or AH traffic through the firewall. The filtering configuration for L2TP is different at the firewall than at the RRAS server, where you are able to use input and output filters. At the firewall, you do not need to create filters for L2TP traffic on UDP port 1701 because, at that point, all L2TP traffic, including tunnel maintenance and tunneled data, is encrypted as an IPSec ESP payload.

exam
🕑 **a t c h**

ESP is used to encrypt the data sent between two communicating computers. AH does not encrypt any data, it only provides authentication and protects the data from modification when in transit between the two communicating computers.

In either case, the security of these filters can be increased by further configuring both the source and destination addresses. For example, when configuring server-to-server VPN connections, you will be aware of the external IP addresses of both VPN servers. These IP addresses can be configured in the destination and source sections of the IP filters to not only limit communication to PPTP and L2TP but also stipulate that only traffic from a single source IP address (that of the remote VPN server) will be permitted.

To this point, all of the filtering configuration that has been discussed has occurred on the firewall. The RRAS snap-in can be used to allow you to configure incoming and outgoing packet filters on the VPN server, adding an increased level of security. Exercise 13-7 teaches you how to configure these packet filters.

EXERCISE 13-7

Configuring PPTP and L2TP Packet Filters

This exercise teaches you how to configure both PPTP and L2TP packet filters and uses the example of the network shown in the following illustration for the purpose of the exercise. Creating packet filters adds one more extra layer of security by only allowing specific protocols, in this case VPN protocols, into the RRAS server.

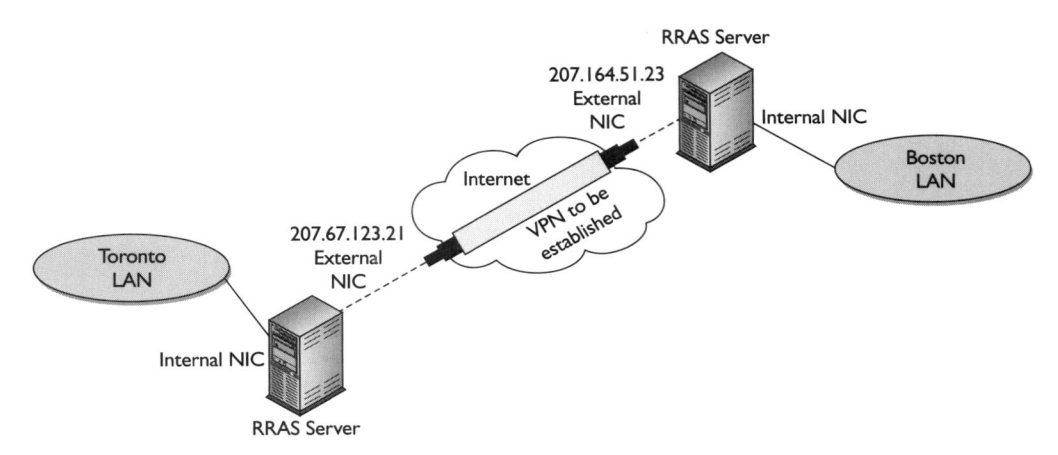

590 Chapter 13: Configuring Remote Access and VPN Connections

[Diagram showing two RRAS Servers connected via the Internet. The Toronto LAN connects through an Internal NIC to an RRAS Server with External NIC 207.67.123.21, across the Internet (with VPN to be established) to an RRAS Server with External NIC 207.164.51.23, then via Internal NIC to the Boston LAN.]

1. On the RRAS server connected to the Toronto LAN, select Start | Programs | Administrative Tools, and click Routing And Remote Access.

2. In RRAS, expand the name of the RRAS server and expand IP Routing. Click General, right-click the external interface, and click Properties to open the external network adapter's Properties dialog box.

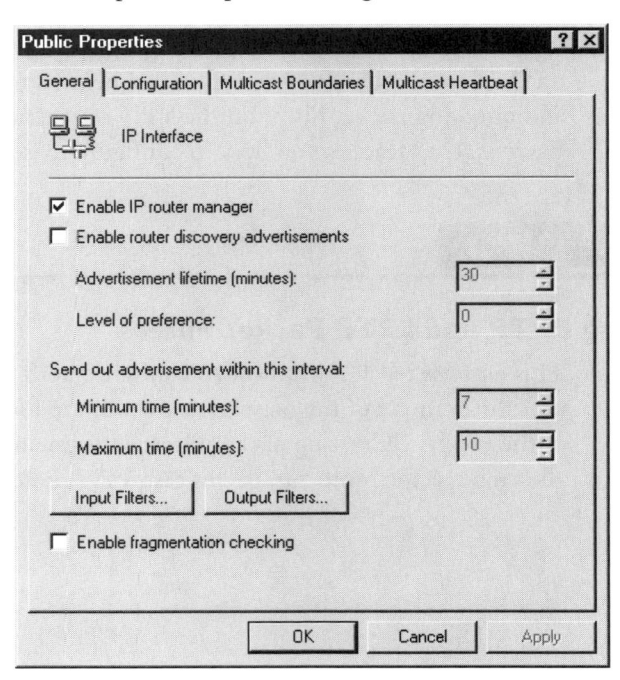

[Screenshot of Public Properties dialog box, General tab, showing IP Interface settings: Enable IP router manager checked, Enable router discovery advertisements unchecked, Advertisement lifetime 30 minutes, Level of preference 0, Minimum time 7 minutes, Maximum time 10 minutes, Input Filters and Output Filters buttons, Enable fragmentation checking unchecked.]

3. Click the Input Filters button and, in the Input Filters dialog box, click Add.

4. To begin the creation of a PPTP filter, select the Destination Network check box, enter the IP address of the external NIC of the local VPN server **207.67.123.21**, and type an IP mask of **255.255.255.255** for the subnet mask. Using this IP mask allows you to enter a specific IP address instead of a destination network or range of addresses, and therefore is more secure by allowing access to only a single IP address. In the Protocol drop-down menu, select TCP, and in the Source Port list box, type **1723**. Click OK. The Add IP Filter dialog box should now look as follows:

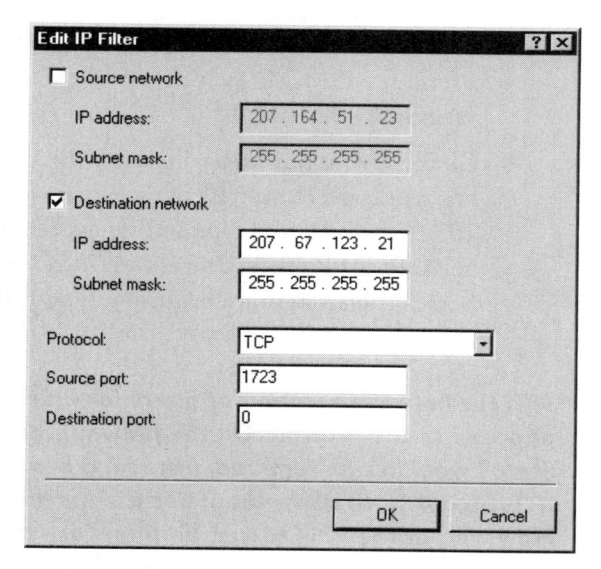

```
Edit IP Filter                                          ? X
  ☐ Source network
     IP address:        207 . 164 . 51 . 23
     Subnet mask:       255 . 255 . 255 . 255

  ☑ Destination network
     IP address:        207 . 67 . 123 . 21
     Subnet mask:       255 . 255 . 255 . 255

  Protocol:             TCP
  Source port:          1723
  Destination port:     0

                              OK        Cancel
```

5. Click the Add button again in the Input Filters dialog box. In the Add IP Filter dialog box, select Other from the Protocol drop-down box, type **47** as the protocol number, and click OK. This will allow GRE through, which is required for PPTP.

6. Click the Add button again in the Input Filters dialog box, select the Destination Network check box, enter the IP address of the external NIC of the local VPN server **207.67.123.21**, and type an IP mask of **255.255.255.255**

for the subnet mask. In the Protocol drop-down menu, select TCP, and in the Destination Port list box, type **1723**. Click OK and click OK again. This will create an outbound PPTP filter, whereas in Step 4 an inbound PPTP filter was created.

7. At this point, you have configured all of the required input filters for PPTP. To add the two remaining input filters for L2TP, click the Input Filters button, click the Add button again, select the Destination Network check box, enter the IP address of the external NIC of the local VPN server **207.67.123.21**, and type an IP mask of **255.255.255.255** for the subnet mask. In the Protocol drop-down menu, select UDP, and in the Source Port and Destination Port boxes, type **500**. Click OK. This will create a filter for ISAKMP, which will allow the IPSec security negotiation to occur.

8. Click the Add button again, select the Destination Network check box, enter the IP address of the external NIC of the local VPN server **207.67.123.21**, and type an IP mask of **255.255.255.255** for the subnet mask. In the Protocol drop-down menu, select UDP, and in the Source Port and Destination Port boxes, type **1701**. Click OK. This will create a filter for L2TP.

on the Job *This is where the creation of filters for IPSec differs on the VPN server as opposed to the firewall. On the firewall, the configuration performed in Step 8 wouldn't be required; instead, a protocol filter would be added for IP protocol 50 to allow the IPSec ESP payload traffic through the firewall. However, at the VPN server, no filters are required for IPSec ESP traffic for IP protocol 50 or 51 because RRAS input and output filters are applied after the IPSec module of TCP/IP removes the ESP header.*

9. In the Input Filters box, change the top option to Drop All Packets Except Those That Meet The Criteria Below and click OK.

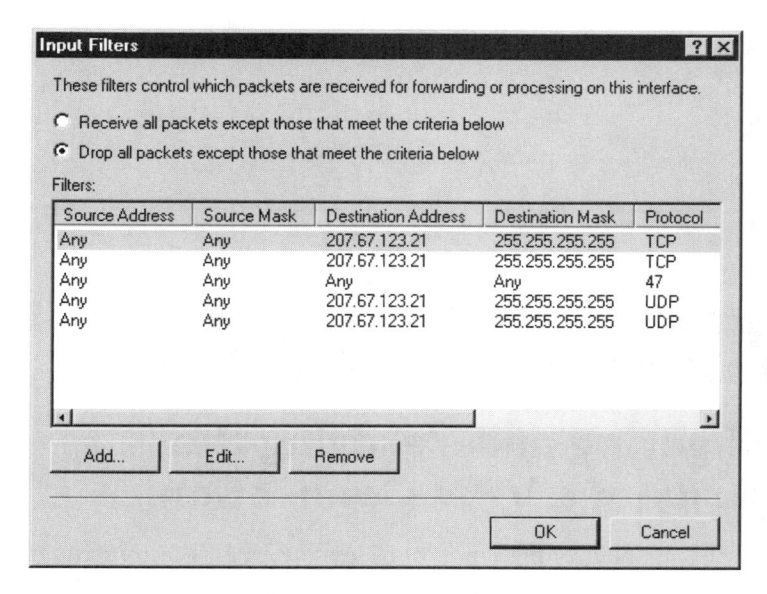

Managing Existing Server-to-Server PPTP and L2TP Connections

10. Now output filters must be created. To do this, click the Output Filters button and add the output filters defined in Table 13-1.

TABLE 13-1 Output Filter Properties

Source Address	Any	207.67.123.21	207.67.123.21	207.67.123.21	207.67.123.21
Source Mask	Any	255.255.255.255	255.255.255.255	255.255.255.255	255.255.255.255
Destination Address	Any	Any	Any	Any	Any
Destination Mask	Any	Any	Any	Any	Any
Protocol	47	TCP	TCP	UDP	UDP
Source Port	Any	1723	Any	500	1701
Destination Port	Any	Any	1723	500	1701
Description	GRE	PPTP Inbound	PPTP Outbound	ISAKMP	L2TP

11. All of the necessary input and output filters are now configured on the Toronto RRAS server. These exact steps should now be performed on the Boston RRAS server, replacing the IP address with the external IP address of the Boston RRAS server.

CERTIFICATION OBJECTIVE 13.05

Configuring and Verifying the Security of a VPN Connection

The configuration of client-side VPN security settings was touched on earlier in this chapter when you learned how to configure a VPN. In Exercise 13-4, you clicked the Advanced button on the Security tab of the VPN client connection dialog box to open the Advanced Security Settings dialog box. This section revisits the settings in that dialog box and explores what each individual setting allows you to accomplish, and in what scenarios it should be used.

Available Authentication Methods

Windows 2000 includes many different authentication methods, all of which we explore in this section. Some of the authentication methods you will be familiar with from other Microsoft Windows operating systems, while others will be new. Table 13-2 lists and describes all of the available authentication methods, starting with the least secure through to the most secure.

on the Job

There are a number of freeware and shareware utilities available to perform brute force attacks on captured network traffic or the SAM database such as Lophtcrack.

TABLE 13-2 Available Authentication Methods

Authentication Method	Description
Password Authentication Protocol (PAP)	PAP allows passwords to be sent in clear text and is the least secure of the authentication protocols. If the password sent by the remote user matches that stored on the RRAS server, access is granted. PAP offers little protection against unauthorized access and should only be enabled when it is required to support legacy clients that offer no other option.
Shiva Password Authentication Protocol (SPAP)	SPAP is a two-way reversible encryption authentication protocol that is included to allow dial-in access from Shiva clients. Like PAP, SPAP is not a secure authentication protocol. SPAP does encrypt the password data sent across the network, but is still not considered secure. Choosing SPAP does not allow you to select the Require encryption option from the data encryption drop-down menu.
Challenge Handshake Authentication Protocol (CHAP)	CHAP is an authentication protocol that allows non-Microsoft clients to communicate with a Windows 2000 server using encryption. It can also be used by a Windows 2000 client to allow communication between a computer running a non-Microsoft OS, again using encryption. CHAP uses a challenge-response authentication process that encrypts the response using Message Digest 5 (MD5), but it does not support mutual authentication. MD5 is an industry-standard hashing algorithm. A hashing algorithm is used to encrypt and decrypt data upon transmission and receipt.
Microsoft CHAP (MS-CHAP)	MS-CHAP is Microsoft's first version of this authentication protocol and is also referred to as NT LAN Manager authentication. Like CHAP, MS-CHAP uses a challenge-response authentication process that encrypts the responses. The security weakness in MS-CHAP is that the user's password is sent across the network during authentication negotiations. Even though the password is encrypted, it could allow a user to sniff the network, capture the encrypted password, and perform a brute-force attack on the encrypted password to decrypt it and obtain the password. MS-CHAP uses MPPE to encrypt data and also only offers one-way authentication.
MS-CHAP v2	MS-CHAP version 2 is the most secure of the standard protocols, as it provides mutual authentication and stronger data encryption keys, and uses different encryption keys for sending and receiving. MS-CHAP v2 also no longer sends the user's encrypted password during authentication negotiations, which prevents it from being sniffed off the network and cracked through a brute-force attack.
Extensible Authentication Protocol (EAP)	EAP is new to Windows 2000 and is not considered one of the "standard" authentication protocols even though EAP and TLS are industry-standard protocols. EAP, as the name implies, provides extensibility to Windows 2000 by providing support for other authentication methods, such as certificates and smart cards. Transport Layer Security (TLS) is used for smart card and other intermediary devices. Smart cards are designed to store the user's certificate and private key electronically. EAP allows for the use of other authentication methods such as token cards.

Default Authentication Protocols

The two default authentication protocols in Windows 2000 are MS-CHAP and MS-CHAP v2. MS-CHAP v2 is supported by a number of different Microsoft OS clients, including Windows 2000, Windows NT 4 with SP4 or higher, Windows 98, XP, Me, and Windows 95 with the Windows Dial-up Networking 1.3 Performance and Security Upgrade. MS-CHAP, the predecessor to MS-CHAP v2, should be used when you have clients that do not support MS-CHAP v2.

Authentication protocols can be configured on both the client and the server. We have seen how to configure these on the client; Exercise 13-8 looks at how to configure them on the server, because in order for a communication connection to be established, both the client and the server must agree on a common authentication protocol.

When multiple authentication methods are configured, Windows 2000 allows attempts to negotiate the most secure authentication settings first and moves down through the list until it finds one that is acceptable on both the client and server computers.

EXERCISE 13-8

Configuring Authentication Protocols on RRAS

This exercise teaches you how to configure authentication protocols on the RRAS server. This will allow you to increase or decrease the level of authentication accepted on the server for incoming connections and even add in support for certificates if required.

1. Select Start | Programs | Administrative Tools, and click Routing And Remote Access.

2. In the RRAS snap-in, right-click the name of your server and select Properties. On the Security tab, click the Authentication Methods button to reveal the Authentication Methods dialog box.

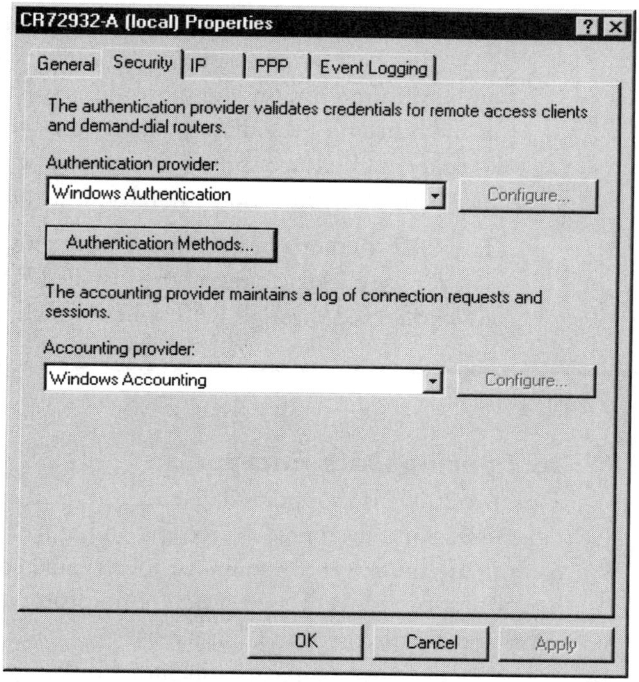
CR72932-A (local) Properties
General
Security
IP
PPP
Event Logging
The authentication provider validates credentials for remote access clients and demand-dial routers.
Authentication provider:
Windows Authentication
Configure...
Authentication Methods...
The accounting provider maintains a log of connection requests and sessions.
Accounting provider:
Windows Accounting
Configure...
OK
Cancel
Apply

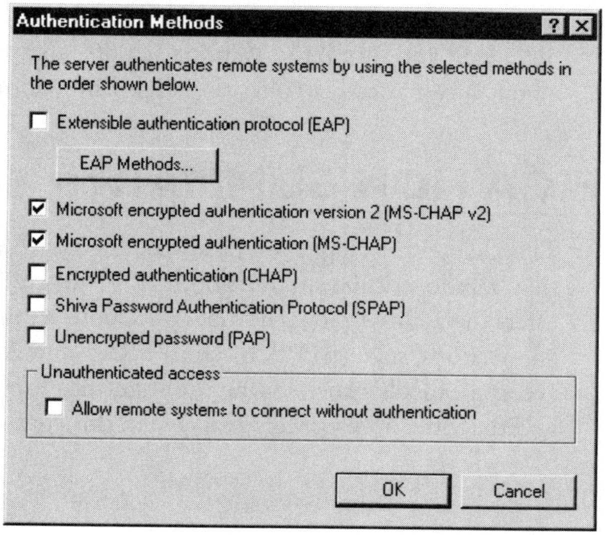
Authentication Methods
The server authenticates remote systems by using the selected methods in the order shown below.
Extensible authentication protocol (EAP)
EAP Methods...
Microsoft encrypted authentication version 2 (MS-CHAP v2)
Microsoft encrypted authentication (MS-CHAP)
Encrypted authentication (CHAP)
Shiva Password Authentication Protocol (SPAP)
Unencrypted password (PAP)
Unauthenticated access
Allow remote systems to connect without authentication
OK
Cancel

3. The two default authentication methods on the server, MS-CHAP and MS-CHAP v2, are the same as the defaults on the client. The other authentication options are the same as well, with one additional option at the bottom of the dialog box, Unauthenticated Access. Use the Unauthenticated Access option when you need to troubleshoot connection problems that you believe are related to encryption.

4. The EAP Methods button in the Authentication Methods dialog box can also be clicked to reveal the installed EAP methods. EAP methods are configured through RAS policy, which is covered in Chapter 14.

Configuring Data Encryption

Windows 2000 also supports data encryption, allowing data to be encrypted on transmission and decrypted on receipt. In highly secure environments, you are able to configure the server to require that encrypted communication be used, and deny the connection if it isn't used. Encryption protocols are enabled in remote access policy and are discussed in Chapter 14.

The data encryption settings included in Windows 2000 are Basic, Strong, and Strongest. Strongest encryption uses 128-bit encryption and requires that you download and install the Windows 2000 High Encryption Pack or install SP2, which automatically applies the High Encryption Pack during installation.

CERTIFICATION SUMMARY

This chapter has taught you how to configure RAS for VPN connections. You learned that Windows 2000 supports both PPTP and L2TP VPN connections and that it offers the ability to use a number of remote access protocols to establish incoming connections, such as PPP, Microsoft RAS, and ARAP. You also learned the remote access protocols available when configuring Windows 2000 as a remote access client and the different protocols available in this configuration.

Turning our attention to the RRAS server configuration, you learned about the two options for configuring IP address allocation. As you saw, RRAS can be configured to use DHCP or can lease out IP addresses from a static pool. You learned about the process RRAS uses when configured to work with DHCP, in which it obtains IP addresses in blocks of ten and manages the entire lease process. Therefore, remote access clients never communicate directly with the DHCP server. This in turn requires that you configure the RRAS server as a DHCP relay agent to enable the remote access clients to obtain all of the scope options defined in DHCP; otherwise, this information would not get to the remote access clients, which could result in name resolution problems since one of your scope options is probably the address of your DNS server. This section also taught you that when RRAS is configured to use DHCP, and a DHCP server is not available when RRAS starts, remote access clients will be leased IP addresses on the 169.254.0.0/16 network through APIPA.

The next section of the chapter taught you what to look for when troubleshooting VPN connectivity problems and discussed a number of the common errors you are likely to run into when working with VPNs, as well as solutions to these common problems.

The last two sections of the chapter explored managing existing PPTP and L2TP connections, including the configuration of firewalls to allow PPTP and L2TP traffic through. Here you learned that PPTP uses IP protocol 47 (GRE) and requires that TCP port 1723 be open. For L2TP connectivity through the firewall, you learned that UDP port 500 and IP protocol 50 for ESP, or 51 for AH, must be opened to allow for L2TP authentication and communication traffic. On the RRAS server, the L2TP input and output filters require that UDP ports 500 and 1701 be opened. We also discussed the standard authentication protocols available in Windows 2000 and the inclusion of EAP, which provides for the use of TLS. In addition to authentication, we also discussed the concept of encryption and how the High Encryption Pack must be installed to allow you to configure 128-bit encryption.

This chapter covers a great deal of information related to VPN connectivity. Be prepared to have your knowledge thoroughly tested on the certification exam, as the majority of the features and technologies discussed in this chapter are either new or are configured differently in Windows 2000 than they were in previous versions.

✓ TWO-MINUTE DRILL

Configuring Client Computer Remote Access Properties

- ❏ There are two sides to remote access connectivity: the client side and the server side. Windows 2000 clients support PPP, Microsoft RAS, and SLIP as available remote access protocols. A Windows 2000 Server running RRAS allows incoming connections via PPP, Microsoft RAS, and ARAP.

- ❏ Windows 2000 supports two types of VPNs: PPTP and L2TP. PPTP is more popular because it has been around longer and is supported by more software and operating systems. L2TP requires IPSec for encryption and authentication, eliminating its availability on computers that do not support IPSec. L2TP is also not configurable through a NAT server.

- ❏ VPNs provide a cost-effective, secure alternative for connecting remote office networks.

- ❏ LCP extensions may prevent you from establishing a connection to a RAS server running older PPP software. Disabling LCP extensions should resolve these connection problems.

- ❏ Selecting to share a connection using ICS requires that all of the computers on the LAN be configured to obtain an IP address through DHCP and will obtain an IP address on the 192.168.0.0/24 network. ICS should not be used in a routed network.

Configuring Remote Access Name Resolution and IP Address Allocation

- ❏ RRAS is installed by default in Windows 2000 but must be enabled and configured.

- ❏ RRAS offers you two configuration choices for the assignment of IP addresses. The first is to assign IP addresses automatically, and the second

- is to assign them from a static address pool. Choosing to assign them automatically requires that a DHCP server exist on the network and that a DHCP relay agent be configured.
- DHCP can be configured to use the Routing and Remote Access user option class, which will allow the remote access clients to receive specific scope options that are different from the LAN clients.
- When you configure RRAS as a VPN server through the wizard, 128 PPTP and L2TP ports are added. When RRAS is configured as a remote access server, five ports are added by default.
- Keep the lease times shorter to reduce the number of required IP addresses.
- If you select to use DHCP, and a DHCP server isn't available when RRAS starts, remote access clients will be leased IP addresses that result from APIPA and are on the 169.254.0.0/16 network.
- RRAS obtains blocks of IP addresses, ten at a time, from DHCP and holds on to those IPs to lease them out to remote access clients. Remote access clients never communicate directly with the DHCP server. The blocks of IP addresses obtained by DHCP are only returned to DHCP when RRAS is restarted.
- Configuring the RRAS server as a DHCP relay agent is highly recommended when you choose to automatically assign IP addresses to RRAS clients, as this will allow additional scope information to be sent to the remote access clients.

Configuring and Troubleshooting Client-to-Server PPTP and L2TP Connections

- Checking the Details tab on the connection's Status dialog box allows you to identify the characteristics of your connection, including the type of encryption, compression, and remote access protocol in use.
- Event Viewer can also be used to look in the System log when troubleshooting VPN connectivity issues.

- ❑ The default number of ports installed by RRAS varies depending on the server configuration you select when you enable and configure RRAS. These defaults can be changed by editing the port configuration.
- ❑ To allow incoming VPN connections either LAN And Demand-Dial Routing or the Remote Access Server option must be selected.
- ❑ For clients to establish a connection, they must be able to agree on an authentication protocol to use and the user must have the required dial-in permission and be permitted access through a RAS policy.
- ❑ PPP logging can be enabled in the RRAS server's Properties dialog box to allow you to collect information about the PPP negotiations and use this information to troubleshoot problems.
- ❑ The successful configuration of L2TP requires that the computer have a machine certificate installed.

Managing Existing Server-to-Server PPTP and L2TP Connections

- ❑ Most corporate RRAS configurations have the RRAS server located behind a firewall. To allow external users access to this computer, packet filters must be configured on the firewall.
- ❑ To allow PPTP through the firewall, TCP port 1723 and IP protocol 47 (GRE) must be permitted through the firewall.
- ❑ To allow L2TP through the firewall, UDP port 500 and IP protocol 50 or 51 must be permitted through the firewall.
- ❑ When configuring input and output filters on the VPN server, UDP protocols 500 and 1701 must be permitted.

- When creating packet filters on the RRAS server, all packet filters should be created on the external network adapter.

Configuring and Verifying the Security of a VPN Connection

- RRAS includes a number of standard authentication protocols. MS-CHAP v2 is the most secure of the standard authentication protocols, but EAP is the most secure out of all of the authentication protocols, as it allows for the use of certificates and smart cards.

- MS-CHAP v2 is not supported on Windows 95 unless the Dial-up Networking 1.3 Performance Upgrade and Security Upgrade has been applied. In this case, Windows 95 can use MS-CHAP v2 but only for VPN connections, not for dial-up connections.

- MS-CHAP is supported by all Microsoft Windows OSs but is less secure than v2 because it sends the user's name across the network in clear text and encrypts only the password, which could allow a hacker sniffing the network to capture the data and perform a brute-force attack on the packets to reveal the password.

- EAP must be enabled to use Transport Layer Security (TLS).

- MS-CHAP v1 and v2 are the two default authentication protocols used in Windows 2000. The Unauthenticated Access option can be useful for troubleshooting, as it allows you to remove authentication as a possible source of the communication problem.

- The strongest data encryption setting requires that the High Encryption Pack or Service Pack 2 be installed, as Service Pack 2 installs the High Encryption Pack by default. This will allow you to use 128-bit encryption.

SELF TEST

The following questions will help you measure your understanding of the material presented in this chapter. Read the questions and answers carefully, and be aware that some questions will provide for more than one correct answer. Choose *all* correct answers for each question.

Configuring Client Computer Remote Access Properties

1. You have configured a dial-up connection on your computer running Windows 2000 to dial your company's UNIX server, which runs an older version of PPP. When attempting to establish a connection, you repeatedly have trouble and are unable to connect. Which of the following solutions is most likely to solve the problem?

    A. Clear the Include Windows Logon Domain check box on the Options tab of the dial-up connection's properties dialog box.

    B. On the Security tab of the dial-up connection's properties dialog box, select the Show Terminal Window option.

    C. In the PPP Settings dialog box, clear the option Enable Software Compression.

    D. In the PPP Settings dialog box, clear the option Enable LCP Extensions.

2. You have configured one of the computers running Windows 2000 with a modem and added a dial-up connection to the local ISP. You want to allow the other two users on the network to use this dial-up ISP connection. What is required to allow for this type of configuration? (Choose all that apply.)

    A. All of the computers on the LAN must have an IP address on the 192.168.0.1/24 network.

    B. All of the users on the LAN must log on with the same username and password.

    C. The dial-up connection must have ICS and on-demand dialing enabled.

    D. All of the users on the LAN must be members of the local Administrators group on the computer configured with ICS.

    E. The computer configured with ICS must be configured for multilink.

Configuring Remote Access Name Resolution and IP Address Allocation

3. You have configured a computer running Windows 2000 as a VPN server, and configured it to allow remote VPN clients access to both the local RRAS server and the LAN. Your remote

access clients report that they are only able to connect to internal LAN computers if they know their IP addresses. You have asked a couple of the users to run the **ipconfig /all** command and report to you the information they receive. All users report back an IP address on the 172.16.0.0/16 network, which is what you have configured the DHCP server to lease out to them, but no other information is reported. What can you do to solve this problem and configure name resolution to work correctly for the remote VPN clients? (Choose two.)

   A. Add a DHCP relay agent on the RRAS server and configure the external network adapter as the interface it listens on.

   B. Add a DHCP relay agent on the RRAS server and configure the internal network adapter as the interface it listens on.

   C. Right-click DHCP relay agent, click Properties, and add in the IP address of the DHCP server.

   D. Right-click the interface you have configured, click Properties, and add in the IP address of the DHCP server.

4. You have configured RRAS to automatically assign IP addresses from an internal DHCP server. You have configured a scope of 200 IP addresses for your remote VPN users. You have also defined the scope options using the Routing and Remote Access User option class. You have to support 250 remote VPN users that do not connect simultaneously and you do not currently have enough available IP addresses. While you work to change the IP addressing scheme, which of the following will help you to maximize the use of the 200 available IP addresses?

   A. Configure the DHCP scope created for remote VPN clients to use shorter leases.

   B. Configure the DHCP scope created for remote VPN clients to use longer leases.

   C. Configure IP address reservations for each of the remote VPN users.

   D. Configure BAP to free up underutilized connections.

5. You have decided to configure your RRAS server to use a static address pool to provide IP addresses to remote access clients. You would like to configure the address pool to include all of the IP addresses on the 192.168.3.0/24 network except for 192.168.3.1, 192.168.3.254, and 192.168.3.100 to 192.168.3.110. Which of the following steps are required to accomplish this? (Choose all that apply.)

   A. Add the IP range 192.168.3.2 through 192.168.3.253.

   B. Add the IP range 192.168.3.2 through 192.168.3.99.

C. Add the IP range 192.168.3.111 through 192.168.3.253.

D. Add the exclusion range 192.168.3.100 through 192.168.3.110.

Configuring and Troubleshooting Client-to-Server PPTP and L2TP Connections

6. You have been experimenting with the configuration of your RRAS server. You would like your RRAS server to accept incoming PPTP connections but are not currently able to get them to work. The properties of the General tab of your RRAS server are shown in Figure 13-15. Based on the current configuration, why are your remote VPN clients not able to connect?

   A. The ports are not configured to accept remote access connections.

   B. There are no PPTP ports installed.

   C. A DHCP relay agent must be installed.

   D. LCP extensions are enabled.

FIGURE 13-15

The General tab of the RRAS Server's Properties dialogue

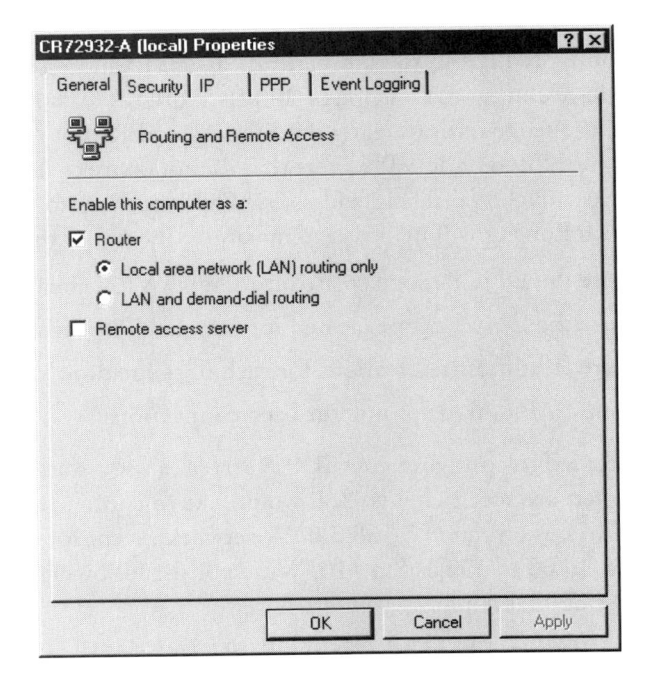

Self Test **607**

7. You have configured a computer running Windows 2000 to establish a dial-up connection to an older PPP server using the default settings. You are having trouble establishing a connection to the RAS server. Which of the following is most likely to resolve the problems and allow you to connect to the older PPP server?

   A. Disable compression.
   B. Disable LCP extensions.
   C. Disable the negotiation of multilink for single-link connections.
   D. Select to use EAP as the authentication protocol.

Managing Existing Server-to-Server PPTP and L2TP Connections

8. You have installed and configured a RRAS server as a VPN server. It is located behind your corporate firewall and you would like external users to be able to establish a VPN connection to the RRAS server using PPTP. Which of the following steps must you perform to allow this to occur? (Select all that apply.)

   A. Configure the firewall to open UCP port 1723.
   B. Configure the firewall to open TCP port 1723.
   C. Configure the firewall to allow IP protocol 17 through.
   D. Configure the firewall to allow IP protocol 47 through.

9. You have configured RRAS as a VPN server that allows a PPTP connection to be established with another remote VPN server at IP address 207.65.31.24. The local RRAS server's external network adapter's IP address is 207.54.20.81. You would like to configure incoming packet filters on the local VPN server that only allow PPTP through the firewall. Which of the following input filters will you create? (Choose all that apply.)

   A. Create an input filter with destination address 207.54.20.81 and destination mask 255.255.255.255 that uses protocol 47.
   B. Create an input filter with destination address 207.54.20.81 and destination mask 255.255.255.255 that uses protocol TCP and source port 1723.
   C. Create an input filter with destination address 207.54.20.81 and destination mask 255.255.255.255 that uses protocol TCP and destination port 1723.

D. Create an input filter with source address 207.54.20.81 and source mask 255.255.255.255 that uses protocol TCP and source port 1723.

E. Create an input filter with source address 207.54.20.81 and source mask 255.255.255.255 that uses protocol TCP and destination port 1723.

Configuring and Verifying the Security of a VPN Connection

10. You have configured your RRAS server as a VPN server that accepts only PPTP connections. You would like to configure the encryption settings to require remote VPN clients to use the highest level of encryption, but the option is not available to you. Which of the following actions will result in this option becoming available to you?

    A. Install Service Pack 2.
    B. Select EAP as the authentication method.
    C. Install the High Encryption Pack.
    D. Configure an IPSec policy that requests security.
    E. Install a machine certificate.

LAB QUESTION

You have been hired as a consultant for a small company that is a supplier to a large steel manufacturing company. The steel manufacturing company is changing its supplier procurement policy and forcing all suppliers to move to a VPN-based system for access to its tenders and inventory database. The steel company has configured a server running Windows 2000 and RRAS to accept up to 60 incoming PPTP connections, one for each of its suppliers. The steel company's RRAS server is connected through a firewall to the Internet with a T1 connection. The IP address of the external adapter at the steel manufacturer is 207.68.91.20. You have been asked to configure a computer at the supplier's office to connect to the steel manufacturer's VPN server.

Answer the following questions to help you define a plan of attack for the configuration of the VPN client at the supplier's location:

1. What Windows 2000 operating system is required to create a PPTP VPN connection to the steel manufacturer's RRAS server?
2. Describe the steps involved in creating the VPN connection at the supplier's location.
3. Once the connection is established, how can you verify the characteristics of the connection?

Answer the following questions as though you were involved in the configuration of the RRAS VPN server at the steel manufacturer's location:

4. How can you configure the DHCP scope properties to help guarantee connectivity for all suppliers?
5. Fill in the following table to show how you will configure the input filters on the RRAS server at the steel manufacturer's location:

Source Address	Source Mask	Destination Address	Destination Mask	Protocol	Source Port	Destination Port

6. How would the configuration of the output filters be different from that of the input filters based on the scenario discussed in the lab question.

SELF TEST ANSWERS

Configuring Client Computer Remote Access Properties

1. ☒ D is correct. The most likely way to resolve the issue of not being able to connect to a remote VPN server is to clear the option Enable LCP Extensions. Older PPP software will sometimes have difficulty accepting connections from clients that have LCP extensions enabled.
   ☒ A is incorrect because the option Include Windows Logon Domain is disabled by default.
   ☒ B is incorrect because the terminal window will appear if required but does not have to be enabled to appear.
   ☒ C is incorrect because enabling software compression should not have any effect on the result.

2. ☑ A and C are correct. Enabling ICS requires that all of the LAN clients have IP addresses on the 192.168.0.1/24 network, and the dial-up connection must have ICS and on-demand dialing enabled.
   ☒ B is incorrect because all users on the LAN do not have to log on with the same username and password.
   ☒ D is incorrect because the users on the LAN do not have to be members of the Administrators group to use the ICS connection.
   ☒ E is incorrect because multilink configuration is not a requirement.

Configuring Remote Access Name Resolution and IP Address Allocation

3. ☑ B and C are correct. The configuration of a DHCP relay agent on the internal interface of the RRAS computer can help to eliminate name resolution problems by allowing DHCP scope information to be sent to the remote access clients. The DHCP server where the scope information is configured is added to the DHCP relay agent by right-clicking the DHCP relay agent in RRAS, selecting Properties, and typing the IP address of the DHCP server. This will allow them to receive the DNS server address in the DHCP scope options sent with the IP address.
   ☒ A is incorrect because the DHCP relay agent should be configured on the internal interface, not the external interface.
   ☒ D is incorrect because right-clicking the interface you have configured will not allow you to add in the IP address of the DHCP server.

4. ☑ A is correct. Keeping the lease times shorter will help you to maximize the use of your limited set of IP addresses. A shorter lease time will allow the lease to become available again

within a short period of time and prevent it from being "tied" to one client for long periods.
☒ B is incorrect because a longer lease time would worsen the situation.
☒ C is incorrect because the creation of IP addresses wouldn't do anything in this case. IP address reservations are used to allow you to ensure that specific IPs are reserved for specific clients; however, in an environment where there are few IPs, reservations are not held if another computer without a reservation requests an IP. When a lease is required, the reservation is ignored.
☒ D is incorrect because BAP is used with physical dial-up remote access connections, not VPN connections.

5. ☑ B and C are correct. The proper way to configure separate IP address ranges in Windows 2000 RRAS is to create multiple address ranges. Unlike Windows NT 4, Windows 2000 RRAS does not allow you to create exclusion ranges, and therefore you must create multiple IP ranges.
☒ A and D are incorrect because they involve creating a single IP address range and then creating an exclusion range. Exclusion ranges cannot be created in Windows 2000 RRAS.

Configuring and Troubleshooting Client-to-Server PPTP and L2TP Connections

6. ☑ B is correct. To allow incoming VPN connections, a minimum of one of the following two settings; *LAN and demand-dial routing* and/or *Remote access server* must be enabled in order for the ports setting to be added to the RRAS server. With the current setting, shown on the General tab, no ports would be installed.
☒ A is incorrect because there are no ports installed that can be configured, so the configuration of the ports is a nonissue until the RRAS server is set up correctly.
☒ C is incorrect because a DHCP relay agent is recommended when automatically assigning IP addresses to RRAS clients, but it is not required.
☒ D is incorrect because LCP extensions are not a requirement.

7. ☑ B is correct. LCP extensions are a known issue when trying to establish a connection with older PPP software. Disabling LCP extensions is the most likely way to allow the connection to succeed.
☒ A is incorrect because compression is not the most likely reason for the connection failure.
☒ C is incorrect because the negotiation of multilink for single-link connections isn't known to cause initial connection problems but can prevent you from establishing additional connections.
☒ D is incorrect because EAP is not required. Selecting to use EAP would only be of value if the older PPP server required certificate or smart card logon.

Managing Existing Server-to-Server PPTP and L2TP Connections

8. ☑ **B and D are correct.** To allow PPTP access through a firewall, IP protocol 47 (GRE) and TCP port 1723 must be allowed through the firewall.
   ☒ **A is incorrect** because PPTP does not use UDP port 1723.
   ☒ **C is incorrect** because IP protocol 17 represents UDP, which is not required by PPTP.

9. ☑ **A, B, and C are correct.** These input filters are required for PPTP. The first should allow IP protocol 47 through, and the other two should allow TCP port 1723 inbound and outbound.
   ☒ **D and E are incorrect.** Source addresses are used when configuring output filters but source addresses are not used in the configuration of input filters. The external IP address of the RRAS server on the local computer is the destination IP address for all incoming traffic.

Configuring and Verifying the Security of a VPN Connection

10. ☑ **A and C are correct.** To allow you to use the highest level of encryption (128-bit), either the High Encryption Pack or Service Pack 2 must be installed.
    ☒ **B is incorrect** because EAP does not have to be used to use 128-bit encryption.
    ☒ **D is incorrect** because an IPSec policy is not required to use MPPE. IPSec is an alternative form of encryption to MPPE but they are mutually exclusive.
    ☒ **E is incorrect** because a machine certificate is only required for L2TP.

LAB ANSWER

The following are the answers for the Lab Question.

1. Any of the Windows 2000 OSs can be used to establish a VPN connection to a Windows 2000 RRAS server. The ideal scenario would be to configure a computer running Windows 2000 Server and create a server-to-server connection, as this would allow the connection to be maintained and allow all users on the LAN to use the connection.

2. The steps involved in creating the client VPN connection include launching the New Connection Wizard, selecting to connect to a private network through the Internet, specifying the IP address of the remote VPN server 207.68.91.20, selecting to use the connection only for yourself, and completing the wizard.

3. After the connection is established, right-click the connection icon in the taskbar and click Status. Click the Details tab to reveal the details of the connection.

4. To help guarantee connectivity for all suppliers, you will want to configure the DHCP scope to use a shorter lease period. This will allow the IP leases to turn around more quickly, making them available for other suppliers.

5. The input filters at the steel manufacturer's location should be configured as shown in the following table:

Source Address	Source Mask	Destination Address	Destination Mask	Protocol	Source Port	Destination Port
Any	Any	Any	Any	47	Any	Any
Any	Any	207.68.91.20	255.255.255.255	TCP	Any	1723
Any	Any	207.68.91.20	255.255.255.255	TCP	1723	Any

6. Based on the scenario in the lab question, the output filters would differ from the input filters by specifying the source address and source mask as 207.68.91.20 and 255.255.255.255 instead of Any. The output filters would also have the destination address and destination mask configured as Any, because specifying only one destination would prevent the other 59 suppliers from establishing a connection. For even tighter security, you could create one output filter for each supplier so that one individual IP address would be affiliated with each supplier.

MCSA
MICROSOFT CERTIFIED SYSTEMS ADMINISTRATOR

14
Troubleshooting Remote Access

CERTIFICATION OBJECTIVES

14.01	Create and Configure Remote Access Policies and Profiles
14.02	Select Appropriate Encryption and Authentication Protocols
14.03	Diagnose RAS Policy Problems Caused by Nested Groups
14.04	Diagnose Problems with Remote Access Policy Priority
✓	Two-Minute Drill
Q&A	Self Test

If you are reading this book sequentially, you have just finished Chapter 13, and you are familiar with the configuration of Routing and Remote Access Service (RRAS). With that knowledge under your belt, this chapter introduces you to the concept of remote access policy. RRAS is not new to Windows 2000, but the concept of remote access policy is. RAS policies provide administrators with the ability to securely configure a computer running Windows 2000 and RRAS. Remote access policies and the three components that make them up include a number of new features and configuration choices, as well as add an additional layer in the RRAS authentication process. I have given RAS policy its own chapter, not simply because of the amount of information that is associated with RAS policy, but also as a way of stressing its importance. As a new feature, you must spend the time required to understand these new concepts so that you are able to apply them effectively at work and are prepared for questions about them on the exam.

CERTIFICATION OBJECTIVE 14.01

Create and Configurie Remote Access Policies and Profiles

In this section, we explore the creation and configuration of RAS policies and profiles, including the three components of a RAS policy and the available settings in each of the three components, but before we jump into the creation and configuration of RAS policy, let's examine what RAS policy allows us to achieve from a macro perspective and examine the authentication process.

Looking at the new RRAS authentication process from a macro perspective reveals that it is comprised of two independent components that, when combined, determine a remote user's access. The first component is the user's dial-in permission, which is granted by editing the user's properties in Active Directory. This component is not new to Windows 2000, as dial-in permissions existed in Windows NT 4. The second component, however, is new, and that is the RAS policy. RAS policies can be broken down into three individual components themselves but are always combined with the user's dial-in permission in order to grant or deny access.

Examining the RRAS Authentication Process

If you are familiar with the Windows NT 4 implementation of RAS, then you are familiar with how to configure remote access on a per-user basis. In Windows NT 4, this is achieved by modifying the Dial-in tab of a user's Properties dialog box in the

Create and Configurie Remote Access Policies and Profiles **617**

SAM database using either User Manager or User Manager for Domains. This concept hasn't changed in Windows 2000. User accounts, stored either locally on a Windows 2000 member server or in Active Directory, have a Dial-in tab that can be modified to allow access to a RAS server. Our focus in this chapter is the configuration of remote access in a domain environment which involves the modification of the user dial-in permission using the Active Directory Users and Computers snap-in. When applying these concepts to a member server with local accounts, the Computer Management snap-in is used to modify the properties of local user accounts.

Configuring Remote Access Permission on the Dial-in Tab of a User's Properties Dialog Box

In an Active Directory domain, the Active Directory Users and Computers snap-in can be used to modify the settings on the Dial-in tab of a user's Properties dialog box, shown in Figure 14-1. This is where access to the RRAS server can be granted or denied and other settings such as a user's callback options can be configured.

FIGURE 14-1

The Dial-in tab of a user's Properties dialog box in Active Directory

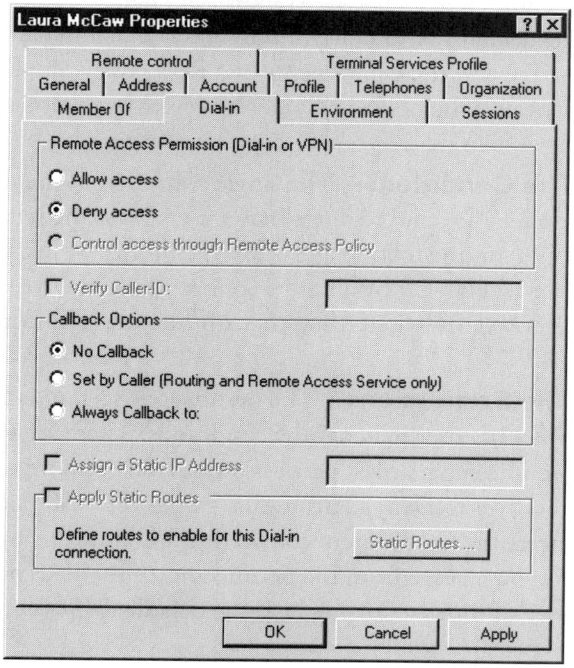

In Figure 14-1, pay particular attention to the topmost section of the dialog box named Remote Access Permission (Dial-in or VPN). In that section, you will notice three choices, of which one is grayed out. The Allow access option is obviously used to grant dial-in access to a user, and the Deny access option is used to deny access. The third, grayed-out option, Control access through remote access policy, is only available when the Active Directory domain is in native mode, so the Dial-in tab is one place to look to determine the mode of the domain. Deny access is the default setting in RRAS in a mixed mode domain. The importance of the access permission granted in the user's properties will become more apparent after we discuss the three components of a RAS policy and the authentication process.

The Three Components of a RAS Policy

RAS policies are comprised of three components: conditions, permissions, and profile settings. The remote access service is installed by default with the installation of Windows 2000, but is not enabled. When an administrator enables remote access, a default RAS policy is created. The default RAS policy can be seen by opening the RRAS snap-in, in Administrative Tools, expanding the RRAS Server, and selecting Remote Access Policies, as shown in Figure 14-2. In the display pane, the name of the default RRAS policy, Allow access if dial-in permission is enabled, appears.

To view the components of a RAS policy, double-click the policy in the display pane and the policy will open to reveal its components, as shown in Figure 14-3.

The Conditions The single condition of the default RAS policy is listed in the top text box and requires that a user access the server between 00:00 on Sunday and 24:00 on the following Saturday. In other words, the condition of 24/7 access is one that will be met by all users connecting to the RAS server. Conditions can be added, removed, or edited using the corresponding buttons.

The Permissions The permissions section is below the conditions text box and titled If a user matches the conditions. There are two conditions to choose from, Grant remote access permission or Deny remote access permission, with the default being set to Deny. This means that as the RAS policy is evaluated, any user that meets the condition of connecting any time during the week will be denied access. As you can see from the permissions of the RAS policy and of the Dial-in tab of the user's Properties dialog box, the default RAS access is to always deny access.

Create and Configurie Remote Access Policies and Profiles **619**

FIGURE 14-2

Viewing the default RRAS policy

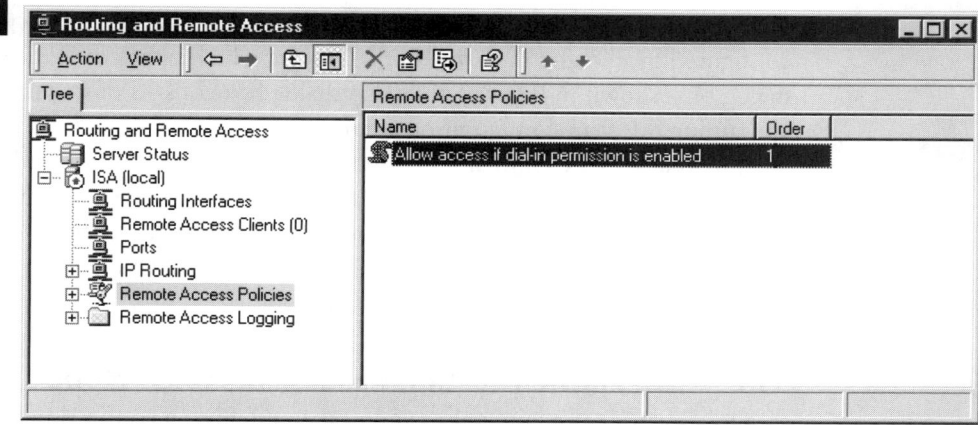

FIGURE 14-3

The components of the default RAS policy

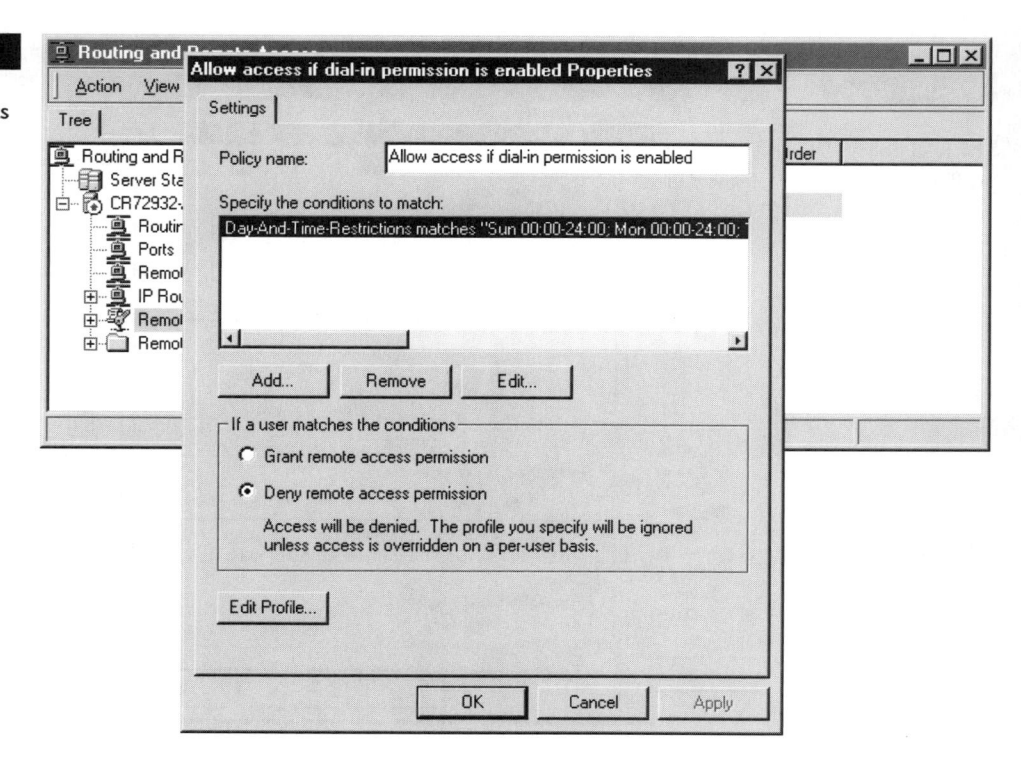

620 Chapter 14: Troubleshooting Remote Access

The Profile The profile is the third component of the RAS policy and can be configured by clicking the Edit Profile button, which opens the Edit Dial-in Profile dialog box, shown in Figure 14-4. This dialog box consists of six tabs, each containing different configuration settings.

Now that you are familiar with all the individual components, let's shift our discussion back to the authentication process and how these components work together to evaluate whether or not you are granted access to the RRAS server. In our examination of the RAS authentication process, we will look at the process in both domain modes, starting with mixed mode.

The RRAS Authentication Process in Mixed Mode

In a mixed mode domain, a user attempts to establish a connection with a RRAS server and is prompted to authenticate via a logon dialog box, which asks for the user's username, password, and domain. The RRAS server queries Active Directory

FIGURE 14-4

The RAS policy profile settings

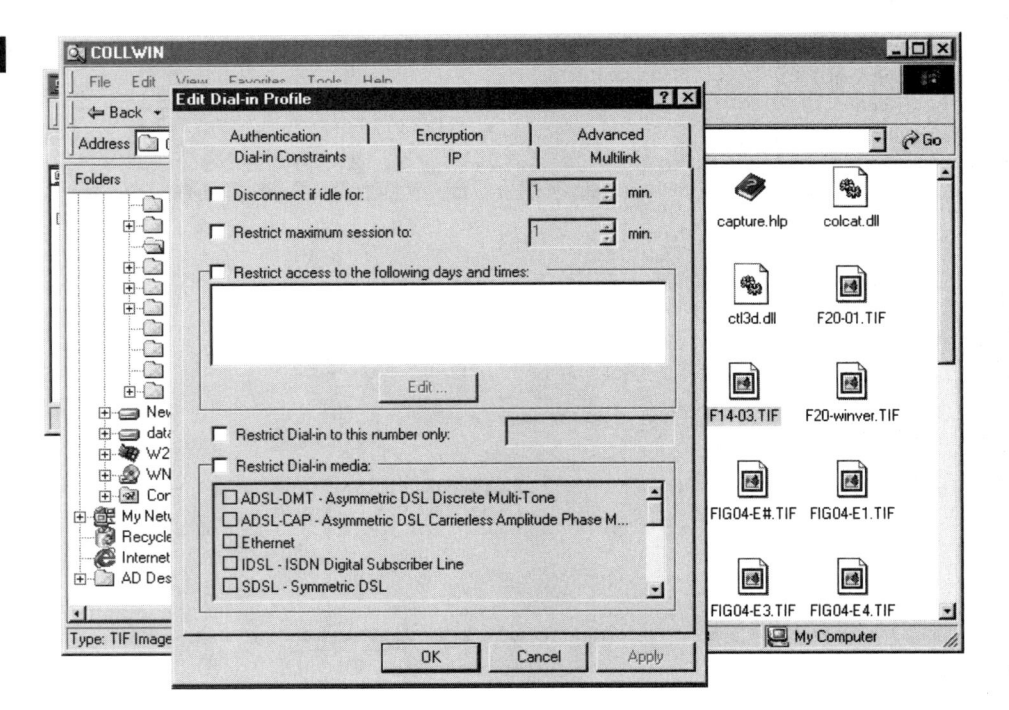

Create and Configurie Remote Access Policies and Profiles   621

to determine the user's dial-in permission, configured on the Dial-in tab of the user's Properties dialog box. In mixed mode, the permission can be set to either Allow access or Deny access. If the user's dial-in permission is set to Deny access, the authentication process stops and the user is denied access.

If the user's dial-in permission is set to Allow access, the RRAS server then checks to see if a RAS policy exists. If no RAS policy exists (in other words, if the default RAS policy has been deleted), then the user is denied access. If a RAS policy exists, RRAS looks to the conditions of the policy, as the user attempting to connect must meet the conditions. If the conditions are met, the RRAS server looks to the profile settings. If the user meets all the profile settings, then access is finally granted. Notice that the permissions of the RAS policy were not evaluated in this example. The reason is that when a user's dial-in permission is set to Allow access, the user's dial-in permission overrides the permission of the RAS policy.

exam
ⓦatch

One RAS policy must exist at all times; otherwise, all connection attempts to a RRAS server will be denied.

To make sure that you are 110 percent comfortable with the authentication process in a mixed mode domain, look to the flowchart in Figure 14-5 that walks you through the various scenarios.

The RRAS Authentication Process in a Native Mode Domain

In a native mode domain, the authentication process can become a little more complicated, because you now have three permission choices on each user's Dial-in tab. In addition to Allow access and Deny access, which were the choices available in mixed mode, the third option Control access through remote access policy, is now also available.

FIGURE 14-5

Authentication scenarios in a mixed mode domain

Domain Mode: Mixed

Dial-in Permission	RAS Policy		Profile	Result
Allow access	Conditions	▸	Profile	Allowed or Denied
Deny access	n/a		n/a	Denied
Control access through remote access policy	n/a		n/a	n/a

FROM THE CLASSROOM

RAS Permissions Could Lead to Logon Problems in Mixed Mode

Implementing RRAS in a mixed mode domain may lead to authentication inconsistencies whereby sometimes a user is granted access and other times the exact same user with the exact same permissions is denied access. The reason for these potential authentication inconsistencies is related to the permissions that you specify when you install Active Directory.

During the domain controller promotion process, which is initiated by executing the **dcpromo.exe** command, you are asked whether you want to set permissions compatible with Windows 2000 servers, as illustrated in the following illustration.

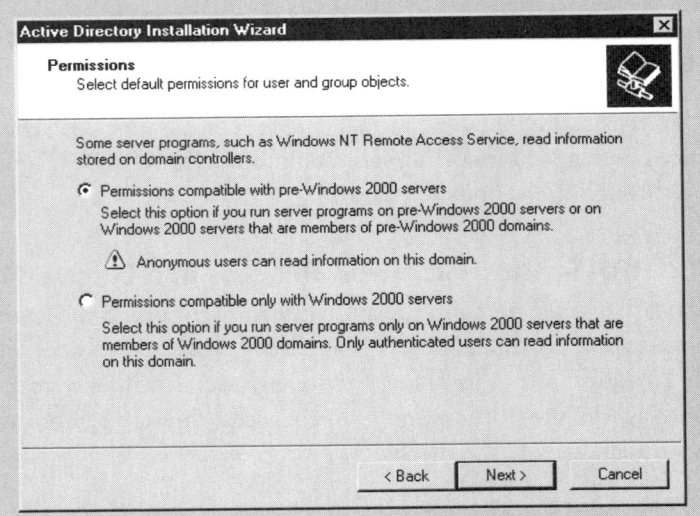

By selecting the option Permissions compatible with pre-Windows 2000 Servers, you can avoid these potential RAS authentication inconsistencies. Selecting this option adds the Everyone group to the built-in Pre-Windows 2000 compatible access group and, by doing so, grants all users the ability to query Active Directory for a user's dial-in permission through a NULL session. A NULL session is a communication session with

FROM THE CLASSROOM

another computer where no username or password is used. Selecting the second option, Permissions compatible only with Windows 2000 servers, increases the default level of security by preventing NULL sessions.

It is when the second option is chosen that RAS authentication inconsistencies can arise. Let's assume that a user is attempting to establish a connection with a server running Windows NT 4 and RAS. If the Windows NT 4 member server tries to query Active Directory to determine the user's dial-in permission (Allow access, Deny access, or Control access through remote access policy) and the Everyone group is not a member of the Pre-Windows 2000 compatible access group, then the user will be denied access, because the Windows NT 4 server running RAS will be unable to determine the user's dial-in permission.

There are three options available to you to resolve these RAS authentication inconsistencies. First, you can allow NULL sessions by adding the Everyone group to the Pre-Windows 2000 compatible access group and force replication throughout the domain. Second, you can upgrade the server running Windows NT 4 and RAS to Windows 2000 and RRAS, as a Windows 2000 server does not use NULL sessions. Your third option, and the one most unlikely to be chosen, is to reinstall the member server running Windows NT 4 as a backup domain controller (BDC). This would allow RAS to query the SAM database on the BDC for the user's dial-in permission and never have to establish a NULL session with an Active Directory domain controller.

—*Rory McCaw*

In a native mode domain, if the permission on the Dial-in tab in your user's Properties dialog box is set to Deny access, the authentication process stops and you are automatically denied. This is the simplest of the scenarios. If you attempt to establish a connection to a RRAS server, and the RRAS server determines that the permission on the Dial-in tab in your user's Properties dialog box is set to Allow access, the RRAS server then looks for a RAS policy. In the RAS policy, the conditions are checked and the user must meet all the conditions in the policy.

If any of the conditions are not met, and there are no more RAS policies, the user is denied. If the user meets all the conditions, then RRAS moves on to the profile settings. When a user's dial-in permission is set to Allow access, in both a mixed or native mode domain, the permissions of the RAS policy are ignored because the user's dial-in permission takes precedence over the RAS policy permissions. RRAS then checks the settings in the profile to ensure that the user meets all of those. If any of the profile settings are not met, the user is denied, but if all the settings are met, the user is granted access.

If you attempt to establish a connection to a RRAS server, and the RRAS server determines that the permission on the Dial-in tab in your user's Properties dialog box is set to Control access through remote access policy, the steps in the authentication process are identical to those described when a user's dial-in permission is set to Allow access, with one exception: the RAS policy permissions are now taken into account.

Let's run through this scenario to make sure you are clear on the difference. If a user attempts to establish a connection to a RRAS server, the RRAS server queries Active Directory for the user's dial-in permission and finds that it is set to Control access through remote access policy. RRAS then looks for a RAS policy. In the RAS policy, the conditions are checked and the user must meet all the conditions in the policy. If any of the conditions are not met, and there are no more RAS policies, the user is denied. If the user meets all the conditions, then the permissions of the RAS policy are checked. RAS policy permissions are a second place in the authentication process where access is either granted or denied, but these permissions are only effective when the user's dial-in permission is set to Control access through remote access policy. In all other instances, the RAS policy permissions are ignored. Assuming that permission is granted, RRAS then checks the settings in the profile to ensure that the user meets all of those. If any of the profile settings are not met, the user is denied, but if all the settings are met, the user is then granted access.

exam
Watch
The Control access through remote access policy setting is only available when the Active Directory domain is in native mode. The permissions defined in a RAS policy are only processed in the authentication process when the user's dial-in permission is set to Control access through remote access policy.

To summarize and review the authentication scenarios available in a native mode domain, look to the flowchart in Figure 14-6.

FIGURE 14-6

Authentication scenarios in a native mode domain

Dial-in Permission	RAS Policy	Result
	Domain Mode: Native	
Allow access	Conditions → Profile	Allowed or Denied
Deny access	n/a n/a	Denied
Control access through remote access policy	Conditions → Profile → Permissions	Allowed or Denied

SCENARIO & SOLUTION

Your domain is in mixed mode and you have granted users the Allow access dial-in permission. Which components of the RAS policy will be evaluated?	When a user's dial-in permission is set to Allow access, only the conditions and profile of a RAS policy are evaluated. The user dial-in permissions override the permissions defined in the RAS policy.
During your configuration of RAS you have deleted the default RAS policy. What is the resulting implication for remote users whose dial-in permission is set to Allow access?	No remote users will be able to connect to the RRAS server if there are no RAS policies. At least one RAS policy must exist, and the remote users must meet the conditions of the policy and the profile settings in order to connect successfully, even if their user dial-in permission is set to Allow access.
You are planning your RAS policies based on the needs in your organization and have identified that some of your policies will require multiple conditions. When a user connects and a policy with multiple conditions is processed, how many of the conditions must the user meet?	A RAS policy with multiple conditions requires that the user meet all the conditions. When multiple conditions exist, they are "ANDed" together, requiring the user to meet all of them.
The Windows NT 4 Server running RRAS is experiencing odd authentication functionality in the mixed mode domain that it operates in. Sometimes authentication succeeds and sometimes it fails for the same users, using the same computers, and no settings have been changed. What can you do to solve this problem?	The likely reason for this problem is that the permissions on the Active Directory domain controllers do not allow the Windows NT 4 RAS server to connect through a NULL session and query AD for the user's dial-in permission. If RAS can't find the user's dial-in permission, the user is denied access. The user is gaining access when the RAS server queries a Windows NT 4 BDC, which does allow NULL sessions. The best way to solve this issue is to upgrade the Windows NT 4 Server to Windows 2000. Another alternative is to lower the default security to permit NULL sessions by adding the Everyone group to the Pre-Windows 2000 compatible access group.

Creating a Remote Access Policy

Now that you are familiar with the three components that make up a RAS policy, let's take a more hands-on approach and look at creating one of our own. Before we jump into the creation process, however, there are a couple of very important points that you should be aware of. First, RAS policies are created and stored locally on RAS servers. Unlike Group Policy Objects (GPOs), which can be created at different levels of the logical and physical Active Directory structure and stored in Active Directory, RAS policies are not stored in Active Directory. The reason for this is the level of granularity available to you in the RAS policy settings. The profile settings of a RAS policy allow you to grant or deny access based on the type of dial-in media over which the incoming connection is trying to connect, such as only allowing ADSL connections.

on the Job — *The Internet Authentication Service (IAS) can be configured to provide authentication for RRAS, IIS, and other services, including non-Microsoft dial-up servers. IAS also allows for RAS policies to be managed from a single location, the server configured with IAS, which can simplify administration in an environment with many RRAS servers because only one set of RAS policies has to be administered.*

RAS policy does tend to create administrative complexity, but the tradeoff in increased security is definitely worth it. RAS policy provides you with the ability to securely configure your Windows 2000 RRAS server to ensure that access is granted to only those clients you specifically identify. In a corporate environment, this can offer you tremendous value, even when RRAS isn't used by a large percentage of your user base. This can offer you a significant value if you configure RRAS for only external administrative access to ensure that you are able to securely connect to your organization's remote offices and provide remote administration through a Terminal Services connection that exists with a VPN tunnel. In this case, RAS policy could be configured to only allow members of the Administrators group access during all times of day or only specific periods and only through VPN connections by restricting dial-in media.

You could also define IP packet filters with the RAS policy profile to only allow packets sent from the external network interface of the RRAS server or firewall at your office, as well as specify the tunnel end points to the external interfaces of the remote office RAS servers or firewalls, depending on the network architecture. The ability to configure very thorough, very advanced, and very secure RAS policies exists. What comes along with those very restrictive policies is added complexity,

Create and Configurie Remote Access Policies and Profiles **627**

particularly when trying to troubleshoot a connectivity problem or when working with a number of RAS policies, all of which are covered in this chapter.

EXERCISE 14-1

Creating a RAS Policy

Creating a RAS policy can be a very easy task, as you will see in this exercise. Configuring it properly to ensure that users are granted the appropriate level of access, however, can be quite complicated. Follow these steps to create a new RAS policy.

1. Select Start | Programs | Administrative Tools, and click the Routing and Remote Access snap-in.

2. In the RRAS snap-in, expand the name of your server, right-click Remote Access Policy, and click New Remote Access Policy.

3. In the Add Remote Access Policy dialog box that appears, enter a friendly name for the new policy, such as **Sales group policy**, and click Next.

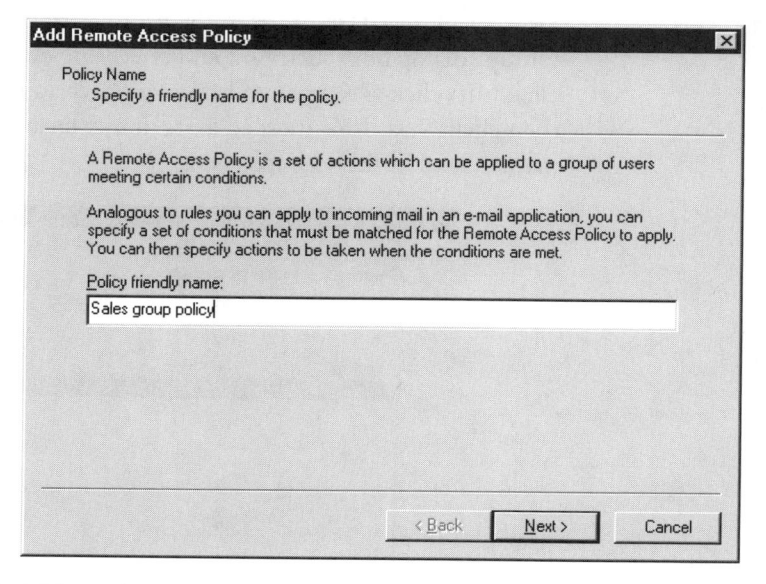

4. Click Add on the Conditions page of the Add Remote Access Policy dialog box to display the Select Attribute dialog box.

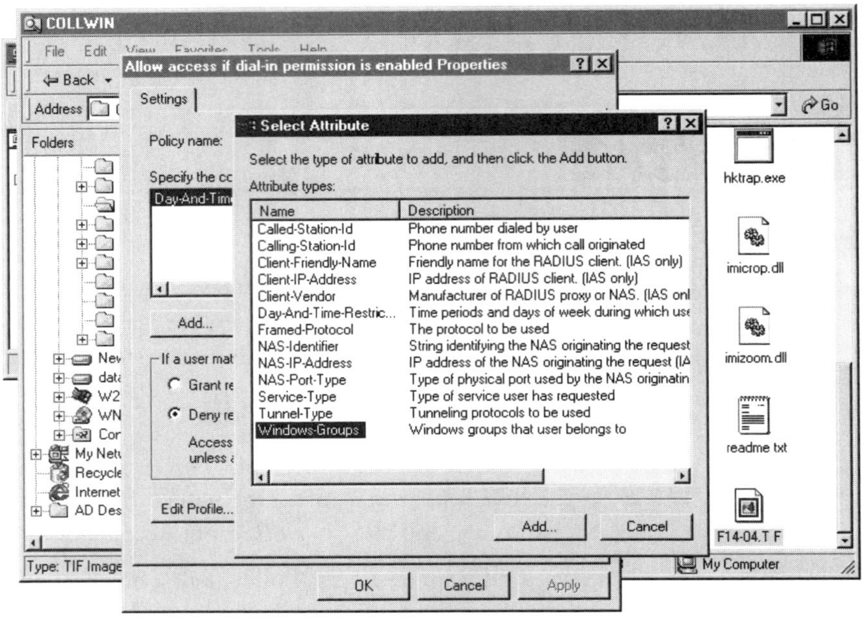

5. Select Windows-Groups from the list of attributes and click Add. In the Groups dialog box, click Add and select one or more groups. Click Add, click OK, click OK again to bring you back to the Conditions page, and then click Next. I have added a previously created global security group named Sales in this example.

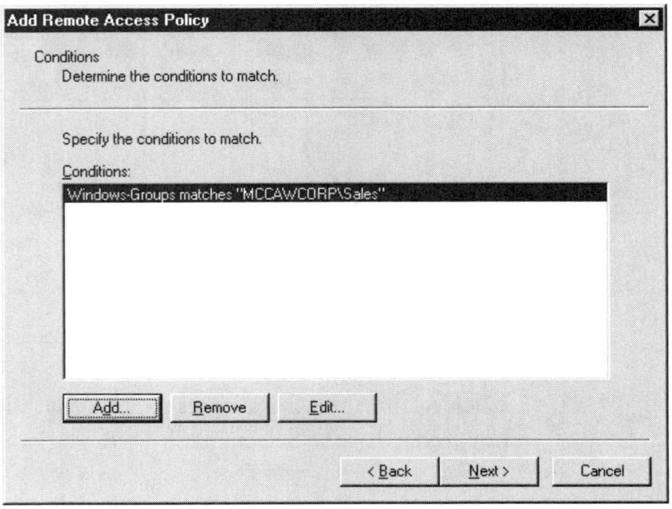

6. On the Permissions page of the Add Remote Access Policy dialog box, specify the permission to be applied to the connecting user if all the conditions in the RAS policy are met. The default is to Deny Remote Access permission, but for this example, select Grant remote access permission and click Next.

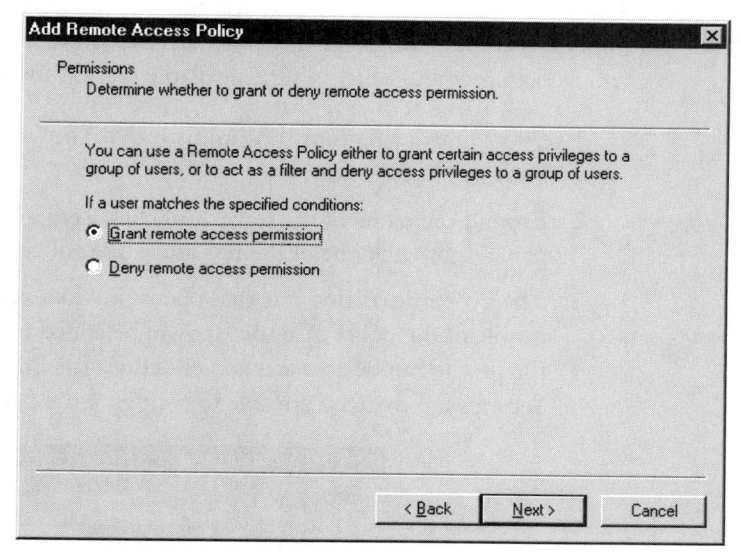

7. In the User Profile page, you can either click the Edit Profile button to open the Edit Dial-in Profile dialog box (shown earlier in Figure 14-4) or click Finish to create the new RAS policy.

Configuring a Remote Access Policy

Now that you have learned how to add a new RAS policy, let's look at how to edit an existing RAS policy and then explore the various options you have to choose from in the conditions and profile components.

on the job

The Netsh command-line utility can be used to dump the current RRAS configuration information in a script form, where it can be cut from the command prompt and pasted into a script file and then executed on another RRAS server, helping to make your administration more efficient.

EXERCISE 14-2

Configure RAS Policies

This exercise teaches you how to configure an existing RAS policy by editing the policy's current settings. This exercise is a lead-in to the next part of this chapter, which examines and describes the available conditions and profile settings.

1. Select Start | Programs | Administrative Tools and click the Routing and Remote Access snap-in.

2. Expand the name of the server and click Remote Access Policies. In the display pane, right-click one of the remote access policies and click Properties.

3. The Properties dialog box that opens provides access to the conditions and the profile of the policy. Conditions can be added by clicking the Add button and the profile can be accessed and edited via the Edit Profile button. It is on the Settings tab that you are able to configure the permissions of the RAS profile.

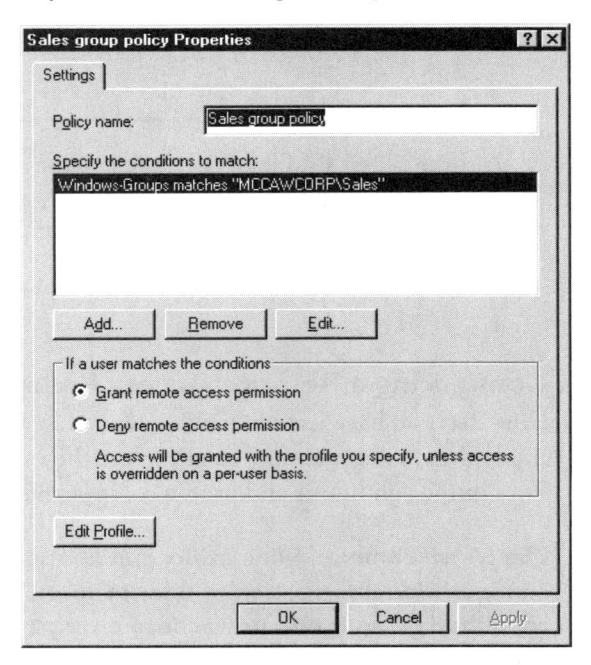

Create and Configurie Remote Access Policies and Profiles 631

Examining RAS Policy Conditions The first component of a RAS policy that is evaluated in the authentication process are the conditions in the policy. If the user's dial-in permission is set to either Allow access or Control access through remote access policy, the next step in the authentication process is to look to the conditions of the first RAS policy. A single policy can have multiple conditions, and when this is the case, the conditions are "ANDed" together, meaning that the user must meet all the conditions. Table 14-1 lists and describes the available conditions (* indicates that the condition applies only to IAS).

exam
Watch
If the computer running Windows 2000 Server and RRAS is configured as a member server, you cannot create a Windows-Groups condition that uses the local groups on the computer running Windows 2000 Server.

TABLE 14-1   RAS Policy Conditions Defined

Condition Attribute Name	Description
Called-Station-ID	The phone number dialed by the user
Calling-Station-ID	The phone number from which the connection originated
Day-and-Time-Restrictions	A schedule for when access is permitted or denied
Framed-Protocol	The protocol to be used
NAS-Port-Type	The physical port type used by the network access server (NAS) on which the request originated
Service-Type	The service type requested by the remote user
Tunnel-Type	The tunneling protocol to be used
Windows-Groups	Membership that allows you to restrict or permit access to only those members of a specific group or groups
Client-Friendly-Name*	The name for the RADIUS client
Client-IP-Address*	The RADIUS client's IP address
Client-Vendor*	The RADIUS proxy of the NAS's manufacturer
NAS-Identifier*	The string of the NAS on which the request originated
NAS-IP-Address*	The IP address of the NAS on which the request originated

Examining RAS Profile Settings Now that you are familiar with the available RAS policy conditions, it is time to examine the RAS profile settings. There are six tabs available for you to configure the settings of a RAS profile, and we are going to examine four of the six and leave the remaining two, Authentication and Encryption, for the next section of this chapter. The first tab that you are presented with when you open the Edit Dial-in Profile dialog box is the Dial-in Constraints tab, shown in Figure 14-7. The dial-in constraints available to you on this tab are listed and defined in Table 14-2.

The second tab in the Edit Dial-in Profile dialog box is the IP tab, shown in Figure 14-8. The IP tab allows you to define two settings: IP Address Assignment Policy and IP Packet Filters. The default IP Address Assignment Policy setting is Server Settings Define Policy, whereby the RRAS server settings define how addresses are assigned; however, it can be changed to either of the other two options.

The IP Packet Filters settings can be defined on both outgoing packets (to client) and incoming packets (from client) but are only in effect during the remote access connection that uses this RAS policy to define its access. Incoming packet filters allow you to ensure that only specific types of traffic enter your network through the RRAS server. The creation of an incoming packet filter requires you to define the

FIGURE 14-7

The Dial-in Constraints tab

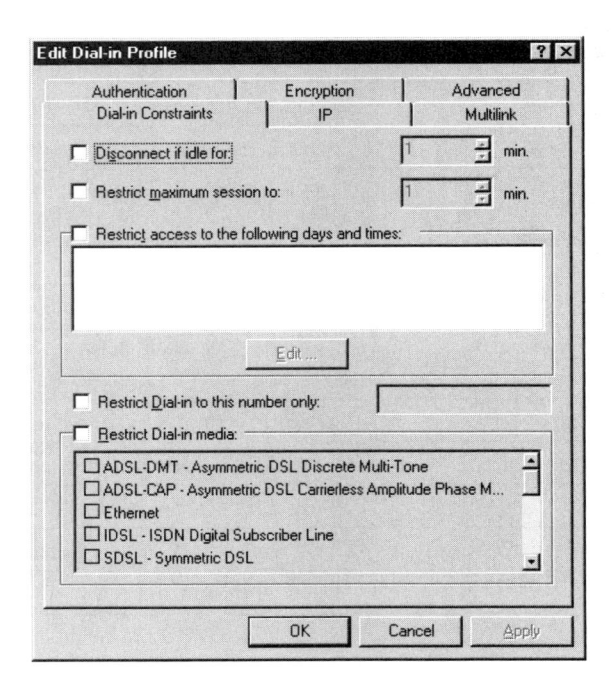

TABLE 14-2 The Settings on the Dial-in Constraints Tab

Dial-in Constraint	Definition
Disconnect if idle for	Defines the amount of time after which the remote access session will be disconnected from the RRAS server.
Restrict maximum session to	Defines the maximum amount of time that a remote access session is allowed to be connected to the RRAS server. Once the defined time is reached, the session is disconnected.
Restrict access to the following days and times	This setting is identical to the day and time restrictions setting available as a condition and allows you to define a schedule for when access is permitted.
Restrict dial-in to this number only	Allows you to specify what number an incoming call must be made from in order to accept the connection.
Restrict dial-in media	Allows you to restrict dial-in connections based on the type of media such as ADSL, Ethernet, or G.3 Fax that is used by the remote user. This can be useful if you know your remote users will only be using a specific media type such as ADSL and will prevent all users, using any other type of media from establishing an authenticated connection.

destination network the packet is destined for, which would normally be your LAN, and then select a specific protocol, such as TCP, and a source and destination port on which the service operates that you wish to block. An example of this might be the destination port for FTP, which would be TCP ports 20 and 21.

This packet filtering capability in the profile component of a RAS policy offers you one more line of defense, and helps you to configure the safest, most secure configuration possible. It isn't uncommon to hear IT people complain or express concern about the use of a single technology or protocol, such as the concern over the effective level of encryption and data protection that a PPTP VPN provides. However, combine the use of PPTP for data encryption with the use of certificates for mutual authentication and encryption and the use of packet filters and you begin to see that multiple layers of security can be applied to increase the effective security.

The Multilink tab shown in Figure 14-9 allows you to configure both multilink and Bandwidth Allocation Protocol (BAP) settings. Multilink is a feature that when enabled allows users with multiple modems, each with separate phone lines to connect using both modems to a RRAS server that is also enabled to accept multilink connections. This allows a remote user to effectively double their connection speed. The multilink settings also allow you to set a limit on the maximum number of ports that any one user can consume at one time. Multilink is a very useful feature

FIGURE 14-8

The IP tab

FIGURE 14-9

The settings on the Multilink tab

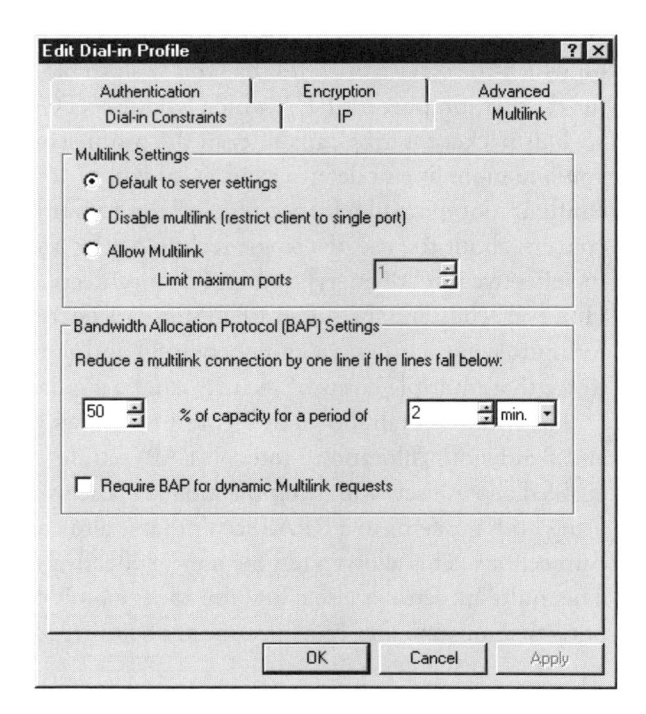

that allows your remote users to increase the speed of their RAS connections and, combined with BAP, can help you prevent one or more users from monopolizing the available pool of incoming connection ports.

> **exam**
> **Watch**
>
> **When configuring a client computer to use multilink, the computer can use modems that are of different speeds such as a 33.6 Kbps and a 56 Kbps modem, however, the multilink connection will only double the speed of the slowest modem which in this case would give you an effective connection speed of 67.2 Kbps.**

The other setting on the Multilink tab allows for the configuration of BAP. If multilink is enabled but incoming ports are at a premium, BAP can be used to monitor incoming connections and drop underutilized multilink connections if the capacity of the connection falls below a threshold that you define. An example of this might be to enable BAP to drop a multilink connection if the line utilization falls below 60 percent for a period of five minutes. This would free up this connection port for other users wanting to connect.

The Advanced tab, shown in Figure 14-10, allows for the configuration of specific connection attributes. The two default connection attributes specify that

FIGURE 14-10

The settings on the Advanced tab

the Framed-Protocol used in the incoming session must be the Point-to-Point Protocol (PPP) and the Service-Type must be Framed. The options for additional attributes are numerous and include generic RADIUS attributes, as well as vendor-specific settings from vendors such as U.S. Robotics, now 3Com.

As you can see, there is a great deal to the creation and configuration of RAS policies. RAS policy offers you a new and much more secure and granular alternative in the configuration of your security and like all new features will be a focus on the certification exam.

SCENARIO & SOLUTION

I have installed RRAS on a server running Windows 2000 and configured six RAS policies. When I install RRAS on a second server running Windows 2000, only the default RAS policy exists. What happened to the six RAS policies I created?	Nothing has happened to the six RAS policies that you have created. If you look at the RRAS snap-in on the original RRAS server, you will see your RAS policies. RAS policies, however, are stored locally on the RAS server, not in Active Directory, so the installation of multiple RRAS servers does not copy over the existing policies from other RRAS servers.
I have created a new RAS policy and configured the permissions to Deny access. The condition defined in the policy applies to all users, so all users should be applying this policy; however, users report that they are still able to gain access. What could be causing this?	This is likely due to the user's dial-in permission. If a user's dial-in permission is set to Allow access, that permission will override the RAS policy permission. The RAS policy permission will only be effective when a user's dial-in permission is set to Control Access through remote access policy.
My organization has more than 15 RRAS servers and I need to be able to monitor all the RAS policies centrally. What options do I have?	Windows 2000 Server can be configured as a RADIUS Server, which would run IAS. IAS manages all the RAS policies centrally on the IAS server and can be configured for both remote access accounting and authentication. IAS can be used to authenticate both Microsoft and non-Microsoft clients.
Is there a command-line tool that would allow me to save the configuration changes I have made to my RRAS server, including RAS policies?	Yes, the Netsh command-line utility can be used to save and then reapply the configuration of an RRAS server.

CERTIFICATION OBJECTIVE 14.02

Select Appropriate Encryption and Authentication Protocols

The remaining two RAS profile tabs are their own objectives on the 70-218 exam and therefore have been given their own section in the chapter. This should immediately demonstrate to you the elevated importance of these two tabs and their significance in the securing of a RRAS connection. Security has become a hot topic again in the media and IT community both in terms of both physical security and network security. The settings that we explore in this section can help you to achieve a more secure RRAS implementation.

The first RAS Edit Dial-in Profile dialog box tab that we focus on is the Encryption tab, shown in Figure 14-11. There are four different settings to choose from on the Encryption tab, and each setting can be configured individually or in combination with another setting:

- **No Encryption**   Provides no encryption, allowing a remote user to send data unencrypted to the RRAS server. This is the least secure choice and should really only be used if you are troubleshooting encryption problems. For the No Encryption setting to be effective, it must be the only setting enabled; otherwise, a more secure choice will always be attempted first.

- **Basic**   The second-least secure method available, as it requires the use of IPSec, 56-bit Digital Encryption Standard (DES) or 40-bit Microsoft Point-to-Point Encryption (MPPE).

- **Strong**   The second-most secure encryption setting, as it requires the use of 56-bit DES for IPSec-based VPN connections or 56-bit MPPE.

- **Strongest**   The most secure encryption setting, as it uses Triple DES (3DES) for IPSec-based VPN connections or 128-bit MPPE.

exam ⓦatch

The Strongest encryption option will only appear if SP2 or the high encryption pack has been applied to the computer running Windows 2000.

As you can see from Figure 14-11, it is possible to have more than one setting enabled. When this is the case, RRAS always attempts to negotiate the most secure encryption setting that is support by both the RRAS server and the connecting client.

FIGURE 14-11

The settings on the Encryption tab

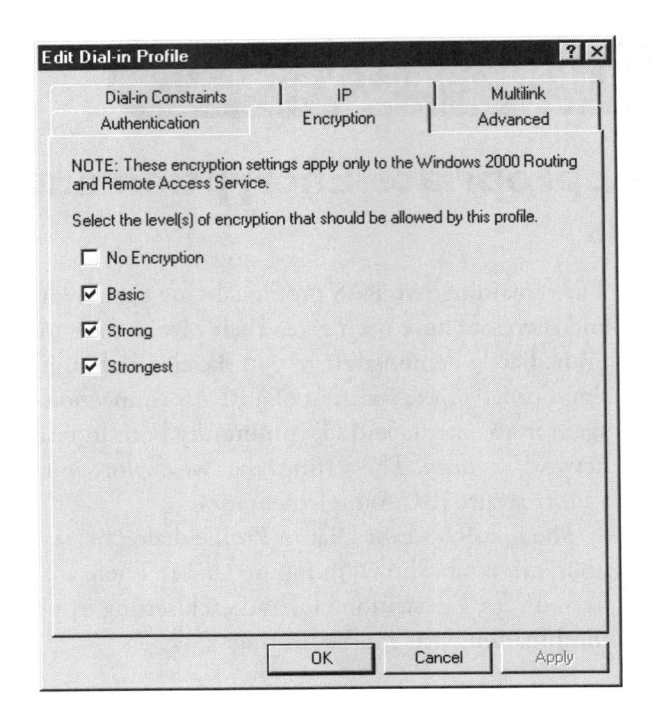

Editing the MaxDenials value in the Registry on the server running RRAS and configuring it with a value greater than 1 will enforce an account lockout policy for remote access connections on the RRAS server. This type of account lockout policy is different from a domain account lockout policy because it locks out the account on the local RRAS server, not in Active Directory. Again, by default, RRAS unlocks locked-out accounts every 48 hours. The MaxDenials value should be added in HKLM\System\CurrentControlSet\Services\RemoteAccess\Parameters\AccountLockout. The amount of time before the Failed Attempts counter resets must also be set in the same Registry path by creating the ResetTime value. The data value for this will represent the number of minutes before the counter resets, with the maximum value being 2880 minutes or 48 hours. To manually reset a locked-out account, delete the Registry subkey that is created that corresponds to the user account.

The last of the RAS Edit Dial-in Profile dialog box tabs is the Authentication tab, shown in Figure 14-12. It is on the Authentication tab that the Extensible Authentication Protocol (EAP) can be enabled. EAP allows for the available means of authentication to be extended to include things like smart cards and certificates. As you can see in Figure 14-12, two authentication methods are enabled by default:

Select Appropriate Encryption and Authentication Protocols 639

FIGURE 14-12

The Authentication tab

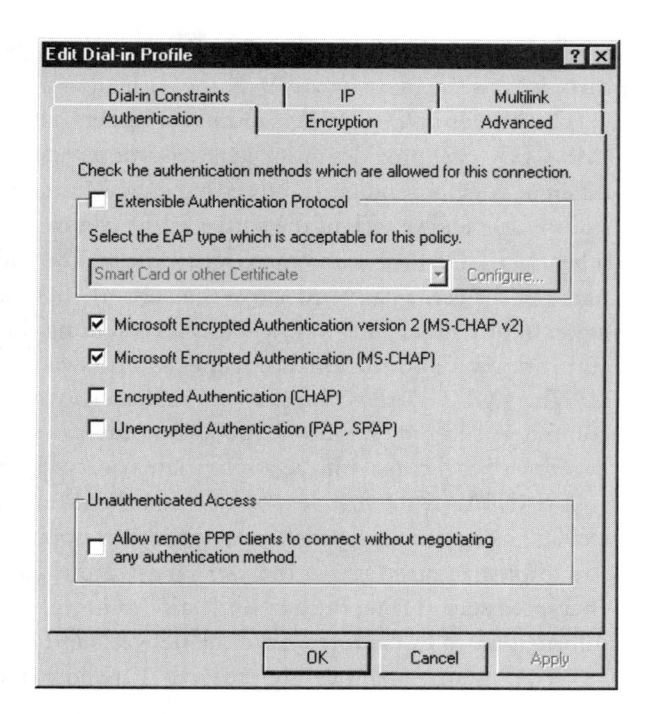

[Screenshot of Edit Dial-in Profile dialog, Authentication tab, showing checkboxes for Extensible Authentication Protocol, Microsoft Encrypted Authentication version 2 (MS-CHAP v2), Microsoft Encrypted Authentication (MS-CHAP), Encrypted Authentication (CHAP), Unencrypted Authentication (PAP, SPAP), and Unauthenticated Access options.]

MS-CHAP versions 1 and 2. Other available authentication options include Challenge Handshake Authentication Protocol (CHAP), Password Authentication Protocol (PAP), Shiva Password Authentication Protocol (SPAP), and Unauthenticated Access. Like encryption settings, multiple authentication methods can be enabled, and when this is the case, RRAS always tries to negotiate the most secure means of authentication first and works its way down the list until a mutually accepted authentication method is found. The Unauthenticated Access option, like the No Encryption setting, is valuable from a troubleshooting perspective because it allows you to rule out connection problems due to authentication, but it should not be enabled in a production environment.

To allow you to make an educated decision about which authentication protocol will best meet your needs, we will examine each of the protocols and what each offers.

EAP is an authentication method that is open ended and provides for the integration of new forms of authentication as they are developed. Enabling EAP allows the server and client to negotiate the actual authentication that is used. This is ideal when you want to authenticate users from outside of your organization through the use of certificates, an industry-standard security alternative. EAP can also allow for secondary checks such as prompting the user for a PIN number in addition to another form of authentication that has been provided, such as a smart card. EAP is the most secure of all the authentication options.

The Microsoft Challenge Handshake Authentication Protocol version 2 (MS-CHAP v2) provides mutual authentication and data encryption and uses different keys for sending and receiving data. Mutual authentication is a nice security feature, as it allows each of the parties in the communication process to identify each other. MS-CHAP v2 is also more secure during the authentication process, as it does not send the user's password across the network, but instead sends a hash of the user's logon information. This way, if someone is sniffing the network and captures the authentication information, usernames and passwords will not be compromised.

When MS-CHAP v2 is used with dial-up networking, it is only available to computers running Windows 2000, computers running Windows NT 4, or Windows 98 clients with the appropriate patches applied.

MS-CHAP is the first version of the authentication protocol and uses a challenge-response process that encrypts the responses. The security weakness in this implementation is that the user's password is sent across the network in an encrypted state during the authentication process, which could allow for that information to be captured from the network and decoded to reveal the password.

CHAP is an authentication protocol that allows for encrypted authentication with non-Microsoft clients or other Microsoft clients that do not support MS-CHAP v2. CHAP also uses a challenge-response authentication process that encrypts the response using Message Digest 5 (MD5), but it does not support mutual authentication. CHAP's reliance on the MD5 hashing scheme also requires that user passwords be stored in Active Directory using reversible encryption. Configuring a user's password to be stored using reversible encryption can be accomplished on the Account tab of the user's Properties dialog box.

EXERCISE 14-3

Configuring Reversible Encryption

The use of CHAP requires that a user's password be stored using reversible encryption. This exercise will show you how to configure a user's password to be stored using reversible encryption.

1. Select Start | Programs | Administrative Tools and click Active Directory Users and Computers.

2. In the Active Directory Users and Computers snap-in, locate the user account that you wish to configure to store its password using reversible encryption. Right-click it and select Properties.

3. Click the Account tab and, in the Account Options section, place a check mark in the box next to Store Passwords Using Reversible Encryption and click OK.

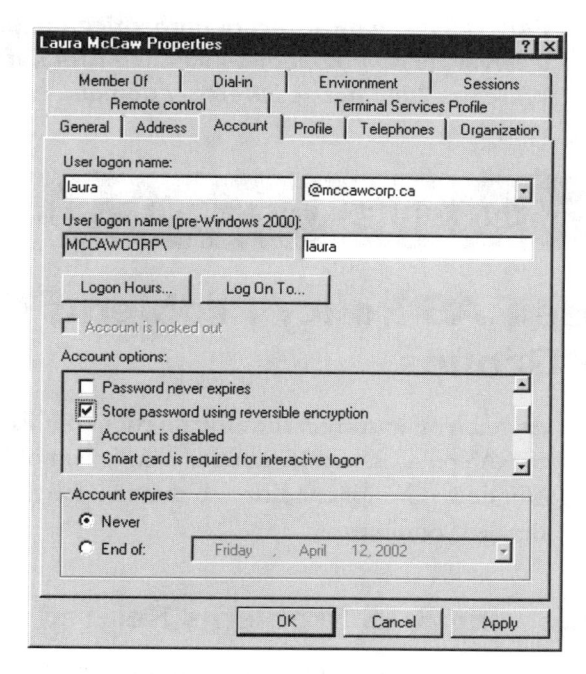

4. Right-click the user's account and click Reset Password. Configuring a user's password to be stored using reversible encryption requires that the user's password be reset in order for the change to take effect.

SPAP is a simple encrypted password authentication protocol supported by Shiva remote access servers. The inherent risk associated with SPAP is that the password is always encrypted the same way, which could allow a hacker to capture the packets from the network, decrypt them, and resend them at a later date and time to impersonate the user or simply use the password to gain access via the user's account.

on the Job *If your password expires, SPAP cannot change passwords during the authentication process.*

PAP is the least restrictive authentication protocol and should only be used when you are not worried about the security of passwords that are sent across the network, as PAP sends passwords in clear text.

exam Watch *EAP-TLS is the most secure authentication protocol but is only supported on a server running Windows 2000 and RRAS, if that server is a member of a Windows 2000 Active Directory domain.*

CERTIFICATON OBJECTIVES 14.03

Diagnose RAS Policy Problems Caused by Nested Groups

As you have learned in the earlier sections of this chapter, there are three components to RAS policies. The conditions component of RAS policy allows you to configure a Windows-Groups condition so that the policy will only apply to users matching the defined condition.

Troubleshooting RAS Problems Related to Nested Groups

One of the features of native mode domains is the ability to nest one global group within another global group. In certain circumstances, this could provide users that you did not intend to grant access to a RRAS server with the rights to connect to the server. For example, if you have a native mode domain with a global security group named Sales and you add another global security group named Sales Assistants to the Sales group, you have nested the Sales Assistants group and all of its members in the Sales group. If a RAS policy is then created with a Windows-Groups condition that requires membership in the Sales group in order to access the RRAS server, now users in both the Sales group and the Sales Assistants group have access to the RRAS server.

User account group memberships are defined through the Active Directory Users and Computers snap-in, in an Active Directory domain. If the server running Windows 2000 is a member server, you cannot use the local computer groups when defining a Windows-Groups condition; only groups in Active Directory can be used.

RAS Policy Storage

Troubleshooting RAS policy problems should begin with the basics by trying to identify exactly what is happening. To this end, one of the first questions that you should ask yourself is, "What RRAS server is the remote client trying to connect to?" The answer is straightforward when you only have a single RAS server, but many large corporate networks have numerous RRAS servers. The answer to this question is useful in troubleshooting, due to how RAS policies are stored. Remember that RAS policies are stored locally on the individual RAS server, meaning that the ten RAS policies you are creating on Server1 are only located on Server1. If your remote user is trying to connect to Server2, only the default policy might exist, which denies the user access based on its default settings.

Identifying Troubleshooting Clues in the Event Viewer

The Windows 2000 event logs can provide you with a number of clues and assist you in troubleshooting RRAS authentication problems, including those related to RAS policy. The Windows 2000 System event log is where you should look for the majority of your RRAS information, warning, and error messages.

EXERCISE 14-4

Identifying RRAS Errors in the System Event Log

A good second step in your troubleshooting efforts is to look at the Windows 2000 System event log, which contains information about system components such as RRAS. The following exercise walks you through the steps involved in accessing the System event log.

1. Select Start | Programs | Administrative Tools and click Computer Management.

2. In the Computer Management snap-in, expand Event Viewer and click System. In the display pane on the right-hand side, you can scroll through the events to locate those related to RRAS.

CERTIFICATION OBJECTIVE 14.04

Diagnose Problems with Remote Access Policy Priority

In the first section of this chapter, we discussed the RRAS authentication process, but in our discussion, we left out one last fundamental variable: having multiple RAS policies. Let's revisit the authentication process and complicate it just a little more by introducing multiple RAS policies.

If multiple RAS policies exist, the authentication process is only slightly augmented. The process still begins with the RRAS server querying Active Directory for the user's dial-in permission. If it is set to either Allow access or Control access through remote access policy, RRAS then looks for a RAS policy. If multiple policies exist, RAS begins with the policy at the top of the list and checks to see if the user meets all the conditions of the policy. If so, RAS continues processing the policy and either allows or denies access based on either the RAS policy permissions (if the domain is in native mode and the user's permission is set to Control access through remote access policy) and the profile settings or only on the profile settings.

If the user does not match the conditions of the first RAS policy, then RRAS looks to the second RAS policy in the list and checks to see if the user meets all the conditions of that policy. This process continues until the RRAS server finds a RAS policy for which the user meets all the defined conditions. Once a RAS policy is found for which the user meets all the conditions, the remainder of that policy (the permissions and profile settings) is processed to determine if the user is granted access. If the user does not meet all the conditions of any RAS policy, then the user is denied access.

As you can see, the order of your RAS policies is critical because the policies are processed from the top of the list through to the bottom, and the first policy for which a user meets all the conditions is the policy that will define the user's access. Due to the importance of RAS policy order, RRAS allows you to define the order of the policies and provides an Order column to the right of the policy to indicate the order as well (refer to Figure 14-2, earlier in the chapter).

> **exam⚠️watch**
>
> *The order in which you structure the RAS policies is very important. In the authentication process, the first RAS policy whose conditions the remote access user meets is the policy that will determine whether that user is allowed or denied access, and no other RAS policies will be evaluated.*

EXERCISE 14-5

Configuring the Order of RAS Policies

The order in which RAS policies are listed is critical because RRAS processes the policies from the top of the list to the bottom. This exercise shows you how to modify the policy order to ensure the settings that you configured become the effective settings.

1. Note the order to the policies shown in the following illustration. If we were to leave the policies in this order, only the default RAS policy would ever be used, because all users, including the users that are members of the Sales group, will meet the condition of the default RAS policy.

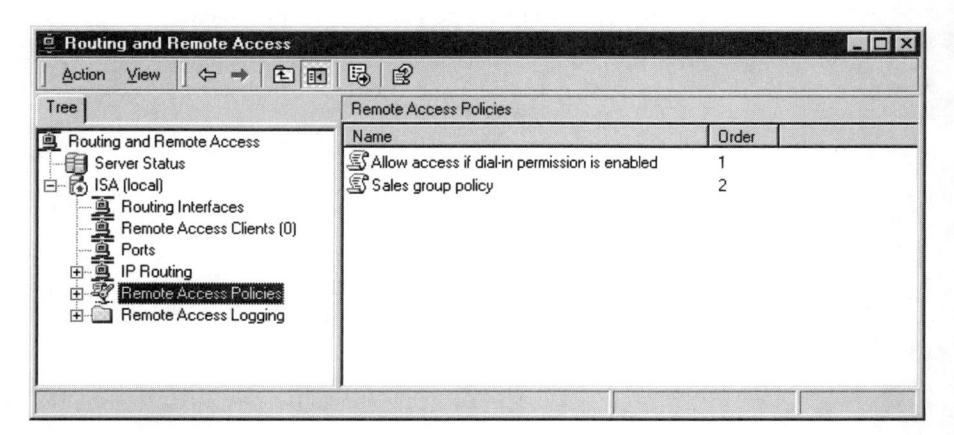

2. To change the order of the policies, right-click the new policy you created (Sales group policy) and click Move Up to move the new policy to the top of the list.

CERTIFICATION SUMMARY

RAS policies are a means of controlling access to Windows 2000 servers running RRAS. The RAS policy settings that are evaluated during the remote authentication process will vary depending on the configuration of a user's dial-in permission. When a user's dial-in permission is set to Allow access or Deny access, only the conditions and the profile of a RAS policy are evaluated. RAS policy permissions are only evaluated when the user's dial-in permission is set to Control access through remote access policy.

RAS policies are created through the Routing and Remote Access snap-in and are stored locally on a RRAS server, not in Active Directory. RAS profile settings allow you to configure specific encryption and authentication settings that allow you to control the security of RRAS connections.

Most organizations will require the use of multiple RAS policies. The order of the RAS policies is significant for successful authentication. The incoming connection request must match all the conditions of at least one policy, and the processing of multiple policies is synchronous, starting with the RAS policy at the top of the list. Once a user meets all the conditions of a policy, the remainder of that policy is processed and no other policies will be evaluated.

✓ TWO-MINUTE DRILL

Create and Configure Remote Access Policies and Profiles

- ❑ RAS policies are comprised of three components: conditions, permissions, and profile.
- ❑ In a mixed mode domain, only the Allow access and Deny access dial-in permissions are available. Control access through remote access policy is only available in native mode.
- ❑ A default RAS policy is created when RRAS is configured and enabled. One RRAS policy must always exist in order for any authentication attempt to succeed.
- ❑ RAS policies are unique to each individual RAS server and are always stored locally on the RRAS server.
- ❑ The RRAS authentication process begins with RRAS querying Active Directory to determine the user's dial-in permission, and if that permission is set to either allow, or control access through RAS policy, RRAS evaluates the RAS policy
- ❑ RAS policy permissions are only used when the user's dial-in permission is set to Control Access Through Remote Access Policy
- ❑ To allow a down-level RRAS server to query Active Directory, the Everyone group must be added to the Pre-Windows 2000 Compatible Access group

Select Appropriate Encryption and Authentication Protocols

- ❑ The Authentication and Encryption tabs in a RAS policy allow for these settings to be configured.
- ❑ There are four available encryption settings to choose from: No Encryption, Basic, Strong, and Strongest. A combination of these settings also can be configured. During the negotiation process, the RRAS server will start with the most secure setting (Strongest) and proceed down the list of enabled encryption settings until a setting that both the client and server support is found.

- Basic encryption uses IPSec, 56-bit DES or 40-bit MPPE, while Strong encryption uses 56-bit DES or 56-bit MPPE, and Strongest uses IPSec, Triple DES, or 128-bit MPPE.
- EAP can be configured on the Authentication tab to include support for smart cards and certificates, but EAP is only supported when the server running Windows 2000 is a member of an Active Directory domain.
- MS-CHAP v1 and v2 are the two default authentication methods, but others include CHAP, PAP, SPAP, and unauthenticated access. When multiple authentication protocols are selected, RRAS always tries to negotiate the most secure authentication protocol first.
- When MS-CHAP v2 is used with dial-up networking, it is only available to computers running Windows 2000, computers running Windows NT 4, or Windows 98 clients with the appropriate patches applied.
- CHAP authentication requires that the user's password be stored using reversible encryption in Active Directory.

Diagnose RAS Policy Problems Caused by Nested Groups

- Nested groups are a feature available in native mode Active Directory domains that can result in a user getting access to a RRAS server that you didn't intend to grant access to.
- Local computer groups on a Windows 2000 server configured as a member server cannot be used in the definition of a RAS policy Windows-Groups condition.
- RAS policies are stored locally on the RAS server, not in Active Directory. RAS policies are not shared or replicated between RRAS servers.
- RRAS information, warning, and error messages can be found in the Windows 2000 event log.

Diagnose Problems with Remote Access Policy Priority

❑ The order of RAS policies is very important because RRAS processes the policies from the top of the list down to the bottom.

❑ When a remote user attempts to connect to a RRAS server, the RRAS server looks for a policy for which the user meets all the defined conditions.

❑ The default RAS policy is included so that users will always meet the conditions of the default policy.

❑ If no RAS policies exist on the RAS server, all connection attempts will be refused.

SELF TEST

The following questions will help you measure your understanding of the material presented in this chapter. Read the questions and answers carefully, and be aware that some questions provide for more than one correct answer. Choose all correct answers for each question.

Create and Configure Remote Access Policies and Profiles

1. You are the administrator of a Windows 2000 server and you have just finished enabling and configuring the server. Your next task is the configuration of permissions in order to test the server. You open Active Directory Users and Computers and select the Dial-in tab of your user account's Properties dialog box, as shown in Figure 14-13. Which of the following is the most likely reason why the option Control Access Through Remote Access Policy is not available?

   A. The RRAS server has not been authorized.
   B. The domain mode has not been changed.
   C. You are not logged on with an account that is a member of the Pre-Windows 2000 Compatible Access group.
   D. A RAS policy must first be created.

2. You are the administrator of a server running Windows 2000 and RRAS. You are testing your configuration after making a couple of changes to the default RAS policy. You have edited the profile of the default RAS policy, as shown in Figure 14-14. You have also configured the dial-in permission of your own account to Allow access, and the domain is in mixed mode. What will be the result when you attempt to log on at 8 P.M. on Monday to test your changes?

   A. You will be granted access due to your dial-in permission.
   B. You will be granted access, but only for 60 minutes, and you will be disconnected if the session is idle for 5 minutes.
   C. You will be denied access because the profile setting conflicts with the condition.
   D. You will be denied access because of the profile day and time restrictions.

3. You have installed Active Directory and selected permissions compatible only with Windows 2000 Server during the domain controller promotion. Your LAN architecture includes a server running Windows NT 4 and RAS. Your domain is in mixed mode and has three Windows NT 4 BDCs and two Active Directory domain controllers. Remote users are experiencing weird results when they attempt to connect remotely to the RAS server. Sometimes they are granted

FIGURE 14-13

The Dial-in tab

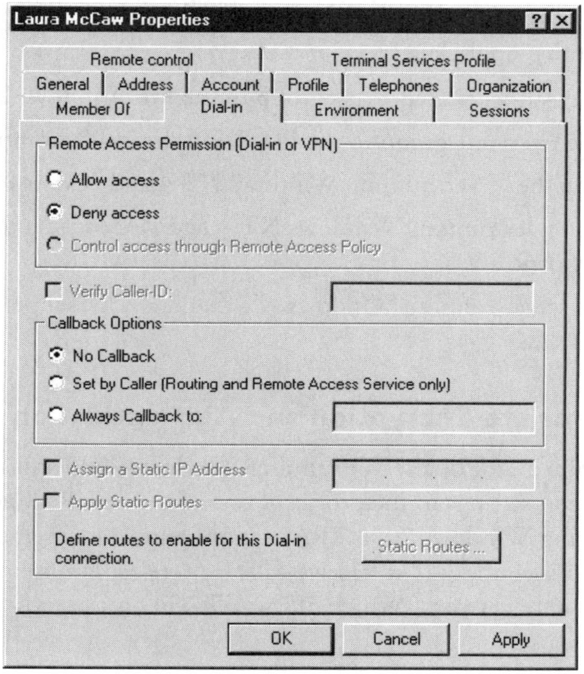

FIGURE 14-14

Edit Dial-in Profile

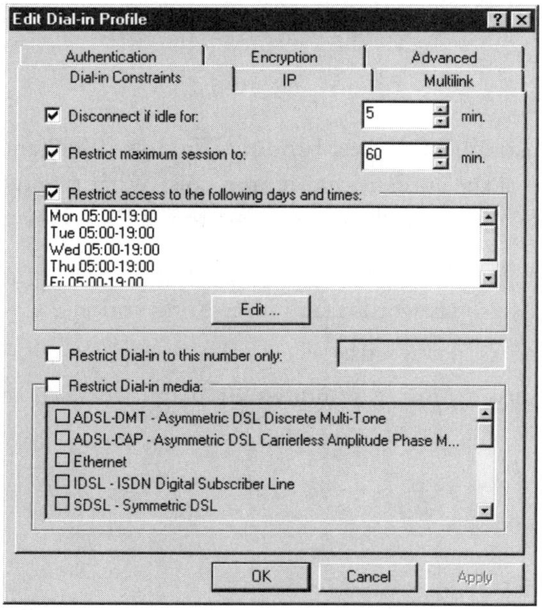

access, and other times they are denied. Which of the following will resolve this problem? (Choose all that apply.)

A. Add the Authenticated Users group to the Pre-Windows 2000 Compatible Access group.

B. Add the Everyone group to the Pre-Windows 2000 Compatible Access group.

C. Upgrade the server running Windows NT 4 and RAS to Windows 2000.

D. On the server running Windows NT 4 and RAS, map a drive to one of the Windows 2000 domain controllers.

E. On the server running Windows NT 4 and RAS, change all users' dial-in permissions to Allow access.

Select Appropriate Encryption and Authentication Protocols

4. As the administrator of a server running Windows 2000 and RRAS, you are configuring the authentication settings in the profile of one of the new RAS policies that you have created. The server running Windows 2000 RRAS is configured as a member server in a workgroup called Remote and is configured to receive calls from telecommuters that require dial-up connectivity to the corporate network. Which of the following is the most secure form of authentication that you can use?

A. MS-CHAP

B. MS-CHAP v2

C. EAP-TLS

D. XML

5. As the administrator of a server running Windows 2000 and RRAS, you have configured CHAP as one of the authentication protocols. What two remaining steps must you perform to allow users to successfully authenticate to the RRAS server using CHAP?

A. Add the Everyone group to the Pre-Windows 2000 Compatible Access group.

B. Store all users' passwords using reverse encryption.

C. Reset all users' passwords.

D. Add the server running Windows 2000 and RRAS to an Active Directory domain.

6. Assuming no additional configuration changes have been made, which of the following operating systems support MS-CHAP v2 as an authentication protocol? (Choose all that apply.)

   A. Windows 2000
   B. Windows 95
   C. Windows XP
   D. Windows NT 4

Diagnose RAS Policy Problems Caused by Nested Groups

7. You are the administrator of a server running Windows 2000 and RRAS and you are planning your strategy for RAS policy creation. The Windows 2000 server is a member server in a workgroup and provides dial-in access to remote users. The computers used by all of the remote users run Windows 2000 Professional, and the RRAS server is configured to use the MS-CHAP v2 authentication protocol. Which of following cannot be configured in this scenario?

   A. User dial-in permissions cannot be set for individual users.
   B. The Windows-Groups condition cannot be used.
   C. The profile settings cannot be configured.
   D. The Control access through remote access policy setting is not available.

8. You are the administrator of all the servers running Windows 2000 and RRAS in your organization. You upgraded the first of your Windows NT 4 RAS servers to Windows 2000 a couple of months ago and created eight new RAS policies to control remote access. All the users in your native mode domain are configured with the dial-in permission Control Access through remote access policy. You have just completed the upgrade of the second RAS server and have asked some of your users to test out the configuration. Users report that they are not allowed access on the new RRAS server but can access the original RRAS server. What is the most likely cause of the problem?

   A. The remote access policies from the original RRAS server have not replicated to the new RRAS server.
   B. You have not added the Everyone group to the Pre-Windows 2000 compatible access group on the new RRAS server.
   C. The RRAS service on the new RRAS server has not been authorized.
   D. You have not created any RAS policies on the new RAS server that allow access.

9. What is the default condition and permission in the default remote access policy? (Choose two.)

   A. Grant access
   B. Deny access
   C. Windows-Groups condition requires membership in the Everyone group
   D. Windows-Groups condition requires membership in the Authenticated Users group
   E. Day and time restriction of 24/7 access

10. You are the administrator of the Windows 2000 RRAS servers in your organization and you are planning the changes to your RAS policies. You currently have two RAS policies in addition to the default policy. The first policy, named Sales, has two conditions: access must be between the hours of 05:00 and 24:00 and membership in the Sales group is required. The second policy is for the Executives group and has two conditions: 24/7 access and membership in the Executives group. Bill Taylor is a member of both the Sales and Executives groups and should get the policy of the Executives group, not the Sales policy. Which of the following is the correct order for the policies in RRAS?

    A. Sales, Executives, Default
    B. Default, Executives, Sales
    C. Default, Sales, Executives
    D. Executives, Sales, Default

LAB QUESTION

You are the administrator responsible for all the servers running Windows 2000 in your organization. Your manager has asked you to enable and configure RAS policies on the one Windows 2000 server in the organization that runs RRAS to ensure all security requirements are met. All users' dial-in permissions are currently configured to Allow access, and the domain is in mixed mode. Your manager has asked you to ensure that a change to native mode will not impact or affect any of the changes you implement. In your organization's Active Directory, each department is represented by a global security group, and all members of each department are members of the corresponding global security group. The configuration settings that you and your manager have discussed that require implementation are defined in Table 14-3.

TABLE 14-3 Required RAS Policy Configuration Settings

Global Security Group	Day and Time Restrictions	Windows-Groups	Tunneling Protocols	Dial-in Constraints
Sales	24/7	Sales	N/A	Disable after 5 minutes of inactivity
Marketing	17:00 – 09:00	Marketing	N/A	Disable after 5 minutes of inactivity
Production	17:00 – 22:00	Production	N/A	Disable after 5 minutes of inactivity
IT	24/7	IT, Administrators	PPTP	Disable after 5 minutes of inactivity
Managers	24/7	Managers	N/A	Disable after 5 minutes of inactivity
Administration	17:00 – 22:00	Office Admins	N/A	Disable after 5 minutes of inactivity

The other factors that you should take into account are that the managers of each of the departments are also members of each of the departmental groups and two users are members of both the Sales and Marketing groups. Based on the settings in Table 14-3, design and order the required RAS policies.

Based on the information provided in the question and in Table 14-3, answer the following questions:

1. How many RAS policies are required to achieve the goals outlined in the question? Create a table with the following column headings: Policy Name, Conditions, Permissions, Profile, and Dial-in Permissions. Add a row to the table for each policy that you would create, and describe each of the different components of the policy in the different columns based on the column header.

2. What component of the RAS policy is most likely to be affected by a change in domain mode from mixed to native? How should this component be configured and why?

3. Once the policies have been created, what last factor should be taken into account that can dramatically affect the authentication outcome?

656 Chapter 14: Troubleshooting Remote Access

SELF TEST ANSWERS

Create and Configure Remote Access Policies and Profiles

1. ☑ B is correct. The domain mode must be changed to native mode in order for the option Control access through remote access policy to be available.
   ☒ A is incorrect because a RRAS server does not require authorization, and even if it were authorized, the option Control access through remote access policy is only available in native mode.
   ☒ C is incorrect because account membership and associated permissions are not the issue.
   ☒ D is incorrect because account membership and associated permissions are not the issue.

2. ☑ D is correct. You will be denied access because of the profile day and time restrictions, which only allow access Monday to Friday between the hours of 05:00 and 19:00.
   ☒ A is incorrect because the RAS policy settings are still evaluated, even when your user dial-in permission is set to Allow access.
   ☒ B is incorrect because the profile time and day restrictions deny you access. Therefore, without access, the other dial-in constraints are mute.
   ☒ C is incorrect because the authentication procedure requires that you meet all defined conditions, and those conditions combine with the profile settings. The most restrictive settings become the effective settings for the connection, which in this case results in access being permitted only between the hours of 05:00 and 19:00.

3. ☑ B and C are correct. Two ways in which you can resolve this problem are to add the Everyone group to the Pre-Windows 2000 compatible access group or upgrade the server running Windows NT 4 and RAS to Windows 2000.
   ☒ A is incorrect because adding the Authenticated Users group to the Pre-Windows 2000 compatible access group will not resolve the problem.
   ☒ D is incorrect because creating a mapped drive will not resolve the problem.
   ☒ E is incorrect because it is not the user's dial-in permission that is causing the problem but rather the inability of the server running Windows NT 4 to establish a NULL session with an Active Directory domain controller to query for and resolve the user's dial-in permission.

Select Appropriate Encryption and Authentication Protocols

4. ☑ B is correct. MS-CHAP v2 is the most secure form of authentication available in this case. EAP is more secure but not available in a workgroup configuration.
   ☒ A is incorrect because MS-CHAP is less secure than MS-CHAP v2.

Self Test Answers **657**

    ☒   **C** is incorrect because although EAP-TLS is the most secure authentication choice available, it can only be used when the RRAS server is a member of an Active Directory domain.

    ☒   **D** is incorrect because XML is not an authentication protocol.

5. ☑   **B** and **C** are correct. The use of CHAP as an authentication protocol requires that all users' passwords be stored using reversible encryption and that the users' passwords be reset after changing the way the passwords are stored.

    ☒   **A** is incorrect because adding the Everyone group to the Pre-Windows 2000 compatible access group is not a requirement of CHAP.

    ☒   **D** is incorrect because adding the server running Windows 2000 and RRAS to an Active Directory domain is not a requirement of CHAP.

6. ☑   **A** and **C** are correct. Both Windows 2000 and Windows XP support MS-CHAP v2 as an authentication protocol without any additional configuration.

    ☒   **B** is incorrect because Windows 95 does not support MS-CHAP v2 as an authentication protocol.

    ☒   **D** is incorrect because Windows NT 4 does not support MS-CHAP v2 as an authentication protocol.

Diagnose RAS Policy Problems Caused by Nested Groups

7. ☑   **B** is correct. The Windows-Groups condition cannot be used with local computer groups.

    ☒   **A** is incorrect because user dial-in permissions can be set for individual users in a workgroup through the Local Users and Groups section in the Computer Management snap-in.

    ☒   **C** is incorrect because RAS policy profile settings can be configured for all RAS policies and are not dependant on the computers membership in a workgroup or domain environment.

    ☒   **D** is incorrect because the Control access through remote access policy setting is available through the Local Users and Groups section in Computer Management.

8. ☑   **D** is correct. You have not created any RAS policies on the new RAS server that Allow access. The default RAS policy on the new server is configured to Deny access.

    ☒   **A** is incorrect because remote access policies do not replicate from one RRAS server to another. If you want to use the same policies, you must either copy them over or re-create them on the new RRAS server.

    ☒   **B** is incorrect because the Everyone group does not have to be added to the Pre-Windows 2000 compatible access group on the new RRAS server; rather, it is done once in Active Directory. However, this is not the issue in this question.

    ☒   **C** is incorrect because the RRAS service does not require authorization.

9. ☑ **B** and **E** are correct. The default condition and permission in the default remote access policy is a day and time restriction of 24/7 access and a permission set to Deny access.
   ☒ **A** is incorrect because the default permission is Deny access.
   ☒ **C** is incorrect because the default RAS policy does not use the Windows-Groups attribute in its list of conditions.
   ☒ **D** is incorrect because the default RAS policy does not use the Windows-Groups attribute in its list of conditions.

10. ☑ **D** is correct. The policies should be ordered Executives, Sales, Default because RAS policies are processed from the top down. When Bill Taylor meets the conditions of the first policy, Executives, no other policies will be processed.
    ☒ **A** is incorrect because ordering the policies Sales, Executives, Default would result in Bill Taylor receiving the Sales policy settings instead of the Executives policy settings.
    ☒ **B** is incorrect because ordering the policies Default, Executives, Sales would result in all users receiving the default policy.
    ☒ **C** is incorrect because ordering the policies Default, Sales, Executives would result in all users receiving the default policy.

Lab Answers

1. The five RAS policies listed in Table 14-4 should be defined to achieve the goals outlined in the lab question. There is no need for a sixth RAS policy for the Managers group because the managers are members of the other groups.

2. One of the other important configuration settings is the permissions of the RAS policy, which in all cases is set to Grant access. In the existing mixed mode domain, these permissions will be ignored, but to plan for the change to native mode, one of the requirements defined in the question is to ensure no changes to the RAS policies would be required. Setting the RAS policy permissions to Grant access will ensure that no changes are required if the user's dial-in permission is changed to Control access through remote access policy.

3. The last factor that you must plan for is the order of the policies, because RAS policies are processed from the top of the list down to the bottom. Because two users are members of both the Sales and Marketing groups and the time and day restrictions are less restrictive for the Sales group, the Sales policy should be at the top of the list, followed by all the others. The order of the remaining policies is not relevant in this scenario because there are no conflicts.

TABLE 14-4 Answer Table

Policy Name	Conditions	Permissions	Profile	Dial-in Permissions
Sales Policy	24/7 time and day restrictions	Grant access	Disable after 5 minutes of inactivity	Allow access
Marketing Policy	17:00–09:00 time and day restrictions	Grant access	Disable after 5 minutes of inactivity	Allow access
Production Policy	17:00–22:00 time and day restrictions	Grant access	Disable after 5 minutes of inactivity	Allow access
IT Policy	24/7 time and day restrictions	Grant access	PPTP Disable after 5 minutes of inactivity	Allow access
Administration Policy	24/7 time and day restrictions	Grant access	Disable after 5 minutes of inactivity	Allow access

15
Implementing Terminal Services for Remote Access

CERTIFICATION OBJECTIVES

15.01　Configure Terminal Services for Remote Administration or Application Server Mode

15.02　Configure Terminal Services for Local Resource Mapping

15.03　Configure Terminal Services User Properties

✓　　Two-Minute Drill

Q&A　Self Test

Windows Terminal Services is included with and closely integrated into Windows 2000, as opposed to earlier versions of Windows NT 4, in which it was available as a special version of the operating system. Terminal Services is a dream come true for administrators who require the ability to remotely administer multiple servers, and with its service improvements and enhanced functionality, it is a valid alternative to other remote administration applications like VNC and PC Anywhere. The benefits of Terminal Services don't stop at remote administration, though; they also include the ability to perform true remote processing, allowing you to leverage older legacy desktop computers and operating systems by allowing them to run their applications remotely on the Terminal Server. The inclusion of Terminal Services with all of the Windows 2000 operating systems adds a tremendous amount of value and goes a long way in helping to demonstrate a return on investment to management. I've given Terminal Services its own chapter—even though its configuration and implementation are fairly straightforward—because Microsoft treats it as a new feature, and therefore it becomes a focus on the certification exam.

When it comes to remote administration of multiple Microsoft operating systems, you have a few alternative administrative strategies to choose from. Telnet can be used to create a telnet session with the Telnet Service on a Windows 2000 server and perform administration from the command line with the command-line tools included in Windows 2000 and the Windows 2000 Server and Professional Resource Kits. Third-party tools such as PC Anywhere and VNC are also available, but some of these come with additional licensing costs. Because all Microsoft operating systems are GUI-based, Terminal Services offers administrators the ability to remotely administer multiple servers through a GUI interface and requires very little in the way of local system resources.

Terminal Services offers two ways in which to establish a connection from a remote computer. The first requires that a Terminal Services client be installed on the remote computer. The Terminal Services client comes in both a 16- and 32-bit format, allowing it to be installed on legacy operating systems such as Windows 95. The second alternative is to install the web interface, known as the Terminal Services Advanced Client (TSAC), which is an ActiveX component that is installed on the Terminal Server running Internet Information Services (IIS) and allows for administration to be conducted through a web browser.

Terminal Services uses the Remote Desktop Protocol (RDP) over TCP/IP to establish and handle all communications between the Terminal Server and the Terminal Services client. RDP is based on the International Telecommunications Union (ITU) T.120 standard for multichannel conferencing and is designed to optimize the transfer of GUI elements from the server to the client. In a Terminal Services session, on the desktop of the Terminal Services client, a Windows 2000 desktop appears, allowing the using to log on using CTRL-ALT-DEL as they normally would in a domain environment, but all of the processing and applications are being run remotely on the Terminal Server, as opposed to locally on the Terminal Services client; hence the idea of a "remote desktop," as shown in Figure 15-1.

on the job

To enable communications through a firewall between a Terminal Server and a Terminal Services client, TCP port 3389 must be open on the firewall, as that is the port that RDP uses. The use of the Citrix ICA protocol is also popular in many existing implementations. Metaframe is a third-party add-on for Terminal Services from Citrix Systems, Inc. that incorporates the Citrix Independent Computing Architecture (ICA) protocol. ICA uses TCP port 1494 for communications between Terminal Services client and server and can extend capabilities for client devices, network connections, and local system resources while also providing additional management tools.

CERTIFICATION OBJECTIVE 15.01

Configure Terminal Services for Remote Administration or Application Server Mode

Terminal Services can operate in one of two modes: Remote Administration mode or Application Server mode. You are asked to specify the mode that you want Terminal Services to run in during the installation of the Terminal Services component. The default mode is Remote Administration mode.

Installing Terminal Services

Terminal Services is not one of the components installed during the default installation of Windows 2000, but it can be added at any time after the installation.

FIGURE 15-1

The mechanics of Terminal Services

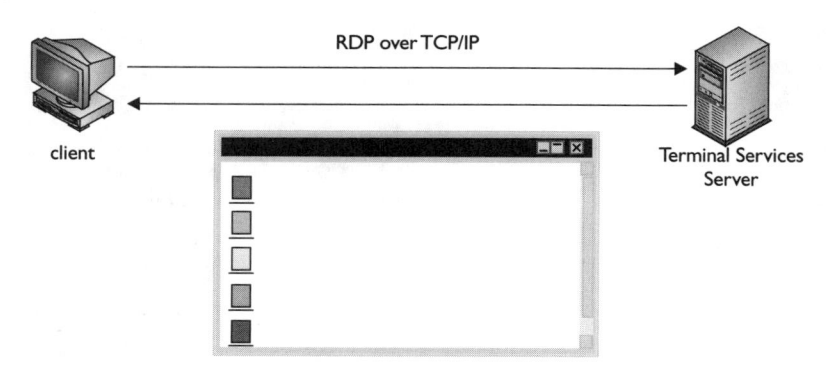

EXERCISE 15-1

Installing Terminal Services

Terminal Services is installed by adding in the Terminal Services component through the Add Windows Components section in Add/Remove Programs in Control Panel. For the purposes of this exercise, I will assume that you will install Terminal Services in Remote Administration mode.

on the Job

Terminal Services and Offline Files are mutually exclusive, meaning that you will not be able to configure the computer running Terminal Services to use Offline Files on other computers.

1. Select Start | Settings | Control Panel, and double-click Add/Remove Programs.
2. In the Add/Remove Programs dialog box, click Add/Remove Windows Components.
3. Scroll through the list of Windows Components and place a check mark in the box to the left of Terminal Services. Installing Terminal Services in Remote Administration mode does not require that Terminal Services Licensing also be selected; however, for the purposes of later exercises, select that option as well. Click Next.
4. On the Terminal Services Setup page of the Windows Components Wizard, confirm that Remote Administration Mode is selected and click Next.

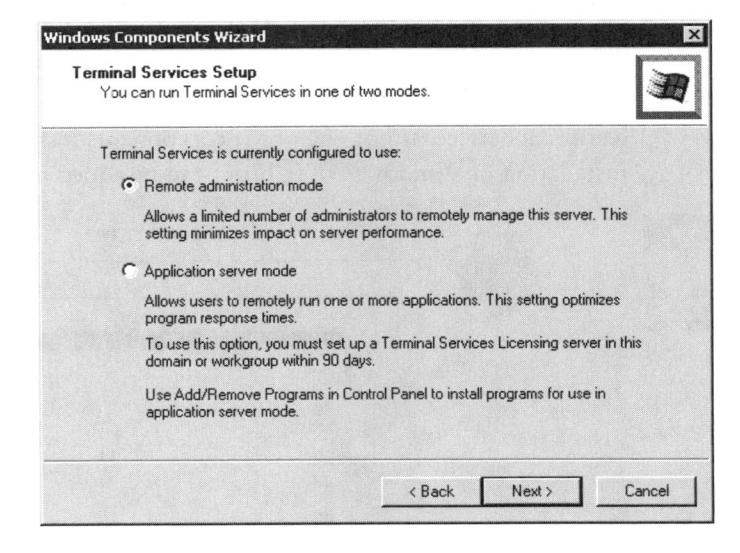

5. The installation of the Terminal Services Licensing component opens a second wizard page that asks you to specify the location of the licensing server database. Accept the default location of c:\Winnt\System32\LServer and click Next.

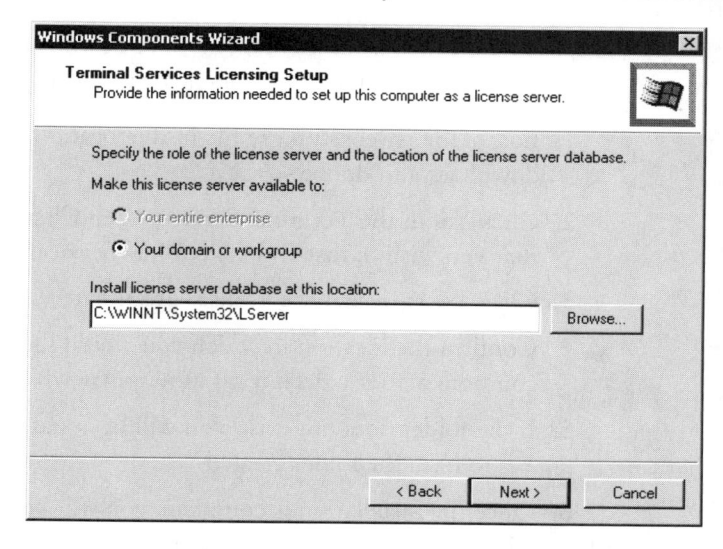

6. You will be prompted during the installation for the installation media; insert the Windows 2000 CD or direct the installation to a path on the network where the installation files can be found.

7. Once the installation is complete, click Finish and click Yes to reboot the computer.

After the release of Windows 2000, Microsoft released an add-on for Terminal Services known as the Terminal Services Advanced Client (TSAC), which extends the types of available client connections to include browser-based Terminal Services connections. TSAC is completely optional and can be downloaded from the Microsoft web site at www.microsoft.com/windows2000/downloads/recommended/TSAC/default.asp.

There are a couple of additional Terminal Server requirements for using TSAC. The Terminal Server must be running IIS 4 or higher. The default Windows 2000 installation includes IIS 5, meaning that this requirement is generally met. The installation of TSAC on the Terminal Server will create a new directory named Tsweb in the path C:\Inetpub\wwwroot\, where all of the web package files will be stored.

EXERCISE 15-2

Installing TSAC

This exercise, which assumes that you have downloaded tswebsetup.exe from the Microsoft web site, walks you through the installation of the add-on:

1. Locate the tswebsetup.exe file in the location you specified during the download and double-click it.

2. Click Yes in the Terminal Services Web Client Setup dialog box, confirming that you wish to install the Terminal Services Web Client package.

3. Click Yes to accept the license agreement.

4. Confirm the location in which you would like to install the TSAC components. The default is C:\inetput\wwwroot\TSWeb. Click OK.

5. If the folder does not exist, you will be asked if you want to create it; click Yes to have the folder created.

6. Once the installation is complete, you will be asked if you want to read the release notes. Click Yes to read the release notes or click No. The release notes are saved in the TSWeb folder and can be read at a later time.

7. To test the installation, open your browser (must be a 32-bit version of Internet Explorer 4.x or higher) and browse to http://*servername*/tsweb, where *servername* is the name of the Terminal Server. The following illustration shows you what the resulting page should look like.

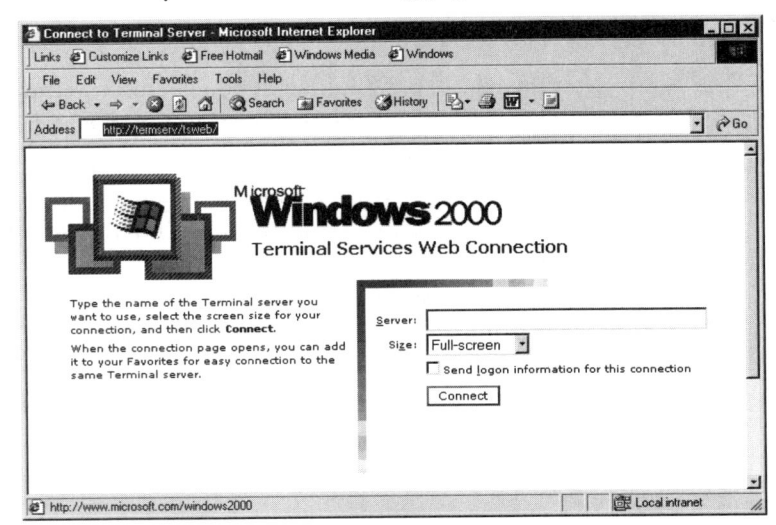

8. Entering the name of the Terminal Server into the logon dialog box and clicking Connect prompts you to download and install the TSAC ActiveX control from the Terminal Server. Clicking Yes installs the control and, when finished, presents you with a logon screen to a Terminal Server in your browser.

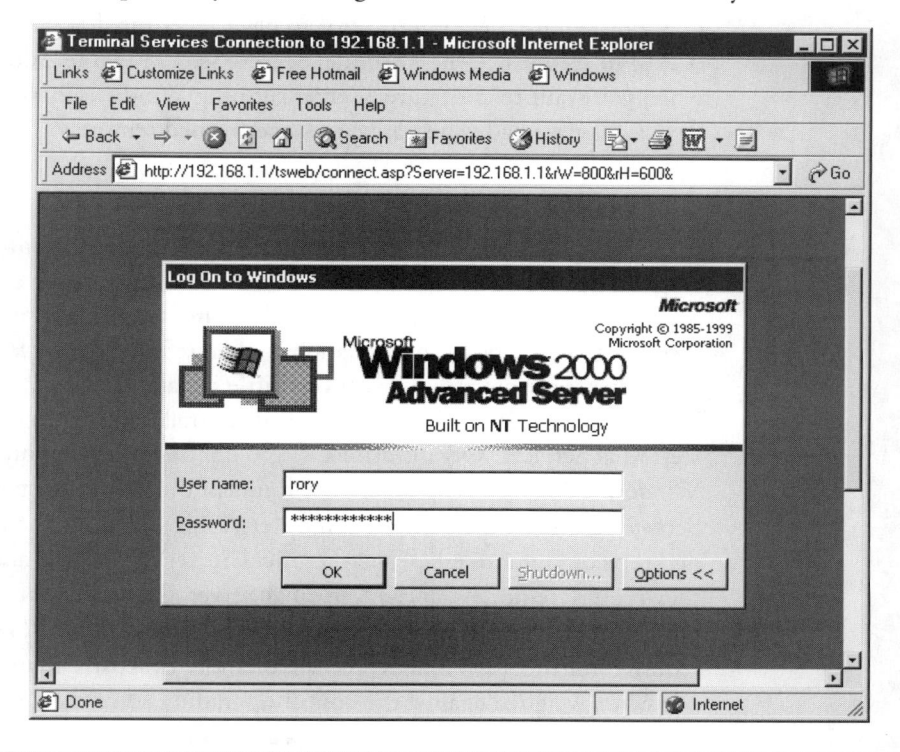

During the installation of Terminal Services, you were asked to choose one of two modes in which to run Terminal Services. The next two sections address each of these modes and will help you to understand the differences, as well as decide which mode to choose based on what you are trying to accomplish.

Remote Administration Mode

Installing Terminal Services in Remote Administration mode allows only members of the Administrators group to connect to the Terminal Server and limits administrative connections to two concurrent connections. Terminal Services Remote Administration mode allows any server running Windows 2000 Server to be administrated remotely with full access to all the built-in GUI-based administrative tools. The desktop on the Terminal Services client makes it appear as though the administrator is sitting locally at the server, performing administrative tasks. Remote administration through the Terminal Services client is possible from a number of client computer operating systems. Another nice feature of Remote Administration mode is that it does not require the administrator to have a Terminal Services client access license (CAL) to connect to the Terminal Server. Select Remote Administration mode when you want to configure a server running Windows 2000 with the ability to have GUI-based administrative tasks performed remotely.

Application Server Mode

Application Server mode is the alternative to Remote Administration mode. Application Server mode is designed to allow users to connect to a Terminal Server and run applications remotely on the Terminal Server, as opposed to on their local computer. This type of configuration is often referred to as a *thin client* environment. Thin clients are computers with very little installed on them in the way of software, because all the applications are installed centrally, in this case on a server running Terminal Services. Organizations with older desktop computers can gain access to a Windows 2000 operating system environment through the installation of the Terminal Services client on the desktop computers. This will allow the user logged on at the desktop computer to establish a Terminal Server connection and run the applications they require remotely on the Terminal Server. The potential for an immediate return on investment is great in this type of configuration. The server hardware required for the Terminal Server will be more expensive than your average server, but when weighed against the cost of upgrading all of the desktops, it will usually pale in comparison. The amount of administration required also has the potential of being reduced, because applications can be deployed and managed from a central location, saving administrators time in their initial development and deployment and in the ongoing maintenance and upgrades.

Configuring Terminal Services in Application Server mode allows all users to connect through remote access, local area network (LAN), or wide area network (WAN) connections from Windows-based, Windows CE-based, or even non-Windows-based clients. As you saw in Exercise 15-1, the Terminal Services Licensing component is required when deploying a Terminal Server in Application Server mode. Each client computer that establishes a connection, regardless of the type of operating system and protocol used to connect to Terminal Services, must also have a Terminal Services CAL as well as a Windows 2000 Server CAL. Windows 2000 Professional and Windows XP Professional both include one Terminal Services CAL, but not a Windows 2000 Server CAL. Accessing Terminal Services from earlier versions of Microsoft Windows, as well as clients using other operating systems, requires that a Terminal Services CAL and Windows 2000 Server CAL, or the appropriate upgrade licenses, be purchased. Connecting to Terminal Services via TSAC also requires that a Windows 2000 Terminal Services Internet Connector license be purchased, but it does not require the remote clients to have a Windows 2000 Server CAL, as the access is browser-based and could be coming in remotely from another network such as the Internet.

Remote troubleshooting and technical support is also possible through Terminal Services when it is running in Application Server mode, and this is a really nice feature! Upon receipt of a call, help desk personnel are able to take remote control of a user's Terminal Services session, assuming the requisite permission has been granted, and guide the user through the resolution of the problem or simply resolve the problem remotely. One important point to stress here is that both the user and the help desk support personnel must be running their own Terminal Services sessions in order for the help desk user to remotely control the other user's session.

FROM THE CLASSROOM

Taking Remote Control of a User's Session

The remote session control feature in Terminal Services can be a big asset to help desk personnel who wish to troubleshoot problems remotely for a user. The scenario here is that the user is connected to a Terminal Server configured in Terminal Services Application Server mode and is presented with an error or problem, such as not being able to print. The help desk receives the call from the user and is able to establish their own connection with the Terminal Server. Once the help desk has a Terminal Server session established, they open the Terminal Services Manager snap-in, found in Administrative Tools, and identify the user's Terminal Server session from the list of existing sessions. By right-clicking the troubled user's session and selecting Remote Control, a dialog box appears, asking the help desk person to select a hot key combination to end the remote control session and then click OK. This generates a request that is sent to the computer of the user having trouble and arrives in the form of a pop-up dialog box. A question is posed in the dialog box, which asks whether the user wishes to allow the help desk personnel to take control of their session remotely. If the user clicks Yes, the help desk person will have remote control of their session and can begin to troubleshoot and correct the problem remotely.

It is interesting to watch this process from the end user's perspective, because the end user can see everything that the remote help desk

FROM THE CLASSROOM

person is doing. When the help desk user clicks the Start button, the Start menu is expanded on the monitors of both the help desk user and the end user. It's a lot like watching an old player piano, you know, the pianos that play all by themselves.

The remote session control feature of Terminal Services is another great way in which to increase return on investment by decreasing the amount of time spent on troubleshooting tickets. This scenario makes the assumption that the default Terminal Services settings have not been changed, as the default settings allow for all of this to take place. The configuration of these settings is discussed in the last section of this chapter, "Configure Terminal Services User Properties."

—*Rory McCaw*

Switching Between Modes

Now that you are familiar with the two modes of Terminal Server operation, let's look at how to switch between modes and why you might need to switch between modes. If you have decided to install Terminal Services in Remote Administration mode on all of your servers for the sole purpose of being able to remotely administer all of your servers, you shouldn't need to concern yourself with switching between modes, but if you have decided to implement a Terminal Server in Application Server mode, this section is critical. In Application Server mode, you are not able to install additional applications. Therefore, to install new applications, apply service packs, or apply service releases on the Terminal Server, you have to switch to Remote Administration mode, perform the installation, and then switch back to Application Server mode to allow your Terminal Services clients to connect and run the applications.

exam ⓦatch

For the exam, be familiar with the two ways available to switch between Terminal Server modes and remember that applications and Windows components can only be installed when the Terminal Server is in Remote Administration mode.

EXERCISE 15-3

Switching Between Terminal Server Modes Using Add/Remove Programs

Switching between Terminal Server modes is quite easy and can be accomplished through Add/Remove Programs or by using the **change user** command. This exercise assumes that you have installed the Terminal Server, following the steps outlined in Exercise 15-1, and have a Terminal Server running in Remote Administration mode. This exercise demonstrates how to switch modes using Add/Remove Programs:

1. Select Start | Settings | Control Panel and double-click Add/Remove Programs.
2. Click Add/Remove Windows Components and scroll down in the list of available Windows Components to Terminal Services. Select Terminal Services, but do not clear the check mark next to Terminal Services, and click Next.
3. The Terminal Services Setup screen in the Windows Components dialog box should appear as shown earlier in Exercise 15-1. Select the mode you wish to change the Terminal Server to and click Next. When the wizard has completed, click Finish, and you have now successfully changed Terminal Server modes.

Terminal Services also allows you to switch between Terminal Server modes using the **change user** command. The **change user** command has three switches:

- **/install** Changes the Terminal Server mode from Application Server mode to Remote Administration mode
- **/execute** Changes the Terminal Server mode from Remote Administration mode to Application Server mode
- **/query** Allows you to identify the current mode of Terminal Services operation

The **change user** command can be run at the command prompt to change modes by using the following syntax:

```
Change user /install
Change user /execute
Change user /query
```

Like most things in Windows, there is another, simpler way to change Terminal Server modes. By using the Add/Remove Programs icon in Control Panel to install your application, the mode will be changed automatically. Much simpler!

Client Installation Options and Requirements

Once the Terminal Server is installed, you must decide how you want the Terminal Services clients to connect to the Terminal Server and establish a connection. Your two choices are to either install a thin, Terminal Services client on each of the computers you wish to connect from or connect through your browser, as discussed earlier in this chapter. Before we address the Terminal Services client installation options, you must first be familiar with the minimum client hardware requirements, which are displayed in Table 15-1. In all cases other than for Windows CE clients, in which the video card is vendor defined, a VGA video card is required to install the Terminal Services client.

Obviously, the minimum requirements are not a standard that you want to follow when designing your organization's computer specifications; rather, the point here is to illustrate that Terminal Services can allow organizations to leverage older hardware in an effort to increase the return on their investment. Now that we have identified the minimum requirements and are confident that our clients meet these requirements, we will examine the available options for installing the Terminal Services client software.

Installing the Terminal Services Client Software

The Windows 2000 Server CD includes two ways in which to install the Terminal Services client software: install it from a set of installation disks, or share the tsclient folder (C:\winnt\system32\clients\tsclient) on the Terminal Server and allow users to perform an over-the-network installation.

TABLE 15-1

Minimum Client Hardware Requirements

Client OS	RAM	Processor
Windows XP	64MB	P2 233 MHz
Windows 2000	64MB	P1 133 MHz
Windows NT 4.0	16MB	486
Windows Me	16MB	Pentium
Windows 98	16MB	486
Windows 95	16MB	386
Windows for Workgroups 3.11	16MB	386
Windows CE	Vendor defined	Vendor defined

EXERCISE 15-4

Creating the Client Installation Disks

1. Select Start | Programs | Administrative Tools and click Terminal Services Client Creator.

2. The Create Installation Disk(s) dialog box appears. Select the appropriate client, either 16- or 32-bit, select the drive letter for the floppy drive, and then click OK.

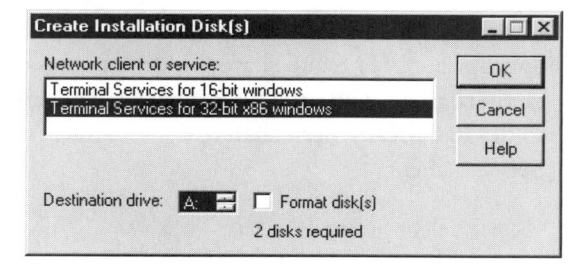

3. Place the first blank floppy disk in the drive and click OK.

4. When prompted, remove the first disk, place the second disk in the floppy drive, and click OK.

5. Once the disks' creation process is complete, you will be notified by a dialog box and asked to click OK.

6. Remove the second disk and click Cancel to close the Create Installation Disk(s) dialog box.

The second and often more convenient way in which to install the Terminal Services client, particularly when you want to install it on a number of client operating systems, is through an over-the-network installation. The additional benefit of this approach is that it can be scripted and scheduled to occur during a time of low network activity, such as after business hours.

on the Job

Terminal Services includes client software in both 16- and 32-bit versions for Windows-based computers. Computers running non-Windows operating systems require a third-party add-on or, alternatively, can use their Internet Explorer browser and use the TSAC web interface.

EXERCISE 15-5

CertCam 15-5

Installing the Terminal Services Client over the Network

To install the Terminal Services client over the network, the tsclient folder (c:\winnt\system32\clients\tsclient) must be shared on the Terminal Server, and the appropriate NTFS and shared folder permissions must be granted to allow users to connect and execute the file setup.exe. This exercise, which assumes that the tsclient folder has already been shared, demonstrates how to install the 32-bit Terminal Services client:

1. Select Start | Run.
2. In the Run dialog box, enter *servername*\tsclient, where *servername* is the name of the Terminal Server with the tsclient share, and click OK.
3. Double-click the Net folder and then double-click the Win32 folder.
4. Inside the win32 folder, double-click setup.exe and, when prompted with the Terminal Services Client Setup dialog box, click Continue.
5. Enter your name and organization information in the Name and Organization Information dialog box and click OK. Click OK again to confirm the information you entered is correct.
6. Click I Agree to agree to the license information.
7. Click the large button in the Terminal Services Client Setup dialog box to start the installation of the Terminal Services client.

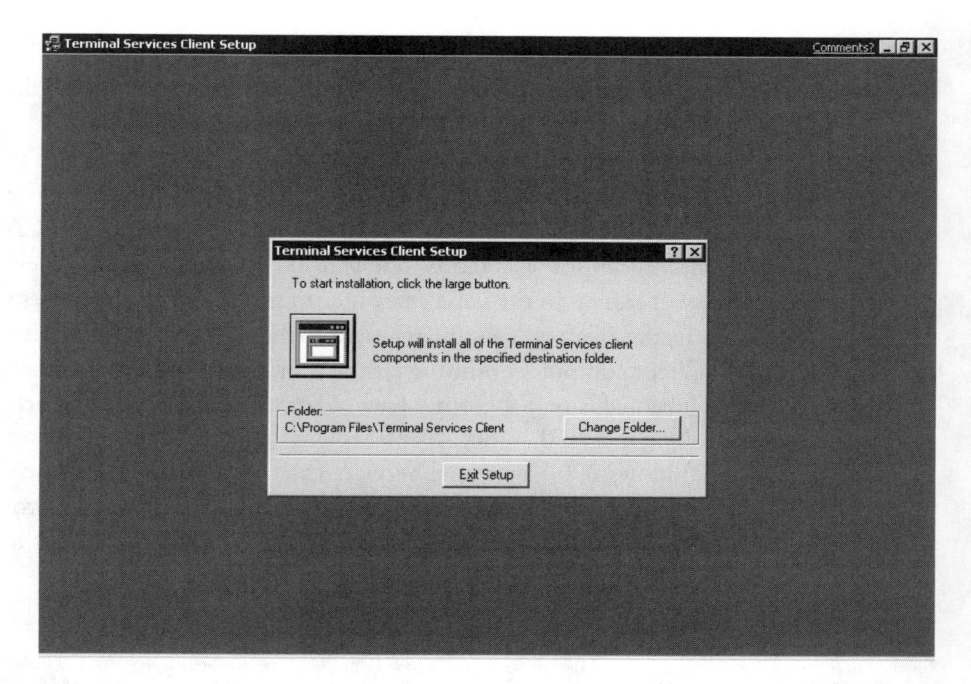

Configure Terminal Services for Remote Administration or Application Server Mode 675

8. At the next dialog box, click Yes to install the Terminal Services client for all users on the client computer, or click No to install it only for the current user.
9. The installation begins; once it is finished, click OK to confirm its success.

A third option also exists that enables you to roll out the Terminal Services client to multiple computers, but it isn't included with the Windows 2000 Server CD and requires Active Directory. Group Policy can be used to assign the Terminal Services client Windows Installer file (Terminal Services client.msi) to the appropriate client computers in an Active Directory domain. The Windows installer file for the Terminal Services client can be downloaded from www.microsoft.com/windows2000/downloads/recommended/TSAC/tsmsi.asp?Lang= as a self-extracting executable named tsmsisetup.exe. This method enables you to deploy the Terminal Services client Windows Installer file to numerous client computers within an Active Directory domain by assigning the application to computers as discussed in Chapter 7.

Licensing

Licensing is a complicated issue with far too many variables to be able to provide one all-encompassing answer to all readers. That being said, use this rule of thumb when considering licensing issues related to Terminal Server: the ability to connect to a Terminal Server running in Application Server mode requires that the user have a Windows 2000 Server CAL and a Terminal Services CAL.

Remember that a client connection to a Terminal Server also results in the client connecting to the Windows 2000 server OS that Terminal Services is operating on. Any client connection to a Windows 2000 server requires a CAL to establish communications with the Windows 2000 server. Should the client initiate a Terminal Services session to the same computer running Terminal Services in Application Server mode, the client will also be required to have a Terminal Services CAL.

Client computers running either Windows 2000 Professional or Windows XP Professional (not XP Home) have a Terminal Services CAL included with the OS, meaning that all that these clients require is a Windows 2000 Server CAL. Alternatively, a Windows 2000 Terminal Services Internet Connector license can be purchased to allow clients to gain access through that. Application service providers (ASPs) or organizations that implement the TSAC are most likely to opt for the Windows 2000 Terminal Services Internet Connector license.

SCENARIO & SOLUTION

You would like to open as few ports as is required to allow Terminal Services communications through your firewall. Which ports are required and for what protocols?	Only TCP port 3389 must be opened on the firewall to allow RDP traffic over TCP/IP to come in and out through the firewall.
You have installed Terminal Services in its default mode on a server configured as a printer server, but when five administrators attempt to establish a Terminal Services session, only two are able. What is causing this?	The default mode for Terminal Services is Remote Administration mode, which only allows two administrative connections to be established with the Terminal Server at any one time.
What are the licensing requirements for clients connecting to a Terminal Server?	Each client that wants to establish a connection with a Terminal Server must have a Terminal Services CAL and a Windows 2000 Server CAL.
You have a computer located in a remote branch office that you wish to install the Terminal Services client on but you do not want to do this over the network. What other options are available?	If you do not want to perform an over-the-network installation, a set of installation boot disks can be created and sent to the remote office to allow the installation of the Terminal Services client to be performed from floppy disks.

Establishing a Connection to the Terminal Server

Now that you are aware of how to install both Terminal Services and the client, we are at the point where we can test Terminal Services to make sure it all works and examine how to create a Terminal Services session.

EXERCISE 15-6

Creating a Terminal Server Session

This exercise walks you through the steps involved in connecting to a Terminal Server located at 192.168.1.253:

1. Select Start | Programs | Terminal Services Client, and then click Terminal Services Client again.

2. The Terminal Services Client dialog box appears. In the Server drop-down list box, enter the name or IP address of the Terminal Server. In the Screen Area drop-down list box, select the resolution you would like for the client connection. If you want to enable data compression and the caching of bitmaps to disk, check the corresponding boxes. Both of these settings are recommended for security and performance reasons.

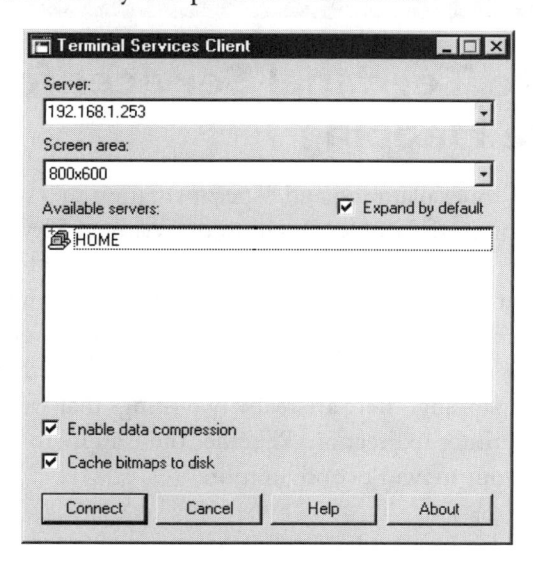

3. Click Connect and, when prompted, enter your username and password in the Logon dialog box and click OK.

Terminating a Connection

Once you have established a connection, you have two options to close that connection: disconnect or log off. By disconnecting from the Terminal Server, the user's session continues to run on the Terminal Server, consuming resources. Disconnecting allows a user to reconnect in the future and resume running the applications that were running previously. Think of disconnecting from a Terminal Server session as being similar to locking a workstation. A disconnect can occur by the user manually selecting to disconnect, but it can also occur as a result of a network or client failure. In either case, when the user logs back into the system, either from the same computer or from a different computer, the user is automatically reconnected to their previously disconnected session.

The second option, which is to log off, is just like logging off a computer locally. All of the resources that were running in the context of that session are stopped, as are all applications, and the session is closed. Reconnecting in the future creates an entirely new session that will require the user to restart any applications that they wish to work with.

CERTIFICATION OBJECTIVE 15.02

Configure Terminal Services for Local Resource Mapping

Proper planning and experimentation in a staging environment is critical to the successful implementation of Terminal Services. This planning and staging will help you to anticipate and resolve problems up front, prior to your production rollout, and can end up saving you many hours, if not days, in the long run. A central component in this planning and staging process is to identify local resource mapping issues and know how to solve and address them. When it comes to local resource mapping, there are really two things that we will focus on: Clipboard mapping and printer redirection. Whether these apply to your own specific scenario depends on your network configuration.

Clipboard Mapping

Clipboard mapping is a new feature of RDP version 5.0 that allows users to cut, copy, and paste text and graphics between applications running on the local Terminal Services client computer and applications running in a Terminal Services session. Text can also be cut, copied, and pasted between Terminal Services sessions. In this scenario, a single client computer might have two Terminal Services connections to two different computers.

exam
Watch

Files and folders cannot be cut, copied, and pasted between a Terminal Services session and the local client computer using the default configuration; only text and graphics can be copied between applications. Look to the Windows 2000 Server Resource Kit for the Rdpclip.exe utility. This utility is an extension to Terminal Services that allows you to copy and paste files and folders between a Terminal Services session and a Terminal Services client.

EXERCISE 15-7

Copying Text from an Application in a Terminal Services Session to an Application on the Terminal Services Client Computer

In this exercise, you will learn how to copy text from an application running in a Terminal Services session to another application running on the Terminal Services client computer.

1. From the Terminal Services client computer, establish a session with a Terminal Server.
2. After successfully logging on, click Start | Run, type **notepad** and click OK.
3. In Notepad, enter some text by typing **This is a test.** Select the text, right-click it, and click Copy.
4. Outside of the Terminal Services session on the client computer, click Start | Run, type **notepad**, and click OK.
5. In Notepad, right-click and click Paste.

Congratulations! You now know how to copy and paste text between an application running in a Terminal Services session and an application running on a Terminal Services client.

Printer Redirection

Accessing local print devices attached to the Terminal Services client has also been simplified thanks to RDP 5. Users are able to print to a print device that is local to the Terminal Services client computer from applications running within a Terminal Services session just as easily as the client computer can print to network print devices, or print devices connected locally to the computer running Terminal Services. Figure 15-2 demonstrates how a user at the Terminal Services client computer named CR72932-A is logged on to a Terminal Services session with the Terminal Server located at 192.168.1.253 and is running the application Notepad. When the user attempts to print from Notepad, which is running within the Terminal Services session, the user has a choice between two print devices: HP5, which is a print device local to the Terminal Services client (CR72932-A), or a network print device named HP with an IP address of 192.168.1.50.

Terminal Services provides *automatic printer redirection,* which allows users to select a print device local to their Terminal Services client, and sends the print jobs from the Terminal Server to the client's local print device queue. This feature is supported on all Win32 client platforms, including Windows 95, 98, and NT 4. When a 32-bit Terminal Services client logs on to a Terminal Server, all print devices attached locally to the Terminal Services client computer via LPT, COM, and USB ports are automatically detected and corresponding print queues created in the user's Terminal Services session.

FIGURE 15-2

Printing from a Terminal Services session

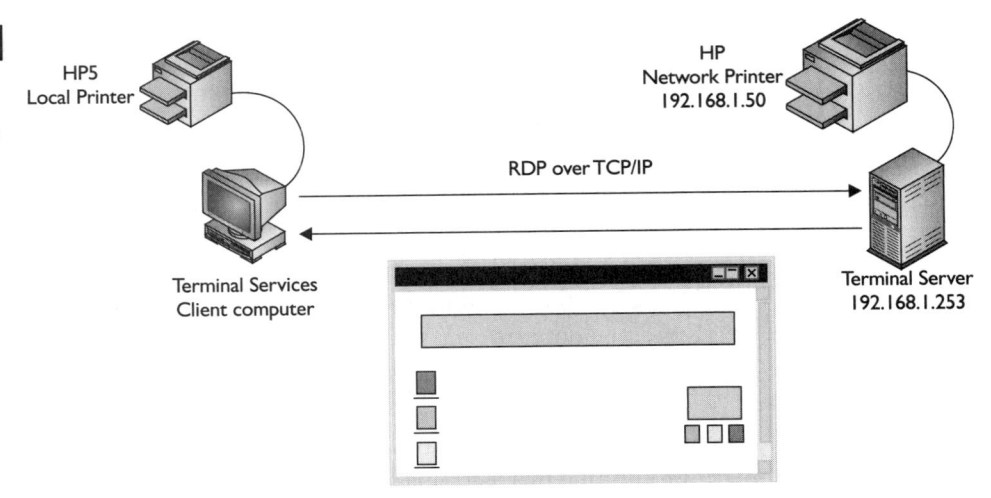

Automatic printer redirection is more evident when taking a closer look at the Print dialog box shown in Figure 15-2. Thus, Figure 15-3 provides an enlarged view of the Print dialog box from Figure 15-2. Pay particular attention to the name of the local print device. HP5 is the name of the printer, which is local to the client computer named CR72932-A; \Session 1 means that this printer has been automatically detected when the user at the Terminal Services client computer CR72932-A logged on to the Terminal Server at 192.168.1.253 and the printer queue for this printer is only available to this session. When the Terminal Services client disconnects or ends the session, the queue will be deleted and all pending print jobs terminated.

Terminal Services also supports a second type of printer redirection known as *manual printer redirection.* Manual printer direction is included to provide support for computers running older, 16-bit operating systems such as Windows for Workgroups 3.11, but really, who is still using Windows for Workgroups 3.11? Manual printer redirection is configured by manually adding the local printer through the Add Printers wizard in Control Panel from within the Terminal Services session.

FIGURE 15-3

Automatic printer redirection

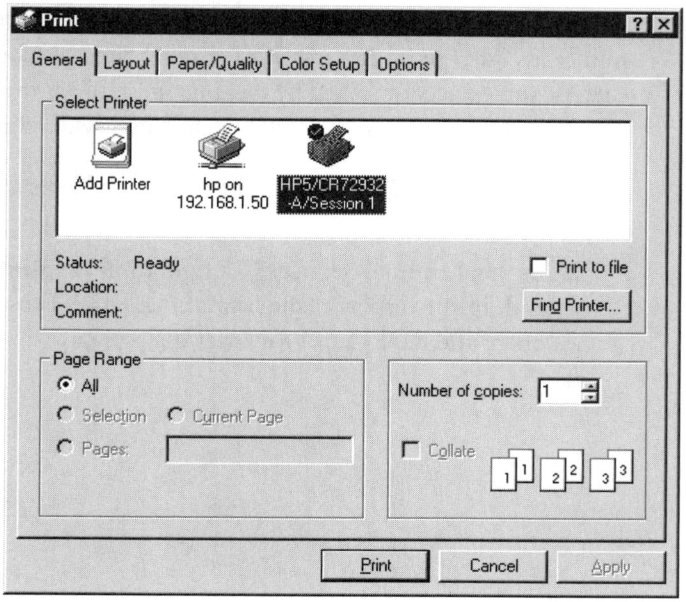

on the job

Before configuring printer redirection, give some thought as to how most users will be establishing Terminal Server connections, particularly what types of network bandwidth connections they will be using. Configuring printer redirection means that when a user prints a large print job to their local printer, that print job will be spooled across the slow link from the Terminal Server to the local printer, which could consume enough bandwidth to reduce the performance of the Terminal Services client. Without printer redirection, your bandwidth requirements only have to accommodate Terminal Services client keystrokes, mouse events, and screen updates.

Printer redirection, whether automatic or manual, can be disabled on a per-connection basis by using the Terminal Services Configuration tool or on a per-user basis by using Active Directory Users and Computers.

EXERCISE 15-8

CertCam 15-8

Configuring Terminal Services Settings on a Per-Connection Basis

In this exercise, you will learn how to configure printer redirection settings and numerous other settings using the Terminal Services Configuration snap-in. This exercise can be accomplished by logging on locally at the Terminal Server or through a Terminal Services session, logged on as a user with administrative permissions.

1. Select Start | Programs | Administrative Tools and click Terminal Services Configuration.

2. In the Terminal Services Configuration snap-in, click the Connections folder and, in the display plane, right-click RDP-Tcp and click Properties. This opens the RDP-Tcp Properties dialog box.

Configure Terminal Services for Local Resource Mapping **683**

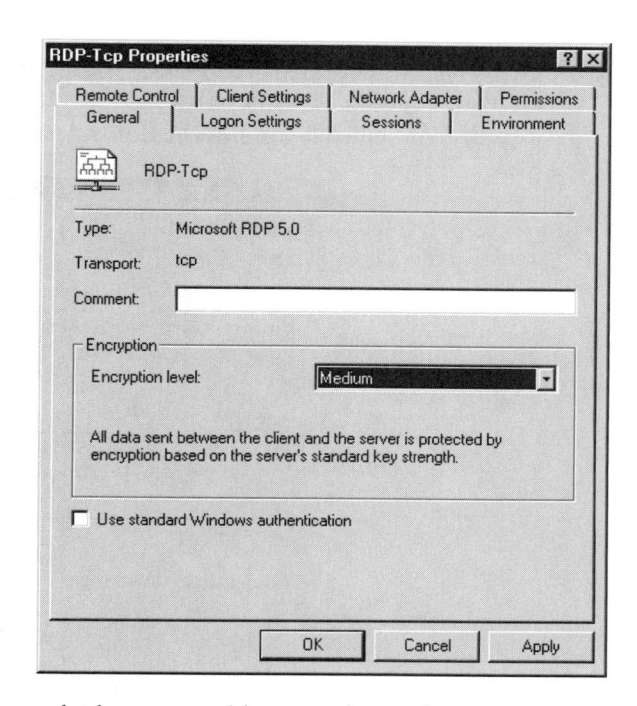

3. On the General tab, you are able to configure the encryption settings for all data sent between the Terminal Services client and Terminal Server. The default Encryption Level setting is Medium; the other two choices are Low and High. The Low setting only protects data sent from the client to the server, not data sent from the server to the client. Both the Medium and High settings encrypt data in both directions, with the difference being that the Medium setting uses the Terminal Server's standard key strength (56-bit) and the High setting uses the Terminal Server's maximum key strength (128-bit). Encryption is important, particularly when the Terminal Server is configured in Remote Administration mode because a hacker sniffing the network could compromise the administrator account information.

on the job — **The 128-bit, maximum key strength is only available after the Windows 2000 High Encryption Pack has been installed on the server or Service Pack 2 is installed. The default installation of Service Pack 2 automatically applies the High Encryption Pack.**

4. Click the Logon Settings tab, on which you can configure automatic logon with a specific account or use the default setting, which is set to use client-provided logon information.

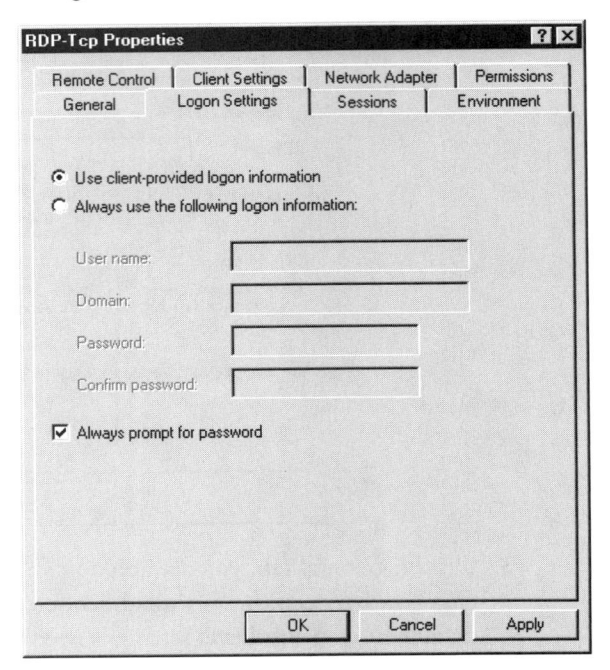

5. Click the Sessions tab, on which you can do the following: configure connection settings that will override the user's personal connection settings configured in Active Directory Users and Computers; specify the amount of time the Terminal Server will wait prior to ending a disconnected session, the

active session limit, and the idle session limit; and configure what the Terminal Server should do when a session limit is reached or when a connection is broken, with the options being to either disconnect from the session or end the session.

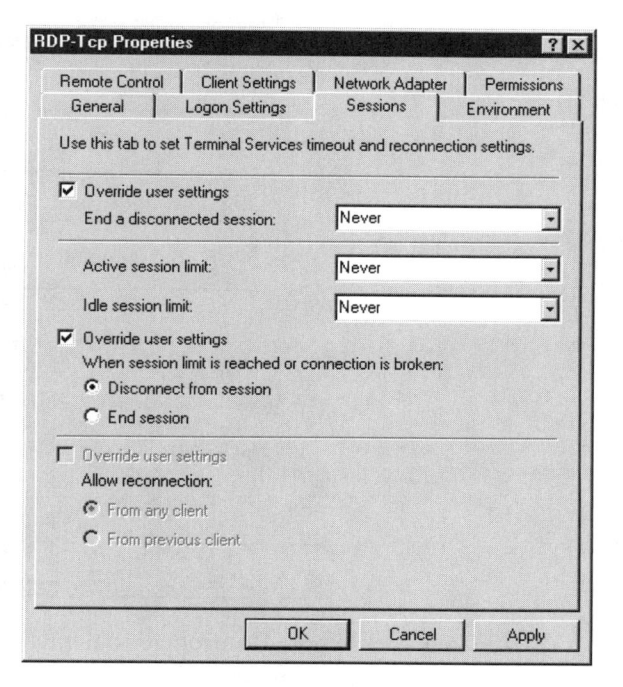

6. Click the Environment tab to configure an application that will run when the user logs on or to disable the use of wallpaper. Because a Terminal Services client's desktop is constantly being redrawn, the use of wallpaper can reduce

performance for both the client and the server. It is a best practice to disable the use of wallpaper for all sessions.

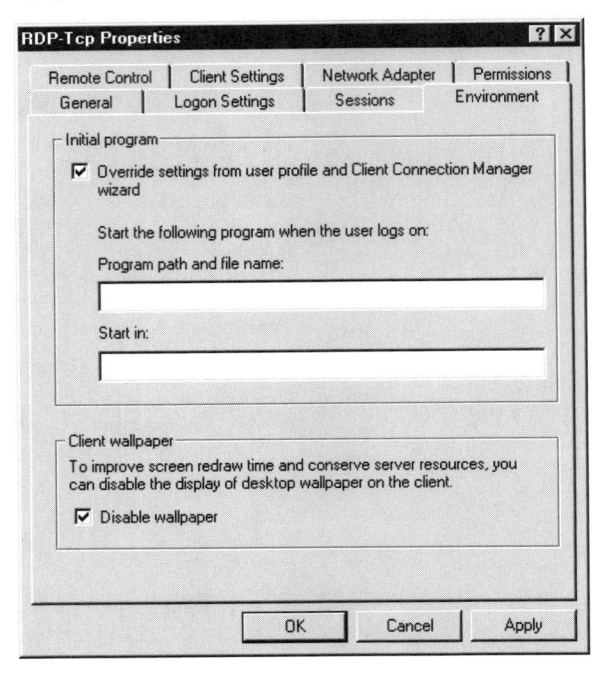

7. Click the Remote Control tab to define the global remote control settings that you wish to use. Here you are able to globally disable remote control or specify the settings to be used for all remote control sessions.

Configure Terminal Services for Local Resource Mapping 687

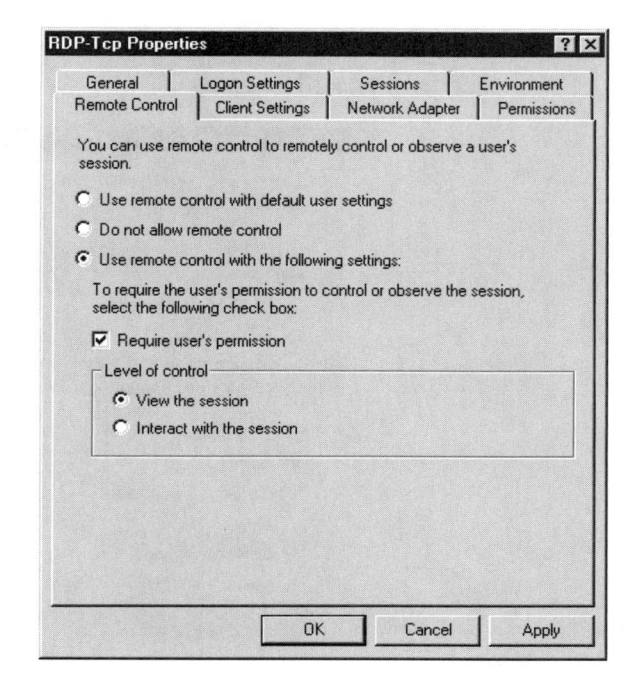

8. Click the Client Settings tab to configure the global client settings. This is where you can define automatic printer redirection by clearing the Connect

client printers at logon check box. This tab is also where you can globally disable Clipboard mapping.

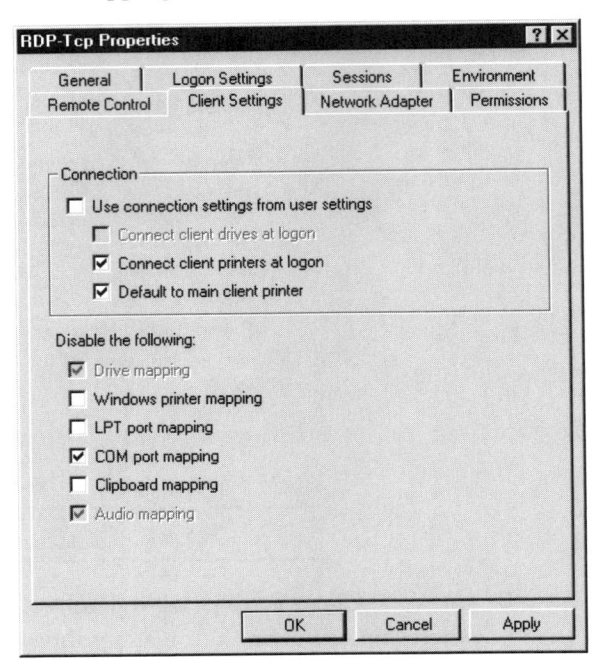

9. Click the Network Adapter tab to define which adapter Terminal Services will listen on. This tab offers you the ability to configure Terminal Services to only listen on one NIC on a multihomed computer.

Configure Terminal Services for Local Resource Mapping

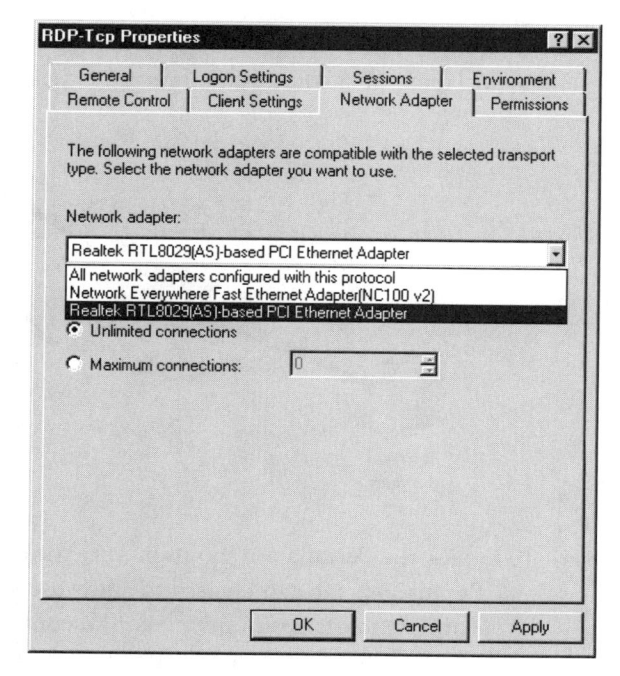

If your Windows 2000 Terminal Server is connected to both the Internet and the LAN, you could establish a security policy requiring all remote administration be performed through a VPN and that only the internal NIC (NIC2) attached to the LAN allow Terminal Services connections to be established. This type of configuration is shown in the following illustration. In this example, any external clients on the Internet wishing to establish a Terminal Services connection would have to first establish a VPN to NIC1, authenticate to the server or domain, and then establish a Terminal Services session with NIC2, which would only be available through the VPN connection or from the LAN. You also can configure on the Network Adapter tab a connection limit for either performance or licensing purposes.

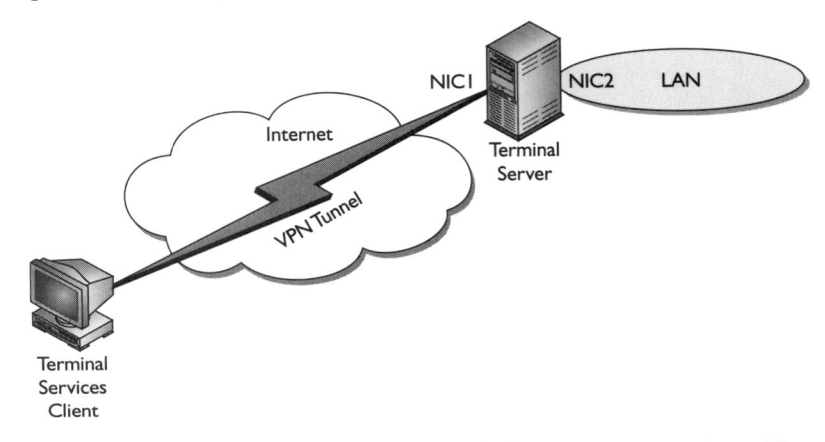

10. Click the Permissions tab to modify the default permission settings. The Permissions tab can be used to allow users that are not members of the Administrators group permission to connect via Terminal Services to a Terminal Server running in Remote Administration mode; however, the same limit of two simultaneous sessions still applies. This offers you a way to allow a specific user, such as the user that performs backups, to establish a Terminal Services connection without adding the user to the Administrators group.

CERTIFICATION OBJECTIVES 15.03

Configure Terminal Services User Properties

The installation and use of Terminal Services requires that you give some consideration to the properties of each user account within your domain or on the local Terminal Server if it is in a workgroup. This section of the chapter deals with the configuration of user properties within the context of an Active Directory domain because that will be the focus on the exam. The configuration of local computer properties can be accomplished through the Local Users and Groups section in the Computer Management snap-in using principles very similar to those used in a domain environment.

Configure Terminal Services User Properties

exam
ⓦatch

Any attribute changes made to a user object with respect to Terminal Services are automatically overridden by the global connection settings, discussed earlier in this chapter, and configured through the Terminal Services Configuration snap-in.

Terminal Services configuration is accomplished through three separate tabs in each user object's Properties dialog box in Active Directory Users and Computers. These three tabs are the Terminal Services Profile tab, the Remote Control tab, and the Sessions tab. The default user property configuration has the Allow logon to terminal server setting enabled (see Figure 15-4), meaning that as soon as you install and configure an Application Server, all users will be able to log on to it.

Additional configuration settings on this tab include the ability to configure each user with a Terminal Services user profile path and a Terminal Services home directory location. It is a recommended best practice to create the profile and home directory folders on the Terminal Server so that the information is available locally on the Terminal Server that users are logging on to. Figure 15-4 shows both a user profile path and home directory path specified using a variable %username%. This

FIGURE 15-4

Configuring a user's Terminal Services profile information

SCENARIO & SOLUTION

You would like to configure a Terminal Services profile for 55 different users. What is the easiest way in which to accomplish this?	To edit the properties of multiple user accounts, select all the accounts you want to edit by holding down the CTRL key and clicking each account and then right-clicking the highlighted accounts and selecting Properties. In the case of the Terminal Services Profile, select the Terminal Services Profile tab and enter the path to where the profiles will be stored, using the %username% variable such as \\termserv1\tsprofiles\%username%. This way, when the changes are applied, the %username% variable will be replaced with the appropriate username. This allows you to make changes to numerous account properties at once and apply to all selected users.
You have created a home directory for all users in the path \\termserv1\tshome. Your users have begun to report that files they have saved to their home directory in previous sessions are no longer there but new files they haven't seen before are.	This occurs because you haven't specified an individual home folder for each user; rather, all users are sharing the same home folder. This means that some users are deleting files that belong to other users. Resolve this by selecting all of the Terminal Server user accounts and changing the home directory path to \\termserv1\tshome\%username%.
As the Active Directory administrator in your organization, you have made several changes to the different users' Terminal Services properties, but when the users establish a connection to the Terminal Server, only certain settings, such as the home directory and profile path, are in effect.	The most likely cause of this is that the user settings are being overridden by global settings made through the Terminal Services Configuration tool. Settings made on a per-connection basis override any user settings. The reason some user settings are effective is that not all user settings can be overridden by the global settings as is the case for the home directory and profile paths.

variable is used in lieu of typing the user's username, as the operating system will replace the variable with the appropriate username when either the Apply or OK buttons is clicked.

The Remote Control tab, shown in Figure 15-5, is used to configure the remote control session settings. This tab enables you to enable or disable the use of session remote control, determine whether or not to require the remote user's permission, and set the level of control. In the Level of control section, you can choose to view "or spy on" a user's session, as well as interact with the session. These settings should

FIGURE 15-5

Configuring a user's Terminal Services remote control settings

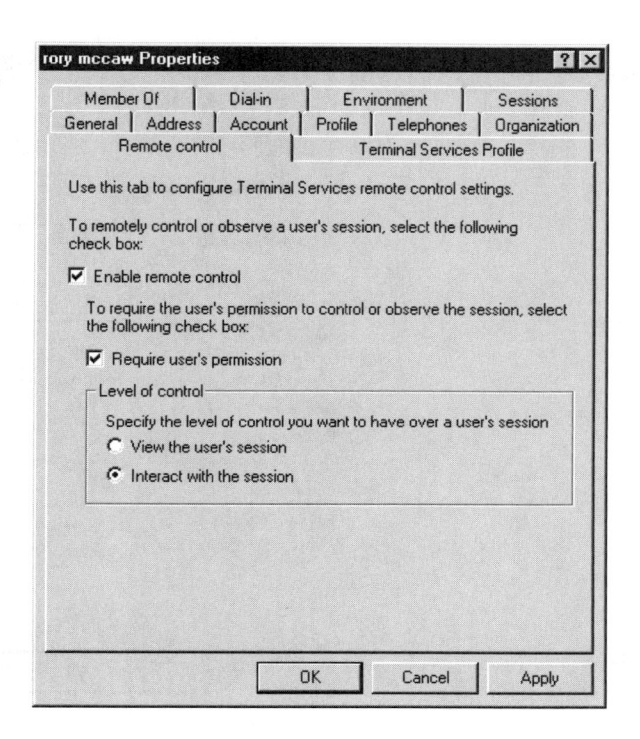

be configured in accordance with your organization's human resources and security policies. Take these settings seriously, as viewing a user's session without their permission could lead to severe corporate punishment, including termination.

The Sessions tab, shown in Figure 15-6, enables you to configure how long after a session is disconnected that the session should be ended, the active session limit, and the idle session limit. This is also where you configure what steps to take when a session limit is reached or the connection is broken, and any limitations with respect to where the reconnection of a broken session can occur.

The configuration of these settings will vary between companies and is dependant on the specific organizational requirements. Setting an active session limit is one way of limiting the amount of time a single user can spend connected. Setting an idle session limit offers a great way to ensure sessions don't continue to consume resumes when they are not in use.

Let's examine how these settings could help you to ensure the best performance on a Terminal Server that must support 48 users but only has the hardware to effectively support 32 concurrent users. In this scenario you have a couple of options. First, you could edit each of the 48 individual users account properties and configure the user connection settings to end disconnected sessions after five minutes. Better yet, you

FIGURE 15-6

Configuring the user's Terminal Services sessions settings

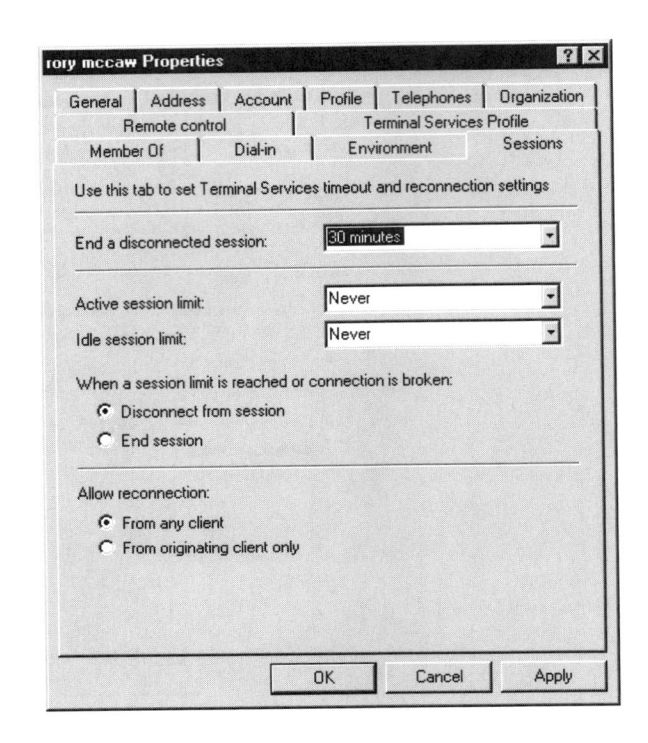

could edit the Terminal Server connection settings to end disconnected sessions after five minutes. This should allow enough time for a user to reconnect without loosing data if their session is lost due to a network problem. The Active Session Limit could be set, but I'll make the assumption that if the session is active, it is being used. The Idle Session Limit, however, could be set to ten minutes, after which time the session would be ended. I would also set the reconnection settings to allow reconnection from any client. By configuring the setting in this manner, I have optimized the Terminal Server to handle the existing connections but have been strict enough in the settings to free up idle and disconnected settings relatively quickly, which allows new sessions to gain access to valuable server resources.

CERTIFICATION SUMMARY

Terminal Services is included with all of the Windows 2000 Server operating systems but is not installed by default. Terminal Services can operate in two modes. Remote Administration mode provides a way for administrators to remotely administer multiple servers using the GUI-based administrative tools. Application Server mode allows users to connect to a Terminal Server and run applications on that server with the results of the user's keyboard and mouse commands sent back to the Terminal Services client by RDP over TCP/IP. This allows the user sitting at the Terminal Services client to receive a Windows 2000 desktop and make it appear as though the applications reside locally on the client when really all of the processing is occurring on the Terminal Server. An additional add-on known as TSAC is available for Terminal Services, which further extends its functionality by allowing Terminal Services sessions to be created through any 32-bit Internet Explorer 4.*x* or higher browser.

Terminal Services sessions, by default, provide users will access to local resources such as printers though automatic printer redirection. The Clipboard-mapping feature can also be used to cut, copy, and paste text and graphics between applications running in a Terminal Services session and applications running on the Terminal Services client.

Terminal Services properties can be configured on either a per-user basis, through Active Directory Users and Computers and the properties of each user account, or a per-connection basis, through the Terminal Services Configuration snap-in. The settings configured on a per-connection basis override the user settings and apply to all RDP connections to a single Terminal Server.

✓ TWO-MINUTE DRILL

Configure Terminal Services for Remote Administration or Application Server Mode

- ❑ Terminal Services uses RDP over TCP/IP but can be configured to use ICA for more efficient communication.
- ❑ RDP uses TCP port 3389 and ICA uses TCP port 1494.
- ❑ Terminal Services can operate in one of two modes: Remote Administration mode or Application Server mode.
- ❑ Terminal Services and Offline Files are mutually exclusive.
- ❑ You are only able to establish two, concurrent administrative connections to Terminal Services when it is operating in Remote Administration mode.
- ❑ Installing Terminal Services in Application Server mode requires that Terminal Services Licensing be installed within the first 90 days.
- ❑ A Terminal Server running IIS can have the Terminal Services Advanced Client installed on it, allowing access to Terminal Services from the Terminal Services client and from within a 32-bit Internet Explorer web browser.
- ❑ Both Windows 2000 Professional and Windows XP Professional include a Terminal Services CAL but both still require a Windows 2000 Server CAL to connect to the server.
- ❑ Both Add/Remove Programs and the **change user** command can be used to switch between Terminal Server modes.
- ❑ The Terminal Services client software can be installed using the client installation disks or by sharing the tsclient folder in C:\winnt\system32\clients.
- ❑ There are two ways to end a Terminal Services session: log off, which terminates the session and releases the consumed resources, or disconnect, which drops the connection but maintains the session on the Terminal Server.

Configure Terminal Services for Local Resource Mapping

- ❑ Clipboard mapping allows text from an application running in a Terminal Services session to be copied and pasted to an application running on the Terminal Services client computer.
- ❑ There are two types of printer redirection: automatic and manual.

- Automatic printer redirection is supported on all Win32 operating systems and allows print devices local to the Terminal Services client to be automatically detected and available to print from within the Terminal Services session.
- Printer redirection can be enabled or disabled on a per-user basis using Active Directory Users and Computers or on a per-connection basis using the Terminal Services Configuration tool.
- Local printers are defined on a per-user basis in a Terminal Services session, therefore, a local printer is available to that user only during their Terminal Services session.
- All data between the client and server is always encrypted when sent over the network, which is the Low encryption setting, but with this setting, data sent from the server to the client is not encrypted.
- The Medium and High encryption settings encrypt data in both directions, with Medium using the 56-bit standard key and High using the 128-bit maximum strength key.
- The use of the maximum-strength key requires that the Windows 2000 High Encryption Pack be installed on the Terminal Server.
- The use of wallpaper is automatically disabled for all Terminal Services connections for performance reasons.
- The Network Adapter tab in Terminal Services configuration allows you to specify that Terminal Services listens on only a single network adapter or all network adapters.

Configure Terminal Services User Properties

- User property settings can be overridden by global connection settings made in the Terminal Services Configuration snap-in.
- Terminal Services user property settings can be configured on a per-user object basis through Active Directory Users and Computers using the three tabs: Sessions, Terminal Services Profile, and Remote Control.
- By default, all users are granted the Allow logon to Terminal Server permission.
- When configuring user profile and home directory paths for Terminal Services connections, the %username% variable can be used in place of the user's username to allow the properties of multiple user accounts to be edited at one time.

SELF TEST

The following questions will help you measure your understanding of the material presented in this chapter. Read the questions and answers carefully, and be aware that some questions will provide for more than one correct answer. Choose all correct answers for each question.

Configure Terminal Services for Remote Administration or Application Server Mode

1. You are the administrator of a Windows 2000 server running Terminal Services. You wish to allow computers running non-Windows-based operating systems access to Terminal Services through a web browser. Which of the following are required on the Terminal Server? (Choose all that apply.)

    A. Internet Explorer 4.01 or higher
    B. Terminal Services Advanced Client
    C. DNS
    D. IIS
    E. Offline Files

2. You are the network administrator in your organization and you have been asked to configure the firewall that separates your DMZ from your LAN to allow Terminal Server communications. Which of the following ports will you open on the firewall?

    A. 1024
    B. 119
    C. 1494
    D. 3389

3. You are a member of the local Administrators group on a member server in your organization's domain. You have installed Terminal Services in Application Server mode on the member server to allow you to run applications remotely. You would like to install a new application on the Terminal Server. Which of the following commands will allow you to change the mode to Remote Administration mode?

    A. change user /install
    B. change user /execute
    C. change user /remote
    D. change user /admin

Configure Terminal Services for Local Resource Mapping

4. You are the administrator of a small office LAN that uses Terminal Services in Application Server mode. Fifteen users connect to the Terminal Server to run applications on a daily basis. Two of the fifteen computers, all of which run Windows 2000 Professional, have local printers attached to them. These computers are named wksprt1 and wksprt2. A third, network printer is available on the network and uses the Terminal Server as its print server. A user calls you in regard to a printing problem. When the user logs on at a computer named wks3, as opposed to their regular computer, wksprt1, and establishes a Terminal Server session, only the network printer is available. What is the most likely reason for this?

   A. Automatic printer redirection has been disabled on wks3.
   B. Only one Terminal Services session is able to use the local printer on wksprt1.
   C. The printer local to wksprt1 isn't being detected when the user establishes a Terminal Server session from wks3.
   D. The use of local printers has been disabled in the global settings, on the Client Settings tab in the RDP-Tcp Properties dialog box.

5. You are the network administrator in your company. You receive a call from a user named Laura who is trying to copy a file from her Terminal Services session to the file system on the computer configured with the Terminal Services client. Laura informs you that she is unable to copy the file and continues to receive an error message. Which of the following is the most likely cause of the problem?

   A. The file system to which Laura is trying to copy the file must be formatted with NTFS.
   B. The file system to which Laura is trying to copy the file must not be compressed.
   C. Laura does not have the proper permissions to copy the file.
   D. Only the text and graphics within the file can be copied, not the file itself.

6. One of the help desk personnel asks you about the copying functionality included by default in Windows 2000 Terminal Server. Which of the following statements are true? (Choose all that apply.)

   A. Text and graphics can be copied from an application running in a Terminal Services session to an application running on a Terminal Services client.
   B. Text and graphics can be copied from an application running in a Terminal Services session to an application running in another Terminal Services session.
   C. A file or folder can be copied from a Terminal Services session to a Terminal Services client.
   D. A file or folder can be copied from one Terminal Services session to another Terminal Services session.

7. You are the administrator of a number of Windows 2000 Terminal Servers. A number of client connections come in to the Terminal Servers from WAN connections, and you want to disable automatic printer redirection on a per-connection basis. Which of the following snap-ins will you use to accomplish this?

    A. Active Directory Users and Computers

    B. Terminal Services Manager

    C. Terminal Services Configuration

    D. Terminal Services Licensing

8. You want to configure your Terminal Server settings to always use the High encryption setting when transmitting data between the Terminal Server and the Terminal Services client. Which of the following does the Terminal Server require to allow for this configuration? (Choose all that apply.)

    A. The Terminal Server must be a member of a domain.

    B. The Terminal Server must be running IE 5 or higher.

    C. The High Encryption Pack must be installed on the Terminal Server.

    D. SP2 must be installed on the Terminal Server.

Configure Terminal Services User Properties

9. You are the administrator of all the servers running Windows 2000 in your department. You have installed Terminal Services on each of the servers. Your company security and human resources privacy policies dictate that a user must be alerted and give consent prior to a network administrator remotely viewing what the user is doing in their Terminal Server session. Which of the following combination of settings will allow you to remotely correct user problems that occur in a Terminal Services session while not breaking any of the corporate policies? (Choose two.)

    A. Edit the Remote Control tab of the RDP-Tcp Properties dialog box on each of the Terminal Servers and select the Use Remote Control With The Following Settings option.

    B. On the Remote Control tab of the RDP-Tcp Properties dialog box on each of the Terminal Servers, enable the Require User's Permission setting and select the Interact With The Session level of control.

    C. On the Remote Control tab of each user's Properties dialog box in Active Directory Users and Computers, enable the Require User's Permission setting and select the Interact With The Session level of control.

Self Test 701

D. Edit the Remote Control tab of the RDP-Tcp Properties dialog box in Active Directory Users and Computers and select the Use Remote Control With The Following Settings option.

E. Edit the Sessions tab of the RDP-Tcp Properties dialog box on each of the Terminal Servers and select the Use Remote Control With The Following Settings option.

10. A user contacts you, complaining that every time he establishes a connection to a Terminal Server and begins working but gets interrupted for a few minutes, his work is lost upon his return and the session is closed. Looking at Figure 15-7, which setting should you change to prevent future data loss in this same type of scenario?

   A. Increase the amount of time for End A Disconnected Session.
   B. Increase the amount of time for Active Session Limit.
   C. Increase the amount of time for Idle Session Limit.
   D. Change the action taken when a session limit is reached or connection is broken to Disconnect From Session.

FIGURE 15-5

Session Settings

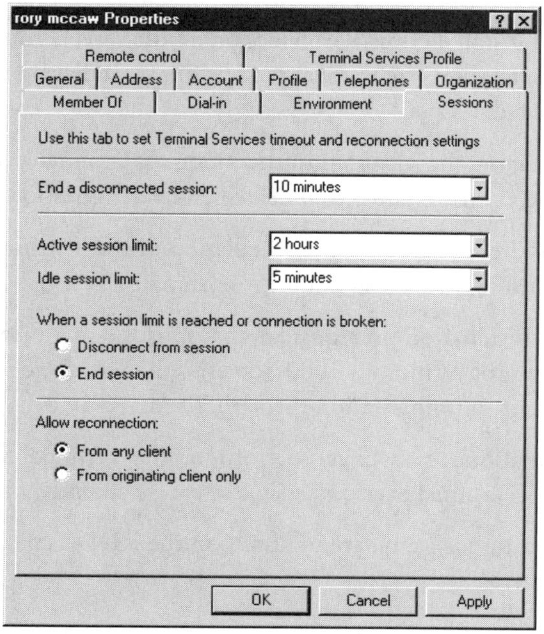

LAB QUESTION

In an effort to streamline administration, you have been asked to install and configure Terminal Services in Remote Administration mode on all servers running Windows 2000 in your organization and install the Terminal Services client on the workstations that you will use to remotely administer the servers. One of the servers on which you are to install Terminal Services is a multihomed computer that runs NAT and provides access to the Internet for users on the LAN. You need to ensure that no Terminal Services connections are permitted on the external interface of the NAT server. Each of the workstations is running Windows 2000 Professional, so you must also ensure that all the licensing requirements are met. Four network administrators, all of whom are members of the Administrators group, and one senior technical support user, who is not a member of the Administrators group, must be able to remotely administer the servers. For security reasons, you do not want to allow any Terminal Services administrative sessions that are disconnected to persist for more than two minutes. This should be enough time for an administrator to reconnect if the session disconnect was a result of a network or client failure. On all the internal servers on the LAN, you also want to configure TSAC to allow for browser-based administration. Answer the following questions to establish the steps involved in implementing this configuration.

1. How will you install Terminal Services on all the servers running Windows 2000? Which mode will you choose? Are there any additional installation requirements based on the mode you have selected?

2. How many licenses are included in the mode that you have selected? Are any additional CALs required based on the architecture described in the question? If so, what are they?

3. What options are available for the installation of the Terminal Services client on each of the computers running Windows 2000 Professional?

4. What are the installation prerequisites that must be met prior to installing TSAC on any of the computers running Windows 2000 Server? What are the client-side browser requirements that will allow remote administration through TSAC?

5. What configuration steps will you perform on the Terminal Server that is running NAT to ensure that incoming Terminal Services sessions are only accepted on the internal network interface?

6. What modifications, if any, are required on the RDP-Tcp connection properties on each Terminal Server?

SELF TEST ANSWERS

Configure Terminal Services for Remote Administration or Application Server Mode

1. ☑ **B** and **D** are correct. To allow non-Windows-based clients access to a Terminal Server through a web browser, the Terminal Server must have both IIS and TSAC installed on it.
   ☒ **A** is incorrect because Internet Explorer is a requirement on the non-Windows-based client that wishes to connect but is not a requirement of the Terminal Server.
   ☒ **C** is incorrect because DNS is not a requirement of Terminal Services. DNS will be required to provide name resolution if a fully qualified domain name is used, as opposed to an IP address.
   ☒ **E** is incorrect because Offline Files and Terminal Services are mutually exclusive, meaning that if the server about to be configured with Terminal Services is using Offline Files, Offline Files will be disabled after Terminal Services in installed.

2. ☑ **D** is correct. To allow Terminal Services communications through a firewall using RDP, TCP port 3389 will have to be opened on the firewall, as that is the port used by Terminal Services.
   ☒ **A** is incorrect because RDP does not use port 1024.
   ☒ **B** is incorrect because RDP does not use port 119. TCP port 119 is used by NNTP.
   ☒ **C** is incorrect because RDP does not use port 1494. TCP port 1494 is used by ICA.

3. ☑ **A** is correct. The **change user /install** command will change the Terminal Server mode from Application Server mode to Remote Administration mode.
   ☒ **B** is incorrect because the **change user /execute** command will change the Terminal Server mode from Remote Administration mode to Application Server mode.
   ☒ **C** is incorrect because the **change user /remote** command is not a valid command.
   ☒ **D** is incorrect because the **change user /admin** command is not a valid command.

Configure Terminal Services for Local Resource Mapping

4. ☑ **C** is correct. Automatic printer redirection is enabled by default, but because the printer is local only to the computer wksprt1, when the user establishes a Terminal Services connection from the computer wks3, the printer will not appear because it is not local to wks3.
   ☒ **A** is incorrect because the printer would not be detected automatically on wks3, whether automatic printer redirection is enabled or disabled.
   ☒ **B** is incorrect because multiple sessions are able to use a local printer, but the multiple sessions would have to be running on the computer to which the printer is local.
   ☒ **D** is incorrect because the printer would not be detected automatically on wks3, whether automatic printer redirection is enabled or disabled for the user or globally.

704 Chapter 15: Implementing Terminal Services for Remote Access

5. ☑ **D** is correct. Only text and graphics within an application running in a Terminal Services session can be copied to an application running on the Terminal Services client. Files and folders cannot be copied by default between the Terminal Services session and the Terminal Services client. Mapped drives, however, can be used to accomplish this.
　☒ **A** is incorrect because the copying of files and folders is not permitted by default, regardless of the format of the file system.
　☒ **B** is incorrect because the copying of files and folders is not permitted by default, regardless of the compression attribute settings of the drive or folder.
　☒ **C** is incorrect because permission to do this is not granted to any user.

6. ☑ **A** and **B** are correct. Text and graphics can be copied from an application running in a Terminal Services session to an application running on a Terminal Services client, as well as between two Terminal Services sessions.
　☒ **C** is incorrect because, by default, a file or folder cannot be copied from a Terminal Services session to a Terminal Services client.
　☒ **D** is incorrect because, by default, a file or folder cannot be copied from one Terminal Services session to another Terminal Services session.

7. ☑ **C** is correct. The Terminal Services Configuration snap-in should be used to configure settings on a per-connection basis.
　☒ **A** is incorrect because Active Directory Users and Computers only allows you to configure settings on a per-user basis.
　☒ **B** is incorrect because Terminal Services Manager does not allow you to configure settings on a per-connection basis.
　☒ **D** is incorrect because Terminal Services Licensing does not allow you to configure settings on a per-connection basis.

8. ☑ **C** and **D** are correct. To enable the High encryption setting, the Windows 2000 High Encryption Pack must be installed on the Terminal Server. Installing Service Pack 2 will also enable High encryption by default during its installation.
　☒ **A** is incorrect because the Terminal Server is not required to be a member of a domain in order to use the High encryption setting.
　☒ **B** is incorrect because the Terminal Server is not required to have IE 5 or higher installed to use the High encryption setting.

Configure Terminal Services User Properties

9. ☑ **A** and **B** are correct. To be able to remotely correct user problems that occur in a Terminal Services session, the Remote Control tab of the RDP-Tcp Properties dialog box on each of the Terminal Servers should be edited and the Use Remote Control With The Following Settings

option selected. The option that should then be selected is the Require User's Permission setting, as well as the level of control setting of Interact With The Session.
☒ C is incorrect because although the Remote Control tab could be used to change each user's properties, it is not the most efficient way to accomplish the task.
☒ D is incorrect because the Remote Control tab in Active Directory Users and Computers does not include any RDP-Tcp properties.
☒ E is incorrect because remote control settings are not found on the Sessions tab.

10. ☑ D is correct. Changing the action taken when a session limit is reached or connection is broken to Disconnect From Session would allow the user to reestablish the connection and find his applications in the same state that they were prior to his being interrupted.
☒ A is incorrect because increasing the amount of time before a disconnected session is ended would not address this problem, because this user's session is being ended after a period of inactivity.
☒ B is incorrect because increasing the amount of time before an active session limit is reached would not apply, because this user's session would be idle when he is attending to other things.
☒ C is incorrect because increasing the amount of time for the idle session limit will only lengthen the amount of time that the user can be away from the session. It does not change the fact that when the new lengthened time expires, the user will loose all of his work that is open in the session.

Lab Answer

1. Installing Terminal Services on all the servers running Windows 2000 can be accomplished by selecting Start | Settings | Control Panel | Add/Remove Programs and clicking the Add/Remove Windows Components button. Choosing to install Terminal Services in Remote Administration mode does not require that you install Terminal Services Licensing.

2. Two administrative licenses are included by default in Remote Administration mode, allowing for a maximum of two concurrent remote administration connections. The computers running Windows 2000 Professional that the five network administrators work from will each require a Windows 2000 Server CAL in order to connect to each of the servers, but no Terminal Services CALs are required. One Terminal Services Internet Connector License will also be required for the computer running the TSAC interface.

3. The installation of the Terminal Services client on each of the computers running Windows 2000 Professional can be accomplished by sharing the tsclient folder on one of the internal Terminal Servers, which is found in the path c:\Winnt\system32\clients\tsclient and will allow for an over-the-network installation of the Terminal Services client to be performed.

4. Installing TSAC on each of the internal servers will require that each server also have IIS installed on it and that TSAC be downloaded from the Microsoft web site. On any of the computers from which the administrator will need to perform browser-based remote administration, the 32-bit version of Internet Explorer 4.x or higher should be installed.

5. To ensure that the Terminal Service installed on the NAT server only listens on the internal network adapter, the Terminal Services Configuration snap-in should be used to edit the RDP-Tcp connection properties on the Network Adapter tab. Here, the internal network adapter should be selected from the drop-down list.

6. To meet the security requirements, the Terminal Services Configuration snap-in should be used to edit the RDP-Tcp connection properties on each Terminal Server. The Sessions tab should be configured to override the user settings and disconnect all idle sessions after five minutes, as well as end all disconnected sessions after two minutes. The Security tab should be accessed and the account of the senior technical support user added and granted Full Control Permission in order to be able to access the server without being made a member of the Administrators group.

MCSA
MICROSOFT CERTIFIED SYSTEMS ADMINISTRATOR

16

Configuring Network Address Translation and Internet Connection Sharing

CERTIFICATION OBJECTIVES

16.01 Configuring Internet Connection Sharing

16.02 Troubleshooting Internet Connection Sharing Problems by Using the IPCONFIG and PING Commands

16.03 Configuring Routing and Remote Access to Perform NAT

✓ Two-Minute Drill

Q&A Self Test

Network Address Translation (NAT) and Internet Connection Sharing (ICS) are two concepts that you must be familiar with to be successful on the certification exam. As with all certification objectives, your knowledge regarding the configuration of shared Internet connections should be both theoretical and hands-on. The more familiarity you have with the Routing and Remote Access Service (RRAS), the better prepared you will be.

The concept of shared Internet connections has widespread application and can be found in both large and small networks. Therefore, knowledge of these concepts is applicable to network administrators in all organizations, regardless of size. This chapter teaches you about the installation and configuration of options, RRAS configuration requirements and discusses specific scenarios in which Windows 2000 can be deployed for either ICS or NAT. Once you have a clear understanding of both options, we will explore how each option works and manages multiple requests from computers on the network, retrieves the requested information on behalf of the internal client, and returns the appropriate response back to the correct internal client.

Both NAT and ICS are new features included in Windows 2000 that were not found in Windows NT 4 and, like all new features, are likely to be a focus on the certification exam. The knowledge that you gain in this chapter can be applied and leveraged in a number of Microsoft certification exams. In addition to the 70-218 exam, you can also apply this knowledge to the Implementing and Administering a Microsoft Windows 2000 Network Infrastructure exam (70-216). This chapter covers all the key points that you need to know to prepare for the exam as well as material that you will require in your daily administration of NAT and ICS.

CERTIFICATION OBJECTIVE 16.01

Configuring Internet Connection Sharing

ICS is the simplest of the available options for configuring shared Internet access in a small organization with a small number of computers and users that require occasional Internet access. This version of ICS is similar to the version included in Windows 98 SE and is designed to allow multiple computers on the same network to access the Internet through a shared connection. ICS is designed for small networks and provides address translation, address assignment, and name resolution to internal computers on the network. The other benefit of ICS is that it is available on both Windows 2000 Professional and Windows 2000 Server. This is beneficial in a small organization that may not have a computer running Windows 2000 Server, as well as for a home user that has more than one computer and would like both computers to share a single Internet connection, be it cable or ADSL.

To configure a computer running either Windows 2000 Professional or Windows 2000 Server to use ICS, a couple of requirements must be met. First, the computer must have a minimum of two adapters, one that is connected to the local area network (LAN) and another that is connected to the Internet, as shown in Figure 16-1. Second, the computers on the LAN must be configured to obtain IP addresses automatically and must be on a single IP segment or subnet. ICS acts as a DHCP server providing IP addresses on the 192.168.0.0/24 network to all LAN clients. This is one of the reasons that an ICS solution is limited to small networks, as it can only work with a single network subnet. The external network adapter on the computer running ICS is the adapter that must be configured to use a valid IP address. The internal LAN clients then use the internal IP address of the computer running ICS as their gateway, DNS forwarder, and shared Internet access point. Pretty simple!

FIGURE 16-1

Typical ICS architecture

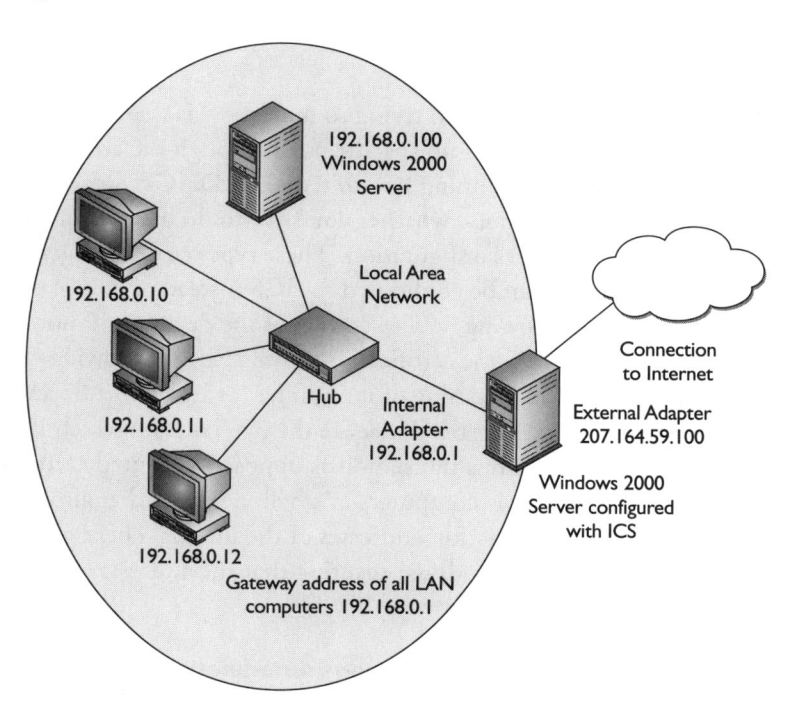

> **exam watch**
>
> *ICS only supports a single external adapter, not multiple external adapters. NAT is the ideal choice for situations where you want to use multiple external adapters.*

ICS is a popular solution for many homes, particularly homes that have more than one computer. It's not uncommon today, with the price of PCs dropping consistently, to find a home with more than one computer—whether there is one for the parents and one for the kids, the requirement and demand is certainly there. One of the configuration issues that you are likely to come across is the need to configure your external network adapter to use DHCP. This is a requirement of most high-speed Internet service providers, such as phone companies and cable companies. Another possible configuration step that is beyond the scope of the certification exam but definitely worth mentioning is the configuration of a home firewall. There are a number of firewall/router manufacturers that sell firewall/router devices, designed for home or small business use for around $100, such as Linksys, DLink, and Cicero. I highly recommend that you add one of these devices to your shopping list to assist in the protection of data on your home PC, particularly if it is directly connected to the Internet. Without one, it is unbelievably easy to get access to your home computer!

The point that I am trying to make here is that with one of these devices, you "may" have to open up specific ports through the creation of a packet filter to allow your computer running ICS to request a DHCP address from your ISP. I use the word "may" because whether you have to do this or not will really depend on your home computer configuration. These types of devices generally include very similar features and can be configured for ICS instead of your computer running Windows 2000. But knowing how to configure the devices and not Windows 2000 isn't going to help you with the certification exam! Use the following configuration to accomplish this. Create an incoming or input filter for UDP port 67 and an outgoing or output filter for UDP port 68. These are the two ports on which DHCP negotiations occur.

ICS uses address translation as opposed to routed connections to provide Internet access to multiple computers in small, networked environments. ICS converts the source and destination addresses of the internal client computers into its own valid external Internet address, ensuring that the addresses of internal clients are not revealed on the Internet.

> **exam watch**
>
> *Use ICS for small office, non-routed networks that have computers running either Windows 2000 Professional or Windows 2000 Server with two network adapters.*

ICS and IP Address Configuration

ICS also includes an implementation of DHCP known as the DHCP Allocator service, as well as a DNS proxy service. The purpose of the DHCP Allocator service is to lease out IP addresses, subnet mask, and gateway information to clients on the local 192.168.0.0/24 subnet. The DHCP Allocator service is not a full implementation of DHCP. The DHCP Allocator service simply allows ICS to lease IP addresses from the default address pool, which is configured to use 192.168.0.2–192.168.0.254. The DNS proxy service is included to allow name resolution to occur by letting the server running ICS to forward the name resolution request to the DNS servers that it is configured to use in the TCP/IP properties of its external network adapter.

exam
Watch

ICS should not be used in a network with Windows 2000 domain controllers, routers, DHCP servers or DHCP relay agents. Nor should it be used in networks that use static IP addresses. In this type of network, use NAT.

Installing ICS

Installing ICS is simple, because it's already installed! By modifying the properties of your external Internet connection, you can configure the connection to use ICS. Using the example of the network shown in Figure 16-1, you would open the Properties dialog box of the external connection on the computer running Windows 2000 Server and configure that adapter to use ICS. Exercise 16-1 walks you through this process.

EXERCISE 16-1

CertCam 16-1

Configuring ICS

This exercise teaches you how to configure ICS on a computer running either Windows 2000 Professional or Windows 2000 Server, as the configuration is the same. This exercise assumes that you are working on a computer that has two network adapters.

1. Open Network and Dial-up Connections, right-click the external Internet connection, and click Properties.

2. Select the Sharing tab, place a check mark in the box next to Enable Internet Connection Sharing For This Connection, and click OK.

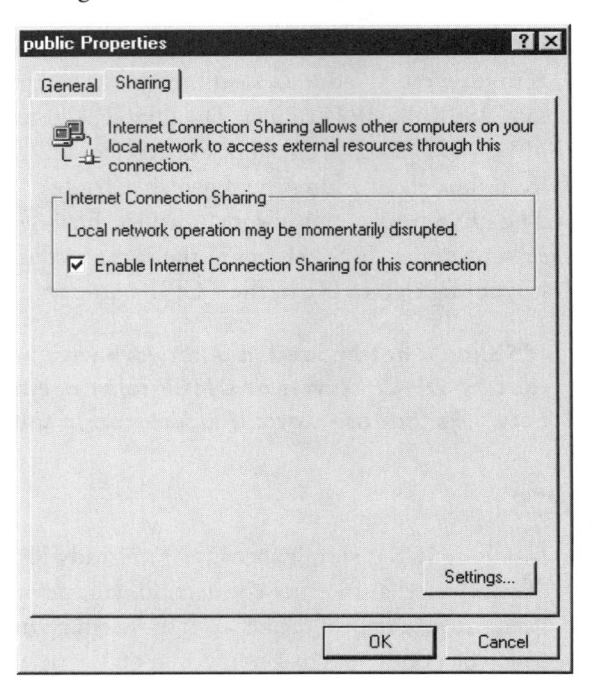

3. If the internal network adapter's interface is configured with an IP address other than 192.168.0.1, the following message will appear. Click Yes, and ICS will automatically configure the internal network adapter with the static IP address 192.168.0.1, and that address will be the gateway used by all internal LAN clients.

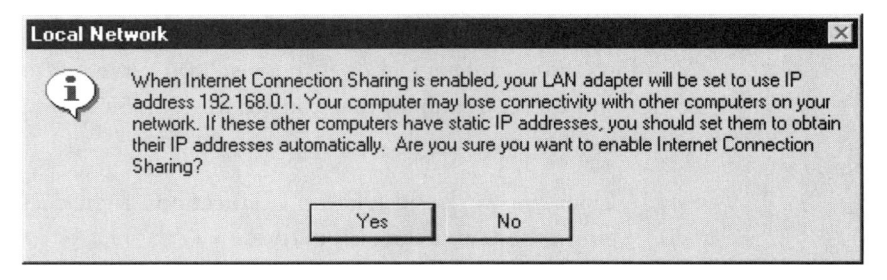

4. If NAT is currently configured on the computer on which you are trying to install ICS, you will receive the following message, informing you that ICS and NAT cannot be installed on the same computer and NAT must first be

removed to configure ICS. Click OK. Remove NAT and repeat the preceding steps to configure ICS.

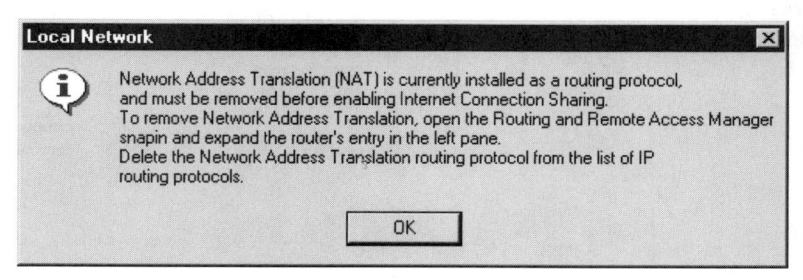

Local Network

Network Address Translation (NAT) is currently installed as a routing protocol, and must be removed before enabling Internet Connection Sharing.
To remove Network Address Translation, open the Routing and Remote Access Manager snapin and expand the router's entry in the left pane.
Delete the Network Address Translation routing protocol from the list of IP routing protocols.

OK

---

exam
Watch

When ICS is installed, it automatically defaults to the private address range 192.168.0.0 with a subnet of 255.255.255.0 and assigns the internal adapter an IP address of 192.168.0.1. Also, NAT and ICS cannot be installed on the same computer.

ICS is designed for two primary applications—the small office user and the home user that have multiple computers and require the ability to share a single Internet connection. ICS can be configured for reverse publishing of both services and applications, which is a feature generally found only in proxy server applications such as Microsoft Proxy or Microsoft Internet Security and Acceleration Server. The key to understanding reverse publishing is to understand that remote clients believe that the service or application they are connecting to is running on the computer with the external IP address, which is always the ICS computer, but in fact it is ICS that is performing reverse address translation and sending the incoming requests to the specified internal computer. The internal computer running the service or application then responds to the computer running ICS, and ICS sends the response on to the remote computer on the Internet, as shown in Figure 16-2. Let's take a look at how these two features can be advantageous to the home user.

Service Publishing

Service publishing allows remote users on the Internet to establish communications with network services running on internal computers on the LAN through the computer running ICS. This is accomplished by clicking the Settings button at the bottom of the Properties dialog box and selecting the Services tab. As you can see in

FIGURE 16-2

Reverse service and application publishing in ICS

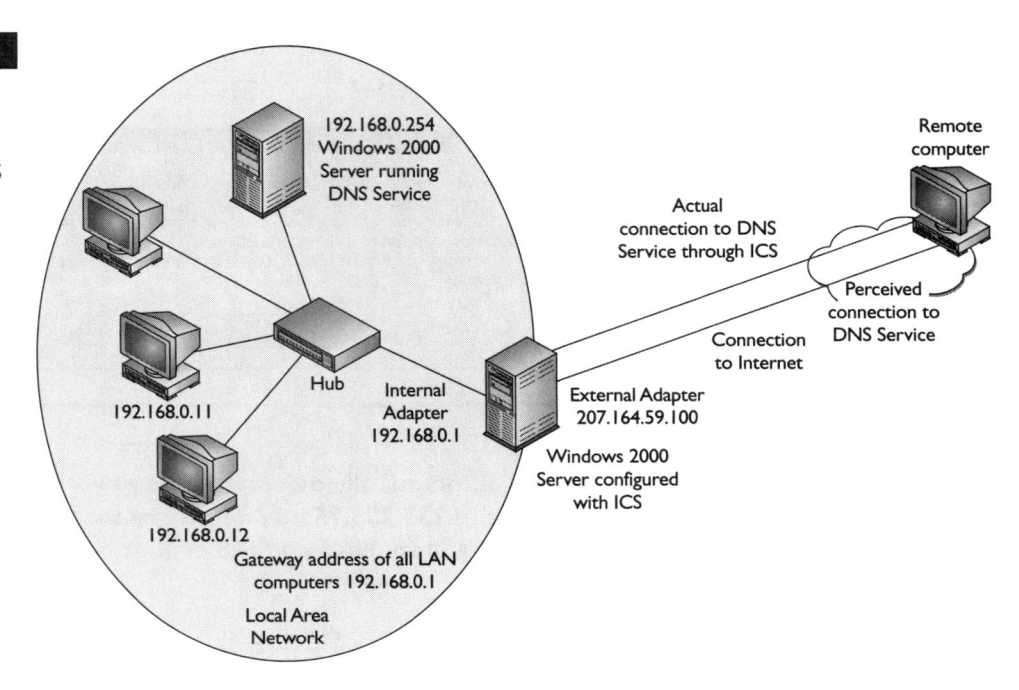

Figure 16-3, a number of the more popular network services are included by default, such as Telnet, POP3, SMTP, and multiple versions of IMAP, and are easily configurable to allow computers on the external network to access computers on the internal network using these protocols.

For example, if you wanted to allow external computers such as mail servers to send mail via SMTP to a computer on your internal network that is configured as an SMTP server, such as an Exchange server, you would select the SMTP choice on the Services tab and click Edit. This would bring up the dialog box shown in Figure 16-4. The name of the service and port number that the service operates on, which is TCP port 25 by default, are already filled in for you. All that's left for you to do is enter the name or IP address of the SMTP server on the LAN, which in this example is mailsrv, and click OK.

If the default list of services doesn't meet your needs and you would like to add your own, click the Add button on the Services tab to open the ICS Service dialog box, shown in Figure 16-5, which allows you to add your own service information. Let's use DNS as an example of a service you want to allow through the computer running ICS to an internal DNS server with the IP address 192.168.0.254. In this case, you will enter **DNS** as the Name Of Service, and **53** as the Service Port

Configuring Internet Connection Sharing 715

FIGURE 16-3

Configuring internal access through ICS for specific network services

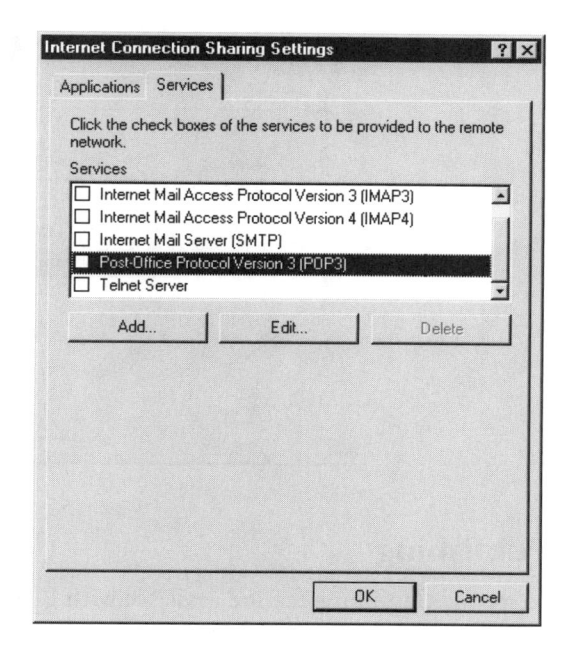

Number. You would then select UDP, enter **192.168.0.254** as the IP address of the DNS server, and click OK. You would then repeat this process using the same information, but instead select TCP. The process must be repeated for network services that use both the TCP and UDP protocol because with ICS there is not an option to select both TCP and UDP.

FIGURE 16-4

Configuring the SMTP service in ICS

FIGURE 16-5

Adding DNS as a new service

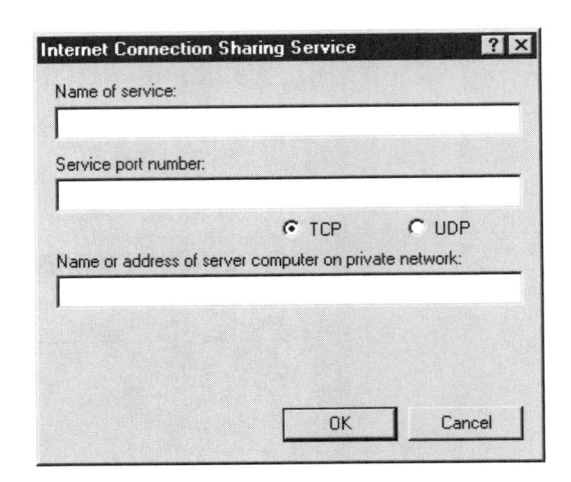

Application Publishing

The second publishing feature available with ICS is application publishing, which allows you to provide access to remote computers on the Internet to specific applications running on a computer on your internal network. An example of such an application might be Windows Media Services running on a Windows Media Server on your LAN.

To allow an external user access to your internal Windows Media application through ICS, select the Applications tab, shown in Figure 16-6, and click Add. This opens the ICS Application dialog box, shown in Figure 16-7, where you enter the required information for the application. If we use Windows Media Services as an example, you would enter Windows Media Services as the Name Of Application. The application name can be any user-friendly name that identifies the application to you, because it will not be seen by any remote users. Type **1755** as the remote server port number. This identifies the port number on the internal server that is running the Windows Media Services application. Choose the TCP radio button in this example as Windows Media Services uses TCP for communication. Some applications will use TCP and others will use UDP. This will differ depending on the application. Type **1755** in the incoming response ports for both TCP and UDP

FIGURE 16-6

The Applications tab

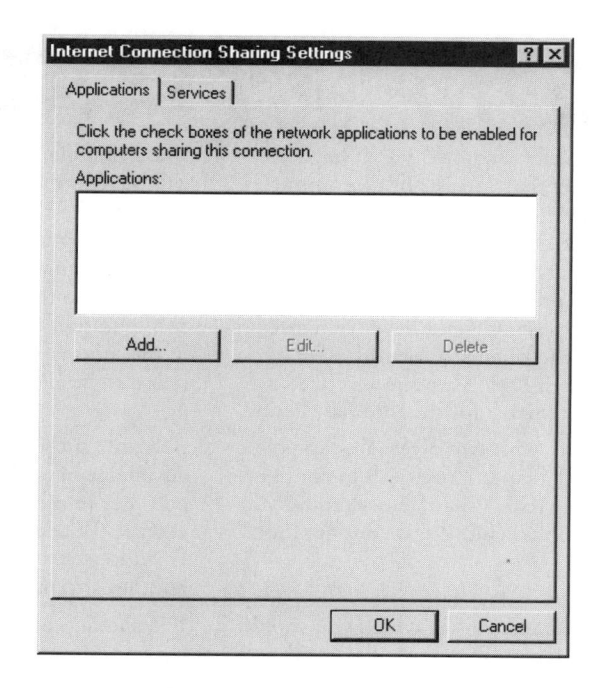

and click OK. The incoming response ports allow you to specify ports for the internal, remote application to listen on. In this example, Windows Media Services listens on both TCP and UDP 1755.

FIGURE 16-7

Adding a new application

SCENARIO & SOLUTION

You are a consultant for a company that has a small, office network that consists of six computers configured in a workgroup. Each of the computers is running Windows 2000 Professional, and the company has just purchased a high-speed Internet access package that provides it with one IP address. You have decided to use ICS and have configured the external adapter to obtain an IP address automatically through DHCP and to use ICS. Are there any requirements for the internal clients?	The five remaining internal client computers will be required to obtain an IP address through DHCP. The DHCP Allocator service running on the computer running ICS will be responsible for the assignment of IP addresses and will assign addresses on the 192.168.0.1/24 network. The configuration of ICS will also change the IP address of the internal adapter to 192.168.0.1 and configure it as a static IP address.
You have a computer with two external adapters and a single internal adapter. You wish to configure this computer to use ICS. What factors should you consider prior to implementing this configuration?	ICS only supports a single external adapter. To take advantage of multiple network adapters, you should consider implementing NAT. If you have two external IP addresses, you are able to bind multiple IP addresses to a single adapter, which offers you another alternative.
Describe a couple of scenarios in which you should not use ICS. What types of network services should you avoid using ICS with?	ICS should not be used in routed networks or networks in which a domain exists. ICS is intended for use in small workgroup-type configurations. Avoid using ICS in networks that have domain controllers, DHCP servers, DHCP relay agents and NAT servers.
Although ICS recommends you configure your clients to obtain an IP address through DHCP, you would like to statically configure all of your client computers with an IP address on the 192.168.0.1/24 network. Is this possible?	Although it is not recommended, it is possible. Client computers can be configured statically to work with ICS as long as their IP addresses are on the 192.168.0.1/24 network. The potential problem that this does represent is a new client being added to the network that obtains an IP address from the DHCP Allocator service that conflict with a statically assigned IP address.

CERTIFICATION OBJECTIVE 16.02

Troubleshooting Internet Connection Sharing Problems by Using the Ipconfig and Ping Commands

ICS problems can often be identified and resolved through the use of some very basic troubleshooting commands, such as **ipconfig** and **ping**. In this section, we look at these commands and discuss how they can be used to troubleshoot problems with ICS.

Troubleshooting with Ipconfig

Ipconfig is the Internet Protocol (IP) configuration command and offers you a number of options when troubleshooting network connectivity issues, whether or not they involve ICS. Executing the **ipconfig** command provides you with some basic output about the IP configuration of the interfaces on the computer, such as the IP addresses bound to each interface, the subnet mask, the default gateway, and the connection-specific DNS suffix. The only two parameters that must be configured for proper IP configuration are the IP address and subnet mask; the rest of the configuration information is optional.

A number of switches can also be used with the **ipconfig** command. The /all switch can be used to display more detailed information about the computer's IP properties, including the computer's hostname, primary DNS suffix, WINS node type, whether IP routing or the WINS proxy is enabled on the computer, and the DNS suffix search list. Additional adapter information is also included, such as the description of the network adapter, the Media Access Control (MAC) address, whether DHCP is enabled, and the DNS server information that is bound to the network adapter. This additional information can be seen in Figure 16-8.

When a network adapter is configured to obtain an IP address from a DHCP server, /release and /renew switches can be used; however, the /renew switch can be used to accomplish both, thereby saving you some time. To release and renew the IP addresses on all adapters on the computer running ICS, which should generally only be the external network adapter, execute the following command:

```
Ipconfig /renew
```

Network connectivity issues are also often related to name resolution problems, and DNS is the primary name resolution service in Windows 2000. Resolved names are stored in the client computer's DNS resolver cache for the Time To Live (TTL) assigned to the record. Should the DNS information change before the TTL expires, the possibility exists that the client will resolve the remote computer to the wrong IP address, thus preventing network connectivity. The **ipconfig** command can be used in these types of circumstances to delete or flush the DNS resolver cache. The following is the command to achieve this:

```
Ipconfig /flushdns
```

Use the /flushdns switch on the computer running ICS and on the client computer when more than one internal computers aren't able to resolve an external

FIGURE 16-8

Results of the ipconfig /all command

```
C:\>ipconfig /all

Windows 2000 IP Configuration

        Host Name . . . . . . . . . . . . : cr72932-a2
        Primary DNS Suffix  . . . . . . . :
        Node Type . . . . . . . . . . . . : Broadcast
        IP Routing Enabled. . . . . . . . : No
        WINS Proxy Enabled. . . . . . . . : No

Ethernet adapter Local Area Connection:

        Connection-specific DNS Suffix  . :
        Description . . . . . . . . . . . : 3Com Megahertz 10/100 LAN CardBus PC
   Card
        Physical Address. . . . . . . . . : 00-50-04-5B-E4-5F
        DHCP Enabled. . . . . . . . . . . : No
        IP Address. . . . . . . . . . . . : 192.168.1.200
        Subnet Mask . . . . . . . . . . . : 255.255.255.0
        Default Gateway . . . . . . . . . : 192.168.1.1
        DNS Servers . . . . . . . . . . . : 192.168.1.50
                                            24.153.32.66

C:\>_
```

computer, such as a web site. This will force the computer running ICS to send out a new DNS query and will result in new information being returned if it exists. If you are interested in seeing the contents of your DNS resolver cache, the **ipconfig** command can also be used to do this using the following command:

```
Ipconfig /displaydns
```

The last of the **ipconfig** switches that you should become familiar with is the /registerdns switch, which accomplishes a couple of tasks: it refreshes all the DHCP leases and, just as important, reregisters the DNS names on the client's preferred DNS server if the DNS zone is configured to allow dynamic updates. Dynamic updates are a feature of many of the newer DNS implementations that can be helpful in reducing the amount of administration associated with DNS by allowing DNS clients to update their name-to-address mappings automatically upon initialization, or upon renewing of the IP address using either the /renew or /registerdns switches.

One of the common outcomes of the **ipconfig** or **ipconfig /all** switch is to find that a network adapter configured to obtain an IP address automatically via DHCP is found to have an IP address on the 169.254.0.0/16 network instead of the 192.168.0.0/24 network required for compatibility with ICS. An IP address on the 169.254.0.0/16 network indicates that the IP address has been automatically assigned. By default, Windows 2000 supports a feature known as Automatic Private IP Addressing (APIPA), which configures a network adapter with an IP address on the 169.254.0.0/16 network when an IP address cannot be obtained from a DHCP server for any number of reasons. APIPA then continues to broadcast out for a DHCP

IP address every five minutes until one is obtained and configured for the client. Finding a client computer with an IP address on the 169.254.0.0/16 network indicates that the DHCP Allocator could not be contacted or does not have any IP addresses to lease out, or that the network cable isn't properly connected. In the case where the DHCP Allocator running on the computer running ICS cannot be contacted, it could suggest a number of possible problems, including network problems, or that the ICS computer is offline. Let's examine how to use **ipconfig** in Exercise 16-2 to determine the current IP configuration of the computer.

on the job

APIPA can be disabled by adding the REG_DWORD data type IPAutoconfigurationEnabled to the HKLM\System\CurrentControlSet\Services\Tcpip\Parameters\Interfaces\AdapterGUID Registry key and configuring it with a data value of 0.

EXERCISE 16-2

Determining a Computer's IP Configuration Using Ipconfig

In this exercise, you will learn how to use the **ipconfig** command to determine a computer's IP configuration. This information can be helpful when troubleshooting communication problems.

1. Select Start | Run, type **cmd**, and click OK.
2. At the command prompt, type **ipconfig /all** and press ENTER.
3. Use this information to determine the number of network adapters installed in the computer, the IP addresses bound to each of the network adapters, and whether each adapter is configured to use DHCP.

Troubleshooting Using PING

If you have determined by using the **ipconfig** command that the IP configuration of the computer appears to be correct, another utility that you can use to troubleshoot communication problems is the **ping** utility. Ping stands for Packet Inter Network Groper utility and is commonly used to try to "grope" a remote computer to get a response. If you are able to receive a response from another computer, you can quickly ascertain that your computer, the remote computer, and any routers in between are all functioning correctly, because the packets could be sent and received through all involved interfaces. The **ping** command can be used with both names and IP addresses and can also offer you a way to determine whether network communication problems are related to name resolution. For example, if you are able to ping a remote computer by IP address but are not able to ping and receive a response from the same remote computer using its hostname, DNS may be the

SCENARIO & SOLUTION

You are the administrator of a number of computers in a small, routed corporate network shown in Figure 16-10. One of the computers on the 192.168.5.0/24 network is unable to communicate with a computer running Windows 2000 Server on another segment with the IP address 192.168.8.21. You have run the **ipconfig /all** command on the client computer. What IP configuration information should you see if communications were working properly?	The client should have an IP address either statically or dynamically configured on the 192.168.5.0/24 network with a subnet of 255.255.255.0. The client should also have a gateway address of 192.168.5.1, the network adapter of the router that is connected to the subnet the client is located on.
When troubleshooting, what command can you run to determine that the local computer, the remote computer, and all devices in between are performing fine?	You can use the **ping** command to test network connectivity. By pinging and receiving a reply from a remote host, you are able to determine that the local computer, remote computer, and all devices in between are operating fine.
You are the administrator of a large corporate network. You have just finished making a number of changes to the name and IP addresses of the intranet servers in your network. Users have started complaining that they are no longer able to reach the intranet servers, but they are able to connect to file and print servers. What commands can you use to resolve this problem on the clients?	You can use the **ipconfig /displaydns** command to show the DNS resolver cache on the client, and if that appears to be what's causing the problem, you can use the **ipconfig /flushdns** command to delete the client's DNS cache.
You are able to successfully ping a remote computer's IP address but not its hostname. Based on this information, where should you focus your troubleshooting?	If you are able to resolve an IP address but not a hostname, this indicates that name resolution could be a problem. First, determine what type of name resolution services are installed on the network, such as WINS or DNS, and begin the troubleshooting process by ensuring that those services are functioning correctly. Another good rule of thumb is to check if other computers are experiencing the same problem. Ruling out other computers allows you to redirect your focus to only the computer experiencing the problem.

cause of the problem. Examples of the **ping** command using both IP address and hostname are shown here:

```
Ping 192.168.1.1
Ping workstation1
```

Another common troubleshooting technique using the **ping** command is to use the –t switch, which runs the **ping** command continuously until you stop it by using the CTRL-C key sequence. By running the **ping** command with the –t switch, as shown next, you are able to make configuration changes on the remote computer and immediately determine if the changes result in communications resuming:

```
Ping 192.168.1.1 -t
```

The results of a basic **ping** command can be seen in Figure 16-9. The **ping** command can be used to ping the local computer as well to test the network adapter to ensure that it is functioning correctly and not the cause of communication problems. To ping the local computer, you can use one of two IP addresses or hostnames. You can use either the IP address bound to the network adapter or hostname configured on the local computer, or the loopback hostname and IP address of 127.0.0.1. Receiving a reply from the loopback name or IP address indicates that the network adapter driver is not the problem. Unfortunately, your network card may still have problems with its network transmitter or receiver circuitry and still respond to a ping request to the loopback address.

A good rule of thumb with the **ping** command is to ping your local gateway or a remote host. By pinging a remote host and receiving a response, you confirm the functionality of the local adapter, gateway, and remote host, because traffic had to have passed through all three successfully to generate a reply on the local computer.

FIGURE 16-9 The results of the ping command

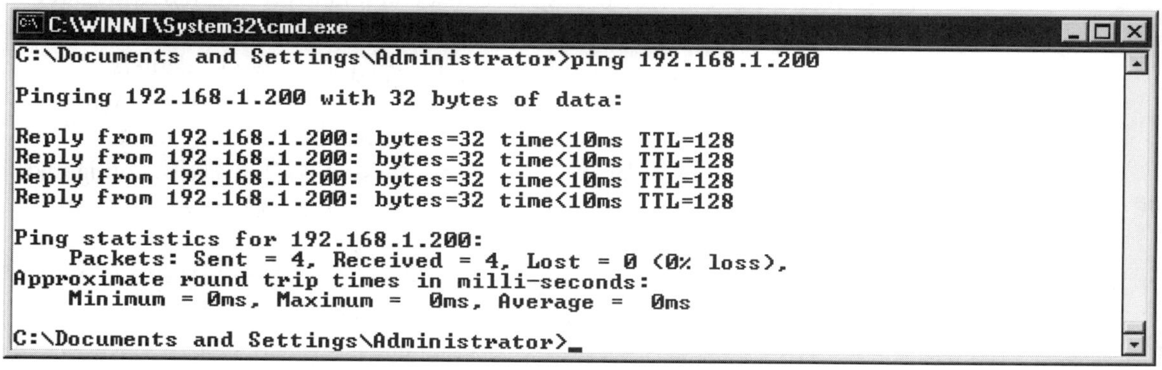

```
C:\WINNT\System32\cmd.exe                                           _ □ ×
C:\Documents and Settings\Administrator>ping 192.168.1.200

Pinging 192.168.1.200 with 32 bytes of data:

Reply from 192.168.1.200: bytes=32 time<10ms TTL=128
Reply from 192.168.1.200: bytes=32 time<10ms TTL=128
Reply from 192.168.1.200: bytes=32 time<10ms TTL=128
Reply from 192.168.1.200: bytes=32 time<10ms TTL=128

Ping statistics for 192.168.1.200:
    Packets: Sent = 4, Received = 4, Lost = 0 (0% loss),
Approximate round trip times in milli-seconds:
    Minimum = 0ms, Maximum =  0ms, Average =  0ms

C:\Documents and Settings\Administrator>_
```

FIGURE 16-10   Routed Network

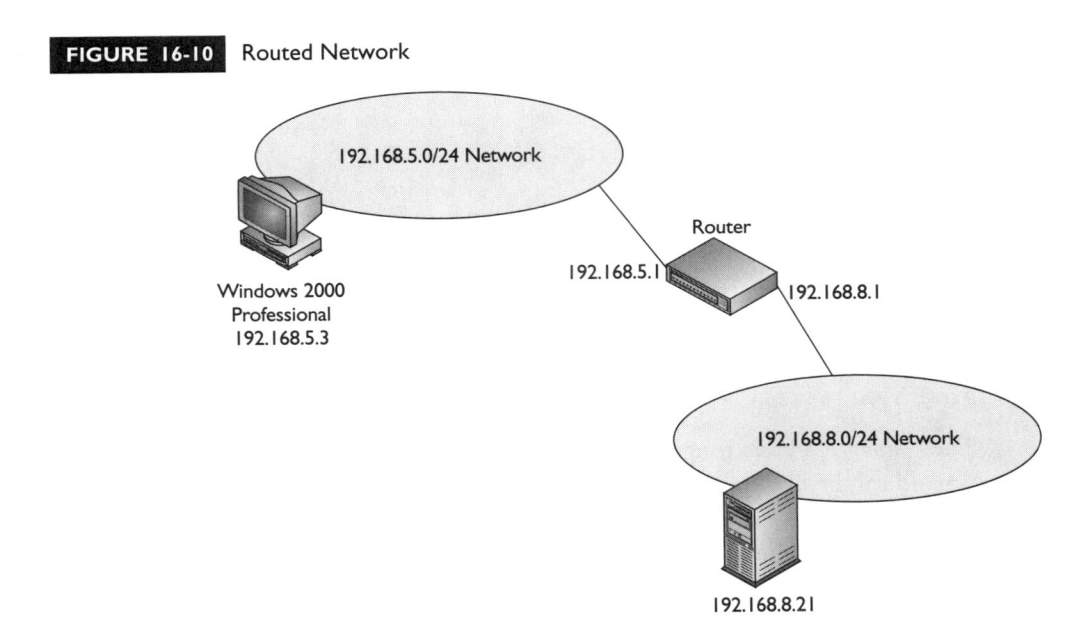

CERTIFICATION OBJECTIVE 16.03

Configuring Routing and Remote Access to Perform NAT

NAT, like ICS, uses translated connections instead of routed connections. NAT's biggest benefit over ICS is that it is more scalable and offers you more configuration options. NAT is intended for larger, routed networks but can also be used in smaller networks.

Unlike ICS, NAT can only be installed on a computer running Windows 2000 Server. It does not run on computers running Windows 2000 Professional. Also unlike ICS, NAT is able to make use of multiple external network adapters to increase network throughput and can operate in a routed network that contains DHCP servers, DHCP relay agents, and domain controllers, making it the recommended alternative for larger corporate networks. NAT can also be configured to use packet filtering on the external adapter to increase the security of your Internet sharing solution.

The advantage of NAT over routing is that, like ICS, it allows the IP addresses of internal client computers to be hidden from the view of external users and computers, increasing the level of security on the network. Like ICS, NAT also allows you to use an unlimited number of internal IP addresses and requires you have fewer valid Internet IP addresses, keeping your costs down.

> **exam**
> **Watch**
>
> **NAT cannot be used for access scenarios that require the use of L2TP VPN support. Knowledge Base articles Q317509 and Q259335 discuss this.**

NAT does have some limitations, and these limitations will be a focus in some of the questions you come across on the exam. If your shared Internet connection scenario requires the ability to cache web pages, restrict users' Internet access or provide support for the IPX protocol, a proxy server would be the recommended approach to meeting these needs, as NAT will not handle them. One last limitation of NAT is that it is not compatible with IP Security (IPSec). This is due to the translation of the computer's IP address in the packet header to that of the NAT server's external interface, all of which is transparent to the user.

> **exam**
> **Watch**
>
> **Be familiar with what NAT can and cannot do. The exam will require that you have a solid understanding of both its uses and its limitations, particularly where you would use it as opposed to ICS.**

Prior to installing NAT, it is important to understand how the TCP/IP information should be configured on the server that is to act as your NAT server. The NAT server must have two network adapters. One or more of these adapters will be configured as external adapters with valid IP addresses, subnet masks, gateway information and DNS information. The internal network adapter's TCP/IP information should include only an internal IP address and subnet mask. Do not configure the internal network adapter with a gateway or DNS server information. An example of this configuration is shown in Figure 16-11.

> **exam**
> **Watch**
>
> **Do not configure DNS or gateway information in the TCP/IP properties of the internal network adapter on the NAT server.**

NAT is installed through the Routing and Remote Access Server snap-in; hence, the RRAS service must be enabled and configured on the computer in order for NAT to be installed. Membership in the Administrators group is required to install NAT and to administer it and other RRAS components. Exercise 16-3 teaches you the steps involved in installing NAT.

FIGURE 16-11 Recommended NAT configuration

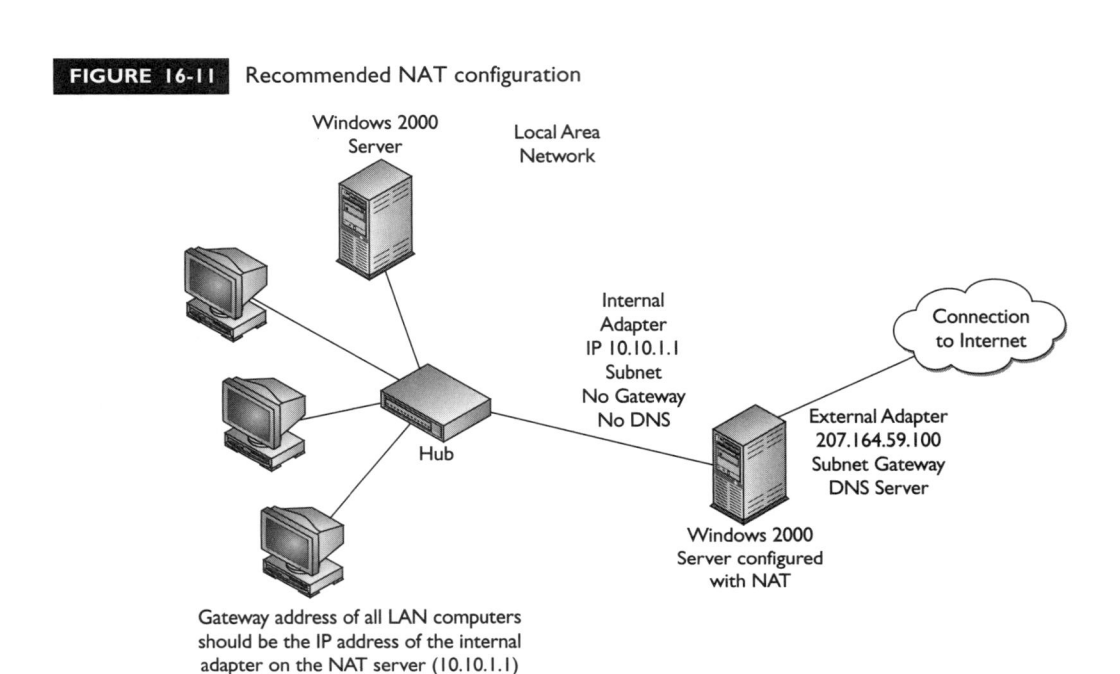

[Diagram showing Windows 2000 Server connected to a Local Area Network via Hub, with client computers. Internal Adapter IP 10.10.1.1, Subnet, No Gateway, No DNS. External Adapter 207.164.59.100, Subnet Gateway, DNS Server. Windows 2000 Server configured with NAT connects to Internet. Gateway address of all LAN computers should be the IP address of the internal adapter on the NAT server (10.10.1.1).]

EXERCISE 16-3

CertCam 16-3

Installing NAT

In this exercise, you will learn how to configure and enable RRAS to install NAT on a computer running Windows 2000 Server:

1. Open Routing and Remote Access, right-click the name of the server that you want to configure, and click Configure And Enable Routing And Remote Access.

2. In the Routing and Remote Access Server Setup Wizard, click Next.

3. On the Common Configurations page, click the Internet Connection Server radio button and click Next.

Configuring Routing and Remote Access to Perform NAT

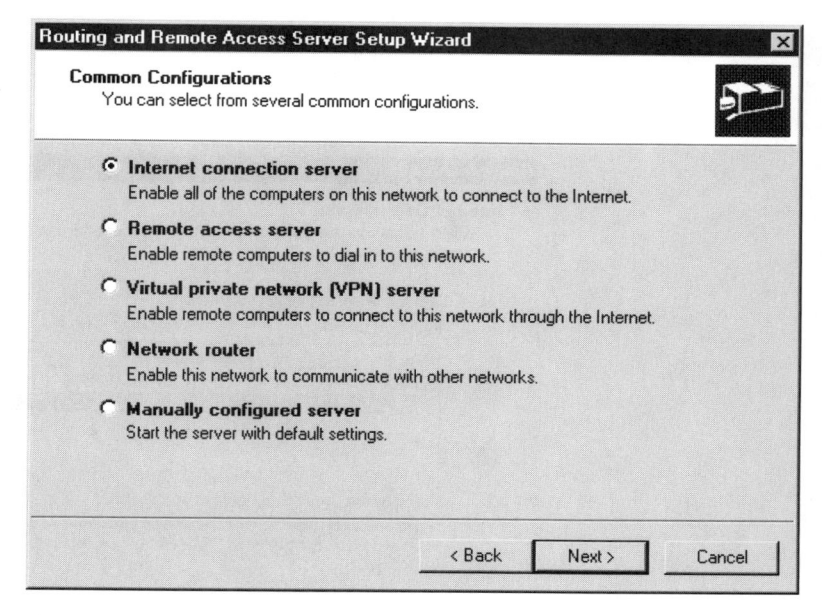

4. On the Internet Connection Server Setup page, click the Set Up A Router With The NAT Routing Protocol radio button and click Next. As you can see, this is also where ICS can be configured on a computer running Windows 2000 Server.

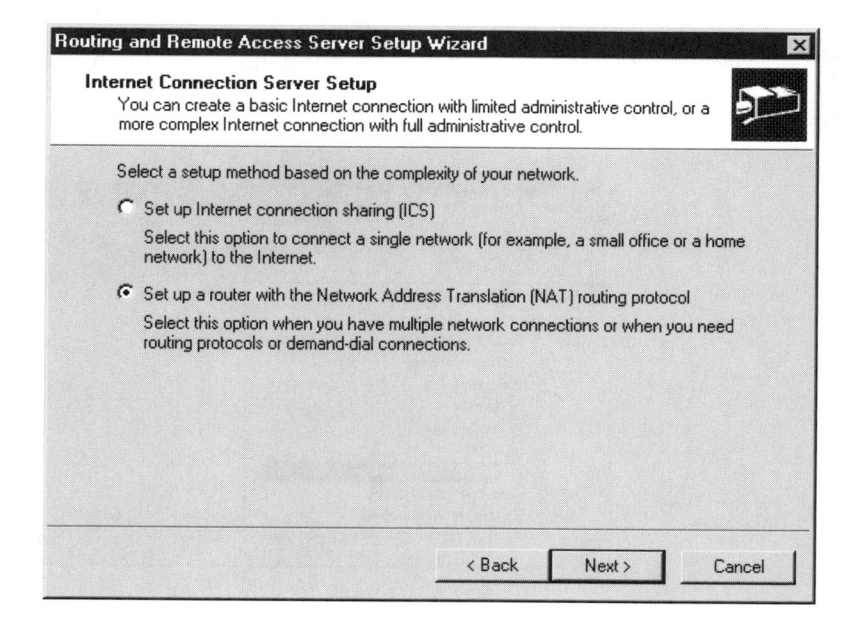

5. On the Internet Connection page, click the network adapter representing the external network interface (in this case, the public connection), and click Next.

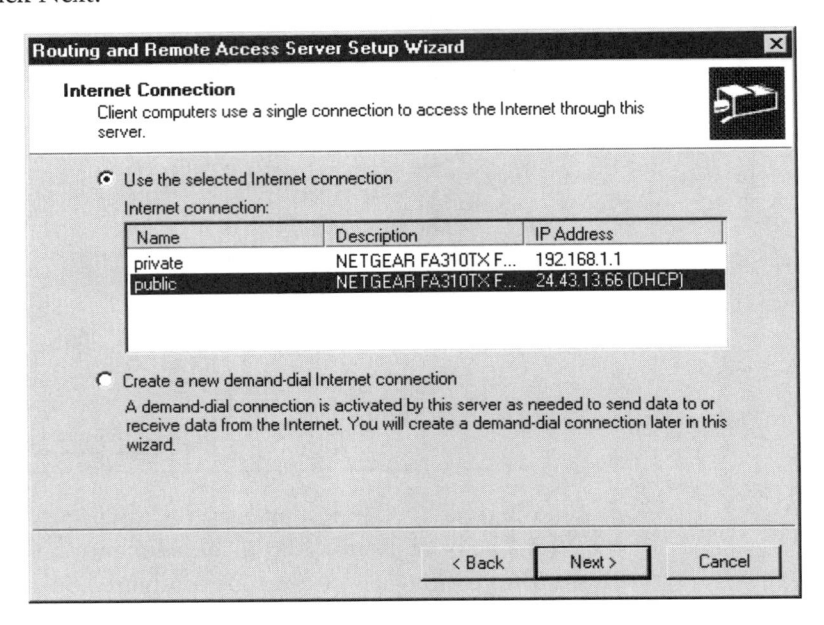

6. On the Summary page of the wizard, click Finish.
7. To confirm that NAT is installed, once the RRAS service starts, expand IP Routing to determine if Network Address Translation (NAT) is displayed in the list of routing protocols.

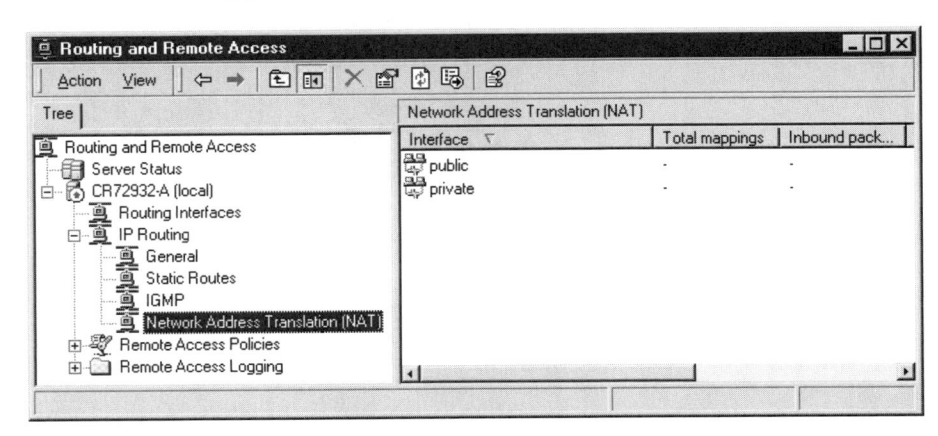

Configuring NAT Properties

Now that you are familiar with how to install NAT, let's take a look at how to configure NAT-specific properties. The configuration of NAT is performed in RRAS by right-clicking NAT, under IP Routing, and selecting Properties. This opens the NAT Properties dialog box, shown in Figure 16-12. The General tab of the NAT Properties dialog box allows you to enable logging options, with the default set to Log Errors Only. The Translation tab allows you to configure the time period, in minutes, after which a TCP mapping is removed. The default is 24 hours. This is the amount of time that a dynamic mapping for a TCP session remains in the Network Address Translation table. The same type of setting is available for the removal of UDP mappings, but as you can see in Figure 16-13, the default for these is much shorter, only a minute, because data sent via UDP is generally less important, as it is sent unguaranteed.

The Translation tab also includes an Applications button. Clicking this button enables you to configure internal applications to be available to external users through reverse publishing, in the same way you learned about earlier with ICS. The configuration is identical to that discussed earlier. Even the Internet Connection Sharing dialog box is the same.

The Address Assignment tab, shown in Figure 16-14, allows you to configure the use of DHCP to lease out IP addresses. The default network ID is set to 192.168.0.0

FIGURE 16-12

Configuring the General tab of the NAT Properties dialog box

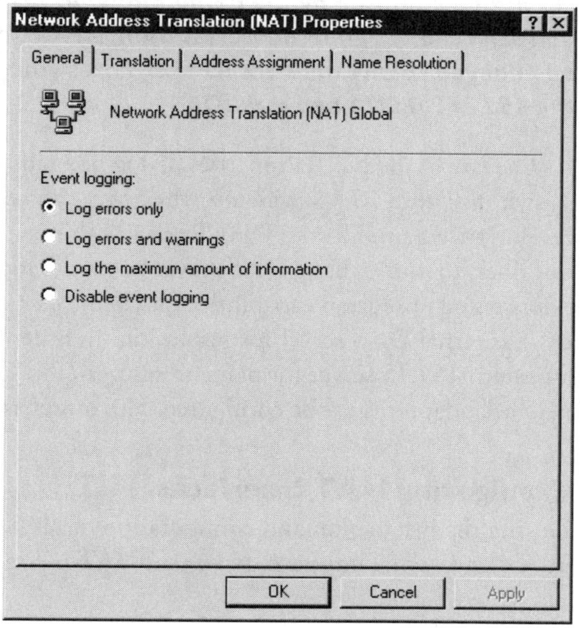

FIGURE 16-13

Configuring the Translation tab of the NAT Properties dialog box

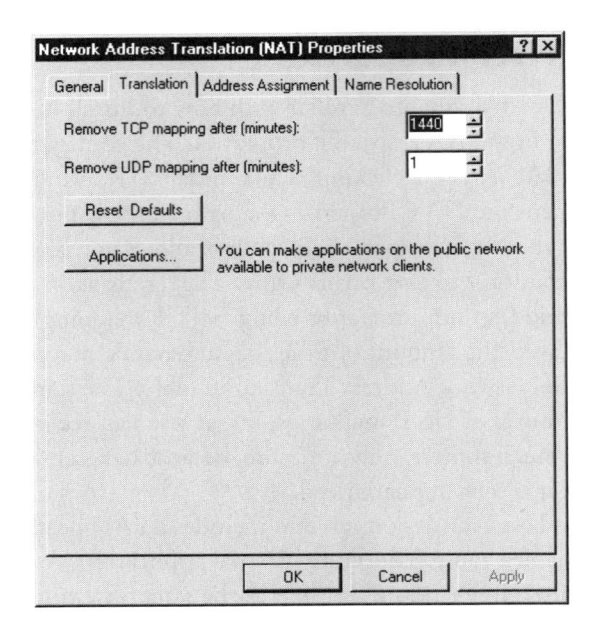

with a subnet mask of 255.255.255.0. An exclusion range can also be configured by clicking the Exclude button. Using the DHCP implementation that is included with NAT in RRAS does not require that a DHCP server be available on the network.

exam
⑩atch

Do not be confused by the default network ID of 192.168.0.0/24 used when you select to assign IP addresses using DHCP. NAT allows this network ID to be changed to any network ID that suites you; only ICS restricts you to using the 192.168.0.0/24 network ID.

The last of the NAT Properties dialog box tabs is the Name Resolution tab, shown in Figure 16-15, which is where you can configure the use of DNS for name resolution. Again, like the DHCP service, this is not a full implementation of DNS nor does it require that a DNS server be on the local network. The NAT protocol offers name resolution capabilities for clients using DNS and forwards the requests to an external DNS server for resolution. In order for NAT to forward requests to an external DNS server for name resolution, the TCP/IP properties of the external network adapter must be configured with a preferred DNS server.

Configuring NAT Interfaces

During the installation and configuration of NAT, you were asked to select the public or external interface. Now that NAT is configured, you are able to modify

FIGURE 16-14

Configuring the Address Assignment tab of the NAT Properties dialog box

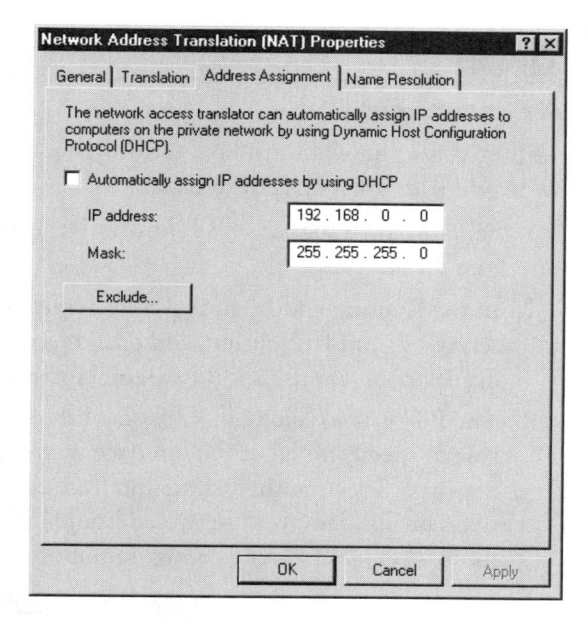

the configuration of the individual NAT interfaces by modifying their properties, or even add additional interfaces. Remember, unlike ICS, NAT can have multiple external interfaces. Exercise 16-4 will teach you the steps involved in configuring the individual NAT interfaces.

FIGURE 16-15

Configuring the Name Resolution tab of the NAT Properties dialog box

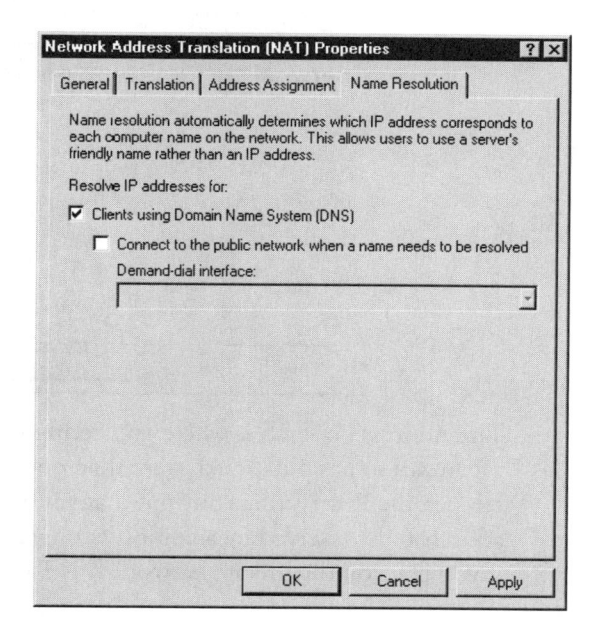

EXERCISE 16-4

Configuring NAT Interfaces

In this exercise, you will learn how to configure the individual NAT interfaces and how to add additional NAT interfaces:

1. Select Start | Programs | Administrative Tools and click Routing And Remote Access.

2. In the Routing and Remote Access Service snap-in, expand the name of your server, expand IP Routing, and click Network Address Translation. In the display pane, right-click the external interface and click Properties.

3. The Properties dialog box consists of three tabs. On the General tab, you are able to specify whether the interface is connected to the public or the private network. Selecting the Private interface connected to the private network radio button removes the two additional tabs from the dialog box. Nothing more is required for the configuration of the private interface.

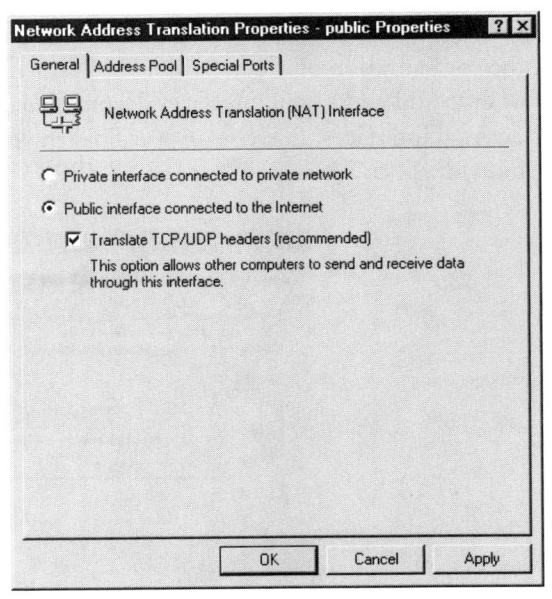

4. The Address Pool tab is where you configure a range of IP addresses if your organization has purchased more than one external IP address. It is on this tab, via the Reservations button, that you would also configure a public address to be reserved by a computer on your private network. This is useful if you have on the private network a mail or web server that you wish to

provide access to from computers on the external network. To add an address pool, click the Add button.

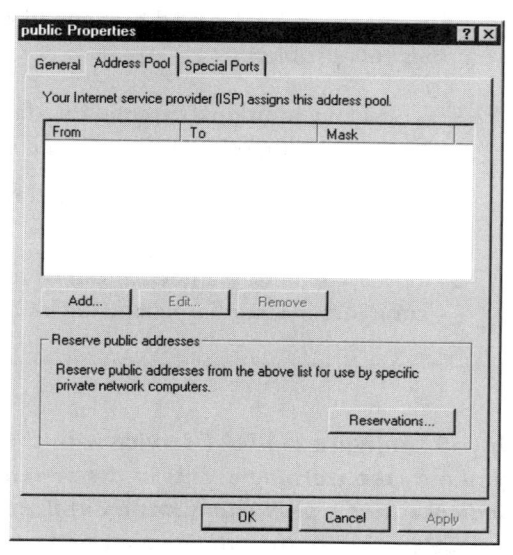

5. The Special Ports tab is used to map specific services from the NAT server to an internal computer on the private network. This is similar to the concept of service publishing discussed in the section on ICS. The addition of multiple network interfaces in the computer running NAT will increase the potential throughput the computer can handle and increase performance.

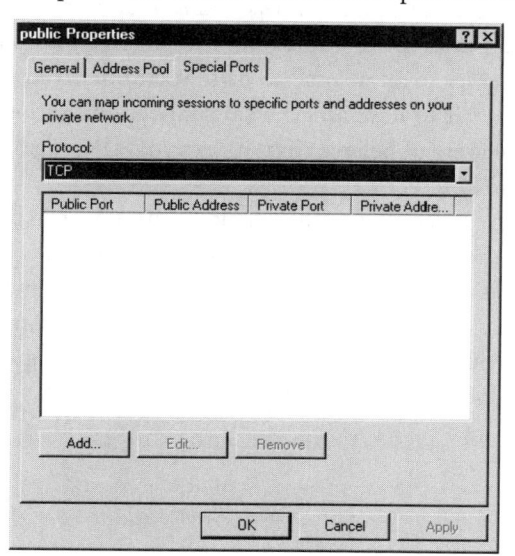

exam
Ⓦatch

If a NAT server detects the presence of a DHCP server on the network, NAT will disable its DHCP Allocator service, allowing the DHCP server to continue to lease out IP addresses and prevent IP address conflicts. KB article Q272076 describes this problem.

6. To add an additional external interface, in the RRAS snap-in, right-click Network Address Translation and click New Interface.

7. Select the interface you wish to add from the list of available new interfaces and click OK.

8. Select whether the interface will be for the public or private network, configure it accordingly, and click OK.

on the
Ⓙob

If you configure the NAT service with the DHCP Allocator service enabled, you may see warning events in the system log with Event ID 30001. These indicate that a LAN client has a duplicate of an IP address found in the NAT DHCP pool. Use the arp –a *command on the NAT computer to determine the client and then manually change its static IP address.*

An example of where you might use the Special Ports tab is in the configuration of your mail server, which is located on the internal network and configured to receive mail on TCP port 25 using the SMTP protocol and to send mail on the same port. NAT allows you to map the incoming and outgoing service ports from an external IP address on the NAT server to the internal IP address of your mail server to allow mail to be sent and received externally without requiring the mail server to have an external connection. Rather, the mail server can allow external mail servers to believe that the external IP address of the computer running NAT is the mail server's IP address.

To configure this, click the Add button on the Special Ports tab of the External interface's Properties dialog box to display the Add Special Port dialog box. Assuming the internal IP address of your mail server is 192.168.1.200 and the external IP address you want to allow incoming mail requests on is the currently selected public interface, you would configure the information in the Add Special Port dialog box as shown in Figure 16-16.

FIGURE 16-16

Configuring incoming mail requests in the Add Special Port dialog box

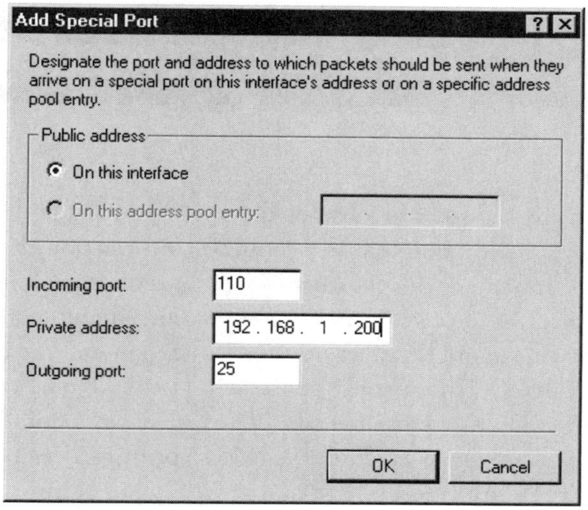

CERTIFICATION SUMMARY

In this chapter, you learned how to configure Internet Connection Sharing, a feature available on both Windows 2000 Professional and Windows 2000 Server operating systems. You learned that two network adapters are required in order to configure ICS, and you learned how to properly configure the IP properties on both the internal and external adapters.

You also learned how to troubleshoot communication problems that can arise when working with ICS using utilities such as **ipconfig** and **ping**, and how to use the switches that are included with these utilities.

The last section of the chapter taught you about Network Address Translation, including how to configure it and where to use it in lieu of ICS. You learned how to configure multiple network interfaces, configure an address pool, and define both the public and private interfaces. Overall, this chapter taught you about the options available in Windows 2000 for establishing shared Internet connections and how to troubleshoot communication problems should they arise.

FROM THE CLASSROOM

NAT Issues

There are a number of issues involved with NAT and its implementation that you should be aware of. Most or all of this information will not be a focus on the certification exam, but is material you should be aware of.

Windows 2000 NAT does not support Netlogon or translate Kerberos. Therefore, if you have legacy clients such as Windows NT 4 or Windows 9*x* that are on a LAN behind a Windows 2000 server running NAT that need to access domain resources, your best bet is to configure a VPN tunnel to allow Netlogon traffic through or to upgrade the clients to Windows 2000. The message you are likely to see indicating this problem is "A domain controller could not be found. You have been logged on with cached credentials."

If you are an MSN Messenger user and enjoy the file transfer and voice features, these are no longer available to you after you install either NAT or ICS to configure shared Internet access. NAT does not include a NAT editor that can correctly translate the IP header information; it only includes NAT editors for FTP, ICMP, and PPTP. This type of problem will arise if a program or protocol stores IP address or TCP/UCP port information within its own headers and a NAT editor isn't included for the program or service to open the packet and translate the address or port information contained in the payload. This problem can often be resolved with the introduction of a proxy server such as ISA Server and the creation of protocol definitions for TCP ports.

The use of NAT may prevent Internet printing if you have a printer installed and shared on the computer running NAT and have disabled File and Printer Sharing on the external adapter on the NAT server, which is the recommended configuration, for security reasons. When a client attempts to connect to http://*servername*/printers, they will likely receive an error message indicating "An error occurred processing your request."

Windows 2000 NAT does not support incoming PPTP traffic from external computers through a NAT server to an internal PPTP server. NAT does include a PPTP NAT editor, which allows an external computer to establish a PPTP VPN tunnel to the external adapter of the NAT server but not tunnel through the NAT server. This is the result of not being able to create a special port mapping for GRE, the protocol used by PPTP, because GRE does not use TCP or UDP headers.

—*Rory McCaw*

✓ TWO-MINUTE DRILL

Configuring Internet Connection Sharing

- ❏ ICS is one of the options available in both Windows 2000 Professional and Windows 2000 Server when configuring shared Internet access.
- ❏ The computer configured with ICS must have two network adapters, one connected to the external or public network and the other connected to the internal network. The computers on the internal network should be configured to obtain an IP address from DHCP and will receive an IP address on the 192.168.0.1/24 network.
- ❏ ICS is designed and intended to be used in small, nonrouted networks that do not have DHCP servers, DHCP relay agents, or domain controllers.
- ❏ ICS only supports a single external adapter. In many cases, to obtain an IP address from an ISP, such as for a high-speed cable or ADSL connection, the external adapter must be configured to obtain an IP address through DHCP..
- ❏ ICS uses address translation as opposed to routed connections to provide shared Internet access.
- ❏ ICS can be configured to provide to external users access to services and applications running on computers on your LAN, in effect behind the computer running ICS. This is accomplished by editing the properties of the shared connection through the Settings button.
- ❏ ICS is able to lease out IP addresses on the 192.168.0.1/24 network through the DHCP Allocator service.

Troubleshooting Internet Connection Sharing Problems by Using the Ipconfig and Ping Commands

- ❏ **Ipconfig** is a utility that can be used to troubleshoot IP configuration and communication problems. There are a number of switches that can be used with **ipconfig**.
- ❏ To release and renew an IP address on a DHCP client computer that is leased from a DHCP server, the **ipconfig /renew** command can be run. The **/registerdns** switch can also be used to renew and reregister your name to IP

address information with a DNS server that is configured with a zone database file that allows dynamic updates.

- The DNS client resolver cache can be deleted on the client using the /flushdns switch to assist in troubleshooting name resolution problems caused from old entries in the client's resolver cache.

- The /all switch can be used with the **ipconfig** command to display all the detailed IP configuration information from all the network adapters on the computer. An IP address on the 169.254.0.0/16 network indicates that the computer was not able to obtain an IP address from a DHCP server and that the client is configured to use APIPA.

- APIPA can be disabled through a Registry edit, but doing so will result in the client receiving an IP address of 0.0.0.0 when it is unable to contact a DHCP server.

- The **ping** utility can also be used to troubleshoot network communication problems.

- Pinging a remote computer and receiving a reply allows you to verify that the local and remote computers and all routers in between the two computers are functioning correctly.

- Pinging a remote computer by hostname allows you to rule out name resolution as a cause of the problem, whereas only being able to ping a remote computer by IP address indicates name resolution might be a problem.

- Pinging a local computer using the reserved localhost name or IP address 127.0.0.1 and receiving a reply indicates that the network adapter isn't the problem.

Configuring Routing and Remote Access to Perform NAT

- NAT is designed to be implemented in larger networks and supports the use of multiple network adapters, both internally and externally.

- NAT can only be installed on a computer running Windows 2000 Server and can either lease out IP addresses through its own DHCP Allocator service or NAT can use a specified address pool or allow a full and separate DHCP server implementation to lease out IPs.

- NAT offers more security options than ICS, including the ability to configure packet filtering, but NAT cannot be used in access solutions that require the use of L2TP.
- NAT does not provide any page caching support, the ability to restrict user access, or support for the IPX protocol; for this type of support, you should look to a proxy server solution. MS Proxy 2.0 supports IPX, but the new version ISA Server does not.
- The internal network adapter should never be configured with a gateway or DNS information; it should only have an IP address and subnet mask.
- NAT is installed and configured through the RRAS snap-in and, like ICS, can be configured to allow external users access to specific applications and services running on computers on the internal network.
- If NAT is installed on a network that already has a DHCP server and NAT detects the presence of the DHCP server, NAT will disable its DHCP Allocator service and let the other DHCP server continue to lease out IP addresses in an effort to reduce IP address conflicts and complexity.

SELF TEST

The following questions will help you measure your understanding of the material presented in this chapter. Read the questions and answers carefully, and be aware that some questions will provide for more than one correct answer. Choose all correct answers for each question.

Configuring Internet Connection Sharing

1. You are the administrator for a small company that has a network with nine computers, all running Windows 2000 Professional. The company has asked you to configure ICS on one of the computers. Which two of the following are required for the computer being configured to run ICS? (Choose two.)

    A. A static IP address on the internal interface of 192.168.1.1.

    B. A static IP address on the internal interface of 192.168.0.1.

    C. Two network adapters.

    D. The Routing and Remote Access Server snap-in.

    E. DNS and gateway information configured on the internal adapter.

2. You are a contract administrator who works for a number of small companies. One of your clients currently has eight computers, seven of which run Windows 2000 Professional and the eighth of which runs Windows 2000 Server and Exchange 5.5. You have configured the company's shared Internet access to use ICS and would like to allow external SMTP servers to communicate with the internal Exchange server at IP address 192.168.0.254. What will you do to accomplish this?

    A. Add the IP address of the Exchange server on the Services tab of the ICS Settings dialog box for the internal adapter.

    B. Add the IP address of the Exchange server on the Services tab of the ICS Settings dialog box for the external adapter.

    C. Add the IP address of the Exchange server on the Applications tab of the ICS Settings dialog box for the internal adapter.

    D. Add the IP address of the Exchange server on the Applications tab of the ICS Settings dialog box for the external adapter

FIGURE 16-17 Home Network Components

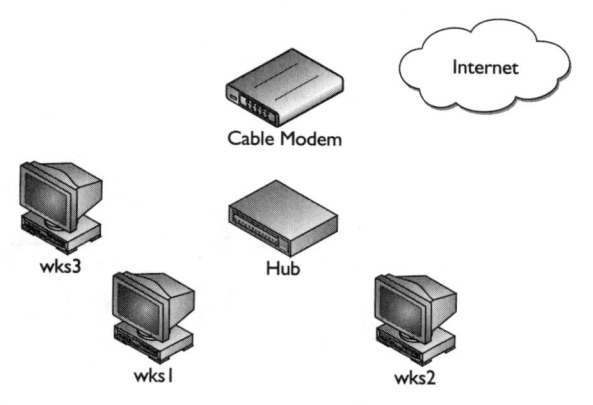

Home Network

3. You have a small network at home, shown in Figure 16-17, that consists of three computers, a hub, and a cable modem that came with your recent purchase of high-speed cable. The high-speed cable package that you bought provides you with one IP address that can only be obtained through DHCP. You would like to configure ICS on wks3, which has two network adapters. Draw the internal network connections on the illustration to create the ideal recommended architecture.

4. You have configured ICS on a computer running Windows 2000 Professional. The internal IP address of the computer is configured statically as 192.168.0.0/24 and the external IP address is 24.34.56.129. All internal computers are configured to obtain an IP address from a DHCP server. You have a computer running an FTP site on the internal network that you would like to allow external users access to. In the external adapter's Properties dialog box on the computer running ICS, you have clicked the Settings button to open the ICS Settings dialog box, shown in Figure 16-18. Which of the following steps must you perform to enable external users to access the internal FTP site through the computer running ICS? (Select all that apply.)

   A. On the Applications tab, click Add.
   B. Edit the FTP Server ICS Services dialog box and enter the name or IP address of the FTP server.
   C. On the Services tab, select FTP server.
   D. Edit the ICS Application dialog box and enter the TCP port range 20 to 21.

FIGURE 16-18

Configuring FTP Access in ICS

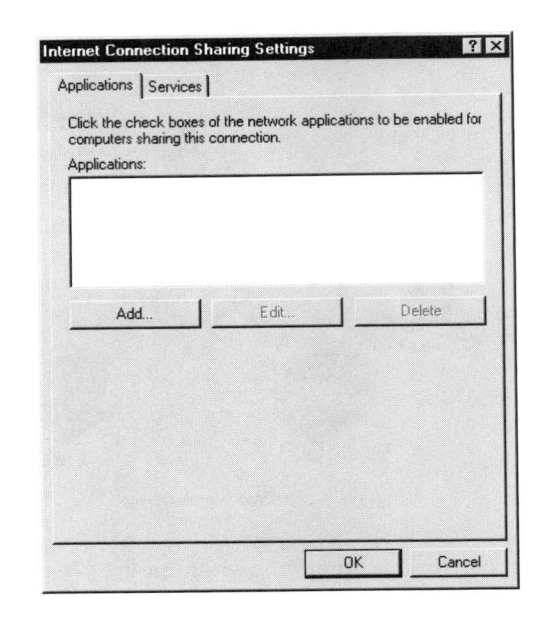

Troubleshooting Internet Connection Sharing Problems by Using the IPCONFIG and PING Commands

5. You are the administrator of a computer running ICS that is having communication problems. You have run the **ipconfig /all** command, which provided the results shown in Figure 16-19. Based on these results, which of the following would most likely resolve the communication problem?

   A. Run the ipconfig /renew command.

   B. Ping the DHCP server.

   C. Disable autoconfiguration by editing the Registry.

   D. Run the ipconfig /flushdns command.

6. You are the administrator of a small network that is having communication problems connecting to the Internet through the computer running ICS. You have run the **ipconfig /all** command on the computer running ICS, which provided the results shown in Figure 16-20. From the results, which of the following best represents the most likely cause of the problem?

   A. The external adapter on the ICS computer is not configured correctly.

   B. The ISP DHCP server is offline.

FIGURE 16-19 The Results of Ipconfig /all

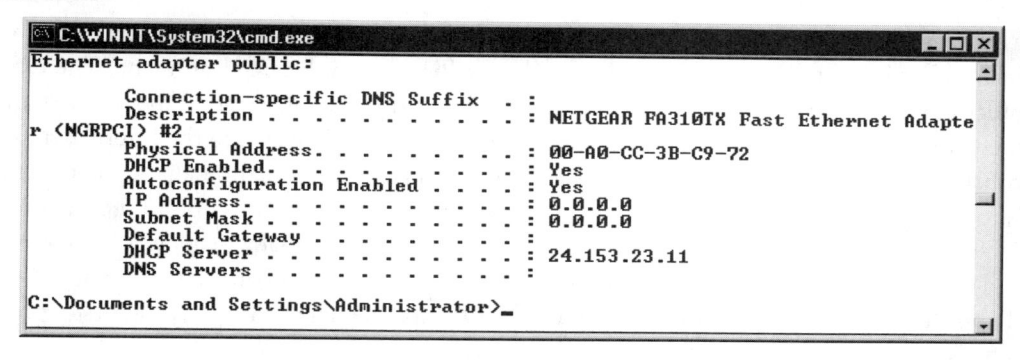

```
C:\WINNT\System32\cmd.exe
Ethernet adapter public:

        Connection-specific DNS Suffix  . :
        Description . . . . . . . . . . . : NETGEAR FA310TX Fast Ethernet Adapte
r (NGRPCI) #2
        Physical Address. . . . . . . . . : 00-A0-CC-3B-C9-72
        DHCP Enabled. . . . . . . . . . . : Yes
        Autoconfiguration Enabled . . . . : Yes
        IP Address. . . . . . . . . . . . : 0.0.0.0
        Subnet Mask . . . . . . . . . . . : 0.0.0.0
        Default Gateway . . . . . . . . . :
        DHCP Server . . . . . . . . . . . : 24.153.23.11
        DNS Servers . . . . . . . . . . . :

C:\Documents and Settings\Administrator>_
```

- C. Autoconfiguration must be disabled in the Registry for the external adapter.
- D. The external network adapter is unplugged.

7. You are the administrator of a computer configured with ICS. You are experiencing name resolution problems on a number of the client computers on the LAN and believe that they might be attributed to the client computers' DNS resolver cache containing outdated records. Which of the following commands would allow you to empty the entries in the DNS client resolver cache?

- A. ipconfig /release
- B. ipconfig /deletedns
- C. ipconfig /purgedns
- D. ipconfig /flushdns

FIGURE 16-20 The Results of Ipconfig /all

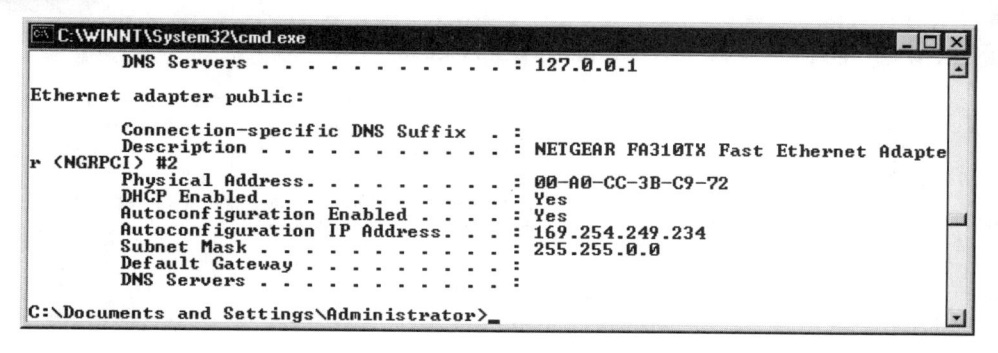

```
C:\WINNT\System32\cmd.exe
        DNS Servers . . . . . . . . . . . : 127.0.0.1
Ethernet adapter public:

        Connection-specific DNS Suffix  . :
        Description . . . . . . . . . . . : NETGEAR FA310TX Fast Ethernet Adapte
r (NGRPCI) #2
        Physical Address. . . . . . . . . : 00-A0-CC-3B-C9-72
        DHCP Enabled. . . . . . . . . . . : Yes
        Autoconfiguration Enabled . . . . : Yes
        Autoconfiguration IP Address. . . : 169.254.249.234
        Subnet Mask . . . . . . . . . . . : 255.255.0.0
        Default Gateway . . . . . . . . . :
        DNS Servers . . . . . . . . . . . :

C:\Documents and Settings\Administrator>_
```

Configuring Routing and Remote Access to Perform NAT

8. You are the administrator of a small corporate network that currently has two locations. The main office is located in Portland and a smaller satellite office is located in Omaha. The Omaha office currently uses a RRAS server to establish a demand-dial connection to the Internet and then create a VPN to the RRAS server in Portland, which is connected to the Internet via a constant ADSL connection. The employees in Omaha are finding that the dial-up connection is too slow. The new budget allocates funds for a constant ADSL connection to the Internet in Omaha. You have been asked to configure the RRAS server in Omaha to allow VPN connections and allow all users in the Omaha office to share the ADSL Internet connection. Figure 16-21 shows the RRAS snap-in on the RRAS server in Omaha. Which of the following best represents how you will add NAT to the existing RRAS server?

   A. In the RRAS snap-in, right-click IP Routing and select New Routing Protocol and add NAT as the new routing protocol.

   B. In the RRAS snap-in, right-click General and select New Routing Protocol and add NAT as the new routing protocol.

   C. In the RRAS snap-in, right-click General and select New Interface and add NAT as the new interface.

   D. In the RRAS snap-in, right-click IP Routing and select New Interface and add NAT as the new interface.

FIGURE 16-21 The RRAS snap-in

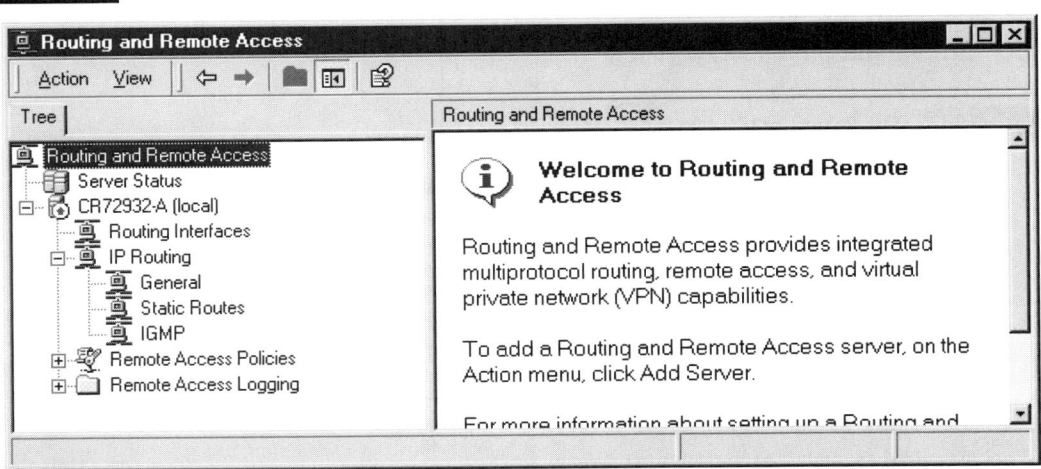

9. The DHCP Allocator service has to be authorized in Active Directory by a member of the Enterprise Admins group if NAT is installed in an Active Directory domain. True or false?

   A. True
   B. False

10. Which of the following statements best represents how you can configure NAT to work with PPTP?

   A. A PPTP tunnel can be created from an external client computer to an internal PPTP server through NAT.
   B. A PPTP tunnel can be created from an external client computer to the internal network adapter on the NAT server.
   C. A PPTP tunnel can be created from an external client computer to the external network adapter on the NAT server.
   D. A PPTP tunnel can only be created when initialized by an internal client computer through the NAT server to an external client computer.

LAB QUESTION

You are the network administrator for a large organization that has many telecommuters. Your organization provides telecommuters with a desktop computer running Windows 2000 Professional and pays for a high-speed connection to the Internet, which allows the users to VPN in to the office and perform all of their work from home. A number of telecommuters have expressed interest in connecting one or more computers at home in order to be able to share the high-speed Internet connection without having to let other family members use the corporate owned and configured computer. Answer the following questions in order to evaluate the possible alternatives and configuration choices.

1. What additional types of hardware would be required by the telecommuters to establish a shared Internet connection? What would be the ideal way in which to share the Internet connection?

2. What other considerations should the telecommuter be made aware of with respect to IP configuration?

3. Draw out the ideal configuration, assuming the telecommuter will have two home computers, one of which is the computer running Windows 2000 Professional.

SELF TEST ANSWERS

Configuring Internet Connection Sharing

1. ☑ **B and C are correct.** The computer configured to run ICS must have two network adapters and the internal adapter's address must be a static address of 192.168.0.1. If the IP address of the internal adapter is different for 192.168.0.1, ICS will change this during the configuration of ICS.
   ☒ **A** is incorrect because the static IP address for the internal network adapter will be configured to be 192.168.0.1, not 192.168.1.1.
   ☒ **D** is incorrect because the RRAS snap-in is not a requirement for the configuration of ICS. ICS can be configured through RRAS but it can also be configured through the properties of the external network adapter in Network and Dial-up Connections.
   ☒ **E** is incorrect because the internal network adapter's TCP/IP properties should not contain DNS or gateway information.

2. ☑ **B is correct.** To allow external SMTP servers the ability to communicate through ICS with the internal Exchange server, you can add the IP address of the Exchange server on the Services tab of the ICS Services dialog box in the external network adapter's properties, as shown in Figure 16-22.
   ☒ **A** is incorrect because the properties of the *external* network adapter must be edited.
   ☒ **C and D** are incorrect because the Services tab, not the Applications tab, should be edited.

3. ☑ Figure 16-23 shows the correct network configuration for this home network type of configuration. The cable modem is connected to the Internet via the cable outlet and also connects to wks3. Wks3 is configured with two network adapters, one external and the other internal. The external adapter is connected to the cable modem, and the internal adapter is connected to the hub. Both other workstations should simply connect to the hub and be configured to obtain an IP address dynamically from the DHCP Allocator service running on wks3.

4. ☑ **B and C are correct.** To enable external users to access an internal DNS server, FTP Server should be selected on the Services tab, and the name or IP address of the FTP server should be added in the FTP Server ICS Services dialog box.
   ☒ **A and D** are incorrect because configuring access to an internal FTP server through ICS is done on the Services tab, not the Applications tab.

Self Test Answers 747

FIGURE 16-22

Configuring Access to Internet Services Through ICS

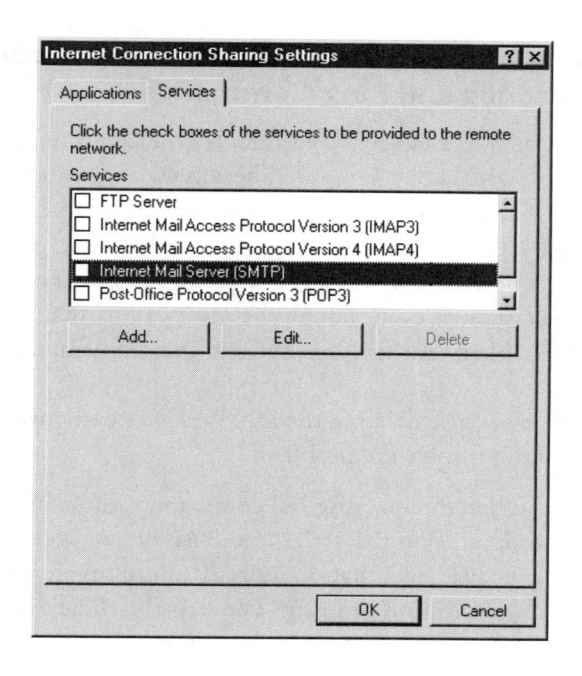

FIGURE 16-23 The Correct Home Network Configuration

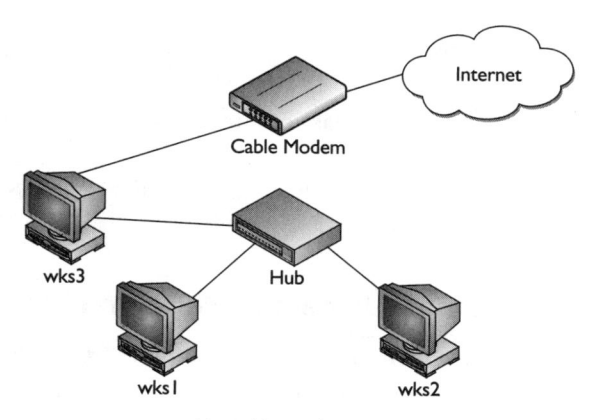

Troubleshooting Internet Connection Sharing Problems by Using the Ipconfig and Ping Commands

5. ☑ **A** is correct. The most likely way to resolve the communication problem would be to renew the IP address for the network adapter, because without an IP address, it will not be able to communicate. The results indicate that the network adapter is configured for DHCP, so a renewal should solve the problem.
☒ **B** is incorrect because without an IP address, the **ping** command will not yield a response.
☒ **C** is incorrect because even though the results show that autoconfiguration is enabled, there is no need to disable it, as this is not causing the problem and disabling it would not resolve the problem.
☒ **D** is incorrect because deleting the DNS resolver cache with the **ipconfig /flushdns** command would not solve the problem.

6. ☑ **B** is correct. When the **ipconfig /all** command returns information indicating that the IP address of the adapter is on the 169.254.0.0/16 network, this generally indicates that the DHCP server is unavailable, that no more IP addresses are available for lease, or that there are network communication problems between the client and the DHCP server.
☒ **A** is incorrect because there is no indication that the external adapter is configured incorrectly.
☒ **C** is incorrect because disabling APIPA would not resolve this problem.
☒ **D** is incorrect because the results would indicate if the adapter was unplugged, but that is not the case here.

7. ☑ **D** is correct. To empty the DNS resolver cache on a client, you can run the command **ipconfig /flushdns**.
☒ **A** is incorrect because the **ipconfig /release** command is used to release a dynamically assigned IP address.
☒ **B** and **C** are incorrect because the /deletedns and /purgedns switches are not valid switches with the **ipconfig** utility.

Configuring Routing and Remote Access to Perform NAT

8. ☑ **B** is correct. To add NAT to a computer already configured as a VPN server, you right-click General in RRAS and select New Routing Protocol and add NAT.
☒ **A** and **D** are incorrect because right-clicking IP Routing will not allow you to add NAT.
☒ **C** is incorrect because right-clicking General and selecting New Interface allows you to add an interface, not a routing protocol such as NAT.

9. ☑ **B** is correct. The DHCP Allocator service does not have to be authorized in Active Directory if NAT is installed in an Active Directory domain.
☒ **A** is incorrect because only a computer running Windows 2000 and DHCP must be authorized in Active Directory by a member of the Enterprise Admins group.

10. ☑ **C** is correct. An external client is only able to create a PPTP tunnel to the external adapter on the NAT server, because it is not possible to create a filter for the GRE protocol in NAT.
☒ **A**, **B**, and **D** are incorrect because a PPTP VPN tunnel can only be created from an external computer to the external interface of the NAT server, not through the NAT server.

LAB ANSWER

1. The telecommuters would require a hub with enough ports for all the home computers, a cable modem to connect to the high-speed cable service, and multiple network cables and network adapters for all computers. Each computer would require a single network adapter, except the computer configured with the shared connection, which would require two network adapters. The ideal way to share the Internet connection would be to configure ICS on the computer running Windows 2000 Professional.

2. ICS requires that the IP addresses of all other home computers be configured to obtain an IP address from a DHCP server. The IP addresses that the other computers will obtain will be on the 192.168.0.0/24 network. Also, if the computer configured with ICS is not powered on, the other computers will not be able to use the Internet connection.

3. Figure 16-24 shows the ideal home configuration using ICS.

FIGURE 16-24

The Ideal Home Configuration

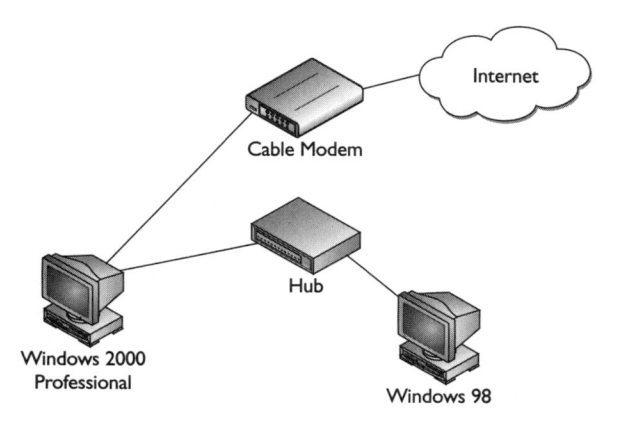

MCSA
MICROSOFT CERTIFIED SYSTEMS ADMINISTRATOR

Part V

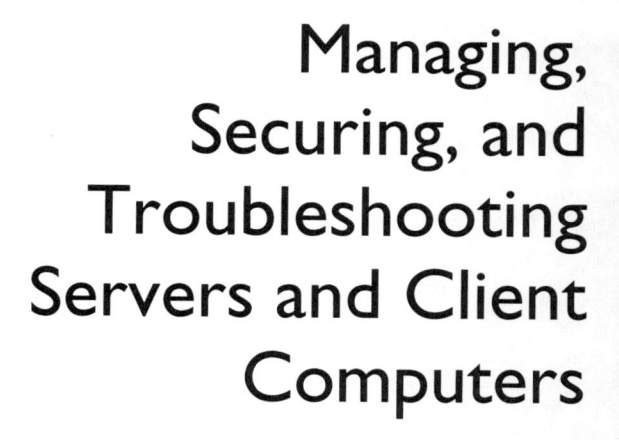

Managing, Securing, and Troubleshooting Servers and Client Computers

CHAPTERS

17 Managing, Securing, and Troubleshooting Servers and Client Computers

18 Troubleshooting Startup Problems

19 Monitoring and Troubleshooting Server Health and Performance

17
Installing and Configuring Server and Client Hardware

CERTIFICATION OBJECTIVES

17.01	Verifying Hardware Compatibility by Using the Qualifier Tools
17.02	Configuring Driver Signing Options
17.03	Verifying Digital Signatures on Existing Driver Files
17.04	Configuring Operating System Support for Legacy Hardware Devices
✓	Two-Minute Drill
Q&A	Self Test

This chapter teaches you about a number of fundamental concepts. Installing and configuring client and server hardware is a constantly evolving part of an administrator's ever-growing list of responsibilities. As new devices appear, the configuration of those devices may change and enhancements to the operating system may help to simplify the process at the same time. This chapter teaches you how to ensure that all of your hardware is compatible with the Windows 2000 operating system and how to bulletproof your drivers once the hardware is installed using driver signing. You will learn how to avert one of the most common causes of system problems, the installation of corrupt or incorrect drivers. This proactive administration can be configured using a new feature, known as *driver signing*, which you are required to be familiar with for the certification exam. You will also learn about other new tools and features, such as Device Manager, a tool that is common to the Windows 9*x* platform but new to Windows 2000. Like all new features, you should anticipate exam questions that focus on these new tools. We wrap up the chapter with a look at how to install and configure legacy devices to work with Windows 2000. The architectural changes, particularly the enhancement of the Plug and Play Manager, greatly simplify device support, but when you are faced with older, non-Plug and Play devices, you will learn the procedure involved in installing and configuring the devices manually.

Before we get into the specifics of installing and configuring client and server hardware, it is important to understand the fundamental architecture that Windows 2000 is built upon. Windows 2000 is divided into two architectural modes: user mode and kernel mode.

User mode is where all user interaction occurs, from logging on through the Windows 2000 security dialog box to running applications in the Win32 subsystem. Kernel mode is the backbone of the Windows 2000 OS and the mode in which all essential processes run. Processes running in kernel mode are protected from direct user interaction, which improves reliability and performance by preventing applications running in user mode from causing system crashes or compromising security. Unlike earlier OSs such as Microsoft 95, 98, and Me, where applications are able to directly access hardware devices, which often leads to systems freezing or crashing, Windows 2000 kernel mode prevents against this. Kernel mode acts as the intermediary between user mode, where applications run, and the physical hardware. Think of kernel mode as the big brother of the OS. As the big brother, kernel mode doesn't allow direct access to its younger brother, hardware, but rather brokers that access to ensure that hardware isn't exploited, monopolized, or overwhelmed.

CERTIFICATION OBJECTIVE 17.01

Verifying Hardware Compatibility by Using the Qualifier Tools

Windows 2000 has some strict hardware requirements. If you aren't able to meet the requirements, at best, some of your components won't operate properly and, at worst, the OS might not even install. There are two basic criteria that you must meet to install and operate Windows 2000: the components must meet the minimum requirements, and the components must be on the Hardware Compatibility List (HCL). Is it possible to have a device work with Windows 2000 that is not on the HCL? Yes, but it is not guaranteed to work, and attempting to install and configure it may result in a stop error on the computer.

on the job

An up-to-date copy of the HCL can be found on the Microsoft web site at www.microsoft.com/hcl.

The minimum requirements for Windows 2000 are listed in Table 17-1.

Use the minimum requirements as a guideline, but don't configure your systems to only meet the minimum guidelines. Other factors, such as the applications and utilization, must be factored in when planning the hardware for your computer systems. With the affordable price of physical memory and hard disks these days, there is very little reason not to greatly exceed the minimum requirements.

The Windows 2000 Readiness Analyzer

Another tool that you can use to verify hardware compatibility is the Windows 2000 Readiness Analyzer. This tool is included on the Windows 2000 CD and can be run prior to installing Windows 2000 by running the following command:

```
winnt32.exe /checkupgradeonly
```

TABLE 17-1

Minimum Hardware Requirements

Component	Minimum Requirement
CPU	Pentium 133 MHz
Memory	64MB for Professional, 128MB for Server
Hard disk	2GB
Display	VGA or better

756 Chapter 17: Installing and Configuring Server and Client Hardware

This command will run a compatibility search and provide you with the results of the command, as shown in Figure 17-1. The report will alert you to any hardware or software that might not be compatible with Windows 2000. If any potential incompatibilities are identified, you can click the Details button to learn more about the specific incompatibilities. This allows you to change, replace, or remove the hardware or software prior to installing Windows 2000.

Device Manager

Another tool that is included with Windows 2000 and can be used to identify hardware incompatibilities is Device Manager. Device Manager is new to Windows 2000 and can be accessed through the Hardware tab in the System Properties dialog box or from within Computer Management. Device Manager is the tool to use when you know what device is causing you the problem, as it displays all of the installed devices and identifies with a yellow exclamation mark devices that are not functioning correctly, as you can see in Figure 17-2. Exercise 17-1 teaches you the process of opening a device's Properties dialog box to begin troubleshooting the problem.

exam
Watch

The only type of device that is not configurable through Device Manager is a print device. Printers are configured through the Printers dialog box.

FIGURE 17-1

Using the Windows 2000 Readiness Analyzer to test compatibility

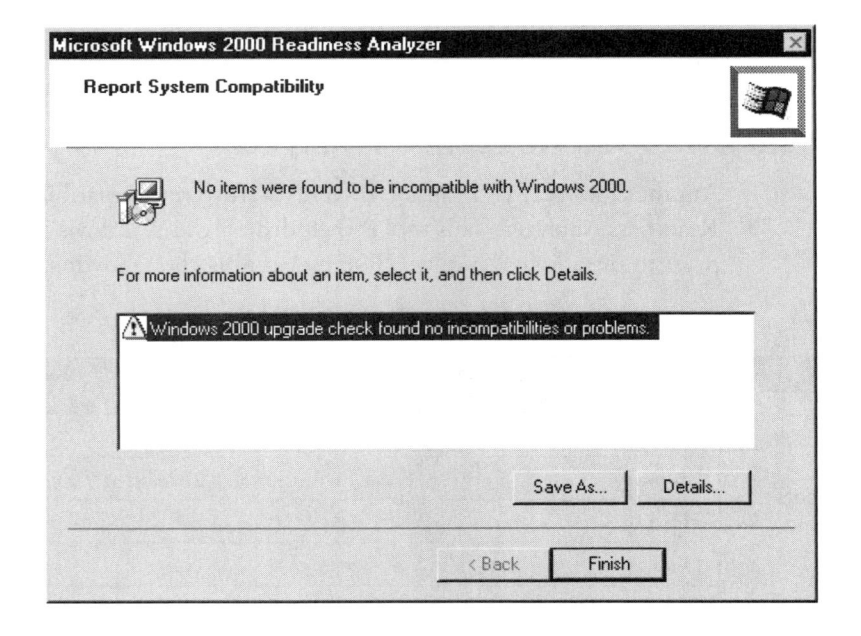

Verifying Hardware Compatibility by Using the Qualifier Tools   **757**

FIGURE 17-2

Identifying nonfunctioning devices in Device Manager

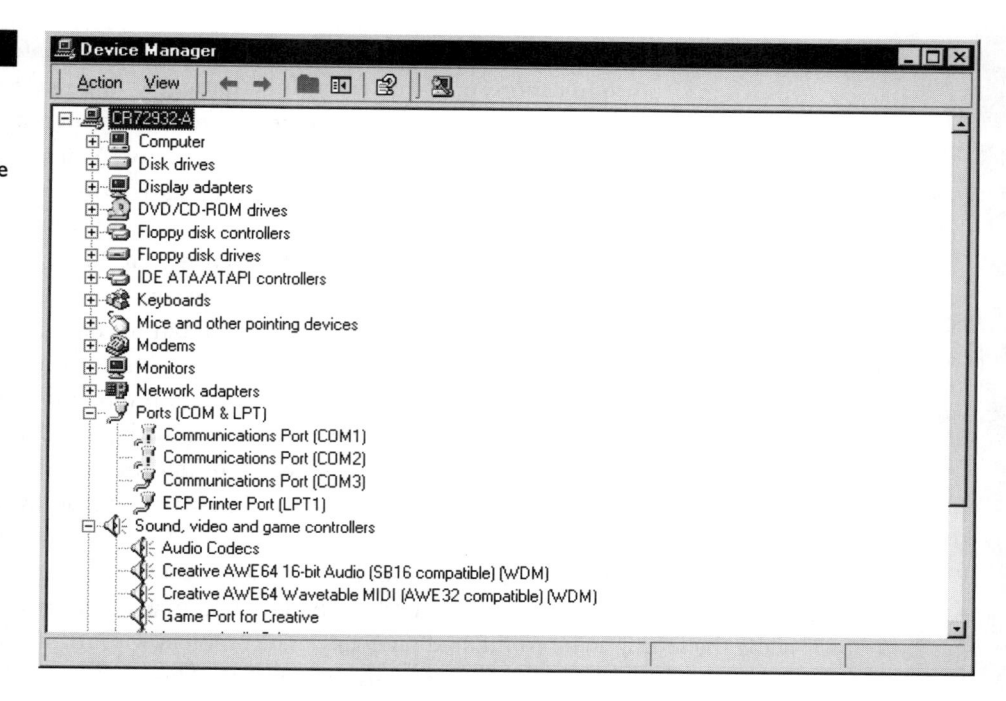

```
Device Manager
Action  View    ←  →    ▣ ▦   ▦

─ 🖳 CR72932-A
  ⊞ 🖳 Computer
  ⊞ 💾 Disk drives
  ⊞ 🖥 Display adapters
  ⊞ 💿 DVD/CD-ROM drives
  ⊞ 💾 Floppy disk controllers
  ⊞ 💾 Floppy disk drives
  ⊞ 💾 IDE ATA/ATAPI controllers
  ⊞ ⌨ Keyboards
  ⊞ 🖱 Mice and other pointing devices
  ⊞ 📞 Modems
  ⊞ 🖥 Monitors
  ⊞ 🖧 Network adapters
  ─ 🜊 Ports (COM & LPT)
      ⚠ Communications Port (COM1)
      ⚠ Communications Port (COM2)
      🜊 Communications Port (COM3)
      🜊 ECP Printer Port (LPT1)
  ─ 🔊 Sound, video and game controllers
      🔊 Audio Codecs
      🔊 Creative AWE64 16-bit Audio (SB16 compatible) (WDM)
      🔊 Creative AWE64 Wavetable MIDI (AWE32 compatible) (WDM)
      🔊 Game Port for Creative
```

EXERCISE 17-1

Opening a Device's Properties Dialog Box in Device Manager

This exercise teaches you how to open a device's Properties dialog box in Device Manager. This is one way in which to troubleshoot a device problem when your device is not functioning properly.

1. Right-click My Computer and click Properties.
2. Click the Hardware tab and click the Device Manager button.
3. Locate the device in Device Manager that is not functioning properly by looking for devices with yellow exclamation marks.

When you double-click a device name that is listed with a yellow exclamation mark in Device Manager, the Properties dialog box of that device or component appears. There are four tabs to this dialog box: General, Port Settings, Driver, and

Resources. The tabs will differ depending on the type of device in question. In this case, it is a communications port that is not functioning, as opposed to a device. On the General tab, shown in Figure 17-3, you are able to quickly identify whether the device is working properly by viewing the Device Status box. You are also able to identify the device type, manufacturer, and location and determine whether the device is enabled or disabled for this profile. In this example it is enabled.

In the case of a communications port, the Port Settings tab allows you to configure the bits per second, data bits, parity, stop bits, and flow control settings. The Driver tab, shown in Figure 17-4, provides you with details about the data provider, driver date, version, and signature. The buttons at the bottom of the Driver tab allow you to see the individual driver files through the Driver Details button, uninstall the device using the Uninstall button, and update the driver using the Update Driver button.

The Resources tab, shown in Figure 17-5, contains information about the resource settings used by the device. These settings are configured automatically for devices and should not be changed unless absolutely necessary. Windows 2000 manages these settings and, in doing so, ensures that conflicts are avoided when new devices are installed. By removing the check mark in the Use Automatic Settings check box, you allow the setting to be configured manually. The problem with manual configuration is that the OS will never change any manual settings. This can be problematic if a new

FIGURE 17-3

Analyzing a device's properties

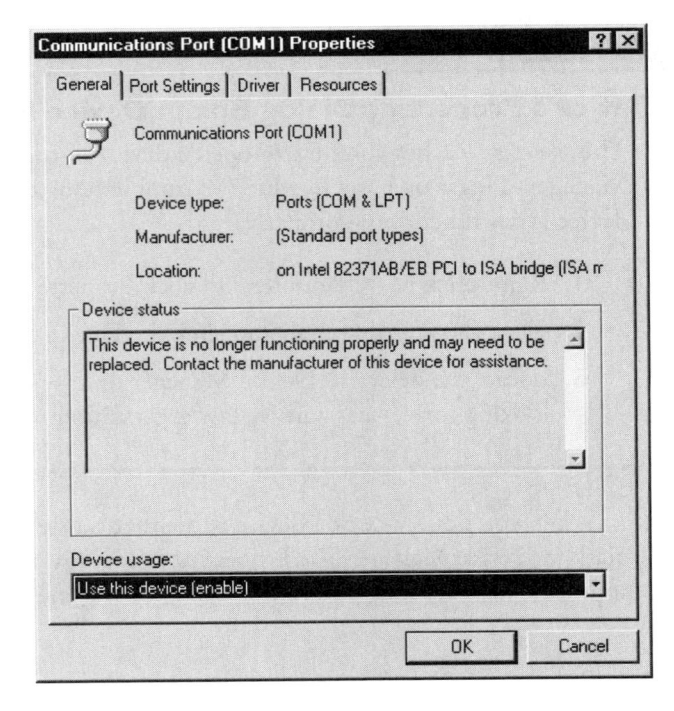

Verifying Hardware Compatibility by Using the Qualifier Tools **759**

FIGURE 17-4

The Driver tab of a device's Properties dialog box

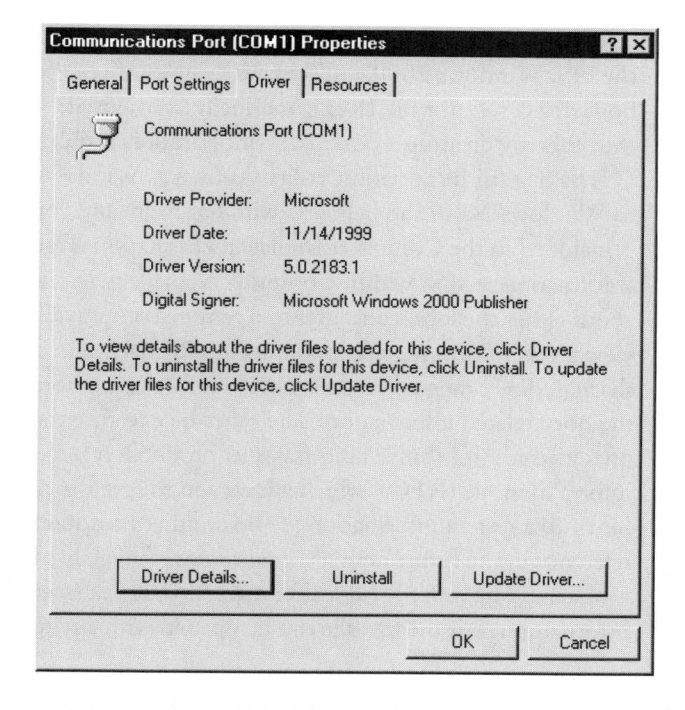

FIGURE 17-5

Configuring the Resources tab for a device

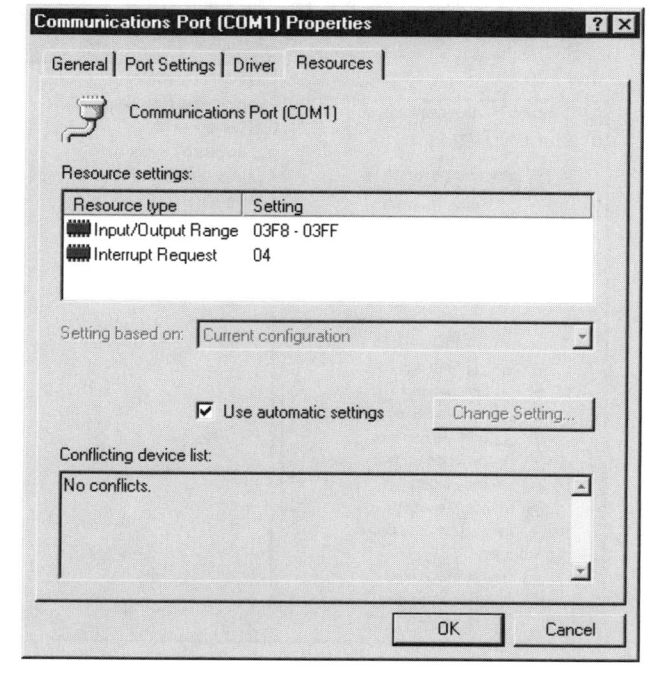

device is installed and it requires the use of a specific IRQ. If that IRQ was assigned by the OS, Windows 2000 could make some configuration changes to accommodate both devices, but if the IRQ is manually configured, Windows 2000 is not able to do this, thereby creating a potential configuration problem.

The System Information utility (known as Windows Diagnostics, or Winmsd, prior to Windows 2000) can help you with hardware and configuration problems. This utility is included in the Computer Management snap-in. Figure 17-6 displays the System Information section within Computer Management and allows you to view information about either the local computer or a remote computer. This allows you to generate and view a system summary or look into specific hardware details, such as IRQ conflicts and sharing, direct memory access (DMA) information, forced hardware, I/O, IRQs, and memory-related information. The other nice feature that can be added to your list of proactive administrative tasks for your production servers is the creation of a system information file (NFO), which allows you to save the computer's configuration to a text file or to a system information file on another computer and can give you a point of reference in the future after a configuration change has begun to cause unexpected problems. The .nfo file extension requires that you open the file using System Information, but the text file can be opened with any text editor.

FIGURE 17-6

Using System Information to identify hardware compatibility

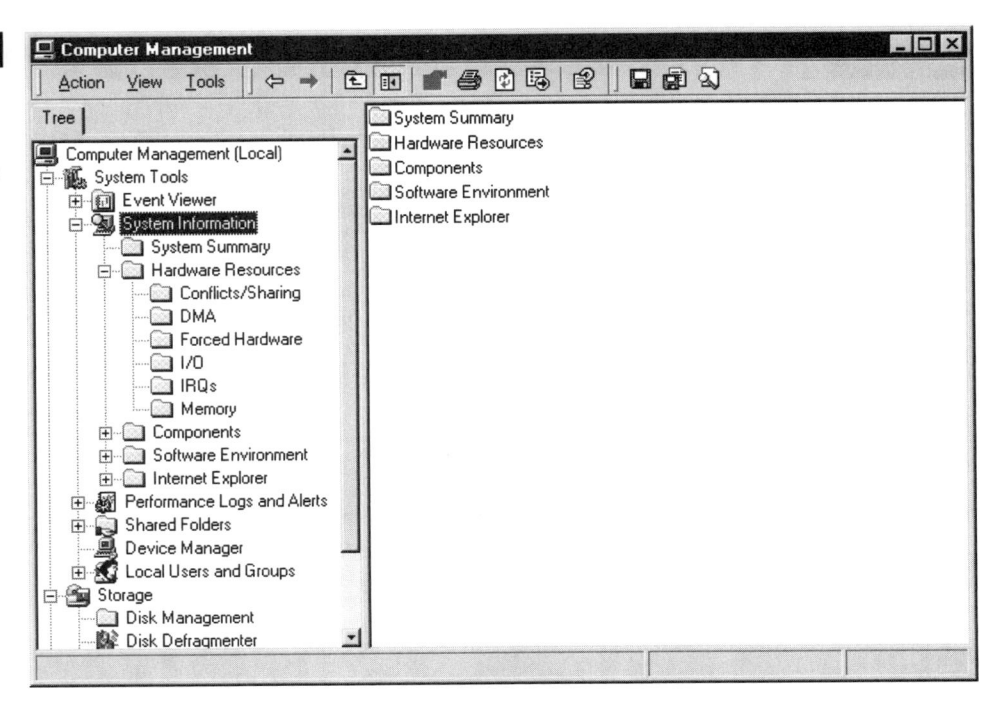

EXERCISE 17-2

Creating a System Information File

This exercise teaches you how to use the System Information utility in Computer Management to generate and save the configuration information of your computer. This information can and should be stored on another computer and can provide you with the functioning configuration information for the computer, which can then be used when troubleshooting in the future.

1. Select Start | Programs | Administrative Tools, and click Computer Management.
2. Expand System Tools and expand System Information.
3. Right-click System Information and click Save As System Information File.
4. In the Save As dialog box, select a location where you wish to save the information, and type a name for the file such as *computername_date*, where *computername* is the name of the computer and *date* is the current date. Click Save.
5. Browse to the location where you selected to save the file using Internet Explorer and double-click the file to open it and view its contents. This file can now be used when the computer begins to experience problems and can provide you with the previous working configuration.

CERTIFICATION OBJECTIVE 17.02

Configuring Driver Signing Options

Drivers are the glue between your OS, applications, and hardware. In a military context, drivers could be likened to officers that give orders to hardware, the front-line soldiers. Applications and the OS are at a higher level, much like generals and admirals who give the orders to the officers who in turn pass those orders on to the soldiers. If the officers fail to pass on the orders from the generals to the soldiers, stop errors (blue screens) result. Drivers allow the OS and applications to talk to hardware. Because of the important role that drivers play, Microsoft has introduced the idea of driver signing in Windows 2000 after its success in Windows 98. Microsoft now signs with its digital signature all drivers that it creates or that it

SCENARIO & SOLUTION

You are responsible for purchasing new computer equipment for your organization. You recently came across a supplier selling 100 video cards at a really good price in an online auction and you want to place a bid. What should you check prior to placing your bid to confirm the video cards will work in your computers running Windows 2000?	You should check the HCL available from the Microsoft site to ensure that the video card is on the list of supported devices, prior to placing your bid.
You are preparing to install Windows 2000 on a number of computers with identical hardware configurations. Prior to installing Windows 2000, you would like to ensure that there are no compatibility issues. What command can you run on one of the computers to avoid potential compatibility issues?	The Windows 2000 Readiness Analyzer can be run using the command **winnt32.exe /checkupgradeonly**. This will alert you to any potential compatibility issues.
You are new to the administration of Windows 2000 and have been asked to look in Device Manager for nonfunctioning devices. What are you looking for?	Device Manager identifies nonfunctioning devices by placing a yellow exclamation mark on the device. The properties of the device can then be accessed by double-clicking the device and accessing the various property tabs.
What major architectural change does Windows 2000 include that makes the installation and configuration of drivers simpler?	The Plug and Play Manager, which provides full support for Plug and Play devices, is the major architectural change included in Windows 2000.

verifies as compatible with the Windows 2000 OS. By digitally signing a driver, Microsoft is guaranteeing that the driver will work with Windows 2000 and that it is free of corruption and viruses. A signed driver is like a stamp of approval for the driver, indicating that it has been tested and confirmed to work on Windows 2000.

on the job

Correlating a specific DLL file by name to a specific application or service can be a difficult task and frustrating when faced with file version conflicts. The DDL Help feature on the Microsoft web site can help you to identify which software installed a specific version of a DLL. Find this handy troubleshooting tool at www.microsoft.com/technet.

Driver signing can be implemented through a number of different means on a computer running Windows 2000. Driver signing can be configured through a local policy, or through a group policy if the computer is a member of a domain. Irregardless of the way in which you implement a driver-signing policy, you have three choices when it comes to how the OS will deal with digitally signed drivers. These three options can be seen in Figure 17-7 and are listed and described next.

FIGURE 17-7

Driver signing options

[Screenshot of Driver Signing Options dialog box with File signature verification options: Ignore, Warn (selected), Block; and Administrator option: Apply setting as system default]

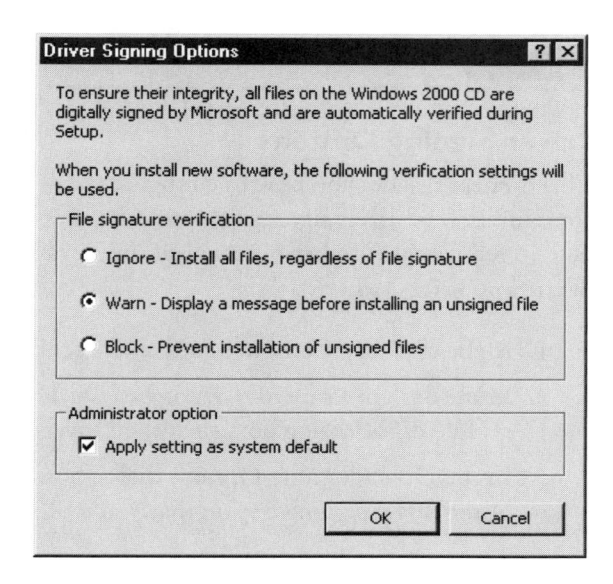

- **Ignore** This option allows any driver file to be installed and does not take into account whether or not the driver is digitally signed. This option is recommended for networks that wish their users to have unrestricted, open access to their computers.

- **Warn** Warning a user by displaying a message before proceeding with the installation of an unsigned driver is the default setting. This option instructs the OS to check the digital signature of the driver as they are installed and warn you if the files are not signed. This provides you with the opportunity to cancel the installation and avoid installing unsigned drivers.

- **Block** This is the most restrictive option and instructs the OS to check the digital signature of the driver and prevent the installation of the driver if it is not signed. This option will ensure that the computer is free of unsigned and possibly corrupt drivers.

exam
⚙atch

Know the three different driver signing options and where and when to use each.

Exercise 17-3 describes how to configure driver signing options on an individual computer and how to configure the settings to prevent other users from changing the driver signing options.

EXERCISE 17-3

Configuring Driver Signing Options

This exercise teaches you how to configure the available driver signing options. The configuration of driver signing options is a preventative administrative task that can help to reduce the number of technical support calls resulting from the installation of corrupt or incorrect drivers.

1. Right-click My Computer and click Properties.
2. In the System Properties dialog box, click the Hardware tab and, in the middle of the dialog box, click the Driver Signing button.
3. In the Driver Signing Options dialog box, click the radio button to the left of the driver signing option that you wish to use.
4. To prevent other users of the computer that are not administrators from overriding your driver signing options, place a check mark in the Apply Setting As System Default check box.
5. Click OK, and click OK again.

Knowing how to configure driver signing options on an individual computer is important, but for the certification exam, and in reality, the focus is more likely to be on driver signing configuration through group policy or local security policy. Another important piece of this puzzle is to known how group policy is applied, as the order of application is critical to determining the effective policy setting.

Group policy can be applied at a number of different levels in the Active Directory logical and physical structure, but it all starts with the local computer policy. The local computer policy is always applied first, but if the computer is a member of an Active Directory domain, group policy can be applied at the site, then the domain, then the OU, and then potentially sub-OU level. The number of OU policies that apply will depend on where the computer object is located in Active Directory. Let's look at an example of this to ensure clarity, as this is something you will have to be comfortable with for the exam.

Let's assume you have an Active Directory structure like that shown in Figure 17-8 and you want to apply a group policy to server1 that prevents unsigned drivers from being installed. Server1 is located in the Finance OU, and according to the way in which GPOs are applied, the settings of the GPO at the Finance OU will be the last

Configuring Driver Signing Options 765

to be applied. This is because the order of GPO application begins with the local computer policy, followed by the site, domain, and OU policies. Therefore, the best place to create the GPO with the setting that prevents unsigned drivers from being installed is at the Finance OU. Also remember that GPO settings are cumulative when they do not conflict, which means that if the local computer policy was configured with the setting to prevent unsigned drivers from being installed, and no other policies had conflicting settings, then that setting would be a part of the effective settings. Exercise 17-4 explains how to configure the setting that prevents unsigned drivers from being installed through local security policy.

exam
Watch

Know that the order of group policy is local, site, domain, and then OU, and that the settings are cumulative unless there is a conflict. In the case of a conflict, the policy setting included in the last-applied group policy is the effective policy setting. Therefore, local computer policy is the most likely to be overridden by policies at other levels.

EXERCISE 17-4

Configuring Driver Signing Options Through Local Security Policy

This exercise teaches you how to configure driver signing options to prevent unsigned drivers from being installed through local security policy. This is a fundamental administrative task that you are likely to perform in a network with multiple computers running Windows 2000.

FIGURE 17-8

Example Active Directory structure

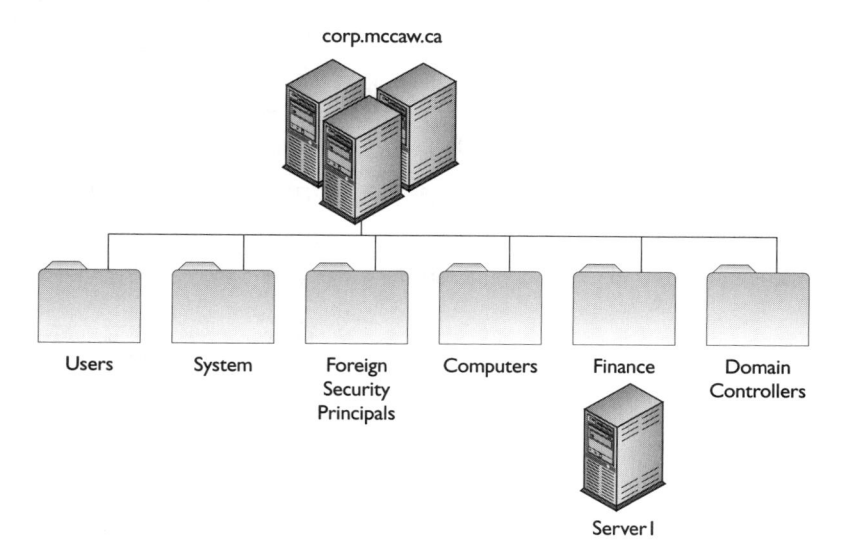

1. Select Start | Programs | Administrative Tools, and click Local Security Policy.
2. In the Local Security Policy dialog box, expand Local Policies and click Security Options. In the display pane, scroll to the bottom of the list of security options, where you will find the Unsigned Driver Installation Behavior and Unsigned Non-Driver Installation Behavior options.

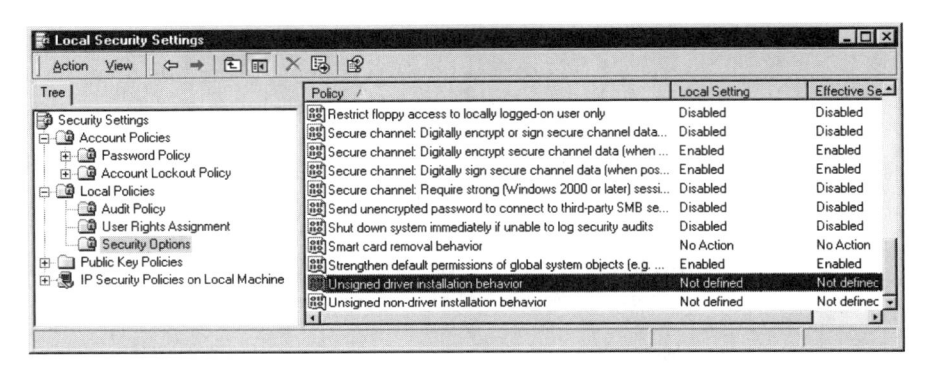

3. To prevent unsigned drivers from being installed on the computer, double-click Unsigned Driver Installation Behavior and, in the Local Policy Setting drop-down box, select Do Not Allow Installation and then click OK. Notice how you are even warned in the dialog box that domain-level policy settings will override these settings if they are defined.

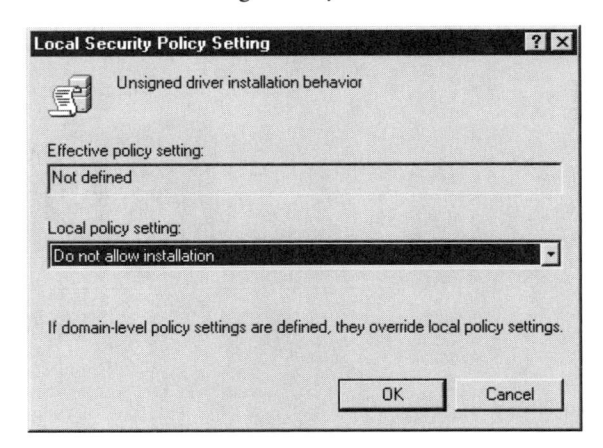

4. Repeat Step 3 for the Unsigned Non-Driver Installation Behavior setting if you wish to configure that, and then close the Local Security Settings dialog box.

The default computer policy settings that make up your computer's effective policy immediately after installation are a result of the settings in the policy templates included with Windows 2000. These built-in policy templates each have unique policy settings, which are beyond the scope of this chapter. What you should know, however, for the exam is that only three security policy templates (hisecws.inf, hisecdc.inf, and securedc.inf) don't allow the installation of unsigned drivers.

exam
🕲 **a t c h**

If a computer is configured with a high-security policy template, you will be prevented from installing unsigned device drivers.

Now that you are familiar with the process of configuring digital signatures, we will shift our focus to the verification of digital signatures.

CERTIFICATION OBJECTIVE 17.03

Verifying Digital Signatures on Existing Driver Files

There are a number of ways available to you to determine if driver signing is enabled on the computer. Oftentimes, it is only during the installation of a device that uses an unsigned driver that you realize that the current driver signing setting prevents you from installing the driver. In this case, the Digital Signature Not Found dialog box will appear, as shown in Figure 17-9, and the option to install the unsigned driver is not available, which prevents it from being installed. If the driver signing options are set to Warn, you will also receive the Digital Signature Not Found dialog box, shown

FIGURE 17-9

The Digital Signature warning that you cannot ignore

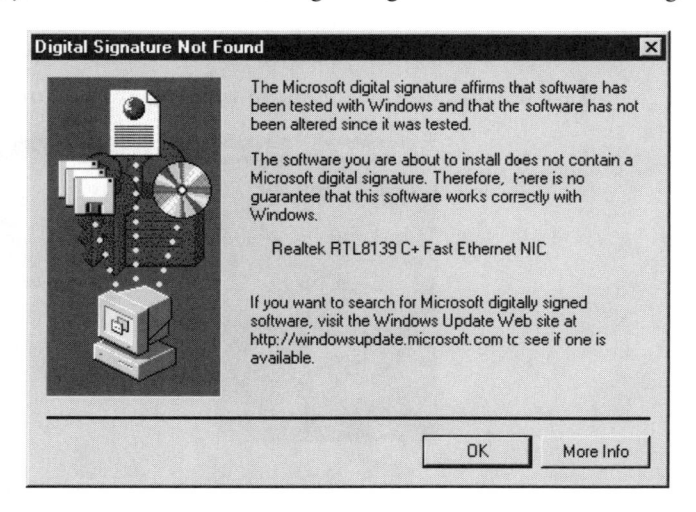

FIGURE 17-10

The Digital Signature warning that you can choose to ignore

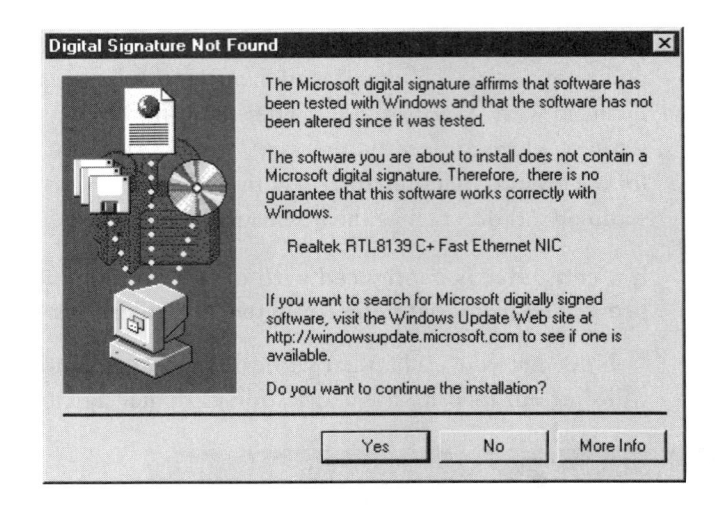

in Figure 17-10, but because the setting is Warn, you are able to click Yes to continue the installation anyway. The File Signature Verification tool can be used to identify unsigned files on the computer and view information about the files, such as the files' name, location, modification date, type, and version number.

EXERCISE 17-5

Using Sigverif.exe

This exercise teaches you how to use the File Signature Verification tool to identify unsigned files on your computer and view the following information about them:

1. Click Start | Run, type **sigverif**, and click OK.
2. Click the Advanced button in the File Signature Verification dialog box.

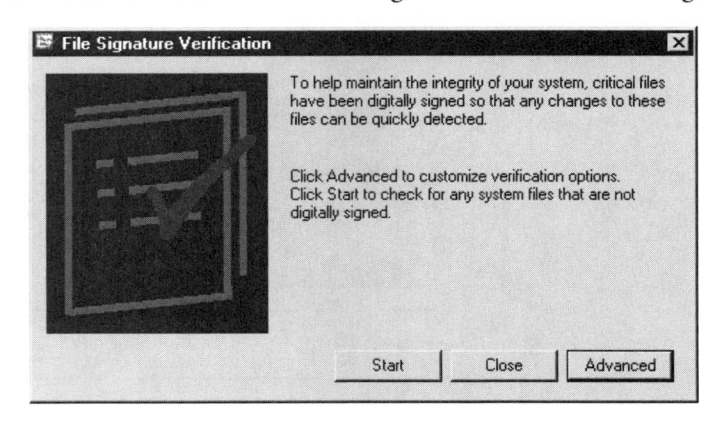

3. In the Advanced File Signature Verification Settings dialog box, choose between the default Notify Me If Any System Files Are Not Signed option and the Look For Other Files That Are Not Digitally Signed, define the search options and the folders in which you wish to look, and click OK.

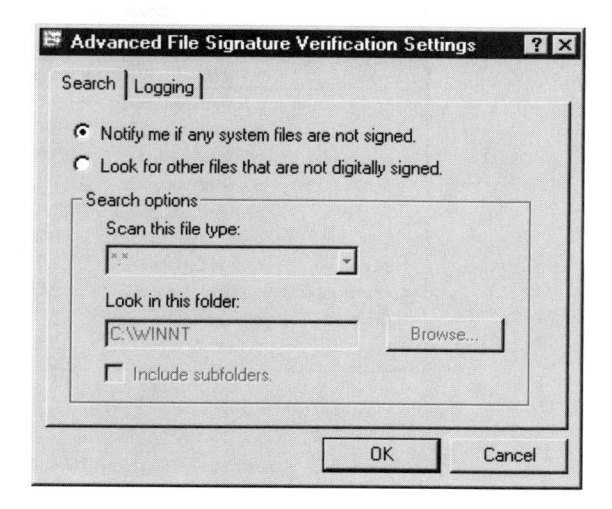

4. Clicking the Logging tab shows the default logging configuration, which is set to save the file signature verification results to a log file named sigverif.txt and overwrite any existing log file should one exist. This file is stored in the %systemroot% directory. Click OK, and then click Start in the main dialog box.

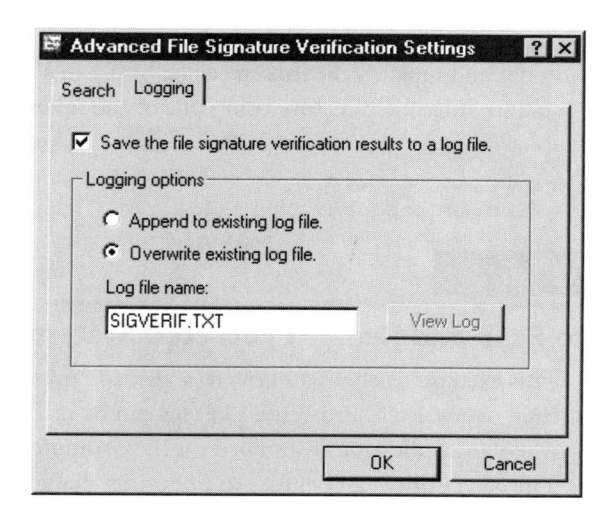

5. Once sigverif has completed its search, the results are displayed, which show the files installed on the local computer that have not been digitally signed.

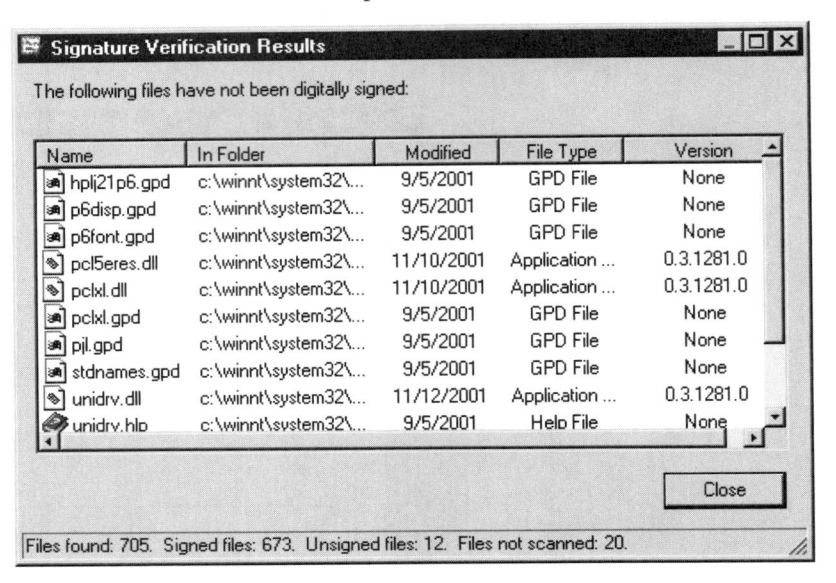

6. Click Close and click Close again.

The System File Checker (Sfc.exe) is another tool available to check for and verify the versions of all protected OS files. This tool requires that you are logged on as a member of the Administrators group. If SFC finds that a protected OS file has been overwritten, it retrieves the correct version from the %systemroot%\system32\dllcache folder and replaces the incorrect file. SFC can also be used to repair the contents of a corrupt dllcache directory using one of the following three commands:

```
Sfc /scannow
Sfc /scanonce
Sfc /scanboot
```

EXERCISE 17-6

Using SFC to Scan and Repair Protected System Files

This exercise teaches you how to scan and replace any protected OS files that have been overwritten. Protected OS files can be inadvertently or intentionally overwritten when an application is installed on the computer. This can result in system instability. The SFC utility can be used to undo this change.

Configuring Operating System Support for Legacy Hardware Devices **771**

1. Click Start | Run, and type **cmd**.

2. At the command prompt, type **sfc /scannow** and press ENTER. This opens the Windows File Protection dialog box. The scanning process can take a few minutes.

   ![Windows File Protection dialog: Please wait while Windows verifies that all protected Windows files are intact and in their original versions. Cancel button.]

3. You may be prompted to insert your Windows 2000 CD to allow Windows File Protection to copy over the required files to the DLL Cache directory. Insert the appropriate CD and click Retry.

on the job

If you receive a message prompting you for the Windows 2000 CD and SFC doesn't like the CD when you click Retry, I strongly suggest that you type sfc /cancel at the command prompt and use Task Manager to end the SFC application. Otherwise, you are likely to find yourself with a frozen and nonfunctioning system upon reboot. This problem can occur when a service pack has been applied to the computer and the CD you have supplied does not include the newer service pack files streamlined into the OS files.

CERTIFICATION OBJECTIVE 17.04

Configuring Operating System Support for Legacy Hardware Devices

Windows 2000 will not detect many legacy devices through a hardware scan using Device Manager. Any device that is not detected must be installed and configured manually. Legacy hardware devices cannot be installed using Device Manager; they must be installed using the Add/Remove Hardware Wizard, found in Control Panel. Device Manager will only allow you to configure those devices that have already been installed.

Legacy devices can be manually installed through the Hardware tab of the System Properties dialog box. Exercise 17-7 explains this process.

SCENARIO & SOLUTION

What options do you have to implement driver signing?	Driver signing can be configured a number of different ways. It can be configured on the local computer through the System icon, or through the Local Security Policy snap-in. It can also be configured through group policy at the site, domain, or OU level.
You would like to configure driver signing options on an individual computer to prevent all users from installing any unsigned drivers. What steps must you perform?	To prevent all users from installing any unsigned drivers, you must configure the Block driver signing option while logged on as a member of the Administrators account. You must also place a check mark in the Apply Setting As System Default box, which prevents other users from changing the driver signing options. Only members of the Administrators group are able to change this setting.
What are the three driver signing options available to you and what is each intended to do? Which option is the default in Windows 2000?	The Ignore option allows you to configure a computer to install all drivers and disregard digital signatures. The Warn option is the default in Windows 2000 and warns the user when it detects an unsigned driver is about to be installed. The user is still able to proceed with the installation but they are warned. The Block option is intended for computers on which you do not want unsigned drivers to be installed. The Block option prevents all unsigned drivers from being installed and jeopardizing the stability of the computer.
You are evaluating the use of different built-in security templates on a number of your production servers. Which templates include default settings that prevent the installation of unsigned drivers?	Three built-in security templates include default settings that prevent the installation of unsigned drivers. These are the hisecws.inf, hisecdc.inf, and securedc.inf templates.

EXERCISE 17-7

Installing a Legacy Device Through the System Properties Dialog Box

This exercise teaches you how to install legacy devices using the System Properties dialog box. Non-Plug and Play devices are considered to be legacy, and these are the devices that cannot be installed through Device Manager.

1. Right-click My Computer and click Properties. Alternatively, you can select Start | Settings | Control Panel and double-click the System icon.

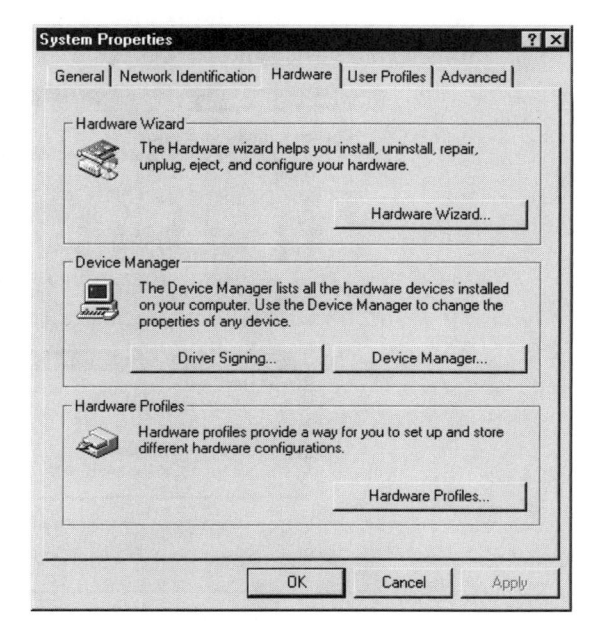

2. Click the Hardware tab and click the Hardware Wizard button.

3. When the Welcome screen of the Add/Remove Hardware Wizard opens, click Next.

4. On the Choose A Hardware Task page, leave the default option Add/Troubleshoot A Device selected and click Next.

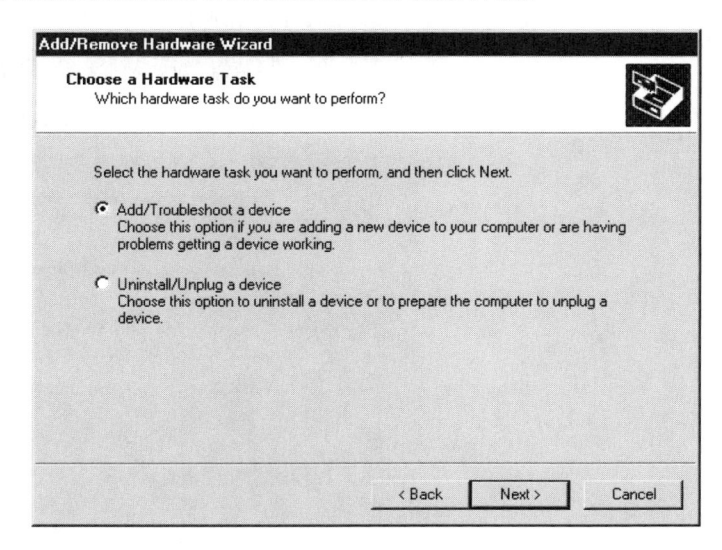

5. The search for new hardware takes place and a list of detected devices appears on the Choose A Hardware Device page. Select Add A New Device to add an undetected device and click Next.

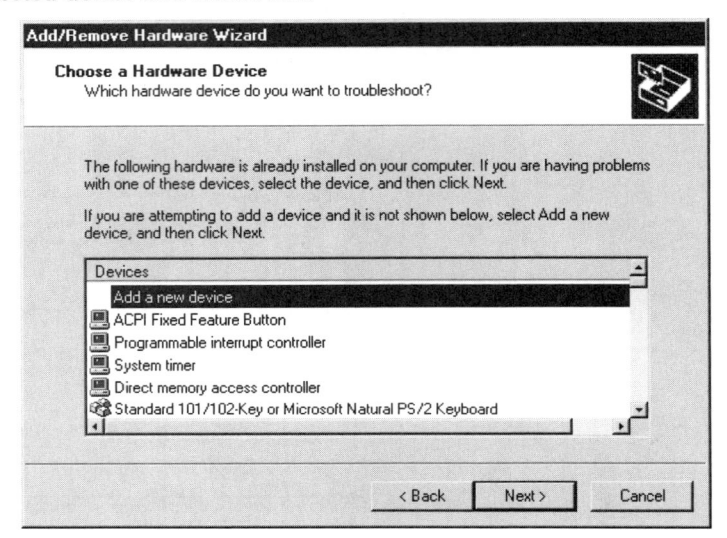

6. On the Find New Hardware screen, you can choose between two options. Yes, Search For New Hardware instructs Windows 2000 to try to detect non-Plug and Play devices. Generally, it is recommended to allow Windows 2000 to detect the hardware, but when you know that the device in question is not going to be detected, you can select the second option, No, I Want To Select The Hardware From A List.

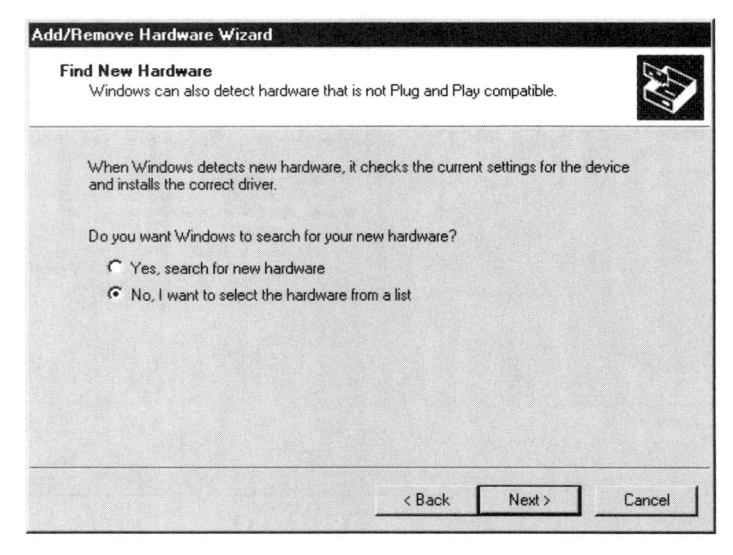

Configuring Operating System Support for Legacy Hardware Devices **775**

7. If you do select Yes on the Find New Hardware screen, the New Hardware Detection page appears. This process can take a couple of minutes.

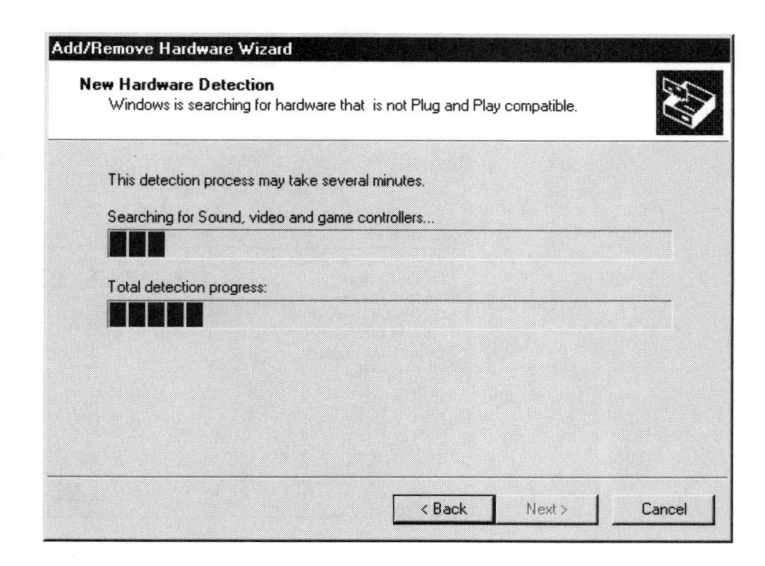

8. If no hardware device is detected, you have the option of manually installing the device on the Hardware Type page. Select the category of device you wish to install from the list of possible device categories and click Next.

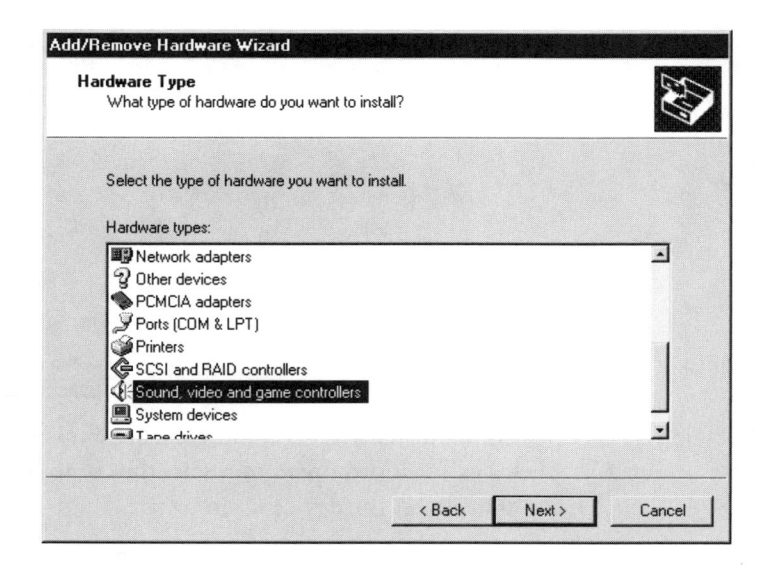

9. On the Select A Device Driver page, select a manufacturer and model for the device you are installing, and click Next.

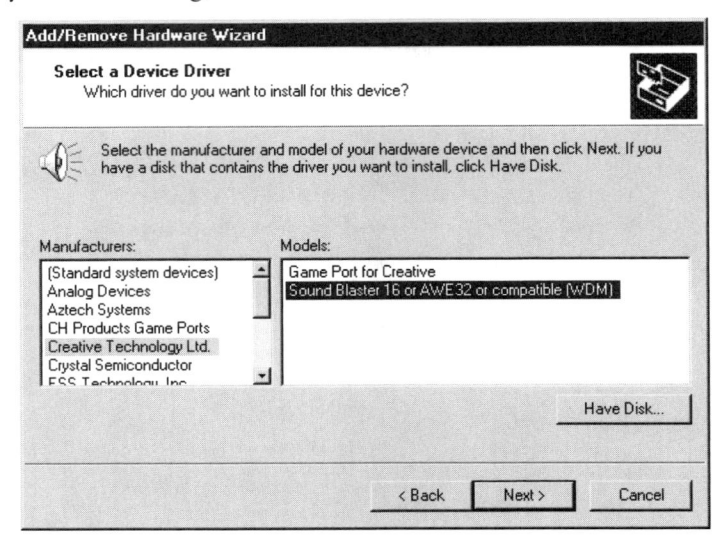

10. On the Start Hardware Installation page, confirm that the correct device is selected, and click Next.

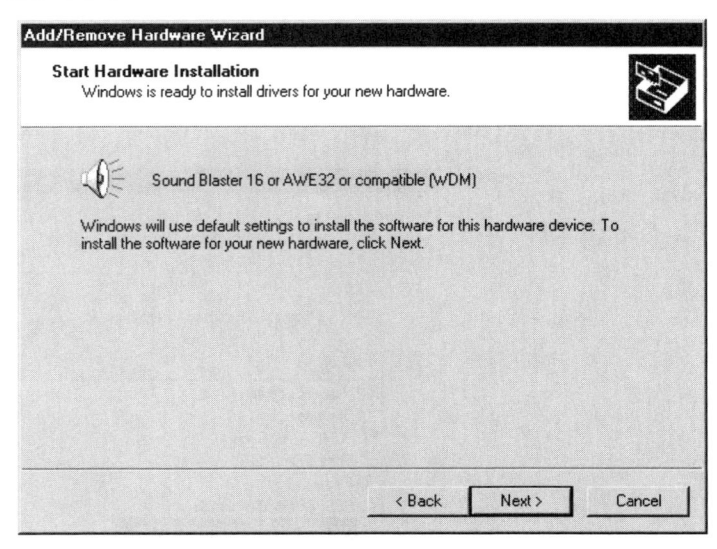

11. When the installation is complete, click Finish to complete the wizard and click Yes when prompted to restart the computer. This will allow Windows 2000 to detect the device upon restart.

FROM THE CLASSROOM

The enhanced architecture of Windows 2000, and in particular its new and improved Plug and Play Manager, has helped to simplify the lives of many administrators. However, with every new advantage often comes an associated disadvantage. In the case of Plug and Play, the disadvantage is that now any user can install Plug and Play hardware devices on their computer and Windows 2000 will automatically detect the devices and configure them.

In more restrictive corporate networks, you may want to prevent this default functionality and require that users have Administrator privileges in Windows 2000 to add new hardware. In order for a device to automatically install in the System context, the following four criteria must be met. If any of these criteria are not met, the device installation will be forced to occur in the User context, which requires administrative permissions.

- A user interface must not be required for the driver installation
- The computer must contain all the driver files (found in driver.cab)
- The driver package must be digitally signed
- The first pass of the installation must return no errors

To prevent automatic installation of hardware, you must ensure that at least one of the preceding criteria cannot be met. The easiest way to accomplish this is to delete the driver.cab file, which is stored in %systemroot%\driver cache\i386. When Windows 2000 determines that the driver.cab file is not available, the device installation will be forced out of the system context and into the user context. In the user context, only members of the local Administrators group have permission to install hardware.

—*Rory McCaw*

CERTIFICATION SUMMARY

In this chapter, you have learned about a number of different ways to verify hardware compatibility by using the HCL or running the Windows 2000 Readiness Analyzer. You learned about the two different architectural modes, user mode and kernel mode, and the benefits of a multitiered architecture. This chapter also taught you what the minimum hardware requirements are for Windows 2000, which is important information for the exam, but I strongly encourage you not to ever build your system configurations based on the minimum requirements. Two new tools that you also learned about in this chapter are Device Manager and System Information, both of which can be used to identify hardware and configuration information. You learned about the benefits of creating a system information file and how this file can be useful when troubleshooting system problems.

Driver signing is yet another new feature that you learned about. We covered the three driver signing options: Ignore, Warn (the default), and Block. You learned how to configure these driver signing options on a local computer through both the System icon and the Local Security Policy snap-in, and how they can be applied through group policy at the site, domain, and OU levels. You were also introduced to the built-in security templates and learned which three templates include default settings that block unsigned drivers.

With an understanding of driver signing configuration under your belt, we shifted our focus to the verification of digital signatures. Here you learned about both the File Signature Verification tool and the System File Checker utility.

This chapter concluded with a look at configuring legacy devices in Windows 2000. You learned that older devices that are not detected by the operating system must be installed through Add/Remove Hardware as opposed to Device Manager.

✓ TWO-MINUTE DRILL

Verifying Hardware Compatibility by Using the Qualifier Tools

- ❑ All components must meet the minimum requirements for Windows 2000 and must be on the Hardware Compatibility List to be supported.
- ❑ The Windows 2000 Readiness Analyzer can be used to determine incompatible hardware and software prior to installing Windows 2000. This tool is run through the command **winnt32.exe /checkupgradeonly**.
- ❑ Device Manager is new to Windows 2000 and can be used to verify hardware compatibility. Nonfunctioning devices are identified with a yellow exclamation mark in Device Manager.
- ❑ Manually configuring a device's resource usage through the device's properties in Device Manager prevents Windows 2000 from changing that resource allocation and can lead to resource conflicts in the future.
- ❑ Printers are the only devices that are not configurable through Device Manager.
- ❑ The System Information utility replaces winmsd.exe and provides you with a view of configuration and diagnostic information and allows you to save a computer's system information to either an NFO or TXT file.

Configuring Driver Signing Options

- ❑ Driver signing is a new feature of Windows 2000 that allows you to restrict driver installation to only files that have been digitally signed by a trusted party such as Microsoft.
- ❑ The three driver signing options are Ignore, Warn, and Block. Ignore allows unsigned drivers to be installed. Warn warns you that you are about to install an unsigned driver, giving you the option to cancel the installation. Block prevents you from installing unsigned drivers.
- ❑ Driver signing can be configured in the local security policy, or at the site, domain, or OU levels. Group policy is also applied in a predefined order, starting with local computer policy, then site, domain, and OU policy. Policy settings are cumulative unless there is a conflict, in which case the last applied policy setting becomes the effective setting.

- When configuring the local computer's driver signing options through the System icon, enabling the Apply Setting As System Default option ensures that the driver signing option you select applies to all users, not just to the currently logged on user.
- Only the high-security policy templates include policy settings that prevent the installation of unsigned drivers. To install an unsigned driver on a computer configured with the High Security template, a less-secure template must be applied, the driver installed, and then the High Security template reapplied to the computer.

Verifying Digital Signatures on Existing Driver Files

- The default driver signing option in Windows 2000 is to warn when a user attempts to install an unsigned driver. This warning message will pop up and alert the user that the driver they are attempting to install is unsigned but will still allow the user to proceed with the installation. If the driver signing option is set to Block, the user will be warned and will not be able to install the unsigned driver.
- The Window File Signature Verification tool (sigverif.exe) can also be used to detect the signed state of both system and driver files.
- The System File Checker tool can also be used to scan and verify the versions of all protected operating system files, but make sure before you run SFC that you have a CD with the operating system and latest service pack. Without one, do *not* run this utility, as it may cause your system to freeze.

Configuring Operating System Support for Legacy Hardware Devices

- Older, non-Plug and Play devices may not be detected automatically by Windows 2000. When this occurs, the device must be installed manually using the Add/Remove Hardware Wizard.
- All users are capable of installing devices that require no manual intervention. It is only when manual intervention is required that the user installing the device must be a member of the Administrators group.

SELF TEST

The following questions will help you measure your understanding of the material presented in this chapter. Read the questions and answers carefully, and be aware that some questions will provide for more than one correct answer. Choose all correct answers for each question.

Verifying Hardware Compatibility by Using the Qualifier Tools

1. Which of the following commands can you run to tell you if any of the hardware or software on a computer running Windows NT 4 isn't compatible with Windows 2000?

    A. innt32.exe /checkupgrade

    B. winnt32.exe /checkupgradeonly

    C. winnt.exe /hcl

    D. winnt32.exe /hcl

    E. winnt.exe /checkupgradeonly

2. You are responsible for purchasing 250 new desktop computers that will have Windows 2000 installed on them. You want to ensure that the computers are fully compatible and thus have asked all interested suppliers to send you a detailed list of the hardware components that will be used in the configuration of the computers. What should you compare this list of components to?

    A. The report generated by the Windows Readiness Analyzer tool

    B. The HCL

    C. The Windows 2000 licensing requirements

    D. The Windows 2000 certified applications list

3. You are the administrator of multiple computers in your network. You are currently logged on at your computer running Windows 2000 Professional and you would like to view the system information of a Windows 2000 Server remotely. You currently have the Computer Management snap-in open, as shown in Figure 17-11. Which of the following actions will allow you to accomplish this?

    A. Right-click System Information and click Connect To Another Computer. In the Select Computer dialog box, type the name of the remote computer and click OK.

    B. Right-click Hardware Resources and click Connect To Another Computer. In the Select Computer dialog box, type the name of the remote computer and click OK.

    C. Right-click System Tools and click Connect To Another Computer. In the Select Computer dialog box, type the name of the remote computer and click OK.

FIGURE 17-11

Computer Management Snap-in

[Screenshot of Computer Management console showing tree with System Tools (Event Viewer, System Information with System Summary, Hardware Resources, Components, Software Environment, Internet Explorer), Performance Logs and Alerts, Shared Folders, Device Manager, Local Users and Groups, Storage, and Services and Applications]

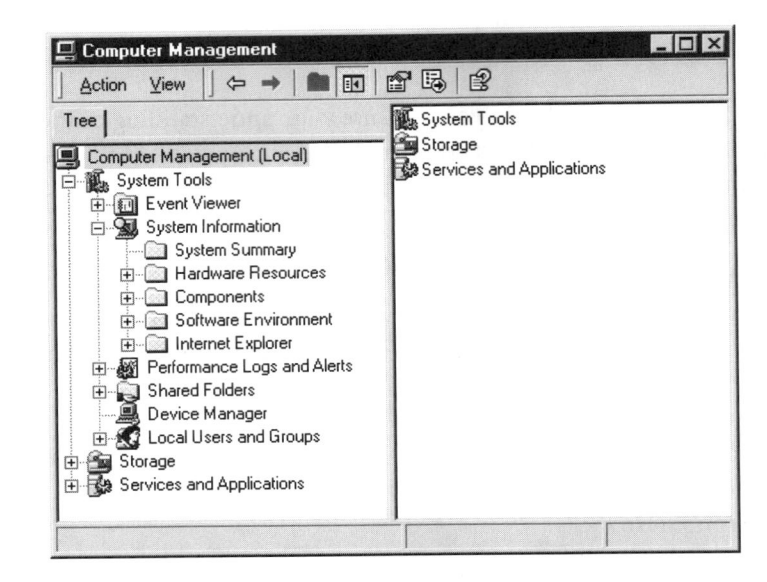

   D. Right-click Computer Management and click Connect To Another Computer. In the Select Computer dialog box, type the name of the remote computer and click OK.

   E. Only the local computer can be managed using the default Computer Management snap-in. To remotely manage a computer, an empty MMC must be opened and the Computer Management snap-in added in.

4. Which of the following are not configurable through Device Manager?

   A. Network adapters

   B. Video cards

   C. Printers

   D. Modems

5. As the administrator of a number of computers running Windows 2000, you have proactively created a system information file for each of the production servers from the System Information utility within Computer Management. You performed this procedure remotely by changing the focus of the snap-in to each of the remote computers in an effort to improve your efficiency. What type of file extension will this file have?

   A. .sif

   B. .txt

   C. .nfo

   D. .udf

Configuring Driver Signing Options

6. You manage a Windows 2000–based network. You have applied the hisecws.inf template to all of the computers running Windows 2000 Professional. One of the users you work with is having problems with a video driver. An old driver was installed and is not working properly. A newer driver is available, but it is unsigned. Which of the following can you do to fix the driver problem?

   A. Install the updated driver, and when the operating system warns you that the driver is unsigned, click OK, and proceed with the installation.
   B. Change the security template on the computer to securews.inf. Update the driver. Then reinstall the hisecws.inf template.
   C. Run sigverif. Then update the driver.
   D. Enable driver signing. Then update the driver.

7. You are the administrator of a Windows 2000–based network. Your organization has a fairly wide-open, unrestrictive policy when it comes to users being able to install and uninstall applications and hardware components. One of your users abuses this unrestrictive policy and on an ongoing basis installs unsigned drivers that cause him problems and require you to assist in the troubleshooting and reconfiguration of his computer. His computer is located in the Finance OU, which is found directly under the domain. You have logged on to his computer and selected the driver signing option shown in Figure 17-12, but somehow the user is still able to install unsigned drivers. What is the most likely cause of the problem?

   A. A policy setting at the domain level is overriding the local policy setting.
   B. A policy setting at the OU level is overriding the local policy setting.

FIGURE 17-12

Driver Signing Options

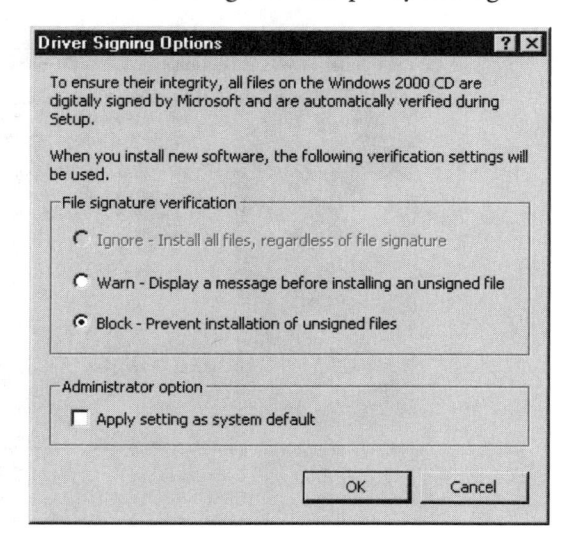

C. The driver signing options you have configured are only valid for your account on the user's computer.

D. The user is disabling the driver signing with the sigverif.exe utility prior to installing unsigned drivers.

8. Which of the following built-in security templates have the driver installation behavior settings set to block by default? (Choose all that apply.)

   A. compatws.inf
   B. hisecws.inf
   C. securedc.inf
   D. ocfiless.inf
   E. securews.inf

9. You are the administrator of a computer running Windows 2000 Server. One of the two network cards has been giving you problems in the computer. You have found an updated driver for the network card on the Internet but it is a beta release. When you attempt to install the driver, you receive the following warning, as shown in Figure 17-13. What must you do to install the driver?

   A. Apply the latest service pack to allow beta drivers to be installed.
   B. Click the More Info button and then click Proceed to continue with the installation.
   C. Click OK and change the driver signing options to Warn from Block.
   D. Click OK and reboot the computer in Safe Mode With Networking and install the driver.

FIGURE 17-13

The Driver Signing Warning dialog box

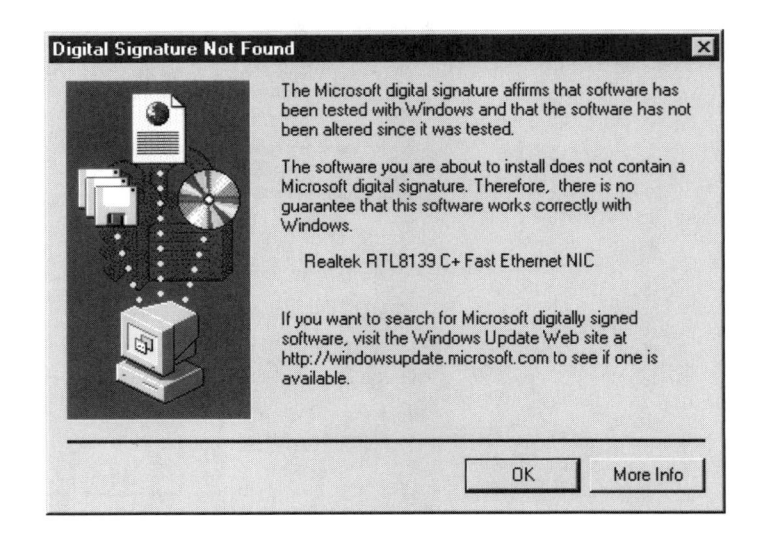

Self Test   785

10. You are the administrator of a computer that is located in the Toronto site. The computer is a member of the canada.corp.mccaw.ca domain and is logically located in the Server OU, which in turn is in the Floor7 OU. The Floor7 OU is located within the root of the canada domain. There are a number of GPOs in place throughout the logical and physical structure. The GPOs at the site and corp domain levels both prevent the installation of unsigned drivers. The GPOs at the canada domain and Server OU level do not include a setting for driver signing. What is the effective driver signing option for the computer you are a member of and where does the setting come from?

   A. The computer's effective driver signing policy will be to prevent the installation of unsigned drivers. This setting will be derived from the site policy.

   B. The computer's effective driver signing policy will be to prevent the installation of unsigned drivers. This setting will be derived from the corp domain policy.

   C. The computer's effective driver signing policy will be to allow the installation of unsigned drivers. This setting will be derived from the Server OU policy.

   D. The computer's effective driver signing policy will be to allow the installation of unsigned drivers. This setting will be derived from the computer's local policy.

Verifying Digital Signatures on Existing Driver Files

11. You are attempting to install an updated driver for a newly purchased device and you receive the following warning dialog box, as shown in Figure 17-14. What is the most likely reason you are receiving this message?

    A. The driver signing properties are set to Ignore.

    B. The driver signing properties are set to Block.

FIGURE 17-14

The Digital Signature Not Found dialog box

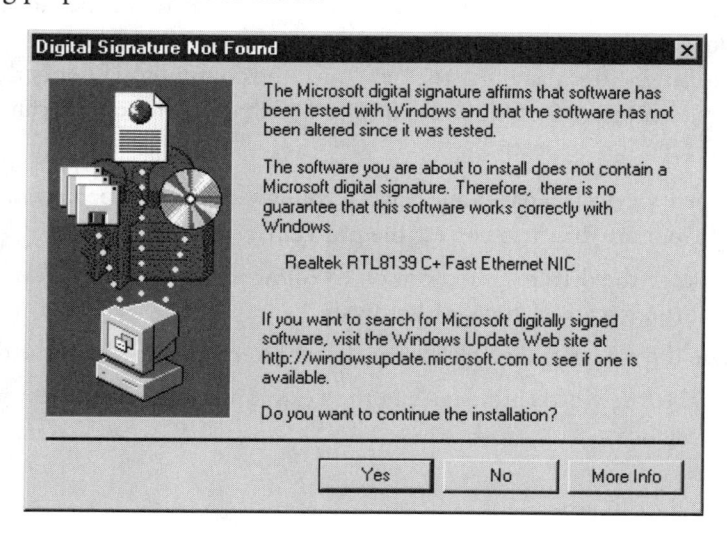

C. The driver signing properties are set to Prevent.

D. The driver signing properties are set to Warn.

12. Which of the following utilities can you use to verify the signed or unsigned state of existing files and save that information to a text file?

    A. Sigverif.exe

    B. Windows 2000 Readiness Analyzer

    C. SFC

    D. Winver.exe

13. You are the administrator of a number of computers running Windows 2000. All of the computers are configured with the default driver signing configuration. You are about to upgrade the drivers for the network cards on some of the computers. Which one of the following tools are you most likely to use to accomplish this task?

    A. Add/Remove Hardware

    B. System Information

    C. Add/Remove Programs

    D. Device Manager

Configuring Operating System Support for Legacy Hardware Devices

14. You are the administrator of a computer running Windows 2000 that is experiencing video problems. You have determined that the problem relates to the video card and have replaced the video card with an older ISA card you had in an older Pentium I computer that you are no longer using. After installing the new card, the computer will only display 16 colors and only appears to support 640×480 resolution. Which of the following can you do to get the video card to function correctly?

    A. Open Device Manager and have Windows 2000 scan for new hardware, and locate the appropriate driver to correct the problem.

    B. Change the driver signing option to Allow for the installation of older, unsigned drivers and run a scan for the new hardware.

    C. Use the Add/Remove Hardware Wizard to manually install the drivers for the device.

    D. Enable the video card device in the default hardware profile through the System Properties dialog box.

15. What can you do to ensure that only administrators are able to install new hardware devices?
    A. In the Local Security Policy, edit the User Rights Assignment and remove the Users group from the Allow PnP Hardware Install policy.
    B. In the Local Security Policy, edit the User Rights Assignment and remove the Everyone group from the Allow PnP Hardware Install policy.
    C. Delete the driver.cab file in %systemroot%\system32\drivers.
    D. Delete the driver.cab file in %systemroot%\driver cache\i386.

LAB QUESTION

You are the administrator of a large corporate network. You are responsible for managing a number of other administrators and coordinating the purchasing of new equipment. You have recently begun accepting bids for 1,000 new desktop computers that your organization is looking to lease for a period of two years. Once a vendor has been selected and the computers have arrived, Windows 2000 will be installed on all the computers. One of the requirements of the tender is to provide a sample computer with the identical hardware configuration of the computers that you will be providing. Four vendors have each couriered over their own configurations and all computers currently have Windows Me installed on them.

You organization has migrated all of its servers to Active Directory and created an empty forest root domain and single child domain that contains all the user and computer accounts. Your organization has a single location, and the plan is to create an OU named Desktops and create all the computer accounts in the Desktops OU. Also part of the plan is to use group policy to restrict the users' ability to install unsigned drivers. You would also like to restrict the ability for any user other than members of the Administrators group to be able to install any hardware device, regardless of Plug and Play compatibility. You also have a small group of users that run an older software application. The application requires support for some older devices that are not Plug and Play compatible but are supported in Windows 2000.

Answer the following questions to help formulate your plan for the new computers that are to run Windows 2000:

1. You would like one of the administrators in your group to test the hardware to ensure that it is compatible with Windows 2000. What options are available for testing for compatibility?
2. Where in the Active Directory structure will you create the GPO with the policy setting that blocks the installation of unsigned drivers?
3. How will you restrict hardware device installation to only members of the Administrators group?
4. Describe the process of installing the older devices in Windows 2000.

788 Chapter 17: Installing and Configuring Server and Client Hardware

SELF TEST ANSWERS

Verifying Hardware Compatibility by Using the Qualifier Tools

1. ☑ **B** is correct. The **winnt32.exe /checkupgradeonly** command can be run on any computer running Windows NT 4 or Windows 9*x* to identify any incompatible hardware or software on the computer without performing an installation of Windows 2000.
   ☒ **A** is incorrect because the **winnt32.exe /checkupgrade** command will not perform a compatibility test.
   ☒ **C** and **D** are incorrect because neither the winnt.exe command nor the winnt32.exe command has an /hcl switch.
   ☒ **E** is incorrect because the **winnt.exe** command does not include a /checkupgradeonly switch.

2. ☑ **B** is correct. The Hardware Compatibility List (HCL) is the list of certified hardware components published by Microsoft. This is the list that you should compare each vendor's components against.
   ☒ **A** is incorrect because the Windows 2000 Readiness Analyzer tool will only create a list of incompatible hardware devices and software applications if run on the local computer. With only a list of the components and no physical computer, you would not be able to run this command.
   ☒ **C** is incorrect because the Windows 2000 licensing requirements have no direct correlation to hardware for a desktop computer.
   ☒ **D** is incorrect because the list of certified applications would not reflect whether or not the hardware would be compatible.

3. ☑ **D** is correct. Right-clicking Computer Management and clicking Connect To Another Computer allows you to type the name of the remote computer in the Select Computer dialog box and click OK. This allows you to remotely view the system information on another computer.
   ☒ **A**, **B**, and **C** are incorrect because right-clicking System Information, Hardware Resources, or System Tools will not allow you to connect to a remote computer.
   ☒ **E** is incorrect because it is possible to change the focus of the default Computer Management snap-in to a remote computer without opening a new MMC by right-clicking Computer Management.

4. ☑ **C** is correct. Printers are the only devices that are not configurable through Device Manager. Printers are configured through the Printers dialog box.
   ☒ **A**, **B**, and **D** are incorrect because network adapters, video cards, and modems are all configurable through Device Manager.

5. ☑ **C** is correct. System information files created through the System Information utility are given an extension of .nfo. This extension is in turn associated with the System Information utility. You can select to save the information to a text file with a .txt extension but this is not an option you have when you select to create a system information file. To create a text file, you would select to save the information to a text file.
☒ **A** is incorrect because the .sif extension is used for setup information files like those used in unattended or scripted operating system installations.
☒ **B** is incorrect because the .txt extension is not what the System Information utility uses, unless you specifically choose to save the information as a text file.
☒ **D** is incorrect because the .udf file extension is used for uniqueness database files. UDF files can be used in conjunction with answer files for an unattended setup.

Configuring Driver Signing Options

6. ☑ **B** is correct. The High Security template (hisecws.inf) blocks the installation of unsigned drivers. You won't be able to install the updated video driver until you lower the security settings on the computer. The Secure template (securews.inf) warns you that a driver is unsigned but it does not prevent its installation.
☒ **A** is incorrect because you will not be given the opportunity to click OK and proceed with the installation.
☒ **C** is incorrect because sigverif.exe does not allow you to change the driver signing options, only generate a list of signed and unsigned drivers.
☒ **D** is incorrect because driver signing is already enabled. That is what is preventing you from installing the driver.

7. ☑ **C** is correct. The driver signing options you have configured are only valid for your account on the user's computer. To apply the Block setting to all users of the computer, you must select the Apply Setting As System Default check box.
☒ **A** and **B** are incorrect because the question states that the corporate policy is unrestrictive. It is possible that a group policy at either the domain or OU level is overriding the local policy setting, but the question does not provide enough information to make that decision. It is also unlikely in an unrestricted environment for there to be policies at the domain and OU levels.
☒ **D** is incorrect because the sigverif.exe utility is used to verify the state (signed or unsigned) of installed files, not to enable or disable driver signing.

8. ☑ **B** and **C** are correct. Both the hisecws.inf and securedc.inf security templates have the unsigned driver installation setting set to Block.
☒ **A**, **D**, and **E** are incorrect because the compatws.inf, ocfiless.inf, and securews.inf security templates do not by default prevent the installation of unsigned drivers. The default setting for each of these security templates is to warn but not block.

9. ☑ **C** is correct. The dialog box shown in the illustration indicates that the driver does not have a digital signature and Windows 2000 is configured to prevent unsigned drivers from being installed.
☒ **A** is incorrect because installing the latest service pack will not solve the problem.
☒ **B** is incorrect because the More Info button will not allow you to click Proceed and continue with the installation.
☒ **D** is incorrect because rebooting the computer in Safe Mode With Networking will not undo the driver signing configuration. You will still not be able to install the driver in Safe Mode.

10. ☑ **A** is correct. The computer's effective driver signing policy will be to prevent the installation of unsigned drivers. This setting will be derived from the site policy, as the site policy is the last policy that has this setting configured.
☒ **B** is incorrect because the server is not a member of the corp domain so it will not inherit GPOs configured at the corp domain level.
☒ **C** and **D** are incorrect because the computer's effective setting will be to prevent, not allow, the installation of unsigned drivers.

Verifying Digital Signatures on Existing Driver Files

11. ☑ **D** is correct. The reason for the message shown in the illustration is that the driver signing policy is set to Warn. When the policy setting is set to Warn, which it is by default, the user will still be able to proceed with the installation.
☒ **A** is incorrect because if the driver signing properties were set to Ignore, no warning message would appear, as the OS would ignore that the driver was unsigned.
☒ **B** is incorrect because if the driver signing properties were set to Block, the user would not be able to proceed with the installation.
☒ **C** is incorrect because there is no Prevent option.

12. ☑ **A** is correct. The File Signature Verification utility (sigverif.exe) can be used to determine the signed or unsigned state of files and save that information to a text file.
☒ **B** is incorrect because the Windows 2000 Readiness Analyzer is used to test for compatibility, not digitally signed files.
☒ **C** is incorrect because the signature file checker (SFC) cannot store the information to a text file.
☒ **D** is incorrect because winver.exe is used to display Windows 2000 version information.

13. ☑ **D** is correct. Device Manager is the tool that is most likely to be used to upgrade device drivers for existing devices.
☒ **A** is incorrect because it is less likely that Add/Remove Hardware would be used to upgrade drivers for existing devices. Add/Remove Hardware is generally used to remove

hardware and to add older, legacy hardware that isn't automatically detected.

☒ **B** is incorrect because the System Information utility will not allow you to upgrade a device driver.

☒ **C** is incorrect because Add/Remove Programs is intended to install applications and Windows Components but not device drivers. The one time this rule could be bent slightly is in the installation of a print device that came with proprietary software.

Configuring Operating System Support for Legacy Hardware Devices

14. ☑ **C** is correct. The driver has to be manually installed from the Hardware Wizard.

    ☒ **A** is incorrect because the Plug and Play manager that the hardware scan uses to detect new devices isn't capable of detecting and installing legacy devices like the older video card.

    ☒ **B** is incorrect because there is no information in the question that indicates that driver signing options are a problem. Furthermore, older device drivers will generally not be signed, and the default setting in Windows 2000 is to warn but not prevent unsigned drivers from being installed.

    ☒ **D** is incorrect because the use of a second hardware profile would not improve the video resolution.

15. ☑ **D** is correct. To prevent all users other than members of the Administrators group from installing any hardware device, you can delete the driver.cab file in the %systemroot%\driver cache\i386 directory. This forces the hardware installation to occur in the User context as opposed to the System context and requires that the user be a member of the Administrators group.

    ☒ **A** and **B** are incorrect because there is no built-in right that the user can be removed from.

    ☒ **C** is incorrect because the driver.cab file only exists in the %systemroot%\driver cache\i386 directory.

LAB ANSWER

1. The administrators have a couple of options to test the hardware to ensure that it is compatible with Windows 2000. The first option is to run the Windows 2000 Readiness Analyzer from the Windows 2000 CD by executing the command **winnt32.exe /checkupgradeonly**. The second option is to install Windows 2000 on the test systems to identify any device issues. A third option is to compare the devices in the computers to the HCL found on the Microsoft site to identify any conflicts or problems.

2. The best place to apply a restrictive driver signing policy setting within a GPO is at the Desktop OU. Applying it at the OU level will ensure that it applies to all the computers in the OU but no computers outside of the OU. The GPO could also be applied at the child domain

level; however, there are two potential issues with this configuration. First, this would require that you filter the GPO to apply only to desktop computers. Otherwise, all computers in the domain would receive the settings included in the GPO. Second, a less-restrictive GPO applied at the OU level could override the settings of the GPO at the domain level, resulting in the effective setting allowing the installation of unsigned drivers.

3. One way in which to restrict hardware device installation to only members of the Administrators group is to delete the driver.cab file located in the %systemroot%\driver cache\i386 directory.

4. Older hardware devices that are detected by Windows 2000 upon physical installation into the computer cannot be added through Device Manager. The Add/Remove Hardware Wizard must be used to accomplish this. The Add/Remove Hardware Wizard can be accessed through the Control Panel or by right-clicking the My Computer icon on the desktop and selecting Properties. On the Hardware tab of the System Properties dialog box, clicking the Hardware Wizard button will launch the wizard.

MCSA
MICROSOFT CERTIFIED SYSTEMS ADMINISTRATOR

18
Troubleshooting Startup Problems

CERTIFICATION OBJECTIVES

18.01	Interpreting the Startup Log File
18.02	Repairing an Operating System by Using Various Startup Options
18.03	Repairing an Operating System by Using the Recovery Console
18.04	Recovering Data from a Hard Disk in the Event that the Operating System Will Not Start
18.05	Restoring an Operating System and Data from Backup
✓	Two-Minute Drill
Q&A	Self Test

Startup problems can occur at any time but generally tend to occur during the least opportune times. This is for the most part attributable to Murphy's Law. This chapter is designed to help you overcome and conquer startup problems and will provide you with a detailed look at the tools, startup, and recovery options, and backup and restoration procedures that you must be familiar with for the certification exam and for your everyday administrative duties.

The content in this chapter is a critical component to an administrator's mental toolkit. Troubleshooting mastery comes down to some basic concepts, such as knowing what steps to take, in what order to take them, and how those steps change depending on the problem. Troubleshooting is a lot like detective work, where you might be presented with a number of clues that must be filtered through to determine the real culprit. In the early troubleshooting stages, you often have a number of potential suspects, but it is only after further investigation that the number of potential suspects is reduced, revealing the true problem.

Before we examine the options available to us when troubleshooting startup problems, let's begin with an examination of the startup process, to provide us with a base level of knowledge to build upon. A basic examination of the startup process reveals that a successful startup consists of three phases: hardware startup, software startup, and load phases. Each of these three phases can be further broken down into multiple subphases. The load phase, for example, consists of four individual load phases: the initial phase, the boot loader phase, the kernel phase, and the logon phase. Should a problem arise during one of these phases, you are likely to experience a stop error or receive an error message. Software viruses are one example of a problem that can cause problems during startup, and often result in a stop error.

The Hardware Startup Phase

The hardware phase is the first phase of any computer initialization process. If the computer hardware prevents you from starting up, these problems must be addressed before the software boot sequence can be examined. The hardware startup phase begins with the computer being powered on. The computer then executes a built-in set of startup routines, known as the basic input/output system (BIOS), and the BIOS executes the power-on self test (POST). The POST routine verifies that critical system components, such as memory, disks, and video cards, are operational. The

POST then sets all of the hardware to a predefined state and finds and loads the file that loads the operating system (ntldr). If a problem occurs during the POST routine, you generally hear a series of beeps. The number of beeps is very important, as each number represents a different problem. For example, a series of eight beeps may indicate a video card problem. Look to your BIOS documentation for the specific beep configuration.

The Software Startup Phase

The second phase is the software startup phase. This and the last phase will be the real focus on the certification exam. The Windows NT/2000 boot process requires access to a number of files in order for the OS to boot properly. Microsoft defines two partitions for the location of these files and differentiates the files into two groups, boot files and system files. The boot files are stored on the system partition, and the system files are stored on the boot partition. (You did read that correctly. As confusing as it appears, this is the way Microsoft documentation refers to the two partitions.) There are always three files; however, with SCSI devices, there may be a fourth file that makes up the required boot files. These three, or potentially four, boot files are stored on what Microsoft refers to as the system partition, and their individual functions are described here:

- **ntldr**   A hidden, read-only system file that initiates the loading of the operating system.
- **boot.ini**   A read-only system file that builds the operating system selection menu. This menu is only visible during the boot process when multiple OSs or the Recovery Console are installed on the computer. When a single OS is installed, the user does not need to make a selection, as there is only one option.
- **ntdetect.com**   A hidden, read-only system file that examines the hardware devices and builds a hardware list. This list is then sent back to Ntldr later in the startup process so it can be added to the Registry.
- **ntbootdd.sys**   A hidden, read-only system file that is the optional fourth file. It is only present on systems that start from a SCSI disk, connected to a SCSI adapter with its BIOS disabled. This file accesses the one or more devices attached to the SCSI adapter during the Windows 2000 startup process. This file is also a requirement in computers that support disk duplexing.

exam watch

Know that Microsoft refers to the partition containing the Windows 2000 system files as the boot partition, and refers to the partition containing the boot files as the system partition. You are reading this correctly. The partitions are named exactly opposite of what you might think. Think of the boot partition as the partition where the OS boots from or, in other words, where the OS files are found. Also remember that the boot and system files can be stored on the same partition.

Problems can arise when one of these critical files is deleted or moved. A missing file will prevent the OS from booting successfully. Viruses and changes to the disk partition structure are two likely causes of files being deleted or moved. The quick solution to this problem is to create a Windows 2000 startup disk to boot the system and then copy over the missing file.

An examination of the boot.ini file reveals that Advanced Risk Computing (ARC) pathnames are used to identify the paths to the locally installed OSs. ARC pathnames use the physical disk partition number as part of the path location of the OS files. The creation of additional partitions may result in a renumbering of the existing partitions, but the OS does not change the corresponding ARC paths in the boot.ini file. Therefore, unless you have made those changes prior to a reboot of your computer, the path indicated in the boot.ini file will be incorrect and your system won't boot properly.

on the job

Look to Knowledge Base article Q102877 for more detailed information on how and why ARC paths change, and look to Q301680 for information on how to create a boot disk for a NTFS or FAT partition in Windows.

The boot partition contains a number of system files that are also critical to the startup process. The boot files are used during the last phase of startup, known as the software load phase, which itself is broken into four subphases. The files accessed in this phase include:

- **ntoskrnl.exe**   The Windows 2000 kernel file, found in the %systemroot%\system32 directory.

- **system.dat**   A collection of system configuration settings that controls which device drivers and services are loaded during the initialization process. This file is part of the Windows 2000 Registry and is found in the %systemroot%\system32\Config folder.

- **device drivers** These files allow individual devices to function. Examples of device driver files include bootvid.dll and ftdisk.sys.
- **hal.dll** The hardware abstraction layer (HAL) file, which protects the kernel and the rest of the Windows 2000 executive from platform-specific hardware differences.

Now that you have an understanding of the files involved in both of the software startup phases, let's put all the components together to see the big picture. As we have seen, there are three distinct phases to this overall process: the hardware startup, software startup, and load phases. Combining all three of these phases into a successful startup results in the following sequence of steps occurring:

1. The hardware startup begins by powering on the computer.
2. The computer executes a built-in set of startup routines known as the BIOS, and the BIOS executes the POST. The POST routine verifies that critical system components such as memory, disks, and video cards are operational. The POST then sets all the hardware to a predefined state and finds and loads the operating system loader (ntldr).
3. The software startup sequence begins with Ntldr, which in turn switches the CPU from real mode to 32-bit flat memory mode. The mini file system drivers, which are built into Ntldr, detect and load Windows 2000. The mini file system drivers are needed in case the system or boot partition is formatted with NTFS.
4. ntldr finds and reads the boot.ini file and displays the boot loader operating system selection menu based on the OSs contained in the boot.ini file.
5. If multiple OSs exist, the user must select one of the available OSs within 30 seconds, or else the default OS is selected and loaded.
6. ntdetect.com is run, which scans the locally installed hardware and returns the list of detected hardware to ntldr.
7. The kernel load phase now begins with ntldr loading ntoskrnl.exe, hal.dll, and system.dat. ntldr loads the Registry key HKEY_LOCAL_MACHINE\SYSTEM\ from %systemroot%\system32\config\system. ntldr then selects a configuration and, if multiple hardware profiles exist, highlights the default profile and prompts the user to select a hardware profile. ntldr then selects the control set that is used to initialize the computer and loads the device drivers that have a start value of 0x0.

8. The kernel initialization phase then executes. The system.dat file is scanned to determine the device drivers configured to start at startup, and those device drivers are loaded.

9. The services load phase occurs, in which Session Manager (smss.exe) loads and starts all remaining Windows 2000 subsystems and services. Session Manager carries out the instructions in several Registry entries and initializes programs configured to run upon initialization as well as the memory management key, which controls the paging file(s).

10. The last load phase, the Win32 subsystem, starts and triggers winlogon.exe, which in turn starts the Local Security Authority (lsass.exe) and displays the CTRL-ALT-DELETE logon dialog box.

The entire startup process is considered complete only after a user successfully logs on to the system, at which time the last known good configuration is overwritten. Now that you have a solid understanding of the three phases of the startup process, let's examine how to troubleshoot various startup problems, beginning with a look at the startup log.

CERTIFICATION OBJECIVE 18.01

Interpreting the Startup Log File

The startup log can be a great place to begin your troubleshooting of startup problems, because it can point you in the direction of the system service or device driver causing the problem. The startup log file is not enabled by default but can be enabled through the Advanced Startup Options by pressing F8 prior to selecting an OS from the boot selection menu. The startup log, named ntbtlog.txt, logs the status of all drivers and services that load (and don't load) during startup. This file is stored by default in the %systemroot% directory.

Don't confuse the ntbtlog.txt file with the memory dump file named memory.dmp, which is configured through the System icon in the Control Panel. Both files can be used to troubleshoot problems, but the memory.dmp file is used to troubleshoot stop errors (blue screens), whereas the ntbtlog.txt file is used to log drivers and services loaded at startup. Exercise 18-1 walks you through the process of enabling boot logging at system initialization, which will allow us to view and interpret the startup log file.

EXERCISE 18-1

Booting a Computer Running Windows Using the Startup Log File Option

In this exercise, you learn how to start your computer using the Enable Boot Logging Advanced Startup feature. This allows the computer to collect information about the drivers loaded into memory during startup and store that information in the ntbtlog.txt file for future examination.

1. Select Start | Shut Down, select Restart from the drop-down dialog box, and click OK.
2. During the initialization of the computer, press F8 to display the Windows 2000 Advanced Options menu. Use the DOWN ARROW key to select the Enable Boot Logging option, and press ENTER.

exam
Watch *Selecting any one of the three Safe Mode options also enables boot logging.*

3. From the operating system boot selection menu, you may be required to choose an OS if more than one option exists on the computer. If this is the case, select the Windows 2000 Advanced Server OS and press ENTER. This step is done automatically if only a single OS selection exists.

Now that you have created a startup log, let's examine its contents. The ntbtlog.txt file can be opened with Notepad and looks similar to Figure 18-1. As you can see in this example, the drivers and services are listed individually on each line in the file as either "Loaded driver" or "Did not load driver" followed by the path to the file associated with the service or driver. Knowing the path to the file that is generating the startup problem allows you to replace that specific file or disable a specific service or device using one of the other troubleshooting utilities, such as the Recovery Console, and resolve the problem.

exam
Watch *The ntbtlog.txt file may not log startup problems that occur very early in the startup process. The ntbtlog.txt file is written to the Registry and then flushed to disk to prevent anything from being written to the hard disk prior to Autocheck and chkdsk finishing.*

FIGURE 18-1

Examining the ntbtlog.txt file using Notepad

```
ntbtlog.txt - Notepad
File Edit Format Help
Loaded driver \SystemRoot\System32\DRIVERS\raspptp.sys
Loaded driver \SystemRoot\System32\DRIVERS\msgpc.sys
Loaded driver \SystemRoot\System32\Drivers\EFS.SYS
Loaded driver \SystemRoot\System32\DRIVERS\psched.sys
Loaded driver \SystemRoot\System32\DRIVERS\ptilink.sys
Loaded driver \SystemRoot\System32\DRIVERS\raspti.sys
Loaded driver \SystemRoot\System32\DRIVERS\parallel.sys
Loaded driver \SystemRoot\System32\DRIVERS\rdpdr.sys
Loaded driver \SystemRoot\System32\DRIVERS\swenum.sys
Loaded driver \SystemRoot\System32\DRIVERS\update.sys
Loaded driver \SystemRoot\System32\DRIVERS\flpydisk.sys
Loaded driver \SystemRoot\System32\DRIVERS\usbhub.sys
Loaded driver \SystemRoot\System32\Drivers\NDProxy.SYS
Did not load driver \SystemRoot\System32\Drivers\NDProxy.SYS
Did not load driver \SystemRoot\System32\Drivers\lbrtfdc.SYS
Did not load driver \SystemRoot\System32\Drivers\Sfloppy.SYS
Did not load driver \SystemRoot\System32\Drivers\Changer.SYS
Did not load driver \SystemRoot\System32\Drivers\Cdaudio.SYS
Loaded driver \SystemRoot\System32\Drivers\Fs_Rec.SYS
```

Another way in which the startup file can be enabled is by modifying the boot.ini file and adding the /bootlog.txt switch to the end of the ARC path. A number of boot.ini file switches are available to further customize the functionality and to potentially assist in your troubleshooting efforts. For more information on the specific switches available for use in the boot.ini file, look to Q170756. Even though this article states that it applies to Windows NT 4, the same switches can be used in the boot.ini file included in Windows 2000. In addition to these existing switches, some new switches, not supported in Windows NT 4, can also be configured in the Windows 2000 boot.ini file. These are discussed at www.microsoft.com/windows2000/techinfo/reskit/en-us/default.asp?url=/WINDOWS2000/techinfo/reskit/en-us/core/fnbb_str_hrhh.asp.

SCENARIO & SOLUTION

What three files are stored on the system partition and must be available for the computer running Windows 2000 to boot successfully?	Microsoft refers to the partition that stores the boot files as the system partition. This partition must contain the boot.ini, ntldr, and ntdetect.com files. The ntbootdd.sys file might also be required if the computer uses SCSI devices that are connected to a SCSI adapter with its BIOS disabled.

SCENARIO & SOLUTION

You wish to enable the boot logging option at startup. What five options are you able to use to accomplish this?	Boot logging can be enabled at startup through the Advanced Startup options by pressing F8 when prompted and selecting any one of the three Safe Mode options or the Enable Boot Logging option. Boot logging can also be enabled by modifying the boot.ini file and adding the /bootlog.txt switch to the end of the OS ARC path and rebooting the system.
What are the name, purpose, and location of the boot log file? How can this file be used to help you troubleshoot startup problems?	The boot log file is named ntbtlog.txt. Its purpose is to log all the system devices and drivers and indicate whether they loaded or didn't load during startup. This can be useful when troubleshooting startup problems because it can allow you to determine what service or device driver is causing the problem. The ntbtlog.txt file is saved by default in the %systemroot% directory.
What boot.ini switch can be enabled to list all the services and devices as they are being configured on the local computer during startup?	The /sos switch can be used in the boot.ini file to list all the services and devices as they are being configured on the local computer during startup.

CERTIFICATION OBJECIVE 18.02

Repairing an Operating System by Using Various Startup Options

When you are faced with a startup problem such as an incompatible driver, extremely poor video resolution, or another device driver problem that is a thorn in your administrative side, the Advanced Startup options might be a way to correct the problem. In this section, you will learn about each of the available Advanced Startup options and where they can be used to help you resolve startup problems.

Exercise 18-1 taught you the steps involved in getting to the Advanced Startup options but focused on only the Enable Boot Logging option. Table 18-1 lists and describes each of the available Advanced Startup options.

Safe Mode

Now that you have an understanding of what each of the options allows you to do, let's take a look at how to use some of these Advanced Startup options, beginning

TABLE 18-1 The Advanced Startup Options

Advanced Startup Option	Description
Safe Mode	This option starts Windows 2000 with only the basic files and drivers, such as mouse (except serial mouse), monitor, keyboard, disks, base video, and default system services, but no networking connections. Use this option to determine if any of the minimal services and devices are causing the problem. If the computer doesn't start successfully in Safe Mode, you may have to use the emergency repair disk (ERD).
Safe Mode with Networking	This option is the same as the first but includes network connectivity. If the computer boots successfully with this option, you can surmise that the basic files and drivers including those for networking are not causing the startup problem.
Safe Mode with Command Prompt	Like the first two options, Windows 2000 is started with only the basic files and drivers, but the command prompt is displayed instead of the normal Windows desktop GUI interface.
Enable Boot Logging	Logs all the drivers and services that were loaded or not loaded by the system to a file named ntbtlog.txt. All Safe Mode startup options enable boot logging by default. This log, as discussed in the first section of this chapter, can be useful in determining the exact cause of the startup problem.
Enable VGA Mode	Uses the basic VGA driver to start Windows 2000 and can be very valuable when you have installed a new driver for your video card that does not allow Windows 2000 to start properly. It is also handy if you have switched monitors and the original monitor's settings do not display correctly on the new monitor. The basic video driver is used in all Safe Mode selections as well.
Last Known Good Configuration	Starts Windows 2000 using the Registry information saved at the last successful shutdown. This can be a handy option when the computer generates a stop error after installing a new driver, because it will roll back the configuration to that of the last successful shutdown. Unfortunately, only a single configuration is saved and that configuration is overwritten at the next successful logon. The last known good configuration will not solve problems that are caused by deleted or missing drivers or files, and any other configuration changes that have been made since the last shutdown will also be lost.
Directory Services Restore Mode	Only applicable to Windows 2000 domain controllers, this option can be used to restore the SYSVOL directory and Active Directory on a Windows 2000 domain controller. This option allows you to reboot a Windows 2000 domain controller, restore from backup a copy of Active Directory, and then, with the ntdsutil.exe tool, perform an authoritative restore.
Debugging Mode	Allows you to start Windows 2000 and send debugging information through a serial cable to another computer. This option can help organizations that write device drivers for the OS identify and resolve problems the drivers are creating.

TABLE 18-1 The Advanced Startup Options *(continued)*

Advanced Startup Option	Description
Boot Normally	Allows you to boot without using any of the advanced options.
Return to OS Choices Menu	Returns you to the original OS choices menu.

with the Safe Mode option. Booting successfully into any one of the Safe Mode Advanced Startup options allows you to conclude that the basic system devices and drivers are not at the root of the startup problem.

EXERCISE 18-2

Starting Your Computer in Safe Mode

This exercise will teach you the steps to perform to start your computer in Safe Mode. If the computer starts successfully in Safe Mode, you can rule out the basic files and drivers as being a cause of the startup problem.

1. Click Start, and click Shut Down.
2. Click Restart, and click OK.
3. As the computer restarts and you see the message Please Select The Operating System To Start, press F8 and use the arrow keys to highlight the Safe Mode option, and press ENTER.
4. Use the arrow keys to highlight an operating system, and press ENTER.

The Last Known Good Configuration

The Last Known Good Configuration, Advanced Startup option is one that can be used to return a computer to its previously functional state. The last known good configuration is simply a copy of the Registry settings that are saved after the last successful shutdown. The last known good configuration can be identified using regedt32.exe to look in the Registry for the Select Registry key found in HKLM\System, shown in Figure 18-2. The LastKnownGood value, in the Select key will allow you to determine the data value which, in this case, is set to 0x2. This indicates that the ControlSet002 key in the same path contains the settings that would be used if you were to boot with the last known good configuration.

The use of the last known good configuration is useful when you experience system problems after making configuration changes prior to logging off and logging back on. For example, if you install a new device driver and your computer generates a stop error, you are able to reboot and select the last known good configuration, which will boot the system using the Registry configuration that existed prior to the configuration changes being made. In effect, the last known good configuration undoes the new changes, allowing you to "roll back" to the previous changes.

Think back to our discussion earlier in this chapter of the boot process and what determines if the boot process is considered complete. A successful startup is considered to be complete only after a successful logon to the computer, which in turn overwrites the last known good configuration with the new configuration changes. This means that if you install a new device driver, reboot the computer, and log on successfully only to be presented with a stop error, the last known good configuration will now consist of the bad device driver configuration settings and will not offer you any value in terms of system recovery.

Directory Services Restore Mode

The Directory Services Restore Mode Advanced Startup feature is one that is only applicable to computers running Windows 2000 that are configured as Active Directory domain controllers. This Advanced Startup option becomes extremely

FIGURE 18-2

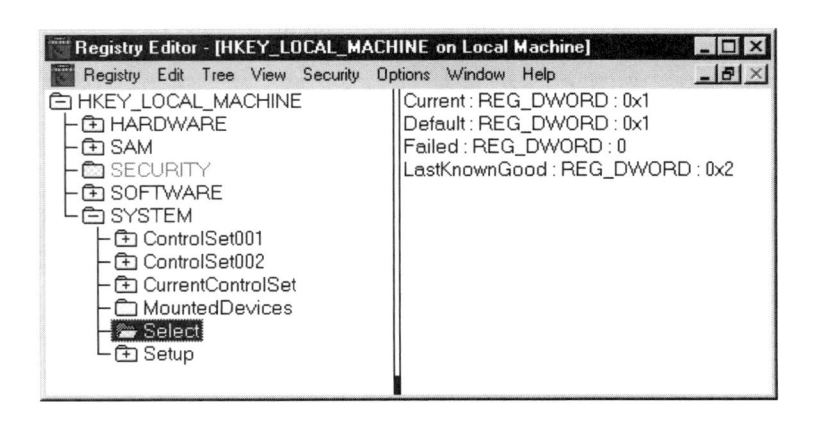

Identifying the last known good configuration in the Registry

important when you or another administrator has deleted an object from Active Directory. Let's assume that your organization has designed Active Directory to use OUs to logically represent the objects found in its different departments. One of the OUs is named Sales and contains all the sales department user accounts, groups, computers, printers, and shared published folders. If that folder is accidentally deleted, performing an ordinary restore from backup would not result in the object being restored. The reason for this has to do with Active Directory replication.

When an object in Active Directory is deleted, the object's tombstone attribute is enabled, which instructs all of the domain controller's replication partners to deactivate, but not delete, the object from their Active Directory database during the next replication cycle. Once Active Directory replication is complete, all domain controllers will have deactivated the object. If the object is restored through an ordinary restore, during the next replication cycle, it will be deactivated again because of the tombstone attribute. To resolve this problem and get the object restored, an authoritative restore must be performed, which can only be performed by rebooting and choosing the Directory Services Restore Mode option. Active Directory objects that are deleted by administrators are actually marked as tombstoned for a default period of 60 days. Only after the tombstone period of 60 days elapses is the object deleted through a "garbage collection" process.

Rebooting the computer into Directory Services Restore Mode appears as though you booted normally (there are no Safe Mode indicators in the corners of the screen or anything else), but this feature allows you to start a domain controller without any domain controller functionality. Once you have logged on, start the Backup utility and restore the system state on the computer. When the restore is complete, open the command prompt and type **ntdsutil** to launch the utility that will allow you to perform an authoritative restore. When the authoritative restore is complete, reboot the server, and after Active Directory replication occurs, the once-deleted object will reappear in Active Directory.

The certification exam requires that you know the process involved in performing an authoritative restore but not the actual syntax of the commands in ntdsutil.exe.

A point worth noting that is beyond the scope of this exam is that when an object in Active Directory is deleted, it is only marked for deletion by enabling the object's tombstone attribute. The deleted object persists in Active Directory for a period of 60 days, by default, after it was originally deleted, allowing for an authoritative restore to recover the object within that 60-day time period.

SCENARIO & SOLUTION

If your computer is experiencing startup problems and you would like to eliminate the basic drivers and services from the list of potential causes, what Advanced Startup option(s) can you use?	If the computer boots successfully with any one of the three Safe Mode options, you can rule out the basic system services and devices as the cause of the problem, as those are all that Safe Mode uses.
You have installed a new device driver on a computer running Windows 2000 Server. After the driver installation, the computer generates a stop error and you realize you've installed the Windows 95 version of the driver, not the Windows 2000 version. What Advanced Startup option will you use to quickly resolve the problem?	This type of problem offers the perfect opportunity to use the Last Known Good Configuration Advanced Startup option. Booting the computer with this option allows it to start up using the system configuration that existed prior to the bad device driver's installation, essentially undoing the device driver's installation and rolling the configuration settings back to a point where the driver has not been installed. When you log on, you can then install the new, correct version of the device driver. It is when a user logs on that the last known good configuration is overwritten.
What is an example of a scenario where you would benefit from selecting the Directory Services Restore Mode Advanced Startup option? How must your computer running Windows 2000 be configured to take advantage of this?	The Directory Services Restore Mode option should be used when you need to perform an authoritative restore of Active Directory or when you would like to start a domain controller without Active Directory running in order to make changes to it in an offline state. Compacting the Active Directory database is an example of this. To take advantage of the Directory Services Restore Mode feature, the computer must be configured as a domain controller. Another example of where you can use this is to move the AD database or log files to a different partition.
What boot.ini file switch can be enabled to allow your computer to boot using basic video drivers as an alternative to selecting the Enable VGA Mode Advanced Startup option? What KB article describes all of the available switches for the boot.ini file?	The /basevideo switch can be added to the OS ARC path in the boot.ini file to enable the basic video drivers. KB article Q170756 describes some of the switches available to be used in the boot.ini file.

CERTIFICATION OBJECIVE 18.03

Repairing an Operating System by Using the Recovery Console

The Recovery Console is a new administrative feature incorporated into Windows 2000 that provides you with an additional administrative recovery option. The only real last-resort recovery option available in Windows NT 4 was the ability to perform a repair using the emergency repair disk (ERD). However, this rolled back the configuration of the computer to the point in time when the ERD was last updated. In a lot of IT departments, that time was the date of the original install, when the ERD was first created. Recovering back to the point of installation doesn't make for much of a recovery. Now, in Windows 2000, the Recovery Console provides you with the ability to stop and start services, reconfigure services, format drives, run **chkdsk** to resolve disk problems, repair a master boot record, copy files from the floppy drive to the local drive, and read and write data on FAT, FAT32, and NTFS file systems.

The use of the Recovery Console is limited to the Administrator account as you do not have the option to specify a username. Logging on to the Recovery Console assumes you are logging on as the administrator and asks for the password for that account. Before we get into the specifics of the Recovery Console, let's start with a look at how to install the Recovery Console.

EXERCISE 18-3

CertCam 18-3

Installing the Recovery Console

This exercise will teach you how to install the Recovery Console from the Windows 2000 installation CD so that it appears as an option in the boot selection menu during the boot process. This procedure should be performed on all production servers in your environment as a proactive recovery measure.

1. Click Start, click Run, and click Browse. With the Windows 2000 CD in the computer, browse to the i386 directory, click winnt32.exe, and click Open.

2. In the Run dialog box, change the command in the Open text box to read *drive*:**\i386\winnt32.exe /cmdcons**, where *drive* is the drive letter of the CD drive, and click OK.

3. In the Windows 2000 Setup dialog box, click Yes.

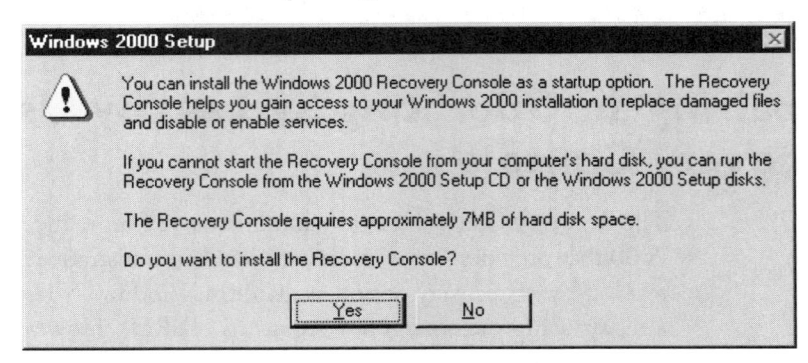

> **Windows 2000 Setup**
>
> You can install the Windows 2000 Recovery Console as a startup option. The Recovery Console helps you gain access to your Windows 2000 installation to replace damaged files and disable or enable services.
>
> If you cannot start the Recovery Console from your computer's hard disk, you can run the Recovery Console from the Windows 2000 Setup CD or the Windows 2000 Setup disks.
>
> The Recovery Console requires approximately 7MB of hard disk space.
>
> Do you want to install the Recovery Console?
>
> [Yes] [No]

4. The Microsoft Windows 2000 Advanced Server Setup dialog box appears and begins the installation. Once the installation is complete, you are presented with an information dialog box confirming the successful installation of the Recovery Console. Click OK. The Recovery Console can be installed on any of the Windows 2000 OSs and from any of the respective OS CDs.

5. To confirm the installation of the Recovery Console, select Start | Programs | Accessories | Windows Explorer.

6. In Windows Explorer, expand My Computer, and click the C drive. Double-click the boot.ini file and confirm that a new line similar to the one highlighted in the following illustration appears and ends with the /cmdcons switch. The appearance of this line indicates the successful installation of the Recovery Console.

```
[boot loader]
timeout=30
default=multi(0)disk(0)rdisk(0)partition(1)\WINNT
[operating systems]
multi(0)disk(0)rdisk(0)partition(1)\WINNT="Microsoft Windows 2000 Advanced Server" /fastdetect
C:\CMDCONS\BOOTSECT.DAT="Microsoft Windows 2000 Recovery Console" /cmdcons
```

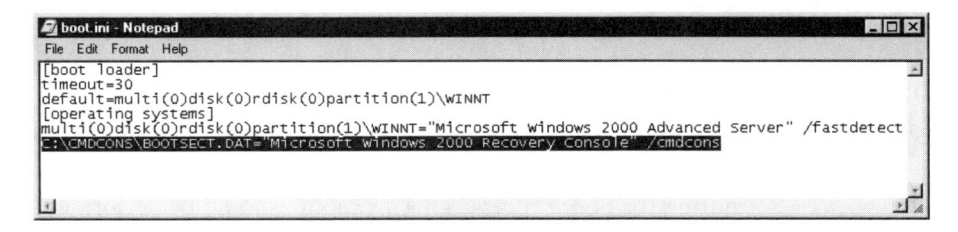

author's note   *Depending on your Windows Explorer settings, you may have to select Tools | Folder Options, click the View tab, click the Show Hidden Files And Folders radio button, and clear the Hide File Extensions For Known File Types and Hide Protected Operating System Files (Recommended) check boxes. Click Yes, click the Like Current Folder button, click Yes again, and click OK. To simplify this process, just press* **CTRL-R**, *type* notepad c:\boot.ini, *and click OK.*

With the Recovery Console installed, you can now reboot your computer and select the Recovery Console from the operating system selection menu.

Exercise 18-3 taught you how to install the Recovery Console, but this assumed that you are proactive and have had the opportunity while the computer is functioning properly to perform the installation. Often times, we aren't as proactive or we find ourselves called into situations where we have not been responsible for a specific server and therefore haven't had the opportunity to configure it as we would have liked for troubleshooting purposes. In situations like these, it is still possible to use the Recovery Console by booting from the Windows 2000 CD and selecting the Recovery option. This is very similar to the process used to access the ERD Recovery option.

EXERCISE 18-4

Accessing the Recovery Console from the Windows 2000 CD

This exercise will teach you how to access the Recovery Console from the Windows CD, which will be required when the Recovery Console hasn't been installed prior to the startup problems occurring.

1. Place the Windows 2000 CD in the computer and configure the BIOS to boot from the CD prior to the hard drive, and restart the computer.

2. When prompted to Press Any Key To Boot From CD, press a key and wait for Setup to initialize.

3. On the Welcome To Setup page in the Windows 2000 Setup, press R to repair a Windows 2000 installation.

4. On the Windows 2000 Repair Options page, press C to repair a Windows 2000 installation by using the recovery console. It is on this screen that you are also given the option to select the emergency repair kit.

5. On the Microsoft Windows 2000 Recovery Console, select the Windows 2000 installation that you would like to log on to. All of the available Windows 2000 installations are listed with a corresponding number to the left of them. If only a single installation exists, click 1 and press ENTER.

6. At the Administrator Password prompt, enter the password for the Administrator account and press ENTER. Upon entering the correct password, you will be presented with the prompt C:\winnt> and you can begin your repair.

Recovery Console Commands

Now that you know how to access the Recovery Console from both the operating system selection menu and the CD, we are ready to look at what the Recovery Console can do. The command available in the Recovery Console can be listed by typing **help** within the Recovery Console. The following table lists the commands available in the Recovery Console, some of the less self-explanatory of which we will expand upon later in the chapter.

ttrib	delete	fixmbr	more
batch	dir	format	rd
cd	disable	help	ren
chdir	diskpart	listsvc	rename
chkdsk	enable	logon	rmdir
cls	exit	map	systemroot
copy	expand	md	type
del	fixboot	mkdir	

If you are familiar with basic DOS commands, you will recognize a number of the Recovery Console commands. The exam is not likely to test your knowledge of any one command's syntax but will require that you know what sorts of tasks you are able to perform using the Recovery Console.

A bad device driver is one of the most likely causes of startup problems, although problems with system services can also create problems. The Recovery Console is a great administrative tool to help you resolve these types of common startup problems. Both the **enable** and **disable** commands can be used to change the startup properties of a device or system service, allowing you to boot successfully and then fix the problem by replacing the driver from within the GUI. To determine the eligible service's use, type the following command in the Recovery Console:

```
listsvc
```

The results of the **listsvc** command is a listing of all the eligible services and drivers along with their corresponding start type value. A driver such as the ACPI driver can then be disabled, if it is causing a problem, using the following command:

```
Disable ACPI
```

Upon reboot, if you find that the ACPI driver was not the problem, back in the Recovery Console, you can enable it and reconfigure it to use the *service_boot_start* start type by using the following command:

```
Enable ACPI service_boot_start
```

Another handy command to help resolve startup problems is the **fixboot** command. This command can be used to fix a corrupted Windows boot sector by writing a new Windows boot sector on the boot partition. The following command would allow you to accomplish this:

```
Fixboot c:
```

The **fixmbr** command can be used to repair the master boot record (MBR) of the system partition. Often times, viruses can damage the MBR, preventing Windows from booting. Executing the following command can repair the MBR, but other steps should be attempted prior to using this option because the **fixmbr** command may damage your partition tables if a virus is present or if a hardware problem exists. This could lead to a whole new problem in which some of the other partitions on the disk become inaccessible.

```
Fixmbr
```

Last but not least, if all else fails, the **format** command can be run as follows to format an individual drive, where c: is the drive to be formatted, *Q* indicates a quick format is to take place, and /FS indicates that the file system should be NTFS:

```
Format c: /Q /FS:NTFS
```

FROM THE CLASSROOM

One of the problems that has arisen with the Recovery Console has to do with the requirement of logging on using the password of the Administrator account. The Recovery Console uses the local Administrator account and its associated password, which is stored in the local security account manager (SAM) database in the Registry of the local computer in the %systemroot%\system32\config directory.

The problem arises if this member server is promoted to be a domain controller. During the Active Directory promotion process triggered by the dcpromo.exe command, you are asked to enter a Directory Services Restore

FROM THE CLASSROOM

Mode Administrator password, as shown in the following illustration. This password is then used by the Recovery Console and is separate from the Administrator password that is now stored in Active Directory once the promotion is complete. When the computer is configured as a domain controller, there is no longer a way, through the GUI to change the password for the Recovery Console Administrator account. Prior to being a domain controller, changing the local Administrator account password would have allowed you to accomplish this.

To change the Recovery Console Administrator password on a Windows 2000 domain controller, restart the domain controller and press F8 to access the Advanced Startup options. Select the Directory Services Restore Mode option and log on using the password you specified during the domain controller promotion. At the command prompt, type **net administrator** * and press ENTER. At the prompt, type the new password and press ENTER. Then, at the confirmation prompt, retype the new password to confirm it's correct and restart the computer.

Another issue with the Recovery Console is that it always prompts you for the password of the Administrator account even if that account has been renamed. In the event the account has been renamed, you must still supply the password from the original, now-renamed Administrator account.

—*Rory McCaw*

Removing the Recovery Console

Removing the Recovery Console requires that you edit the boot.ini file, which is stored on the root of your system partition, generally C. The boot.ini file has the read-only attribute enabled by default; therefore, you must remove this prior to making any changes you wish to save.

EXERCISE 18-5

Removing the Recovery Console

I can't think of any really good reason to remove the Recovery Console, as its sole purpose is to assist in troubleshooting. Provided you have designed your network and computer configurations with security in mind, only users that know the password for the Administrator account are able to use the Recovery Console. This is something you should know for your daily administration as well as something you must know for the exam.

1. Press CTRL-E to launch Windows Explorer.
2. Double-click the C drive in the display pane, right-click the boot.ini file, and click Properties. If you do not see any files on the C drive, you will have to change the view settings by selecting Tools | Folder Options, clicking the View tab, and selecting Show Hidden Files.

3. In the Properties dialog box of the boot.ini file, remove the check mark from the Read-only box and click OK.

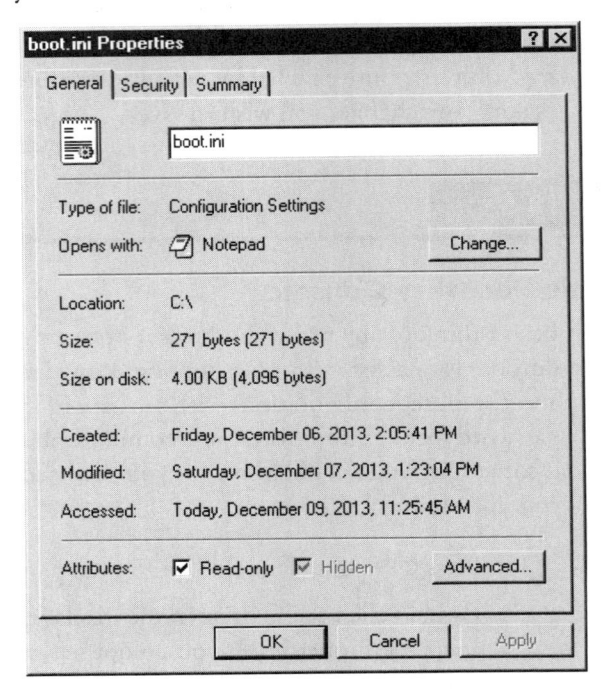

4. Double-click the boot.ini file and, in Notepad, remove the line in the boot.ini file that includes the /cmdcons switch.

5. Close Notepad, and click Yes to save the changes.

6. Re-enable the read-only attribute at this point, which is not required but highly recommended. To do that, repeat Step 3, but this time enable the read-only attribute.

7. In Windows Explorer, delete the cmdcons folder on the C drive and close Windows Explorer.

As a new feature included in Windows 2000, you will be required to know what options are available in the Recovery Console and how and when to use this option to assist with startup problems.

SCENARIO & SOLUTION

What two options are available for accessing the Recovery Console?	The Recovery Console can be installed from the Windows 2000 CD by executing the command winnt32.exe /cmdcons and then accessed from the operating system boot selection menu. It can also be accessed by booting from the Windows 2000 CD, running Setup, and selecting to repair an existing installation as opposed to installing a new copy of the OS.
You are the administrator of a computer that runs Windows 2000 Server. You have booted the computer using the Enable Boot Logging Advanced Startup option but the system generates a stop error prior to reaching the logon screen. How can you use the Recovery Console to assist in the troubleshooting and resolution of this problem? What command within the Recovery Console can be used to see the computer's eligible services and their respective startup parameter?	Using the Recovery Console will allow you to use the type command to view the contents of the ntbtlog.txt file to determine the service or driver causing the problem. The disable command could then be used to disable the problem service or device driver. The listsvc command can be used in the Recovery Console to see the computer's eligible services and their respective startup parameter.
You administer a number of computers running Windows 2000, three of which are domain controllers. One of the domain controllers was taken offline for maintenance and now fails to start. What password will you use to log on to the Recovery Console on the domain controller?	As a domain controller, there are no longer local accounts on the computer, so the password for the local Administrator account is not a valid option. During the domain controller promotion, however, you were asked to specify a password for the Directory Services Restore Mode Advanced Startup option. This password is now used to log on to the Recovery Console.
List three commands that could be used to help you correct disk-related problems in the Recovery Console?	Recovery Console commands that could be used to correct disk-related problems include diskpart, format, fixmbr, fixboot, and chkdsk.

CERTIFICATION OBJECIVE 18.04

Recovering Data from a Hard Disk in the Event that the Operating System Will Not Start

This is not a situation I wish upon anyone, but it is one that can be resolved like any other. Hopefully, you have done your proactive administrative duties and are in possession of a recent backup of the data on the failed system, which in the worst case will allow you to reinstall Windows 2000 and restore the data from backup. If you don't have a current backup, you may want to consider updating your resume.

In the event the OS will not start, you are faced with the task of troubleshooting the problem and trying to identify the source and make the required changes. In your troubleshooting efforts, I strongly encourage you to try not to overlook the obvious. Remember the KISS principal (Keep It Simple Smartguy). Just last week, one of the computers in my lab wouldn't boot and the problem had nothing to do with software; rather, a failed power supply was causing the problem. The morale of this story is to start with the basics. It sounds so simple, but the basics often are overlooked.

I think the funniest thing I have come across happened a couple of years ago at a small business I had worked with. I received a frantic call Monday morning asking if I was available, because their server was offline and would not boot. I arrived to find the server located under a hanging plant, and it was obvious that someone overwatered the plant and then the server. I don't ever recall a server manual that stated servers require water, but the cleaning staff obviously overlooked that minor point when watering the plant. Again, this goes right back to the basics—physical server security and proper physical location is not something to overlook!

A good place to start, then, is with the hardware in the computer. Take off the case, or pull it out of the rack, and make sure that everything is connected properly and that when you turn it on, everything sounds and acts as it should. Confirm that your CPU fan(s) is working and that no BIOS-related beeping occurs upon startup.

The Windows 2000 Boot Disk

If you are fairly certain that it isn't a hardware problem, reboot the computer to identify what error message is displayed. The error message can often help to point you in the correct troubleshooting direction. The following are some common startup error messages that can generally be resolved through the use of a Windows 2000 boot disk:

```
Boot: Couldn't find NTLDR. Please insert another disk.
NTDETECT V5.0 Checking Hardware… NTDETECT failed.
Windows 2000 could not start because the following file is
missing or corrupt: %systemroot%\system32\ntoskrnl.exe. Please
re-install a copy of the above file.
I/O Error accessing boot sector file
multi(0)disk(0)rdisk(0)partition(1)
```

In the event of any one of these messages, you have a number of options available to you. First, you can create and boot from a Windows 2000 boot disk and copy the missing file(s) to the hard drive. If that doesn't work, you can boot into the Recovery

Console and view the contents of the boot.ini and compare the ARC pathnames to those displayed in the Recovery Console when you execute the **map** command. A third option is to boot using the Windows 2000 CD and select to perform a repair using the ERD. This option requires that you have created an ERD recently. The following exercises will walk you through some of these options.

EXERCISE 18-6

CertCam 18-6

Creating a Windows 2000 Boot Disk

In this exercise, you will learn the steps involved in creating a Windows 2000 boot disk. This boot disk can help you boot a computer running Windows 2000 that is experiencing startup problems.

1. Insert a floppy disk into the floppy drive of a functioning computer running Windows 2000 and click Start, click Run, and type **cmd**.

2. At the command prompt, type **format a:** and press ENTER.

3. At the prompt, press ENTER to start the format operation. When prompted for a volume label, type **bootdsk** and press ENTER.

4. When prompted to format another disk, type **n** and press ENTER

5. Once the format is complete, close the command prompt and press CTRL-E.

on the Job

The formatting of the disk on a computer running Windows 2000 or Windows NT is critical. Skipping this step will not result in the creation of a Windows 2000 boot disk.

6. In Windows Explorer, click the C drive. In the display pane, hold down the CTRL key and click the boot.ini file, followed by the ntldr file, then the ntdetect.com file, and, if it exists, the ntbootdd.sys file. Right-click one of the selected files and click Copy.

7. Right-click the A drive and click Paste.

Congratulations! You have now created a Windows 2000 boot disk.

Now that you have created a Windows 2000 boot disk, you may have to make one additional change if the startup problem is related to any of the startup files, such as boot.ini, ntldr, or ntdetect.com not being found. This type of error generally indicates that the ARC paths on the computer do not match those in the boot.ini file. If you think this is the case, edit the paths in the boot.ini file on the Windows 2000 startup disk to reflect what you think they are on the computer, and then try to boot with the startup disk. If you are successful, copy the boot.ini file from the startup disk to the hard drive and try a reboot without the startup disk.

Windows NT and Windows 2000 assign partition numbers to all primary partitions before assigning partition numbers to any logical drives within an extended partition. Where this could introduce problems is when a disk is partitioned as shown in Figure 18-3, where the boot files are stored on the D drive and then a new primary partition is created in the area of free disk space.

In Figure 18-3, the partitions are numbered as follows: the C drive is partition 1 and the D drive is partition 2.

Figure 18-4 shows the disk after the new primary partition is created. What changes during the creation of the second primary partition is the partition number: the C drive remains partition 1, the D drive becomes partition 3, and the E drive becomes the new partition 2.

The Emergency Repair Disk

Maintaining current system documentation can assist you tremendously when faced with a system problem. In the case of a system startup failure, you can reference the documentation to determine when the ERD was updated last. If the ERD hasn't been updated since the original installation, I would suggest holding off on using this potential recovery option until you have exhausted all others. If you have a recent ERD on floppy or have simply updated the repair folder on the hard drive, this might be the first place to start your recovery.

on the job

Unlike in Windows NT 4, you are no longer able to use the rdisk command to create an ERD; it must be done through the Backup utility.

FIGURE 18-3

A partitioned disk

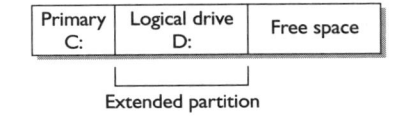

| Primary C: | Logical drive D: | Free space |

Extended partition

Recovering Data from a Hard Disk in the Event that the Operating System Will Not Start **819**

FIGURE 18-4

The new partition numbers

Primary C:	Logical drive D:	New Primary E:

Extended partition

EXERCISE 18-7

CertCam 18-7

Creating an ERD

In this exercise, you will learn the steps involved in creating an emergency repair disk and updating the repair folder in the %systemroot% directory at the same time. This is something that, unfortunately, cannot be scheduled with only the tools included with the OS, but can be scheduled through the use of third-party tools like Aelita's ERDisk. The ERD is something that should be updated prior to making any system configuration changes, and another new disk should be created after the configuration changes have been made. Let's explore how to do just that:

1. Place a blank, formatted floppy disk in the floppy drive (A) and select Start | Programs | Accessories | System Tools | Backup.

2. On the Welcome tab of the Backup utility, click the button to the left of Emergency Repair Disk.

3. In the Emergency Repair Diskette dialog box, place a check mark in the box and click OK.

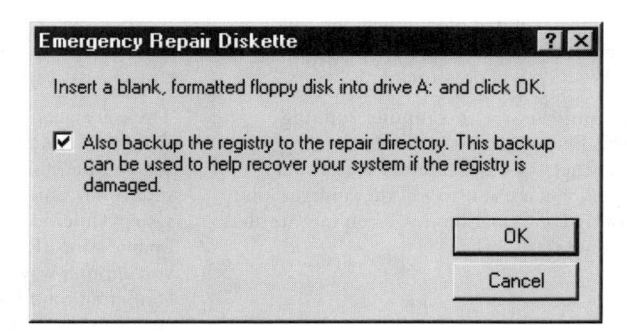

4. The ERD creation occurs, and you are alerted to the successful creation of the ERD. Click OK.

The ERD is not a bootable disk, so to use it in the repair process, you must boot the computer from the Windows 2000 CD, launching the OS setup, and then select the Repair option.

exam⚠️watch

The ERD is computer-specific, meaning that an ERD created on one computer cannot be used in the recovery of another.

The recovery steps described thus far are not the only options available to you when you are trying to recover data from the hard drive of your computer that will not boot. You can use a third-party utility, such as Lost and Found; you can install a new version of Windows 2000 to another directory on the computer, if disk space permits; or you can remove the hard drive from the problem computer and install it in another functioning computer as a second drive. The latter two options would allow you to try to access the data from another functioning version of the OS and transfer the files off the problem hard drive. When it comes to recovering your critical business data, the old adage "where there's a will, there's a way" definitely applies!

SCENARIO & SOLUTION

You have made some partition changes to your computer running Windows 2000 and forgot to edit the boot.ini file prior to rebooting the computer. You are now experiencing startup problems that you believe you can resolve with a modified boot.ini file on a Windows 2000 boot disk. You have copied the three required files to the floppy and attempted a reboot, but it doesn't appear to be booting off the floppy. What do you need to do?	There are a couple of things that you might need to do. First, you should check the BIOS to confirm the boot order is configured to read from the floppy disk before it reads from the hard drive. Second, you need to format the floppy disk on a computer running Windows NT or 2000 and then recopy the three required files (boot.ini, ntldr, and ntdetect.com) to the disk. Finally, you must edit the boot.ini file to reflect the correct ARC path, and reboot the computer.
You are the administrator of a computer running Windows 2000. Before making a number of configuration changes to the computer, you would like to ensure that you are able to roll the configuration back to its existing configuration if you run into trouble. What should you do?	There are a couple of preventative administration steps that you should take. First, back up the data and system state on the computer and confirm that the backup was successful. This will allow you to completely restore the system should something catastrophic occur. Second, update your ERD through the Backup utility. This offers you another way in which to try and restore the existing configuration if something goes wrong. A third, optional step is to install the Recovery Console. This is less important than the first two because it can always be accessed from the Windows 2000 CD.

SCENARIO & SOLUTION

You are the administrator of a computer running Windows 2000. The computer has gone offline unexpectedly. After trying a number of different things, you are unable to start the computer. You must retrieve the data that is on the hard disk. What other options do you have?	One option that is available to you, if disk space permits, is to install another copy of the OS on the drive and access the data through the new OS installation. Another option is to remove the disk from the problem computer and install it as an additional disk in another computer and try to access the data.
You are the administrator of a number of computers in your organization. The computers run a combination of Windows NT 4 and Windows 2000 OSs. You have been using **rdisk** to create ERDs for each of the computers running Windows NT 4 but are unable to create them on the computers running Windows 2000. What is causing this problem and how can you resolve it?	The **rdisk** command is not supported in Windows 2000, hence the problem. The ERD can only be created using the Ntbackup utility in Windows 2000.

CERTIFICATION OBJECIVE 18.05

Restoring an Operating System and Data from Backup

The most important and proactive administrative recovery task is the regular creation of a good backup. A "good" backup includes many things in a network environment, including all of your business data, all directory data such as the Active Directory and SYSVOL, and all critical server configurations. A good backup strategy can help to get things back up and running and restore business data. A bad backup can cost you not only your job but the entire business. I recall reading an article a few years ago, during the dot com frenzy, that listed the stats of companies that lost their business data and what percentage of those companies failed. Not astonishing, more than 50 percent of companies that didn't have a recent backup of their business data were out of business within two years of losing the information. The lesson is that backups are critical—hence the success of companies like Veritas that make enterprise backup software.

The Backup utility included with Windows 2000 offers many improvements over that included with Windows NT 4. One of the nicest new features is the ability to back up to any type of backup media, including the hard drive, CDRW, removable storage, and good old tape. If you are not familiar with the Backup utility, you can follow along with the guided wizard; however, I am going to assume that you are familiar with the Backup utility and walk you through using the default interface.

822 Chapter 18: Troubleshooting Startup Problems

EXERCISE 18-8

Backing Up Your Computer

This exercise will teach you how to back up your entire computer, including the system state, Registry, and all other important information.

1. Select Start | Programs | Accessories | System Tools | Backup. Notice on the Welcome tab of the Backup dialog box that you can launch either the backup or restore wizard or create your ERD.

on the Job

The Backup utility is the only location where your ERD can be created in Windows 2000. Whereas in Windows NT 4 you had the option to run the rdisk command, that option is no longer available in Windows 2000.

2. Select the Backup tab and place a check mark in the boxes to the left of what you would like to back up, as shown in the following illustration. Pay particular attention to the box to the left of System State. The system state includes the Registry, the COM+ database, and the system startup files, but depending on the configuration of the computer, such as the domain controller, it could also include the certificate services database, Active Directory, and SYSVOL folder.

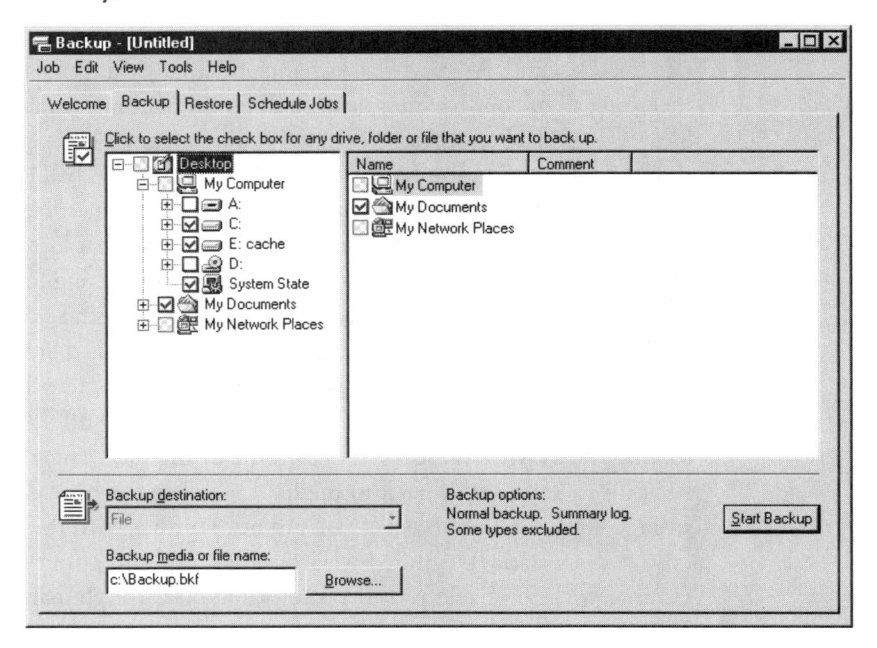

Restoring an Operating System and Data from Backup **823**

3. Once you have selected everything you wish to back up, select a location where you want the information to be backed up to. You'll notice that it defaults to your floppy drive. Can you imagine the number of floppies that would require!

4. Click the Start Backup button, which presents you with the Backup Job Information dialog box. Here, you are able to select to append this backup to the backup media which allows you to keep existing backup information and add the new data to the additional space on the backup media. Alternatively, you can choose to replace the old backup data with the new backup information. The frequency of your backups and the amount of free space will help you to decide which choice is best for you.

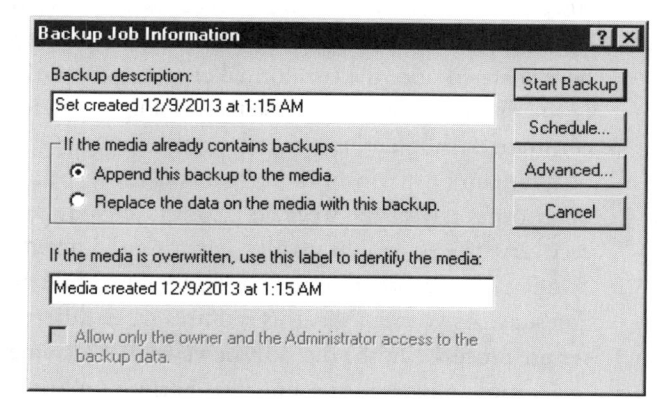

5. To start the backup, click Start Backup. To further configure the backup job, you can select the Schedule or Advanced buttons. The Schedule button opens the Task Scheduler, allowing you to schedule the job to run in the future. The Advanced button allows you to select the backup type and additional options.

Backup Types

There are a number of configuration options available to you when setting up your backups. One of the most important is the type of backup you would like to perform. There are a number of backup types to choose from, and the default is a full backup, which backs up everything. Using the full backup all the time, however, may not be suitable in your network environment. Normal backups generally take longer than any other backup type, and your systems may not be able to support the potential downtime that is required. Other backup choices to consider are the incremental and differential backups. Both of these can be combined with the normal backup in your daily backup schedules to reduce the amount of time required to back up on a daily basis. Don't get hung up, however, on the amount of time required to back up. The amount of time required to restore your systems should be what you are trying to minimize. With that in mind, you might consider running a normal backup on Sundays and early Thursday mornings, and incremental or differential backups on each of the other days.

An incremental backup backs up only those files that have been created or changed since the last normal or incremental backup; hence the name incremental—it only backs up the increments. A differential backup is one that backs up or copies files that have changed since the last normal or incremental backup. To get a better understanding of the difference between these two backup types, let's take a look at a couple of common backup and associated restore strategies.

Company A performs a normal backup on Sundays and an incremental backup every other day of the week. If a computer were to fail on Wednesday morning, the recovery process would involve restoring the normal backup created the previous Sunday first and then restoring the incremental backups from Monday, and then Tuesday. As you can see, this requires three different restores, which slows down the restore process. On the flip side, however, the incremental backups occur quite quickly.

Company B performs a normal backup on Sundays and a differential backup every other day of the week. If a computer were to fail on Wednesday morning, the recovery process in this case would involve restoring the normal backup created the previous Sunday, followed by the differential backup from Tuesday. This allows the restore process to occur more quickly, which is what you are generally looking for in a recovery strategy.

Once your data has been backed up, you are then able to restore the information at any time in the future. Data can easily be restored by selecting the Restore tab in the Backup utility, selecting what you would like to restore, and specifying a location where you wish to restore the data to. A very good habit to get into is to test backed-up data through regular trial restores. Should the day come when you need to perform a restore and you find that the backups have not been working, you'll be kicking yourself for not attempting a trial restore. One important point relating to trial restores is to make sure you choose to restore to an alternate location so that you don't override the current data!

Restoring an Operating System and Data from Backup **825**

> **on the job**
>
> *You should also try restoring your data to a different machine than the machine that was used to create the backup tapes. While rare, it is possible for a tape drive to malfunction in such a way that it can read its own backup tapes, but no other tape drive can read them.*

EXERCISE 18-9

Performing a Restore

This exercise will teach you the steps involved in performing a restore. This is critical to being able to get your system back up and running in as little time as possible. A system or data restore can be performed using the same Ntbackup utility used to perform the backup.

1. Select Start | Programs | Accessories | System Tools | Backup.

2. Click the Restore tab of the Backup dialog box and select the media catalog file that you wish to use to restore from. When performing a restore, you are able to restore everything that was originally backed up, or only a specific file or folder. Select what you would like to restore and select a location from the drop-down list box shown in the illustration and then select where you would like to restore the data to.

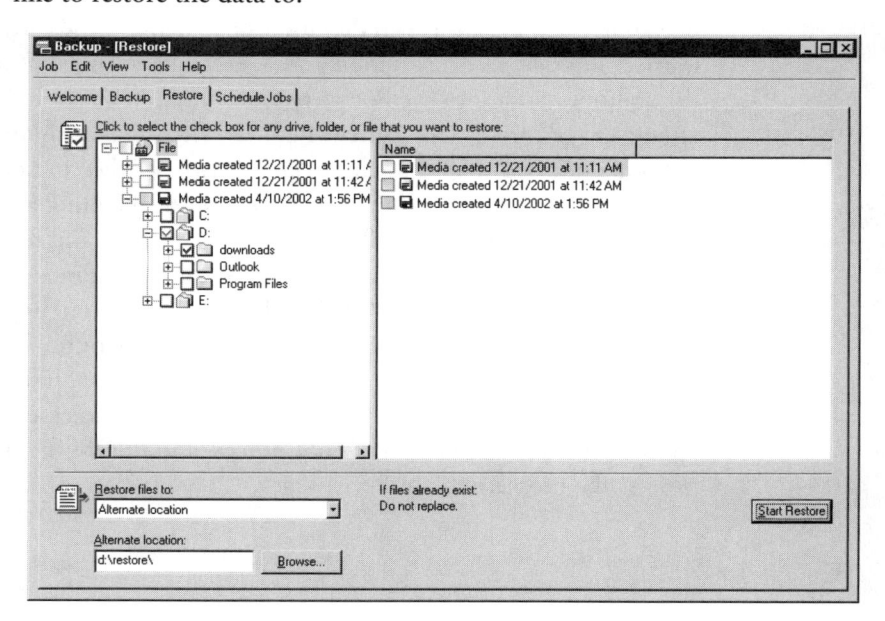

author's note: *When performing a trial restore, make sure you do not restore to the original location.*

3. Click Start Restore to begin the restoration and then click OK. Confirm the path and name of the backup file and click OK.

CERTIFICATION SUMMARY

In this chapter, you have learned how to troubleshoot startup problems using the features included with Windows 2000. You learned about the Windows 2000 startup process and the steps involved in starting your computer. Understanding the sequential boot sequence set the foundation for troubleshooting startup problems by allowing you to analyze the problem and pinpoint at which stage it is likely occurring.

We began our look into troubleshooting with the startup log file (ntbtlog.txt), examining how this can be used to identify a specific device driver or system file that is causing the problem, and continued on with a look at the available Advanced Startup options. You learned what each of the Advanced Startup options allows you to do and when each of the options can and should be used in a recovery.

One of the new features included in Windows 2000 is the Recovery Console, and like all new features, this will definitely be a focus on the certification exam. As you learned, this new recovery option gives a user who knows the administrator password the ability to boot into the Recovery Console and run a number of commands in an attempt to restore the computer's functionality, such as **chkdsk**, **listsvc**, **format**, **fixboot**, and **fixmbr**, and to enable and disable services and devices.

The last two sections of the chapter looked at the other available recovery options, the most critical being the ability to back up and restore using the Backup utility as a proactive administrative task. We also examined the use of the ERD, and how to create a Windows 2000 boot disk to allow you to boot the system when the correct partition numbers are not reflective in the boot.ini file.

This chapter has provided you with a look at all the options available to assist you in both system and data recovery, both proactively and reactively. It also provided you with the knowledge of the boot process and the ability to identify where in the process the problem might be arising.

✓ TWO-MINUTE DRILL

Interpreting the Startup Log File

- ❑ The startup log is not enabled by default. Enable it by choosing any of the Safe Mode options or by selecting the Enable Boot Logging Advanced Startup option.
- ❑ The startup log can also be enabled by modifying the boot.ini file and adding the switch /bootlog.txt to the end of the ARC path.
- ❑ The startup log is named ntbtlog.txt and is saved to the %systemroot% directory.
- ❑ The startup log logs all eligible devices and services on the local computer and indicates whether they loaded or failed to load.
- ❑ Use the startup log to determine which specific driver or service is causing the startup problems.

Repairing an Operating System by Using Various Startup Options

- ❑ Advanced Startup options can be accessed during system initialization by pressing the F8 key.
- ❑ Successfully booting with the Safe Mode options tells you that the basic system and device drivers are not the root of the problem.
- ❑ The Directory Services Restore Mode option is only applicable to computers configured as Windows 2000 domain controllers and can be used to perform an authoritative restore.
- ❑ The Enable VGA Mode option allows you to boot a computer on which you are experiencing video-related issues such as indecipherable resolution. When the computer is booted with this option, it boots using base video resolution.
- ❑ The Last Known Good Configuration option can be used to roll back the configuration settings of a computer to those saved during the last successful shutdown. The last known good configuration is stored in the Registry and overwritten during a successful logon. The Select Registry key in HKLM\System allows you to determine which Registry key contains the last known good configuration settings.
- ❑ The Debugging Mode option allows you to send debugging information through a serial cable to another computer.

Repairing an Operating System by Using the Recovery Console

- The Recovery Console can be installed using the **winnt32.exe /cmdcons** command and then accessed from the operating system selection menu, or it can be accessed by booting the computer from the Windows 2000 CD and selecting the Repair option.
- The Recovery Console requires that you log on with the password of the built-in Administrator account. On a domain controller, this password will be the password you specified for the Directory Services Restore Mode during the domain controller promotion.
- Use the Recovery Console to list the local system services and device drivers and their startup values, enable or disable services or device drivers, fix the MBR, format a drive, and to run **chkdsk** to identify bad sectors. The Recovery Console can also be used to identify the ARC paths on the computer.
- The Recovery Console can be removed by editing the boot.ini file and removing the entry with the /cmdcons switch at the end of the ARC path.

Recovering Data from a Hard Disk in the Event that the Operating System Won't Start

- Start with the computer hardware and eliminate that as the source of the problem.
- Create a Windows 2000 boot disk to start the system when presented with errors that indicate files are missing or paths to existing files appear incorrect. Three critical files must be copied to the boot disk: boot.ini, ntldr, and ntdetect.com.
- The ERD can be used to recover a computer and restore its configuration to that stored on the ERD. The ERD can be updated only through the Backup utility in Windows 2000 and should be updated after any configuration change is made on the computer.

Restoring an Operating System and Data from Backup

- The Ntbackup utility is found in the System Tools folder and can be used to back up and restore system information and data and is also where the ERD is created in Windows 2000.
- Backups can be scheduled to occur on specific days and at specific times. The scheduler is integrated into the Backup utility and backups can now be saved to a variety of storage media.

- ❑ Backing up the system state backs up the important OS information, including the Registry, COM+ database, and system startup files, and potentially the certificate services database, Active Directory, and SYSVOL folder, depending on the configuration of the computer.

- ❑ Backup types include normal, incremental, differential, and copy. Incremental backups only back up what has changed since the last backup and therefore reduce the amount of time to back up. Differential backups back up everything that has changed since the last normal backup and reduce the amount of time required to restore. Normal backups back up everything and take the longest amount of time to back up, but they take the least amount of time to completely restore because only the last normal backup has to be restored. A copy backup allows you to make a copy of the data using the backup utility, but it doesn't affect the archive attribute which ensures that it does not affect other ongoing backups. A daily backup backs up all the files that were changed during the day of the daily backup.

SELF TEST

The following questions will help you measure your understanding of the material presented in this chapter. Read the questions and answers carefully, and be aware that some questions will provide for more than one correct answer. Choose *all* correct answers for each question.

Interpreting the Startup Log File

1. As the administrator of a computer running Windows 2000 that is experiencing startup problems, you have enabled the boot logging options in the Advanced Startup options. After startup failed to boot successfully, you started the computer using the Recovery Console and would like to look at the contents of the boot log file. What is the name of the boot log file?

    A. ntbootlog.txt
    B. bootlog.txt
    C. ntlog.txt
    D. ntbtlog.txt

2. You want to enable the startup log option to create a log file during all system startups. How can you accomplish this?

    A. Edit the boot.ini file and append the /sos switch to the end of the OS ARC path.
    B. Install the Recovery Console.
    C. Change the default startup properties in the System icon in the Control Panel to create a dump file.
    D. Edit the boot.ini file and append the /bootlog.txt switch to the end of the OS ARC path.
    E. Edit the boot.ini file and append the /ntbtlog.txt switch to the end of the OS ARC path.

Repairing an Operating System by Using Various Startup Options

3. You are the administrator of a computer running Windows 2000 Server. You are interested in determining the Registry key that contains the last known good configuration. You open regedt32 as shown in Figure 18-5. Which Registry will tell you what key contains the last known good configuration?

    A. Select
    B. CurrentControlSet

FIGURE 18-5

Identifying the location of the last known good configuration

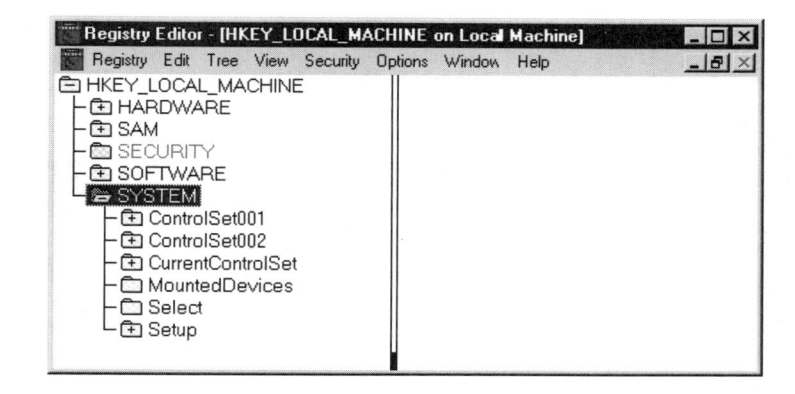

[Screenshot: Registry Editor - HKEY_LOCAL_MACHINE on Local Machine, showing HKEY_LOCAL_MACHINE expanded with HARDWARE, SAM, SECURITY, SOFTWARE, SYSTEM (expanded to show ControlSet001, ControlSet002, CurrentControlSet, MountedDevices, Select, Setup)]

    C. Setup

    D. ControlSet001

    E. ControlSet002

4. You are the administrator of a computer running Windows 2000 Server configured as a domain controller. You have accidentally deleted an OU within Active Directory and need to perform an authoritative restore. Place the following steps in the correct order to successfully perform an authoritative restore. (Choose only those answers that apply.)

    A. Use Active Directory Sites and Services to force replication.

    B. Reboot the computer.

    C. Reboot the computer in Directory Services Restore Mode.

    D. Run **ntdsutil** to perform an authoritative restore.

    E. Restore the system state from backup.

Repairing an Operating System by Using the Recovery Console

5. You are the administrator of a computer running Windows 2000 on which you have installed the Recovery Console. This computer is a member of the mccaw.ca domain. You are a member of the local Administrators group on the computer but not a member of the Domain Admins group. You are logged on as a user named JohnS with a password of password. You are trying to log on to the Recovery Console, but it will not accept the password for your account. What is the most likely cause of the problem?

    A. CAPS LOCK is on.

    B. To use another account, you must use the **logon** command.

832   Chapter 18:   Troubleshooting Startup Problems

    C. You must use the password of the local Administrator account.

    D. You must be a member of the Domain Admins group.

    E. You must use the password of the Domain Administrator account.

6. You are the local administrator of a computer running Windows 2000. You have used the Local Security Settings snap-in, shown in Figure 18-6, to rename the local Administrator account. You have created a new Administrator account that has no rights and permissions and is a member of only the Guests group. Weeks later, your computer has begun to experience startup problems after you have made some configuration changes. You would like to use the Recovery Console to try and resolve the problems. What account's password will you use to log on?

    A. Use the password of the new Administrator account.

    B. Use the password of the renamed Administrator account.

    C. Use your own password, as your account is a member of the Administrators group.

    D. Use the password for the Domain Administrator account.

Recovering Data from a Hard Disk in the Event that the Operating System Won't Start

7. You are the administrator of a number of computers running Windows 2000. The OS on one of the computers does not allow you to start the computer. You are presented with an error message "Boot: Couldn't find NTLDR. Please insert another disk." Which of the following is the most likely cause of the problem?

    A. The ERD was recently updated.

    B. Recent changes were made to the disk partitions.

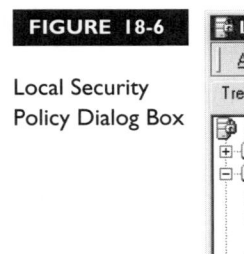

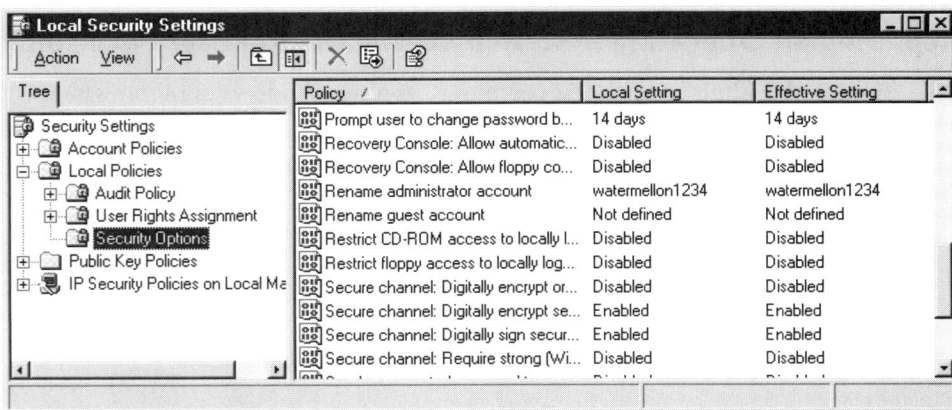

FIGURE 18-6

Local Security Policy Dialog Box

Self Test **833**

C. The Administrator account was recently renamed.

D. Installing the Recovery Console has changed the ARC paths in the boot.ini file.

8. Which command or utility can be used to identify the partition numbers on basic disks in Windows 2000?

A. Disk Management

B. dskmgmt.msc

C. The **map** command in the Recovery Console

D. The **chkdsk** command run at the Windows 2000 command prompt

Restoring an Operating System and Data from Backup

9. You are the administrator of a computer running Windows 2000. You would like to back up all the information on your computer to allow you to restore the computer's configuration and data in the event of an unrecoverable system failure. In the Backup dialog box, as shown in Figure 18-7, what check boxes would you check to accomplish this?

A. All of the check boxes

B. Only the Desktop check box, as that would enable all others

FIGURE 18-7

Windows 2000 Backup Dialog Box

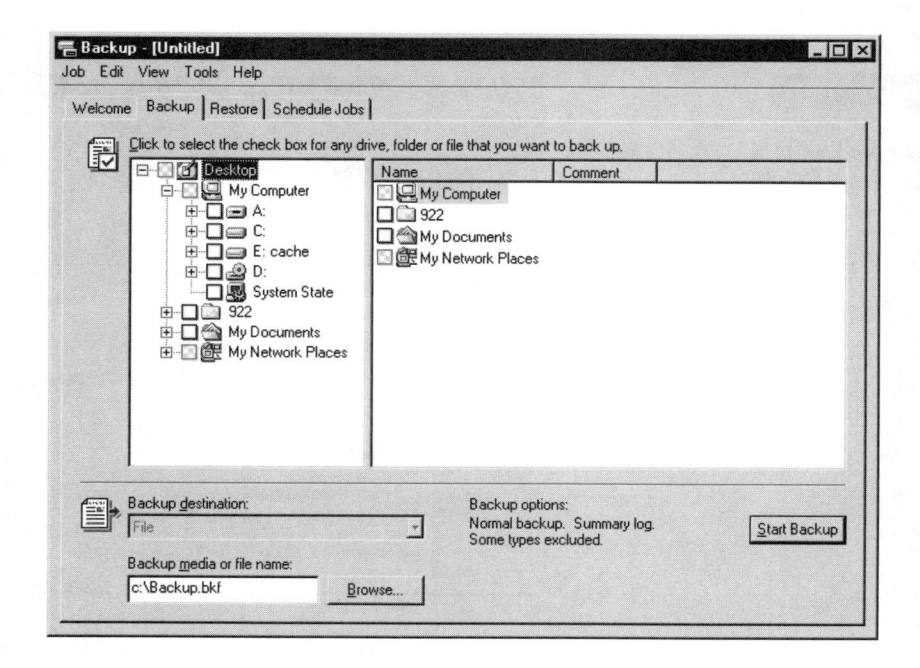

834 Chapter 18: Troubleshooting Startup Problems

    C. Only the C, E, and System State check boxes

    D. Only the System State check box

10. You are the administrator of a computer running Windows 2000 Server. You have scheduled daily normal backups on the computer to back up the system state. All files for the system state are stored on a 4GB hard disk. You have noticed, though, that the size of your backups are larger than 4GB in size. You look to the advanced backup options shown in Figure 18-8 to try to determine what might be causing this problem. What is the most likely cause of the problem?

    A. The catalogs on the media have grown so large, due to repeated backups, that they are taking up the extra space.

    B. Backing up the contents of mounted drives is causing the problem.

    C. The selection information on the media is consuming the extra space.

    D. Because the verification option is not enabled, the data is backed up twice, which is causing the size increase.

LAB QUESTION

You are the administrator of all the computers running Windows 2000 in your organization. You are evaluating your backup and recovery strategy to try to be as proactive as possible. Your goal for the new

FIGURE 18-8

Advanced Backup Options

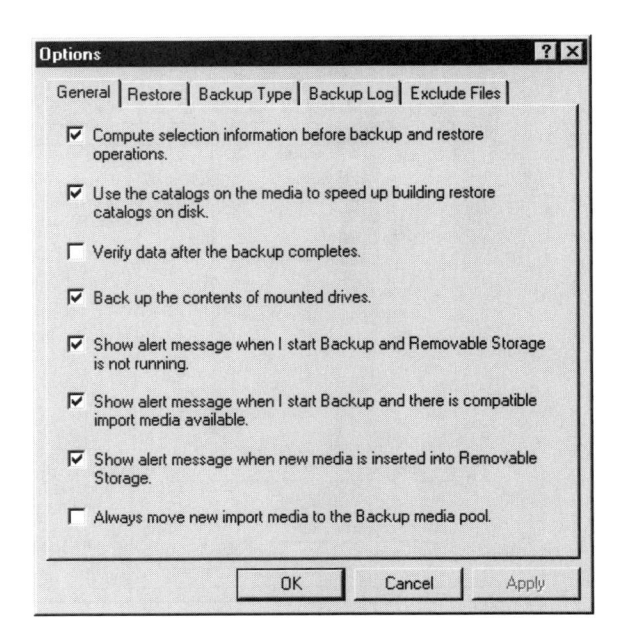

strategy is to be able to reduce the amount of time required to recover from a system failure. Answer the following questions to help you in the development of this new backup and recovery strategy.

1. What proactive steps can you take that may help you plan for a system failure and recover scenario?

2. Describe the steps involved in creating a Windows 2000 boot disk. Describe a scenario that would require the ntbootdd.sys file to also be copied over to the Windows 2000 boot disk.

3. Describe the different backup types that you can choose from when using the Windows Backup utility and describe an example of when to use each type.

4. Assuming all of your recovery attempts fail to recover the failed system and you do not have a recent backup, what other options are available to you to recover the data on the disk?

836 Chapter 18: Troubleshooting Startup Problems

SELF TEST ANSWERS

Interpreting the Startup Log File

1. ☑ **D** is correct. The name of the boot log file is ntbtlog.txt.
   ☒ **A** is incorrect because ntbootlog.txt is not the name of the boot log file.
   ☒ **B** is incorrect because bootlog.txt is not the name of the boot log file. The \bootlog.txt switch can be used in the boot.ini file to enable boot logging.
   ☒ **C** is incorrect because ntlog.txt is not the correct filename either.

2. ☑ **D** is correct. Editing the boot.ini file and appending the /bootlog.txt switch to the end of the OS ARC path will enable the boot log file during all startups.
   ☒ **A** is incorrect because, although the /sos switch can be used in the boot.ini file to display all the drivers and system services at startup on the monitor, this does not create the boot log file.
   ☒ **B** is incorrect because the installation of the Recovery Console does not affect the use or configuration of the boot log file.
   ☒ **C** is incorrect because changing the startup properties in the System icon in the Control Panel can allow you to configure the memory.dmp file but not the boot log file.
   ☒ **E** is incorrect because the .ntbtlog.txt file is not a valid switch in the boot.ini file.

Repairing an Operating System by Using Various Startup Options

3. ☑ **A** is correct. The LastKnownGood value found in the Select key in the Registry can be used to determine the Registry key that contains the last known good configuration.
   ☒ **B** is incorrect because the CurrentControlSet key contains the configuration information pertaining to the current configuration.
   ☒ **C** is incorrect because the Setup Registry key does not contain this information.
   ☒ **D** and **E** are incorrect because neither the ControlSet001 nor the ControlSet002 Registry key contains information to determine the key containing the last known good configuration.

4. ☑ **C, E, D, B** is the correct order of the steps required to perform an authoritative restore. To perform an authoritative restore, reboot the computer in Directory Services Restore Mode, restore the system state from backup, run **ntdsutil** to perform the authoritative restore, and then reboot the computer.
   ☒ **A** is incorrect because using Active Directory Sites and Services is not required, because replication will occur automatically.

Self Test Answers **837**

Repairing an Operating System by Using the Recovery Console

5. ☑ C is correct. The Recovery Console requires that you use the password of the local Administrator account to log on.
☒ A is incorrect because, although CAPS LOCK could be a valid reason if you were using the correct account password, the user is logging on with his own account password, which, even if correct, will not be accepted by the Recovery Console.
☒ B is incorrect because you must log on successfully before using the **logon** command.
☒ D and E are incorrect because you are not required to be a member of the Domain Admins group or use the Domain Administrators password to log on to the Recovery Console.

6. ☑ B is correct. To log on to the Recovery Console, the password of the renamed Administrator account must be used even though the prompt asked for the password for the Administrator account.
☒ A is incorrect because the password of the new Administrator account will not log you on.
☒ C is incorrect because you must log on using the password of the original Administrator account. Using the password of an account that is a member of the Administrators group will not log you on.
☒ D is incorrect because the password of the Domain Administrator account will not log you on.

Recovering Data from a Hard Disk in the Event that the Operating System Won't Start

7. ☑ B is correct. The most likely cause of this type of problem is a recent change to the disk partitions without a corresponding partition numbering change being made to the boot.ini file.
☒ A is incorrect because updating the ERD will not affect the computer's partition numbering.
☒ C is incorrect because renaming the Administrator account will not affect the partition configuration.
☒ D is incorrect because installing the Recovery Console will not affect the partition configuration.

8. ☑ C is correct. The **map** command can be used from within the Recovery Console to display the partition numbers on basic disks in Windows 2000.
☒ A is incorrect because Disk Management does not identify the partition numbers of basic disks.
☒ B is incorrect because dskmgmt.msc isn't a valid file for an MMC extension.
☒ D is incorrect because **chkdsk** does not display the disk partition numbers.

Restoring an Operating System and Data from Backup

9. ☑ **C** is correct. Enabling only the C, E, and System State check boxes would also enable 922 and My Documents, as that information is stored on the C drive in the Documents and Settings folder.
☒ **A** is incorrect because enabling all the check boxes would back up information in the CD and floppy drive, which is not necessary.
☒ **B** is incorrect because the Desktop check box is grayed out, preventing you from enabling it.
☒ **D** is incorrect because enabling only the System State check box would not back up your data.

10. ☑ **B** is correct. The most likely cause of this problem is that the option to back up the contents of mounted drives is enabled.
☒ **A** is incorrect because the catalogs on the media would not take up that much space.
☒ **C** is incorrect because the selection information will not dramatically affect the space consumed.
☒ **D** is incorrect because data is never backed up twice, regardless of the verification option.

LAB ANSWER

1. Perform a backup of all production servers that include the data and system state information. Test the backup to verify that it was successful. Install the Recovery Console using the **winnt32.exe /cmdcons** command and edit the ARC path in the boot.ini file to add in the /bootlog.txt switch. This will enable the ntbtlog.txt file to be created at every system boot and accessed using the **type** command in the Recovery Console during a startup failure. Create an updated copy of the ERD using the Backup utility and select to also back up the repair folder on the hard disk. Create a Windows 2000 boot disk for each of the production servers and store these in a safe and secure location with any ERDs that you create.

2. To create a Windows 2000 boot disk, format a floppy disk on a computer running Windows NT or 2000 and copy over the files boot.ini, ntldr, and ntdetect.com. The ntbootdd.sys file may also have to be copied over to the Windows 2000 boot disk if the computer uses SCSI devices connected to SCSI adapters that have their BIOS disabled.

3. There are five backup types to choose from: normal, copy, differential, incremental, and daily. The normal backup backs up all the data that you select and enables the archive attribute to indicate that the file has been backed up. This allows another backup type such as incremental to be combined with the normal backups and allows the incremental backup to know what files have changed since the last normal backup. Any file that has changed will no longer have its archive attribute enabled, indicating to the incremental backup that the file should be backed up. The copy backup copies all selected files but doesn't enable the archive attribute.

This is useful if you want to back up all files between a normal and incremental backup without affecting the archive attributes. The differential backup backs up files that have been created or changed since the last normal or incremental backup but does not change the archive attribute. Restoring requires that both the last normal and differential backups be used in the restore process. An incremental backup backs up only those files created or changed since the last normal or incremental backup and changes the archive attribute on the files to indicate they have been backed up. Restoring requires that you have the last normal backup as well as all incremental backups during the restore process. A daily backup backs up all selected files that have been modified on the day the daily backup is performed. Daily backups do not enable the archive attribute and can be used without affecting a combined normal and incremental backup schedule.

4. Three other available recovery options include installing a new copy of the OS and getting access to the data through this new installation; removing the failed drive and adding it to another functioning computer as an additional drive; and using a third-party disk utility that is designed to recover lost data.

19
Monitoring and Troubleshooting Server Health and Performance

CERTIFICATION OBJECTIVES

19.01	Monitoring and Interpreting Real-Time Performance by Using System Monitor and Task Manager
19.02	Configuring System Monitor Alerts and Logging
19.03	Diagnosing Server Health Problems with Event Viewer
19.04	Identifying and Disabling Unnecessary Services
✓	Two-Minute Drill
Q&A	Self Test

In this chapter, you will learn how to monitor and interpret the performance of your computers running Windows 2000 Server or Professional using a number of built-in tools and utilities such as System Monitor, Task Manager, Event Viewer, and Computer Management. Being a good systems or network administrator is a lot like being a good detective or doctor. In all professions, you are provided with, or must evaluate, the symptoms and interpret those symptoms to determine the possible causes. A number of times, the causes themselves may initially appear to be the problem, but upon further investigation, you often find that one cause leads to another, and by solving the true problem, all the other subsequent problems disappear as well.

A great example of where I have seen this lately is in my golf swing. In an effort to improve my golf game, I have begun to take some lessons. In my first lesson, my instructor pointed out a number of problems with my swing. But where we started to make the changes and address the problem was from the absolute beginning, with my stance. As it turns out, my original poor stance was leading to five or more of the problems he noticed. Correcting that made a number of the other subsequent problems disappear. Knowing how to improve my golf game won't help you on the certification exam but it does demonstrate that the same concepts can be applied across a number of disciplines.

To pass the certification exam, you must be very familiar with the monitoring tools included with Windows 2000 that allow you to interpret performance data. What you will notice throughout the chapter is that a number of the tools are identical in name to those found in Windows NT 4, though some have been improved or modified slightly. We'll begin with a look at monitoring real-time performance data with System Monitor, which used to be Performance Monitor and Task Manager.

CERTIFICATION OBJECTIVE 19.01

Monitoring and Interpreting Real-Time Performance by Using System Monitor and Task Manager

Knowing how to monitor real-time performance information is a critical piece of knowledge as a systems or network administrator. Windows 2000 provides two tools that allow you to do this, System Monitor and Windows Task Manager, both of which you will learn your way around in this section.

Windows Task Manager

Task Manager is a utility that you can use to determine real-time information about the programs and processes running on your computer. Task Manager is a great tool to use when you want to monitor key indicators of your computer's performance, such as memory and CPU usage, which it will show to you in both percentage and graph form. Task Manager can be accessed in a number of different ways, but the two most common are pressing the CTRL-ALT-DELETE key sequence or right-clicking the Start bar, usually at the bottom of the screen.

Pressing CTRL-ALT-DELETE opens the Windows Security dialog box, allowing you to select the Task Manager button, whereas right-clicking the taskbar opens a context menu from which you can select Task Manager. In either case, the Windows Task Manager dialog box appears, as shown in Figure 19-1.

As you can see from Figure 19-1, data is divided into three tabs, with the focus in Figure 9-1 being on the Applications tab. The other two tabs are the Processes and Performance tabs. The Applications tab allows you to quickly determine the status of the application on the local computer. A status message of Running indicates that the application is functioning correctly, whereas a status of Not Responding indicates that the program is frozen. Task Manager allows you to select the nonresponding application, and click the End Task button.

By selecting the Performance tab, shown in Figure 19-2, you are able to see a graphical view of both CPU and memory usage as well as a percentage indication at the bottom of the dialog box and to the left of the CPU graph. One way in which to

FIGURE 19-1

Windows Task Manager

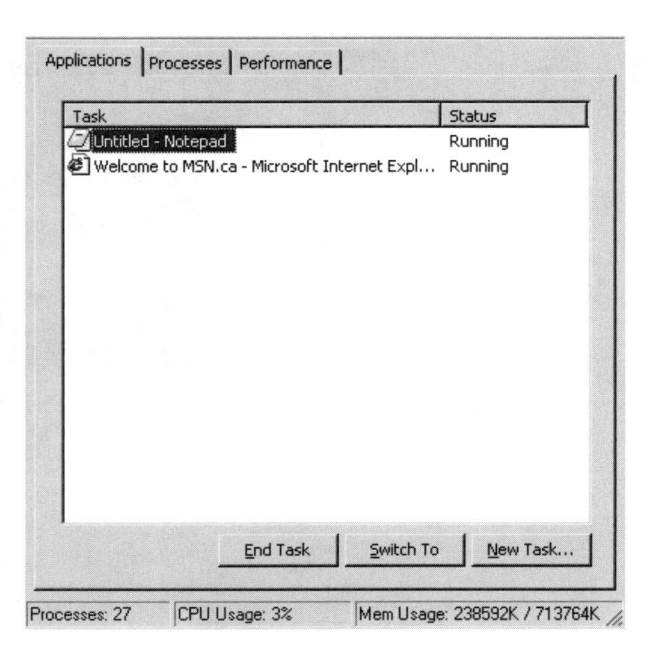

determine the performance of the computer is to monitor the CPU and memory usage. The Performance tab provides you with a great deal of valuable information in the four boxes at the bottom of the dialog box. The Totals section contains information on the number of handles, threads, and processes. The Physical Memory section shows you the total memory in the computer, the amount available, and the amount used by the system cache. The Kernel Memory section shows you the total amount of memory that the operating system is using and then breaks it down into paged and nonpaged memory. Paged memory is memory the OS can temporarily swap to disk if the OS requires the physical memory. The Commit Charge box shows how much memory is allocated to application and system programs. It shows the total memory, the limit, which is the maximum available memory (total physical memory plus virtual memory), and the peak usage since Task Manager started.

The Processes tab, shown in Figure 19-3, allows you to view the system resource consumption for each individual process that is running on the computer. The Processes tab displays the information in a tabular format with columns for the name of the process, the processor ID, CPU, CPU Time, and Memory Usage. Select View | Select Columns to open the Select Columns dialog box, shown in Figure 19-4, and customize the information that is displayed.

FIGURE 19-2

The Performance tab of Windows Task Manager

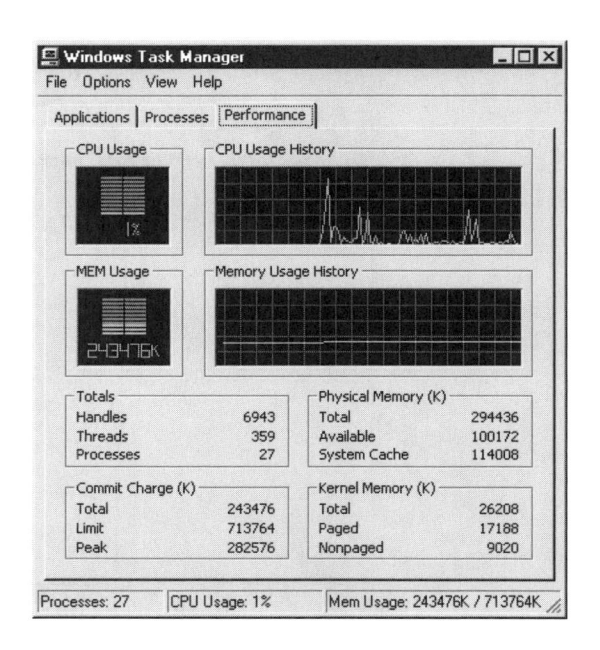

FIGURE 19-3

The Processes tab of Windows Task Manager

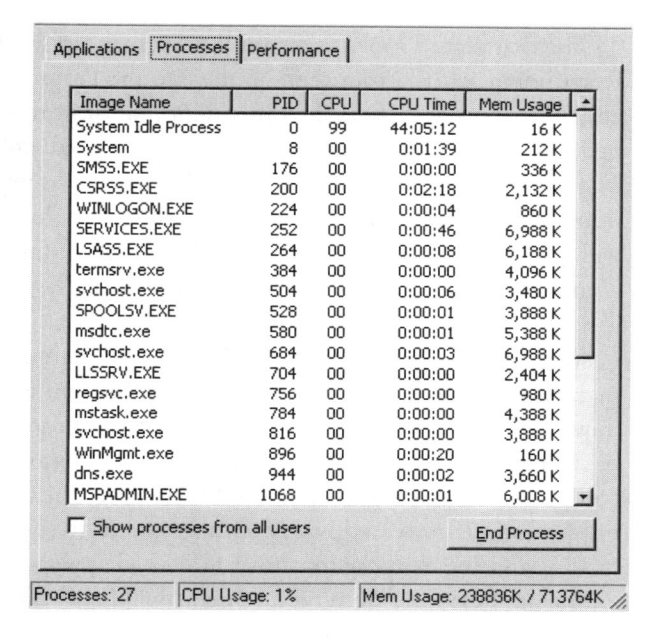

I like to think of Task Manager as the first stop on the path to troubleshooting system resources, particularly if I am asked to troubleshoot a system that I am not that familiar with, as is often the case in a consulting engagement. I use Task Manager first, because it is easy to get to and with its "always on top" configuration, you can generally get to it even when a process or application has frozen and everything else on the system is sluggish.

FIGURE 19-4

Customizing the view of the Processes tab

The first place I look is the Applications tab, to see if any applications have a Not Responding status. From there, I move to the Performance tab to look at the CPU and memory usage. If either component is at or near its peak, and appears to be operating at that level consistently, I have some valuable information. What would be even more valuable is what the level of activity is normally. This type of information can be found from your performance logs, the configuration which we will discuss later in this chapter. The Performance tab also allows you to get a click glimpse of what you are dealing with in terms of system resources. You can quickly identify the total and available amounts of physical memory and virtual memory.

Microsoft operating systems and applications are notorious for requiring more memory, and have a growing memory requirement with each new release. Knowing how much memory is in the computer allows you to compute how much should be in the computer when the OS and applications are factored in. For example, a computer running Windows 2000 Server should really have a minimum of 256MB of physical memory. Add in applications such as Exchange, SMS, SQL, MOM, or ISA, and the memory for those individual applications must also be factored in. Knowing these minimum requirements will help you to plan for the correct amount of memory for your computer.

System Monitor

System Monitor is another useful tool that can be used for real-time system monitoring. Once you have gathered the basic troubleshooting information that Task Manager is able to provide you, System Monitor can be used to dig deeper into a specific object that you suspect is causing the problem. A basic installation of Windows 2000 installs a number of performance objects and counters for each object and also allows you to specify certain instances where multiple objects exist. Examples of performance objects include physical components such as Processor and Memory and represent the software or device that is being monitored. An object may have multiple instances in the case of a computer with two CPUs. A *counter* is a specific statistic of an object, such as % Processor Time in the case of the Processor object. An instance is the specific occurrence of an object you wish to monitor, such as CPU 0 and CPU 1 in the case of a multiprocessor computer. System Monitor also allows you to monitor services such as Terminal Services, DNS, and the Web Publishing Service.

There are four methods available for collecting data, one of which is the System Monitor. The other three are available through Performance Logs and Alerts and include counter logs, trace logs, and alerts. This section of the chapter focuses on the System Monitor as that is the tool you use for real-time monitoring, although it too can be configured to save logged data to a file. Later in this chapter, you will learn about the other three available methods included with Performance Logs and Alerts.

System Monitor is found in the Administrative Tools menu under Performance. Exercise 19-1 looks at opening System Monitor and configuring it to view real-time system information.

EXERCISE 19-1

CertCam 19-1

Using System Monitor to View Real-Time System Information

This exercise teaches you the steps involved in configuring System Monitor to analyze real-time information in a graphical format. Knowing how to use System Monitor can assist you in troubleshooting performance problems.

1. Select Start | Programs | Administrative Tools, and click Performance.

2. After the Performance snap-in opens, select System Monitor in the left pane and click the + sign on the menu bar to display the Add Counters dialog box.

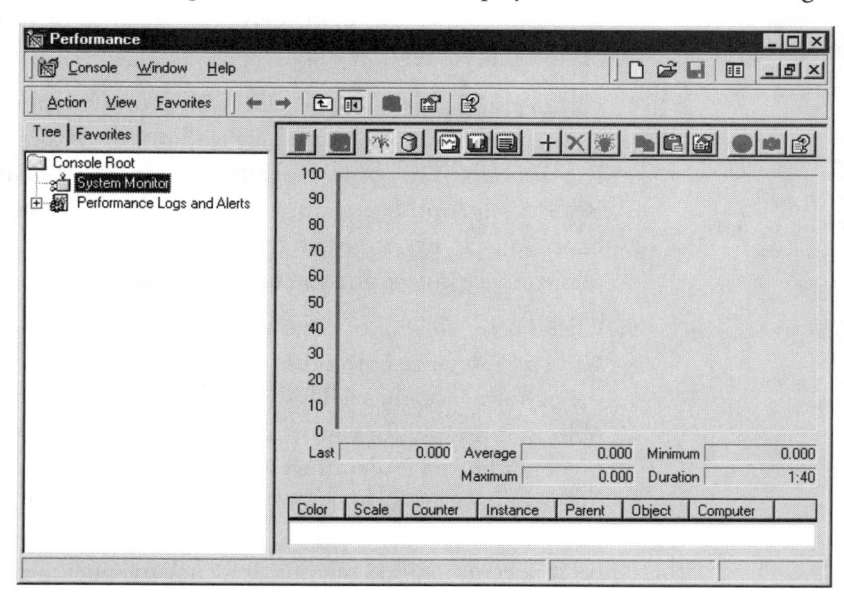

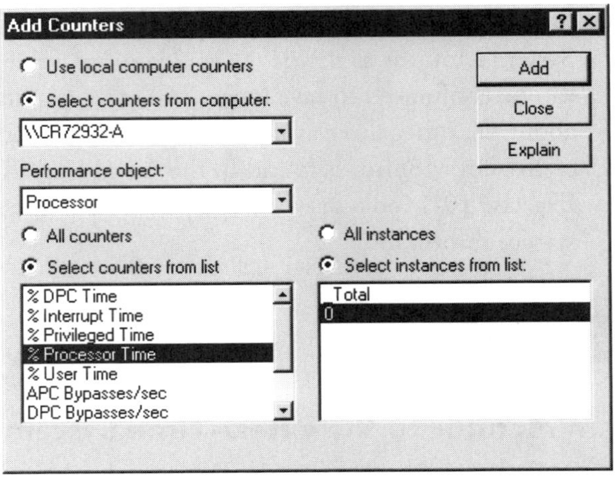

3. In the Add Counters dialog box, you are able to monitor system resources on the local computer as well as remote computers by selecting other computers from the drop-down menu. You also have a choice of performance objects to choose from and then a choice of counters and instances for each performance object. In this exercise, choose the Processor performance object and the % Processor Time counter. The computer that I am using for this exercise only has a single processor, so the selection I make in the Instances section won't make a difference.
4. Click Add. Before you close the Add Counters dialog box, I want to draw your attention to one of the nice features, the Explain button. Click the Explain button to see an explanation of what the counter is intended to do. Realistically, unless you work with the System Monitor on a very regular basis, you can't be expected to know exactly what each counter for each performance object does, so use the Explain button when you are unsure.
5. Click Close. Now notice that the graph in System Monitor begins to chart the CPU performance object that you added and uses a unique color to represent the performance object. This way, if you are monitoring multiple performance objects, it is easier for you to identify the different performance objects. The highlight button is identified on the rebar (the reaction bar, where the buttons in the snap-in are located such as the + sign) by the light bulb icon which can be used to highlight a specific counter. Select the counter in the list in the bottom portion of the snap-in and click the highlight (light bulb) button.

6. System Monitor also provides you with three viewing options. You have seen the graph option. The other two options are histogram and report. These can be selected from the menu bar. Histogram view is identified by the icon with the bar graphs on a flip chart, and report view is identified by the icon that looks like a notepad that appears to the left of the + sign.

on the job

The Windows 2000 disk counters differ from the Windows NT 4 disk counters. In Windows NT 4, no disk counters were initialized on startup. Windows 2000 does initialize disk counters on startup for the PhysicalDisk counters but not the LogicalDisk counters.

Counters for the LogicalDisk performance object are not enabled by default, requiring you to enable them if you wish to monitor logical disk activity. The **diskperf** command can be used to enable, disable, and identify the counters that are currently installed on the computer. Running **diskperf** to enable or disable a counter requires that the computer be restarted for the change to take effect. Running the **diskperf** command by itself with no switches will allow you to see what counters are currently turned on, as shown in Figure 19-5.

To enable the Logical Disk counter, open the command prompt and run the **diskperf –yv** command, as shown in Figure 19-6.

The **diskperf** command can also be used to disable both the Physical and Logical Disk counters. To do this, use the **diskperf –n** command.

You can also use the **diskperf /?** command to list all of the available **diskperf** switches. In addition to disk counters, you might also consider enabling the network segment monitors. These require an add-on utility that is available only in System Management Server (SMS) 2.0, but these are beyond the scope of the certification exam.

FIGURE 19-5

Using diskperf to identify installed performance counters

```
C:\WINNT\System32\cmd.exe
Microsoft Windows 2000 [Version 5.00.2195]
(C) Copyright 1985-2000 Microsoft Corp.

C:\Documents and Settings\Administrator>diskperf

Physical Disk Performance counters on this system are currently set to start at
boot.
```

FIGURE 19-6

Enabling the logical counters

```
C:\WINNT\System32\cmd.exe
C:\Documents and Settings\Administrator>diskperf -yv
Both Logical and Physical Disk Performance counters on this system
        are now set to start at boot.
C:\Documents and Settings\Administrator>_
```

FROM THE CLASSROOM

Enabling Network Segment Monitors

There are two types of network counters to choose from when monitoring network performance: Network Interface counters and Network Segment counters. As the name implies, Network Interface counters allow you to monitor the network interface cards (NICs) and the information that passes through them. These counters are valuable if you wish to monitor the network performance of a specific NIC, but usually the Network Segment counters are of greater value.

The Network Segment counters allow you to monitor the performance of the entire physical network segment that the card is attached to, which allows you to measure your network bandwidth utilization. Knowing your network bandwidth utilization is useful when you are planning network changes, such as the upgrade to Active Directory, SMS, or Exchange, as it tells you how much bandwidth you are currently using. You can then forecast how much bandwidth the proposed new technology will require and determine whether you have enough bandwidth or need to increase the amount required. Once the new technology has been implemented, you can then continue to monitor network bandwidth utilization and determine if your forecasts were accurate and form a baseline for future decisions.

Now that you have seen how useful this can be, I will tell you the bad news. This functionality isn't available with only the Windows 2000 OS. The monitoring of network segments requires that you install the full version of Network Monitor and the corresponding Network Monitor driver, which is only included with the full version of SMS 2.0. If you are questioning this requirement, because you remember seeing the Network Monitor driver option in Windows 2000, you are not entirely wrong—there is a version included but it is the light version. The Network Monitor driver included with Windows 2000 only allows you to monitor the network traffic where your computer is the source or destination, but it will not provide you with statistics on the network segment.

—*Rory McCaw*

CERTIFICATION OBJECTIVE 19.02

Configuring System Monitor Alerts and Logging

The first section of the chapter introduced you to System Monitor and taught you how to configure real-time monitoring. System Monitor is not a tool that is of great use when faced with trying to determine resource usage over an extended period. In this section, you will learn how to use Performance Logs and Alerts to collect and examine data over a longer time period. Logging is the best configuration option available to continuously monitor one or more computers in an effort to establish a performance baseline. The information you collect will allow you to analyze system performance and establish a baseline, which can be used when evaluating hardware and software upgrade options. Performance Logs and Alerts can be configured to create two types of logs, counter logs and trace logs, as well as alerts.

Counter Logs

Counter logs provide you with the ability to monitor data in much the same way you do with System Monitor. The creation of a counter log requires that you select specific objects, counters, and instances, again much like you would with System Monitor. With a counter log, you can also specify the polling frequency, which is the interval at which the log polls the system for information. The default interval is every 15 seconds, but if you are polling over a long period of time, you might want to change this to every minute to still provide you with valid data but prevent the log files from taking up too much space on the hard drive. Counter logs can also be configured to log at specific times, such as between the hours of 6 A.M. and 6 P.M. You are also able to configure as many logs as you like, to capture different information to different log files as a way of separating the logged information. This can be useful if you need to log something temporarily, such as network bandwidth consumption, and you don't want to modify one of your existing counters. The other nice benefit of logging is that it doesn't take up very much system overhead, which allows you to gather valid data samples without polluting the data with system resource consumption generated by the logging components.

Microsoft has included a sample counter log known as the System Overview log, which is installed by default with Windows 2000 Server. This allows you to activate the log and begin logging immediately even if you don't thoroughly grasp the logging process. It also gives you the ability to examine the counter log configuration and use it as a guide in creating your own counter logs. Exercise 19-2 teaches you the process of creating your own counter log.

EXERCISE 19-2

CertCam 19-2

Creating a Counter Log

This exercise teaches you how to create a counter log in Performance Logs and Alerts and how to configure each of the tabs to meet your requirements. Use counter logs to collect data on one or more computers over an extended period of time to create a performance baseline.

1. Select Start | Programs | Administrative Tools, and click Performance.

2. In the Performance dialog box, expand Performance Logs and Alerts, right-click Counter Logs, and click New Log Settings.

3. In the New Log Settings dialog box, type the name of the log you wish to create, such as **new**, and click OK. This will generate and display the new dialog box.

4. On the General tab, click Add to add the counters that you wish to add to the log, and click Close to close the Select Counters dialog box when you are finished adding counters.

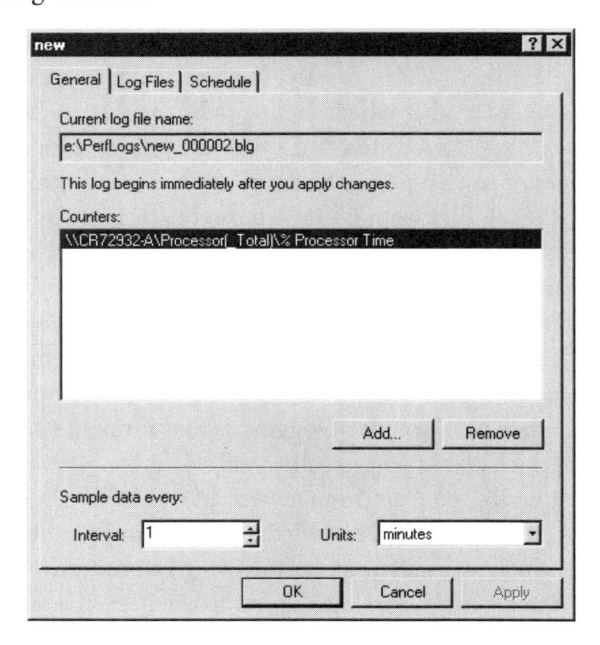

5. At the bottom on the General tab, configure the sampling interval and click Apply.

6. Select the Log Files tab. This is where you specify the location of the log files, modify the filename, and select the log file type. Best practices suggest that you store the log files on a partition other than the partition with the OS files. In the Log File Type drop-down box, you have the choice of a CSV, TSV, binary, or binary circular file. The binary circular option configures the log to overwrite itself when it reaches its maximum size. It is on the Log Files tab that you can also specify a maximum size for the log file. This is a good step to take to prevent the log from getting too big.

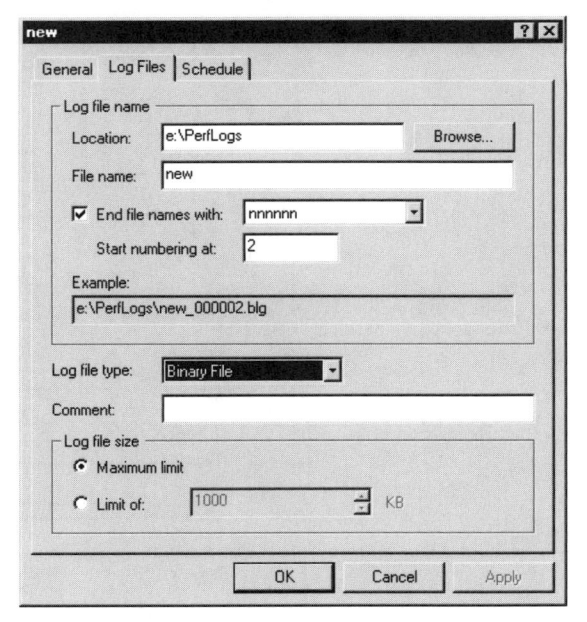

7. On the Schedule tab, you can configure the log to start and stop at a specific date and time, or to stop after a specific period of time, such as one day. When you select to stop the log after a specific period of time, the options of what to do when the log file closes become available and allow you to start a new log file or to run a command. If you have configured logging for a one-week period

854 Chapter 19: Monitoring and Troubleshooting Server Health and Performance

on a specific server, you might want to configure a batch file to run, and in the batch file, configure the **net send** command to send you a message alerting you to the log closing and reminding you to check the log. Another possible command to execute might be the **xcopy** command, which could be used to move the log to a different location where it will be analyzed. In this case, you could create a batch file that maps a drive, copies the file, and then deletes the drive mapping.

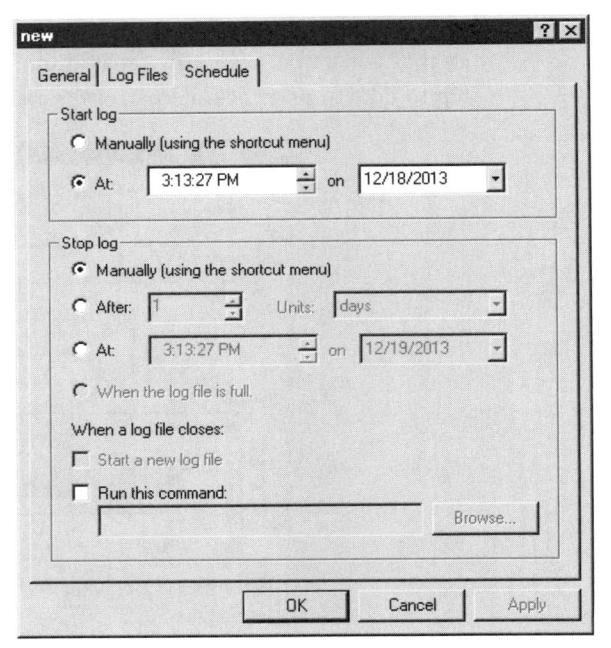

Once you have created your new log, you will notice that the icons to the left of the counter logs are different colors—the System Overview log is red while the New log is green. These colors indicate the state of the log files, with green indicating that the log has started and red indicating that the log has stopped. To start or stop a log, right-click the log and, in the context menu, click either Start or Stop. If on the Schedule tab you chose the manual start option, you have to manually start the log.

Once the log has been created, you have a number of different options available to analyze it. You can open binary formats with System Monitor or use Excel if you chose to store the log in the CSV format. If you selected the TSV option, almost any word processing or spreadsheet application should allow you to open the TSV file. Should you decide to open the log with System Monitor, as you will learn in Exercise 19-3, you must remember that the data is static and you will not be able to add counters to the view that are not contained within the log file.

EXERCISE 19-3

CertCam 19-3

Opening a Log with System Monitor

This exercise teaches you how to open a log file using System Monitor and examine its contents. Once you have generated a number of logged events, you need to view those logs, which is what you learn how to do in this exercise.

1. Select Start | Programs | Administrative Tools, and click Performance.
2. In the Performance dialog box, click System Monitor and click the Properties button on the menu. This opens the System Monitor Properties dialog box.

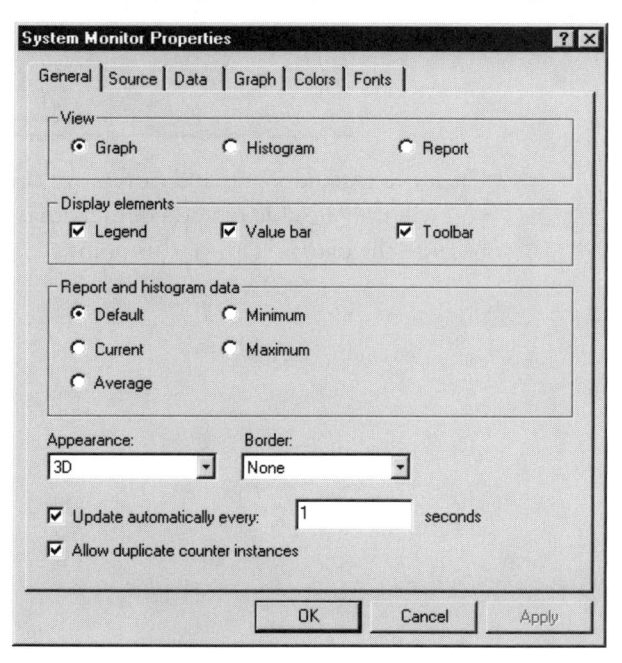

3. Click the Source tab, and in the Data Source section, select the Log File option and click Browse to browse for the log file you wish to view. If you want to see only a portion of the total time the log file spans, click the Time Range button and drag the blocks on either side toward the center until you reach the desired range.

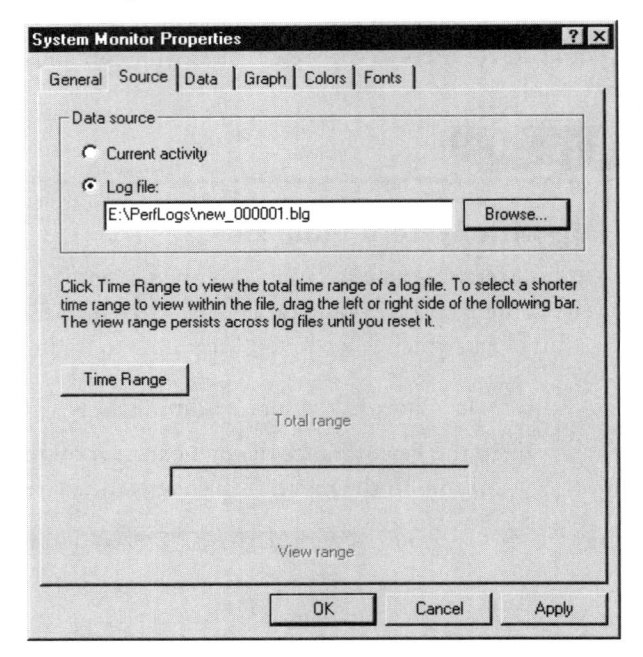

4. Click the Data tab, and add or remove counters as desired. Remember that you will only be able to add counters that you logged in the first place, because the data is static at this point.

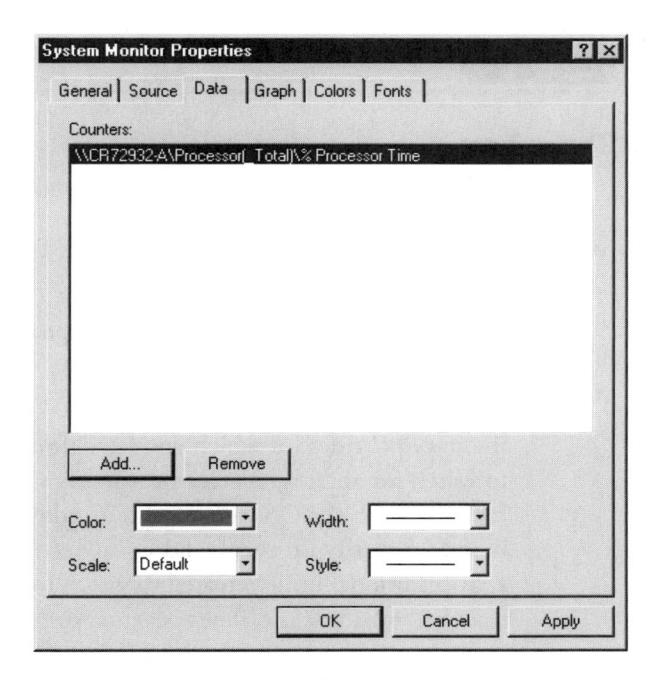

Configuring System Monitor Alerts and Logging **857**

5. Click OK to return to the graph you have just configured.

Trace Logs

Trace logs are the second type of logging available to you in Performance Logs and Alerts. Trace logs are new to Windows 2000, so you should anticipate a question on them on the certification exam. Trace logs require special third-party tools to analyze them, so they aren't extremely useful unless you have some tools to analyze them. Windows 2000 does not include a trace log parser with the operating system.

Trace logs differ from counter logs in what you configure them to monitor. Counter logs are configured to monitor certain resources, such as CPU, memory, or a service such as DNS. Trace logs are configured to monitor certain events. Exercise 19-4 teaches you the steps involved in creating a trace log.

exam
Watch — *Counter logs monitor certain system resources, and trace logs monitor certain events.*

EXERCISE 19-4

Creating a Trace Log

This exercise teaches you how to create and configure the properties of a trace log.

1. Select Start | Programs | Administrative Tools, and expand Performance Tools and Alerts. Right-click Trace Logs and click New Log Settings.

2. In the New Log Settings dialog box, type **newtrace** as the name of the trace log you wish to create and click OK.

3. The newtrace dialog box appears. The General tab allows you to configure the trace provider for which you have three choices, as well as the event types to watch for and log. A trace provider is a piece of software that may be included with the OS, such as the Windows 2000 Kernel Trace Provider, NTLM Security Protocol, and Local Security Authority, or may be provided as an additional utility created to watch for specific types of events. Each trace provider tracks different events, such as disk input or output, and user logon events. Choosing the Events Logged By System Provider radio button allows you to choose which events you want logged.

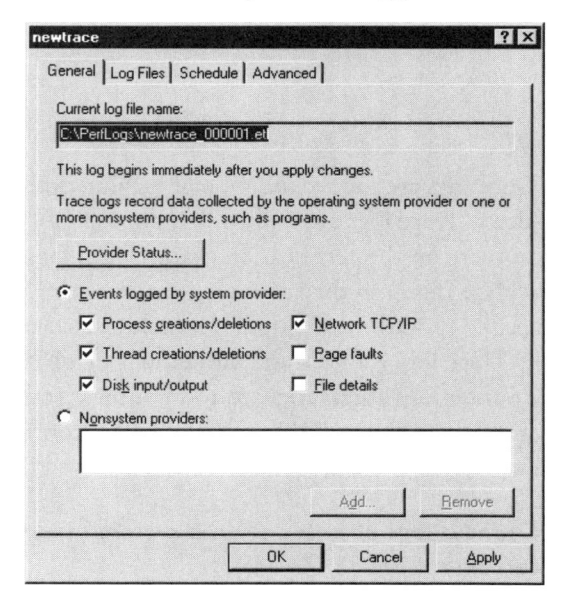

on the job *If you need to track events with more than one provider, you have to create more than one trace log.*

4. Click the Log Files tab, and you will notice that it is very similar to the Log Files tab in the counter log's Properties dialog box, with the key difference being that the trace log file type can only be a sequential trace file or circular trace file.

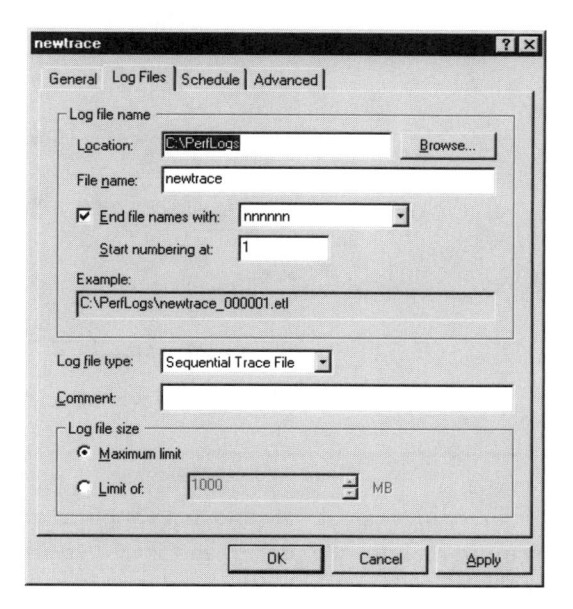

5. Click the Schedule tab to configure the scheduling properties. This tab is identical to the Scheduling tab found in the counter log's Properties dialog box.

6. Click the Advanced tab to configure the memory buffer number and size. The memory buffers are where the event data is captured prior to writing the information to the log file. It is at the bottom of the Advanced tab that you are able to specify how often to transfer this information from the buffers to the log file.

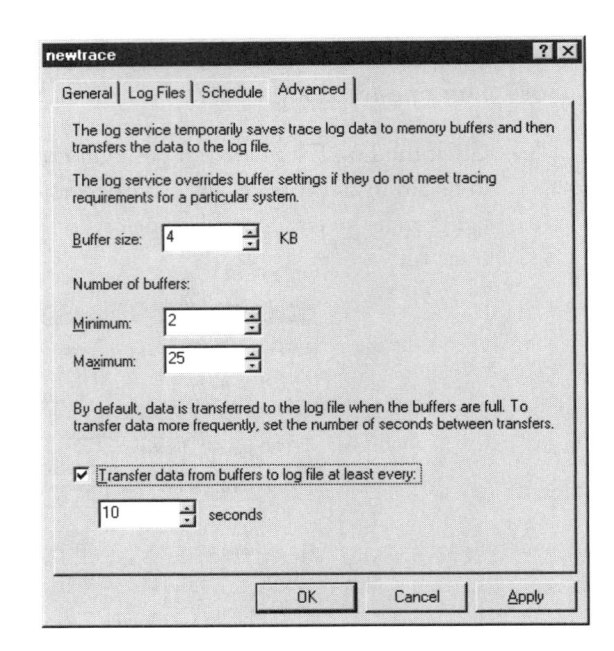

7. Click OK, and the new log will appear and be started.

Trace logs can be valuable in an application development environment where you want to monitor the process and thread creations and deletions that are associated with a specific application.

Configuring Alerts

The configuration of alerts within the Performance snap-in can offer you a way to proactively monitor the computers in your network environment. Most larger organizations already have existing applications, such as HP OpenView, Tivoli, or Microsoft's new Operations Manager product, that allow them to gather event information and configure alerts based on certain performance thresholds being met. The whole idea of proactively monitoring the computers in your network is to allow you to respond to issues before they become critical and threaten to cause server downtime. There are numerous examples of these types of events, too many to list individually, but let's look at a couple of examples.

Over the last ten years, the use of e-mail within the corporate market has grown tremendously. Few organizations in developed countries don't have the ability to send and receive e-mail. This increase in e-mail usage has resulted in many

Configuring System Monitor Alerts and Logging **861**

organizations requiring large amounts of storage space on corporate servers. As in every facet of life, some people are more organized than others and some people prefer to keep all of their e-mail, whereas others tend to delete it once it has been dealt with. I must admit that I fall within the "saver" category. As a religious subscriber to a number of IT-related mailing lists, I save a number of postings so that I can refer to them at a future time. If your organization has a number of "savers," then your server's disk space needs inevitably will grow. Being alerted to your disks' capacity as they hit the 70, 80, or 90 percent capacity level can help you to resolve this issue before it affects your users and becomes another fire to put out. This is where alerts become extremely useful.

If you work in a smaller network environment and don't have the budget, human resources, or immediate need for an enterprise monitoring application, you can take advantage of the Performance Logs and Alerts tool that is included with Windows 2000. So, now that you know that the purpose of alerts is to monitor certain objects and alert you when they reach specified performance thresholds, let's explore how to configure these alerts and, even more exciting, how you can automate the response taken when the alert is triggered.

EXERCISE 19-5

CertCam 19-5

Configuring Alerts

In this exercise, you learn how to configure alerts to occur when specific thresholds are met and what actions can be configured to occur at that time.

1. Select Start | Programs | Administrative Tools, and click Performance.

2. In the Performance dialog box, expand Performance Logs and Alerts, right-click Alerts, and click New Alert Settings.

3. In the New Alert Settings dialog box, type **diskalert** as the name of the alert and click OK.

4. The diskalert dialog box appears, which consists of three tabs. On the General tab, you can enter a comment for the alert, and click Add to add the counters that will help to define the alert. In this example, choose the LogicalDisk performance object, which you enabled earlier using the **diskperf –yn** command, select the %Free Space counter, and select the C drive as the

instance, if that is the drive where your system files are located. Click Add and then Close.

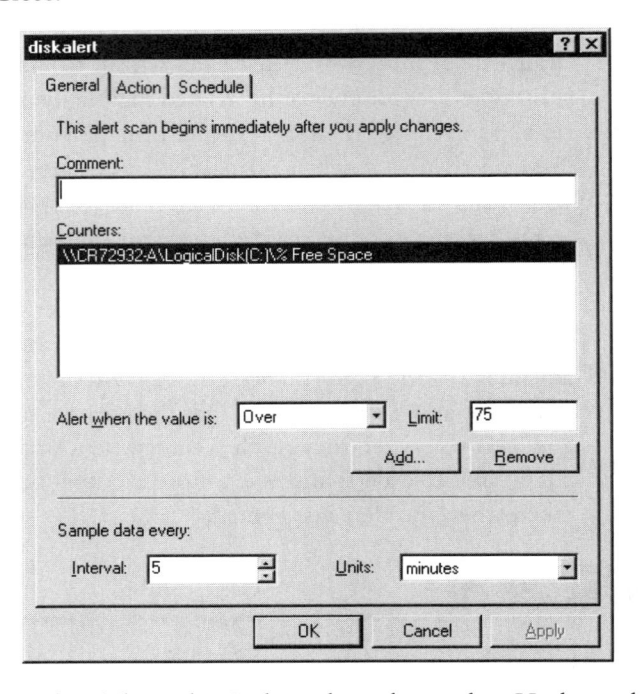

5. In the Alert When The Value Is drop-down box, select Under and enter the limit you would like to define, such as 25, which in the case of % Free Space represents 25 percent. At the bottom of the dialog box, set the sampling interval. In the case of free disk space, you can select a longer interval, such as 5 minutes, and click Apply.

6. On the Action tab, the default setting logs an entry in the Application event log, but you are also able to configure additional actions to be taken, such as sending a network message using the messenger service in the form of a pop-up window, starting a Performance Data log, which can allow you to trigger the collection of data for this specific circumstance, or running a specific program for which you are also able to specify command-line arguments. In the case of a disk space alert, sending a network message to the administrator may be the action you would like taken.

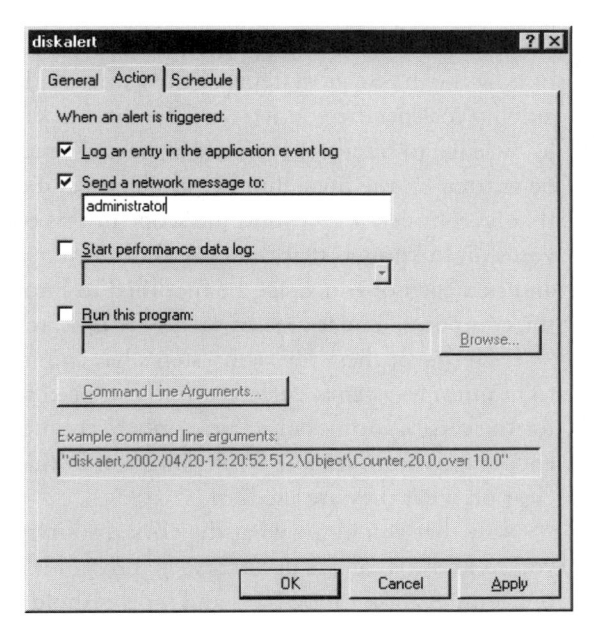

Configuring System Monitor Alerts and Logging 863

7. The Schedule tab also allows you to configure when and how to start and stop the scan. The default is to start the scan now and allow it to run until it is stopped manually.

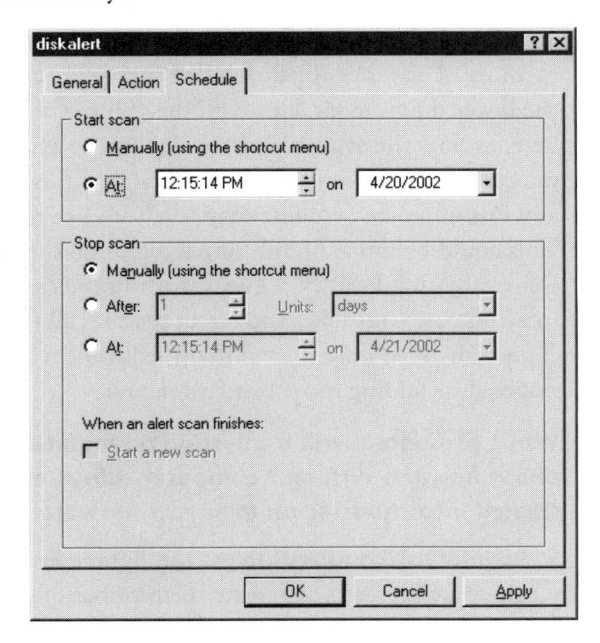

A discussion about logging alerts isn't complete unless you have an understanding of how the major subsystems of the computer interact and what acceptable levels of activity for specific counters are. Gathering statistical data without the ability or knowledge to interpret it results in wasted time and resources. An entire book could be written on the huge number of objects and even greater number of counters, and that level of detail is beyond the scope of this book and the certification exam. What you should know is that there are four primary subsystems that interact with one another, each of which can be modified to improve or degrade the performance of the computer. The four subsystems are disk, memory, processor, and network.

Each one of these four subsystems has counters that are useful when you want to monitor a system's performance. You need to be familiar with these key counters for the certification exam. These critical counters are listed in Table 19-1, and I encourage you to use the Explain button in the Performance snap-in if you are not clear on what they are used for.

Now that you know what the critical subsystem counters are, it is important for you to know what the performance thresholds are for each of the counters. Some of the counters don't have hard and set thresholds, but rather rules of thumb to keep in mind when evaluating your performance data.

When monitoring PhysicalDisk counters such as Disk Reads and Writes per second, % Disk Time, and Avg. Disk Queue length, you are looking for the numbers or percentages to be lower rather than higher. Factors to consider here are the actual speed and type of disks in the computer and the amount of physical memory. The faster the disk RPM speed, the better the performance should be and the lower the number, although the volume of incoming requests also plays a role here, as does the available physical memory and disk adapter configuration. For example, a computer with multiple SCSI disks but only 128MB of physical memory and lots of request volume may result in disk reads and writes being extremely high. This could be more a result of paging to disk than poor hardware performance. Remembering that all the subsystems in the computer work together will help you to avoid costly mistakes such as upgrading all the SCSI disks to even faster, more expensive disks, only to find that the problem still exists and might have been resolved by adding more physical memory.

exam
⚠ Watch

When presented with a question on monitoring system performance, think about how the different computer subsystems work together, to avoid being tricked into choosing an incorrect answer.

LogicalDisk counters such as the % Free Space counter help you to determine when you will need to increase the number of disks or the disk size of the individual

TABLE 19-1 Critical Subsystem Counters

Subsystem	What It Monitors	Important Counters
Disk	Disk usage	PhysicalDisk\Disk Reads/sec PhysicalDisk\Disk Writes/sec LogicalDisk\% Free Space LogicalDisk\% Disk Time LogicalDisk\% Idle Time
Disk	Disk bottlenecks	PhysicalDisk\Avg. Disk Queue Length (all instances)
Memory	Memory usage	Memory\Available Bytes Memory\Cache Bytes
Memory	Memory bottlenecks	Memory\Pages/sec Memory\Page reads/sec Memory\Transition Faults/sec Memory\Pool Paged Bytes Memory\Pool Nonpaged Bytes Paging File\% Usage (all instances) Cache\Data Map Hits % Server\Pool Paged Bytes Server\Pool Nonpaged Bytes
Network	Network usage	Network Segment\% Net Utilization
Network	Throughput/bottlenecks	Network Interface\Bytes total/sec Network Interface\Packets/sec Server\Bytes Total/sec
CPU	CPU usage	Processor\% Processor Time (all instances)
CPU	CPU bottlenecks	System\Processor Queue Length (all instances) Processor\Interrupts/sec

disks. LogicalDisk counters may also alert you to the need for a storage area network (SAN). You are looking for lower as opposed to higher values when monitoring your LogicalDisk counters.

When examining memory counters, you can begin with a look at available bytes. A good rule of thumb here is that if this number is less than 4MB, you should be looking to increase the physical memory in the computer.

Memory bottlenecks can also be identified with the Pages per second counter. Results above 20 indicate that the memory is not large enough to store the data that is being requested, resulting in virtual memory being accessed on the hard disk.

The pages/sec counter gives a more quantifiable value to a potential memory bottleneck than the Page reads/sec counter, but the Page reads/sec counter can be used in conjunction to identify the number of times the disk needed to be read to resolve a hard page fault.

The Transition Faults/sec counter is not a counter to look at in isolation, as it is used to identify the number of times page faults were recovered by locating the data in another location in memory, different from where it was marked as being located. Large numbers of transition faults can be common on a very busy computer, but when they occur in conjunction with other memory issues, they should be given more attention.

Keep an eye on both the Pool Paged Bytes and Pool Nonpaged Bytes counters in comparison to total memory. If the percentage of either of these counters is a significant percentage of total memory, it may indicate a memory bottleneck.

When looking at the Paging File\% Usage counter, the higher the number the better, as a high value indicates that the page file is sized correctly. If the number is low, before jumping to conclusions, ask yourself if the page file has been resized recently, as this could result in a low value. If it hasn't been resized recently, then the file could be set too large.

The Cache\Data Map Hits % counter is another counter that can't be looked at in isolation, as it shows the ratio of positive hits to memory. It can indicate a bottleneck if the number is small and other memory counters lead you to the same conclusion.

The Server\Pool Paged Bytes and Memory\Pool Paged Bytes counters can be useful in determining where the majority of a memory bottleneck is located. If both the Server and Memory counters are high, this would indicate that the amount of memory being used by network requests is generating the bottleneck.

The Network Interface\Bytes Total/sec counter can help you to access the total throughput for the interface and help you to assess whether additional interfaces are required to handle the volume of requests and responses. This is a great counter to use for general capacity planning.

The Processor counter % Processor Time should not continuously exceed 75 percent in a computer with a single processor. In a multiprocessor computer, this value should not continuously exceed 50 percent. This is one of those counters that could result in an inaccurate conclusion being drawn if read in isolation. A high value could indicate a CPU bottleneck, but could also indicate a lack of memory, with the high utilization due to the paging to disk that is required. When looking at your processor metrics, also look to the System\Processor Queue Length counter. A constant queue greater than two generally indicates a processor bottleneck. Remember that a single queue exists regardless of the number of processors in the computer. The Interrupts/sec counter can be useful in helping you to determine hardware problems when you compare it to the baseline for the computer in question. A significant increase in the number of interrupts may indicate hardware problems.

on the job

For detailed information on performance tuning and how to identify bottlenecks, search for **Performance Tuning** *at www.microsoft.com/windows2000.*

SCENARIO & SOLUTION

You would like to enable the LogicalDisk counters on your computer running Windows 2000. What can you do to accomplish this?	Running the **diskperf –yv** command and then rebooting the computer will enable the LogicalDisk counters on your computer running Windows 2000.
You would like to configure your computer running Windows 2000 to notify you when thresholds that you define are reached, such as the % Free Space counter moving below 20 percent. How will you configure this?	Configure an alert in Performance Logs and Alerts. Add the % Free Space in counters to the alert and set the threshold to alert you when it moves below 20 percent. Then, configure an action to be taken when the threshold is exceeded. Confirm that the alert appears and is green in color, indicating that it has started.
What is the difference between a trace log and a counter log?	A trace log is used to monitor certain events or thresholds, whereas a counter log is used to monitor performance objects and specific counters over a period of time. Counter logs are generally used to collect information and allow you to create a performance baseline. Trace logs are new to Windows 2000 and require special third-party log parser tools to analyze them. Windows 2000 does not include a trace log parser. You can find one from Sand Stone at www.sand-stone.com, known as Meta-S.
You would like to create performance baselines on a number of different production servers in your network. How would you configure this?	Here you have a couple of options. You can configure individual counter logs on each of the production servers or you can configure individual logs on a single computer to have all of the information collected and saved to a central location.

CERTIFICATION OBJECTIVE 19.03

Diagnosing Server Health Problems with Event Viewer

Event Viewer and its built-in event logs can be helpful in the identification of pending and existing problems. Event Viewer separates messages into five types—Information, Warning, Error, Success, and Failure—three of which you can see in Figure 19-7, which shows the System event log on a member server. The Success and Failure events are only found within the Security log. These events are used to represent successful or failed security access attempts and require that auditing is configured. In the case of the object access auditing selection, you are also required to set NTFS permissions at the file and folder level. NTFS isn't required to audit object access for shares and printers.

Depending on the version of the Windows 2000 OS and the installed services, the number of event logs will vary, but regardless of the configuration, there will always be a minimum of three logs: Application, Security, and System. The Application log is used to log events generated by applications installed on the computer. The Security

FIGURE 19-7

Event Viewer messages

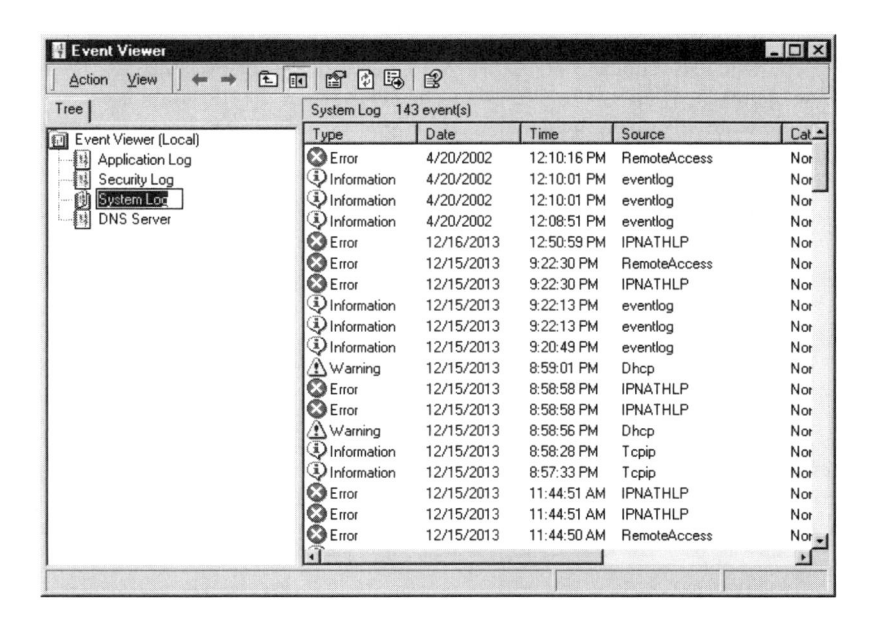

log is used to log security-related events, which are generated by the configuration of auditing. If you don't use auditing and it is therefore not configured on your computer, you will not find any events in the Security log. The System log is used to log system-related service messages for system services such as DHCP and RRAS, for the startup and shutdown of services, and for the installation of service packs or hotfixes. Not all network services report all of their information to the System log—the exceptions are Active Directory, File Replication Service, and DNS, each of which have their own logs if they are installed on the computer.

Event Viewer can be accessed a number of different ways, including by selecting Start | Run and typing **eventvwr**, by accessing the Event Viewer snap-in on the Administrative Tools menu, or by using the Computer Management snap-in. I prefer to access it through the Computer Management snap-in, because a number of other administrative tools are available there, in one location, for troubleshooting. The other nice feature of Event Viewer is the ability to connect to another computer and view the logs on a remote computer, making remote troubleshooting a lot easier and more efficient.

on the Job
The Windows 2000 Server Resource Kit includes an Access database file named w2000events.mdb that lists a number of Windows 2000 events, event IDs, and, in some cases, methods of resolution. This file can be useful in helping to provide you with a solution to a common error message.

EXERCISE 19-6

CertCam 19-6

Examining Event Viewer Events

In this exercise, you learn how to examine events in Event Viewer. This is particularly useful while troubleshooting system problems, as multiple events can help direct you to the source of the problem and individual events can provide you with information to help you solve individual problems.

1. Select Start | Programs | Administrative Tools, and click Computer Management. Under System Tools, expand Event Viewer and select the System log.

2. Double-click one of the events in the details pane to open the Event Properties dialog box, providing you with detailed information about the specific event.

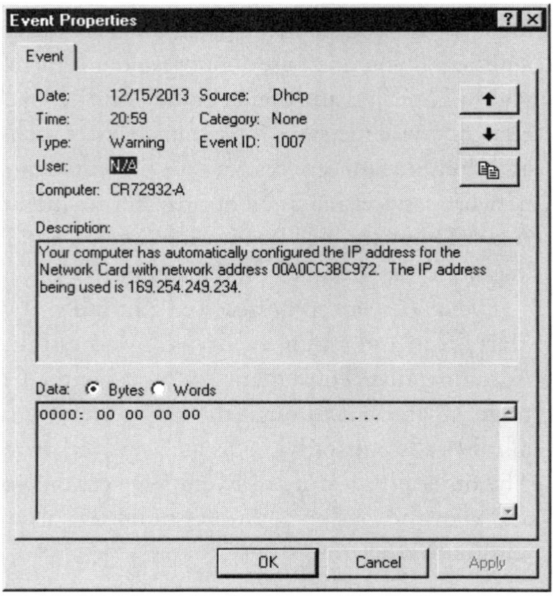
Event Properties
Event
Date: 12/15/2013 Source: Dhcp
Time: 20:59 Category: None
Type: Warning Event ID: 1007
User: N/A
Computer: CR72932-A
Description:
Your computer has automatically configured the IP address for the Network Card with network address 00A0CC3BC972. The IP address being used is 169.254.249.234.
Data: Bytes Words
0000: 00 00 00 00 ....
OK
Cancel
Apply

3. You can see within the individual event properties the date and time the event occurred, that it's a Warning event, the source is the DHCP service, the category, the event ID, the user, and the computer on which it was generated. The middle of the dialog box provides a description of the event, and the bottom of the dialog box provides some data that corresponds to the event. Some other nice, new features included in Windows 2000 are the up and down arrows that allow you to move up and down through the list of events, and the Copy button that allows you to copy the event information so that it can be pasted in another application, allowing you to keep your own company knowledge base.

You are also able to configure the properties of your event logs by right-clicking the individual log, such as the Application log, and clicking Properties. This opens the General tab of the Application Properties dialog box, shown in Figure 19-8. On this tab, you are able to configure the maximum log file size, the action to take when this size is reached, and, using the Clear Log button, delete the contents of the log.

The Filter tab, shown in Figure 19-9, allows you to search the log file for specific types of events using a number of different search criteria, including the event type, source, category, event ID, user, computer, and a time and date range.

FIGURE 19-8

Configuring the Application log properties

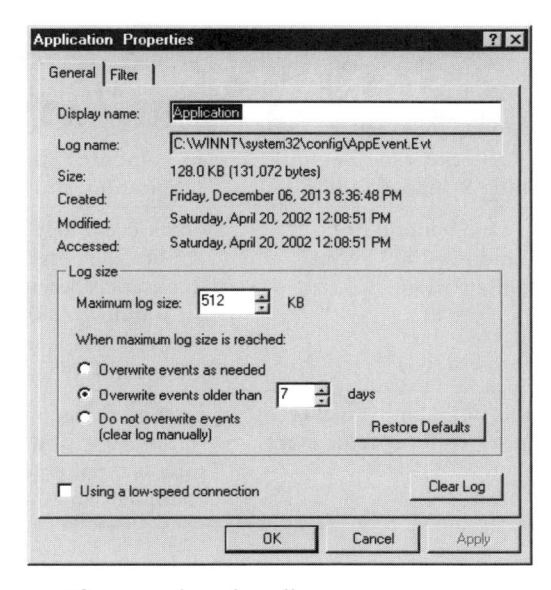

Right-clicking a specific event log also allows you to open a new log, save an existing log, and clear all the log's events. Whether you save your event logs on an occasional or regular basis is a decision you will have to make based on your own goals and requirements. It can be a good habit to get into, particularly when it comes to the Security log if you would like the ability to compare older logs against newer logs to allow you to perform a comparative analysis.

FIGURE 19-9

Filtering for specific events

SCENARIO & SOLUTION

What are the three, default event logs found on all computers running Windows 2000?	All computers running Windows 2000 have the System, Application, and Security event logs.
What other event logs can be found on computers running Windows 2000 Server depending on their configuration?	Other event logs include the Directory Service, File Replication Service, and DNS Service logs. The File Replication Service and Directory Service logs are found on Windows 2000 domain controllers. The DNS Service log is found on computers running Windows 2000 and DNS.
What option is available in the individual event logs that allows you to search for specific event IDs and error types?	Each event log offers the ability to filter the events contained within the log based on certain criteria, such as event type, source, category, event ID, user, computer, and dates of occurrence.

CERTIFICATION OBJECTIVE 19.04

Identifying and Disabling Unnecessary Services

A critical component of computer performance optimization involves ensuring that only the required services are installed on the computer, freeing up resources for those required services, and preventing resources from listening for unwanted requests.

To optimize the performance of your computer, a good place to start is with the removal of unneeded components, followed by tuning the paging file, which often means making it bigger and moving it to a different disk, and lastly by tuning the server service. The server service is the service responsible for responding to all incoming network requests for file, print, and named pipe sharing. In other words, stopping and disabling the Server service results will prevent remote users from accessing resources on the computer.

Within the Computer Management snap-in, in the Services and Applications section, you will find Services, as shown in Figure 19-10. Selecting Services displays all the services installed on the computer as well as their status, startup type, and how they are configured to log on as, which by default is the LocalSystem.

Double-clicking a service such as the Alerter service brings up the service's Properties dialog box, as shown in Figure 19-11. On the General tab, you are able to configure the display name, description, and startup type. The three available

FIGURE 19-10

The Services utility

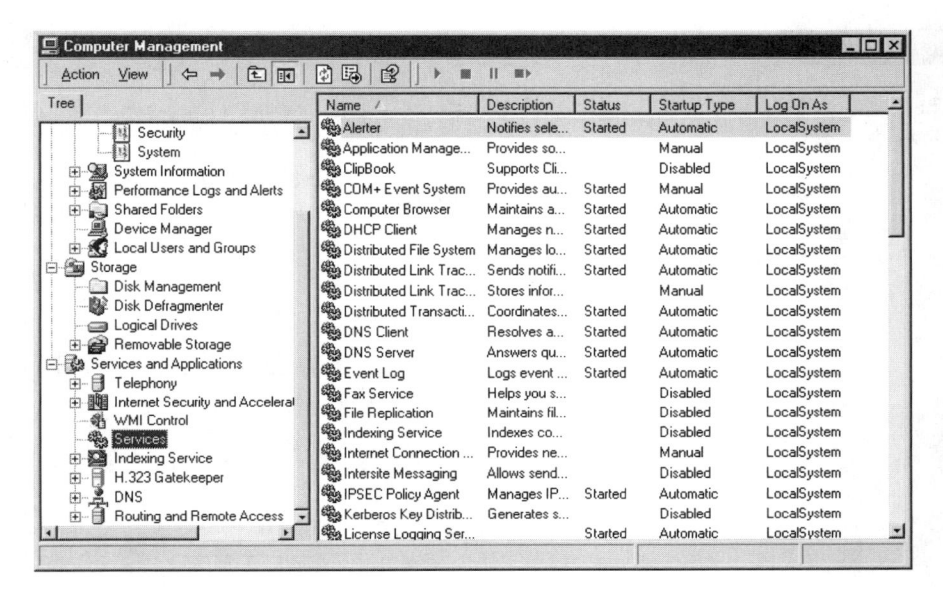

startup types are Automatic, Manual, and Disabled. This is also where the service can be started, stopped, paused, or resumed using the respective button. It is on the General tab that you can also identify the path to the service's executable, which generally is located in the %systemroot%\system32 directory.

Before making any changes to a service's startup type or service state, it is a good idea to look at the Dependencies tab, shown in Figure 19-12. The Dependencies tab

FIGURE 19-11

The Alerter service Properties dialog box

FIGURE 19-12

The Dependencies tab

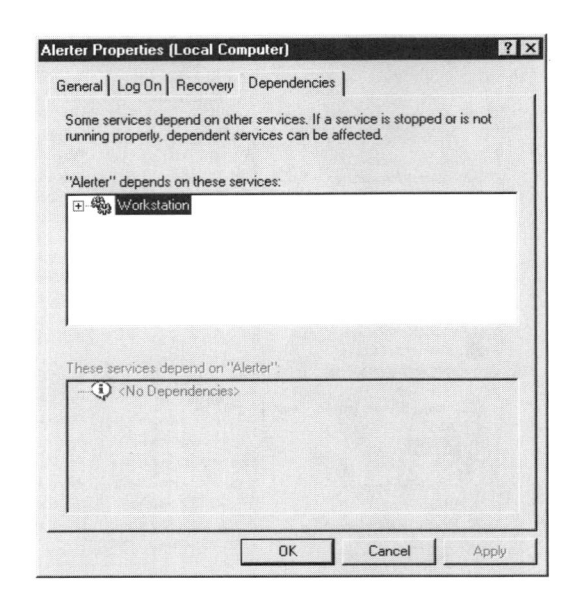

alerts you to any other services that are dependent on the current service and that would be affected by changes to the startup type or service state you decide to make. In this example, you can see that no other services depend on the Alerter service, but that the Alerter service does depend on the Workstation service. This means that if the Workstation service is stopped, the Alerter service will not be able to function. The Dependencies tab is extremely valuable in helping to prevent you from disabling services that adversely affect other services. This tab is new to Windows 2000.

The Log On tab, shown in Figure 19-13, allows you to configure the account used by the service to log on. By default, this is the LocalSystem account, though this can differ for other applications added to the computer such as Exchange or MOM. If you wish to specify a different account, select the This Account radio button and specify the account and password. On the Log On tab, you are also able to configure the service to start or stop based on a specific hardware profile. Hardware profiles can be useful in the case of notebook users, where you can create docked and undocked profiles and disable all nonessential services in the undocked profile to lengthen the life of the battery. Hardware profiles can also be valuable in test lab environments where you must test applications on computers with different hardware configurations. In this type of environment, you can create individual hardware profiles for each of the hardware configurations and boot using the different profiles when you are testing.

FIGURE 19-13

Configuring the Log On tab properties

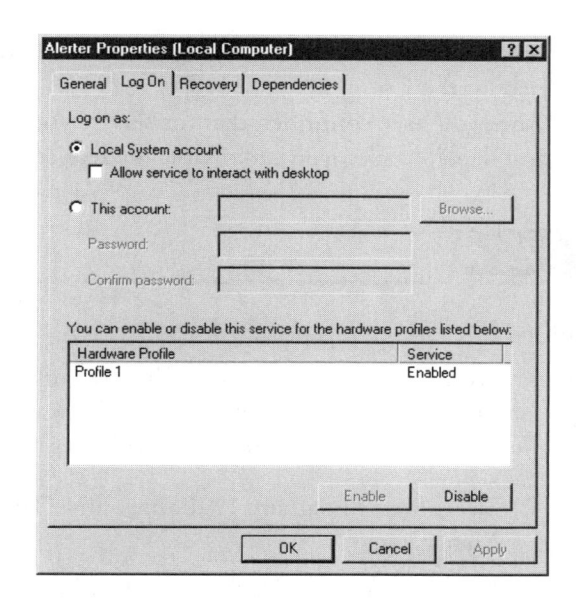

The last tab that is handy from a problem-resolution perspective is the Recovery tab, shown in Figure 19-14. On the Recovery tab, you are able to configure an action to be taken upon first service failure, second service failure, and subsequent

FIGURE 19-14

Configuring the Recovery tab

failures. Options here include Take No Action, Restart the Service, Run a File, or Reboot the Computer.

Once you have confirmed that the service you wish to disable doesn't have any critical dependencies, you can disable the service, as described in Exercise 19-7.

EXERCISE 19-7

CertCam 19-7

Disabling Services

This exercise teaches you how to disable system services in an effort to optimize the performance of your computer. This should be performed on all production servers to allow peak performance and avoid resources being consumed by unused services.

1. Select Start | Programs | Administrative Tools, and click Computer Management.

2. In the Computer Management snap-in, expand Services And Applications and click Services.

3. Double-click the service that you wish to disable and, in the Service Properties dialog box, click the Dependencies tab to confirm that there aren't any dependencies.

4. Once you have confirmed that no other services depend on the service you wish to disable, click the General tab and stop the service if it is running. Then, in the Startup Type drop-down box, click Disabled.

✓ TWO-MINUTE DRILL

Monitoring and Interpreting Real-Time Performance by Using System Monitor and Task Manager

- ❑ Windows 2000 Task Manager is accessible through the CTRL-ALT-DELETE key sequence or by right-clicking the taskbar and selecting Task Manager.
- ❑ Task Manager is comprised of three tabs: Applications, Processes, and Performance.
- ❑ Use Task Manager to stop applications with a Not Responding status, view resource consumption on a per-process basis, and view CPU and memory performance in real time.
- ❑ System Monitor can be configured to view real-time data in chart, histogram, or report views. Counters from multiple performance objects can be added and configured.
- ❑ Some counters are not enabled by default, such as the LogicalDisk counters, but can be enabled using the **diskperf** command.
- ❑ Network segment monitors can also be configured but require an add-on utility only available in SMS 2.0.

Configuring System Monitor Alerts and Logging

- ❑ System Monitor can be used to configure logging and alerts in addition to viewing a computer's performance in real time.
- ❑ Two types of logs can be configured in Performance Logs and Alerts: counter logs and trace logs. A sample counter log known as the System Overview log is included with the default installation of Windows 2000.
- ❑ Use counter logs to monitor certain system resources over a period of time by selecting specific performance objects, object counters, and instances that you wish to monitor.
- ❑ Use trace logs to monitor certain events. Windows 2000 does not include a log parser to read trace logs.
- ❑ Alerts can be configured in Performance Logs and Alerts as a way of proactively monitoring the computers in your network and alerting you when defined thresholds have been met.

- There are four computer subsystems that you will want to monitor using various counters to troubleshoot and identify system bottlenecks: disk, memory, processor, and network.

Diagnosing Server Health Problems with Event Viewer

- There are always a minimum of three Event Viewer logs: Application, System, and Security. Additional event logs are added when those services are installed on the computer, services such as DNS, Active Directory, and File Replication Service.

- System-related events are stored in the System log, such as the starting and stopping of services. Audited events are stored in the Security log but auditing must be enabled for these events to be logged. The Application log stores events related to application-specific information and errors.

- You can search the event logs for specific types of events by filtering events using specific criteria such as username, computer, or Event ID.

- The support.microsoft.com web site can be searched based on the event ID to identify ways in which to solve the problem.

- The event logs can also be saved for future review or comparative analysis.

Identifying and Disabling Unnecessary Services

- The Services utility in the Control Panel or in the Computer Management snap-in can be used to view and modify the properties of a service.

- The Properties dialog box of a service includes a Dependencies tab that allows you to determine what other services depend on the service you wish to disable.

- The Recovery tab in the Service Properties dialog box allows you to configure the actions to take should the service fail. Options include restarting the service, running a file, and rebooting the computer.

SELF TEST

The following questions will help you measure your understanding of the material presented in this chapter. Read the questions and answers carefully, and be aware that some questions will provide for more than one correct answer. Choose *all* correct answers for each question.

Monitoring and Interpreting Real-Time Performance by Using System Monitor and Task Manager

1. There is a significant difference between the disk counters' initialization settings in Windows NT 4 and Windows 2000. Which of the following statements best represents these differences?

    A. No disk counters are initialized in Windows 2000.

    B. Only LogicalDisk counters are initialized in Windows 2000.

    C. Only PhysicalDisk counters are initialized in Windows 2000.

    D. Both logical and PhysicalDisk counters are initialized in Windows 2000.

2. You have been hired as a consultant for a large organization that is looking to gather performance-related information on its production servers over a period of two weeks to create a performance baseline. What type of logging would you recommend for this type of project?

    A. Configure System Monitor to gather the information by adding the appropriate counters and save the information through an OBDC connection to a database to allow for real-time analysis.

    B. Configure a counter log in System Monitor to log the information to a daily log file on a partition other than that which contains the system files.

    C. Configure a counter log in Performance Logs and Alerts to log the information to a daily log file.

    D. Configure a trace log in Performance Logs and Alerts to log the information to a daily log file.

3. You would like to enable the LogicalDisk counters on a computer running Windows 2000 to allow you to capture information in Performance Logs and Alerts and System Monitor. Which of the following will allow you to accomplish this?

   A. Do nothing; the LogicalDisk counters are installed by default.

   B. Run the **diskperf –yv** command.

   C. Run the **diskperf –yn** command.

   D. Run the **diskperf –n** command.

Configuring System Monitor Alerts and Logging

4. You are the administrator of a number of servers running Windows 2000. Your organization is planning the introduction of some new applications and Active Directory. You would like to begin collecting some performance information to create a performance baseline for your production servers. You are new to Performance Logs and Alerts but understand Windows 2000 includes a sample log file. Which of the following describes how you will access the sample log file?

   A. In the Performance snap-in, expand Performance Logs and Alerts and select Counter Logs. In the Display pane, right-click the log named System Sample and select Properties. Edit the configuration settings and start the log.

   B. In the Performance snap-in, expand Performance Logs and Alerts and select Counter Logs. In the Display pane, right-click the log named System Overview and select Properties. Edit the configuration settings and start the log.

   C. In the Performance snap-in, expand Performance Logs and Alerts and select Trace Logs. In the Display pane, right-click the log named System Sample and select Properties. Edit the configuration settings and start the log.

   D. In the Performance snap-in, expand Performance Logs and Alerts and select Trace Logs. In the Display pane, right-click the log named System Overview and select Properties. Edit the configuration settings and start the log.

5. You are the administrator of a computer running Windows 2000 and IIS. The server is configured as an FTP server and the ftproot directory has been granted write permission to allow contractors to upload reports as they complete them. You would like to use Performance

Logs and Alerts, to notify you when the hard disk that the ftproot directory is located on exceeds 70 percent capacity. This will allow you to move existing data or add another drive without affecting the remote users. How will you achieve this? (Select all of the steps required.)

A. Right-click Alerts and create a new alert using the PhysicalDisk object and % Free Space counter.

B. Right-click Alerts and create a new alert using the LogicalDisk object and % Free Space counter.

C. Run **diskperf –yv** to enable the LogicalDisk counters.

D. Run **diskperf –yd** to enable the PhysicalDisk counters.

6. You have been monitoring a computer running Windows 2000 for a one-week period and, upon your investigation of the log file, have noticed that the values for Disk Time and Disk Queue Length are continuously quite high. The Memory\Pages per second counter is consistently around 50 and the % Processor Time is consistently above 90 percent. Which of the following is most likely to correct the existing problem?

A. Add a faster CPU.

B. Add more memory.

C. Increase the size of the page file.

D. Add a faster hard drive.

7. Which of the following steps can be taken to improve performance if excessive paging is occurring on your server? (Choose all that apply.)

A. Add more memory.

B. Reduce the size of the paging file.

C. Defragment the page file.

D. Move the page file off of the disk that contains the operating system files.

8. You are the administrator of a computer running Windows 2000 that has a disk-duplexing RAID device installed. The computer has begun to experience performance problems and you

are wondering if they are associated with this device. Which of the following performance counters would offer you the best information to confirm or deny your hunch?

A. % Disk Time
B. Disk Queue Length
C. Average Disk Queue Length
D. Current Disk Queue Length

Diagnosing Server Health Problems with Event Viewer

9. You would like to search the System event log for the events generated by a specific user. Which of the following will allow you to do this?

    A. In Event Viewer, right-click the System log and save the log file. Log on as the user for whom you would like to search for specific events and then open the saved event log. Only events generated by that user will appear.
    B. In Event Viewer, right-click the System log and select Properties. On the General tab, specify the user for whom you want to search for events, and click Search.
    C. In Event Viewer, right-click the System log and select Properties. On the Filter tab, enter in the User box the name of the user for whom you want to search for events, and click OK.
    D. Right-click Event Viewer and select Properties. On the Filter tab, enter in the User box the name of the user for whom you want to search for events, and click OK.

Identifying and Disabling Unnecessary Services

10. You are the administrator of a computer running Windows 2000 Server and IIS. The web development group in your organization has written a new web application and, after successful testing on a staging server, you have moved it to the production server. The new application is not performing well on the new production server and is causing the web publishing service to stop at irregular intervals. You have been manually restarting the service each time this happens but would like to automate the process. Which of the following will accomplish that for you with the least interruption to the other applications running on the server?

    A. In Services, open the Properties dialog box of the web publishing service and select the Recovery tab. Change the values in the first, second, and subsequent failures to Run A File and browse to %systemroot%\inetpub\iisreset.exe.

- B. In Services, open the Properties dialog box of the web publishing service and select the Recovery tab. Change the values in the first, second, and subsequent failures to Reboot The Computer.
- C. In Services, open the Properties dialog box of the web publishing service and select the Recovery tab. Change the values in the first, second, and subsequent failures to Run A File and browse to %systemroot%\inetsrv\iisreset.exe.
- D. In Services, open the Properties dialog box of the web publishing service and select the Recovery tab. Change the values in the first, second, and subsequent failures to Restart The Service.

LAB QUESTION

You are tasked with troubleshooting a computer running Windows 2000 that is experiencing performance problems. You are running multiple applications on the computer, and one of the applications has frozen. You would like to stop this application. You are also noticing that the hard drive light is always blinking and that the system is sluggish. You would like to use the built-in tools available to troubleshoot these problems. To further improve the performance of the computer, you would like to disable all the services that are not required to be running on the computer, without affecting those services that are critical to the proper functioning of the computer. You would also like to ensure that no errors or warnings exist, and if any do exist, that they are rectified. Answer the following questions to help you put together an action plan that will solve the preceding issues:

1. What application can you use to stop or end applications that are not responding? Describe the steps involved in accomplishing this task.
2. What tools will you use to troubleshoot the performance of the system? What objects and counters can provide useful information and lead you to the real problem?
3. How will you identify the interdependencies of different services? What utility will you use to do this and what are two ways this utility can be accessed?
4. Where will you look to identify any errors being generated on the computer? How can you find out more-detailed information about specific errors?

SELF TEST ANSWERS

Monitoring and Interpreting Real-Time Performance by Using System Monitor and Task Manager

1. ☑ **C** is correct. Windows 2000 does initialize disk counters on startup but for only the PhysicalDisk counters, not the LogicalDisk counters.
   ☒ **A** is incorrect because Windows 2000 does initialize the PhysicalDisk counters.
   ☒ **B** is incorrect because the LogicalDisk counters are not initialized at startup.
   ☒ **D** is incorrect because only the PhysicalDisk counters are initialized at startup.

2. ☑ **C** is correct. To log information over a two-week period, the ideal configuration would be to create a counter log in Performance Logs and Alerts and log the information daily to a log file stored on a partition other than that which contains the system files.
   ☒ **A** is incorrect because System Monitor does not allow you to log to a database through an ODBC connection. Logging using System Monitor would require you to sit in front of the monitor for the two-week period, noting the results, as they are not captured anywhere.
   ☒ **B** is incorrect because counter logs can only be created in Performance Logs and Alerts.
   ☒ **D** is incorrect because a trace log allows you to log for performance thresholds but will not provide you with data that you can use to establish a performance baseline.

3. ☑ **B** is correct. To enable the Logical Disk counters on a computer running Windows 2000, you can run the **diskperf –yv** command and then restart the computer for the settings to take effect.
   ☒ **A** is incorrect because doing nothing would not result in the counters starting. In Windows 2000, only the PhysicalDisk counters are started by default.
   ☒ **C** is incorrect because the **diskperf –yn** command is not a valid command.
   ☒ **D** is incorrect because the **diskperf –n** command is used to disable both the logical and physical counters.

Configuring System Monitor Alerts and Logging

4. ☑ **B** is correct. To configure the sample log named System Overview, you would open the Performance snap-in, expand Performance Logs and Alerts, and select Counter Logs. In the Display pane, right-click the log named System Overview and select Properties. Edit the configuration settings and start the log.
   ☒ **A** is incorrect because the sample counter log is named System Overview, not System Sample.
   ☒ **C** and **D** are incorrect because there is no sample trace log included with Windows 2000.

5. ☑ **B** and **C** are correct. The LogicalDisk performance object counters must be enabled first using the **diskperf –yv** command. The computer must then be restarted and a new alert created using the LogicalDisk object and the % Free Space counter.
☒ **A** is incorrect because the PhysicalDisk performance object does not include a % Free Space counter.
☒ **D** is incorrect because the PhysicalDisk performance object counters are enabled by default in Windows 2000.

6. ☑ **B** is correct. Adding more physical memory is the most likely way to solve this problem. When the disk queue length and CPU are showing consistently high values, it can generally be attributed to a lack of physical memory.
☒ **A** is incorrect because high CPU utilization is one of the side effects of the real problem. With more physical memory, the requirements of the CPU should drop dramatically.
☒ **C** is incorrect because a larger page file would not reduce disk or CPU utilization.
☒ **D** is incorrect because adding a faster hard drive wouldn't address the true problem.

7. ☑ **A** and **D** are correct. Adding more memory and moving the page file off of the disk that contains the OS files are two ways to improve the performance of the computer. A third way is to distribute multiple page files across multiple disks, if the computer has multiple disks.
☒ **B** is incorrect because decreasing the size of the page file will not improve performance.
☒ **C** is incorrect because defragmenting the page file will not dramatically improve performance.

8. ☑ **C** is correct. The Average Disk Queue Length counter should be used to determine how many system requests are waiting for access to the disk. This will help you to determine if the disk-duplexing RAID controller is causing the performance problems.
☒ **A** is incorrect because the % Disk Time counter will indicate the load on a hard disk but should not be used on computers with RAID devices, as it can contain values greater than 100 percent, which can skew the results.
☒ **B** is incorrect because the Disk Queue Length counter wouldn't be representative of all the disks.
☒ **D** is incorrect because the Current Disk Queue Length is an instantaneous length, not an average over the time interval.

Diagnosing Server Health Problems with Event Viewer

9. ☑ **C** is correct. You are able to specify filters when searching for events in the event logs. Right-click the System log and select Properties. On the Filter tab, enter in the User box the

name of the user for whom you want to search for events, and click OK.

☒ A is incorrect because you do not need to save the log first, prior to searching, nor do you need to be logged on as the user for whom you are searching.

☒ B is incorrect because there are no filtering or searching options on the General tab of the System log's Properties dialog box.

☒ D is incorrect because there are no options other than Help and Open Log File when you right-click Event Viewer.

Identifying and Disabling Unnecessary Services

10. ☑ D is correct. If you are experiencing problems with a single service, one option you have is to open Services, double-click the web publishing service to access its Properties dialog box, and select the Recovery tab. Change the values in the first, second, and subsequent failures to Restart The Service. This will allow the service to be restarted automatically and no longer require manual intervention.

☒ A and C are incorrect because, although the intended action is correct, the path to the iisreset.exe file is incorrect. Iisreset.exe is stored in the %systemroot%\system32 directory.

☒ B is incorrect because rebooting the computer would affect the other applications running on the server.

LAB ANSWER

1. Task Manager can be used to end an application that is not responding. To accomplish this, access the Windows 2000 Security dialog box by holding down the CTRL-ALT-DELETE keys and clicking the Task Manager button. On the Applications tab, select the application that is identified as Not Responding and click End Task.

2. Both Task Manager and System Monitor can be used to help troubleshoot the system's sluggishness. The Performance tab in Task Manager can give you a quick look at the memory and CPU utilization and also tell you the total amount of physical memory and page file space in the computer. System Monitor can also be used to monitor the following objects and counters to help troubleshoot the problem:

Object	Counters
Physical disk	Disk Reads per second, Disk Writes per second, % Disk Time, and Avg. Disk Queue Length
Memory	Pages per second, Page reads/sec, Pool Paged Bytes, and Pool Nonpaged bytes
Paging file	% Usage
Processor	% Processor Time

3. The System utility found in either the Control Panel or the Computer Management snap-in can be used to identify service interdependencies. Double-click the service and click the Dependencies tab to reveal the services that the current service depends on and the services that depend on the current service.

4. Event Viewer, also found within the Computer Management snap-in, can be used to identify errors and warnings on the computer. The System event log is where you will find information, warnings, and error messages relating to drivers and system services. The Application log is where you should look for the same types of messages but generated by applications running on the OS. The Security log will only contain Success or Failure events as they relate to auditing, if auditing has been configured on the computer. In addition to the information that you can find when you double-click an event, the Windows 2000 Server Resource Kit includes a file named w2000events.mdb that can be used to find more information about specific events.

Appendix

ABOUT THE CD

The CD-ROM included with this book comes complete with MasterExam, MasterSim, CertCam movie clips, the electronic version of the book along with a bonus Chapter 20 covering Installing and Managing Service Packs and Hotfixes, the Glossary, and Session #1 of LearnKey's on-line training for MCSA. The software is easy to install on any Windows 98/NT/2000 computer and must be installed to access the MasterExam and MasterSim features. You may, however, browse the electronic book and CertCams directly from the CD without installation. To register for LearnKey's online training and a second bonus MasterExam, simply click the Online Training link on the Main Page and follow the directions to the free online registration.

System Requirements

Software requires Windows 98 or higher and Internet Explorer 5.0 or above and 20 MB of hard disk space for full installation. The Electronic book requires Adobe Acrobat Reader. To access the Online Training from LearnKey you must have RealPlayer Basic 8 or Real1 Plugin, which will be automatically installed when you launch the on-line training.

LearnKey Online Training

The **LearnKey Online Training** link will allow you to access online training from Osborne.Onlineexpert.com. The first session of this course is provided at no charge. Additional Session for this course and other courses may be purchased directly from www.LearnKey.com or by calling 800 865-0165.

The first time that you run the Training, you will required to Register with the online product. Follow the instructions for a first time user. Please make sure to use a valid e-mail address.

Prior to running the Online Training you will need to add the Real Plugin and the RealCBT plugin to your system. This will automatically be facilitated to your system when you run the training the first time.

Installing and Running MasterExam and MasterSim

If your computer CD-ROM drive is configured to auto run, the CD-ROM will automatically start up upon inserting the disk. From the opening screen you may install MasterExam or MasterSim by pressing the *MasterExam* or *MasterSim* buttons. This will begin the installation process and create a program group named

"LearnKey." To run MasterExam or MasterSim use START | PROGRAMS | LEARNKEY. If the auto run feature did not launch your CD, browse to the CD and Click on the "RunInstall" icon.

MasterExam

MasterExam provides you with a simulation of the actual exam. The number of questions, the type of questions, and the time allowed are intended to be an accurate representation of the exam environment. You have the option to take an open book exam (including hints, references, and answers), a closed book exam, or the timed MasterExam simulation.

When you launch MasterExam, a digital clock display will appear in the upper left-hand corner of your screen. The clock will continue to count down to zero unless you choose to end the exam before the time expires.

MasterSim

The MasterSim is a set of interactive labs that will provide you with a wide variety of tasks to allow the user to experience the software environment even if the software is not installed. Once you have installed the MasterSim, you may access it quickly through this CD launch page or you may also access it through START | PROGRAMS | LEARNKEY.

Electronic Book

You can access the bonus Chapter 20, Installing and Managing Service Packs and Hotfixes, by selecting the chapter under the Electronic Book menu off of the main CD interface. The Glossary is also included only on the CD-ROM. The entire contents of the Study Guide are provided in PDF. Adobe's Acrobat Reader has been included on the CD.

CertCam

CertCam .AVI clips provide detailed examples of key certification objectives. These clips walk you step-by-step through various system configurations. You can access the clips directly from the CertCam table of contents by pressing the CertCam button on the Main Page.

The CertCam .AVI clips are recorded and produced using TechSmith's Camtasia Producer. Since .AVI clips can be very large, ExamSim uses TechSmith's special AVI Codec to compress the clips. The file named tsccvid.dll is copied to your Windows\System folder during the first auto run. If the .AVI clip runs with audio but no video, you may need to re-install the file from the CD-ROM. Browse to the PROGRAMS | CERTCAMS folder, and run TSCC.

Help

A help file is provided through the help button on the main page in the lower left hand corner. Individual help features are also available through MasterExam, MasterSim, and LearnKey's Online Training.

Removing Installation(s)

MasterExam and MasterSim are installed to your hard drive. For BEST results for removal of programs use the START | PROGRAMS | LEARNKEY | UNINSTALL options to remove MasterExam or MasterSim.

If you desire to remove the Real Player use the Add/Remove Programs Icon from your Control Panel. You may also remove the LearnKey training program from this location.

Technical Support

For questions regarding the technical content of the electronic book, MasterExam, or CertCams, please visit www.osborne.com or email customer.service@mcgraw-hill.com. For customers outside the 50 United States, email: international_cs@mcgraw-hill.com.

LearnKey Technical Support

For technical problems with the software (installation, operation, removing installations), and for questions regarding LearnKey Online Training and MasterSim content, please visit www.learnkey.com or email techsupport@learnkey.com.

INDEX

A

Access, configuring routing and remote, 724–735
Access database files, 869
Access scenarios, NAT cannot be used for, 725
Access servers, Shiva remote, 641
Account Policies, 307–309
Accounts
    AD (Active Directory) user, 257–260
    adding computer, 254–257
    computer, 253
    creating two user, 258–260
Active Directory; *See also* AD (Active Directory)
Active Directory-integrated zones, 125
Active Directory Service (ADS), 231
Active Directory Services Interface (ADSI), 238
AD (Active Directory)
    benefits of, 238
    configuring and implementing, 229–290
    implementing intersite replication, 433–438
    installing DNS without, 128
    is both flexible and scalable, 426
    publishing shared resources in, 377–380
    sites, 232
    user accounts, 257–260
AD (Active Directory) computers and users, administering, 253–261
    AD (Active Directory) user accounts, 257–260
    joining computers to domains, 260–261
AD (Active Directory) concepts, understanding, 231–243
    AD logical structure, 232–237
    AD physical layout, 231–232
    global catalog, 240–243
    OUs (organizational units), 237–240
AD (Active Directory), configuring and implementing
    administering AD (Active Directory) computers and users, 253–261
    creating and managing OUs (organizational units), 261–268
    delegating control, 268–278
    managing AD (Active Directory) groups, 243–247
    understanding AD (Active Directory) concepts, 231–243
AD (Active Directory) groups, managing, 243–247
    builtin groups, 248–249
    creating security groups, 251–252
    nesting groups, 249–250
    predefined groups, 247
    security group scopes, 244–246

AD (Active Directory), managing and troubleshooting, 425–452
    configuring Active Directory replication, 431–438
    managing Active Directory objects, 426–431
    troubleshooting AD replication, 438–442
AD (Active Directory) objects, managing, 426–431
AD computers, finding shared printers in, 376–377
AD-integrated DNS, installing, 125–128
AD-integrated zones (Active Directory-integrated zones), 123
AD logical structure, 232–237
    domains, 232–233
    forests, 235
    transitive trusts, 235–237
    trees, 233–234
AD objects
    linking group policies to, 329–332
    searching for, 379
AD permissions, managing, 271–277
AD physical layout, 231–232
AD replication, troubleshooting, 438–442
    checking replication topology, 440–441
    minimizing replication overhead, 440
    replication between sites fails, 439
    replication has slowed down, 439–440
AD users, finding shared printers in, 376–377
Adapters, ICS only supports single external, 710
Add/remove programs, 670–671
Adding
    computer accounts, 254–257
    more space to existing volumes, 459
    packages to group policy, 398–401
Address allocation, configuring IP, 571–576
Address assignment, automatic IP, 575–576
Address configuration, ICS and IP, 711
Address pool, static, 576
Address Resolution Protocol (ARP), 45
Address/subnet mask combination, IP, 7
Address translation, ICS uses, 710
Addresses
    assign IP, 577
    assigning IP, 730
    automatically assign IP, 574
    broadcast, 10
    Class A, B and C, 8–10
    classed IP, 9
    classful IP, 9
    control of IP, 8

893

default gateway, 11–12
determining valid IP, 17–23
distinguishing sites by IP, 488
finding valid IP, 18–21
getting IP, 7–8
hardware, 4–5
Internet, 5
IP, 5–12, 41
IP network, 10
limited broadcast, 33
logical, 5
multicast, 33, 100
physical, 40
ping default gateway, 43
ping loopback, 42–43
ping more distant IP, 44
ping nearby IP, 44
ping your own IP, 43
slash 26, 14
standard Class C, 17
static IP, 201, 206
subnet, 10
subnet Class C, 17
Addresses on hosts, dynamic, 13
Addresses on servers, static IP, 13
Administrative Templates, 320–322
Administrators
    enterprise, 184
    folder redirection provides benefits to, 318
ADS (Active Directory Service), 231
ADSI (Active Directory Services Interface), 238
Advanced Published option, 397
Advanced Risk Computing (ARC), 796
Agents
    DHCP relay, 198–199
    Windows 2000 DHCP relay, 199
    WINS proxy, 91
Alerts and logging, configuring System Monitor, 851–867
Alerts, configuring, 860–867
Allocation, configuring IP address, 571–579
Allocator service, DHCP, 734
Analysis, command-line, 534–535
Anonymous authentication, 493
API (application programming interface), 65
APIPA (Automatic Private IP Addressing), 207, 575
    disabling with Registry hack, 207
    note on, 207
AppleTalk Remote Access Protocol (ARAP), 550, 552
Application programming interface (API), 65
Application publishing, 716–717
Application Server mode, 668–669
    configuring Terminal Services for, 663–678
Applications
    categorizing, 400
    enabling ISAPI, 497–498
    publishing, 392
Applying security templates, 529

ARAP (AppleTalk Remote Access Protocol), 550, 552
ARC (Advanced Risk Computing), 796
ARP (Address Resolution Protocol), 45
ARP, troubleshooting with, 45
Assigned option, 397
Attribute changes made to user objects, 691
Audit, choosing objects to, 521–523
Audit policies
    creating, 519
    defined, 519
Auditing
    enabling, 519–520
    setting up on Domain Controllers, 520–521
Auditing does eat up some resources, 522
Auditing Failure events, 522
Auditing security, 518–523
    configuring and, 516–525
Authentication
    anonymous, 493
    basic, 494
    digest, 494
Authentication, integrated Windows, 495
Authentication limitations, getting around FTP's, 495
Authentication methods, 493–495, 594–598
Authentication processes
    examining RRAS, 616–625
    RRAS, 620–621, 621–625
Authentication protocols
    configuring on RRAS, 596–598
    default, 596
    EAP-TLS is most secure, 642
    problems, 583–586
    selecting encryption and, 637–642
    SPAP is encrypted password, 641
Authoritative restore, performing, 805
Authority, subdomains and delegation of, 145–146
Automatic IP address assignment, 575–576
Automatic printer redirection, 680, 681
Automatic Private IP Addressing (APIPA), 207, 575
    disabling with Registry hack, 207
    note on, 207

B

B-node clients, name resolution for, 90
B-node, Microsoft-enhanced, 74
Backing up
    and restoring IIS, 499–500
    WINS database, 84–85
    your computer, 822–823
Backup domain controller (BDC), 231
Backup tapes, 825
Backup types, 823–825
Backup utility, 818, 822
Backups
    incremental, 824
    restoring OS (operating system) from, 821–826

Index

Bandwidth Allocation Protocol (BAP), 633
Bandwidth connections, network, 682
BAP (Bandwidth Allocation Protocol), 633
Basic authentication, 494
Basic disks, 456
Basic input/output system (BIOS), 794
BDC (backup domain controller), 231
Binary and decimal, converting between, 15–17
BIOS (basic input/output system), 794
Block inheritance options, no override and, 293–295
Board, Ethernet, 5
Boot disks
    creating Windows 2000, 817
    Windows 2000, 816–818
Boot logging, 799
Boot partition defined, 796
Booting computers, 799
BOOTP (Bootstrap Protocol), 196
BOOTP-compliant routers, 197
BOOTP forwarding, 196–198
Bootstrap Protocol (BOOTP), 196
Bridgehead servers, defining, 437
Broadcast, 67
Broadcast addresses, 10, 33
Broadcasting, 22–23
Broadcasts rarely cross routers, 91
Builtin groups, 248–249
    local, 248
Builtin Local, 248
Builtin local groups, domain, 249
Burst cache, 89
Burst handling, 89
Burst mode, 89
Burst mode, configuring, 88–89
Business routing scenario, small, 24–25

C

CA (certificate authority), 498
Cache entries, negative, 162
Caches
    burst, 89
    NetBIOS name, 66–67
Caching-only DNS name servers, 151–152
CAL (client access license), 668
Calculator, subnet, 21
Card, Ethernet, 5
Catalog, global, 240–243
Categories tab, 400
CD, accessing Recovery Console from Windows 2000, 809
Certificate authority (CA), 498
Certificate services and SSL, using, 498–499
Challenge Handshake Authentication Protocol (CHAP), 639
Changer user command, 671
CHAP (Challenge Handshake Authentication Protocol), 639
Child domains, 233
CIDR (Classless Inter-domain Routing), 13–15

Class A, B and C addresses, 8–10
Class C addresses
    standard, 17
    subnet, 17
Classed IP addresses, 9
Classful IP addresses, 9
Classless Inter-domain Routing (CIDR), 13–15
Client access license (CAL), 668
Client computer name resolution properties, configuring, 153–159
Client computer remote access properties, configuring, 550–570
Client computers
    configuring to use multilinks, 635
    Terminal Services, 679
Client DNS registration options, 159
Client hardware
    configuring server and, 753–792
    installing server and, 753–792
Client installation disks, creating, 673
Client installation options and requirements, 671–675
Client, non-WINS, 79
Client reservations, DHCP, 191–193
Client settings, configuring VPN, 563–569
Client software, installing Terminal Services, 672–674
Client-to-server L2TP connections
    configuring, 579–587
    troubleshooting, 579–587
Client-to-server PPTP connections
    configuring, 579–587
    troubleshooting, 579–587
Clients
    commands for managing, 205–207
    configuring DHCP, 202–207
    configuring dial-up connections on remote access, 553–556
    configuring DNS, 154–156
    configuring DNS suffix options on, 157–159
    configuring TCP/IP on servers and, 4–17
    configuring to use DHCP, 203–204
    configuring WINS, 80–82
    DHCP, 180
    downlevel, 194
    downlevel DHCP, 201
    installing Terminal Services, 674–675
    name registration for non-WINS, 92–93
    name resolution for b-node, 90
    remote access, 574
    supporting downlevel, 143–144
    supporting non-WINS, 90–93
    troubleshooting WINS, 102–103
Clipboard mapping, 679
Clues, troubleshooting, 643
Command-line analysis and configuration, 534–535
Commands
    changer user, 671
    compact, 88
    disable, 810
    diskperf, 849
    diskperf-n, 849

diskperf-yy, 849
enable, 810
fixboot, 811
fixmbr, 811
format, 811
ipconfig, 718–724
ipconfig/all, 39, 41, 74, 204
ipconfig/registerdns, 208
ipconfig/release, 208
ipconfig/renew, 208
jetpack, 88
listsvc, 810
for managing clients, 205–207
movetree, 429
NSLOOKUP, 160–161
ping, 44, 718–724
rdisk, 818
Recovery Console, 810–811
route, 38
route change, 38
route print, 31
secedit, 535
Compact command, 88
Compatibility, verifying hardware, 755–761
Compressed, files can be, 464
Computer accounts, 253
Computer accounts, adding, 254–257
Computer name, checking out your, 68
Computer name resolution properties, client, 153–159
Computer objects, moving, 428
Computer remote access properties, configuring client, 550–570
Computernames, 67, 71
Computers
    backing up your, 822–823
    booting, 799
    configuration settings and remote, 499
    configuring direct connections to other, 557–558
    deploying hotfixes on new, 412
    ESP and communicating between, 589
    finding shared printers in, 376–377
    installing service packs on new, 409–411
    joining to domains, 260–261
    logging on to, 517
    multihomed, 30
    multiple, 675
    running non-Windows operating systems, 674
    starting in Safe Mode, 803
    Terminal Services client, 679
    Windows-based, 674
Computers and users, administering AD (Active Directory), 253–261
Computer's IP configuration, determining using ipconfig, 721
Computer's routing table, viewing, 34
Computers to use multilinks, configuring client, 635
Configuration
    analyzing current, 530–534
    checking IP, 42
    command-line analysis and, 534–535
    computer's IP, 721
    ICS and IP addresses, 711
    Last Known Good, 803–804
    settings and remote computers, 499
    Terminal Services, 691
Configuring
    Active Directory replication, 431–438
    alerts, 860–867
    and auditing security, 516–525
    authentication protocols on RRAS, 596–598
    burst mode, 88–89
    client computer name resolution properties, 153–159
    client computers to use multilinks, 635
    client-to-server L2TP connections, 579–587
    client-to-server PPTP connections, 579–587
    clients to use DHCP, 203–204
    data encryption, 598
    DDNS, 140–143
    DHCP clients, 202–207
    DHCP-DDNS integration, 201–202
    DHCP relay agent, 577–578
    DHCP scopes, 186–202
    DHCP servers, 186–202
    dial-up connections on remote access clients, 553–556
    direct connections to other computers, 557–558
    disks and volumes, 456–459
    DNS, 117–178
    DNS clients, 154–156
    DNS server properties, 138–152
    DNS suffix options on clients, 157–159
    DNS zones, creating and, 118–132
    driver signing options, 761, 764, 765–766
    and enforcing disk quotas, 459–462
    Event Viewer, 523–524
    ICS, 711–713
    ICS (Internet Connection Sharing), 707, 708–718
    and implementing Active Directory (AD), 229–290
    and implementing WINS, 78–100
    Internet Information Services (IIS), 481–513
    IP address allocation, 571–579
    IP address allocation in Windows 2000, 571–576
    L2TP filtering, 588–594
    L2TP packet filters, 589–594
    NAT interfaces, 730–735
    NAT (Network Address Translation), 707
    NAT properties, 729–735
    NAT service, 734
    NetBIOS name resolution, 70–78
    order of RAS policies, 645
    OS (operating system) support, 771–777
    PPTP filtering, 588–594
    PPTP packet filters, 589–594
    printer redirection, 682
    printers, 373–375
    printers, sharing and, 371
    quota limits, 462

Index

RAS policies, 630
remote access connections, 549–613
remote access name resolution, 571–579, 576–578
remote access permission, 617
remote access policies, 629
remote access policies and profiles, 616–636
reversible encryption, 640–641
routing, 23–39
routing and remote access, 724–735
routing tables, 34–37
RRAS as VPN server, 571–574
security of VPN connections, 594–599
server and client hardware, 753–792
slave servers, 151
System Monitor alerts and logging, 851–867
TCP/IP on servers, 12–15
TCP/IP on servers and clients, 4–17
Terminal Services for Application Server mode, 663–678
Terminal Services for local resource mapping, 678–690
Terminal Services for Remote Administration mode, 663–678
Terminal Services settings on per-connection basis, 682–690
Terminal Services user properties, 690–694
and troubleshooting DHCP, 179–226
and troubleshooting TCP/IP, 3–61
VPN client settings, 563–569
VPN connections, 549–613
WINS clients, 80–82
WINS intervals, 85–86
WINS replication partnerships, 95–99
Connect Directly To Another Computer option, 556
Connection object, 431
Connection object, KCC-created, 433
Connection-specific DNS suffix, 40
Connections
    configuring client-to-server L2TP, 579–587
    configuring client-to-server PPTP, 579–587
    configuring direct, 557–558
    configuring remote access, 549–613
    configuring security of VPN, 594–599
    configuring VPN, 549–613
    creating VPN, 559–561
    dial-up, 552–558
    establishing Terminal Server, 682
    establishing to Terminal Server, 677–678
    managing existing server-to-server L2TP, 588–594
    managing existing server-to-server PPTP, 588–594
    network bandwidth, 682
    terminating, 678
    troubleshooting client-to-server L2TP, 579–587
    troubleshooting client-to-server PPTP, 579–587
    verifying security of VPN, 594–599
    VPN (virtual private network), 558–570
Connectivity errors, L2TP, 586–587
Connectivity, VPN, 579–581

Console
    DNS, 129
    installing Recovery, 807–808
    Recovery, 807
    removing Recovery, 813–814
    repairing OS (operating system) by using Recovery, 807–815
    WINS management, 82
Contacts, creating, 266
Containers, LostAndFound, 430, 431
Control Access Through Remote Access Policy setting, 624
Control, delegating, 268–278
    delegating control to users, 270
    managing AD permissions, 271–277
Control, delegating to users, 270
Controllers
    setting up auditing on Domain, 520–521
    upgrading all domain, 245
Controlling replication, sites are strictly for, 434
Corporate scenario, 26–27
Counter defined, 846
Counter logs, 851–857
Counter logs monitor certain system resources, 857
Counters
    Windows 2000 disk, 849
    Windows NT 4 disk, 849
Create GPOs, delegating authority to, 338–341
Creating
    audit policies, 519
    client installation disks, 673
    and configuring, DNS zones, 118–132
    contacts, 266
    counter logs, 852–854
    distribution points, 393–394
    domain Dfs root, 467
    ERDs, 819
    and filtering GPO, 405–406
    folders, 356
    forward lookup zones, 129–130
    FTP sites, 490–492
    GPOs, 395–398
    GPOs (Group Policy Objects), 304–328
    and implementing group policies, 291–351
    LMHOSTS files, 74–78
    and managing, OUs (organizational units), 261–268
    new templates, 528–529
    objects in OUs, 264
    OUs (organizational units), 262–264
    RAS policies, 627–629
    remote access policies, 626–636
    remote access policies and profiles, 616–636
    reverse lookup zones, 130–132
    security databases, 533–534
    site links, 434–436
    stand-alone GPO, 327–328
    stand-alone GPOs, 322–328
    System Information file, 761

Terminal Server session, 677–678
trace logs, 858–860
two user accounts, 258–260
virtual directories, 484–485
virtual web servers, 487–489
VPN connections, 559–561
web sites, 482–490
Windows 2000 boot disk, 817
Current configuration, analyzing, 530–534
Cycle, software life, 395

D

Data
    ESP is used to encrypt, 589
    restoring, 825
    restoring from backup, 821–826
Data encryption, configuring, 598
Data, recovering from hard disks, 815–821
    ERDs (Emergency Repair Disks), 818–820
    Windows 2000 boot disk, 816–818
Data storage, managing, 455–480
    configuring and enforcing disk quotas, 459–462
    configuring disks and volumes, 456–459
    implementing and managing Distributed File System (Dfs), 465–469
    using Encrypting File System (EFS), 463–464
Database files, Access, 869
Database name, 88
    temporary, 88
Database records, managing DNS, 132–138
Databases
    backing up WINS, 84–85
    compacting WINS, 87–88
    creating security, 533–534
    managing WINS, 82–89
    restoring WINS, 84–85
    viewing records in WINS, 83
DC (domain controllers), 231–232
DC (domain controllers), upgrading all, 245
DCs, replication traffic between specific, 437
DDNS aging and scavenging properties, 141–143
DDNS, configuring, 140–143
DDNS (dynamic DNS), 140, 199
DDNS integration
    configuring DHCP-, 201–202
    DHCP-, 199–202
Decimal, converting between binary and, 15–17
Decimal notation, dotted, 6
Default authentication protocols, 596
Default gateway, 22, 41, 586
Default gateway address, ping, 43
Default gateway addresses, 11–12
Delegation Wizard, 274

Deleted objects, 431
Deploying hotfixes, note on, 411–412
Deploying hotfixes on new computers, 412
Deploying software, 409
Deployment
    testing, 402
    testing software, 410
DES (Digital Encryption Standard), 637
Description defined, 40
Destination defined, 36
Device Manager, 756–760
Devices
    installing legacy, 772–776
    legacy hardware, 771–777
Dfs
    domain-based, 465
    fault-tolerant, 465
    replication, 466
    topology, 468
Dfs (Distributed File System), implementing and managing, 465–469
Dfs root, creating domain, 467
DHCP
    assigning IP address using, 730
    installing, 182–183
DHCP Allocator service, 734
DHCP client reservations, 191–193
DHCP clients, 180
DHCP clients, configuring, 202–207
    commands for managing clients, 205–207
    note on APIPA, 207
DHCP clients, downlevel, 201
DHCP, configuring and troubleshooting, 179–226
    configuring DHCP clients, 202–207
    configuring DHCP scopes, 186–202
    configuring DHCP servers, 186–202
    installing and authorizing DHCP servers, 180–186
    troubleshooting DHCP, 207–212
DHCP, configuring clients to use, 203–204
DHCP-DDNS integration, 199–202
DHCP-DDNS integration, configuring, 201–202
DHCP (Dynamic Host Configuration Protocol), 5, 180, 182
DHCP enabled, 41
DHCP-enabled defined, 210
DHCP leases, 181–182
DHCP load balancing and redundancy, 194–199
    BOOTP forwarding, 196–198
    DHCP relay agents, 198–199
DHCP relay agent, configuring, 577–578
DHCP relay agents, 198–199
DHCP scopes, configuring, 186–202
DHCP servers, 575
    authorizing, 183–184
    checking for rogue, 211
    configuring, 186–202

Index

enterprise administrators authorizing, 184
installing and authorizing, 180–186
multiple, 210
NAT servers detecting presence of, 734
rogue, 183
DHCP service
   authorizing, 184–186
   installing, 184–186
DHCP, troubleshooting, 207–212
   detecting rogue servers, 210–212
Diagnostics, Windows, 760
Dial-in tab of user's Properties dialog box, 617
Dial-up connections, 552–558
Dial-up connections, configuring on remote access clients, 553–556
Dialog boxes
   Dial-in tab of user's Properties, 617
   Digital Signature Not Found, 767
   opening device's Properties, 757
   printers are configured through Printers, 756
   Properties, 400
   System Properties, 772–776
Digest authentication, 494
Digital Encryption Standard (DES), 637
Digital Signature Not Found dialog box, 767
Digital signatures, verifying on existing driver files, 767–771
Direct connections, configuring to other computers, 557–558
Direct memory access (DMA), 760
Directories, creating virtual, 484–485
Directories (web sharing), defining virtual, 483–486
Directory (NTFS) permissions, file and, 358–361
Directory Services Restore Mode, 804–805
Disable command, 810
Disk counters
   Windows 2000, 849
   Windows NT 4, 849
Disk Quota Limit policy, Enforce, 462
Disk quotas
   configuring and enforcing, 459–462
   enabling, 460–461
Disk quotas are features of NTFS, 464
Diskperf command, 849
Diskperf-n command, 849
Diskperf-yy command, 849
Disks
   basic, 456, 457–458
   converting basic disk to dynamic, 457–458
   creating client installation, 673
   creating Windows 2000 boot, 817
   dynamic, 456
   recovering data from hard, 815–821
   Windows 2000 boot, 816–818
Disks and volumes, configuring, 456–459
Distributed File System (Dfs), implementing and managing, 465–469

Distribution points
   creating, 393–394
   setting up software, 393–394
DLL file, 762
DMA (direct memory access), 760
DNS clients, configuring, 154–156
DNS console, 129
DNS database records, managing, 132–138
DNS (Domain Name System), 64, 69, 118, 468
   configuring, 117–178
   installing AD-integrated, 125–128
   installing without Active Directory, 128
   managing, 117–178
   troubleshooting, 117–178
   troubleshooting with IPCONFIG, 161–162
   workings of, 120–121
DNS forwarder, 150
DNS forwarding servers, 150
DNS name resolution, troubleshooting, 159–164
DNS name servers
   caching-only, 151–152
   local, 120
   multihomed, 146–147
   remote, 120
DNS or gateway information, do not configure, 725
DNS registration options, client, 159
DNS server properties, configuring, 138–152
   alternative DNS server roles, 147–152
   configuring DDNS, 140–143
   multihomed DNS name servers, 146–147
   subdomains and delegation of authority, 145–146
   supporting downlevel clients, 143–144
DNS server roles, alternative, 147–152
DNS servers, 41
DNS suffix, connection-specific, 40
DNS suffix options, configuring on clients, 157–159
DNS suffix, primary, 40
DNS zones, creating and configuring, 118–132
   DNS zones of authority, 122
   how DNS works, 120–121
   types of zones, 122–125
DNS zones of authority, 122
Document web site, 495
#DOM (domain) tag, 76
Domain-based Dfs, 465
Domain builtin local groups, 249
Domain controllers (DC), 231–232
Domain Controllers, setting up auditing on, 520–521
Domain Dfs root, creating, 467
Domain, local, 440
Domain local group, 440
Domain Name System (DNS), 64, 69, 118, 468
Domain names, unqualified, 157
Domain trees, 233, 234

Domains, 232–233
    child, 233
    joining computers to, 260–261
    moving objects across, 428–431
    moving objects within, 426
    RRAS authentication process in native mode, 621–625
Domains; *see also* subdomains, 145
Dotted decimal notation, 6
Dotted quad format, 6
Downlevel clients, 194
    supporting, 143–144
Downlevel DHCP clients, 201
Driver files, verifying digital signatures on existing, 767–771
Driver signing defined, 754
Driver signing options, 763
Driver signing options, configuring, 761, 764, 765–766
Drivers, installing for NIC, 41
Dump file, memory, 798
Dynamic addresses on hosts, 13
Dynamic disks, 456
    converting basic disks to, 457–458
Dynamic DNS (DDNS), 140, 199
Dynamic Host Configuration Protocol (DHCP), 5, 180, 182

E

EAP, open-ended authentication method, 639
EAP-TLS is most secure authentication protocol, 642
Edit GPOs, delegating authority to, 342
EFS are features of NTFS, 464
EFS (Encrypting File System), 463–464
Emergency Repair Disks (ERDs), 818–820
Enable command, 810
Encrypt data, ESP is used to, 589
Encrypted, files can be, 464
Encrypted password authentication protocol, 641
Encrypting File System (EFS), 463–464
Encryption
    and authentication protocols, 637–642
    configuring data, 598
    configuring reversible, 640–641
Encryption Pack, High, 683
Enforce Disk Quota Limit policy, 462
Enterprise administrators authorizing DHCP servers, 184
Environment, non-WINS, 77
ERD and recovery, 820
ERD is computer-specific, 820
ERDs, creating, 819
ERDs (Emergency Repair Disks), 818–820
Errors
    identifying RRAS, 643
    L2TP connectivity, 586–587
    no-answer, 581–583
ESE (Extensible Storage Engine), 87
ESP and communicating between computers, 589

ESP (Encapsulating Security Payload) protocol, 588
ESP is used to encrypt data, 589
Ethernet
    board, 5
    card, 5
Event logs, identifying RRAS errors in System, 643
Event Viewer
    configuring, 523–524
    diagnosing server health problems with, 868–872
    identifying troubleshooting clues in, 643
Event Viewer events, examining, 869–870
Events
    auditing Failure, 522
    examining Event Viewer, 869–870
    trace logs monitor certain, 857
    tracking, 859
    Windows 2000, 869
Exclusions, 187
Expiring passwords, 642
Extensible Storage Engine (ESE), 87
Extensions, LCP (Link Control Protocol), 569
External adapters, ICS only supports single, 710

F

Failure events, auditing, 522
Fast transfers, 164
FAT (File Allocation Table), 458
FAT file systems, NTFS and, 458
FAT partitions, 458
Fault tolerance, 25
Fault-tolerant Dfs, 465
File Allocation Table (FAT), 458
File and directory (NTFS) permissions, 358–361
File inheritance, 363–364
File option, running Window using startup log, 799
File systems, NTFS and FAT, 458
File Transfer Protocol (FTP), 482, 490
Files
    Access database, 869
    can be compressed, 464
    can be encrypted, 464
    creating LMHOSTS, 74–78
    creating System Information, 761
    DLL, 762
    and folders, 679
    HOSTS, 70, 159
    interpreting startup log, 798–801
    LMHOSTS, 67
    memory dump, 798
    ntbtlog.txt, 798, 799
    offline, 367–370
    root hints, 121
    SAM (Security Accounts Manager), 248
    scan and repair protected system, 770–771

Index

SDB (security configuration database), 531
sharing folders and, 355–370
Terminal Services and Offline, 664
verifying digital signatures on existing driver, 767–771
Windows 2000 system, 796
Filtering
    configuring L2TP, 588–594
    configuring PPTP, 588–594
Filtering problems, troubleshooting TCP/IP, 500–501
Filters
    configuring L2TP packet, 589–594
    configuring PPTP packet, 589–594
    creation of, 592
    defining IP packet, 626
Firewalls, 437
Fixboot command, 811
Fixmbr command, 811
Flat namespace, 71
Folder inheritance, 363–364
Folder permissions, shared, 357–361
Folder Redirection, 318–319
Folder redirection provides benefits to administrators, 318
Folders
    creating, 356
    encrypting, 463
    files and, 679
    publishing shared, 377–379
    sharing, 356
    %systemroot%\inf, 526
    SYSVOL, 306
Folders and files, sharing, 355–370
    combining permissions, 361–363
    file inheritance, 363–364
    folder inheritance, 363–364
    hidden shares, 365–367
    shared folder permissions, 357–361
    taking ownership, 364–365
Folders, sharing and publishing, 353–390
    sharing folders and files, 355–370
Forests, 235
Format command, 811
Format, dotted quad, 6
Forward lookup zone, 129
Forwarder, DNS, 150
Forwarding, BOOTP, 196–198
Forwarding servers, DNS, 150
FQDN (fully qualified domain name), 7, 69, 118
Frames, 11
Freeware utilities, 594
FTP (File Transfer Protocol), 482, 490
FTP sites
    creating, 490–492
    securing web and, 493–499
FTP's authentication limitations, getting around, 495
Fully qualified domain name (FQDN), 7, 69, 118

G

Gateway address, ping default, 43
Gateway, default, 11–12, 22, 41, 586
Gateway defined, 36
Gateway information, do not configure DNS or, 725
Generic Routing Encapsulation (GRE), 588
Global catalog, 240–243
Global security groups, 250
GPO links, delegating authority to manage, 338
GPOs, creating stand-alone
    choosing policy settings for GPO, 324–326
    disabling unused policy settings, 326
GPOs (Group Policy Objects), 292, 392, 626
    choosing policy settings for, 324–326
    creating, 395–398
    creating and filtering, 405–406
    creating stand-alone, 322–328, 327–328
    delegating authority to create, 338–341
    delegating authority to edit, 342
    delegating control of Start Menu Icons, 340
    filtering Start Menu Icons, 336
    linking at site level, 330
    linking Start Menu Icons, 331–332
    linking to OUs, 330
    modifying existing, 296–301
    viewing existing, 296–301
GPOs (Group Policy Objects), creating, 304–328
    Administrative Templates, 320–322
    creating stand-alone GPOs, 322–328
    software settings, 305
    Windows settings, 305–319
GRE (Generic Routing Encapsulation), 588
Group, domain local, 440
Group membership, user account, 642–643
Group policies
    adding packages to, 398–401
    applying to OUs, 264
    deploying software with, 392–402
    enforcing quota limits through, 461–462
    filtering, 333–337
    and installing new software, 395
    linking to AD objects, 329–332
    order of, 765
Group policies, creating and implementing, 291–351
    creating GPOs (Group Policy Objects), 304–328
    delegating control of group policies, 337–342
    filtering group policies, 333–337
    implementing group policies, 292–303
    linking group policies to AD objects, 329–332
Group policies, delegating control of, 337–342
    delegating authority to create GPOs, 338–341
    delegating authority to edit GPOs, 342
    delegating authority to manage GPO links, 338
Group policies, implementing, 292–303

group policy concepts, 293–296
managing multiple policy links, 301–303
modifying existing GPOs, 296–301
viewing existing GPOs, 296–301
Group policies, importance of, 316
Group policy concepts, 293–296
group policy timing and refresh intervals, 296
no override and block inheritance options, 293–295
Group policy, managing software with, 391–423
deploying service packs, 409–412
deploying software with group policy, 392–402
maintaining and upgrading software, 402
Group Policy Objects (GPOs), 626
Group policy timing, 296
Groups
builtin, 248–249
creating security, 251–252
domain builtin local, 249
global security, 250
local builtin, 248
nested, 642, 642–643
nesting, 249–250
predefined, 247
Restricted, 517, 518
security, 440

H

HAL (hardware abstraction layer), 797
Handling, burst, 89
Hard disks, recovering data from, 815–821
Hardware
addresses, 4–5
configuring server and client, 753–792
installing server and client, 753–792
startup phase, 794–795
Hardware abstraction layer (HAL), 797
Hardware Compatibility List (HCL), 755
Hardware compatibility, verifying, 755–761
Device Manager, 756–760
Windows 2000 Readiness Analyzer, 755–756
Hardware devices, legacy, 771–777
HCL (Hardware Compatibility List), 755
HCL, up-to-date copy of, 755
Headers, distinguishing sites by host, 488–489
Hidden shares, 365–367
Hierarchical namespace, 118
High Encryption Pack, 683
Hints file, root, 121
Host (A) records, 135
Host headers, distinguishing sites by, 488–489
Hostnames, pinging, 44–45
Hosts, dynamic addresses on, 13
HOSTS file, 70, 159
Hotfixes
deploying on new computers, 412
note on deploying, 411–412

I

IAS (Internet Authentication Service), 626
ICA (Independent Computing Architecture), 663
Icons GPO, delegating control of Start Menu, 340
ICS
configuring, 711–713
installing, 711–713
ICS and IP address configuration, 711
ICS and networks, 711
ICS (Internet Connection Sharing), 550, 708
configuring, 707, 708–718
troubleshooting problems, 718–724
ICS only supports single external adapters, 710
ICS uses address translation, 710
ID
network, 10
subnet, 10
Identifiers, NetBIOS service, 72–73
IETF (Internet Engineering Task Force), 4
IGMP (Internet Group Management Protocol), 100
IIS (Internet Information Services), 482
backing up and restoring, 499–500
maintaining and troubleshooting, 499–501
remotely administering, 496
IIS (Internet Information Services), configuring, 481–513
creating FTP sites, 490–492
creating web sites, 482–490
maintaining and troubleshooting IIS, 499–501
securing web and FTP sites, 493–499
Implementing
Active Directory (AD), configuring, and, 229–290
group policies, 292–303
group policies, creating, and, 291–351
intersite Active Directory replication, 433–438
security, 515–546
Terminal Services for remote access, 661–706
and troubleshooting name resolution, 63–116
WINS, configuring, and, 78–100
Independent Computing Architecture (ICA), 663
Infrastructure, NetBIOS, 144
Inheritance
file, 363–364
folder, 363–364
Inheritance options, no override and block, 293–295
Installation, basic Windows 2000 Server, 482
Installer packages, 392
Installing
AD-integrated DNS, 125–128
and authorizing DHCP servers, 180–186
DHCP, 182–183
DHCP service, 184–186
DNS without Active Directory, 128
drivers for NIC, 41
ICS, 711–713
legacy devices, 772–776
NAT, 726–728
new software, group policies and, 395

Index 903

Recovery Console, 807–808
server and client hardware, 753–792
service packs on new computers, 409–411
Terminal Services, 663–665, 664–665
Terminal Services client software, 672–674
Terminal Services clients over networks, 674–675
TSAC, 666–667
WINS server, 79–80
Integrated Windows authentication, 495
Integration
configuring DHCP-DDNS, 201–202
DHCP-DDNS, 199–202
Interface defined, 36
Interfaces
configuring NAT, 730–735
NetBIOS is legacy network, 64
International Telecommunications Union (ITU), 662
Internet address, 5
Internet Authentication Service (IAS), 626
Internet Engineering Task Force (IETF), 4
Internet Group Management Protocol (IGMP), 100
Internet Information Services (IIS), 482
Internet service providers (ISPs), 23, 69, 148
Intersite Active Directory replication, implementing, 433–438
Intersite replication, 433
Intervals
configuring WINS, 85–86
refresh, 296
renewal, 181
Intrasite replication defined, 431
IP address allocation
configuring, 571–579
configuring in Windows 2000, 571–576
IP address, assigning using DHCP, 730
IP address assignment, automatic, 575–576
IP address configuration, ICS and, 711
IP address, ping your own, 43
IP address/subnet mask combination, 7
IP addresses, 5, 5–12, 41
assign in RRAS, 577
automatically assign, 574
broadcast addresses, 10
Class A, B and C addresses, 8–10
classed, 9
classful, 9
control of, 8
default gateway addresses, 11–12
distinguishing sites by, 488
finding valid, 18–21
getting, 7–8
of name servers, 148
ping more distant, 44
ping nearby, 44
static, 201, 206
subnet addresses, 10
subnet masks, 6–7

IP addresses, determining valid, 17–23
broadcasting, 22–23
finding valid IP addresses, 18–21
subnetting, 17–18
IP addresses on servers, static, 13
IP configuration
checking, 42
computer's, 721
IP network address, 10
IP packet filters, defining, 626
IP routing enabled, 40
IP transport, 434
Ipaddress, ping, 44
IPCONFIG
troubleshooting DNS with, 161–162
troubleshooting with, 39–42
Ipconfig/all command, 39, 41, 74, 204
Ipconfig commands, 718–724
Ipconfig, determining computer's IP configuration using, 721
Ipconfig/registerdns command, 208
Ipconfig/release, 204
command, 208
releases, 206
Ipconfig/renew command, 208
Ipconfig switches, 720
Ipconfig, troubleshooting with, 719–721
IPSec, creating of filters for, 592
IPSec (IP Security), 725
ISAPI applications, enabling, 497–498
ISPs (Internet service providers), 23, 69, 148
Iterative query defined, 120
ITU (International Telecommunications Union), 662

J

Jetpack command, 88

K

KCC-created connection object, 433
KCC (Knowledge Consistency Checker), 431
KDC (Key Distribution Center), 308
Keep It Simple Smartguy (KISS), 816
Key Distribution Center (KDC), 308
Kit, Windows 2000 Server Resource, 869
Knowledge Consistency Checker (KCC), 431

L

L2TP connections
configuring client-to-server, 579–587
managing existing server-to-server, 588–594
troubleshooting client-to-server, 579–587
L2TP connectivity errors, 586–587
L2TP filtering, configuring, 588–594

L2TP (Layer Two Tunneling Protocol), 561, 562–563
L2TP packet filters, configuring, 589–594
LANs (Local Area Networks), 30, 501, 668, 709
Last Known Good Configuration, 803–804
Law, Murphy's, 794
Layer Two Tunneling Protocol (L2TP), 561
Layout, AD physical, 231–232
LCP (Link Control Protocol) extensions, 569
LDAP (Lightweight Directory Access Protocol), 231
Leases, DHCP, 181–182
Legacy devices, installing, 772–776
Legacy hardware devices, 771–777
Licensing, 675–676
Life cycle, software, 395
Lightweight Directory Access Protocol (LDAP), 231
Limited broadcast address, 33
Linking
    GPOs at site levels, 330
    GPOs to OUs, 330
    group policies to AD objects, 329–332
    Start Menu Icons GPO to OUs, 331–332
Links
    bridging site, 436
    creating site, 434–436
    delegating authority to manage GPO, 338
    managing multiple policy, 301–303
    WAN, 426
Lists, members, 517
Listsvc command, 810
LMHOSTS file, 67
LMHOSTS files, creating, 74–78
Load balancing and redundancy, DHCP, 194–199
Local Area Networks (LANs), 30, 501, 668, 709
Local, Builtin, 248
Local builtin groups, 248
Local DNS name server, 120
Local domain, 440
Local groups
    domain, 440
    domain builtin, 249
Local policies, 309–311
Local security policies, 292
Local settings, comparing policy settings to, 531
Local sites, accessing, 486
Localhost, 70
Log file option, running Window using startup, 799
Log files, interpreting startup, 798–801
Logging
    boot, 799
    on to computers, 517
    configuring System Monitor alerts and, 851–867
Logical address, 5
Logon problems in mixed mode, 622–623

Logs
    counter, 851–857
    creating counter, 852–854
    creating trace, 858–860
    identifying RRAS errors in System event, 643
    opening with System Monitor, 855–857
    trace, 857, 857–860
Lookup zone, forward, 129
Loopback address, ping, 42–43
LostAndFound container, 430, 431

M

M defined, 36
Manage GPO links, delegating authority to, 338
Management console, WINS, 82
Management tasks, simplify, 395
Manager, Device, 756–760
Managing
    Active Directory objects, 426–431
    AD permissions, 271–277
    clients, commands for, 205–207
    DNS, 117–178
    DNS database records, 132–138
    existing server-to-server L2TP connections, 588–594
    existing server-to-server PPTP connections, 588–594
    multiple policy links, 301–303
    OUs (organizational units), creating, and, 261–268
    software with group policy, 391–423
    and troubleshooting AD (Active Directory), 425–452
Mandatory upgrade, 403
Manual printer redirection, 681
Mapping
    clipboard, 679
    configuring Terminal Services for local resource, 678–690
Mappings, static, 92–93
Mask combination, IP address/subnet, 7
Masks defined, 18
Masks, subnet, 6–7, 41
MaxDenials value, editing in Registry, 638
MD5 (Message Digest 5), 640
Media, streaming, 100
Member server defined, 231
Members list, 517
Membership, user account group, 642–643
Memory dump file, 798
Memory.dmp, 798
Menu Icons GPO, delegating control of Start, 340
Message Digest 5 (MD5), 640
Methods, authentication, 493–495
Microsoft-Enhanced b-Node, 74
Microsoft Management Console (MMC), 82, 129
Microsoft Patch (MSP), 392
Microsoft Point-to-Point Encryption (MPPE), 637

Microsoft RAS (Remote Access Service), 551
Microsoft Software Installation (MSI), 392
Microsoft Transform (MST), 392
Mixed mode, 245, 250
    logon problems in, 622–623
    RRAS authentication process in, 620–621
MMC (Microsoft Management Console), 82, 129
Mode domain, RRAS authentication process in native, 621–625
Modes
    Application Server, 668–669
    burst, 89
    configuring burst, 88–89
    configuring Terminal Services for Application Server, 663–678
    configuring Terminal Services for Remote Administration, 663–678
    Directory Services Restore, 804–805
    logon problems in mixed, 622–623
    mixed, 245, 250
    native, 245, 250
    Remote Administration, 667–668
    RRAS authentication process in mixed, 620–621
    switching between, 670–671
    switching between Terminal Server, 670–671
    switching to native, 245–246
Modes, Safe, 801–803
Modifying existing GPOs, 296–301
Monitor
    enabling Network Segment, 850
    See also System Monitor
Monitoring
    server health and performance, 841–887
    system performance, 864
Mount points, 458–459
Movetree command, 429
MPPE (Microsoft Point-to-Point Encryption), 637
MS-CHAP v2 (Microsoft Challenge Handshake Authentication Protocol version 2), 640
MSI (Microsoft Software Installation), 392
MSP (Microsoft Patch), 392
MST (Microsoft Transform), 392
Multicast address, 33, 100
Multicast routers, 100
Multicasting and IGMP, 100
Multihomed
    computer, 30
    DNS name servers, 146–147
    machine, 206
Multilinks, configuring client computers to use, 635
Multimaster replication, 231
Multimaster zone replication, 125
Multiple computers, 675
Multiple policy links, managing, 301–303
Multiple WINS servers, setting up, 93–99
Murphy's Law, 794

N

Name cache, NetBIOS, 66–67
Name registration for non-WINS clients, 92–93
Name resolution, configuring NetBIOS, 70–78
    creating LMHOSTS files, 74–78
    NetBIOS name resolution sequences, 74
    NetBIOS names, 71–72
    NetBIOS service identifiers, 72–73
Name resolution, configuring remote access, 571–579, 576–578
Name resolution for b-node clients, 90
Name resolution, implementing and troubleshooting, 63–116
    configuring and implementing WINS, 78–100
    configuring NetBIOS name resolution, 70–78
    troubleshooting NetBIOS name resolution, 100–103
    understanding name resolution, 64–70
Name resolution problems, 45
Name resolution resources, 65–70
    broadcast, 67
    Domain Name System (DNS), 69
    HOSTS file, 70
    LMHOSTS file, 67
    local host (HOSTNAME), 66
    NetBIOS name cache, 66–67
    WINS (Windows Internet Naming Service), 68
Name resolution sequences, NetBIOS, 74
Name resolution, troubleshooting DNS, 159–164
Name resolution, troubleshooting NetBIOS, 100–103
    troubleshooting WINS clients, 102–103
    troubleshooting WINS servers, 102
Name resolution, understanding, 64–70
Name server lookup (NSLOOKUP), 160
Name Server (NS) records, 133–135
Name servers
    caching-only DNS, 151–152
    IP addresses of, 148
    local DNS, 120
    multihomed DNS, 146–147
    remote DNS, 120
    standard primary, 124–125
    standard secondary, 124–125
    testing, 163
Names
    checking out your computer, 68
    database, 88
    NetBIOS, 71–72
    peeking at some NetBIOS, 76
    short, 159
    temporary database, 88
    unqualified domain, 157
Namespaces
    DNS (Domain Name System), 468
    flat, 71
    hierarchical, 118
NAT cannot be used for access scenarios, 725

NAT interfaces, configuring, 730–735
NAT (Network Address Translation), 9, 550, 708, 728
    installing, 726–728
    performing, 724–735
NAT (Network Address Translation), configuring, 707
NAT properties, configuring, 729–735
NAT server detecting presence of DHCP server, 734
NAT service, configuring, 734
NAT uses and limitations, 725
Native mode, 245, 250
    domain, 621–625
    switching to, 245–246
Native package, 392
NBNS (NetBIOS name server), 74, 78
Negative cache entries, 162
Nested groups, 642, 642–643
Nesting groups, 249–250
NetBEUI (NetBIOS Extended User Interface), 71
NetBIOS
    infrastructure, 144
    is legacy network interface, 64
    name cache, 66–67
NetBIOS Extended User Interface (NetBEUI), 71
NetBIOS name resolution, configuring, 70–78
    creating LMHOSTS files, 74–78
    NetBIOS name resolution sequences, 74
    NetBIOS names, 71–72
    NetBIOS service identifiers, 72–73
NetBIOS name resolution sequences, 74
NetBIOS name resolution, troubleshooting, 100–103
    troubleshooting WINS clients, 102–103
    troubleshooting WINS servers, 102
NetBIOS name server (NBNS), 74, 78
NetBIOS names, 71–72, 76
NetBIOS (Network Basic Input/Output System), 551
NetBIOS service identifiers, 72–73
Netsh command-line utility, 629
Network address, IP, 10
Network Address Translation (NAT), 9, 550
Network bandwidth connections, 682
Network Basic Input/Output System (NetBIOS), 551
Network ID, 10
Network interface, NetBIOS is legacy, 64
Network News Transfer Protocol (NNTP), 482
Network, remote, 24
Network Segment monitors, enabling, 850
Networks
    ICS and, 711
    installing Terminal Services clients over, 674–675
    traffic and remote, 586
New computers
    deploying hotfixes on, 412
    installing service packs on, 409–411
New registrations, 124
New Scope Wizard, 193
New software, group policies and installing, 395

New templates, creating, 528–529
NIC, installing drivers for, 41
NICs (network interface cards), 850
NNTP (Network News Transfer Protocol), 482
No-answer errors, 581–583
Node clients, name resolution for b-, 90
Node, Microsoft-enhanced b-, 74
Node type, 40
Non-Windows operating systems, computers running, 674
Non-WINS client, 79
Non-WINS clients
    name registration for, 92–93
    supporting, 90–93
Non-WINS environment, 77
Notation, dotted decimal, 6
NSLOOKUP
    command, 160–161
    testing forward and reverse lookups with, 161
NSLOOKUP (name server lookup), 160
Ntbtlog.txt file, 798, 799
NTFS
    disk quotas are features of, 464
    EFS are features of, 464
    and FAT file systems, 458
    partitions, 458
Numbers, assigning partition, 818

O

Objects
    attribute changes made to user, 691
    choosing to audit, 521–523
    connection, 431
    creating in OUs, 264
    deleted, 431
    finding existing, 266–268
    KCC-created connection, 433
    linking group policies to AD, 329–332
    managing Active Directory, 426–431
    moving across domains, 428–431
    moving computer, 428
    moving to OUs, 264–265
    moving within domains, 426
    searching for AD, 379
Offline files, 367–370
Offline Files, Terminal Services and, 664
Open Shortest Path First (OSPF), 38
Operating system; *See* OS (operating system)
Optional upgrade, 403
Options
    Advanced Published, 397
    Assigned, 397
    client DNS registration, 159
    client installation, 671–675
    configuring driver signing, 761, 764, 765–766
    Connect Directly To Another Computer, 556

Index

driver signing, 763
no override and block inheritance, 293–295
repairing OS (operating system) by using various startup, 801–807
running Window using startup log file, 799
server, 193–194
server options vs. scope, 193–194
three Safe Mode, 799
verifying VPN connectivity, 579–581
OS (operating system)
computers running non-Windows, 674
configuring support for hardware devices, 771–777
not starting, 815–821
repairing by using Recovery Console, 807–815
repairing by using startup options, 801–807
restoring from backup, 821–826
OS (operating system), repairing by using various startup options
Directory Services Restore Mode, 804–805
Last Known Good Configuration, 803–804
OSPF (Open Shortest Path First), 38
OU Admins, allowing to log on locally, 312–314
OUs (organizational units), 237–240
applying group policies to, 264
creating objects in, 264
linking GPOs to, 330
linking Start Menu Icons GPO to, 331–332
moving objects to, 264, 264–265
OUs (organizational units), creating, 262–264
OUs (organizational units), creating and managing, 261–268
creating contacts, 266
creating objects in OUs, 264
creating OUs (organizational units), 262–264
finding existing objects, 266–268
moving objects to OUs, 264–265
Overhead, minimizing replication, 440
Override and block inheritance options, no, 293–295
Ownership, taking, 364–365

P

Pack 2, Service, 683
Pack, High Encryption, 683
Package, native, 392
Packages
adding to group policy, 398–401
installer, 392
Packet filters
configuring L2TP, 589–594
configuring PPTP, 589–594
defining IP, 626
Packet Inter Network Groper (ping), 721
Packet Internet Groper (ping), 42
Packets, 11
PAP (Password Authentication Protocol), 639
Partition numbers, assigning, 818

Partitions
boot, 796
FAT, 458
NTFS, 458
Partners
push/pull, 95
replication, 94
Partnerships, configuring WINS replication, 95–99
Password Authentication Protocol (PAP), 639
Password authentication protocol, SPAP is encrypted, 641
Passwords, expiring, 642
PATHPING, troubleshooting with, 48–49
PDC (primary domain controller), 231
Performance
monitoring and interpreting real-time, 842–850
monitoring server health and, 841–887
monitoring system, 864
tuning web site, 489–490
Permissions
combining, 361–363
configuring remote access, 617
controlling site access through, 496–498
defined, 243
file and directory (NTFS), 358–361
managing AD, 271–277
RAS, 622–623
setting shared printer, 373
share, 357–358
shared folder, 357–361
Phases
hardware startup, 794–795
software startup, 795–798
Physical address, 40
Physical layout, AD, 231–232
Ping command, 44, 723
Ping commands, 718–724
Ping default gateway address, 43
Ping ipaddress, 44
Ping loopback address, 42–43
Ping more distant IP addresses, 44
Ping nearby IP addresses, 44
Ping (Packet Inter Network Groper), 721
Ping (Packet Internet Groper), 42
Ping, troubleshooting using, 721–724
PING, troubleshooting with, 42–45
Ping your own IP address, 43
Pinging hostnames, 44–45
Platforms, TCP/IP-enabled, 65
Point-to-Point Protocol (PPP), 550, 551, 636
Point-to-Point Tunneling Protocol (PPTP), 561
Pointer (PTR) records, 136
Points
creating distribution, 393–394
mount, 458–459
setting up software distribution, 393–394

Policies
    Account, 307–309
    audit, 519
    configuring order of RAS, 645
    configuring RAS, 630
    configuring remote access, 629
    creating audit, 519
    creating RAS, 627–629
    creating remote access, 626–636
    delegating control of Group, 337–342
    Enforce Disk Quota Limit, 462
    importance of Group, 316
    local, 309–311
    local security, 292, 765–766
    order of group, 765
    structuring RAS, 645
Policies and profiles
    configuring remote access, 616–636
    creating remote access, 616–636
Policies, three components of RAS, 618–620
    conditions, 618
    permissions, 618
    profile, 620
Policy conditions, examining RAS, 631
Policy links, managing multiple, 301–303
Policy priority, diagnosing problems with remote access, 644–645
Policy problems, diagnosing remote access, 642–643
Policy settings
    choosing for GPO, 324–326
    comparing to local settings, 531
    disabling unused, 326
Policy storage, RAS, 643
Policy timing, group, 296
Port Settings tab, 758
Ports
    distinguishing sites by, 488
    not enough available, 583
    and UDP, 139
    well-known, 488
POST (power-on self test), 794
Power-on self test (POST), 794
PPP (Point-to-Point Protocol), 550, 551, 636
PPTP connections
    configuring client-to-server, 579–587
    managing existing server-to-server, 588–594
    troubleshooting client-to-server, 579–587
PPTP filtering, configuring, 588–594
PPTP packet filters, configuring, 589–594
PPTP (Point-to-Point Tunneling Protocol), 561, 562
#PRE (preload) tag, 77
Predefined groups, 247
Primary DNS suffix, 40
Primary domain controller (PDC), 231
Primary name servers, standard, 124–125
Primary zones, standard, 122
Print command, route, 31

Printer permissions, setting shared, 373
Printer redirection, 680–690
    automatic, 680, 681
    configuring, 682
    manual, 681
Printers
    are configured through Printers dialog box, 756
    configuring, 373–375
    finding shared, 376–377
    managing remotely, 487
    publishing shared, 379
Printers dialog box, printers are configured through, 756
Printers, sharing, 372
Printers, sharing and configuring, 371
    configuring printers, 373–375
    setting shared printer permissions, 373
Printers, sharing and publishing, 353–390
    sharing and configuring printers, 371
Problems
    authentication protocol, 583–586
    diagnosing remote access policy, 642–643
    diagnosing server health, 868–872
    diagnosing with remote access policy priority, 644–645
    logon, 622–623
    name resolution, 45
    troubleshooting ICS (Internet Connection Sharing), 718–724
    troubleshooting RAS, 642
    troubleshooting startup, 793–839
    troubleshooting TCP/IP filtering, 500–501
Profile settings, examining RAS, 632–636
Profiles
    configuring remote access policies and, 616–636
    creating remote access policies and, 616–636
Programs, add/remove, 670–671
Properties
    configuring client computer name resolution, 153–159
    configuring client computer remote access, 550–570
    configuring DNS server, 138–152
    configuring NAT, 729–735
    configuring Terminal Services user, 690–694
    DDNS aging and scavenging, 141–143
Properties dialog box, 400, 757
Protected system files, scan and repair, 770–771
Protocol problems, authentication, 583–586
Protocols
    configuring authentication, 596–598
    default authentication, 596
    EAP-TLS is most secure authentication, 642
    ESP (Encapsulating Security Payload), 588
    remote access, 550–552
    selecting encryption and authentication, 637–642
    SPAP is encrypted password authentication, 641
Proxy agent, WINS, 91
Proxy enabled, WINS, 40
Proxy servers, troubleshooting problems with, 501
Proxy, WINS, 90

Index

Public Switched Telephone Network (PSTN), 552
Published option, Advanced, 397
Publishing
    application, 716–717
    service, 713–716
    shared folders, 377–379
    shared printers, 379
    shared resources in AD (Active Directory), 377–380
Pull relationship, 94
Pull Replication tab, 98
Push/pull partners, 95
Push relationship, 94
Push trigger, 97

Q

Quad format, dotted, 6
Qualifier tools, 755–761
Queries
    iterative, 120
    recursive, 120
Quota Limit policy, Enforce Disk, 462
Quota limits
    configuring, 462
    enforcing through group policy, 461–462
Quotas, 461
    configuring and enforcing disk, 459–462

R

RAS permissions, 622–623
RAS policies
    configuring, 630
    configuring order of, 645
    creating, 627–629
    structuring, 645
RAS policies, three components of, 618–620
    conditions, 618
    permissions, 618
    profile, 620
RAS policy conditions, examining, 631
RAS policy exists at all times, 621
RAS policy storage, 643
RAS problems, troubleshooting, 642
RAS profile settings, examining, 632–636
RAS (Remote Access Service), 551
Rdisk command, 818
RDP (Remote Desktop Protocol), 662
Readiness Analyzer, Windows 2000, 755–756
Real-time performance, monitoring and interpreting, 842–850
Real-time system information, 847–849
Rebinding State, 181
Rebinding Time Value, 181

Records
    host (A), 135
    managing DNS database, 132–138
    miscellaneous resource, 136–138
    Name Server (NS), 133–135
    Pointer (PTR), 136
    Start of Authority (SOA), 133
    viewing in WINS database, 83
    viewing resource, 134–135
Recovery Console, 807
    accessing from Windows 2000 CD, 809
    commands, 810–811
    installing, 807–808
    removing, 813–814
    repairing OS (operating system) by using, 807–815
Recovery, ERD and, 820
Recursive query, 120
Redirection
    automatic printer, 680, 681
    configuring printer, 682
    Folder, 318–319
    manual printer, 681
    printer, 680–690
Redundancy, DHCP load balancing and, 194–199
Referral response defined, 121
Refresh intervals, 296
/refreshpolicy switch, 535
Registration options, client DNS, 159
Registrations
    name, 92–93
    new, 124
Registry, editing MaxDenials value in, 638
Registry hack, disabling APIPA with, 207
Relationships
    pull, 94
    push, 94
Relay agents
    configuring DHCP, 577–578
    DHCP, 198–199
    Windows 2000 DHCP, 199
/release switch, 206
Releases
    ipconfig, 204
    ipconfig/release, 206
Remote access
    configuring policies and profiles, 616–636
    configuring routing and, 724–735
    creating policies and profiles, 616–636
    implementing Terminal Services for, 661–706
Remote access clients, 574
Remote access clients, configuring dial-up connections on, 553–556
Remote access connections, configuring, 549–613
    configuring client computer remote access properties, 550–570

configuring client-to-server L2TP connections, 579–587
configuring client-to-server PPTP connections, 579–587
configuring IP address allocation, 571–579
configuring L2TP filtering, 588–594
configuring PPTP filtering, 588–594
configuring remote access name resolution, 571–579
configuring security of VPN connections, 594–599
managing existing server-to-server L2TP connections, 588–594
managing existing server-to-server PPTP connections, 588–594
troubleshooting client-to-server L2TP connections, 579–587
troubleshooting client-to-server PPTP connections, 579–587
verifying security of VPN connections, 594–599
Remote access name resolution, configuring, 571–579, 576–578
Remote access permission, configuring, 617
Remote access policies
    configuring, 629
    creating, 626–636
Remote access policy priority, diagnosing problems with, 644–645
Remote access policy problems, diagnosing, 642–643
Remote Access Policy setting, Control Access Through, 624
Remote access properties, configuring client computer, 550–570
Remote access protocols, 550–552
Remote access servers, Shiva, 641
Remote Access Service (RAS), 551
Remote access, troubleshooting, 615–659
    configuring remote access policies and profiles, 616–636
    creating remote access policies and profiles, 616–636
    diagnosing problems with remote access policy priority, 644–645
    diagnosing remote access policy problems, 642–643
    nested groups, 642–643
    selecting encryption and authentication protocols, 637–642
    user account group membership, 642–643
Remote Administration mode, 667–668
    configuring Terminal Services for, 663–678
Remote computers, configuration settings and, 499
Remote Desktop Protocol (RDP), 662
Remote DNS name server, 120
Remote Installation Services (RIS), 316–317
Remote network, 24
Remote networks, traffic and, 586
Remote Procedure Calls (RPCs), 434, 438
Remote troubleshooting, 669
Remove programs, add, 670–671
/renew switch, 206
Renewal interval, 181
Repair protected system files, scan and, 770–771
Repairing OS (operating system)
    by using Recovery Console, 807–815
    by using startup options, 801–807
Replication
    configuring Active Directory, 431–438
    Dfs, 466
    has slowed down, 439–440
    how it takes place, 432
    implementing intersite Active Directory, 433–438
    intersite, 433
    intrasite, 431
    multimaster, 231
    multimaster zone, 125
    partners, 94
    sites are strictly for controlling, 434
    between sites fails, 439
    traffic between specific DCs, 437
    WINS, 95–99
Replication overhead, minimizing, 440
Replication schedule, changing, 433
Replication topology, checking, 440–441
Requests for Comments (RFCs), 4
Reservations, DHCP client, 191–193
Resolution
    configuring NetBIOS name, 70–78
    configuring remote access name, 571–579, 576–578
    implementing and troubleshooting name, 63–116
    troubleshooting DNS name, 159–164
Resolution problems, name, 45
Resolution properties, client computer name, 153–159
Resolver defined, 120
Resource mapping, Terminal Services for local, 678–690
Resource records
    miscellaneous, 136–138
    viewing, 134–135
Resource records (RR), 133
Resources
    auditing does eat up some, 522
    counter logs monitor certain system, 857
    publishing shared, 377–380
Resources tab, 758
Response, referral, 121
Restore Mode, Directory Services, 804–805
Restores
    performing, 825–826
    performing authoritative, 805
    performing trial, 826
Restoring
    data, 825
    data from backup, 821–826
    IIS, backing up and, 499–500
    OS (operating system) from backup, 821–826
    WINS database, 84–85
Restricted Groups, 517, 518
Reverse lookup zones, creating, 130–132
Reversible encryption, configuring, 640–641
RFCs (Requests for Comments), 4
Right defined, 243
RIP (Routing Information Protocol), 38
RIS (Remote Installation Services), 316–317
Rogue DHCP servers, 183, 211
Rogue servers, detecting, 210–212

Index **911**

Root, creating domain Dfs, 467
Root hints file, 121
Route change command, 38
Route command, 38
Route print command, 31
Routers, 22
    BOOTP-compliant, 197
    broadcasts rarely cross, 91
    multicast, 100
    working of, 30
Routes
    static, 36
    tracing, 46–47
Routing, 22
Routing and remote access, configuring, 724–735
Routing and Remote Access Service (RRAS), 550, 616
Routing, configuring, 23–39
    building Windows 2000 router, 27–30
    configuring routing tables, 34–37
    corporate scenario, 26–27
    how routing conflicts are handled, 37–38
    how routing works, 30
    managing routing tables, 38–39
    small business routing scenario, 24–25
    viewing computer's routing table, 34
    viewing routing tables, 30–34
Routing conflicts, 37–38
Routing enabled, IP, 40
Routing Information Protocol (RIP), 38
Routing scenario, small business, 24–25
Routing tables
    configuring, 34–37
    managing, 38–39
    viewing, 30–34
    viewing computer's, 34
Routing, troubleshooting TCP/IP and, 39–49
    troubleshooting with ARP, 45
    troubleshooting with IPCONFIG, 39–42
    troubleshooting with PATHPING, 48–49
    troubleshooting with PING, 42–45
    troubleshooting with tracert, 45–48
RPCs (Remote Procedure Calls), 434, 438
RR (resource records), 133
RRAS authentication process
    examining, 616–625
    in mixed mode, 620–621
    in native mode domain, 621–625
RRAS errors, identifying in System event logs, 643
RRAS is installed by default in Windows 2000, 572
RRAS (Routing and Remote Access Service), 550, 616, 708
    assign IP addresses in, 577
    configuring as VPN server, 571–574
    configuring authentication protocols on, 596–598
Running Window using startup log file option, 799

S

Safe Mode, 801–803
    starting computer in, 803
Safe Mode options, three, 799
SAM (Security Accounts Manager), 248, 811
Scan and repair protected system files, 770–771
Scenarios
    corporate, 26–27
    small business routing, 24–25
Schedules, changing replication, 433
Scope options, server options vs., 193–194
Scopes
    configuring DHCP, 186–202
    defining, 187–191
    security group, 244–246
Scripts, 305–307
Secedit command, 535
Secondary name servers, standard, 124–125
Secondary zones, standard, 122–123
Secure Sockets Layer (SSL), 493
Security
    auditing, 518–523
    configuring and auditing, 516–525
    configuring of VPN connections, 594–599
    verifying of VPN connections, 594–599
Security databases, creating, 533–534
Security group scopes, 244–246
Security groups, 440
    creating, 251–252
    global, 250
Security, implementing and analyzing, 515–546
    administering security templates, 525–530
    analyzing security settings, 530–536
    configuring and auditing security, 516–525
Security Log, reviewing, 525
Security policies, local, 292, 765–766
Security Settings, 307–311
Security settings, analyzing, 530–536
    analyzing current configuration, 530–534
    command-line analysis and configuration, 534–535
Security templates, administering, 525–530
    creating new templates, 528–529
Security templates, applying, 529
Security templates defined, 525
Security Templates snap-in, 527–528
Serial Line Internet Protocol (SLIP), 550, 552
Server and client hardware
    configuring, 753–792
    installing, 753–792
Server detecting presence of DHCP server, NAT, 734
Server health and performance, monitoring, 841–887
    configuring System Monitor alerts and logging, 851–867

diagnosing server health problems with Event Viewer, 868–872
disabling unnecessary services, 872–876
identifying unnecessary services, 872–876
monitoring and interpreting real-time performance, 842–850
using System Monitor and Task Manager, 842–850
Server health and performance, troubleshooting, 841–887
configuring System Monitor alerts and logging, 851–867
diagnosing server health problems with Event Viewer, 868–872
disabling unnecessary services, 872–876
identifying unnecessary services, 872–876
monitoring and interpreting real-time performance, 842–850
using System Monitor and Task Manager, 842–850
Server health problems, diagnosing with Event Viewer, 868–872
Server installation, basic Windows 2000, 482
Server mode, configuring Terminal Services for Application, 663–678
Server options vs. scope options, 193–194
Server properties, configuring DNS, 138–152
Server Resource Kit, Windows 2000, 869
Server roles, alternative DNS, 147–152
Server statistics, viewing WINS, 102
Server-to-server L2TP connections, 588–594
Server-to-server PPTP connections, 588–594
Servers
authorizing DHCP, 183–184
caching-only DNS name, 151–152
checking for rogue DHCP, 211
configuring DHCP, 186–202
configuring RRAS as VPN, 571–574
configuring slave, 151
configuring TCP/IP on, 12–15
creating virtual web, 487–489
defining bridgehead, 437
detecting rogue, 210–212
DHCP, 575
DNS, 41
DNS forwarding, 150
enterprise administrators authorizing DHCP, 184
establishing connections to Terminal, 677–678
installing and authorizing DHCP, 180–186
installing WINS, 79–80
IP addresses of name, 148
local DNS name, 120
member, 231
multihomed DNS name, 146–147
multiple DHCP, 210
NAT server detecting presence of DHCP, 734
remote DNS name, 120
rogue DHCP, 183
Shiva remote access, 641
standard primary name, 124–125
standard secondary name, 124–125
static IP addresses on, 13
testing name, 163
troubleshooting problems with proxy, 501
troubleshooting WINS, 102
virtual, 487
WINS, 68, 144
Servers and clients, configuring TCP/IP on, 4–17
Servers, setting up multiple WINS, 93–99
configuring WINS replication partnerships, 95–99
pull relationship, 94
push/pull partners, 95
push relationship, 94
Service
authorizing DHCP, 184–186
DHCP Allocator, 734
installing DHCP, 184–186
Service identifiers, NetBIOS, 72–73
Service Pack 2, 683
Service packs
deploying, 409–412
installing on new computers, 409–411
Service publishing, 713–716
Services
disabling, 876
disabling unnecessary, 872–876
identifying unnecessary, 872–876
Sessions
copying text from applications in Terminal Services, 679
taking remote control of user's, 669–670
Settings
analyzing security, 530–536
comparing policy settings to local, 531
configuring VPN client, 563–569
Control Access Through Remote Access Policy, 624
disabling unused policy, 326
examining RAS profile, 632–636
policy, 531
Security, 307–311
Software, 305
Windows, 305–319
SFC, using, 770–771
Sfc.exe (System File Checker), 770
Share permissions, 357–358
Shared folders
permissions, 357–361
publishing, 377–379
Shared printer permissions, setting, 373
Shared printers, publishing, 379
Shared resources in AD(Active Directory), publishing, 377–380
Shares, hidden, 365–367
Shareware utilities, 594
Sharing
folders, 356
printers, 372
Shiva Password Authentication Protocol (SPAP), 639
Shiva remote access servers, 641

Index

Short names, 159
Signing, driver, 754
Signing options, driver, 763
Sigverif.exe, 768–770
Site access, controlling through permissions, 496–498
Site level, linking GPO at, 330
Site links
    bridging, 436
    creating, 434–436
Sites
    accessing local, 486
    AD (Active Directory), 232
    are strictly for controlling replication, 434
    creating FTP, 490–492
    creating web, 482–490
    distinguishing by host headers, 488–489
    distinguishing by IP addresses, 488
    distinguishing by ports, 488
    document web, 495
    securing web and FTP, 493–499
Sites fail, replication between, 439
Slash 26 address, 14
Slave servers, configuring, 151
SLIP (Serial Line Internet Protocol), 550, 552
Small business routing scenario, 24–25
SMS (System Management Server), 849
SMTP transport, 434
Snap-in, Security Templates, 527–528
Sockets, Windows, 65
Software
    deploying, 409
    deploying with group policy, 392–402
    group policies and installing new, 395
    installing Terminal Services client, 672–674
    life cycle, 395
    maintaining and upgrading, 402
    managing with group policy, 391–423
    redeploying, 407
    removing, 407
    startup phase, 795–798
    upgrading, 403–406
Software deployments
    planning, 408
    testing, 410
Software distribution points, setting up, 393–394
Software Settings, 305
Space, adding to existing volumes, 459
SPAP, 642
SPAP is encrypted password authentication protocol, 641
SPAP (Shiva Password Authentication Protocol), 639
SSL (Secure Sockets Layer), 493
SSL, using certificate services and, 498–499
Stand-alone GPOs, creating, 322–328, 327–328
Standard primary zones, 122
Standard secondary zones, 122–123

Start Menu Icons GPO
    delegating control of, 340
    filtering, 336
    linking to OUs, 331–332
Start of Authority (SOA) records, 133
Starting your computer in Safe Mode, 803
Startup log file option, running Window using, 799
Startup log files, interpreting, 798–801
Startup options, repairing OS (operating system), 801–807
Startup phase
    hardware, 794–795
    software, 795–798
Startup problems can occur at any time, 794
Startup problems, troubleshooting, 793–839
    interpreting startup log files, 798–801
    OS (operating systems) not start, 815–821
    recovering data from hard disks, 815–821
    repairing OS (operating system), 801–807, 807–815
    restoring data from backup, 821–826
    restoring OS (operating system) from backup, 821–826
    Safe Mode, 801–803
State, Rebinding, 181
Static address pool, 576
Static IP addresses, 201, 206
    on servers, 13
Static mappings, 92–93
Static routes, 36
Statistics, viewing WINS server, 102
Storage, RAS policy, 643
Streaming media, 100
Subdomains and delegation of authority, 145–146
Subnet
    addresses, 10
    calculator, 21
    Class C address, 17
    defined, 36
    ID, 10
    masks, 6–7, 41
Subnetting, 10, 17–18, 21
Suffix options, configuring DNS, 157–159
Suffixes
    connection-specific DNS, 40
    primary DNS, 40
Switches
    ipconfig, 720
    /refreshpolicy, 535
    /release, 206
    /renew, 206
Synchronous defined, 306
System event logs, identifying RRAS errors in, 643
System File Checker (Sfc.exe), 770
System files
    scan and repair protected, 770–771
    Windows 2000, 796
System Information file, creating, 761

System Information utility, 760
System information, view real-time, 847–849
System Management Server (SMS), 849
System Monitor, 846–850
    opening logs with, 855–857
    using to view real-time system information, 847–849
System Monitor alerts and logging, configuring, 851–867
System Monitor and Task Manager, using, 842–850
System performance, monitoring, 864
System Properties dialog box, 772–776
System resources, counter logs monitor certain, 857
%systemroot%\inf folder, 526
SYSVOL folder, 306

T

Tab of user's Properties dialog box, Dial-in, 617
Tables
    configuring routing, 34–37
    managing routing, 38–39
    viewing computer's routing, 34
    viewing routing, 30–34
Tabs
    Categories, 400
    Port Settings, 758
    Pull Replication, 98
    Resources, 758
Tags
    #DOM (domain), 76
    #PRE (preload), 77
Tapes, backup, 825
Task Manager
    using System Monitor and, 842–850
    Windows, 842–846
Tasks, simplify management, 395
TCP/IP
    configuring on servers, 12–15
    configuring on servers and clients, 4–17
TCP/IP and routing, troubleshooting, 39–49
    troubleshooting with ARP, 45
    troubleshooting with IPCONFIG, 39–42
    troubleshooting with PATHPING, 48–49
    troubleshooting with PING, 42–45
    troubleshooting with tracert, 45–48
TCP/IP, configuring and troubleshooting, 3–61
    configuring routing, 23–39
    configuring TCP/IP on servers and clients, 4–17
    determining valid IP addresses, 17–23
    troubleshooting TCP/IP and routing, 39–49
TCP/IP-enabled platforms, 65
TCP/IP filtering problems, troubleshooting, 500–501
TCP (Transmission Control Protocol), 139
Templates
    administering security, 525–530
    Administrative, 320–322
    applying security, 529
    creating new, 528–529
    Security, 527–528
Temporary database name, 88
Terminal Server connections, establishing, 682
Terminal Server, establishing connections to, 677–678
Terminal Server modes, switching between, 670–671
Terminal Server session, creating, 677–678
Terminal Services
    configuring for Application Server mode, 663–678
    configuring for local resource mapping, 678–690
    configuring for Remote Administration mode, 663–678
    implementing for remote access, 661–706
    installing, 663–665, 664–665
Terminal Services Advanced Client (TSAC), 662, 665
Terminal Services and Offline Files, 664
Terminal Services client computer, 679
Terminal Services client software, installing, 672–674
Terminal Services clients, installing over networks, 674–675
Terminal Services configuration, 691
Terminal Services session, copying text from application in, 679
Terminal Services settings, configuring on per-connection basis, 682–690
Terminal Services user properties, configuring, 690–694
Testing
    name servers, 163
    software deployment, 410
Text, copying from application in Terminal Services session, 679
TGT (Ticket-Granting Ticket), 309
3DES (Triple DES), 637
Ticket-Granting Ticket (TGT), 309
Time To Live (TTL), 181
Time Value, Rebinding, 181
Timing, group policy, 296
Tools, qualifier, 755–761
Topology, checking replication, 440–441
Topology, Dfs, 468
Trace logs, 857–860
    creating, 858–860
    monitor certain events, 857
Tracert (Trace Route), 45
Tracert, troubleshooting with, 45–48
Tracing routes, 46–47
Traffic and remote networks, 586
Traffic, replication, 437
Traffic sent over VPN, 586
Transfers
    fast, 164
    troubleshooting zone, 164
    zone, 125
Transitive trusts, 235–237
Translation, ICS uses address, 710
Transmission Control Protocol (TCP), 139
Transport
    IP, 434
    SMTP, 434

Index

Trees, 233–234
    domain, 233, 234
Trial restore, performing, 826
Triggers, push, 97
Triple DES (3DES), 637
Troubleshooting
    AD (Active Directory), 425–452
    AD replication, 438–442
    with ARP, 45
    client-to-server L2TP connections, 579–587
    client-to-server PPTP connections, 579–587
    DHCP, 179–226, 207–212
    DNS, 117–178
    DNS name resolution, 159–164
    DNS with IPCONFIG, 161–162
    ICS (Internet Connection Sharing) problems, 718–724
    IIS, 499–501
    with IPCONFIG, 39–42
    with ipconfig, 719–721
    name resolution, 63–116
    NetBIOS name resolution, 100–103
    with PATHPING, 48–49
    with PING, 42–45
    problems with proxy servers, 501
    RAS problems, 642
    remote, 669
    remote access, 615–659
    server health and performance, 841–887
    startup problems, 793–839
    TCP/IP, 3–61
    TCP/IP and routing, 39–49
    TCP/IP filtering problems, 500–501
    with tracert, 45–48
    using ping, 721–724
    WINS clients, 102–103
    WINS servers, 102
    zone transfers, 164
Troubleshooting clues, identifying in Event Viewer, 643
Trusts, transitive, 235–237
TSAC, installing, 666–667
TSAC (Terminal Services Advanced Client), 662, 665
TTL (Time To Live), 181, 719
Types
    backup, 823–825
    node, 40

U

UDP, ports and, 139
UDP (User Datagram Protocol), 139
Unqualified domain names, 157
Update sequence number (USN), 432
Upgrades
    mandatory, 403
    optional, 403

Upgrading
    all DC (domain controllers), 245
    software, 402, 403–406
User account group membership, 642–643
User accounts
    AD (Active Directory), 257–260
    creating two, 258–260
User Datagram Protocol (UDP), 139
User objects, attribute changes made to, 691
User properties, configuring Terminal Services, 690–694
Users
    administering AD (Active Directory) computers and, 253–261
    delegating control to, 270
    finding shared printers in AD, 376–377
User's Properties dialog box, Dial-in tab of, 617
User's session, taking remote control of, 669–670
USN (update sequence number), 432
Utilities
    Backup, 818, 822
    freeware, 594
    Netsh command-line, 629
    shareware, 594
    System Information, 760

V

Viewing existing GPOs, 296–301
Virtual directories, creating, 484–485
Virtual directories (web sharing), defining, 483–486
Virtual private networks (VPNs), 550
Virtual servers, 487
Virtual web servers, creating, 487–489
Volumes
    adding more space to existing, 459
    configuring disks and, 456–459
VPN client settings, configuring, 563–569
VPN connections
    creating, 559–561
    verifying security of, 594–599
VPN connections, configuring, 549–613
    configuring client computer remote access properties, 550–570
    configuring client-to-server L2TP connections, 579–587
    configuring client-to-server PPTP connections, 579–587
    configuring IP address allocation, 571–579
    configuring L2TP filtering, 588–594
    configuring PPTP filtering, 588–594
    configuring remote access name resolution, 571–579
    configuring security of VPN connections, 594–599
    managing existing server-to-server L2TP connections, 588–594
    managing existing server-to-server PPTP connections, 588–594
    troubleshooting client-to-server L2TP connections, 579–587
    troubleshooting client-to-server PPTP connections, 579–587
VPN connections, configuring security of, 594–599

VPN connectivity options, verifying, 579–581
VPN server, configuring RRAS as, 571–574
VPN, traffic sent over, 586
VPN (virtual private network) connections, 558–570
VPNs (virtual private networks), 550

W

WAN link, 426
WANs (wide area networks), 668
Web and FTP sites, securing, 493–499
web servers, creating virtual, 487–489
web site performance, tuning, 489–490
web sites
    creating, 482–490
    document, 495
WebDAV (Web Distributed Authoring and Versioning), 495
Well-known port, 488
Wide area networks (WANs), 668
Windows 2000
    boot disk, 816–818
    configuring IP address allocation in, 571–576
    disk counters, 849
    events, 869
    Readiness Analyzer, 755–756
    RRAS is installed by default in, 572
    Server installation, 482
    Server Resource Kit, 869
    system files, 796
Windows 2000 boot disk, creating, 817
Windows 2000 CD, accessing Recovery Console from, 809
Windows authentication, integrated, 495
Windows-based computers, 674
Windows Diagnostics, 760
Windows Internet Naming Service (WINS), 68, 78
Windows NT 4 disk counters, 849
Windows settings, 305–319
    Folder Redirection, 318–319
    RIS (Remote Installation Services), 316–317
    scripts, 305–307
    Security Settings, 307–311
Windows Sockets, 65
Windows Task Manager, 842–846
Winmsd, 760
WINS clients
    configuring, 80–82
    name registration for non-, 92–93
    non, 79
    troubleshooting, 102–103
WINS, configuring and implementing, 78–100
    configuring WINS clients, 80–82
    installing WINS server, 79–80

managing WINS database, 82–89
setting up multiple WINS servers, 93–99
supporting non-WINS clients, 90–93
WINS database
    backing up, 84–85
    compacting, 87–88
    restoring, 84–85
    viewing records in, 83
WINS database, managing, 82–89
    backing up WINS database, 84–85
    compacting WINS database, 87–88
    configuring burst mode, 88–89
    configuring WINS intervals, 85–86
    manual scavenging, 87
    manual tombstoning, 87
    restoring WINS database, 84–85
WINS environment, non-, 77
WINS intervals, configuring, 85–86
WINS, management console, 82
WINS, proxy, 90
WINS, proxy agent, 91
WINS, proxy enabled, 40
WINS replication partnerships, configuring, 95–99
WINS server statistics, viewing, 102
WINS servers, 68, 144
    installing, 79–80
    troubleshooting, 102
WINS servers, setting up multiple
    configuring WINS replication partnerships, 95–99
    push/pull partners, 95
WINS, servers, setting up multiple, 93–99
    pull relationship, 94
    push relationship, 94
WINS (Windows Internet Naming Service), 68, 78
Winsock, 65
Wizard, Delegation, 274
Wizard, New Scope, 193

Z

Zone replication, multimaster, 125
Zone transfers
    defined, 125
    troubleshooting, 164
Zones
    Active Directory-integrated, 125
    creating forward lookup, 129–130
    creating reverse lookup, 130–132
    standard primary, 122
    standard secondary, 122–123

INTERNATIONAL CONTACT INFORMATION

AUSTRALIA
McGraw-Hill Book Company Australia Pty. Ltd.
TEL +61-2-9415-9899
FAX +61-2-9415-5687
http://www.mcgraw-hill.com.au
books-it_sydney@mcgraw-hill.com

CANADA
McGraw-Hill Ryerson Ltd.
TEL +905-430-5000
FAX +905-430-5020
http://www.mcgrawhill.ca

GREECE, MIDDLE EAST, NORTHERN AFRICA
McGraw-Hill Hellas
TEL +30-1-656-0990-3-4
FAX +30-1-654-5525

MEXICO (Also serving Latin America)
McGraw-Hill Interamericana Editores S.A. de C.V.
TEL +525-117-1583
FAX +525-117-1589
http://www.mcgraw-hill.com.mx
fernando_castellanos@mcgraw-hill.com

SINGAPORE (Serving Asia)
McGraw-Hill Book Company
TEL +65-863-1580
FAX +65-862-3354
http://www.mcgraw-hill.com.sg
mghasia@mcgraw-hill.com

SOUTH AFRICA
McGraw-Hill South Africa
TEL +27-11-622-7512
FAX +27-11-622-9045
robyn_swanepoel@mcgraw-hill.com

UNITED KINGDOM & EUROPE (Excluding Southern Europe)
McGraw-Hill Education Europe
TEL +44-1-628-502500
FAX +44-1-628-770224
http://www.mcgraw-hill.co.uk
computing_neurope@mcgraw-hill.com

ALL OTHER INQUIRIES Contact:
Osborne/McGraw-Hill
TEL +1-510-549-6600
FAX +1-510-883-7600
http://www.osborne.com
omg_international@mcgraw-hill.com

"Like the Book? You'll Love the Movie!"

Try out the interactive resources on the enclosed CD!

IMAGINE . . .

- Imagine Internet-based learning that allows you to engage in dynamic multi-media instruction with a connection as low as 56.6 kbps

- Imagine learning from an expert through uninterrupted video instruction, full motion graphics and interactive lab exercises

- Imagine a Web-based learning environment that includes personal study plans, online mentoring, labs, references, testing, and all the resources you need for certification success

Stop Imagining!
Insert the enclosed CD and experience it Today!

CD Contains:
- Online Course Link
- Step-by-Step Video Clips
- Lab Simulations
- Test Prep
- Electronic Book

1.800.865.0165 • **learnkey.com/osborne**

© 2002 LearnKey, Inc. LK022102

LearnKey.
Learn From The Experts™

What's on the enclosed CD?

- Step-by-step training from proven experts
- Simulation Exercises that reinforce certification objectives
- Test Prep tools to help you prepare for the certification exam
- Electronic version of the this Study Guide
- Your link to comprehensive Online Training Resources from LearnKey

With online MCSA training from LearnKey, you'll gain access to interactive instruction from experts to help you successfully manage and troubleshoot Windows 2000 networks and prepare to pass MCSA exam 70-218. Media-rich content is delivered to your desktop with full motion video and audio to give you a practical and engaging learning experience.

Load the enclosed CD for dynamic Online instruction from LearnKey and McGraw Hill/Osborne. Your first Session is FREE!

PLUS! Special Online Discounts for Osborne Customers!
Because you purchased an Osborne Study Guide with a MediaPoint CD, you are entitled to incredible savings on LearnKey online training courses.

Save up to 60% on Online Training!
Purchase the complete course and get 12 months access to all of the online training materials including:

- Media-rich Courseware
- Test Prep Software
- Study Plans
- Online Mentoring
- Reference Material and more!

This is a limited time offer so don't delay. Get started on your online training today!

For additional Online training contact LearnKey.

1.800.865.0165 • **learnkey.com/osborne**

© 2002 LearnKey, Inc.   LK022102

Learn From The Experts™

LICENSE AGREEMENT

THIS PRODUCT (THE "PRODUCT") CONTAINS PROPRIETARY SOFTWARE, DATA AND INFORMATION (INCLUDING DOCUMENTATION) OWNED BY THE McGRAW-HILL COMPANIES, INC. ("McGRAW-HILL") AND ITS LICENSORS. YOUR RIGHT TO USE THE PRODUCT IS GOVERNED BY THE TERMS AND CONDITIONS OF THIS AGREEMENT.

LICENSE: Throughout this License Agreement, "you" shall mean either the individual or the entity whose agent opens this package. You are granted a non-exclusive and non-transferable license to use the Product subject to the following terms:
(i) If you have licensed a single user version of the Product, the Product may only be used on a single computer (i.e., a single CPU). If you licensed and paid the fee applicable to a local area network or wide area network version of the Product, you are subject to the terms of the following subparagraph (ii).
(ii) If you have licensed a local area network version, you may use the Product on unlimited workstations located in one single building selected by you that is served by such local area network. If you have licensed a wide area network version, you may use the Product on unlimited workstations located in multiple buildings on the same site selected by you that is served by such wide area network; provided, however, that any building will not be considered located in the same site if it is more than five (5) miles away from any building included in such site. In addition, you may only use a local area or wide area network version of the Product on one single server. If you wish to use the Product on more than one server, you must obtain written authorization from McGraw-Hill and pay additional fees.
(iii) You may make one copy of the Product for back-up purposes only and you must maintain an accurate record as to the location of the back-up at all times.

COPYRIGHT; RESTRICTIONS ON USE AND TRANSFER: All rights (including copyright) in and to the Product are owned by McGraw-Hill and its licensors. You are the owner of the enclosed disc on which the Product is recorded. You may not use, copy, decompile, disassemble, reverse engineer, modify, reproduce, create derivative works, transmit, distribute, sublicense, store in a database or retrieval system of any kind, rent or transfer the Product, or any portion thereof, in any form or by any means (including electronically or otherwise) except as expressly provided for in this License Agreement. You must reproduce the copyright notices, trademark notices, legends and logos of McGraw-Hill and its licensors that appear on the Product on the back-up copy of the Product which you are permitted to make hereunder. All rights in the Product not expressly granted herein are reserved by McGraw-Hill and its licensors.

TERM: This License Agreement is effective until terminated. It will terminate if you fail to comply with any term or condition of this License Agreement. Upon termination, you are obligated to return to McGraw-Hill the Product together with all copies thereof and to purge all copies of the Product included in any and all servers and computer facilities.

DISCLAIMER OF WARRANTY: THE PRODUCT AND THE BACK-UP COPY ARE LICENSED "AS IS." McGRAW-HILL, ITS LICENSORS AND THE AUTHORS MAKE NO WARRANTIES, EXPRESS OR IMPLIED, AS TO THE RESULTS TO BE OBTAINED BY ANY PERSON OR ENTITY FROM USE OF THE PRODUCT, ANY INFORMATION OR DATA INCLUDED THEREIN AND/OR ANY TECHNICAL SUPPORT SERVICES PROVIDED HEREUNDER, IF ANY ("TECHNICAL SUPPORT SERVICES"). McGRAW-HILL, ITS LICENSORS AND THE AUTHORS MAKE NO EXPRESS OR IMPLIED WARRANTIES OF MERCHANTABILITY OR FITNESS FOR A PARTICULAR PURPOSE OR USE WITH RESPECT TO THE PRODUCT. McGRAW-HILL, ITS LICENSORS, AND THE AUTHORS MAKE NO GUARANTEE THAT YOU WILL PASS ANY CERTIFICATION EXAM WHATSOEVER BY USING THIS PRODUCT. NEITHER McGRAW-HILL, ANY OF ITS LICENSORS NOR THE AUTHORS WARRANT THAT THE FUNCTIONS CONTAINED IN THE PRODUCT WILL MEET YOUR REQUIREMENTS OR THAT THE OPERATION OF THE PRODUCT WILL BE UNINTERRUPTED OR ERROR FREE. YOU ASSUME THE ENTIRE RISK WITH RESPECT TO THE QUALITY AND PERFORMANCE OF THE PRODUCT.

LIMITED WARRANTY FOR DISC: To the original licensee only, McGraw-Hill warrants that the enclosed disc on which the Product is recorded is free from defects in materials and workmanship under normal use and service for a period of ninety (90) days from the date of purchase. In the event of a defect in the disc covered by the foregoing warranty, McGraw-Hill will replace the disc.

LIMITATION OF LIABILITY: NEITHER McGRAW-HILL, ITS LICENSORS NOR THE AUTHORS SHALL BE LIABLE FOR ANY INDIRECT, SPECIAL OR CONSEQUENTIAL DAMAGES, SUCH AS BUT NOT LIMITED TO, LOSS OF ANTICIPATED PROFITS OR BENEFITS, RESULTING FROM THE USE OR INABILITY TO USE THE PRODUCT EVEN IF ANY OF THEM HAS BEEN ADVISED OF THE POSSIBILITY OF SUCH DAMAGES. THIS LIMITATION OF LIABILITY SHALL APPLY TO ANY CLAIM OR CAUSE WHATSOEVER WHETHER SUCH CLAIM OR CAUSE ARISES IN CONTRACT, TORT, OR OTHERWISE. Some states do not allow the exclusion or limitation of indirect, special or consequential damages, so the above limitation may not apply to you.

U.S. GOVERNMENT RESTRICTED RIGHTS: Any software included in the Product is provided with restricted rights subject to subparagraphs (c), (1) and (2) of the Commercial Computer Software-Restricted Rights clause at 48 C.F.R. 52.227-19. The terms of this Agreement applicable to the use of the data in the Product are those under which the data are generally made available to the general public by McGraw-Hill. Except as provided herein, no reproduction, use, or disclosure rights are granted with respect to the data included in the Product and no right to modify or create derivative works from any such data is hereby granted.

GENERAL: This License Agreement constitutes the entire agreement between the parties relating to the Product. The terms of any Purchase Order shall have no effect on the terms of this License Agreement. Failure of McGraw-Hill to insist at any time on strict compliance with this License Agreement shall not constitute a waiver of any rights under this License Agreement. This License Agreement shall be construed and governed in accordance with the laws of the State of New York. If any provision of this License Agreement is held to be contrary to law, that provision will be enforced to the maximum extent permissible and the remaining provisions will remain in full force and effect.